Corporate Finance:
A Focused Approach

Corporate Finance:

A Focused Approach

FOURTH EDITION

MICHAEL C. EHRHARDT
University of Tennessee

EUGENE F. BRIGHAM
University of Florida

Australia • Brazil • Japan • Korea • Mexico • Singapore • Spain • United Kingdom • United States

Corporate Finance: A Focused Approach, Fourth Edition

Michael C. Ehrhardt and Eugene F. Brigham

VP/Editorial Director: Jack W. Calhoun

Publisher: Joe Sabatino

Executive Editor: Mike Reynolds

Developmental Editor: Michael Guendelsberger

Senior Editorial Assistant: Adele Scholtz

Marketing Manager: Nathan Anderson

Marketing Coordinator: Suellen Ruttkay

Content Project Manager: Jacquelyn K Featherly

Technology Production Analyst: Starratt Alexander

Senior Manufacturing Coordinator: Kevin Kluck

Production House/Compositor: Integra Software Services Pvt. Ltd.

Senior Art Director: Michelle Kunkler

Cover and Internal Designer: Rokusek Design

Cover Images: © Lael Henderson/Stock Illustration Source/Getty Images, Inc.

Library of Congress Control Number: 2009942955
Student Edition ISBN 13: 978-1-4390-7811-2
Student Edition ISBN 10: 1-4390-7811-6

South-Western Cengage Learning
5191 Natorp Boulevard
Mason, OH 45040
USA

Cengage Learning products are represented in Canada by Nelson Education, Ltd.

For your course and learning solutions, visit **www.cengage.com**

Purchase any of our products at your local college store or at our preferred online store **www.CengageBrain.com**

Printed in China
2 3 4 5 13 12 11 10

Brief Contents

Contents

Preface

Be sure to visit the Corporate Finance: A Focused Approach (4th Edition) *Web site at* **www.cengage.com/finance/ehrhardt**. *This site provides access for instructors and students.*

When we wrote the first edition of *Corporate Finance: A Focused Approach*, we had four goals: (1) to create a book that would help managers make better financial decisions; (2) to motivate students by demonstrating that finance is both interesting and relevant; (3) to make the book clear enough for students to go through the material without wasting time trying to figure out what we were trying to say; and (4) to provide a book that covers the core material necessary for a one-semester introductory MBA course but without all the other interesting-but-not-essential material that is contained in most MBA texts.

The collapse of the sub-prime mortgage market, the financial crisis, and the global economic crisis make it more important than ever for students and managers to understand the role that finance plays in a global economy, in their own companies, and in their own lives. So, in addition to the four goals just listed, this edition has a fifth goal: to prepare students for a changed world.

Intrinsic Valuation as a Unifying Theme

Our emphasis throughout the book is on the actions that a manager can and should take to increase the intrinsic value of the firm. Structuring the book around intrinsic valuation enhances continuity and helps students see how various topics are related to one another.

This book combines theory and practical applications. An understanding of finance theory is absolutely essential for anyone developing and/or implementing effective financial strategies. But theory alone isn't sufficient, so we provide numerous examples in the book and the accompanying *Excel* spreadsheets to illustrate how theory is applied in practice. Indeed, we believe that the ability to analyze financial problems using *Excel* is absolutely essential for a student's successful job search and subsequent career. Therefore, many exhibits in the book come directly from the accompanying *Excel* spreadsheets. Many of the spreadsheets also provide brief "tutorials" by way of detailed comments on *Excel* features that we have found to be especially useful, such as Goal Seek, Tables, and many financial functions.

The book begins with fundamental concepts, including background on the economic and financial environment, financial statements (with an emphasis on cash flows), the time value of money, bond valuation, risk analysis, and stock valuation. With this background, we go on to discuss how specific techniques and decision rules can be used to help maximize the value of the firm. This organization provides four important advantages:

1. Managers should try to maximize the intrinsic value of a firm, which is determined by cash flows as revealed in financial statements. Our early coverage of financial statements thus helps students see how particular financial decisions affect the various parts of the firm and the resulting cash flow. Also, financial statement analysis provides an excellent vehicle for illustrating the usefulness of spreadsheets.

2. Covering time value of money early helps students see how and why expected future cash flows determine the value of the firm. Also, it takes time for students to digest TVM concepts and to learn how to do the required calculations, so it is good to cover TVM concepts early and often.
3. Most students—even those who do not plan to major in finance—are interested in investments. The ability to learn is a function of individual interest and motivation, so our early coverage of securities and security markets is pedagogically sound.
4. Once basic concepts have been established, it is easier for students to understand both how and why corporations make specific decisions in the areas of capital budgeting, raising capital, working capital management, mergers, and the like.

Intended Market and Use

Corporate Finance is designed primarily for use in the introductory MBA finance course and as a reference text in follow-on case courses and after graduation. The book can also be used as an undergraduate introductory text with exceptionally good students.

Improvements in the Fourth Edition

As in every revision, we updated and clarified materials throughout the text and reviewed the entire book for completeness, ease of exposition, and currency. We made hundreds of small changes to keep the text up-to-date, with particular emphasis on updating the real-world examples and including the latest changes in the financial environment and financial theory. In addition, we made a number of larger changes. Some of them affect all chapters, some involve reorganizing sections among chapters, and some modify material covered within specific chapters.

Changes That Affect All Chapters

The global economic crisis. In virtually every chapter we use real-world examples to show how the chapter's topics are related to some aspect of the global economic crisis. In addition, many chapters contain new "Global Economic Crisis" features that focus on particularly important issues related to the crisis.

The big picture. Students often fail to see the forest for the trees, and this is especially true in finance because they must learn new vocabularies and analytical tools. To help students understand the big picture and integrate the different parts into an overall framework, we have added a graphic at the beginning of each chapter (and in the *PowerPoint* shows) that clearly illustrates where the chapter's topics fit into the big picture. Here is an example from Chapter 9:

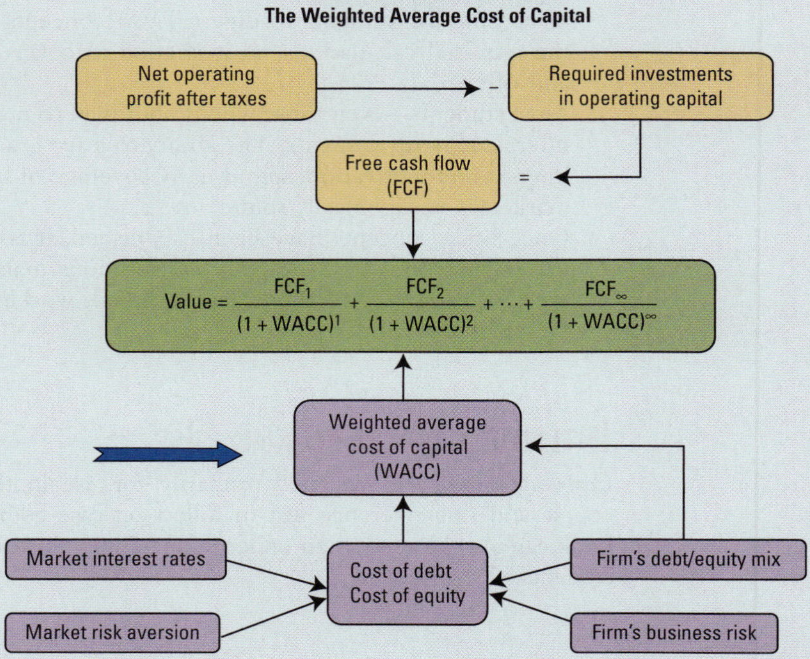

Additional integration of the textbook and the accompanying* Excel Tool Kit *spreadsheet models for each chapter. Many figures in the textbook are actually screen shots from the chapter's *Excel **Tool Kit*** model. This makes the analysis more transparent to the students and better enables them to follow the analysis in the *Excel* model.

Significant Reorganization of Some Chapters

Financial markets and performance measures. Chapter 1 still addresses the financial environment, but now it is followed by two chapters that focus on measuring the firm's performance in the financial environment by understanding financial statements, calculating free cash flow, and analyzing ratios.

Time value of money and bond valuation. Chapter 4 covers the time value of money, and Chapter 5 applies these concepts to bond pricing. Thus, students learn a tool and then immediately use the tool.

Dividends and stock repurchases before capital structure decisions. We now cover dividends and stock repurchases in Chapter 14 so that students will already understand stock repurchases when we discuss recapitalizations in Chapter 15.

Notable Changes within Selected Chapters

We made too many small improvements within each chapter to mention them all, but some of the more notable ones are discussed below.

Chapter 1: An Overview of Financial Management and the Financial Environment. We updated and extended a box on globalization, "Columbus Was Wrong, the World Is Flat! And Hot, and Crowded," and added a new box on the global economic crisis, "Say Hello to the Global Economic Crisis!" We completely rewrote the section on financial securities, including a discussion of securitization, and added a new section on the global crisis. New figures showing the national debt, trade balances, federal budget deficits and the Case-Shiller real estate index help us better illustrate different aspects of the global crisis.

Chapter 2: Financial Statements, Cash Flow, and Taxes. A new opening vignette shows the cash that several different companies generated and the different ways that they used the cash flow. We added a new box on the global economic crisis that explains the problems associated with off–balance sheet assets, "Let's Play Hide-and-Seek!" We added a new figure illustrating the uses of free cash flow. We now have two end-of-chapter spreadsheet problems: one focusing on the articulation between the income statement and statement of cash flows, and one focusing on free cash flow.

Chapter 3: Analysis of Financial Statements. We added a new box on marking to market, "The Price is Right! (Or Wrong!)," as well as a new box on international accounting standards, "The World Might be Flat, but Global Accounting is Bumpy! The Case of IFRS versus FASB." We added a brief discussion explaining how to use the statement of cash flows in financial analysis.

Chapter 4: Time Value of Money. We added three new boxes: (1) "Hints on Using Financial Calculators," (2) "Variable Annuities: Good or Bad?" and (3) "An Accident Waiting to Happen: Option Reset Adjustable Rate Mortgages."

Chapter 5: Bonds, Bond Valuation, and Interest Rates. We added four new boxes related to the global economic crisis: (1) "Betting with or against the U.S. Government: The Case of Treasury Bond Credit Default Swaps," (2) "Insuring with Credit Default Swaps: Let the Buyer Beware!" (3) "Might the U.S. Treasury Bond Be Downgraded?" and (4) "Are Investors Rational?" We also added a new table summarizing corporate bond default rates and annual changes in ratings.

Chapter 6: Risk, Return, and the Capital Asset Pricing Model. The new opening vignette discusses the recent stock market and compares the market's returns to GE's returns. We added a new box on the risk that remains even for long-term investors, "What Does Risk Really Mean?" We added two additional boxes on risk, "How Risky Is a Large Portfolio of Stocks?" and "Another Kind of Risk: The Bernie Madoff Story."

Chapter 7: Stocks, Stock Valuation, and Stock Market Equilibrium. A new opening vignette discusses buy- and sell-side analysts. We added a new box on behavioral issues, "Rational Behavior versus Animal Spirits, Herding, and Anchoring Bias." We added a new section, "The Market Stock Price versus Intrinsic Value."

Chapter 8: Financial Options and Applications in Corporate Finance. We completely rewrote the description of the binomial option pricing model. In addition to the hedge portfolio, we also discuss replicating portfolios. We now provide the binomial formula and show the complete solution to the two-period model. To provide greater continuity, the company used to illustrate the binomial example is now the same company used to illustrate the Black-Scholes model. Our discussion of put options now includes the Black-Scholes put formula.

Chapter 9: The Cost of Capital. We added a new figure to highlight the similarities and differences among capital structure weights based on book values, market values, and target values. We added a new box, "GE and Warren Buffett: The Cost of Preferred Stock." We completely rewrote our discussion of the market risk premium, which now includes the impact of stock repurchases on estimating the market risk premium. We also present data from surveys identifying the market risk premia used by CFOs and professors.

Chapter 10: The Basics of Capital Budgeting: Evaluating Cash Flows. We added a new box, "Why NPV Is Better Than IRR."

Chapter 11: Cash Flow Estimation and Risk Analysis. We now show how to use tornado diagrams in sensitivity analysis. We rewrote our discussion of Monte Carlo simulation and show how to conduct a simulation analysis without using add-ins but instead using only *Excel*'s built-in features (Data Tables and random number generators). We have included an example of replacement analysis and an example of a decision tree showing abandonment. We added a new box, "Are Bank Stress Tests Stressful Enough?"

Chapter 12: Financial Planning and Forecasting Financial Statements. It is difficult to do financial planning without using spreadsheet software, so we completely rewrote the chapter and explicitly integrated the text and the *Excel* ***Tool Kit*** model. We illustrate the ways that financial policies (i.e., dividend payout and capital structure choices) affect financial projections, including ways to ensure that balance sheets balance. The *Excel* ***Tool Kit*** model now demonstrates a simple way to incorporate financing feedback effects.

Chapter 13: Corporate Valuation, Value-Based Management, and Corporate Governance. The new opening vignette discusses the role of corporate governance in the global economic crisis. We also added three new boxes. The first describes corporate governance issues at IBM, "Let's Go to Miami! IBM's 2009 Annual Meeting." The second discusses leadership at bailout recipients, "Would the U.S. Government Be an Effective Board Director?" The third discusses the 2009 proxy season, "Shareholder Reactions to the Crisis."

Chapter 14: Distributions to Shareholders: Dividends and Repurchases. We consolidated the coverage of stock repurchases that was previously spread over two chapters and located it here, which now precedes our discussion of capital structure in Chapter 15. We also use the FCF valuation model to illustrate the different impacts of stock repurchases versus dividend payments. We added two new boxes. The first discusses recent dividend cuts, "Will Dividends Ever Be the Same?" and the second discusses Sun Microsystems' stock splits and recent reverse split, "Talk About a Split Personality!"

Chapter 15: Capital Structure Decisions: The Basics. The new opening vignette discusses recent bankruptcies and Black & Decker's efforts to reduce liquidity risk by refinancing short-term debt with long-term debt. Because stock repurchases are now covered in the preceding chapter, we were able to improve our discussion of recapitalizations within the context of the FCF valuation model. We added a new box on "Deleveraging" that discusses the changes in leverage many companies and individuals are making in light of the global economic crisis.

Chapter 16: Working Capital Management. We reorganized the chapter so that we now discuss working capital holdings and financing before discussing the cash conversion cycle. We rewrote our coverage of the cash conversion cycle to explain the general concepts and then apply them to actual financial statement data. We added a new box entitled "Some Firms Operate with Negative Working Capital!" and a new section on the cost of bank loans.

Chapter 17: Multinational Financial Management. We added a new opening vignette on the global economic crisis and its impact on world economies, foreign direct investment, and cross-border M&As.

Aplia Finance

Aplia Finance, an interactive learning system, engages students in course concepts, ensures they practice on a regular basis, and helps them prepare to learn finance through a series of tutorials. Created by an instructor to help students excel, book-specific problem sets have instant grades and detailed feedback, ensuring students have the opportunity to learn from and improve with every question.

Chapter assignments use the same language and tone of the course textbook, giving students a seamless experience in and out of the classroom. Problems are automatically graded and offer detailed explanations, helping students learn from every question.

Aplia Finance offers:

- *Problem Sets:* Chapter-specific problem sets ensure that students are completing finance assignments on a regular basis.
- *Preparing for Finance Tutorials:* Hands-on tutorials solve math, statistics, economics, and accounting roadblocks before they become a problem in the course, and financial calculator tutorials help students learn to use the tools needed in a finance course.
- *News Analyses:* Students connect course theories to real-world events by reading relevant news articles and answering graded questions about the article.
- *Course Management System*
- *Digital Textbook*

For more information, visit **http://www.aplia.com/finance**.

Thomson ONE—Business School Edition

To access Thomson ONE—BSE, go to **http://tobsefin.swlearning.com** *and follow the instructions shown there. You will need the serial number that came on the card in your textbook.*

Thomson ONE—Business School Edition is an online database that draws from the world-acclaimed Thomson Financial data sources, including the SEC Disclosure, Datastream, First Call, and Worldscope databases. Now you can give your students the opportunity to practice with a business school version of the same Internet-based database that brokers and analysts around the world use every day. Thomson ONE—BSE provides (1) one-click download of financial statements to *Excel*, (2) data from domestic *and* international companies, (3) 10 years of financial data; and (4) one-click Peer Set analyses.

Many chapters have suggested problems based on data available at Thomson ONE—BSE. Following is a brief description of the data provided by Thomson ONE—BSE.

I/B/E/S Consensus Estimates. Includes consensus estimates—averages, means, and medians; analyst-by-analyst earnings coverage; analysts' forecasts based on 15 industry standard measures; and current and historic coverage for the selected 500 companies. Current coverage is five years forward plus historic data from 1976 for U.S. companies and from 1987 for international companies, with current data updated daily and historic data updated monthly.

Worldscope. Includes company profiles, financials, accounting results, and market per share data for the selected 500 companies going back to 1980, all updated daily.

Disclosure SEC Database. Includes company profiles, annual and quarterly company financials, pricing information, and earnings estimates for selected U.S. and Canadian companies—annually from 1987, quarterly for the last 10 years, and monthly for prices; all updated weekly.

DataStream Pricing. Daily international pricing, including share price information (open, high, low, close, P/E) plus index and exchange rate data, for the last 10 years.

ILX Systems Delayed Quotes. Includes 20-minute delayed quotes of equities and indices from U.S. and global tickers covering 130 exchanges in 25 developed countries.

Comtex Real-Time News. Includes current news releases.

SEC Edgar Filings and Global Image Source Filings. Includes regulatory and nonregulatory filings for both corporate and individual entities. Edgar filings are real-time and go back 10 years; image filings are updated daily and go back 7 years.

Make It Yours:

Your course is unique; create a casebook that reflects it. Let us help you put together a quality casebook simply, quickly, and affordably.

We want to help you focus on the most important thing – teaching. That's why we have made this as simple as possible for you. We have aligned best-selling cases from our Klein/Brigham and Brigham/Buzzard series at the chapter level to Ehrhardt/Brigham. We encourage you to visit **http://www.cengage.com/custom/makeityours/Ehrhardt Brigham** and select the cases to include in a custom case book. The cases are listed under each chapter title. To review cases, simply click on "view abstract" next to each case title. If you would like to review the full case, contact your Cengage Learning representative or fill out the form and we will contact you.

For more information about custom publishing options, visit **www.cengage.com/custom**.

The Instructional Package: An Integrated Learning System

Corporate Finance includes a broad range of ancillary materials designed to enhance students' learning and to make it easier for instructors to prepare for and conduct classes. All resources available to students are, of course, also available to instructors; in addition, instructors have access to the course management tools.

Learning Tools Available to Students and Instructors

The Cengage Global Economic Watch (GEW) Resource Center. This is your source for turning today's challenges into tomorrow's solutions. This online portal houses the most current and up-to-date content concerning the economic crisis. Organized by discipline, the GEW Resource Center offers the solutions instructors and students need in an easy-to-use format. Included are an overview and timeline of the historical events leading up to the crisis, links to the latest news and resources, discussion and testing content, an instructor feedback forum, and a Global Issues Database.

In addition to these resources and the items noted previously, many other resources are available on the Web at *Corporate Finance*'s Web site. These ancillaries include the following.

Excel Tool Kits. Proficiency with spreadsheets is an absolute necessity for all MBA students. With that in mind, for each chapter we created *Excel* spreadsheets, called *Tool Kits*, to show how the calculations used in the chapter were actually done. The *Tool Kit* models include explanations and screen shots that show students how to use many of the features and functions of *Excel*, enabling the *Tool Kits* to serve as self-taught tutorials.

An e-Library: Web Extensions. Many chapters have Adobe PDF "appendices" that provide more detailed coverage of topics that were addressed in the chapter.

End-of-Chapter Spreadsheet Problems. Each chapter has a *Build a Model* problem, where students start with a spreadsheet that contains financial data plus general instructions about solving a specific problem. The model is partially completed, with headings but no formulas, so the student must literally build a model. This structure guides the student through the problem, minimizes unnecessary typing and data entry, and also makes it easy to grade the work, since all students' answers are in the same locations on the spreadsheet. The partial spreadsheets for the *Build a Model* problems are available to students on the book's Web site; the completed models are in files on the Instructor's portion of the Web site.

Thomson ONE—BSE Problem Sets. The book's Web site has a set of problems that require accessing the Thomson ONE—Business School Edition Web data. Using real-world data, students are better able to develop the skills they will need before seeking employment.

Interactive Study Center. The textbook's Web site contains links to all Web sites that are cited in each chapter.

Course Management Tools Available Only to Instructors

Instructors have access to all of the materials listed above in addition to course management tools. These tools are available at *Corporate Finance*'s Instructor companion Web site and on the Instructor's Resource CD. These materials include the following resources.

Solutions Manual. This comprehensive manual contains worked-out solutions to all end-of-chapter materials. It is available in both print and electronic forms at the Instructor's Web site.

PowerPoint Slides. There is a Mini Case at the end of each chapter. These cases cover all the essential issues presented in the chapter, and they provide the structure for our class lectures. For each Mini Case, we developed a set of *PowerPoint* slides that present graphs, tables, lists, and calculations for use in lectures. Although based on the Mini Cases, the slides are completely self-contained in the sense that they can be used for lectures regardless of whether students have read the Mini Cases. Also, instructors can easily customize the slides, and they can be converted quickly into any *PowerPoint* Design Template.[1] Copies of these files are on the Instructor's Web site and the CengageNOW site.

---

[1]To convert into *PowerPoint*, select Format, Apply Design Template, and then pick any template. Always double-check the conversion; some templates use differently sized fonts, which can cause some slide titles to run over their allotted space.

Mini Case Spreadsheets. In addition to the *PowerPoint* slides, we also provide *Excel* spreadsheets that perform the calculations required in the Mini Cases. These spreadsheets are similar to the *Tool Kits* except (a) the numbers correspond to the Mini Cases rather than the chapter examples, and (b) we added some features that enable "what if" analysis on a real-time basis in class. We usually begin our lectures with the *PowerPoint* presentation, but after we have explained a basic concept we "toggle" to the Mini Case *Excel* file and show how the analysis can be done in *Excel*.[2] For example, when teaching bond pricing, we begin with the *PowerPoint* show and cover the basic concepts and calculations. Then we toggle to *Excel* and use a sensitivity-based graph to show how bond prices change as interest rates and time to maturity vary. More and more students are bringing their laptops to class—they can follow along and do the "what if" analysis for themselves.

Solutions to End-of-Chapter Spreadsheet Problems. The partial spreadsheets for the *Build a Model* problems are available to students, and the completed models are in files on the Instructor's Web site.

Solutions to Thomson ONE—BSE Problem Sets. The Thomson ONE—BSE problem sets require students to use real-world data. Although the solutions change daily as the data change, we provide instructors with "representative" answers.

Test Bank. The *Test Bank* contains more than 1,200 class-tested questions and problems. Information regarding the topic and degree of difficulty, along with the complete solution for all numerical problems, is provided with each question. The *Test Bank* is available in three forms: (1) in a printed book; (2) in Microsoft *Word* files; and (3) in a computerized test bank software package, Exam View, which has many features that make test preparation, scoring, and grade recording easy—including the ability to generate different versions of the same problem. Exam View is easily able to export pools into Blackboard and WebCT.

Textchoice, the Cengage Learning Online Case Library. More than a hundred cases written by Eugene F. Brigham, Linda Klein, and Chris Buzzard are now available via the Internet, and new cases are added every year. These cases are in a database that allows instructors to select cases and create their own customized casebooks. Most of the cases have accompanying spreadsheet models that, although not essential for working the case, do reduce number crunching and thus leave more time for students to consider conceptual issues. The models also illustrate how computers can be used to make better financial decisions. Cases that we have found particularly useful for the different chapters are listed in the end-of-chapter references. The cases, case solutions, and spreadsheet models can be previewed and ordered by instructors at **http://www.textchoice2.com**.

Cengage/South-Western will provide complimentary supplements or supplement packages to those adopters qualified under Cengage's adoption policy. Please contact your sales representative to learn how you may qualify. If, as an adopter or potential user, you receive supplements you do not need, please return them to your sales representative.

---

[2]To toggle between two open programs, such as *Excel* and *PowerPoint*, hold the Alt key down and hit the Tab key until you have selected the program you want to show.

Acknowledgments

This book reflects the efforts of a great many people over a number of years. First, we would like to thank the following reviewers of the Third Edition for their suggestions:

ANNE ANDERSON
Lehigh University

OMAR M. BENKATO
Ball State University

RAHUL BISHNOI
Hofstra University

JONATHAN CLARKE
Georgia Institute of Technology

SHARON H. GARRISON
University of Arizona

HASSAN MOUSSAWI
Wayne State University

A. JON SAXON
Loyola Marymount University

JOSEPH VU
DePaul University–Lincoln

In addition, we appreciate the many helpful comments and suggestions, which were incorporated into this edition, that were offered by Richard M. Burns, Greg Faulk, John Harper, Robert Irons, Joe Walker, Barry Wilbratte, and Serge Wind.

Many professors and professionals who are experts on specific topics reviewed earlier versions of individual chapters or groups of chapters, and we are grateful for their insights; in addition, we would like to thank those whose reviews and comments on earlier editions and companion books have contributed to this edition: Mike Adler, Syed Ahmad, Sadhana M. Alangar, Ed Altman, Mary Schary Amram, Bruce Anderson, Ron Anderson, Bob Angell, Vince Apilado, Henry Arnold, Nasser Arshadi, Bob Aubey, Abdul Aziz, Gil Babcock, Peter Bacon, Kent Baker, Tom Bankston, Les Barenbaum, Charles Barngrover, Michael Barry, Bill Beedles, Moshe Ben-Horim, Bill Beranek, Tom Berry, Bill Bertin, Roger Bey, Dalton Bigbee, John Bildersee, Eric Blazer, Russ Boisjoly, Keith Boles, Gordon R. Bonner, Geof Booth, Kenneth Boudreaux, Helen Bowers, Oswald Bowlin, Don Boyd, G. Michael Boyd, Pat Boyer, Ben S. Branch, Joe Brandt, Elizabeth Brannigan, Greg Brauer, Mary Broske, Dave Brown, Kate Brown, Bill Brueggeman, Kirt Butler, Robert Button, Chris Buzzard, Bill Campsey, Bob Carleson, Severin Carlson, David Cary, Steve Celec, Don Chance, Antony Chang, Susan Chaplinsky, Jay Choi, S. K. Choudhury, Lal Chugh, Maclyn Clouse, Margaret Considine, Phil Cooley, Joe Copeland, David Cordell, John Cotner, Charles Cox, David Crary, John Crockett, Roy Crum, Brent Dalrymple, Bill Damon, Joel Dauten, Steve Dawson, Sankar De, Miles Delano, Fred Dellva, Anand Desai, Bernard Dill, Greg Dimkoff, Les Dlabay, Mark Dorfman, Gene Drycimski, Dean Dudley, David Durst, Ed Dyl, Dick Edelman, Charles Edwards, John Ellis, Dave Ewert, John Ezzell, Richard Fendler, Michael Ferri, Jim Filkins, John Finnerty, Susan Fischer, Mark Flannery, Steven Flint, Russ Fogler, E. Bruce Frederickson, Dan French, Tina Galloway, Partha Gangopadhyay, Phil Gardial, Michael Garlington, Jim Garvin, Adam Gehr, Jim Gentry, Stuart Gillan, Philip Glasgo, Rudyard Goode, Myron Gordon, Walt Goulet, Bernie Grablowsky, Theoharry Grammatikos, Ed Grossnickle, John Groth, Alan Grunewald, Manak Gupta, Sam Hadaway, Don Hakala, Janet Hamilton, Sally Hamilton, Gerald Hamsmith, William Hardin, John Harris, Paul Hastings, Patty Hatfield, Bob Haugen, Steve Hawke, Del Hawley, Hal Heaton, Robert Hehre, John Helmuth, George Hettenhouse, Hans Heymann, Kendall Hill, Roger Hill, Tom Hindelang, Linda Hittle, Ralph Hocking, J. Ronald Hoffmeister, Jim Horrigan, John Houston, John Howe, Keith Howe, Hugh Hunter, Steve Isberg, Jim Jackson, Vahan Janjigian, Kurt Jesswein, Kose John, Craig Johnson,

Keith Johnson, Steve Johnson, Ramon Johnson, Ray Jones, Manuel Jose, Gus Kalogeras, Mike Keenan, Bill Kennedy, Joe Kiernan, Robert Kieschnick, Rick Kish, Linda Klein, Don Knight, Dorothy Koehl, Theodor Kohers, Jaroslaw Komarynsky, Duncan Kretovich, Harold Krogh, Charles Kroncke, Lynn Phillips Kugele, Joan Lamm, P. Lange, Howard Lanser, Martin Laurence, Ed Lawrence, Richard LeCompte, Wayne Lee, Jim LePage, Ilene Levin, Jules Levine, John Lewis, James T. Lindley, Chuck Linke, Bill Lloyd, Susan Long, Judy Maese, Bob Magee, Ileen Malitz, Phil Malone, Terry Maness, Chris Manning, Terry Martell, D. J. Masson, John Mathys, John McAlhany, Andy McCollough, Tom McCue, Bill McDaniel, Robin McLaughlin, Jamshid Mehran, Ilhan Meric, Larry Merville, Rick Meyer, Stuart E. Michelson, Jim Millar, Ed Miller, John Mitchell, Carol Moerdyk, Bob Moore, Barry Morris, Gene Morris, Fred Morrissey, Chris Muscarella, Stu Myers, David Nachman, Tim Nantell, Don Nast, Bill Nelson, Bob Nelson, Bob Niendorf, Tom O'Brien, Dennis O'Connor, John O'Donnell, Jim Olsen, Robert Olsen, Frank O'Meara, David Overbye, R. Daniel Pace, Coleen Pantalone, Jim Pappas, Stephen Parrish, Pam Peterson, Glenn Petry, Jim Pettijohn, Rich Pettit, Dick Pettway, Hugo Phillips, John Pinkerton, Gerald Pogue, Ralph A. Pope, R. Potter, Franklin Potts, R. Powell, Chris Prestopino, Jerry Prock, Howard Puckett, Herbert Quigley, George Racette, Bob Radcliffe, Allen Rappaport, Bill Rentz, Ken Riener, Charles Rini, John Ritchie, Jay Ritter, Pietra Rivoli, Fiona Robertson, Antonio Rodriguez, E. M. Roussakis, Dexter Rowell, Mike Ryngaert, Jim Sachlis, Abdul Sadik, Thomas Scampini, Kevin Scanlon, Frederick Schadler, James Schallheim, Mary Jane Scheuer, Carl Schweser, John Settle, Alan Severn, Sol Shalit, Elizabeth Shields, Frederic Shipley, Dilip Shome, Ron Shrieves, Neil Sicherman, J. B. Silvers, Clay Singleton, Joe Sinkey, Stacy Sirmans, Jaye Smith, Steve Smith, Don Sorenson, David Speairs, Ken Stanly, John Stansfield, Ed Stendardi, Alan Stephens, Don Stevens, Jerry Stevens, G. Bennett Stewart, Mark Stohs, Glen Strasburg, Robert Strong, Philip Swensen, Ernie Swift, Paul Swink, Eugene Swinnerton, Robert Taggart, Gary Tallman, Dennis Tanner, Craig Tapley, Russ Taussig, Richard Teweles, Ted Teweles, Andrew Thompson, Jonathan Tiemann, Sheridan Titman, George Trivoli, George Tsetsekos, Alan L. Tucker, Mel Tysseland, David Upton, Howard Van Auken, Pretorious Van den Dool, Pieter Vanderburg, Paul Vanderheiden, David Vang, Jim Verbrugge, Patrick Vincent, Steve Vinson, Susan Visscher, John Wachowicz, Mark D. Walker, Mike Walker, Sam Weaver, Kuo Chiang Wei, Bill Welch, Gary R. Wells, Fred Weston, Norm Williams, Tony Wingler, Ed Wolfe, Larry Wolken, Don Woods, Thomas Wright, Michael Yonan, Zhong-guo Zhou, David Ziebart, Dennis Zocco, and Kent Zumwalt.

Special thanks are due to Dana Clark, Susan Whitman, Amelia Bell, Stephanie Hodge, and Kirsten Benson, who provided invaluable editorial support; to Joel Houston and Phillip Daves, whose work with us on other books is reflected in this text; and to Lou Gapenski, our past co-author, for his many contributions.

Our colleagues and our students at the Universities of Florida and Tennessee gave us many useful suggestions, and the Cengage/South-Western staff—especially Mike Guendelsberger, Scott Fidler, Jacquelyn Featherly, Nate Anderson, and Mike Reynolds—helped greatly with all phases of text development, production, and marketing.

Errors in the Text

At this point, authors generally say something like this: "We appreciate all the help we received from the people listed above, but any remaining errors are, of course, our own responsibility." And in many books, there are plenty of remaining errors. Having experienced difficulties with errors ourselves, both as students and as instructors, we resolved to avoid this problem in *Corporate Finance*. As a result of our error detection procedures, we are convinced that the book is relatively free of mistakes.

Partly because of our confidence that few such errors remain, but primarily because we want to detect any errors in the textbook that may have slipped by so we can correct them in subsequent printings, we decided to offer a reward of $10 per error to the first person who reports a textbook error to us. For purposes of this reward, errors in the textbook are defined as misspelled words, nonrounding numerical errors, incorrect statements, and any other error that inhibits comprehension. Typesetting problems such as irregular spacing and differences in opinion regarding grammatical or punctuation conventions do not qualify for this reward. Also, given the ever-changing nature of the Internet, changes in Web addresses do not qualify as errors, although we would appreciate reports of changed Web addresses. Finally, any qualifying error that has follow-through effects is counted as two errors only. **Please report any errors to Michael C. Ehrhardt at the e-mail address given below.**

Conclusion

Finance is, in a real sense, the cornerstone of the free enterprise system. Good financial management is therefore vitally important to the economic health of business firms and hence to the nation and the world. Because of its importance, corporate finance should be thoroughly understood. However, this is easier said than done—the field is relatively complex, and it is undergoing constant change in response to shifts in economic conditions. All of this makes corporate finance stimulating and exciting but also challenging and sometimes perplexing. We sincerely hope that *Corporate Finance: A Focused Approach* will help readers understand and solve the financial problems faced by businesses today.

Michael C. Ehrhardt
University of Tennessee
Ehrhardt@utk.edu

Eugene F. Brigham
University of Florida
Gene.Brigham@cba.ufl.edu

January 2010

PART 1

Fundamental Concepts of Corporate Finance

Chapter 1
An Overview of Financial Management and the Financial Environment

Chapter 2
Financial Statements, Cash Flow, and Taxes

Chapter 3
Analysis of Financial Statements

CHAPTER 1

An Overview of Financial Management and the Financial Environment

In a global beauty contest for companies, the winner is ... Apple.

Or at least Apple is the most admired company in the world, according to Fortune *magazine's annual survey. The others in the global top ten are Berkshire Hathaway, Toyota, Google, Johnson & Johnson, Procter & Gamble, FedEx, Southwest Airlines, General Electric, and Microsoft. What do these companies have that separates them from the rest of the pack?*

See **http://money.cnn.com/magazines/fortune/** *for updates on the ranking.*

According to a survey of executives, directors, and security analysts, these companies have very high average scores across nine attributes: (1) innovativeness, (2) quality of management, (3) long-term investment value, (4) social responsibility, (5) employee talent, (6) quality of products and services, (7) financial soundness, (8) use of corporate assets, and (9) effectiveness in doing business globally. After culling weaker companies, the final rankings are then determined by over 3,700 experts from a wide variety of industries.

What do these companies have in common? First, they have an incredible focus on using technology to understand their customers, reduce costs, reduce inventory, and speed up product delivery. Second, they continually innovate and invest in ways to differentiate their products. Some are known for game-changing products, such as Apple's touch screen iPhone or Toyota's hybrid Prius. Others continually introduce small improvements, such as Southwest Airline's streamlined boarding procedures.

In addition to their acumen with technology and customers, they are also on the leading edge when it comes to training employees and providing a workplace in which people can thrive.

In a nutshell, these companies reduce costs by having innovative production processes, they create value for customers by providing high-quality products and services, and they create value for employees by training and fostering an environment that allows employees to utilize all of their skills and talents.

Do investors benefit from this focus on processes, customers, and employees? During the most recent 5-year period, these ten companies posted an average annual stock return of 6.9%, which is not too shabby when compared with the −4.1% average annual return of the S&P 500. These superior returns are due to superior cash flow generation. But, as you will see throughout this book, a company can generate cash flow only if it also creates value for its customers, employees, and suppliers.

The textbook's Web site has tools for teaching, learning, and conducting financial research.

This chapter should give you an idea of what financial management is all about, including an overview of the financial markets in which corporations operate. Before going into details, let's look at the big picture. You're probably in school because you want an interesting, challenging, and rewarding career. To see where finance fits in, here's a five-minute MBA.

1.1 The Five-Minute MBA

Okay, we realize you can't get an MBA in five minutes. But just as an artist quickly sketches the outline of a picture before filling in the details, we can sketch the key elements of an MBA education. The primary objective of an MBA program is to provide managers with the knowledge and skills they need to run successful companies, so we start our sketch with some common characteristics of successful companies. In particular, all successful companies are able to accomplish two main goals:

1. All successful companies identify, create, and deliver products or services that are highly valued by customers—so highly valued that customers choose to purchase from them rather than from their competitors.
2. All successful companies sell their products/services at prices that are high enough to cover costs and to compensate owners and creditors for the use of their money and their exposure to risk.

It's easy to talk about satisfying customers and investors, but it's not so easy to accomplish these goals. If it were, then all companies would be successful, and you wouldn't need an MBA!

The Key Attributes of Successful Companies

First, *successful companies have skilled people* at all levels inside the company, including leaders, managers, and a capable workforce.

Second, *successful companies have strong relationships* with groups outside the company. For example, successful companies develop win–win relationships with suppliers and excel in customer relationship management.

Third, *successful companies have enough funding* to execute their plans and support their operations. Most companies need cash to purchase land, buildings, equipment, and materials. Companies can reinvest a portion of their earnings, but most growing companies must also raise additional funds externally by some combination of selling stock and/or borrowing in the financial markets.

Just as a stool needs all three legs to stand, a successful company must have all three attributes: skilled people, strong external relationships, and sufficient capital.

The MBA, Finance, and Your Career

Consult **http://www.careers-in-finance.com** *for an excellent site containing information on a variety of business career areas, listings of current jobs, and other reference materials.*

To be successful, a company must meet its first main goal: identifying, creating, and delivering highly valued products and services to its customers. This requires that it possess all three of the key attributes mentioned above. Therefore, it's not surprising that most of your MBA courses are directly related to these attributes. For example, courses in economics, communication, strategy, organizational behavior, and human resources should prepare you for a leadership role and enable you to effectively manage your company's workforce. Other courses, such as marketing, operations management, and information technology, increase your knowledge of specific disciplines, enabling you to develop the efficient business processes and strong external relationships your company needs. Portions of *this* finance course will address

THE GLOBAL ECONOMIC CRISIS

Say Hello to the Global Economic Crisis!

Imagine a story of greed and reckless daring, of fortunes made and fortunes lost, of enormous corporations failing and even governments brought to the brink of ruin. No, this isn't a box-office blockbuster, but instead is the situation facing the world's financial markets and economies as we write this in mid-2009.

What exactly is the crisis? At the risk of oversimplification, many of the world's individuals, financial institutions, and governments borrowed too much money and used those borrowed funds to make speculative investments. As those investments are turning out to be worth less than the amounts owed by the borrowers, widespread bankruptcies, buyouts, and restructurings for both borrowers and lenders are occurring. This in turn is reducing the supply of available funds that financial institutions normally lend to creditworthy individuals, manufacturers, and retailers. Without access to credit, consumers are buying less, manufacturers are producing less, and retailers are selling less—all of which leads to layoffs. Because of falling consumption, shrinking production, and higher unemployment, the National Bureau of Economic Research declared that the United States entered a recession in December 2007. In fact, this is a global downturn, and most economists expect it to be severe and lengthy.

As we progress through this chapter and the rest of the book, we will discuss different aspects of the crisis. For real-time updates, go to the Global Economic Crisis (GEC) Resource Center at **http://www.cengage.com/gec** and log in.

raising the capital your company needs to implement its plans. In short, your MBA courses will give you the skills you need to help a company achieve its first goal: producing goods and services that customers want.

Recall, though, that it's not enough just to have highly valued products and satisfied customers. Successful companies must also meet their second main goal, which is generating enough cash to compensate the investors who provided the necessary capital. To help your company accomplish this second goal, you must be able to evaluate any proposal, whether it relates to marketing, production, strategy, or any other area, and implement only the projects that add value for your investors. For this, you must have expertise in finance, no matter your major. Thus, finance is a critical part of an MBA education, and it will help you throughout your career.

Self-Test

What are the goals of successful companies?
What are the three key attributes common to all successful companies?
How does expertise in finance help a company become successful?

1.2 The Corporate Life Cycle

Many major corporations, including Apple Computer and Hewlett-Packard, began life in a garage or basement. How is it possible for such companies to grow into the giants we see today? No two companies develop in exactly the same way, but the following sections describe some typical stages in the corporate life cycle.

Starting Up as a Proprietorship

Many companies begin as a **proprietorship**, which is an unincorporated business owned by one individual. Starting a business as a proprietor is easy—one merely begins business operations after obtaining any required city or state business licenses. The proprietorship has three important advantages: (1) it is easily and inexpensively

Columbus Was Wrong—the World *Is* Flat! And Hot, and Crowded!

In his best-selling book *The World Is Flat,* Thomas L. Friedman argues that many of the barriers that long protected businesses and employees from global competition have been broken down by dramatic improvements in communication and transportation technologies. The result is a level playing field that spans the entire world. As we move into the information age, any work that can be digitized will flow to those able to do it at the lowest cost, whether they live in San Jose's Silicon Valley or Bangalore, India. For physical products, supply chains now span the world. For example, raw materials might be extracted in South America, fabricated into electronic components in Asia, and then used in computers assembled in the United States, with the final product being sold in Europe.

Similar changes are occurring in the financial markets, as capital flows across the globe to those who can best use it. Indeed, China raised more money through initial public offerings than any other country in 2006, and the euro is becoming the currency of choice for denominating global bond issues.

Unfortunately, a dynamic world can bring runaway growth, which can lead to significant environmental problems and energy shortages. Friedman describes these problems in another bestseller, *Hot, Flat, and Crowded.* In a flat world, the keys to success are knowledge, skills, and a great work ethic. In a flat, hot, and crowded world, these factors must be combined with innovation and creativity to deal with truly global problems.

formed, (2) it is subject to few government regulations, and (3) its income is not subject to corporate taxation but is taxed as part of the proprietor's personal income.

However, the proprietorship also has three important limitations: (1) it may be difficult for a proprietorship to obtain the capital needed for growth; (2) the proprietor has unlimited personal liability for the business's debts, which can result in losses that exceed the money invested in the company (creditors may even be able to seize a proprietor's house or other personal property!); and (3) the life of a proprietorship is limited to the life of its founder. For these three reasons, sole proprietorships are used primarily for small businesses. In fact, proprietorships account for only about 13% of all sales, based on dollar values, even though about 80% of all companies are proprietorships.

More Than One Owner: A Partnership

Some companies start with more than one owner, and some proprietors decide to add a partner as the business grows. A **partnership** exists whenever two or more persons or entities associate to conduct a noncorporate business for profit. Partnerships may operate under different degrees of formality, ranging from informal, oral understandings to formal agreements filed with the secretary of the state in which the partnership was formed. Partnership agreements define the ways any profits and losses are shared between partners. A partnership's advantages and disadvantages are generally similar to those of a proprietorship.

Regarding liability, the partners can potentially lose all of their personal assets, even assets not invested in the business, because under partnership law, each partner is liable for the business's debts. Therefore, in the event the partnership goes bankrupt, if any partner is unable to meet his or her pro rata liability then the remaining partners must make good on the unsatisfied claims, drawing on their personal assets to the extent necessary. To avoid this, it is possible to limit the liabilities of some of the partners by establishing a **limited partnership**, wherein certain partners are designated **general partners** and others **limited partners**. In a limited partnership, the limited partners can lose only the amount of their investment in the partnership, while the general partners have unlimited liability. However, the limited partners typically have no control—it rests solely with the general partners—and their returns are likewise limited. Limited partnerships are common in real estate, oil, equipment leasing ventures, and venture capital. However, they are not widely used in general business situations because usually no one partner is willing to be the general partner and thus accept the majority of the business's risk, and none of the others are willing to be limited partners and give up all control.

In both regular and limited partnerships, at least one partner is liable for the debts of the partnership. However, in a **limited liability partnership (LLP)**, sometimes called a **limited liability company (LLC)**, all partners enjoy limited liability with regard to the business's liabilities, and their potential losses are limited to their investment in the LLP. Of course, this arrangement increases the risk faced by an LLP's lenders, customers, and suppliers.

Many Owners: A Corporation

Most partnerships have difficulty attracting substantial amounts of capital. This is generally not a problem for a slow-growing business, but if a business's products or services really catch on, and if it needs to raise large sums of money to capitalize on its opportunities, then the difficulty in attracting capital becomes a real drawback. Thus, many growth companies, such as Hewlett-Packard and Microsoft, began life as a proprietorship or partnership, but at some point their founders decided to convert to a corporation. On the other hand, some companies, in anticipation of growth, actually begin as corporations. A **corporation** is a legal entity created under state laws, and it is separate and distinct from its owners and managers. This separation gives the corporation three major advantages: (1) *unlimited life*—a corporation can continue after its original owners and managers are deceased; (2) *easy transferability of ownership interest*—ownership interests are divided into shares of stock, which can be transferred far more easily than can proprietorship or partnership interests; and (3) *limited liability*—losses are limited to the actual funds invested.

To illustrate limited liability, suppose you invested $10,000 in a partnership that then went bankrupt and owed $1 million. Because the owners are liable for the debts of a partnership, you could be assessed for a share of the company's debt, and you could be held liable for the entire $1 million if your partners could not pay their shares. On the other hand, if you invested $10,000 in the stock of a corporation that went bankrupt, your potential loss on the investment would be limited to your $10,000 investment.[1] Unlimited life, easy transferability of ownership interest, and limited liability make it much easier for corporations than proprietorships or partnerships to raise money in the financial markets and grow into large companies.

The corporate form offers significant advantages over proprietorships and partnerships, but it also has two disadvantages: (1) Corporate earnings may be subject to double taxation—the earnings of the corporation are taxed at the corporate level, and then earnings paid out as dividends are taxed again as income to the stockholders. (2) Setting up a corporation involves preparing a charter, writing a set of bylaws, and filing the many required state and federal reports, which is more complex and time-consuming than creating a proprietorship or a partnership.

The **charter** includes the following information: (1) name of the proposed corporation, (2) types of activities it will pursue, (3) amount of capital stock, (4) number of

[1]In the case of very small corporations, the limited liability may be fiction because lenders frequently require personal guarantees from the stockholders.

directors, and (5) names and addresses of directors. The charter is filed with the secretary of the state in which the firm will be incorporated, and when it is approved, the corporation is officially in existence.[2] After the corporation begins operating, quarterly and annual employment, financial, and tax reports must be filed with state and federal authorities.

The **bylaws** are a set of rules drawn up by the founders of the corporation. Included are such points as (1) how directors are to be elected (all elected each year or perhaps one-third each year for 3-year terms); (2) whether the existing stockholders will have the first right to buy any new shares the firm issues; and (3) procedures for changing the bylaws themselves, should conditions require it.

There are actually several different types of corporations. Professionals such as doctors, lawyers, and accountants often form a **professional corporation (PC)** or a **professional association (PA)**. These types of corporations do not relieve the participants of professional (malpractice) liability. Indeed, the primary motivation behind the professional corporation was to provide a way for groups of professionals to incorporate and thus avoid certain types of unlimited liability yet still be held responsible for professional liability.

Finally, if certain requirements are met, particularly with regard to size and number of stockholders, owners can establish a corporation but elect to be taxed as if the business were a proprietorship or partnership. Such firms, which differ not in organizational form but only in how their owners are taxed, are called **S corporations**.

Growing and Managing a Corporation

Once a corporation has been established, how does it evolve? When entrepreneurs start a company, they usually provide all the financing from their personal resources, which may include savings, home equity loans, or even credit cards. As the corporation grows, it will need factories, equipment, inventory, and other resources to support its growth. In time, the entrepreneurs usually deplete their own resources and must turn to external financing. Many young companies are too risky for banks, so the founders must sell stock to outsiders, including friends, family, private investors (often called angels), or venture capitalists. If the corporation continues to grow, it may become successful enough to attract lending from banks, or it may even raise additional funds through an **initial public offering (IPO)** by selling stock to the public at large. After an IPO, corporations support their growth by borrowing from banks, issuing debt, or selling additional shares of stock. In short, a corporation's ability to grow depends on its interactions with the financial markets, which we describe in much more detail later in this chapter.

For proprietorships, partnerships, and small corporations, the firm's owners are also its managers. This is usually not true for a large corporation, which means that large firms' stockholders, who are its owners, face a serious problem. What is to prevent managers from acting in their own best interests, rather than in the best interests of the stockholder/owners? This is called an **agency problem**, because managers are hired as agents to act on behalf of the owners. Agency problems can be addressed by a company's **corporate governance**, which is the set of rules that control the company's behavior towards its directors, managers, employees, shareholders, creditors, customers, competitors, and community. We will have much more to say about

---

[2]More than 60% of major U.S. corporations are chartered in Delaware, which has, over the years, provided a favorable legal environment for corporations. It is not necessary for a firm to be headquartered, or even to conduct operations, in its state of incorporation, or even in its country of incorporation.

agency problems and corporate governance throughout the book, especially in Chapters 13 and 14.[3]

Self-Test

What are the key differences between proprietorships, partnerships, and corporations?

Describe some special types of partnerships and corporations, and explain the differences among them.

1.3 The Primary Objective of the Corporation: Value Maximization

Shareholders are the owners of a corporation, and they purchase stocks because they want to earn a good return on their investment without undue risk exposure. In most cases, shareholders elect directors, who then hire managers to run the corporation on a day-to-day basis. Because managers are supposed to be working on behalf of shareholders, they should pursue policies that enhance shareholder value. Consequently, throughout this book we operate on the assumption that management's primary objective is *stockholder wealth maximization*.

The **market price** is the stock price that we observe in the financial markets. We later explain in detail how stock prices are determined, but for now it is enough to say that a company's market price incorporates the information available to investors. If the market price reflects all *relevant* information, then the observed price is also the **intrinsic**, or **fundamental, price**. However, investors rarely have all relevant information. For example, companies report most major decisions, but they sometimes withhold selected information to prevent competitors from gaining strategic advantages.

Unfortunately, some managers deliberately mislead investors by taking actions to make their companies appear more valuable than they truly are. Sometimes these actions are illegal, such as those taken by the senior managers at Enron. Sometimes the actions are legal but are taken to push the current market price above its fundamental price in the short term. For example, suppose a utility's stock price is equal to its fundamental price of $50 per share. What would happen if the utility substantially reduced its tree-trimming program but didn't tell investors? This would lower current costs and thus boost current earnings and current cash flow, but it would also lead to major expenditures in the future when falling limbs damage the lines. If investors were told about the major repair costs facing the company, the market price would immediately drop to a new fundamental value of $45. But if investors were kept in the dark, they might misinterpret the higher-than-expected current earnings, and the market price might go up to $52. Investors would eventually understand the situation when the company later incurred large costs to repair the damaged lines; when that happened, the price would fall to its fundamental value of $45.

Consider this hypothetical sequence of events. A company's managers deceived investors, and the price rose to $52 when it would have fallen to $45 if not for the deception. Of course, this benefited those who owned the stock at the time of the deception, including managers with stock options. But when the deception came to light, those

[3]The classic work on agency theory is Michael C. Jensen and William H. Meckling's "Theory of the Firm, Managerial Behavior, Agency Costs, and Ownership Structure," *Journal of Financial Economics*, October 1976, 305–360. Another article by Jensen specifically addresses these issues; see "Value Maximization, Stakeholder Theory, and the Corporate Objective Function," *Journal of Applied Corporate Finance*, Fall 2001, 8–21. For an overview of corporate governance, see Stuart Gillan, "Recent Developments in Corporate Governance: An Overview," *Journal of Corporate Finance*, June 2006, 381–402.

Ethics for Individuals and Businesses

A firm's commitment to business ethics can be measured by the tendency of its employees, from the top down, to adhere to laws, regulations, and moral standards relating to product safety and quality, fair employment practices, fair marketing and selling practices, the use of confidential information for personal gain, community involvement, and illegal payments to obtain business.

Ethical Dilemmas

When conflicts arise between profits and ethics, sometimes legal and ethical considerations make the choice obvious. At other times the right choice isn't clear. For example, suppose Norfolk Southern's managers know that its trains are polluting the air, but the amount of pollution is within legal limits and further reduction would be costly, causing harm to their shareholders. Are the managers ethically bound to reduce pollution? Aren't they also ethically bound to act in their shareholders' best interests? This is clearly a dilemma.

Ethical Responsibility

Over the past few years, illegal ethical lapses have led to a number of bankruptcies, which have raised this question: Were the *companies* unethical, or was it just a few of their *employees*? Arthur Andersen, an accounting firm, audited Enron, WorldCom, and several other companies that committed accounting fraud. The U.S. Justice Department concluded that Andersen itself was guilty because it fostered a climate in which unethical behavior was permitted, and it built an incentive system that made such behavior profitable to both the perpetrators and the firm itself. As a result, Andersen went out of business. Anderson was later judged to be not guilty, but by the time the judgment was rendered the company was already out of business. People simply did not want to deal with a tainted accounting firm.

Protecting Ethical Employees

If employees discover questionable activities or are given questionable orders, should they obey their bosses' orders, refuse to obey those orders, or report the situation to a higher authority, such as the company's board of directors, its auditors, or a federal prosecutor? In 2002 Congress passed the Sarbanes-Oxley Act, with a provision designed to protect "whistle-blowers." If an employee reports corporate wrongdoing and later is penalized, he or she can ask the Occupational Safety and Health Administration to investigate the situation, and if the employee was improperly penalized, the company can be required to reinstate the person, along with back pay and a sizable penalty award. Several big awards have been handed out since the act was passed.

stockholders who still owned the stock suffered a significant loss, ending up with stock worth less than its original fundamental value. If the managers cashed in their stock options prior to this, then only the stockholders were hurt by the deception. Because the managers were hired to act in the interests of stockholders, their deception was a breach of their fiduciary responsibility. In addition, the managers' deception would damage the company's reputation, making it harder to raise capital in the future.

Therefore, when we say management's objective should be to maximize stockholder wealth, we really mean it is to *maximize the fundamental price of the firm's common stock*, not just the current market price. Firms do, of course, have other objectives; in particular, the managers who make the actual decisions are interested in their own personal satisfaction, in their employees' welfare, and in the good of their communities and of society at large. Still, for the reasons set forth in the following sections, *maximizing intrinsic stock value is the most important objective for most corporations.*

Intrinsic Stock Value Maximization and Social Welfare

If a firm attempts to maximize its intrinsic stock value, is this good or bad for society? In general, it is good. Aside from such illegal actions as fraudulent accounting, ex-

The Security Industry Association's Web site, **http://www.sifma.org**, is a great source of information. To find data on stock ownership, go to its Web page, click on Research, choose Surveys, then Equity/Bond Ownership in America. You can purchase the most recent data, or look at the prior year for free.

ploiting monopoly power, violating safety codes, and failing to meet environmental standards, *the same actions that maximize intrinsic stock values also benefit society*. Here are some of the reasons:

1. **To a large extent, the owners of stock *are* society.** Seventy-five years ago this was not true, because most stock ownership was concentrated in the hands of a relatively small segment of society consisting of the wealthiest individuals. Since then, there has been explosive growth in pension funds, life insurance companies, and mutual funds. These institutions now own more than 61% of all stock, which means that most individuals have an indirect stake in the stock market. In addition, more than 47% of all U.S. households now own stock or bonds directly, as compared with only 32.5% in 1989. Thus, most members of society now have an important stake in the stock market, either directly or indirectly. Therefore, when a manager takes actions to maximize the stock price, this improves the quality of life for millions of ordinary citizens.
2. **Consumers benefit.** Stock price maximization requires efficient, low-cost businesses that produce high-quality goods and services at the lowest possible cost. This means that companies must develop products and services that consumers want and need, which leads to new technology and new products. Also, companies that maximize their stock price must generate growth in sales by creating value for customers in the form of efficient and courteous service, adequate stocks of merchandise, and well-located business establishments.

   People sometimes argue that firms, in their efforts to raise profits and stock prices, increase product prices and gouge the public. In a reasonably competitive economy, which we have, prices are constrained by competition and consumer resistance. If a firm raises its prices beyond reasonable levels, it will simply lose its market share. Even giant firms such as Dell and Coca-Cola lose business to domestic and foreign competitors if they set prices above the level necessary to cover production costs plus a "normal" profit. Of course, firms *want* to earn more, and they constantly try to cut costs, develop new products, and so on, and thereby earn above-normal profits. Note, though, that if they are indeed successful and do earn above-normal profits, those very profits will attract competition, which will eventually drive prices down. So again, the main long-term beneficiary is the consumer.
3. **Employees benefit.** There are situations where a stock increases when a company announces plans to lay off employees, but viewed over time this is the exception rather than the rule. In general, companies that successfully increase stock prices also grow and add more employees, thus benefiting society. Note too that many governments across the world, including U.S. federal and state governments, are privatizing some of their state-owned activities by selling these operations to investors. Perhaps not surprisingly, the sales and cash flows of recently privatized companies generally improve. Moreover, studies show that newly privatized companies tend to grow and thus require more employees when they are managed with the goal of stock price maximization.

   One of *Fortune* magazine's key criteria in determining its list of most-admired companies is a company's ability to attract, develop, and retain talented people. The results consistently show high correlations among admiration for a company, its ability to satisfy employees, and its creation of value for shareholders. Employees find that it is both fun and financially rewarding to work for successful companies. Thus, successful companies get the cream of the employee crop, and skilled, motivated employees are one of the keys to corporate success.

Managerial Actions to Maximize Shareholder Wealth

What types of actions can managers take to maximize shareholder wealth? To answer this question, we first need to ask, "What determines a firm's value?" In a nutshell, it is *a company's ability to generate cash flows now and in the future.*

We address different aspects of this in detail throughout the book, but we can lay out three basic facts now: (1) any financial asset, including a company's stock, is valuable only to the extent that it generates cash flows; (2) the timing of cash flows matters—cash received sooner is better; and (3) investors are averse to risk, so all else equal, they will pay more for a stock whose cash flows are relatively certain than for one whose cash flows are more risky. Because of these three facts, managers can enhance their firm's value by increasing the size of the expected cash flows, by speeding up their receipt, and by reducing their risk.

The cash flows that matter are called **free cash flows (FCF)**, not because they are free, but because they are available (or free) for distribution to all of the company's investors, including creditors and stockholders. You will learn how to calculate free cash flows in Chapter 2, but for now you should know that free cash flows depend on three factors: (1) sales revenues, (2) operating costs and taxes, and (3) required new investments in operating capital. In particular, free cash flow is equal to:

$$\begin{aligned}\text{FCF} = \text{Sales revenues} &- \text{Operating costs} - \text{Operating taxes}\\ &- \text{Required new investments in operating capital}\end{aligned}$$

Brand managers and marketing managers can increase sales (and prices) by truly understanding their customers and then designing goods and services that customers want. Human resource managers can improve productivity through training and employee retention. Production and logistics managers can improve profit margins, reduce inventory, and improve throughput at factories by implementing supply chain management, just-in-time inventory management, and lean manufacturing. In fact, all managers make decisions that can increase free cash flows.

One of the financial manager's roles is to help others see how their actions affect the company's ability to generate cash flow and, hence, its intrinsic value. Financial managers also must decide *how to finance the firm.* In particular, they must choose the mix of debt and equity that should be used and the specific types of debt and equity securities that should be issued. They must also decide what percentage of current earnings should be retained and reinvested rather than paid out as dividends. Along with these financing decisions, the general level of interest rates in the economy, the risk of the firm's operations, and stock market investors' overall attitude toward risk determine the rate of return that is required to satisfy a firm's investors. This rate of return from an investor's perspective is a cost from the company's point of view. Therefore, the rate of return required by investors is called the **weighted average cost of capital (WACC)**.

The relationship between a firm's fundamental value, its free cash flows, and its cost of capital is defined by the following equation:

$$\text{Value} = \frac{\text{FCF}_1}{(1+\text{WACC})^1} + \frac{\text{FCF}_2}{(1+\text{WACC})^2} + \frac{\text{FCF}_3}{(1+\text{WACC})^3} + \cdots + \frac{\text{FCF}_\infty}{(1+\text{WACC})^\infty} \quad \text{(1-1)}$$

We will explain how to use this equation in later chapters, but for now note that (1) a growing firm often needs to raise external funds in the financial markets and

Corporate Scandals and Maximizing Stock Price

The list of corporate scandals seems to go on forever: Sunbeam, Enron, ImClone, WorldCom, Tyco, Adelphia .... At first glance, it's tempting to say, "Look what happens when managers care only about maximizing stock price." But a closer look reveals a much different story. In fact, if these managers were trying to maximize stock price, they failed dismally, given the resulting values of these companies.

Although details vary from company to company, a few common themes emerge. First, managerial compensation was linked to the *short-term* performance of the stock price via poorly designed stock option and stock grant programs. This provided managers with a powerful incentive to drive up the stock price at the option vesting date without worrying about the future. Second, it is virtually impossible to take *legal and ethical* actions that drive up the stock price in the short term without harming it in the long term because the value of a company is based on all of its future free cash flows and not just cash flows in the immediate future. Because legal and ethical actions to quickly drive up the stock price didn't exist (other than the old-fashioned ones, such as increasing sales, cutting costs, or reducing capital requirements), these managers began bending a few rules. Third, as they initially got away with bending rules, it seems that their egos and hubris grew to such an extent that they felt they were above all rules, so they began breaking even more rules.

Stock prices did go up, at least temporarily, but as Abraham Lincoln said, "You can't fool all of the people all of the time." As the scandals became public, the stocks' prices plummeted, and in some cases the companies were ruined.

There are several important lessons to be learned from these examples. First, people respond to incentives, and poorly designed incentives can cause disastrous results. Second, ethical violations usually begin with small steps, so if stockholders want managers to avoid large ethical violations, then they shouldn't let them make the small ones. Third, there is no shortcut to creating lasting value. It takes hard work to increase sales, cut costs, and reduce capital requirements, but this is the formula for success.

(2) the actual price of a firm's stock is determined in those markets. Therefore, the rest of this chapter focuses on financial markets.

Self-Test

What should be management's primary objective?
How does maximizing the fundamental stock price benefit society?
Free cash flow depends on what three factors?
How is a firm's fundamental value related to its free cash flows and its cost of capital?

1.4 An Overview of the Capital Allocation Process

Businesses often need capital to implement growth plans; governments require funds to finance building projects; and individuals frequently want loans to purchase cars, homes, and education. Where can they get this money? Fortunately, there are some individuals and firms with incomes greater than their expenditures. In contrast to William Shakespeare's advice, most individuals and firms are both borrowers and lenders. For example, an individual might borrow money with a car loan or a home mortgage but might also lend money through a bank savings account. In the aggregate, individuals are net savers and provide most of the funds ultimately used by nonfinancial corporations. Although most nonfinancial corporations own some financial securities, such as short-term Treasury bills, nonfinancial corporations are net borrowers in the aggregate. It should be no surprise to you that in the United States federal, state, and local governments are also net borrowers in the aggregate (although many foreign governments, such as those of China and oil-producing countries, are actually net lenders). Banks and other financial corporations raise money with one hand and invest it with the other. For example, a bank might raise money from individuals in the form of a savings account and then lend most of that money to business customers. In the aggregate, financial corporations borrow slightly more than they lend.

Transfers of capital between savers and those who need capital take place in three different ways. Direct transfers of money and securities, as shown in Panel 1 of Figure 1-1, occur when a business (or government) sells its securities directly to savers. The business delivers its securities to savers, who in turn provide the firm with the money it needs. For example, a privately held company might sell shares of stock directly to a new shareholder, or the U.S. government might sell a Treasury bond directly to an individual investor.

As shown in Panel 2, indirect transfers may go through an **investment banking house** such as Goldman Sachs, which *underwrites* the issue. An underwriter serves as a middleman and facilitates the issuance of securities. The company sells its stocks or bonds to the investment bank, which in turn sells these same securities to savers. Because new securities are involved and the corporation receives the proceeds of the sale, this is a "primary" market transaction.

Transfers can also be made through a **financial intermediary** such as a bank or mutual fund, as shown in Panel 3. Here the intermediary obtains funds from savers in exchange for its own securities. The intermediary then uses this money to purchase and then hold businesses' securities. For example, a saver might give dollars to a bank and receive a certificate of deposit, and then the bank might lend the money to a small business, receiving in exchange a signed loan. Thus, intermediaries literally create new types of securities.

FIGURE 1-1 Diagram of the Capital Allocation Process

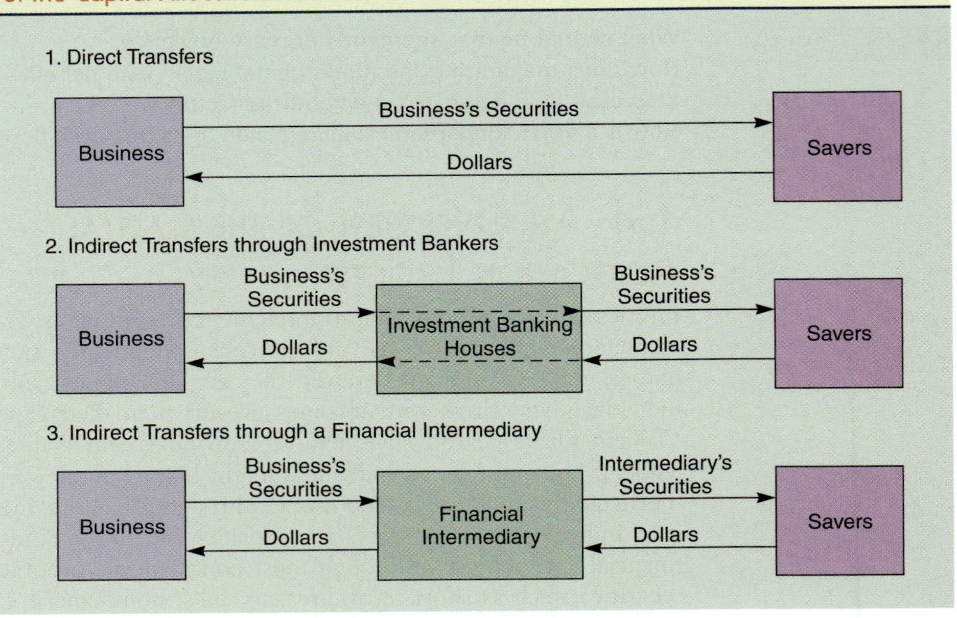

There are three important characteristics of the capital allocation process. First, new financial securities are created. Second, financial institutions are often involved. Third, allocation between providers and users of funds occurs in financial markets. The following sections discuss each of these characteristics.

Self-Test

Identify three ways that capital is transferred between savers and borrowers.
Distinguish between the roles played by investment banking houses and financial intermediaries.

WWW

You can access current and historical interest rates and economic data from the Federal Reserve Economic Data (FRED) site at **http://www.stls.frb.org/fred/**.

1.5 Financial Securities

The variety of financial securities is limited only by human creativity, ingenuity, and governmental regulations. At the risk of oversimplification, we can classify most financial securities by the type of claim and the time until maturity. In addition, some securities actually are created from packages of other securities. We discuss the key aspects of financial securities in this section.

Type of Claim: Debt, Equity, or Derivatives

Financial securities are simply pieces of paper with contractual provisions that entitle their owners to specific rights and claims on specific cash flows or values. Debt instruments typically have specified payments and a specified maturity. For example, an Alcoa bond might promise to pay 10% interest for 30 years, at which time it promises to make a $1,000 principal payment. If debt matures in more than a year, it is called a *capital market security*. Thus, the Alcoa bond in this example is a capital market security.

If the debt matures in less than a year, it is a *money market security*. For example, Home Depot might expect to receive $300,000 in 75 days, but it needs cash now. Home Depot might issue commercial paper, which is essentially an IOU. In this example, Home Depot might agree to pay $300,000 in 75 days in exchange for $297,000 today. Thus, commercial paper is a money market security.

Equity instruments are a claim upon a residual value. For example, Alcoa's stockholders are entitled to the cash flows generated by Alcoa after its bondholders, creditors, and other claimants have been satisfied. Because stock has no maturity date, it is a capital market security.

For an overview of derivatives, see **Web Extension 1A** *on the textbook's Web site.*

Notice that debt and equity represent claims upon the cash flows generated by real assets, such as the cash flows generated by Alcoa's factories and operations. In contrast, **derivatives** are securities whose values depend on, or are *derived* from, the values of some other traded assets. For example, options and futures are two important types of derivatives, and their values depend on the prices of other assets. An option on Alcoa stock or a futures contract to buy pork bellies are examples of derivatives. We discuss options in Chapter 8 and in ***Web Extension 1A***, which provides a brief overview of options and other derivatives.

Some securities are a mix of debt, equity, and derivatives. For example, preferred stock has some features like debt and some like equity, while convertible debt has both debt-like and option-like features.

We discuss these and other financial securities in detail later in the book, but Table 1-1 provides a summary of the most important conventional financial securities. We discuss rates of return later in this chapter, but notice now in Table 1-1 that interest rates tend to increase with the maturity and risk of the security.

TABLE 1-1 Summary of Major Financial Instruments

INSTRUMENT	MAJOR PARTICIPANTS	RISK	ORIGINAL MATURITY	RATES OF RETURN ON 1/08/09[a]
U.S. Treasury bills	Sold by U.S. Treasury	Default-free	91 days to 1 year	0.41%
Bankers' acceptances	A firm's promise to pay, guaranteed by a bank	Low if strong bank guarantees	Up to 180 days	1.5%
Commercial paper	Issued by financially secure firms to large investors	Low default risk	Up to 270 days	0.28%
Negotiable certificates of deposit (CDs)	Issued by major banks to large investors	Depends on strength of issuer	Up to 1 year	1.58%
Money market mutual funds	Invest in short-term debt; held by individuals and businesses	Low degree of risk	No specific maturity (instant liquidity)	1.27%
Eurodollar market time deposits	Issued by banks outside U.S.	Depends on strength of issuer	Up to 1 year	2.60%
Consumer credit loans	Loans by banks/credit unions/finance companies	Risk is variable	Variable	Variable
Commercial loans	Loans by banks to corporations	Depends on borrower	Up to 7 years	Tied to prime rate (3.25%) or LIBOR (2.02%)[b]
U.S. Treasury notes and bonds	Issued by U.S. government	No default risk, but price falls if interest rates rise	2 to 30 years	3.04%
Mortgages	Loans secured by property	Risk is variable	Up to 30 years	5.02%
Municipal bonds	Issued by state and local governments to individuals and institutions	Riskier than U.S. government bonds, but exempt from most taxes	Up to 30 years	5.02%
Corporate bonds	Issued by corporations to individuals and institutions	Riskier than U.S. government debt; depends on strength of issuer	Up to 40 years[c]	5.03%
Leases	Similar to debt; firms lease assets rather than borrow and then buy them	Risk similar to corporate bonds	Generally 3 to 20 years	Similar to bond yields
Preferred stocks	Issued by corporations to individuals and institutions	Riskier than corporate bonds	Unlimited	6% to 9%
Common stocks[d]	Issued by corporations to individuals and institutions	Riskier than preferred stocks	Unlimited	9% to 15%

[a]Data are from *The Wall Street Journal* (**http://online.wsj.com**) or the *Federal Reserve Statistical Release* (**http://www.federalreserve.gov/releases/H15/update**). Bankers' acceptances assume a 3-month maturity. Money market rates are for the Merrill Lynch Ready Assets Trust. The corporate bond rate is for AAA-rated bonds.

[b]The prime rate is the rate U.S. banks charge to good customers. LIBOR (London Interbank Offered Rate) is the rate that U.K. banks charge one another.

[c]A few corporations have issued 100-year bonds; however, most have issued bonds with maturities of less than 40 years.

[d]Common stocks are expected to provide a "return" in the form of dividends and capital gains rather than interest. Of course, if you buy a stock, your *actual* return may be considerably higher or lower than your *expected* return.

Some securities are created from packages of other securities, a process called *securitization*. The misuse of securitized assets is one of the primary causes of the global financial crisis, so we discuss securitization next.

The Process of Securitization

Many types of assets can be securitized, but we will focus on mortgages because they played such an important role in the global financial crisis. At one time, most mortgages were made by **savings and loan associations (S&Ls)**, which took in the vast majority of their deposits from individuals who lived in nearby neighborhoods. The S&Ls pooled these deposits and then lent money to people in the neighborhood in the form of fixed-rate mortgages, which were pieces of paper signed by borrowers promising to make specified payments to the S&L. The new homeowners paid principal and interest to the S&L, which then paid interest to its depositors and reinvested the principal repayments in other mortgages. This was clearly better than having individuals lend directly to aspiring homeowners, because a single individual might not have enough money to finance an entire house nor the expertise to know if the borrower was creditworthy. Note that the S&Ls were government-chartered institutions, and they obtained money in the form of immediately withdrawable deposits and then invested most of it in the form of mortgages with fixed interest rates and on individual homes. Also, initially the S&Ls were not permitted to have branch operations—they were limited to one office so as to maintain their local orientation.

These restrictions had important implications. First, in the 1950s there was a massive migration of people to the west, so there was a strong demand for funds in that area. However, the wealthiest savers were in the east. That meant that mortgage interest rates were much higher in California and other western states than in New York and the east. This created disequilibrium, something that can't exist forever in financial markets.

Second, note that the S&Ls' assets consisted mainly of long-term, fixed-rate mortgages, but their liabilities were in the form of deposits that could be withdrawn immediately. The combination of long-term assets and short-term liabilities created another problem. If the overall level of interest rates increased, the S&Ls would have to increase the rates they paid on deposits or else savers would take their money elsewhere. However, the S&Ls couldn't increase the rates on their outstanding mortgages because these mortgages had fixed interest rates. This problem came to a head in the 1960s, when the Vietnam War led to inflation, which pushed up interest rates. At this point, the "money market fund" industry was born, and it literally sucked money out of the S&Ls, forcing many of them into bankruptcy.

The government responded by giving the S&Ls broader lending powers, permitting nationwide branching, and allowing them to obtain funds as long-term debt in addition to immediately withdrawable deposits. Unfortunately, these changes had another set of unintended consequences. S&L managers who had previously dealt with a limited array of investments and funding choices in local communities were suddenly allowed to expand their scope of operations. Many of these inexperienced S&L managers made poor business decisions and the result was disastrous—virtually the entire S&L industry collapsed, with many S&Ls going bankrupt or being acquired in shotgun mergers with commercial banks.

The demise of the S&Ls created another financial disequilibrium—a higher demand for mortgages than the supply of available funds from the mortgage lending industry. Savings were accumulating in pension funds, insurance companies, and other institutions, not in S&Ls and banks, the traditional mortgage lenders.

This situation led to the development of "mortgage securitization," a process whereby banks, the remaining S&Ls, and specialized mortgage originating firms would originate mortgages and then sell them to investment banks, which would bundle them into packages and then use these packages as collateral for bonds that could be sold to pension funds, insurance companies, and other institutional investors. Thus, individual loans were bundled and then used to back a bond—a "security"—that could be traded in the financial markets.

Congress facilitated this process by creating two stockholder-owned but government-sponsored entities, the Federal National Mortgage Association (Fannie Mae) and the Federal Home Loan Mortgage Corporation (Freddie Mac). Fannie Mae and Freddie Mac were financed by issuing a relatively small amount of stock and a huge amount of debt.

To illustrate the securitization process, suppose an S&L or bank is paying its depositors 5% but is charging its borrowers 8% on their mortgages. The S&L can take hundreds of these mortgages, put them in a pool, and then sell the pool to Fannie Mae. The mortgagees can still make their payments to the original S&L, which will then forward the payments (less a small handling fee) to Fannie Mae.

Consider the S&L's perspective. First, it can use the cash it receives from selling the mortgages to make additional loans to other aspiring homeowners. Second, the S&L is no longer exposed to the risk of owning mortgages. The risk hasn't disappeared—it has been transferred from the S&L (and its federal deposit insurers) to Fannie Mae. This is clearly a better situation for aspiring homeowners and perhaps also for taxpayers.

Fannie Mae can take the mortgages it just bought, put them into a very large pool, and sell bonds backed by the pool to investors. The homeowner will pay the S&L, the S&L will forward the payment to Fannie Mae, and Fannie Mae will use the funds to pay interest on the bonds it issued, to pay dividends on its stock, and to buy additional mortgages from S&Ls, which can then make additional loans to aspiring homeowners. Notice that the mortgage risk has been shifted from Fannie Mae to the investors who now own the mortgage-backed bonds.

How does the situation look from the perspective of the investors who own the bonds? In theory, they own a share in a large pool of mortgages from all over the country, so a problem in a particular region's real estate market or job market won't affect the whole pool. Therefore, their expected rate of return should be very close to the 8% rate paid by the home-owning mortgagees. (It will be a little less due to handling fees charged by the S&L and Fannie Mae and to the small amount of expected losses from the homeowners who could be expected to default on their mortgages.) These investors could have deposited their money at an S&L and earned a virtually risk-free 5%. Instead, they chose to accept more risk in hopes of the higher 8% return. Note too that mortgage-backed bonds are more liquid than individual mortgage loans, so the securitization process increases liquidity, which is desirable. The bottom line is that risk has been reduced by the pooling process and then allocated to those who are willing to accept it in return for a higher rate of return.

Thus, in theory it is a win–win–win situation: More money is available for aspiring homeowners, S&Ls (and taxpayers) have less risk, and there are opportunities for investors who are willing to take on more risk to obtain higher potential returns. Although the securitization process began with mortgages, it is now being used with car loans, student loans, credit card debt, and other loans. The details vary for different assets, but the processes and benefits are similar to those with mortgage securitization: (1) increased supplies of lendable funds; (2) transfer of risk to those who are willing to bear it; and (3) increased liquidity for holders of the debt.

Mortgage securitization was a win–win situation in theory, but as practiced in the last decade it has turned into a lose–lose situation. We will have more to say about securitization and the global economic crisis later in this chapter, but first let's take a look at the cost of money.

1.6 The Cost of Money

In a free economy, capital from those with available funds is allocated through the price system to users who have a need for funds. The interaction of the providers' supply and the users' demand determines the cost (or price) of money, which is the rate users pay to providers. For debt, we call this price the **interest rate**. For equity, we call it the **cost of equity**, and it consists of the dividends and capital gains stockholders expect. Keep in mind that the "price" of money is a cost from a user's perspective but a return from the provider's point of view.

Notice in Table 1-1 that a financial instrument's rate of return generally increases as its maturity and risk increase. We will have much more to say about the relationships among an individual security's features, risk, and return later in the book, but there are some fundamental factors and economic conditions that affect all financial instruments.

Fundamental Factors That Affect the Cost of Money

The four most fundamental factors affecting the cost of money are **(1) production opportunities, (2) time preferences for consumption, (3) risk**, and **(4) inflation**. By production opportunities, we mean the ability to turn capital into benefits. If a business raises capital, the benefits are determined by the expected rates of return on its production opportunities. If a student borrows to finance his or her education, the benefits are higher expected future salaries (and, of course, the sheer joy of learning!). If a homeowner borrows, the benefits are the pleasure from living in his or her own home, plus any expected appreciation in the value of the home. Observe that the expected rates of return on these "production opportunities" put an upper limit on how much users can pay to providers.

Providers can use their current funds for consumption or saving. By saving, they give up consumption now in the expectation of having more consumption in the future. If providers have a strong preference for consumption now, then it takes high interest rates to induce them to trade current consumption for future consumption. Therefore, the time preference for consumption has a major impact on the cost of money. Notice that the time preference for consumption varies for different individuals, for different age groups, and for different cultures. For example, people in Japan have a lower time preference for consumption than those in the United States, which partially explains why Japanese families tend to save more than U.S. families even though interest rates are lower in Japan.

If the expected rate of return on an investment is risky, then providers require a higher expected return to induce them to take the extra risk, which drives up the cost of money. As you will see later in this book, the risk of a security is determined by market conditions and the security's particular features.

Inflation also leads to a higher cost of money. For example, suppose you earned 10% one year on your investment but inflation caused prices to increase by 20%. This means you can't consume as much at the end of the year as when you originally invested your money. Obviously, if you had expected 20% inflation, you would have required a higher rate of return than 10%.

Economic Conditions and Policies That Affect the Cost of Money

Economic conditions and policies also affect the cost of money. These include: (1) Federal Reserve policy; (2) the federal budget deficit or surplus; (3) the level of

The home page for the Board of Governors of the Federal Reserve System can be found at **http://www.federalreserve.gov**. *You can access general information about the Federal Reserve, including press releases, speeches, and monetary policy.*

business activity; and (4) international factors, including the foreign trade balance, the international business climate, and exchange rates.

Federal Reserve Policy. If the Federal Reserve Board wants to stimulate the economy, it most often uses open market operations to purchase Treasury securities held by banks. Because banks are selling some of their securities, the banks will have more cash, which increases their supply of loanable funds, which in turn makes banks willing to lend more money at lower interest rates. In addition, the Fed's purchases represent an increase in the demand for Treasury securities. As for anything that is for sale, increased demand causes Treasury securities' prices to go up and interest rates to go down (we explain the mathematical relationship between higher prices and lower interest rates in Chapter 4; for now, just trust us when we say that a security's price and its interest rate move in opposite directions). The net result is a reduction in interest rates, which stimulates the economy by making it less costly for companies to borrow for new projects or for individuals to borrow for major purchases or other expenditures.

When banks sell their holdings of Treasury securities to the Fed, the banks' reserves go up, which increases the money supply. A larger money supply ultimately leads to an increase in expected inflation, which eventually pushes interest rates up. Thus, the Fed can stimulate the economy in the short term by driving down interest rates and increasing the money supply, but this creates longer-term inflationary pressures. This is exactly the dilemma facing the Fed in early 2009 as it attempts to stimulate the economy to prevent another great depression.

If the Fed wishes to slow down the economy and reduce inflation, the Fed reverses the process. Instead of purchasing Treasury securities, the Fed sells Treasury securities to banks, which causes an increase in short-term interest rates but a decrease in long-term inflationary pressures.

Budget Deficits or Surpluses. If the federal government spends more than it takes in from tax revenues then it's running a deficit, and that deficit must be covered either by borrowing or by printing money (increasing the money supply). The government borrows by issuing new Treasury securities. All else held equal, this creates a greater supply of Treasury securities, which leads to lower security prices and higher interest rates. Other federal government actions that increase the money supply also increase expectations for future inflation, which drives up interest rates. Thus, the larger the federal deficit, other things held constant, the higher the level of interest rates. As shown in Figure 1-2, the federal government has run large budget deficits for 12 of the past 16 years, and even larger deficits are predicted for at least several years into the future. These deficits contributed to the cumulative federal debt, which stood at over $11 trillion at the beginning of 2009.

Business Activity. Figure 1-3 shows interest rates, inflation, and recessions. Notice that interest rates and inflation typically rise prior to a recession and fall afterward. There are several reasons for this pattern.

Consumer demand slows during a recession, keeping companies from increasing prices, which reduces price inflation. Companies also cut back on hiring, which reduces wage inflation. Less disposable income causes consumers to reduce their purchases of homes and automobiles, reducing consumer demand for loans. Companies reduce investments in new operations, which reduces their demand for funds. The cumulative effect is downward pressure on inflation and interest rates. The Federal Reserve is also active during recessions, trying to stimulate the economy by driving down interest rates.

FIGURE 1-2 Federal Budget Surplus/Deficits and Trade Balances (Billions of Dollars)

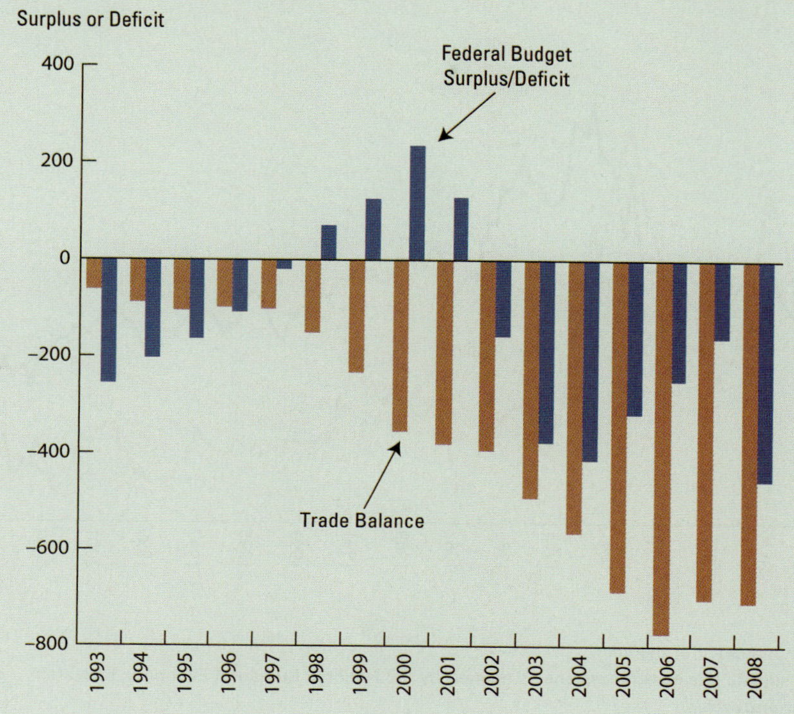

Notes:

1. Years are for federal government fiscal years, which end on September 30.
2. Federal budget surplus/deficit data are from the Congressional Budget Office, **http://www.cbo.gov/**.
3. Data for international trade balances are from the St. Louis Federal Reserve Web site known as FRED: **http://research.stlouisfed.org/fred/**.

International Trade Deficits or Surpluses. Businesses and individuals in the United States buy from and sell to people and firms in other countries. If we buy more than we sell (that is, if we import more than we export), we are said to be running a *foreign trade deficit.* When trade deficits occur, they must be financed, and the main source of financing is debt. In other words, if we import $200 billion of goods but export only $90 billion, we run a trade deficit of $110 billion, and we will probably borrow the $110 billion.[4] Therefore, the larger our trade deficit, the more we must borrow, and increased borrowing drives up interest rates. Also, international investors are willing to hold U.S. debt if and only if the risk-adjusted rate paid on this debt is competitive with interest rates in other countries. Therefore, if the Federal Reserve attempts to lower interest rates in the United States, causing our rates to fall below rates abroad (after adjustments for expected changes in the exchange rate), then international investors will sell U.S. bonds, which will depress bond prices and result in higher U.S. rates. Thus, if the trade deficit is large relative to the size of

[4]The deficit could also be financed by selling assets, including gold, corporate stocks, entire companies, and real estate. The United States has financed its massive trade deficits by all of these means in recent years, but the primary method has been by borrowing from foreigners.

FIGURE 1-3 Business Activity, Interest Rates, and Inflation

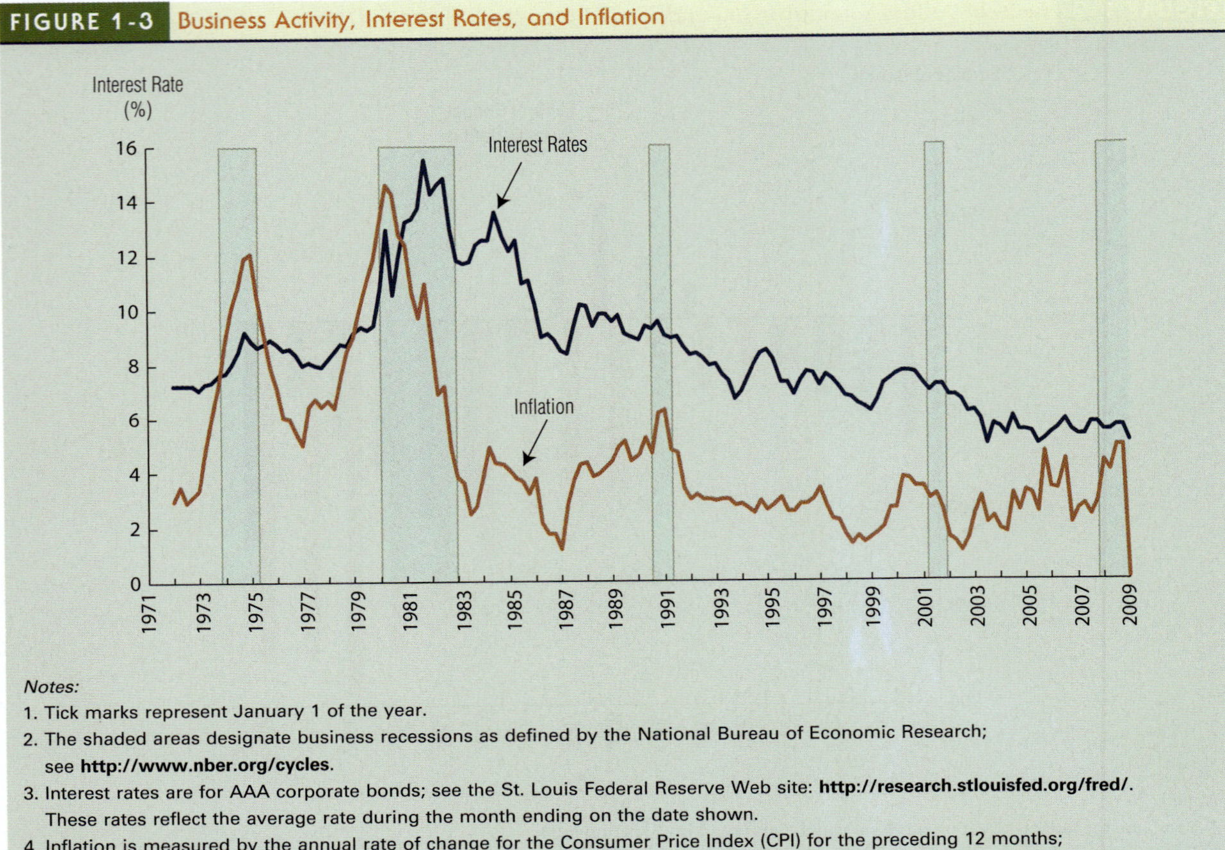

Notes:

1. Tick marks represent January 1 of the year.
2. The shaded areas designate business recessions as defined by the National Bureau of Economic Research; see **http://www.nber.org/cycles**.
3. Interest rates are for AAA corporate bonds; see the St. Louis Federal Reserve Web site: **http://research.stlouisfed.org/fred/**. These rates reflect the average rate during the month ending on the date shown.
4. Inflation is measured by the annual rate of change for the Consumer Price Index (CPI) for the preceding 12 months; see **http://research.stlouisfed.org/fred/**.

the overall economy, it will hinder the Fed's ability to reduce interest rates and combat a recession.

The United States has been running annual trade deficits since the mid-1970s; see Figure 1-2 for recent years. The cumulative effect of trade deficits and budget deficits is that the United States has become the largest debtor nation of all time. As noted earlier, this federal debt has exceeded *$11 trillion!* As a result, our interest rates are very much influenced by interest rates in other countries around the world.

WWW

Transparency International provides a ranking of countries based on their levels of perceived corruption. See **http://www.transparency.org/policy_research/surveys_indices/cpi/2008**. *The U.S. Department of State provides thorough descriptions of countries' business climates at* **http://www.state.gov/e/eeb/ifd/2008/**.

International Country Risk. International risk factors may increase the cost of money that is invested abroad. **Country risk** is the risk that arises from investing or doing business in a particular country, and it depends on the country's economic, political, and social environment. Countries with stable economic, social, political, and regulatory systems provide a safer climate for investment and therefore have less country risk than less stable nations. Examples of country risk include the risk associated with changes in tax rates, regulations, currency conversion, and exchange rates. Country risk also includes the risk that (1) property will be expropriated without adequate compensation; (2) the host country will impose new stipulations concerning local production, sourcing, or hiring practices; and (3) there might be damage or destruction of facilities due to internal strife.

Exchange Rate Risk. International securities frequently are denominated in a currency other than the dollar, which means that the value of an investment depends on what happens to exchange rates. This is known as **exchange rate risk**. For example, if a U.S. investor purchases a Japanese bond, interest will probably be paid in Japanese yen, which must then be converted to dollars if the investor wants to spend his or her money in the United States. If the yen weakens relative to the dollar, then the yen will buy fewer dollars when it comes time for the investor to convert the Japanese bond's payout. Alternatively, if the yen strengthens relative to the dollar, the investor will earn higher dollar returns. It therefore follows that the effective rate of return on a foreign investment will depend on both the performance of the foreign security in its home market and on what happens to exchange rates over the life of the investment. We discuss exchange rates in detail in Chapter 17.

Self-Test

What four fundamental factors affect the cost of money?

Name some economic conditions that influence interest rates and explain their effects.

1.7 Financial Institutions

When raising capital, direct transfers of funds from individuals to businesses are most common for small businesses or in economies where financial markets and institutions are not well developed. Businesses in developed economies usually find it more efficient to enlist the services of one or more financial institutions to raise capital. Most financial institutions don't compete in a single line of business but instead provide a wide variety of services and products, both domestically and globally. The following sections describe the major types of financial institutions and services, but keep in mind that the dividing lines among them are often blurred. Also, note that the global financial crisis we are now going through is changing the structure of our financial institutions, and new regulations are certain to affect those that remain. Finance today is dynamic, to say the least!

Investment Banks and Brokerage Activities

Investment banking houses help companies raise capital. Such organizations underwrite security offerings, which means they (1) advise corporations regarding the design and pricing of new securities, (2) buy these securities from the issuing corporation, and (3) resell them to investors. Although the securities are sold twice, this process is really one primary market transaction, with the investment banker acting as a facilitator to help transfer capital from savers to businesses. An investment bank often is a division or subsidiary of a larger company. For example, JPMorgan Chase & Co. is a very large financial services firm, with over $2 *trillion* in managed assets. One of its holdings is J.P. Morgan, an investment banking house.

In addition to security offerings, investment banks also provide consulting and advisory services, such as merger and acquisition (M&A) analysis and investment management for wealthy individuals.

Most investment banks also provide brokerage services for institutions and individuals (called "retail" customers). For example, Merrill Lynch (acquired in 2008 by Bank of America) has a large retail brokerage operation that provides advice and executes trades for its individual clients. Similarly, J.P. Morgan helps execute trades for institutional customers, such as pension funds.

At one time, most investment banks were partnerships, with income generated primarily by fees from their underwriting, M&A consulting, asset management, and brokering activities. When business was good, investment banks generated high fees and paid big bonuses to their partners. When times were tough, investment banks paid no bonuses and often fired employees. In the 1990s, however, most investment banks were reorganized into publicly traded corporations (or were acquired and then operated as subsidiaries of public companies). For example, in 1994 Lehman Brothers sold some of its own shares of stock to the public via an IPO. Like most corporations, Lehman Brothers was financed by a combination of equity and debt. A relaxation of regulations in the 2000s allowed investment banks to undertake much riskier activities than at any time since the Great Depression. Basically, the new regulations allowed investment banks to use an unprecedented amount of debt to finance their activities—Lehman used roughly $30 of debt for every dollar of equity. In addition to their fee-generating activities, most investment banks also began trading securities for their own accounts. In other words, they took the borrowed money and invested it in financial securities. If you are earning 12% on your investments while paying 8% on your borrowings, then the more money you borrow, the more profit you make. But if you are leveraged 30 to 1 and your investments decline in value by even 3.33%, your business will fail. This is exactly what happened to Bear Stearns, Lehman Brothers, and Merrill Lynch in the fall of 2008. In short, they borrowed money, used it to make risky investments, and then failed when the investments turned out to be worth less than the amount they owed. Notice that it was not their traditional investment banking activities that caused the failure, but the fact that they borrowed so much and used those funds to speculate in the market.

Deposit-Taking Financial Intermediaries

Some financial institutions take deposits from savers and then lend most of the deposited money to borrowers. Following is a brief description of such intermediaries.

Savings and Loan Associations (S&Ls). As we explained in Section 1.5, S&Ls originally accepted deposits from many small savers and then loaned this money to home buyers and consumers. Later, they were allowed to make riskier investments, such as real estate development. **Mutual savings banks (MSBs)** are similar to S&Ls, but they operate primarily in the northeastern states. Today, most S&Ls and MSBs have been acquired by banks.

Credit Unions. **Credit unions** are cooperative associations whose members have a common bond, such as being employees of the same firm or living in the same geographic area. Members' savings are loaned only to other members, generally for auto purchases, home improvement loans, and home mortgages. Credit unions are often the cheapest source of funds available to individual borrowers.

Commercial Banks. **Commercial banks** raise funds from depositors and by issuing stock and bonds to investors. For example, someone might deposit money in a checking account. In return, that person can write checks, use a debit card, and even receive interest on the deposits. Those who buy the banks' stocks expect to receive dividends and interest payments. Unlike nonfinancial corporations, most commercial banks are highly leveraged in the sense that they owe much more to their depositors and creditors than they raised from stockholders. For example, a typical bank has about $90 of debt for every $10 of stockholders' equity. If the bank's assets are worth $100, we can calculate its equity capital by subtracting the $90 of liabilities from the $100 of assets: Equity capital = $100 − $90 = $10. But if the assets drop in value by 5% to $95, the equity drops to $5 = $95 − $90, a 50% decline.

Banks are critically important to a well-functioning economy, and their high leverage makes them risky. As a result, banks are more highly regulated than nonfinancial firms. Given the high risk, banks might have a hard time attracting and retaining deposits unless the deposits were insured, so the Federal Deposit Insurance Corporation (FDIC), which is backed by the U.S. government, insures up to $250,000 per depositor. As a result of the global economic crisis, this insured amount was increased from $100,000 in 2008 to reassure depositors.

Without such insurance, if depositors believed that a bank was in trouble, they would rush to withdraw funds. This is called a "bank run," which is exactly what happened in the United States during the Great Depression, causing many bank failures and leading to the creation of the FDIC in an effort to prevent future bank runs. Not all countries have their own versions of the FDIC, so international bank runs are still possible. In fact, a bank run occurred in September 2008 at the U.K. bank Northern Rock, leading to its nationalization by the government.

Most banks are small and locally owned, but the largest banks are parts of giant financial services firms. For example, JPMorgan Chase Bank, commonly called Chase Bank, is owned by JPMorgan Chase & Co., and Citibank is owned by Citicorp (at the time we write this, but perhaps not when you read this—the financial landscape is changing daily).

Investment Funds

At some financial institutions, savers have an ownership interest in a pool of funds rather than owning a deposit account. Examples include mutual funds, hedge funds, and private equity funds.

Mutual Funds. **Mutual funds** are corporations that accept money from savers and then use these funds to buy financial instruments. These organizations pool funds, which allows them to reduce risks by diversification and achieve economies of scale in analyzing securities, managing portfolios, and buying/selling securities. Different funds are designed to meet the objectives of different types of savers. Hence, there are bond funds for those who desire safety and stock funds for savers who are willing to accept risks in the hope of higher returns. There are literally thousands of different mutual funds with dozens of different goals and purposes. Some funds are actively managed, with their managers trying to find undervalued securities, while other funds are passively managed and simply try to minimize expenses by matching the returns on a particular market index.

Money market funds invest in short-term, low-risk securities, such as Treasury bills and commercial paper. Many of these funds offer interest-bearing checking accounts with rates that are greater than those offered by banks, so many people invest in mutual funds as an alternative to depositing money in a bank. Note, though, that money market funds are not required to be insured by the FDIC and so are riskier than bank deposits.

Most traditional mutual funds allow investors to redeem their share of the fund only at the close of business. A special type of mutual fund, the **exchange traded fund (ETF)**, allows investors to sell their share at any time during normal trading hours. ETFs usually have very low management expenses and are rapidly gaining in popularity.

Hedge Funds. **Hedge funds** raise money from investors and engage in a variety of investment activities. Unlike typical mutual funds, which can have thousands of investors, hedge funds are limited to institutional investors and a relatively small number of high–net-worth individuals. Because these investors are supposed to be sophisticated, hedge funds are much less regulated than mutual funds. The first hedge funds literally tried to hedge their bets by forming portfolios of conventional securities and derivatives in such a way as to limit their potential losses without sacrificing too much of their potential gains. Recently, though, most hedge funds began to lever their positions by borrowing heavily. Many hedge funds had spectacular rates of return during the 1990s. This success attracted more investors, and thousands of new hedge funds were created. Much of the low-hanging fruit had already been picked, however, so the hedge funds began pursuing much riskier (and unhedged) strategies. Perhaps not surprisingly (at least in retrospect), some funds have produced spectacular losses. For example, many hedge fund investors suffered huge losses in 2007 and 2008 when large numbers of sub-prime mortgages defaulted.

Private Equity Funds. **Private equity funds** are similar to hedge funds in that they are limited to a relatively small number of large investors, but they differ in that they own stock (equity) in other companies and often control those companies, whereas hedge funds usually own many different types of securities. In contrast to a mutual fund, which might own a small percentage of a publicly traded company's stock, a private equity fund typically owns virtually all of a company's stock. Because the company's stock is not traded in the public markets, it is called "private equity." In fact, private equity funds often take a public company (or subsidiary) and turn it private, such as the 2007 privatization of Chrysler by Cerberus. The general partners who manage the private equity funds usually sit on the boards of the companies the funds owns and guide the firms' strategies with the goal of later selling them for a profit. For example, The Carlyle Group, Clayton Dubilier & Rice, and Merrill Lynch Global Private Equity bought Hertz from Ford on December 22, 2005, and then sold shares of Hertz in an IPO less than a year later.

Chapter 15 provides additional discussion of private equity funds, but it is important to note here that many private equity funds experienced high rates of return in the last decade, and those returns attracted enormous sums from investors. A few funds, most notably The Blackstone Group, actually went public themselves through an IPO. Just as with hedge funds, the performance of many private equity funds faltered. For example, shortly after its IPO in June 2007, Blackstone's stock price was over $31 per share; by early 2009, it had fallen to about $4.

Life Insurance Companies and Pension Funds

Life insurance companies take premiums, invest these funds in stocks, bonds, real estate, and mortgages, and then make payments to beneficiaries. Life insurance companies also offer a variety of tax-deferred savings plans designed to provide retirement benefits.

Traditional **pension funds** are retirement plans funded by corporations or government agencies. Pension funds invest primarily in bonds, stocks, mortgages, hedge funds, private equity, and real estate. Most companies now offer self-directed retirement plans, such as 401(k) plans, as an addition to or substitute for traditional pension plans. In traditional plans, the plan administrators determine how to invest the funds; in self-directed plans, all individual participants must decide how to invest their own funds. Many companies are switching from traditional plans to self-directed plans, partly because this shifts the risk from the company to the employee.

Regulation of Financial Institutions

With the notable exception of investment banks, hedge funds, and private equity funds, financial institutions have been heavily regulated to ensure their safety and thus protect investors and depositors. Historically, many of these regulations—which have included a prohibition on nationwide branch banking, restrictions on the types of assets the institutions could buy, ceilings on the interest rates they could pay, and limitations on the types of services they could provide—tended to impede the free flow of capital and thus hurt the efficiency of our capital markets. Recognizing this fact, policymakers took several steps from the 1970s to the 1990s to deregulate financial services companies. For example, the barriers that restricted banks from expanding nationwide were eliminated. Likewise, regulations that once forced a strict separation of commercial and investment banking were relaxed.

The result of the ongoing regulatory changes has been a blurring of the distinctions between the different types of institutions. Indeed, the trend in the United States was toward huge financial services corporations, which own banks, S&Ls, investment banking houses, insurance companies, pension plan operations, and mutual funds and which have branches across the country and around the world.

For example, Citigroup combined one of the world's largest commercial banks (Citibank), a huge insurance company (Travelers), and a major investment bank (Smith Barney), along with numerous other subsidiaries that operate throughout the world. This structure was similar to that of major institutions in Europe, Japan, and elsewhere around the globe. Among the world's largest world banking companies, only one (Citigroup) is based in the United States. While U.S. banks have grown dramatically as a result of recent mergers, they are still relatively small by global standards.

However, the global economic crisis is causing regulators and financial institutions to rethink the wisdom of conglomerate financial services corporations. For example, in late 2008 Merrill Lynch sold itself to Bank of America to avoid bankruptcy. That was supposed to strengthen BofA, but Merrill brought with it billions of "toxic" loans, and now BofA is in danger of bankruptcy. Then, in early 2009 Citigroup was reorganizing itself in preparation for spinning off several lines of business into separate companies, again with the bankruptcy gun pointed straight at its head. Thus, the two largest U.S. banks are in danger of failure, and their continued survival is due primarily to support from the U.S. government. Congress and the new Obama administration are currently (mid-2009) considering new regulations on a variety of financial institutions, and more bank failures are a certainty. As the crisis unfolds, it will be interesting to see how regulations and the structure of financial institutions evolve to reshape our financial infrastructure, both in the U.S. and around the globe.

Self-Test

What is the difference between a pure commercial bank and a pure investment bank?

List the major types of financial institutions, and briefly describe the original purpose of each.

What are some important differences between mutual funds and hedge funds? How are they similar?

1.8 Financial Markets

Financial markets bring together people and organizations needing money with those having surplus funds. There are many different financial markets in a developed economy. Each market deals with a somewhat different type of instrument, customer, or geographic location. Here are some ways to classify markets:

1. **Physical asset markets** (also called "tangible" or "real" asset markets) are those for such products as wheat, autos, real estate, computers, and machinery. **Financial asset markets**, on the other hand, deal with stocks, bonds, notes, mortgages, derivatives, and other **financial instruments**.
2. **Spot markets** and **futures markets** are markets where assets are being bought or sold for "on-the-spot" delivery (literally, within a few days) or for delivery at some future date, such as 6 months or a year into the future.
3. **Money markets** are the markets for short-term, highly liquid debt securities, while **capital markets** are the markets for corporate stocks and debt maturing more than a year in the future. The New York Stock Exchange is an example of a capital market. When describing debt markets, "short term" generally means less than 1 year, "intermediate term" means 1 to 5 years, and "long term" means more than 5 years.
4. **Mortgage markets** deal with loans on residential, agricultural, commercial, and industrial real estate, while **consumer credit markets** involve loans for autos, appliances, education, vacations, and so on.
5. **World, national, regional**, and **local markets** also exist. Thus, depending on an organization's size and scope of operations, it may be able to borrow or lend all around the world, or it may be confined to a strictly local, even neighborhood, market.
6. **Primary markets** are the markets in which corporations raise new capital. If Microsoft were to sell a new issue of common stock to raise capital, this would be a primary market transaction. The corporation selling the newly created stock receives the proceeds from such a transaction. The **initial public offering (IPO) market** is a subset of the primary market. Here firms "go public" by offering shares to the public for the first time. Microsoft had its IPO in 1986. Previously, Bill Gates and other insiders owned all the shares. In many IPOs, the insiders sell some of their shares and the company sells newly created shares to raise additional capital. **Secondary markets** are markets in which existing, already outstanding securities are traded among investors. Thus, if you decided to buy 1,000 shares of AT&T stock, the purchase would occur in the secondary market. The New York Stock Exchange is a secondary market, since it deals in outstanding (as opposed to newly issued) stocks. Secondary markets also exist for bonds, mortgages, and other financial assets. The corporation whose securities are being traded is not involved in a secondary market transaction and, thus, does not receive any funds from such a sale.
7. **Private markets**, where transactions are worked out directly between two parties, are differentiated from **public markets**, where standardized contracts are traded on organized exchanges. Bank loans and private placements of debt with insurance companies are examples of private market transactions. Since these transactions are private, they may be structured in any manner that appeals to the two parties. By contrast, securities that are issued in public markets (for example, common stock and corporate bonds) are ultimately held by a large number of individuals. Public securities must have fairly standardized contractual features because public investors cannot afford the time to study unique, nonstandardized contracts. Hence private market securities are more tailor-made but less liquid, whereas public market securities are more liquid but subject to greater standardization.

The distinctions among markets are often blurred. For example, it makes little difference if a firm borrows for 11, 12, or 13 months and thus whether such borrowing is a "money" or "capital" market transaction. You should recognize the big differences among types of markets, but don't get hung up trying to distinguish them at the boundaries.

Self-Test

Distinguish between (1) physical asset markets and financial asset markets, (2) spot and futures markets, (3) money and capital markets, (4) primary and secondary markets, and (5) private and public markets.

1.9 Trading Procedures in Financial Markets

A huge volume of trading occurs in the secondary markets. Although there are many secondary markets for a wide variety of securities, we can classify their trading procedures along two dimensions: location and method of matching orders.

Physical Location versus Electronic Network

A secondary market can be either a **physical location exchange** or a **computer/telephone network**. For example, the New York Stock Exchange, the American Stock Exchange (AMEX), the Chicago Board of Trade (the CBOT trades futures and options), and the Tokyo Stock Exchange are all physical location exchanges. In other words, the traders actually meet and trade in a specific part of a specific building.

In contrast, Nasdaq, which trades a number of U.S. stocks, is a network of linked computers. Other network examples are the markets for U.S. Treasury bonds and foreign exchange, which are conducted via telephone and/or computer networks. In these electronic markets, the traders never see one another except maybe for cocktails after work.

By their very nature, networks are less transparent than physical location exchanges. For example, credit default swaps are traded directly between buyers and sellers, and there is no easy mechanism for recording, aggregating, and reporting the transactions or the net positions of the buyers and sellers.

Matching Orders: Auctions, Dealers, and ECNs

The second dimension is the way orders from sellers and buyers are matched. This can occur through an open outcry **auction** system, through dealers, or by automated order matching. An example of an outcry auction is the CBOT, where traders actually meet in a pit and sellers and buyers communicate with one another through shouts and hand signals.

In a **dealer market**, there are "market makers" who keep an inventory of the stock (or other financial instrument) in much the same way that any merchant keeps an inventory. These dealers list bid and ask quotes, which are the prices at which they are willing to buy or sell. Computerized quotation systems keep track of all bid and asked prices, but they don't actually match buyers and sellers. Instead, traders must contact a specific dealer to complete the transaction. Nasdaq (U.S. stocks) is one such market, as are the London SEAQ (U.K. stocks) and the Neuer Market (stocks of small German companies).

The third method of matching orders is through an **electronic communications network (ECN)**. Participants in an ECN post their orders to buy and sell, and the ECN automatically matches orders. For example, someone might place an order to buy 1,000 shares of IBM stock—this is called a "market order" since it is to buy the stock at the current market price. Suppose another participant had placed an order to sell 1,000 shares of IBM, but only at a price of $91 per share, and this was the lowest price of any "sell" order. The ECN would automatically match these two orders, execute the trade, and notify both participants that the trade has occurred. The $91 sell price was a "limit order" as opposed to a market order because the action was limited by the seller. Note that orders can also be limited with regard to their duration. For example, someone might stipulate that they are willing to buy 1,000 shares of IBM at $90 per share if the price falls that low during the next two hours. In other words, there are limits on the price and/or the duration of the order. The ECN will execute the limit order only if both conditions are met. Two of the largest ECNs for trading U.S. stocks are Instinet (now owned by Nasdaq) and Archipelago (now owned by the NYSE). Other large ECNs include Eurex, a Swiss–German ECN that trades futures contracts, and SETS, a U.K. ECN that trades stocks.

Self-Test

What are the major differences between physical location exchanges and computer/telephone networks?

What are the differences among open outcry auctions, dealer markets, and ECNs?

1.10 Types of Stock Market Transactions

Because the primary objectives of financial management are to maximize the firm's intrinsic value and then help ensure that the current stock price equals that value, knowledge of the stock market is important to anyone involved in managing a business. We can classify stock market transactions into three distinct types: (1) initial public offerings, (2) seasoned equity offerings, and (3) secondary market transactions.

Whenever stock is offered to the public for the first time, the company is said to be **going public**. This primary market transaction is called the initial public offering (IPO) market. If a company later decides to sell (i.e., issue) additional shares to raise new equity capital, this is still a primary market, but it is called a **seasoned equity offering**. Trading in the outstanding shares of established, publicly owned companies are secondary market transactions. For example, if the owner of 100 shares of publicly held stock sells his or her stock, the trade is said to have occurred in the secondary market. Thus, the market for outstanding shares, or used shares, is the secondary market. The company receives no new money when sales occur in this market.

For more on issuing stock, see **Web Extension 1B** *on the textbook's Web site.*

Here is a brief description of recent IPO activity. The 662 total global IPOs in 2008 was a huge decline from the 1,711 in 2007. Proceeds also plummeted, to $77 billion from $279 billion. The Americas raised more money than any other region in the world, with the United States having 33 IPOs that raised a total of $26.4 billion. Visa's IPO was the largest in the world, bringing in over $19 billion.

WWW

For updates on IPO activity, see **http://www.ipohome.com/IPOHome/Review/2008main.aspx** *or* **http://www.hoovers.com/global/ipoc/index.xhtml**. The Wall Street Journal *also provides IPO data in its Year-End Review of Markets & Finance at* **http://online.wsj.com**. *See Professor Jay Ritter's Web site for additional IPO data and analysis,* **http://bear.cba.ufl.edu/ritter/ipodata.htm**.

In the United States, the average first-day return was around 5.3% in 2008. However, some firms had spectacular first-day price run-ups, such as Intrepid Potash's 57% gain on its first day of trading and Grand Canyon Education's 59.7% gain for the year. However, not all companies fared so well—indeed, Intrepid Potash fell 30% for the year, despite its great first-day return. Some lost even more, including GT Solar International, which lost 11.6% on its first day and a total of 82.5% for the year.

Even if you are able to identify a "hot" issue, it is often difficult to purchase shares in the initial offering. In strong markets, these deals are generally oversubscribed, which means that the demand for shares at the offering price exceeds the number of shares issued. In such instances, investment bankers favor large institutional investors (who are their best customers), and small investors find it hard, if not impossible, to get in on the ground floor. They can buy the stock in the aftermarket, but evidence

Rational Exuberance?

The Daily Planet Ltd. made history on May 1, 2003, by becoming the world's first publicly traded brothel. Technically, the Daily Planet owns only property, including a hotel with 18 rooms, each with a different theme, but all have multi-person showers and very large beds. The Daily Planet charges guests a room fee of 115 Australian dollars (A$) per hour; clients also pay a fee of A$115 directly to individual members of the staff.

The IPO was for 7.5 million shares of stock, initially priced at A$0.50. However, the price ended the first day of trading at A$1.09 for a first-day return of 118%. The price closed the second day at A$1.56 for a two-day return of 212%, one of the largest returns since the days of the dot-com boom. Institutional investors normally buy about 60% to 70% of the stock in an IPO, but they didn't participate in this offering.

The company is named after the fictitious newspaper for which comic strip character Clark Kent was a reporter. All receptionists have "Lois Lane" nametags, and there is a telephone booth in the lobby. What would Superman think!

suggests that if you do not get in on the ground floor, the average IPO underperforms the overall market over the long run.[5]

Before you conclude that it isn't fair to let only the best customers have the stock in an initial offering, think about what it takes to become a best customer. Best customers are usually investors who have done lots of business in the past with the investment banking firm's brokerage department. In other words, they have paid large sums as commissions in the past, and they are expected to continue doing so in the future. As is so often true, there is no free lunch—most of the investors who get in on the ground floor of an IPO have, in fact, paid for this privilege.

Self-Test

Differentiate between an IPO, a seasoned equity offering, and a secondary transaction.

Why is it often difficult for the average investor to make money during an IPO?

1.11 The Secondary Stock Markets

The two leading U.S. stock markets today are the New York Stock Exchange and the Nasdaq stock market.

The New York Stock Exchange

WWW

You can access the home pages of the major U.S. stock markets at **http://www.nyse.com** *or* **http://www.nasdaq.com**. *These sites provide background information as well as the opportunity to obtain individual stock quotes.*

Before March of 2006, the **New York Stock Exchange (NYSE)** was a privately held firm owned by its members. It then merged with Archipelago, a publicly traded company that was one of the world's largest ECNs. NYSE members received approximately 70% of the shares in the combined firm, with Archipelago shareholders receiving 30%. The combined firm, which also owned the Pacific Exchange, was known as The NYSE Group, Inc., and was traded publicly under the ticker symbol NYX. It continued to operate the New York Stock Exchange (a physical location exchange located on Wall Street) and Arca (comprising the Pacific Exchange and the ECN formerly known as Archipelago). In 2007 The NYSE Group merged with Euronext, a European company that operates stock exchanges (called bourses) in Paris, Amsterdam, Brussels, and Lisbon. The combined company is called NYSE Euronext.

[5]See Jay R. Ritter, "The Long-Run Performance of Initial Public Offerings," *Journal of Finance*, March 1991, pp. 3–27.

For more on stock markets, see **Web Extension 1B** *on the textbook's Web site.*

The NYSE still has over 300 member organizations, which are corporations, partnerships, or LLCs. Membership prices were as high as $4 million in 2005, and the last sale before the Euronext merger was $3.5 million. Member organizations are registered broker-dealers, but they may not conduct trading on the floor of the exchange unless they also hold a trading license issued by the NYSE. Before going public, the equivalent to the trading license was called a "seat," although there was very little sitting on the floor of the exchange. Trading licenses are now leased by member organizations from the exchange, with an annual fee of $40,000 for 2009. The NYSE has leased most of its 1,500 available trading licenses.

Most of the larger investment banking houses operate *brokerage departments* and are members of the NYSE with leased trading rights. The NYSE is open on all normal working days, and members meet in large rooms equipped with electronic equipment that enables each member to communicate with his or her firm's offices throughout the country. For example, Merrill Lynch (now owned by Bank of America) might receive an order in its Atlanta office from a customer who wants to buy shares of Procter & Gamble stock. Simultaneously, Edward Jones' St. Louis office might receive an order from a customer wishing to sell shares of P&G. Each broker communicates electronically with the firm's representative on the NYSE. Other brokers throughout the country also communicate with their own exchange members. The exchange members with *sell orders* offer the shares for sale, and they are bid for by the members with *buy orders*. Thus, the NYSE operates as an *auction market*.[6]

The Nasdaq Stock Market

The **National Association of Securities Dealers (NASD)** is a self-regulatory body that licenses brokers and oversees trading practices. The computerized network used by the NASD is known as the NASD Automated Quotation System, or Nasdaq. Nasdaq started as just a quotation system, but it has grown to become an organized securities market with its own listing requirements. Nasdaq lists about 5,000 stocks, although not all trade through the same Nasdaq system. For example, the Nasdaq National Market lists the larger Nasdaq stocks, such as Microsoft and Intel, while the Nasdaq SmallCap Market lists smaller companies with the potential for high growth. Nasdaq also operates the Nasdaq OTC Bulletin Board, which lists quotes

[6]The NYSE is actually a modified auction market, wherein people (through their brokers) bid for stocks. Originally—about 200 years ago—brokers would literally shout, "I have 100 shares of Erie for sale; how much am I offered?" and then sell to the highest bidder. If a broker had a buy order, he or she would shout, "I want to buy 100 shares of Erie; who'll sell at the best price?" The same general situation still exists, although the exchanges now have members known as *specialists* who facilitate the trading process by keeping an inventory of shares of the stocks in which they specialize. If a buy order comes in at a time when no sell order arrives, the specialist will sell off some inventory. Similarly, if a sell order comes in, the specialist will buy and add to inventory. The specialist sets a *bid price* (the price the specialist will pay for the stock) and an *asked price* (the price at which shares will be sold out of inventory). The bid and asked prices are set at levels designed to keep the inventory in balance. If many buy orders start coming in because of favorable developments or sell orders come in because of unfavorable events, the specialist will raise or lower prices to keep supply and demand in balance. Bid prices are somewhat lower than asked prices, with the difference, or *spread*, representing the specialist's profit margin.

Special facilities are available to help institutional investors such as mutual funds or pension funds sell large blocks of stock without depressing their prices. In essence, brokerage houses that cater to institutional clients will purchase blocks (defined as 10,000 or more shares) and then resell the stock to other institutions or individuals. Also, when a firm has a major announcement that is likely to cause its stock price to change sharply, it will ask the exchanges to halt trading in its stock until the announcement has been made and digested by investors. See ***Web Extension 1B*** on the textbook's Web site for more on specialists and trading off the exchange floor.

Measuring the Market

A *stock index* is designed to show the performance of the stock market. Here we describe some leading indexes.

Dow Jones Industrial Average

Begun in 1896, the Dow Jones Industrial Average (DJIA) now includes 30 widely held stocks that represent almost a fifth of the market value of all U.S. stocks. See **http://www.dowjones.com** for more information.

S&P 500 Index

Created in 1926, the S&P 500 Index is widely regarded as the standard for measuring large-cap U.S. stocks' market performance. It is value weighted, so the largest companies (in terms of value) have the greatest influence. The S&P 500 Index is used as a comparison benchmark by 97% of all U.S. money managers and pension plan sponsors. See **http://www2.standardandpoors.com** for more information.

Nasdaq Composite Index

The Nasdaq Composite Index measures the performance of all common stocks listed on the Nasdaq stock market. Currently, it includes more than 3,200 companies, many of which are in the technology sector. Microsoft, Cisco Systems, and Intel account for a high percentage of the index's value-weighted market capitalization. For this reason, substantial movements in the same direction by these three companies can move the entire index. See **http://www.nasdaq.com** for more information.

NYSE Composite Index

The NYSE Composite Index measures the performance of all common stocks listed on the NYSE. It is a value-weighted index based on just over 2,000 stocks that represent 77% of the total market capitalization of all publicly traded companies in the United States. See **http://www.nyse.com** for more information.

Trading the Market

Through the use of exchange traded funds (ETFs), it is now possible to buy and sell the market in much the same way as an individual stock. For example, the Standard & Poor's depository receipt (SPDR) is a share of a fund that holds the stocks of all the companies in the S&P 500. SPDRs trade during regular market hours, making it possible to buy or sell the S&P 500 any time during the day. There are hundreds of other ETFs, including ones for the Nasdaq, the Dow Jones Industrial Average, gold stocks, utilities, and so on.

Recent Performance

Go to the Web site **http://finance.yahoo.com/**. Enter the symbol for any of the indexes (^DJI for the Dow Jones, ^SPC for the S&P 500, ^IXIC for the Nasdaq, and ^NYA for the NYSE) and then click GO. This will bring up the current value of the index, shown in a table. Click Basic Chart in the panel on the left, which will bring up a chart showing the historical performance of the index. Directly above the chart is a series of buttons that allows you to choose the number of years and to plot the relative performance of several indexes on the same chart. You can even download the historical data in spreadsheet form by clicking Historical Prices in the left panel.

for stocks that are registered with the Securities and Exchange Commission (SEC) but are not listed on any exchange, usually because the company is too small or not sufficiently profitable.[7] Finally, Nasdaq operates the Pink Sheets, which provide quotes on companies that are not registered with the SEC.

[7]OTC stands for over-the-counter. Before Nasdaq, the quickest way to trade a stock that was not listed at a physical location exchange was to find a brokerage firm that kept shares of that stock in inventory. The stock certificates were actually kept in a safe and were literally passed over the counter when bought or sold. Nowadays the certificates for almost all listed stocks and bonds in the United States are stored in a vault, beneath Manhattan, that is operated by the Depository Trust and Clearing Corporation (DTCC). Most brokerage firms have an account with the DTCC, and most investors leave their stocks with their brokers. Thus, when stocks are sold, the DTCC simply adjusts the accounts of the brokerage firms that are involved, and no stock certificates are actually moved.

"Liquidity" is the ability to trade quickly at a net price (i.e., after any commissions) that is close to the security's recent market price. In a dealer market, such as Nasdaq, a stock's liquidity depends on the number and quality of the dealers who make a market in the stock. Nasdaq has more than 400 dealers, most of whom make markets in a large number of stocks. The typical stock has about 10 market makers, but some stocks have more than 50 market makers. Obviously, there are more market makers, and hence there is more liquidity, for the Nasdaq National Market than for the SmallCap Market. Stocks listed on the OTC Bulletin Board or the Pink Sheets have much less liquidity.

Competition in the Secondary Markets

For updates, see **http://www.world-exchanges.org/statistics/time-series/market-capitalization** *at the World Federation of Exchanges.*

There is intense competition between the NYSE, Nasdaq, and other international stock exchanges—they all want the larger, more profitable companies to list on their exchange. Since most of the largest U.S. companies trade on the NYSE, the market capitalization of NYSE-traded stocks is much higher than for stocks traded on Nasdaq (about \$15.7 trillion compared with \$4.0 trillion at the end of 2007). However, reported volume (number of shares traded) is often larger on Nasdaq, and more companies are listed on Nasdaq.[8] For comparison, the market capitalizations for global exchanges are \$4.3 trillion in Tokyo, \$3.9 trillion in London, \$3.7 trillion in Shanghai, \$2.7 trillion in Hong Kong, \$2.1 trillion in Germany, and \$1.8 trillion in Bombay.

Interestingly, many high-tech companies such as Microsoft and Intel have remained on Nasdaq even though they easily meet the listing requirements of the NYSE. At the same time, however, other high-tech companies such as Gateway and Iomega have left Nasdaq for the NYSE. Despite these defections, Nasdaq's growth over the past decade has been impressive. In an effort to become even more competitive with the NYSE and with international markets, Nasdaq acquired one of the leading ECNs, Instinet, in 2005. Moreover, in early 2006 Nasdaq made an offer to acquire the London Stock Exchange (LSE), was rejected by the LSE, withdrew the offer but retained the right to make a subsequent offer, and busily acquired additional shares of stock in the LSE. In late 2006, Nasdaq made a second offer for the LSE and again was rejected. Nasdaq ultimately ended up by selling most of its LSE shares to Bourse Dubai, which owns about 28% of the LSE. Nasdaq did acquire the Nordic exchange OMX, giving it an international presence. The combined company is now known as the NASDAQ OMX Group.

Despite all the shifting ownerships of exchanges, one thing is clear—there will be a continued consolidation in the securities exchange industry, with a blurring of the lines between physical location exchanges and electronic exchanges.

Self-Test

What are some major differences between the NYSE and the Nasdaq stock market?

1.12 Stock Market Returns

During the period 1968–2008, the average annual return for the stock market, as measured by total returns (dividends plus capital gains) on the S&P 500 index, was about 10.6%, but this average does not reflect the considerable annual variation. Notice in Panel A of Figure 1-4 that the market was relatively flat in the 1970s, increased somewhat in the 1980s, and has been a roller coaster ever since. In fact, the market in early 2009 dipped to a level last seen in 1995. Panel B highlights the

---

[8]One transaction on Nasdaq generally shows up as two separate trades (the buy and the sell). This "double counting" makes it difficult to compare the volume between stock markets.

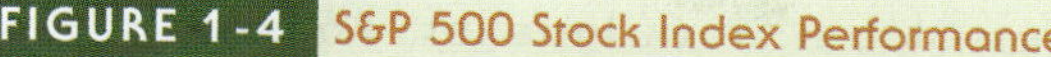

Panel A: End-of-Month Index Value

Panel B: Total Annual Returns: Dividend Yield + Capital Gain or Loss

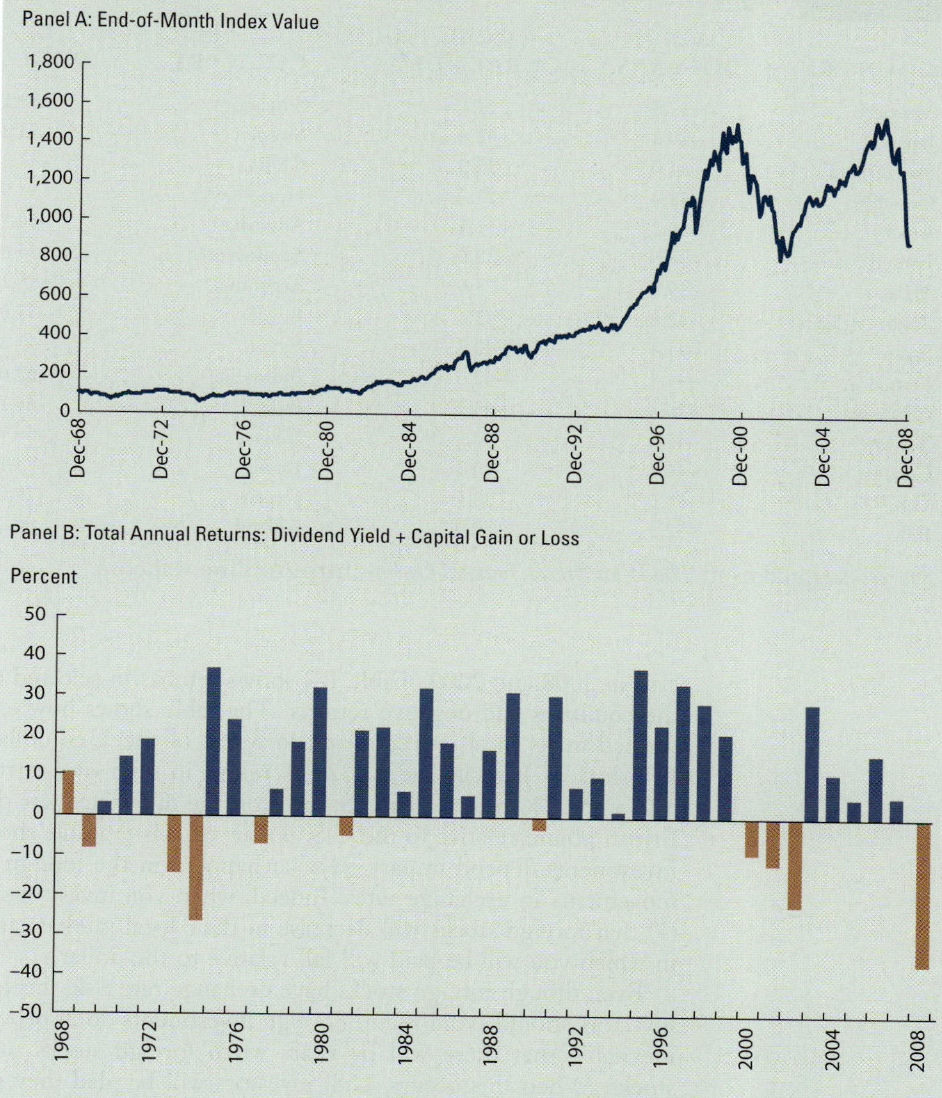

Sources: Returns data are from various issues of *The Wall Street Journal*, "Investment Scoreboard" section; the index level is from **http://finance.yahoo.com.**

year-to-year risk by showing annual returns. Notice that stocks have had positive returns in most years, but there have been several years with large losses. Stocks lost more than 40% of their value during 1973–1974 and again during 2000–2002, and they lost 37% of their value in 2008 alone. We will examine risk in more detail later in the book, but even a cursory glance at Figure 1-4 shows just how risky stocks can be!

U.S. stocks amount to only about 40% of the world's stocks, and this is prompting many U.S. investors to also hold foreign stocks. Analysts have long touted the benefits of investing overseas, arguing that foreign stocks improve diversification and provide good growth opportunities. This has been true for many years, but it wasn't the

TABLE 1-2 2008 Performance of Selected Dow Jones Global Stock Indexes, Ranked Highest to Lowest

COUNTRY	U.S. DOLLARS	LOCAL CURRENCY	COUNTRY	U.S. DOLLARS	LOCAL CURRENCY
Morocco	−17.5%	−14.1%	Singapore	−53.1%	−53.0%
Japan	−29.3	−42.6	Sweden	−53.2	−42.7
Switzerland	−31.0	−35.0	China	−53.3	−53.6
Colombia	−31.4	−23.5	Hong Kong	−53.9	−54.2
Israel	−36.2	−37.4	Australia	−54.5	−42.7
United States	−38.6	−38.6	South Korea	−55.6	−40.3
Mexico	−39.8	−23.6	Argentina	−56.1	−51.9
South Africa	−42.8	−22.6	Brazil	−57.0	−43.7
Spain	−43.4	−40.5	Egypt	−57.2	−57.3
France	−45.5	−42.6	Indonesia	−63.0	−57.1
Germany	−46.3	−43.5	India	−66.7	−58.9
Taiwan	−47.6	−46.9	Ireland	−68.7	−67.1
Canada	−49.1	−36.3	Russia	−73.1	−66.6
U.K.	−51.2	−32.5	Cyprus	−79.0	−77.9
Italy	−52.5	−50.0	Iceland	−96.2	−92.6

Source: Adapted from *The Wall Street Journal Online*, **http://online.wsj.com**.

case in 2008 and 2009. Table 1-2 shows returns in selected countries. Notice that all the countries had negative returns. The table shows how each country's stocks performed in its local currency and in terms of the U.S. dollar. For example, in 2008 British (U.K.) stocks had a −32.5% return in their own currency, but that translated into a −51.2% return to a U.S. investor; the difference was due to depreciation in the British pound relative to the U.S. dollar. As this example shows, the results of foreign investments depend in part on what happens in the foreign economy and in part on movements in exchange rates. Indeed, when you invest overseas, you face two risks: (1) that foreign stocks will decrease in their local markets and (2) that the currencies in which you will be paid will fall relative to the dollar.

Even though foreign stocks have exchange rate risk, this by no means suggests that investors should avoid them. Foreign investments do improve diversification, and it is inevitable that there will be years when foreign stocks outperform U.S. domestic stocks. When this occurs, U.S. investors will be glad they put some of their money in overseas markets.

Self-Test

Explain how exchange rates affect the rate of return on international investments.

1.13 The Global Economic Crisis

Although the global economic crisis has many causes, mortgage securitization in the 2000s is certainly one culprit, so we begin with it.

The Globalization of Mortgage Market Securitization

A national TV program ran a documentary on the travails of Norwegian retirees resulting from defaults on Florida mortgages. Your first reaction might be to wonder how Norwegian retirees became financially involved with risky Florida mortgages.

We will break the answer to that question into two parts. First, we will identify the different links in the financial chain between the retirees and mortgagees. Second, we will explain why there were so many weak links.

In the movie *Jerry Maguire*, Tom Cruise said "Show me the money!" That's a good way to start identifying the financial links, starting with a single home purchase in Florida.

1. Home Purchase. In exchange for cash, a seller in Florida turned over ownership of a house to a buyer.

2. Mortgage Origination. To get the cash used to purchase the house, the home buyer signed a mortgage loan agreement and gave it to an "originator." Years ago the originator would probably have been an S&L or a bank, but more recently the originators have been specialized mortgage brokers, which was true in this case. The broker gathered and examined the borrower's credit information, arranged for an independent appraisal of the house's value, handled the paperwork, and received a fee for these services.

3. Securitization and Resecuritization. In exchange for cash, the originator sold the mortgage to a securitizing firm. For example, Merrill Lynch's investment banking operation was a major player in securitizing loans. It would bundle large numbers of mortgages into pools and then create new securities that had claims on the pools' cash flows. Some claims were simple, such as a proportional share of a pool, and some claims were more complex, such as a claim on all interest payments during the first five years or a claim on only principal payments. More complicated claims were entitled to a fixed payment, while other claims would receive payments only after the "senior" claimants had been paid. These slices of the pool were called "tranches," which comes from a French word for slice.

Some of the tranches were themselves re-combined and then re-divided into securities called "collateralized debt obligations (CDOs)", some of which were themselves combined and subdivided into other securities, commonly called CDOs-squared. For example, Lehman Brothers often bought different tranches, split them into CDOs of differing risk, and then had the different CDOs rated by an agency like Moody's or Standard & Poor's.

There are two very important points to notice. First, the process didn't change the *total amount of risk* embedded in the mortgages, but it did make it possible to create some securities that were less risky than average and some that were more risky. Second, each time a new security was created or rated, fees were being earned by the investment banks and rating agencies.

4. The Investors. In exchange for cash, the securitizing firms sold the newly created securities to individual investors, hedge funds, college endowments, insurance companies, and other financial institutions, including a pension fund in Norway. Keep in mind that financial institutions are themselves funded by individuals, so cash begins with individuals and flows through the system until it is eventually received by the seller of the home. If all goes according to plan, payments on the mortgages eventually return to the individuals who originally provided the cash. But in this case, the chain was broken by a wave of mortgage defaults, resulting in problems for Norwegian retirees.

Students and managers often ask us, "What happened to all the money?" The short answer is "It went from investors to home sellers, with fees being skimmed off all along the way."

Although the process is complex, in theory there is nothing inherently wrong with it. In fact, it should, in theory, provide more funding for U.S. home purchasers, and it should allow risk to be shifted to those best able to bear it. Unfortunately, this isn't the end of the story.

The Dark Side of Securitization: The Sub-Prime Mortgage Meltdown

What caused the financial crisis? Entire books are now being written on this subject, but we can identify a few of the culprits.

Regulators Approved Sub-Prime Standards. In the 1980s and early 1990s, regulations did not permit a nonqualifying mortgage to be securitized, so most originators mandated that borrowers meet certain requirements, including having at least a certain minimum level of income relative to the mortgage payments and a minimum down payment relative to the size of the mortgage. But in the mid-1990s, Washington politicians wanted to extend home ownership to groups that traditionally had difficulty obtaining mortgages. To accomplish this, regulations were relaxed so that nonqualifying mortgages could be securitized. Such loans are commonly called sub-prime or Alt-A mortgages. Thus, riskier mortgages were soon being securitized and sold to investors. Again, there was nothing inherently wrong, provided the two following questions were being answered in the affirmative: One, were home buyers making sound decisions regarding their ability to repay the loans? And two, did the ultimate investors recognize the additional risk? We now know that the answer to both questions is a resounding "no." Homeowners were signing mortgages that they could not hope to repay, and investors treated these mortgages as if they were much safer than they actually were.

The Fed Helped Fuel the Real Estate Bubble. With more people able to get a mortgage, including people who should not have obtained one, the demand for homes increased. This alone would have driven up house prices. However, the Fed also slashed interest rates to historic lows after 9/11 to prevent a recession, and it kept them low for a long time. These low rates made mortgage payments lower, which made home ownership seem even more affordable, again contributing to an increase in the demand for housing. Figure 1-5 shows that the combination of lower mortgage qualifications and lower interest rates caused house prices to skyrocket. Thus, the Fed contributed to an artificial bubble in real estate.

Home Buyers Wanted More for Less. Even with low interest rates, how could sub-prime borrowers afford the mortgage payments, especially with house prices rising? First, most sub-prime borrowers chose an adjustable rate mortgage (ARM) with an interest rate based on a short-term rate, such as that on 1-year Treasury bonds, to which the lender added a couple of percentage points. Because the Fed had pushed short-term rates so low, the initial rates on ARMs were very low.

With a traditional fixed-rate mortgage, the payments remain fixed over time. But with an ARM, an increase in market interest rates triggers higher monthly payments, so an ARM is riskier than a fixed-rate mortgage. However, many borrowers chose an *even riskier* mortgage, the "option ARM," where the borrower can choose to make such low payments during the first couple of years that they don't even cover the interest, causing the loan balance to actually increase each month! At a later date, the payments would be reset to reflect both the current market interest rate and the higher loan balance. For example, in some cases a monthly payment of $948 for the first

FIGURE 1-5 The Real Estate Boom: Housing Prices and Mortgage Rates

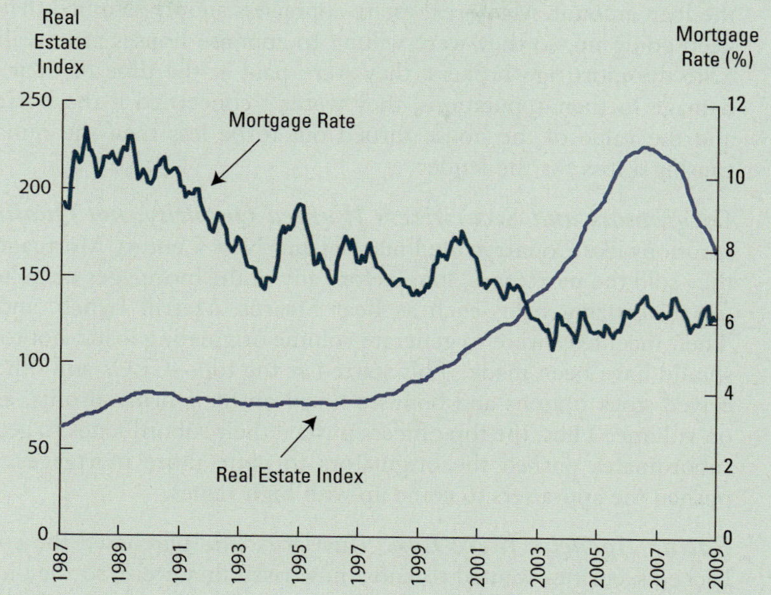

Notes:

1. The real estate index is the Case-Shiller composite index for house prices in 10 real estate markets, available at **http://www2.standardandpoors.com/spf/pdf/index/CSHomePrice_History_012724.xls.**
2. Interest rates are for 30-year conventional fixed rate mortgages, available from the St. Louis Federal Reserve: **http://research.stlouisfed.org/fred/.**

32 months was reset to \$2,454 for the remaining 328 months (we provide the calculations for this example in Chapter 4).

Why would anyone who couldn't afford to make a \$2,454 monthly payment choose an option ARM? Here are three possible reasons. First, some borrowers simply didn't understand the situation and were victims of predatory lending practices by brokers eager to earn fees regardless of the consequences. Second, some borrowers thought that the home price would go up enough to allow them to sell at a profit or else refinance with another low-payment loan. Third, some people were simply greedy and shortsighted, and they wanted to live in a better home than they could afford.

Mortgage Brokers Didn't Care. Years ago, S&Ls and banks had a vested interest in the mortgages they originated because they held them for the life of the loan—up to 30 years. If a mortgage went bad, the bank or S&L would lose money, so they were careful to verify that the borrower would be able to repay the loan. In the bubble years, though, over 80% of mortgages were arranged by independent mortgage brokers who received a commission. Thus, the broker's incentive was to complete deals even if the borrowers couldn't make the payments after the soon-to-come reset. So it's easy to understand (but not to approve!) why brokers pushed deals onto borrowers who were almost certain to default eventually.

Real Estate Appraisers Were Lax. The relaxed regulations didn't require the mortgage broker to verify the borrower's income, so these loans were called "liar loans" because the borrowers could overstate their income. But even in these cases the broker had to get an appraisal showing that the house's value was greater than the loan amount. Many real estate appraisers simply assumed that house prices would keep going up, so they were willing to appraise houses at unrealistically high values. Like the mortgage brokers, they were paid at the time of their service. Other than damage to their reputations, they weren't concerned if the borrower later defaulted and the value of the house turned out to be less than the remaining loan balance, causing a loss for the lender.

Originators and Securitizers Wanted Quantity, not Quality. Originating institutions like Countrywide Financial and New Century Mortgage made money when they sold the mortgages, long before any of the mortgages defaulted. The same is true for securitizing firms such as Bear Stearns, Merrill Lynch, and Lehman Brothers. Their incentives were to generate volume originating loans, not to make sure the loans should have been made. This started at the top—CEOs and other top executives received stock options and bonuses based on their firms' profits, and profits depended on volume. Thus, the top officers pushed their subordinates to generate volume, those subordinates pushed the originators to write more mortgages, and the originators pushed the appraisers to come up with high values.

Rating Agencies Were Lax. Investors who purchased the complicated mortgage backed securities wanted to know how risky they were, so they insisted on seeing the bonds' "ratings." Rating agencies were paid to investigate the details of each bond and to assign a rating which reflected the security's risk. The securitizing firms paid the rating agencies to do the ratings. For example, Lehman Brothers hired Moody's to rate some of their CDOs. Indeed, the investment banks would actually pay for advice from the rating agencies as they were designing the securities. The rating and consulting activities were extremely lucrative for the agencies, which ignored the obvious conflict of interest: The investment bank wanted a high rating, the rating agency got paid to help design securities that would qualify for a high rating, and high ratings led to continued business for the raters.

Insurance Wasn't Insurance. To provide a higher rating and make these mortgage-backed securities look even more attractive to investors, the issuers would frequently purchase a type of insurance policy on the security called a **credit default swap**. For example, suppose you had wanted to purchase a CDO from Lehman Brothers but were worried about the risk. What if Lehman Brothers had agreed to pay an annual fee to an insurance company like AIG, which would guarantee the CDO's payments if the underlying mortgages defaulted? You probably would have felt confident enough to buy the CDO.

But any similarity to a conventional insurance policy ends here. Unlike home insurance, where there is a single policyholder and a single insurer, totally uninvolved speculators can also make bets on your CDO by either selling or purchasing credit default swaps on the CDO. For example, a hedge fund could buy a credit default swap on your CDO if it thinks the CDO will default; or an investment bank like Bear Stearns could sell a swap, betting that the CDO won't default. In fact, the International Swaps and Derivatives Association estimates that in mid-2008 there was about $54 trillion in credit default swaps. This staggering amount is approximately 7 times the value of all U.S. mortgages, over 4 times the level of the U.S. national debt, and over twice the value of the entire U.S. stock market.

Another big difference is that home insurance companies are highly regulated, but there was virtually no regulation in the credit default swap market. The players traded directly among themselves, with no central clearinghouse. It was almost impossible to tell how much risk any of the players had taken on, making it impossible to know whether or not counterparties like AIG would be able to fulfill their obligations in the event of a CDO default. And that made it impossible to know the value of CDOs held by many banks, which in turn made it impossible to judge whether or not those banks were de facto bankrupt.

Rocket Scientists Had Poor Rearview Mirrors. Brilliant financial experts, often trained in physics and hired from rocket science firms, built elegant models to determine the value of these new securities. Unfortunately, a model is only as good as its inputs. The experts looked at the high growth rates of recent real estate prices (see Figure 1-5) and assumed that future growth rates also would be high. These high growth rates caused models to calculate very high CDO prices, at least until the real estate market crumbled.

Investors Wanted More for Less. In the early 2000s, low-rated debt (including mortgage-backed securities), hedge funds, and private equity funds produced great rates of return. Many investors jumped into this debt to keep up with the Joneses. As shown in Chapter 5 when we discuss bond ratings and bond spreads, investors began lowering the premium they required for taking on extra risk. Thus, investors focused primarily on returns and largely ignored risk. In fairness, some investors assumed the credit ratings were accurate, and they trusted the representatives of the investment banks selling the securities. In retrospect, however, Warren Buffett's maxim that "I only invest in companies I understand" seems wiser than ever.

The Emperor Has No Clothes. In 2006, many of the option ARMs began to reset, borrowers began to default, and home prices first leveled off and then began to fall. Things got worse in 2007 and 2008, and by early 2009, almost 1 out of 10 mortgages was in default or foreclosure, resulting in displaced families and virtual ghost towns of new subdivisions. As homeowners defaulted on their mortgages, so did the CDOs backed by the mortgages. That brought down the counterparties like AIG who had insured the CDOs via credit default swaps. Virtually overnight, investors realized that mortgage-backed security default rates were headed higher and that the houses used as collateral were worth less than the mortgages. Mortgage-backed security prices plummeted, investors quit buying newly securitized mortgages, and liquidity in the secondary market disappeared. Thus, the investors who owned these securities were stuck with pieces of paper that were substantially lower than the values reported on their balance sheets.

From Sub-Prime Meltdown to Liquidity Crisis to Economic Crisis

Like the Andromeda strain, the sub-prime meltdown went viral, and it ended up infecting almost all aspects of the economy. Financial institutions were the first to fall. Many originating firms had not sold all of their sub-prime mortgages, and they failed. For example, New Century declared bankruptcy in 2007, IndyMac was placed under FDIC control in 2008, and Countrywide was acquired by Bank of America in 2008 to avoid bankruptcy.

Securitizing firms also crashed, partly because they kept some of the new securities they created. For example, Fannie Mae and Freddie Mac had huge losses on their portfolio assets, causing them to be virtually taken over by the Federal Housing

Finance Agency in 2008. In addition to big losses on their own sub-prime portfolios, many investment banks also had losses related to their positions in credit default swaps. Thus, Lehman Brothers was forced into bankruptcy, Bear Stearns was sold to JPMorgan Chase, and Merrill Lynch was sold to Bank of America, with huge losses to their stockholders.

Because Lehman Brothers defaulted on some of its commercial paper, investors in the Reserve Primary Fund, a big money market mutual fund, saw the value of its investments "break the buck," dropping to less than a dollar per share. To avoid panic and a total lockdown in the money markets, the U.S. Treasury agreed to insure some investments in money market funds.

AIG was the number one backer of credit default swaps, and it operated worldwide. In 2008 it became obvious that AIG could not honor its commitments as a counterparty, so the Fed effectively nationalized AIG to avoid a domino effect in which AIG's failure would topple hundreds of other financial institutions.

In normal times, banks provide liquidity to the economy and funding for creditworthy businesses and individuals. These activities are absolutely crucial for a well-functioning economy. However, the financial contagion spread to commercial banks because some owned mortgage-backed securities, some owned commercial paper issued by failing institutions, and some had exposure to credit default swaps. As banks worried about their survival in the fall of 2008, they stopped providing credit to other banks and businesses. The market for commercial paper dried up to such an extent that the Fed began buying new commercial paper from issuing companies.

Banks also began hoarding cash rather than lending it. The Fed requires banks to keep 10% of the funds they raise from depositors on "reserve." Banks use the other 90% to make loans or to buy securities. In aggregate, there usually has been about $9 billion in excess reserves—that is, reserves over and above the 10% they are required to keep on hand. However, at the end of 2008, banks held over $770 billion in excess reserves compared to $75 billion in required reserves. This hoarding may have reduced the banks' risk, but it deprived the economy of a much needed capital.

Consequently, there has been a reduction in construction, manufacturing, retailing, and consumption, all of which caused job losses in 2008 and 2009, with more expected in the future. In short, this has led to a serious recession in the United States and most of the developed world, a recession that brings back memories of the Great Depression of the 1930s.

Self-Test

Briefly describe some of the mistakes that were made by participants in the sub-prime mortgage process.

1.14 The Big Picture

Finance has a lot of vocabulary and tools that might be new to you. To help you avoid getting bogged down in the trenches, Figure 1-6 presents the "big picture." A manager's primary job is to increase the company's intrinsic value, but how exactly does one go about doing that? The equation in the center of Figure 1-6 shows that intrinsic value is the present value of the firm's expected free cash flows, discounted at the weighted average cost of capital. Thus, there are two approaches for increasing intrinsic value: Improve FCF or reduce the WACC. Observe that several factors affect FCF and several factors affect the WACC. In the rest of the book's chapters, we will typically focus on only one of these factors, systematically building the vocabu-

FIGURE 1-6 The Determinants of Intrinsic Value: The Big Picture

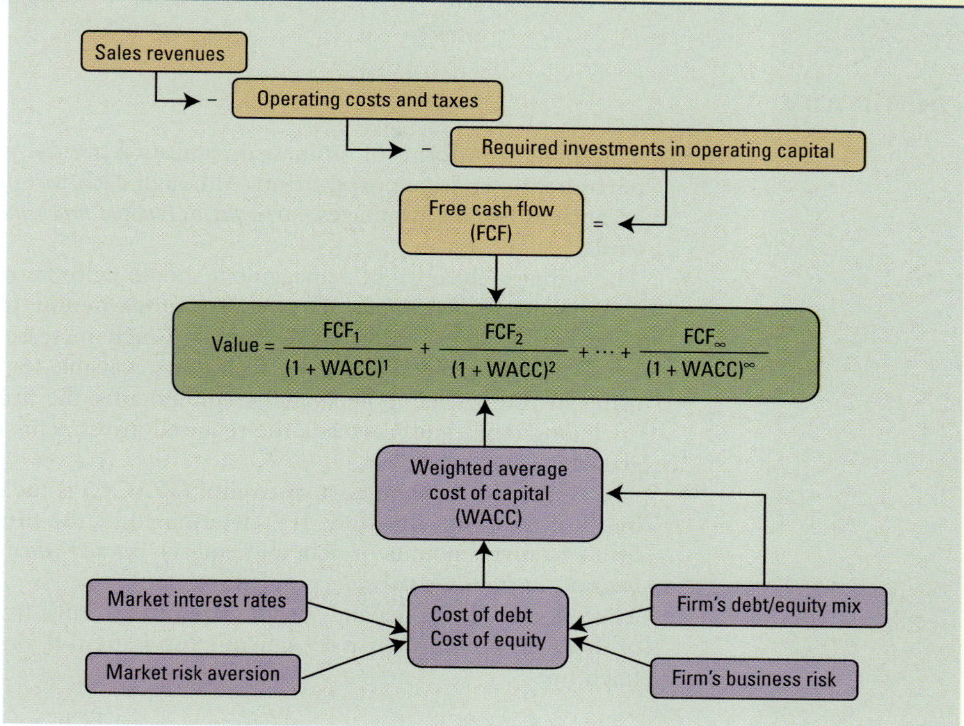

lary and tools that you will use after graduation to improve your company's intrinsic value. It is true that every manager needs to understand financial vocabulary and be able to apply financial tools, but really successful managers also understand how their decisions affect the big picture. So as you read this book, keep in mind where each topic fits into the big picture.

e-Resources

The textbook's Web site contains several types of files that will be helpful to you:

1. It contains *Excel* files, called *Tool Kits*, that provide well-documented models for almost all of the text's calculations. Not only will these *Tool Kits* help you with this finance course, they also will serve as tool kits for you in other courses and in your career.
2. There are problems at the end of the chapters that require spreadsheets, and the Web site contains the models you will need to begin work on these problems.

When we think it might be helpful for you to look at one of the Web site's files, we'll show an icon in the margin like the one shown here.

Other resources are also on the Web site, including Cyberproblems and problems that use the Thomson ONE—Business School Edition Web site. The textbook's Web site also contains an electronic library that contains Adobe PDF files for "extensions" to many chapters that cover additional useful material related to the chapter.

Summary

- The three main forms of business organization are the **proprietorship**, the **partnership**, and the **corporation**. Although each form of organization offers advantages and disadvantages, *corporations conduct much more business than the other forms.*
- The primary objective of management should be to *maximize stockholders' wealth*, and this means *maximizing the company's* **fundamental**, or **intrinsic, stock price**. Legal actions that maximize stock prices usually increase social welfare.
- **Free cash flows (FCFs)** are the cash flows available for distribution to all of a firm's investors (shareholders and creditors) after the firm has paid all expenses (including taxes) and has made the required investments in operations to support growth.
- The **weighted average cost of capital (WACC)** is the average return required by all of the firm's investors. It is determined by the firm's *capital structure* (the firm's relative amounts of debt and equity), *interest rates*, the firm's *risk*, and the *market's attitude toward risk.*
- The value of a firm depends on the size of the firm's free cash flows, the timing of those flows, and their risk. A **firm's fundamental**, or **intrinsic**, **value** is defined by

$$\text{Value} = \frac{FCF_1}{(1+WACC)^1} + \frac{FCF_2}{(1+WACC)^2} + \frac{FCF_3}{(1+WACC)^3} + \cdots + \frac{FCF_\infty}{(1+WACC)^\infty}$$

- Transfers of capital between borrowers and savers take place (1) by **direct transfers** of money and securities; (2) by transfers through **investment banking houses**, which act as go-betweens; and (3) by transfers through **financial intermediaries**, which create new securities.
- Four fundamental factors affect the cost of money: (1) **production opportunities**, (2) **time preferences for consumption**, (3) **risk**, and (4) **inflation**.
- **Derivatives**, such as options, are claims on other financial securities. In **securitization**, new securities are created from claims on packages of other securities.
- Major financial institutions include **commercial banks**, **savings and loan associations**, **mutual savings banks**, **credit unions**, **pension funds**, **life insurance companies**, **mutual funds**, **money market funds**, **hedge funds**, and **private equity funds**.
- **Spot markets** and **futures markets** are terms that refer to whether the assets are bought or sold for "on-the-spot" delivery or for delivery at some future date.
- **Money markets** are the markets for debt securities with maturities of less than a year. **Capital markets** are the markets for long-term debt and corporate stocks.
- **Primary markets** are the markets in which corporations raise new capital. **Secondary markets** are markets in which existing, already outstanding securities are traded among investors.
- Orders from buyers and sellers can be matched in one of three ways: (1) in an open outcry **auction**, (2) through **dealers**, and (3) automatically through an **electronic communications network (ECN)**.

- There are two basic types of markets—the physical location exchanges (such as the NYSE) and computer/telephone networks (such as Nasdaq).
- ***Web Extension 1A*** discusses derivatives, and ***Web Extension 1B*** provides additional coverage of stock markets.

Questions

(1–1) Define each of the following terms:

a. Proprietorship; partnership; corporation
b. Limited partnership; limited liability partnership; professional corporation
c. Stockholder wealth maximization
d. Money market; capital market; primary market; secondary market
e. Private markets; public markets; derivatives
f. Investment banker; financial services corporation; financial intermediary
g. Mutual fund; money market fund
h. Physical location exchanges; computer/telephone network
i. Open outcry auction; dealer market; electronic communications network (ECN)
j. Production opportunities; time preferences for consumption
k. Foreign trade deficit

(1–2) What are the three principal forms of business organization? What are the advantages and disadvantages of each?

(1–3) What is a firm's fundamental, or intrinsic, value? What might cause a firm's intrinsic value to be different than its actual market value?

(1–4) Edmund Enterprises recently made a large investment to upgrade its technology. Although these improvements won't have much of an impact on performance in the short run, they are expected to reduce future costs significantly. What impact will this investment have on Edmund Enterprises's earnings per share this year? What impact might this investment have on the company's intrinsic value and stock price?

(1–5) Describe the different ways in which capital can be transferred from suppliers of capital to those who are demanding capital.

(1–6) What are financial intermediaries, and what economic functions do they perform?

(1–7) Is an initial public offering an example of a primary or a secondary market transaction?

(1–8) Differentiate between dealer markets and stock markets that have a physical location.

(1–9) Identify and briefly compare the two leading stock exchanges in the United States today.

Mini Case

Assume that you recently graduated and have just reported to work as an investment advisor at the brokerage firm of Balik and Kiefer Inc. One of the firm's clients is Michelle DellaTorre, a professional tennis player who has just come to the United States from Chile. DellaTorre is a highly ranked tennis player who would like to start a company to produce and market apparel she designs. She also expects to invest substantial amounts of money through Balik and Kiefer.

DellaTorre is very bright, and she would like to understand in general terms what will happen to her money. Your boss has developed the following set of questions you must answer to explain the U.S. financial system to DellaTorre.

a. Why is corporate finance important to all managers?
b. Describe the organizational forms a company might have as it evolves from a start-up to a major corporation. List the advantages and disadvantages of each form.
c. How do corporations go public and continue to grow? What are agency problems? What is corporate governance?
d. What should be the primary objective of managers?

   (1) Do firms have any responsibilities to society at large?
   (2) Is stock price maximization good or bad for society?
   (3) Should firms behave ethically?

e. What three aspects of cash flows affect the value of any investment?
f. What are free cash flows?
g. What is the weighted average cost of capital?
h. How do free cash flows and the weighted average cost of capital interact to determine a firm's value?
i. Who are the providers (savers) and users (borrowers) of capital? How is capital transferred between savers and borrowers?
j. What do we call the price that a borrower must pay for debt capital? What is the price of equity capital? What are the four most fundamental factors that affect the cost of money, or the general level of interest rates, in the economy?
k. What are some economic conditions (including international aspects) that affect the cost of money?
l. What are financial securities? Describe some financial instruments.
m. List some financial institutions.
n. What are some different types of markets?
o. How are secondary markets organized?

   (1) List some physical location markets and some computer/telephone networks.
   (2) Explain the differences between open outcry auctions, dealer markets, and electronic communications networks (ECNs).

p. Briefly explain mortgage securitization and how it contributed to the global economic crisis.

CHAPTER 2
Financial Statements, Cash Flow, and Taxes

Even in today's era of financial crises, $14.6 billion is a lot of money. This is the amount of cash flow that Hewlett-Packard's (HP) operations generated in 2008, up from $9.6 billion in 2007, despite the recession. The ability to generate cash flow is the lifeblood of a company and the basis for its fundamental value. How did HP use this cash flow? HP invested for the future by making over $11 billion in acquisitions.

Other companies also generated large cash flows from operations in 2008, but they used the money differently. For example, Walgreens generated over $3 billion from its operations and used over $2 billion for capital expenditures, much of it on new stores and the purchase of worksite health centers.

Procter & Gamble generated $15.8 billion. P&G made relatively small capital expenditures (abut $3 billion) and returned the lion's share (over $12 billion) to shareholders as dividends or through stock repurchases.

Apple generated about $9.6 billion (up from $5.5 billion the previous year) but made relatively small capital expenditures, acquisitions, or distributions to shareholders. Instead, it put about $9.1 billion into short-term financial securities like T-bills.

These four well-managed companies used their operating cash flows in four different ways: HP made acquisitions, Walgreens spent on a mix of internal and external growth, P&G returned cash to shareholders, and Apple saved for a rainy day. Which company made the right choice? Only time will tell, but keep these companies and their different cash flow strategies in mind as you read this chapter.

Intrinsic Value, Free Cash Flow, and Financial Statements

In Chapter 1, we told you that managers should strive to make their firms more valuable and that the intrinsic value of a firm is determined by the present value of its free cash flows (FCF) discounted at the weighted average cost of capital (WACC). This chapter focuses on FCF, including its calculation from financial statements and its interpretation when evaluating a company and manager.

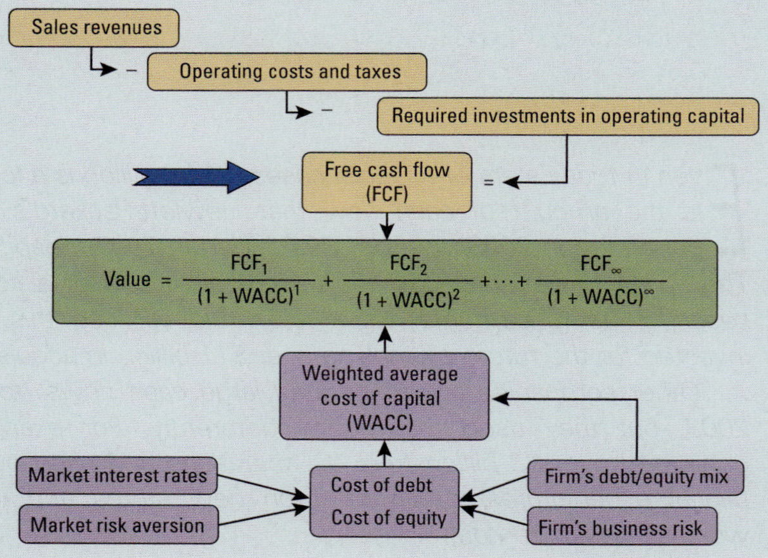

The textbook's Web site contains an Excel file that will guide you through the chapter's calculations. The file for this chapter is **Ch02 Tool Kit.xls**, and we encourage you to open the file and follow along as you read the chapter.

A manager's primary goal is to maximize the fundamental, or intrinsic, value of the firm's stock. This value is based on the stream of cash flows the firm is expected to generate in the future. But how does an investor go about estimating future cash flows, and how does a manager decide which actions are most likely to increase cash flows? The first step is to understand the financial statements that publicly traded firms must provide to the public. Thus, we begin with a discussion of financial statements, including how to interpret them and how to use them. Because value depends on usable, after-tax cash flows, we highlight the difference between accounting income and cash flow. In fact, it is *after-tax* cash flow that is important, so we also provide an overview of the federal income tax system.

A source for links to the annual reports of many companies is **http://www.annualreportservice.com**.

2.1 Financial Statements and Reports

A company's **annual report** usually begins with the chairman's description of the firm's operating results during the past year and a discussion of new developments that will affect future operations. The annual report also presents four basic financial statements—the *balance sheet*, the *income statement*, the *statement of stockholders' equity*, and the *statement of cash flows*.[1]

[1]Firms also provide less comprehensive quarterly reports. Larger firms file even more detailed statements, giving breakdowns for each major division or subsidiary, with the Securities and Exchange Commission (SEC). These reports, called *10-K reports*, are available on the SEC's Web site at **http://www.sec.gov** under the heading "EDGAR."

The quantitative and written materials are equally important. The financial statements report *what has actually happened* to assets, earnings, dividends, and cash flows during the past few years, whereas the written materials attempt to explain why things turned out the way they did.

For illustrative purposes, we use a hypothetical company, MicroDrive Inc., which produces hard drives for microcomputers. Formed in 1982, MicroDrive has grown steadily and has a reputation as one of the best firms in the microcomputer components industry.

Self-Test

What is the annual report, and what two types of information are given in it?
What four types of financial statements are typically included in the annual report?

2.2 The Balance Sheet

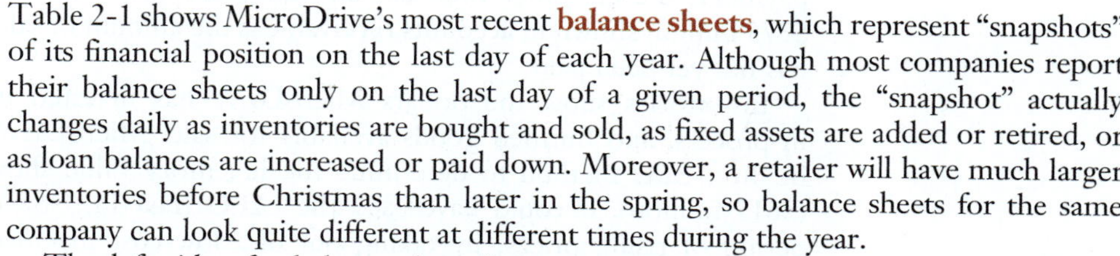

See **Ch02 Tool Kit.xls** for details.

Table 2-1 shows MicroDrive's most recent **balance sheets**, which represent "snapshots" of its financial position on the last day of each year. Although most companies report their balance sheets only on the last day of a given period, the "snapshot" actually changes daily as inventories are bought and sold, as fixed assets are added or retired, or as loan balances are increased or paid down. Moreover, a retailer will have much larger inventories before Christmas than later in the spring, so balance sheets for the same company can look quite different at different times during the year.

The left side of a balance sheet lists assets, which are the "things" the company owns. They are listed in order of "liquidity," or length of time it typically takes to convert them to cash at fair market values. The right side lists the claims that various groups have against the company's value, listed in the order in which they must be paid. For example, suppliers may have a claim called "accounts payable" that is due within 30 days, banks may have claims called "notes payable" that are due within 90 days, and bondholders may have claims that are not due for 20 years or more.

Stockholders come last, for two reasons. First, their claim represents ownership (or equity) and need never be "paid off." Second, they have a residual claim in the sense that they may receive payments only if the other claimants have already been paid. The nonstockholder claims are liabilities from the stockholders' perspective. The amounts shown on the balance sheets are called **book values** because they are based on the amounts recorded by bookkeepers when assets are purchased or liabilities are issued. As you will see throughout this textbook, book values may be very different from **market values**, which are the current values as determined in the marketplace.

TABLE 2-1 MicroDrive Inc.: December 31 Balance Sheets (Millions of Dollars)

ASSETS	2010	2009	LIABILITIES AND EQUITY	2010	2009
Cash and equivalents	$ 10	$ 15	Accounts payable	$ 60	$ 30
Short-term investments	0	65	Notes payable	110	60
Accounts receivable	375	315	Accruals	140	130
Inventories	615	415	Total current liabilities	$ 310	$ 220
Total current assets	$1,000	$ 810	Long-term bonds	754	580
Net plant and equipment	1,000	870	Total liabilities	$1,064	$ 800
			Preferred stock (400,000 shares)	40	40
			Common stock (50,000,000 shares)	130	130
			Retained earnings	766	710
			Total common equity	$ 896	$ 840
Total assets	$2,000	$1,680	Total liabilities and equity	$2,000	$1,680

The following sections provide more information about specific asset, liability, and equity accounts.

Assets

Cash, short-term investments, accounts receivable, and inventories are listed as current assets because MicroDrive is expected to convert them into cash within a year. All assets are stated in dollars, but only cash represents actual money that can be spent. Some marketable securities mature very soon, and these can be converted quickly into cash at prices close to their book values. Such securities are called "cash equivalents" and are included with cash. Therefore, MicroDrive could write checks for a total of $10 million. Other types of marketable securities have a longer time until maturity, and their market values are less predictable. These securities are classified as "short-term investments."

When MicroDrive sells its products to a customer but doesn't demand immediate payment, the customer then has an obligation called an "account receivable." The $375 million shown in accounts receivable is the amount of sales for which MicroDrive has not yet been paid.

Inventories show the dollars MicroDrive has invested in raw materials, work-in-process, and finished goods available for sale. MicroDrive uses the **FIFO (first-in, first-out)** method to determine the inventory value shown on its balance sheet ($615 million). It could have used the **LIFO (last-in, first-out)** method. During a period of rising prices, by taking out old, low-cost inventory and leaving in new, high-cost items, FIFO will produce a higher balance sheet inventory value but a lower cost of goods sold on the income statement. (This is strictly used for accounting; companies actually use older items first.) Because MicroDrive uses FIFO and because inflation has been occurring: (1) its balance sheet inventories are higher than they would have been had it used LIFO, (2) its cost of goods sold is lower than it would have been under LIFO, and (3) its reported profits are therefore higher. In MicroDrive's case, if the company had elected to switch to LIFO, then its balance sheet would have inventories of $585 million rather than $615 million and its earnings (discussed in the next section) would have been reduced by $18 million. Thus, the inventory valuation method can have a significant effect on financial statements, which is important to know when comparing different companies.

Rather than treat the entire purchase price of a long-term asset (such as a factory, plant, or equipment) as an expense in the purchase year, accountants "spread" the purchase cost over the asset's useful life.[2] The amount they charge each year is called the **depreciation** expense. Some companies report an amount called "gross plant and equipment," which is the total cost of the long-term assets they have in place, and another amount called "accumulated depreciation," which is the total amount of depreciation that has been charged on those assets. Some companies, such as MicroDrive, report only net plant and equipment, which is gross plant and equipment less accumulated depreciation. Chapter 11 provides a more detailed explanation of depreciation methods.

Liabilities and Equity

Accounts payable, notes payable, and accruals are listed as current liabilities because MicroDrive is expected to pay them within a year. When MicroDrive purchases supplies but doesn't immediately pay for them, it takes on an obligation called an account payable. Similarly, when MicroDrive takes out a loan that must be repaid within a year, it signs an IOU called a note payable. MicroDrive doesn't pay its taxes

[2]This is called *accrual accounting*, which attempts to match revenues to the periods in which they are earned and expenses to the periods in which the effort to generate income occurred.

THE GLOBAL ECONOMIC CRISIS

Let's Play Hide-and-Seek!

In a shameful lapse of regulatory accountability, banks and other financial institutions were allowed to use "structured investment vehicles" (SIVs) to hide assets and liabilities off their balance sheets and simply not report them. Here's how SIVs worked and why they subsequently failed. The SIV was set up as a separate legal entity that the bank owned and managed. The SIV would borrow money in the short-term market (backed by the credit of the bank) and then invest in long-term securities. As you might guess, many SIVs invested in mortgage-backed securities. When the SIV paid only 3% on its borrowings but earned 10% on its investments, the managing bank was able to report fabulous earnings, especially if it also earned fees for creating the mortgage securities that went into the SIV.

But this game of hide-and-seek doesn't have a happy ending. Mortgage-backed securities began defaulting in 2007 and 2008, causing the SIVs to pass losses through to the banks. SunTrust, Citigroup, Bank of America, and Northern Rock are just a few of the many banks that reported enormous losses in the SIV game. Investors, depositors, and the government eventually found the hidden assets and liabilities, but by then the assets were worth a lot less than the liabilities.

In a case of too little and too late, regulators are closing these loopholes, and it doesn't look like there will be any more SIVs in the near future. But the damage has been done, and the entire financial system is at risk in large part because of this high-stakes game of hide-and-seek.

or its employees' wages daily, and the amount it owes on these items at any point in time is called an "accrual" or an "accrued expense." Long-term bonds are also liabilities because they, too, reflect a claim held by someone other than a stockholder.

Preferred stock is a hybrid, or a cross between common stock and debt. In the event of bankruptcy, preferred stock ranks below debt but above common stock. Also, the preferred dividend is fixed, so preferred stockholders do not benefit if the company's earnings grow. Most firms do not use much, or even any, preferred stock, so "equity" usually means "common equity" unless the words "total" or "preferred" are included.

When a company sells shares of stock, the proceeds are recorded in the common stock account.[3] Retained earnings are the cumulative amount of earnings that have not been paid out as dividends. The sum of common stock and retained earnings is called "common equity," or sometimes just equity. If a company's assets could actually be sold at their book value, and if the liabilities and preferred stock were actually worth their book values, then a company could sell its assets, pay off its liabilities and preferred stock, and the remaining cash would belong to common stockholders. Therefore, common equity is sometimes called **net worth**—it's the assets net of the liabilities.

Self-Test

What is the balance sheet, and what information does it provide?
What determines the order of the information shown on the balance sheet?
Why might a company's December 31 balance sheet differ from its June 30 balance sheet?
A firm has $8 million in total assets. It has $3 million in current liabilities, $2 million in long-term debt, and $1 million in preferred stock. What is the total value of common equity? ($2 million)

[3]Companies sometimes break the total proceeds into two parts, one called "par" and the other called "paid-in capital" or "capital surplus." For example, if a company sells shares of stock for $10, it might record $1 of par and $9 of paid-in capital. For most purposes, the distinction between par and paid-in capital is not important, and most companies use no-par stock.

See **Ch02 Tool Kit.xls** for details.

2.3 The Income Statement

Table 2-2 shows the **income statements** for MicroDrive. Income statements can cover any period of time, but they are usually prepared monthly, quarterly, and annually. Unlike the balance sheet, which is a snapshot of a firm at a point in time, the income statement reflects performance during the period.

Subtracting operating costs from net sales but excluding depreciation and amortization results in **EBITDA**, which stands for earnings before interest, taxes, depreciation, and amortization. Depreciation and amortization are annual charges that reflect the estimated costs of the assets used up each year. Depreciation applies to tangible

TABLE 2-2 MicroDrive Inc.: Income Statements for Years Ending December 31 (Millions of Dollars, Except for Per Share Data)

	2010	2009
Net sales	$3,000.0	$2,850.0
Operating costs excluding depreciation and amortization	2,616.2	2,497.0
Earnings before interest, taxes, depreciation, and amortization (EBITDA)	$ 383.8	$ 353.0
Depreciation	100.0	90.0
Amortization	0.0	0.0
Depreciation and amortization	$ 100.0	$ 90.0
Earnings before interest and taxes (EBIT, or operating income)	$ 283.8	$ 263.0
Less interest	88.0	60.0
Earnings before taxes (EBT)	$ 195.8	$ 203.0
Taxes (40%)	78.3	81.2
Net income before preferred dividends	$ 117.5	$ 121.8
Preferred dividends	4.0	4.0
Net income	$ 113.5	$ 117.8
Additional Information		
Common dividends	$ 57.5	$ 53.0
Addition to retained earnings	$ 56.0	$ 64.8
Per Share Data		
Common stock price	$ 23.00	$ 26.00
Earnings per share (EPS)	$ 2.27	$ 2.36
Dividends per share (DPS)	$ 1.15	$ 1.06
Book value per share (BVPS)	$ 17.92	$ 16.80
Cash flow per share (CFPS)	$ 4.27	$ 4.16

Notes: There are 50,000,000 shares of common stock outstanding. Note that EPS is based on earnings after preferred dividends—that is, on net income available to common stockholders. Calculations of the most recent EPS, DPS, BVPS, and CFPS values are as follows:

$$\text{Earnings per share} = \text{EPS} = \frac{\text{Net income}}{\text{Common shares outstanding}} = \frac{\$113{,}500{,}000}{50{,}000{,}000} = \$\ 2.27$$

$$\text{Dividends per share} = \text{DPS} = \frac{\text{Dividends paid to common stockholders}}{\text{Common shares outstanding}} = \frac{\$57{,}500{,}000}{50{,}000{,}000} = \$\ 1.15$$

$$\text{Book value per share} = \text{BVPS} = \frac{\text{Total common equity}}{\text{Common shares outstanding}} = \frac{\$896{,}000{,}000}{50{,}000{,}000} = \$17.92$$

$$\text{Cash flow per share} = \text{CFPS} = \frac{\text{Net income} + \text{Depreciation} + \text{Amortization}}{\text{Common shares outstanding}} = \frac{\$213{,}500{,}000}{50{,}000{,}000} = \$\ 4.27$$

assets, such as plant and equipment, whereas amortization applies to intangible assets such as patents, copyrights, trademarks, and goodwill.[4] Because neither depreciation nor amortization is paid in cash, some analysts claim that EBITDA is a better measure of financial strength than is net income. However, as we show later in the chapter, EBITDA is not as important as free cash flow. In fact, some financial wags have stated that EBITDA really stands for "earnings before anything bad happens."

The net income available to common shareholders, which is revenues less expenses, taxes, and preferred dividends (but before paying common dividends), is generally referred to as **net income**, although it is also called **profit** or **earnings**, particularly in the news or financial press. Dividing net income by the number of shares outstanding gives earnings per share (EPS), which is often called "the bottom line." Throughout this book, unless otherwise indicated, net income means net income available to common stockholders.[5]

Self-Test

What is an income statement, and what information does it provide?

What is often called "the bottom line?"

What is EBITDA?

Regarding the time period reported, how does the income statement differ from the balance sheet?

A firm has $2 million in earnings before taxes. The firm has an interest expense of $300,000 and depreciation of $200,000; it has no amortization. What is its EBITDA? **($2.5 million)**

2.4 Statement of Stockholders' Equity

See **Ch02 Tool Kit.xls** *for details.*

Changes in stockholders' equity during the accounting period are reported in the **statement of stockholders' equity**. Table 2-3 shows that MicroDrive earned $113.5 million during 2010, paid out $57.5 million in common dividends, and plowed $56 million back into the business. Thus, the balance sheet item "Retained earnings" increased from $710 million at year-end 2009 to $766 million at year-end 2010.[6] The last column shows the beginning stockholders' equity, any changes, and the end-of-year stockholders' equity.

Note that "retained earnings" does not represent assets but is instead a *claim against assets.* In 2010, MicroDrive's stockholders allowed it to reinvest $56 million instead of distributing the money as dividends, and management spent this money

---

[4]The accounting treatment of goodwill resulting from mergers has changed in recent years. Rather than an annual charge, companies are required to periodically evaluate the value of goodwill and reduce net income only if the goodwill's value has decreased materially ("become impaired," in the language of accountants). For example, in 2002 AOL Time Warner wrote off almost $100 billion associated with the AOL merger. It doesn't take too many $100 billion expenses to really hurt net income!

[5]Companies also report "comprehensive income," which is the sum of net income and any "comprehensive" income item, such as unrealized gain or loss when an asset is marked-to-market. For our examples, we assume that there are no comprehensive income items.

Some companies also choose to report "pro forma income." For example, if a company incurs an expense that it doesn't expect to recur, such as the closing of a plant, it might calculate pro forma income as though it had not incurred the one-time expense. There are no hard-and-fast rules for calculating pro forma income, so many companies find ingenious ways to make pro forma income higher than traditional income. The SEC and the Public Company Accounting Oversight Board (PCAOB) are taking steps to reduce deceptive uses of pro forma reporting.

[6]If they had been applicable, then columns would have been used to show "Additional Paid-in Capital" and "Treasury Stock." Also, additional rows would have contained information on such things as new issues of stock, treasury stock acquired or reissued, stock options exercised, and unrealized foreign exchange gains or losses.

TABLE 2-3 MicroDrive Inc.: Statement of Stockholders' Equity, December 31, 2010 (Millions of Dollars)

	COMMON STOCK (MILLIONS)			
	SHARES	AMOUNT	RETAINED EARNINGS	TOTAL EQUITY
Balances, Dec. 31, 2009	50	$130.0	$710.0	$840.0
Net income			$113.5	$113.5
Cash dividends			(57.5)	(57.5)
Issuance of common stock	0	0.0		
Balances, Dec. 31, 2010	50	$130.0	$766.0	$896.0

Note: Here and throughout the book, parentheses are used to denote negative numbers.

on new assets. Thus, retained earnings, as reported on the balance sheet, does not represent cash and is not "available" for the payment of dividends or anything else.[7]

Self-Test

What is the statement of stockholders' equity, and what information does it provide?
Why do changes in retained earnings occur?
Explain why the following statement is true: "The retained earnings reported on the balance sheet does not represent cash and is not available for the payment of dividends or anything else."
A firm had a retained earnings balance of $3 million in the previous year. In the current year, its net income is $2.5 million. If it pays $1 million in common dividends in the current year, what is its resulting retained earnings balance? **($4.5 million)**

2.5 Net Cash Flow

A business's **net cash flow** generally differs from its *accounting profit* because some of the revenues and expenses listed on the income statement were not received or paid in cash during the year. The relationship between net cash flow and net income is:

$$\text{Net cash flow} = \text{Net income} - \text{Noncash revenues} + \text{Noncash charges} \quad (2\text{-}1)$$

The primary examples of noncash charges are depreciation and amortization. These items reduce net income but are not paid out in cash, so we add them back to net income when calculating net cash flow. Another example of a noncash charge is deferred taxes. In some instances, companies are allowed to defer tax payments to a later date even though the tax payment is reported as an expense on the income statement. Therefore, deferred tax payments are added to net income when calculat-

[7]The amount reported in the retained earnings account is *not* an indication of the amount of cash the firm has. Cash (as of the balance sheet date) is found in the cash account, an asset account. A positive number in the retained earnings account indicates only that in the past the firm earned some income, but its dividends paid were less than its earnings. Even though a company reports record earnings and shows an increase in its retained earnings account, it still may be short of cash.

The same situation holds for individuals. You might own a new BMW (no loan), lots of clothes, and an expensive stereo—and hence have a high net worth—but if you have only 23 cents in your pocket plus $5 in your checking account, you will still be short of cash.

ing net cash flow.[8] Sometimes a customer will purchase services or products that extend beyond the reporting date, such as iPhone subscriptions at Apple. Even if the company collects the cash at the time of the purchase, the company will spread the reported revenues over the life of the purchase. This causes income to be lower than cash flow in the first year and higher in any subsequent years, so adjustments are made when calculating net cash flow.

Depreciation and amortization usually are the largest noncash items, and in many cases the other noncash items roughly net out to zero. For this reason, many analysts assume that net cash flow equals net income plus depreciation and amortization:

$$\text{Net cash flow} = \text{Net income} + \text{Depreciation and amortization} \tag{2-2}$$

We will generally assume that Equation 2-2 holds. However, you should remember that Equation 2-2 will not accurately reflect net cash flow when there are significant noncash items other than depreciation and amortization.

We can illustrate Equation 2-2 with 2010 data for MicroDrive taken from Table 2-2:

$$\text{Net cash flow} = \$113.5 + \$100.0 = \$213.5 \text{ million}$$

To illustrate depreciation's effect, suppose a machine with a life of 5 years and zero expected salvage value was purchased in late 2009 for $100,000 and placed into service in early 2010. This $100,000 cost is not expensed in the purchase year; rather, it is charged against production over the machine's 5-year depreciable life. If the depreciation expense were not taken, then profits would be overstated and taxes would be too high. Therefore, the annual depreciation charge is deducted from sales revenues, along with such other costs as labor and raw materials, to determine income. However, because the $100,000 was actually expended back in 2009, the depreciation charged against income in 2010 and subsequent years is not a cash outflow. *Depreciation is a noncash charge, so it must be added back to net income to obtain the net cash flow.* If we assume that all other noncash items (including amortization) sum to zero, then net cash flow is simply equal to net income plus depreciation.

Self-Test

Differentiate between net cash flow and accounting profit.

A firm has net income of $5 million. Assuming that depreciation of $1 million is its only noncash expense, what is the firm's net cash flow? ($6 million)

2.6 Statement of Cash Flows

Even if a company reports a large net income during a year, the *amount of cash* reported on its year-end balance sheet may be the same or even lower than its beginning cash. The reason is that its net income can be used in a variety of ways, not just kept as cash in the bank. For example, the firm may use its net income to pay dividends, to increase inventories, to finance accounts receivable, to invest in fixed assets, to reduce debt, or to buy back common stock. Indeed, the company's *cash position* as reported on its balance sheet is affected by a great many factors, which include the following.

1. **Net income before preferred dividends.** Other things held constant, a positive net income will lead to more cash in the bank. However, as we shall discuss, other things generally are not held constant.

[8] Deferred taxes may arise, for example, if a company uses accelerated depreciation for tax purposes but straight-line depreciation for reporting its financial statements to investors. If deferred taxes are increasing, then the company is paying less in taxes than it reports to the public.

Financial Analysis on the WEB

A wide range of valuable financial information is available on the Web. With just a couple of clicks, an investor can easily find the key financial statements for most publicly traded companies. Here's a partial (by no means a complete) list of places you can go to get started.

- One of the very best sources of financial information is Thomson Financial. Go to the textbook's Web site and follow the directions to access Thomson ONE—Business School Edition. An especially useful feature is the ability to download up to 10 years of financial statements in spreadsheet form. First, enter the ticker for a company and click Go. From the top tab (in dark blue), select Financials. This will show a second row of items (in light blue). Selecting More from this row will reveal a drop-down menu. Select SEC Database Reports & Charts. This will bring up another drop-down menu that includes the 10-year balance sheets, income statements, and statement of cash flows. To download the financial statements into a spreadsheet, first select one of the statements, such as the 10YR Balance Sheet. The balance sheets will then be displayed on your browser page. To download, click on the *Excel* icon toward the right of the light blue row at the top of the Thomson ONE panel. This will bring up a dialog box that lets you download the *Excel* file to your computer.
- Try Yahoo! Finance's Web site, **http://finance.yahoo.com**. Here you will find updated market information along with links to a variety of interesting research sites. Enter a stock's ticker symbol, click GO, and you will see the stock's current price along with recent news about the company. The panel on the left has links to key statistics and to the company's income statement, balance sheet, statement of cash flows, and more. The Web site also has a list of insider transactions, so you can tell if a company's CEO and other key insiders are buying or selling their company's stock. In addition, there is a message board where investors share opinions about the company, and there is a link to the company's filings with the SEC. Note that, in most cases, a more complete list of the SEC filings can be found at **http://www.sec.gov**.
- Other sources for up-to-date market information are **http://money.cnn.com** and **http://www.zacks.com**. These sites also provide financial statements in standardized formats.
- Both **http://www.bloomberg.com** and **http://www.marketwatch.com** have areas where you can obtain stock quotes along with company financials, links to Wall Street research, and links to SEC filings.
- If you are looking for charts of key accounting variables (for example, sales, inventory, depreciation and amortization, and reported earnings) as well as financial statements, take a look at **http://www.smartmoney.com**.
- Another good place to look is **http://www.investor.reuters.com**. Here you can find links to analysts' research reports along with the key financial statements.
- Zacks (already mentioned) and **http://www.hoovers.com** have free research available along with more detailed information provided to subscribers.

In addition to this information, you may be looking for sites that provide opinions regarding the direction of the overall market and views regarding individual stocks. Two popular sites in this category are The Motley Fool's Web site, **http://www.fool.com**, and the Web site for The Street.com, **http://www.thestreet.com**.

2. **Noncash adjustments to net income.** To calculate cash flow, it is necessary to adjust net income to reflect noncash revenues and expenses, such as depreciation and deferred taxes, as shown previously in the calculation of net cash flow.
3. **Changes in working capital.** Increases in current assets other than cash (such as inventories and accounts receivable) decrease cash, whereas decreases in

these accounts increase cash. For example, if inventories are to increase, then the firm must use some of its cash to acquire the additional inventory. Conversely, if inventories decrease, this generally means the firm is selling inventories and not replacing all of them, hence generating cash. On the other hand, if payables increase then the firm has received additional credit from its suppliers, which saves cash, but if payables decrease, this means it has used cash to pay off its suppliers. Therefore, increases in current liabilities such as accounts payable increase cash, whereas decreases in current liabilities decrease cash.

4. **Investments.** If a company invests in fixed assets or short-term financial investments, this will reduce its cash position. On the other hand, if it sells some fixed assets or short-term investments, this will increase cash.
5. **Security transactions and dividend payments.** If a company issues stock or bonds during the year, the funds raised will increase its cash position. On the other hand, if the company uses cash to buy back outstanding stock or to pay off debt, or if it pays dividends to its shareholders, this will reduce cash.

Each of these five factors is reflected in the **statement of cash flows**, which summarizes the changes in a company's cash position. The statement separates activities into three categories, plus a summary section, as follows.

1. **Operating activities,** which includes net income, depreciation, changes in current assets and liabilities other than cash, short-term investments, and short-term debt.
2. **Investing activities,** which includes investments in or sales of fixed assets and short-term financial investments.
3. **Financing activities,** which includes raising cash by issuing short-term debt, long-term debt, or stock. Also, because dividend payments, stock repurchases, and principal payments on debt reduce a company's cash, such transactions are included here.

Accounting texts explain how to prepare the statement of cash flows, but the statement is used to help answer questions such as these: Is the firm generating enough cash to purchase the additional assets required for growth? Is the firm generating any extra cash that can be used to repay debt or to invest in new products? Such information is useful both for managers and investors, so the statement of cash flows is an important part of the annual report.

Table 2-4 shows MicroDrive's statement of cash flows as it would appear in the company's annual report. The top section shows cash generated by and used in operations—for MicroDrive, operations provided net cash flows of *minus* \$2.5 million. This subtotal, the minus \$2.5 million net cash flow provided by operating activities, is in many respects the most important figure in any of the financial statements. Profits as reported on the income statement can be "doctored" by such tactics as depreciating assets too slowly, not recognizing bad debts promptly, and the like. However, it is far more difficult to simultaneously doctor profits and the working capital accounts. Therefore, it is not uncommon for a company to report positive net income right up to the day it declares bankruptcy. In such cases, however, the net cash flow from operations almost always began to deteriorate much earlier, and analysts who kept an eye on cash flow could have predicted trouble. Therefore, if you are ever analyzing a company and are pressed for time, look first at the trend in net cash flow provided by operating activities, because it will tell you more than any other number.

See **Ch02 Tool Kit.xls** for details.

TABLE 2-4 MicroDrive Inc.: Statement of Cash Flows for 2010 (Millions of Dollars)

	CASH PROVIDED OR USED
Operating Activities	
Net income before preferred dividends	$117.5
Adjustments:	
Noncash adjustments:	
Depreciation[a]	100.0
Due to changes in working capital:[b]	
Increase in accounts receivable	(60.0)
Increase in inventories	(200.0)
Increase in accounts payable	30.0
Increase in accruals	10.0
Net cash provided (used) by operating activities	($ 2.5)
Investing Activities	
Cash used to acquire fixed assets[c]	($230.0)
Sale of short-term investments	$ 65.0
Net cash provided (used) by investing activities	($165.0)
Financing Activities	
Increase in notes payable	$ 50.0
Increase in bonds outstanding	174.0
Payment of preferred and common dividends	(61.5)
Net cash provided (used) by financing activities	$162.5
Summary	
Net change in cash	($ 5.0)
Cash at beginning of year	15.0
Cash at end of year	$ 10.0

[a]Depreciation is a noncash expense that was deducted when calculating net income. It must be added back to show the correct cash flow from operations.

[b]An increase in a current asset *decreases* cash. An increase in a current liability *increases* cash. For example, inventories increased by $200 million and therefore reduced cash by a like amount.

[c]The net increase in fixed assets is $130 million; however, this net amount is after a deduction for the year's depreciation expense. Depreciation expense would have to be added back to find the increase in gross fixed assets. From the company's income statement, we see that the 2010 depreciation expense is $100 million; thus, expenditures on fixed assets were actually $230 million.

The second section shows investing activities. MicroDrive purchased fixed assets totaling $230 million and sold $65 million of short-term investments, for a net cash flow from investing activities of *minus* $165 million.

The third section, financing activities, includes borrowing from banks (notes payable), selling new bonds, and paying dividends on common and preferred stock. MicroDrive raised $224 million by borrowing, but it paid $61.5 million in preferred and common dividends. Therefore, its net inflow of funds from financing activities was $162.5 million.

In the summary, when all of these sources and uses of cash are totaled, we see that MicroDrive's cash outflows exceeded its cash inflows by $5 million during 2010; that is, its net change in cash was a *negative* $5 million.

MicroDrive's statement of cash flows should be worrisome to its managers and to outside analysts. The company had a $2.5 million cash shortfall from operations, it spent an additional $230 million on new fixed assets, and it paid out another $61.5 million in dividends. It covered these cash outlays by borrowing heavily and by liquidating $65 million of short-term investments. Obviously, this situation cannot continue year after year, so something will have to be done. In Chapter 12, when we discuss financial planning, we consider some of the actions that MicroDrive's financial staff might recommend.[9]

Self-Test

What types of questions does the statement of cash flows answer?

Identify and briefly explain the three different categories of activities shown in the statement of cash flows.

A firm has inventories of $2 million for the previous year and $1.5 million for the current year. What impact does this have on net cash provided by operations? **(Increase of $500,000)**

2.7 Modifying Accounting Data for Managerial Decisions

Thus far in the chapter we have focused on financial statements as they are presented in the annual report. When you studied income statements in accounting, the emphasis was probably on the firm's net income, which is its **accounting profit**. However, the intrinsic value of a company's operations is determined by the stream of cash flows that the operations will generate now and in the future. To be more specific, the value of operations depends on all the future expected **free cash flows (FCF)**, defined as after-tax operating profit minus the amount of new investment in working capital and fixed assets necessary to sustain the business. *Therefore, the way for managers to make their companies more valuable is to increase free cash flow now and in the future.*

Notice that FCF is the cash flow *available for distribution to all the company's investors after the company has made all investments necessary to sustain ongoing operations.* How well have MicroDrive's managers done in generating FCF? In this section, we will calculate MicroDrive's FCF and evaluate the performance of MicroDrive's managers.

Figure 2-1 shows the five steps in calculating free cash flow. As we explain each individual step in the following sections, refer back to Figure 2-1 to keep the big picture in mind.

Net Operating Profit after Taxes (NOPAT)

If two companies have different amounts of debt and hence different amounts of interest charges, they could have identical operating performances but different net incomes—the one with more debt would have a lower net income. Net income is certainly important, but it does not always reflect the true performance of a company's operations or the effectiveness of its operating managers. A better measurement for comparing managers' performance is **net operating profit after taxes**, or **NOPAT**, which is the amount of profit a company would generate if it had no debt and held no financial assets. NOPAT is defined as follows:[10]

---

[9]For a more detailed discussion of financial statement analysis, see Lyn M. Fraser and Aileen Ormiston, *Understanding Financial Statements*, 9th ed. (Upper Saddle River, NJ: Prentice-Hall, 2010).

[10]For firms with a more complicated tax situation, it is better to define NOPAT as follows: NOPAT = (Net income before preferred dividends) + (Net interest expense)(1 − Tax rate). Also, if firms are able to defer paying some of their taxes, perhaps by the use of accelerated depreciation, then NOPAT should be adjusted to reflect the taxes that the company actually paid on its operating income. See P. Daves, M. Ehrhardt, and R. Shrieves, *Corporate Valuation: A Guide for Managers and Investors* (Mason, OH: Thomson South-Western, 2004) for a detailed explanation of these and other adjustments. Also see Tim Koller, Marc Goedhart, and David Wessels, *Valuation: Measuring and Managing the Value of Companies* (Hoboken, NJ: Wiley, 2005), and G. Bennett Stewart, *The Quest for Value* (New York: Harper Collins, 1991).

FIGURE 2-1 Calculating Free Cash Flow

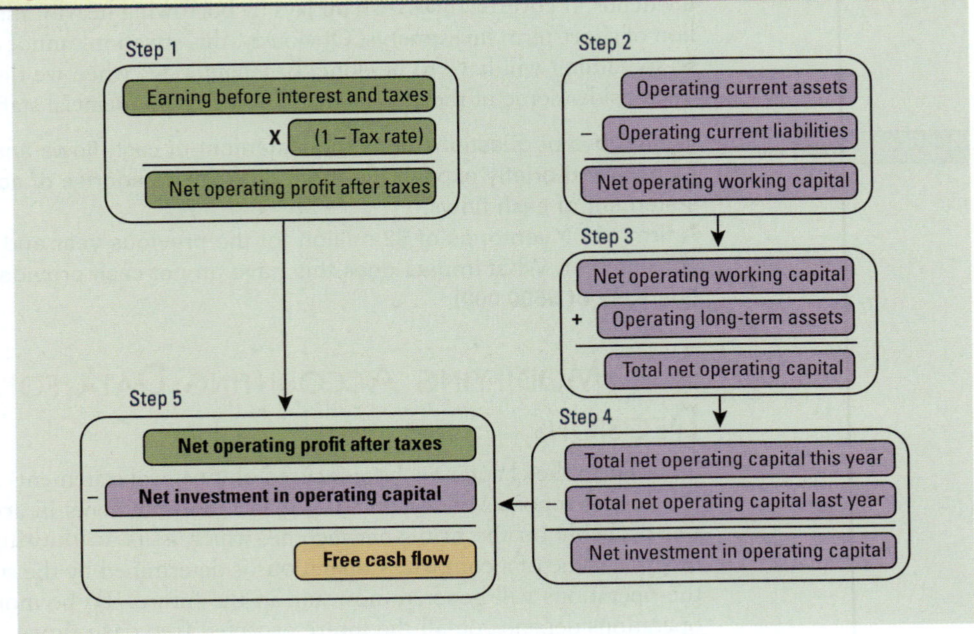

$$\text{NOPAT} = \text{EBIT}(1 - \text{Tax rate}) \tag{2-3}$$

Using data from the income statements of Table 2-2, MicroDrive's 2010 NOPAT is

$$\text{NOPAT} = \$283.8(1 - 0.4) = \$283.8(0.6) = \$170.3 \text{ million}$$

This means MicroDrive generated an after-tax operating profit of \$170.3 million, a little better than its previous NOPAT of \$263(0.6) = \$157.8 million. However, the income statements in Table 2-2 show that MicroDrive's earnings per share actually declined. This decrease in EPS was caused by an increase in interest expense, and not by a decrease in operating profit.

Net Operating Working Capital

Most companies need some current assets to support their operating activities. For example, all companies must carry some cash to "grease the wheels" of their operations. Companies continuously receive checks from customers and write checks to suppliers, employees, and so on. Because inflows and outflows do not coincide perfectly, a company must keep some cash in its bank account. In other words, some cash is required to conduct operations. The same is true for most other current assets, such as inventory and accounts receivable, which are required for normal operations. The short-term assets normally used in a company's operating activities are called **operating current assets**.

Not all current assets are operating current assets. For example, holdings of short-term securities generally result from investment decisions made by the treasurer and not as a natural consequence of operating activities. Therefore, short-term investments are **nonoperating assets** and normally are excluded when calculating operating current assets.[11] A useful rule of thumb is that if an asset pays interest, it should not be classified as an operating asset.

Some current liabilities—especially accounts payable and accruals—arise in the normal course of operations. Such short-term liabilities are called **operating current liabilities**. Not all current liabilities are operating current liabilities. For example, consider the current liability shown as notes payable to banks. The company could have raised an equivalent amount as long-term debt or could have issued stock, so the choice to borrow from the bank was a financing decision and not a consequence of operations. Again, the rule of thumb is that if a liability charges interest, it is not an operating liability.

If you are ever uncertain about whether an item is an operating asset or operating liability, ask yourself whether the item is a natural consequence of operations or if it is a discretionary choice, such as a particular method of financing or an investment in a particular financial asset. If it is discretionary, then the item is not an operating asset or liability.

Notice that each dollar of operating current liabilities is a dollar that the company does not have to raise from investors in order to conduct its short-term operating activities. Therefore, we define **net operating working capital (NOWC)** as operating current assets minus operating current liabilities. In other words, net operating working capital is the working capital acquired with investor-supplied funds. Here is the definition in equation form:

$$\text{Net operating working capital} = \text{Operating current assets} - \text{Operating current liabilities} \quad \text{(2-4)}$$

We can apply these definitions to MicroDrive, using the balance sheet data given in Table 2-1. Here is its net operating working capital at year-end 2010:

$$\begin{aligned}\text{NOWC} &= \text{Operating current assets} - \text{Operating current liabilities}\\ &= (\text{Cash} + \text{Accounts receivable} + \text{Inventories})\\ &\quad - (\text{Accounts payable} + \text{Accruals})\\ &= (\$10 + \$375 + \$615) - (\$60 + \$140)\\ &= \$800 \text{ million}\end{aligned}$$

For the previous year, net operating working capital was

$$\begin{aligned}\text{NOWC} &= (\$15 + \$315 + \$415) - (\$30 + \$130)\\ &= \$585 \text{ million}\end{aligned}$$

Total Net Operating Capital

In addition to working capital, most companies also use long-term assets to support their operations. These include land, buildings, factories, equipment, and the like. **Total net operating capital** is the sum of NOWC and operating long-term assets:

$$\text{Total net operating capital} = \text{NOWC} + \text{operating long-term assets} \quad \text{(2-5)}$$

[11] If the marketable securities are held as a substitute for cash and therefore reduce the cash requirements, then they may be classified as part of operating working capital. Generally, though, large holdings of marketable securities are held as a reserve for some contingency or else as a temporary "parking place" for funds prior to an acquisition, a major capital investment program, or the like.

Because MicroDrive's operating long-term assets consist only of net plant and equipment, its total net operating capital at year-end 2010 was

$$\begin{aligned}\text{Total net operating capital} &= \$800 + \$1{,}000\\ &= \$1{,}800 \text{ million}\end{aligned}$$

For the previous year, its total net operating capital was

$$\begin{aligned}\text{Total net operating capital} &= \$585 + \$870\\ &= \$1{,}455 \text{ million}\end{aligned}$$

Notice that we have defined total net operating capital as the sum of net operating working capital and operating long-term assets. In other words, our definition is in terms of operating assets and liabilities. However, we can also calculate total net operating capital by adding up the funds provided by investors, such as notes payable, long-term bonds, preferred stock, and common equity. For MicroDrive, the total capital provided by investors at year-end 2009 was $60 + $580 + $40 + $840 = $1,520 million. Of this amount, $65 million was tied up in short-term investments, which are not directly related to MicroDrive's operations. Therefore, only $1,520 − $65 = $1,455 million of investor-supplied capital was used in operations. Notice that this is exactly the same value as calculated before. This shows that we can calculate total net operating capital either from net operating working capital and operating long-term assets or from the investor-supplied funds. We usually base our calculations on operating data because this approach allows us to analyze a division, factory, or work center, whereas the approach based on investor-supplied capital is applicable only for the entire company.

The expression "total net operating capital" is a mouthful, so we often call it *operating capital* or even just *capital.* Also, unless we specifically say "investor-supplied capital," we are referring to total net operating capital.

Net Investment in Operating Capital

As calculated previously, MicroDrive had $1,455 million of total net operating capital at the end of 2009 and $1,800 million at the end of 2010. Therefore, during 2010, it made a **net investment in operating capital** of

$$\text{Net investment in operating capital} = \$1{,}800 - \$1{,}455 = \$345 \text{ million}$$

Most of this investment was made in net operating working capital, which rose from $585 million to $800 million, or by $215 million. This 37% increase in net operating working capital, in view of a sales increase of only 5% (from $2,850 to $3,000 million), should set off warning bells in your head: Why did MicroDrive tie up so much additional cash in working capital? Is the company gearing up for a big increase in sales, or are inventories not moving and receivables not being collected? We will address these questions in detail in Chapter 3, when we cover ratio analysis.

Calculating Free Cash Flow

Free cash flow is defined as

$$\text{FCF} = \text{NOPAT} - \text{Net investment in operating capital} \qquad \textbf{(2-6)}$$

MicroDrive's free cash flow in 2010 was

$$\begin{aligned}\text{FCF} &= \$170.3 - (\$1{,}800 - \$1{,}455)\\ &= \$170.3 - \$345\\ &= -\$174.7 \text{ million}\end{aligned}$$

Financial Bamboozling: How to Spot It

Recent accounting frauds by Enron, WorldCom, Xerox, Merck, Arthur Andersen, Tyco, and many others have shown that analysts can no longer blindly assume that a firm's published financial statements are the best representation of its financial position. Clearly, many companies were "pushing the envelope" if not outright lying in an effort to make their companies look better.

A recent *Fortune* article points out that there are only three basic ways to manipulate financial statements: moving earnings from the future to the present, avoiding taxes, or hiding debt. For example, suppose one telecom firm (think WorldCom or Global Crossing) sold the right to use parts of its fiber-optic network for 10 years to another telecom firm for $100 million. The seller would immediately record revenues of $100 million. The buyer, however, could spread the expense over 10 years and report an expense of only $10 million this year. The buyer would simultaneously sell similar rights to the original seller for $100 million. This way, no cash changes hands, both companies report an extra $100 million in revenue, but each reports a cost of only $10 million. Thus, both companies "created" an extra $90 million in pre-tax profits without actually doing anything. Of course, both companies will have to report an extra $10 million expense each year for the remaining 9 years, but they have each boosted short-term profits and thus this year's executive bonuses. To boost earnings next year, all they have to do is play the same game, but on a bigger scale.

For hiding debt, it's hard to beat Enron's special purpose entities (SPEs). These SPEs owed hundreds of millions of dollars, and it turned out that Enron was responsible for this debt, even though it never showed up on Enron's financial statements.

How can you spot bamboozling? Here are some tips. When companies have lots of write-offs or charges for restructuring, it could be that they are planning on managing earnings in the future. In other words, they sandbag this year to pad next year's earnings. Beware of serial acquirers, especially if they use their own stock to buy other companies. This can increase reported earnings, but it often erodes value since the acquirer usually pays a large premium for the target. Watch out for companies that depreciate their assets much more slowly than others in the industry (this is shown in the financial statements' footnotes). This causes their current earnings to look larger than their competitors', even though they aren't actually performing any better. Perhaps the best evidence of bamboozling is if earnings are consistently growing faster than cash flows, which almost always indicates a financial scam.

Sources: Geoffrey Colvin, "Bamboozling: A Field Guide," *Fortune*, July 8, 2002, 51; and Shawn Tully, "Don't Get Burned," *Fortune*, February 18, 2002, 87–90.

Although we prefer this approach to calculating FCF, sometimes the financial press calculates FCF with a different approach. The results are the same either way, but you should be aware of this alternative approach. The difference lies in how depreciation is treated. To see this, notice that net fixed assets rose from \$870 to \$1,000 million, or by \$130 million. However, MicroDrive reported \$100 million of depreciation, so its gross investment in fixed assets was \$130 + \$100 = \$230 million for the year. With this background, the **gross investment in operating capital** is

$$\text{Gross investment in operating capital} = \text{Net investment in operating capital} + \text{Depreciation} \quad \text{(2-7)}$$

For MicroDrive, the gross investment in operating capital was:

$$\text{Gross investment in operating capital} = \$345 + \$100 = \$445 \text{ million}$$

Because depreciation is a noncash expense, some analysts calculate **operating cash flow** as

$$\text{Operating cash flow} = \text{NOPAT} + \text{Depreciation} \tag{2-8}$$

MicroDrive's most recent operating cash flow is

$$\text{Operating cash flow} = \text{NOPAT} + \text{Depreciation} = \$170.3 + \$100 = \$270.3$$

An algebraically equivalent expression for free cash flow in terms of operating cash flow and gross investment in operating capital is

$$\begin{aligned} \text{FCF} &= \begin{pmatrix} \text{NOPAT} \\ + \text{Depreciation} \end{pmatrix} - \begin{pmatrix} \text{Net investment} \\ \text{in operating capital} \\ + \text{Depreciation} \end{pmatrix} \\ &= \begin{matrix} \text{Operating} \\ \text{cash flow} \end{matrix} - \begin{matrix} \text{Gross investment} \\ \text{in operating capital} \end{matrix} \\ &= \begin{matrix} \text{Operating} \\ \text{cash flow} \end{matrix} - \begin{matrix} \text{Gross investment} \\ \text{in long-term} \\ \text{operating assets} \end{matrix} - \begin{matrix} \text{Investment} \\ \text{in NOWC} \end{matrix} \end{aligned} \tag{2-9}$$

For MicroDrive, this definition produces FCF of –\$174.7, the same value as found earlier:

$$\begin{aligned} \text{FCF} &= (\$170.3 + \$100) - \$445 \\ &= -\$174.7 \text{ million} \end{aligned}$$

Equations 2-6 and 2-9 are equivalent because depreciation is added to both NOPAT and net investment in Equation 2-6 to arrive at Equation 2-9. We usually use Equation 2-6, because it saves us this step, but you should be aware of this alternative approach.

The Uses of FCF

Recall that free cash flow (FCF) is the amount of cash that is available for distribution to all investors, including shareholders and debtholders. There are five good uses for FCF:

1. Pay interest to debtholders, keeping in mind that the net cost to the company is the after-tax interest expense.
2. Repay debtholders; that is, pay off some of the debt.
3. Pay dividends to shareholders.
4. Repurchase stock from shareholders.
5. Buy short-term investments or other nonoperating assets.

Consider MicroDrive, with its FCF of –\$174.7 million in 2010. How did MicroDrive use the FCF?

MicroDrive's income statement shows an interest expense of \$88 million. With a tax rate of 40%, the after-tax interest payment for the year is

$$\text{After-tax interest payment} = \$88(1 - 40\%) = \$52.8 \text{ million}$$

The net amount of debt that is repaid is equal to the amount at the beginning of the year minus the amount at the end of the year. This includes notes payable and long-term debt. If the amount of ending debt is less than the beginning debt, the company paid down some of its debt. But if the ending debt is greater than the beginning debt, the company actually borrowed additional funds from creditors. In that case, it would be a negative use of FCF. For MicroDrive, the net debt repayment for 2010 is

$$\text{Net reduction in debt} = (\$60 + \$580) - (\$754 - \$110) = -\$224 \text{ million}$$

This is a "negative use" of FCF because it increased the debt balance. This is typical of most companies because growing companies usually add debt each year.

MicroDrive paid \$4 million in preferred dividends and \$57.5 in common dividends for a total of

$$\text{Dividend payments} = \$4 + \$57.5 = \$61.5 \text{ million}$$

The net amount of stock that is repurchased is equal to the amount at the beginning of the year minus the amount at the end of the year. This includes preferred stock and common stock. If the amount of ending stock is less than the beginning stock, then the company made net repurchases. But if the ending stock is greater than the beginning stock, the company actually made net issuances. In that case, it would be a negative use of FCF. Even though MicroDrive neither issued nor repurchased stock during the year, many companies use FCF to repurchase stocks as a replacement for or supplement to dividends, as we discuss in Chapter 14.

The amount of net purchases of short-term investments is equal to the amount at the end of the year minus the amount at the beginning of the year. If the amount of ending investments is greater than the beginning investments, then the company made net purchases. But if the ending investments are less than the beginning investments, the company actually sold investments. In that case, it would be a negative use of FCF. MicroDrive's net purchases of short-term investments in 2010 is:

$$\text{Net purchases of short-term investments} = \$0 - \$65 = -\$65 \text{ million}$$

Notice that this is a "negative use" because MicroDrive sold short-term investments instead of purchasing them.

We combine these individual uses of FCF to find the total uses.

1. After-tax interest:	\$ 52.8
2. Net debt repayments:	–224.0
3. Dividends:	61.5
4. Net stock repurchases:	0.0
5. Net purchases of ST investments:	–65.0
Total uses of FCF:	–\$174.7

The –\$174.7 total for uses of FCF is identical to the value of FCF from operations that we calculated previously. If it were not equal, then we would have made an error somewhere in our calculations.

Observe that a company does not use FCF to acquire operating assets, because the calculation of FCF already takes into account the purchase of operating assets needed to support growth. Unfortunately, there is evidence to suggest that some companies with high FCF tend to make unnecessary investments that don't add value, such as paying too much to acquire another company. Thus, high FCF can cause waste if managers fail to act in the best interests of shareholders. As discussed in Chapter 1, this is called an agency cost, since managers are hired as agents to act on behalf of stockholders. We discuss agency costs and ways to control them in Chapter 13, where we discuss value-based management and corporate governance, and in Chapter 15, where we discuss the choice of capital structure.

FCF and Corporate Value

Free cash flow is the amount of cash available for distribution to investors; so the fundamental value of a company to its investors depends on the present value of its expected future FCFs, discounted at the company's weighted average cost of capital (WACC). Subsequent chapters will develop the tools needed to forecast FCFs and evaluate their risk. Chapter 13 ties all this together with a model that is used to calculate the value of a company. Even though you do not yet have all the tools to apply the model, it's important that you understand this basic concept: *FCF is the cash flow available for distribution to investors. Therefore, the fundamental value of a firm primarily depends on its expected future FCF.*

Evaluating FCF, NOPAT, and Operating Capital

Even though MicroDrive had a positive NOPAT, its very high investment in operating assets resulted in a negative FCF. Because free cash flow is the cash flow available for distribution to investors, MicroDrive's negative FCF meant that MicroDrive had to sell short-term investments and so investors actually had to provide *additional* money to keep the business going.

Is a negative free cash flow always bad? The answer is, "Not necessarily; it depends on why the free cash flow was negative." It's a bad sign if FCF was negative because NOPAT was negative, since then the company is probably experiencing operating problems. However, many high-growth companies have positive NOPAT but negative FCF because they are making large investments in operating assets to support growth. There is nothing wrong with profitable growth, even if it causes negative cash flows.

One way to determine whether growth is profitable is by examining the **return on invested capital (ROIC)**, which is the ratio of NOPAT to total operating capital. If the ROIC exceeds the rate of return required by investors, then a negative free cash flow caused by high growth is nothing to worry about. Chapter 13 discusses this in detail.

To calculate the ROIC, we first calculate NOPAT and operating capital. The return on invested capital is a performance measure that indicates how much NOPAT is generated by each dollar of operating capital:

$$\text{ROIC} = \frac{\text{NOPAT}}{\text{Operating capital}} \tag{2-10}$$

If ROIC is greater than the rate of return that investors require, which is the weighted average cost of capital (WACC), then the firm is adding value.

As noted previously, a negative FCF is not necessarily bad, provided it is due to high, profitable growth.[12] For example, Qualcomm's sales grew by 26% in 2008, which led to large capital investments and a FCF of *negative* \$4.6 billion. However, its ROIC was about 29%, so the growth was profitable. At some point Qualcomm's growth will slow and will not require large capital investments. If Qualcomm maintains a high ROIC, then its FCF will become positive and very large as growth slows.

MicroDrive had an ROIC in 2010 of 9.46% (\$170.3/\$1,800 = 0.0946). Is this enough to cover its cost of capital? We'll answer that question in the next section.

---

[12] If g is the growth rate in capital, then with a little (or a lot of!) algebra, free cash flow is

$$\text{FCF} = \text{Capital}\left(\text{ROIC} - \frac{g}{1+g}\right)$$

This shows that when the growth rate gets almost as high as ROIC, then FCF will be negative.

Self-Test

What is net operating working capital? Why does it exclude most short-term investments and also notes payable?
What is total net operating capital? Why is it important for managers to calculate a company's capital requirements?
Why is NOPAT a better performance measure than net income?
What is free cash flow? Why is it important?
A firm's total net operating capital for the previous year was $2 million. For the current year, its total net operating capital is $2.5 million and its NOPAT is $1.2 million. What is its free cash flow for the current year? **($700,000)**

2.8 MVA AND EVA

Neither traditional accounting data nor the modified data discussed in the preceding section incorporates stock prices, even though the primary goal of management is to maximize the firm's stock price. Financial analysts have therefore developed two additional performance measures, Market Value Added (MVA) and Economic Value Added (EVA). These concepts are discussed in this section.[13]

Market Value Added (MVA)

The primary goal of most firms is to maximize shareholders' wealth. This goal obviously benefits shareholders, but it also helps to ensure that scarce resources are allocated efficiently, which benefits the economy. Shareholder wealth is maximized by maximizing the *difference* between the market value of the firm's stock and the amount of equity capital that was supplied by shareholders. This difference is called the **Market Value Added (MVA)**:

$$\begin{aligned} \text{MVA} &= \text{Market value of stock} - \text{Equity capital supplied by shareholders} \\ &= (\text{Shares outstanding})(\text{Stock price}) - \text{Total common equity} \end{aligned} \quad (2\text{-}11)$$

WWW

For an updated estimate of Coca-Cola's MVA, go to **http://finance.yahoo.com**, *enter KO, and click GO. This shows the market value of equity, called Mkt Cap. To get the book value of equity, select Balance Sheet from the left panel.*

To illustrate, consider Coca-Cola. In January 2009, its total market equity value was $103.2 billion while its balance sheet showed that stockholders had put up only $23.7 billion. Thus, Coca-Cola's MVA was $103.2 – $23.7 = $79.5 billion. This $79.5 billion represents the difference between the money that Coca-Cola's stockholders have invested in the corporation since its founding—including indirect investment by retaining earnings—and the cash they could get if they sold the business. The higher its MVA, the better the job management is doing for the firm's shareholders.

Sometimes MVA is defined as the total market value of the company minus the total amount of investor-supplied capital:

$$\begin{aligned} \text{MVA} &= \text{Total market value} - \text{Total investor-supplied capital} \\ &= (\text{Market value of stock} + \text{Market value of debt}) \\ &\quad - \text{Total investor-supplied capital} \end{aligned} \quad (2\text{-}11\text{a})$$

---

[13]The concepts of EVA and MVA were developed by Joel Stern and Bennett Stewart, co-founders of the consulting firm Stern Stewart & Company. Stern Stewart copyrighted the terms "EVA" and "MVA," so other consulting firms have given other names to these values. Still, EVA and MVA are the terms most commonly used in practice.

For most companies, the total amount of investor-supplied capital is the sum of equity, debt, and preferred stock. We can calculate the total amount of investor-supplied capital directly from their reported values in the financial statements. The total market value of a company is the sum of the market values of common equity, debt, and preferred stock. It is easy to find the market value of equity, since stock prices are readily available, but it is not always easy to find the market value of debt. Hence, many analysts use the value of debt that is reported in the financial statements, which is the debt's book value, as an estimate of its market value.

For Coca-Cola, the total amount of reported debt was about \$24.4 billion, and Coca-Cola had no preferred stock. Using this as an estimate of the market value of debt, Coke's total market value was \$103.2 + \$24.4 = \$127.6 billion. The total amount of investor-supplied funds was \$23.7 + \$24.4 = \$48.1 billion. Using these total values, the MVA was \$127.6 − \$48.1 = \$79.5 billion. Note that this is the same answer as when we used the previous definition of MVA. Both methods will give the same result if the market value of debt is approximately equal to its book value.

Economic Value Added (EVA)

Whereas MVA measures the effects of managerial actions since the very inception of a company, **Economic Value Added (EVA)** focuses on managerial effectiveness in a given year. The basic EVA formula is:

$$\begin{aligned} \text{EVA} &= \text{Net operating profit after taxes (NOPAT)} \\ &\quad - \text{After-tax dollar cost of capital used to support operations} \\ &= \text{EBIT}(1 - \text{Tax rate}) - (\text{Total net operating capital})(\text{WACC}) \end{aligned} \tag{2-12}$$

We can also calculate EVA in terms of ROIC:

$$\text{EVA} = (\text{Operating capital})(\text{ROIC} - \text{WACC}) \tag{2-13}$$

As this equation shows, a firm adds value—that is, has a positive EVA—if its ROIC is greater than its WACC. If WACC exceeds ROIC, then new investments in operating capital will reduce the firm's value.

Economic Value Added is an estimate of a business's true economic profit for the year, and it differs sharply from accounting profit.[14] EVA represents the residual income that remains after the cost of *all* capital, including equity capital, has been deducted, whereas accounting profit is determined without imposing a charge for equity capital. As we discuss in Chapter 9, equity capital has a cost because shareholders give up the opportunity to invest and earn returns elsewhere when they provide capital to the firm. This cost is an *opportunity cost* rather than an *accounting cost*, but it is quite real nevertheless.

Note that when calculating EVA we do not add back depreciation. Although it is not a cash expense, depreciation is a cost because worn-out assets must be replaced, and it is therefore deducted when determining both net income and EVA. Our calculation of

[14]The most important reason EVA differs from accounting profit is that the cost of equity capital is deducted when EVA is calculated. Other factors that could lead to differences include adjustments that might be made to depreciation, to research and development costs, to inventory valuations, and so on. These other adjustments also can affect the calculation of investor-supplied capital, which affects both EVA and MVA. See Stewart, *The Quest for Value*, cited in footnote 10.

EVA assumes that the true economic depreciation of the company's fixed assets exactly equals the depreciation used for accounting and tax purposes. If this were not the case, adjustments would have to be made to obtain a more accurate measure of EVA.

Economic Value Added measures the extent to which the firm has increased shareholder value. Therefore, if managers focus on EVA, this will help to ensure that they operate in a manner that is consistent with maximizing shareholder wealth. Note too that EVA can be determined for divisions as well as for the company as a whole, so it provides a useful basis for determining managerial performance at all levels. Consequently, EVA is being used by an increasing number of firms as the primary basis for determining managerial compensation.

Table 2-5 shows how MicroDrive's MVA and EVA are calculated. The stock price was $23 per share at year-end 2010, down from $26 per share the previous year. Its WACC, which is the percentage after-tax cost of capital, was 10.8% in 2009 and 11.0% in 2010, and its tax rate was 40%. Other data in Table 2-5 were given in the basic financial statements provided earlier in the chapter.

Note first that the lower stock price and the higher book value of equity (due to retaining earnings during 2010) combined to reduce the MVA. The 2010 MVA is still positive, but $460 – $254 = $206 million of stockholders' value was lost during the year.

Economic Value Added for 2009 was just barely positive, and in 2010 it was negative. Operating income (NOPAT) rose, but EVA still declined, primarily because the amount of capital rose more sharply than NOPAT—by about 26% versus 8%—and the cost of this additional capital pulled EVA down.

Recall also that net income fell, but not nearly so dramatically as the decline in EVA. Net income does not reflect the amount of equity capital employed, but EVA

See **Ch02 Tool Kit.xls** for details.

TABLE 2-5 MVA and EVA for MicroDrive Inc. (Millions of Dollars)

	2010	2009
MVA Calculation		
Price per share	$ 23.0	$ 26.0
Number of shares (millions)	50.0	50.0
Market value of equity = Share price × Number of shares	$1,150.0	$1,300.0
Book value of equity	$ 896.0	$ 840.0
MVA = Market value – Book value	$ 254.0	$ 460.0
EVA Calculation		
EBIT	$ 283.8	$ 263.0
Tax rate	40.0%	40.0%
NOPAT = EBIT(1 – T)	$ 170.3	$ 157.8
Total investor-supplied operating capital[a]	$1,800.0	$1,455.0
Weighted average cost of capital, WACC (%)	11.0%	10.8%
Dollar cost of capital = Operating capital × WACC	$ 198.0	$ 157.1
EVA = NOPAT – Dollar cost of capital	($ 27.7)	$ 0.7
ROIC = NOPAT ÷ Operating capital	9.46%	10.85%
ROIC – Cost of capital = ROIC – WACC	(1.54%)	0.05%
EVA = Operating capital × (ROIC – WACC)	($ 27.7)	$ 0.7

[a]Investor-supplied operating capital equals the sum of notes payable, long-term debt, preferred stock, and common equity, less short-term investments. It could also be calculated as total liabilities and equity minus accounts payable, accruals, and short-term investments. It is also equal to total net operating capital.

Sarbanes-Oxley and Financial Fraud

Investors need to be cautious when they review financial statements. Although companies are required to follow generally accepted accounting principles (GAAP), managers still have quite a lot of discretion in deciding how and when to report certain transactions. Consequently, two firms in exactly the same operating situation may report financial statements that convey different impressions about their financial strength. Some variations may stem from legitimate differences of opinion about the correct way to record transactions. In other cases, managers may choose to report numbers in a way that helps them present either higher earnings or more stable earnings over time. As long as they follow GAAP, such actions are not illegal, but these differences make it harder for investors to compare companies and gauge their true performances.

Unfortunately, there have also been cases where managers overstepped the bounds and reported fraudulent statements. Indeed, a number of high-profile executives have faced criminal charges because of their misleading accounting practices. For example, in June 2002 it was discovered that WorldCom (now called MCI) had committed the most massive accounting fraud of all time by recording over $7 billion of ordinary operating costs as capital expenditures, thus overstating net income by the same amount.

WorldCom's published financial statements fooled most investors—investors bid the stock price up to $64.50, and banks and other lenders provided the company with more than $30 billion of loans. Arthur Andersen, the firm's auditor, was faulted for not detecting the fraud. WorldCom's CFO and CEO were convicted, and Arthur Andersen went bankrupt. But that didn't help the investors who relied on the published financial statements.

In response to these and other abuses, Congress passed the Sarbanes-Oxley Act of 2002. One of its provisions requires both the CEO and the CFO to sign a statement certifying that the "financial statements and disclosures fairly represent, in all material respects, the operations and financial condition" of the company. This will make it easier to haul off in handcuffs a CEO or CFO who has been misleading investors. Whether this will prevent future financial fraud remains to be seen.

does. Because of this omission, net income is not as useful as EVA for setting corporate goals and measuring managerial performance.

We will have more to say about both MVA and EVA later in the book, but we can close this section with two observations. First, there is a relationship between MVA and EVA, but it is not a direct one. If a company has a history of negative EVAs, then its MVA will probably be negative; conversely, its MVA probably will be positive if the company has a history of positive EVAs. However, the stock price, which is the key ingredient in the MVA calculation, depends more on expected future performance than on historical performance. Therefore, a company with a history of negative EVAs could have a positive MVA, provided investors expect a turnaround in the future.

The second observation is that when EVAs or MVAs are used to evaluate managerial performance as part of an incentive compensation program, EVA is the measure that is typically used. The reasons are: (1) EVA shows the value added during a given year, whereas MVA reflects performance over the company's entire life, perhaps even including times before the current managers were born; and (2) EVA can be applied to individual divisions or other units of a large corporation, whereas MVA must be applied to the entire corporation.

Self-Test

Define "Market Value Added (MVA)" and "Economic Value Added (EVA)."

How does EVA differ from accounting profit?

A firm has $100 million in total net operating capital. Its return on invested capital is 14%, and its weighted average cost of capital is 10%. What is its EVA? **($4 million)**

2.9 The Federal Income Tax System

The value of any financial asset (including stocks, bonds, and mortgages), as well as most real assets such as plants or even entire firms, depends on the after-tax stream of cash flows produced by the asset. The following sections describe the key features of corporate and individual taxation.

Corporate Income Taxes

The corporate tax structure, shown in Table 2-6, is relatively simple. The **marginal tax rate** is the rate paid on the last dollar of income, while the **average tax rate** is the average rate paid on all income. To illustrate, if a firm had \$65,000 of taxable income, its tax bill would be

$$\begin{aligned}\text{Taxes} &= \$7{,}500 + 0.25(\$65{,}000 - \$50{,}000)\\ &= \$7{,}500 + \$3{,}750 = \$11{,}250\end{aligned}$$

Its marginal rate would be 25%, and its average tax rate would be \$11,250/\$65,000 = 17.3%. Note that corporate income above \$18,333,333 has an average and marginal tax rate of 35%.[15]

TABLE 2-6 Corporate Tax Rates as of January 2008

IF A CORPORATION'S TAXABLE INCOME IS	IT PAYS THIS AMOUNT ON THE BASE OF THE BRACKET	PLUS THIS PERCENTAGE ON THE EXCESS OVER THE BASE	AVERAGE TAX RATE AT TOP OF BRACKET
Up to \$50,000	\$0	15%	15.0%
\$50,000–\$75,000	\$7,500	25	18.3
\$75,000–\$100,000	\$13,750	34	22.3
\$100,000–\$335,000	\$22,250	39	34.0
\$335,000–\$10,000,000	\$113,900	34	34.0
\$10,000,000–\$15,000,000	\$3,400,000	35	34.3
\$15,000,000–\$18,333,333	\$5,150,000	38	35.0
Over \$18,333,333	\$6,416,667	35	35.0

[15]Prior to 1987, many large, profitable corporations such as General Electric and Boeing paid no income taxes. The reasons for this were as follows: (1) expenses, especially depreciation, were defined differently for calculating taxable income than for reporting earnings to stockholders, so some companies reported positive profits to stockholders but losses—hence no taxes—to the Internal Revenue Service; and (2) some companies that did have tax liabilities used various tax credits to offset taxes that would otherwise have been payable. This situation was effectively eliminated in 1987.

The principal method used to eliminate this situation is the Alternative Minimum Tax (AMT). Under the AMT, both corporate and individual taxpayers must figure their taxes in two ways, the "regular" way and the AMT way, and then pay the higher of the two. The AMT is calculated as follows: (1) Figure your regular taxes. (2) Take your taxable income under the regular method and then add back certain items, especially income on certain municipal bonds, depreciation in excess of straight-line depreciation, certain research and drilling costs, itemized or standard deductions (for individuals), and a number of other items. (3) The income determined in (2) is defined as AMT income, and it must then be multiplied by the AMT tax rate to determine the tax due under the AMT system. An individual or corporation must then pay the higher of the regular tax or the AMT tax. In 2008, there were two AMT tax rates for individuals (26% and 28%, depending on the level of AMT income and filing status). Most corporations have an AMT of 20%. However, there is no AMT for very small companies, defined as those that have had average sales of less than \$7.5 million for the past 3 years.

Interest and Dividend Income Received by a Corporation. Interest income received by a corporation is taxed as ordinary income at regular corporate tax rates. However, *70% of the dividends received by one corporation from another is excluded from taxable income, while the remaining 30% is taxed at the ordinary tax rate.*[16] Thus, a corporation earning more than $18,333,333 and paying a 35% marginal tax rate would pay only (0.30)(0.35) = 0.105 = 10.5% of its dividend income as taxes, so its effective tax rate on dividends received would be 10.5%. If this firm had $10,000 in pre-tax dividend income, then its after-tax dividend income would be $8,950:

$$\begin{aligned}\text{After-tax income} &= \text{Before-tax income} - \text{Taxes}\\ &= \text{Before-tax income} - (\text{Before-tax income})\ (\text{Effective tax rate})\\ &= \text{Before-tax income}\ (1 - \text{Effective tax rate})\\ &= \$10{,}000[1 - (0.30)(0.35)]\\ &= \$10{,}000(1 - 0.105) = \$10{,}000(0.895) = \$8{,}950.\end{aligned}$$

See **Ch02 Tool Kit.xls** *for details.*

If the corporation pays its own after-tax income out to its stockholders as dividends, then the income is ultimately subjected to *triple taxation:* (1) the original corporation is first taxed, (2) the second corporation is then taxed on the dividends it received, and (3) the individuals who receive the final dividends are taxed again. This is the reason for the 70% exclusion on intercorporate dividends.

If a corporation has surplus funds that can be invested in marketable securities, the tax treatment favors investment in stocks, which pay dividends, rather than in bonds, which pay interest. For example, suppose GE had $100,000 to invest, and suppose it could buy either bonds that paid interest of $8,000 per year or preferred stock that paid dividends of $7,000. GE is in the 35% tax bracket; therefore, its tax on the interest, if it bought bonds, would be 0.35($8,000) = $2,800, and its after-tax income would be $5,200. If it bought preferred (or common) stock, its tax would be 0.35[(0.30)($7,000)] = $735, and its after-tax income would be $6,265. Other factors might lead GE to invest in bonds, but the tax treatment certainly favors stock investments when the investor is a corporation.[17]

Interest and Dividends Paid by a Corporation. A firm's operations can be financed with either debt or equity capital. If the firm uses debt then it must pay interest on this debt, but if the firm uses equity then it is expected to pay dividends to the equity investors (stockholders). The interest *paid* by a corporation is deducted from its operating income to obtain its taxable income, but dividends paid are not deductible. Therefore, a firm needs $1 of pre-tax income to pay $1 of interest, but if it is in

---

[16]The size of the dividend exclusion actually depends on the degree of ownership. Corporations that own less than 20% of the stock of the dividend-paying company can exclude 70% of the dividends received; firms that own more than 20% but less than 80% can exclude 80% of the dividends; and firms that own more than 80% can exclude the entire dividend payment. We will, in general, assume a 70% dividend exclusion.

[17]This illustration demonstrates why corporations favor investing in lower-yielding preferred stocks over higher-yielding bonds. When tax consequences are considered, the yield on the preferred stock, [1 − 0.35(0.30)](7.0%) = 6.265%, is higher than the yield on the bond, (1 − 0.35)(8.0%) = 5.2%. Also, note that corporations are restricted in their use of borrowed funds to purchase other firms' preferred or common stocks. Without such restrictions, firms could engage in *tax arbitrage*, whereby the interest on borrowed funds reduces taxable income on a dollar-for-dollar basis while taxable income is increased by only $0.30 per dollar of dividend income. Thus, current tax laws reduce the 70% dividend exclusion in proportion to the amount of borrowed funds used to purchase the stock.

the 40% federal-plus-state tax bracket, it must earn \$1.67 of pre-tax income to pay \$1 of dividends:

$$\text{Pre-tax income needed to pay \$1 of dividends} = \frac{\$1}{1 - \text{Tax rate}} = \frac{\$1}{0.60} = \$1.67$$

Working backward, if a company has \$1.67 in pre-tax income, it must pay \$0.67 in taxes: (0.4)(\$1.67) = \$0.67. This leaves the firm with after-tax income of \$1.00.

Of course, it is generally not possible to finance exclusively with debt capital, and the risk of doing so would offset the benefits of the higher expected income. Still, *the fact that interest is a deductible expense has a profound effect on the way businesses are financed: Our corporate tax system favors debt financing over equity financing*. This point is discussed in more detail in Chapters 9 and 15.

Corporate Capital Gains. Before 1987, corporate long-term capital gains were taxed at lower rates than corporate ordinary income, so the situation was similar for corporations and individuals. Under current law, however, corporations' capital gains are taxed at the same rates as their operating income.

Corporate Loss Carryback and Carryforward. Ordinary corporate operating losses can be carried back **(carryback)** to each of the preceding 2 years and forward **(carryforward)** for the next 20 years and thus be used to offset taxable income in those years. For example, an operating loss in 2010 could be carried back and used to reduce taxable income in 2008 and 2009 as well as forward, if necessary, to reduce taxes in 2011, 2012, and so on, to the year 2030. After carrying back 2 years, any remaining loss is typically carried forward first to the next year, then to the one after that, and so on, until losses have been used up or the 20-year carryforward limit has been reached.

To illustrate, suppose Apex Corporation had \$2 million of *pre-tax* profits (taxable income) in 2008 and 2009, and then, in 2010, Apex lost \$12 million. Also, assume that Apex's federal-plus-state tax rate is 40%. As shown in Table 2-7, the company would use the carryback feature to recompute its taxes for 2008, using \$2 million of the 2010 operating losses to reduce the 2008 pre-tax profit to zero. This would permit it to recover the taxes paid in 2008. Therefore, in 2010 Apex would receive a refund of its 2008 taxes because of the loss experienced in 2010. Because \$10 million of the

TABLE 2-7 Apex Corporation: Calculation of \$12 Million Loss Carryback and Amount Available for Carryforward

	PAST YEAR 2008	PAST YEAR 2009	CURRENT YEAR 2010
Original taxable income	\$2,000,000	\$2,000,000	–\$12,000,000
Carryback credit	2,000,000	2,000,000	
Adjusted profit	\$ 0	\$ 0	
Taxes previously paid (40%)	800,000	800,000	
Difference = Tax refund due	\$ 800,000	\$ 800,000	
Total tax refund received			\$ 1,600,000
Amount of loss carryforward available			
Current loss			–\$12,000,000
Carryback losses used			4,000,000
Carryforward losses still available			–\$ 8,000,000

See **Ch02 Tool Kit.xls** for details.

unrecovered losses would still be available, Apex would repeat this procedure for 2009. Thus, in 2010 the company would pay zero taxes for 2010 and also would receive a refund for taxes paid in 2008 and 2009. Apex would still have $8 million of unrecovered losses to carry forward, subject to the 20-year limit. This $8 million could be used to offset future taxable income. The purpose of this loss treatment is to avoid penalizing corporations whose incomes fluctuate substantially from year to year.

Improper Accumulation to Avoid Payment of Dividends. Corporations could refrain from paying dividends and thus permit their stockholders to avoid personal income taxes on dividends. To prevent this, the Tax Code contains an **improper accumulation** provision that states that earnings accumulated by a corporation are subject to penalty rates *if the purpose of the accumulation is to enable stockholders to avoid personal income taxes*. A cumulative total of $250,000 (the balance sheet item "retained earnings") is by law exempted from the improper accumulation tax for most corporations. This is a benefit primarily to small corporations.

The improper accumulation penalty applies only if the retained earnings in excess of $250,000 are *shown by the IRS to be unnecessary to meet the reasonable needs of the business*. A great many companies do indeed have legitimate reasons for retaining more than $250,000 of earnings. For example, earnings may be retained and used to pay off debt, to finance growth, or to provide the corporation with a cushion against possible cash drains caused by losses. How much a firm should be allowed to accumulate for uncertain contingencies is a matter of judgment. We shall consider this matter again in Chapter 14, which deals with corporate dividend policy.

Consolidated Corporate Tax Returns. If a corporation owns 80% or more of another corporation's stock, then it can aggregate income and file one consolidated tax return; thus, the losses of one company can be used to offset the profits of another. (Similarly, one division's losses can be used to offset another division's profits.) No business ever wants to incur losses (you can go broke losing $1 to save 35¢ in taxes), but tax offsets do help make it more feasible for large, multidivisional corporations to undertake risky new ventures or ventures that will suffer losses during a developmental period.

Taxes on Overseas Income. Many U.S. corporations have overseas subsidiaries, and those subsidiaries must pay taxes in the countries where they operate. Often, foreign tax rates are lower than U.S. rates. As long as foreign earnings are reinvested overseas, no U.S. tax is due on those earnings. However, when foreign earnings are repatriated to the U.S. parent, they are taxed at the applicable U.S. rate, less a credit for taxes paid to the foreign country. As a result, U.S. corporations such as IBM, Coca-Cola, and Microsoft have been able to defer billions of dollars of taxes. This procedure has stimulated overseas investments by U.S. multinational firms—they can continue the deferral indefinitely, but only if they reinvest the earnings in their overseas operations.[18]

Taxation of Small Businesses: S Corporations

The Tax Code provides that small businesses that meet certain restrictions may be set up as corporations and thus receive the benefits of the corporate form of organization—especially limited liability—yet still be taxed as proprietorships or partnerships rather

[18]This is a contentious political issue. U.S. corporations argue that our tax system is similar to systems in the rest of the world, and if they were taxed immediately on all overseas earnings then they would be at a competitive disadvantage vis-à-vis their global competitors. Others argue that taxation encourages overseas investments at the expense of domestic investments, contributing to the jobs outsourcing problem and also to the federal budget deficit.

than as corporations. These corporations are called **S corporations**. ("Regular" corporations are called C corporations.) If a corporation elects S corporation status for tax purposes, then all of the business's income is reported as personal income by its stockholders, on a pro rata basis, and thus is taxed at the rates that apply to individuals. This is an important benefit to the owners of small corporations in which all or most of the income earned each year will be distributed as dividends, because then the income is taxed only once, at the individual level.

Personal Taxes

See **Web Extension 2A** *on the textbook's Web site for details concerning personal taxation.*

Web Extension 2A provides a more detailed treatment of individual taxation, but the key elements are presented here. **Ordinary income** consists primarily of wages or profits from a proprietorship or partnership, plus investment income. For the 2009 tax year, individuals with less than $8,350 of taxable income are subject to a federal income tax rate of 10%. For those with higher income, tax rates increase and go up to 35%, depending on the level of income. This is called a **progressive tax**, because the higher one's income, the larger the percentage paid in taxes.

As noted before, individuals are taxed on investment income as well as earned income, but with a few exceptions and modifications. For example, interest received from most state and local government bonds, called **municipals** or **"munis,"** is not subject to federal taxation. However, interest earned on most other bonds or lending is taxed as ordinary income. This means that a lower-yielding muni can provide the same after-tax return as a higher-yielding corporate bond. For a taxpayer in the 35% marginal tax bracket, a muni yielding 5.5% provides the same after-tax return as a corporate bond with a pre-tax yield of 8.46%: 8.46%(1 − 0.35) = 5.5%.

Assets such as stocks, bonds, and real estate are defined as capital assets. If you own a capital asset and its price goes up, then your wealth increases, but you are not liable for any taxes on your increased wealth until you sell the asset. If you sell the asset for more than you originally paid, the profit is called a **capital gain**; if you sell it for less, then you suffer a **capital loss**. The length of time you owned the asset determines the tax treatment. If held for less than one year, then your gain or loss is simply added to your other ordinary income. If held for more than a year, then gains are called *long-term capital gains* and are taxed at a lower rate. See ***Web Extension 2A*** for details, but the long-term capital gains rate is 15% for most situations.

Under the 2003 tax law changes, dividends are now taxed as though they were capital gains. As stated earlier, corporations may deduct interest payments but not dividends when computing their corporate tax liability, which means that dividends are taxed twice, once at the corporate level and again at the personal level. This differential treatment motivates corporations to use debt relatively heavily and to pay small (or even no) dividends. The 2003 tax law did not eliminate the differential treatment of dividends and interest payments from the corporate perspective, but it did make the tax treatment of dividends more similar to that of capital gains from investors' perspectives. To see this, consider a company that doesn't pay a dividend but instead reinvests the cash it could have paid. The company's stock price should increase, leading to a capital gain, which would be taxed at the same rate as the dividend. Of course, the stock price appreciation isn't actually taxed until the stock is sold, whereas the dividend is taxed in the year it is paid, so dividends will still be more costly than capital gains for many investors.

Finally, note that the income of S corporations *and* noncorporate businesses is reported as income by the firms' owners. Since there are far more S corporations, partnerships, and proprietorships than C corporations (which are subject to the corporate tax), individual tax considerations play an important role in business finance.

Self-Test

Explain what is meant by this statement: "Our tax rates are progressive."
If a corporation has $85,000 in taxable income, what is its tax liability? **($17,150)**
Explain the difference between marginal tax rates and average tax rates.
What are municipal bonds, and how are these bonds taxed?
What are capital gains and losses, and how are they taxed?
How does the federal income tax system treat dividends received by a corporation versus those received by an individual?
What is the difference in the tax treatment of interest and dividends paid by a corporation? Does this factor favor debt or equity financing?
Briefly explain how tax loss carryback and carryforward procedures work.

Summary

The primary purposes of this chapter were (1) to describe the basic financial statements, (2) to present some background information on cash flows, and (3) to provide an overview of the federal income tax system. The key concepts covered are listed below.

- The four basic statements contained in the **annual report** are the balance sheet, the income statement, the statement of stockholders' equity, and the statement of cash flows.
- The **balance sheet** shows assets on the left-hand side and liabilities and equity, or claims against assets, on the right-hand side. (Sometimes assets are shown at the top and claims at the bottom of the balance sheet.) The balance sheet may be thought of as a snapshot of the firm's financial position at a particular point in time.
- The **income statement** reports the results of operations over a period of time, and it shows earnings per share as its "bottom line."
- The **statement of stockholders' equity** shows the change in retained earnings between balance sheet dates. Retained earnings represent a claim against assets, not assets per se.
- The **statement of cash flows** reports the effect of operating, investing, and financing activities on cash flows over an accounting period.
- **Net cash flow** differs from **accounting profit** because some of the revenues and expenses reflected in accounting profits may not have been received or paid out in cash during the year. Depreciation is typically the largest noncash item, so net cash flow is often expressed as net income plus depreciation.
- **Operating current assets** are the current assets that are used to support operations, such as cash, inventory, and accounts receivable. They do not include short-term investments.
- **Operating current liabilities** are the current liabilities that occur as a natural consequence of operations, such as accounts payable and accruals. They do not include notes payable or any other short-term debts that charge interest.
- **Net operating working capital** is the difference between operating current assets and operating current liabilities. Thus, it is the working capital acquired with investor-supplied funds.
- **Operating long-term assets** are the long-term assets used to support operations, such as net plant and equipment. They do not include any long-term investments that pay interest or dividends.

- **Total net operating capital** (which means the same as **operating capital** and **net operating assets**) is the sum of net operating working capital and operating long-term assets. It is the total amount of capital needed to run the business.
- **NOPAT** is net operating profit after taxes. It is the after-tax profit a company would have if it had no debt and no investments in nonoperating assets. Because it excludes the effects of financial decisions, it is a better measure of operating performance than is net income.
- **Free cash flow (FCF)** is the amount of cash flow remaining after a company makes the asset investments necessary to support operations. In other words, FCF is the amount of cash flow available for distribution to investors, so *the value of a company is directly related to its ability to generate free cash flow*. FCF is defined as NOPAT minus the net investment in operating capital.
- **Market Value Added (MVA)** represents the difference between the total market value of a firm and the total amount of investor-supplied capital. If the market values of debt and preferred stock equal their values as reported on the financial statements, then MVA is the difference between the market value of a firm's stock and the amount of equity its shareholders have supplied.
- **Economic Value Added (EVA)** is the difference between after-tax operating profit and the total dollar cost of capital, including the cost of equity capital. EVA is an estimate of the value created by management during the year, and it differs substantially from accounting profit because no charge for the use of equity capital is reflected in accounting profit.
- Interest income received by a corporation is taxed as **ordinary income**; however, 70% of the dividends received by one corporation from another are excluded from **taxable income**.
- Because interest paid by a corporation is a **deductible expense** whereas dividends are not, our tax system favors debt over equity financing.
- Ordinary corporate operating losses can be **carried back** to each of the preceding 2 years and **carried forward** for the next 20 years in order to offset taxable income in those years.
- **S corporations** are small businesses that have the limited-liability benefits of the corporate form of organization yet are taxed as partnerships or proprietorships.
- In the United States, tax rates are **progressive**—the higher one's income, the larger the percentage paid in taxes.
- Assets such as stocks, bonds, and real estate are defined as **capital assets**. If a capital asset is sold for more than its cost, the profit is called a **capital gain**; if the asset is sold for a loss, it is called a **capital loss**. Assets held for more than a year provide **long-term gains** or **losses**.
- Dividends are taxed as though they were capital gains.
- **Personal taxes** are discussed in more detail in ***Web Extension 2A***.

Questions

(2–1) Define each of the following terms:

a. Annual report; balance sheet; income statement
b. Common stockholders' equity, or net worth; retained earnings
c. Statement of stockholders' equity; statement of cash flows
d. Depreciation; amortization; EBITDA
e. Operating current assets; operating current liabilities; net operating working capital; total net operating capital

f. Accounting profit; net cash flow; NOPAT; free cash flow
g. Market Value Added; Economic Value Added
h. Progressive tax; taxable income; marginal and average tax rates
i. Capital gain or loss; tax loss carryback and carryforward
j. Improper accumulation; S corporation

(2–2) What four statements are contained in most annual reports?

(2–3) If a "typical" firm reports $20 million of retained earnings on its balance sheet, can the firm definitely pay a $20 million cash dividend?

(2–4) Explain the following statement: "Whereas the balance sheet can be thought of as a snapshot of the firm's financial position *at a point in time*, the income statement reports on operations *over a period of time*."

(2–5) What is operating capital, and why is it important?

(2–6) Explain the difference between NOPAT and net income. Which is a better measure of the performance of a company's operations?

(2–7) What is free cash flow? Why is it the most important measure of cash flow?

(2–8) If you were starting a business, what tax considerations might cause you to prefer to set it up as a proprietorship or a partnership rather than as a corporation?

Self-Test Problem

Solution Appears in Appendix A

(ST–1) Net Income, Cash Flow, and EVA

Last year Cole Furnaces had $5 million in operating income (EBIT). The company had a net depreciation expense of $1 million and an interest expense of $1 million; its corporate tax rate was 40%. The company has $14 million in operating current assets and $4 million in operating current liabilities; it has $15 million in net plant and equipment. It estimates that it has an after-tax cost of capital of 10%. Assume that Cole's only noncash item was depreciation.

a. What was the company's net income for the year?
b. What was the company's net cash flow?
c. What was the company's net operating profit after taxes (NOPAT)?
d. Calculate net operating working capital and total net operating capital for the current year.
e. If total net operating capital in the previous year was $24 million, what was the company's free cash flow (FCF) for the year?
f. What was the company's Economic Value Added (EVA)?

Problems

Answers Appear in Appendix B

Note: By the time this book is published, Congress may have changed rates and/or other provisions of current tax law—as noted in the chapter, such changes occur fairly often. Work all problems on the assumption that the information in the chapter is applicable.

EASY PROBLEMS 1–6

(2–1) Personal After-Tax Yield

An investor recently purchased a corporate bond that yields 9%. The investor is in the 36% combined federal and state tax bracket. What is the bond's after-tax yield?

(2–2) Personal After-Tax Yield

Corporate bonds issued by Johnson Corporation currently yield 8%. Municipal bonds of equal risk currently yield 6%. At what tax rate would an investor be indifferent between these two bonds?

(2–3) Income Statement

Little Books Inc. recently reported $3 million of net income. Its EBIT was $6 million, and its tax rate was 40%. What was its interest expense? (*Hint:* Write out the headings for an income statement and then fill in the known values. Then divide $3 million net income by 1 – T = 0.6 to find the pre-tax income. The difference between EBIT and taxable income must be the interest expense. Use this same procedure to work some of the other problems.)

(2–4) Income Statement

Pearson Brothers recently reported an EBITDA of $7.5 million and net income of $1.8 million. It had $2.0 million of interest expense, and its corporate tax rate was 40%. What was its charge for depreciation and amortization?

(2–5) Net Cash Flow

Kendall Corners Inc. recently reported net income of $3.1 million and depreciation of $500,000. What was its net cash flow? Assume it had no amortization expense.

(2–6) Statement of Retained Earnings

In its most recent financial statements, Newhouse Inc. reported $50 million of net income and $810 million of retained earnings. The previous retained earnings were $780 million. How much in dividends was paid to shareholders during the year?

INTERMEDIATE PROBLEMS 7–11

(2–7) Corporate Tax Liability

The Talley Corporation had a taxable income of $365,000 from operations after all operating costs but before (1) interest charges of $50,000, (2) dividends received of $15,000, (3) dividends paid of $25,000, and (4) income taxes. What are the firm's income tax liability and its after-tax income? What are the company's marginal and average tax rates on taxable income?

(2–8) Corporate Tax Liability

The Wendt Corporation had $10.5 million of taxable income.

a. What is the company's federal income tax bill for the year?
b. Assume the firm receives an additional $1 million of interest income from some bonds it owns. What is the tax on this interest income?
c. Now assume that Wendt does not receive the interest income but does receive an additional $1 million as dividends on some stock it owns. What is the tax on this dividend income?

(2–9) Corporate After-Tax Yield

The Shrieves Corporation has $10,000 that it plans to invest in marketable securities. It is choosing among AT&T bonds, which yield 7.5%, state of Florida muni bonds, which yield 5% (but are not taxable), and AT&T preferred stock, with a dividend yield of 6%. Shrieves's corporate tax rate is 35%, and 70% of the dividends received are tax exempt. Find the after-tax rates of return on all three securities.

(2–10) Cash Flows

The Moore Corporation has operating income (EBIT) of $750,000. The company's depreciation expense is $200,000. Moore is 100% equity financed, and it faces a 40% tax rate. What is the company's net income? What is its net cash flow?

(2–11) Income and Cash Flow Analysis

The Berndt Corporation expects to have sales of $12 million. Costs other than depreciation are expected to be 75% of sales, and depreciation is expected to be $1.5 million. All sales revenues will be collected in cash, and costs other than depreciation must be paid for during the year. Berndt's federal-plus-state tax rate is 40%. Berndt has no debt.

a. Set up an income statement. What is Berndt's expected net cash flow?
b. Suppose Congress changed the tax laws so that Berndt's depreciation expenses doubled. No changes in operations occurred. What would happen to reported profit and to net cash flow?
c. Now suppose that Congress, instead of doubling Berndt's depreciation, reduced it by 50%. How would profit and net cash flow be affected?
d. If this were your company, would you prefer Congress to cause your depreciation expense to be doubled or halved? Why?

CHALLENGING PROBLEMS
12–13

(2–12)
Free Cash Flows

Using Rhodes Corporation's financial statements (shown below), answer the following questions.

a. What is the net operating profit after taxes (NOPAT) for 2010?
b. What are the amounts of net operating working capital for both years?
c. What are the amounts of total net operating capital for both years?
d. What is the free cash flow for 2010?
e. What is the ROIC for 2010?
f. How much of the FCF did Rhodes use for each of the following purposes: after-tax interest, net debt repayments, dividends, net stock repurchases, and net purchases of short-term investments? (*Hint:* Remember that a net use can be negative.)

Rhodes Corporation: Income Statements for Year Ending December 31 (Millions of Dollars)

	2010	2009
Sales	$11,000	$10,000
Operating costs excluding depreciation	9,360	8,500
Depreciation	380	360
Earnings before interest and taxes	$ 1,260	$ 1,140
Less interest	120	100
Earnings before taxes	$ 1,140	$ 1,040
Taxes (40%)	456	416
Net income available to common stockholders	$ 684	$ 624
Common dividends	$ 220	$ 200

Rhodes Corporation: Balance Sheets as of December 31 (Millions of Dollars)

	2010	2009
Assets		
Cash	$ 550	$ 500
Short-term investments	110	100
Accounts receivable	2,750	2,500
Inventories	1,650	1,500
Total current assets	$5,060	$4,600
Net plant and equipment	3,850	3,500
Total assets	$8,910	$8,100

	2010	2009
Liabilities and Equity		
Accounts payable	$1,100	$1,000
Accruals	550	500
Notes payable	384	200
Total current liabilities	$2,034	$1,700
Long-term debt	1,100	1,000
Total liabilities	$3,134	$2,700
Common stock	4,312	4,400
Retained earnings	1,464	1,000
Total common equity	$5,776	$5,400
Total liabilities and equity	$8,910	$8,100

(2–13) Loss Carryback and Carryforward

The Bookbinder Company has made $150,000 before taxes during each of the last 15 years, and it expects to make $150,000 a year before taxes in the future. However, in 2010 the firm incurred a loss of $650,000. The firm will claim a tax credit at the time it files its 2010 income tax return, and it will receive a check from the U.S. Treasury. Show how it calculates this credit, and then indicate the firm's tax liability for each of the next 5 years. Assume a 40% tax rate on *all* income to ease the calculations.

Spreadsheet Problems

(2-14) Build a Model: Free Cash Flows, EVA, and MVA

Begin with the partial model in the file ***Ch02 P14 Build a Model.xls*** on the textbook's Web site.

a. Cumberland Industries's 2010 sales were $455,000,000; operating costs (excluding depreciation) were equal to 85% of sales; net fixed assets were $67,000,000; depreciation amounted to 10% of net fixed assets; interest expenses were $8,550,000; the state-plus-federal corporate tax rate was 40%; and Cumberland paid 25% of its net income out in dividends. Given this information, construct Cumberland's 2010 income statement. Also calculate total dividends and the addition to retained earnings. (*Hint:* Start with the partial model in the file and report all dollar figures in thousands to reduce clutter.)

b. Cumberland Industries's partial balance sheets are shown below. Cumberland issued $10,000,000 of new common stock in 2010. Using this information and the results from part a, fill in the missing values for common stock, retained earnings, total common equity, and total liabilities and equity.

Cumberland Industries: Balance Sheets as of December 31 (Thousands of Dollars)

	2010	2009
Assets		
Cash	$ 91,450	$ 74,625
Short-term investments	11,400	15,100
Accounts receivable	108,470	85,527
Inventories	38,450	34,982
Total current assets	$249,770	$210,234
Net fixed assets	67,000	42,436
Total assets	$316,770	$252,670

	2010	2009
Liabilities and Equity		
Accounts payable	$ 30,761	$ 23,109
Accruals	30,405	22,656
Notes payable	12,717	14,217
Total current liabilities	$ 73,883	$ 59,982
Long-term debt	80,263	63,914
Total liabilities	$154,146	$123,896
Common stock	?	$ 90,000
Retained earnings	?	38,774
Total common equity	?	$128,774
Total liabilities and equity	?	$252,670

c. Construct the statement of cash flows for 2010.

(2–15)
Build a Model: Free Cash Flows, EVA, and MVA

Begin with the partial model in the file ***Ch02 P15 Build a Model.xls*** on the textbook's Web site.

a. Using the financial statements shown below for Lan & Chen Technologies, calculate net operating working capital, total net operating capital, net operating profit after taxes, free cash flow, and return on invested capital for 2010. (*Hint:* Start with the partial model in the file and report all dollar figures in thousands to reduce clutter.)

b. Assume there were 15 million shares outstanding at the end of 2010, the year-end closing stock price was $65 per share, and the after-tax cost of capital was 8%. Calculate EVA and MVA for 2010.

Lan & Chen Technologies: Income Statements for Year Ending December 31 (Thousands of Dollars)

	2010	2009
Sales	$945,000	$900,000
Expenses excluding depreciation and amortization	812,700	774,000
EBITDA	$132,300	$126,000
Depreciation and amortization	33,100	31,500
EBIT	$ 99,200	$ 94,500
Interest expense	10,470	8,600
EBT	$ 88,730	$ 85,900
Taxes (40%)	35,492	34,360
Net income	$ 53,238	$ 51,540
Common dividends	$ 43,300	$ 41,230
Addition to retained earnings	$ 9,938	$ 10,310

Lan & Chen Technologies: December 31 Balance Sheets (Thousands of Dollars)

	2010	2009
Assets		
Cash and cash equivalents	$ 47,250	$ 45,000
Short-term investments	3,800	3,600
Accounts receivable	283,500	270,000
Inventories	141,750	135,000
Total current assets	$476,300	$453,600
Net fixed assets	330,750	315,000
Total assets	$807,050	$768,600
Liabilities and equity		
Accounts payable	$ 94,500	$ 90,000
Accruals	47,250	45,000
Notes payable	26,262	9,000
Total current liabilities	$168,012	$144,000
Long-term debt	94,500	90,000
Total liabilities	$262,512	$234,000
Common stock	444,600	444,600
Retained earnings	99,938	90,000
Total common equity	$544,538	$534,600
Total liabilities and equity	$807,050	$768,600

THOMSON ONE | Business School Edition Problem

Use the Thomson ONE—Business School Edition online database to work this chapter's questions.

EXPLORING STARBUCKS'S FINANCIAL STATEMENTS WITH THOMSON ONE—BUSINESS SCHOOL EDITION

Over the past decade, Starbucks coffee shops have become an increasingly familiar part of the urban landscape. The Thomson ONE—Business School Edition online database can provide a wealth of financial information for companies such as Starbucks. Begin by entering the company's ticker symbol, SBUX, and then selecting GO. The opening screen includes a summary of what Starbucks does, a chart of its recent stock price, EPS estimates, some recent news stories, and a list of key financial data and ratios.

For recent stock price performance, look at the top of the Stock Price Chart and click on the section labeled Interactive Chart. From this point, we are able to obtain a chart of the company's stock price performance relative to the overall market, as measured by the S&P 500. To obtain a 10-year chart, go to Time Frame, click on the down arrow, and select 10 years. Then click on Draw, and a 10-year price chart should appear.

You can also find Starbucks's recent financial statements. Near the top of your screen, click on the Financials tab to find the company's balance sheet, income statement, and statement of cash flows for the past 5 years. Clicking on the Microsoft *Excel* icon downloads these statements directly to a spreadsheet.

Thomson ONE—BSE Discussion Questions

1. Looking at the most recent year available, what is the amount of total assets on Starbucks's balance sheet? What percentage is fixed assets, such as plant and equipment, and what percentage is current assets? How much has the company grown over the years shown?
2. Does Starbucks have a lot of long-term debt? What are Starbucks's primary sources of financing?
3. Looking at the statement of cash flows, what factors can explain the change in the company's cash position over the last couple of years?
4. Looking at the income statement, what are the company's most recent sales and net income? Over the past several years, what has been the sales growth rate? What has been the growth rate in net income?

Mini Case

Donna Jamison, a graduate of the University of Tennessee with four years of banking experience, was recently brought in as assistant to the chairman of the board of Computron Industries, a manufacturer of electronic calculators.

The company doubled its plant capacity, opened new sales offices outside its home territory, and launched an expensive advertising campaign. Computron's results were not satisfactory, to put it mildly. Its board of directors, which consisted of its president and vice-president plus its major stockholders (who were all local businesspeople), was most upset when directors learned how the expansion was going. Suppliers were being paid late and were unhappy, and the bank was complaining about the deteriorating situation and threatening to cut off credit. As a result, Al Watkins, Computron's president, was informed that changes would have to be made—and quickly—or he would be fired. At the board's insistence, Donna Jamison was given the job of assistant to Fred Campo, a retired banker who was Computron's chairman and largest stockholder. Campo agreed to give up a few of his golfing days and to help nurse the company back to health, with Jamison's assistance.

Jamison began by gathering financial statements and other data.

	2009	2010
Balance Sheets		
Assets		
Cash	$ 9,000	$ 7,282
Short-term investments	48,600	20,000
Accounts receivable	351,200	632,160
Inventories	715,200	1,287,360
Total current assets	$1,124,000	$1,946,802
Gross fixed assets	491,000	1,202,950
Less: Accumulated depreciation	146,200	263,160
Net fixed assets	$ 344,800	$ 939,790
Total assets	$1,468,800	$2,886,592
Liabilities and Equity		
Accounts payable	$ 145,600	$ 324,000
Notes payable	200,000	720,000
Accruals	136,000	284,960
Total current liabilities	$ 481,600	$1,328,960

	2009	2010
Long-term debt	323,432	1,000,000
Common stock (100,000 shares)	460,000	460,000
Retained earnings	203,768	97,632
Total equity	$ 663,768	$ 557,632
Total liabilities and equity	$1,468,800	$2,886,592

	2009	2010
Income Statements		
Sales	$3,432,000	$5,834,400
Cost of goods sold	2,864,000	4,980,000
Other expenses	340,000	720,000
Depreciation	18,900	116,960
Total operating costs	$3,222,900	$5,816,960
EBIT	$ 209,100	$ 17,440
Interest expense	62,500	176,000
EBT	$ 146,600	($ 158,560)
Taxes (40%)	58,640	(63,424)
Net income	$ 87,960	($ 95,136)
Other Data		
Stock price	$ 8.50	$ 6.00
Shares outstanding	100,000	100,000
EPS	$ 0.880	($ 0.951)
DPS	$ 0.220	$ 0.110
Tax rate	40%	40%

	2010
Statement of Cash Flows	
Operating Activities	
Net income	($ 95,136)
Adjustments:	
Noncash adjustments:	
Depreciation	116,960
Changes in working capital:	
Change in accounts receivable	(280,960)
Change in inventories	(572,160)
Change in accounts payable	178,400
Change in accruals	148,960
Net cash provided (used) by operating activities	($ 503,936)
Investing Activities	
Cash used to acquire fixed assets	($ 711,950)
Change in short-term investments	28,600
Net cash provided (used) by investing activities	($ 683,350)

	2010
Financing Activities	
Change in notes payable	$ 520,000
Change in long-term debt	676,568
Change in common stock	—
Payment of cash dividends	(11,000)
Net cash provided (used) by financing activities	$1,185,568
Summary	
Net change in cash	($ 1,718)
Cash at beginning of year	9,000
Cash at end of year	$ 7,282

Assume that you are Jamison's assistant and that you must help her answer the following questions for Campo.

a. What effect did the expansion have on sales and net income? What effect did the expansion have on the asset side of the balance sheet? What effect did it have on liabilities and equity?
b. What do you conclude from the statement of cash flows?
c. What is free cash flow? Why is it important? What are the five uses of FCF?
d. What is Computron's net operating profit after taxes (NOPAT)? What are operating current assets? What are operating current liabilities? How much net operating working capital and total net operating capital does Computron have?
e. What is Computron's free cash flow (FCF)? What are Computron's "net uses" of its FCF?
f. Calculate Computron's return on invested capital. Computron has a 10% cost of capital (WACC). Do you think Computron's growth added value?
g. Jamison also has asked you to estimate Computron's EVA. She estimates that the after-tax cost of capital was 10% in both years.
h. What happened to Computron's Market Value Added (MVA)?
i. Assume that a corporation has $100,000 of taxable income from operations plus $5,000 of interest income and $10,000 of dividend income. What is the company's federal tax liability?
j. Assume that you are in the 25% marginal tax bracket and that you have $5,000 to invest. You have narrowed your investment choices down to California bonds with a yield of 7% or equally risky ExxonMobil bonds with a yield of 10%. Which one should you choose and why? At what marginal tax rate would you be indifferent to the choice between California and ExxonMobil bonds?

CHAPTER 3

Analysis of Financial Statements

To guide or not to guide, that is the question. Or at least it's the question many companies are wrestling with regarding earnings forecasts. Should a company provide earnings estimates to investors? In 2006, Best Buy answered this question by announcing that it would no longer provide quarterly earnings forecasts. It's no coincidence that Best Buy's decision came shortly after its actual earnings came in just 2 cents below the forecast, yet its stock price fell by 12%. Coca-Cola, Motorola, and Citigroup are among the growing number of companies that no longer provide quarterly earnings forecasts.

Virtually no one disputes that investors need as much information as possible to accurately evaluate a company, and academic studies show that companies with greater transparency have higher valuations. However, greater disclosure often brings the possibility of lawsuits if investors have reason to believe that the disclosure is fraudulent. Although the Private Securities Litigation Reform Act of 1995 helped prevent "frivolous" lawsuits, many companies still chose not to provide information directly to all investors. Instead, before 2000, many companies provided earnings information to brokerage firms' analysts, and the analysts then forecast their own earnings expectations. In 2000 the SEC adopted Reg FD (Regulation Fair Disclosure), which prevented companies from disclosing information only to select groups, such as analysts. Reg FD led many companies to begin providing quarterly earnings forecasts directly to the public, and a survey by the National Investors Relations Institute showed that 95% of respondents in 2006 provided either annual or quarterly earnings forecasts, up from 45% in 1999.

Two trends are now in evidence. First, the number of companies reporting quarterly earnings forecasts is falling, but the number reporting annual forecasts is increasing. Second, many companies are providing other types of forward-looking information, including key operating ratios plus qualitative information about the company and its industry. Ratio analysis can help investors use such information, so keep that in mind as you read this chapter.

Sources: Adapted from Joseph McCafferty, "Guidance Lite," CFO, *June 2006, 16–17, and William F. Coffin and Crocker Coulson, "Is Earnings Guidance Disappearing in 2006?" 2006, White Paper, available at* ***http://www.ccgir.com/ccgir/white_papers/pdf/Earnings%20Guidance%202006.pdf.***

Intrinsic Value and Analysis of Financial Statements

The intrinsic value of a firm is determined by the present value of the expected future free cash flows (FCF) when discounted at the weighted average cost of capital (WACC). This chapter explains how to use financial statements to evaluate a company's profitability, required capital investments, business risk, and mix of debt and equity.

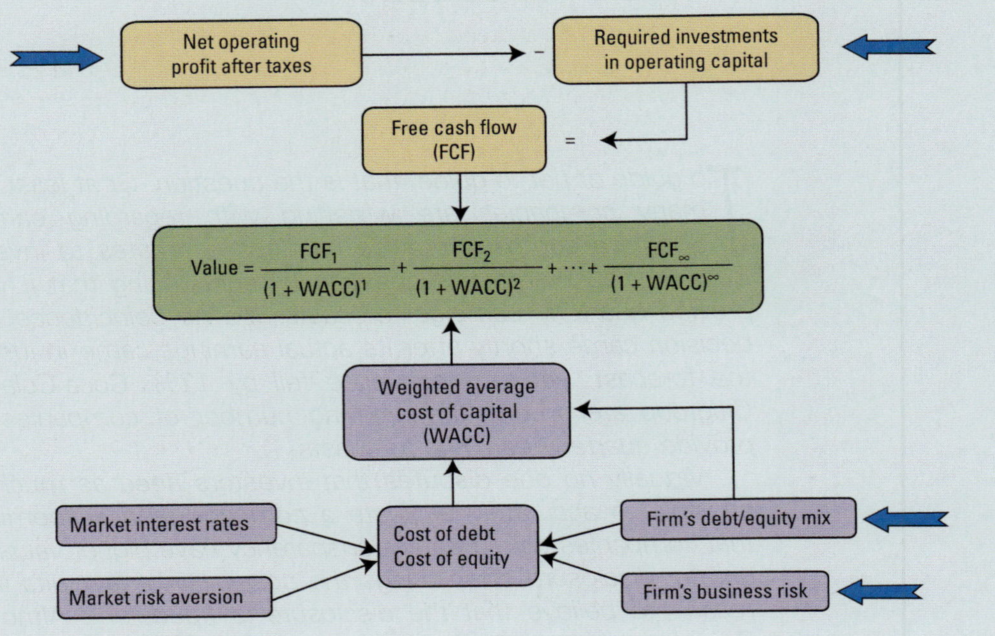

Financial statement analysis involves (1) comparing a firm's performance with that of other firms in the same industry and (2) evaluating trends in the firm's financial position over time. Managers use financial analysis to identify situations needing attention; potential lenders use financial analysis to determine whether a company is creditworthy; and stockholders use financial analysis to help predict future earnings, dividends, and free cash flow. As we explain in this chapter, there are similarities and differences among these uses.[1]

The textbook's Web site contains an Excel *file that will guide you through the chapter's calculations. The file for this chapter is* **Ch03 Tool Kit.xls**, *and we encourage you to open the file and follow along as you read the chapter.*

3.1 Financial Analysis

When we perform a financial analysis, we conduct the following steps.

Gather Data

See **http://www.zacks.com** *for a source of standardized financial statements.*

The first step in financial analysis is to gather data. As we discussed in Chapter 2, financial statements can be downloaded from many different Web sites. One of our favorites is Zacks Investment Research, which provides financial statements in

[1] Widespread accounting fraud has cast doubt on whether all firms' published financial statements can be trusted. New regulations by the SEC and the exchanges, as well as new laws enacted by Congress, have improved oversight of the accounting industry and increased the criminal penalties on management for fraudulent reporting.

a standardized format. If you cut and paste financial statements from Zacks into a spreadsheet and then perform a financial analysis, you can quickly repeat the analysis on a different company by simply pasting that company's financial statements into the same cells as the original company's statements. In other words, there is no need to reinvent the wheel each time you analyze a company.

Examine the Statement of Cash Flows

Some financial analysis can be done with virtually no calculations. For example, we always look to the statement of cash flows first, particularly the net cash provided by operating activities. Downward trends or negative net cash flow from operations almost always indicate problems. The statement of cash flows section on investing activities shows whether the company has made a big acquisition, especially when compared with the prior years' net cash flows from investing activities. A quick look at the section on financing activities also reveals whether or not a company is issuing debt or buying back stock; in other words, is the company raising capital from investors or returning it to them?

Calculate and Examine the Return on Invested Capital

After examining the statement of cash flows, we calculate the return on invested capital (ROIC) as described in Chapter 2. The ROIC provides a vital measure of a firm's overall performance. If ROIC is greater than the company's weighted average cost of capital (WACC), then the company usually is adding value. If ROIC is less than WACC, then the company usually has serious problems. No matter what ROIC tells us about the firm's overall performance, it is important to examine specific areas within the firm, and for that we use ratios.

Begin Ratio Analysis

Financial ratios are designed to extract important information that might not be obvious simply from examining a firm's financial statements. For example, suppose Firm A owes $5 million of debt while Firm B owes $50 million of debt. Which company is in a stronger financial position? It is impossible to answer this question without first standardizing each firm's debt relative to total assets, earnings, and interest. Such standardized comparisons are provided through *ratio analysis*.

We will calculate the 2010 financial ratios for MicroDrive Inc., using data from the balance sheets and income statements given in Table 3-1. We will also evaluate the ratios in relation to the industry averages. Note that dollar amounts are in millions.

3.2 Liquidity Ratios

See **Ch03 Tool Kit.xls** *for all calculations.*

As shown in Table 3-1, MicroDrive has current liabilities of $310 million that must be paid off within the coming year. Will it have trouble satisfying those obligations? **Liquidity ratios** attempt to answer this type of question: We discuss two commonly used liquidity ratios in this section.

The Current Ratio

The **current ratio** is calculated by dividing current assets by current liabilities:

$$\text{Current ratio} = \frac{\text{Current assets}}{\text{Current liabilities}}$$

TABLE 3-1 MicroDrive Inc.: Balance Sheets and Income Statements for Years Ending December 31 (Millions of Dollars, Except for Per Share Data)

ASSETS	2010	2009	LIABILITIES AND EQUITY	2010	2009
Cash and equivalents	$ 10	$ 15	Accounts payable	$ 60	$ 30
Short-term investments	0	65	Notes payable	110	60
Accounts receivable	375	315	Accruals	140	130
Inventories	615	415	Total current liabilities	$ 310	$ 220
Total current assets	$1,000	$ 810	Long-term bonds[a]	754	580
Net plant and equipment	1,000	870	Total liabilities	$1,064	$ 800
			Preferred stock (400,000 shares)	40	40
			Common stock (50,000,000 shares)	130	130
			Retained earnings	766	710
			Total common equity	$ 896	$ 840
Total assets	$2,000	$1,680	Total liabilities and equity	$2,000	$1,680

	2010	2009
Net sales	$3,000.0	$2,850.0
Operating costs excluding depreciation and amortization[b]	2,616.2	2,497.0
Earnings before interest, taxes, depreciation, and amortization (EBITDA)	$ 383.8	$ 353.0
Depreciation	100.0	90.0
Amortization	0.0	0.0
Depreciation and amortization	$ 100.0	$ 90.0
Earnings before interest and taxes (EBIT, or operating income)	$ 283.8	$ 263.0
Less interest	88.0	60.0
Earnings before taxes (EBT)	$ 195.8	$ 203.0
Taxes (40%)	78.3	81.2
Net income before preferred dividends	$ 117.5	$ 121.8
Preferred dividends	4.0	4.0
Net income	$ 113.5	$ 117.8
Common dividends	$ 57.5	$ 53.0
Addition to retained earnings	$ 56.0	$ 64.8
Per-Share Data		
Common stock price	$ 23.00	$ 26.00
Earnings per share (EPS)	$ 2.27	$ 2.36
Book value per share (BVPS)	$ 17.92	$ 16.80
Cash flow per share (CFPS)	$ 4.27	$ 4.16

[a]The bonds have a sinking fund requirement of $20 million a year.
[b]The costs include lease payments of $28 million a year.

$$= \frac{\$1,000}{\$310} = 3.2$$

$$\text{Industry average} = 4.2$$

Current assets normally include cash, marketable securities, accounts receivable, and inventories. Current liabilities consist of accounts payable, short-term notes payable, current maturities of long-term debt, accrued taxes, and other accrued expenses.

MicroDrive has a lower current ratio than the average for its industry. Is this good or bad? Sometimes the answer depends on who is asking the question. For example, suppose a supplier is trying to decide whether to extend credit to MicroDrive. In general, creditors like to see a high current ratio. If a company is getting into financial difficulty, it will begin paying its bills (accounts payable) more slowly, borrowing from its bank, and so on, so its current liabilities will be increasing. If current liabilities are rising faster than current assets then the current ratio will fall, and this could spell trouble. Because the current ratio provides the best single indicator of the extent to which the claims of short-term creditors are covered by assets that are expected to be converted to cash fairly quickly, it is the most commonly used measure of short-term solvency.

Now consider the current ratio from the perspective of a shareholder. A high current ratio could mean that the company has a lot of money tied up in nonproductive assets, such as excess cash or marketable securities. Or perhaps the high current ratio is due to large inventory holdings, which might well become obsolete before they can be sold. Thus, shareholders might not want a high current ratio.

An industry average is not a magic number that all firms should strive to maintain—in fact, some very well-managed firms will be above the average, while other good firms will be below it. However, if a firm's ratios are far removed from the averages for its industry, this is a red flag, and analysts should be concerned about why the variance occurs. For example, suppose a low current ratio is traced to low inventories. Is this a competitive advantage resulting from the firm's mastery of just-in-time inventory management, or is it an Achilles' heel that is causing the firm to miss shipments and lose sales? Ratio analysis doesn't answer such questions, but it does point to areas of potential concern.

The Quick, or Acid Test, Ratio

The **quick**, or **acid test**, **ratio** is calculated by deducting inventories from current assets and then dividing the remainder by current liabilities:

$$\text{Quick, or acid test, ratio} = \frac{\text{Current assets} - \text{Inventories}}{\text{Current liabilities}}$$

$$= \frac{\$385}{\$310} = 1.2$$

$$\text{Industry average} = 2.1$$

A **liquid asset** is one that trades in an active market and hence can be converted quickly to cash at the going market price. Inventories are typically the least liquid of a firm's current assets; hence they are the current assets on which losses are most likely to occur in a bankruptcy. Therefore, a measure of the firm's ability to pay off short-term obligations without relying on the sale of inventories is important.

The industry average quick ratio is 2.1, so MicroDrive's 1.2 ratio is low in comparison with other firms in its industry. Still, if the accounts receivable can be collected, the company can pay off its current liabilities without having to liquidate its inventory.

Self-Test

Identify two ratios that are used to analyze a firm's liquidity position, and write out their equations.

What are the characteristics of a liquid asset? Give some examples.

Which current asset is typically the least liquid?

A company has current liabilities of $800 million, and its current ratio is 2.5. What is its level of current assets? **($2,000 million)** If this firm's quick ratio is 2, how much inventory does it have? **($400 million)**

3.3 Asset Management Ratios

Asset management ratios measure how effectively a firm is managing its assets. If a company has excessive investments in assets, then its operating capital will be unduly high, which will reduce its free cash flow and ultimately its stock price. On the other hand, if a company does not have enough assets then it will lose sales, which will hurt profitability, free cash flow, and the stock price. Therefore, it is important to have the *right* amount invested in assets. Ratios that analyze the different types of assets are described in this section.

Evaluating Inventories: The Inventory Turnover Ratio

The **inventory turnover ratio** is defined as sales divided by inventories:

$$\text{Inventory turnover ratio} = \frac{\text{Sales}}{\text{Inventories}}$$

$$= \frac{\$3{,}000}{\$615} = 4.9$$

$$\text{Industry average} = 9.0$$

As a rough approximation, each item of MicroDrive's inventory is sold out and restocked, or "turned over," 4.9 times per year.[2]

MicroDrive's turnover of 4.9 is much lower than the industry average of 9.0. This suggests that MicroDrive is holding too much inventory. High levels of inventory add to net operating working capital (NOWC), which reduces FCF, which leads to lower stock prices. In addition, MicroDrive's low inventory turnover ratio makes us wonder whether the firm is actually holding obsolete goods not worth their stated value.[3]

Note that sales occur over the entire year, whereas the inventory figure is measured at a single point in time. For this reason, it is better to use an average inventory measure.[4] If the firm's business is highly seasonal, or if there has been a strong upward or downward sales trend during the year, then it is especially useful to make some such adjustment. To maintain comparability with industry averages, however, we did not use the average inventory figure.

---

[2]"Turnover" is a term that originated many years ago with the old Yankee peddler who would load up his wagon with goods and then go off to peddle his wares. If he made 10 trips per year, stocked 100 pans, and made a gross profit of $5 per pan, his annual gross profit would be (100)($5)(10) = $5,000. If he "turned over" (i.e., sold) his inventory faster and made 20 trips per year, then his gross profit would double, other things held constant. So, his turnover directly affected his profits.

[3]A problem arises when calculating and analyzing the inventory turnover ratio. Sales are stated at market prices, so if inventories are carried at cost, as they generally are, then the calculated turnover overstates the true turnover ratio. Therefore, it would be more appropriate to use cost of goods sold in place of sales in the formula's numerator. However, established compilers of financial ratio statistics such as Dun & Bradstreet use the ratio of sales to inventories carried at cost. To develop a figure that can be compared with those published by Dun & Bradstreet and similar organizations, it is necessary to measure inventory turnover with sales in the numerator, as we do here.

[4]Preferably, the average inventory value should be calculated by summing the monthly figures during the year and dividing by 12. If monthly data are not available, one can add the beginning and ending annual figures and divide by 2. However, most industry ratios are calculated as shown here, using end-of-year values.

THE GLOBAL ECONOMIC CRISIS

The Price is Right! (Or Wrong!)

How much is an asset worth if no one is buying or selling? The answer to that question matters because an accounting practice called "mark to market" requires that some assets be adjusted on the balance sheet to reflect their "fair market value." The accounting rules are complicated, but the general idea is that if an asset is available for sale, then the balance sheet would be most accurate if it showed the asset's market value. For example, suppose a company purchased $100 million of Treasury bonds and the value of those bonds later fell to $90 million. With mark to market, the company would report the bonds' value on the balance sheet as $90 million, not the original purchase price of $100 million. Notice that marking to market can have a significant impact on financial ratios and thus on investors' perception of a firm's financial health.

But what if the assets are mortgage-backed securities that were originally purchased for $100 million? As defaults increased during 2008, the value of such securities fell rapidly, and then investors virtually stopped trading them. How should the company report them? At the $100 million original price, at a $60 million price that was observed before the market largely dried up, at $25 million when a hedge fund in desperate need for cash to avoid a costly default sold a few of these securities, or at $0, since there are no current quotes? Or should they be reported at a price generated by a computer model or in some other manner?

The answer to this question has vital implications for the global financial crisis. In early 2009, Congress, the SEC, FASB, and the U.S. Treasury all are working to find the right answers. If they come up with a price that is too low, it could cause investors mistakenly to believe that some companies are worth much less than their intrinsic values, and this could trigger runs on banks and bankruptcies for companies that might otherwise survive. But if the price is too high, some "walking dead" or "zombie" companies could linger on and later cause even larger losses for investors, including the U.S. government, which is now the largest investor in many financial institutions. Either way, an error in pricing could perhaps trigger a domino effect that might topple the entire financial system. So let's hope the price is right!

Evaluating Receivables: The Days Sales Outstanding

Days sales outstanding (DSO), also called the "average collection period" (ACP), is used to appraise accounts receivable, and it is calculated by dividing accounts receivable by average daily sales to find the number of days' sales that are tied up in receivables.[5] Thus, the DSO represents the average length of time that the firm must wait after making a sale before receiving cash, which is the average collection period. MicroDrive has 46 DSO, well above the 36-day industry average:

$$\text{DSO} = \frac{\text{Days sales}}{\text{outstanding}} = \frac{\text{Receivables}}{\text{Average sales per day}} = \frac{\text{Receivables}}{\text{Annual sales}/365}$$

$$= \frac{\$375}{\$3{,}000/365} = \frac{\$375}{\$8.2192} = 45.6 \text{ days} \approx 46 \text{ days}$$

$$\text{Industry average} = 36 \text{ days}$$

MicroDrive's sales terms call for payment within 30 days. The fact that 46 days of sales are outstanding indicates that customers, on average, are not paying their bills

[5]It would be better to use *average* receivables, but we have used year-end values for comparability with the industry average.

on time. As with inventory, high levels of accounts receivable cause high levels of NOWC, which hurts FCF and stock price.

A customer who is paying late may well be in financial trouble, in which case MicroDrive may have a hard time ever collecting the receivable. Therefore, if the trend in DSO has been rising but the credit policy has not been changed, steps should be taken to review credit standards and to expedite the collection of accounts receivable.

Evaluating Fixed Assets: The Fixed Assets Turnover Ratio

The **fixed assets turnover ratio** measures how effectively the firm uses its plant and equipment. It is the ratio of sales to net fixed assets:

$$\text{Fixed assets turnover ratio} = \frac{\text{Sales}}{\text{Net fixed assets}}$$

$$= \frac{\$3{,}000}{\$1{,}000} = 3.0$$

$$\text{Industry average} = 3.0$$

MicroDrive's ratio of 3.0 is equal to the industry average, indicating that the firm is using its fixed assets about as intensively as are other firms in its industry. Therefore, MicroDrive seems to have about the right amount of fixed assets in relation to other firms.

A potential problem can exist when interpreting the fixed assets turnover ratio. Recall from accounting that fixed assets reflect the historical costs of the assets. Inflation has caused the current value of many assets that were purchased in the past to be seriously understated. Therefore, if we were comparing an old firm that had acquired many of its fixed assets years ago at low prices with a new company that had acquired its fixed assets only recently, we would probably find that the old firm had the higher fixed assets turnover ratio. However, this would be more reflective of the difficulty accountants have in dealing with inflation than of any inefficiency on the part of the new firm. You should be alert to this potential problem when evaluating the fixed assets turnover ratio.

Evaluating Total Assets: The Total Assets Turnover Ratio

The **total assets turnover ratio** is calculated by dividing sales by total assets:

$$\text{Total assets turnover ratio} = \frac{\text{Sales}}{\text{Total assets}}$$

$$= \frac{\$3{,}000}{\$2{,}000} = 1.5$$

$$\text{Industry average} = 1.8$$

MicroDrive's ratio is somewhat below the industry average, indicating that the company is not generating a sufficient volume of business given its total asset investment. Sales should be increased, some assets should be sold, or a combination of these steps should be taken.

Self-Test

Identify four ratios that are used to measure how effectively a firm is managing its assets, and write out their equations.

What problem might arise when comparing different firms' fixed assets turnover ratios?

A firm has annual sales of $200 million, $40 million of inventory, and $60 million of accounts receivable. What is its inventory turnover ratio? **(5)** What is its DSO based on a 365-day year? **(109.5 days)**

3.4 Debt Management Ratios

The extent to which a firm uses debt financing, or **financial leverage,** has three important implications: (1) By raising funds through debt, stockholders can maintain control of a firm without increasing their investment. (2) If the firm earns more on investments financed with borrowed funds than it pays in interest, then its shareholders' returns are magnified, or "leveraged," but their risks are also magnified. (3) Creditors look to the equity, or owner-supplied funds, to provide a margin of safety, so the higher the proportion of funding supplied by stockholders, the less risk creditors face. Chapter 15 explains the first two points in detail, while the following ratios examine leverage from a creditor's point of view.

How the Firm is Financed: Total Liabilities to Total Assets

The ratio of total liabilities to total assets is called the **debt ratio**, or sometimes the **total debt ratio**. It measures the percentage of funds provided by current liabilities and long-term debt:

$$\text{Debt ratio} = \frac{\text{Total liabilities}}{\text{Total assets}}$$

$$= \frac{\$310 + \$754}{\$2{,}000} = \frac{\$1{,}064}{\$2{,}000} = 53.2\%$$

$$\text{Industry average} = 40.0\%$$

Creditors prefer low debt ratios because the lower the ratio, the greater the cushion against creditors' losses in the event of liquidation. Stockholders, on the other hand, may want more leverage because it magnifies their return, as we explain in Section 3.8 when we discuss the Du Pont model.

MicroDrive's debt ratio is 53.2% but its debt ratio in the previous year was 47.6%, which means that creditors are now supplying more than half the total financing. In addition to an upward trend, the level of the debt ratio is well above the industry average. Creditors may be reluctant to lend the firm more money because a high debt ratio is associated with a greater risk of bankruptcy.

Some sources report the debt-to-equity ratio, defined as:

$$\text{Debt-to-equity ratio} = \frac{\text{Total liabilities}}{\text{Total assets} - \text{Total liabilities}}$$

$$= \frac{\$310 + \$754}{\$2{,}000 - (\$310 + \$754)} = \frac{\$1{,}064}{\$936} = 1.14$$

$$\text{Industry average} = 0.67$$

The debt-to-equity ratio and the debt ratio contain the same information but present that information slightly differently.[6] The debt-to-equity ratio shows that MicroDrive has $1.14 of debt for every dollar of equity, whereas the debt ratio shows that 53.2% of MicroDrive's financing is in the form of liabilities. We find it more

---

[6]The debt ratio and debt-to-equity ratios are simply transformations of each other:

$$\text{Debt-to-equity} = \frac{\text{Debt ratio}}{1 - \text{Debt ratio}} \text{ and Debt ratio} = \frac{\text{Debt-to-equity}}{1 + \text{Debt-to-equity}}$$

intuitive to think about the percentage of the firm that is financed with debt, so we usually use the debt ratio. However, the debt-to-equity ratio is also widely used, so you should know how to interpret it.

Sometimes it is useful to express debt ratios in terms of market values. It is easy to calculate the market value of equity, which is equal to the stock price multiplied by the number of shares. MicroDrive's market value of equity is $23(50) = $1,150. Often it is difficult to estimate the market value of liabilities, so many analysts define the market debt ratio as

$$\text{Market debt ratio} = \frac{\text{Total liabilities}}{\text{Total liabilities} + \text{Market value of equity}}$$

$$= \frac{\$1,064}{\$1,064 + (\$23 \times 50)} = \frac{\$1,064}{\$2,214} = 48.1\%$$

MicroDrive's market debt ratio in the previous year was 38.1%. The big increase was due to two major factors: Liabilities increased and the stock price fell. The stock price reflects a company's prospects for generating future cash flows, so a decline in stock price indicates a likely decline in future cash flows. Thus, the market debt ratio reflects a source of risk that is not captured by the conventional book debt ratio.

If you use a debt ratio that you did not calculate yourself, be sure to find out how the ratio was defined. Some sources provide the ratio of long-term debt to total assets, and some provide the ratio of all debt to equity, so be sure to check your source's definition.

Ability to Pay Interest: Times-Interest-Earned Ratio

The **times-interest-earned (TIE) ratio**, also called the **interest coverage ratio**, is determined by dividing earnings before interest and taxes (EBIT in Table 3-1) by the interest expense:

$$\text{Times-interest-earned (TIE) ratio} = \frac{\text{EBIT}}{\text{Interest expense}}$$

$$= \frac{\$283.8}{\$88} = 3.2$$

$$\text{Industry average} = 6.0$$

The TIE ratio measures the extent to which operating income can decline before the firm is unable to meet its annual interest costs. Failure to meet this obligation can bring legal action by the firm's creditors, possibly resulting in bankruptcy. Note that earnings before interest and taxes, rather than net income, is used in the numerator. Because interest is paid with pre-tax dollars, the firm's ability to pay current interest is not affected by taxes.

MicroDrive's interest is covered 3.2 times. The industry average is 6, so MicroDrive is covering its interest charges by a relatively low margin of safety. Thus, the TIE ratio reinforces the conclusion from our analysis of the debt ratio that MicroDrive would face difficulties if it attempted to borrow additional funds.

Ability to Service Debt: EBITDA Coverage Ratio

The TIE ratio is useful for assessing a company's ability to meet interest charges on its debt, but this ratio has two shortcomings: (1) Interest is not the only fixed financial charge—companies must also reduce debt on schedule, and many firms lease assets and thus must make lease payments. If they fail to repay debt or meet lease payments, they can be forced into bankruptcy. (2) EBIT does not represent all the cash flow available to service debt, especially if a firm has high depreciation and/or amortization charges. The **EBITDA coverage ratio** accounts for these deficiencies:[7]

$$\text{EBITDA coverage ratio} = \frac{\text{EBITDA} + \text{Lease payments}}{\text{Interest} + \text{Principal payments} + \text{Lease payments}}$$

$$= \frac{\$383.8 + \$28}{\$88 + \$20 + \$28} = \frac{\$411.8}{\$136} = 3.0$$

$$\text{Industry average} = 4.3$$

MicroDrive had $383.8 million of earnings before interest, taxes, depreciation, and amortization (EBITDA). Also, lease payments of $28 million were deducted while calculating EBITDA. That $28 million was available to meet financial charges; hence it must be added back, bringing the total available to cover fixed financial charges to $411.8 million. Fixed financial charges consisted of $88 million of interest, $20 million of sinking fund payments, and $28 million for lease payments, for a total of $136 million.[8] Therefore, MicroDrive covered its fixed financial charges by 3.0 times. However, if EBITDA declines then the coverage will fall, and EBITDA certainly can decline. Moreover, MicroDrive's ratio is well below the industry average, so again the company seems to have a relatively high level of debt.

The EBITDA coverage ratio is most useful for relatively short-term lenders such as banks, which rarely make loans (except real estate-backed loans) for longer than about 5 years. Over a relatively short period, depreciation-generated funds can be used to service debt. Over a longer time, those funds must be reinvested to maintain the plant and equipment or else the company cannot remain in business. Therefore, banks and other relatively short-term lenders focus on the EBITDA coverage ratio, whereas long-term bondholders focus on the TIE ratio.

Self-Test

How does the use of financial leverage affect current stockholders' control position?

Explain the following statement: "Analysts look at both balance sheet and income statement ratios when appraising a firm's financial condition."

Name three ratios that are used to measure the extent to which a firm uses financial leverage, and write out their equations.

A company has EBITDA of $600 million, interest payments of $60 million, lease payments of $40 million, and required principal payments (due this year) of $30 million. What is its EBITDA coverage ratio? **(4.9)**

---

[7]Different analysts define the EBITDA coverage ratio in different ways. For example: some omit the lease payment information; others "gross up" principal payments by dividing them by 1 − T since these payments are not tax deductions and hence must be made with after-tax cash flows. We included lease payments because for many firms they are quite important, and failing to make them can lead to bankruptcy just as surely as can failure to make payments on "regular" debt. We did not gross up principal payments because, if a company is in financial difficulty, then its tax rate will probably be zero; hence the gross up is not necessary whenever the ratio is really important.

[8]A sinking fund is a required annual payment designed to reduce the balance of a bond or preferred stock issue.

3.5 Profitability Ratios

Profitability is the net result of a number of policies and decisions. The ratios examined thus far provide useful clues as to the effectiveness of a firm's operations, but the **profitability ratios** go on to show the combined effects of liquidity, asset management, and debt on operating results.

Net Profit Margin

The **net profit margin**, which is also called the **profit margin on sales**, is calculated by dividing net income by sales. It gives the profit per dollar of sales:

$$\text{Net profit margin} = \frac{\text{Net income available to common stockholders}}{\text{Sales}}$$

$$= \frac{\$113.5}{\$3{,}000} = 3.8\%$$

$$\text{Industry average} = 5.0\%$$

MicroDrive's net profit margin is below the industry average of 5%, but why is this so? Is it due to inefficient operations, high interest expenses, or both?

Instead of just comparing net income to sales, many analysts also break the income statement into smaller parts to identify the sources of a low net profit margin. For example, the **operating profit margin** is defined as

$$\text{Operating profit margin} = \frac{\text{EBIT}}{\text{Sales}}$$

The operating profit margin identifies how a company is performing with respect to its operations before the impact of interest expenses is considered. Some analysts drill even deeper by breaking operating costs into their components. For example, the **gross profit margin** is defined as

$$\text{Gross profit margin} = \frac{\text{Sales} - \text{Cost of goods sold}}{\text{Sales}}$$

The gross profit margin identifies the gross profit per dollar of sales before any other expenses are deducted.

Rather than calculate each type of profit margin here, later in the chapter we will use common size analysis and percent change analysis to focus on different parts of the income statement. In addition, we will use the Du Pont equation to show how the ratios interact with one another.

Sometimes it is confusing to have so many different types of profit margins. To help simplify the situation, we will focus primarily on the net profit margin throughout the book and simply call it the "profit margin."

Basic Earning Power (BEP) Ratio

The **basic earning power (BEP) ratio** is calculated by dividing earnings before interest and taxes (EBIT) by total assets:

The World Might be Flat, but Global Accounting is Bumpy! The Case of IFRS versus FASB

In a flat world, distance is no barrier. Work flows to where it can be accomplished most efficiently, and capital flows to where it can be invested most profitably. If a radiologist in India is more efficient than one in the United States, then images will be e-mailed to India for diagnosis; if rates of return are higher in Brazil, then investors throughout the world will provide funding for Brazilian projects. One key to "flattening" the world is agreement on common standards. For example, there are common Internet standards so that users throughout the world are able to communicate.

A glaring exception to standardization is in accounting. The Securities and Exchange Commission (SEC) in the United States requires firms to comply with standards set by the Financial Accounting Standards Board (FASB). But the European Union requires all EU-listed companies to comply with the International Financial Reporting Standards (IFRS) as defined by the International Accounting Standards Board (IASB).

IFRS tends to rely on general principles, whereas FASB standards are rules-based. As the recent accounting scandals demonstrate, many U.S. companies have been able to comply with U.S. rules while violating the principle, or intent, underlying the rules. The United States is likely to adopt IFRS, or a slightly modified IFRS, but the question is "When?" The SEC estimated that a large company is likely to incur costs of up to $32 million when switching to IFRS. So even though a survey by the accounting firm KPMG indicates that most investors and analysts favor adoption of IFRS, the path to adoption is likely to be bumpy.

Sources: See the Web sites of the IASB and the FASB, **http://www.iasb.org.uk** and **http://www.fasb.org**. Also see David M. Katz and Sarah Johnson, "Top Obama Advisers Clash on Global Accounting Standards," January 15, 2009, at **http://www.cfo.com**; and "Survey Favors IFRS Adoption," February 3, 2009, at **http://www.webcpa.com**.

$$\text{Basic earning power (BEP) ratio} = \frac{\text{EBIT}}{\text{Total assets}}$$

$$= \frac{\$283.8}{\$2{,}000} = 14.2\%$$

$$\text{Industry average} = 17.2\%$$

This ratio shows the raw earning power of the firm's assets before the influence of taxes and leverage, and it is useful for comparing firms with different tax situations and different degrees of financial leverage. Because of its low turnover ratios and low profit margin on sales, MicroDrive is not getting as high a return on its assets as is the average company in its industry.[9]

Return on Total Assets

The ratio of net income to total assets measures the **return on total assets (ROA)** after interest and taxes. This ratio is also called the **return on assets** and is defined as follows:

[9]Notice that EBIT is earned throughout the year, whereas the total assets figure is an end-of-the-year number. Therefore, it would be better, conceptually, to calculate this ratio as EBIT/(Average assets) = EBIT/[(Beginning assets + Ending assets)/2]. We have not made this adjustment because the published ratios used for comparative purposes do not include it. However, when we construct our own comparative ratios, we do make this adjustment. The same adjustment would also be appropriate for the next two ratios, ROA and ROE.

$$\text{Return on total assets} = \text{ROA} = \frac{\text{Net income available to common stockholders}}{\text{Total assets}}$$

$$= \frac{\$113.5}{\$2{,}000} = 5.7\%$$

$$\text{Industry average} = 9.0\%$$

MicroDrive's 5.7% return is well below the 9% average for the industry. This low return is due to (1) the company's low basic earning power and (2) high interest costs resulting from its above-average use of debt; both of these factors cause MicroDrive's net income to be relatively low.

Return on Common Equity

The ratio of net income to common equity measures the **return on common equity (ROE):**

$$\text{Return on common equity} = \text{ROE} = \frac{\text{Net income available to common stockholders}}{\text{Common equity}}$$

$$= \frac{\$113.5}{\$896} = 12.7\%$$

$$\text{Industry average} = 15.0\%$$

Stockholders invest to earn a return on their money, and this ratio tells how well they are doing in an accounting sense. MicroDrive's 12.7% return is below the 15% industry average, but not as far below as its return on total assets. This somewhat better result is due to the company's greater use of debt, a point that we explain in detail later in the chapter.

Self-Test

Identify and write out the equations for four profitability ratios.
Why is the basic earning power ratio useful?
Why does the use of debt lower ROA?
What does ROE measure?
A company has $200 billion of sales and $10 billion of net income. Its total assets are $100 billion, financed half by debt and half by common equity. What is its profit margin? **(5%)** What is its ROA? **(10%)** What is its ROE? **(20%)** Would ROA increase if the firm used less leverage? **(Yes)** Would ROE increase? **(No)**

3.6 Market Value Ratios

Market value ratios relate a firm's stock price to its earnings, cash flow, and book value per share. Market value ratios are a way to measure the value of a company's stock relative to that of another company.

Price/Earnings Ratio

The **price/earnings (P/E) ratio** shows how much investors are willing to pay per dollar of reported profits. MicroDrive's stock sells for $23, so with an earnings per share (EPS) of $2.27 its P/E ratio is 10.1:

$$\text{Price/earnings (P/E) ratio} = \frac{\text{Price per share}}{\text{Earnings per share}}$$

$$= \frac{\$23.00}{\$2.27} = 10.1$$

$$\text{Industry average} = 12.5$$

Price/earnings ratios are higher for firms with strong growth prospects, other things held constant, but they are lower for riskier firms. Because MicroDrive's P/E ratio is below the average, this suggests that the company is regarded as being somewhat riskier than most, as having poorer growth prospects, or both. In early 2009, the average P/E ratio for firms in the S&P 500 was 12.54, indicating that investors were willing to pay $12.54 for every dollar of earnings.

Price/Cash Flow Ratio

Stock prices depend on a company's ability to generate cash flows. Consequently, investors often look at the **price/cash flow ratio,** where cash flow is defined as net income plus depreciation and amortization:

$$\text{Price/cash flow ratio} = \frac{\text{Price per share}}{\text{Cash flow per share}}$$

$$= \frac{\$23.00}{\$4.27} = 5.4$$

$$\text{Industry average} = 6.8$$

MicroDrive's price/cash flow ratio is also below the industry average, once again suggesting that its growth prospects are below average, its risk is above average, or both.

The **price/EBITDA ratio** is similar to the price/cash flow ratio, except the price/EBITDA ratio measures performance before the impact of interest expenses and taxes, making it a better measure of operating performance. MicroDrive's EBITDA per share is $383.8/50 = $7.676, so its price/EBITDA is $23/$7.676 = 3.0. The industry average price/EBITDA ratio is 4.6, so we see again that MicroDrive is below the industry average.

Note that some analysts look at other multiples as well. For example, depending on the industry, some may look at measures such as price/sales or price/customers. Ultimately, though, value depends on free cash flows, so if these "exotic" ratios do not forecast future free cash flow, they may turn out to be misleading. This was true in the case of the dot-com retailers before they crashed and burned in 2000, costing investors many billions.

Market/Book Ratio

The ratio of a stock's market price to its book value gives another indication of how investors regard the company. Companies with relatively high rates of return on equity generally sell at higher multiples of book value than those with low returns. First, we find MicroDrive's book value per share:

$$\text{Book value per share} = \frac{\text{Common equity}}{\text{Shares outstanding}}$$

$$= \frac{\$896}{50} = \$17.92$$

Now we divide the market price by the book value to get a **market/book (M/B) ratio** of 1.3 times:

$$\text{Market/book ratio} = \text{M/B} = \frac{\text{Market price per share}}{\text{Book value per share}}$$

$$= \frac{\$23.00}{\$17.92} = 1.3$$

$$\text{Industry average} = 1.7$$

Investors are willing to pay relatively little for a dollar of MicroDrive's book value.

The average company in the S&P 500 had a market/book ratio of about 2.50 in early 2009. Since M/B ratios typically exceed 1.0, this means that investors are willing to pay more for stocks than their accounting book values. The book value is a record of the past, showing the cumulative amount that stockholders have invested, either directly by purchasing newly issued shares or indirectly through retaining earnings. In contrast, the market price is forward-looking, incorporating investors' expectations of future cash flows. For example, in early 2009 Alaska Air had a market/book ratio of only 0.81, reflecting the airline industry's problems, whereas Apple's market/book ratio was 3.45, indicating that investors expected Apple's past successes to continue.

Table 3-2 summarizes MicroDrive's financial ratios. As the table indicates, the company has many problems.

Self-Test

Describe three ratios that relate a firm's stock price to its earnings, cash flow, and book value per share, and write out their equations.

What does the price/earnings (P/E) ratio show? If one firm's P/E ratio is lower than that of another, what are some factors that might explain the difference?

How is book value per share calculated? Explain why book values often deviate from market values.

A company has $6 billion of net income, $2 billion of depreciation and amortization, $80 billion of common equity, and 1 billion shares of stock. If its stock price is $96 per share, what is its price/earnings ratio? **(16)** Its price/cash flow ratio? **(12)** Its market/book ratio? **(1.2)**

3.7 Trend Analysis, Common Size Analysis, and Percentage Change Analysis

Trends give clues as to whether a firm's financial condition is likely to improve or deteriorate. To do a **trend analysis**, you examine a ratio over time, as shown in Figure 3-1. This graph shows that MicroDrive's rate of return on common equity has been declining since 2007, even though the industry average has been relatively stable. All the other ratios could be analyzed similarly.

In a **common size analysis**, all income statement items are divided by sales and all balance sheet items are divided by total assets. Thus, a common size income state-

TABLE 3-2 MicroDrive Inc.: Summary of Financial Ratios (Millions of Dollars)

RATIO	FORMULA	CALCULATION	RATIO	INDUSTRY AVERAGE	COMMENT
Liquidity					
Current	$\frac{\text{Current assets}}{\text{Current liabilities}}$	$\frac{\$1,000}{\$310} =$	3.2	4.2	Poor
Quick	$\frac{\text{Current assets} - \text{Inventories}}{\text{Current liabilities}}$	$\frac{\$385}{\$310} =$	1.2	2.1	Poor
Asset Management					
Inventory turnover	$\frac{\text{Sales}}{\text{Inventories}}$	$\frac{\$3,000}{\$615} =$	4.9	9.0	Poor
Days sales outstanding (DSO)	$\frac{\text{Receivables}}{\text{Annual sales/365}}$	$\frac{\$375}{\$8.219} =$	45.6	36.0	Poor
Fixed assets turnover	$\frac{\text{Sales}}{\text{Net fixed assets}}$	$\frac{\$3,000}{\$1,000} =$	3.0	3.0	OK
Total assets turnover	$\frac{\text{Sales}}{\text{Total assets}}$	$\frac{\$3,000}{\$2,000} =$	1.5	1.8	Poor
Debt Management					
Debt ratio	$\frac{\text{Total liabilities}}{\text{Total assets}}$	$\frac{\$1,064}{\$2,000} =$	53.2%	40.0%	High (risky)
Times-interest-earned (TIE)	$\frac{\text{Earnings before interest and taxes (EBIT)}}{\text{Interest charges}}$	$\frac{\$283.8}{\$88} =$	3.2	6.0	Low (risky)
EBITDA coverage	$\frac{\text{EBITDA} + \text{Lease pmts.}}{\text{Interest} + \text{Principal payments} + \text{Lease pmts.}}$	$\frac{\$411.8}{\$136} =$	3.0	4.3	Low (risky)
Profitability					
Profit margin on sales	$\frac{\text{Net income available to common stockholders}}{\text{Sales}}$	$\frac{\$113.5}{\$3,000} =$	3.8%	5.0%	Poor
Basic earning power (BEP)	$\frac{\text{Earnings before interest and taxes (EBIT)}}{\text{Total assets}}$	$\frac{\$283.8}{\$2,000} =$	14.2%	17.2%	Poor
Return on total assets (ROA)	$\frac{\text{Net income available to common stockholders}}{\text{Total assets}}$	$\frac{\$113.5}{\$2,000} =$	5.7%	9.0%	Poor
Return on common equity (ROE)	$\frac{\text{Net income available to common stockholders}}{\text{Common equity}}$	$\frac{\$113.5}{\$896} =$	12.7%	15.0%	Poor
Market Value					
Price/earnings (P/E)	$\frac{\text{Price per share}}{\text{Earnings per share}}$	$\frac{\$23.00}{\$2.27} =$	10.1	12.5	Low
Price/cash flow	$\frac{\text{Price per share}}{\text{Cash flow per share}}$	$\frac{\$23.00}{\$4.27} =$	5.4	6.8	Low
Market/book (M/B)	$\frac{\text{Market price per share}}{\text{Book value per share}}$	$\frac{\$23.00}{\$17.92} =$	1.3	1.7	Low

FIGURE 3-1 Rate of Return on Common Equity, 2006–2010

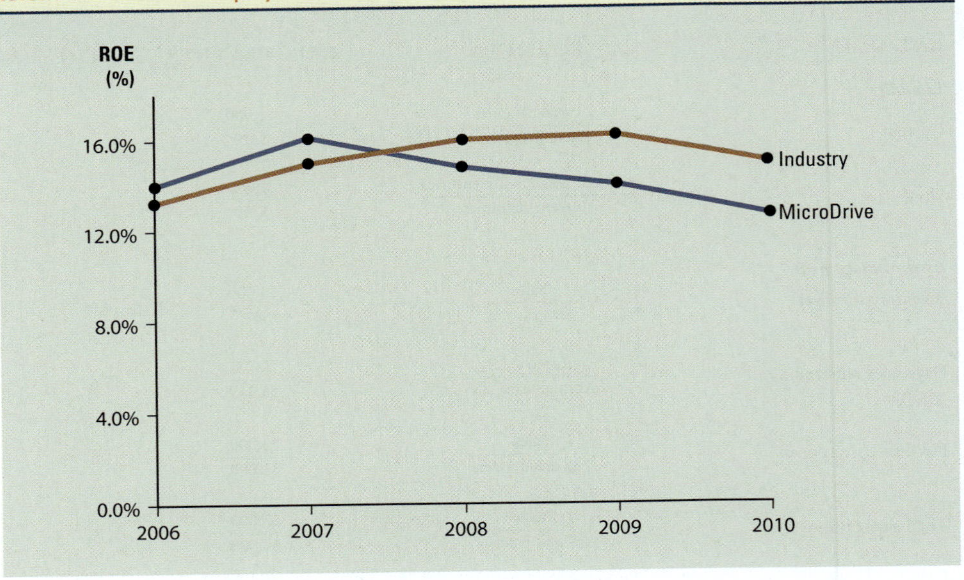

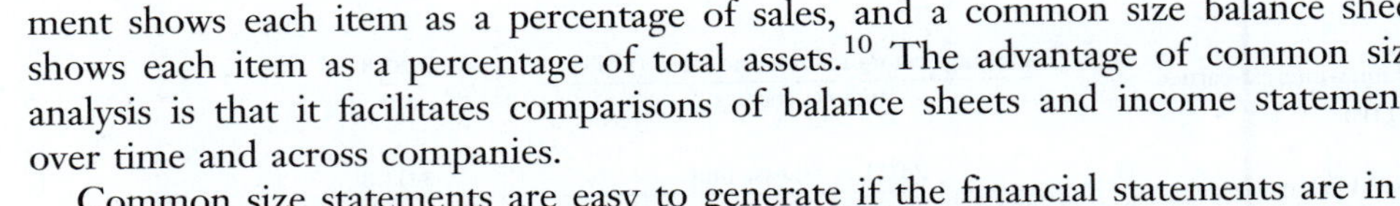

ment shows each item as a percentage of sales, and a common size balance sheet shows each item as a percentage of total assets.[10] The advantage of common size analysis is that it facilitates comparisons of balance sheets and income statements over time and across companies.

Common size statements are easy to generate if the financial statements are in a spreadsheet. In fact, if you obtain your data from a source that uses standardized financial statements, then it is easy to cut and paste the data for a new company over your original company's data, and all of your spreadsheet formulas will be valid for the new company. We generated Figure 3-2 in the *Excel* file ***Ch03 Tool Kit.xls***. Figure 3-2 shows MicroDrive's 2009 and 2010 common size income statements, along with the composite statement for the industry. (*Note:* Rounding may cause addition/subtraction differences in Figures 3-2, 3-3, and 3-4.) MicroDrive's EBIT is slightly below average, and its interest expenses are slightly above average. The net effect is a relatively low profit margin.

Figure 3-3 shows MicroDrive's common size balance sheets along with the industry composite. Its accounts receivable are significantly higher than the industry average, its inventories are significantly higher, and it uses much more debt than the average firm.

In **percentage change analysis**, growth rates are calculated for all income statement items and balance sheet accounts relative to a base year. To illustrate, Figure 3-4 contains MicroDrive's income statement percentage change analysis for 2010 relative to 2009. Sales increased at a 5.3% rate during 2010, but EBITDA increased by 8.7%. This "good news" was offset by a 46.7% increase in interest expense. The significant growth in interest expense caused growth in net income to be negative. Thus, the percentage change analysis points out that the decrease in net income in 2010 resulted almost exclusively from an increase in interest expense. This conclusion could be reached by analyzing dollar

[10]Some sources of industry data, such as Risk Management Associates (formerly known as Robert Morris Associates), are presented exclusively in common size form.

FIGURE 3-2 MicroDrive Inc.: Common Size Income Statement

	A B C	D	E	F
167		Industry Composite		
168			MicroDrive	
169		2010	2010	2009
170	Net sales	100.0%	100.0%	100.0%
171	Operating costs	87.6%	87.2%	87.6%
172	Earnings before interest, taxes, depr. & amort. (EBITDA)	12.4%	12.8%	12.4%
173	Depreciation and amortization	2.8%	3.3%	3.2%
174	Earnings before interest and taxes (EBIT)	9.6%	9.5%	9.2%
175	Less interest	1.3%	2.9%	2.1%
176	Earnings before taxes (EBT)	8.3%	6.5%	7.1%
177	Taxes (40%)	3.3%	2.6%	2.8%
178	Net income before preferred dividends	5.0%	3.9%	4.3%
179	Preferred dividends	0.0%	0.1%	0.1%
180	Net income available to common stockholders (profit margin)	5.0%	3.5%	4.1%

FIGURE 3-3 MicroDrive Inc.: Common Size Balance Sheet

	A B	C	D	E
185		Industry Composite	MicroDrive	
186		2010	2010	2009
187	*Assets*			
188	Cash and equivalents	1.0%	0.5%	0.9%
189	Short-term investments	2.2%	0.0%	3.9%
190	Accounts receivable	17.8%	18.8%	18.8%
191	Inventories	19.8%	30.8%	24.7%
192	Total current assets	40.8%	50.0%	48.2%
193	Net plant and equipment	59.2%	50.0%	51.8%
194	Total assets	100.0%	100.0%	100.0%
195				
196	*Liabilities and equity*			
197	Accounts payable	1.8%	3.0%	1.8%
198	Notes payable	4.4%	5.5%	3.6%
199	Accruals	3.6%	7.0%	7.7%
200	Total current liabilities	9.8%	15.5%	13.1%
201	Long-term bonds	30.2%	37.7%	34.5%
202	Total liabilities	40.0%	53.2%	47.6%
203	Preferred stock	0.0%	2.0%	2.4%
204	Total common equity	60.0%	44.8%	50.0%
205	Total liabilities and equity	100.0%	100.0%	100.0%
206				

See **Ch03 Tool Kit.xls** *for details.*

amounts, but percentage change analysis simplifies the task. We apply the same type of analysis to the balance sheets (see the file ***Ch03 Tool Kit.xls***), which shows that inventories grew at a whopping 48.2% rate. With only a 5.3% growth in sales, the extreme growth in inventories should be of great concern to MicroDrive's managers.

Self-Test

What is a trend analysis, and what important information does it provide?
What is common size analysis?
What is percentage change analysis?

FIGURE 3-4 MicroDrive Inc.: Income Statement Percentage Change Analysis

See **Ch03 Tool Kit.xls** *for details.*

	A	B	C	D
213	Base Year = 2009			Percent Change in 2010
214				
215	Net sales			5.3%
216	Operating costs			4.8%
217	Earnings before interest, taxes, depr. & amort. (EBITDA)			8.7%
218	Depreciation and amortization			11.1%
219	Earnings before interest and taxes (EBIT)			7.9%
220	Less interest			46.7%
221	Earnings before taxes (EBT)			(3.5%)
222	Taxes (40%)			(3.5%)
223	Net income before preferred dividends			(3.5%)
224	Preferred dividends			0.0%
225	Net income available to common stockholders			(3.7%)
226				

3.8 Tying the Ratios Together: The Du Pont Equation

In ratio analysis, it is sometimes easy to miss the forest for all the trees. The **Du Pont equation** provides a framework that ties together a firm's profitability, asset efficiency, and use of debt. The return on assets (ROA) can be expressed as the profit margin multiplied by the total assets turnover ratio:

$$\begin{aligned} \text{ROA} &= \text{Profit margin} \times \text{Total assets turnover} \\ &= \frac{\text{Net income}}{\text{Sales}} \times \frac{\text{Sales}}{\text{Total assets}} \end{aligned} \tag{3-1}$$

For MicroDrive, the ROA is

$$\text{ROA} = 3.8\% \times 1.5 = 5.7\%$$

MicroDrive made 3.8%, or 3.8 cents, on each dollar of sales, and its assets were turned over 1.5 times during the year. Therefore, the company earned a return of 5.7% on its assets.

To find the return on equity (ROE), multiply the ROA by the *equity multiplier*, which is the ratio of assets to common equity:

$$\text{Equity multiplier} = \frac{\text{Total assets}}{\text{Common equity}} \tag{3-2}$$

Firms that have a lot of leverage (i.e., a lot of liabilities or preferred stock) have a high equity multiplier because the assets are financed with a relatively smaller amount of equity. Therefore, the return on equity (ROE) depends on the ROA and the use of leverage:

$$\begin{aligned} \text{ROE} &= \text{ROA} \times \text{Equity multiplier} \\ &= \frac{\text{Net income}}{\text{Total assets}} \times \frac{\text{Total assets}}{\text{Common equity}} \end{aligned} \tag{3-3}$$

MicroDrive's ROE is

$$\begin{aligned} \text{ROE} &= 5.7\% \times \$2{,}000/\$896 \\ &= 5.7\% \times 2.23 \\ &= 12.7\% \end{aligned}$$

Combining Equations 3-1 and 3-3 gives the *extended, or modified, Du Pont equation*, which shows how the profit margin, the total assets turnover ratio, and the equity multiplier combine to determine the ROE:

$$\begin{aligned} \text{ROE} &= (\text{Profit margin})(\text{Total assets turnover})(\text{Equity multiplier}) \\ &= \frac{\text{Net income}}{\text{Sales}} \times \frac{\text{Sales}}{\text{Total assets}} \times \frac{\text{Total assets}}{\text{Common equity}} \end{aligned} \tag{3-4}$$

For MicroDrive, we have

$$\begin{aligned} \text{ROE} &= (3.8\%)(1.5)(2.23) \\ &= 12.7\% \end{aligned}$$

The insights provided by the Du Pont model are valuable, and the model can be used for "quick and dirty" estimates of the impact that operating changes have on returns. For example, holding all else equal, if MicroDrive can implement lean production techniques and increase to 1.8 its ratio of sales to total assets, then its ROE will improve to (3.8%)(1.8)(2.23) = 15.25%. For a more complete "what if" analysis, most companies use a forecasting model such as the one described in Chapter 12.

Self-Test

Explain how the extended, or modified, Du Pont equation can be used to reveal the basic determinants of ROE.

What is the equity multiplier?

A company has a profit margin of 6%, a total asset turnover ratio of 2, and an equity multiplier of 1.5. What is its ROE? (18%)

3.9 Comparative Ratios and Benchmarking

Ratio analysis involves comparisons. A company's ratios are compared with those of other firms in the same industry—that is, with industry average figures. However, like most firms, MicroDrive's managers go one step further: they also compare their ratios with those of a smaller set of the leading computer companies. This technique is called **benchmarking**, and the companies used for the comparison are called **benchmark companies**. For example, MicroDrive benchmarks against five other firms that its management considers to be the best-managed companies with operations similar to its own.

Many companies also benchmark various parts of their overall operation against top companies, whether they are in the same industry or not. For example, MicroDrive has a division that sells hard drives directly to consumers through catalogs and the Internet. This division's shipping department benchmarks against L.L.Bean, even though they are in different industries, because L.L.Bean's shipping department is one of the best. MicroDrive wants its own shippers to strive to match L.L.Bean's record for on-time shipments.

TABLE 3-3 Comparative Ratios for Apple Inc., the Computer Hardware Industry, the Technology Sector, and the S&P 500

RATIO	APPLE	COMPUTER HARDWARE INDUSTRY[a]	TECHNOLOGY SECTOR[b]	S&P 500
P/E ratio	15.92	7.88	8.75	17.93
Market to book	3.60	3.12	2.90	6.84
Price to tangible book	3.70	4.41	3.87	8.73
Price to cash flow	14.30	6.70	4.58	12.01
Net profit margin	14.88	3.32	4.92	11.18
Quick ratio	2.43	1.86	1.97	1.04
Current ratio	2.46	2.21	2.36	1.28
Long-term debt to equity	0.00	20.05	18.28	151.80
Total debt to equity	0.00	30.32	27.38	197.45
Interest coverage (TIE)[c]	—	0.15	1.12	31.97
Return on assets	14.89	4.07	4.90	8.05
Return on equity	27.19	8.27	7.68	19.09
Inventory turnover	49.90	12.99	3.09	9.71
Asset turnover	1.00	0.37	0.46	0.79

[a]The computer hardware industry is composed of fifty firms, including IBM, Dell, Apple, Sun Microsystems, Gateway, and Silicon Graphics.
[b]The technology sector contains eleven industries, including communications equipment, computer hardware, computer networks, semiconductors, and software and programming.
[c]Apple had more interest income than interest expense.

Source: Adapted from **http://www.investor.reuters.com**, January 17, 2009.

To find quick information about a company, go to **http://www.investor.reuters.com.** Here you can find company profiles, stock price and share information, and several key ratios.

Comparative ratios are available from a number of sources, including *Value Line*, Dun and Bradstreet (D&B), and the *Annual Statement Studies* published by Risk Management Associates, which is the national association of bank loan officers. Table 3-3 reports selected ratios from Reuters for Apple and its industry, revealing that Apple has a much higher profit margin and lower debt ratio than its peers.

Each data-supplying organization uses a somewhat different set of ratios designed for its own purposes. For example, D&B deals mainly with small firms, many of which are proprietorships, and it sells its services primarily to banks and other lenders. Therefore, D&B is concerned largely with the creditor's viewpoint, and its ratios emphasize current assets and liabilities, not market value ratios. So, when you select a comparative data source, you should be sure that your own emphasis is similar to that of the agency whose ratios you plan to use. Additionally, there are often definitional differences in the ratios presented by different sources, so before using a source, be sure to verify the exact definitions of the ratios to ensure consistency with your own work.

Self-Test

Differentiate between trend analysis and comparative ratio analysis.
What is benchmarking?

3.10 Uses and Limitations of Ratio Analysis

Ratio analysis provides useful information concerning a company's operations and financial condition, but it has limitations that necessitate care and judgment. Some potential problems include the following.

Ratio Analysis on the Web

A great source for comparative ratios is **http://www.investor.reuters.com**. You have to register to use the site, but registration is free. Once you register and log in, select Stocks; enter a company's ticker symbol, select the Symbol ratio button, and then click the Go button. This brings up a table with the stock quote, company information, and additional links. Select Ratios, which brings up a page with a detailed ratio analysis for the company and includes comparative ratios for other companies in the same sector, the same industry, and the S&P 500.

1. Many large firms operate different divisions in different industries, and for such companies it is difficult to develop a meaningful set of industry averages. Therefore, industry averages are more applicable to small, narrowly focused firms than to large, multidivisional ones.
2. To set goals for high-level performance, it is best to benchmark on the industry *leaders'* ratios rather than the industry *average* ratios.
3. Inflation may have badly distorted firms' balance sheets—reported values are often substantially different from "true" values. Further, because inflation affects depreciation charges and inventory costs, reported profits are also affected. Thus, inflation can distort a ratio analysis for one firm over time or a comparative analysis of firms of different ages.
4. Seasonal factors can also distort a ratio analysis. For example, the inventory turnover ratio for a food processor will be radically different if the balance sheet figure used for inventory is the one just before versus the one just after the close of the canning season. This problem can be minimized by using monthly averages for inventory (and receivables) when calculating turnover ratios.
5. Firms can employ **"window dressing" techniques** to make their financial statements look stronger. To illustrate, suppose a company takes out a 2-year loan in late December. Because the loan is for more than one year, it is not included in current liabilities even though the cash received through the loan is reported as a current asset. This improves the current and quick ratios and makes the year-end balance sheet look stronger. If the company pays the loan back in January, then the transaction was strictly window dressing.
6. Companies' choices of different accounting practices can distort comparisons. For example, choices of different inventory valuation and depreciation methods affect financial statements differently, making comparisons among companies less meaningful. As another example, if one firm leases a substantial amount of its productive equipment, then its assets may appear low relative to sales (because leased assets often do not appear on the balance sheet) and its debt may appear low (because the liability associated with the lease obligation may not be shown as debt).[11]

In summary, conducting ratio analysis in a mechanical, unthinking manner is dangerous, but when ratio analysis is used intelligently and with good judgment, it can provide useful insights into a firm's operations and identify the right questions to ask.

[11]This may change when FASB and IASB complete their joint project on leasing. But it may be a while before this happens; in early 2009, the estimated project completion date was 2011. See **http://72.3.243.42/project/leases.shtml** for updates.

Self-Test List several potential problems with ratio analysis.

3.11 Looking Beyond the Numbers

Sound financial analysis involves more than just calculating and comparing ratios—qualitative factors must be considered. Here are some questions suggested by the American Association of Individual Investors (AAII).

1. To what extent are the company's revenues tied to one key customer or to one key product? To what extent does the company rely on a single supplier? Reliance on single customers, products, or suppliers increases risk.
2. What percentage of the company's business is generated overseas? Companies with a large percentage of overseas business are exposed to risk of currency exchange volatility and political instability.
3. What are the probable actions of current competitors and the likelihood of additional new competitors?
4. Do the company's future prospects depend critically on the success of products currently in the pipeline or on existing products?
5. How does the legal and regulatory environment affect the company?

Self-Test What are some qualitative factors that analysts should consider when evaluating a company's likely future financial performance?

Summary

This chapter explained techniques used by investors and managers to analyze financial statements. The key concepts covered are listed below.

- **Liquidity ratios** show the relationship of a firm's current assets to its current liabilities and thus its ability to meet maturing debts. Two commonly used liquidity ratios are the **current ratio** and the **quick,** or **acid test, ratio.**
- **Asset management ratios** measure how effectively a firm is managing its assets. These ratios include **inventory turnover, days sales outstanding, fixed assets turnover,** and **total assets turnover.**
- **Debt management ratios** reveal (1) the extent to which the firm is financed with debt and (2) its likelihood of defaulting on its debt obligations. They include the **debt ratio,** the **times-interest-earned ratio,** and the **EBITDA coverage ratio.**
- **Profitability ratios** show the combined effects of liquidity, asset management, and debt management policies on operating results. They include the **net profit margin** (also called the **profit margin on sales**), the **basic earning power ratio**, the **return on total assets**, and the **return on common equity.**
- **Market value ratios** relate the firm's stock price to its earnings, cash flow, and book value per share, thus giving management an indication of what investors think of the company's past performance and future prospects. These include the **price/earnings ratio,** the **price/cash flow ratio,** and the **market/book ratio.**
- **Trend analysis,** in which one plots a ratio over time, is important because it reveals whether the firm's condition has been improving or deteriorating over time.
- The **Du Pont system** is designed to show how the profit margin on sales, the assets turnover ratio, and the use of debt all interact to determine the rate of

return on equity. The firm's management can use the Du Pont system to analyze ways of improving performance.

- **Benchmarking** is the process of comparing a particular company with a group of similar successful companies.

Ratio analysis has limitations, but when used with care and judgment it can be very helpful.

Questions

(3–1) Define each of the following terms:

a. *Liquidity ratios:* current ratio; quick, or acid test, ratio
b. Asset management ratios: inventory turnover ratio; days sales outstanding (DSO); fixed assets turnover ratio; total assets turnover ratio
c. *Financial leverage ratios:* debt ratio; times-interest-earned (TIE) ratio; coverage ratio
d. *Profitability ratios:* profit margin on sales; basic earning power (BEP) ratio; return on total assets (ROA); return on common equity (ROE)
e. Market value ratios: price/earnings (P/E) ratio; price/cash flow ratio; market/book (M/B) ratio; book value per share
f. Trend analysis; comparative ratio analysis; benchmarking
g. Du Pont equation; window dressing; seasonal effects on ratios

(3–2) Financial ratio analysis is conducted by managers, equity investors, long-term creditors, and short-term creditors. What is the primary emphasis of each of these groups in evaluating ratios?

(3–3) Over the past year, M. D. Ryngaert & Co. has realized an increase in its current ratio and a drop in its total assets turnover ratio. However, the company's sales, quick ratio, and fixed assets turnover ratio have remained constant. What explains these changes?

(3–4) Profit margins and turnover ratios vary from one industry to another. What differences would you expect to find between a grocery chain such as Safeway and a steel company? Think particularly about the turnover ratios, the profit margin, and the Du Pont equation.

(3–5) How might (a) seasonal factors and (b) different growth rates distort a comparative ratio analysis? Give some examples. How might these problems be alleviated?

(3–6) Why is it sometimes misleading to compare a company's financial ratios with those of other firms that operate in the same industry?

Self-Test Problems

Solutions Appear in Appendix A

(ST–1) Debt Ratio

Argent Corporation had earnings per share of $4 last year, and it paid a $2 dividend. Total retained earnings increased by $12 million during the year, and book value per share at year-end was $40. Argent has no preferred stock, and no new common stock was issued during the year. If Argent's year-end debt (which equals its total liabilities) was $120 million, what was the company's year-end debt/assets ratio?

(ST–2) Ratio Analysis

The following data apply to Jacobus and Associates (millions of dollars):

Cash and marketable securities	$ 100.00
Fixed assets	$ 283.50
Sales	$1,000.00
Net income	$ 50.00
Quick ratio	2.0
Current ratio	3.0
DSO	40.55 days
ROE	12%

Jacobus has no preferred stock—only common equity, current liabilities, and long-term debt.

a. Find Jacobus's (1) accounts receivable, (2) current liabilities, (3) current assets, (4) total assets, (5) ROA, (6) common equity, and (7) long-term debt.
b. In part a, you should have found Jacobus's accounts receivable = $111.1 million. If Jacobus could reduce its DSO from 40.55 days to 30.4 days while holding other things constant, how much cash would it generate? If this cash were used to buy back common stock (at book value), thus reducing the amount of common equity, how would this affect (1) the ROE, (2) the ROA, and (3) the ratio of total debt to total assets?

Problems

Answers Appear in Appendix B

Easy Problems 1–5

(3–1) Days Sales Outstanding

Greene Sisters has a DSO of 20 days. The company's average daily sales are $20,000. What is the level of its accounts receivable? Assume there are 365 days in a year.

(3–2) Debt Ratio

Vigo Vacations has an equity multiplier of 2.5. The company's assets are financed with some combination of long-term debt and common equity. What is the company's debt ratio?

(3–3) Market/Book Ratio

Winston Washers's stock price is $75 per share. Winston has $10 billion in total assets. Its balance sheet shows $1 billion in current liabilities, $3 billion in long-term debt, and $6 billion in common equity. It has 800 million shares of common stock outstanding. What is Winston's market/book ratio?

(3–4) Price/Earnings Ratio

A company has an EPS of $1.50, a cash flow per share of $3.00, and a price/cash flow ratio of 8.0. What is its P/E ratio?

(3–5) ROE

Needham Pharmaceuticals has a profit margin of 3% and an equity multiplier of 2.0. Its sales are $100 million and it has total assets of $50 million. What is its ROE?

Intermediate Problems 6–10

(3–6) Du Pont Analysis

Donaldson & Son has an ROA of 10%, a 2% profit margin, and a return on equity equal to 15%. What is the company's total assets turnover? What is the firm's equity multiplier?

(3–7) Current and Quick Ratios

Ace Industries has current assets equal to $3 million. The company's current ratio is 1.5, and its quick ratio is 1.0. What is the firm's level of current liabilities? What is the firm's level of inventories?

(3–8) Profit Margin and Debt Ratio

Assume you are given the following relationships for the Clayton Corporation:

Sales/total assets	1.5
Return on assets (ROA)	3%
Return on equity (ROE)	5%

Calculate Clayton's profit margin and debt ratio.

(3–9) Current and Quick Ratios

The Nelson Company has $1,312,500 in current assets and $525,000 in current liabilities. Its initial inventory level is $375,000, and it will raise funds as additional notes payable and use them to increase inventory. How much can Nelson's short-term debt (notes payable) increase without pushing its current ratio below 2.0? What will be the firm's quick ratio after Nelson has raised the maximum amount of short-term funds?

(3–10) Times-Interest-Earned Ratio

The Manor Corporation has $500,000 of debt outstanding, and it pays an interest rate of 10% annually: Manor's annual sales are $2 million, its average tax rate is 30%, and its net profit margin on sales is 5%. If the company does not maintain a TIE ratio of at least 5 to 1, then its bank will refuse to renew the loan and bankruptcy will result. What is Manor's TIE ratio?

CHALLENGING PROBLEMS 11–14

(3–11) Balance Sheet Analysis

Complete the balance sheet and sales information in the table that follows for Hoffmeister Industries using the following financial data:

Debt ratio: 50%
Quick ratio: 0.80
Total assets turnover: 1.5
Days sales outstanding: 36.5 days[a]
Gross profit margin on sales: (Sales − Cost of goods sold)/Sales = 25%
Inventory turnover ratio: 5.0

[a]Calculation is based on a 365-day year.

Balance Sheet

Cash	______	Accounts payable	______
Accounts receivable	______	Long-term debt	60,000
Inventories	______	Common stock	______
Fixed assets	______	Retained earnings	97,500
Total assets	$300,000	Total liabilities and equity	______
Sales	______	Cost of goods sold	______

(3–12) Comprehensive Ratio Calculations

The Kretovich Company had a quick ratio of 1.4, a current ratio of 3.0, an inventory turnover of 6 times, total current assets of $810,000, and cash and marketable securities of $120,000. What were Kretovich's annual sales and its DSO? Assume a 365-day year.

(3–13) Comprehensive Ratio Analysis

Data for Morton Chip Company and its industry averages follow.

a. Calculate the indicated ratios for Morton.
b. Construct the extended Du Pont equation for both Morton and the industry.
c. Outline Morton's strengths and weaknesses as revealed by your analysis.
d. Suppose Morton had doubled its sales as well as its inventories, accounts receivable, and common equity during 2010. How would that information affect the validity of your ratio analysis? (*Hint:* Think about averages and the effects of rapid growth on ratios if averages are not used. No calculations are needed.)

Morton Chip Company: Balance Sheet as of December 31, 2010 (Thousands of Dollars)

Cash	$ 77,500	Accounts payable	$129,000
Receivables	336,000	Notes payable	84,000
Inventories	241,500	Other current liabilities	117,000
Total current assets	$655,000	Total current liabilities	$330,000
Net fixed assets	292,500	Long-term debt	256,500
		Common equity	361,000
Total assets	$947,500	Total liabilities and equity	$947,500

Morton Chip Company: Income Statement for Year Ended December 31, 2010 (Thousands of Dollars)

Sales	$1,607,500
Cost of goods sold	1,392,500
Selling, general, and administrative expenses	145,000
Earnings before interest and taxes (EBIT)	$ 70,000
Interest expense	24,500
Earnings before taxes (EBT)	$ 45,500
Federal and state income taxes (40%)	18,200
Net income	$ 27,300

Ratio	Morton	Industry Average
Current assets/Current liabilities	________	2.0
Days sales outstanding[a]	________	35.0 days
Sales/Inventory	________	6.7
Sales/Fixed assets	________	12.1
Sales/Total assets	________	3.0
Net income/Sales	________	1.2%
Net income/Total assets	________	3.6%
Net income/Common equity	________	9.0%
Total debt/Total assets	________	60.0%

[a]Calculation is based on a 365-day year.

(3–14) Comprehensive Ratio Analysis

The Jimenez Corporation's forecasted 2011 financial statements follow, along with some industry average ratios.

a. Calculate Jimenez's 2011 forecasted ratios, compare them with the industry average data, and comment briefly on Jimenez's projected strengths and weaknesses.
b. What do you think would happen to Jimenez's ratios if the company initiated cost-cutting measures that allowed it to hold lower levels of inventory and substantially decreased the cost of goods sold? No calculations are necessary: Think about which ratios would be affected by changes in these two accounts.

Jimenez Corporation: Forecasted Balance Sheet as of December 31, 2011

Assets	
Cash	$ 72,000
Accounts receivable	439,000
Inventories	894,000
Total current assets	$1,405,000
Fixed assets	431,000
Total assets	$1,836,000
Liabilities and Equity	
Accounts and notes payable	$ 432,000
Accruals	170,000
Total current liabilities	$ 602,000
Long-term debt	404,290
Common stock	575,000
Retained earnings	254,710
Total liabilities and equity	$1,836,000

Jimenez Corporation: Forecasted Income Statement for 2011

Sales	$4,290,000
Cost of goods sold	3,580,000
Selling, general, and administrative expenses	370,320
Depreciation	159,000
Earnings before taxes (EBT)	$ 180,680
Taxes (40%)	72,272
Net income	$ 108,408
Per Share Data	
EPS	$ 4.71
Cash dividends per share	$ 0.95
P/E ratio	5
Market price (average)	$ 23.57
Number of shares outstanding	23,000
Industry Financial Ratios (2010)[a]	
Quick ratio	1.0
Current ratio	2.7
Inventory turnover[b]	7.0
Days sales outstanding[c]	32 days
Fixed assets turnover[b]	13.0
Total assets turnover[b]	2.6
Return on assets	9.1%
Return on equity	18.2%
Debt ratio	50.0%
Profit margin on sales	3.5%
P/E ratio	6.0
Price/Cash flow ratio	3.5

[a]Industry average ratios have been constant for the past 4 years.
[b]Based on year-end balance sheet figures.
[c]Calculation is based on a 365-day year.

SPREADSHEET PROBLEM

(3-15)
Build a Model: Ratio Analysis

Start with the partial model in the file ***Ch03 P15 Build a Model.xls*** from the textbook's Web site. Joshua & White (J&W) Technologies's financial statements are also shown below. Answer the following questions. (*Note:* Industry average ratios are provided in ***Ch03 P15 Build a Model.xls***.)

a. Has J&W's liquidity position improved or worsened? Explain.
b. Has J&W's ability to manage its assets improved or worsened? Explain.
c. How has J&W's profitability changed during the last year?
d. Perform an extended Du Pont analysis for J&W for 2009 and 2010. What do these results tell you?
e. Perform a common size analysis. What has happened to the composition (that is, percentage in each category) of assets and liabilities?
f. Perform a percentage change analysis. What does this tell you about the change in profitability and asset utilization?

Joshua & White Technologies: December 31 Balance Sheets (Thousands of Dollars)

Assets	2010	2009	*Liabilities & Equity*	2010	2009
Cash and cash equivalents	$ 21,000	$ 20,000	Accounts payable	$ 33,600	$ 32,000
Short-term investments	3,759	3,240	Accruals	12,600	12,000
Accounts receivable	52,500	48,000	Notes payable	19,929	6,480
Inventories	84,000	56,000	Total current liabilities	$ 66,129	$ 50,480
Total current assets	$161,259	$127,240	Long-term debt	67,662	58,320
Net fixed assets	218,400	200,000	Total liabilities	$133,791	$108,800
Total assets	$379,659	$327,240	Common stock	183,793	178,440
			Retained earnings	62,075	40,000
			Total common equity	$245,868	$218,440
			Total liabilities & equity	$379,659	$327,240

Joshua & White Technologies December 31 Income Statements (Thousands of Dollars)

	2010	2009
Sales	$420,000	$400,000
Expenses excluding depr. & amort.	327,600	320,000
EBITDA	$ 92,400	$ 80,000
Depreciation and amortization	19,660	18,000
EBIT	$ 72,740	$ 62,000

	2010	2009
Interest expense	5,740	4,460
EBT	$67,000	$57,540
Taxes (40%)	26,800	23,016
Net income	$40,200	$34,524
Common dividends	$18,125	$17,262

Other Data	2010	2009
Year-end stock price	$ 90.00	$ 96.00
Number of shares (Thousands)	4,052	4,000
Lease payment (Thousands of Dollars)	$20,000	$20,000
Sinking fund payment (Thousands of Dollars)	$ 0	$ 0

THOMSON ONE Business School Edition Problem

Use the Thomson ONE—Business School Edition online database to work this chapter's questions.

Analysis of Ford's Financial Statements with Thomson ONE—Business School Edition

Use Thomson ONE to analyze Ford Motor Company. Enter Ford's ticker symbol (F) and select GO. By selecting the tab at the top labeled Financials, you can find Ford's key financial statements for the past several years. At the Financials screen on the second line of tabs, select the Fundamental Ratios tab. If you then select the SEC Database Ratios from the pull-down menu, you can select either annual or quarterly ratios.

Under annual ratios, there is an in-depth summary of Ford's various ratios over the past three years.

Click on the Peers tab (on the first line of tabs) near the top of the screen for a summary of financial information for Ford and a few of its peers. If you click on the Peer Sets tab (second line of tabs), you can modify the list of peer firms. The default setup is "Peers set by SIC Code." To obtain a comparison of many of the key ratios presented in the text, just click on Financials (second line of tabs) and select Key Financial Ratios from the drop-down menu.

Thomson ONE—BSE Discussion Questions

1. What has happened to Ford's liquidity position over the past 3 years? How does Ford's liquidity compare with its peers? (*Hint:* You may use both the peer key financial ratios and liquidity comparison to answer this question.)
2. Take a look at Ford's inventory turnover ratio. How does this ratio compare with its peers? Have there been any interesting changes over time in this measure? Do you consider Ford's inventory management to be a strength or a weakness?
3. Construct a simple Du Pont analysis for Ford and its peers. What are Ford's strengths and weaknesses relative to its competitors?

Mini Case

The first part of the case, presented in Chapter 2, discussed the situation of Computron Industries after an expansion program. A large loss occurred in 2010, rather than the expected profit. As a result, its managers, directors, and investors are concerned about the firm's survival.

Donna Jamison was brought in as assistant to Fred Campo, Computron's chairman, who had the task of getting the company back into a sound financial position. Computron's 2009 and 2010 balance sheets and income statements, together with projections for 2011, are shown in the following tables. The tables also show the 2009 and 2010 financial ratios, along with industry average data. The 2011 projected financial statement data represent Jamison's and Campo's best guess for 2011 results, assuming that some new financing is arranged to get the company "over the hump."

Balance Sheets

	2009	2010	2011E
Assets			
Cash	$ 9,000	$ 7,282	$ 14,000
Short-term investments	48,600	20,000	71,632
Accounts receivable	351,200	632,160	878,000
Inventories	715,200	1,287,360	1,716,480
Total current assets	$1,124,000	$1,946,802	$2,680,112
Gross fixed assets	491,000	1,202,950	1,220,000
Less: Accumulated depreciation	146,200	263,160	383,160
Net fixed assets	$ 344,800	$ 939,790	$ 836,840
Total assets	$1,468,800	$2,886,592	$3,516,952
Liabilities and Equity			
Accounts payable	$ 145,600	$ 324,000	$ 359,800
Notes payable	200,000	720,000	300,000
Accruals	136,000	284,960	380,000
Total current liabilities	$ 481,600	$1,328,960	$1,039,800
Long-term debt	323,432	1,000,000	500,000
Common stock (100,000 shares)	460,000	460,000	1,680,936
Retained earnings	203,768	97,632	296,216
Total equity	$ 663,768	$ 557,632	$1,977,152
Total liabilities and equity	$1,468,800	$2,886,592	$3,516,952

Note: "E" denotes "estimated"; the 2011 data are forecasts.

Jamison must prepare an analysis of where the company is now, what it must do to regain its financial health, and what actions should be taken. Your assignment is to help her answer the following questions. Provide clear explanations, not yes or no answers.

a. Why are ratios useful? What three groups use ratio analysis and for what reasons?
b. Calculate the 2011 current and quick ratios based on the projected balance sheet and income statement data. What can you say about the company's liquidity position in 2009, 2010, and as projected for 2011? We often think of ratios as being useful (1) to managers to help run the business, (2) to bankers for credit analysis, and (3) to stockholders for stock valuation. Would these different types of analysts have an equal interest in the liquidity ratios?
c. Calculate the 2011 inventory turnover, days sales outstanding (DSO), fixed assets turnover, and total assets turnover. How does Computron's utilization of assets stack up against that of other firms in its industry?

Income Statements

	2009	2010	2011E
Sales	$3,432,000	$5,834,400	$7,035,600
Cost of goods sold	2,864,000	4,980,000	5,800,000
Other expenses	340,000	720,000	612,960
Depreciation	18,900	116,960	120,000
Total operating costs	$3,222,900	$5,816,960	$6,532,960
EBIT	$ 209,100	$ 17,440	$ 502,640
Interest expense	62,500	176,000	80,000
EBT	$ 146,600	($ 158,560)	$ 422,640
Taxes (40%)	58,640	(63,424)	169,056
Net income	$ 87,960	($ 95,136)	$ 253,584
Other Data			
Stock price	$ 8.50	$ 6.00	$ 12.17
Shares outstanding	100,000	100,000	250,000
EPS	$ 0.880	($ 0.951)	$ 1.014
DPS	$ 0.220	0.110	0.220
Tax rate	40%	40%	40%
Book value per share	$ 6.638	$ 5.576	$ 7.909
Lease payments	$ 40,000	$ 40,000	$ 40,000

Note: "E" denotes "estimated"; the 2011 data are forecasts.

Ratio Analysis

	2009	2010	2011E	Industry Average
Current	2.3	1.5	______	2.7
Quick	0.8	0.5	______	1.0
Inventory turnover	4.8	4.5	______	6.1
Days sales outstanding	37.3	39.6	______	32.0
Fixed assets turnover	10.0	6.2	______	7.0
Total assets turnover	2.3	2.0	______	2.5
Debt ratio	54.8%	80.7%	______	50.0%
TIE	3.3	0.1	______	6.2
EBITDA coverage	2.6	0.8	______	8.0
Profit margin	2.6%	-1.6%	______	3.6%
Basic earning power	14.2%	0.6%	______	17.8%
ROA	6.0%	-3.3%	______	9.0%
ROE	13.3%	-17.1%	______	17.9%
Price/Earnings (P/E)	9.7	-6.3	______	16.2
Price/Cash flow	8.0	27.5	______	7.6
Market/Book	1.3	1.1	______	2.9

Note: "E" denotes "estimated."

d. Calculate the 2011 debt, times-interest-earned, and EBITDA coverage ratios. How does Computron compare with the industry with respect to financial leverage? What can you conclude from these ratios?
e. Calculate the 2011 profit margin, basic earning power (BEP), return on assets (ROA), and return on equity (ROE). What can you say about these ratios?
f. Calculate the 2011 price/earnings ratio, price/cash flow ratio, and market/book ratio. Do these ratios indicate that investors are expected to have a high or low opinion of the company?

g. Perform a common size analysis and percentage change analysis. What do these analyses tell you about Computron?
h. Use the extended Du Pont equation to provide a summary and overview of Computron's financial condition as projected for 2011. What are the firm's major strengths and weaknesses?
i. What are some potential problems and limitations of financial ratio analysis?
j. What are some qualitative factors that analysts should consider when evaluating a company's likely future financial performance?

Selected Additional Cases

The following cases from Textchoice, *Cengage Learning's online library, cover many of the concepts discussed in this chapter and are available at* ***http://www.textchoice2.com***.

Klein-Brigham Series:

Case 35, "Mark X Company (A)," which illustrates the use of ratio analysis in the evaluation of a firm's existing and potential financial positions; Case 36, "Garden State Container Corporation," which is similar in content to Case 35; Case 51, "Safe Packaging Corporation," which updates Case 36; Case 68, "Sweet Dreams Inc.," which also updates Case 36; and Case 71, "Swan-Davis, Inc.," which illustrates how financial analysis—based on both historical statements and forecasted statements—is used for internal management and lending decisions.

4.1 Time Lines

resource

The textbook's Web site contains an Excel file that will guide you through the chapter's calculations. The file for this chapter is **Ch04 Tool Kit.xls**, *and we encourage you to open the file and follow along as you read the chapter.*

The first step in a time value analysis is to set up a **time line** to help you visualize what's happening in the particular problem. To illustrate, consider the following diagram, where PV represents $100 that is in a bank account today and FV is the value that will be in the account at some future time (3 years from now in this example):

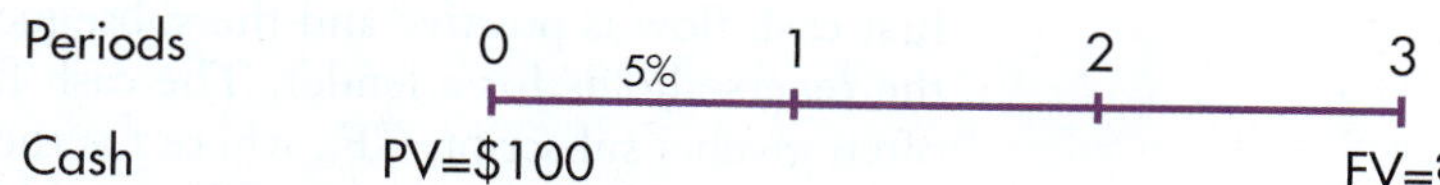

The intervals from 0 to 1, 1 to 2, and 2 to 3 are time periods such as years or months. Time 0 is today, and it is the beginning of Period 1; Time 1 is one period from today, and it is both the end of Period 1 and the beginning of Period 2; and so on. In our example the periods are years, but they could also be quarters or months or even days. Note again that each tick mark corresponds to both the *end* of one period and the *beginning* of the next one. Thus, if the periods are years, the tick mark at Time 2 represents both the end of Year 2 and the beginning of Year 3.

Cash flows are shown directly below the tick marks, and the relevant interest rate is shown just above the time line. Unknown cash flows, which you are trying to find, are indicated by question marks. Here the interest rate is 5%; a single cash outflow, $100, is invested at Time 0; and the Time-3 value is unknown and must be found. In this example, cash flows occur only at Times 0 and 3, with no flows at Times 1 or 2. We will, of course, deal with situations where multiple cash flows occur. Note also that in our example the interest rate is constant for all 3 years. The interest rate is generally held constant, but if it varies then in the diagram we show different rates for the different periods.

Time lines are especially important when you are first learning time value concepts, but even experts use them to analyze complex problems. Throughout the book, our procedure is to set up a time line to show what's happening, provide an equation that must be solved to find the answer, and then explain how to solve the equation with a regular calculator, a financial calculator, and a computer spreadsheet.

Self-Test

Do time lines deal only with years, or could other periods be used?

Set up a time line to illustrate the following situation: You currently have $2,000 in a 3-year certificate of deposit (CD) that pays a guaranteed 4% annually. You want to know the value of the CD after 3 years.

4.2 Future Values

A dollar in hand today is worth more than a dollar to be received in the future—if you had the dollar now you could invest it, earn interest, and end up with more than one dollar in the future. The process of going forward, from **present values (PVs)** to **future values (FVs),** is called **compounding.** To illustrate, refer back to our 3-year time line and assume that you have $100 in a bank account that pays a guaranteed 5% interest each year. How much would you have at the end of Year 3? We first define some terms, after which we set up a time line and show how the future value is calculated.

PV = Present value, or beginning amount. In our example, PV = \$100.

FV_N = Future value, or ending amount, in the account after N periods. Whereas PV is the value *now*, or the *present value*, FV_N is the value N periods into the *future*, after interest earned has been added to the account.

CF_t = Cash flow. Cash flows can be positive or negative. For a borrower, the first cash flow is positive and the subsequent cash flows are negative, and the reverse holds for a lender. The cash flow for a particular period is often given a subscript, CF_t, where t is the period. Thus, CF_0 = PV = the cash flow at Time 0, whereas CF_3 would be the cash flow at the end of Period 3. In this example the cash flows occur *at the ends* of the periods, but in some problems they occur at the beginning.

I = Interest rate earned per year. (Sometimes a lowercase i is used.) Interest earned is based on the balance at the beginning of each year, and we assume that interest is paid at the end of the year. Here I = 5% or, expressed as a decimal, 0.05. Throughout this chapter, we designate the interest rate as I (or I/YR, for interest rate per year) because that symbol is used on most financial calculators. Note, though, that in later chapters we use the symbol "r" to denote the rate because r (for *rate* of return) is used more often in the finance literature. Also, in this chapter we generally assume that interest payments are guaranteed by the U.S. government and hence are riskless (i.e., certain). In later chapters we will deal with risky investments, where the rate actually earned might be different from its expected level.

INT = Dollars of interest earned during the year = (Beginning amount) × I. In our example, INT = \$100(0.05) = \$5 for Year 1, but it rises in subsequent years as the amount at the beginning of each year increases.

N = Number of periods involved in the analysis. In our example, N = 3. Sometimes the number of periods is designated with a lowercase n, so both N and n indicate number of periods.

We can use four different procedures to solve time value problems.[3] These methods are described next.

Step-by-Step Approach

The time line itself can be modified and used to find the FV of \$100 compounded for 3 years at 5%, as shown below:

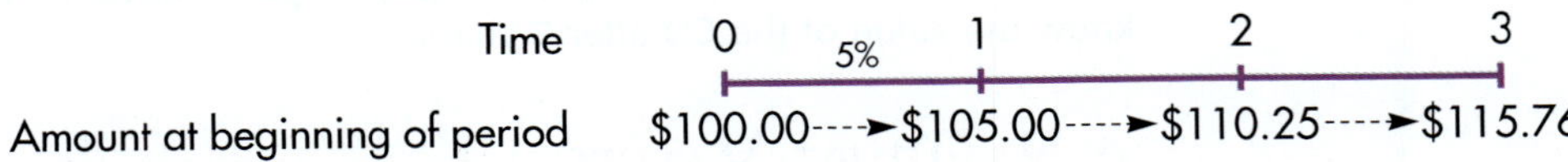

[3]A fifth procedure is called the *tabular approach*, which uses tables that provide "interest factors;" this procedure was used before financial calculators and computers became available. Now, though, calculators and spreadsheets such as *Excel* are programmed to calculate the specific factor needed for a given problem, which is then used to find the FV. This is much more efficient than using the tables. Also, calculators and spreadsheets can handle fractional periods and fractional interest rates. For these reasons, tables are not used in business today; hence we do not discuss them in the text. However, because some professors cover the tables for pedagogic purposes, we discuss them in ***Web Extension 4A***, on the textbook's Web site.

We start with $100 in the account, which is shown at t = 0. We then multiply the initial amount, and each succeeding beginning-of-year amount, by (1 + I) = (1.05).

- You earn $100(0.05) = $5 of interest during the first year, so the amount at the end of Year 1 (or at t = 1) is

$$\begin{aligned} FV_1 &= PV + INT \\ &= PV + PV(I) \\ &= PV(1 + I) \\ &= \$100(1 + 0.05) = \$100(1.05) = \$105 \end{aligned}$$

- We begin the second year with $105, earn 0.05($105) = $5.25 on the now larger beginning-of-period amount, and end the year with $110.25. Interest during Year 2 is $5.25, and it is higher than the first year's interest, $5, because we earned $5(0.05) = $0.25 interest on the first year's interest. This is called "compounding," and interest earned on interest is called "compound interest."
- This process continues, and because the beginning balance is higher in each successive year, the interest earned each year increases.
- The total interest earned, $15.76, is reflected in the final balance, $115.76.

The step-by-step approach is useful because it shows exactly what is happening. However, this approach is time-consuming, especially if the number of years is large and you are using a calculator rather than *Excel*, so streamlined procedures have been developed.

Formula Approach

In the step-by-step approach, we multiplied the amount at the beginning of each period by (1 + I) = (1.05). Notice that the value at the end of Year 2 is

$$\begin{aligned} FV_2 &= FV_1(1 + I) \\ &= PV(1 + I)(1 + I) \\ &= PV(1 + I)^2 \\ &= 100(1.05)^2 = \$110.25 \end{aligned}$$

If N = 3, then we multiply PV by (1 + I) three different times, which is the same as multiplying the beginning amount by $(1 + I)^3$. This concept can be extended, and the result is this key equation:

$$FV_N = PV(1 + I)^N \quad \text{(4-1)}$$

We can apply Equation 4-1 to find the FV in our example:

$$FV_3 = \$100(1.05)^3 = \$115.76$$

Equation 4-1 can be used with any calculator, even a nonfinancial calculator that has an exponential function, making it easy to find FVs no matter how many years are involved.

Financial Calculators

Financial calculators were designed specifically to solve time value problems. First, note that financial calculators have five keys that correspond to the five variables in the basic time value equations. Equation 4-1 has only four variables, but we will shortly deal with situations where a fifth variable (a set of periodic additional payments) is involved. We show the inputs for our example above their keys in the following diagram, and the output, which is the FV, below its key. Since in this example there are no periodic payments, we enter 0 for PMT. We describe the keys in more detail below the diagram.

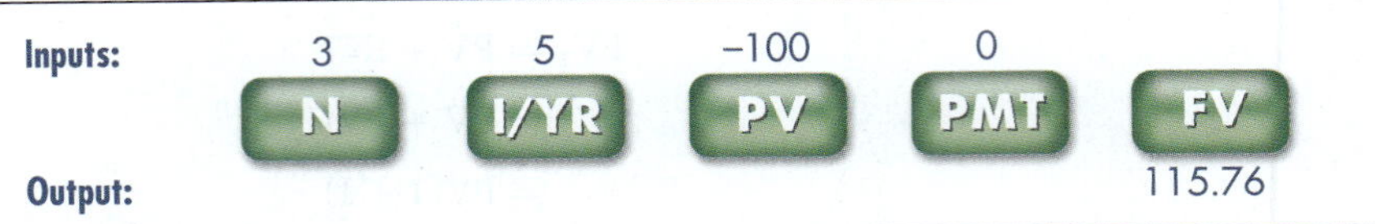

N = Number of periods = 3. Some calculators use n rather than N.

I/YR = Interest rate per period = 5. Some calculators use i or I rather than I/YR. Calculators are programmed to automatically convert the 5 to the decimal 0.05 before doing the arithmetic.

PV = Present value = 100. In our example we begin by making a deposit, which is an outflow of 100, so the PV is entered with a negative sign. On most calculators you must enter the 100, then press the +/− key to switch from +100 to −100. If you enter −100 directly, this will subtract 100 from the last number in the calculator, which will give you an incorrect answer unless the last number was zero.

PMT = Payment. This key is used if we have a series of equal, or constant, payments. Since there are no such payments in our current problem, we enter PMT = 0. We will use the PMT key later in this chapter.

FV = Future value. In our example, the calculator automatically shows the FV as a positive number because we entered the PV as a negative number. If we had entered the 100 as a positive number, then the FV would have been negative. Calculators automatically assume that either the PV or the FV must be negative.

As noted in our example, you first enter the four known values (N, I/YR, PMT, and PV) and then press the FV key to get the answer, FV = 115.76.

Spreadsheets

resource

See **Ch04 Tool Kit.xls** *for all calculations.*

Spreadsheets are ideally suited for solving many financial problems, including those dealing with the time value of money.[4] Spreadsheets are obviously useful for calculations, but they can also be used like a word processor to create exhibits like our Figure 4-1, which includes text, drawings, and calculations. We use this figure to show that four methods can be used to find the FV of $100 after 3 years at an interest rate of 5%. The time line on Rows 43 to 45 is useful for visualizing the problem, after which the spreadsheet calculates the required answer. Note that the letters across the top designate columns, the numbers down the left column designate rows, and the rows and columns jointly designate cells. Thus, cell C39 shows the amount of the investment, $100, and it is given a minus sign because it is an outflow.

[4]The file ***Ch04 Tool Kit.xls*** on the book's Web site does the calculations in the chapter using *Excel*. We *highly recommend* that you go through this ***Tool Kit***. This will give you practice with *Excel*, and that will help tremendously in later courses, in the job market, and in the workplace. Also, going through the models will improve your understanding of financial concepts.

Hints on Using Financial Calculators

When using a financial calculator, make sure your machine is set up as indicated below. Refer to your calculator manual or to our calculator tutorial on the text's Web site for information on setting up your calculator.

- **One payment per period.** Many calculators "come out of the box" assuming that 12 payments are made per year; that is, they assume monthly payments. However, in this book we generally deal with problems in which only one payment is made each year. *Therefore, you should set your calculator at one payment per year and leave it there. See our tutorial or your calculator manual if you need assistance.* We will show you how to solve problems with more than 1 payment per year in Section 4.15.
- **End mode.** With most contracts, payments are made at the *end* of each period. However, some contracts call for payments at the *beginning* of each period. You can switch between "End Mode" and "Begin Mode" depending on the problem you are solving. *Because most of the problems in this book call for end-of-period payments, you should return your calculator to End Mode after you work a problem in which payments are made at the beginning of periods.*
- **Negative sign for outflows.** When first learning how to use financial calculators, students often forget that one cash flow must be negative. Mathematically, financial calculators solve a version of this equation:

$$PV(1+I)^N + FV_N = 0 \quad (4\text{-}2)$$

Notice that for reasonable values of I, either PV or FV_N must be negative, and the other one must be positive to make the equation equal 0. This is reasonable because, in all realistic situations, one cash flow is an outflow (which should have a negative sign) and one is an inflow (which should have a positive sign). For example, if you make a deposit (which is an outflow, and hence should have a negative sign) then you will expect to make a later withdrawal (which is an inflow with a positive sign). *The bottom line is that one of your inputs for a cash flow must be negative and one must be positive. This generally means typing the outflow as a positive number and then pressing the +/– key to convert from + to – before hitting the enter key.*

- **Decimal places.** When doing arithmetic, calculators use a great many decimal places. However, they allow you to show from 0 to 11 decimal places on the display. When working with dollars, we generally specify two decimal places. When dealing with interest rates, we generally specify two places if the rate is expressed as a percentage, like 5.25%, but we specify four places if the rate is expressed as a decimal, like 0.0525.
- **Interest rates.** *For arithmetic operations with a nonfinancial calculator, the rate 5.25% must be stated as a decimal, .0525. However, with a financial calculator you must enter 5.25, not .0525, because financial calculators are programmed to assume that rates are stated as percentages.*

It is useful to put all of the problem's inputs in a section of the spreadsheet designated "Inputs." In Figure 4-1 we put the inputs in the range A38:C41, with C39 being the cell where we specify the investment, C40 the interest rate, and C41 the number of periods. We can use these three cell references, rather than the fixed numbers themselves, in the formulas in the remainder of the model. This makes it easy to modify the problem by changing the inputs and then having the new data automatically used in the calculations.

Time lines are important for solving finance problems because they help us visualize what's happening. When we work a problem by hand we usually draw a time line, and when we work a problem with *Excel*, we actually set the model up as a time line. For example, in Figure 4-1 Rows 43 to 45 are indeed a time line. It's easy

FIGURE 4-1 Alternative Procedures for Calculating Future Values

	A	B	C	D	E	F	G
38	INPUTS:						
39	Investment	$= CF_0 = PV =$	–$100.00				
40	Interest rate	= I =	5.00%				
41	No. of periods	= N =	3				
42							
43	Setup of the problem as a		Periods:	0 5%	1	2	3
44	Time Line						
45			Cash Flow:	–$100	0	0	FV = ?
46							
47	1.Step-by-Step: Multiply $100 by (1 + I)			$100 →	$105.00 →	$110.25 →	$115.76
48							
49	2. Formula: $FV_N = PV(1 + I)^N$			$FV_3 =$	$\$100(1.05)^3$	=	$115.76
50							
51			3	5	–$100.00	$0	
52	3. Financial Calculator:		N	I/YR	PV	PMT	FV
53							$115.76
54							
55	4. *Excel* Spreadsheet:		FV Function:	$FV_N =$	= FV(I,N,0,PV)		
56			Fixed inputs:	$FV_N =$	= FV(0.05,3,0,–100)		$115.76
57			Cell references:	$FV_N =$	= FV(C40,C41,0,C39)		$115.76
58	In the *Excel* formula, the terms are entered in the sequence: interest, periods, 0 to indicate no periodic cash flows, and then the PV. The data can be entered as fixed numbers or, better yet, as cell references.						

to construct time lines with *Excel*, with each column designating a different period on the time line.

On Row 47 we use *Excel* to go through the step-by-step calculations, multiplying the beginning-of-year values by (1 + I) to find the compounded value at the end of each period. Cell G47 shows the final result of the step-by-step approach.

We illustrate the formula approach in Row 49, using *Excel* to solve Equation 4-1 to find the FV. Cell G49 shows the formula result, $115.76. As it must, it equals the step-by-step result.

Rows 51 to 53 illustrate the financial calculator approach, which again produces the same answer, $115.76.

The last section, in Rows 55 to 58, illustrates *Excel*'s future value (FV) function. You can access the function wizard by clicking the f_x symbol in *Excel*'s formula bar. Then select the category for Financial functions, and then the FV function, which is **=FV(I,N,0,PV)**, as shown in Cell E55.[5] Cell E56 shows how the formula would look with numbers as inputs; the actual function itself is entered in Cell G56, but it shows up in the table as the answer, $115.76. If you access the model and put the pointer on Cell G56, you will see the full formula. Finally, Cell E57 shows how the formula would look with cell references rather than fixed values as inputs, with

[5]All functions begin with an equal sign. The third entry is zero in this example, which indicates that there are no periodic payments. Later in this chapter we will use the FV function in situations where we have nonzero periodic payments. Also, for inputs we use our own notation, which is similar but not identical to *Excel*'s notation.

the actual function again in Cell G57. We generally use cell references as function inputs because this makes it easy to change inputs and see how those changes affect the output. This is called "sensitivity analysis." Many real-world financial applications use sensitivity analysis, so it is useful to get in the habit of setting up an input data section and then using cell references rather than fixed numbers in the functions.

When entering interest rates in *Excel*, you can use either actual numbers or percentages, depending on how the cell is formatted. For example, in cell C40, we first formatted to Percentage, and then typed in 5, which showed up as 5%. However, *Excel* uses 0.05 for the arithmetic. Alternatively, we could have formatted C40 as a Number, in which case we would have typed "0.05." If C40 is formatted to Number and you enter 5, then *Excel* would think you meant 500%. Thus, *Excel*'s procedure is quite different from the convention used in financial calculators.

Comparing the Procedures

The first step in solving any time value problem is to understand what is happening and then to diagram it on a time line. Woody Allen said that 90% of success is just showing up. With time value problems, 90% of success is correctly setting up the time line.

After you diagram the problem on a time line, your next step is to pick one of the four approaches shown in Figure 4-1 to solve the problem. Any may be used, but your choice of method will depend on the particular situation.

All business students should know Equation 4-1 by heart and should also know how to use a financial calculator. So, for simple problems such as finding the future value of a single payment, it is generally easiest and quickest to use either the formula approach or a financial calculator. However, for problems that involve several cash flows, the formula approach usually is time-consuming, so either the calculator or spreadsheet approach would generally be used. Calculators are portable and quick to set up, but if many calculations of the same type must be done, or if you want to see how changes in an input such as the interest rate affect the future value, then the spreadsheet approach is generally more efficient. If the problem has many irregular cash flows, or if you want to analyze alternative scenarios using different cash flows or interest rates, then the spreadsheet approach definitely is the most efficient procedure.

Spreadsheets have two additional advantages over calculators. First, it is easier to check the inputs with a spreadsheet—they are visible, whereas with a calculator they are buried somewhere in the machine. Thus, you are less likely to make a mistake in a complex problem when you use the spreadsheet approach. Second, with a spreadsheet, you can make your analysis much more transparent than you can when using a calculator. This is not necessarily important when all you want is the answer, but if you need to present your calculations to others, like your boss, it helps to be able to show intermediate steps, which enables someone to go through your exhibit and see exactly what you did. Transparency is also important when you must go back, sometime later, and reconstruct what you did.

You should understand the various approaches well enough to make a rational choice, given the nature of the problem and the equipment you have available. In any event, you must understand the concepts behind the calculations, and you must also know how to set up time lines in order to work complex problems. This is true for stock and bond valuation, capital budgeting, lease analysis, and many other important financial problems.

The Power of Compound Interest

Assume that you are 26 and just received your MBA. After reading the introduction to this chapter, you decide to start investing in the stock market for your retirement. Your goal is to have $1 million when you retire at age 65. Assuming you earn 10% annually on your stock investments, how much must you invest at the end of each year in order to reach your goal?

The answer is $2,491, but this amount depends critically on the return earned on your investments. If your return drops to 8%, the required annual contribution would rise to $4,185. On the other hand, if the return rises to 12%, you would need to put away only $1,462 per year.

What if you are like most 26-year-olds and wait until later to worry about retirement? If you wait until age 40, you will need to save $10,168 per year to reach your $1 million goal, assuming you can earn 10%, but $13,679 per year if you earn only 8%. If you wait until age 50 and then earn 8%, the required amount will be $36,830 per year!

Although $1 million may seem like a lot of money, it won't be when you get ready to retire. If inflation averages 5% a year over the next 39 years, then your $1 million nest egg would be worth only $149,148 in today's dollars. If you live for 20 years after retirement and earn a real 3% rate of return, your annual retirement income in today's dollars would be only $9,733 before taxes. So, after celebrating your graduation and new job, start saving!

Graphic View of the Compounding Process

See **Ch04 Tool Kit.xls** *for all calculations.*

Figure 4-2 shows how a $100 investment grows (or declines) over time at different interest rates. Interest rates are normally positive, but the "growth" concept is broad enough to include negative rates. We developed the curves by solving Equation 4-1 with different values for N and I. The interest rate is a growth rate: If money is deposited and earns 5% per year, then your funds will grow by 5% per year. Note also that time value concepts can be applied to anything that grows—sales, population, earnings per share, or your future salary. Also, as noted before, the "growth rate" can be negative, as was sales growth for a number of auto companies in recent years.

Simple Interest versus Compound Interest

As explained earlier, when interest is earned on the interest earned in prior periods, we call it **compound interest.** If interest is earned only on the principal, we call it **simple interest.** The total interest earned with simple interest is equal to the principal multiplied by the interest rate times the number of periods: PV(I)(N). The future value is equal to the principal plus the interest: FV = PV + PV(I)(N). For example, suppose you deposit $100 for 3 years and earn simple interest at an annual rate of 5%. Your balance at the end of 3 years would be:

$$\begin{aligned} FV &= PV + PV(I)(N) \\ &= \$100 + \$100(5\%)(3) \\ &= \$100 + \$15 = \$115 \end{aligned}$$

Notice that this is less than the $115.76 we calculated earlier using compound interest. Most applications in finance are based on compound interest, but you should be aware that simple interest is still specified in some legal documents.

Self-Test

Explain why this statement is true: "A dollar in hand today is worth more than a dollar to be received next year, assuming interest rates are positive."

What is compounding? What would the future value of $100 be after 5 years at 10% *compound* interest? **($161.05)**

FIGURE 4-2 Growth of $100 at Various Interest Rates and Time Periods

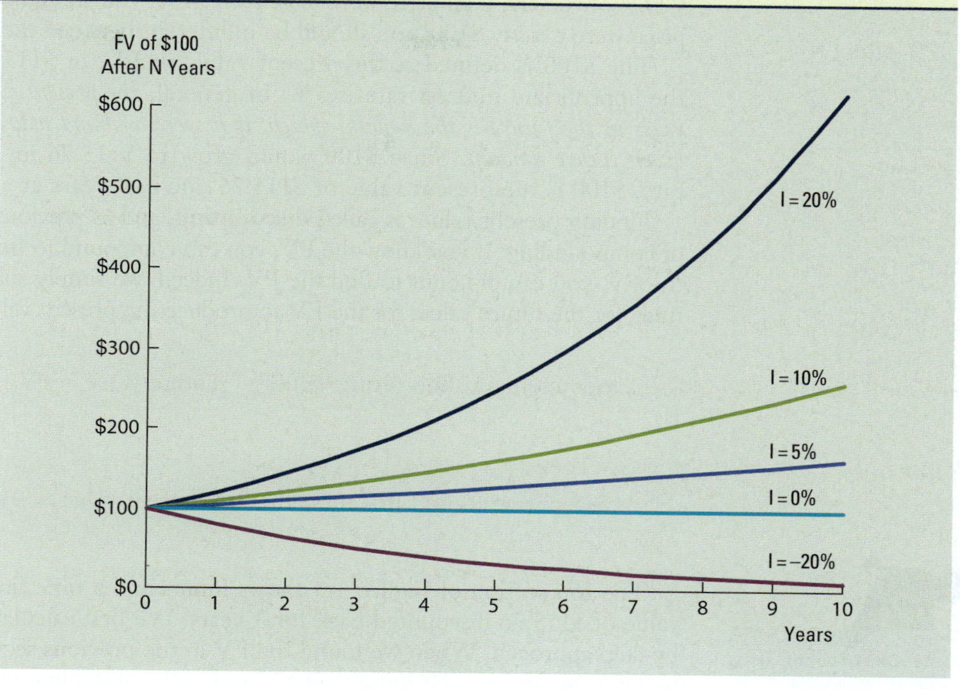

Suppose you currently have $2,000 and plan to purchase a 3-year certificate of deposit (CD) that pays 4% interest, compounded annually. How much will you have when the CD matures? **($2,249.73)** How would your answer change if the interest rate were 5%, or 6%, or 20%? (*Hint*: With a calculator, enter N = 3, I/YR = 4, PV = –2000, and PMT = 0; then press FV to get 2,249.73. Then, enter I/YR = 5 to override the 4% and press FV again to get the second answer. In general, you can change one input at a time to see how the output changes.) **($2,315.25; $2,382.03; $3,456.00)**

A company's sales in 2009 were $100 million. If sales grow by 8% annually, what will they be 10 years later? **($215.89 million)** What would they be if they decline by 8% per year for 10 years? **($43.44 million)**

How much would $1, growing at 5% per year, be worth after 100 years? **($131.50)** What would FV be if the growth rate were 10%? **($13,780.61)**

4.3 Present Values

Suppose you have some extra money and want to make an investment. A broker offers to sell you a bond that will pay a guaranteed $115.76 in 3 years. Banks are currently offering a guaranteed 5% interest on 3-year certificates of deposit (CDs), and if you don't buy the bond you will buy a CD. The 5% rate paid on the CD is defined as your **opportunity cost,** or the rate of return you would earn on an alternative investment of similar risk if you don't invest in the security under consideration. Given these conditions, what's the most you should pay for the bond?

First, recall from the future value example in the last section that if you invested $100 at 5% in a CD, it would grow to $115.76 in 3 years. You would also have $115.76 after 3 years if you bought the bond. Therefore, the most you should pay for the bond is $100—this is its "fair price," which is also its intrinsic, or fundamental, value. If you could buy the bond for *less than* \$100, then you should buy it rather than invest in the CD. Conversely, if its price were *more than* \$100, you should buy the CD. If the bond's price were exactly \$100, you should be indifferent between the bond and the CD.

The \$100 is defined as the present value, or PV, of \$115.76 due in 3 years when the appropriate interest rate is 5%. In general, *the present value of a cash flow due N years in the future is the amount which, if it were on hand today, would grow to equal the given future amount.* Since \$100 would grow to \$115.76 in 3 years at a 5% interest rate, \$100 is the present value of \$115.76 due in 3 years at a 5% rate.

Finding present values is called **discounting**, and as previously noted, it is the reverse of compounding: If you know the PV, you can compound to find the FV; or if you know the FV, you can discount to find the PV. Indeed, we simply solve Equation 4-1, the formula for the future value, for the PV to produce the present value equation as follows.

$$\text{Compounding to find future values: } \quad \text{Future value} = FV_N = PV(1+I)^N \tag{4-1}$$

$$\text{Discounting to find present values: } \quad \text{Present value} = PV = \frac{FV_N}{(1+I)^N} \tag{4-3}$$

resource

See **Ch04 Tool Kit.xls** *for all calculations.*

The top section of Figure 4-3 shows inputs and a time line for finding the present value of \$115.76 discounted back for 3 years. We first calculate the PV using the step-by-step approach. When we found the FV in the previous section, we worked from left to right, *multiplying* the initial amount and each subsequent amount by (1 + I). To find

FIGURE 4-3 Alternative Procedures for Calculating Present Values

	A	B	C	D	E	F	G
109	INPUTS:						
110	Future payment	= CF_N = FV =	\$115.76				
111	Interest rate	= I =	5.00%				
112	No. of periods	= N =	3				
113							
114	Problem as a Time Line		Periods:	0	1	2	3
115							
116			Cash Flow Time Line:	PV = ?			\$115.76
117							
118	1.Step-by-Step:			\$100.00 ←	\$105.00 ←	\$110.25 ←	\$115.76
119							
120	2. Formula: $FV_N = PV/(1+I)^N$				PV = \$115.76(1.05)^3	=	\$100.00
121							
122			3	5		\$0	\$115.76
123	3. Financial Calculator:		N	I/YR	PV	PMT	FV
124					−\$100.00		
125							
126			PV Function:	PV =	= PV(I,N,0,FV)		
127	4. *Excel* Spreadsheet:		Fixed inputs:	PV =	= PV(0.05,3,0,115.76) =		−\$100.00
128			Cell references:	PV =	= PV(C111,C112,0,C110) =		−\$100.00
129	In the *Excel* formula, the terms are entered in the sequence: interest, periods, 0 to indicate no periodic cash flows, and then the FV. The data can be entered as fixed numbers or, better yet, as cell references.						

present values, we work backwards, or from right to left, *dividing* the future value and each subsequent amount by (1 + I), with the present value of $100 shown in Cell D118. The step-by-step procedure shows exactly what's happening, and that can be quite useful when you are working complex problems or trying to explain a model to others. However, it's inefficient, especially if you are dealing with more than a year or two.

A more efficient procedure is to use the formula approach in Equation 4-3, simply dividing the future value by $(1 + I)^N$. This gives the same result, as we see in Figure 4-3, Cell G120.

Equation 4-2 is actually programmed into financial calculators. As shown in Figure 4-3, Rows 122 to 124, we can find the PV by entering values for N=3, I/YR=5, PMT=0, and FV=115.76, and then pressing the PV key to get −100.

Excel also has a function that solves Equation 4-3—this is the PV function, and it is written as =**PV(I,N,0,FV)**.[6] Cell E126 shows the inputs to this function. Next, Cell E127 shows the *Excel* function with fixed numbers as inputs, with the actual function and the resulting −$100 in Cell G127. Cell E128 shows the *Excel* function using cell references, with the actual function and the resulting −$100 in Cell G128.

The fundamental goal of financial management is to maximize the firm's intrinsic value, and the intrinsic value of a business (or any asset, including stocks and bonds) is the *present value* of its expected future cash flows. Because present value lies at the heart of the valuation process, we will have much more to say about it in the remainder of this chapter and throughout the book.

Graphic View of the Discounting Process

Figure 4-4 shows that the present value of a sum to be received in the future decreases and approaches zero as the payment date is extended further and further into the future; it also shows that, the higher the interest rate, the faster the present value falls. At relatively high rates, funds due in the future are worth very little today, and even at relatively

FIGURE 4-4 Present Value of $1 at Various Interest Rates and Time Periods

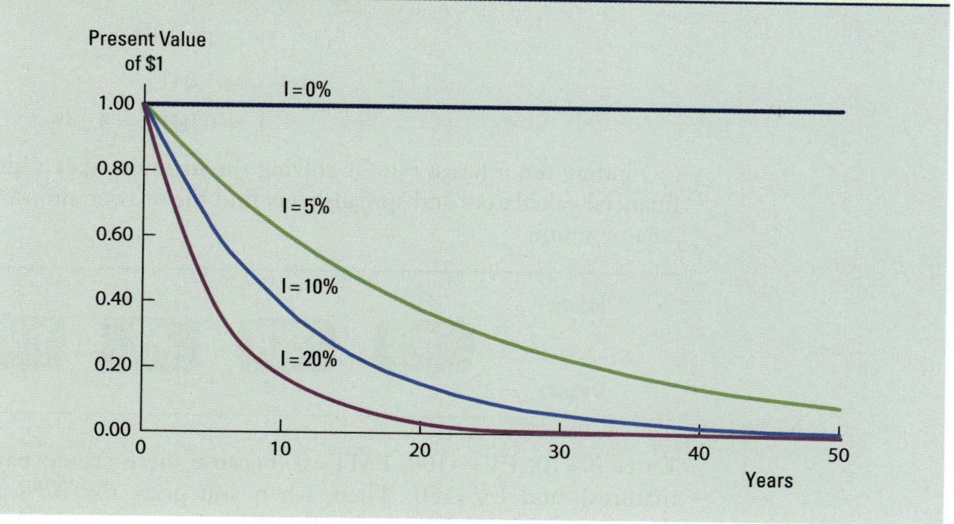

[6]The third entry in the PV function is zero to indicate that there are no intermediate payments in this particular example.

low rates present values of sums due in the very distant future are quite small. For example, at a 20% discount rate, $1 million due in 100 years would be worth just over 1 cent today. (However, 1 cent would grow to almost $1 million in 100 years at 20%.)

Self-Test

What is "discounting," and how is it related to compounding? How is the future value equation (4-1) related to the present value equation (4-3)?

How does the present value of a future payment change as the time to receipt is lengthened? As the interest rate increases?

Suppose a risk-free bond promises to pay $2,249.73 in 3 years. If the going risk-free interest rate is 4%, how much is the bond worth today? **($2,000)** How would your answer change if the bond matured in 5 rather than 3 years? **($1,849.11)** If the risk-free interest rate is 6% rather than 4%, how much is the 5-year bond worth today? **($1,681.13)**

How much would $1 million due in 100 years be worth today if the discount rate were 5%? **($7,604.49)** What if the discount rate were 20%? **($0.0121)**

4.4 Finding the Interest Rate, I

Thus far we have used Equations 4-1, 4-2, and 4-3 to find future and present values. Those equations have four variables, and if we know three of them, then we (or our calculator or *Excel*) can solve for the fourth. Thus, if we know PV, I, and N, we can solve Equation 4-1 for FV, or if we know FV, I, and N, we can solve Equation 4-3 to find PV. That's what we did in the preceding two sections.

Now suppose we know PV, FV, and N, and we want to find I. For example, suppose we know that a given security has a cost of $100 and that it will return $150 after 10 years. Thus, we know PV, FV, and N, and we want to find the rate of return we will earn if we buy the security. Here's the solution using Equation 4-1:

$$\begin{aligned} FV &= PV(1+I)^N \\ \$150 &= \$100(1+I)^{10} \\ \$150/\$100 &= (1+I)^{10} \\ (1+I)^{10} &= 1.5 \\ (1+I) &= 1.5^{(1/10)} \\ 1+I &= 1.0414 \\ I &= 0.0414 = 4.14\%. \end{aligned}$$

Finding the interest rate by solving the formula takes a little time and thought, but financial calculators and spreadsheets find the answer almost instantly. Here's the calculator setup:

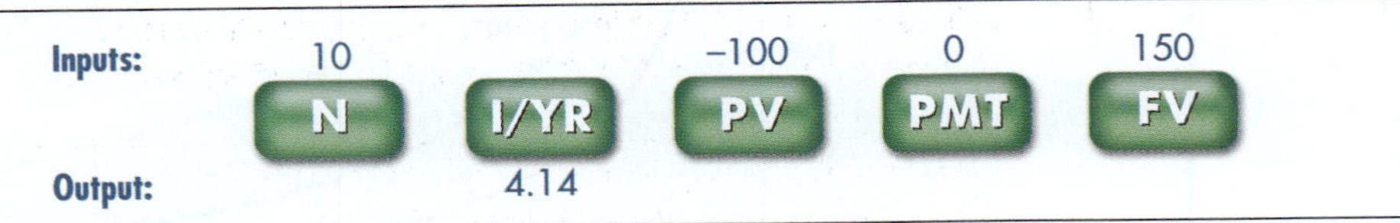

Enter N=10, PV=−100, PMT=0 (because there are no payments until the security matures), and FV=150. Then, when you press the I/YR key, the calculator gives the answer, 4.14%. Notice that the PV is a negative value because it is a cash outflow (an investment) and the FV is positive because it is a cash inflow (a return of the investment). If you enter both PV and FV as positive numbers (or both as negative numbers), you will get an error message rather than the answer.

In *Excel*, the **RATE** function can be used to find the interest rate: **=RATE(N,PMT, PV,FV)**. For this example, the interest rate is found as **=RATE(10,0,–100,150)** = 0.0414 = 4.14%. See the file ***Ch04 Tool Kit.xls*** on the textbook's Web site for an example.

Self-Test

Suppose you can buy a U.S. Treasury bond that makes no payments until the bond matures 10 years from now, at which time it will pay you $1,000.[7] What interest rate would you earn if you bought this bond for $585.43? **(5.5%)** What rate would you earn if you could buy the bond for $550? **(6.16%)** For $600? **(5.24%)**

Microsoft earned $0.33 per share in 1997. Ten years later, in 2007, it earned $1.42. What was the growth rate in Microsoft's earnings per share (EPS) over the 10-year period? **(15.71%)** If EPS in 2007 had been $1.00 rather than $1.42, what would the growth rate have been? **(11.72%)**

4.5 Finding the Number of Years, N

We sometimes need to know how long it will take to accumulate a specific sum of money, given our beginning funds and the rate we will earn. For example, suppose we now have $500,000 and the interest rate is 4.5%. How long will it be before we have $1 million?

Here's Equation 4-1, showing all the known variables.

$$\$1{,}000{,}000 = \$500{,}000(1 + 0.045)^N \tag{4-1}$$

We need to solve for N, and we can use three procedures: a financial calculator, *Excel* (or some other spreadsheet), or by working with natural logs. As you might expect, the calculator and spreadsheet approaches are easier.[8] Here's the calculator setup:

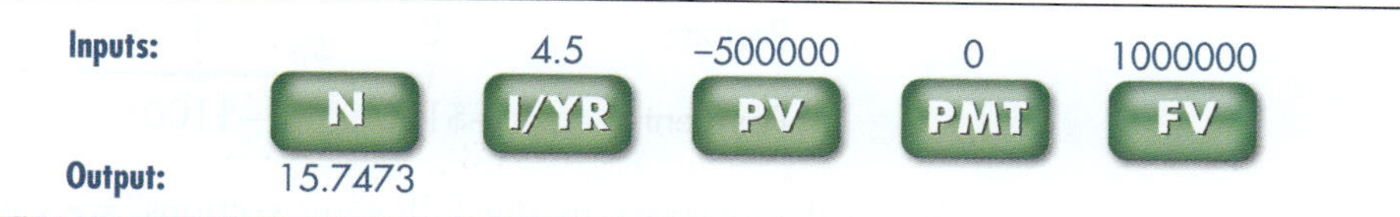

Enter I/YR = 4.5, PV = –500000, PMT = 0, and FV = 1000000. We press the N key to get the answer, 15.7473 years. In *Excel*, we would use the **NPER** function: **=NPER (I,PMT,PV,FV)**. Inserting data, we have **=NPER(0.045,0,–500000,1000000)** = 15.7473. The chapter's tool kit, ***Ch04 Tool Kit.xls,*** shows this example.

Self-Test

How long would it take $1,000 to double if it were invested in a bank that pays 6% per year? **(11.9 years)** How long would it take if the rate were 10%? **(7.27 years)**

Microsoft's 2007 earnings per share were $1.42, and its growth rate during the prior 10 years was 15.71% per year. If that growth rate were maintained, how long would it take for Microsoft's EPS to double? **(4.75 years)**

---

[7]This is a STRIP bond, which we explain in Chapter 5.

[8]Here's the setup for the log solution. First, transform Equation 4-1 as indicated, then find the natural logs using a financial calculator, and then solve for N:

$$\$1{,}000{,}000 = \$500{,}000(1 + 0.045)^N$$
$$2 = (1 + 0.045)^N$$
$$\ln(2) = N[\ln(1.045)]$$
$$N = 0.6931/0.0440 = 15.7473 \text{ years}$$

4.6 ANNUITIES

Thus far we have dealt with single payments, or "lump sums." However, assets such as bonds provide a series of cash inflows over time, and obligations such as auto loans, student loans, and mortgages call for a series of payments. If the payments are equal and are made at fixed intervals, then we have an **annuity.** For example, $100 paid at the end of each of the next 3 years is a 3-year annuity.

If payments occur at the *end* of each period, then we have an **ordinary** (or **deferred) annuity.** Payments on mortgages, car loans, and student loans are generally made at the ends of the periods and thus are ordinary annuities. If the payments are made at the *beginning* of each period, then we have an **annuity due.** Rental lease payments, life insurance premiums, and lottery payoffs (if you are lucky enough to win one!) are examples of annuities due. Ordinary annuities are more common in finance, so when we use the term "annuity" in this book, you may assume that the payments occur at the ends of the periods unless we state otherwise.

Next we show the time lines for a $100, 3-year, 5%, ordinary annuity and for the same annuity on an annuity due basis. With the annuity due, each payment is shifted back (to the left) by 1 year. In our example, we assume that a $100 payment will be made each year, so we show the payments with minus signs.

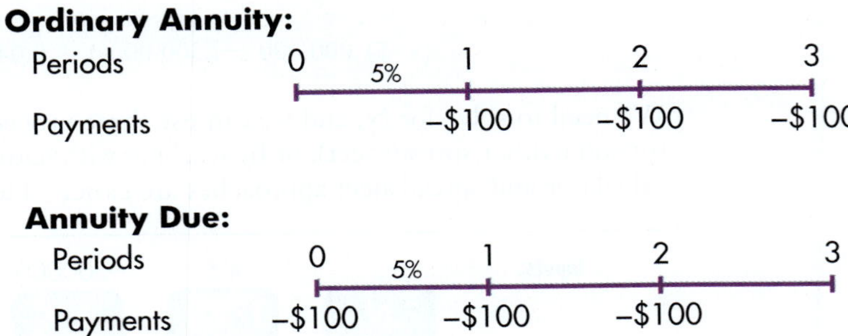

As we demonstrate in the following sections, we can find an annuity's future value, present value, the interest rate built into the contracts, how long it takes to reach a financial goal using the annuity, and, if we know all of those values, the size of the annuity payment. Keep in mind that annuities must have *constant payments* and a *fixed number of periods*. If these conditions don't hold, then the series is not an annuity.

Self-Test

What's the difference between an ordinary annuity and an annuity due?
Why should you prefer to receive an *annuity due* with payments of $10,000 per year for 10 years than an otherwise similar *ordinary annuity*?

4.7 FUTURE VALUE OF AN ORDINARY ANNUITY

Consider the ordinary annuity whose time line was shown previously, where you deposit $100 at the *end* of each year for 3 years and earn 5% per year. Figure 4-5 shows how to calculate the **future value of the annuity, FVA_N,** using the same approaches we used for single cash flows.

As shown in the step-by-step section of Figure 4-5, we compound each payment out to Time 3, then sum those compounded values in Cell F226 to find the annuity's FV, FVA_3 = $315.25. The first payment earns interest for two periods, the second for

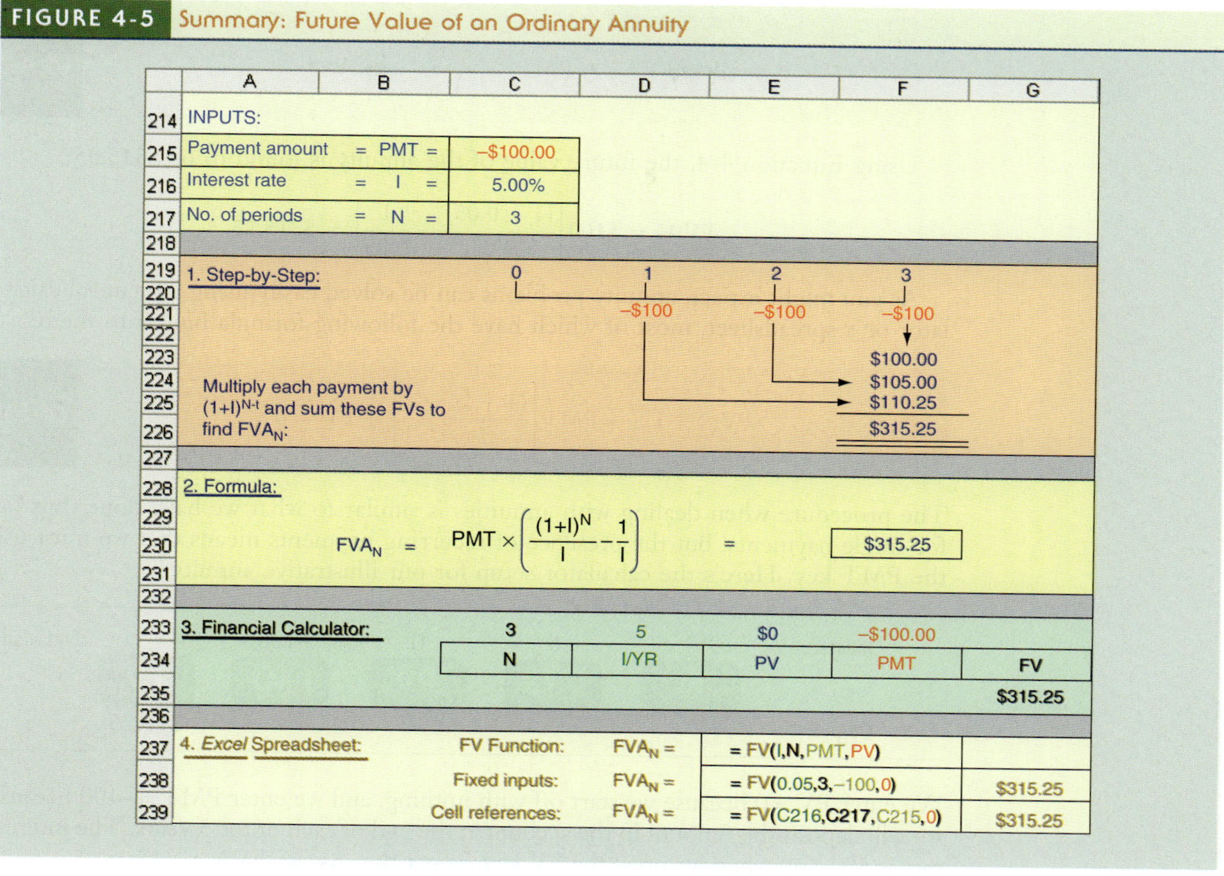

FIGURE 4-5 Summary: Future Value of an Ordinary Annuity

one period, and the third earns no interest because it is made at the end of the annuity's life. This approach is straightforward, but if the annuity extends out for many years, it is cumbersome and time-consuming.

As you can see from the time line diagram, with the step-by-step approach we apply the following equation with N = 3 and I = 5%:

$$\begin{aligned} FVA_N &= PMT(1+I)^{N-1} + PMT(1+I)^{N-2} + PMT(1+I)^{N-3} \\ &= \$100(1.05)^2 + \$100(1.05)^1 + \$100(1.05)^0 \\ &= \$315.25 \end{aligned}$$

For the general case, the future value of an annuity is

$$FVA_N = PMT(1+I)^{N-1} + PMT(1+I)^{N-2} + PMT(1+I)^{N-3} + \cdots + PMT(1+I)^0$$

As shown in ***Web Extension 4B*** on the textbook's Web site, the future value of an annuity can be written as follows:[9]

[9]Section 4.11 shows that the present value of an infinitely long annuity, called a perpetuity, is equal to PMT/I. The cash flows of an ordinary annuity of N periods are equal to the cash flows of a perpetuity minus the cash flows of a perpetuity that begins at year N+1. Therefore, the future value of an N-period annuity is equal to the future value (as of year N) of a perpetuity minus the value (as of year N) of a perpetuity that begins at year N+1. See ***Web Extension 4B*** on the textbook's Web site for details regarding derivations of Equation 4-4.

$$FVA_N = PMT\left[\frac{(1+I)^N}{I} - \frac{1}{I}\right] \quad (4\text{-}4)$$

Using Equation 4-4, the future value of the annuity is found to be \$315.25:

$$FVA_3 = \$100\left[\frac{(1+0.05)^3}{0.05} - \frac{1}{0.05}\right] = \$315.25$$

As you might expect, annuity problems can be solved easily using a financial calculator or a spreadsheet, most of which have the following formula built into them:

$$PV(1+I)^N + PMT\left[\frac{(1+I)^N}{I} - \frac{1}{I}\right] + FV = 0 \quad (4\text{-}5)$$

The procedure when dealing with annuities is similar to what we have done thus far for single payments, but the presence of recurring payments means that we must use the PMT key. Here's the calculator setup for our illustrative annuity:

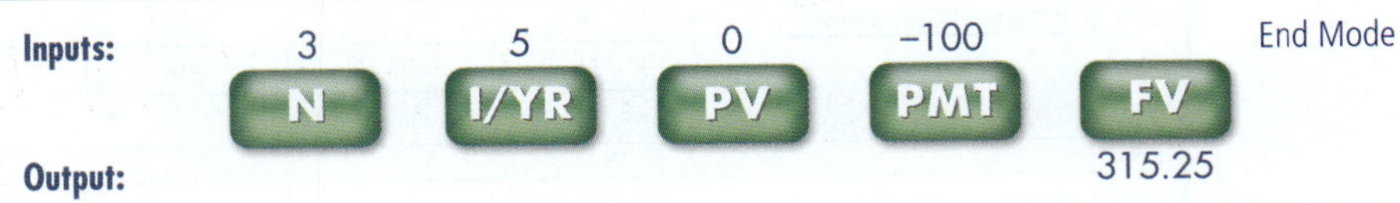

We enter PV = 0 because we start off with nothing, and we enter PMT = –100 because we will deposit this amount in the account at the end of each of the 3 years. The interest rate is 5%, and when we press the FV key we get the answer, FVA_3 = 315.25.

Since this is an ordinary annuity, with payments coming at the *end* of each year, we must set the calculator appropriately. As noted earlier, most calculators "come out of the box" set to assume that payments occur at the end of each period—that is, to deal with ordinary annuities. However, there is a key that enables us to switch between ordinary annuities and annuities due. For ordinary annuities, the designation "End Mode" or something similar is used, while for annuities due the designator is "Begin," "Begin Mode," "Due," or something similar. If you make a mistake and set your calculator on Begin Mode when working with an ordinary annuity, then each payment will earn interest for one extra year, which will cause the compounded amounts, and thus the FVA, to be too large.

See **Ch04 Tool Kit.xls** *for all calculations.*

The spreadsheet approach uses *Excel*'s FV function, **=FV(I,N,PMT,PV)**. In our example, we have **=FV(0.05,3,–100,0)**, and the result is again \$315.25.

Self-Test

For an ordinary annuity with 5 annual payments of \$100 and a 10% interest rate, for how many years will the *first payment* earn interest, and what is the compounded value of this payment at the end? **(4 years, \$146.41)** Answer this same question for the fifth payment. **(0 years, \$100)**

Assume that you plan to buy a condo 5 years from now, and you estimate that you can save \$2,500 per year toward a down payment. You plan to deposit the money in a bank that pays 4% interest, and you will make the first deposit at the end of this year. How much will you have after 5 years? **(\$13,540.81)** How would your answer change if the bank's interest rate were increased to 6%, or decreased to 3%? **(\$14,092.73; \$13,272.84)**

4.8 Future Value of an Annuity Due

Because each payment occurs one period earlier with an annuity due, the payments will all earn interest for one additional period. Therefore, the FV of an annuity due will be greater than that of a similar ordinary annuity.

If you went through the step-by-step procedure, you would see that our illustrative annuity due has a FV of $331.01 versus $315.25 for the ordinary annuity. See ***Ch04 Tool Kit.xls*** on the textbook's Web site for a summary of future value calculations.

With the formula approach, we first use Equation 4-4, but since each payment occurs one period earlier, we multiply the Equation 4-4 result by (1 + I):

$$FVA_{due} = FVA_{ordinary}(1 + I) \quad (4\text{-}6)$$

Thus, for the annuity due, FVA_{due} = $315.25(1.05) = $331.01, which is the same result as found with the step-by-step approach.

With a calculator we input the variables just as we did with the ordinary annuity, but we now set the calculator to Begin Mode to get the answer, $331.01.

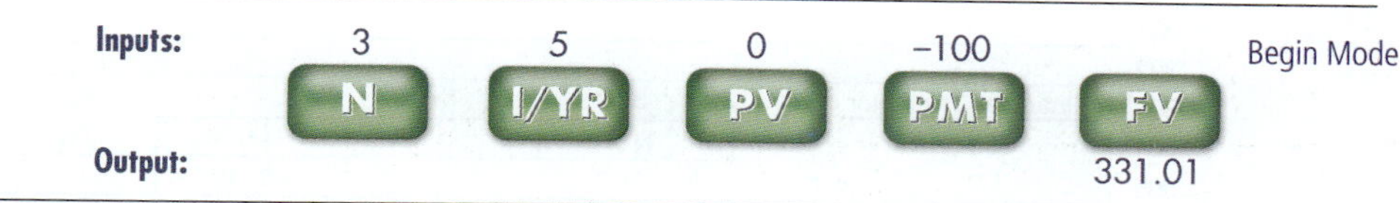

See **Ch04 Tool Kit.xls** for all calculations.

In *Excel*, we still use the FV function, but we must indicate that we have an annuity due. The function is **=FV(I,N,PMT,PV,Type)**, where "Type" indicates the type of annuity. If Type is omitted then *Excel* assumes that it is 0, which indicates an ordinary annuity. For an annuity due, Type = 1. As shown in ***Ch04 Tool Kit.xls,*** the function is **=FV(0.05,3,−100,0,1)** = $331.01.

Self-Test

Why does an annuity due always have a higher future value than an ordinary annuity?

If you know the value of an ordinary annuity, explain why you could find the value of the corresponding annuity due by multiplying by (1+I).

Assume that you plan to buy a condo 5 years from now and that you need to save for a down payment. You plan to save $2,500 per year, with the first payment being made *immediately* and deposited in a bank that pays 4%. How much will you have after 5 years? **($14,082.44)** How much would you have if you made the deposits at the *end* of each year? **($13,540.81)**

4.9 Present Value of Ordinary Annuities and Annuities Due

The present value of any annuity, **PVA_N,** can be found using the step-by-step, formula, calculator, or spreadsheet methods. We begin with ordinary annuities.

Present Value of an Ordinary Annuity

See Figure 4-6 for a summary of the different approaches for calculating the present value of an ordinary annuity.

FIGURE 4-6 Summary: Present Value of an Ordinary Annuity

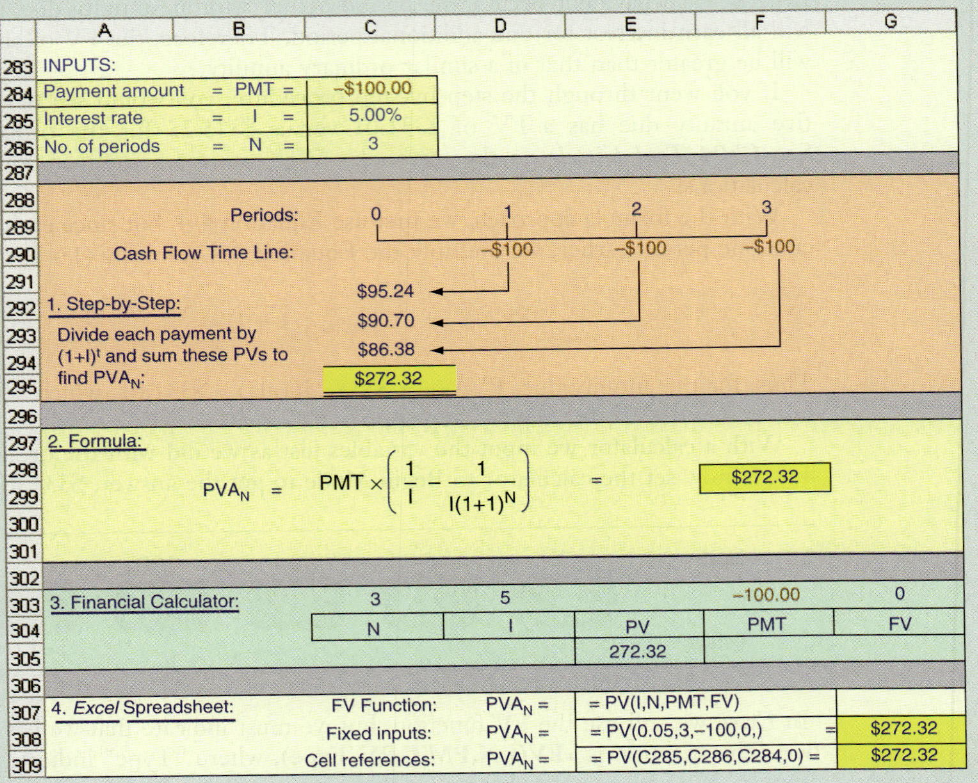

As shown in the step-by-step section of Figure 4-6, we discount each payment back to Time 0, then sum those discounted values to find the annuity's PV, PVA_3 = \$272.32. This approach is straightforward, but if the annuity extends out for many years, it is cumbersome and time-consuming.

The time line diagram shows that with the step-by-step approach we apply the following equation with N = 3 and I = 5%:

$$PVA_N = PMT/(1+I)^1 + PMT/(1+I)^2 + \cdots + PMT/(1+I)^N$$

The present value of an annuity can be written as[10]

$$PVA_N = PMT\left[\frac{1}{I} - \frac{1}{I(1+I)^N}\right] \qquad (4\text{-}7)$$

For our illustrative annuity, the present value is

$$PVA_3 = PMT\left[\frac{1}{0.05} - \frac{1}{0.05(1+0.05)^3}\right] = \$272.32$$

[10]See *Web Extension 4B* on the textbook's Web site for details of this derivation.

Financial calculators are programmed to solve Equation 4-7, so we merely input the variables and press the PV key, *first making sure the calculator is set to End Mode.* The calculator setup is shown below:

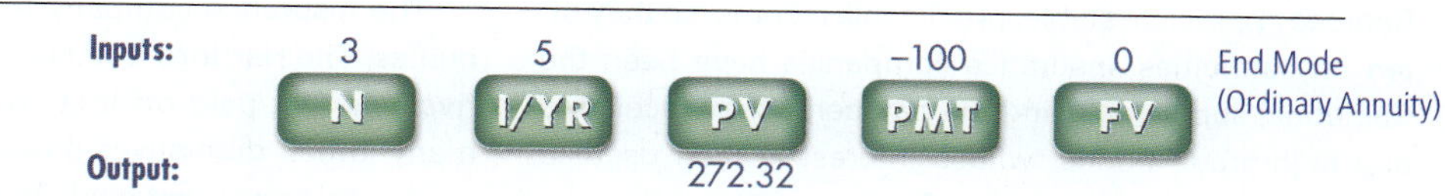

Section 4 of Figure 4-6 shows the spreadsheet solution using *Excel*'s built-in PV function: **=PV(I,N,PMT,FV)**. In our example, we have **=PV(0.05,3,–100,0)** with a resulting value of $272.32.

Present Value of Annuities Due

Because each payment for an annuity due occurs one period earlier, the payments will all be discounted for one less period. Therefore, the PV of an annuity due must be greater than that of a similar ordinary annuity.

If you went through the step-by-step procedure, you would see that our illustrative annuity due has a PV of $285.94 versus $272.32 for the ordinary annuity. See ***Ch04 Tool Kit.xls*** for this and the other calculations.

With the formula approach, we first use Equation 4-7 to find the value of the ordinary annuity and then, since each payment now occurs one period earlier, we multiply the Equation 4-7 result by (1 + I):

$$PVA_{due} = PVA_{ordinary}(1 + I) \tag{4-8}$$

$$PVA_{due} = \$272.32(1.05) = \$285.94$$

With a financial calculator, the inputs are the same as for an ordinary annuity, except you must set the calculator to Begin Mode:

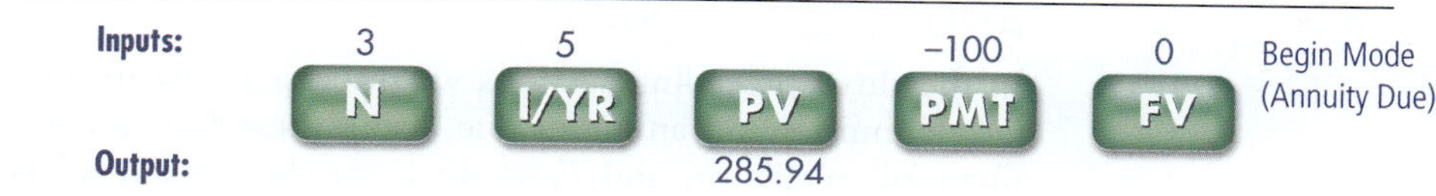

In *Excel*, we again use the PV function, but now we must indicate that we have an annuity due. The function is now **=PV(I,N,PMT,FV,Type)**, where "Type" is the type of annuity. If Type is omitted then *Excel* assumes that it is 0, which indicates an ordinary annuity; for an annuity due, Type = 1. As shown in ***Ch04 Tool Kit.xls***, the function for this example is **=PV(0.05,3,–100,0,1)** = $285.94.

Self-Test

Why does an annuity due have a higher present value than an ordinary annuity?

If you know the present value of an ordinary annuity, what's an easy way to find the PV of the corresponding annuity due?

What is the PVA of an ordinary annuity with 10 payments of $100 if the appropriate interest rate is 10%? **($614.46)** What would the PVA be if the interest rate were 4%? **($811.09)** What if the interest rate were 0%? **($1,000.00)** What would the PVAs be if we were dealing with annuities due? **($675.90, $843.53, and $1,000.00)**

Variable Annuities: Good or Bad?

Retirees appreciate stable, predictable income, so they often buy annuities. Insurance companies have been the traditional suppliers, using the payments they receive to buy high-grade bonds, whose interest is then used to make the promised payments. Such annuities were quite safe and stable and provided returns of around 7.5%. However, returns on stocks (dividends plus capital gains) have historically exceeded bonds' returns (interest). Therefore, some insurance companies in the 1990s began to offer *variable annuities*, which were backed by stocks instead of bonds. If stocks earned in the future as much as they had in the past, then variable annuities could offer returns of about 9%, better than the return on a fixed rate annuities. If stock returns turned out to be lower in the future than they had been in the past (or even had negative returns), then the variable annuities promised a *guaranteed minimum payment* of about 6.5%. Variable annuities appealed to many retirees, so companies that offered them had a significant competitive advantage.

The insurance company that pioneered variable annuities, The Hartford, tried to hedge its position with derivatives that paid off if stocks went down. But like so many other derivatives-based risk management programs, this one went awry in 2008 because stock losses exceeded the assumed worst-case scenario. The Hartford, which was founded in 1810 and was one of the oldest and largest U.S. insurance companies at the beginning of 2008, saw its stock fall from $85.54 to $4.16. Because of the general stock market crash, investors feared that The Hartford would be unable to make good on its variable annuity promises, which would lead to bankruptcy. The company was bailed out by the economic stimulus package, but this 199-year-old firm will never be the same again.

Source: Leslie Scism and Liam Pleven, "Hartford Aims to Take Risk Out of Annuities," *Online Wall Street Journal*, January 13, 2009.

Assume that you are offered an annuity that pays $100 at the end of each year for 10 years. You could earn 8% on your money in other equally risky investments. What is the most you should pay for the annuity? **($671.01)** If the payments began immediately, then how much would the annuity be worth? **($724.69)**

4.10 Finding Annuity Payments, Periods, and Interest Rates

In the three preceding sections we discussed how to find the FV and PV of ordinary annuities and annuities due, using these four methods: step-by-step, formula, financial calculator, and *Excel*. Five variables are involved—N, I, PMT, FV, and PV—and if you know any four, you can find the fifth by solving either 4-4 (4-6 for annuities due) or 4-7 (4-8 for annuities due). However, a trial-and-error procedure is generally required to find N or I, and that can be quite tedious. Therefore, we discuss only the financial calculator and spreadsheet approaches for finding N and I.

Finding Annuity Payments, PMT

We need to accumulate $10,000 and have it available 5 years from now. We can earn 6% on our money. Thus, we know that FV = 10,000, PV = 0, N = 5, and I/YR = 6. We can enter these values in a financial calculator and then press the PMT key to find our required deposits. However, the answer depends on whether we make deposits at the end of each year (ordinary annuity) or at the beginning (annuity due), so the mode must be set properly. Here are the results for each type of annuity:

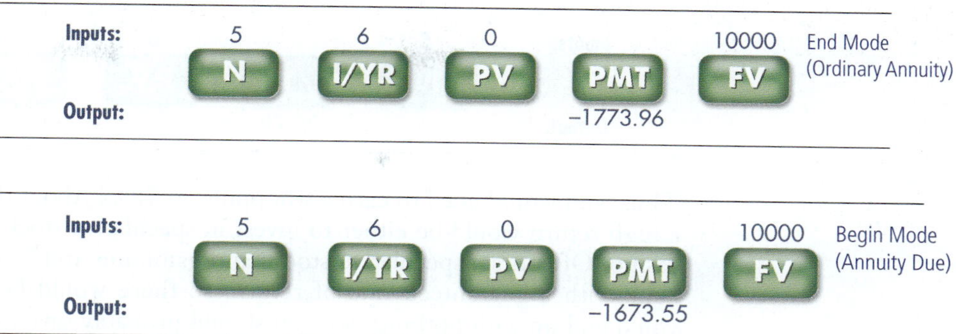

Thus, you must put away $1,773.96 per year if you make payments at the *end* of each year, but only $1,673.55 if the payments begin *immediately*. Finally, note that the required payment for the annuity due is the ordinary annuity payment divided by (1 + I): $1,773.96/1.06 = $1,673.55.

Excel can also be used to find annuity payments, as shown below for the two types of annuities. For end-of-year (ordinary) annuities, "Type" can be left blank or a 0 can be inserted. For beginning-of-year annuities (annuities due), the same function is used but now Type is designated as 1. Here is the setup for the two types of annuities.

$$\begin{aligned}&\textbf{Function:} && = \textbf{PMT(I, N, PV, FV, Type)} &&\\ &\textbf{Ordinary annuity:} && = \textbf{PMT(0.06, 5, 0, 10000)} && = \textbf{\$1,773.96}\\ &\textbf{Annuity due} && = \textbf{PMT(0.06, 5, 0, 10000, 1)} && = \textbf{\$1,673.55}\end{aligned}$$

Finding the Number of Periods, N

Suppose you decide to make end-of-year deposits, but you can save only $1,200 per year. Again assuming that you would earn 6%, how long would it take you to reach your $10,000 goal? Here is the calculator setup:

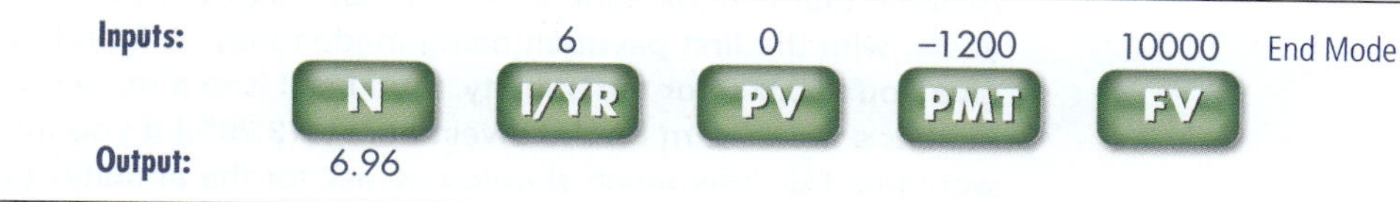

With these smaller deposits, it would take 6.96 years, not 5 years, to reach the $10,000 target. If you began the deposits immediately, then you would have an annuity due and N would be slightly less, 6.63 years.

With *Excel*, you can use the NPER function: **=NPER(I,PMT,PV,FV, Type)**. For our ordinary annuity example, Type is left blank (or 0 is inserted) and the function is **=NPER(0.06,−1200,0,10000)** = 6.96. If we put in 1 for type, we would find N = 6.63.

Finding the Interest Rate, I

Now suppose you can save only $1,200 annually, but you still need to have the $10,000 in 5 years. What rate of return would you have to earn to reach your goal? Here is the calculator setup:

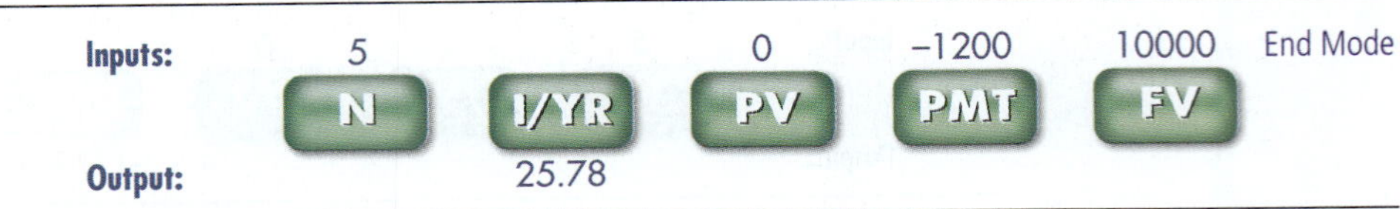

Thus, you would need to earn a whopping 25.78%! About the only way to earn such a high return would be either to invest in speculative stocks or head to a Las Vegas casino. Of course, speculative stocks and gambling aren't like making deposits in a bank with a guaranteed rate of return, so there would be a high probability that you'd end up with nothing. So, you should probably save more, lower your $10,000 target, or extend your time horizon. It might be appropriate to seek a somewhat higher return, but trying to earn 25.78% in a 6% market would involve speculation, not investing.

In *Excel*, you can use the RATE function: **=RATE(N,PMT,PV,FV,Type)**. For our example, the function is **=RATE(5,−1200,0,10000)** = 0.2578 = 25.78%. If you decide to make the payments beginning immediately then the required rate of return would decline sharply, to 17.54%.

Self-Test

Suppose you inherited $100,000 and invested it at 7% per year. How large of a withdrawal could you make at the *end* of each of the next 10 years and end up with zero? **($14,237.75)** How would your answer change if you made withdrawals at the *beginning* of each year? **($13,306.31)**

If you had $100,000 that was invested at 7% and you wanted to withdraw $10,000 at the end of each year, how long would your funds last? **(17.8 years)** How long would they last if you earned 0%? **(10 years)** How long would they last if you earned the 7% but limited your withdrawals to $7,000 per year? **(forever)**

Your rich uncle named you as the beneficiary of his life insurance policy. The insurance company gives you a choice of $100,000 today or a 12-year annuity of $12,000 at the end of each year. What rate of return is the insurance company offering? **(6.11%)**

Assume that you just inherited an annuity that will pay you $10,000 per year for 10 years, with the first payment being made today. A friend of your mother offers to give you $60,000 for the annuity. If you sell it to him, what rate of return will your mother's friend earn on the investment? **(13.70%)** If you think a "fair" rate of return would be 6%, how much should you ask for the annuity? **($78,016.92)**

4.11 Perpetuities

In the previous section we dealt with annuities whose payments continue for a specific number of periods—for example, $100 per year for 10 years. However, some securities promise to make payments forever. For example, in the mid-1700s the British government issued some bonds that never matured and whose proceeds were used to pay off other British bonds. Since this action consolidated the government's debt, the new bonds were called "consols." The term stuck, and now any bond that promises to pay interest perpetually is called a **consol,** or a perpetuity. The interest rate on the consols was 2.5%, so a consol with a face value of $1,000 would pay $25 per year in perpetuity.[11]

[11]The consols actually pay interest in pounds, but we discuss them in dollar terms for simplicity.

Using the Internet for Personal Financial Planning

People continually face important financial decisions that require an understanding of the time value of money. Should we buy or lease a car? How much and how soon should we begin to save for our children's education? How expensive a house can we afford? Should we refinance our home mortgage? How much must we save each year if we are to retire comfortably?

The answers to these questions are often complicated, and they depend on a number of factors, such as projected housing and education costs, interest rates, inflation, expected family income, and stock market returns. Hopefully, after completing this chapter, you will have a better idea of how to answer such questions. Note, though, that a number of online resources are available to help with financial planning. A good place to start is **http://www.smartmoney.com**. *Smartmoney* is a personal finance magazine produced by the publishers of *The Wall Street Journal*. If you go to *Smartmoney*'s Web site you will find a section entitled "Tools." This section has a number of financial calculators, spreadsheets, and descriptive materials that cover a wide range of personal finance issues.

A consol, or **perpetuity**, is simply an annuity whose promised payments extend out forever. Since the payments go on forever, you can't apply the step-by-step approach. However, it's easy to find the PV of a perpetuity with the following formula:[12]

$$\text{PV of a perpetuity} = \frac{\text{PMT}}{\text{I}} \tag{4-9}$$

We can use Equation 4-9 to find the value of a British consol with a face value of $1,000 that pays $25 per year in perpetuity. The answer depends on the interest rate being earned on investments of comparable risk at the time the consol is being valued. Originally, the "going rate" as established in the financial marketplace was 2.5%, so originally the consol's value was $1,000:

$$\text{Consol's value}_{\text{Originally}} = \$25/0.025 = \$1,000$$

The annual payment is still $25 today, but the going interest rate has risen to about 5.2%, causing the consol's value to fall to $480.77:

$$\text{Consol's value}_{\text{Today}} = \$25/0.052 = \$480.77$$

Note, though, that if interest rates decline in the future, say to 2%, then the value of the consol will rise to $1,250.00:

$$\text{Consol's value if rates decline to 2\%} = \$25/0.02 = \$1,250.00$$

These examples demonstrate an important point: *When interest rates change, the prices of outstanding bonds also change, but inversely to the change in rates. Thus, bond prices* **decline** *if rates* **rise,** *and prices* **increase** *if rates* **fall**. *This holds for all bonds, both consols and those with finite maturities.* We will discuss this point in more detail in Chapter 5, where we cover bonds in depth.

Self-Test

What is the present value of a perpetuity that pays $1,000 per year, beginning 1 year from now, if the appropriate interest rate is 5%? **($20,000)** What would the value be if

[12] See ***Web Extension 4B*** on the textbook's Web site for a derivation of the perpetuity formula.

the annuity began its payments immediately? **($21,000)** (*Hint:* Just add the $1,000 to be received immediately to the formula value of the annuity.)

Do bond prices move directly or inversely with interest rates—that is, what happens to the value of a bond if interest rates increase or decrease?

4.12 Uneven, or Irregular, Cash Flows

The definition of an annuity includes the term *constant payment*—in other words, annuities involve a set of identical payments over a given number of periods. Although many financial decisions do involve constant payments, many others involve cash flows that are **uneven** or **irregular.** For example, the dividends on common stocks are typically expected to increase over time, and investments in capital equipment almost always generate cash flows that vary from year to year. Throughout the book, we use the term *payment* (PMT) in situations where the cash flows are constant and thus an annuity is involved; we use the term *cash flow* (CF_t), where the t designates the period in which the particular cash flow occurs, if the cash flows are irregular.

There are two important classes of uneven cash flows: (1) those in which the cash flow stream consists of a series of annuity payments plus an additional final lump sum in Year N, and (2) all other uneven streams. Bonds are an instance of the first type, while stocks and capital investments illustrate the second type. Here's an example of each type.

Stream 1. Annuity plus additional final payment:

Periods	0 (I = 12%)	1	2	3	4	5
Cash flows	$0	$100	$100	$100	$100	$ 100 $ 1,000 $1,100

Stream 2. Irregular cash flows:

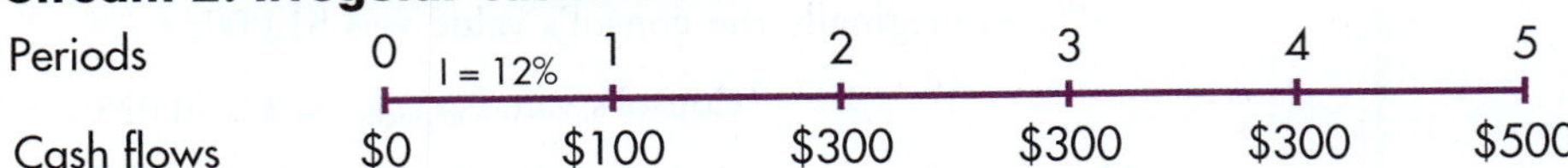

Equation 4-10 can be used, following the step-by-step procedure, to find the PV of either stream. However, as we shall see, the solution process differs significantly for the two types.

$$PV = \frac{CF_1}{(1+I)^1} + \frac{CF_2}{(1+I)^2} + \cdots + \frac{CF_N}{(1+I)^N} = \sum_{t=1}^{N} \frac{CF_t}{(1+I)^t} \quad \text{(4-10)}$$

Annuity Plus Additional Final Payment

First, consider Stream 1 and notice that it is a 5-year, 12%, ordinary annuity plus a final payment of $1,000. We can find the PV of the annuity, find the PV of the final payment, and then sum them to get the PV of the stream. Financial calculators are programmed do this for us—we use all five time value of money (TVM) keys, entering the data for the four known values as shown below, and then pressing the PV key to get the answer, $927.90:

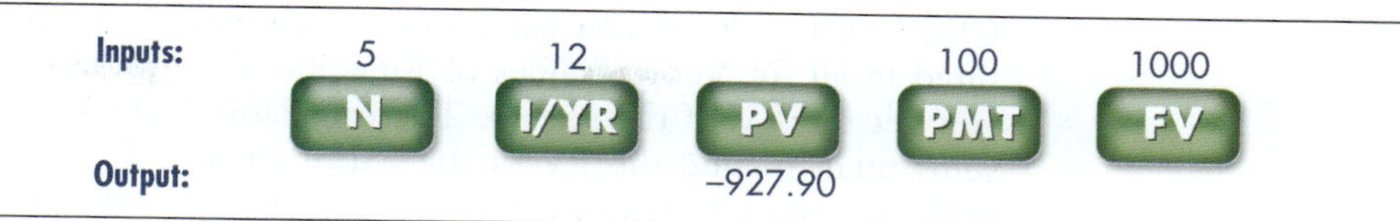

Similarly, we could use *Excel*'s PV function, **=PV(I,N,PMT,FV)** = **PV(0.12,5,100,1000)** = –$927.90. Note that the process is similar to that for annuities, except we now have a nonzero value for FV.

Irregular Cash Flow Stream

Now consider the irregular stream, which is analyzed in Figure 4-7. The top section shows the basic time line, which contains the inputs, and we first use the step-by-step approach to find PV = $1,016.35. Note that we show the PV of each cash flow directly below the cash flow, and then we sum these PVs to find the PV of the stream. This setup saves space as compared with showing the individual PVs in a column, and it is also transparent and thus easy to understand.

Now consider the financial calculator approach. The cash flows don't form an annuity, so you can't use the annuity feature on the calculator. You could, of course, use the calculator in the step-by-step procedure, but financial calculators have a feature—the cash flow register—that allows you to find the present value more efficiently. First, you input the individual cash flows, in chronological

FIGURE 4-7 Present Value of an Irregular Cash Flow Stream

	A	B	C	D	E	F	G
470	Step-by-step:						
471	Interest rate	= I =	12%				
472	Periods:	0	1	2	3	4	5
473							
474	CF Time Line:	$0.00	$100.00	$300.00	$300.00	$300.00	$500.00
475	PVs of the CFs:		$89.29	$239.16	$213.53	$190.66	$283.71
476							
477	Σ C477:G477 =	$1,016.35	= Sum of the individual PVs = PV of the irregular CF stream.				
478							
479	Here we put the PVs of each individual CF under the CF itself and then summed them to find the PV of						
480	the entire stream, rather than show them all in Column C as was done in Figure 4-6. This setup takes						
481	up less space and also makes the calculations quite transparent, which is useful, especially when the						
482	table must be explained to people who did not develop it. People appreciate transparency and clarity.						
483							
484	Calculator:	You could enter the cash flows into the cash flow register of a financial calculator, enter I/YR, and then press the NPV key to find the answer.					$1,016.35
485	*Excel* Function:		Fixed inputs:	NPV =	=NPV(0.12,100,300,300,300,500)		$1,016.35
486			Cell references:	NPV =	=NPV(C471,C474:G474)		$1,016.35
487							
488	Our Excel formula ignores the initial cash flow (in Year 0). When entering a cash flow range, Excel						
489	assumes that the first value occurs at the end of the first year. As we will see later, if there is an initial						
490	cash flow, it must be added seperately to complete the NPV formula result. Notice too that you can						
491	enter cash flows one-by-one, but if the cash flows appear in consecutive cells, you can enter the cell						
492	range, as we did here.						

order, into the cash flow register.[13] Cash flows are designated CF_0, CF_1, CF_2, CF_3,..., CF_N. Next, you enter the interest rate, I. At this point, you have substituted in all the known values of Equation 4-10, so when you press the NPV key you get the PV of the stream. The calculator finds the PV of each cash flow and sums them to find the PV of the entire stream. To input the cash flows for this problem, enter 0 (because $CF_0 = 0$), 100, 300, 300, 300, and 500 in that order into the cash flow register, enter I=12, and then press NPV to obtain the answer, $1,016.35.

Two points should be noted. First, when dealing with the cash flow register, the calculator uses the term "NPV" rather than "PV." The N stands for "net," so NPV is the abbreviation for "net present value," which is simply the net present value of a series of positive and negative cash flows, including any cash flow at time zero. The NPV function will be used extensively when we get to capital budgeting, where CF_0 is generally the cost of the project.

The second point to note is that repeated cash flows with identical values can be entered into the cash flow register more efficiently by using the Nj key. In this illustration, you would enter $CF_0=0$, $CF_1=100$, $CF_2=300$, Nj=3 (which tells the calculator that the 300 occurs 3 times), and $CF_5=500$.[14] Then enter I=12, press the NPV key, and 1,016.35 will appear in the display. Also, note that numbers entered into the cash flow register remain in the register until they are cleared. Thus, if you previously worked a problem with eight cash flows, then moved to one with only four cash flows, the calculator would simply add the cash flows from the second problem to those of the first problem, and you would get an incorrect answer. Therefore, you must be sure to clear the cash flow register before starting a new problem.

Spreadsheets are especially useful for solving problems with uneven cash flows. You enter the cash flows in the spreadsheet as shown in Figure 4-7 on Row 474. To find the PV of these cash flows without going through the step-by-step process, you would use the NPV function. First put the cursor on the cell where you want the answer to appear, Cell G486, click Financial, scroll down to NPV, and click OK to get the dialog box. Then enter C471 (or 0.12) for Rate and enter either the individual cash flows or the range of cells containing the cash flows, C474:G474, for Value 1. Be very careful when entering the range of cash flows. With a financial calculator, you begin by entering the Time-0 cash flow. With *Excel*, you do *not* include the Time-0 cash flow; instead, you begin with the Year-1 cash flow. Now, when you click OK, you get the PV of the stream, $1,016.35. Note that you can use the PV function if the payments are constant, but you must use the NPV function if the cash flows are not constant. Finally, note that *Excel* has a major advantage over financial calculators in that you can see the cash flows, which makes it easy to spot data entry errors. With a calculator, the numbers are buried in the machine, making it harder to check your work.

---

[13]We cover the calculator mechanics in the tutorial, and we discuss the process in more detail in Chapter 10, where we use the NPV calculation to analyze proposed projects. If you don't know how to use the cash flow register of your calculator, you should to go to our tutorial or your calculator manual, learn the steps, and be sure you can make this calculation. You will have to know how to do it eventually, and now is a good time to learn.

[14]On some calculators, instead of entering $CF_5 = 500$, you enter $CF_3 = 500$, because this is the next cash flow *different* from 300.

Self-Test

Could you use Equation 4-3, once for each cash flow, to find the PV of an uneven stream of cash flows?

What is the present value of a 5-year ordinary annuity of $100 plus an additional $500 at the end of Year 5 if the interest rate is 6%? **($794.87)** How would the PV change if the $100 payments occurred in Years 1 through 10 and the $500 came at the end of Year 10? **($1,015.21)**

What is the present value of the following uneven cash flow stream: $0 at Time 0, $100 at the end of Year 1 (or at Time 1), $200 at the end of Year 2, $0 at the end of Year 3, and $400 at the end of Year 4—assuming the interest rate is 8%? **($558.07)**

Would a "typical" common stock provide cash flows more like an annuity or more like an uneven cash flow stream?

4.13 Future Value of an Uneven Cash Flow Stream

The future value of an uneven cash flow stream (sometimes called the **terminal,** or **horizon, value**) is found by compounding each payment to the end of the stream and then summing the future values:

$$FV = CF_0(1+I)^N + CF_1(1+I)^{N-1} + CF_2(1+I)^{N-2} + \cdots + CF_{N-1}(1+I) + CF_N = \sum_{t=0}^{N} CF_t(1+I)^{N-t} \quad (4\text{-}11)$$

The future value of our illustrative uneven cash flow stream is $1,791.15, as shown in Figure 4-8.

Most financial calculators have a net future value (NFV) key which, after the cash flows and interest rate have been entered, can be used to obtain the future value of an uneven cash flow stream. If your calculator doesn't have the NFV feature, you can first find the net present value of the stream, then find its net future value as $NFV = NPV(1 + I)^N$. In the illustrative problem, we find PV = 1,016.35 using the cash flow register and I=12. Then we use the TVM register, entering N=5, I=12, PV = −1016.35, and PMT = 0. When we press FV, we find FV = 1,791.15, which is

FIGURE 4-8 Future Value of an Irregular Cash Flow Stream

	A	B	C	D	E	F	G
503	Step-by-step:						
504	Periods:	0	1	2	3	4	5
505	Interest rate	= I = 12%					
506							
507	CF Time Line:	$0	$100	$300	$300	$300	$500
508	FV of each CF:	$0.00	$157.35	$421.48	$376.32	$336.00	$500
509			Sum of the Cash Flows' FVs = FV of the stream =				$1,791.15
510							
511	Calculator:	You could enter the cash flows into the cash flow register of a financial					$1,791.15
512							
513	Excel:	Step 1. Find NPV:				=NPV(C505,C507:G507)	$1,016.35
514		Step 2. Compound NPV to find NFV:				=FV(C505,G504,0,−G513)	$1,791.15

the same as the value shown on the time line in Figure 4-8. As Figure 4-8 also shows, this same procedure can be used with *Excel*.

Self-Test

What is the future value of this cash flow stream: $100 at the end of 1 year, $150 after 2 years, and $300 after 3 years, assuming the appropriate interest rate is 15%? **($604.75)**

4.14 Solving for I with Irregular Cash Flows

Before financial calculators and spreadsheets existed, it was *extremely difficult* to find I if the cash flows were uneven. However, with spreadsheets and financial calculators it's easy to find I. If you have an *annuity plus a final lump sum*, you can input values for N, PV, PMT, and FV into the calculator's TVM registers and then press the I/YR key. Here's the setup for Stream 1 from Section 4.12, assuming we must pay $927.90 to buy the asset:

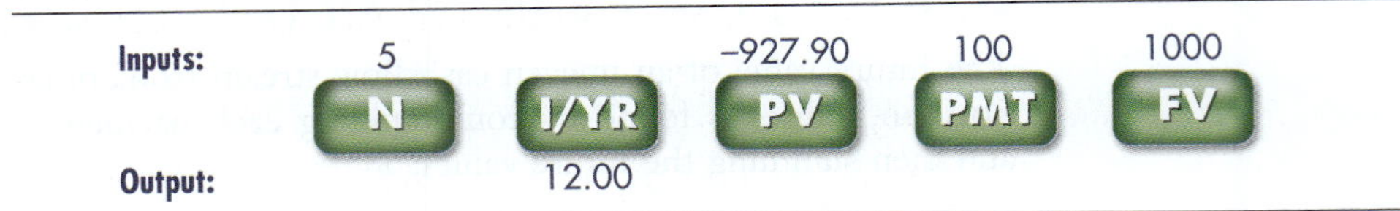

The rate of return on the $927.90 investment is 12%.

Finding the interest rate for an *irregular cash flow stream* with a calculator is a bit more complicated. Figure 4-9 shows Stream 2 from Section 4.12, assuming a required investment of CF_0 = –$1,000. First, note that there is no simple step-by-step method for finding the rate of return—finding the rate for this investment requires a trial-and-error process, which is terribly time consuming. Therefore, we really need a financial calculator or a spreadsheet. With a calculator, we would enter the CFs into the cash flow register and then press the IRR key to get the answer. IRR stands for "internal rate of return," and it is the rate of return the investment provides. The investment is the cash flow at Time 0, and it must be entered as a negative number. When we enter those cash flows in the calculator's cash flow register and press the IRR key, we get the rate of return on the $1,000 investment, 12.55%. Finally, note that once you have entered the cash flows in the calculator's register, you can find both the investment's net present value (NPV) and its internal rate of return. For investment decisions, we typically want both of these numbers. Therefore, we generally enter the data once and then find both the NPV and the IRR.

You would get the same answer using *Excel*'s IRR function, as shown in Figure 4-9. Notice that when using the IRR—unlike using the NPV function—you must include all cash flows, including the Time-0 cash flow.

FIGURE 4-9 IRR of an Uneven Cash Flow Stream

	A	B	C	D	E	F	G
547	Periods:	0	1	2	3	4	5
548		├	┼	┼	┼	┼	┤
549	CF Time Line:	–$1,000	$100	$300	$300	$300	$500
550	Calculator:	You could enter the cash flows into the cash flow register of a financial calculator and then press the IRR key to find the answer.					12.55%
551	*Excel* IRR Function:		Cell references:	IRR =	=IRR(B549:G549)		12.55%

Self-Test

An investment costs $465 now and is expected to produce cash flows of $100 at the end of each of the next 4 years, plus an extra lump-sum payment of $200 at the end of the fourth year. What is the expected rate of return on this investment? **(9.05%)**

An investment costs $465 and is expected to produce cash flows of $100 at the end of Year 1, $200 at the end of Year 2, and $300 at the end of Year 3. What is the expected rate of return on this investment? **(11.71%)**

4.15 Semiannual and Other Compounding Periods

In most of our examples thus far, we assumed that interest is compounded once a year, or annually. This is **annual compounding.** Suppose, however, that you put $1,000 into a bank that pays a 6% annual interest rate but credits interest each 6 months. This is **semiannual compounding.** If you leave your funds in the account, how much would you have at the end of 1 year under semiannual compounding? Note that you will receive $60 of interest for the year, but you will receive $30 of it after only 6 months and the other $30 at the end of the year. You will earn interest on the first $30 during the second 6 months, so you will end the year with more than the $60 you would have had under annual compounding. You would be even better off under quarterly, monthly, weekly, or daily compounding. Note also that virtually all bonds pay interest semiannually; most stocks pay dividends quarterly; most mortgages, student loans, and auto loans involve monthly payments; and most money fund accounts pay interest daily. Therefore, it is essential that you understand how to deal with nonannual compounding.

Types of Interest Rates

When we move beyond annual compounding, we must deal with the following four types of interest rates:

- Nominal annual rates, given the symbol $\mathbf{I_{NOM}}$
- Annual percentage rates, termed **APR** rates
- Periodic rates, denoted as $\mathbf{I_{PER}}$
- Effective annual rates, given the symbol **EAR** or **EFF%**

Nominal (or Quoted) Rate, I_{NOM}.[15] This is the rate quoted by banks, brokers, and other financial institutions. So, if you talk with a banker, broker, mortgage lender, auto finance company, or student loan officer about rates, the nominal rate is the one he or she will normally quote you. However, to be meaningful, the quoted nominal rate must also include the number of compounding periods per year. For example, a bank might offer you a CD at 6% compounded daily, while a credit union might offer 6.1% compounded monthly.

Note that the nominal rate is never shown on a time line, and it is never used as an input in a financial calculator (except when compounding occurs only once a year). If more frequent compounding occurs, you must use periodic rates.

Periodic Rate, I_{PER}. This is the rate charged by a lender or paid by a borrower each period. It can be a rate per year, per 6 months (semiannually), per quarter, per month, per day, or per any other time interval. For example, a bank might charge 1.5% per month on

[15]The term *nominal rate* as it is used here has a different meaning than the way it was used in Chapter 1. There, nominal interest rates referred to stated market rates as opposed to real (zero-inflation) rates. In this chapter, the term *nominal rate* means the stated, or quoted, annual rate as opposed to the effective annual rate, which we explain later. In both cases, though, *nominal* means *stated*, or *quoted*, as opposed to some sort of adjusted rate.

its credit card loans, or a finance company might charge 3% per quarter on installment loans.

We find the periodic rate as follows:

$$\text{Periodic rate } I_{PER} = I_{NOM}/M \tag{4-12}$$

where I_{NOM} is the nominal annual rate and M is the number of compounding periods per year. Thus, a 6% nominal rate with semiannual payments results in a periodic rate of

$$\text{Periodic rate } I_{PER} = 6\%/2 = 3.00\%.$$

If only one payment is made per year then M = 1, in which case the periodic rate would equal the nominal rate: 6%/1 = 6%.

The periodic rate is the rate shown on time lines and used in calculations.[16] To illustrate, suppose you invest $100 in an account that pays a nominal rate of 12%, compounded quarterly, or 3% per period. How much would you have after 2 years if you leave the funds on deposit? First, here is the time line for the problem:

0	1	2	3	4	5	6	7	8	Quarters
3%									
−100								FV=?	

To find the FV, we would use this modified version of Equation 4-1:

$$FV_N = PV(1 + I_{PER})^{\text{Number of periods}} = PV\left(1 + \frac{I_{NOM}}{M}\right)^{MN} \tag{4-13}$$

$$= \$100\left(1 + \frac{0.12}{4}\right)^{4\times 2} = \$100(1 + 0.03)^8 = \$126.68.$$

With a financial calculator, we find the FV using these inputs: N = 4 × 2 = 8, I = 12/4 = 3, PV = −100, and PMT = 0. The result is again FV = $126.68.[17]

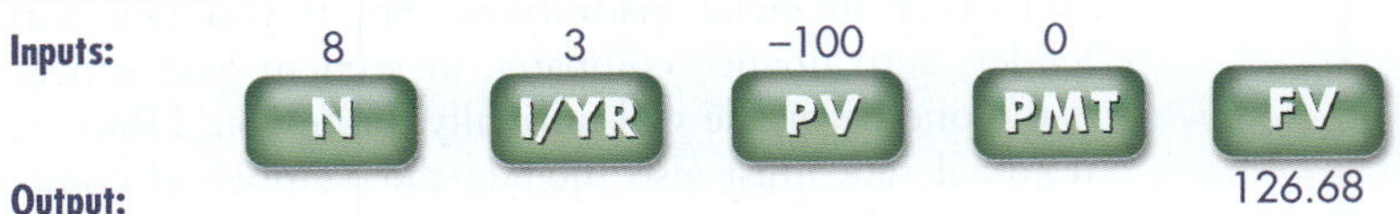

[16]The only exception is in cases where (1) annuities are involved *and* (2) the payment periods do not correspond to the compounding periods. In such cases—for example, if you are making quarterly payments into a bank account to build up a specified future sum but the bank pays interest on a daily basis—then the calculations are more complicated. For such problems, the simplest procedure is to determine the periodic (daily) interest rate by dividing the nominal rate by 365 (or by 360 if the bank uses a 360-day year), then compound each payment over the exact number of days from the payment date to the terminal point, and then sum the compounded payments to find the future value of the annuity. This is what is generally done in the real world, because with a computer it's a simple process.

[17]Most financial calculators have a feature that allows you to set the number of payments per year and then use the nominal annual interest rate. However, students tend to make fewer errors when using the periodic rate with their calculators set for one payment per year (i.e., per period), so this is what we recommend. Note also that a normal time line cannot be used unless you use the periodic rate.

Effective (or Equivalent) Annual Rate (EAR or EFF%). This is the annual (interest once a year) rate that produces the same final result as compounding at the periodic rate for M times per year. The EAR, also called EFF% (for effective percentage rate), is found as follows:[18]

$$\text{EAR} = \text{EFF\%} = \left(1 + \frac{I_{NOM}}{M}\right)^{M} - 1.0 \tag{4-14}$$

Here I_{NOM}/M is the periodic rate and M is the number of periods per year. If a bank would lend you money at a nominal rate of 12%, compounded quarterly, then the EFF% rate would be 12.5509%:

$$\textbf{Rate on bank loan: } \text{EFF\%} = (1 + 0.03)^4 - 1.0 = (1.03)^4 - 1.0$$
$$= 1.125509 - 1.0 = 0.125509 = 12.5509\%$$

To see the importance of the EFF%, suppose that—as an alternative to the bank loan—you could borrow on a credit card that charges 1% per month. Would you be better off using the bank loan or credit card loan? *To answer this question, the cost of each alternative must be expressed as an EFF%.* We just saw that the bank loan's effective cost is 12.5509%. The cost of the credit card loan, with monthly payments, is slightly higher, 12.6825%:

$$\textbf{Credit card loan: } \text{EFF\%} = (1 + 0.01)^{12} - 1.0 = (1.01)^{12} - 1.0$$
$$= 1.126825 - 1.0 = 0.126825 = 12.6825\%$$

This result is logical: Both loans have the same 12% nominal rate, yet you would have to make the first payment after only one month on the credit card versus three months under the bank loan.

The EFF% rate is rarely used in calculations. *However, it must be used to compare the effective costs of different loans or rates of return on different investments when payment periods differ*, as in our example of the credit card versus a bank loan.

The Result of Frequent Compounding

What would happen to the future value of an investment if interest were compounded annually, semiannually, quarterly, or some other less-than-annual period? Because interest will be earned on interest more often, you should expect higher future values the more frequently compounding occurs. Similarly, you should expect the effective annual rate to increase with more frequent compounding. As Figure 4-10 shows, these results do occur—the future value and the EFF% do increase as the frequency of compounding increases. Notice that the biggest increase in FV (and in EFF%) occurs when compounding goes from annual to semiannual, and notice also that moving from monthly to daily compounding has a relatively small impact. Although Figure 4-10 shows daily compounding as the smallest interval, it is possible to compound even more frequently. At the limit, compounding can occur **continuously.** This is explained in ***Web Extension 4C*** on the textbook's Web site.

[18]You could also use the "interest conversion feature" of a financial calculator. Most financial calculators are programmed to find the EFF% or, given the EFF%, to find the nominal rate; this is called "interest rate conversion." You enter the nominal rate and the number of compounding periods per year, then press the EFF% key to find the effective annual rate. However, we generally use Equation 4-14 because it's easy and because using the equation reminds us of what we are really doing. If you do use the interest rate conversion feature on your calculator, don't forget to reset your settings afterward. Interest conversion is discussed in our calculator tutorials.

Truth in Lending: What Loans Really Cost

Congress passed the Consumer Credit Protection Act in 1968. The Truth in Lending provisions in the Act require banks and other lenders to disclose the **annual percentage rate (APR)** they are charging. For example, suppose you plan to buy a fancy TV set that costs $3,000, and the store offers you credit for one year at an "add-on" quoted rate of 8%. Here we first find the total dollars of interest by multiplying the $3,000 you are borrowing times 8%, getting $240. This interest is then added to the $3,000 cost of the TV, resulting in a total loan of $3,240. The total loan is divided by 12 to get the monthly payments: $3,240/12 = $270 per month, with the first payment made at the time of purchase. Therefore, we have a 12-month annuity due with payments of $270. Is your cost really the 8% that you were quoted?

To find the APR, you first set your calculator to Begin Mode, then enter N = 12, PV = 3000, PMT = −270, and FV = 0. Then, when you press the I/YR key, you get the periodic rate, 1.4313%. You then multiply by 12 to get the APR, 17.1758%. You could also find the EFF%, which is 18.5945%. We show these calculations using both the calculator and *Excel*, along with a time line that helps us visualize what's happening, in the chapter's *Excel* Tool Kit.

The 17.1758% APR that the dealer is required to report is a much better indicator of the loan's cost than the 8% nominal rate, but it still does not reflect the true cost, which is the 18.5945% effective annual rate. Thus, buying the TV on time would really cost you 18.5945%. If you don't know what's happening when you buy on time or borrow, you may pay a lot more than you think!

FIGURE 4-10 Effect on $100 of Compounding More Frequently Than Once a Year

	A	B	C	D	E	F	G
566	Frequency of Compounding	Nominal Annual Rate	Number of periods per year (M)[a]	Periodic Interest Rate	Effective Annual Rate[b]	Future Value[c]	Percentage increase in FV
567	Annual	12%	1	12.0000%	12.0000%	$112.00	
568	Semiannual	12%	2	6.0000%	12.3600%	$112.36	0.32%
569	Quarterly	12%	4	3.0000%	12.5509%	$112.55	0.17%
570	Monthly	12%	12	1.0000%	12.6825%	$112.68	0.12%
571	Daily	**12%**	365	0.0329%	12.7475%	$112.75	0.06%
572							
573	[a] We used 365 days per year in the calculations.						
574	[b] The EFF% is calculated using text Equation 4-14.						
575	[c] The Future Value is calculated using text Equation 4-1.						

Self-Test

Would you rather *invest* in an account that pays a 7% nominal rate with annual compounding or with monthly compounding? If you *borrowed* at a nominal rate of 7%, would you rather make annual or rather monthly payments? Why?

What is the *future value* of $100 after 3 years if the appropriate interest rate is 8%, compounded annually? **($125.97)** Compounded monthly? **($127.02)**

What is the *present value* of $100 due in 3 years if the appropriate interest rate is 8%, compounded annually? **($79.38)** Compounded monthly? **($78.73)**

Define the following terms: "annual percentage rate, or APR"; "effective annual rate, or EFF%"; and "nominal interest rate, I_{NOM}."

A bank pays 5% with daily compounding on its savings accounts. Should it advertise the nominal or effective rate if it is seeking to attract new deposits?

Credit card issuers must by law print their annual percentage rate on their monthly statements. A common APR is 18%, with interest paid monthly. What is the EFF% on such a loan? **(19.56%)**

Some years ago banks weren't required to reveal the rate they charged on credit cards. Then Congress passed a "truth in lending" law that required them to publish their APR rate. Is the APR rate really the "most truthful" rate, or would the EFF% be even "more truthful"?

4.16 Fractional Time Periods[19]

Thus far we have assumed that payments occur at either the beginning or the end of periods, but not *within* periods. However, we occasionally encounter situations that require compounding or discounting over fractional periods. For example, suppose you deposited \$100 in a bank that pays a nominal rate of 10%, compounded daily, based on a 365-day year. How much would you have after 9 months? The answer of \$107.79 is found as follows:[20]

$$\text{Periodic rate} = I_{PER} = 0.10/365 = 0.000273973 \text{ per day}$$

$$\text{Number of days} = (9/12)(365) = 0.75(365)$$
$$= 273.75 \text{ days, rounded to } 274$$

$$\text{Ending amount} = \$100(1.000273973)^{274} = \$107.79$$

Now suppose that instead you borrow \$100 at a nominal rate of 10% per year, *simple interest*, which means that interest is not earned on interest. If the loan is outstanding for 274 days (or 9 months), how much interest would you have to pay? The interest owed is equal to the principal multiplied by the interest rate times the number of periods. In this case, the number of periods is equal to a fraction of a year: N = 274/365 = 0.7506849.

$$\text{Interest owed} = \$100(10\%)(0.7506849) = \$7.51$$

Another approach would be to use the daily rate rather than the annual rate and thus to use the exact number of days rather than the fraction of the year:

$$\text{Interest owed} = \$100(0.000273973)(274) = \$7.51$$

You would owe the bank a total of \$107.51 after 274 days. This is the procedure most banks actually use to calculate interest on loans, except that they generally require borrowers to pay the interest on a monthly basis rather than after 274 days; this more frequent compounding raises the EFF% and thus the total amount of interest paid.

Self-Test

Suppose a company borrowed \$1 million at a rate of 9%, simple interest, with interest paid at the end of each month. The bank uses a 360-day year. How much interest would the firm have to pay in a 30-day month? **(\$7,500.00)** What would the interest be if the bank used a 365-day year? **(\$7,397.26)**

Suppose you deposited \$1,000 in a credit union that pays 7% with daily compounding and a 365-day year. What is the EFF%? **(7.250098%)** How much could you withdraw after 7 months, assuming this is 7/12 of a year? **(\$1,041.67)**

---

[19]This section is interesting and useful, but relatively technical. It can be omitted, at the option of the instructor, without loss of continuity.

[20]We assume that these 9 months constitute 9/12 of a year. Also, bank deposit and loan contracts specifically state whether they are based on a 360-day or a 365-day year. If a 360-day year is used, then the daily rate is higher, so the effective rate is also higher. Here we assumed a 365-day year. Finally, note that banks' computers, like *Excel*, have built-in calendars, so they can calculate the exact number of days.

Note also that banks often treat such loans as follows. (1) They require monthly payments, and they figure the interest for the month as the periodic rate multiplied by the beginning-of-month balance times the number of days in the month. This is called "simple interest." (2) The interest for the month is either added to the next beginning of month balance, or else the borrower must actually pay the earned interest. In this case, the EFF% is based on 12 compounding periods, not 365 as is assumed in our example.

4.17 Amortized Loans

An extremely important application of compound interest involves loans that are paid off in installments over time. Included are automobile loans, home mortgage loans, student loans, and many business loans. A loan that is to be repaid in equal amounts on a monthly, quarterly, or annual basis is called an **amortized loan.**[21] For example, suppose a company borrows $100,000, with the loan to be repaid in 5 equal payments at the end of each of the next 5 years. The lender charges 6% on the balance at the beginning of each year.

Here's a picture of the situation:

Our task is to find the amount of the payment, PMT, such that the sum of their PVs equals the amount of the loan, $100,000:

$$\$100,000 = \frac{PMT}{(1.06)^1} + \frac{PMT}{(1.06)^2} + \frac{PMT}{(1.06)^3} + \frac{PMT}{(1.06)^4} + \frac{PMT}{(1.06)^5} = \sum_{t=1}^{5} \frac{PMT}{(1.06)^t}$$

It is possible to solve the annuity formula, Equation 4-7, for PMT, but it is much easier to use a financial calculator or spreadsheet. With a financial calculator, we insert values as shown below to get the required payments, $23,739.64.

Inputs:	5	6	100000		0
	N	I/YR	PV	PMT	FV
Output:				−23739.64	

With *Excel*, you would use the PMT function: **=PMT(I,N,PV,FV)** = **PMT(0.06, 5,100000,0)** = −$23,739.64. Thus, we see that the borrower must pay the lender $23,739.64 per year for the next 5 years.

Each payment will consist of two parts—part interest and part repayment of principal. This breakdown is shown in the **amortization schedule** given in Figure 4-11. The interest component is relatively high in the first year, but it declines as the loan balance decreases. For tax purposes, the borrower would deduct the interest component while the lender would report the same amount as taxable income. Over the 5 years, the lender will earn 6% on its investment and also recover the amount of its investment.

Self-Test

Consider again the example in Figure 4-11. If the loan were amortized over 5 years with 60 equal monthly payments, how much would each payment be, and how would the first payment be divided between interest and principal? **(Each payment would be $1,933.28; the first payment would have $500 of interest and $1,433.28 of principal repayment.)**

Suppose you borrowed $30,000 on a student loan at a rate of 8% and now must repay it in three equal installments at the end of each of the next 3 years. How large would your payments be, how much of the first payment would represent

[21] The word *amortized* comes from the Latin *mors*, meaning "death," so an amortized loan is one that is "killed off" over time.

FIGURE 4-11 Loan Amortization Schedule, $100,000 at 6% for 5 Years

	A	B	C	D	E	F
644		Amount borrowed:	$100,000			
645		Years:	5			
646		Rate:	6%			
647		PMT:	$23,739.64 = PMT(C646,C645,-C644)			
648	Year	Beginning Amount (1)	Payment (2)	Interest[a] (3)	Repayment of Principal[b] (2) - (3) = (4)	Ending Balance (1) - (4) = (5)
649	1	$100,000.00	$23,739.64	$6,000.00	$17,739.64	$82,260.36
650	2	$82,260.36	$23,739.64	$4,935.62	$18,804.02	$63,456.34
651	3	$63,456.34	$23,739.64	$3.807.38	$19,932.26	$43,524.08
652	4	$43,524.08	$23,739.64	$2,611.44	$21,128.20	$22,395.89
653	5	$22,395.89	$23,739.64	$1,343.75	$22,395.89	$0.00

654 [a]Interest in each period is calculated by multiplying the loan balance at the beginning
655 of the year by the interest rate. Therefore, interest in Year 1 is $100,000(0.06) = $6,000; in
656 Year 2 it is $82,260.36(0.06) = $4,935.62; and so on.

657 [b]Repayment of principal is the $23,739.64 annual payment minus the interest charges for
658 the year, $17,739.64 for Year 1.

interest and how much would be principal, and what would your ending balance be after the first year? **(PMT = $11,641.01; interest = $2,400; principal = $9,241.01; balance at end of Year 1 = $20,758.99)**

4.18 Growing Annuities[22]

Normally, an annuity is defined as a series of *constant* payments to be received over a specified number of periods. However, the term **growing annuity** is used to describe a series of payments that grow at a constant rate.

Example 1: Finding a Constant Real Income

Growing annuities are often used in the area of financial planning, where a prospective retiree wants to determine the maximum constant *real*, or *inflation-adjusted*, withdrawals that he or she can make over a specified number of years. For example, suppose a 65-year-old is contemplating retirement, expects to live for another 20 years, has a $1 million nest egg, expects the investments to earn a nominal annual rate of 6%, expects inflation to average 3% per year, and wants to withdraw a constant *real* amount annually over the next 20 years so as to maintain a constant standard of living. If the first withdrawal is to be made today, what is the amount of that initial withdrawal?

See **Ch04 Tool Kit.xls** for all calculations.

This problem can be solved in three ways. (1) Set up a spreadsheet model that is similar to an amortization table, where the account earns 6% per year, withdrawals rise at the 3% inflation rate, and *Excel*'s Goal Seek function is used to find the initial inflation-adjusted withdrawal. A zero balance will be shown at the end of the twentieth year. (2) Use a financial calculator, where we first calculate the real rate of return,

---

[22]This section is interesting and useful, but relatively technical. It can be omitted, at the option of the instructor, without loss of continuity.

THE GLOBAL ECONOMIC CRISIS

An Accident Waiting to Happen: Option Reset Adjustable Rate Mortgages

Option reset adjustable rate mortgages (ARMs) give the borrower some choices regarding the initial monthly payment. One popular option ARM allowed borrowers to make a monthly payment equal to only half of the interest due in the first month. Because the monthly payment was less than the interest charge, the loan balance grew each month. When the loan balance exceeded 110% of the original principal, the monthly payment was reset to fully amortize the now-larger loan at the prevailing market interest rates.

Here's an example. Someone borrows $325,000 for 30 years at an initial rate of 7%. The interest accruing in the first month is (7%/12)($325,000) = $1,895.83. Therefore, the initial monthly payment is 50%($1,895.83) = $947.92. Another $947.92 of deferred interest is added to the loan balance, taking it up to $325,000 + $947.92 = $325,947.82. Because the loan is now larger, interest in the second month is higher, and both interest and the loan balance will continue to rise each month. The first month after the loan balance exceeds 110%($325,000) = $357,500, the contract calls for the payment to be reset so as to fully amortize the loan at the then-prevailing interest rate.

First, how long would it take for the balance to exceed $357,500? Consider this from the lender's perspective: the lender initially pays out $325,000, receives $947.92 each month, and then would receive a payment of $357,500 if the loan were payable when the balance hit that amount, with interest accruing at a 7% annual rate and with monthly compounding. We enter these values into a financial calculator: I = 7%/12, PV = −325000, PMT = 947.92, and FV = 357500. We solve for N = 31.3 months, rounded up to 32 months. Thus, the borrower will make 32 payments of $947.92 before the ARM resets.

The payment after the reset depends upon the terms of the original loan and the market interest rate at the time of the reset. For many borrowers, the initial rate was a lower-than-market "teaser" rate, so a higher-than-market rate would be applied to the remaining balance. For this example, we will assume that the original rate wasn't a teaser and that the rate remains at 7%. Keep in mind, though, that for many borrowers the reset rate was higher than the initial rate. The balance after the 32nd payment can be found as the future value of the original loan and the 32 monthly payments, so we enter these values in the financial calculator: N = 32, I = 7%/12, PMT = 947.92, PV = −325000, and then solve for FV = $358,242.84. The number of remaining payments to amortize the $358,424.84 loan balance is 360 − 32 = 328, so the amount of each payment is found by setting up the calculator as: N = 328, I = 7%/12, PV = 358242.84 and FV = 0. Solving, we find that PMT = $2,453.94.

Even if interest rates don't change, the monthly payment jumps from $947.92 to $2,453.94 and would increase even more if interest rates were higher at the reset. This is exactly what happened to millions of American homeowners who took out option reset ARMS in the early 2000s. When large numbers of resets began in 2007, defaults ballooned. The accident caused by option reset ARMs didn't wait very long to happen!

adjusted for inflation, and use it for I/YR when finding the payment for an annuity due. (3) Use a relatively complicated and obtuse formula to find this same amount.[23] We will focus on the first two approaches.

[23]For example, the formula used to find the payment of a growing annuity due is shown below. If g = annuity growth rate and r = nominal rate of return on investment, then

$$\text{PVIF of a growing annuity due} = \text{PVIFGA}_{\text{Due}} = \{1 - [(1+g)/(1+r)]^N\}[(1+r)/(r-g)]$$

$$\text{PMT} = \text{PV}/\text{PVIFGA}_{\text{Due}}$$

where PVIF denotes "present value interest factor." Similar formulas are available for growing ordinary annuities.

We illustrate the spreadsheet approach in the chapter model, ***Ch04 Tool Kit.xls***. The spreadsheet model provides the most transparent picture of what's happening, since it shows the value of the retirement portfolio, the portfolio's annual earnings, and each withdrawal over the 20-year planning horizon—especially if you include a graph. A picture is worth a thousand numbers, and graphs make it easy to explain the situation to people who are planning their financial futures.

To implement the calculator approach, we first find the expected *real* rate of return, where r_r is the real rate of return and r_{NOM} the nominal rate of return. The real rate of return is the return that we would see if there were no inflation. We calculate the real rate as:

$$\text{Real rate} = r_r = [(1 + r_{NOM})/(1 + \text{Inflation})] - 1.0 \quad \textbf{(4-15)}$$

$$= [1.06/1.03] - 1.0 = 0.029126214 = 2.9126214\%$$

Using this real rate of return, we solve the annuity due problem exactly as we did earlier in the chapter. We set the calculator to Begin Mode, after which we input N=20, I/YR = real rate=2.9126214, PV=–1,000,000, and FV=0; then we press PMT to get $64,786.88. This is the amount of the initial withdrawal at Time 0 (today), and future withdrawals will increase at the inflation rate of 3%. These withdrawals, growing at the inflation rate, will provide the retiree with a constant real income over the next 20 years—provided the inflation rate and the rate of return do not change.

In our example we assumed that the first withdrawal would be made immediately. The procedure would be slightly different if we wanted to make end-of-year withdrawals. First, we would set the calculator to End Mode. Second, we would enter the same inputs into the calculator as just listed, including the real interest rate for I/YR. The calculated PMT would be $66,673.87. However, that value is in beginning-of-year terms, and since inflation of 3% will occur during the year, we must make the following adjustment to find the inflation-adjusted initial withdrawal:

$$\begin{aligned}\text{Initial end-of-year withdrawal} &= \$66{,}673.87(1 + \text{Inflation})\\ &= \$66{,}673.87(1.03)\\ &= \$68{,}674.09.\end{aligned}$$

Thus the first withdrawal at the *end* of the year would be $68,674.09; it would grow by 3% per year; and after the 20th withdrawal (at the end of the 20th year) the balance in the retirement fund would be zero.

We also demonstrate the solution for this end-of-year payment example in ***Ch04 Tool Kit.xls***. There we set up a table showing the beginning balance, the annual withdrawals, the annual earnings, and the ending balance for each of the 20 years. This analysis confirms the $68,674.09 initial end-of-year withdrawal derived previously.

Example 2: Initial Deposit to Accumulate a Future Sum

As another example of growing annuities, suppose you need to accumulate $100,000 in 10 years. You plan to make a deposit in a bank now, at Time 0, and then make 9 more deposits at the beginning of each of the following 9 years, for a total of 10 deposits. The bank pays 6% interest, you expect inflation to be 2% per year, and you plan to increase your annual deposits at the inflation rate. How much must you deposit initially? First, we calculate the real rate:

$$\text{Real rate} = r_r = [1.06/1.02] - 1.0 = 0.0392157 = 3.9215686\%$$

Next, since inflation is expected to be 2% per year, in 10 years the target \$100,000 will have a real value of

$$\$100{,}000/(1 + 0.02)^{10} = \$82{,}034.83.$$

Now we can find the size of the required initial payment by setting a financial calculator to the Begin Mode and then inputting N = 10, I/YR = 3.9215686, PV = 0, and FV = 82,034.83. Then, when we press the PMT key, we get PMT = −6,598.87. Thus, a deposit of \$6,598.87 made at time 0 and growing by 2% per year will accumulate to \$100,000 by Year 10 if the interest rate is 6%. Again, this result is confirmed in the chapter's ***Tool Kit.*** The key to this analysis is to express I/YR, FV, and PMT in real, not nominal, terms.

Self-Test

Differentiate between a "regular" and a "growing" annuity.

What three methods can be used to deal with growing annuities?

If the nominal interest rate is 10% and the expected inflation rate is 5%, what is the expected real rate of return? **(4.7619%)**

Summary

Most financial decisions involve situations in which someone makes a payment at one point in time and receives money later. Dollars paid or received at two different points in time are different, and this difference is dealt with using *time value of money (TVM) analysis.*

- **Compounding** is the process of determining the **future value (FV)** of a cash flow or a series of cash flows. The compounded amount, or future value, is equal to the beginning amount plus interest earned.
- Future value of a single payment = $FV_N = PV(1 + I)^N$.
- **Discounting** is the process of finding the **present value (PV)** of a future cash flow or a series of cash flows; discounting is the reciprocal, or reverse, of compounding.
- Present value of a payment received at the end of Time $N = PV = \dfrac{FV_N}{(I+I)^N}$.
- An **annuity** is defined as a series of equal periodic payments (PMT) for a specified number of periods.
- An annuity whose payments occur at the *end* of each period is called an **ordinary annuity.**
- Future value of an (ordinary) annuity $FVA_N = PMT\left[\dfrac{(1+I)^N}{I} - \dfrac{1}{I}\right]$.
- Present value of an (ordinary) annuity $PVA_N = PMT\left[\dfrac{1}{I} - \dfrac{1}{I(1+I)^N}\right]$.
- If payments occur at the *beginning* of the periods rather than at the end, then we have an **annuity due.** The PV of each payment is larger, because each payment is discounted back one year less, so the PV of the annuity is also larger. Similarly, the FV of the annuity due is larger because each payment is compounded for an extra year. The following formulas can be used to convert the PV and FV of an ordinary annuity to an annuity due:

$$PVA_{due} = PVA_{ordinary}(1 + I)$$
$$FVA_{due} = FVA_{ordinary}(1 + I)$$

- A **perpetuity** is an annuity with an infinite number of payments.

$$\text{Value of a perpetuity} = \frac{PMT}{I}$$

- To find the PV or FV of an uneven series, find the PV or FV of each individual cash flow and then sum them.
- If you know the cash flows and the PV (or FV) of a cash flow stream, you can **determine its interest rate.**
- When compounding occurs more frequently than once a year, the nominal rate must be converted to a periodic rate, and the number of years must be converted to periods:

$$\text{Periodic rate}(I_{PER}) = \text{Nominal annual rate} \div \text{Periods per year}$$
$$\text{Number of Periods} = \text{Years} \times \text{Periods per year}$$

The periodic rate and number of periods is used for calculations and is shown on time lines.

- If you are comparing the costs of alternative loans that require payments more than once a year, or the rates of return on investments that pay interest more than once a year, then the comparisons should be based on **effective** (or **equivalent) rates** of return. Here is the formula:

$$EAR = EFF\% = \left(1 + \frac{I_{NOM}}{M}\right)^{M} - 1.0$$

- The general equation for finding the future value of a current cash flow (PV) for any number of compounding periods per year is

$$FV_N = PV(1 + I_{PER})^{\text{Number of periods}} = PV\left(1 + \frac{I_{NOM}}{M}\right)^{MN}$$

where

$$I_{NOM} = \text{Nominal quoted interest rate}$$
$$M = \text{Number of compounding periods per year}$$
$$N = \text{Number of years}$$

- An **amortized loan** is one that is paid off with equal payments over a specified period. An **amortization schedule** shows how much of each payment constitutes interest, how much is used to reduce the principal, and the unpaid balance at the end of each period. The unpaid balance at Time N must be zero.
- A **"Growing Annuity"** is a stream of cash flows that grows at a constant rate for a specified number of years. The present and future values of growing annuities can be found with relatively complicated formulas or, more easily, with an *Excel* model.
- ***Web Extension 4A*** explains the **tabular approach.**
- ***Web Extension 4B*** provides derivations of the annuity formulas.
- ***Web Extension 4C*** explains **continuous compounding.**

Questions

(4–1) Define each of the following terms:

a. PV; I; INT; FV_N; PVA_N; FVA_N; PMT; M; I_{NOM}
b. Opportunity cost rate
c. Annuity; lump-sum payment; cash flow; uneven cash flow stream
d. Ordinary (or deferred) annuity; annuity due
e. Perpetuity; consol
f. Outflow; inflow; time line; terminal value
g. Compounding; discounting
h. Annual, semiannual, quarterly, monthly, and daily compounding
i. Effective annual rate (EAR or EFF%); nominal (quoted) interest rate; APR; periodic rate
j. Amortization schedule; principal versus interest component of a payment; amortized loan

(4–2) What is an *opportunity cost rate?* How is this rate used in discounted cash flow analysis, and where is it shown on a time line? Is the opportunity rate a single number that is used to evaluate all potential investments?

(4–3) An *annuity* is defined as a series of payments of a fixed amount for a specific number of periods. Thus, \$100 a year for 10 years is an annuity, but \$100 in Year 1, \$200 in Year 2, and \$400 in Years 3 through 10 does *not* constitute an annuity. However, the entire series *does contain* an annuity. Is this statement true or false?

(4–4) If a firm's earnings per share grew from \$1 to \$2 over a 10-year period, the *total growth* would be 100%, but the *annual growth rate* would be *less than* 10%. True or false? Explain.

(4–5) Would you rather have a savings account that pays 5% interest compounded semiannually or one that pays 5% interest compounded daily? Explain.

Self-Test Problems

Solutions Appear in Appendix A

(ST–1) Future Value

Assume that 1 year from now you plan to deposit \$1,000 in a savings account that pays a nominal rate of 8%.

a. If the bank compounds interest annually, how much will you have in your account 4 years from now?
b. What would your balance be 4 years from now if the bank used quarterly compounding rather than annual compounding?
c. Suppose you deposited the \$1,000 in 4 payments of \$250 each at the end of Years 1, 2, 3, and 4. How much would you have in your account at the end of Year 4, based on 8% annual compounding?
d. Suppose you deposited 4 equal payments in your account at the end of Years 1, 2, 3, and 4. Assuming an 8% interest rate, how large would each of your payments have to be for you to obtain the same ending balance as you calculated in part a?

(ST–2) Time Value of Money

Assume that 4 years from now you will need \$1,000. Your bank compounds interest at an 8% annual rate.

a. How much must you deposit 1 year from now to have a balance of $1,000 at Year 4?
b. If you want to make equal payments at the end of Years 1 through 4 to accumulate the $1,000, how large must each of the 4 payments be?
c. If your father were to offer either to make the payments calculated in part b ($221.92) or to give you a lump sum of $750 one year from now, which would you choose?
d. If you will have only $750 at the end of Year 1, what interest rate, compounded annually, would you have to earn to have the necessary $1,000 at Year 4?
e. Suppose you can deposit only $186.29 each at the end of Years 1 through 4, but you still need $1,000 at the end of Year 4. What interest rate, with annual compounding, is required to achieve your goal?
f. To help you reach your $1,000 goal, your father offers to give you $400 one year from now. You will get a part-time job and make 6 additional deposits of equal amounts each 6 months thereafter. If all of this money is deposited in a bank that pays 8%, compounded semiannually, how large must each of the 6 deposits be?
g. What is the effective annual rate being paid by the bank in part f?

(ST–3) Effective Annual Rates

Bank A pays 8% interest, compounded quarterly, on its money market account. The managers of Bank B want its money market account's effective annual rate to equal that of Bank A, but Bank B will compound interest on a monthly basis. What nominal, or quoted, rate must Bank B set?

Problems

Answers Appear in Appendix B

Easy Problems 1–8

(4–1) Future Value of a Single Payment

If you deposit $10,000 in a bank account that pays 10% interest annually, how much will be in your account after 5 years?

(4–2) Present Value of a Single Payment

What is the present value of a security that will pay $5,000 in 20 years if securities of equal risk pay 7% annually?

(4–3) Interest Rate on a Single Payment

Your parents will retire in 18 years. They currently have $250,000, and they think they will need $1 million at retirement. What annual interest rate must they earn to reach their goal, assuming they don't save any additional funds?

(4–4) Number of Periods of a Single Payment

If you deposit money today in an account that pays 6.5% annual interest, how long will it take to double your money?

(4–5) Number of Periods for an Annuity

You have $42,180.53 in a brokerage account, and you plan to deposit an additional $5,000 at the end of every future year until your account totals $250,000. You expect to earn 12% annually on the account. How many years will it take to reach your goal?

(4–6) Future Value: Ordinary Annuity versus Annuity Due

What is the future value of a 7%, 5-year ordinary annuity that pays $300 each year? If this were an annuity due, what would its future value be?

(4–7) Present and Future Value of an Uneven Cash Flow Stream

An investment will pay $100 at the end of each of the next 3 years, $200 at the end of Year 4, $300 at the end of Year 5, and $500 at the end of Year 6. If other investments of equal risk earn 8% annually, what is this investment's present value? Its future value?

(4-8) Annuity Payment and EAR

You want to buy a car, and a local bank will lend you $20,000. The loan would be fully amortized over 5 years (60 months), and the nominal interest rate would be 12%, with interest paid monthly. What is the monthly loan payment? What is the loan's EFF%?

INTERMEDIATE PROBLEMS 9–29

(4-9) Present and Future Values of Single Cash Flows for Different Periods

Find the following values, *using the equations*, and then work the problems using a financial calculator to check your answers. Disregard rounding differences. (*Hint:* If you are using a financial calculator, you can enter the known values and then press the appropriate key to find the unknown variable. Then, without clearing the TVM register, you can "override" the variable that changes by simply entering a new value for it and then pressing the key for the unknown variable to obtain the second answer. This procedure can be used in parts b and d, and in many other situations, to see how changes in input variables affect the output variable.)

a. An initial $500 compounded for 1 year at 6%
b. An initial $500 compounded for 2 years at 6%
c. The present value of $500 due in 1 year at a discount rate of 6%
d. The present value of $500 due in 2 years at a discount rate of 6%

(4-10) Present and Future Values of Single Cash Flows for Different Interest Rates

Use both the TVM equations and a financial calculator to find the following values. See the Hint for Problem 4-9.

a. An initial $500 compounded for 10 years at 6%
b. An initial $500 compounded for 10 years at 12%
c. The present value of $500 due in 10 years at a 6% discount rate
d. The present value of $500 due in 10 years at a 12% discount rate

(4-11) Time for a Lump Sum to Double

To the closest year, how long will it take $200 to double if it is deposited and earns the following rates? [*Notes:* (1) See the Hint for Problem 4-9. (2) This problem cannot be solved exactly with some financial calculators. For example, if you enter PV = –200, PMT = 0, FV = 400, and I = 7 in an HP-12C and then press the N key, you will get 11 years for part a. The correct answer is 10.2448 years, which rounds to 10, but the calculator rounds up. However, the HP-10B gives the exact answer.]

a. 7%
b. 10%
c. 18%
d. 100%

(4-12) Future Value of an Annuity

Find the *future value* of the following annuities. The first payment in these annuities is made at the *end* of Year 1, so they are *ordinary annuities.* (*Notes:* See the Hint to Problem 4-9. Also, note that you can leave values in the TVM register, switch to Begin Mode, press FV, and find the FV of the annuity due.)

a. $400 per year for 10 years at 10%
b. $200 per year for 5 years at 5%
c. $400 per year for 5 years at 0%
d. Now rework parts a, b, and c assuming that payments are made at the *beginning* of each year; that is, they are *annuities due.*

(4–13) Present Value of an Annuity

Find the *present value* of the following *ordinary annuities* (see the Notes to Problem 4-12).

a. $400 per year for 10 years at 10%
b. $200 per year for 5 years at 5%
c. $400 per year for 5 years at 0%
d. Now rework parts a, b, and c assuming that payments are made at the *beginning* of each year; that is, they are *annuities due.*

(4–14) Uneven Cash Flow Stream

Find the present values of the following cash flow streams. The appropriate interest rate is 8%. (*Hint:* It is fairly easy to work this problem dealing with the individual cash flows. However, if you have a financial calculator, read the section of the manual that describes how to enter cash flows such as the ones in this problem. This will take a little time, but the investment will pay huge dividends throughout the course. Note that, when working with the calculator's cash flow register, you must enter $CF_0 = 0$. Note also that it is quite easy to work the problem with *Excel*, using procedures described in the Chapter 4 ***Tool Kit***.)

Year	Cash Stream A	Cash Stream B
1	$100	$300
2	400	400
3	400	400
4	400	400
5	300	100

b. What is the value of each cash flow stream at a 0% interest rate?

(4–15) Effective Rate of Interest

Find the interest rate (or rates of return) in each of the following situations.

a. You *borrow* $700 and promise to pay back $749 at the end of 1 year.
b. You *lend* $700 and receive a promise to be paid $749 at the end of 1 year.
c. You borrow $85,000 and promise to pay back $201,229 at the end of 10 years.
d. You borrow $9,000 and promise to make payments of $2,684.80 at the end of each of the next 5 years.

(4–16) Future Value for Various Compounding Periods

Find the amount to which $500 will grow under each of the following conditions.

a. 12% compounded annually for 5 years
b. 12% compounded semiannually for 5 years
c. 12% compounded quarterly for 5 years
d. 12% compounded monthly for 5 years

(4–17) Present Value for Various Compounding Periods

Find the present value of $500 due in the future under each of the following conditions.

a. 12% nominal rate, semiannual compounding, discounted back 5 years
b. 12% nominal rate, quarterly compounding, discounted back 5 years
c. 12% nominal rate, monthly compounding, discounted back 1 year

(4–18) Future Value of an Annuity for Various Compounding Periods

Find the future values of the following ordinary annuities.

a. FV of $400 each 6 months for 5 years at a nominal rate of 12%, compounded semiannually
b. FV of $200 each 3 months for 5 years at a nominal rate of 12%, compounded quarterly

c. The annuities described in parts a and b have the same total amount of money paid into them during the 5-year period, and both earn interest at the same nominal rate, yet the annuity in part b earns $101.75 more than the one in part a over the 5 years. Why does this occur?

(4–19) Effective versus Nominal Interest Rates

Universal Bank pays 7% interest, compounded annually, on time deposits. Regional Bank pays 6% interest, compounded quarterly.

a. Based on effective interest rates, in which bank would you prefer to deposit your money?
b. Could your choice of banks be influenced by the fact that you might want to withdraw your funds during the year as opposed to at the end of the year? In answering this question, assume that funds must be left on deposit during an entire compounding period in order for you to receive any interest.

(4–20) Amortization Schedule

a. Set up an amortization schedule for a $25,000 loan to be repaid in equal installments at the end of each of the next 5 years. The interest rate is 10%.
b. How large must each annual payment be if the loan is for $50,000? Assume that the interest rate remains at 10% and that the loan is still paid off over 5 years.
c. How large must each payment be if the loan is for $50,000, the interest rate is 10%, and the loan is paid off in equal installments at the end of each of the next 10 years? This loan is for the same amount as the loan in part b, but the payments are spread out over twice as many periods. Why are these payments not half as large as the payments on the loan in part b?

(4–21) Growth Rates

Sales for Hanebury Corporation's just-ended year were $12 million. Sales were $6 million 5 years earlier.

a. At what rate did sales grow?
b. Suppose someone calculated the sales growth for Hanebury in part a as follows: "Sales doubled in 5 years. This represents a growth of 100% in 5 years; dividing 100% by 5 results in an estimated growth rate of 20% per year." Explain what is wrong with this calculation.

(4–22) Expected Rate of return

Washington-Pacific invested $4 million to buy a tract of land and plant some young pine trees. The trees can be harvested in 10 years, at which time W-P plans to sell the forest at an expected price of $8 million. What is W-P's expected rate of return?

(4–23) Effective Rate of Interest

A mortgage company offers to lend you $85,000; the loan calls for payments of $8,273.59 at the end of each year for 30 years. What interest rate is the mortgage company charging you?

(4–24) Required Lump-Sum Payment

To complete your last year in business school and then go through law school, you will need $10,000 per year for 4 years, starting next year (that is, you will need to withdraw the first $10,000 one year from today). Your rich uncle offers to put you through school, and he will deposit in a bank paying 7% interest a sum of money that is sufficient to provide the 4 payments of $10,000 each. His deposit will be made today.

a. How large must the deposit be?
b. How much will be in the account immediately after you make the first withdrawal? After the last withdrawal?

(4–25) Repaying a Loan

While Mary Corens was a student at the University of Tennessee, she borrowed \$12,000 in student loans at an annual interest rate of 9%. If Mary repays \$1,500 per year, then how long (to the nearest year) will it take her to repay the loan?

(4–26) Reaching a Financial Goal

You need to accumulate \$10,000. To do so, you plan to make deposits of \$1,250 per year—with the first payment being made a year from today—into a bank account that pays 12% annual interest. Your last deposit will be less than \$1,250 if less is needed to round out to \$10,000. How many years will it take you to reach your \$10,000 goal, and how large will the last deposit be?

(4–27) Present Value of a Perpetuity

What is the present value of a perpetuity of \$100 per year if the appropriate discount rate is 7%? If interest rates in general were to double and the appropriate discount rate rose to 14%, what would happen to the present value of the perpetuity?

(4–28) PV and Effective Annual Rate

Assume that you inherited some money. A friend of yours is working as an unpaid intern at a local brokerage firm, and her boss is selling securities that call for 4 payments of \$50 (1 payment at the end of each of the next 4 years) plus an extra payment of \$1,000 at the end of Year 4. Your friend says she can get you some of these securities at a cost of \$900 each. Your money is now invested in a bank that pays an 8% nominal (quoted) interest rate but with quarterly compounding. You regard the securities as being just as safe, and as liquid, as your bank deposit, so your required effective annual rate of return on the securities is the same as that on your bank deposit. You must calculate the value of the securities to decide whether they are a good investment. What is their present value to you?

(4–29) Loan Amortization

Assume that your aunt sold her house on December 31, and to help close the sale she took a second mortgage in the amount of \$10,000 as part of the payment. The mortgage has a quoted (or nominal) interest rate of 10%; it calls for payments every 6 months, beginning on June 30, and is to be amortized over 10 years. Now, 1 year later, your aunt must inform the IRS and the person who bought the house about the interest that was included in the two payments made during the year. (This interest will be income to your aunt and a deduction to the buyer of the house.) To the closest dollar, what is the total amount of interest that was paid during the first year?

Challenging Problems 30–34

(4–30) Loan Amortization

Your company is planning to borrow \$1 million on a 5-year, 15%, annual payment, fully amortized term loan. What fraction of the payment made at the end of the second year will represent repayment of principal?

(4–31) Nonannual Compounding

a. It is now January 1. You plan to make a total of 5 deposits of \$100 each, one every 6 months, with the first payment being made *today*. The bank pays a nominal interest rate of 12% but uses *semiannual* compounding. You plan to leave the money in the bank for 10 years. How much will be in your account after 10 years?

b. You must make a payment of \$1,432.02 in 10 years. To get the money for this payment, you will make 5 equal deposits, beginning today and for the following 4 quarters, in a bank that pays a nominal interest rate of 12% with *quarterly compounding*. How large must each of the 5 payments be?

(4–32) Nominal Rate of return

Anne Lockwood, manager of Oaks Mall Jewelry, wants to sell on credit, giving customers 3 months to pay. However, Anne will have to borrow from her bank to carry the accounts receivable. The bank will charge a nominal rate of 15% and will compound monthly. Anne wants to quote a nominal rate to her customers (all of whom are expected to pay on time) that will exactly offset her financing costs. What nominal annual rate should she quote to her credit customers?

(4–33) Required Annuity Payments

Assume that your father is now 50 years old, that he plans to retire in 10 years, and that he expects to live for 25 years after he retires—that is, until age 85. He wants his first retirement payment to have the same purchasing power at the time he retires as $40,000 has today. He wants all of his subsequent retirement payments to be equal to his first retirement payment. (Do not let the retirement payments grow with inflation: Your father realizes that the real value of his retirement income will decline year by year after he retires.) His retirement income will begin the day he retires, 10 years from today, and he will then receive 24 additional annual payments. Inflation is expected to be 5% per year from today forward. He currently has $100,000 saved up; and he expects to earn a return on his savings of 8% per year with annual compounding. To the nearest dollar, how much must he save during each of the next 10 years (with equal deposits being made at the end of each year, beginning a year from today) to meet his retirement goal? (*Note:* Neither the amount he saves nor the amount he withdraws upon retirement is a growing annuity.)

(4–34) Growing Annuity Payments

You want to accumulate $1 million by your retirement date, which is 25 years from now. You will make 25 deposits in your bank, with the first occurring *today*. The bank pays 8% interest, compounded annually. You expect to get annual raises of 3%, which will offset inflation, and you will let the amount you deposit each year also grow by 3% (i.e., your second deposit will be 3% greater than your first, the third will be 3% greater than the second, etc.). How much must your first deposit be if you are to meet your goal?

Spreadsheet Problem

(4-35) Build a Model: The Time Value of Money

See **Ch04 Tool Kit.xls** for all calculations.

Start with the partial model in the file ***Ch04 P35 Build a Model.xls*** from the textbook's Web site. Answer the following questions, using a spreadsheet model to do the calculations.

a. Find the FV of $1,000 invested to earn 10% annually 5 years from now. Answer this question first by using a math formula and then by using the *Excel* function wizard.
b. Now create a table that shows the FV at 0%, 5%, and 20% for 0, 1, 2, 3, 4, and 5 years. Then create a graph with years on the horizontal axis and FV on the vertical axis to display your results.
c. Find the PV of $1,000 due in 5 years if the discount rate is 10% per year. Again, work the problem with a formula and also by using the function wizard.
d. A security has a cost of $1,000 and will return $2,000 after 5 years. What rate of return does the security provide?
e. Suppose California's population is 30 million people and its population is expected to grow by 2% per year. How long would it take for the population to double?
f. Find the PV of an ordinary annuity that pays $1,000 at the end of each of the next 5 years if the interest rate is 15%. Then find the FV of that same annuity.
g. How would the PV and FV of the above annuity change if it were an annuity due rather than an ordinary annuity?
h. What would the FV and PV for parts a and c be if the interest rate were 10% with *semiannual* compounding rather than 10% with *annual* compounding?

i. Find the PV and FV of an investment that makes the following end-of-year payments. The interest rate is 8%.

Year	Payment
1	$100
2	200
3	400

j. Suppose you bought a house and took out a mortgage for $50,000. The interest rate is 8%, and you must amortize the loan over 10 years with equal end-of-year payments. Set up an amortization schedule that shows the annual payments and the amount of each payment that repays the principal and the amount that constitutes interest expense to the borrower and interest income to the lender.

1. Create a graph that shows how the payments are divided between interest and principal repayment over time.
2. Suppose the loan called for 10 years of monthly payments, 120 payments in all, with the same original amount and the same nominal interest rate. What would the amortization schedule show now?

Mini Case

Assume that you are nearing graduation and have applied for a job with a local bank. As part of the bank's evaluation process, you have been asked to take an examination that covers several financial analysis techniques. The first section of the test addresses discounted cash flow analysis. See how you would do by answering the following questions.

a. Draw time lines for (1) a $100 lump sum cash flow at the end of Year 2, (2) an ordinary annuity of $100 per year for 3 years, and (3) an uneven cash flow stream of –$50, $100, $75, and $50 at the end of Years 0 through 3.

b. 1. What's the *future value* of an initial $100 after 3 years if it is invested in an account paying 10% annual interest?
2. What's the *present value* of $100 to be received in 3 years if the appropriate interest rate is 10%?

c. We sometimes need to find out how long it will take a sum of money (or anything else) to grow to some specified amount. For example, if a company's sales are growing at a rate of 20% per year, how long will it take sales to double?

d. If you want an investment to double in 3 years, what interest rate must it earn?

e. What's the difference between an ordinary annuity and an annuity due? What type of annuity is shown below? How would you change the time line to show the other type of annuity?

f. 1. What's the future value of a 3-year ordinary annuity of $100 if the appropriate interest rate is 10%?
2. What's the present value of the annuity?
3. What would the future and present values be if the annuity were an annuity due?

g. What is the present value of the following uneven cash flow stream? The appropriate interest rate is 10%, compounded annually.

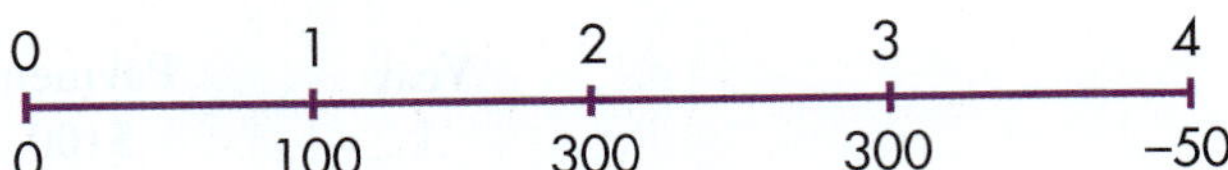

h. 1. Define the stated (quoted) or nominal rate I_{NOM} as well as the periodic rate I_{PER}.

2. Will the future value be larger or smaller if we compound an initial amount more often than annually—for example, every 6 months, or *semiannually*—holding the stated interest rate constant? Why?

3. What is the future value of $100 after 5 years under 12% annual compounding? Semiannual compounding? Quarterly compounding? Monthly compounding? Daily compounding?

4. What is the effective annual rate (EAR or EFF%)? What is the EFF% for a nominal rate of 12%, compounded semiannually? Compounded quarterly? Compounded monthly? Compounded daily?

i. Will the effective annual rate ever be equal to the nominal (quoted) rate?

j. 1. Construct an amortization schedule for a $1,000, 10% annual rate loan with 3 equal installments.

2. During Year 2, what is the annual interest expense for the borrower, and what is the annual interest income for the lender?

k. Suppose that on January 1 you deposit $100 in an account that pays a nominal (or quoted) interest rate of 11.33463%, with interest added (compounded) daily. How much will you have in your account on October 1, or 9 months later?

l. 1. What is the value at the end of Year 3 of the following cash flow stream if the quoted interest rate is 10%, compounded semiannually?

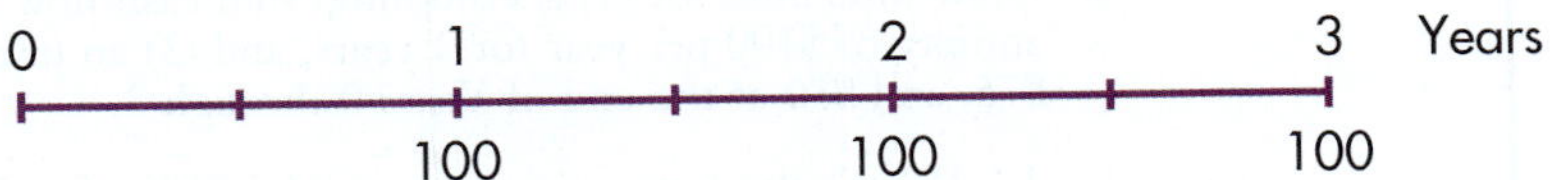

2. What is the PV of the same stream?

3. Is the stream an annuity?

4. An important rule is that you should never show a nominal rate on a time line or use it in calculations unless what condition holds? (*Hint:* Think of annual compounding, when I_{NOM} = EFF% = I_{PER}.) What would be wrong with your answers to parts (1) and (2) if you used the nominal rate of 10% rather than the periodic rate, $I_{NOM}/2$ = 10%/2 = 5%?

m. Suppose someone offered to sell you a note calling for the payment of $1,000 in 15 months. They offer to sell it to you for $850. You have $850 in a bank time deposit that pays a 6.76649% nominal rate with daily compounding, which is a 7% effective annual interest rate, and you plan to leave the money in the bank unless you buy the note. The note is not risky—you are sure it will be paid on schedule. Should you buy the note? Check the decision in three ways: (1) by comparing your future value if you buy the note versus leaving your money in the bank; (2) by comparing the PV of the note with your current bank account; and (3) by comparing the EFF% on the note with that of the bank account.

CHAPTER 5

Bonds, Bond Valuation, and Interest Rates

A lot of U.S. bonds have been issued, and we mean a lot! *According to the Federal Reserve, there are about $5.7 trillion of outstanding U.S. Treasury securities, more than $2.6 trillion of municipal securities, $3.7 trillion of corporate bonds, and more than $1.4 billion of foreign bonds held in the United States. Not only is the dollar amount mind-boggling, but so is the variety. Bonds come in many shapes and flavors, and one even has a negative interest rate.*

How can a bond have a negative rate? First, consider a bond that makes no payments before it comes due. For example, an investor might buy a bond today for $558 in exchange for the promise of $1,000 in 10 years. The investor would not receive any cash interest payments, but the 10-year increase from the original purchase price to the $1,000 repayment would provide a 6% annual return on the investment. Although there are no annual cash interest payments, the government still allows corporate issuers to deduct an imputed annual interest expense from their taxable income based on the bond's annual appreciation in value. Thus, the company gets a tax deduction each year, even though it isn't making actual interest payments.

Berkshire Hathaway (chaired by Warren Buffett) issued bonds with a negative *interest rate in 2002. Technically, Berkshire's bonds called for a 3% interest payment, but they also had an attached warrant that would allow an investor to purchase shares of Berkshire Hathaway stock at a fixed price in the future. If the stock price rises above the specified price, then investors can profit by exercising the warrants. However, Berkshire Hathaway didn't just give away the warrants—it required investors to make annual installment payments equal to 3.75% of the bond's face value. Thus, investors receive a 3% interest payment but must then pay a 3.75% warrant fee, for a net interest rate of negative 0.75%. Berkshire Hathaway can deduct the 3% interest payment for tax purposes, but the 3.75% warrant fee is not taxable, further increasing Berkshire Hathaway's annual after-tax cash flow.*

Think about the implications of these and other bonds as you read this chapter.

Source: "*Flow of Funds Accounts of the United States, Section L.2, Credit Market Debt Owed by Nonfinancial Sectors,*" ***http://www.federalreserve.gov/releases/Z1/current/***.

Intrinsic Value and the Cost of Debt

This chapter explains bond pricing and bond risk, which affect the return demanded by a firm's bondholders. A bondholder's return is a cost from the company's point of view. This cost of debt affects the firm's weighted average cost of capital (WACC), which in turn affects the company's intrinsic value. Therefore, it is important for all managers to understand the cost of debt, which we explain in this chapter.

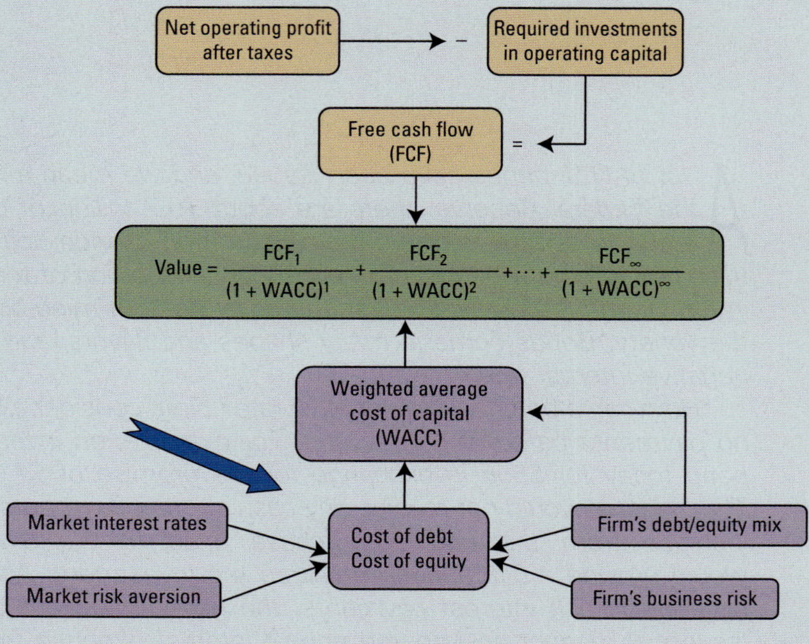

Growing companies must acquire land, buildings, equipment, inventory, and other operating assets. The debt markets are a major source of funding for such purchases. Therefore, every manager should have a working knowledge of the types of bonds that companies and government agencies issue, the terms that are contained in bond contracts, the types of risks to which both bond investors and issuers are exposed, and procedures for determining the values of and rates of return on bonds.

resource

The textbook's Web site contains an Excel file that will guide you through the chapter's calculations. The file for this chapter is **Ch05 Tool Kit.xls**, *and we encourage you to open the file and follow along as you read the chapter.*

5.1 Who Issues Bonds?

A **bond** is a long-term contract under which a borrower agrees to make payments of interest and principal, on specific dates, to the holders of the bond. For example, on January 5, 2011, MicroDrive Inc. borrowed \$50 million by issuing \$50 million of bonds. For convenience, we assume that MicroDrive sold 50,000 individual bonds for \$1,000 each. Actually, it could have sold one \$50 million bond, 10 bonds with a \$5 million face value, or any other combination that totals to \$50 million. In any event, MicroDrive received the \$50 million, and in exchange it promised to make annual interest payments and to repay the \$50 million on a specified maturity date.

Investors have many choices when investing in bonds, but bonds are classified into four main types: Treasury, corporate, municipal, and foreign. Each type differs with respect to expected return and degree of risk.

Treasury bonds, sometimes referred to as *government bonds*, are issued by the U.S. federal government.[1] It is reasonable to assume that the federal government will make good on its promised payments, so these bonds have almost no default risk. However, Treasury bond prices decline when interest rates rise, so they are not free of all risks.

Federal agencies and other government-sponsored entities (GSEs) include the Tennessee Valley Authority, the Small Business Administration, Fannie Mae, Freddie Mac, and the Federal Home Loan Bank System, among others. **Agency debt** and **GSE debt** are not officially backed by the full faith and credit of the U.S. government, but investors assume that the government implicitly guarantees this debt, so these bonds carry interest rates only slightly higher than Treasury bonds. In 2008, the implicit guarantee became much more explicit as the government placed several GSEs into conservatorship, including Fannie Mae and Freddie Mac.

Corporate bonds, as the name implies, are issued by corporations. Unlike Treasury bonds, corporate bonds are exposed to default risk—if the issuing company gets into trouble, it may be unable to make the promised interest and principal payments. Different corporate bonds have different levels of default risk, depending on the issuing company's characteristics and the terms of the specific bond. Default risk is often referred to as "credit risk," and the larger the credit risk, the higher the interest rate the issuer must pay.

Municipal bonds, or "munis," are issued by state and local governments. Like corporate bonds, munis have default risk. However, munis offer one major advantage: The interest earned on most municipal bonds is exempt from federal taxes and also from state taxes if the holder is a resident of the issuing state. Consequently, municipal bonds carry interest rates that are considerably lower than those on corporate bonds with the same default risk.

Foreign bonds are issued by foreign governments or foreign corporations. Foreign corporate bonds are, of course, exposed to default risk, and so are some foreign government bonds. An additional risk exists if the bonds are denominated in a currency other than that of the investor's home currency. For example, if a U.S. investor purchases a corporate bond denominated in Japanese yen and if the yen subsequently falls relative to the dollar, then the investor will lose money even if the company does not default on its bonds.

Self-Test

What is a bond?
What are the four main types of bonds?
Why are U.S. Treasury bonds not riskless?
To what types of risk are investors of foreign bonds exposed?

5.2 Key Characteristics of Bonds

Although all bonds have some common characteristics, they do not always have identical contractual features, as described below.

[1] The U.S. Treasury actually issues three types of securities: "bills," "notes," and "bonds." A bond makes an equal payment every 6 months until it matures, at which time it makes an additional lump-sum payment. If the maturity at the time of issue is less than 10 years, the security is called a note rather than a bond. A T-bill has a maturity of 52 weeks or less at the time of issue, and it makes no payments at all until it matures. Thus, T-bills are sold initially at a discount to their face, or maturity, value.

THE GLOBAL ECONOMIC CRISIS

Betting With or Against the U.S. Government: The Case of Treasury Bond Credit Default Swaps

It might be hard to believe, but there is actually a market for U.S. Treasury bond insurance. In early 2009, a credit default swap (CDS) on a 5-year T-bond was selling for 71 basis points (a basis point is 1 percentage point). This means that you could pay $7.10 a year to a counterparty who would promise to insure $1,000 of T-bond principal against default. Considering that the T-bond pays only $18.75 a year in interest, the insurance would eat up a lot of the annual interest for an investor who owned the bond. However, most of the trading in this CDS is by speculators and hedgers who don't even own the T-bond but are simply betting for or against the financial soundness of the U.S. government.

But it does make you wonder: "If the United States fails, who will be around to pay off the CDS?"!

Par Value

The **par value** is the stated face value of the bond; for illustrative purposes, we generally assume a par value of $1,000. In practice, some bonds have par values that are multiples of $1,000 (for example, $5,000) and some have par values of less than $1,000 (Treasury bonds can be purchased in multiples of $100). The par value generally represents the amount of money the firm borrows and promises to repay on the maturity date.

An excellent site for information on many types of bonds is the Yahoo! Finance bond site, which can be found at **http://finance.yahoo.com/bonds**. *The site has a great deal of information about corporates, municipals, Treasuries, and bond funds. It includes free bond searches, through which the user specifies the attributes desired in a bond and then the search returns the publicly traded bonds meeting the criteria. The site also includes a bond calculator and an excellent glossary of bond terminology.*

Coupon Interest Rate

MicroDrive's bonds require the company to pay a fixed number of dollars of interest every year (or, more typically, every 6 months). When this **coupon payment,** as it is called, is divided by the par value, the result is the **coupon interest rate.** For example, MicroDrive's bonds have a $1,000 par value, and they pay $100 in interest each year. The bond's coupon interest is $100, so its coupon interest rate is $100/$1,000 = 10%. The coupon payment, which is fixed at the time the bond is issued, remains in force during the life of the bond.[2] Typically, at the time a bond is issued, its coupon payment is set at a level that will enable the bond to be issued at or near its par value.

In some cases, a bond's coupon payment will vary over time. For these **floating-rate bonds,** the coupon rate is set for, say, the initial 6-month period, after which it is adjusted every 6 months based on some market rate. Some corporate issues are tied to the Treasury bond rate; other issues are tied to other rates, such as LIBOR (the London Interbank Offered Rate). Many additional provisions can be included in floating-rate issues. For example, some are convertible to fixed-rate debt, whereas others have upper and lower limits ("caps" and "floors") on how high or low the rate can go.

Floating-rate debt is popular with investors who are worried about the risk of rising interest rates, since the interest paid on such bonds increases whenever market

[2]At one time, bonds literally had a number of small coupons attached to them, and on each interest payment date the owner would clip off the coupon for that date and either cash it at the bank or mail it to the company's paying agent, who would then mail back a check for the interest. For example, a 30-year, semiannual bond would start with 60 coupons. Today, most new bonds are *registered*—no physical coupons are involved, and interest checks are mailed automatically to the registered owners.

rates rise. This causes the market value of the debt to be stabilized, and it also provides institutional buyers, such as banks, with income that is better geared to their own obligations. Banks' deposit costs rise with interest rates, so the income on floating-rate loans they have made rises at the same time as their deposit costs rise. The savings and loan industry was almost destroyed as a result of its former practice of making fixed-rate mortgage loans but borrowing on floating-rate terms. If you are earning 6% fixed but paying 10% floating (which they were), you will soon go bankrupt (which they did). Moreover, floating-rate debt appeals to corporations that want to issue long-term debt without committing themselves to paying a historically high interest rate for the entire life of the loan.

For more on zero coupon bonds, including U.S. Treasury STRIP bonds, see **Web Extension 5A** *on the textbook's Web site.*

Some bonds pay no coupons at all but are offered at a substantial discount below their par values and hence provide capital appreciation rather than interest income. These securities are called **zero coupon bonds** ("zeros"). Most zero coupon bonds are Treasury bonds, although a few corporations, such as Coca-Cola, have zero coupon bonds outstanding. Some bonds are issued with a coupon rate too low for the bond to be issued at par, so the bond is issued at a price less than its par value. In general, any bond originally offered at a price significantly below its par value is called an **original issue discount (OID) bond**.

Some bonds don't pay cash coupons but pay coupons consisting of additional bonds (or a percentage of an additional bond). These are called **payment-in-kind bonds,** or just **PIK bonds**. PIK bonds are usually issued by companies with cash flow problems, which makes them risky.

Some bonds have a step-up provision: If the company's bond rating is downgraded, then it must increase the bond's coupon rate. Step-ups are more popular in Europe than in the United States, but that is beginning to change. Note that a step-up is quite dangerous from the company's standpoint. The downgrade means that it is having trouble servicing its debt, and the step-up will exacerbate the problem. This combination has led to a number of bankruptcies.

Maturity Date

Bonds generally have a specified **maturity date** on which the par value must be repaid. MicroDrive bonds issued on January 5, 2011, will mature on January 5, 2026; thus, they have a 15-year maturity at the time they are issued. Most bonds have **original maturities** (the maturity at the time the bond is issued) ranging from 10 to 40 years, but any maturity is legally permissible.[3] Of course, the effective maturity of a bond declines each year after it has been issued. Thus, MicroDrive's bonds have a 15-year original maturity, but in 2012, a year later, they will have a 14-year maturity, and so on.

Provisions to Call or Redeem Bonds

Most corporate bonds contain a **call provision**, which gives the issuing corporation the right to call the bonds for redemption.[4] The call provision generally states that the company must pay the bondholders an amount greater than the par value if they are called. The additional sum, which is termed a **call premium**, is often set equal to 1 year's interest if the bonds are called during the first year, and the

[3] In July 1993, Walt Disney Co., attempting to lock in a low interest rate, issued the first 100-year bonds to be sold by any borrower in modern times. Soon after, Coca-Cola became the second company to stretch the meaning of "long-term bond" by selling $150 million of 100-year bonds.

[4] A majority of municipal bonds also contain call provisions. Although the U.S. Treasury no longer issues callable bonds, some past Treasury issues were callable.

premium declines at a constant rate of INT/N each year thereafter (where INT = annual interest and N = original maturity in years). For example, the call premium on a $1,000 par value, 10-year, 10% bond would generally be $100 if it were called during the first year, $90 during the second year (calculated by reducing the $100, or 10%, premium by one-tenth), and so on. However, bonds are often not callable until several years (generally 5 to 10) after they are issued. This is known as a **deferred call**, and the bonds are said to have **call protection**.

Suppose a company sold bonds when interest rates were relatively high. Provided the issue is callable, the company could sell a new issue of low-yielding securities if and when interest rates drop. It could then use the proceeds of the new issue to retire the high-rate issue and thus reduce its interest expense. This process is called a **refunding operation.**

A call provision is valuable to the firm but potentially detrimental to investors. If interest rates go up, the company will not call the bond, and the investor will be stuck with the original coupon rate on the bond, even though interest rates in the economy have risen sharply. However, if interest rates fall, the company *will* call the bond and pay off investors, who then must reinvest the proceeds at the current market interest rate, which is lower than the rate they were getting on the original bond. In other words, the investor loses when interest rates go up but doesn't reap the gains when rates fall. To induce an investor to take this type of risk, a new issue of callable bonds must provide a higher coupon rate than an otherwise similar issue of noncallable bonds.

Bonds that are **redeemable at par** at the holder's option protect investors against a rise in interest rates. If rates rise, the price of a fixed-rate bond declines. However, if holders have the option of turning their bonds in and having them redeemed at par, then they are protected against rising rates. If interest rates have risen, holders will turn in the bonds and reinvest the proceeds at a higher rate.

Event risk is the chance that some sudden event will occur and increase the credit risk of a company, hence lowering the firm's bond rating and the value of its outstanding bonds. Investors' concern over event risk means that those firms deemed most likely to face events that could harm bondholders must pay extremely high interest rates. To reduce this interest rate, some bonds have a covenant called a **super poison put,** which enables a bondholder to turn in, or "put," a bond back to the issuer at par in the event of a takeover, merger, or major recapitalization.

Some bonds have a **make-whole call provision.** This allows a company to call the bond, but it must pay a call price that is essentially equal to the market value of a similar noncallable bond. This provides companies with an easy way to repurchase bonds as part of a financial restructuring, such as a merger.

Sinking Funds

Some bonds include a **sinking fund provision** that facilitates the orderly retirement of the bond issue. On rare occasions the firm may be required to deposit money with a trustee, which invests the funds and then uses the accumulated sum to retire the bonds when they mature. Usually, though, the sinking fund is used to buy back a certain percentage of the issue each year. A failure to meet the sinking fund requirement causes the bond to be thrown into default, which may force the company into bankruptcy.

In most cases, the firm is given the right to administer the sinking fund in either of two ways.

1. The company can call in for redemption (at par value) a certain percentage of the bonds each year; for example, it might be able to call 5% of the total original amount of the issue at a price of $1,000 per bond. The bonds are numbered serially, and those called for redemption are determined by a lottery administered by the trustee.
2. The company may buy the required number of bonds on the open market.

The firm will choose the least-cost method. If interest rates have risen, causing bond prices to fall, then it will buy bonds in the open market at a discount; if interest rates have fallen, it will call the bonds. Note that a call for sinking fund purposes is quite different from a refunding call as discussed previously. A sinking fund call typically requires no call premium, but only a small percentage of the issue is normally callable in any one year.[5]

Although sinking funds are designed to protect bondholders by ensuring that an issue is retired in an orderly fashion, you should recognize that sinking funds can work to the detriment of bondholders. For example, suppose that the bond carries a 10% interest rate but that yields on similar bonds have fallen to 7.5%. A sinking fund call at par would require an investor to give up a bond that pays $100 of interest and then to reinvest in a bond that pays only $75 per year. This obviously harms those bondholders whose bonds are called. On balance, however, bonds that have a sinking fund are regarded as being safer than those without such a provision, so at the time they are issued sinking fund bonds have lower coupon rates than otherwise similar bonds without sinking funds.

Other Provisions and Features

Owners of **convertible bonds** have the option to convert the bonds into a fixed number of shares of common stock. Convertibles offer investors the chance to share in the upside if a company does well, so investors are willing to accept a lower coupon rate on convertibles than on an otherwise identical but nonconvertible bond.

Warrants are options that permit the holder to buy stock at a fixed price, thereby providing a gain if the price of the stock rises. Some bonds are issued with warrants. As with convertibles, bonds with warrants have lower coupon rates than straight bonds.

An **income bond** is required to pay interest only if earnings are high enough to cover the interest expense. If earnings are not sufficient, then the company is not required to pay interest and the bondholders do not have the right to force the company into bankruptcy. Therefore, from an investor's standpoint, income bonds are riskier than "regular" bonds.

Indexed bonds, also called **purchasing power bonds,** first became popular in Brazil, Israel, and a few other countries plagued by high inflation rates. The interest payments and maturity payment rise automatically when the inflation rate rises, thus protecting the bondholders against inflation. In January 1997, the U.S. Treasury began issuing indexed bonds called TIPS, short for Treasury Inflation-Protected Securities. Later in this chapter we show how TIPS can be used to estimate the risk-free rate.

Bond Markets

Corporate bonds are traded primarily in electronic/telephone markets rather than in organized exchanges. Most bonds are owned by and traded among a relatively small

[5]Some sinking funds require the issuer to pay a call premium.

number of very large financial institutions, including banks, investment banks, life insurance companies, mutual funds, and pension funds. Although these institutions buy and sell very large blocks of bonds, it is relatively easy for bond dealers to arrange transactions because there are relatively few players in this market as compared with stock markets.

Information on bond trades is not widely published, but a representative group of bonds is listed and traded on the bond division of the NYSE and is reported on the bond market page of *The Wall Street Journal.* Bond data are also available on the Internet at sites such as **http://finance.yahoo.com**.

Self-Test

Define "floating-rate bonds" and "zero coupon bonds."

Why is a call provision advantageous to a bond issuer?

What are the two ways a sinking fund can be handled? Which method will be chosen by the firm if interest rates have risen? If interest rates have fallen?

Are securities that provide for a sinking fund regarded as being riskier than those without this type of provision? Explain.

What are income bonds and indexed bonds?

Why do bonds with warrants and convertible bonds have lower coupons than similarly rated bonds that do not have these features?

5.3 Bond Valuation

The value of any financial asset—a stock, a bond, a lease, or even a physical asset such as an apartment building or a piece of machinery—is simply the present value of the cash flows the asset is expected to produce. The cash flows from a specific bond depend on its contractual features as described in the previous section. For a standard coupon-bearing bond such as the one issued by MicroDrive, the cash flows consist of interest payments during the life of the bond plus the amount borrowed when the bond matures (usually a $1,000 par value):

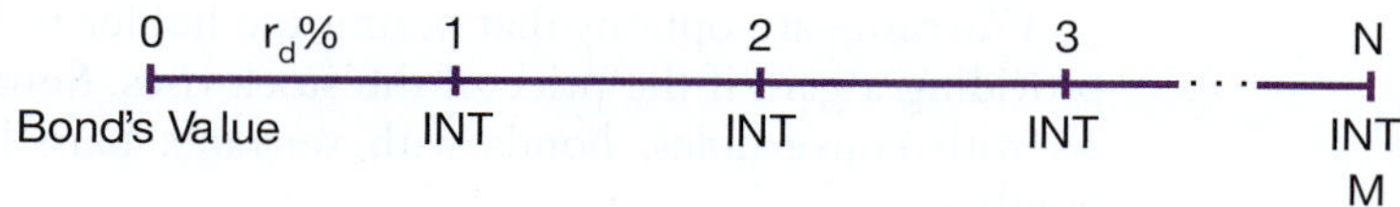

The notation in the time line is explained below.

r_d = The bond's required rate of return, which is the market rate of interest for that type of bond. This is the discount rate that is used to calculate the present value of the bond's cash flows. It is also called the "yield" or "going rate of interest." Note that r_d is *not* the coupon interest rate. It is equal to the coupon rate only if (as in this case) the bond is selling at par. Generally, most coupon bonds are issued at par, which implies that the coupon rate is set at r_d. Thereafter, interest rates, as measured by r_d, will fluctuate, but the coupon rate is fixed, so r_d will equal the coupon rate only by chance. We use the term "i" or "I" to designate the interest rate for many calculations because those terms are used on financial calculators, but "r," with the subscript "d" to designate the rate on a debt security, is normally used in finance.

N = Number of years before the bond matures. Note that N declines each year after the bond was issued, so a bond that had a maturity of 15 years when it was issued (original maturity = 15) will have N = 14 after 1 year, N = 13 after 2 years, and so on. Note also that for the sake of simplicity we assume the bond pays interest once a year, or annually, so N is measured in years. We consider bonds with semiannual payment bonds later in the chapter.

INT = Dollars of interest paid each year = (Coupon rate)(Par value). For a bond with a 10% coupon and a $1,000 par value, the annual interest is 0.10($1,000) = $100. In calculator terminology, INT = PMT = 100. If the bond had been a semiannual payment bond, the payment would have been $50 every 6 months.

M = Par, or maturity, value of the bond. This amount must be paid off at maturity, and it is often equal to $1,000.

The following general equation, written in several forms, can be used to find the value of any bond, V_B:

$$\begin{aligned} V_B &= \frac{INT}{(1+r_d)^1} + \frac{INT}{(1+r_d)^2} + \cdots + \frac{INT}{(1+r_d)^N} + \frac{M}{(1+r_d)^N} \\ &= \sum_{t=1}^{N} \frac{INT}{(1+r_d)^t} + \frac{M}{(1+r_d)^N} \\ &= INT\left[\frac{1}{r_d} - \frac{1}{r_d(1+r_d)^N}\right] + \frac{M}{(1+r_d)^N} \end{aligned} \tag{5-1}$$

Observe that the cash flows consist of an annuity of N years plus a lump-sum payment at the end of Year N. Equation 5-1 can be solved by using (1) a formula, (2) a financial calculator, or (3) a spreadsheet.

Solving for the Bond Price

Recall that MicroDrive issued a 15-year bond with an annual coupon rate of 10% and a par value of $1,000. To find the value of MicroDrive's bond by using a formula, insert values for MicroDrive's bond into Equation 5-1:

$$\begin{aligned} V_B &= \sum_{t=1}^{15} \frac{\$100}{(1+0.10)^t} + \frac{\$1,000}{(1+0.10)^{15}} \\ &= \$100\left[\frac{1}{0.10} - \frac{1}{0.10(1+0.10)^{15}}\right] + \frac{\$1,000}{(1+0.10)^{15}} \\ &= \$1,000 \end{aligned} \tag{5-1a}$$

You could use the first line of Equation 5-1a to discount each cash flow back to the present and then sum these PVs to find the bond's value; see Figure 5-1. This procedure is not very efficient, especially if the bond has many years to maturity.

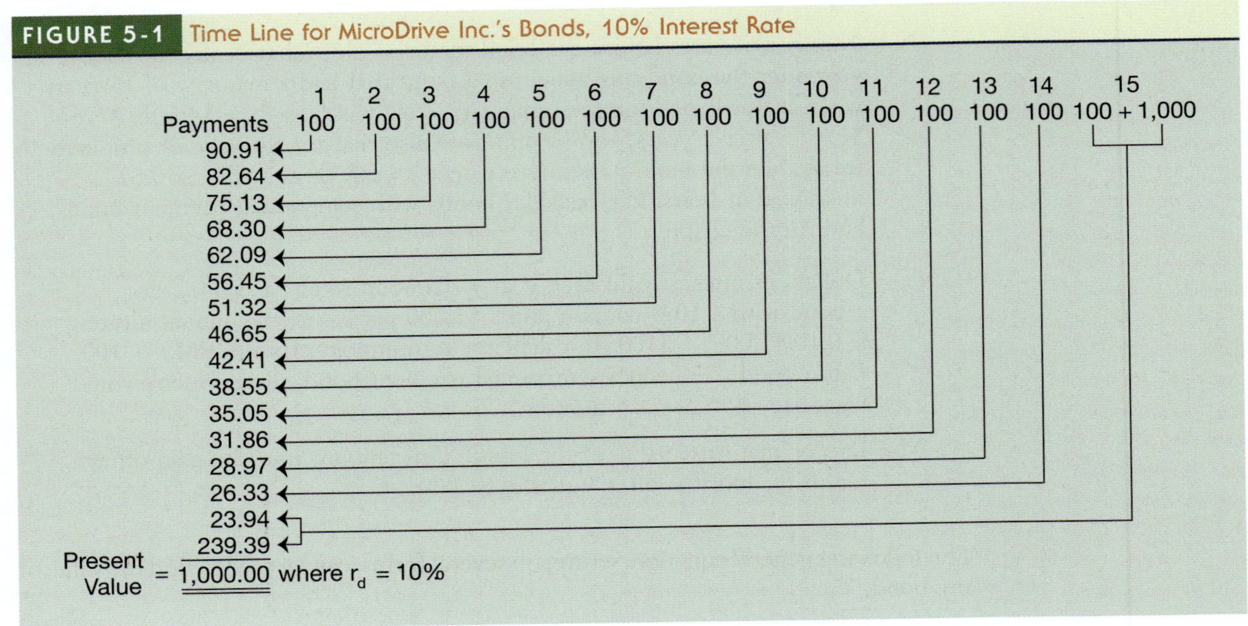

FIGURE 5-1 Time Line for MicroDrive Inc.'s Bonds, 10% Interest Rate

Alternatively, you could use the formula in the second line of Equation 5-1a with a simple or scientific calculator, although this would still be somewhat cumbersome.

A financial calculator is ideally suited for finding bond values. Here is the setup for MicroDrive's bond:

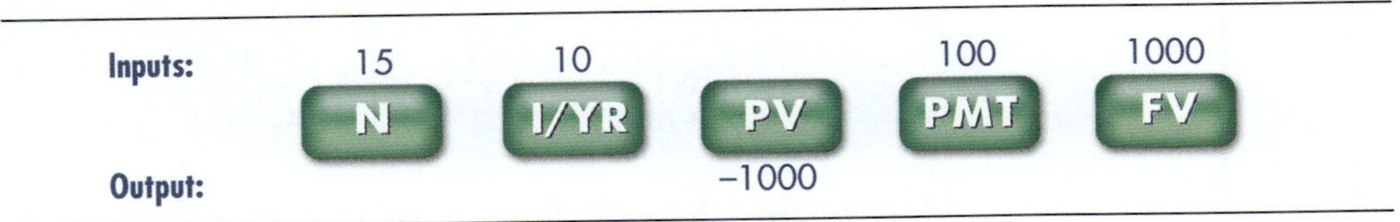

Input N = 15, I/YR = r_d = 10, INT = PMT = 100, and M = FV = 1000; then press the PV key to find the value of the bond, $1,000. Since the PV is an outflow to the investor, it is shown with a negative sign. The calculator is programmed to solve Equation 5-1: It finds the PV of an annuity of $100 per year for 15 years, discounted at 10%, then it finds the PV of the $1,000 maturity payment, and then it adds these two PVs to find the value of the bond. Notice that even though the time line in Figure 5-1 shows a total of $1,100 at Year 15, you should not enter FV = 1100! When you entered N = 15 and PMT = 100, you told the calculator that there is a $100 payment at Year 15. Thus, setting FV = 1000 accounts for any *extra* payment at Year 15, above and beyond the $100 payment.

With *Excel*, it is easiest to use the PV function: **=PV(I,N,PMT,FV,0)**. For MicroDrive's bond, the function is **=PV(0.10,15,100,1000,0)** with a result of –$1,000. Like the financial calculator solution, the bond value is negative because PMT and FV are positive.

Excel also provides specialized functions for bond prices based on actual dates. For example, in *Excel* you could find the MicroDrive bond value as of the date it was issued by using the function wizard to enter this formula:

=PRICE(DATE(2011,1,5),DATE(2026,1,5),10%,10%,100,1,1)

The first two arguments in the function are *Excel's* DATE function. The DATE function takes the year, month, and day as inputs and converts them into a date. The first argument is the date on which you want to find the price, and the second argument is the maturity date. The third argument in the PRICE function is the bond's coupon rate, followed by the required return on the bond, r_d. The fifth argument, 100, is the redemption value of the bond at maturity per $100 of face value; entering "100" means that the bond pays 100% of its face value when it matures. The sixth argument is the number of payments per year. The last argument, 1, tells the program to base the price on the actual number of days in each month and year. This function produces a result based upon a face value of $100. In other words, if the bond pays $100 of face value at maturity, then the PRICE function result is the price of the bond. Because MicroDrive's bond pays $1,000 of face value at maturity, we must multiply the PRICE function's result by 10. In this example, the PRICE function returns a result of $100. When we multiply it by 10, we get the actual price of $1,000. This function is essential if a bond is being evaluated between coupon payment dates. See ***Ch05 Tool Kit.xls*** on the textbook's Web site for an example.[6]

Interest Rate Changes and Bond Prices

In this example, the bond is selling at a price equal to its par value. Whenever the going market rate of interest, r_d, is equal to the coupon rate, a *fixed-rate* bond will sell at its par value. Normally, the coupon rate is set at the going rate when a bond is issued, causing it to sell at par initially.

The coupon rate remains fixed after the bond is issued, but interest rates in the market move up and down. Looking at Equation 5-1, we see that an *increase* in the market interest rate (r_d) will cause the price of an outstanding bond to *fall*, whereas a *decrease* in rates will cause the bond's price to *rise*. For example, if the market interest rate on MicroDrive's bond increased to 15% immediately after it was issued, we would recalculate the price with the new market interest rate as follows:

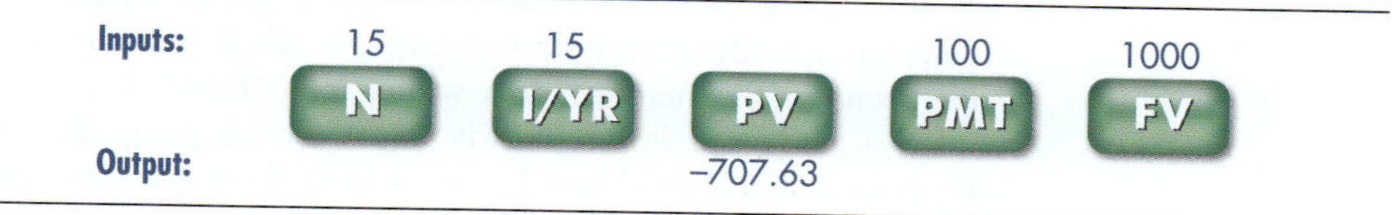

The price would fall to $707.63. Notice that the bond would then sell at a price below its par value. Whenever the going rate of interest *rises above* the coupon rate, a fixed-rate bond's price will *fall below* its par value, and it is called a **discount bond.**

[6]The bond prices quoted by brokers are calculated as described. However, if you bought a bond between interest payment dates, you would have to pay the basic price plus accrued interest. Thus, if you purchased a MicroDrive bond 6 months after it was issued, your broker would send you an invoice stating that you must pay $1,000 as the basic price of the bond plus $50 interest, representing one-half the annual interest of $100. The seller of the bond would receive $1,050. If you bought the bond the day before its interest payment date, you would pay $1,000 + (364/365)($100) = $1,099.73. Of course, you would receive an interest payment of $100 at the end of the next day. For more on the valuation of bonds between payment dates, see Richard Taylor, "The Valuation of Semiannual Bonds between Interest Payment Dates," *The Financial Review*, August 1988, pp. 365–368, and K. S. Maurice Tse and Mark A. White, "The Valuation of Semiannual Bonds between Interest Payment Dates: A Correction," *Financial Review*, November 1990, pp. 659–662.

On the other hand, bond prices rise when market interest rates fall. For example, if the market interest rate on MicroDrive's bond decreased to 5%, then we would once again recalculate its price:

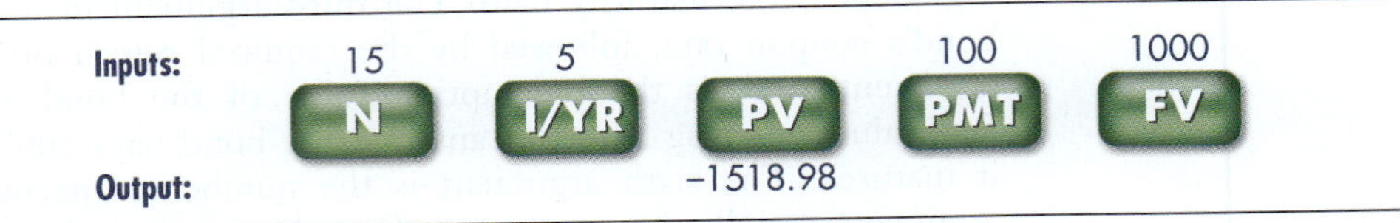

In this case, the price rises to $1,518.98. In general, whenever the going interest rate *falls below* the coupon rate, a fixed-rate bond's price will *rise above* its par value, and it is called a **premium bond.**

Self-Test

Why do the prices of fixed-rate bonds fall if expectations for inflation rise?

What is a discount bond? A premium bond?

A bond that matures in 6 years has a par value of $1,000, an annual coupon payment of $80, and a market interest rate of 9%. What is its price? **($955.14)**

A bond that matures in 18 years has a par value of $1,000, an annual coupon of 10%, and a market interest rate of 7%. What is its price? **($1,301.77)**

5.4 Changes in Bond Values over Time

At the time a coupon bond is issued, the coupon is generally set at a level that will cause the market price of the bond to equal its par value. If a lower coupon were set then investors would not be willing to pay $1,000 for the bond, and if a higher coupon were set then investors would clamor for the bond and bid its price up over $1,000. Investment bankers can judge quite precisely the coupon rate that will cause a bond to sell at its $1,000 par value.

A bond that has just been issued is known as a **new issue.** (Investment bankers classify a bond as a new issue for about a month after it has first been issued. New issues are usually actively traded and are called "on-the-run" bonds.) Once the bond has been on the market for a while, it is classified as an **outstanding bond,** also called a **seasoned issue.** Newly issued bonds generally sell very close to par, but the prices of seasoned bonds vary widely from par. Except for floating-rate bonds, coupon payments are constant, so when economic conditions change, a 10% coupon bond with a $100 coupon that sold at par when it was issued will sell for more or less than $1,000 thereafter.

MicroDrive's bonds with a 10% coupon rate were originally issued at par. If r_d remained constant at 10%, what would the value of the bond be 1 year after it was issued? Now the term to maturity is only 14 years—that is, N = 14. With a financial calculator, just override N = 15 with N = 14, press the PV key, and you find a value of $1,000. If we continued, setting N = 13, N = 12, and so forth, we would see that the value of the bond will remain at $1,000 as long as the going interest rate remains constant at the coupon rate, 10%.

Now suppose interest rates in the economy fell after the MicroDrive bonds were issued and, as a result, r_d *fell below the coupon rate,* decreasing from 10% to 5%. Both the coupon interest payments and the maturity value remain constant, but now 5% would have to be used for r_d in Equation 5-1. The value of the bond at the end of the first year would be $1,494.93:

$$
\begin{aligned}
V_B &= \sum_{t=1}^{14} \frac{\$100}{(1+0.05)^t} + \frac{\$1,000}{(1+0.05)^{14}} \\
&= \$100\left[\frac{1}{0.05} - \frac{1}{0.05(1+0.05)^{14}}\right] + \frac{\$1,000}{(1+0.05)^{14}} \\
&= \$1,494.93
\end{aligned}
$$

With a financial calculator, just change r_d = I/YR from 10 to 5, and then press the PV key to get the answer, \$1,494.93. Thus, if r_d fell *below* the coupon rate, the bond would sell *above* par, or at a **premium.**

The arithmetic of the bond value increase should be clear, but what is the logic behind it? Because r_d has fallen to 5%, with \$1,000 to invest you could buy new bonds like MicroDrive's (every day some ten to twelve companies sell new bonds), except that these new bonds would pay \$50 of interest each year rather than \$100. Naturally, you would prefer \$100 to \$50, so you would be willing to pay more than \$1,000 for a MicroDrive bond to obtain its higher coupons. All investors would react similarly; as a result, the MicroDrive bonds would be bid up in price to \$1,494.93, at which point they would provide the same 5% rate of return to a potential investor as the new bonds.

Assuming that interest rates remain constant at 5% for the next 14 years, what would happen to the value of a MicroDrive bond? It would fall gradually from \$1,494.93 at present to \$1,000 at maturity, when MicroDrive will redeem each bond for \$1,000. This point can be illustrated by calculating the value of the bond 1 year later, when it has 13 years remaining to maturity. With a financial calculator, simply input the values for N, I/YR, PMT, and FV, now using N = 13, and press the PV key to find the value of the bond, \$1,469.68. Thus, the value of the bond will have fallen from \$1,494.93 to \$1,469.68, or by \$25.25. If you were to calculate the value of the bond at other future dates, the price would continue to fall as the maturity date approached.

Note that if you purchased the bond at a price of \$1,494.93 and then sold it 1 year later with r_d still at 5%, you would have a capital loss of \$25.25, or a total return of \$100.00 – \$25.25 = \$74.75. Your percentage rate of return would consist of the rate of return due to the interest payment (called the **current yield**) and the rate of return due to the price change (called the **capital gains yield**). This total rate of return is often called the bond yield, and it is calculated as follows:

$$
\begin{aligned}
\text{Interest, or current, yield} &= \$100/\$1,494.93 = 0.0669 = 6.69\% \\
\text{Capital gains yield} &= -\$25.25/\$1,494.93 = -0.0169 = \underline{-1.69\%} \\
\text{Total rate of return, or yield} &= \$74.75/\$1,494.93 = 0.0500 = \underline{\underline{5.00\%}}
\end{aligned}
$$

Had interest rates risen from 10% to 15% during the first year after issue (rather than falling from 10% to 5%), then you would enter N = 14, I/YR = 15, PMT = 100, and FV = 1000, and then press the PV key to find the value of the bond, \$713.78. In this case, the bond would sell below its par value, or at a discount. The total expected future return on the bond would again consist of an expected return due to interest and an expected return due to capital gains or capital losses. In this situation, the capital gains yield would be *positive.* The total return would be 15%. To see this, calculate the price of the bond with 13 years left to maturity, assuming that interest rates remain at 15%. With a calculator, enter N = 13, I/YR = 15, PMT = 100, and FV = 1000; then press PV to obtain the bond's value, \$720.84.

Note that the capital gain for the year is the difference between the bond's value at Year 2 (with 13 years remaining) and the bond's value at Year 1 (with 14 years remaining), or $720.84 - $713.78 = $7.06. The interest yield, capital gains yield, and total yield are calculated as follows:

$$\text{Interest, or current, yield} = \$100/\$713.78 = 0.1401 = 14.01\%$$

$$\text{Capital gains yield} = \$7.06/\$713.78 = 0.0099 = \underline{0.99\%}$$

$$\text{Total rate of return, or yield} = \$107.06/\$713.78 = 0.1500 = \underline{\underline{15.00\%}}$$

Figure 5-2 graphs the value of the bond over time, assuming that interest rates in the economy (1) remain constant at 10%, (2) fall to 5% and then remain constant at that level, or (3) rise to 15% and remain constant at that level. Of course, if interest rates do *not* remain constant, then the price of the bond will fluctuate. However, regardless of what future interest rates do, the bond's price will approach $1,000 as it nears the maturity date (barring bankruptcy, in which case the bond's value might fall dramatically).

Figure 5-2 illustrates the following key points.

1. Whenever the going rate of interest, r_d, is equal to the coupon rate, a *fixed-rate* bond will sell at its par value. Normally, the coupon rate is set equal to the going rate when a bond is issued, causing it to sell at par initially.
2. Interest rates do change over time, but the coupon rate remains fixed after the bond has been issued. Whenever the going rate of interest *rises above* the coupon rate, a fixed-rate bond's price will *fall below* its par value. Such a bond is called a discount bond.
3. Whenever the going rate of interest *falls below* the coupon rate, a fixed-rate bond's price will *rise above* its par value. Such a bond is called a premium bond.
4. Thus, an *increase* in interest rates will cause the prices of outstanding bonds to *fall*, whereas a *decrease* in rates will cause bond prices to *rise*.

See **Ch05 Tool Kit.xls** *for all calculations.*

FIGURE 5-2 Time Path of the Value of a 10% Coupon, $1,000 Par Value Bond When Interest Rates Are 5%, 10%, and 15%

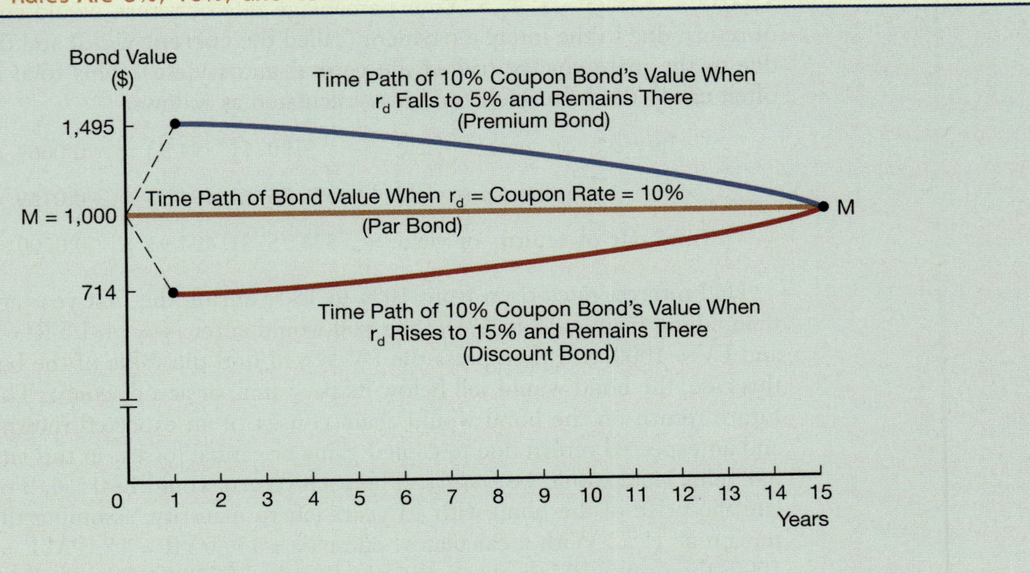

Note: The curves for 5% and 15% have a slight bow.

Drinking Your Coupons

In 1996, Chateau Teyssier, an English vineyard, was looking for some cash to purchase additional vines and to modernize its production facilities. Their solution? With the assistance of a leading underwriter, Matrix Securities, the vineyard issued 375 bonds, each costing 2,650 British pounds. The issue raised nearly 1 million pounds, or roughly $1.5 million.

What makes these bonds interesting is that, instead of paying with something boring like money, they paid their investors back with wine. Each June until 2002, when the bond matured, investors received their "coupons." Between 1997 and 2001, each bond provided six cases of the vineyard's rosé or claret. Starting in 1998 and continuing through maturity in 2002, investors also received four cases of its prestigious Saint Emilion Grand Cru. Then, in 2002, they got their money back.

The bonds were not without risk. The vineyard's owner, Jonathan Malthus, acknowledged that the quality of the wine "is at the mercy of the gods."

Source: Steven Irvine, "My Wine Is My Bond, and I Drink My Coupons," *Euromoney,* July 1996, p. 7.

5. The market value of a bond will always approach its par value as its maturity date approaches, provided the firm does not go bankrupt.

These points are very important, for they show that bondholders may suffer capital losses or make capital gains depending on whether interest rates rise or fall after the bond is purchased.

Self-Test

What is meant by the terms "new issue" and "seasoned issue"?
Last year, a firm issued 30-year, 8% annual coupon bonds at a par value of $1,000. (1) Suppose that 1 year later the going rate drops to 6%. What is the new price of the bonds, assuming that they now have 29 years to maturity? **($1,271.81)** (2) Suppose instead that 1 year after issue the going interest rate increases to 10% (rather than dropping to 6%). What is the price? **($812.61)**

5.5 Bonds with Semiannual Coupons

Although some bonds pay interest annually, the vast majority actually pay interest semiannually. To evaluate semiannual payment bonds, we must modify the valuation model as follows.

1. Divide the annual coupon interest payment by 2 to determine the dollars of interest paid every 6 months.
2. Multiply the years to maturity, N, by 2 to determine the number of semiannual periods.
3. Divide the nominal (quoted) interest rate, r_d, by 2 to determine the periodic (semiannual) interest rate.

By making these changes, we obtain the following equation for finding the value of a bond that pays interest semiannually:

$$V_B = \sum_{t=1}^{2N} \frac{INT/2}{(1 + r_d/2)^t} + \frac{M}{(1 + r_d/2)^{2N}} \quad \text{(5-2)}$$

To illustrate, assume now that MicroDrive's bonds pay $50 interest every 6 months rather than $100 at the end of each year. Each semiannual interest payment is only half as large, but there are twice as many of them. The nominal, or quoted, coupon rate is "10%, semiannual payments."[7]

When the going (nominal) rate of interest is 5% with semiannual compounding, the value of this 15-year bond is found as follows:

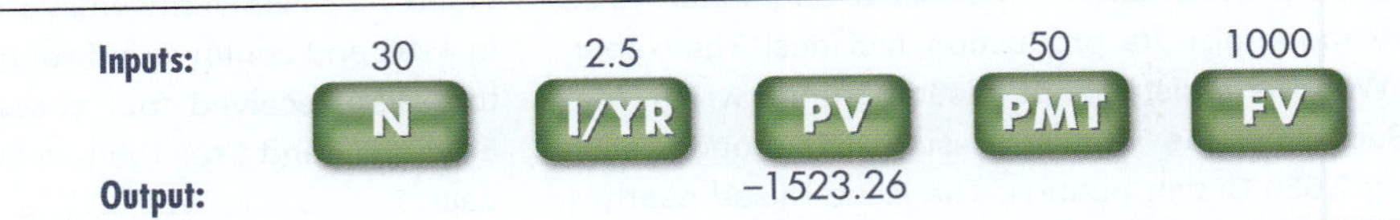

Enter N = 30, r_d = I/YR = 2.5, PMT = 50, FV = 1000, and then press the PV key to obtain the bond's value, $1,523.26. The value with semiannual interest payments is slightly larger than $1,518.98, the value when interest is paid annually. This higher value occurs because interest payments are received somewhat faster under semiannual compounding.

Self-Test

Describe how the annual bond valuation formula is changed to evaluate semiannual coupon bonds. Write out the revised formula.

A bond has a 25-year maturity, an 8% annual coupon paid semiannually, and a face value of $1,000. The going nominal *annual* interest rate (r_d) is 6%. What is the bond's price? **($1,257.30)**

5.6 Bond Yields

Unlike the coupon interest rate, which is fixed, the bond's *yield* varies from day to day depending on current market conditions. Moreover, the yield can be calculated in three different ways, and three "answers" can be obtained. These different yields are described in the following sections.

Yield to Maturity

Suppose you were offered a 14-year, 10% annual coupon, $1,000 par value bond at a price of $1,494.93. What rate of interest would you earn on your investment if you bought the bond and held it to maturity? This rate is called the bond's **yield to maturity (YTM),** and it is the interest rate generally discussed by investors when they talk about rates of return. The yield to maturity is usually the same as the market rate of interest, r_d. To find the YTM for a bond with annual interest payments, you must solve Equation 5-1 for r_d:[8]

$$\text{Bond price} = \sum_{t=1}^{N} \frac{\text{INT}}{(1+\text{YTM})^t} + \frac{M}{(1+\text{YTM})^N} \qquad (5\text{-}3)$$

[7]In this situation, the coupon rate of "10% paid semiannually" is the rate that bond dealers, corporate treasurers, and investors generally would discuss. Of course, if this bond were issued at par, then its *effective annual rate* would be higher than 10%:

$$\text{EAR} = \text{EFF\%} = \left(1+\frac{r_{NOM}}{M}\right)^M - 1 = \left(1+\frac{0.10}{2}\right)^2 - 1 = (1.05)^2 - 1 = 10.25\%$$

Because 10% with annual payments is quite different from 10% with semiannual payments, we have assumed a change in effective rates in this section from the situation described in Section 5.3, where we assumed 10% with annual payments.

[8]If the bond has semiannual payments, you must solve Equation 5-2 for r_d.

For MicroDrive's yield, you must solve this equation:

$$\$1,494.93 = \frac{\$100}{(1+r_d)^1} + \dots + \frac{\$100}{(1+r_d)^{14}} + \frac{\$1,000}{(1+r_d)^{14}}$$

You could substitute values for r_d until you found a value that "works" and forces the sum of the PVs on the right side of the equal sign to equal $1,494.93, but this would be tedious and time-consuming.[9] As you might guess, it is much easier with a financial calculator. Here is the setup:

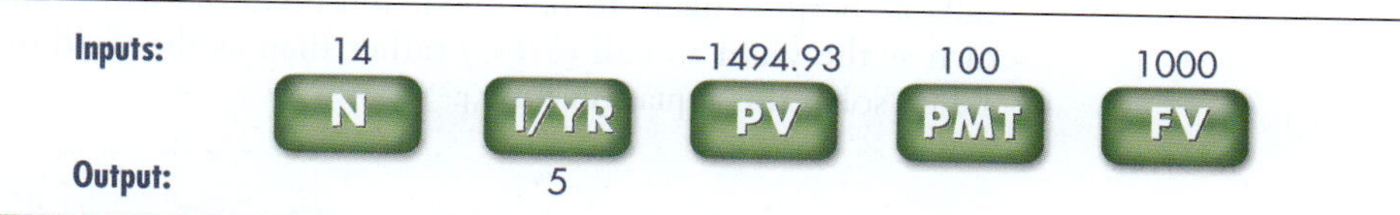

Simply enter N = 14, PV = −1494.93, PMT = 100, and FV = 1000, and then press the I/YR key for the answer of 5%.

You could also find the YTM with a spreadsheet. In *Excel*, you would use the RATE function for this bond, inputting N = 14, PMT = 100, PV = −1494.93, FV = 1000, 0 for Type, and leave Guess blank: **=RATE(14,100,−1494.93,1000,0)**. The result is 5%. The RATE function works only if the current date is immediately after either the issue date or a coupon payment date. To find bond yields on other dates, use *Excel's* YIELD function. See the ***Ch05 Tool Kit.xls*** file for an example.

See **Ch05 Tool Kit.xls** *on the textbook's Web site.*

The yield to maturity can be viewed as the bond's *promised rate of return*, which is the return that investors will receive if all the promised payments are made. However, the yield to maturity equals the *expected rate of return* only if (1) the probability of default is zero and (2) the bond cannot be called. If there is some default risk or if the bond may be called, then there is some probability that the promised payments to maturity will not be received, in which case the calculated yield to maturity will differ from the expected return.

The YTM for a bond that sells at par consists entirely of an interest yield, but if the bond sells at a price other than its par value then the YTM will consist of the interest yield plus a positive or negative capital gains yield. Note also that a bond's yield to maturity changes whenever interest rates in the economy change, and this is almost daily. If you purchase a bond and hold it until it matures, you will receive the YTM that existed on the purchase date but the bond's calculated YTM will change frequently between the purchase date and the maturity date.[10]

---

[9]Alternatively, you can substitute values of r_d into the third form of Equation 5-1 until you find a value that works.

[10]We often are asked by students if the purchaser of a bond will receive the YTM if interest rates subsequently change. The answer is definitely "yes" provided the question means "Is the realized rate of return on the investment in the bond equal to the YTM?" This is because the realized rate of return on an investment is the rate that sets the present value of the realized cash flows equal to the price. If instead the question means "Is the realized rate of return on the investment in the bond and the subsequent reinvestment of the coupons equal to the YTM?" then the answer is definitely "no." Thus, the question really is one about strategy and timing. The bond, in combination with a reinvestment strategy, is really two investments, and clearly the realized rate on this combined strategy depends on the reinvestment rate (see ***Web Extension 5C*** for more on investing for a target future value). For the rest of the book, we assume that an investment in a bond is just that, an investment only in the bond, and not a combination of the bond and a reinvestment strategy; this means the investor earns the expected YTM if the bond is held to maturity.

Yield to Call

If you purchased a bond that was callable and the company called it, you would not have the option of holding the bond until it matured. Therefore, the yield to maturity would not be earned. For example, if MicroDrive's 10% coupon bonds were callable and if interest rates fell from 10% to 5%, then the company could call in the 10% bonds, replace them with 5% bonds, and save $100 – $50 = $50 interest per bond per year. This would be good for the company but not for the bondholders.

If current interest rates are well below an outstanding bond's coupon rate, then a callable bond is likely to be called, and investors will estimate its expected rate of return as the **yield to call (YTC)** rather than as the yield to maturity. To calculate the YTC, solve this equation for r_d:

$$\text{Price of callable bond} = \sum_{t=1}^{N} \frac{\text{INT}}{(1 + r_d)^t} + \frac{\text{Call price}}{(1 + r_d)^N} \qquad (5\text{-}4)$$

Here N is the number of years until the company can call the bond, r_d is the YTC, and "Call price" is the price the company must pay in order to call the bond (it is often set equal to the par value plus 1 year's interest).

To illustrate, suppose MicroDrive's bonds had a provision that permitted the company, if it desired, to call the bonds 10 years after the issue date at a price of $1,100. Suppose further that 1 year after issuance the going interest rate had declined, causing the price of the bonds to rise to $1,494.93. Here is the time line and the setup for finding the bond's YTC with a financial calculator:

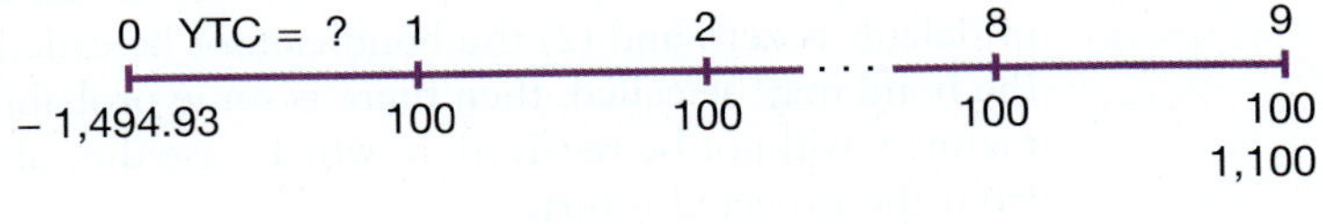

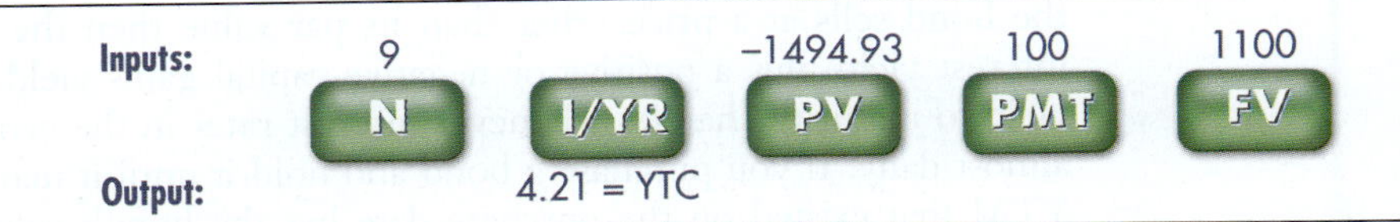

The YTC is 4.21%—this is the return you would earn if you bought the bond at a price of $1,494.93 and it was called 9 years from today. (The bond could not be called until 10 years after issuance, and 1 year has gone by, so there are 9 years left until the first call date.)

Do you think MicroDrive *will* call the bonds when they become callable? MicroDrive's actions depend on the going interest rate when the bonds become callable. If the going rate remains at r_d = 5%, then MicroDrive could save 10% – 5% = 5%, or $50 per bond per year, by calling them and replacing the 10% bonds with a new 5% issue. There would be costs to the company to refund the issue, but the interest savings would probably be worth the cost, so MicroDrive would probably refund the bonds. Therefore, you would probably earn YTC = 4.21% rather than YTM = 5% if you bought the bonds under the indicated conditions.

In the balance of this chapter, we assume that bonds are not callable unless otherwise noted. However, some of the end-of-chapter problems deal with yield to call.

Current Yield

If you examine brokerage house reports on bonds, you will often see reference to a bond's **current yield**. The current yield is the annual interest payment divided by the bond's current price. For example, if MicroDrive's bonds with a 10% coupon were currently selling at $985, then the bond's current yield would be $100/$985 = 0.1015 = 10.15%.

Unlike the yield to maturity, the current yield does not represent the rate of return that investors should expect on the bond. The current yield provides information regarding the amount of cash income that a bond will generate in a given year, but it does not provide an accurate measure of the bond's total expected return, the yield to maturity. In fact, here is the relation between current yield, capital gains yield (which can be negative for a capital loss), and the yield to maturity:

$$\text{Current yield} + \text{Capital gains yield} = \text{Yield to maturity} \tag{5-5}$$

The Cost of Debt and Intrinsic Value

The "Intrinsic Value Box" at the beginning of this chapter highlights the cost of debt, which affects the weighted average cost of capital (WACC), which in turn affects the company's intrinsic value. The pre-tax cost of debt from the company's perspective is the required return from the debtholder's perspective. Therefore, the pre-tax cost of debt is the yield to maturity (or the yield to call if a call is likely). But why do different bonds have different yields to maturity? The following sections answer this question.

Self-Test

Explain the difference between the yield to maturity and the yield to call.
How does a bond's current yield differ from its total return?
Could the current yield exceed the total return?
A bond currently sells for $850. It has an 8-year maturity, an annual coupon of $80, and a par value of $1,000. What is its yield to maturity? **(10.90%)** What is its current yield? **(9.41%)**
A bond currently sells for $1,250. It pays a $110 annual coupon and has a 20-year maturity, but it can be called in 5 years at $1,110. What are its YTM and its YTC? **(8.38%, 6.85%)** Is the bond likely to be called if interest rates don't change?

5.7 The Pre-Tax Cost of Debt: Determinants of Market Interest Rates

Up until now we have given you r_d, the going market rate. But as we showed in Chapter 1, different debt securities often have very different market rates. What explains these differences? In general, the quoted (or nominal) interest rate on a debt security, r_d, is composed of a real risk-free rate of interest, r*, plus several premiums that reflect inflation, the risk of the security, and the security's marketability (or liquidity). A conceptual framework is shown below:

$$\begin{aligned}\text{Quoted market interest rate} = r_d &= r^* + IP + DRP + LP + MRP \\ &= r_{RF} + DRP + LP + MRP\end{aligned} \tag{5-6}$$

Here are definitions of the variables in Equation 5-6:

r_d = Quoted, or nominal, rate of interest on a given security.[11] There are many different securities and hence many different quoted interest rates.

r^* = Real risk-free rate of interest. Pronounced "r-star," r^* is the rate that would exist on a riskless security if zero inflation were expected.

IP = Inflation premium, which is equal to the average expected inflation rate over the life of the security. The expected future inflation rate is not necessarily equal to the current inflation rate, so IP is not necessarily equal to current inflation.

r_{RF} = r^* + IP, and it is the quoted risk-free rate of interest on a security such as a U.S. Treasury bill, which is very liquid and also free of most risks. Note that r_{RF} includes the premium for expected inflation because $r_{RF} = r^* + IP$.

DRP = Default risk premium. This premium reflects the possibility that the issuer will not pay interest or principal at the stated time and in the stated amount. The DRP is zero for U.S. Treasury securities, but it rises as the riskiness of issuers increases.

LP = Liquidity, or marketability, premium. This is a premium charged by lenders to reflect the fact that some securities cannot be converted to cash on short notice at a "reasonable" price. The LP is very low for Treasury securities and for securities issued by large, strong firms, but it is relatively high on securities issued by very small firms.

MRP = Maturity risk premium. As we will explain later, longer-term bonds (even Treasury bonds) are exposed to a significant risk of price declines, and a maturity risk premium is charged by lenders to reflect this risk.

We discuss the components whose sum makes up the quoted, or nominal, rate on a given security in the following sections.

Self-Test

Write out an equation for the nominal interest rate on any debt security.

5.8 The Real Risk-Free Rate of Interest, r*

WWW

See **http://www.bloomberg.com** *and select MARKET DATA. Then select RATES AND BONDS for a partial listing of indexed Treasury bonds and their interest rates. See* **http://online.wsj.com** *for a complete set of Treasury quotes. See* **http://www.treasurydirect.gov/indiv/products/products.htm** *for a complete listing of all Treasury securities.*

The **real risk-free rate of interest, r***, is defined as the interest rate that would exist on a riskless security if no inflation were expected, and it may be thought of as the rate of interest on *short-term* U.S. Treasury securities in an inflation-free world. The real risk-free rate is not static—it changes over time depending on economic

[11]The term *nominal* as it is used here means the *stated* rate as opposed to the *real* rate, which is adjusted to remove inflation effects. Suppose you bought a 10-year Treasury bond with a quoted, or nominal, rate of about 4.6%. If inflation averages 2.5% over the next 10 years, then the real rate would be about 4.6% – 2.5% = 2.1%. To be technically correct, we should find the real rate by solving for r^* in the following equation: $(1 + r^*)(1 + 0.025) = (1 + 0.046)$. Solving the equation, we find $r^* = 2.05\%$. Since this is very close to the 2.1% just calculated, we will continue to approximate the real rate in this chapter by subtracting inflation from the nominal rate.

conditions, especially (1) the rate of return corporations and other borrowers expect to earn on productive assets and (2) people's time preferences for current versus future consumption.[12]

In addition to its regular bond offerings, in 1997 the U.S. Treasury began issuing **indexed bonds**, with payments linked to inflation. These bonds are called **TIPS**, short for **Treasury Inflation-Protected Securities**. Because the payments (including the principal) are tied to inflation, the yield on TIPS is a good estimate of the risk-free rate. In early 2009, the TIPS with about 1 year remaining until maturity had a 1.54% yield.[13] This is a pretty good estimate of the real risk-free rate, r*, although ideally we would prefer a TIPS with an even shorter time until maturity. We will have more to say about how to use TIPS when we discuss the inflation premium in the next section. For details on how TIPS are adjusted to protect against inflation, see ***Web Extension 5B*** on the textbook's Web site.

Self-Test

What security provides a good estimate of the real risk-free rate?

5.9 The Inflation Premium (IP)

Inflation has a major effect on interest rates because it erodes the purchasing power of the dollar and lowers the real rate of return on investments. To illustrate, suppose you invest $3,000 in a default-free zero coupon bond that matures in 1 year and pays a 5% interest rate. At the end of the year, you will receive $3,150—your original $3,000 plus $150 of interest. Now suppose that the inflation rate during the year is 10% and that it affects all items equally. If gas had cost $3 per gallon at the beginning of the year, it would cost $3.30 at the end of the year. Therefore, your $3,000 would have bought $3,000/$3 = 1,000 gallons at the beginning of the year but only $3,150/$3.30 = 955 gallons at the end. In *real terms*, you would be worse off—you would receive $150 of interest, but it would not be sufficient to offset inflation. You would thus be better off buying 1,000 gallons of gas (or some other storable asset) than buying the default-free bond.

Investors are well aware of inflation's effects on interest rates, so when they lend money, they build in an **inflation premium (IP)** equal to the average expected inflation rate over the life of the security. For a short-term, default-free U.S. Treasury bill, the actual interest rate charged, $r_{T\text{-bill}}$, would be the real risk-free rate, r*, plus the inflation premium (IP):

$$r_{T\text{-bill}} = r_{RF} = r^* + IP$$

[12]The real rate of interest as discussed here is different from the *current* real rate as often discussed in the press. The current real rate is often estimated as the current interest rate minus the current (or most recent) inflation rate, whereas the real rate, as used here (and in the fields of finance and economics generally) without the word "current," is the current interest rate minus the *expected future* inflation rate over the life of the security. For example, suppose the current quoted rate for a 1-year Treasury bill is 5%, inflation during the previous year was 2%, and inflation expected for the coming year is 4%. Then the *current* real rate would be approximately 5% − 2% = 3%, but the *expected* real rate would be approximately 5% − 4% = 1%.

[13]Negative *nominal* rates are pretty much impossible—investors would just hold cash instead of investing in a negative-rate bond. But negative real rates are possible. In spring 2008, the combination of stagnant economic growth, a high level of investor uncertainty, fears of inflation, and the Federal Reserve's reduction in nominal short-term interest rates caused the real rate to fall below zero, as measured by negative yields on several short-term TIPS.

Therefore, if the real short-term risk-free rate of interest were $r^* = 0.6\%$ and if inflation were expected to be 1.0% (and hence IP = 1.0%) during the next year, then the quoted rate of interest on 1-year T-bills would be 0.6% + 1.0% = 1.6%.

It is important to note that the inflation rate built into interest rates is *the inflation rate expected in the future*, not the rate experienced in the past. Thus, the latest reported figures might show an annual inflation rate of 2%, but that is for the *past* year. If people on average expect a 6% inflation rate in the future, then 6% would be built into the current interest rate.

Note also that the inflation rate reflected in the quoted interest rate on any security is the *average rate of inflation expected over the security's life*. Thus, the inflation rate built into a 1-year bond is the expected inflation rate for the next year, but the inflation rate built into a 30-year bond is the average rate of inflation expected over the next 30 years. If I_t is the expected inflation during year t, then the inflation premium for an N-year bond's yield (IP_N) can be approximated as

$$IP_N = \frac{I_1 + I_2 + \ldots + I_N}{N} \tag{5-7}$$

For example, if investors expect inflation to average 3% during Year 1 and 5% during Year 2, then the inflation premium built into a 2-year bond's yield can be approximated by[14]

$$IP_2 = \frac{I_1 + I_2}{2} = \frac{3\% + 5\%}{2} = 4\%$$

In the previous section, we saw that the yield on an inflation-indexed Treasury bond (TIPS) is a good estimate of the real interest rate. We can also use TIPS to estimate inflation premiums. For example, in early 2009 the yield on a 5-year nonindexed T-bond was 1.91% and the yield on a 5-year TIPS was 1.41%. Thus, the 5-year inflation premium was 1.91% − 1.41% = 0.50%, implying that investors expected inflation to average 0.50% over the next 5 years.[15] Similarly, the rate on a 20-year nonindexed T-bond was 3.93% and the rate on a 20-year indexed T-bond was 2.44%. Thus, the 20-year inflation premium was approximately 3.93% − 2.44% = 1.49%, implying that investors expected inflation to average 1.49% over the long term.[16] These calculations are summarized below:

---

[14]To be theoretically correct, we should take the *geometric average*: $(1 + IP_2)^2 = (1 + I_1)(1 + I_2)$. In this example, we have $(1 + IP_2)^2 = (1 + 0.03)(1 + 0.05)$. Solving for IP_2 yields 3.9952, which is close to our approximation of 4%.

[15]To be theoretically precise, we should use a *geometric average* by solving the following equation: (1 + IP)(1.0141) = 1.0191. Solving for IP gives IP = 0.493%, which is the same as our approximation.

Note, though, that the difference in yield between a T-bond and a TIPS of the same maturity reflects both the expected inflation *and* any risk premium for bearing inflation risk. So the difference in yields is really an upper limit on the expected inflation.

[16]There are several other sources for the estimated inflation premium. The Congressional Budget Office regularly updates the estimates of inflation that it uses in its forecasted budgets; see **http://www.cbo.gov/**; select Economic Projections. A second source is the University of Michigan's Institute for Social Research, which regularly polls consumers regarding their expectations for price increases during the next year; see **http://www.isr.umich.edu/home/**; select Inst for Social Research; then search for Consumers to get the survey.

We prefer using inflation premiums derived from indexed and nonindexed Treasury securities, as described in the text, since these are based on how investors actually spend their money, not on theoretical models or opinions.

	Maturity	
	5 Years	20 Years
Yield on nonindexed U.S. Treasury bond	1.91%	3.93%
Yield on TIPS	1.41	2.44
Inflation premium	0.50%	1.49%

Expectations for future inflation are closely, but not perfectly, correlated with rates experienced in the recent past. Therefore, if the inflation rate reported for last month increases, people often raise their expectations for future inflation, and this change in expectations will cause an increase in interest rates.

Note that Germany, Japan, and Switzerland have, over the past several years, had lower inflation rates than the United States, so their interest rates have generally been lower than ours. South Africa, Brazil, and most South American countries have experienced higher inflation, which is reflected in their interest rates.

Self-Test

Explain how a TIPS and a nonindexed Treasury security can be used to estimate the inflation premium.

The yield on a 15-year TIPS is 3% and the yield on a 15-year Treasury bond is 5%. What is the inflation premium for a 15-year security? **(2%)**

5.10 The Nominal, or Quoted, Risk-Free Rate of Interest, r_{RF}

The **nominal**, or **quoted, risk-free rate, r_{RF}**, is the real risk-free rate plus a premium for expected inflation: $r_{RF} = r^* + IP$. To be strictly correct, the risk-free rate should mean the interest rate on a totally risk-free security—one that has no risk of default, no maturity risk, no liquidity risk, no risk of loss if inflation increases, and no risk of any other type. There is no such security, so there is no observable truly risk-free rate. When the term "risk-free rate" is used without either the modifier "real" or the modifier "nominal," people generally mean the quoted (nominal) rate, and we will follow that convention in this book. Therefore, when we use the term "risk-free rate, r_{RF}," we mean the nominal risk-free rate, which includes an inflation premium equal to the average expected inflation rate over the life of the security. In general, we use the T-bill rate to approximate the short-term risk-free rate and use the T-bond rate to approximate the long-term risk-free rate (even though it also includes a maturity premium). So, whenever you see the term "risk-free rate," assume that we are referring either to the quoted U.S. T-bill rate or to the quoted T-bond rate.

Since $r_{RF} = r^* + IP$, we can express the quoted rate as

$$\text{Nominal, or quoted, rate} = r_d = r_{RF} + DRP + LP + MRP$$

Self-Test

What security is a good approximation of the nominal risk-free rate?

5.11 The Default Risk Premium (DRP)

If the issuer defaults on a payment, investors receive less than the promised return on the bond. The quoted interest rate includes a default risk premium (DRP)—the greater the default risk, the higher the bond's yield to maturity.[17] The default risk

[17]Suppose two bonds have the same promised cash flows, coupon rate, maturity, liquidity, and inflation exposure, but one bond has more default risk than the other. Investors will naturally pay less for the bond with the greater chance of default. As a result, bonds with higher default risk will have higher interest rates.

on Treasury securities is virtually zero, but default risk can be substantial for corporate and municipal bonds. In this section, we consider some issues related to default risk.

Bond Contract Provisions That Influence Default Risk

Default risk is affected by both the financial strength of the issuer and the terms of the bond contract, especially whether collateral has been pledged to secure the bond. Several types of contract provisions are discussed next.

Bond Indentures. An **indenture** is a legal document that spells out the rights of both bondholders and the issuing corporation, and a **trustee** is an official (usually a bank) who represents the bondholders and makes sure the terms of the indenture are carried out. The indenture may be several hundred pages in length, and it will include **restrictive covenants** that cover such points as the conditions under which the issuer can pay off the bonds prior to maturity, the levels at which certain ratios must be maintained if the company is to issue additional debt, and restrictions against the payment of dividends unless earnings meet certain specifications.

The Securities and Exchange Commission (1) approves indentures and (2) makes sure that all indenture provisions are met before allowing a company to sell new securities to the public. A firm will have different indentures for each of the major types of bonds it issues, but a single indenture covers all bonds of the same type. For example, one indenture will cover a firm's first mortgage bonds, another its debentures, and a third its convertible bonds.

Mortgage Bonds. A corporation pledges certain assets as security for a **mortgage bond**. The company might also choose to issue *second-mortgage bonds* secured by the same assets that were secured by a previously issued mortgage bond. In the event of liquidation, the holders of these second mortgage bonds would have a claim against the property, but only after the first mortgage bondholders had been paid off in full. Thus, second mortgages are sometimes called *junior mortgages*, because they are junior in priority to the claims of *senior mortgages*, or *first-mortgage bonds*. All mortgage bonds are subject to an indenture that usually limits the amount of new bonds that can be issued.

Debentures and Subordinated Debentures. A **debenture** is an unsecured bond, and as such it provides no lien against specific property as security for the obligation. Debenture holders are, therefore, general creditors whose claims are protected by property not otherwise pledged.

The term *subordinate* means "below," or "inferior to"; thus, in the event of bankruptcy, subordinated debt has claims on assets only after senior debt has been paid off. **Subordinated debentures** may be subordinated either to designated notes payable (usually bank loans) or to all other debt. In the event of liquidation or reorganization, holders of subordinated debentures cannot be paid until all senior debt, as named in the debentures' indentures, has been paid.

Development Bonds. Some companies may be in a position to benefit from the sale of either **development bonds** or **pollution control bonds**. State and local governments may set up both *industrial development agencies* and *pollution control agencies*. These agencies are allowed, under certain circumstances, to sell **tax-exempt bonds** and then make the proceeds available to corporations for specific uses deemed (by Congress) to be in the public interest. For example, a Detroit pollution control agency might sell bonds to provide Ford with funds for purchasing pollution control equipment. Because the income from the bonds would be tax exempt, the bonds would have a relatively low interest rates. Note, how-

THE GLOBAL ECONOMIC CRISIS

Insuring with Credit Default Swaps: Let the Buyer Beware!

Recall that a credit default swap (CDS) is like an insurance policy. The purchaser of the CDS agrees to make annual payments to a counterparty that agrees to pay if a particular bond defaults. During the 2000s, investment banks often would purchase CDS for the mortgage-backed securities (MBS) they were creating in order to make the securities more attractive to investors. But how good was this type of insurance? As it turned out, not very. For example, Lehman Brothers might have bought a CDS from AIG in order to sell a Lehman-created MBS to an investor. But when the MBS began defaulting, neither Lehman nor AIG was capable of making full restitution to the investor.

ever, that these bonds are guaranteed by the corporation that will use the funds, not by a governmental unit, so their rating reflects the credit strength of the corporation using the funds.

Municipal Bond Insurance. Municipalities can have their bonds insured, which means that an insurance company guarantees to pay the coupon and principal payments should the issuer default. This reduces risk to investors, who will thus accept a lower coupon rate for an insured bond than for a comparable but uninsured one. Even though the municipality must pay a fee to have its bonds insured, its savings due to the lower coupon rate often make insurance cost effective. Keep in mind that the insurers are private companies, and the value added by the insurance depends on the creditworthiness of the insurer. The larger insurers are strong companies, and their own ratings are AAA.

Bond Ratings

Since the early 1900s, bonds have been assigned quality ratings that reflect their probability of going into default. The three major rating agencies are Moody's Investors Service (Moody's), Standard & Poor's Corporation (S&P), and Fitch Ratings. As shown in Columns (3) and (4) of Table 5-1, triple-A and double-A bonds are extremely safe, rarely defaulting even within 5 years of being assigned a rating. Single-A and triple-B bonds are also strong enough to be called **investment-grade bonds**, and they are the lowest-rated bonds that many banks and other institutional investors are permitted by law to hold. Double-B and lower bonds are speculative, or **junk bonds**. These bonds have a significant probability of defaulting.

Bond Rating Criteria, Upgrades, and Downgrades

Bond ratings are based on both quantitative and qualitative factors, as we describe below.

1. **Financial Ratios**. Many ratios potentially are important, but the return on assets, debt ratio, and interest coverage ratio are particularly valuable for predicting financial distress. For example, Columns 5 and 6 in Table 5-1 show a strong relationship between ratings and the return on capital and the debt ratio.
2. **Bond Contract Terms**. Important provisions for determining the bond's rating include whether the bond is secured by a mortgage on specific assets, whether the bond is subordinated to other debt, any sinking fund provisions, guarantees by some other party with a high credit ranking, and *restrictive covenants* such as requirements that the firm keep its debt ratio below a given level or that it keep its times interest earned ratio above a given level.

TABLE 5-1 Bond Ratings, Default Risk, and Yields

RATING AGENCY[a]		PERCENT DEFAULTING WITHIN:[b]		MEDIAN RATIOS[c]		PERCENT UPGRADED OR DOWNGRADED IN 2008[b]		
S&P AND FITCH (1)	MOODY'S (2)	1 YEAR (3)	5 YEARS (4)	RETURN ON CAPITAL (5)	TOTAL DEBT/ TOTAL CAPITAL (6)	DOWN (7)	UP (8)	YIELD[d] (9)
Investment-grade bonds								
AAA	Aaa	0.0%	0.0%	27.6%	12.4%	13.6%	NA	5.50%
AA	Aa	0.0	0.1	27.0	28.3	21.8	0.0	5.62
A	A	0.1	0.6	17.5	37.5	8.0	1.8	5.79
BBB	Baa	0.3	2.9	13.4	42.5	6.4	2.6	7.53
Junk bonds								
BB	Ba	1.4	8.2	11.3	53.7	15.1	6.8	11.62
B	B	1.8	9.2	8.7	75.9	10.8	5.6	13.70
CCC	Caa	22.3	36.9	3.2	113.5	26.1	8.7	26.30

Notes: [a]The ratings agencies also use "modifiers" for bonds rated below triple-A. S&P and Fitch use a plus and minus system; thus, A+ designates the strongest A-rated bonds and A– the weakest. Moody's uses a 1, 2, or 3 designation, with 1 denoting the strongest and 3 the weakest; thus, within the double-A category, Aa1 is the best, Aa2 is average, and Aa3 is the weakest.

[b]Default data are from Fitch Ratings Global Corporate Finance 2008 Transition and Default Study, March 5, 2009: see **http://www.fitchratings.com/corporate/reports/report_frame.cfm?rpt_id=428182**.

[c]Median ratios are from Standard & Poor's 2006 Corporate Ratings Criteria, April 23, 2007: see **http://www2.standardandpoors .com/spf/pdf/fixedincome/Corporate_Ratings_2006.pdf**.

[d]Composite yields for AAA, AA, and A bonds can be found at **http://finance.yahoo.com/bonds/composite_bond_rates**. Representative yields for BBB, BB, B, and CCC bonds can be found using the bond screener at **http://screen.yahoo .com/bonds.html**.

3. **Qualitative Factors.** Included here would be such factors as sensitivity of the firm's earnings to the strength of the economy, how it is affected by inflation, whether it is having or is likely to have labor problems, the extent of its international operations (including the stability of the countries in which it operates), potential environmental problems, potential antitrust problems, and so on. Today (2009), a critical factor is exposure to sub-prime loans, including the difficulty of determining the extent of this exposure owing to the complexity of the assets backed by such loans.

Rating agencies review outstanding bonds on a periodic basis and re-rate if necessary. Columns (7) and (8) in Table 5-1 show the percentages of companies in each rating category that were downgraded or upgraded in 2008 by Fitch Ratings. The year 2008 was a difficult one, as more bonds were downgraded than upgraded.

Over the long run, ratings agencies have done a reasonably good job of measuring the average credit risk of bonds and of changing ratings whenever there is a significant change in credit quality. However, it is important to understand that ratings do not adjust immediately to changes in credit quality, and in some cases there can be a considerable lag between a change in credit quality and a change in rating. For example, Enron's bonds still carried an investment-grade rating on a Friday in December 2001, but the company declared bankruptcy two days later, on Sunday. Many other abrupt downgrades occurred in 2007 and 2008, leading to calls by Congress and the SEC for changes in rating agencies and the way they rate bonds. Clearly, improvements can be made, but there will always be occasions when completely unexpected information about a company is released, leading to a sudden change in its rating.

THE GLOBAL ECONOMIC CRISIS

Might the U.S. Treasury Bond Be Downgraded?

The worsening recession that began at the end of 2007 led Congress to pass a huge economic stimulus package in early 2009. The combination of the stimulus package and the government's bailouts of financial institutions is causing the U.S. government to increase its borrowing. Moody's, the bond rating agency, projects that federal debt will rise from $5.8 trillion (41% of GDP) at the beginning of 2009 to $9 trillion (62% of GDP) by the end of 2010. This is a lot of money, even by Washington standards!

Moody's rates sovereign debt as well as corporate debt, and the United States has always ranked right at the top. However, Moody's essentially put America on "credit watch" starting February 13, 2009. Moody's predicted that the U.S. ranking will go from the strongest to near the bottom of the most developed nations' rankings (Canada, Britain, France, Germany, and the Scandinavian countries). It even stated that the U.S.'s "triple A rating isn't assured forever."

A downgrade might cause lenders in China and elsewhere around the globe to sell many of their T-bonds. Massive selling pressure would cause T-bond interest rates to go up, which would increase the government's cost of borrowing. The sellers would want to convert into their own currency the dollars they receive from selling T-bonds. This means they would "sell" dollars for their own currency, and this selling pressure would cause the value of the dollar to fall. If the Chinese and others didn't want to hold dollar denominated debt, who would buy the extra $3.2 trillion of bonds the United States must sell to fund the stimulus package?

A downgrading would also have a huge effect on the finance profession—we would no longer have a proxy for the riskless rate, which is an important element of financial theory and practice. Clearly, though, that would be a very small problem compared to the damage a downgrade would do to our economy.

Bond Ratings and the Default Risk Premium

Why are bond ratings so important? First, most bonds are purchased by institutional investors rather than individuals, and many institutions are restricted to investment-grade securities. Thus, if a firm's bonds fall below BBB, it will have a difficult time selling new bonds because many potential purchasers will not be allowed to buy them. Second, many bond covenants stipulate that the coupon rate on the bond automatically increases if the rating falls below a specified level. Third, because a bond's rating is an indicator of its default risk, the rating has a direct, measurable influence on the bond's yield. Column (9) of Table 5-1 shows that a AAA bond has a yield of 5.50% and that yields increase as the rating falls. In fact, an investor would earn 26.3% on a CCC bond if it didn't default!

A **bond spread** is the difference between a bond's yield and the yield on some other security of the same maturity. Unless specified differently, the term "spread" generally means the difference between a bond's yield and the yield on a Treasury bond of similar maturity.

Figure 5-3 shows the spreads between an index of AAA bonds and a 10-year Treasury bond; it also shows spreads for an index of BBB bonds relative to the T-bond. Figure 5-3 illustrates three important points. First, the BAA spread always is greater than the AAA spread. This is because a BAA bond is riskier than an AAA bond, so BAA investors require extra compensation for their extra risk. The same is true for other ratings: Lower-rated bonds have higher yields.

FIGURE 5-3 Bond Spreads

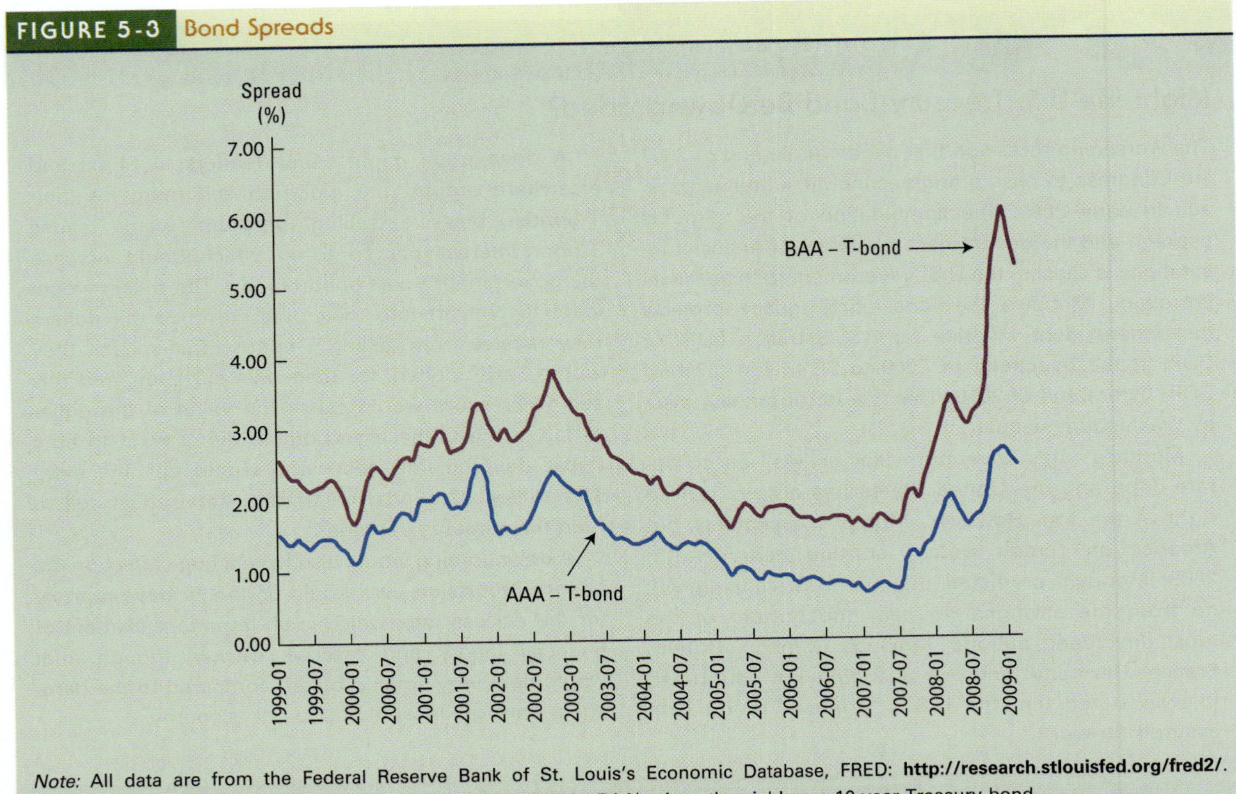

Note: All data are from the Federal Reserve Bank of St. Louis's Economic Database, FRED: **http://research.stlouisfed.org/fred2/**. The spreads are defined as the yield on the risky bond (AAA or BAA) minus the yield on a 10-year Treasury bond.

Second, the spreads are not constant over time. For example, look at the AAA spread. It was exceptionally low during the boom years of 2005–2007 but rose dramatically as the economy subsequently declined.

Third, the difference between the BAA spread and the AAA spread isn't constant over time. The two spreads were quite close to one another in early 2000 but were very far apart in early 2009. In other words, BAA investors didn't require much extra return over that of an AAA bond to induce them to take on that extra risk for most of the decade, but now (2009) they are requiring a very large risk premium.

Not only do spreads vary with the rating of the security, they also usually increase as maturity increases. This should make sense. If a bond matures soon, investors are able to forecast the company's performance fairly well. But if a bond has a long time until it matures, investors have a difficult time forecasting the likelihood that the company will fall into financial distress. This extra uncertainty creates additional risk, so investors demand a higher required return.

Self-Test

Differentiate between mortgage bonds and debentures.

Name the major rating agencies, and list some factors that affect bond ratings.

What is a bond spread?

How do bond ratings affect the default risk premium?

A 10-year T-bond has a yield of 6%. A 10-year corporate bond with a rating of AA has a yield of 7.5%. If the corporate bond has excellent liquidity, what is an estimate of the corporate bond's default risk premium? **(1.5%)**

THE GLOBAL ECONOMIC CRISIS

Are Investors Rational?

The figure in this box shows the yield on junk bonds during the recent past. Observe that the yields were less than 10% from mid-2003 through the end of 2008. During this period, 10-year T-bonds yielded an average of about 4.4%. Thus, the spread on junk bonds over Treasuries was only about 5.4% during these boom years, which is exceptionally low by historic standards. In other words, investors had a voracious appetite for risk and simply didn't require much extra return to induce them to buy very risky securities—investors almost ignored risk during the boom years. But as the economy began to deteriorate in 2008, investors reversed course and became extremely risk averse, with junk-bond yields climbing as high as 25% and the spread exceeding 21%. Such drastic changes in investors' risk aversion are hard to reconcile with careful, deliberate, and rational behavior!

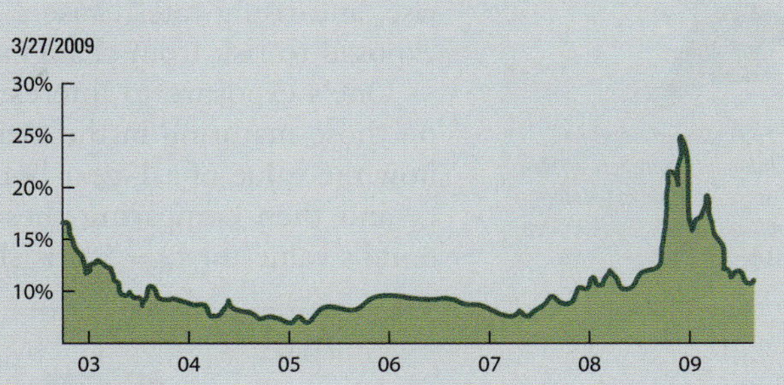

Source: Financial Industry Regulatory Authority, March 27, 2009, High Yield Index (NBBH) Yields: see **http://cxa.marketwatch.com/finra/BondCenter/ActiveUSCorpBond.aspx**. Copyright © 2009 FINRA. All rights reserved. FINRA is a registered trademark of the Financial Industry Regulatory Authority, Inc. Reprinted with permission from FINRA.

5.12 The Liquidity Premium (LP)

A "liquid" asset can be converted to cash quickly and at a "fair market value." Financial assets are generally more liquid than real assets. Because liquidity is important, investors include **liquidity premiums (LPs)** when market rates of securities are established. Although it is difficult to measure liquidity premiums accurately, a differential of at least 2 percentage points (and perhaps up to 4 or 5 percentage points) exists between the least liquid and the most liquid financial assets of similar default risk and maturity. Corporate bonds issued by small companies are traded less frequently than those issued by large companies, so small-company bonds tend to have a higher liquidity premium.

As discussed in Chapter 1, liquidity in the market for mortgage-backed securities evaporated in 2008 and early 2009. The few transactions that occurred were priced such that the yields on these MBS were extremely high, which was partially due to a much higher liquidity premium caused by the extremely low liquidity of MBS.

Self-Test

Which bond usually will have a higher liquidity premium: one issued by a large company or one issued by a small company?

5.13 The Maturity Risk Premium (MRP)

All bonds, even Treasury bonds, are exposed to two additional sources of risk: interest rate risk and reinvestment risk. The net effect of these two sources of risk upon a bond's yield is called the **maturity risk premium, MRP**. The following sections explain how interest rate risk and reinvestment risk affect a bond's yield.

Interest Rate Risk

Interest rates go up and down over time, and an increase in interest rates leads to a decline in the value of outstanding bonds. This risk of a decline in bond values due to rising interest rates is called **interest rate risk**. To illustrate, suppose you bought some 10% MicroDrive bonds at a price of $1,000 and then interest rates rose in the following year to 15%. As we saw earlier, the price of the bonds would fall to $713.78, so you would have a loss of $286.22 per bond.[18] Interest rates can and do rise, and rising rates cause a loss of value for bondholders. Thus, bond investors are exposed to risk from changing interest rates.

For more on bond risk, including duration analysis, see **Web Extension 5C** *on the textbook's Web site.*

One's exposure to interest rate risk is higher on bonds with long maturities than on those maturing in the near future.[19] This point can be demonstrated by showing how the value of a 1-year bond with a 10% annual coupon fluctuates with changes in r_d and then comparing these changes with those on a 25-year bond. The 1-year bond's value for r_d = 5% is shown below:

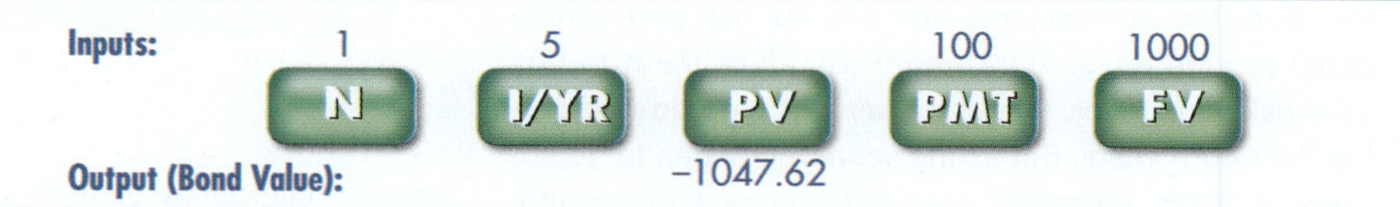

Using either a calculator or a spreadsheet, you could calculate the bond values for a 1-year and a 25-year bond at several current market interest rates; these results are plotted in Figure 5-4. Note how much more sensitive the price of the 25-year bond is to changes in interest rates. At a 10% interest rate, both the 25-year and the 1-year bonds are valued at $1,000. When rates rise to 15%, the 25-year bond falls to $676.79 but the 1-year bond falls only to $956.52.

For bonds with similar coupons, this differential sensitivity to changes in interest rates always holds true: The longer the maturity of the bond, the more its price changes in response to a given change in interest rates. Thus, even if the risk of default on two bonds is exactly the same, the one with the longer maturity is exposed to more risk from a rise in interest rates.

The explanation for this difference in interest rate risk is simple. Suppose you bought a 25-year bond that yielded 10%, or $100 a year. Now suppose interest rates on bonds of comparable risk rose to 15%. You would be stuck with only $100 of interest for the next 25 years. On the other hand, had you bought a 1-year bond, you would have a low return for only 1 year. At the end of the year, you would get your $1,000 back, and you could then reinvest it and receive a 15% return ($150) for the next year. Thus, interest rate risk reflects the length of time one is committed to a given investment.

[18]You would have an *accounting* (and tax) loss only if you sold the bond; if you held it to maturity, you would not have such a loss. However, even if you did not sell, you would still have suffered a *real economic loss in an opportunity cost sense* because you would have lost the opportunity to invest at 15% and would be stuck with a 10% bond in a 15% market. In an economic sense, "paper losses" are just as bad as realized accounting losses.

[19]Actually, a bond's maturity and coupon rate each affect interest rate risk. Low coupons mean that most of the bond's return will come from repayment of principal, whereas on a high-coupon bond with the same maturity, more of the cash flows will come in during the early years because of the relatively large coupon payments. A measurement called "duration," which finds the average number of years that the bond's PV of cash flows remains outstanding, has been developed to combine maturity and coupons. A zero coupon bond, which has no interest payments and whose payments all come at maturity, has a duration equal to the bond's maturity. Coupon bonds all have durations that are shorter than maturity, and the higher the coupon rate, the shorter the duration. Bonds with longer duration are exposed to more interest rate risk. *Excel*'s DURATION function provides an easy way to calculate a bond's duration. See ***Web Extension 5C*** and ***Ch05 Tool Kit.xls*** for more on duration.

FIGURE 5-4 Value of Long- and Short-Term 10% Annual Coupon Bonds at Different Market Interest Rates

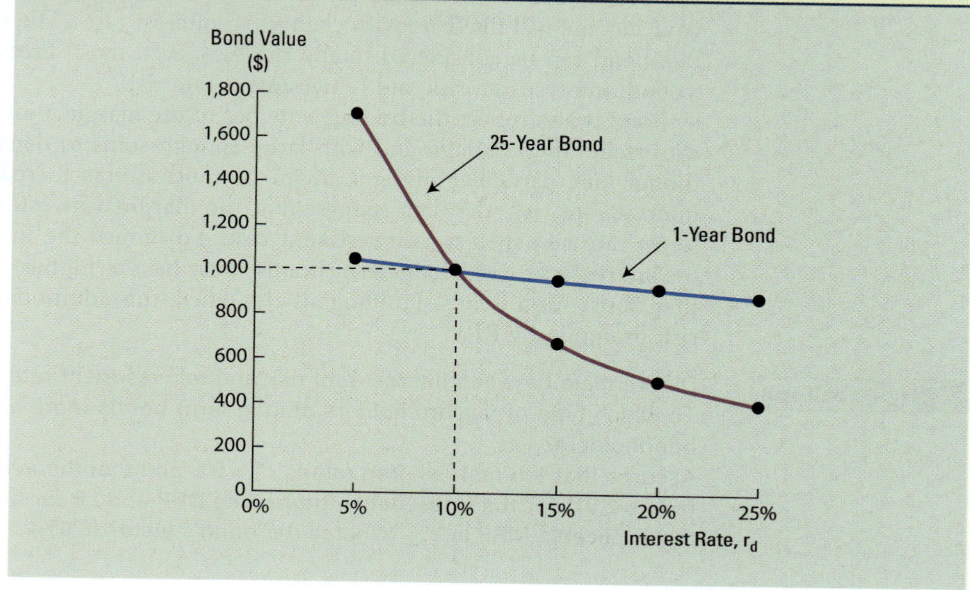

Reinvestment Rate Risk

As we saw in the preceding section, an *increase* in interest rates will hurt bondholders because it will lead to a decline in the value of a bond portfolio. But can a *decrease* in interest rates also hurt bondholders? The answer is "yes," because if interest rates fall then a bondholder may suffer a reduction in his or her income. For example, consider a retiree who has a portfolio of bonds and lives off the income they produce. The bonds, on average, have a coupon rate of 10%. Now suppose that interest rates decline to 5%. The short-term bonds will mature, and when they do, they will have to be replaced with lower-yielding bonds. In addition, many of the remaining long-term bonds may be called, and as calls occur, the bondholder will have to replace 10% bonds with 5% bonds. Thus, our retiree will suffer a reduction of income.

The risk of an income decline due to a drop in interest rates is called **reinvestment rate risk**. Reinvestment rate risk is obviously high on callable bonds. It is also high on short-maturity bonds, because the shorter the maturity of a bond, the fewer the years when the relatively high old interest rate will be earned and the sooner the funds will have to be reinvested at the new low rate. Thus, retirees whose primary holdings are short-term securities, such as bank CDs and short-term bonds, are hurt badly by a decline in rates, but holders of long-term bonds continue to enjoy their old high rates.

Comparing Interest Rate Risk and Reinvestment Rate Risk: The Maturity Risk Premium

Note that interest rate risk relates to the *value* of the bonds in a portfolio, while reinvestment rate risk relates to the *income* the portfolio produces. If you hold long-term bonds then you will face a lot of interest rate risk, because the value of your bonds will decline if interest rates rise; but you will not face much reinvestment rate risk, so your income will be stable. On the other hand, if you hold short-term bonds, you will not be exposed to much interest rate risk because the value of your portfolio will be stable, but you will be exposed to considerable reinvestment rate risk because your income will fluctuate with changes in interest rates. We see, then, that no fixed-rate bond can be considered totally riskless—even most Treasury bonds are exposed to both interest rate risk and reinvestment rate risk.[20]

Bond prices reflect the trading activities of the marginal investors, defined as those who trade often enough and with large enough sums to determine bond prices. Although one particular investor might be more averse to reinvestment risk than to interest rate risk, the data suggest that the marginal investor is more averse to interest rate risk than to reinvestment risk. To induce the marginal investor to take on interest rate risk, long-term bonds must have a higher expected rate of return than short-term bonds. Holding all else equal, this additional return is the maturity risk premium (MRP).

Self-Test

Differentiate between interest rate risk and reinvestment rate risk.

To which type of risk are holders of long-term bonds more exposed? Short-term bondholders?

Assume that the real risk-free rate is r* = 3% and that the average expected inflation rate is 2.5% for the foreseeable future. The DRP and LP for a bond are each 1%, and the applicable MRP is 2%. What is the bond's yield? **(9.5%)**

5.14 The Term Structure of Interest Rates

The **term structure of interest rates** describes the relationship between long-term and short-term rates. The term structure is important both to corporate treasurers deciding whether to borrow by issuing long-term or short-term debt and to investors who are deciding whether to buy long-term or short-term bonds.

Interest rates for bonds with different maturities can be found in a variety of publications, including *The Wall Street Journal* and the *Federal Reserve Bulletin*, as well as on a number of Web sites, including Bloomberg, Yahoo!, CNN Financial, and the Federal Reserve Board. Using interest rate data from these sources, we can determine the term structure at any given point in time. For example, Figure 5-5 presents interest rates for different maturities on three different dates. The set of data for a given date, when plotted on a graph such as Figure 5-5, is called the **yield curve** for that date.

As the figure shows, the yield curve changes both in position and in slope over time. In March 1980, all rates were quite high because high inflation was expected. However, the rate of inflation was expected to decline, so the inflation premium (IP) was larger for short-term bonds than for long-term bonds. This caused short-term yields to be higher than long-term yields, resulting in a *downward-sloping* yield curve. By February 2000, inflation had indeed declined and thus all rates were lower. The yield curve had become **humped**—medium-term rates were higher than either short- or long-term rates. By March 2009, all rates had fallen below the 2000 levels. Because short-term rates had dropped below long-term rates, the yield curve was *upward sloping*.

Historically, long-term rates are generally higher than short-term rates owing to the maturity risk premium, so the yield curve usually slopes upward. For this reason, people often call an upward-sloping yield curve a **"normal" yield curve** and a yield

---

[20]Although indexed Treasury bonds are almost riskless, they pay a relatively low real rate. Note also that risks have not disappeared—they have simply been transferred from bondholders to taxpayers.

FIGURE 5-5 U.S. Treasury Bond Interest Rates on Different Dates

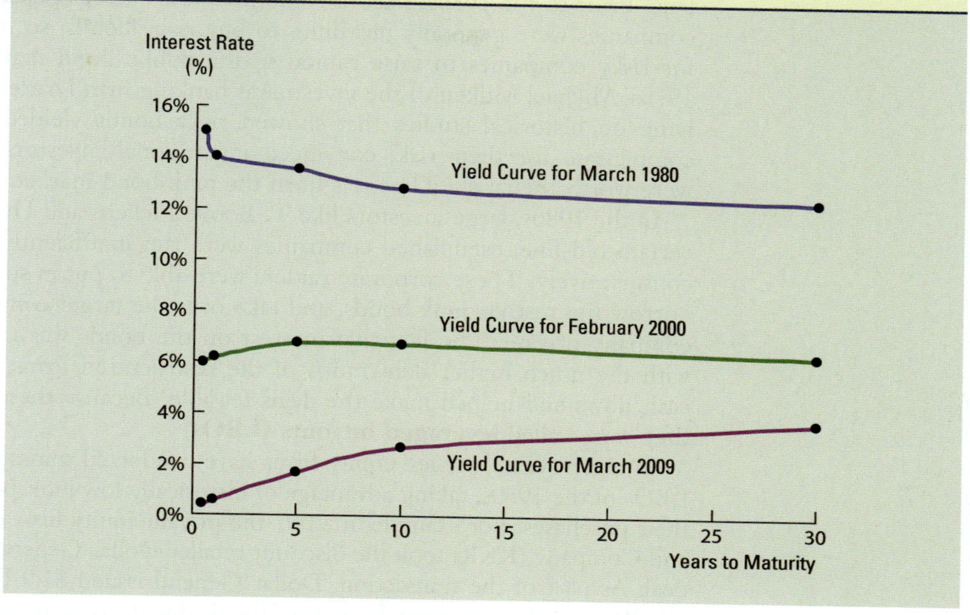

curve that slopes downward an **inverted**, or **"abnormal," curve**. Thus, in Figure 5-5 the yield curve for March 1980 was inverted whereas the yield curve in March 2009 was normal. As stated above, the February 2000 curve was humped.

A few academics and practitioners contend that large bond traders who buy and sell securities of different maturities each day dominate the market. According to this view, a bond trader is just as willing to buy a 30-year bond to pick up a short-term profit as to buy a 3-month security. Strict proponents of this view argue that the shape of the yield curve is therefore determined only by market expectations about future interest rates, a position that is called the **pure expectations theory**, or sometimes just the **expectations theory**. If this were true, then the maturity risk premium (MRP) would be zero and long-term interest rates would simply be a weighted average of current and expected future short-term interest rates. See ***Web Extension 5D*** for a more detailed discussion of the expectations theory.

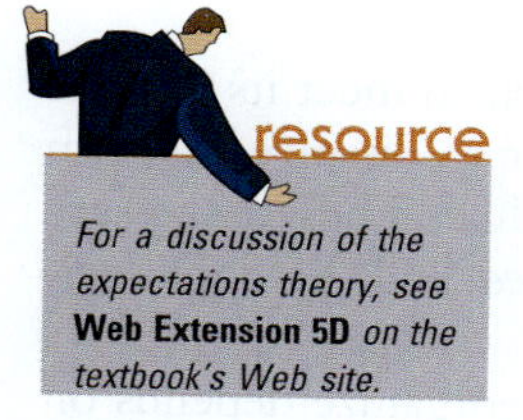

For a discussion of the expectations theory, see **Web Extension 5D** *on the textbook's Web site.*

Self-Test

What is a yield curve, and what information would you need to draw this curve?

Distinguish among the shapes of a "normal" yield curve, an "abnormal" curve, and a "humped" curve.

If the interest rates on 1-, 5-, 20-, and 30-year bonds are (respectively) 4%, 5%, 6%, and 7%, then how would you describe the yield curve? How would you describe it if the rates were reversed?

5.15 Financing with Junk Bonds

Recall that bonds rated less than BBB are noninvestment-grade debt, also called junk bonds or high-yield debt. There are two ways that a bond can become a junk bond. First, the bond might have been investment-grade debt when it was issued but its rating declined because the issuing corporation had fallen on hard times. Such bonds are called "fallen angels," and there are many such bonds as we write this in 2009.

Some bonds are junk bonds at the time they are issued, but this was not always true. Prior to the 1980s, fixed-income investors such as pension funds and insurance companies were generally unwilling to buy risky bonds, so it was almost impossible for risky companies to raise capital in the public bond markets. Then, in the late 1970s, Michael Milken of the investment banking firm Drexel Burnham Lambert, relying on historical studies that showed risky bonds yielded more than enough to compensate for their risk, convinced institutional investors that junk bond yields were worth their risk. Thus was born the junk bond market.

In the 1980s, large investors like T. Boone Pickens and Henry Kravis thought that certain old-line, established companies were run inefficiently and were financed too conservatively. These corporate raiders were able to put in some of their own money, borrow the rest via junk bonds, and take over the target company, usually taking the company private. The fact that interest on the bonds was tax deductible, combined with the much higher debt ratios of the restructured firms, also increased after-tax cash flows and helped make the deals feasible. Because these deal used lots of debt, they were called **leveraged buyouts (LBOs)**.

In recent years, private equity firms have conducted transactions very similar to the LBOs of the 1980s, taking advantage of historically low junk-bond rates to help finance their purchases. For example, in 2007 the private equity firm Kohlberg Kravis Roberts and Company (KKR) took the discount retailer Dollar General private in a $6.9 billion deal. As part of the transaction, Dollar General issued $1.9 billion in junk bonds. So KKR financed approximately 73% of the deal with its own cash (coming from its own equity and from money it had borrowed on its own account) and about 27% of the deal with money that Dollar General raised. Dollar General's sales have been soaring during the early part of the current recession, making KKR's purchase look like a winner.

Self-Test What are junk bonds?

5.16 Bankruptcy and Reorganization

When a business becomes *insolvent*, it does not have enough cash to meet its interest and principal payments. A decision must then be made whether to dissolve the firm through *liquidation* or to permit it to *reorganize* and thus stay alive. These issues are addressed in Chapters 7 and 11 of the federal bankruptcy statutes, and the final decision is made by a federal bankruptcy court judge.

The decision to force a firm to liquidate versus permit it to reorganize depends on whether the value of the reorganized firm is likely to be greater than the value of the firm's assets if they are sold off piecemeal. In a reorganization, the firm's creditors negotiate with management on the terms of a potential reorganization. The reorganization plan may call for a *restructuring* of the firm's debt, in which case the interest rate may be reduced, the term to maturity lengthened, or some of the debt may be exchanged for equity. The point of the restructuring is to reduce the financial charges to a level that the firm's cash flows can support. Of course, the common stockholders also have to give up something: they often see their position diluted as a result of additional shares being given to debtholders in exchange for accepting a reduced amount of debt principal and interest. In fact, the original common stockholders often end up with nothing. A trustee may be appointed by the court to oversee the reorganization, but generally the existing management is allowed to retain control.

Liquidation occurs if the company is deemed to be too far gone to be saved—if it is worth more dead than alive. If the bankruptcy court orders liquidation, then assets are sold off and the cash obtained is distributed as specified in Chapter 7 of the Bankruptcy Act. Here is the priority of claims: (1) past-due property taxes; (2) secured creditors who are entitled to the proceeds from the sale of collateral; (3) the trustee's costs of administering and operating the bankrupt firm; (4) expenses incurred after bankruptcy was filed; (5) wages due workers, up to a limit of $2,000 per worker; (6) claims for unpaid contributions to employee benefit plans (with wages and claims not to exceed $2,000 per worker); (7) unsecured claims for customer deposits up to $900 per customer; (8) federal, state, and local taxes due; (9) unfunded pension plan liabilities (although some limitations exist); (10) general unsecured creditors; (11) preferred stockholders (up to the par value of their stock); and (12) common stockholders (although usually nothing is left).

The key points for you to know are: (1) the federal bankruptcy statutes govern both reorganization and liquidation, (2) bankruptcies occur frequently, and (3) a priority of the specified claims must be followed when distributing the assets of a liquidated firm.

Self-Test

Differentiate between a Chapter 7 liquidation and a Chapter 11 reorganization.
List the priority of claims for the distribution of a liquidated firm's assets.

Summary

This chapter described the different types of bonds that governments and corporations issue, explained how bond prices are established, and discussed how investors estimate the rates of return they can expect to earn. The rate of return required by debtholders is the company's pre-tax cost of debt, and this rate depends on the risk that investors face when they buy bonds.

- A **bond** is a long-term promissory note issued by a business or governmental unit. The issuer receives money in exchange for promising to make interest payments and to repay the principal on a specified future date.
- Some special types of long-term financing include **zero coupon bonds**, which pay no annual interest but are issued at a discount; see ***Web Extension 5A*** for more on zero coupon bonds. Other types are **floating-rate debt**, whose interest payments fluctuate with changes in the general level of interest rates; and **junk bonds**, which are high-risk, high-yield instruments issued by firms that use a great deal of financial leverage.
- A **call provision** gives the issuing corporation the right to redeem the bonds prior to maturity under specified terms, usually at a price greater than the maturity value (the difference is a **call premium**). A firm will typically call a bond if interest rates fall substantially below the coupon rate.
- A **sinking fund** is a provision that requires the corporation to retire a portion of the bond issue each year. The purpose of the sinking fund is to provide for the orderly retirement of the issue. A sinking fund typically requires no call premium.
- The **value of a bond** is found as the present value of an **annuity** (the interest payments) plus the present value of a lump sum (the **principal**). The bond is evaluated at the appropriate periodic interest rate over the number of periods for which interest payments are made.
- The equation used to find the value of an annual coupon bond is

$$V_B = \sum_{t=1}^{N} \frac{INT}{(1 + r_d)^t} + \frac{M}{(1 + r_d)^N}$$

- An adjustment to the formula must be made if the bond pays interest **semiannually**: divide INT and r_d by 2, and multiply N by 2.

- The expected rate of return on a bond held to maturity is defined as the bond's **yield to maturity (YTM)**:

$$\text{Bond price} = \sum_{t=1}^{N} \frac{\text{INT}}{(1+\text{YTM})^t} + \frac{\text{M}}{(1+\text{YTM})^N}$$

- The expected rate of return on a callable bond held to its call date is defined as the **yield to call (YTC)**.
- The **nominal** (or **quoted) interest rate** on a debt security, r_d, is composed of the real risk-free rate, r^*, plus premiums that reflect inflation (IP), default risk (DRP), liquidity (LP), and maturity risk (MRP):

$$r_d = r^* + \text{IP} + \text{DRP} + \text{LP} + \text{MRP}$$

- The **risk-free rate of interest, r_{RF}**, is defined as the real risk-free rate, r^*, plus an inflation premium, IP: $r_{RF} = r^* + \text{IP}$.
- **Treasury Inflation-Protected Securities (TIPS)** are U.S. Treasury bonds that have no inflation risk. See ***Web Extension 5B*** for more discussion of TIPS.
- The longer the maturity of a bond, the more its price will change in response to a given change in interest rates; this is called **interest rate risk.** However, bonds with short maturities expose investors to high **reinvestment rate risk,** which is the risk that income from a bond portfolio will decline because cash flows received from bonds will be rolled over at lower interest rates.
- **Duration** is a measure of interest rate risk. See ***Web Extension 5C*** for a discussion of duration.
- Corporate and municipal bonds have **default risk**. If an issuer defaults, investors receive less than the promised return on the bond. Therefore, investors should evaluate a bond's default risk before making a purchase.
- Bonds are assigned **ratings** that reflect the probability of their going into default. The highest rating is AAA, and they go down to D. The higher a bond's rating, the lower its risk and therefore its interest rate.
- The relationship between the yields on securities and the securities' maturities is known as the **term structure of interest rates**, and the **yield curve** is a graph of this relationship.
- The shape of the yield curve depends on two key factors: (1) *expectations about future inflation* and (2) *perceptions about the relative risk of securities with different maturities.*
- The yield curve is normally **upward sloping**—this is called a **normal yield curve**. However, the curve can slope downward (an **inverted yield curve**) if the inflation rate is expected to decline. The yield curve also can be **humped**, which means that interest rates on medium-term maturities are higher than rates on both short- and long-term maturities.
- The **expectations theory** states that yields on long-term bonds reflect expected future interest rates. ***Web Extension 5D*** discusses this theory.

Questions

(5–1) Define each of the following terms:

a. Bond; Treasury bond; corporate bond; municipal bond; foreign bond
b. Par value; maturity date; coupon payment; coupon interest rate
c. Floating-rate bond; zero coupon bond; original issue discount bond (OID)

d. Call provision; redeemable bond; sinking fund
e. Convertible bond; warrant; income bond; indexed, or purchasing power, bond
f. Premium bond; discount bond
g. Current yield (on a bond); yield to maturity (YTM); yield to call (YTC)
h. Indentures; mortgage bond; debenture; subordinated debenture
i. Development bond; municipal bond insurance; junk bond; investment-grade bond
j. Real risk-free rate of interest, r*; nominal risk-free rate of interest, r_{RF}
k. Inflation premium (IP); default risk premium (DRP); liquidity; liquidity premium (LP)
l. Interest rate risk; maturity risk premium (MRP); reinvestment rate risk
m. Term structure of interest rates; yield curve
n. "Normal" yield curve; inverted ("abnormal") yield curve

(5–2) "Short-term interest rates are more volatile than long-term interest rates, so short-term bond prices are more sensitive to interest rate changes than are long-term bond prices." Is this statement true or false? Explain.

(5–3) The rate of return you would get if you bought a bond and held it to its maturity date is called the bond's yield to maturity. If interest rates in the economy rise after a bond has been issued, what will happen to the bond's price and to its YTM? Does the length of time to maturity affect the extent to which a given change in interest rates will affect the bond's price?

(5–4) If you buy a *callable* bond and interest rates decline, will the value of your bond rise by as much as it would have risen if the bond had not been callable? Explain.

(5–5) A sinking fund can be set up in one of two ways. Discuss the advantages and disadvantages of each procedure from the viewpoint of both the firm and its bondholders.

Self-Test Problem

Solution Appears in Appendix A

(ST–1)
Bond Valuation

The Pennington Corporation issued a new series of bonds on January 1, 1987. The bonds were sold at par ($1,000), had a 12% coupon, and matured in 30 years on December 31, 2016. Coupon payments are made semiannually (on June 30 and December 31).

a. What was the YTM on the date the bonds were issued?
b. What was the price of the bonds on January 1, 1992 (5 years later), assuming that interest rates had fallen to 10%?
c. Find the current yield, capital gains yield, and total yield on January 1, 1992, given the price as determined in part b.
d. On July 1, 2010 (6.5 years before maturity), Pennington's bonds sold for $916.42. What are the YTM, the current yield, and the capital gains yield for that date?
e. Now assume that you plan to purchase an outstanding Pennington bond on March 1, 2010, when the going rate of interest given its risk is 15.5%. How large a check must you write to complete the transaction? (*Hint:* Don't forget the accrued interest.)

Problems

Answers Appear in Appendix B

EASY PROBLEMS 1–6

(5–1) Bond Valuation with Annual Payments

Jackson Corporation's bonds have 12 years remaining to maturity. Interest is paid annually, the bonds have a \$1,000 par value, and the coupon interest rate is 8%. The bonds have a yield to maturity of 9%. What is the current market price of these bonds?

(5–2) Yield to Maturity for Annual Payments

Wilson Wonders's bonds have 12 years remaining to maturity. Interest is paid annually, the bonds have a \$1,000 par value, and the coupon interest rate is 10%. The bonds sell at a price of \$850. What is their yield to maturity?

(5–3) Current Yield for Annual Payments

Heath Foods's bonds have 7 years remaining to maturity. The bonds have a face value of \$1,000 and a yield to maturity of 8%. They pay interest annually and have a 9% coupon rate. What is their current yield?

(5–4) Determinant of Interest Rates

The real risk-free rate of interest is 4%. Inflation is expected to be 2% this year and 4% during the next 2 years. Assume that the maturity risk premium is zero. What is the yield on 2-year Treasury securities? What is the yield on 3-year Treasury securities?

(5–5) Default Risk Premium

A Treasury bond that matures in 10 years has a yield of 6%. A 10-year corporate bond has a yield of 9%. Assume that the liquidity premium on the corporate bond is 0.5%. What is the default risk premium on the corporate bond?

(5–6) Maturity Risk Premium

The real risk-free rate is 3%, and inflation is expected to be 3% for the next 2 years. A 2-year Treasury security yields 6.3%. What is the maturity risk premium for the 2-year security?

INTERMEDIATE PROBLEMS 7–20

(5–7) Bond Valuation with Semiannual Payments

Renfro Rentals has issued bonds that have a 10% coupon rate, payable semiannually. The bonds mature in 8 years, have a face value of \$1,000, and a yield to maturity of 8.5%. What is the price of the bonds?

(5–8) Yield to Maturity and Call with Semiannual Payments

Thatcher Corporation's bonds will mature in 10 years. The bonds have a face value of \$1,000 and an 8% coupon rate, paid semiannually. The price of the bonds is \$1,100. The bonds are callable in 5 years at a call price of \$1,050. What is their yield to maturity? What is their yield to call?

(5–9) Bond Valuation and Interest Rate Risk

The Garraty Company has two bond issues outstanding. Both bonds pay \$100 annual interest plus \$1,000 at maturity. Bond L has a maturity of 15 years, and Bond S has a maturity of 1 year.

a. What will be the value of each of these bonds when the going rate of interest is (1) 5%, (2) 8%, and (3) 12%? Assume that there is only one more interest payment to be made on Bond S.
b. Why does the longer-term (15-year) bond fluctuate more when interest rates change than does the shorter-term bond (1 year)?

(5–10) Yield to Maturity and Required Returns

The Brownstone Corporation's bonds have 5 years remaining to maturity. Interest is paid annually, the bonds have a \$1,000 par value, and the coupon interest rate is 9%.

a. What is the yield to maturity at a current market price of (1) $829 or (2) $1,104?
b. Would you pay $829 for one of these bonds if you thought that the appropriate rate of interest was 12%—that is, if r_d = 12%? Explain your answer.

(5–11) Yield to Call and Realized Rates of Return

Seven years ago, Goodwynn & Wolf Incorporated sold a 20-year bond issue with a 14% annual coupon rate and a 9% call premium. Today, G&W called the bonds. The bonds originally were sold at their face value of $1,000. Compute the realized rate of return for investors who purchased the bonds when they were issued and who surrender them today in exchange for the call price.

(5–12) Bond Yields and Rates of Return

A 10-year, 12% semiannual coupon bond with a par value of $1,000 may be called in 4 years at a call price of $1,060. The bond sells for $1,100. (Assume that the bond has just been issued.)

a. What is the bond's yield to maturity?
b. What is the bond's current yield?
c. What is the bond's capital gain or loss yield?
d. What is the bond's yield to call?

(5–13) Yield to Maturity and Current Yield

You just purchased a bond that matures in 5 years. The bond has a face value of $1,000 and has an 8% annual coupon. The bond has a current yield of 8.21%. What is the bond's yield to maturity?

(5–14) Current Yield with Semiannual Payments

A bond that matures in 7 years sells for $1,020. The bond has a face value of $1,000 and a yield to maturity of 10.5883%. The bond pays coupons semiannually. What is the bond's current yield?

(5–15) Yield to Call, Yield to Maturity, and Market Rates

Absalom Motors's 14% coupon rate, semiannual payment, $1,000 par value bonds that mature in 30 years are callable 5 years from now at a price of $1,050. The bonds sell at a price of $1,353.54, and the yield curve is flat. Assuming that interest rates in the economy are expected to remain at their current level, what is the best estimate of the nominal interest rate on new bonds?

(5–16) Interest Rate Sensitivity

A bond trader purchased each of the following bonds at a yield to maturity of 8%. Immediately after she purchased the bonds, interest rates fell to 7%. What is the percentage change in the price of each bond after the decline in interest rates? Fill in the following table:

	Price @ 8%	Price @ 7%	Percentage Change
10-year, 10% annual coupon	________	________	________
10-year zero	________	________	________
5-year zero	________	________	________
30-year zero	________	________	________
$100 perpetuity	________	________	________

(5–17) Bond Value as Maturity Approaches

An investor has two bonds in his portfolio. Each bond matures in 4 years, has a face value of $1,000, and has a yield to maturity equal to 9.6%. One bond, Bond C, pays an annual coupon of 10%; the other bond, Bond Z, is a zero coupon bond. Assuming that the yield to maturity of each bond remains at 9.6% over the next 4 years, what will be the price of each of the bonds at the following time periods? Fill in the following table:

t	Price of Bond C	Price of Bond Z
0	______	______
1	______	______
2	______	______
3	______	______
4	______	______

(5–18) Determinants of Interest Rates

The real risk-free rate is 2%. Inflation is expected to be 3% this year, 4% next year, and then 3.5% thereafter. The maturity risk premium is estimated to be 0.0005 × (t – 1), where t = number of years to maturity. What is the nominal interest rate on a 7-year Treasury security?

(5–19) Maturity Risk Premiums

Assume that the real risk-free rate, r*, is 3% and that inflation is expected to be 8% in Year 1, 5% in Year 2, and 4% thereafter. Assume also that all Treasury securities are highly liquid and free of default risk. If 2-year and 5-year Treasury notes both yield 10%, what is the difference in the maturity risk premiums (MRPs) on the two notes; that is, what is MRP_5 minus MRP_2?

(5–20) Inflation Risk Premiums

Because of a recession, the inflation rate expected for the coming year is only 3%. However, the inflation rate in Year 2 and thereafter is expected to be constant at some level above 3%. Assume that the real risk-free rate is r* = 2% for all maturities and that there are no maturity premiums. If 3-year Treasury notes yield 2 percentage points more than 1-year notes, what inflation rate is expected after Year 1?

Challenging Problems 21–23

(5–21) Bond Valuation and Changes in Maturity and Required Returns

Suppose Hillard Manufacturing sold an issue of bonds with a 10-year maturity, a $1,000 par value, a 10% coupon rate, and semiannual interest payments.

a. Two years after the bonds were issued, the going rate of interest on bonds such as these fell to 6%. At what price would the bonds sell?
b. Suppose that, 2 years after the initial offering, the going interest rate had risen to 12%. At what price would the bonds sell?
c. Suppose, as in part a, that interest rates fell to 6% 2 years after the issue date. Suppose further that the interest rate remained at 6% for the next 8 years. What would happen to the price of the bonds over time?

(5–22) Yield to Maturity and Yield to Call

Arnot International's bonds have a current market price of $1,200. The bonds have an 11% annual coupon payment, a $1,000 face value, and 10 years left until maturity. The bonds may be called in 5 years at 109% of face value (call price = $1,090).

a. What is the yield to maturity?
b. What is the yield to call if they are called in 5 years?
c. Which yield might investors expect to earn on these bonds, and why?
d. The bond's indenture indicates that the call provision gives the firm the right to call them at the end of each year beginning in Year 5. In Year 5, they may be called at 109% of face value, but in each of the next 4 years the call percentage will decline by 1 percentage point. Thus, in Year 6 they may be called at 108% of face value, in Year 7 they may be called at 107% of face value, and so on. If the yield curve is horizontal and interest rates remain at their current level, when is the latest that investors might expect the firm to call the bonds?

(5–23) Determinants of Interest Rates

Suppose you and most other investors expect the inflation rate to be 7% next year, to fall to 5% during the following year, and then to remain at a rate of 3% thereafter. Assume that the real risk-free rate, r*, will remain at 2% and that maturity risk premiums on Treasury securities rise from zero on very short-term securities (those that mature in a few days) to a level of 0.2 percentage points for 1-year securities. Furthermore, maturity risk premiums increase 0.2 percentage points for each year to maturity, up to a limit of 1.0 percentage point on 5-year or longer-term T-notes and T-bonds.

a. Calculate the interest rate on 1-, 2-, 3-, 4-, 5-, 10-, and 20-year Treasury securities, and plot the yield curve.
b. Now suppose ExxonMobil's bonds, rated AAA, have the same maturities as the Treasury bonds. As an approximation, plot an ExxonMobil yield curve on the same graph with the Treasury bond yield curve. (*Hint:* Think about the default risk premium on ExxonMobil's long-term versus its short-term bonds.)
c. Now plot the approximate yield curve of Long Island Lighting Company, a risky nuclear utility.

Spreadsheet Problem

(5–24) Build a Model: Bond Valuation

Start with the partial model in the file ***Ch05 P24 Build a Model.xls*** on the textbook's Web site. A 20-year, 8% semiannual coupon bond with a par value of $1,000 may be called in 5 years at a call price of $1,040. The bond sells for $1,100. (Assume that the bond has just been issued.)

a. What is the bond's yield to maturity?
b. What is the bond's current yield?
c. What is the bond's capital gain or loss yield?
d. What is the bond's yield to call?
e. How would the price of the bond be affected by a change in the going market interest rate? (*Hint:* Conduct a sensitivity analysis of price to changes in the going market interest rate for the bond. Assume that the bond will be called if and only if the going rate of interest *falls below* the coupon rate. This is an oversimplification, but assume it anyway for purposes of this problem.)
f. Now assume the date is October 25, 2010. Assume further that a 12%, 10-year bond was issued on July 1, 2010, pays interest semiannually (on January 1 and July 1), and sells for $1,100. Use your spreadsheet to find the bond's yield.

Mini Case

Sam Strother and Shawna Tibbs are vice presidents of Mutual of Seattle Insurance Company and co-directors of the company's pension fund management division. An important new client, the North-Western Municipal Alliance, has requested that Mutual of Seattle present an investment seminar to the mayors of the represented cities, and Strother and Tibbs, who will make the actual presentation, have asked you to help them by answering the following questions

a. What are the key features of a bond?
b. What are call provisions and sinking fund provisions? Do these provisions make bonds more or less risky?

c. How does one determine the value of any asset whose value is based on expected future cash flows?
d. How is the value of a bond determined? What is the value of a 10-year, \$1,000 par value bond with a 10% annual coupon if its required rate of return is 10%?
e. (1) What would be the value of the bond described in part d if, just after it had been issued, the expected inflation rate rose by 3 percentage points, causing investors to require a 13% return? Would we now have a discount or a premium bond?
   (2) What would happen to the bond's value if inflation fell and r_d declined to 7%? Would we now have a premium or a discount bond?
   (3) What would happen to the value of the 10-year bond over time if the required rate of return remained at 13%? If it remained at 7%? (*Hint:* With a financial calculator, enter PMT, I/YR, FV, and N, and then change N to see what happens to the PV as the bond approaches maturity.)
f. (1) What is the yield to maturity on a 10-year, 9% annual coupon, \$1,000 par value bond that sells for \$887.00? That sells for \$1,134.20? What does the fact that a bond sells at a discount or at a premium tell you about the relationship between r_d and the bond's coupon rate?
   (2) What are the total return, the current yield, and the capital gains yield for the discount bond? (Assume the bond is held to maturity and the company does not default on the bond.)
g. How does the equation for valuing a bond change if semiannual payments are made? Find the value of a 10-year, semiannual payment, 10% coupon bond if the nominal $r_d = 13\%$.
h. Suppose a 10-year, 10% semiannual coupon bond with a par value of \$1,000 is currently selling for \$1,135.90, producing a nominal yield to maturity of 8%. However, the bond can be called after 5 years for a price of \$1,050.
   (1) What is the bond's *nominal* yield to call (YTC)?
   (2) If you bought this bond, do you think you would be more likely to earn the YTM or the YTC? Why?
i. Write a general expression for the yield on any debt security (r_d) and define these terms: real risk-free rate of interest (r*), inflation premium (IP), default risk premium (DRP), liquidity premium (LP), and maturity risk premium (MRP).
j. Define the nominal risk-free rate (r_{RF}). What security can be used as an estimate of r_{RF}?
k. Describe a way to estimate the inflation premium (IP) for a t-Year bond.
l. What is a *bond spread* and how is it related to the default risk premium? How are bond ratings related to default risk? What factors affect a company's bond rating?
m. What is *interest rate* (or *price*) *risk?* Which bond has more interest rate risk: an annual payment 1-year bond or a 10-year bond? Why?
n. What is *reinvestment rate risk?* Which has more reinvestment rate risk: a 1-year bond or a 10-year bond?
o. How are interest rate risk and reinvestment rate risk related to the maturity risk premium?
p. What is the term structure of interest rates? What is a yield curve?
q. Briefly describe bankruptcy law. If a firm were to default on its bonds, would the company be liquidated immediately? Would the bondholders be assured of receiving all of their promised payments?

SELECTED ADDITIONAL CASES

The following cases from Textchoice, *Cengage Learning's online library, cover many of the concepts discussed in this chapter and are available at* **http://www.textchoice2.com**.

Klein-Brigham Series:
Case 3, "Peachtree Securities, Inc. (B)"; Case 72, "Swan Davis"; and Case 78, "Beatrice Peabody."

Brigham-Buzzard Series:
Case 3, "Powerline Network Corporation (Bonds and Preferred Stock)."

PART 3

Stocks and Options

CHAPTER 6

Risk, Return, and the Capital Asset Pricing Model

As sung by the Grateful Dead, "What a long, strange trip it's been!" The chart below provides some insights into the stock market's risks and returns. The top portion shows the relative changes in price since 1994 for General Electric (GE), General Motors (GM), and the S&P 500 Index. The bottom portion shows the price/earnings ratio for GE.

WWW

Updates on stock prices can be found at many Web sites, including **http://finance.yahoo.com**. *For updates on P/E ratios, see Yahoo!, Value Line Investment Survey, or GE's annual reports.*

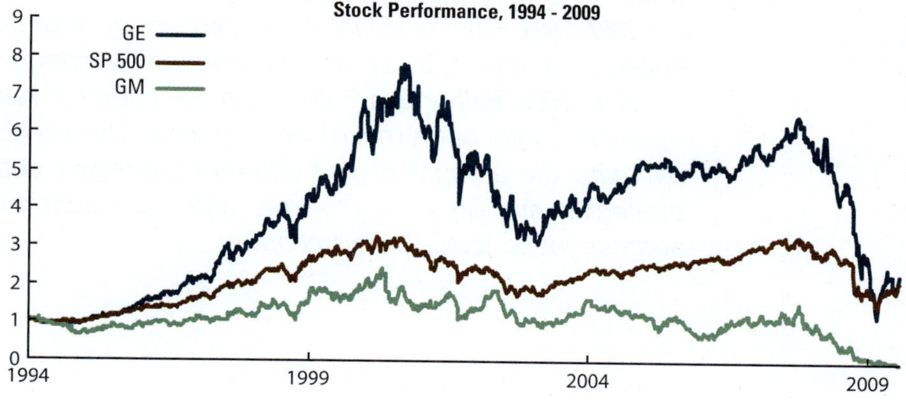

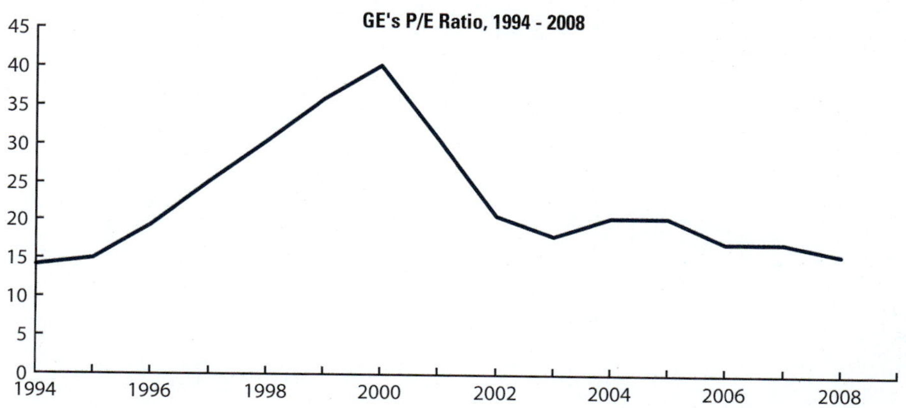

Let's take a look at several sub-periods.

1996–2000. *These years were wonderful for GE, great for the S&P stocks, and pretty good even for GM. The dramatic increase in P/E ratios indicated that stock prices were going up more as a result of increasing expectations than actual earnings, which was a dangerous sign. Alan Greenspan, Chairman of the Federal Reserve Board at that time, stated that the market was suffering from "irrational exuberance," but investors paid no attention and kept roaring ahead.*

2001–2003. *Greenspan was right. The bubble started to leak in 2001, the 9/11 terrorist attacks on the World Trade Center knocked stocks down further, and in 2002 fears of another attack plus a recession drove the market down even more. Those three years cost the average investor almost 50% of his or her beginning-of-2000 market value. P/E ratios plunged, reflecting investors' declining expectations.*

2004–2007. *Investors had overreacted, so in 2004 the market as measured by the S&P 500 began a rebound, remaining strong through 2007. The economy was robust, profits were rising rapidly, and the Federal Reserve encouraged a bull market by cutting interest rates eleven times. In 2007 the S&P hit an all-time high.*

2007–2009. *The financial crisis caused by mortgage-backed securities spilled over into the stock markets and the economy, causing a recession.*

After 2009: Bull or Bear? *We wish we knew! Investing in stocks can be quite profitable, but it means bearing risks. The key to smart investing is to estimate the amount of risk different strategies entail, the returns those strategies are likely to produce, and your own tolerance for risk. We address these topics in this chapter.*

Intrinsic Value, Risk, and Return

The intrinsic value of a company is the present value of its expected future free cash flows (FCF) discounted at the weighted average cost of capital (WACC). This chapter shows you how to measure a firm's risk and the rate of return expected by shareholders, which affects the weighted average cost of capital (WACC). All else held equal, higher risk increases the WACC, which reduces the firm's value.

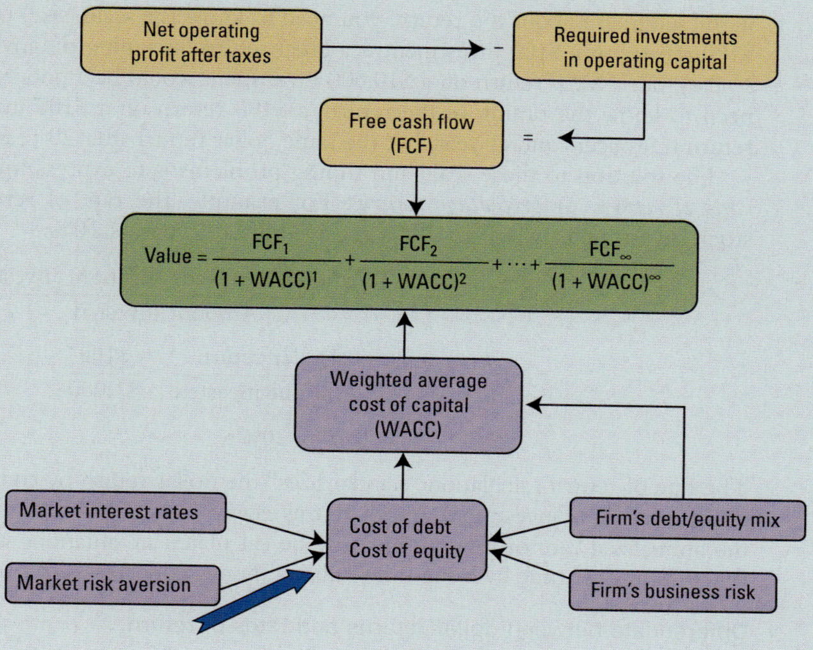

The textbook's Web site contains an Excel file that will guide you through the chapter's calculations. The file for this chapter is **Ch06 Tool Kit.xls,** *and we encourage you to open the file and follow along as you read the chapter.*

In this chapter, we start from the basic premise that investors like returns and dislike risk. Therefore, people will invest in relatively risky assets only if they expect to receive relatively high returns—the higher the perceived risk, the higher the expected rate of return an investor will demand. We define exactly what the term *risk* means as it relates to investments, we examine procedures used to measure risk, and we discuss more precisely the relationship between risk and required returns. In later chapters we extend these relationships to show how risk and return interact to determine security prices. Managers must understand and apply these concepts as they plan the actions that will shape their firms' futures, and investors must understand them in order to make appropriate investment decisions.

6.1 Returns on Investments

With most investments, an individual or business spends money today with the expectation of earning even more money in the future. The concept of *return* provides investors with a convenient way to express the financial performance of an investment. To illustrate, suppose you buy 10 shares of a stock for $1,000. The stock pays no dividends, but at the end of 1 year you sell the stock for $1,100. What is the return on your $1,000 investment?

One way to express an investment's return is in *dollar terms:*

$$\begin{aligned}\text{Dollar return} &= \text{Amount to be received} - \text{Amount invested}\\ &= \$1{,}100 - \$1{,}000\\ &= \$100\end{aligned}$$

If at the end of the year you sell the stock for only $900, your dollar return will be –$100.

Although expressing returns in dollars is easy, two problems arise: (1) to make a meaningful judgment about the return, you need to know the scale (size) of the investment; a $100 return on a $100 investment is a great return (assuming the investment is held for 1 year), but a $100 return on a $10,000 investment would be a poor return. (2) You also need to know the timing of the return; a $100 return on a $100 investment is a great return if it occurs after 1 year, but the same dollar return after 20 years is not very good.

The solution to these scale and timing problems is to express investment results as *rates of return,* or *percentage returns.* For example, the rate of return on the 1-year stock investment, when $1,100 is received after 1 year, is 10%:

$$\begin{aligned}\text{Rate of return} &= \frac{\text{Amount received} - \text{Amount invested}}{\text{Amount invested}}\\ &= \frac{\text{Dollar return}}{\text{Amount invested}} = \frac{\$100}{\$1{,}000}\\ &= 0.10 = 10\%\end{aligned}$$

The rate of return calculation "standardizes" the dollar return by considering the annual return per unit of investment. Although this example has only one outflow and one inflow, the annualized rate of return can easily be calculated in situations where multiple cash flows occur over time by using time value of money concepts as discussed in Chapter 4.

Self-Test

Differentiate between dollar returns and rates of return.

Why are rates of return superior to dollar returns when comparing different potential investments? (*Hint:* Think about size and timing.)

If you pay $500 for an investment that returns $600 in one year, what is your annual rate of return? **(20%)**

6.2 Stand-Alone Risk

Risk is defined in *Webster's* as "a hazard; a peril; exposure to loss or injury." Thus, risk refers to the chance that some unfavorable event will occur. If you go skydiving, you are taking a chance with your life—skydiving is risky. If you bet on horse races, you are risking your money. If you invest in speculative stocks (or, really, *any* stock), then you are taking a risk in the hope of earning an appreciable return.

An asset's risk can be analyzed in two ways: (1) on a stand-alone basis, where the asset is considered in isolation, and (2) on a portfolio basis, where the asset is held as one of a number of assets in a portfolio. Thus, an asset's **stand-alone risk** is the risk an investor would face if she held only this one asset. Obviously, most assets are held in portfolios, but it is necessary to understand stand-alone risk in order to understand risk in a portfolio context.

To begin, suppose an investor buys $100,000 of short-term Treasury bills with an expected return of 5%. In this case, the rate of return on the investment, 5%, can be estimated quite precisely, and the investment is defined as being essentially *risk free.* However, if the $100,000 were invested in the stock of a company just being organized to prospect for oil in the mid-Atlantic, then the investment's return could not be estimated precisely. One might analyze the situation and conclude that the *expected* rate of return, in a statistical sense, is 20%, but the investor should recognize that the *actual* rate of return could range from, say, +1,000% to −100%. Because there is a significant danger of actually earning much less than the expected return, this stock would be relatively risky.

No investment should be undertaken unless the expected rate of return is high enough to compensate for the perceived risk. In our example, it is clear that few if any investors would be willing to buy the oil company's stock if its expected return were 5%, the same as that of the T-bill.

Risky assets rarely produce their exact expected rates of return; in general, risky assets earn either more or less than was originally expected. Indeed, if assets always produced their expected returns, they would not be risky. Investment risk, then, is related to the probability of actually earning a low or negative return: The greater the chance of a low or negative return, and the larger the potential loss, the riskier the investment. However, risk can be defined more precisely, and we do so in the next section.

Distributions

An event's *probability* is defined as the chance that the event will occur. For example, a weather forecaster might state: "There is a 40% chance of rain today and a 60% chance that it will not rain." If all possible events, or outcomes, are listed, and if a probability is assigned to each event, then the listing is called a **probability distribution**. Keep in mind that the probabilities must sum to 1.0, or 100%.

With this in mind, consider the possible rates of return—due to dividends or stock price changes—that you might earn next year on a $10,000 investment in the stock of either Sale.com or Basic Foods Inc. Sale.com is an Internet company that offers deep discounts on factory seconds and overstocked merchandise. Because it faces intense competition, its new services may or may not be competitive in the marketplace, so its future earnings cannot be predicted very well. Indeed, some new company could develop better services and literally bankrupt Sale.com. Basic Foods, on the other hand, distributes essential food staples to grocery stores, and its sales and profits are relatively stable and predictable.

The rate-of-return probability distributions for the two companies are shown in Figure 6-1. There is a 30% chance of strong demand, in which case both companies will have high earnings, pay high dividends, and enjoy capital gains. There is a 40% probability of normal demand and moderate returns and a 30% probability of weak demand, which will mean low earnings and dividends as well as capital losses. Notice, however, that Sale.com's rate of return could vary far more widely than that of Basic Foods. There is a fairly high probability that the value of Sale.com's stock will drop substantially, resulting in a 70% loss, while there is a much smaller possible loss for Basic Foods.[1]

Expected Rate of Return

If we multiply each possible outcome by its probability of occurrence and then sum these products, as in Figure 6-2, the result is a *weighted average* of outcomes. The weights are the probabilities, and the weighted average is the **expected rate of return, $\hat{r}$,** called "r-hat."[2] The expected rates of return for both Sale.com and Basic Foods are shown in Figure 6-2 to be 15%. This type of table is known as a *payoff matrix*.

[1]Note that the following discussion of risk applies to all random variables, not just stock returns.

[2]In other chapters, we will use $\hat{r}_d$ and $\hat{r}_s$ to signify expected returns on bonds and stocks, respectively. However, this distinction is unnecessary in this chapter, so we just use the general term, $\hat{r}$, to signify the expected return on an investment.

FIGURE 6-1 Probability Distributions for Sale.com and Basic Foods

	A	B	C	D
26	Demand for the	Probability of this	Rate of Return on Stock	
27	Company's Products	Demand Occurring	if this Demand Occurs	
28			Sale.com	Basic Foods
29	Strong	0.30	90%	45%
30	Normal	0.40	15%	15%
31	Weak	0.30	−60%	−15%
32		1.00		
33				

FIGURE 6-2 Calculation of Expected Rates of Return: Payoff Matrix

	A	B	C	D	E	F
41	Demand for the	Probability of this	Sale.com		Basic Foods	
42	Company's Products (1)	Demand Occuring (2)	Rate of Return (3)	Product (2) x (3) = (4)	Rate of Return (5)	Product (2) x (5) = (6)
43						
44	Strong	0.3	90%	27.0%	45%	13.0%
45	Normal	0.4	15%	6.0%	15%	6.0%
46	Weak	0.3	−60%	−18.0%	−15%	−4.5%
47		1.0				
48	Expected Rate of Return = Sum of Products =		$\hat{r}$ =	15.0%	$\hat{r}$ =	15.0%
49						

See **Ch06 Tool Kit.xls** on the textbook's Web site.

The calculation for expected rate of return can also be expressed as an equation that does the same thing as the payoff matrix table:

$$\text{Expected rate of return} = \hat{r} = P_1r_1 + P_2r_2 + \cdots + P_nr_n = \sum_{i=1}^{n} P_ir_i \tag{6-1}$$

Here r_i is the return if outcome i occurs, P_i is the probability that outcome i occurs, and n is the number of possible outcomes. Thus, $\hat{r}$ is a weighted average of the possible outcomes (the r_i values), with each outcome's weight being its probability of occurrence. Using the data for Sale.com, we obtain its expected rate of return as follows:

$$\begin{aligned}\hat{r} &= P_1(r_1) + P_2(r_2) + P_3(r_3)\\ &= 0.3(90\%) + 0.4(15\%) + 0.3(-60\%)\\ &= 15\%\end{aligned}$$

Basic Foods's expected rate of return is also 15%:

$$\begin{aligned}\hat{r} &= 0.3(45\%) + 0.4(15\%) + 0.3(-15\%)\\ &= 15\%\end{aligned}$$

FIGURE 6-3 Probability Distributions of Sale.com's and Basic Foods's Rates of Return

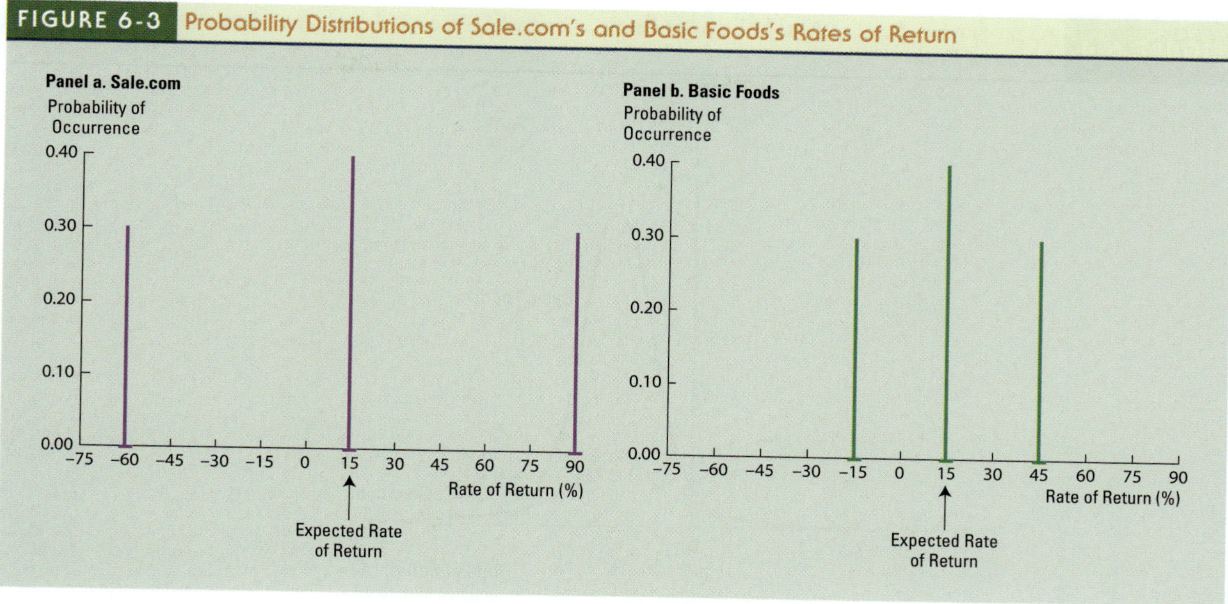

We can graph the rates of return to obtain a picture of the variability of possible outcomes; this is shown in the bar charts of Figure 6-3. The height of each bar signifies the probability that a given outcome will occur. The range of probable returns for Sale.com is from –60% to +90%, with an expected return of 15%. The expected return for Basic Foods is also 15%, but its range is much narrower.

Thus far, we have assumed that only three situations can exist: strong, normal, and weak demand. Actually, of course, demand could range from a deep depression to a fantastic boom, and there are unlimited possibilities in between. Suppose we had the time and patience to assign a probability to each possible level of demand (with the sum of the probabilities still equaling 1.0) and to assign a rate of return to each stock for each level of demand. We would have a table similar to Figure 6-2, except it would have many more entries in each column. This table could be used to calculate expected rates of return using the same approach as shown previously. In fact, the probabilities and outcomes could be approximated by continuous curves such as those presented in Figure 6-4.

The tighter (or more peaked) the probability distribution, the more likely it is that the actual outcome will be close to the expected value, and hence the less likely it is that the actual return will end up far below the expected return. Thus, *the tighter the probability distribution, the lower the risk assigned to a stock.* Since Basic Foods has a relatively tight probability distribution, its *actual return* is likely to be closer to its 15% *expected return* than that of Sale.com.

Measuring Stand-Alone Risk: The Standard Deviation

Risk is a difficult concept to grasp, and a great deal of controversy has surrounded attempts to define and measure it. However, a common definition that is satisfactory for many purposes is stated in terms of probability distributions such as those presented in Figure 6-4: *The tighter the probability distribution of expected future returns, the smaller the risk of a given investment.* According to this definition, Basic Foods is

FIGURE 6-4 Approximate Continuous Probability Distributions of Sale.com's and Basic Foods's Rates of Return

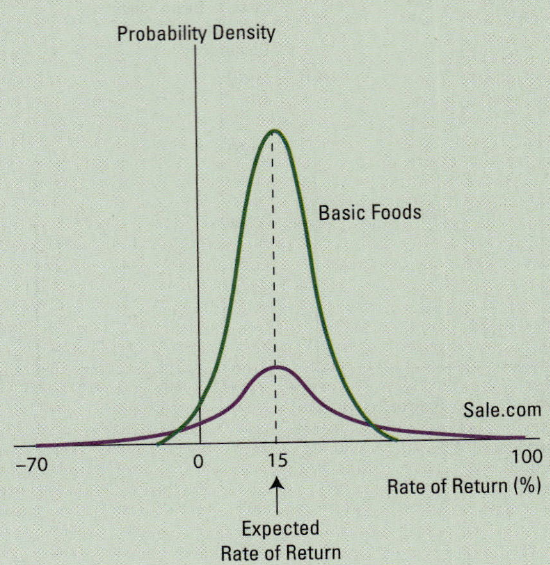

Note: The assumptions regarding the probabilities of various outcomes have been changed from those in Figure 6-3. There the probability of obtaining exactly 15% was 40%; here it is *much smaller* because there are many possible outcomes instead of just three. With continuous distributions, it is more appropriate to ask what the probability is of obtaining at least some specified rate of return than to ask what the probability is of achieving exactly that rate. This topic is covered in detail in statistics courses.

less risky than Sale.com because there is a smaller chance that its actual return will end up far below its expected return.

To be most useful, any measure of risk should have a definite value—we need a measure of the tightness of the probability distribution. One such measure is the **standard deviation**, the symbol for which is **σ**, pronounced "sigma." The smaller the standard deviation, the tighter the probability distribution and, accordingly, the less risky the stock. To calculate the standard deviation, we proceed as shown in Figure 6-5, taking the following steps.[3]

1. Calculate the expected rate of return:

$$\text{Expected rate of return} = \hat{r} = \sum_{i=1}^{n} P_i r_i$$

   For Sale.com, we previously found $\hat{r}$ = 15%.

2. Subtract the expected rate of return ($\hat{r}$) from each possible outcome (r_i) to obtain a set of deviations about $\hat{r}$ as shown in Column 4 of Figure 6-5:

$$\text{Deviation}_i = r_i - \hat{r}$$

[3]These equations are valid for any random variable from a discrete probability distribution, not just for returns.

FIGURE 6-5 Calculating Sale.com's and Basic Foods's Standard Deviations

	A	B	C	D	E	F
89						
90	Panel a.			Sale.com		
91	Probability of Occurring (1)	Rate of Return on Stock (2)	Expected Return (3)	Deviation from Expected Return (2) – (3) = (4)	Squared Deviation $(4)^2 = (5)$	Sq. Dev. × Prob. (5) × (1) = (6)
92	0.3	90%	15%	75.0%	56.25%	16.88%
93	0.4	15%	15%	0.0%	0.00%	0.00%
94	0.3	–60%	15%	–75.0%	56.25%	16.88%
95	1.0				Sum = Variance =	33.75%
96				Std. Dev. = Square root of variance =		58.09%
97						
98	Panel b.			Basic Foods		
99	Probability of Occurring (1)	Rate of Return on Stock (2)	Expected Return (3)	Deviation from Expected Return (2) – (3) = (4)	Squared Deviation $(4)^2 = (5)$	Sq. Dev. × Prob. (5) × (1) = (6)
100	0.3	45%	15%	30.0%	9.00%	2.70%
101	0.4	15%	15%	0.0%	0.00%	0.00%
102	0.3	–15%	15%	–30.0%	9.00%	2.70%
103	1.0				Sum = Variance =	5.40%
104				Std. Dev. = Square root of variance =		23.24%
105						

See **Ch06 Tool Kit.xls** *on the textbook's Web site.*

3. Square each deviation as shown in Column 5. Then multiply the squared deviations in Column 5 by the probability of occurrence for its related outcome; these products are shown in Column 6. Sum these products to obtain the **variance** of the probability distribution:

$$\text{Variance} = \sigma^2 = \sum_{i=1}^{n} (r_i - \hat{r})^2 P_i \qquad \text{(6-2)}$$

4. Finally, find the square root of the variance to obtain the standard deviation:

resource

See **Ch06 Tool Kit.xls** *on the textbook's Web site for all calculations.*

$$\text{Standard deviation} = \sigma = \sqrt{\sum_{i=1}^{n} (r_i - \hat{r})^2 P_i} \qquad \text{(6-3)}$$

Thus, the standard deviation is essentially a weighted average of the deviations from the expected value, and it provides an idea of how far above or below the expected value the actual value is likely to be. If we use this procedure, Sale.com's standard deviation is seen in Figure 6-5 to be σ = 58.09%; we likewise find Basic Foods's standard deviation to be 23.24%. Sale.com has the larger standard deviation,

FIGURE 6-6 Probability Ranges for a Normal Distribution

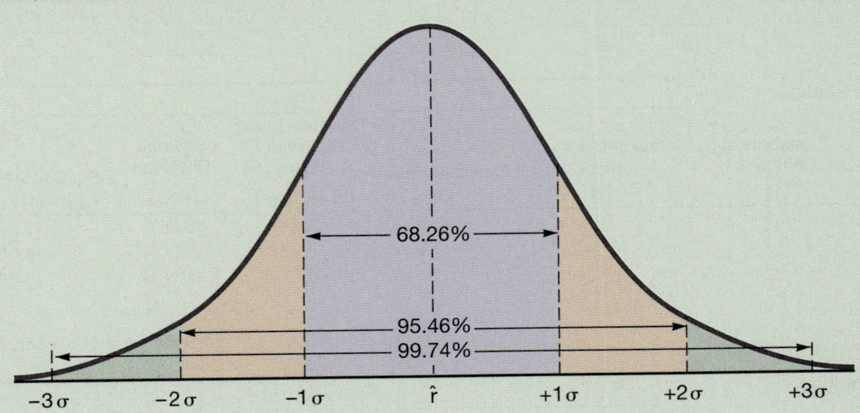

Notes:

a. The area under the normal curve always equals 1.0, or 100%. Thus, the areas under any pair of normal curves drawn on the same scale, whether they are peaked or flat, must be equal.

b. Half of the area under a normal curve is to the left of the mean, indicating that there is a 50% probability that the actual outcome will be less than the mean, and half is to the right of $\hat{r}$, indicating a 50% probability that it will be greater than the mean.

c. Of the area under the curve, 68.26% is within ±1σ of the mean, indicating that the probability is 68.26% that the actual outcome will be within the range $\hat{r}$ σ to $\hat{r} + \sigma$.

For more discussion of probability distributions, see **Web Extension 6A,** *available on the textbook's Web site.*

which indicates a greater variation of returns and thus a greater chance that the actual return will turn out to be substantially lower than the expected return. Therefore, Sale.com is a riskier investment than Basic Foods when held alone.[4]

If we have a **normal distribution**, then the *actual* return will be within ±1 standard deviation of the *expected* return 68.26% of the time. Figure 6-6 illustrates this point, and it also shows the situation for ±2σ and ±3σ. For Sale.com, $\hat{r}$ = 15% and σ = 58.09%, whereas for Basic Foods $\hat{r}$ = 15% and σ = 23.24%. Thus, if the two distributions were normal, there would be a 68.26% probability that Sale.com's actual return would be in the range of 15% ± 58.09%, or from −43.09% to 73.09%. For Basic Foods, the 68.26% range is 15% ± 23.24%, or from −8.24% to 38.24%.

[4]As *Ch06 Tool Ki.xls* shows, it is easy to calculate the standard deviation in *Excel.* Calculating by hand is tedious and error-prone:

$$\sigma = \sqrt{(0.3)(0.90 - 0.15)^2 + (0.4)(0.15 - 0.15)^2 + (0.3)(-0.60 - 0.15)^2} = 0.5809$$

Most financial calculators have no built-in formula for finding the expected value or variance for discrete probability distributions, except for the special case in which the probabilities for all outcomes are equal. Therefore, you must go through the processes outlined in Figure 6-2 and 6-5 (i.e., Equations 6-1 and 6-3). For an example of this process using a financial calculator, see Richard W. Taylor, "Discrete Probability Analysis with the BAII Plus Professional Calculator," *Journal of Financial Education*, Winter 2005, pp. 100–106.

What Does Risk Really Mean?

As explained in the text, the probability of being within 1 standard deviation of the expected return is 68.26%, so the probability of being further than 1 standard deviation from the mean is 31.74%. There is an equal probability of being above or below the range, so there is a 15.87% chance of being more than one standard deviation below the mean, which is roughly equal to a 1 in 6 chance (1 in 6 is 16.67%).

For the average firm listed on the New York Stock Exchange, σ has been in the range of 35% to 40% in recent years, with an expected return of around 8% to 12%. One standard deviation below this expected return is about 10% − 35% = −25%. This means that, for a typical stock in typical year, there is about a 1 in 6 chance of having a 25% loss. You might be thinking that 1 in 6 is a pretty low probability, but what if your chance of getting hit by a car when you crossed a street were 1 in 6? When put that way, 1 in 6 sounds pretty scary.

You might also correctly be thinking that there would be a 1 in 6 chance of getting a return higher than 1 standard deviation above the mean, which would be about 45% for a typical stock. A 45% return is great, but human nature is such that most investors would dislike a 25% loss a whole lot more than they would enjoy a 45% gain.

You might also be thinking that you'll be OK if you hold stock long enough. But even if you buy and hold a diversified portfolio for 10 years, there is still roughly a 10% chance that you will lose money. If you hold it for 20 years, there is about a 4% chance of losing. Such odds wouldn't be worrisome if you were engaged in a game of chance that could be played multiple times, but you have only one life to live and just a few rolls of the dice.

We aren't suggesting that investors shouldn't buy stocks; indeed, we own stock ourselves. But we do believe investors should understand more clearly exactly how much risk stock investing entails.

Using Historical Data to Measure Risk

In our previous example, we described the procedure for finding the mean and standard deviation when the data are in the form of a known probability distribution. This implies that the distribution includes all data points, not a sample of data points from a broader universe of returns. Suppose, however, that only a sample of returns over some past period is available. These past **realized rates of return** are denoted as $\bar{r}_t$ ("r bar t"), where t designates the time period. The average annual return over the last n years is then denoted as $\bar{r}_{Avg}$:

$$\bar{r}_{Avg} = \frac{\sum_{t=1}^{n} \bar{r}_t}{n} \qquad (6\text{-}4)$$

The standard deviation of the sample of returns can then be estimated using this formula:[5]

$$\text{Estimated } \sigma = S = \sqrt{\frac{\sum_{t=1}^{n} (\bar{r}_t - \bar{r}_{Avg})^2}{n-1}} \qquad (6\text{-}5)$$

[5]Because we are estimating the standard deviation from a sample of observations, the denominator in Equation 6-5 is "n − 1" and not just "n." Equations 6-4 and 6-5 are built into all financial calculators. For example, to find the sample standard deviation, enter the rates of return into the calculator and press the key marked S (or S_x) to get the standard deviation. See our tutorials on the textbook's Web site or your calculator's manual for details.

FIGURE 6-7 Standard Deviation Based on a Sample of Historical Data

	A	B	C	D
120				Realized
121			Year	return
122			2008	15.0%
123			2009	–5.0%
124			2010	20.0%
125				
126			Average = AVERAGE(D122:D124) =	10.0%
127			Standard deviation = STDEV(D122:D124) =	13.2%
128				

See **Ch06 Tool Kit.xls** *on the textbook's Web site.*

When estimated from past data, the standard deviation is often denoted by S.

To illustrate, consider the historical returns in Figure 6-7. Using Equations 6-4 and 6-5, the estimated average and standard deviation are, respectively,

$$\bar{r}_{Avg} = \frac{15\% - 5\% + 20\%}{3} = 10.0\%$$

$$\text{Estimated}\,\sigma\,(\text{or S}) = \sqrt{\frac{(15\% - 10\%)^2 + (-5\% - 10\%)^2 + (20\% - 10\%)^2}{3-1}}$$

$$= 13.2\%$$

The average and standard deviation can also be calculated using *Excel*'s built-in functions, shown below using numerical data rather than cell ranges as inputs:

$$= \textbf{AVERAGE(0.15,–0.05,0.20)} = \textbf{10.0\%}$$
$$= \textbf{STDEV(0.15,–0.05,0.20)} = \textbf{13.2\%}$$

The historical standard deviation is often used as an estimate of the future variability. Because past variability is likely to be repeated, past variability may be a reasonably good estimate of future risk. However, it is usually incorrect to use $\bar{r}_{Avg}$ based on a past period as an estimate of $\hat{r}$, the expected future return. For example, just because a stock had a 75% return in the past year, there is no reason to expect a 75% return this year.

Measuring Stand-Alone Risk: The Coefficient of Variation

If a choice has to be made between two investments that have the same expected returns but different standard deviations, most people would choose the one with the lower standard deviation and, therefore, the lower risk. Similarly, given a choice between two investments with the same risk (standard deviation) but different expected returns, investors would generally prefer the investment with the higher expected return. To most people, this is common sense—return is "good," risk is "bad," and consequently investors want as much return and as little risk as possible. But how do we choose between two investments if one has a higher expected return and the other a lower standard deviation? To help answer this question, we often use another measure of risk, the **coefficient of variation (CV)**, which is the standard deviation divided by the expected return:

$$\text{Coefficient of variation} = \text{CV} = \frac{\sigma}{\hat{r}} \qquad \textbf{(6-6)}$$

The Trade-off between Risk and Return

The table accompanying this box summarizes the historical trade-off between risk and return for different classes of investments. The assets that produced the highest average returns also had the highest standard deviations and the widest ranges of returns. For example, small-company stocks had the highest average annual return, but their standard deviation of returns was also the highest. In contrast, U.S. Treasury bills had the lowest standard deviation, but they also had the lowest average return.

Note that a T-bill is riskless *if you hold it until maturity,* but if you invest in a rolling portfolio of T-bills and hold the portfolio for a number of years, then your investment income will vary depending on what happens to the level of interest rates in each year. You can be sure of the return you will earn on an individual T-bill, but you cannot be sure of the return you will earn on a portfolio of T-bills held over a number of years.

Distribution of Realized Returns, 1926–2008

	Small Company Stocks	Large Company Stocks	Long-Term Corporate Bonds	Long-Term Government Bonds	U.S. Treasury Bills	Inflation
Average return	16.4%	11.7%	6.2%	6.1%	3.8%	3.1%
Standard deviation	33.0	20.6	8.4	9.4	3.1	4.2
Excess return over T-bonds[a]	10.3	5.6	0.1			

[a]The excess return over T-bonds is called the "historical risk premium." This excess return will also be the current risk premium that is reflected in security prices if and only if investors expect returns in the future to be similar to returns earned in the past.

Sources: Based on *Stocks, Bonds, Bills, and Inflation: Valuation Edition 2009 Yearbook* (Chicago: Ibbotson Associates, 2009).

The coefficient of variation shows the risk per unit of return, and it provides a more meaningful basis for comparison than σ when the expected returns on two alternatives are different. Since Basic Foods and Sale.com have the same expected return, 15%, the coefficient of variation is not necessary in this case: The firm with the larger standard deviation, Sale.com, must have the larger coefficient of variation when the means are equal. In fact, the coefficient of variation for Sale.com is 58.09/15 = 3.87 and that for Basic Foods is 23.24/15 = 1.55. Thus, Sale.com is more than three times as risky as Basic Foods on the basis of this criterion. Because the coefficient of variation captures the effects of both risk and return, it is a better measure than the standard deviation when evaluating stand-alone risk in situations in which different investments have substantially different expected returns.

Risk Aversion and Required Returns

Suppose you have worked hard and saved $1 million, which you now plan to invest for 1 year. You can buy a 5% U.S. Treasury security, and at the end of the year you will have a sure $1.05 million, which is your original investment plus $50,000 in interest. Alternatively, you can buy stock in Genetic Advances Inc. If Genetic Advances's research programs are successful, your stock will increase in value to $2.1 million. However, if the research is a failure, the value of your stock will go to zero, and you will be penniless. You regard Genetic Advances's chances of success or failure as being 50-50, so the expected value of the stock investment is 0.5($0) + 0.5($2,100,000) = $1,050,000. Subtracting the $1 million cost of the stock leaves an expected profit of $50,000, or an expected (but risky) 5% rate of return: $50,000/$1,000,000 = 0.05 = 5%.

Thus, you have a choice between a sure $50,000 profit (representing a 5% rate of return) on the Treasury security and a risky expected $50,000 profit (also representing a 5% expected rate of return) on the Genetic Advances stock. Which one would you choose? *If you choose the less risky investment, you are risk averse. Most investors are indeed risk averse, and certainly the average investor is risk averse with regard to his "serious money." Because this is a well-documented fact, we shall assume* **risk aversion** *throughout the remainder of the book.*

What are the implications of risk aversion for security prices and rates of return? The answer is that, other things held constant, the higher a security's risk, the lower its price and the higher its required return. To see how risk aversion affects security prices, consider again Basic Foods and Sale.com. Suppose each stock is expected to pay an annual dividend of $15 forever. We know that the dividend could be higher or lower, but $15 is our best guess. Under these conditions, the price of each stock can be found as the present value of a perpetuity. If each stock had an expected return of 15%, then each stock's price must be P = $15/0.15 = $100. However, investors are averse to risk, so under these conditions there would be a general preference for Basic Foods—it has the same expected return as Sale.com but less risk. People with money to invest would bid for Basic Foods rather than Sale.com stock, and Sale.com stockholders would start selling their stock and using the money to buy Basic Foods. Buying pressure would drive up Basic Foods's stock price, and selling pressure would simultaneously cause Sale.com's price to decline.

These price changes, in turn, would cause changes in the expected rates of return on the two securities. Suppose, for example, that Basic Foods's stock price was bid up from $100 to $150, whereas Sale.com's stock price declined from $100 to $75. This would cause Basic Foods's expected return to fall to 10%, while Sale.com's expected return would rise to 20%.[6] The difference in returns, 20% − 10% = 10%, is a **risk premium, RP**, which represents the additional compensation investors require for assuming the additional risk of Sale.com stock.

This example demonstrates a fundamentally important principle: *In a market dominated by risk-averse investors, riskier securities must have higher expected returns, as estimated by the marginal investor, than less risky securities. If this situation does not already exist, then buying and selling in the marketplace will force it to occur.* We will consider the question of how much higher the returns on risky securities must be later in the chapter, after we see how diversification affects risk and the way it should be measured. Then, in later chapters, we will see how risk-adjusted rates of return affect the prices that investors are willing to pay for bonds and stocks.

Self-Test

What does "investment risk" mean?

Set up an illustrative probability distribution for an investment.

What is a payoff matrix?

---

[6]Recall that the present value of a perpetuity is P = PMT/I, where PMT is the constant annual cash flow of the perpetuity and I is the rate of return. For stocks, we use r for the expected rate of return. Solving for r, the expected return for Basic Foods is $15/$150 = 0.10 = 10% and that for Sale.com is $15/$75 = 0.20 = 20%.

Which of the two stocks graphed in Figure 6-4 is less risky? Why?
How does one calculate the standard deviation?
Which is a better measure of risk when assets have different expected returns: (1) the standard deviation or (2) the coefficient of variation? Why?
Discuss the following statement: "Most investors are risk averse."
How does risk aversion affect rates of return on securities?
An investment has a 20% chance of producing a 25% return, a 60% chance of producing a 10% return, and a 20% chance of producing a −15% return. What is its expected return? **(8%)** What is its standard deviation? **(12.9%)**
A stock's returns for the past 3 years were 10%, −15%, and 35%. What is the historical average return? **(10%)** What is the historical sample standard deviation? **(25%)**
An investment has an expected return of 15% and a standard deviation of 30%. What is its coefficient of variation? **(2.0)**

6.3 Risk in a Portfolio Context

In the preceding section we considered the risk of assets held in isolation. Now we analyze the risk of assets held in portfolios. As we shall see, an asset held as part of a portfolio is less risky than the same asset held in isolation. Therefore, most financial assets are actually held as parts of portfolios. Banks, pension funds, insurance companies, mutual funds, and other financial institutions are required by law to hold diversified portfolios. Even individual investors—at least those whose security holdings constitute a significant part of their total wealth—generally hold portfolios, not the stock of only one firm. This being the case, from an investor's standpoint the fact that a particular stock goes up or down is not the key issue: What's important are the portfolio's return and its risk. Logically, then, the risk and return of an individual security should be analyzed in terms of how that security affects the risk and return of the portfolio in which it is held.

To illustrate, Pay Up Inc. collects debts for other firms and operates nationwide through 37 offices. The company is not well known, its stock is not very liquid, its earnings have fluctuated quite a bit in the past, and it doesn't pay a dividend. All this suggests that Pay Up is risky and that the required rate of return on its stock should be relatively high. However, Pay Up's required rate of return in 2008, and all other years, was quite low relative to those of most other companies. Thus, investors regard Pay Up as being a low-risk company in spite of its uncertain profits. This is counterintuitive, but it is caused by diversification and its effect on risk. Pay Up's earnings rise during recessions, whereas most other companies' earnings tend to decline when the economy slumps. The stock is like a fire insurance policy—it pays off when other things go badly. Therefore, adding Pay Up to a portfolio of "normal" stocks tends to stabilize returns on the entire portfolio, thus making the portfolio less risky.

Portfolio Returns

The **expected return on a portfolio**, $\hat{r}_p$, is simply the weighted average of the expected returns on the individual assets in the portfolio. Suppose there are n stocks. The expected return on Stock i is $\hat{r}_i$. The fraction of the portfolio's dollar value invested in Stock i (that is, the value of the investment in Stock i divided by the total value of the portfolio) is w_i, and all the w_i must sum to 1.0. The expected return on the portfolio is

FIGURE 6-8 Expected Returns on a Portfolio of Stocks

	A	B	C	D	E
150	Stock	Amount of Investment	Portfolio Weight	Expected Return	Weighted Expected Return
151	Southwest Airlines	\$300,000	0.3	15.0%	4.5%
152	Starbucks	\$100,000	0.1	12.0%	1.2%
153	FedEx	\$200,000	0.2	10.0%	2.0%
154	Dell	\$400,000	0.4	9.0%	3.6%
155	Total investment =	\$1,000,000	1.0		
156					
157			Portfolio's Expected Return =		11.3%

See **Ch06 Tool Kit.xls** *on the textbook's Web site.*

$$\hat{r}_p = w_1\hat{r}_1 + w_2\hat{r}_2 + \cdots + w_n\hat{r}_n = \sum_{i=1}^{n} w_i\hat{r}_i \tag{6-7}$$

To illustrate, assume that a security analyst estimated the upcoming year's returns on the stocks of four large companies, as shown in Figure 6-8. A client wishes to invest \$1 million, divided among the stocks as shown in the figure. Notice that the \$300,000 investment in Southwest Airlines means that its weight in the portfolio is 0.3 = \$3,000,000/\$1,000,000. The expected portfolio return is:

$$\begin{aligned}\hat{r}_p &= w_1\hat{r}_1 + w_2\hat{r}_2 + w_3\hat{r}_3 + w_4\hat{r}_4 \\ &= 0.3(15\%) + 0.1(12\%) + 0.2(10\%) + 0.4(9\%) \\ &= 11.3\%\end{aligned}$$

Of course, the actual realized rates of return almost certainly will be different from their expected values, so the realized portfolio return, $\bar{r}_p$, will be different from the expected return. For example, Starbucks might double and provide a return of +100%, whereas Dell might have a terrible year, fall sharply, and have a return of –75%. Note, though, that those two events would be somewhat offsetting, so the portfolio's return might still be close to its expected return.

Portfolio Risk

As we just saw, the expected return on a portfolio is simply the weighted average of the expected returns on the individual assets in the portfolio. However, unlike returns, the risk of a portfolio, σ_p, is generally not the weighted average of the standard deviations of the individual assets in the portfolio. Indeed, the portfolio's standard deviation will (almost always) be smaller than the assets' weighted standard deviations, and it is theoretically possible to combine stocks that are individually quite risky as measured by their standard deviations and form a portfolio that is completely riskless, with σ_p = 0.

To illustrate the effect of combining assets, consider first the situation in Figure 6-9. The bottom section gives data on rates of return for Stocks W and M as well as for a

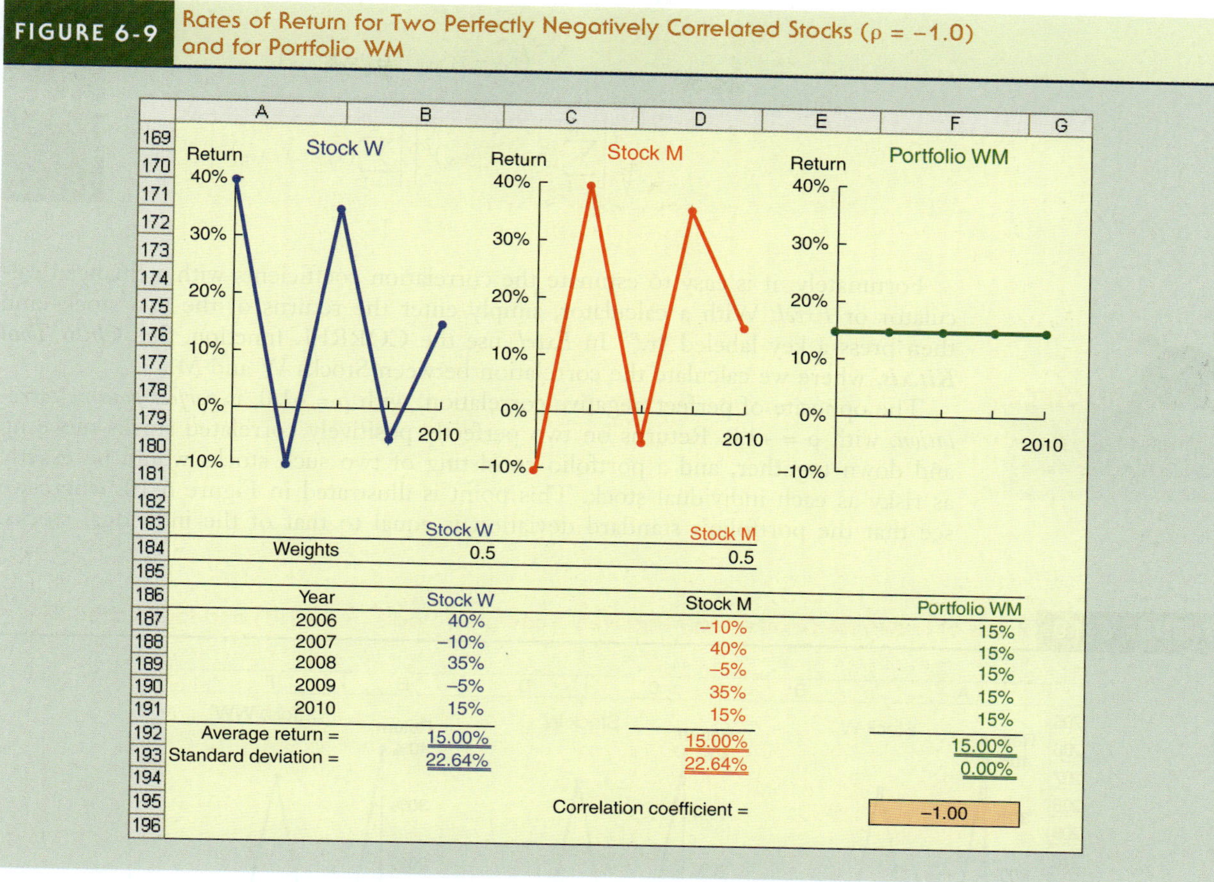

	Stock W	Stock M
Weights	0.5	0.5

Year	Stock W	Stock M	Portfolio WM
2006	40%	–10%	15%
2007	–10%	40%	15%
2008	35%	–5%	15%
2009	–5%	35%	15%
2010	15%	15%	15%
Average return =	15.00%	15.00%	15.00%
Standard deviation =	22.64%	22.64%	0.00%

Correlation coefficient =	–1.00

FIGURE 6-9 Rates of Return for Two Perfectly Negatively Correlated Stocks (ρ = –1.0) and for Portfolio WM

resource

See **Ch06 Tool Kit.xls** *on the textbook's Web site.*

portfolio invested 50% in each stock. (*Note:* These stocks are called W and M because the graphs of their returns in Figure 6-9 resemble a W and an M.) The three graphs plot the data in a time-series format. Note that the portfolio's return is 15% in every year. Therefore, although the two stocks would be quite risky if they were held in isolation, when combined to form Portfolio WM they are not risky at all.

The reason Stocks W and M can be combined to form a riskless portfolio is that their returns move countercyclically to each other—when W's returns fall, those of M rise, and vice versa. The tendency of two variables to move together is called **correlation**, and the **correlation coefficient** measures this tendency.[7] The symbol for the correlation coefficient is the Greek letter rho, ρ (pronounced roe). In statistical terms, we say that the returns on Stocks W and M are *perfectly negatively correlated*, with ρ = –1.0.

The estimate of correlation from a sample of historical data is often called "R." Here is the formula to estimate the correlation between stocks i and j ($\bar{r}_{i,t}$ is the actual return for Stock i in period t, and $\bar{r}_{i,Avg}$ is the average return during the n-period sample; similar notation is used for stock j):

[7] The correlation coefficient, ρ, can range from +1.0, denoting that the two variables move up and down in perfect synchronization, to –1.0, denoting that the variables always move in exactly opposite directions. A correlation coefficient of zero indicates that the two variables are not related to each other—that is, changes in one variable are independent of changes in the other.

$$\text{Estimated } \rho = R = \frac{\sum_{t=1}^{n}(\bar{r}_{i,t} - \bar{r}_{i,Avg})(\bar{r}_{j,t} - \bar{r}_{j,Avg})}{\sqrt{\left[\sum_{t=1}^{n}(\bar{r}_{i,t} - \bar{r}_{i,Avg})^2\right]\left[\sum_{t=1}^{n}(\bar{r}_{j,t} - \bar{r}_{j,Avg})^2\right]}} \tag{6-8}$$

See **Ch06 Tool Kit.xls** *on the textbook's Web site.*

Fortunately, it is easy to estimate the correlation coefficients with a financial calculator or *Excel.* With a calculator, simply enter the returns of the two stocks and then press a key labeled "r."[8] In *Excel,* use the CORREL function. See ***Ch06 Tool Kit.xls,*** where we calculate the correlation between Stocks W and M.

The opposite of perfect negative correlation, with ρ = −1.0, is *perfect positive correlation,* with ρ = +1.0. Returns on two perfectly positively correlated stocks move up and down together, and a portfolio consisting of two such stocks would be exactly as risky as each individual stock. This point is illustrated in Figure 6-10, where we see that the portfolio's standard deviation is equal to that of the individual stocks.

FIGURE 6-10 Rates of Return for Two Perfectly Positively Correlated Stocks (ρ = +1.0) and for Portfolio WW'

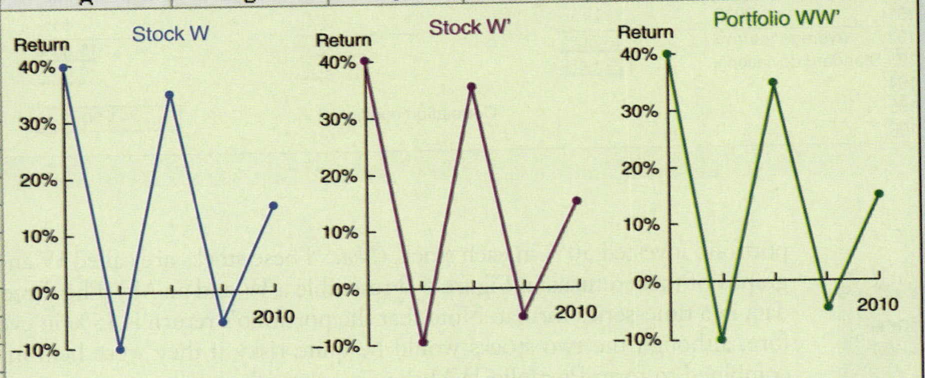

	Stock W	Stock W'	Portfolio WW'
Weights	0.5	0.5	
Year	**Stock W**	**Stock W'**	**Portfolio WW'**
2006	40%	40%	40%
2007	−10%	−10%	−10%
2008	35%	35%	35%
2009	−5%	−5%	−5%
2010	15%	15%	15%
Average return =	15.00%	15.00%	15.00%
Standard deviation =	22.64%	22.64%	22.64%
Correlation coefficient =			1.00

---

[8]See our tutorial or your calculator manual for the exact steps. Also, note that the correlation coefficient is often denoted by the term "r." We use ρ here to avoid confusion with r, which is used to denote the rate of return.

FIGURE 6-11 Rates of Return for Two Partially Correlated Stocks (ρ = +0.35) and for Portfolio WY

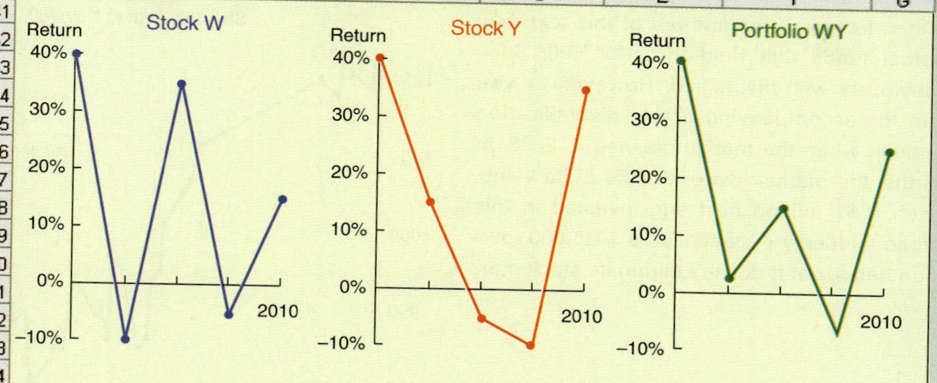

Stock W | Stock Y | Portfolio WY
(Return charts: vertical axis −10% to 40%, horizontal axis ending 2010)

	Stock W	Stock Y
Weights	0.5	0.5

Year	Stock W	Stock Y	Portfolio WY
2006	40%	40%	40.00%
2007	−10%	15%	2.50%
2008	35%	−5%	15.00%
2009	−5%	−15%	7.50%
2010	15%	35%	25.00%
Average return =	15.00%	15.00%	15.00%
Standard deviation =	22.64%	22.64%	18.62%

Correlation coefficient = 0.35

See **Ch06 Tool Kit.xls** *on the textbook's Web site.*

Thus, *diversification does nothing to reduce risk if the portfolio consists of stocks that are perfectly positively correlated.*

Figures 6-9 and 6-10 show that when stocks are perfectly negatively correlated (ρ = −1.0), all risk can be diversified away, but when stocks are perfectly positively correlated (ρ = +1.0), diversification does no good whatsoever. In reality, virtually all stocks are positively correlated, but not perfectly so. Past studies have estimated that, on average, the correlation coefficient for the monthly returns on two randomly selected stocks is in the range of 0.28 to 0.35.[9] *Under this condition, combining stocks into portfolios reduces but does not completely eliminate risk.* Figure 6-11 illustrates this point with two stocks whose correlation coefficient is ρ = +0.35. The portfolio's average return is 15%, which is exactly the same as the average return for our other two illustrative portfolios, but its standard deviation is 18.6%, which is between the other two portfolios' standard deviations.

[9]During the period 1968–1998, the average correlation coefficient between two randomly selected stocks was 0.28, while the average correlation coefficient between two large-company stocks was 0.33; see Louis K. C. Chan, Jason Karceski, and Josef Lakonishok, "On Portfolio Optimization: Forecasting Covariance and Choosing the Risk Model," *The Review of Financial Studies*, Vol. 12, No. 5, Winter 1999, pp. 937–974. The average correlation fell from around 0.35 in the late 1970s to less than 0.10 by the late 1990s; see John Y. Campbell, Martin Lettau, Burton G. Malkiel, and Yexiao Xu, "Have Individual Stocks Become More Volatile? An Empirical Exploration of Idiosyncratic Risk," *Journal of Finance*, February 2001, pp. 1–43.

How Risky Is a Large Portfolio of Stocks?

Many investors, including the authors of this text, buy "index" mutual funds that hold the S&P 500. Such funds are obviously well diversified. However, as you can see from the accompanying graph, diversification didn't help much when the market crashed in 2008. In just 2½ months, the market lost over 40% of its value. Someone with a $1 million nest egg invested in this "safe" portfolio suddenly experienced a $411,000 loss. Diversification helps, but it doesn't eliminate stock market risk.

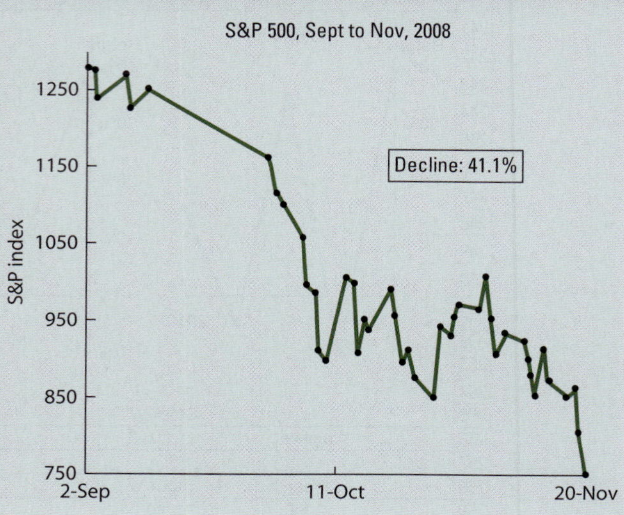

These examples demonstrate that in one extreme case ($\rho = -1.0$), risk can be completely eliminated, while in the other extreme case ($\rho = +1.0$), diversification does not affect risk at all. The real world lies between these extremes, so combining stocks into portfolios reduces—but does not eliminate—the risk inherent in the individual stocks. Also, we should note that in the real world it is *impossible* to find stocks like W and M, whose returns are expected to be perfectly negatively correlated. Therefore, *it is impossible to form completely riskless stock portfolios.* Diversification can reduce risk but not eliminate it, so the real world is similar to the situation depicted in Figure 6-11.

What would happen if we included more than two stocks in the portfolio? As a rule, *the risk of a portfolio declines as the number of stocks in the portfolio increases.* If we added enough partially correlated stocks, could we completely eliminate risk? The answer is "no," but adding stocks to a portfolio reduces its risk to an extent that depends on the *degree of correlation* among the stocks: The smaller the stocks' correlation coefficients, the lower the portfolio's risk. If we could find stocks with correlations of −1.0, all risk could be eliminated. However, *in the real world the correlations among the individual stocks are generally positive but less than +1.0, so some (but not all) risk can be eliminated.*

In general, there are higher correlations between the returns on two companies in the same industry than for two companies in different industries. There are also higher correlations among similar "style" companies, such as large versus small and growth versus value. Thus, to minimize risk, portfolios should be diversified across industries and styles.

Diversifiable Risk versus Market Risk

As already mentioned, it's difficult if not impossible to find stocks whose expected returns are negatively correlated—most stocks tend to do well when the national economy is strong and badly when it is weak. Thus, even very large portfolios end up with a substantial amount of risk, but not as much risk as if all the money were invested in only one stock.

To see more precisely how portfolio size affects portfolio risk, consider Figure 6-12, which shows how portfolio risk is affected by forming larger and larger portfolios of randomly selected New York Stock Exchange (NYSE) stocks. Standard deviations are plotted for an average one-stock portfolio, an average two-stock portfolio, and so on, up to a portfolio consisting of all 2,000-plus common stocks that were listed on the NYSE at the time the data were plotted. The graph illustrates that, in general, the risk of a portfolio consisting of large-company stocks tends to decline and to approach some limit as the size of the portfolio increases. According to data accumulated in recent years, σ_1, the standard deviation of a one-stock portfolio (or an average stock), is approximately 35%. However, a portfolio consisting of all stocks, which is called the **market portfolio**, would have a standard deviation, σ_M, of only about 20%, which is shown as the horizontal dashed line in Figure 6-12.

Thus, *almost half of the risk inherent in an average individual stock can be eliminated if the stock is held in a reasonably well-diversified portfolio, which is one containing forty or more stocks in a number of different industries.* Some risk always remains—terrorists can attack, recessions can get out of hand, meteors can strike, and so forth—so it is impossible to diversify away the effects of broad stock market movements that affect virtually all stocks.

FIGURE 6-12 Effects of Portfolio Size on Portfolio Risk for Average Stocks

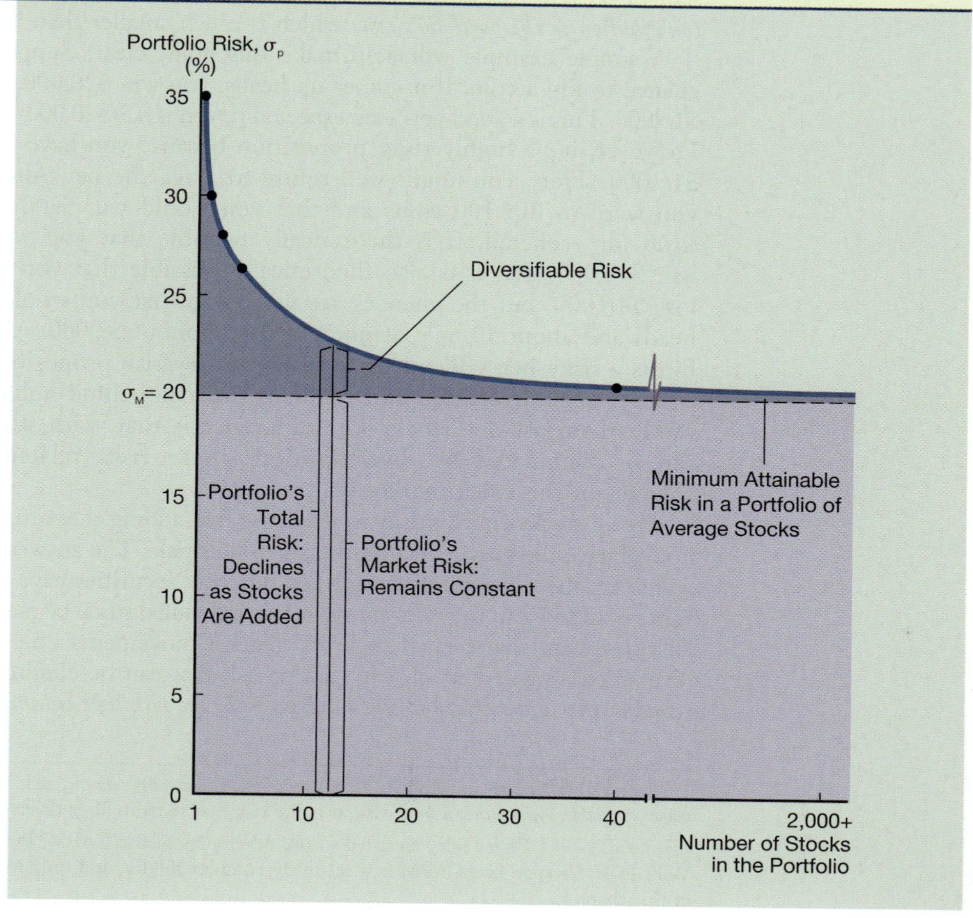

The part of a stock's risk that *can* be eliminated is called *diversifiable risk*, while the part that *cannot* be eliminated is called *market risk*.[10] The fact that a large part of the risk of any individual stock can be eliminated is vitally important, because rational investors *will* eliminate it and thus render it irrelevant.

Diversifiable risk is caused by such random events as lawsuits, strikes, successful and unsuccessful marketing programs, winning or losing a major contract, and other events that are unique to a particular firm. Because these events are random, their effects on a portfolio can be eliminated by diversification—bad events in one firm will be offset by good events in another. **Market risk**, on the other hand, stems from factors that systematically affect most firms: war, inflation, recessions, and high interest rates. Because most stocks are negatively affected by these factors, market risk cannot be eliminated by diversification.

We know that investors demand a premium for bearing risk; that is, the higher the risk of a security, the higher its expected return must be to induce investors to buy (or to hold) it. However, if investors are primarily concerned with the risk of their *portfolios* rather than the risk of the individual securities in the portfolio, then how should the risk of an individual stock be measured? One answer is provided by the **Capital Asset Pricing Model (CAPM)**, an important tool used to analyze the relationship between risk and rates of return.[11] The primary conclusion of the CAPM is this: *The relevant risk of an individual stock is its contribution to the risk of a well-diversified portfolio.* A stock might be quite risky if held by itself, but—since about half of its risk can be eliminated by diversification—the stock's **relevant risk** is its *contribution to the portfolio's risk*, which is much smaller than its stand-alone risk.

A simple example will help make this point clear. Suppose you are offered the chance to flip a coin. If it comes up heads, you win $20,000, but if it's tails, you lose $16,000. This is a good bet—the expected return is 0.5($20,000) + 0.5(–$16,000) = $2,000. However, it's a highly risky proposition because you have a 50% chance of losing $16,000. Thus, you might well refuse to make the bet. Alternatively, suppose that you were to flip 100 coins and that you would win $200 for each head but lose $160 for each tail. It is theoretically possible that you would flip all heads and win $20,000, and it is also theoretically possible that you would flip all tails and lose $16,000, but the chances are very high that you would actually flip about 50 heads and about 50 tails, winning a net of about $2,000. Although each individual flip is a risky bet, collectively you have a low-risk proposition because most of the risk has been diversified away. This is the idea behind holding portfolios of stocks rather than just one stock. The difference is that, with stocks, not all of the risk can be eliminated by diversification—those risks related to broad, systematic changes in the stock market will remain.

Are all stocks equally risky in the sense that adding them to a well-diversified portfolio will have the same effect on the portfolio's risk? The answer is "no." Different stocks will affect the portfolio differently, so different securities have different degrees of relevant risk. How can the relevant risk of an individual stock be measured? As we have seen, all risk except that related to broad market movements can, and presumably will, be diversified away. After all, why accept risk that can be eliminated easily? *The risk that remains after diversifying is called market risk, the risk that is inherent in the market.* In the

---

[10]Diversifiable risk is also known as *company-specific*, or *unsystematic*, risk. Market risk is also known as *nondiversifiable*, *systematic*, or *beta*, risk; it is the risk that remains after diversification.

[11]Indeed, Nobel Prizes were awarded to the developers of the CAPM, Professors Harry Markowitz and William F. Sharpe. The CAPM is a relatively complex theory, and only its basic elements are presented in this chapter.

The Benefits of Diversifying Overseas

Figure 6-12 shows that an investor can significantly reduce portfolio risk by holding a large number of stocks. The figure accompanying this box suggests that investors may be able to reduce risk even further by holding stocks from all around the world, because the returns on domestic and international stocks are not perfectly correlated.

Although U.S. investors have traditionally been relatively reluctant to hold international assets, it is a safe bet that in the years ahead U.S. investors will shift more and more of their assets to overseas investments.

Source: For further reading, see Kenneth Kasa, "Measuring the Gains from International Portfolio Diversification," *Federal Reserve Bank of San Francisco Weekly Letter,* no. 94–14 (April 8, 1994).

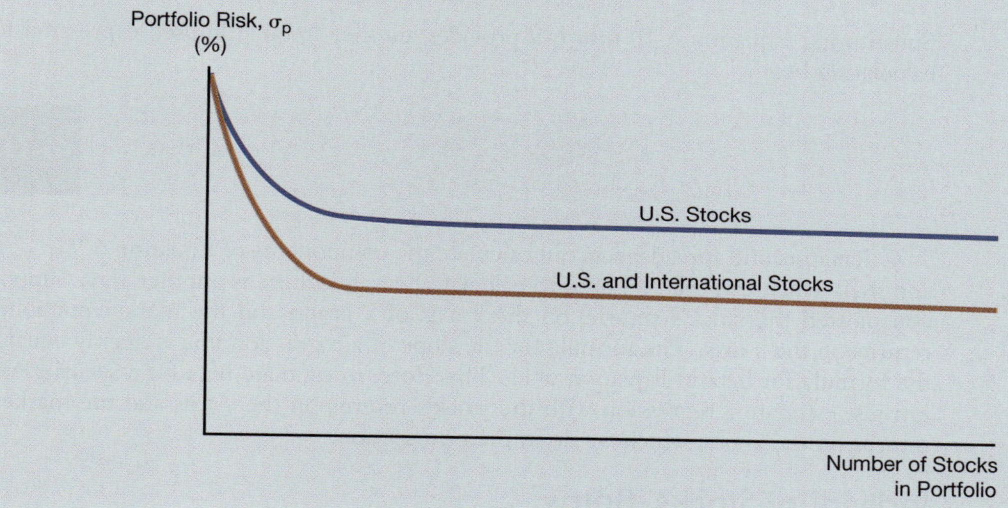

next section, we develop a measure of a stock's market risk and then, in a later section, we introduce an equation for determining the required rate of return on a stock, given its market risk.

Contribution to Market Risk: Beta

The primary conclusion reached in the preceding section is that the relevant risk of an individual stock is the amount of risk the stock contributes to a well-diversified portfolio. The benchmark for a well-diversified stock portfolio is the market portfolio, which is a portfolio containing all stocks. Therefore, the relevant risk of an individual stock, which is measured by its **beta coefficient**, is defined under the CAPM as the amount of risk that the stock contributes to the market portfolio. In CAPM terminology, ρ_{iM} is the correlation between Stock i's return and the market return, σ_i is the standard deviation of Stock i's return, and σ_M is the standard deviation of the market's return. The beta coefficient of Stock i, denoted by b_i, is found as follows:

$$b_i = \left(\frac{\sigma_i}{\sigma_M}\right)\rho_{iM} \quad (6\text{-}9)$$

This tells us that a stock with a high standard deviation, σ_i, will tend to have a high beta, which means that, other things held constant, the stock contributes a lot of risk to a well-diversified portfolio. This makes sense, because a stock with high stand-alone risk will tend to destabilize the portfolio. Note too that a stock with a high correlation with the market, ρ_{iM}, will also tend to have a large beta and hence be risky. This also makes sense, because a high correlation means that diversification is not helping much, with most of the stock's risk affecting the portfolio's risk.

It is also useful to transform the variables in Equation 6-9 to form the **covariance between Stock i and the market, COV_{iM},** defined as[12]

$$COV_{iM} = \rho_{iM}\sigma_i\sigma_M \qquad (6\text{-}10)$$

Substituting Equation 6-10 into 6-9 provides another frequently used expression for calculating beta:

$$b_i = \frac{COV_{iM}}{\sigma_M^2} \qquad (6\text{-}11)$$

Calculators and spreadsheets can calculate the components of Equation 6-9 (ρ_{iM}, σ_i, and σ_M), which can then be used to calculate beta, but there is another way. Suppose you plotted the stock's returns on the y-axis of a graph and the market portfolio's returns on the x-axis. The formula for the slope of a regression line is exactly equal to the formula for beta in Equation 6-11. Therefore, to estimate beta for a security, you can just estimate a regression with the stock's returns on the y-axis and the market's returns on the x-axis, which we do in the next section.

Individual Stocks' Betas

The tendency of a stock to move up and down with the market is reflected in its beta coefficient. An *average-risk stock* is defined as one with a beta equal to 1 (b = 1.0). Such a stock's returns tend to move up and down, on average, with the market, which is measured by some index such as the S&P 500 Index. A portfolio of such b = 1.0 stocks will move up and down with the broad market indexes, and it will be just as risky as the market. A portfolio of b = 0.5 stocks tends to move in the same direction as the market, but to a lesser degree. On the other hand, a portfolio of b = 2.0 stocks also tends to move with the market, but it will have even bigger swings than the market.

Figure 6-13 shows a graph of the historical returns of three stocks versus the market. The data below the graph show that in Year 1 the "market," defined as a portfolio consisting of all stocks, had a total return (dividend yield plus capital gains yield) of $\bar{r}_M$ = 19% and that Stocks H, A, and L (for High, Average, and Low risk) had returns of 26%, 19%, and 12%, respectively. In Year 2, the market went up sharply,

---

[12]Using historical data, the sample covariance can be calculated as

$$\text{Sample covariance from historical data} = COV_{iM} = \frac{\sum_{t=1}^{n}(\bar{r}_{i,t} - \bar{r}_{i,Avg})(\bar{r}_{M,t} - \bar{r}_{M,Avg})}{n-1}$$

Calculating the covariance is somewhat easier than calculating the correlation. So if you have already calculated the standard deviations, it is easier to calculate the covariance and then calculate the correlation as $\rho_{iM} = COV_{iM}/(\sigma_i\sigma_M)$.

FIGURE 6-13 Relative Returns of Stocks H, A, and L

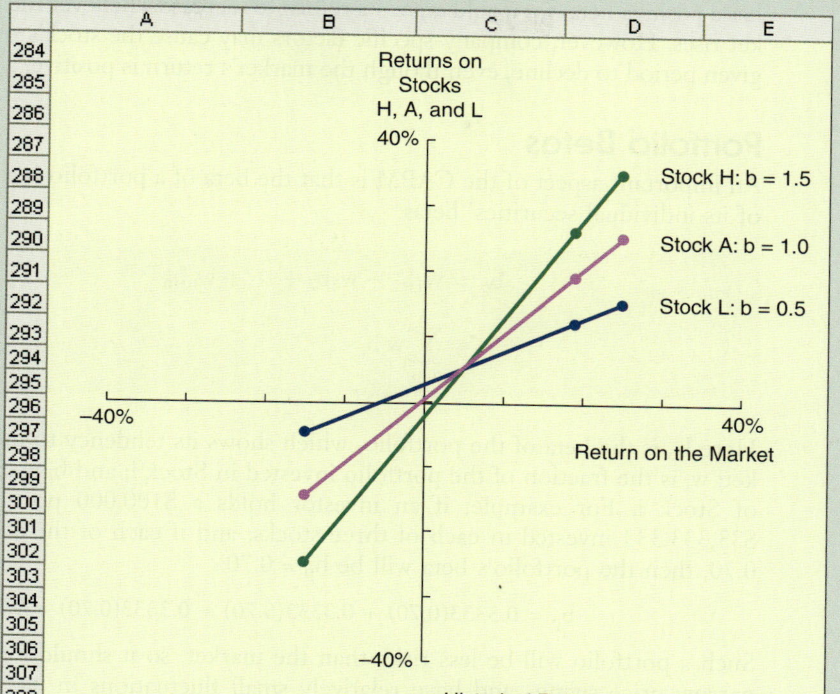

Returns on Stocks H, A, and L

Stock H: b = 1.5

Stock A: b = 1.0

Stock L: b = 0.5

40%

−40%

−40%

40%

Return on the Market

Historical Returns

Year	Market	Stock H	Stock A	Stock L
1	19.0%	26.0%	19.0%	12.0%
2	25.0%	35.0%	25.0%	15.0%
3	−15.0%	−25.0%	−15.0%	−5.0%
Average =	9.7%	12.0%	9.7%	7.3%
Standard deviation =	21.6%	32.4%	21.6%	10.8%
Beta =		1.5	1.0	0.5

Note: These three stocks plot exactly on their regression lines. This indicates that they are exposed only to market risk. Portfolios that concentrate on stocks with betas of 1.5, 1.0, and 0.5 have patterns similar to those shown in the graph.

See **Ch06 Tool Kit.xls** *on the textbook's Web site.*

and the return on the market portfolio was $\bar{r}_M$ = 25%. Returns on the three stocks also went up: H soared to 35%; A went up to 25%, the same as the market; and L went up only to 15%. The market dropped in Year 3, when the market return was $\bar{r}_M$ = −15%. The three stocks' returns also fell: H plunging to −25%, A falling to −15%, and L going down to $\bar{r}_L$ = −5%. Thus, the three stocks all moved in the same direction as the market, but H was by far the most volatile; A was just as volatile as the market; and L was less volatile than the market.

Beta measures a stock's tendency to move up and down with the market. By definition, then, the market has b = 1.0. As noted previously, the slope of a regression line shows how a stock moves in response to a movement in the general market. Most stocks have betas in the range of 0.50 to 1.50, and the average beta for all stocks is 1.0 by definition.

Theoretically, it is possible for a stock to have a negative beta. In this case, the stock's returns would tend to rise whenever the returns on other stocks fall. In practice, few if any stocks have a negative beta. Keep in mind that a stock in a given period may move counter to the overall market even though the stock's "true" beta is positive. If a stock has a positive beta, we would *expect* its return to increase whenever the overall stock market rises. However, company-specific factors may cause the stock's realized return in a given period to decline, even though the market's return is positive.

Portfolio Betas

An important aspect of the CAPM is that the beta of a portfolio is a weighted average of its individual securities' betas:

$$\begin{aligned} b_p &= w_1 b_1 + w_2 b_2 + \cdots + w_n b_n \\ &= \sum_{i=1}^{n} w_i b_i \end{aligned} \tag{6-12}$$

Here b_p is the beta of the portfolio, which shows its tendency to move with the market; w_i is the fraction of the portfolio invested in Stock i; and b_i is the beta coefficient of Stock i. For example, if an investor holds a \$100,000 portfolio consisting of \$33,333.333 invested in each of three stocks, and if each of the stocks has a beta of 0.70, then the portfolio's beta will be $b_p = 0.70$:

$$b_p = 0.3333(0.70) + 0.3333(0.70) + 0.3333(0.70) = 0.70$$

Such a portfolio will be less risky than the market, so it should experience relatively narrow price swings and have relatively small fluctuations in its rates of return. In terms of Figure 6-13, the slope of its regression line would be 0.70, which is less than that for a portfolio of average stocks.

Now suppose that one of the existing stocks is sold and replaced by a stock with $b_i = 2.00$. This action will increase the beta of the portfolio from $b_{p1} = 0.70$ to $b_{p2} = 1.13$:

$$\begin{aligned} b_{p2} &= 0.3333(0.70) + 0.3333(0.70) + 0.3333(2.00) \\ &= 1.13 \end{aligned}$$

Had a stock with $b_i = 0.20$ been added, the portfolio beta would have declined from 0.70 to 0.53. Adding a low-beta stock, therefore, would reduce the risk of the portfolio. Consequently, adding new stocks to a portfolio can change the risk of that portfolio. *Since a stock's beta measures its contribution to the risk of a portfolio, beta is the theoretically correct measure of the stock's risk.*

Some Other Points Related to Beta

The preceding analysis of risk in a portfolio context is part of the CAPM, and we highlight the key points below.

1. A stock's risk consists of two components, market risk and diversifiable risk.
2. Diversifiable risk can be eliminated by diversification, and most investors do indeed diversify, either by holding large portfolios or by purchasing shares in a mutual fund. We are left, then, with market risk, which is caused by general movements in the stock market and which reflects the fact that most stocks are systematically affected by events like war, recessions, and inflation. Market risk is the only risk relevant to a rational, diversified investor because such an investor can eliminate diversifiable risk.

3. Investors must be compensated for bearing risk: The greater the risk of a stock, the higher its required return. However, compensation is required only for risk that cannot be eliminated by diversification. If stocks had risk premiums due to diversifiable risk, then well-diversified investors would start buying those securities (which the investors would not consider especially risky) and bidding up their prices. The stocks' final (equilibrium) expected returns would reflect only nondiversifiable market risk.
4. The market risk of a stock is measured by its beta coefficient, and beta is the proper measure of the stock's relevant risk. If b equals 1.0, then the stock is about as risky as the market, assuming it is held in a diversified portfolio. If b is less than 1.0 then the stock is less risky than the market; if beta is greater than 1.0, the stock is more risky.
5. The beta of a portfolio is a weighted average of the individual securities' betas.
6. *Since a stock's beta coefficient determines how the stock affects the risk of a diversified portfolio, beta is the most relevant measure of any stock's risk.*

Self-Test

Explain the following statement: "An asset held as part of a portfolio is generally less risky than the same asset held in isolation."

What is meant by *perfect positive correlation, perfect negative correlation,* and *zero correlation?*

In general, can the risk of a portfolio be reduced to zero by increasing the number of stocks in the portfolio? Explain.

What is the average beta? If a stock has the average beta, what does that imply about its risk relative to the market?

Why is beta the theoretically correct measure of a stock's risk?

If you plotted the returns on a particular stock versus those on the Dow Jones Index over the past 5 years, what would the slope of the regression line tell you about the stock's market risk?

An investor has a three-stock portfolio with $25,000 invested in Dell, $50,000 invested in Ford, and $25,000 invested in Wal-Mart. Dell's beta is estimated to be 1.20, Ford's beta is estimated to be 0.80, and Wal-Mart's beta is estimated to be 1.0. What is the estimated beta of the investor's portfolio? (0.95)

6.4 Calculating Beta Coefficients

The CAPM is an *ex ante* model, which means that all of the variables represent before-the-fact, *expected* values. In particular, the beta coefficient used by investors should reflect the relationship between a stock's expected return and the market's return during some *future* period. However, people generally calculate betas using data from some *past* period and then assume that the stock's risk will be the same in the future as it was in the past.

Table 6-1 shows the betas for some well-known companies as provided by two different financial organizations, Zacks and Yahoo! Finance. Notice that their estimates of beta usually differ because they calculate it in slightly different ways. Given these differences, many analysts choose to calculate their own betas or else average the published betas.

Recall from Figure 6-13 how betas can be calculated. The actual historical returns for a company are plotted on the y-axis and the market portfolio's returns are plotted on the x-axis. A regression line is then fitted through the points, and the slope of that line provides an estimate of the stock's beta. It is possible to compute beta coefficients with a calculator, but in the real world a computer is typically used, either with a statistical

WWW

To see updated estimates, go to **http://www.zacks.com** *and enter the ticker symbol; select Detailed Quotes for beta. Or go to* **http://finance.yahoo.com** *and enter the ticker symbol. When the results page comes up, select Key Statistics from the left panel to find beta.*

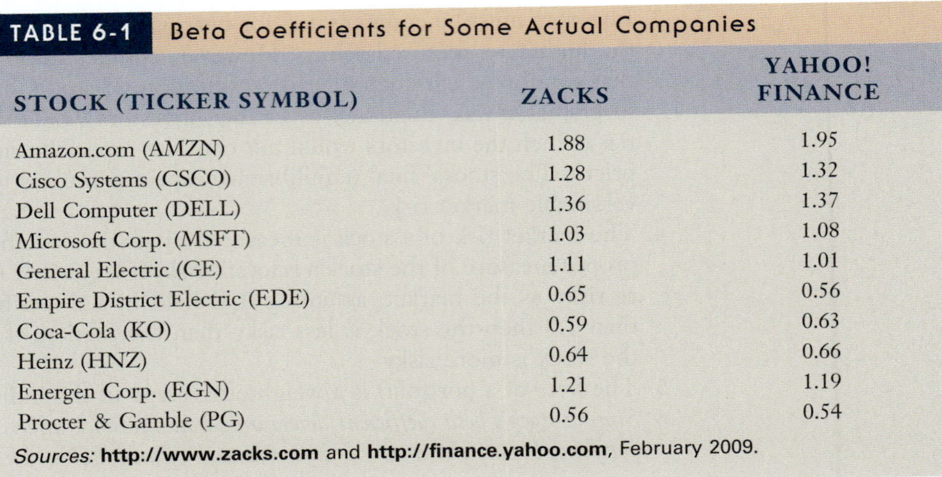

TABLE 6-1 Beta Coefficients for Some Actual Companies

STOCK (TICKER SYMBOL)	ZACKS	YAHOO! FINANCE
Amazon.com (AMZN)	1.88	1.95
Cisco Systems (CSCO)	1.28	1.32
Dell Computer (DELL)	1.36	1.37
Microsoft Corp. (MSFT)	1.03	1.08
General Electric (GE)	1.11	1.01
Empire District Electric (EDE)	0.65	0.56
Coca-Cola (KO)	0.59	0.63
Heinz (HNZ)	0.64	0.66
Energen Corp. (EGN)	1.21	1.19
Procter & Gamble (PG)	0.56	0.54

Sources: **http://www.zacks.com** and **http://finance.yahoo.com**, February 2009.

software program or a spreadsheet program. The chapter's *Excel* ***Tool Kit*** model shows how GE's beta can be calculated using *Excel*'s regression function.[13]

See **Ch06 Tool Kit.xls** *on the textbook's Web site.*

The first step in a regression analysis is getting the data. Most analysts use 4 to 5 years of monthly data, although some use 52 weeks of weekly data. We decided to use 4 years (48 months) of monthly data, so we began by downloading 49 months of stock prices for GE from the Yahoo! Finance Web site (we needed 49 months of data to get 48 rates of return). We used the S&P 500 Index as the market portfolio because it is representative of the market and because many analysts use this index. Figure 6-14 shows a portion of these data; the full data set is in the chapter's ***Tool Kit***.

The second step is to convert the stock prices into rates of return. For example, to find the March 2009 return for GE, we find the percentage change from the previous month: ($10.11 – $8.51)/$8.51 = 0.188 = 18.8%.[14] We also find the percent change of the S&P Index level and use this as the market return.

As the lower portion of Figure 6-14 shows, GE had an average annual return of –22.9% during this 4-year period, while the market had an average annual return of –8.5%. As we noted before, it is usually unreasonable to think that the future expected return for a stock will equal its average historical return over a relatively short period, such as 4 years. If this were not true, then why would anyone buy either the S&P or GE if they expected the same negative returns as were earned in the past? However, we might well expect past volatility to be a reasonable estimate of fu-

[13]For an explanation of computing beta with a financial calculator, see ***Web Extension 6B*** on the textbook's Web site.

[14]The prices reported in Yahoo! Finance are adjusted for dividends and stock splits, so we can calculate the return as the percentage change in the adjusted price. If you use a source that reports actual market prices, then you must make the adjustment yourself when calculating returns. For example, suppose the stock price is $100 in January, the company has a 2-for-1 split, and the actual price is then $60 in February. The reported adjusted price for February would be $60, but the reported adjusted price for January would be lowered to $50 to reflect the stock split. This gives an accurate stock return of 20%: ($60 – $50)/$50 = 20%, the same as if there had not been a split, in which case the return would have been ($120 – $100)/$100 = 20%. Or suppose the actual price in March was $50, the company paid a $10 dividend, and the actual price in April was $60. Shareholders have earned a return of ($60 + $10 – $50)/$50 = 40%. Yahoo! Finance reports an adjusted price of $60 for April and an adjusted price of $42.857 for March, which gives a return of ($60 – $42.857)/$42.857 = 40%. Again, the percentage change in the adjusted price accurately reflects the actual return.

FIGURE 6-14 Stock Return Data for General Electric and the S&P 500 Index

	A	B	C	D	E
395	Month	Market Level (S&P 500 Index) at Month End	Market's Return	GE Adjusted Stock Price at Month End	GE's Return
396	March 2009	797.87	8.5%	$10.11	18.8%
397	February 2009	735.09	−11.0%	$8.51	−27.8%
398	January 2009	825.88	8.6%	$11.78	−25.2%
399	December 2008	903.25	0.8%	$15.74	−3.8%
441	June 2005	1,191.33	0.0%	$29.68	−4.4%
442	May 2005	1,191.50	3.0%	$31.05	0.07%
443	April 2005	1,156.85	−20%	$30.82	0.4%
444	March 2005	1,180.59	NA	$30.70	NA
445					
446	Description of Data				
447	Average return (annual):		−8.5%		−22.9%
448	Standard deviation (annual):		15.9%		28.9%
449	Minimum monthly return:		−16.8%		−27.8%
450	Maximum monthly return:		8.5%		18.8%
451	Correlation between GE and the market:				0.76
452	Beta: $b_{GE} = \rho_{GE,M}(\sigma_{GE}/\sigma_M)$				1.37

Note: The data for July 2005 through November 2008 are not shown but are included in all calculations.

You can get historical stock returns for GE and the S&P 500 index (its symbol is ^SPX) from **http://finance.yahoo.com.**

ture volatility, at least during the next couple of years. Note that the annualized standard deviation for GE's return during this period was 28.9% versus 15.9% for the market. The range between GE's minimum and maximum returns is also greater than the corresponding range for the market. Thus, GE's volatility is greater than the market's volatility. This is what we would expect, since the market is a well-diversified portfolio and so much of its risk has been diversified away. The correlation between GE's stock returns and the market returns is 0.76, which is somewhat higher than the correlation between a typical stock and the market.

We obtained inputs from Figure 6-14 and used Equation 6-9 to approximate GE's beta:

$$b_i = \left(\frac{\sigma_i}{\sigma_M}\right)\rho_{iM} = \left(\frac{0.289}{0.159}\right)(0.76) = 1.38 \approx 1.37$$

Other than a small difference due to rounding in intermediate steps, this is the same result reported in Figure 6-14.

A picture is worth a thousand words, so Figure 6-15 shows a plot of GE's returns against the market returns. As you will notice if you look in the *Excel* ***Tool Kit*** file, we used the *Excel* chart feature to add a trend line and to display the equation and R^2 value on the chart itself. We also could have used the *Excel* regression analysis feature, which would have provided more detailed data.

Figure 6-15 indicates that GE's estimated beta is about 1.37, as shown by the slope coefficient in the regression equation displayed on the chart. This means that GE's beta is greater than the 1.0 average beta. Therefore, GE's returns tend to move up and down (on average) by more than the market's returns. Note, however, that the points are only loosely clustered around the regression line. Sometimes GE does much better than the

FIGURE 6-15 Stock Return Data for General Electric and the S&P 500 Index

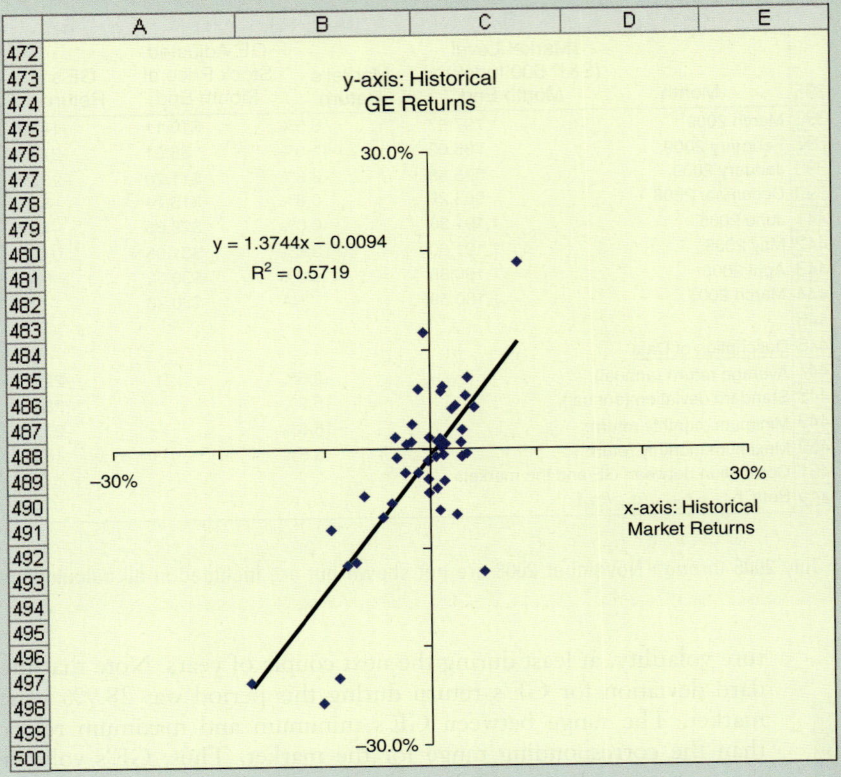

market, while at other times it does much worse. The R^2 value shown in the chart measures the degree of dispersion about the regression line. Statistically speaking, it measures the percentage of the variance that is explained by the regression equation. An R^2 of 1.0 indicates that all points lie exactly on the line and hence that all of the variations in the y-variable are explained by the x-variable. GE's R^2 is about 0.57, which is somewhat higher than the typical stock R^2 of 0.32. This indicates that about 57% of the variance in GE's returns is explained by the market returns versus only 32% of the explained variance of a typical stock. If we had done a similar analysis for a portfolio of forty randomly selected stocks, then the points would probably have been clustered tightly around the regression line and the R^2 probably would have exceeded 0.90.

Finally, observe that the intercept shown in the regression equation on the chart is –0.0094. This indicates that GE's average monthly return was –0.94% less than that of a typical company during these 4 years, or 12(–0.94%) = –11.28% less per year as a result of factors other than the general decline in stock prices.

Self-Test

What types of data are needed to calculate a beta coefficient for an actual company? What does the R^2 measure? What is the R^2 for a typical company?

6.5 The Relationship between Risk and Return

In the preceding section we saw that, under the CAPM theory, beta is the proper measure of a stock's relevant risk. However, we need to quantify how risk affects required returns: For a given level of risk as measured by beta, what rate of return do investors require to compensate them for bearing that risk? To begin, let us define the following terms.

$\hat{r}_i$ = *Expected* rate of return on Stock i.

r_i = *Required* rate of return on Stock i. This is the minimum expected return that is required to induce an average investor to purchase the stock.

$\bar{r}$ = Realized, after-the-fact return.

r_{RF} = Risk-free rate of return. In this context, r_{RF} is generally measured by the expected return on long-term U.S. Treasury bonds.

b_i = Beta coefficient of Stock i.

r_M = Required rate of return on a portfolio consisting of all stocks, which is called the *market portfolio.*

RP_M = Risk premium on "the market." $RP_M = (r_M - r_{RF})$ is the additional return over the risk-free rate required to induce an average investor to invest in the market portfolio.

RP_i = Risk premium on Stock i: $RP_i = (RP_M)b_i$.

The **market risk premium, RP_M,** is the premium that investors require for bearing the risk of an average stock, and it depends on the degree of risk aversion that investors on average have. Assume that Treasury bonds yield r_{RF} = 6% and that the stock market has a required return of r_M = 11%. Under these conditions, the market risk premium, RP_M, is 5%:

$$RP_M = r_M - r_{RF} = 11\% - 6\% = 5\%$$

We can measure a stock's relative risk by its beta coefficient and then calculate its individual risk premium as follows:

$$\text{Risk premium for Stock i} = RP_i = (RP_M)b_i \qquad (6\text{-}13)$$

For example, if b_i = 0.5 and RP_M = 5%, then RP_i is 2.5%:

$$\begin{aligned} RP_i &= (5\%)(0.5) \\ &= 2.5\% \end{aligned}$$

The required return for any investment can be expressed in general terms as

$$\text{Required return} = \text{Risk-free return} + \text{Premium for risk}$$

Here the risk-free return includes a premium for expected inflation, and we assume that the assets under consideration have similar maturities and liquidity. Under these conditions, the relationship between risk and required returns can be found as specified in the **Security Market Line (SML):**

$$\text{SML equation}: \begin{matrix}\text{Required return}\\ \text{on Stock i}\end{matrix} = \begin{matrix}\text{Risk-free}\\ \text{rate}\end{matrix} + \begin{pmatrix}\text{Market risk}\\ \text{premium}\end{pmatrix}\begin{pmatrix}\text{Beta of}\\ \text{Stock i}\end{pmatrix} \qquad (6\text{-}14)$$

$$\begin{aligned} r_i &= r_{RF} + (r_M - r_{RF})b_i \\ &= r_{RF} + (RP_M)b_i \end{aligned}$$

The required return for our illustrative Stock i is then found as follows:

$$
\begin{aligned}
r_i &= 6\% + 5\%(0.5) \\
&= 8.5\%
\end{aligned}
$$

If some other Stock j were riskier than Stock i and had $b_j = 2.0$, then its required rate of return would be 16%:

$$r_j = 6\% + (5\%)2.0 = 16\%$$

An average stock, with b = 1.0, would have a required return of 11%, the same as the market return:

$$r_A = 6\% + (5\%)1.0 = 11\% = r_M$$

Equation 6-14 is called the Security Market Line (SML) equation, and it is often expressed in graph form; see Figure 6-16, which shows the SML when $r_{RF} = 6\%$ and $RP_M = 5\%$. Note the following points.

1. Required rates of return are shown on the vertical axis, while risk as measured by beta is shown on the horizontal axis. This graph is quite different from the one shown in Figure 6-13, where the returns on individual stocks were plotted on the vertical axis and returns on the market index were shown on the horizontal axis. The slopes of the three lines in Figure 6-13 were used to calculate the three stocks' betas, and those betas were then plotted as points on the horizontal axis of Figure 6-16.

FIGURE 6-16 The Security Market Line (SML)

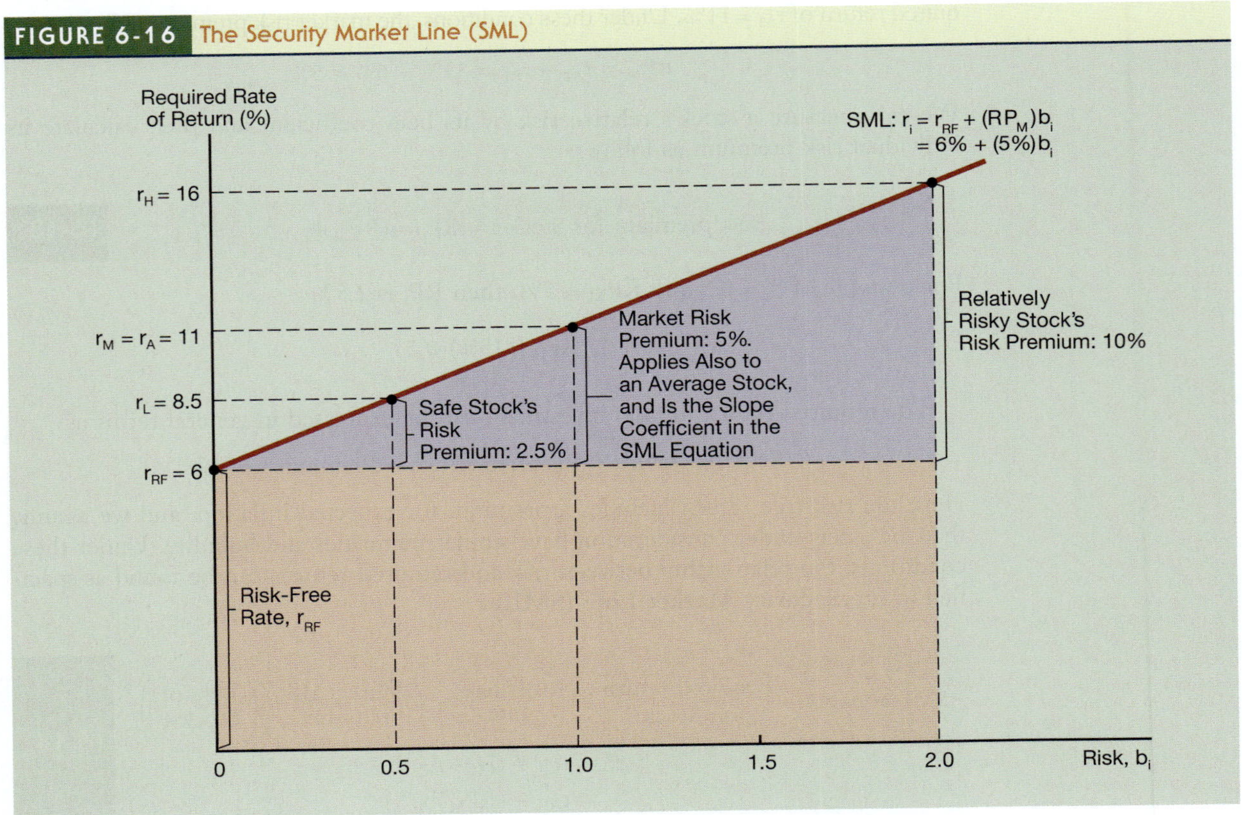

2. Riskless securities have $b_i = 0$; therefore, r_{RF} appears as the vertical axis intercept in Figure 6-16. If we could construct a portfolio that had a beta of zero, then it would have a required return equal to the risk-free rate.
3. The slope of the SML (5% in Figure 6-16) reflects the degree of risk aversion in the economy: The greater the average investor's aversion to risk, then (a) the steeper the slope of the line, (b) the greater the risk premium for all stocks, and (c) the higher the required rate of return on all stocks.[15] These points are discussed further in a later section.
4. The values we worked out for stocks with $b_i = 0.5$, $b_i = 1.0$, and $b_i = 2.0$ agree with the values shown on the graph for r_L, r_A, and r_H.
5. Negative betas are rare, but they can occur. For example, some stocks associated with gold, such as a mining operation, occasionally have a negative beta. Based on the SML, a stock with a negative beta should have a required return less than the risk-free rate. In fact, a stock with a very large but negative beta might have negative required return! This means that when the market is doing well, this stock will do poorly. But it also implies the opposite: When the market is doing poorly, a negative-beta stock should have a positive return. In other words, the negative-beta stock acts like an insurance policy. Therefore, an investor might be willing to accept a negative return on the stock during good times if it is likely to provide a positive return in bad times.

What would happen if a stock's expected return, $\hat{r}_i$, were greater than its required return, r_i? In other words, suppose investors thought they could get a 14% return even though the stock's risk only justified an 11% return? If all investors felt this way, then demand for the stock would soar as investors tried to purchase it. But if everyone tried to buy the stock, its price would go up. As the price went up, the extra expected returns would evaporate until the expected return equaled the required return. The reverse would happen if the expected return were less than the required return. Therefore, it seems reasonable to expect that investors' actions would tend to drive the expected return toward the required return.

Unexpected news about a stock's cash flow prospects would certainly change the stock's expected return. A stock's required return can also change because the Security Market Line and a company's position on it can change over time as a result of changes in interest rates, investors' aversion to risk, and individual companies' betas. Such changes are discussed in the following sections.

The Impact of Changes in Inflation and Interest Rates

Interest is the same as "rent" on borrowed money, or the price of money. Thus, r_{RF} is the price of money to a riskless borrower. The risk-free rate as measured by the rate on U.S. Treasury securities is called the *nominal,* or *quoted, rate,* and it consists of two elements: (1) a *real inflation-free rate of return, r**; and (2) an *inflation premium, IP,* equal to the anticipated rate of inflation.[16] Thus, $r_{RF} = r^* + IP$. The real rate on

[15]Students sometimes confuse beta with the slope of the SML. This is a mistake. The slope of any straight line is equal to the "rise" divided by the "run," or $(Y_1 - Y_0)/(X_1 - X_0)$. Consider Figure 6-16. If we let Y = r and X = beta and if we go from the origin to b = 1.0, then we see that the slope is $(r_M - r_{RF})/(b_M - b_{RF}) = (11\% - 6\%)/(1 - 0) = 5\%$. Thus, the slope of the SML is equal to $(r_M - r_{RF})$, the market risk premium. In Figure 6-16, $r_i = 6\% + 5\%(b_i)$, so an increase of beta from 1.0 to 2.0 would produce a 5-percentage-point increase in r_i.

[16]In addition to anticipated inflation, the inflation premium may also include a premium for bearing inflation risk. Long-term Treasury bonds also contain a maturity risk premium, MRP. Here we include the MRP in r* to simplify the discussion. See Chapter 5 for more on bond pricing and bond risk premiums.

long-term Treasury bonds has historically ranged from 2% to 4% with a mean of about 3%. Therefore, the 6% r_{RF} shown in Figure 6-16 might be thought of as consisting of a 3% real risk-free rate of return plus a 3% inflation premium: $r_{RF} = r^* + IP = 3\% + 3\% = 6\%$.

The nominal risk-free rate could change as a result of changes in anticipated inflation or changes in the real interest rate. Consider a recession, such as the one that began in 2007. If consumers and businesses decide to cut back on spending, this will reduce the demand for funds, and that will, other things held constant, lower the risk-free rate and thus the required return on other investments.[17] A key point to note is that a change in r_{RF} will not necessarily cause a change in the market risk premium. Thus, as r_{RF} changes, so will the required return on the market, and this will, other things held constant, keep the market risk premium stable.

Suppose the risk-free interest rate increases to 8% from some combination of an increase in real rates and in anticipated inflation. Such a change is shown in Figure 6-17. Notice that, under the CAPM, the increase in r_{RF} leads to an *identical* increase in the rate of return on all assets, because the same risk-free rate is built into the required rate of return on all assets. For example, the rate of return on an average stock, r_M, increases from 11% to 13%. Other risky securities' returns also rise by 2 percentage points.

FIGURE 6-17 Shift in the SML Caused by an Increase in Interest Rates

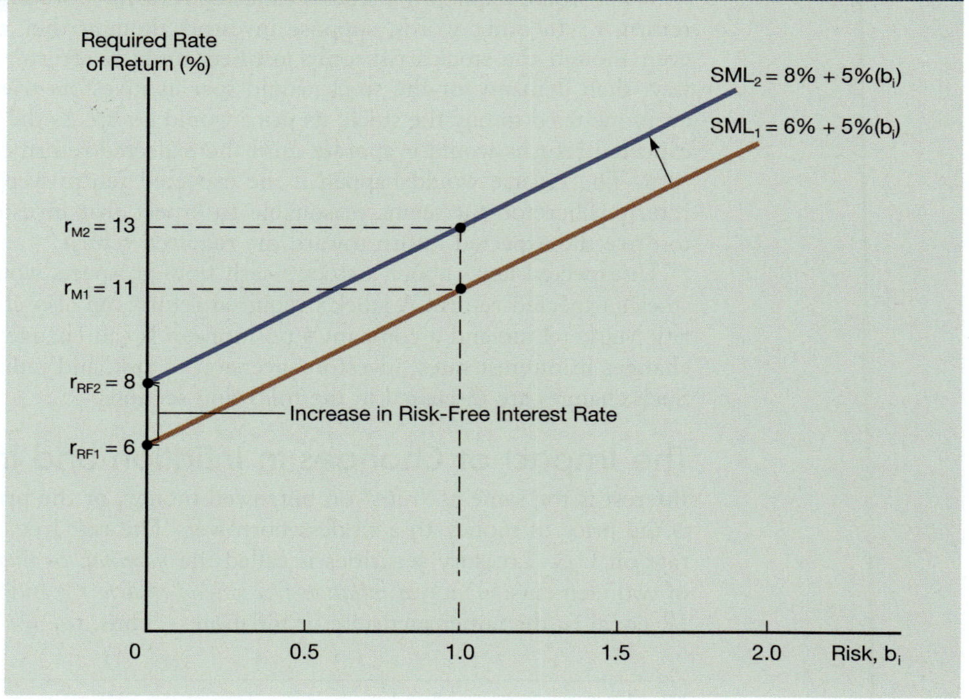

[17]Think of a sailboat floating in a harbor. The distance from the ocean floor to the ocean surface is like the risk-free rate, and it moves up and down with the tides. The distance from the top of the ship's mast to the ocean floor is like the required market return: It too moves up and down with the tides. The distance from the mast-top to the ocean surface is like the market risk premium—it also stays the same, even though tides move the ship up and down. Thus, other things held constant, a change in the risk-free rate also causes an identical change in the required market return, r_M, resulting in a relatively stable market risk premium, $r_M - r_{RF}$.

Changes in Risk Aversion

The slope of the Security Market Line reflects the extent to which investors are averse to risk: The steeper the slope of the line, the greater the average investor's aversion to risk. Suppose all investors were indifferent to risk—that is, suppose they were *not* risk averse. If r_{RF} were 6%, then risky assets would also provide an expected return of 6%, because if there were no risk aversion then there would be no risk premium, and the SML would be plotted as a horizontal line. As risk aversion increases, so does the risk premium, and this causes the slope of the SML to become steeper.

Figure 6-18 illustrates an increase in risk aversion. The market risk premium rises from 5% to 7.5%, causing r_M to rise from r_{M1} = 11% to r_{M2} = 13.5%. The returns on other risky assets also rise, and the effect of this shift in risk aversion is greater for riskier securities. For example, the required return on a stock with b_i = 0.5 increases by only 1.25 percentage points, from 8.5% to 9.75%; that on a stock with b_i = 1.0 increases by 2.5 percentage points, from 11.0% to 13.5%; and that on a stock with b_i = 1.5 increases by 3.75 percentage points, from 13.5% to 17.25%.

Changes in a Stock's Beta Coefficient

Given risk aversion and a positively sloped SML as in Figure 6-18, the higher a stock's beta, the higher its required rate of return. As we shall see later in the book, a firm can influence its beta through changes in the composition of its assets and also through its use of debt: Acquiring riskier assets will increase beta, as will a change in capital structure that calls for a higher debt ratio. A company's beta can also change as a result of external factors such as increased competition in its industry, the expiration of basic patents, and the like. When such changes lead to a higher or lower beta, the required rate of return will also change.

FIGURE 6-18 Shift in the SML Caused by Increased Risk Aversion

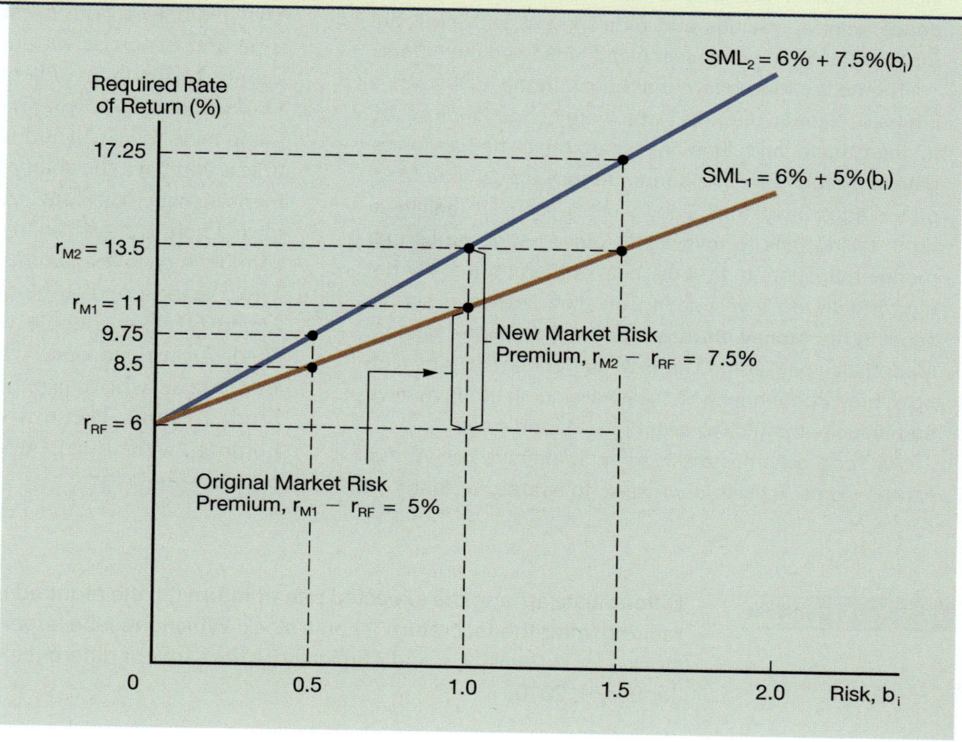

Another Kind of Risk: The Bernie Madoff Story

In the fall of 2008, Bernard Madoff's massive Ponzi scheme was exposed, revealing an important type of risk that's not dealt with in this chapter. Madoff was a money manager in the 1960s, and apparently through good luck he produced above-average results for several years. His clients then told their friends about Madoff's success, and those friends sent in money for him to invest. Madoff's actual returns then dropped, but he didn't tell his clients that they were losing money. Rather, he told them that returns were holding up well, and he used new incoming money to pay dividends and meet withdrawal requests. The idea of using new money to pay off old investors is called a Ponzi scheme, named after Charles Ponzi, a Bostonian who set up the first widely publicized such scheme in the early 1900s.

Madoff perfected the system, ran his scheme for about 40 years, and attracted about $50 billion of investors' funds. His investors ranged from well-known billionaires to retirees who invested their entire life savings. His advertising was strictly word-of-mouth, and clients telling potential clients about the many wealthy and highly regarded people who invested with him certainly helped. All of his investors assumed that someone else had done the "due diligence" and found the operation to be clean. A few investors who actually did some due diligence were suspicious and didn't invest with him, but for the most part people just blindly followed the others.

The hedge fund boom that began in the 1990s was a big help. "Funds of funds," which are hedge funds set up to investigate and then invest in other hedge funds, gained momentum, and some of those funds were Madoff's biggest investors. They were a scam in their own right, taking fees to investigate other hedge funds and money managers to find the best of them, but really doing virtually no investigating on their own and simply sending the money entrusted to them to Bernie Madoff. Madoff also paid some "finders" to frequent country club bars, brag about how well they were doing in the market, and induce other fish to swim into Madoff's net.

All Ponzi schemes crash when something occurs that causes some investors to seek to withdraw funds in amounts greater than the incoming funds from new investors. Someone tries to get out, can't do it, tells others who worry and try to get out too, and almost overnight the scam unravels. That happened to Madoff in 2008, when the stock market crash caused some of his investors to seek withdrawals and few new dollars were coming in. In the end, his investors lost billions; some lost their entire life savings, and several have committed suicide. Moreover, the Madoff revelations have led to the exposure of other, similar (but smaller), frauds. Indeed, people—especially the rich and famous—are reluctant to admit they've been taken, so it's likely that lots of frauds are never reported.

How can you guard against a fraud like Madoff's? For a scheme as sophisticated as that of Madoff, it's not easy, but there are some steps that can and should be taken.

1. *Use your basic financial knowledge and some common sense.* Earlier in this chapter we gave you an idea about the kinds of returns that have been earned in the past on different classes of investments with different risk profiles. If someone offers you an investment that seems too good to be true, it probably is, so you should drill deep to see if it is really what its sponsor says it is before you invest. If you don't have the time and expertise for such investigation, you should probably avoid the investment.
2. *Deal with reputable institutions.* We hate to recommend avoiding small and new organizations, but unless you have the ability to check out an investment manager carefully, that's probably a good idea. There are institutions with the expertise to conduct such investigations, so you might be wise to leave the too-good-to-be-true investments to them.
3. *Diversify.* Many people were burned by Bernie Madoff, but the ones who were hurt worst were those who trusted most or all of their funds to him. Those who diversified their holdings were hurt, but they weren't wiped out. So diversify!

Self-Test

Differentiate among the expected rate of return ($\hat{r}$), the required rate of return (r), and the realized, after-the-fact return ($\hat{r}$) on a stock. Which must be larger to get you to buy the stock, $\hat{r}$ or r? Would $\hat{r}$, r, and $\bar{r}$ typically be the same or different for a given company, say on January 1, 2010?

What are the differences between the relative returns graph (Figure 6-13), where "betas are made," and the SML graph (Figure 6-16), where "betas are used"? Discuss both how the graphs are constructed and the information they convey.

What happens to the SML graph in Figure 6-16 when inflation increases or decreases?

What happens to the SML graph when risk aversion increases or decreases? What would the SML look like if investors were completely indifferent to risk—that is, had zero risk aversion?

How can a firm influence its market risk as reflected in its beta?

A stock has a beta of 1.4. Assume that the risk-free rate is 5.5% and that the market risk premium is 5%. What is the stock's required rate of return? **(12.5%)**

WWW

Kenneth French's Web site, **http://mba.tuck.dartmouth.edu/pages/faculty/ken.french/index.html** *is an excellent resource for data and information regarding factors related to stock returns.*

6.6 Some Concerns about Beta and the CAPM

The Capital Asset Pricing Model is more than just an abstract theory described in textbooks. It has great intuitive appeal, and it is widely used by analysts, investors, and corporations. However, a number of recent studies have raised concerns about its validity. For example, a study by Eugene Fama of the University of Chicago and Kenneth French of Dartmouth found no historical relationship between stocks' returns and their market betas, confirming a position long held by some professors and stock market analysts.[18]

As an alternative to the traditional CAPM, researchers and practitioners are developing models with more explanatory variables than just beta. These multi-factor models represent an attractive generalization of the traditional CAPM model's insight that market risk—risk that cannot be diversified away—underlies the pricing of assets. In the multi-variable models, risk is assumed to be caused by a number of different factors, including size of firm, market/book ratios, measures of liquidity, and the like, whereas the CAPM gauges risk only relative to returns on the market portfolio. The multi-variable models represent a potentially important step forward in finance theory, but they also have some deficiencies when applied in practice. As a result, the basic CAPM is still the most widely used method for thinking about required rates of return on stocks.

Self-Test

Have there been any studies that question the validity of the CAPM? Explain.

6.7 Some Concluding Thoughts: Implications for Corporate Managers and Investors

The connection between risk and return is an important concept, and it has numerous implications for both corporate managers and investors. As we will see in later chapters, corporate managers spend a great deal of time assessing the risk and returns of individual projects. Indeed, given their concerns about the risk of individual projects, it might be fair to ask why we spend so much time discussing the riskiness of stocks. Why not begin by looking at the riskiness of such business assets as plant and equipment? The reason is that, *for a management whose primary goal is to maximize*

[18]See Eugene F. Fama and Kenneth R. French, "The Cross-Section of Expected Stock Returns," *Journal of Finance*, Vol. 47 (1992), pp. 427–465; and Eugene F. Fama and Kenneth R. French, "Common Risk Factors in the Returns on Stocks and Bonds," *Journal of Financial Economics*, Vol. 33 (1993), pp. 3–56. They found that stock returns are related to firm size and market/book ratios. Small firms and those firms with low market/book ratios had higher returns; however, they found no relationship between returns and beta.

intrinsic value, the overriding consideration is the riskiness of the firm's stock, and the relevant risk of any physical asset must be measured in terms of its effect on the stock's risk as seen by investors. For example, suppose Goodyear is considering a major investment in a new product, recapped tires. Sales of recaps and hence earnings on the new operation are highly uncertain, so on a stand-alone basis the new venture appears to be quite risky. However, suppose returns in the recap business are negatively correlated with Goodyear's other operations: When times are good and people have plenty of money, they buy new cars with new tires, but when times are bad, they tend to keep their old cars and buy recaps for them. Therefore, returns would be high on regular operations and low on the recap division during good times, but the opposite would be true during recessions. The result might be a pattern like that shown earlier in Figure 6-9 for Stocks W and M. Thus, what appears to be a risky investment when viewed on a stand-alone basis might not be so risky when viewed within the context of the company as a whole.

This analysis can be extended to the corporation's stockholders. Because Goodyear's stock is owned by diversified stockholders, the real issue each time management makes an investment decision is this: How will this investment affect the risk of our stockholders? Again, the stand-alone risk of an individual project may look quite high; however, when viewed in the context of the project's effect on stockholder risk, it may not be as large. We will address this issue again in Chapter 11, where we examine the effects of capital budgeting on companies' beta coefficients and thus on stockholders' risks.

These concepts are obviously important for individual investors, but they are also important for corporate managers. Here we summarize some key ideas that all investors should consider.

1. *There is a trade-off between risk and return.* The average investor likes higher returns but dislikes risk. It follows that higher-risk investments need to offer investors higher expected returns. Put another way: If you are seeking higher returns, you must be willing to assume higher risks.
2. *Diversification is crucial.* By diversifying wisely, investors can dramatically reduce risk without reducing their expected returns. Don't put all of your money in one or two stocks, or in one or two industries. A huge mistake many people make is to invest a high percentage of their funds in their employer's stock. Then, if the company goes bankrupt, they lose not only their job but also their invested capital. Although no stock is completely riskless, you can smooth out the bumps somewhat by holding a well-diversified portfolio.
3. *Real returns are what matters.* All investors should understand the difference between nominal and real returns. When assessing performance, the real return (what you have left after inflation) is what really matters. It follows that, as expected inflation increases, investors need to earn higher nominal returns.
4. *The risk of an investment often depends on how long you plan to hold the investment.* Common stocks, for example, can be extremely risky for short-term investors. However, over the long haul the bumps tend to even out, so stocks are less risky when held as part of a long-term portfolio. Indeed, in his best-selling book *Stocks for the Long Run*, Jeremy Siegel of the University of Pennsylvania concludes: "The safest long-term investment for the preservation of purchasing power has clearly been stocks, not bonds."
5. The past gives us insights into the risk and returns on various investments, but *there is no guarantee that the future will repeat the past.* Stocks that have performed well in recent years might tumble, while stocks that have struggled may rebound.

The same thing can hold true for the stock market as a whole. Even Jeremy Siegel, who has preached that stocks have historically been good long-term investments, has also argued that there is no assurance that returns in the future will be as strong as they have been in the past. More importantly, when purchasing a stock you always need to ask: "Is this stock fairly valued, or is it currently priced too high?" We discuss this issue more completely in the next chapter.

Self-Test

Explain the following statement: "The stand-alone risk of an individual corporate project may be quite high, but viewed in the context of its effect on stockholders' risk, the project's true risk may be much lower."

How does the correlation between returns on a project and returns on the firm's other assets affect the project's risk?

What are some important concepts for individual investors to consider when evaluating the risk and returns of various investments?

Summary

This chapter focuses on the trade-off between risk and return. We began by discussing how to estimate risk and return for both individual assets and portfolios. In particular, we differentiated between stand-alone risk and risk in a portfolio context, and we explained the benefits of diversification. Finally, we introduced the CAPM, which describes how risk affects rates of return. In the chapters that follow, we will give you the tools to estimate the required rates of return for bonds, preferred stock, and common stock, and we will explain how firms use these rates of return to estimate their costs of capital. As you will see, the cost of capital is a basic element in the capital budgeting process. The key concepts covered in this chapter are listed below.

- **Risk** can be defined as the chance that some unfavorable event will occur.
- The risk of an asset's cash flows can be considered on a **stand-alone basis** (each asset all by itself) or in a **portfolio context**, in which the investment is combined with other assets and its risk is reduced through **diversification**.
- Most rational investors hold **portfolios of assets**, and they are more concerned with the risk of their portfolios than with the risk of individual assets.
- The **expected return** on an investment is the mean value of its probability distribution of returns.
- The **greater the probability** that the actual return will be far below the expected return, the **greater the asset's stand-alone risk**.
- The average investor is **risk averse**, which means that he or she must be compensated for holding risky assets. Therefore, riskier assets have higher required returns than less risky assets.
- An asset's risk has two components: (1) **diversifiable risk**, which can be eliminated by diversification, and (2) **market risk**, which cannot be eliminated by diversification.
- Market risk is measured by the standard deviation of returns on a well-diversified portfolio, one that consists of all stocks traded in the market. Such a portfolio is called the **market portfolio**.
- The **relevant risk** of an individual asset is its contribution to the risk of a well-diversified portfolio. Since market risk cannot be eliminated by diversification, investors must be compensated for bearing it.
- A stock's **beta coefficient, b**, is a measure of its market risk. Beta measures the extent to which the stock's returns move relative to the market.

- A **high-beta stock** has stock returns that tend to move up and down by more than the returns on an average stock, while the opposite is true for a **low-beta stock**. An average stock has b = 1.0, as does the market portfolio.
- The **beta of a portfolio** is a **weighted average** of the betas of the individual securities in the portfolio.
- The **Security Market Line (SML)** equation shows the relationship between a security's market risk and its required rate of return. The return required for any security i is equal to the **risk-free rate** plus the **market risk premium** multiplied by the security's **beta**: $r_i = r_{RF} + (RP_M)b_i$.
- In equilibrium, the expected rate of return on a stock must equal its required return. However, a number of things can happen to cause the required rate of return to change: (1) **the risk-free rate can change** because of changes in either real rates or expected inflation, (2) **a stock's beta can change**, and (3) **investors' aversion to risk can change**.
- Because returns on assets in different countries are not perfectly correlated, **global diversification** may result in lower risk for multinational companies and globally diversified portfolios.
- The CAPM is conceptually based on **expected returns.** However, only historical returns are available to test it. Various tests have been conducted, and none has "proved" that the CAPM actually describes how investors behave. Indeed, evidence exists to suggest that investors regard factors other than just beta when analyzing risk. The 2008–2009 market crash suggests that, in addition to risk as measured by beta, liquidity is important as well.
- Two web extensions accompany this chapter: ***Web Extension 6A*** provides a discussion of **continuous probability distributions**, and ***Web Extension 6B*** shows how to calculate beta with a financial calculator.

Questions

(6–1) Define the following terms, using graphs or equations to illustrate your answers where feasible.

a. Risk in general; stand-alone risk; probability distribution and its relation to risk
b. Expected rate of return, $\hat{r}$
c. Continuous probability distribution
d. Standard deviation, σ; variance, σ^2; coefficient of variation, CV
e. Risk aversion; realized rate of return, $\bar{r}$
f. Risk premium for Stock i, RP_i; market risk premium, RP_M
g. Capital Asset Pricing Model (CAPM)
h. Expected return on a portfolio, $\hat{r}_p$; market portfolio
i. Correlation as a concept; correlation coefficient, ρ
j. Market risk; diversifiable risk; relevant risk
k. Beta coefficient, b; average stock's beta
l. Security Market Line (SML); SML equation
m. Slope of SML and its relationship to risk aversion

(6–2) The probability distribution of a less risky return is more peaked than that of a riskier return. What shape would the probability distribution have for (a) completely certain returns and (b) completely uncertain returns?

(6–3) Security A has an expected return of 7%, a standard deviation of returns of 35%, a correlation coefficient with the market of –0.3, and a beta coefficient of –1.5. Security B has an expected return of 12%, a standard deviation of returns of 10%, a correlation with the market of 0.7, and a beta coefficient of 1.0. Which security is riskier? Why?

(6–4) Suppose you owned a portfolio consisting of $250,000 of U.S. government bonds with a maturity of 30 years.

a. Would your portfolio be riskless?
b. Now suppose you hold a portfolio consisting of $250,000 of 30-day Treasury bills. Every 30 days your bills mature, and you reinvest the principal ($250,000) in a new batch of bills. Assume that you live on the investment income from your portfolio and that you want to maintain a constant standard of living. Is your portfolio truly riskless?
c. Can you think of any asset that would be completely riskless? What security comes closest to being riskless? Explain.

(6–5) If investors' aversion to risk *increased*, would the risk premium on a high-beta stock increase by more or less than that on a low-beta stock? Explain.

(6–6) If a company's beta were to double, would its expected return double?

(6–7) In the real world, is it possible to construct a portfolio of stocks that has an expected return equal to the risk-free rate?

Self-Test Problems

Solutions Appear in Appendix A

(ST–1) Realized Rates of Return

Stocks A and B have the following historical returns:

Year	$\bar{r}_A$	$\bar{r}_B$
2006	–18%	–24%
2007	44	24
2008	–22	–4
2009	22	8
2010	34	56

a. Calculate the average rate of return for each stock during the 5-year period. Assume that someone held a portfolio consisting of 50% of Stock A and 50% of Stock B. What would have been the realized rate of return on the portfolio in each year? What would have been the average return on the portfolio for the 5-year period?
b. Now calculate the standard deviation of returns for each stock and for the portfolio. Use Equation 6-5.
c. Looking at the annual returns data on the two stocks, would you guess that the correlation coefficient between returns on the two stocks is closer to 0.8 or to –0.8?
d. If you added more stocks at random to the portfolio, which of the following is the most accurate statement of what would happen to σ_p?
   (1) σ_p would remain constant.
   (2) σ_p would decline to somewhere in the vicinity of 20%.
   (3) σ_p would decline to zero if enough stocks were included.

(ST–2) Beta and Required Rate of Return

ECRI Corporation is a holding company with four main subsidiaries. The percentage of its business coming from each of the subsidiaries, and their respective betas, are as follows:

Subsidiary	Percentage of Business	Beta
Electric utility	60%	0.70
Cable company	25	0.90
Real estate	10	1.30
International/special projects	5	1.50

a. What is the holding company's beta?
b. Assume that the risk-free rate is 6% and that the market risk premium is 5%. What is the holding company's required rate of return?
c. ECRI is considering a change in its strategic focus: It will reduce its reliance on the electric utility subsidiary so that the percentage of its business from this subsidiary will be 50%. At the same time, ECRI will increase its reliance on the international/special projects division, and the percentage of its business from that subsidiary will rise to 15%. What will be the shareholders' required rate of return if management adopts these changes?

Problems

Answers Appear in Appendix B

Easy Problems 1–3

(6–1) Portfolio Beta

An individual has $35,000 invested in a stock with a beta of 0.8 and another $40,000 invested in a stock with a beta of 1.4. If these are the only two investments in her portfolio, what is her portfolio's beta?

(6–2) Required Rate of Return

Assume that the risk-free rate is 6% and that the expected return on the market is 13%. What is the required rate of return on a stock that has a beta of 0.7?

(6–3) Required Rates of Return

Assume that the risk-free rate is 5% and that the market risk premium is 6%. What is the required return on the market, on a stock with a beta of 1.0, and on a stock with a beta of 1.2?

Intermediate Problems 4–9

(6–4) Expected Return: Discrete Distribution

A stock's return has the following distribution:

Demand for the Company's Products	Probability of This Demand Occurring	Rate of Return If This Demand Occurs (%)
Weak	0.1	−50%
Below average	0.2	(5)
Average	0.4	16
Above average	0.2	25
Strong	0.1	60
	1.0	

Calculate the stock's expected return, standard deviation, and coefficient of variation.

(6–5) Expected Returns: Discrete Distribution

The market and Stock J have the following probability distributions:

Probability	r_M	r_J
0.3	15%	20%
0.4	9	5
0.3	18	12

a. Calculate the expected rates of return for the market and Stock J.
b. Calculate the standard deviations for the market and Stock J.
c. Calculate the coefficients of variation for the market and Stock J.

(6–6) Required Rate of Return

Suppose $r_{RF} = 5\%$, $r_M = 10\%$, and $r_A = 12\%$.

a. Calculate Stock A's beta.
b. If Stock A's beta were 2.0, then what would be A's new required rate of return?

(6–7) Required Rate of Return

Suppose $r_{RF} = 9\%$, $r_M = 14\%$, and $b_i = 1.3$.

a. What is r_i, the required rate of return on Stock i?
b. Now suppose r_{RF} (1) increases to 10% or (2) decreases to 8%. The slope of the SML remains constant. How would this affect r_M and r_i?
c. Now assume r_{RF} remains at 9% but r_M (1) increases to 16% or (2) falls to 13%. The slope of the SML does not remain constant. How would these changes affect r_i?

(6–8) Portfolio Beta

Suppose you hold a diversified portfolio consisting of a $7,500 investment in each of 20 different common stocks. The portfolio's beta is 1.12. Now, suppose you sell one of the stocks with a beta of 1.0 for $7,500 and use the proceeds to buy another stock whose beta is 1.75. Calculate your portfolio's new beta.

(6–9) Portfolio Required Return

Suppose you manage a $4 million fund that consists of four stocks with the following investments:

Stock	Investment	Beta
A	$ 400,000	1.50
B	600,000	−0.50
C	1,000,000	1.25
D	2,000,000	0.75

If the market's required rate of return is 14% and the risk-free rate is 6%, what is the fund's required rate of return?

Challenging Problems 10–13

(6–10) Portfolio Beta

You have a $2 million portfolio consisting of a $100,000 investment in each of 20 different stocks. The portfolio has a beta of 1.1. You are considering selling $100,000 worth of one stock with a beta of 0.9 and using the proceeds to purchase another stock with a beta of 1.4. What will the portfolio's new beta be after these transactions?

(6–11) Required Rate of Return

Stock R has a beta of 1.5, Stock S has a beta of 0.75, the expected rate of return on an average stock is 13%, and the risk-free rate is 7%. By how much does the required return on the riskier stock exceed that on the less risky stock?

(6–12) Historical Realized Rates of Return

Stocks A and B have the following historical returns:

Year	$\bar{r}_A$	$\bar{r}_B$
2006	−18.00%	−14.50%
2007	33.00	21.80
2008	15.00	30.50
2009	−0.50	−7.60
2010	27.00	26.30

a. Calculate the average rate of return for each stock during the 5-year period.
b. Assume that someone held a portfolio consisting of 50% of Stock A and 50% of Stock B. What would have been the realized rate of return on the portfolio in each year? What would have been the average return on the portfolio during this period?
c. Calculate the standard deviation of returns for each stock and for the portfolio.
d. Calculate the coefficient of variation for each stock and for the portfolio.
e. If you are a risk-averse investor then, assuming these are your only choices, would you prefer to hold Stock A, Stock B, or the portfolio? Why?

(6–13) Historical Returns: Expected and Required Rates of Return

You have observed the following returns over time:

Year	Stock X	Stock Y	Market
2006	14%	13%	12%
2007	19	7	10
2008	−16	−5	−12
2009	3	1	1
2010	20	11	15

Assume that the risk-free rate is 6% and the market risk premium is 5%.

a. What are the betas of Stocks X and Y?
b. What are the required rates of return on Stocks X and Y?
c. What is the required rate of return on a portfolio consisting of 80% of Stock X and 20% of Stock Y?
d. If Stock X's expected return is 22%, is Stock X under- or overvalued?

Spreadsheet Problem

(6-14) Evaluating Risk and Return

Start with the partial model in the file ***Ch06 P14 Build a Model.xls*** on the textbook's Web site. The file contains hypothetical data for working this problem. Bartman Industries's and Reynolds Incorporated's stock prices and dividends, along with the Market Index, are shown below. Stock prices are reported for December 31 of each year, and dividends reflect those paid during the year. The market data are adjusted to include dividends.

	Bartman Industries		Reynolds Incorporated		Market Index
Year	Stock Price	Dividend	Stock Price	Dividend	Includes Dividends
2010	$17.25	$1.15	$48.75	$3.00	11,663.98
2009	14.75	1.06	52.30	2.90	8,785.70
2008	16.50	1.00	48.75	2.75	8,679.98
2007	10.75	0.95	57.25	2.50	6,434.03
2006	11.37	0.90	60.00	2.25	5,602.28
2005	7.62	0.85	55.75	2.00	4,705.97

a. Use the data given to calculate annual returns for Bartman, Reynolds, and the Market Index, and then calculate average annual returns for the two stocks and the index. (*Hint:* Remember, returns are calculated by subtracting the beginning price from the ending price to get the capital gain or loss, adding the dividend to the capital gain or loss, and then dividing the result by the beginning price. Assume that dividends are already included in the index. Also, you cannot calculate the rate of return for 2005 because you do not have 2004 data.)

b. Calculate the standard deviations of the returns for Bartman, Reynolds, and the Market Index. (*Hint:* Use the sample standard deviation formula given in the chapter, which corresponds to the STDEV function in *Excel.*)

c. Now calculate the coefficients of variation for Bartman, Reynolds, and the Market Index.

d. Construct a scatter diagram graph that shows Bartman's returns on the vertical axis and the Market Index's returns on the horizontal axis. Construct a similar graph showing Reynolds's stock returns on the vertical axis.

e. Estimate Bartman's and Reynolds's betas as the slopes of regression lines with stock return on the vertical axis (y-axis) and market return on the horizontal axis (x-axis). (*Hint:* Use *Excel*'s SLOPE function.) Are these betas consistent with your graph?

f. The risk-free rate on long-term Treasury bonds is 6.04%. Assume that the market risk premium is 5%. What is the required return on the market? Now use the SML equation to calculate the two companies' required returns.

g. If you formed a portfolio that consisted of 50% Bartman stock and 50% Reynolds stock, what would be its beta and its required return?

h. Suppose an investor wants to include some Bartman Industries stock in his portfolio. Stocks A, B, and C are currently in the portfolio, and their betas are 0.769, 0.985, and 1.423, respectively. Calculate the new portfolio's required return if it consists of 25% Bartman, 15% Stock A, 40% Stock B, and 20% Stock C.

THOMSON ONE | Business School Edition Problem

Use the Thomson ONE—Business School Edition online database to work this chapter's questions.

Using Past Information to Estimate Required Returns

In the Capital Asset Pricing Model (CAPM) discussion, beta is identified as the correct measure of risk for diversified shareholders. Recall that beta measures the extent to which the returns of a given stock move with the stock market. When using the

CAPM to estimate required returns, we would ideally like to know how the stock will move with the market in the future, but since we don't have a crystal ball we generally use historical data to estimate this relationship.

As noted in the chapter, beta can be estimated by regressing the individual stock's returns against the returns of the overall market. As an alternative to running our own regressions, we can instead rely on reported betas from a variety of sources. These published sources make it easy to obtain beta estimates for most large publicly traded corporations. However, a word of caution is in order. Beta estimates can often be quite sensitive to the time period in which the data are estimated, the market index used, and the frequency of the data used. Therefore, it is not uncommon to find a wide range of beta estimates among the various published sources. Indeed, Thomson ONE reports multiple beta estimates. These multiple estimates reflect the fact that Thomson ONE puts together data from a variety of different sources.

Thomson ONE—BSE Discussion Questions

1. Begin by taking a look at the historical performance of the overall stock market. If you want to see, for example, the performance of the S&P 500, select INDICES and enter S&PCOMP. Click on PERFORMANCE and you will immediately see a quick summary of the market's performance in recent months and years. How has the market performed over the past year? The past 3 years? The past 5 years? The past 10 years?
2. Now let's take a closer look at the stocks of four companies: Colgate Palmolive (CL), Gillette (G), Heinz (HNZ), and Microsoft (MSFT). Before looking at the data, which of these companies would you expect to have a relatively high beta (greater than 1.0), and which of these companies would you expect to have a relatively low beta (less than 1.0)?
3. Select one of the four stocks listed in question 2 by selecting COMPANIES, entering the company's ticker symbol, and clicking on GO. On the overview page, you should see a chart that summarizes how the stock has done relative to the S&P 500 over the past 6 months. Has the stock outperformed or underperformed the overall market during this time period?
4. Return to the overview page for the stock you selected. If you scroll down the page you should see an estimate of the company's beta. What is the company's beta? What was the source of the estimated beta?
5. Click on the tab labeled PRICES. What is the company's current dividend yield? What has been its total return to investors over the past 6 months? Over the past year? Over the past 3 years? (Remember that total return includes the dividend yield plus any capital gains or losses.)
6. What is the estimated beta on this page? What is the source of the estimated beta? Why might different sources produce different estimates of beta? (*Note:* if you want to see even more beta estimates, click OVERVIEWS on the second line of tabs and then select SEC DATABASE MARKET DATA. Scroll through the STOCK OVERVIEW SECTION and you will see a range of different beta estimates.)
7. Select a beta estimate that you believe is best. (If you are not sure, you may want to consider an average of the given estimates.) Assume that the risk-free rate is 5% and that the market risk premium is 6%. What is the required return on the company's stock?

8. Repeat the same exercise for each of the three remaining companies. Do the reported betas confirm your earlier intuition? In general, do you find that the higher-beta stocks tend to do better in up markets and worse in down markets? Explain.

Mini Case

Assume that you recently graduated with a major in finance and that you just landed a job as a financial planner with Barney Smith Inc., a large financial services corporation. Your first assignment is to invest $100,000 for a client. Because the funds are to be invested in a new business that the client plans to start at the end of 1 year, you have been instructed to plan for a 1-year holding period. Further, your boss has restricted you to the investment alternatives shown in the table below. (Disregard for now the items at the bottom of the data; you will fill in the blanks later.)

Barney Smith's economic forecasting staff has developed probability estimates for the state of the economy, and its security analysts have developed a sophisticated computer program that was used to estimate the rate of return on each alternative under each state of the economy. Alta Industries is an electronics firm; Repo Men Inc. collects past-due debts; and American Foam manufactures mattresses and various other foam products. Barney Smith also maintains an "index fund" that owns a market-weighted fraction of all publicly traded stocks; you can invest in that fund and thus obtain average stock market results. Given the situation as described, answer the following questions.

Estimated Returns on Alternative Investments

State of the Economy	Probability	T-Bills	Alta Industries	Repo Men	American Foam	Market Portfolio	2-Stock Portfolio
Recession	0.1	8.0%	−22.0%	28.0%	10.0%[a]	−13.0%	3.0%
Below average	0.2	8.0	−2.0	14.7	−10.0	1.0	
Average	0.4	8.0	20.0	0.0	7.0	15.0	10.0
Above average	0.2	8.0	35.0	−10.0	45.0	29.0	
Boom	0.1	8.0	50.0	−20.0	30.0	43.0	15.0
$\hat{r}$		8.0%	___	1.7%	13.8%	15.0%	___
σ		0.0%	___	13.4%	18.8%	15.3%	___
CV			___	7.9	1.4	1.0	___
b			___	−0.86	0.68		___

[a]Note that the estimated returns of American Foam do not always move in the same direction as the overall economy. For example, when the economy is below average, consumers purchase fewer mattresses than they would if the economy were stronger. However, if the economy is in a flat-out recession, a large number of consumers who were planning to purchase a more expensive inner spring mattress may purchase, instead, a cheaper foam mattress. Under these circumstances, we would expect American Foam's stock price to be higher if there is a recession than if the economy was just below average.

a. What are investment returns? What is the return on an investment that costs $1,000 and is sold after 1 year for $1,100?

b. (1) Why is the T-bill's return independent of the state of the economy? Do T-bills promise a completely risk-free return? (2) Why are Alta Industries's returns expected to move with the economy whereas Repo Men's are expected to move counter to the economy?
c. Calculate the expected rate of return on each alternative and fill in the blanks in the row for $\hat{r}$ in the table.
d. You should recognize that basing a decision solely on expected returns is appropriate only for risk-neutral individuals. Because your client, like virtually everyone, is risk averse, the riskiness of each alternative is an important aspect of the decision. One possible measure of risk is the standard deviation of returns. (1) Calculate this value for each alternative, and fill in the blank in the row for σ in the table. (2) What type of risk is measured by the standard deviation? (3) Draw a graph that shows *roughly* the shape of the probability distributions for Alta Industries, American Foam, and T-bills.
e. Suppose you suddenly remembered that the coefficient of variation (CV) is generally regarded as being a better measure of stand-alone risk than the standard deviation when the alternatives being considered have widely differing expected returns. Calculate the missing CVs, and fill in the blanks in the row for CV in the table. Does the CV produce the same risk rankings as the standard deviation?
f. Suppose you created a two-stock portfolio by investing $50,000 in Alta Industries and $50,000 in Repo Men. (1) Calculate the expected return ($\hat{r}_p$), the standard deviation (σ_p), and the coefficient of variation (CV_p) for this portfolio and fill in the appropriate blanks in the table. (2) How does the risk of this two-stock portfolio compare with the risk of the individual stocks if they were held in isolation?
g. Suppose an investor starts with a portfolio consisting of one randomly selected stock. As more and more randomly selected stocks are added to the portfolio, what happens to the portfolio's risk and its expected return? What is the implication for investors? Draw a graph of the two portfolios to illustrate your answer.
h. (1) Should portfolio effects influence how investors think about the risk of individual stocks? (2) If you decided to hold a one-stock portfolio and consequently were exposed to more risk than diversified investors, could you expect to be compensated for all of your risk; that is, could you earn a risk premium on that part of your risk that you could have eliminated by diversifying?
i. How is market risk measured for individual securities? How are beta coefficients calculated?
j. Suppose you have the following historical returns for the stock market and for the company P. Q. Unlimited. Explain how to calculate beta, and use the historical stock returns to calculate the beta for PQU. Interpret your results.

Year	Market	PQU
1	25.7%	40.0%
2	8.0	−15.0
3	−11.0	−15.0
4	15.0	35.0
5	32.5	10.0
6	13.7	30.0
7	40.0	42.0
8	10.0	−10.0
9	−10.8	−25.0
10	−13.1	25.0

k. The expected rates of return and the beta coefficients of the alternatives, as supplied by Barney Smith's computer program, are as follows:

Security	Return ($\hat{r}$)	Risk (Beta)
Alta Industries	17.4%	1.29
Market	15.0	1.00
American Foam	13.8	0.68
T-bills	8.0	0.00
Repo Men	1.7	−0.86

(1) Do the expected returns appear to be related to each alternative's market risk? (2) Is it possible to choose among the alternatives on the basis of the information developed thus far?

l. (1) Write out the Security Market Line (SML) equation, use it to calculate the required rate of return on each alternative, and then graph the relationship between the expected and required rates of return. (2) How do the expected rates of return compare with the required rates of return? (3) Does it make sense that Repo Men has an expected return that is less than the T-bill rate? (4) What would be the market risk and the required return of a 50-50 portfolio of Alta Industries and Repo Men? Of Alta Industries and American Foam?

m. (1) Suppose investors raised their inflation expectations by 3 percentage points over current estimates as reflected in the 8% T-bill rate. What effect would higher inflation have on the SML and on the returns required on high- and low-risk securities? (2) Suppose instead that investors' risk aversion increased enough to cause the market risk premium to increase by 3 percentage points. (Assume inflation remains constant.) What effect would this have on the SML and on returns of high- and low-risk securities?

Selected Additional Cases

The following cases from Textchoice, Cengage Learning's online library, cover many of the concepts discussed in this chapter and are available at ***http://www.textchoice2.com.***

Klein-Brigham Series:
Case 2, "Peachtree Securities, Inc. (A)."
Brigham-Buzzard Series:
Case 2, "Powerline Network Corporation (Risk and Return)."

CHAPTER 7

Stocks, Stock Valuation, and Stock Market Equilibrium

The opening chart in Chapter 6 showed General Electric's stock rising by almost eight-fold from 1994 to 2000 but then, from 2000 to 2003, experiencing a sickening fall, losing over half of its value. GE had recovered about half of this decline by 2008, but then it plummeted again and in early 2009 hit a 20-year low.

What led to those wild swings? In a nutshell, risk and expected cash flows. Until 2000, GE was regarded as a low-risk company capable of sustaining fast-growing cash flows. Investors' perceptions of low risk and high expected cash flow growth propelled it up, and investors' subsequent reduced expectations drove it down.

In this chapter we will see how stocks are valued in the marketplace. For the most part, professional security analysts do the work, using the techniques described in this chapter. "Sell side" analysts work for investment banks and brokerages. They write reports that are distributed to investors, generally through brokers. "Buy side" analysts work for mutual funds, hedge funds, pension funds, and other institutional investors. Those institutions obtain information from the buy-side analysts, but they also do their own research and ignore the buy side if they disagree.

The analysts on both sides generally focus on specific industries, and many of them were hired as analysts after working for a time in the industry they cover. Physics PhDs are often electronics analysts, biologists analyze biotech stocks, and so on. The analysts pore over financial statements, but they also go on the road and talk with company officials, companies' customers, and their suppliers. The point of all this work is to try to predict corporate earnings, dividends, and free cash flow—and thus stock prices.

How good are analysts' predictions and hence their ability to forecast stock prices? A look back at the opening chart in Chapter 6 would suggest "not very good"—if they had seen the crash coming then they would have sold before the peaks and bought at the troughs, thus smoothing out the graphs. However, some analysts are better than others, and the material in this chapter can help you be better than average.

Corporate Valuation and Stock Prices

In Chapter 1, we told you that managers should strive to maximize intrinsic value and that the value of a firm is determined by the size, timing, and risk of its free cash flows (FCF). Recall that one use of FCF is to pay dividends. One way to estimate the intrinsic value of stock is to discount the cash flows to stockholders (dividends, D_t) at the rate of return required by stockholders (r_s). The result is the intrinsic value to stockholders

You may say, "But what about capital gains? Don't investors buy stocks expecting to realize capital gains?" The answer is "yes," but we will see that the this equation actually incorporates capital gains.

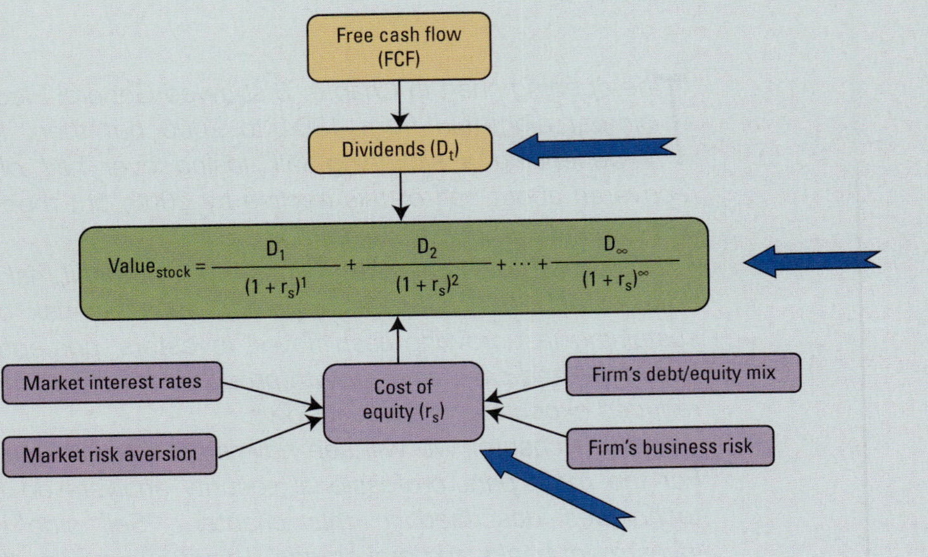

The textbook's Web site contains an Excel file that will guide you through the chapter's calculations. The file for this chapter is **Ch07 Tool Kit.xls**, *and we encourage you to open the file and follow along as you read the chapter.*

In Chapter 6 we examined stocks' risks and the factors that affect their required returns. In this chapter we use those findings to estimate the *intrinsic value* of a stock. The concepts and models developed here will also be used when we estimate the cost of capital in Chapter 9 a key concept used in many important decisions, especially decisions to invest or not invest in new assets.

Some companies are so small that their common stocks are not actively traded; they are owned by only a few people, usually the companies' managers. The stock in such firms is said to be closely held. In contrast, the stocks of most large companies are owned by many investors, most of whom are not active in management. These are publicly held stocks. Institutions such as pension plans, mutual funds, hedge funds, foreign investors, and insurance companies hold about half the market value of all stocks and buy and sell relatively actively. As a result, they account for about 75% of all transactions and thus have a heavy influence on the valuation of individual stocks. But before plunging into stock valuation, it is useful to begin with a closer look at what it means to be a stockholder.

7.1 Legal Rights and Privileges of Common Stockholders

The common stockholders are the *owners* of a corporation, and as such they have certain rights and privileges as discussed in this section.

Control of the Firm

A firm's common stockholders have the right to elect its directors, who, in turn, elect the officers who manage the business. In a small firm, the largest stockholder typically serves as president and chairperson of the board. In a large, publicly owned firm, the managers typically have some stock, but their personal holdings are generally insufficient to give them voting control. Thus, the managers of most publicly owned firms can be removed by the stockholders if the management team is not effective.

State and federal laws stipulate how stockholder control is to be exercised. First, corporations must hold periodic elections to select directors, usually once a year, with the vote taken at the annual meeting. Frequently, one-third of the directors are elected each year for a 3-year term. Each share of stock has one vote, so the owner of 1,000 shares has 1,000 votes for each director.[1] Stockholders can appear at the annual meeting and vote in person, but typically they transfer their right to vote to another party by means of a **proxy**. Management always solicits stockholders' proxies and usually gets them. However, if earnings are poor and stockholders are dissatisfied, an outside group may solicit the proxies in an effort to overthrow management and take control of the business. This is known as a **proxy fight**. Proxy fights are discussed in detail in Chapter 13.

The Preemptive Right

Common stockholders often have the right, called the **preemptive right**, to purchase any additional shares sold by the firm. In some states, the preemptive right is automatically included in every corporate charter; in others, it is used only if it is specifically inserted into the charter.

The preemptive right enables current stockholders to maintain control, and it also prevents a transfer of wealth from current stockholders to new stockholders. If it were not for this safeguard, the management of a corporation could issue additional shares at a low price and purchase these shares itself. Management could thereby seize control of the corporation and steal value from the current stockholders. For example, suppose 1,000 shares of common stock, each with a price of $100, were outstanding, making the total market value of the firm $100,000. If an additional 1,000 shares were sold at $50 a share, or for $50,000, this would raise the total market value to $150,000. When total market value is divided by new total shares outstanding, a value of $75 a share is obtained. The old stockholders thus lose $25 per share, and the new stockholders have an instant profit of $25 per share. Thus, selling common stock at a price below the market value would dilute its price and transfer wealth from the present stockholders to those who were allowed to purchase the new shares. The preemptive right prevents such occurrences.

Self-Test

What is a proxy fight?
What are the two primary reasons for using preemptive rights?

7.2 Types of Common Stock

Although most firms have only one type of common stock, in some instances **classified stock** is used to meet a company's special needs. Generally, when special

[1]In the situation described, a 1,000-share stockholder could cast 1,000 votes for each of three directors if there were three contested seats on the board. An alternative procedure that may be prescribed in the corporate charter calls for *cumulative voting*. Here the 1,000-share stockholder would get 3,000 votes if there were three vacancies, and he or she could cast all of them for one director. Cumulative voting helps minority stockholders (i.e., those who do not own a majority of the shares) get representation on the board.

WWW

Note that **http://finance.yahoo.com** *provides an easy way to find stocks meeting specified criteria. Under the Investing tab, select Stocks and then Stock Screener. To find the largest companies in terms of market value, for example, choose More Preset Screens, then select Largest Market Cap. You can also create custom screens to find stocks meeting other criteria.*

classifications are used, one type is designated *Class A*, another *Class B*, and so on. Small, new companies seeking funds from outside sources frequently use different types of common stock. For example, when Genetic Concepts went public, its Class A stock was sold to the public and paid a dividend, but this stock had no voting rights for 5 years. Its Class B stock, which was retained by the firm's organizers, had full voting rights for 5 years, but the legal terms stated that dividends could not be paid on the Class B stock until the company had established its earning power and built up retained earnings to a designated level. The use of classified stock thus enabled the public to take a position in a conservatively financed growth company without sacrificing income, while the founders retained absolute control during the crucial early stages of the firm's development. At the same time, outside investors were protected against excessive withdrawals of funds by the original owners. As is often the case in such situations, the Class B stock was called **founders' shares**.[2]

As these examples illustrate, the right to vote is often a distinguishing characteristic between different classes of stock. Suppose two classes of stock differ in only one respect: One class has voting rights but the other does not. As you would expect, the stock with voting rights would be more valuable. In the United States, which has a legal system with fairly strong protection for minority stockholders (that is, noncontrolling stockholders), voting stock typically sells at a price 4% to 6% above that of otherwise similar nonvoting stock. Thus, if a stock with no voting rights sold for $50, then one with voting rights would probably sell for $52 to $53. In countries with legal systems that provide less protection for minority stockholders, the right to vote is far more valuable. For example, voting stock on average sells for 45% more than nonvoting stock in Israel and for 82% more in Italy.

Some companies have multiple lines of business, with each line having very different growth prospects. Because cash flows for all business lines are mingled on financial statements, some companies worry that investors are not able to value the high-growth business lines correctly. To separate the cash flows and to allow separate valuations, occasionally a company will have classes of stock with dividends tied to a particular part of a company. This is called **tracking stock**, or **target stock**. For example, in 2002 Loews Corporation, a holding company with property and casualty insurance, oil and gas drilling, and tobacco subsidiaries, issued Carolina Group tracking stock tied to the performance of its Lorillard tobacco subsidiary.

However, many analysts are skeptical as to whether tracking stock increases a company's total market value. Companies still report consolidated financial statements for the entire company and have considerable leeway in allocating costs, deploying capital, and reporting the financial results for the various divisions, even those with tracking stock. Thus, a tracking stock is far from identical to the stock of an independent, stand-alone company.

Self-Test

What are some reasons why a company might use classified stock?

7.3 The Market Stock Price versus Intrinsic Value

We saw in Chapter 1 that managers should seek to maximize the value of their firms' stocks. In that chapter, we also emphasized the difference between stock price and intrinsic value. The stock price is simply the current market price, and it is easily observed for publicly traded companies. By contrast, intrinsic value, which represents

[2]Note that "Class A," "Class B," and so on have no standard meanings. Most firms have no classified shares, but a firm that does could designate its Class B shares as founders' shares and its Class A shares as those sold to the public and another firm might reverse these designations.

FIGURE 7-1 Determinants of Intrinsic Values and Stock Prices

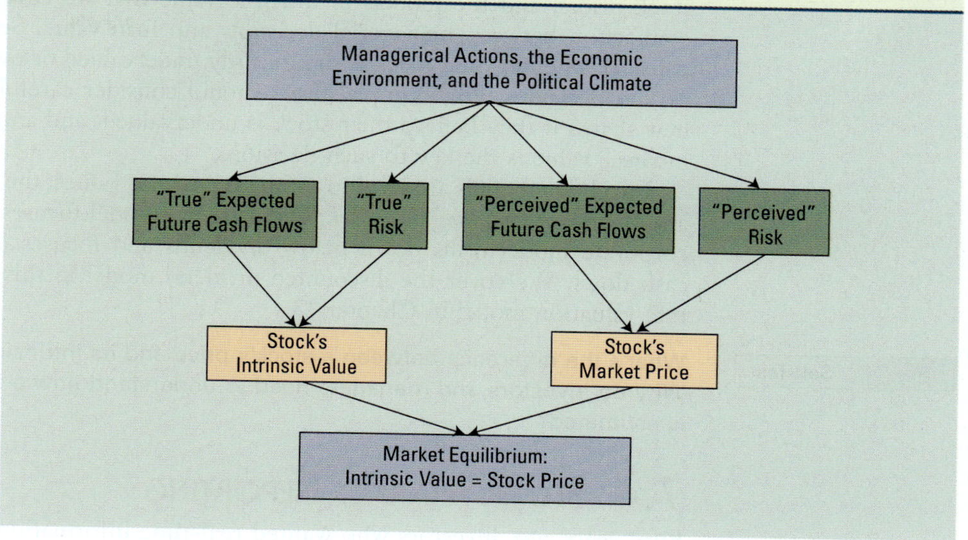

the "true" value of the company's stock, cannot be directly observed and must instead be estimated. Figure 7-1 illustrates the connection between stock price and intrinsic value.

As the figure suggests, market equilibrium occurs when the stock's price equals its intrinsic value. If the stock market is reasonably efficient, then gaps between the stock price and intrinsic value should not be very large and they should not persist for very long. However, there are cases when an individual stock price may be much higher or lower than its intrinsic value, and such divergence may persist for quite a while. During several years leading up to the crash of 2008–2009, most of the large investment banks were reporting record profits and selling at record prices. However, much of those earnings were illusory in that they did not reflect the huge risks that existed in the sub-prime mortgages they were buying. So, with hindsight, we now know that the market prices of most financial firms' stocks exceeded their intrinsic values just prior to 2008. Then, when the market realized what was happening, those stock prices crashed. Citigroup, Merrill Lynch, and others lost over 80% of their value in a few short months, and others suffered even worse declines. It clearly pays to question market prices at times!

Why Do Investors and Companies Care about Intrinsic Value?

The remainder of this chapter focuses primarily on different approaches for estimating a stock's intrinsic value. Before describing these approaches, it is worth asking why it is important for investors and companies to understand how to estimate intrinsic values.

When investing in common stocks, the goal is to purchase stocks that are undervalued (i.e., the price is below the stock's intrinsic value) and avoid stocks that are overvalued. Consequently, Wall Street analysts, institutional investors who control mutual funds and pension funds, and even many individual investors are quite interested in finding reliable models that help predict intrinsic value. Investors obviously care about intrinsic value, but managers also must understand how intrinsic value is estimated. First, managers need to know how alternative actions are likely to affect stock prices, and the models of intrinsic value that we cover help demonstrate the connection between managerial decisions and firm value. Second, managers should consider whether their stock is significantly undervalued or overvalued before making certain decisions. For example, firms should consider carefully the decision to issue new shares if they believe their stock is undervalued, and an estimate of their stock's intrinsic value is the key to such decisions.

Two basic models are used to estimate intrinsic values: the *discounted dividend model* and the *corporate valuation model*. The dividend model focuses on dividends, while the corporate model drills down below dividends and focuses on sales, costs, and free cash flows. We cover the discounted dividend model in this chapter and the corporate valuation model in Chapter 13.

Self-Test

What's the difference between a stock's price and its intrinsic value?

Why do investors and managers need to understand how a firm's intrinsic value is estimated?

7.4 Stock Market Reporting

Fifty years ago, investors who wanted real-time information would sit in brokerage firms' offices watching a "ticker tape" go by that displayed prices of stocks as they were traded. Those who did not need current information could find the previous day's prices from the business section of a daily newspaper like *The Wall Street Journal*. Today, though, one can get quotes throughout the day from many different Internet sources, including Yahoo!.[3] Figure 7-2 shows the quote for General Electric, which is traded on the NYSE under the symbol GE, on February 13, 2009. GE ended the regular trading day (4 p.m. EST) at $11.44, down $0.24, which was a 2.05% decline from the previous day. However, the stock rose by 9 cents in after-hours trading. The data also show that GE opened the day at $11.55 and traded in a range from $11.35 to $11.74. If this quote had been obtained during

FIGURE 7-2 Stock Quote and Other Key Data for GE, February 13, 2009

GEN ELECTRIC CO (NYSE: GE)

After Hours: 11.53 ↑ 0.09 (0.79%) 7:59PM ET

Last Trade:	**11.44**	Day's Range:	**11.35 - 11.74**
Trade Time:	**Feb 13**	52wk Range:	**10.66 - 38.52**
Change:	↓ 0.24 (2.05%)	Volume:	**86,594,997**
Prev Close:	**11.68**	Avg Vol (3m):	**119,828,000**
Open:	**11.55**	Market Cap:	**119.67B**
Bid:	**N/A**	P/E (ttm):	**6.66 x**
Ask:	**N/A**	EPS (ttm):	**1.72**
1y Target Est:	**14.81**	Div & Yield:	**1.24 (10.80%)**

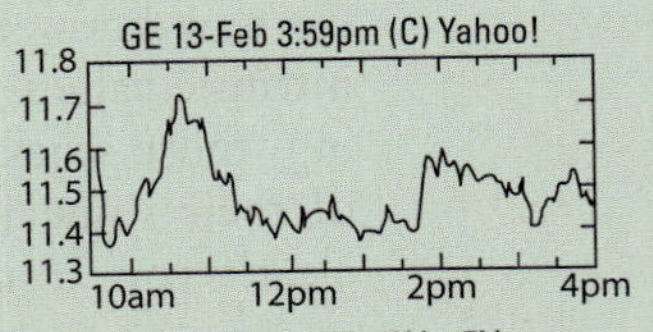

GE 13-Feb 3:59pm (C) Yahoo!

11.8 11.7 11.6 11.5 11.4 11.3

10am 12pm 2pm 4pm

1d 5d 3m 6m 1Y 2Y 5Y max

customize chart

Add GE to Your Portfolio

Set Alert for GE

Download Data

Download Annual Report

Add Quotes to your Web Site

Source: **http://finance.yahoo.com/.**

[3]Most free sources actually provide quotes that are delayed by 20 minutes, but if you subscribe to a paid site like the *Online Wall Street Journal*, or if you have a brokerage account, you can generally get online real time quotes.

trading hours, it would also have provided information about the quotes at which the stock could be bought (the Ask quote) or sold (the Bid quote). During the past year, the price hit a high of $38.52 and a low of $10.66. A total of 86.59 million GE shares traded that day, which was a little below the average trading volume of 119.8 million shares.

The screen with the stock quote information also gives the total market value of GE's common stock (the Market Cap); the dividend and dividend yield; the most recent "ttm," or "trailing twelve months," EPS and P/E ratios; and a graph showing the stock's performance during the day. (However, the graph can be changed to show the stock's performance over a number of time periods up to and including 5 years.) In addition to this information, the Web page has links to financial statements, research reports, historical ratios, analysts' forecasts of EPS and EPS growth rates, and a wealth of other data.

Self-Test What information is provided on the Internet in addition to the stock's latest price?

7.5 Valuing Common Stocks

Common stocks are expected to provide a stream of future cash flows, and a stock's value is found the same way as the values of other financial assets—namely, as the present value of its expected future cash flow stream. The expected cash flows consist of two elements: (1) the dividends expected in each year and (2) the price investors expect to receive when they sell the stock. The expected final stock price includes the return of the original investment plus an expected capital gain.

Definitions of Terms Used in Stock Valuation Models

We saw in Chapter 1 that a manager should seek to maximize the intrinsic value of the firm's stock. To do this, a manager needs to know how her actions are likely to affect the stock's price. Therefore, we develop some models in this section to show how the value of a share of stock is determined, and we begin by defining some key terms as follows.

D_t = Dividend the stockholder *expects* to receive at the end of Year t. D_0 is the most recent dividend, which has already been paid; D_1 is the first dividend expected, which will be paid at the end of this year; D_2 is the dividend expected at the end of Year 2; and so forth. D_1 represents the first cash flow that a new purchaser of the stock will receive, because D_0 has just been paid. D_0 is known with certainty, but all future dividends are expected values, so the estimate of D_t may differ among investors.[4]

P_0 = Actual **market price** of the stock today.

[4]Stocks generally pay dividends quarterly, so theoretically we should evaluate them on a quarterly basis. However, in stock valuation, most analysts work on an annual basis because the data generally are not precise enough to warrant refinement to a quarterly model. For additional information on the quarterly model, see Charles M. Linke and J. Kenton Zumwalt, "Estimation Biases in Discounted Cash Flow Analysis of Equity Capital Cost in Rate Regulation," *Financial Management*, Autumn 1984, pp. 15–21. Also see Robert Brooks and Billy Helms, "An N-Stage, Fractional Period, Quarterly Dividend Discount Model," *Financial Review*, November 1990, pp. 651–657.

$\hat{P}_t$ = Expected price of the stock at the end of each Year t (pronounced "P hat t"). $\hat{P}_0$ is the **intrinsic**, or **fundamental, value** of the stock today as seen by the particular investor doing the analysis; $\hat{P}_1$ is the price expected at the end of one year; and so on. Note that $\hat{P}_0$ is the intrinsic value of the stock today based on a particular investor's estimate of the stock's expected dividend stream and the risk of that stream. Hence, whereas the market price P_0 is fixed and is identical for all investors, $\hat{P}_0$ could differ among investors depending on how optimistic they are regarding the company. The caret, or "hat," is used to indicate that $\hat{P}_t$ is an estimated future value. $\hat{P}_0$, the individual investor's estimate of the intrinsic value today, could be above or below P_0, the current stock price, but an investor would buy the stock only if his estimate of $\hat{P}_0$ were equal to or greater than P_0.

Since there are many investors in the market, there can be many values for $\hat{P}_0$. However, we can think of a group of "average," or "marginal," investors whose actions actually determine the market price. For these marginal investors, P_0 must equal $\hat{P}_0$; otherwise, a disequilibrium would exist, and buying and selling in the market would cause P_0 to change until $P_0 = \hat{P}_0$ as seen by the marginal investor.

D_1/P_0 = Expected **dividend yield** during the coming year. If the stock is expected to pay a dividend of D_1 = $1 during the next 12 months and if its current price is P_0 = $10, then the expected dividend yield is $1/$10 = 0.10 = 10%.

$\frac{\hat{P}_1 - P_0}{P_0}$ = Expected **capital gains yield** during the coming year. If the stock sells for $10 today and if it is expected to rise to $10.50 at the end of one year, then the expected capital gain is $\hat{P}_1 - P_0$ = $10.50 – $10.00 = $0.50, and the expected capital gains yield is $0.50/$10 = 0.05 = 5%.

g = Expected **growth rate** in dividends as predicted by a marginal investor. If dividends are expected to grow at a constant rate, then g is also the expected rate of growth in earnings and the stock's price. Different investors may use different values of g to evaluate a firm's stock, but the market price, P_0, is set on the basis of g as estimated by the marginal investor.

r_s = Minimum acceptable return, or **required rate of return**, on the stock, considering both its risk and the returns available on other investments. Again, this term generally relates to the marginal investor. The primary determinants of r_s include the real rate of return, expected inflation, and risk.

$\hat{r}_s$ = **Expected rate of return** that an investor who buys the stock expects to receive in the future. $\hat{r}_s$ (pronounced "r hat s") could be above or below r_s, but one would buy the stock only if $\hat{r}_s \geq r_s$. Note that the expected return ($\hat{r}_s$) is equal to the expected dividend yield (D_1/P_0) plus the expected capital gains yield ($[\hat{P}_1 - P_0]/P_0$). In our example, $\hat{r}_s$ = 10% + 5% = 15%.

$\bar{r}_s$ = **Actual**, or **realized**, *after-the-fact* **rate of return**, pronounced "r bar s." You may *expect* to obtain a return of $\hat{r}_s$ = 15% if you buy ExxonMobil today, but if the market declines then you may end up next year with an actual realized return that is much lower and perhaps even negative.

Expected Dividends as the Basis for Stock Values

Like all financial assets, the value of a stock is estimated by finding the present value of a stream of expected future cash flows. What are the cash flows that corporations are expected to provide to their stockholders? First, think of yourself as an investor who buys a stock with the intention of holding it (in your family) forever. In this case, all that you (and your heirs) will receive is a stream of dividends, and the value of the stock today is calculated as the present value of an infinite stream of dividends:

$$\begin{aligned}\text{Value of stock} = \hat{P}_0 &= \text{PV of expected future dividends}\\ &= \frac{D_1}{(1+r_s)^1} + \frac{D_2}{(1+r_s)^2} + \cdots + \frac{D_\infty}{(1+r_s)^\infty}\\ &= \sum_{t=1}^{\infty} \frac{D_t}{(1+r_s)^t}\end{aligned} \tag{7-1}$$

What about the more typical case, where you expect to hold the stock for a finite period and then sell it—what is the value of $\hat{P}_0$ in this case? Unless the company is likely to be liquidated or sold and thus to disappear, *the value of the stock is again determined by Equation 7-1.* To see this, recognize that for any individual investor, the expected cash flows consist of expected dividends plus the expected sale price of the stock. However, the sale price a current investor receives will depend on the dividends some future investor expects. Therefore, for all present and future investors in total, expected cash flows must be based on expected future dividends. Put another way, unless a firm is liquidated or sold to another concern, the cash flows it provides to its stockholders will consist only of a stream of dividends. Therefore, the value of a share of its stock must be the present value of that expected dividend stream.

The general validity of Equation 7-1 can also be confirmed by solving the following problem. Suppose I buy a stock and expect to hold it for 1 year. I will receive dividends during the year plus the value $\hat{P}_1$ when I sell at the end of the year. But what will determine the value of $\hat{P}_1$? The answer is that it will be determined as the present value of the dividends expected during Year 2 plus the stock price at the end of that year, which, in turn, will be determined as the present value of another set of future dividends and an even more distant stock price. This process can be continued ad infinitum, and the ultimate result is Equation 7-1.[5]

Self-Test

What are the two components of most stocks' expected total return?

How does one calculate the capital gains yield and the dividend yield of a stock?

If D_1 = \$3.00, P_0 = \$50, and $\hat{P}_1$ = \$52, what are the stock's expected dividend yield, expected capital gains yield, and expected total return for the coming year? (6%, 4%, 10%)

[5]It is ironic that investors periodically lose sight of the long-run nature of stocks as investments and forget that, in order to sell a stock at a profit, one must find a buyer who will pay the higher price. If you analyze a stock's value in accordance with Equation 7-1, conclude that the stock's market price exceeds a reasonable value, and then buy the stock anyway, then you would be following the "bigger fool" theory of investment—you think that you may be a fool to buy the stock at its excessive price, but you think that when you get ready to sell it, you can find someone who is an even bigger fool. The bigger fool theory was widely followed in the spring of 2000, just before the Nasdaq market lost more than one-third of its value.

7.6 Valuing a Constant Growth Stock

Equation 7-1 is a generalized stock valuation model in that the time pattern of D_t can be anything: D_t can be rising, falling, fluctuating randomly, or even zero for several years, yet Equation 7-1 will still hold. With a computer spreadsheet we can easily use this equation to find a stock's intrinsic value for any pattern of dividends.[6] In practice, the hard part is getting an accurate forecast of the future dividends. However, in many cases the stream of dividends is expected to grow at a constant rate, and if so then Equation 7-1 can be rewritten as follows:

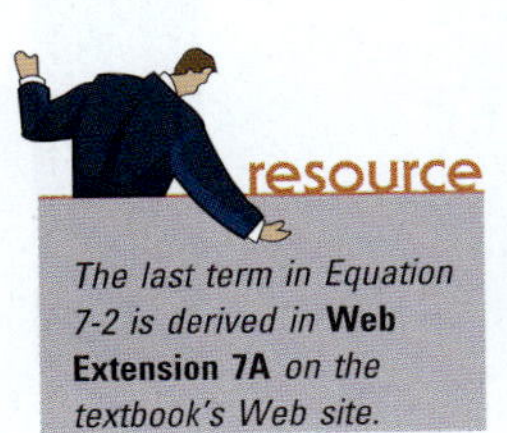

The last term in Equation 7-2 is derived in **Web Extension 7A** on the textbook's Web site.

$$\begin{aligned}\hat{P}_0 &= \frac{D_0(1+g)^1}{(1+r_s)^1} + \frac{D_0(1+g)^2}{(1+r_s)^2} + \cdots + \frac{D_0(1+g)^\infty}{(1+r_s)^\infty} \\ &= D_0 \sum_{t=1}^{\infty} \frac{(1+g)^t}{(1+r_s)^t} \\ &= \frac{D_0(1+g)}{r_s - g} = \frac{D_1}{r_s - g}\end{aligned} \quad (7\text{-}2)$$

The last term of Equation 7-2 is called the **constant growth model**, or the **Gordon model**, after Myron J. Gordon, who did much to develop and popularize it.

A necessary condition for the validity of Equation 7-2 is that r_s be greater than g. Look back at the second form of Equation 7-2. If g is larger than r_s, then $(1 + g)^t/(1 + r_s)^t$ must always be greater than 1. In this case, the second line of Equation 7-2 is the sum of an infinite number of terms, with each term being larger than 1. Therefore, if r_s were constant and greater than g, the resulting stock price would be infinite! Since no company is worth an infinite amount, it is impossible to have a constant growth rate that is greater than r_s forever. Similarly, a student will occasionally plug a value for g that is greater than r_s into the last form of Equation 7-2 and report a negative stock price. This is nonsensical. The last form of Equation 7-2 is valid only when g is less than r_s. *If g is greater than r_s then the constant growth model cannot be used, and the answer you would get from using Equation 7-2 would be wrong and misleading.*

Illustration of a Constant Growth Stock

Assume that MicroDrive just paid a dividend of \$1.15 (that is, D_0 = \$1.15). Its stock has a required rate of return, r_s, of 13.4%, and investors expect the dividend to grow at a constant 8% rate in the future. The estimated dividend 1 year hence would be D_1 = \$1.15(1.08) = \$1.24; D_2 would be \$1.34; and the estimated dividend 5 years hence would be \$1.69:

$$D_t = D_0(1+g)^t = \$1.15(1.08)^5 = \$1.69$$

We could use this procedure to estimate each future dividend and then use Equation 7-1 to determine the current stock value, $\hat{P}_0$. In other words, we could find each expected future dividend, calculate its present value, and then sum all the present values to find the intrinsic value of the stock.

Such a process would be time-consuming, but we can take a shortcut—just insert the illustrative data into Equation 7-2 to find the stock's intrinsic value, \$23:

[6]Actually, we can only find an approximate price. However, if we project dividends for 100 or so years, the present value of that finite dividend stream is approximately equal to the present value of the infinite dividend stream.

FIGURE 7-3 Present Value of Dividends of a Constant Growth Stock Where D_0 = $1.15, g = 8%, and r_s = 13.4%

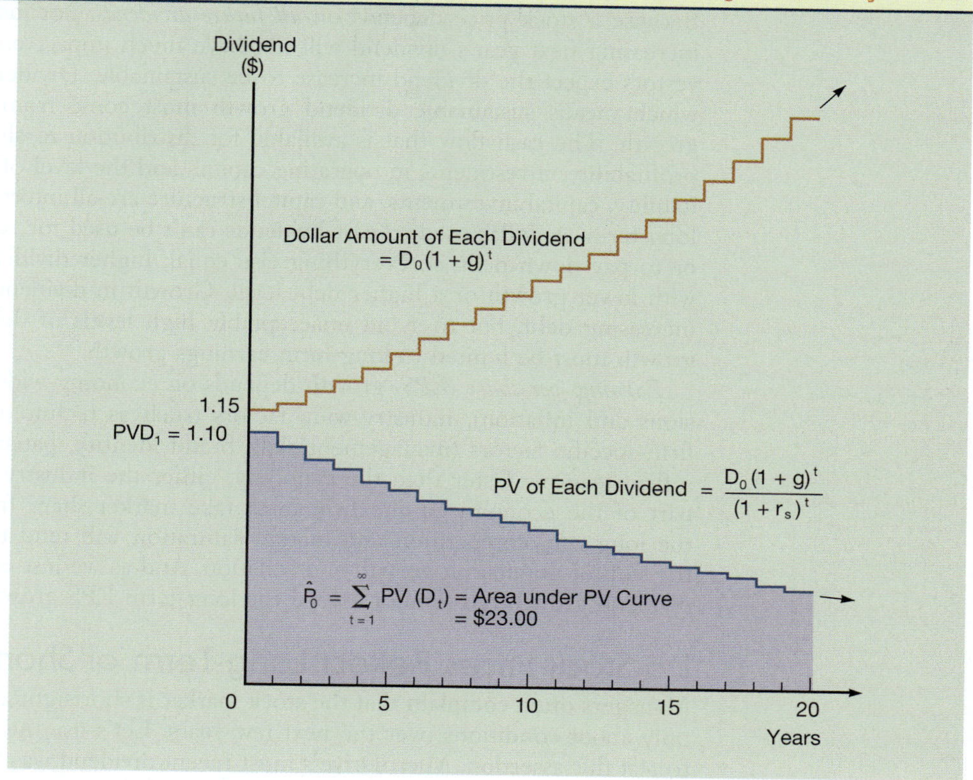

$$\hat{P}_0 = \frac{\$1.15(1.08)}{0.134 - 0.08} = \frac{\$1.242}{0.054} = \$23.00$$

The concept underlying the valuation process for a constant growth stock is graphed in Figure 7-3. Dividends are growing at the rate g = 8%, but because $r_s > g$, the present value of each future dividend is declining. For example, the dividend in Year 1 is $D_1 = D_0(1 + g)^1 = \$1.15(1.08) = \$1.242$. However, the present value of this dividend, discounted at 13.4%, is $PV(D_1) = \$1.242/(1.134)^1 = \$1.095$. The dividend expected in Year 2 grows to $1.242(1.08) = $1.341, but the present value of this dividend falls to $1.043. Continuing, D_3 = $1.449 and $PV(D_3)$ = $0.993, and so on. Thus, the expected dividends are growing, but the present value of each successive dividend is declining, because the dividend growth rate (8%) is less than the rate used for discounting the dividends to the present (13.4%).

If we summed the present values of each future dividend, this summation would be the value of the stock, $\hat{P}_0$. When g is a constant, this summation is equal to $D_1/(r_s - g)$, as shown in Equation 7-2. Therefore, if we extended the lower step-function curve in Figure 7-3 on out to infinity and added up the present values of each future dividend, the summation would be identical to the value given by Equation 7-2, $23.00.

Although Equation 7-2 assumes there are *infinite* time periods, most of the value is based on dividends during a *finite* time period. In our example, 70% of the value is attributed to the first 25 years, 91% to the first 50 years, and 99.4% to the first 100 years. This means that companies don't have to survive forever to justify using the Gordon growth model.

Dividend and Earnings Growth

Because a stock price depends on *all future dividends*, not just next year's dividend, increasing next year's dividend will not have much impact on stock price unless investors expect the dividend increase to be sustainable. Dividends are paid with cash, which means sustainable dividend growth must come from sustainable cash flow growth. The cash flow that is available for distribution to shareholders depends on profitability, investments in operating capital, and the level of debt. Dividends, profitability, capital investments, and capital structure are all interrelated, especially in the long term. A dollar used to pay dividends can't be used for reinvestment in the firm or to pay down debt, so everything else equal, higher dividends must be associated with lower growth or a higher debt level. Growth in dividends can be supported by increasing debt, but to avoid unacceptably high levels of debt, long-term dividend growth must be limited to long-term earnings growth.

Earnings per share (EPS) growth depends on economy-wide factors (such as recessions and inflation), industry-wide factors (such as technological innovations), and firm-specific factors (management skill, brand identity, patent protection, etc.). For a firm to grow faster than the economy, either the industry must become a bigger part of the economy or the firm must take market share from its competitors. In the long run, competition and market saturation will tend to limit EPS growth to the sum of population growth and inflation. And as we just explained, the long-term dividend growth rate cannot exceed the long-term EPS growth rate.

Do Stock Prices Reflect Long-Term or Short-Term Events?

Managers often complain that the stock market is shortsighted and that investors care only about conditions over the next few years. Let's use the constant growth model to test this assertion. MicroDrive's most recent dividend was \$1.15, and it is expected to grow at a rate of 8% per year. Since we know the growth rate, we can forecast the dividends for each of the next 5 years and then find their present values:

$$
\begin{aligned}
\text{PV} &= \frac{D_0(1+g)^1}{(1+r_s)^1} + \frac{D_0(1+g)^2}{(1+r_s)^2} + \frac{D_0(1+g)^3}{(1+r_s)^3} + \frac{D_0(1+g)^4}{(1+r_s)^4} + \frac{D_0(1+g)^5}{(1+r_s)^5} \\
&= \frac{\$1.15(1.08)^1}{(1.134)^1} + \frac{\$1.15(1.08)^2}{(1.134)^2} + \frac{\$1.15(1.08)^3}{(1.134)^3} + \frac{\$1.15(1.08)^4}{(1.134)^4} + \frac{\$1.15(1.08)^5}{(1.134)^5} \\
&= \frac{\$1.242}{(1.134)^1} + \frac{\$1.341}{(1.134)^2} + \frac{\$1.449}{(1.134)^3} + \frac{\$1.565}{(1.134)^4} + \frac{\$1.690}{(1.134)^5} \\
&= 1.095 + 1.043 + 0.993 + 0.946 + 0.901 \\
&\approx \$5.00
\end{aligned}
$$

Recall that MicroDrive's stock price is \$23.00. Therefore, only \$5.00, or \$5/\$23 = 0.22 = 22%, of the \$23.00 stock price is attributable to short-term cash flows. This means that MicroDrive's managers will affect the stock price more by working to increase long-term cash flows than by focusing on short-term flows. This situation holds for most companies. Indeed, a number of professors and consulting firms have used actual company data to show that more than 80% of a typical company's stock price is due to cash flows expected farther than 5 years in the future.

This brings up an interesting question. If most of a stock's value is due to long-term cash flows, then why do managers and analysts pay so much attention to quarterly earnings? Part of the answer lies in the information conveyed by short-term earnings.

For example, when actual quarterly earnings are lower than expected not because of fundamental problems but only because a company has increased its research and development (R&D) expenditures, studies have shown that the stock price probably won't decline and may actually increase. This makes sense, because R&D should increase future cash flows. On the other hand, if quarterly earnings are lower than expected because customers don't like the company's new products, then this new information will have negative implications for future values of g, the long-term growth rate. As we show later in this chapter, even small changes in g can lead to large changes in stock prices. Therefore, quarterly earnings themselves might not be that important, but the information they convey about future prospects can be extremely important.

Another reason many managers focus on short-term earnings is that some firms pay managerial bonuses on the basis of current earnings rather than stock prices (which reflect future earnings). For these managers, the concern with quarterly earnings is not due to their effect on stock prices—it's due to their effect on bonuses.[7]

When Can the Constant Growth Model Be Used?

The constant growth model is most appropriate for mature companies with a stable history of growth. Expected growth rates vary somewhat among companies, but dividend growth for most mature firms is generally expected to continue in the future at about the same rate as nominal gross domestic product (real GDP plus inflation). On this basis, one might expect the dividends of an average, or "normal," company to grow at a rate of 5% to 8% a year. Note, though, that the 2008–2009 recession has caused many analysts to lower their expectations for long-run growth, and those lowered expectations contributed mightily to the stock market crash.

Note too that Equation 7-2 is sufficiently general to handle the case of a **zero growth stock**, where the dividend is expected to remain constant over time. If g = 0, then Equation 7-2 reduces to Equation 7-3:

$$\hat{P}_0 = \frac{D}{r_s} \quad (7\text{-}3)$$

This is essentially the equation for a perpetuity, and it is simply the dividend divided by the discount rate.

Self-Test

Write out and explain the valuation formula for a constant growth stock.
Are stock prices affected more by long-term or short-term performance? Explain.
A stock is expected to pay a dividend of $2 at the end of the year. The required rate of return is r_s = 12%. What would the stock's price be if the constant growth rate in dividends were 4%? ($25.00) What would the price be if g = 0%? ($16.67)

7.7 Expected Rate of Return on a Constant Growth Stock

When using Equation 7-2, we first estimated D_0 and r_s, the *required* rate of return on the stock; then we solved for the stock's intrinsic value, which we compared to its actual market price. We can also reverse the process, observing the actual stock price,

[7]Many apparent puzzles in finance can be explained either by managerial compensation systems or by peculiar features of the Tax Code. So, if you can't explain a firm's behavior in terms of economic logic, look to compensation procedures or taxes as possible explanations.

substituting it into Equation 7-2, and solving for the rate of return. In doing so, we are finding the *expected* rate of return, which will also equal the *required* rate of return, $\hat{r}_s = r_s$, if the market is in equilibrium:[8]

$$\begin{aligned}\hat{r}_s = \text{Expected rate of return} &= \text{Expected dividend yield} + \text{Expected capital gains yield} \\ &= \text{Expected dividend yield} + \text{Expected growth rate} \\ &= \frac{D_1}{P_0} + g\end{aligned} \tag{7-4}$$

Thus, if you buy a stock for a price P_0 = \$23, and if you expect the stock to pay a dividend D_1 = \$1.242 one year from now and to grow at a constant rate g = 8% in the future, then your expected rate of return will be 13.4%:

$$\hat{r}_s = \frac{\$1.242}{\$23} + 8\% = 5.4\% + 8\% = 13.4\%$$

In this form, we see that $\hat{r}_s$ is the *expected total return* and that it consists of an *expected dividend yield*, D_1/P_0 = 5.4%, plus an *expected growth rate* (which is also the *expected capital gains yield*) of g = 8%.

Suppose that the current price, P_0, is equal to \$23 and that the Year-1 expected dividend, D_1, is equal to \$1.242. What is the expected price at the end of the first year, immediately after D_1 has been paid? First, we can estimate the expected Year-2 dividend as $D_2 = D_1(1 + g)$ = \$1.242(1.08) = \$1.3414. Then we can apply a version of Equation 7-2 that is shifted ahead by 1 year, using D_2 instead of D_1 and solving for $\hat{P}_1$ instead of $\hat{P}_0$:

$$\hat{P}_1 = \frac{D_2}{r_s - g} = \frac{\$1.3414}{0.134 - 0.08} = \$24.84$$

Even easier, notice that $\hat{P}_1$ must be 8% larger than \$23, the price found 1 year earlier for P_0:

$$\$23(1.08) = \$24.84$$

WWW

The popular Motley Fool Web site **http://www.fool.com/school/introductiontovaluation.htm** *provides a good description of some benefits and drawbacks of a few of the more commonly used valuation procedures.*

Either way, we expect a capital gain of \$24.84 – \$23.00 = \$1.84 during the year, which is a capital gains yield of 8%:

$$\text{Capital gains yield} = \frac{\text{Capital gain}}{\text{Beginning price}} = \frac{\$1.84}{\$23.00} = 0.08 = 8\%$$

We could extend the analysis, and in each future year the expected capital gains yield would always equal g, the expected dividend growth rate.

The dividend yield during the year could be estimated as follows:

$$\text{Dividend yield} = \frac{D_2}{\hat{P}_1} = \frac{\$1.3414}{\$24.84} = 0.054 = 5.4\%$$

The dividend yield for the following year could also be calculated, and again it would be 5.4%. Thus, *for a constant growth stock*, the following conditions must hold.

[8]We say that a stock is in *equilibrium* when $r_s = \hat{r}_s$ and $\hat{P}_0 = P_0$. We discuss this in more detail later in the chapter.

1. The dividend is expected to grow forever at a constant rate, g.
2. The stock price will also grow at this same rate.
3. The expected dividend yield is constant.
4. The expected capital gains yield is also constant and is equal to g, the dividend (and stock price) growth rate.
5. The expected total rate of return, $\hat{r}_s$, is equal to the expected dividend yield plus the expected growth rate: $\hat{r}_s$ = dividend yield + g.

The term *expected* should be clarified—it means "expected" in a probabilistic sense, as the "statistically expected" outcome. Thus, if we say the growth rate is expected to remain constant at 8%, we mean that the best prediction for the growth rate in any future year is 8%, not that we literally expect the growth rate to be exactly 8% in each future year. In this sense, the constant growth assumption is a reasonable one for many large, mature companies.

Self-Test

What conditions must hold in order for a stock to be evaluated using the constant growth model?

What does the term "expected" mean when we say "expected growth rate"?

If D_0 = \$4.00, r_s = 9%, and g = 5% for a constant growth stock, what are the stock's expected dividend yield and capital gains yield for the coming year? **(4%, 5%)**

7.8 Valuing Nonconstant Growth Stocks

For many companies, it is not appropriate to assume that dividends will grow at a constant rate. Firms typically go through *life cycles*. During their early years, their growth is much faster than that of the economy as a whole; then they match the economy's growth; and finally their growth is slower than that of the economy.[9] Automobile manufacturers in the 1920s, software companies such as Microsoft in the 1990s, and technology firms such as Cisco in the 2000s are examples of firms in the early part of the cycle; these firms are called **supernormal**, or **nonconstant, growth** firms. Figure 7-4 illustrates nonconstant growth and also compares it with normal growth, zero growth, and negative growth.[10]

In Figure 7-4, the dividends of the supernormal growth firm are expected to grow at a 30% rate for 3 years, after which the growth rate is expected to fall to 8%, the assumed average for the economy. The value of this firm, like any other, is the present value of its expected future dividends as determined by Equation 7-1. When D_t is growing at a constant rate, we simplify Equation 7-1 to $\hat{P}_0 = D_1/(r_s - g)$. In the supernormal case, however, the expected growth rate is not a constant—it declines at the end of the supernormal growth period.

[9]The concept of life cycles could be broadened to *product cycle*, which would include both small start-up companies and large companies like Apple, which periodically introduce new products that give sales and earnings a boost. We should also mention *business cycles*, which alternately depress and boost sales and profits. The growth rate just after a major new product has been introduced, or just after a firm emerges from the depths of a recession, is likely to be much higher than the "expected long-run average growth rate," which is the number that should be used in a DCF analysis.

[10]A negative growth rate indicates a declining company. A mining company whose profits are falling because of a declining ore body is an example. Someone buying such a company would expect its earnings, and consequently its dividends and stock price, to decline each year, and this would lead to capital losses rather than capital gains. Obviously, a declining company's stock price will be relatively low, and its dividend yield must be high enough to offset the expected capital loss and still produce a competitive total return. Students sometimes argue that they would never be willing to buy a stock whose price was expected to decline. However, if the annual dividends are large enough to *more than offset* the falling stock price, the stock could still provide a good return.

FIGURE 7-4 Illustrative Dividend Growth Rates

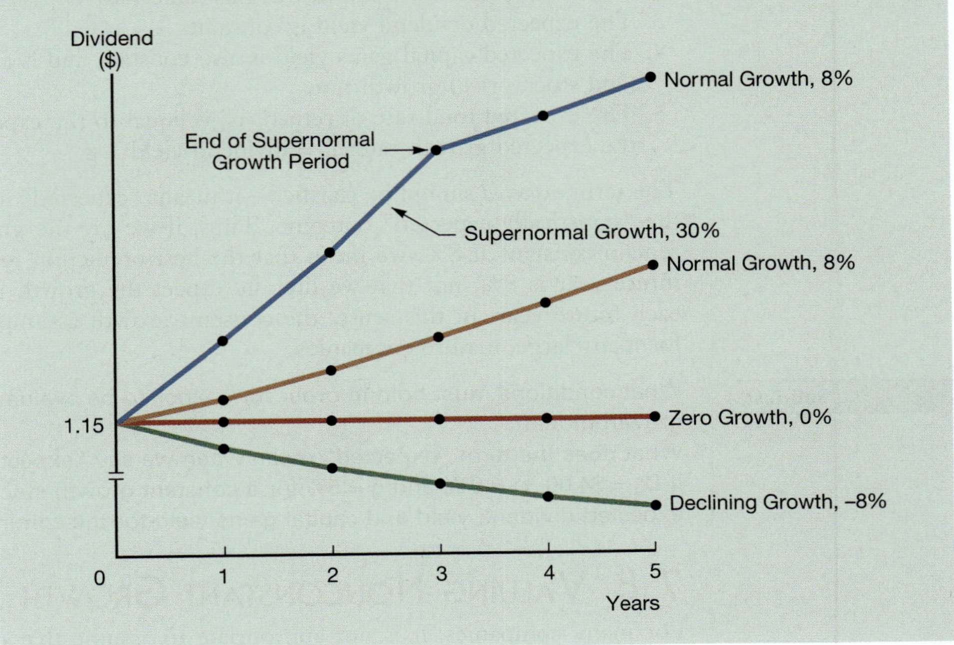

Because Equation 7-2 requires a constant growth rate, we obviously cannot use it to value stocks that have nonconstant growth. However, assuming a company currently enjoying supernormal growth will eventually slow down and become a constant growth stock, we can use Equation 7-2 to help find the stock's value. First, we assume that the dividend will grow at a nonconstant rate (generally a relatively high rate) for N periods, after which it will grow at a constant rate, g. Often N is called the **horizon date** or the **terminal date**.

Recall that a stock's current intrinsic value, $\hat{P}_0$, is the present value of all dividends after Time 0, discounted back to Time 0. Similarly, the intrinsic value of a stock at Time N is the present value of all dividends beyond Time N, discounted back to Time N. When dividends beyond Time N are expected to grow at a constant rate, we can use a variation of the constant growth formula, Equation 7-2, to estimate the stock's intrinsic value at Time N. The intrinsic value at Time N is often called the **horizon value** or the **terminal value**:

$$\text{Horizon value} = \hat{P}_N = \frac{D_{N+1}}{r_s - g} = \frac{D_N(1+g)}{r_s - g} \qquad (7\text{-}5)$$

A stock's intrinsic value today, $\hat{P}_0$, is the present value of the dividends during the nonconstant growth period plus the present value of the dividends after the horizon date:

$$\hat{P}_0 = \frac{D_1}{(1+r_s)^1} + \frac{D_2}{(1+r_s)^2} + \cdots + \frac{D_N}{(1+r_s)^N} + \frac{D_{N+1}}{(1+r_s)^{N+1}} + \cdots + \frac{D_\infty}{(1+r_s)^\infty}$$

$$= \underbrace{\text{PV of dividends during the nonconstant growth period } t = 1 \text{ to } N}_{} + \underbrace{\text{PV of dividends during the constant growth period } t = N+1 \text{ to } \infty}_{}$$

The horizon value is the value of all dividends beyond Time N discounted back to Time N. Discounting the horizon value from Time N to Time 0 provides an estimate of the present value of all dividends beyond the nonconstant growth period. Thus, the stock's current intrinsic value is the present value of all dividends during the nonconstant growth period plus the present value of the horizon value:

$$\hat{P}_0 = \left[\frac{D_1}{(1+r_s)^1} + \frac{D_2}{(1+r_s)^2} + \cdots + \frac{D_N}{(1+r_s)^N}\right] + \frac{\hat{P}_N}{(1+r_s)^N}$$
$$= \left[\frac{D_1}{(1+r_s)^1} + \frac{D_2}{(1+r_s)^2} + \cdots + \frac{D_N}{(1+r_s)^N}\right] + \frac{[(D_{N+1})/(r_s - g)]}{(1+r_s)^N} \qquad \text{(7-6)}$$

To implement Equation 7-6, we go through the following three steps.

1. Estimate the expected dividends for each year during the period of nonconstant growth.
2. Find the expected price of the stock at the end of the nonconstant growth period, at which point it has become a constant growth stock.
3. Find the present values of the expected dividends during the nonconstant growth period and the present value of the expected stock price at the end of the nonconstant growth period. Their sum is the intrinsic value of the stock, $\hat{P}_0$.

To illustrate the process for valuing nonconstant growth stocks, we make the following assumptions.

r_s = Stockholders' required rate of return = 13.4%. This rate is used to discount all the cash flows.

N = Years of supernormal growth = 3.

g_s = Rate of growth in both earnings and dividends during the supernormal growth period = 30%. This rate is shown directly on the time line. (*Note:* The growth rate during the supernormal growth period could vary from year to year. Also, there could be several different supernormal growth periods—for example, 30% for 3 years, then 20% for 3 years, and then a constant 8%.)

g_L = Rate of normal, constant growth after the supernormal period = 8%. This rate is also shown on the time line, between Periods 3 and 4.

D_0 = Last dividend the company paid = \$1.15.

FIGURE 7-5 Process for Finding the Value of a Supernormal Growth Stock

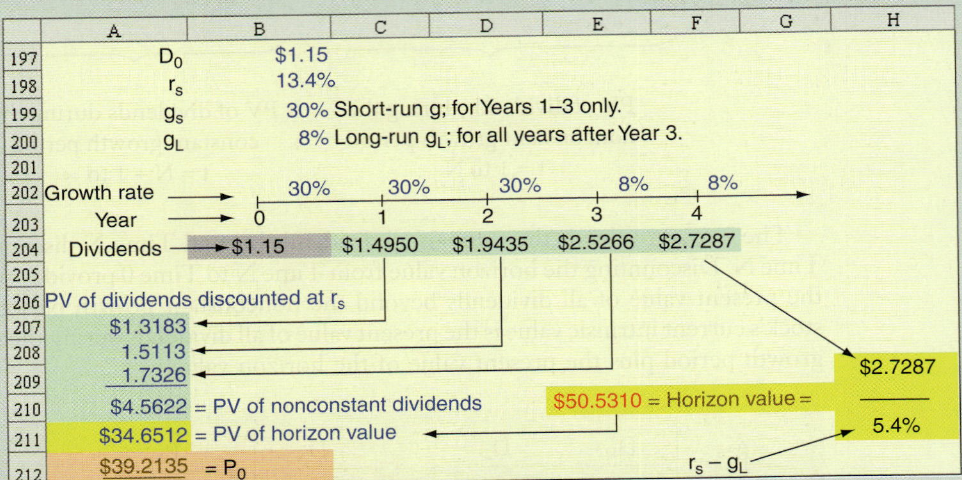

Notes:

Step 1. Calculate the dividends expected at the end of each year during the nonconstant growth period. Calculate the first dividend, $D_1 = D_0(1 + g_s) = \$1.15(1.30) = \$1.4950$. Here g_s is the growth rate (30%) during the 3-year supernormal growth period. Show the \$1.4950 on the time line as the cash flow at Time 1. Then calculate $D_2 = D_1(1 + g_s) = \$1.4950(1.30) = \$1.9435$ and then $D_3 = D_2(1 + g_s) = \$1.9435(1.30) = \$2.52655$ (the figure shows the values rounded to 4 decimal places, but all calculations used nonrounded values). Show these values on the time line as the cash flows at Time 2 and Time 3. Note that D_0 is used only to calculate D_1.

Step 2. At Time 3, the stock becomes a constant growth stock. Therefore, we can use the constant growth formula to find $\hat{P}_3$, which is the PV of the dividends from Time 4 to infinity as evaluated at Time 3. First we determine $D_4 = \$2.52655(1.08) = \$2.7287$ for use in the formula, and then we calculate $\hat{P}_3$ as follows:

$$\hat{P}_3 = \frac{D_4}{r_s - g_L} = \frac{\$2.7287}{0.134 - 0.08} = \$50.5310$$

We show this \$50.5310 on the time line as a second cash flow at Time 3. The \$50.5310 is a Time-3 cash flow in the sense that the owner of the stock could sell it for \$50.5310 at Time 3 and also in the sense that \$50.5310 is the value at Time 3 of the dividend cash flows from Time 4 to infinity.

Step 3. Now that the cash flows have been placed on the time line, we can discount each cash flow at the required rate of return, $r_s = 13.4\%$. This produces the PVs shown to the left below the time line, and the sum of the PVs is the value of the supernormal growth stock, \$39.21.

In the figure we show the setup for an *Excel* solution. With a financial calculator, you could use the cash flow (CFLO) register of your calculator. Enter 0 for CF_0 because you get no cash flow at Time 0, $CF_1 = 1.495$, $CF_2 = 1.9435$, and $CF_3 = 2.52655 + 50.531 = 53.0576$. Then enter I/YR = 13.4 and press the NPV key to find the value of the stock, \$39.21.

See **Ch07 Tool Kit.xls** *on the textbook's Web site.*

The valuation process as diagrammed in Figure 7-5 is explained in the steps set forth below the time line. The estimated value of the supernormal growth stock is \$39.21.

Self-Test

Explain how one would find the value of a supernormal growth stock.

Explain what is meant by the terms "horizon (terminal) date" and "horizon (terminal) value."

Suppose $D_0 = \$5.00$ and $r_s = 10\%$. The expected growth rate from Year 0 to Year 1 ($g_{0 \text{ to } 1}$) = 20%, the expected growth rate from Year 1 to Year 2 ($g_{1 \text{ to } 2}$) = 10%, and the constant rate beyond Year 2 is $g_L = 5\%$. What are the expected dividends for Year 1 and Year 2? **(\$6.00 and \$6.60)** What is the expected horizon value price at Year 2 ($\hat{P}_2$)? **(\$138.60)** What is $\hat{P}_0$? **(\$125.45)**

7.9 Stock Valuation by the Free Cash Flow Approach

The box at the beginning of the chapter showed that the value of a firm is the present value of its future expected free cash flows (FCFs) discounted at the weighted average cost of capital (WACC). The following example illustrates how the firm's total value can be used to find the value of its stock.

Suppose Crum Inc. had a free cash flow of $200 million at the end of the most recent year. Chapter 12 shows how to forecast financial statements and free cash flows, but for now let's assume that Crum's FCFs are expected to grow at a constant rate of 5% per year forever. Chapter 9 explains how to estimate the weighted average cost of capital, but for now let's assume that Crum's WACC is 9%. The present value of the expected future free cash flows is the PV of a growing annuity, so we can use a variation of Equation 7-2, the value of a constantly growing stream of dividends:

$$V = \frac{FCF(1+g)}{WACC-g} = \frac{\$200(1.05)}{0.09-0.05} = \$5{,}250 \text{ million} \tag{7-7}$$

FCF is the cash flow available for distribution to *all* of the firm's investors, bondholders as well as stockholders. Also, the WACC is the average rate of return required by *all* of the firm's investors, not just shareholders. Therefore, V is the value of the entire firm's operations, not just the value of its equity. If the firm had any nonoperating assets, such as short-term investments in marketable securities, then we would add them to V to find the firm's total value. Crum has no nonoperating assets, so its total value is $5,250 million. To find the value of its equity, subtract the value of claims held by all groups other than common shareholders, such as debtholders and preferred stockholders. If the value of debt plus preferred stock is $2,000 million, then Crum's common equity has a value of $5,250 – $2,000 = $3,250 million. If 325 million shares of stock are outstanding, then the intrinsic value of the stock is $3,250/325 = $10 per share. This example should give you the general idea behind the free cash flow approach to stock price valuation, but see Chapter 13 for a more comprehensive example, including a situation in which free cash flows are growing at a nonconstant rate.

Self-Test

Explain how to find a firm's stock price using the free cash flow approach.

7.10 Market Multiple Analysis

If a company is publicly traded, then we can simply look up its most recent stock price to get an estimate of the stock's value. However, we must take another approach if the firm is privately owned. We could estimate the firm's cost of equity based on data for a sample of companies, forecast its earnings and dividends, and apply the DCF method to find the value of its stock. However, another method, **market multiple analysis**, can and generally would be used. Here we would take a metric for the firm—say, its EPS—and then multiply by a market-determined multiple such as the average P/E ratio for the S&P 500. This would give us an estimate of the stock's intrinsic value. Market multiples can also be applied to total net income, to sales, to book value, or to number of subscribers for businesses such as cable TV or cellular telephone systems. Whereas the discounted dividend method applies valuation concepts in a precise manner by focusing on expected cash flows, market multiple analysis is more judgmental.

To illustrate the concept, suppose Tapley Products is a privately held firm whose forecasted earnings per share are \$7.70, and suppose the average price/earnings (P/E) ratio for a set of similar publicly traded companies is 12. To estimate the intrinsic value of Tapley's stock we would simply multiply its \$7.70 EPS by the multiple 12, obtaining the value \$7.70(12) = \$92.40.

Another commonly used metric is *earnings before interest, taxes, depreciation, and amortization (EBITDA)*. The EBITDA *multiple* is the total value of a company (the market value of its equity plus that of its debt) divided by EBITDA. This multiple is based on total value, since EBITDA is used to compensate the firm's stockholders and bondholders. Therefore, it is called an **entity multiple**. The EBITDA market multiple is the average EBITDA multiple for a group of similar publicly traded companies. This procedure gives an estimate of the company's total value, and to find the estimated intrinsic value of the stock we would subtract the value of the debt from total value and then divide by the shares of stock outstanding.

As suggested previously, in some businesses, such as cable TV and cellular telephone, a critical factor is the number of customers the company has. For example, when a telephone company acquires a cellular operator, it might pay a price that is based on the number of customers. Managed care companies such as HMOs have applied similar logic in acquisitions, basing valuations primarily on the number of people insured. Some Internet companies have been valued by the number of "eyeballs," which is the number of hits on the site.

If you examine the prospectus for a firm that is having an IPO, or information regarding the acquisition of one firm by another, you will almost certainly see references to market multiple analysis. Security analysts also use this approach, sometimes as a primary measure and sometimes as a supplement to a DCF analysis, when estimating firms' intrinsic values.

Self-Test

What is market multiple analysis?
What is an entity multiple?

7.11 Preferred Stock

Preferred stock is a *hybrid*—it's similar to bonds in some respects and to common stock in others. Like bonds, preferred stock has a par value, and a fixed amount of dividends must be paid before dividends can be paid on the common stock. However, if the preferred dividend is not earned, the directors can omit (or "pass") it without throwing the company into bankruptcy. So, although preferred stock has a fixed payment like bonds, a failure to make this payment will not lead to bankruptcy.

The dividends on preferred stocks are fixed, and if they are scheduled to go on forever, the issue is a perpetuity whose value is found as follows:

$$V_{ps} = \frac{D_{ps}}{r_{ps}} \tag{7-8}$$

V_{ps} is the value of the preferred stock, D_{ps} is the preferred dividend, and r_{ps} is the required rate of return. MicroDrive has preferred stock outstanding that pays a dividend of \$10 per year. If the required rate of return on this preferred stock is 10%, then its value is \$100:

$$V_{ps} = \frac{\$10.00}{0.10} = \$100.00$$

If we know the current price of a preferred stock and its dividend, we can transpose terms and solve for the expected rate of return as follows:

$$\hat{r}_{ps} = \frac{D_{ps}}{V_{ps}} \tag{7-9}$$

Some preferred stocks have a stated maturity, say, 50 years. If a firm's preferred stock matures in 50 years, pays a $10 annual dividend, has a par value of $100, and has a required return of 8%, then we can find its price using a financial calculator: Enter N = 50, I/YR = 8, PMT = 10, and FV = 100. Then press PV to find the price, V_{ps} = $124.47. If you know the price of a share of preferred stock, you can solve for I/YR to find the expected rate of return, $\hat{r}_{ps}$.

Most preferred stocks pay dividends quarterly. This is true for MicroDrive, so we could find the effective rate of return on its preferred stock as follows:

$$\text{EFF\%} = \text{EAR} = \left(1 + \frac{r_{NOM}}{M}\right)^M - 1 = \left(1 + \frac{0.10}{4}\right)^4 - 1 = 10.38\%$$

If an investor wanted to compare the returns on MicroDrive's bonds and its preferred stock, it would be best to convert the nominal rates on each security to effective rates and then compare these "equivalent annual rates."

Self-Test

Explain the following statement: "Preferred stock is a hybrid security."

Is the equation used to value preferred stock more like the one used to evaluate perpetual bonds or the one used for common stock? Explain.

A preferred stock has an annual dividend of $5. The required return is 8%. What is the V_{ps}? **($62.50)**

7.12 Stock Market Equilibrium

Recall that r_i, the required return on Stock i, can be found using the Capital Asset Pricing Model (CAPM) as discussed in Chapter 6:

$$r_i = r_{RF} + (RP_M)b_i$$

If the risk-free rate of return is 8%, the market risk premium, RP_M, is 4%, and Stock i has a beta of 2, then its required rate of return is 16%:

$$\begin{aligned} r_i &= 8\% + (4\%)2.0 \\ &= 16\% \end{aligned}$$

The **marginal investor** will want to buy Stock i if its expected rate of return is more than 16%, will want to sell it if the expected rate of return is less than 16%, and will be indifferent—and hence will hold but not buy or sell it—if the expected rate of return is exactly 16%.

Now suppose a typical investor's portfolio contains Stock i, and suppose she analyzes the stock's prospects and concludes that its earnings, dividends, and price can be expected to grow at a constant rate of 5% per year. The last dividend was D_0 = $2.8571, so the next expected dividend is

$$D_1 = \$2.8571(1.05) = \$3$$

Our investor observes that the present price of the stock, P_0, is $30. Should she purchase more of Stock i, sell the stock, or maintain the present position?

The investor can calculate Stock i's *expected rate of return* as follows:

$$\hat{r}_i = \frac{D_1}{P_0} + g = \frac{\$3}{\$30} + 5\% = 15\%$$

Because the expected rate of return, 15%, is less than the required return, 16%, the investor would want to sell the stock, as would most other holders if this one is typical. However, few people would want to buy at the $30 price, so the present owners would be unable to find buyers unless they cut the price of the stock. Thus, the price would decline, and this decline would continue until the price reached $27.27, at which point the stock would be in **equilibrium**, defined as the price at which the expected rate of return, 16%, is equal to the required rate of return as seen by the marginal investor:

$$\hat{r}_i = \frac{\$3}{\$27.27} + 5\% = 11\% + 5\% = 16\% = r_i$$

Had the stock initially sold for less than $27.27, say, for $25, then events would have been reversed. Investors would have wanted to buy the stock because its expected rate of return would have exceeded its required rate of return, and buy orders would have driven the stock's price up to $27.27.

To summarize, in equilibrium two related conditions must hold.

1. A stock's expected rate of return as seen by the marginal investor must equal its required rate of return: $\hat{r}_i = r_i$.
2. The actual market price of the stock must equal its intrinsic value as estimated by the marginal investor: $P_0 = \hat{P}_0$.

Of course, some individual investors probably believe that $\hat{r}_i > r_i$ and $\hat{P}_0 > P_0$, hence they would invest in the stock, while other investors have the opposite view and would sell all of their shares. However, it is the marginal investor who establishes the actual market price, and for the marginal investor we must have $\hat{r}_i = r_i$ and $P_0 = \hat{P}_0$. if these conditions do not hold, trading will occur until they do.

Changes in Equilibrium Stock Prices and Market Volatility

Stock prices are not constant—as we demonstrated earlier in this chapter and elsewhere, they undergo violent changes at times. Indeed, many stocks declined by 80% or more during 2008, and a few enjoyed gains of up to 200% or even more. At the risk of understatement, the stock market is volatile!

To see how such changes can occur, assume that Stock i is in equilibrium, selling at a price of $27.27. If all expectations are met exactly, during the next year the price would gradually rise by 5%, to $28.63. However, many different events could occur to cause a change in the equilibrium price. To illustrate, consider again the set of inputs used to develop Stock i's price of $27.27, along with a new set of expected inputs:

	Variable Value	
	Original	**New**
Risk-free rate, r_{RF}	8%	7%
Market risk premium, $r_M - r_{RF}$	4%	3%
Stock i's beta coefficient, b_i	2.0	1.0
Stock i's expected growth rate, g_i	5%	6%
D_0	$ 2.8571	$2.8571
Price of Stock i	$27.27	?

Now give yourself a test: Would each of the indicated changes, by itself, lead to an increase, a decrease, or no change in the price, and what is your guess as to the new stock price?

Every change, taken alone, would lead to a higher price. Taken together, the first three would lower r_i from 16% to 10%:

$$\text{Original } r_i = 8\% + 4\%(2.0) = 16\%$$
$$\text{New } r_i = 7\% + 3\%(1.0) = 10\%$$

Using these values together with the new g = 6%, we find that $\hat{P}_0$ rises from \$27.27 to \$75.71:[11]

$$\text{Original } \hat{P}_0 = \frac{\$2.8571(1.05)}{0.16 - 0.05} = \frac{\$3}{0.11} = \$27.27$$

$$\text{New } \hat{P}_0 = \frac{\$2.8571(1.06)}{0.10 - 0.06} = \frac{\$3.0285}{0.04} = \$75.71$$

At the new price, the expected and required rates of return are equal:[12]

$$\hat{r}_i = \frac{\$3.0285}{\$75.71} + 6\% = 10\% = r_i$$

This indicates that the stock is in equilibrium at the new and higher price. As this example illustrates, even small changes in the size of expected future dividends or in their risk, as reflected in the required return, can cause large changes in stock prices as the price moves from one equilibrium condition to another. What might cause investors to change their expectations about future dividends? It could be new information about the company, such as preliminary results for an R&D program, initial sales of a new product, or the discovery of harmful side effects from the use of an existing product. Or new information that will affect many companies could arrive, such as the collapse of the debt markets in 2008. Given the existence of computers and telecommunications networks, new information hits the market on an almost continuous basis, and it causes frequent and sometimes large changes in stock prices. In other words, *ready availability of information causes stock prices to be volatile.*

If a stock's price is stable, this probably means that little new information is arriving. But if you think it's risky to invest in a volatile stock, imagine how risky it would be to invest in a company that rarely releases new information about its sales or operations. It may be bad to see your stock's price jump around, but it would be a lot worse to see a stable quoted price most of the time and then to see huge moves on the rare days when new information is released.[13] Fortunately, in our economy timely information is readily available, and evidence suggests that stocks—especially those of large companies—adjust

---

[11]A price change of this magnitude is by no means rare. The prices of *many* stocks double or halve during any given year. For example, Emergent Biosolutions went up 416% in 2008, even as the market crashed, on the development of a new anthrax vaccine, while Fannie Mae, the government-sponsored mortgage company, lost 98.1% of its value.

[12]It should be obvious by now that *actual realized* rates of return are not necessarily equal to expected and required returns. Thus, an investor might have *expected* to receive a return of 15% if he had bought Emergent Biosolutions stock, but after the fact, the realized return was far above 15% in 2008. On the other hand, the 2008 actual realized return on Fannie Mae stock was far below 15%.

[13]Note, however, that if information came out infrequently, stock prices would probably be stable for a time and then experience large price swings when news did come out. This would be a bit like not having a lot of little earthquakes (frequent new information) that relieve stress along the fault and instead building up stress for a number of years before a massive earthquake.

rapidly to new information. Consequently, equilibrium ordinarily exists for any given stock, and required and expected returns are generally equal. Stock prices certainly change, sometimes violently and rapidly, but this simply reflects changing conditions and expectations.

There are times, of course, when a stock appears to react for several months to favorable or unfavorable developments. However, this does not necessarily signify a long adjustment period; rather, it could simply indicate that, as more new pieces of information about the situation come out, the market adjusts to them. The ability of the market to adjust to new information is discussed in the next section.

Self-Test

What two conditions must hold for a stock to be in equilibrium?
Why doesn't a volatile stock price imply irrational pricing?

7.13 The Efficient Markets Hypothesis

A body of theory called the **Efficient Markets Hypothesis (EMH)** asserts that (1) stocks are always in equilibrium and (2) it is impossible for an investor to "beat the market" and consistently earn a higher rate of return than is justified by the stock's risk. Those who believe in the EMH note that there are 100,000 or so full-time, highly trained, professional analysts and traders operating in the market, while there are fewer than 3,000 major stocks. Therefore, if each analyst followed 30 stocks (which is about right, as analysts tend to specialize in a specific industry), there would on average be 1,000 analysts following each stock. Furthermore, these analysts work for organizations such as Morgan Stanley, Goldman Sachs, CALPERS, Prudential Financial, and the like, which have billions of dollars available with which to take advantage of bargains. In addition, as a result of SEC disclosure requirements and electronic information networks, as new information about a stock becomes available, these analysts generally receive and evaluate it at the same time. Therefore, the price of a stock will adjust almost immediately to any new development. That, in a nutshell, is the logic behind the efficient markets hypothesis. However, there are variations on the theory, as we discuss next.

Weak-Form Efficiency

Technical analysts believe that past trends or patterns in stock prices can be used to predict future stock prices. In contrast, those who believe in the **weak form** of the EMH argue that all information contained in past price movements is fully reflected in current market prices. If the weak form were true, then information about recent trends in stock prices would be of no use in selecting stocks—the fact that a stock has risen for the past three days, for example, would give us no useful clues as to what it will do today or tomorrow. Those who believe that weak-form efficiency exists also believe that technical analysts, also known as "chartists," are wasting their time.

To illustrate the arguments, after studying the past history of the stock market, a technical analyst might "discover" the following pattern: If a stock falls for three consecutive days, its price typically rises by 10% the following day. The technician would then conclude that investors could make money by purchasing a stock whose price has fallen three consecutive days.

Weak-form advocates argue that if this pattern truly existed then other investors would soon discover it, and if so, why would anyone be willing to sell a stock after it had fallen for three consecutive days? In other words, why sell if you know that the price is going to increase by 10% the next day? Those who believe in weak-form efficiency argue that if the stock were really likely to rise to $44 tomorrow, then its price *today, right now,* would actually rise to somewhere close to $44, thereby eliminating the trading opportunity. Consequently, weak-form efficiency implies that any information that comes from past stock prices is rapidly incorporated into the current stock price.

Semistrong-Form Efficiency

The **semistrong form** of the EMH states that current market prices reflect all *publicly available* information. Therefore, if semistrong-form efficiency exists, it would do no good to pore over annual reports or other published data because market prices would have adjusted to any good or bad news contained in such reports back when the news came out. With semistrong-form efficiency, investors should expect to earn the returns predicted by the SML, but they should not expect to do any better or worse other than by chance.

Another implication of semistrong-form efficiency is that whenever information is released to the public, stock prices will respond only if the information is different from what had been expected. For example, if a company announces a 30% increase in earnings and if that increase is about what analysts had been expecting, then the announcement should have little or no effect on the company's stock price. On the other hand, the stock price would probably fall if analysts had expected earnings to increase by more than 30%, but it probably would rise if they had expected a smaller increase.

Strong-Form Efficiency

The **strong form** of the EMH states that current market prices reflect all pertinent information, whether publicly available or privately held. If this form holds, even insiders would find it impossible to earn consistently abnormal returns in the stock market.

Is the Stock Market Efficient?

Many empirical studies have been conducted to test the validity of the three forms of market efficiency. Most empirical studies are joint tests of the EMH and an asset pricing model (usually the CAPM or the Fama-French three-factor model). They are joint tests in the sense that they examine whether a particular strategy can beat the market, where "beating the market" means earning a return higher than that predicted by the particular asset pricing model. Most studies suggest that the stock market is highly efficient in the weak form and reasonably efficient in the semistrong form, at least for the larger and more widely followed stocks.[14] The evidence

[14]The vast majority of academic studies have shown that no excess returns (defined as returns above those predicted by the CAPM or other asset pricing models) can be earned with technical analysis—that is, using past stock prices to predict future stock prices—especially after considering transactions costs. A possible exception is in the area of long-term reversals, where several studies show that portfolios of stocks with poor past long-term performance tend to do slightly better than average in the future long term, and vice versa. Another possible exception is in the area of momentum, where studies show that stocks with strong performance in the short-term past tend to do slightly better than average in the short-term future, and likewise for weak performance. For example, see N. Jegadeesh and S. Titman, "Returns to Buying Winners and Selling Losers: Implications for Stock Market Efficiency," *Journal of Finance*, March 1993, pp. 69–91, and W. F. M. DeBondt and R. H. Thaler, "Does the Stock Market Overreact?" *Journal of Finance*, July 1985, pp. 793–808. However, when a way to "beat" the market becomes known, the actions of investors tend to eliminate it.

suggests that the strong form EMH does not hold, because those who possessed inside information could and did (illegally) make abnormal profits.

However, skeptics of the EMH point to the stock market bubbles that burst in 2000 and 2008 and suggest that, at the height of these booms, the stocks of many companies—especially in the technology sector—vastly exceeded their intrinsic values. These skeptics suggest that investors are not simply machines that rationally process all available information; rather, a variety of psychological and perhaps irrational factors also come into play. Indeed, researchers have begun to incorporate elements of cognitive psychology in an effort to better understand how individuals and entire markets respond to different circumstances. In other words, if people aren't rational in their daily decisions, why should we expect them to be rational in their financial decisions? For example, studies show that investors tend to hold on too long to stocks that have performed poorly in the past (i.e., losers) but that they sell winners too quickly. This field of study is called *behavioral finance.*[15]

Keep in mind that the EMH does not assume that all investors are rational. Instead, it assumes that stock market prices track intrinsic values fairly closely. As we described earlier, new information should cause a stock's intrinsic value to move rapidly to a new level that reflects the new information. The EMH also assumes that if stock prices deviate from their intrinsic values, investors will *quickly* take advantage of this mispricing by buying undervalued stocks and selling overvalued stocks. Thus, investors' actions work to drive prices to their new equilibrium level based on new information. Even if some investors behave irrationally, as by holding losers too long and/or selling winners too quickly, this does not imply that the markets are not efficient. Thus, it is possible to have irrational investors in a rational market.

On the other hand, if the market itself is inherently irrational (i.e., if mispricings persist for long periods), then rational investors can lose a lot of money even if they are ultimately proven to be correct. For example, a "rational" investor in mid-1999 might have concluded that the Nasdaq was overvalued when it was trading at 3,000. If such an investor had acted on that assumption and sold stock short, he would have lost a lot of money the following year, when the Nasdaq soared to over 5,000 as "irrational exuberance" pushed the prices of already overvalued stocks to even higher levels. Ultimately, if our "rational investor" had the courage, patience, and financial resources to hold on, he would have been vindicated in the long run, because the Nasdaq subsequently fell from over 5,000 to about 1,300. But as the economist John Maynard Keynes said, "In the long run we are all dead."

What is the bottom line on market efficiency? Based on our reading of the evidence, we believe that for most stocks, for most of the time, it is generally safe to assume that the market is reasonably efficient in the sense that the intrinsic price is approximately equal to the actual market price ($\hat{P}_0 \approx P_0$). However, major shifts can and do occur periodically, causing most stocks to move strongly up or down. In the early 1980s, inflation was running over 10% per year and interest rates on AAA corporate bonds hit 15%. That knocked most stocks way below their intrinsic

---

[15]Three noteworthy sources for students interested in behavioral finance are: Richard H. Thaler, Editor, *Advances in Behavioral Finance* (New York: Russell Sage Foundation, 1993); Andrei Shleifer, *Inefficient Markets: An Introduction to Behavioral Finance* (New York: Oxford University Press, 2000); and Nicholas Barberis and Richard Thaler, "A Survey of Behavioral Finance," Chapter 18 in *Handbook of the Economics of Finance*, edited by George Constantinides, Milt Harris, and René Stulz (Amsterdam: Elsevier/North-Holland, 2003). Students interested in learning more about the Efficient Markets Hypothesis should consult Burton G. Malkiel, *A Random Walk Down Wall Street* (New York: W.W. Norton & Company, 2007).

Rational Behavior versus Animal Spirits, Herding, and Anchoring Bias

If investors were completely rational, they would carefully analyze all the available information about stocks and then make well-informed decisions to buy, sell, or hold them. Most academics have argued that investors with enough clout to move the market behave in this manner. However, the stock market bubbles of 2000 and 2008 suggest that something other than pure rationality is alive and well.

The great economist John Maynard Keynes, writing during the 1920s and 1930s, suggested that **animal spirits** influence markets. After a period of rising prosperity and stock prices, Keynes believed that investors begin to think that the good times will last forever, a feeling that is driven by happy talk and high spirits rather than cool reasoning. Indeed, psychologists have demonstrated that many people do in fact anchor too closely on recent events when predicting future events, a phenomenon called **anchoring bias**. Therefore, when the market is performing better than average, they tend to think it will continue to perform better than average. Even worse, when one group of investors does well, other investors begin to emulate them, acting like a herd of sheep following one another merrily down the road. Such **herding behavior** makes it easy for hedge funds to raise enormous sums and for con men like Bernie Madoff to find new marks.

Overinflated markets and bubbles eventually burst, and when they do, the same psychological factors act in reverse, often causing bigger declines than can be explained by rational models. Eventually, though, markets bottom out, and before long the next bubble starts to inflate. Historically, such cycles have existed for as far back as our data go, and these cycles are inconsistent with the idea of rational, data-driven investors. This is the realm of behavioral finance as discussed earlier in the chapter.

How can we reconcile theories that assume investors and decision makers are rational and data-driven with the fact that businesses and the stock market are influenced by people subject to animal spirits and herding instincts? Our conclusion is that there is some truth in both theories—markets are rational to a large extent, but they are also subject to irrational behavior at times. Our advice is to do careful, rational analyses, using the tools and techniques described in this book, but also to recognize that actual prices can differ from intrinsic values—sometimes by large amounts and for long periods. That's the bad news. The good news is that differences between actual prices and intrinsic values provide wonderful opportunities for those able to capitalize on them.

values, so when inflation fears receded, stock prices roared ahead. A similar situation, but in reverse, may be occurring in 2008 and 2009. Stock prices have fallen sharply, perhaps to a level below their intrinsic values. In other words, we may be in a "reverse bubble."

Implications of Market Efficiency for Financial Decisions

What bearing does the EMH have on financial decisions? First, many investors have given up trying to beat the market because the professionals who manage mutual fund portfolios, on average, do not outperform the overall stock market as measured by an index like the S&P 500.[16] Indeed, the relatively poor performance of actively managed mutual funds helps explain the growing popularity of index funds, where administrative costs are lower than for actively managed funds. Rather than spending time and money trying to find undervalued stocks, index funds try instead to match overall market returns by buying the basket of stocks that makes up a particular index, such as the S&P 500.

[16]For a discussion of the performance of actively managed funds, see Jonathan Clements, "Resisting the Lure of Managed Funds," *The Wall Street Journal*, February 27, 2001, p. C1.

Second, market efficiency also has important implications for managerial decisions, especially stock issues, stock repurchases, and tender offers. If the market prices stocks fairly, then managerial decisions based on the premise that a stock is undervalued or overvalued might not make sense. Managers may have better information about their own companies than outsiders, but it would be illegal to use this information for their own advantage, and they cannot deliberately defraud investors by knowingly putting out false information.

Self-Test

What is the Efficient Markets Hypothesis (EMH)?
What are the differences among the three forms of the EMH?
What are the implications of the EMH for financial decisions?

Summary

Corporate decisions should be analyzed in terms of how alternative courses of action are likely to affect a firm's value. However, it is necessary to know how stock prices are established before attempting to measure how a given decision will affect a firm's value. This chapter showed how stock values are determined and also how investors go about estimating the rates of return they expect to earn. The key concepts covered are listed below.

- A **proxy** is a document that gives one person the power to act for another, typically the power to vote shares of common stock. A **proxy fight** occurs when an outside group solicits stockholders' proxies in an effort to overthrow the current management.
- A **takeover** occurs when a person or group succeeds in ousting a firm's management and takes control of the company.
- Stockholders often have the right to purchase any additional shares sold by the firm. This right, called the **preemptive right**, protects the present stockholders' control and prevents dilution of their value.
- Although most firms have only one type of common stock, in some instances **classified stock** is used to meet the special needs of the company. One type is **founders' shares**. This is stock owned by the firm's founders that carries sole voting rights but restricted dividends for a specified number of years.
- A **closely held company** is one whose stock is owned by a few individuals who are typically associated with the firm's management.
- A **publicly held company** is one whose stock is owned by a relatively large number of individuals who are not actively involved in the firm's management. Publicly held companies are generally regulated by the SEC or other governmental bodies.
- The **intrinsic value of a share of stock** is calculated as the **present value of the stream of dividends** the stock is expected to provide in the future.
- The equation used to find the **intrinsic**, or **expected, value of a constant growth stock** is

$$\hat{P}_0 = \frac{D_1}{r_s - g}$$

Web Extension 7A provides a derivation of this formula.

- The **expected total rate of return** from a stock consists of an **expected dividend yield** plus an **expected capital gains yield**. For a constant growth firm, both the dividend yield and the capital gains yield are expected to remain constant in the future.
- The equation for $\hat{r}_s$, the **expected rate of return on a constant growth stock**, is

$$\hat{r}_s = \frac{D_1}{P_0} + g$$

- A **zero growth stock** is one whose future dividends are not expected to grow at all. A **supernormal growth stock** is one whose earnings and dividends are expected to grow much faster than the economy as a whole over some specified time period and then to grow at the "normal" rate.
- To find the **present value of a supernormal growth stock**, (1) find the dividends expected during the supernormal growth period, (2) find the price of the stock at the end of the supernormal growth period, (3) discount the dividends and the projected price back to the present, and (4) sum these PVs to find the current intrinsic, or expected, value of the stock, $\hat{P}_0$.
- The **horizon (terminal) date** is the date when individual dividend forecasts are no longer made because the dividend growth rate is assumed to be constant thereafter.
- The **horizon (terminal) value** is the value at the horizon date of all future dividends after that date:

$$\hat{P}_N = \frac{D_{N+1}}{r_s - g}$$

- **Preferred stock** is a hybrid security having some characteristics of debt and some of equity.
- The **value of a share of perpetual preferred stock** is found as the dividend divided by the required rate of return:

$$V_{ps} = \frac{D_{ps}}{r_{ps}}$$

- **Preferred stock** that has a finite maturity is evaluated with a formula that is identical in form to the bond value formula.
- The **marginal investor** is a representative investor whose actions reflect the beliefs of those people who are currently trading a stock. It is the marginal investor who determines a stock's price.
- **Equilibrium** is the condition under which the expected return on a security as seen by the marginal investor is just equal to its required return, $\hat{r}_s = r_s$. Also, the stock's intrinsic value must be equal to its market price, $\hat{P}_0 = P_0$.
- The **Efficient Markets Hypothesis (EMH)** holds that (1) stocks are always in equilibrium and (2) it is impossible for an investor who does not have inside information to consistently "beat the market." Therefore, according to the EMH, stocks are always fairly valued ($\hat{P}_0 = P_0$) and have a required return equal to their expected return ($r_s = \hat{r}_s$).
- **Animal spirits** refers to the tendency of investors to become excited and let their emotions affect their behavior; **herding instincts** refers to the tendency of investors to follow the crowd, relying on others rather than their own analysis; and **anchoring bias** is the human tendency to "anchor" too closely on recent events when predicting future events. These three factors can interfere with our desire to base decisions on pure rational analysis.

Questions

(7–1) Define each of the following terms:

a. Proxy; proxy fight; takeover; preemptive right; classified stock; founders' shares
b. Closely held stock; publicly owned stock
c. Intrinsic value ($\hat{P}_0$); market price (P_0)
d. Required rate of return, r_s; expected rate of return, $\hat{r}_s$; actual, or realized, rate of return, $\bar{r}_s$
e. Capital gains yield; dividend yield; expected total return
f. Normal, or constant, growth; supernormal, or nonconstant, growth; zero growth stock
g. Preferred stock
h. Equilibrium; Efficient Markets Hypothesis (EMH); three forms of EMH
i. Purely rational behavior; animal spirits; herding instincts; anchoring; behavioral finance

(7–2) Two investors are evaluating General Electric's stock for possible purchase. They agree on the expected value of D_1 and also on the expected future dividend growth rate. Further, they agree on the risk of the stock. However, one investor normally holds stocks for 2 years and the other normally holds stocks for 10 years. On the basis of the type of analysis done in this chapter, they should both be willing to pay the same price for General Electric's stock. True or false? Explain.

(7–3) A bond that pays interest forever and has no maturity date is a perpetual bond, also called a perpetuity or a consol. In what respect is a perpetual bond similar to (1) a no-growth common stock and (2) a share of preferred stock?

(7–4) In this chapter and elsewhere we have argued that a stock's market price can deviate from its intrinsic value. Discuss the following question: If all investors attempt to behave in an entirely rational manner, could these differences still exist? In answering this question, think about information that's available to insiders versus outsiders, the fact that historical probabilities of financial events are "fuzzier" than probabilities related to physical items, and the validity of the concepts of animal spirits, herding, and anchoring.

Self-Test Problems

Solutions Appear in Appendix A

(ST–1) Constant Growth Stock Valuation

Ewald Company's current stock price is \$36, and its last dividend was \$2.40. In view of Ewald's strong financial position and its consequent low risk, its required rate of return is only 12%. If dividends are expected to grow at a constant rate g in the future, and if r_s is expected to remain at 12%, then what is Ewald's expected stock price 5 years from now?

(ST–2) Supernormal Growth Stock Valuation

Snyder Computer Chips Inc. is experiencing a period of rapid growth. Earnings and dividends are expected to grow at a rate of 15% during the next 2 years, at 13% in the third year, and at a constant rate of 6% thereafter. Snyder's last dividend was \$1.15, and the required rate of return on the stock is 12%.

a. Calculate the value of the stock today.
b. Calculate $\hat{P}_1$ and $\hat{P}_2$.
c. Calculate the dividend yield and capital gains yield for Years 1, 2, and 3.

Problems

Answers Appear in Appendix B

EASY PROBLEMS 1–5

(7–1) DPS Calculation

Thress Industries just paid a dividend of \$1.50 a share (i.e., D_0 = \$1.50). The dividend is expected to grow 5% a year for the next 3 years and then 10% a year thereafter. What is the expected dividend per share for each of the next 5 years?

(7–2) Constant Growth Valuation

Boehm Incorporated is expected to pay a \$1.50 per share dividend at the end of this year (i.e., D_1 = \$1.50). The dividend is expected to grow at a constant rate of 7% a year. The required rate of return on the stock, r_s, is 15%. What is the value per share of Boehm's stock?

(7–3) Constant Growth Valuation

Woidtke Manufacturing's stock currently sells for \$20 a share. The stock just paid a dividend of \$1.00 a share (i.e., D_0 = \$1.00), and the dividend is expected to grow forever at a constant rate of 10% a year. What stock price is expected 1 year from now? What is the required rate of return on Woidtke's stock?

(7–4) Preferred Stock Valuation

Nick's Enchiladas Incorporated has preferred stock outstanding that pays a dividend of \$5 at the end of each year. The preferred sells for \$50 a share. What is the stock's required rate of return?

(7–5) Nonconstant Growth Valuation

A company currently pays a dividend of \$2 per share (D_0 = \$2). It is estimated that the company's dividend will grow at a rate of 20% per year for the next 2 years, then at a constant rate of 7% thereafter. The company's stock has a beta of 1.2, the risk-free rate is 7.5%, and the market risk premium is 4%. What is your estimate of the stock's current price?

INTERMEDIATE PROBLEMS 6–16

(7–6) Constant Growth Rate, g

A stock is trading at \$80 per share. The stock is expected to have a year-end dividend of \$4 per share (D_1 = \$4), and it is expected to grow at some constant rate g throughout time. The stock's required rate of return is 14%. If markets are efficient, what is your forecast of g?

(7–7) Constant Growth Valuation

You are considering an investment in Crisp Cookware's common stock. The stock is expected to pay a dividend of \$2 a share at the end of this year (D_1 = \$2.00); its beta is 0.9; the risk-free rate is 5.6%; and the market risk premium is 6%. The dividend is expected to grow at some constant rate g, and the stock currently sells for \$25 a share. Assuming the market is in equilibrium, what does the market believe will be the stock's price at the end of 3 years (i.e., what is $\hat{P}_3$)?

(7–8) Preferred Stock Rate of Return

What is the nominal rate of return on a preferred stock with a \$100 par value, a stated dividend of 8% of par, and a current market price of (a) \$60, (b) \$80, (c) \$100, and (d) \$140?

(7–9) Declining Growth Stock Valuation

Brushy Mountain Mining Company's ore reserves are being depleted, so its sales are falling. Also, its pit is getting deeper each year, so its costs are rising. As a result, the company's earnings and dividends are declining at the constant rate of 4% per year. If D_0 = \$5 and r_s = 15%, what is the value of Brushy Mountain's stock?

(7–10) Rates of Return and Equilibrium

The beta coefficient for Stock C is $b_C = 0.4$ and that for Stock D is $b_D = -0.5$. (Stock D's beta is negative, indicating that its rate of return rises whenever returns on most other stocks fall. There are very few negative-beta stocks, although collection agency and gold mining stocks are sometimes cited as examples.)

a. If the risk-free rate is 9% and the expected rate of return on an average stock is 13%, what are the required rates of return on Stocks C and D?
b. For Stock C, suppose the current price, P_0, is \$25; the next expected dividend, D_1, is \$1.50; and the stock's expected constant growth rate is 4%. Is the stock in equilibrium? Explain, and describe what would happen if the stock were not in equilibrium.

(7–11) Nonconstant Growth Stock Valuation

Assume that the average firm in your company's industry is expected to grow at a constant rate of 6% and that its dividend yield is 7%. Your company is about as risky as the average firm in the industry, but it has just successfully completed some R&D work that leads you to expect that its earnings and dividends will grow at a rate of 50% [$D_1 = D_0(1 + g) = D_0(1.50)$] this year and 25% the following year, after which growth should return to the 6% industry average. If the last dividend paid (D_0) was \$1, what is the value per share of your firm's stock?

(7–12) Nonconstant Growth Stock Valuation

Simpkins Corporation is expanding rapidly, and it does not pay any dividends because it currently needs to retain all of its earnings. However, investors expect Simpkins to begin paying dividends, with the first dividend of \$1.00 coming 3 years from today. The dividend should grow rapidly—at a rate of 50% per year—during Years 4 and 5. After Year 5, the company should grow at a constant rate of 8% per year. If the required return on the stock is 15%, what is the value of the stock today?

(7–13) Preferred Stock Valuation

Several years ago, Rolen Riders issued preferred stock with a stated annual dividend of 10% of its \$100 par value. Preferred stock of this type currently yields 8%. Assume dividends are paid annually.

a. What is the value of Rolen's preferred stock?
b. Suppose interest rate levels have risen to the point where the preferred stock now yields 12%. What would be the new value of Rolen's preferred stock?

(7–14) Return on Common Stock

You buy a share of The Ludwig Corporation stock for \$21.40. You expect it to pay dividends of \$1.07, \$1.1449, and \$1.2250 in Years 1, 2, and 3, respectively, and you expect to sell it at a price of \$26.22 at the end of 3 years.

a. Calculate the growth rate in dividends.
b. Calculate the expected dividend yield.
c. Assuming that the calculated growth rate is expected to continue, you can add the dividend yield to the expected growth rate to obtain the expected total rate of return. What is this stock's expected total rate of return?

(7–15) Constant Growth Stock Valuation

Investors require a 15% rate of return on Brooks Sisters's stock (r_s = 15%).

a. What would the value of Brooks's stock be if the previous dividend was D_0 = \$2 and if investors expect dividends to grow at a constant annual rate of (1) –5%, (2) 0%, (3) 5%, and (4) 10%?
b. Using data from part a, what is the Gordon (constant growth) model's value for Brooks Sisters's stock if the required rate of return is 15% and the expected growth rate is (1) 15% or (2) 20%? Are these reasonable results? Explain.
c. Is it reasonable to expect that a constant growth stock would have $g > r_s$?

(7–16) Equilibrium Stock Price

The risk-free rate of return, r_{RF}, is 11%; the required rate of return on the market, r_M, is 14%; and Schuler Company's stock has a beta coefficient of 1.5.

a. If the dividend expected during the coming year, D_1, is \$2.25, and if g is a constant 5%, then at what price should Schuler's stock sell?
b. Now suppose that the Federal Reserve Board increases the money supply, causing a fall in the risk-free rate to 9% and in r_M to 12%. How would this affect the price of the stock?
c. In addition to the change in part b, suppose investors' risk aversion declines; this fact, combined with the decline in r_{RF}, causes r_M to fall to 11%. At what price would Schuler's stock now sell?
d. Suppose Schuler has a change in management. The new group institutes policies that increase the expected constant growth rate to 6%. Also, the new management stabilizes sales and profits and thus causes the beta coefficient to decline from 1.5 to 1.3. Assume that r_{RF} and r_M are equal to the values in part c. After all these changes, what is Schuler's new equilibrium price? (*Note:* D_1 goes to \$2.27.)

Challenging Problems 17–19

(7–17) Constant Growth Stock Valuation

Suppose a firm's common stock paid a dividend of \$2 *yesterday*. You expect the dividend to grow at the rate of 5% per year for the next 3 years; if you buy the stock, you plan to hold it for 3 years and then sell it.

a. Find the expected dividend for each of the next 3 years; in other words, calculate D_1, D_2, and D_3. Note that D_0 = \$2.
b. Given that the appropriate discount rate is 12% and that the first of these dividend payments will occur 1 year from now, find the present value of the dividend stream; that is, calculate the PV of D_1, D_2, and D_3, and then sum these PVs.
c. You expect the price of the stock 3 years from now to be \$34.73 (i.e., you expect $\hat{P}_3$= \$34.73). Discounted at a 12% rate, what is the present value of this expected future stock price? In other words, calculate the PV of \$34.73.
d. If you plan to buy the stock, hold it for 3 years, and then sell it for \$34.73, what is the most you should pay for it?
e. Use Equation 7-2 to calculate the present value of this stock. Assume that g = 5% and is constant.
f. Is the value of this stock dependent on how long you plan to hold it? In other words, if your planned holding period were 2 years or 5 years rather than 3 years, would this affect the value of the stock today, $\hat{P}_0$? Explain your answer.

(7–18) Nonconstant Growth Stock Valuation

Reizenstein Technologies (RT) has just developed a solar panel capable of generating 200% more electricity than any solar panel currently on the market. As a result, RT is expected to experience a 15% annual growth rate for the next 5 years. By the end of 5 years, other firms will have developed comparable technology, and RT's growth rate will slow to 5% per year indefinitely. Stockholders require a return of 12% on RT's stock. The most recent annual dividend (D_0), which was paid yesterday, was \$1.75 per share.

a. Calculate RT's expected dividends for t = 1, t = 2, t = 3, t = 4, and t = 5.
b. Calculate the intrinsic value of the stock today, $\hat{P}_0$. Proceed by finding the present value of the dividends expected at t = 1, t = 2, t = 3, t = 4, and t = 5 plus the present value of the stock price that should exist at t = 5, $\hat{P}_5$. The $\hat{P}_5$ stock price can be found by using the constant growth equation. Note that to find $\hat{P}_5$ you use the dividend expected at t = 6, which is 5% greater than the t = 5 dividend.

c. Calculate the expected dividend yield ($D_1/\hat{P}_0$), the capital gains yield expected during the first year, and the expected total return (dividend yield plus capital gains yield) during the first year. (Assume that $\hat{P}_0 = P_0$, and recognize that the capital gains yield is equal to the total return minus the dividend yield.) Also calculate these same three yields for t = 5 (e.g., $D_6/\hat{P}_5$).

d. If your calculated intrinsic value differed substantially from the current market price, and if your views are consistent with those of most investors (the marginal investor), what would happen in the marketplace? What would happen if your views were *not* consistent with those of the marginal investor and you turned out to be correct?

(7–19) Supernormal Growth Stock Valuation

Taussig Technologies Corporation (TTC) has been growing at a rate of 20% per year in recent years. This same supernormal growth rate is expected to last for another 2 years ($g_1 = g_2 = 20\%$).

a. If $D_0 = \$1.60$, $r_s = 10\%$, and $g_L = 6\%$, then what is TTC's stock worth today? What is its expected dividend yield and its capital gains yield at this time?

b. Now assume that TTC's period of supernormal growth is to last another 5 years rather than 2 years ($g_1 = g_2 = g_3 = g_4 = g_5 = 20\%$). How would this affect its price, dividend yield, and capital gains yield? Answer in words only.

c. What will TTC's dividend yield and capital gains yield be once its period of supernormal growth ends? (*Hint:* These values will be the same regardless of whether you examine the case of 2 or 5 years of supernormal growth, and the calculations are very easy.)

d. Of what interest to investors is the relationship over time between dividend yield and capital gains yield?

Spreadsheet Problem

(7-20) Build a Model: Supernormal Growth and Corporate Valuation

Start with the partial model in the file ***Ch07 P20 Build a Model.xls*** on the textbook's Web site. Rework parts a, b, and c of Problem 7-19 using a spreadsheet model. For part b, calculate the price, dividend yield, and capital gains yield as called for in the problem.

THOMSON ONE | Business School Edition Problem

Use the Thomson ONE—Business School Edition online database to work this chapter's questions.

Estimating ExxonMobil's Intrinsic Stock Value with Thomson ONE—Business School Edition

In this chapter we described the various factors that influence stock prices and the approaches analysts use to estimate a stock's intrinsic value. By comparing these intrinsic value estimates to the current price, an investor can assess whether it makes sense to buy or sell a particular stock. Stocks trading at a price far below their estimated intrinsic values may be good candidates for purchase, whereas stocks trading at prices far in excess of their intrinsic value may be good stocks to avoid or sell.

Although estimating a stock's intrinsic value is a complex exercise that requires reliable data and good judgment, we can use the data available in Thomson ONE to arrive at a quick "back of the envelope" calculation of intrinsic value.

Thomson ONE—BSE Discussion Questions

1. For purposes of this exercise, let's take a closer look at the stock of ExxonMobil Corporation (XOM). Looking at the COMPANY OVERVIEW, we can immediately see the company's current stock price and its performance relative to the overall market in recent months. What is ExxonMobil's current stock price? How has the stock performed relative to the market over the past few months?
2. Click on the "NEWS" tab to see the recent news stories for the company. Have there been any recent events affecting the company's stock price, or have things been relatively quiet?
3. To provide a starting point for gauging a company's relative valuation, analysts often look at a company's price-to-earnings (P/E) ratio. Returning to the COMPANY OVERVIEW page, you can see XOM's current P/E ratio. To put this number in perspective, it is useful to compare this ratio with other companies in the same industry and to take a look at how this ratio has changed over time. If you want to see how XOM's P/E ratio stacks up to its peers, click on the tab labeled PEERS. Click on FINANCIALS on the next row of tabs and then select KEY FINANCIAL RATIOS. Toward the bottom of the table you should see information on the P/E ratio in the section titled Market Value Ratios. Toward the top, you should see an item that says CLICK HERE TO SELECT NEW PEER SET—do this if you want to compare XOM to a different set of firms.

   For the most part, is XOM's P/E ratio above or below that of its peers? Off the top of your head, can these factors explain why XOM's P/E ratio differs from its peers?
4. To see how XOM's P/E ratio has varied over time, return to the COMPANY OVERVIEW page. Next click FINANCIALS—GROWTH RATIOS and then select WORLDSCOPE—INCOME STATEMENT RATIOS. Is XOM's current P/E ratio well above or well below its historical average? If so, do you have any explanation for why the current P/E deviates from its historical trend? On the basis of this information, does XOM's current P/E suggest that the stock is undervalued or overvalued? Explain.
5. In the text, we discussed using the dividend growth model to estimate a stock's intrinsic value. To keep things as simple as possible, let's assume at first that XOM's dividend is expected to grow at some constant rate over time. Then its intrinsic value would equal $D_1/(r_s - g)$, where D_1 is the expected annual dividend 1 year from now, r_s is the stock's required rate of return, and g is the dividend's constant growth rate. To estimate the dividend growth rate, it's helpful first to look at XOM's dividend history. Staying on the current Web page (WORLDSCOPE—INCOME STATEMENT RATIOS), you should immediately find the company's annual dividend for the past several years. On the basis of this information, what has been the average annual dividend growth rate? Another way to obtain estimates of dividend growth rates is to look at analysts' forecasts for future dividends, which can be found on the ESTIMATES tab. Scrolling down the page, you should see an area marked Consensus Estimates and a tab under Available Measures. Here you click on the down arrow key and select Dividends Per Share (DPS). What is the median year-end dividend forecast? You can use this as an estimate of D_1 in

your measure of intrinsic value. You can also use this forecast along with the historical data to arrive at a measure of the forecasted dividend growth rate, g.

6. The required return on equity, r_s, is the final input needed to estimate intrinsic value. For our purposes you can either assume a number (say, 8% or 9%) or use the CAPM to calculate an estimated cost of equity using the data available in Thomson ONE. (For more details, take a look at the Thomson ONE exercise for Chapter 2). Having decided on your best estimates for D_1, r_s, and g, you can then calculate XOM's intrinsic value. How does this estimate compare with the current stock price? Does your preliminary analysis suggest that XOM is undervalued or overvalued? Explain.
7. Often it is useful to perform a sensitivity analysis, in which you show how your estimate of intrinsic value varies according to different estimates of D_1, r_s, and g. To do so, recalculate your intrinsic value estimate for a range of different estimates for each of these key inputs. One convenient way to do this is to set up a simple data table in *Excel*. Refer to the *Excel* tutorial accessed through the textbook's Web site for instructions on data tables. On the basis of this analysis, what inputs justify the current stock price?
8. On the basis of the dividend history you uncovered in question 5 and your assessment of XOM's future dividend payout policies, do you think it is reasonable to assume that the constant growth model is a good proxy for intrinsic value? If not, how would you use the available data in Thomson ONE to estimate intrinsic value using the nonconstant growth model?
9. Finally, you can also use the information in Thomson ONE to value the entire corporation. This approach requires that you estimate XOM's annual free cash flows. Once you estimate the value of the entire corporation, you subtract the value of debt and preferred stock to arrive at an estimate of the company's equity value. Divide this number by the number of shares of common stock outstanding, which yields an alternative estimate of the stock's intrinsic value. This approach may take some more time and involve more judgment concerning forecasts of future free cash flows, but you can use the financial statements and growth forecasts in Thomson ONE as useful starting points. Go to Worldscope's Cash Flow Ratios Report (which you find by clicking on FINANCIALS, FUNDAMENTAL RATIOS, and WORLDSCOPE RATIOS) to find an estimate of "free cash flow per share." Although this number is useful, Worldscope's definition of free cash flow subtracts out dividends per share; therefore, to make it comparable to the measure used in this text, you must add back dividends. To see Worldscope's definition of free cash flow (or any term), click on SEARCH FOR COMPANIES from the left toolbar and then select the ADVANCED SEARCH tab. In the middle of your screen, on the right-hand side, you will see a dialog box with terms. Use the down arrow to scroll through the terms, highlighting the term for which you would like to see a definition. Then, click on the DEFINITION button immediately below the dialog box.

Mini Case

Sam Strother and Shawna Tibbs are senior vice presidents of Mutual of Seattle. They are co-directors of the company's pension fund management division, with Strother having responsibility for fixed income securities (primarily bonds) and Tibbs responsible for equity investments. A major new client, the Northwestern Municipal Alliance, has requested that Mutual of Seattle present an investment seminar to the mayors of the cities in the association, and Strother and Tibbs, who will make the actual presentation, have asked you to help them.

To illustrate the common stock valuation process, Strother and Tibbs have asked you to analyze the Temp Force Company, an employment agency that supplies word processor operators and computer programmers to businesses with temporarily heavy workloads. You are to answer the following questions.

a. Describe briefly the legal rights and privileges of common stockholders.

b. (1) Write out a formula that can be used to value any stock, regardless of its dividend pattern.

(2) What is a constant growth stock? How are constant growth stocks valued?

(3) What happens if a company has a constant g that exceeds its r_s? Will many stocks have expected $g > r_s$ in the short run (i.e., for the next few years)? In the long run (i.e., forever)?

c. Assume that Temp Force has a beta coefficient of 1.2, that the risk-free rate (the yield on T-bonds) is 7.0%, and that the market risk premium is 5%. What is the required rate of return on the firm's stock?

d. Assume that Temp Force is a constant growth company whose last dividend (D_0, which was paid yesterday) was $2.00 and whose dividend is expected to grow indefinitely at a 6% rate.

(1) What is the firm's expected dividend stream over the next 3 years?

(2) What is the firm's current intrinsic stock price?

(3) What is the stock's expected value 1 year from now?

(4) What are the expected dividend yield, the expected capital gains yield, and the expected total return during the first year?

e. Now assume that the stock is currently selling at $30.29. What is its expected rate of return?

f. What would the stock price be if the dividends were expected to have zero growth?

g. Now assume that Temp Force's dividend is expected to experience supernormal growth of 30% from Year 0 to Year 1, 20% from Year 1 to Year 2, and 10% from Year 2 to Year 3. After Year 3, dividends will grow at a constant rate of 6%. What is the stock's intrinsic value under these conditions? What are the expected dividend yield and capital gains yield during the first year? What are the expected dividend yield and capital gains yield during the fourth year (from Year 3 to Year 4)?

h. Is the stock price based more on long-term or short-term expectations? Answer this by finding the percentage of Temp Force's current stock price that is based on dividends expected more than 3 years in the future.

i. Suppose Temp Force is expected to experience zero growth during the first 3 years and then to resume its steady-state growth of 6% in the fourth year. What is the stock's intrinsic value now? What is its expected dividend yield and its capital gains yield in Year 1? In Year 4?

j. Now suppose that Temp Force's earnings and dividends are expected to decline by a constant 6% per year forever—that is, $g = -6\%$. Why would anyone be willing to buy such a stock, and at what price should it sell? What would be the dividend yield and capital gains yield in each year?

k. What is market multiple analysis?

l. Temp Force recently issued preferred stock that pays an annual dividend of $5 at a price of $50 per share. What is the expected return to an investor who buys this preferred stock?

m. Why do stock prices change? Suppose the expected D_1 is $2, the growth rate is 5%, and r_s is 10%. Using the constant growth model, what is the stock's price? What is the impact on the stock price if g falls to 4% or rises to 6%? If r_s increases to 9% or to 11%?

n. What does market equilibrium mean?

o. If equilibrium does not exist, how will it be established?

p. What is the Efficient Markets Hypothesis, what are its three forms, and what are its implications?

q. Assume that all the growth rates used in the preceding answers were averages of the growth rates published by well-known and respected security analysts. Would you then say that your results are based on a purely rational analysis? If not, what factors might have led to "irrational results?"

SELECTED ADDITIONAL CASES

The following cases from Textchoice, *Cengage Learning's online library, cover many of the concepts discussed in this chapter and are available at* ***http://www.textchoice2.com***.

Klein-Brigham Series:
Case 3, "Peachtree Securities, Inc. (B)"; Case 71, "Swan Davis"; Case 78, "Beatrice Peabody"; and Case 101, "TECO Energy."
Brigham-Buzzard Series:
Case 4, "Powerline Network Corporation (Stocks)."

CHAPTER 8

Financial Options and Applications in Corporate Finance

In 2008, Cisco had almost 1.2 billion outstanding employee stock options and about 5.9 billion outstanding shares of stock. If all these options are exercised, then the option holders will own 16.9% of Cisco's stock: 1.2/(5.9+1.2) = 0.169. Many of these options never may be exercised, but any way you look at it, 1.2 billion is a lot of options. Cisco isn't the only company with mega-grants: Pfizer, Time Warner, Ford, and Bank of America are among the many companies that have granted to their employees options to buy more than 100 million shares. Whether your next job is with a high-tech firm, a financial service company, or a manufacturer, you will probably receive stock options, so it's important that you understand them.

In a typical grant, you receive options allowing you to purchase shares of stock at a fixed price, called the strike price or exercise price, on or before a stated expiration date. Most plans have a vesting period, during which you can't exercise the options. For example, suppose you are granted 1,000 options with a strike price of $50, an expiration date 10 years from now, and a vesting period of 3 years. Even if the stock price rises above $50 during the first 3 years, you can't exercise the options because of the vesting requirement. After 3 years, if you are still with the company then you have the right to exercise the options. For example, if the stock goes up to $110, you could pay the company $50(1,000) = $50,000 and receive 1,000 shares of stock worth $110,000. However, if you don't exercise the options within 10 years, they will expire and thus be worthless.

Even though the vesting requirement prevents you from exercising the options the moment they are granted to you, the options clearly have some immediate value. Therefore, if you are choosing between different job offers where options are involved, you will need a way to determine the value of the alternative options. This chapter explains how to value options, so read on.

The Intrinsic Value of Stock Options

In previous chapters we showed that the intrinsic value of an asset is the present value of its cash flows. This time value of money approach works great for stocks and bonds, but we must use another approach for options and derivatives. If we can find a portfolio of stocks and risk-free bonds that replicates an option's cash flows, then the intrinsic value of the option must be identical to the value of the replicating portfolio.

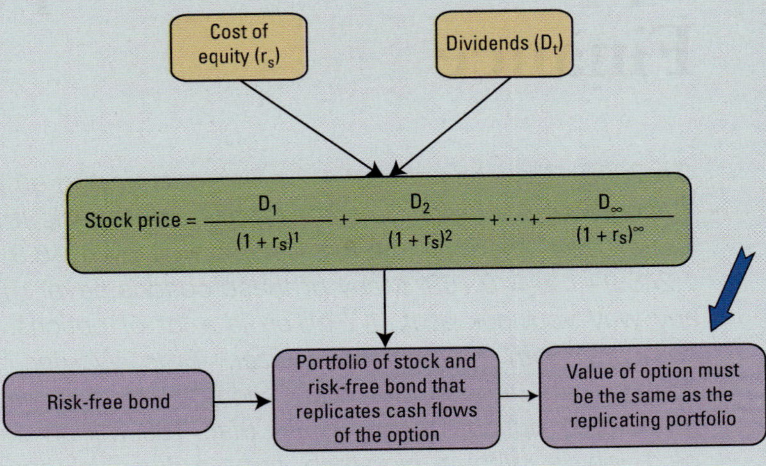

There are two fundamental approaches to valuing assets. The first is the *discounted cash flow* (DCF) approach, which we covered in previous chapters: An asset's value is the present value of its cash flows. The second is the *option pricing* approach. It is important that every manager understands the basic principles of option pricing, for the following reasons. First, many projects allow managers to make strategic or tactical changes in plans as market conditions change. The existence of these "embedded options" often means the difference between a successful project and a failure. Understanding basic financial options can help you manage the value inherent in these real options. Second, many companies use derivatives to manage risk; many derivatives are types of financial options, so an understanding of basic financial options is necessary before tackling derivatives. Third, option pricing theory provides insights into the optimal debt/equity choice, especially when convertible securities are involved. And fourth, understanding financial options will help you better understand any employee stock options that you receive.

The textbook's Web site contains an Excel file that will guide you through the chapter's calculations. The file for this chapter is **Ch08 Tool Kit.xls**, *and we encourage you to open the file and follow along as you read the chapter.*

8.1 Overview of Financial Options

In general, an **option** is a contract that gives its owner the right to buy (or sell) an asset at some predetermined price within a specified period of time. However, there are many types of options and option markets.[1] Consider the options reported in Table 8-1, which is an extract from a Listed Options Quotations table as it might appear on a Web site or in a daily newspaper. The first column reports the closing

[1]For an in-depth treatment of options, see Don M. Chance, *An Introduction to Derivatives and Risk Management* (Mason, OH: Thomson/South-Western, 2007), or John C. Hull, *Options, Futures, and Other Derivatives*, 7th ed. (Upper Saddle River, NJ: Prentice-Hall, 2009).

TABLE 8-1 Listed Options Quotations for January 8, 2010

CLOSING PRICE	STRIKE PRICE	CALLS—LAST QUOTE			PUTS—LAST QUOTE		
		FEBRUARY	MARCH	MAY	FEBRUARY	MARCH	MAY
General Computer Corporation (GCC)							
53.50	50	4.25	4.75	5.50	0.65	1.40	2.20
53.50	55	1.30	2.05	3.15	2.65	r	4.50
53.50	60	0.30	0.70	1.50	6.65	r	8.00

Note: r means not traded on January 8.

stock price. For example, the table shows that General Computer Corporation's (GCC) stock price closed at $53.50 on January 8, 2010.

A **call option** gives its owner the right to *buy* a share of stock at a fixed price, which is called the **strike price** (sometimes called the **exercise price** because it is the price at which you exercise the option). A **put option** gives its owner the right to *sell* a share of stock at a fixed strike price. For example, the first row in Table 8-1 is for GCC's options that have a $50 strike price. Observe that the table has columns for call options and for put options with this strike price.

Each option has an **expiration date**, after which the option may not be exercised. Table 8-1 reports data for options that expire in February, March, and May (the expiration date is the Friday before the third Saturday of the exercise month). If the option can be exercised any time before the expiration, then it is called an **American option**; if it can be exercised only on its expiration date, it is a **European option**. All of GCC's options are American options. The first row shows that GCC has a call option with a strike price of $50 that expires on May 14 (the third Saturday in May 2010 is the 15th). The quoted price for this option is $5.50.[2]

When the current stock price is greater than the strike price, the option is **in-the-money**. For example, GCC's $50 (strike) May call option is in-the-money by $53.50 − $50 = $3.50. Thus, if the option were immediately exercised, it would have a payoff of $3.50. On the other hand, GCC's $55 (strike) May call is **out-of-the-money** because the current $53.50 stock price is below the $55 strike price. Obviously, you currently would not want to exercise this option by paying the $55 strike price for a share of stock selling for $53.50. Therefore, the **exercise value**, which is any profit from immediately exercising an option, is[3]

$$\text{Exercise value} = \text{MAX}[\text{Current price of the stock} - \text{Strike price}, 0] \tag{8-1}$$

An option's price always will be greater than (or equal to) its exercise value. If the option's price were less, you could buy the option and immediately exercise it, reaping a sure gain. For example, GCC's May call with a $50 strike price sells for $5.50, which is greater than its exercise value of $3.50. Also, GCC's out-of-the-money May call with a strike price of $55 sells for $3.15 even though it would be worthless if it had to be exercised immediately. An option always will be worth more than zero as

[2]Option contracts are generally written in 100-share multiples, but we focus on the cost and payoffs of a single option.

[3]MAX means choose the maximum. For example, MAX[15, 0] = 15 and MAX[−10, 0] = 0.

long as there is still any chance at all that it will end up in-the-money: Where there is life, there is hope! The difference between the option's price and its exercise value is called the **time value** because it represents the extra amount over the option's immediate exercise value that a purchaser will pay for the chance the stock price will appreciate over time.[4] For example, GCC's May call with a $50 strike price sells for $5.50 and has an exercise value of $3.50, so its time value is $5.50 – $3.50 = $2.00.

Suppose you bought GCC's $50 (strike) May call option for $5.50 and then the stock price increased to $60. If you exercised the option by purchasing the stock for the $50 strike price, you could immediately sell the share of stock at its market price of $60, resulting in a payoff of $60 – $50 = $10. Notice that the stock itself had a return of 12.1% = ($60 – $53.50)/$53.50, but the option's return was 81.8% = ($10 – $5.50)/$5.50. Thus, the option offers the possibility of a higher return.

However, if the stock price fell to $50 and stayed there until the option expired, the stock would have a return of –6.5% = ($50.00 – $53.50)/$53.50, but the option would have a 100% loss (it would expire worthless). As this example shows, call options are a lot riskier than stocks. This works to your advantage if the stock price goes up but to your disadvantage if the stock price falls.

Suppose you bought GCC's May put option (with a strike price of $50) for $2.20 and then the stock price fell to $45. You could buy a share of stock for $45 and exercise the put option, which would allow you to sell the share of stock at its strike price of $50. Your payoff from exercising the put would be $5 = $50 – $45. Stockholders would lose money because the stock price fell, but a put holder would make money. In this example, your rate of return would be 127.3% = ($5 – $2.20)/$2.20. So if you think a stock price is going to fall, you can make money by purchasing a put option. On the other hand, if the stock price doesn't fall below the strike price of $50 before the put expires, you would lose 100% of your investment in the put option.[5]

Options are traded on a number of exchanges, with the Chicago Board Options Exchange (CBOE) being the oldest and the largest. Existing options can be traded in the secondary market in much the same way that existing shares of stock are traded in secondary markets. But unlike new shares of stock that are issued by corporations, new options can be "issued" by investors. This is called **writing** an option.

For example, you could write a call option and sell it to some other investor. You would receive cash from the option buyer at the time you wrote the option, but you would be obligated to sell a share of stock at the strike price if the option buyer later decided to exercise the option.[6] Thus, each option has two parties, the writer and the buyer, with the CBOE (or some other exchange) acting as an intermediary. Other than commissions, the writer's profits are exactly opposite those of the buyer. An investor who writes call options against stock held in his or her portfolio is said to be selling **covered options**. Options sold without the stock to back them up are called **naked options**.

WWW

The Chicago Board Options Exchange provides 20-minute delayed quotes for equity, index, and LEAPS options at **http://www.cboe.com**.

In addition to options on individual stocks, options are also available on several stock indexes such as the NYSE Index and the S&P 100 Index. Index options permit one to hedge (or bet) on a rise or fall in the general market as well as on individual stocks.

---

[4]Among traders, an option's market price is also called its "premium." This is particularly confusing since for all other securities the word *premium* means the excess of the market price over some base price. To avoid confusion, we will not use the word *premium* to refer to the option price.

[5]Most investors don't actually exercise an option prior to expiration. If they want to cash in the option's profit or cut its losses, they sell the option to some other investor. As you will see later in the chapter, the cash flow from selling the option before its expiration is always greater than (or equal to) the profit from exercising the option.

[6]Your broker would require collateral to ensure that you kept this obligation.

Financial Reporting for Employee Stock Options

When granted to executives and other employees, options are a "hybrid" form of compensation. At some companies, especially small ones, option grants may be a substitute for cash wages: employees are willing to take lower cash salaries if they have options. Options also provide an incentive for employees to work harder. Whether issued to motivate employees or to conserve cash, options clearly have value at the time they are granted, and they transfer wealth from existing shareholders to employees to the extent that they do not reduce cash expenditures or increase employee productivity enough to offset their value at the time of issue.

Companies like the fact that an option grant requires no immediate cash expenditure, although it might dilute shareholder wealth if later it is exercised. Employees, and especially CEOs, like the potential wealth that they receive when they are granted options. When option grants were relatively small, they didn't show up on investors' radar screens. However, as the high-tech sector began making mega-grants in the 1990s, and as other industries followed suit in the heavy use of options, stockholders began to realize that large grants were making some CEOs filthy rich at the stockholders' expense.

Before 2005, option grants were barely visible in companies' financial reports. Even though such grants are clearly a wealth transfer to employees, companies were required only to footnote the grants and could ignore them when reporting their income statements and balance sheets. The Financial Accounting Standards Board now requires companies to show option grants as an expense on the income statement. To do this, the value of the options is estimated at the time of the grant and then expensed during the vesting period, which is the amount of time the employee must wait before being allowed to exercise the options. For example, if the initial value is $100 million and the vesting period is 2 years, the company would report a $50 million expense for each of the next 2 years. This approach isn't perfect, because the grant is not a cash expense; nor does the approach take into account changes in the option's value after the initial grant. However, it does make the option grant more visible to investors, which is a good thing.

The leverage involved in option trading makes it possible for speculators with just a few dollars to make a fortune almost overnight. Also, investors with sizable portfolios can sell options against their stocks and earn the value of the option (less brokerage commissions) even if the stock's price remains constant. Most important, though, options can be used to create *hedges* that protect the value of an individual stock or portfolio.[7]

Conventional options are generally written for 6 months or less, but a type of option called a **Long-Term Equity AnticiPation Security (LEAPS)** is different. Like conventional options, LEAPS are listed on exchanges and are available on both individual stocks and stock indexes. The major difference is that LEAPS are long-term options, having maturities of up to almost 3 years. One-year LEAPS cost about twice as much as the matching 3-month option, but because of their much longer time to expiration, LEAPS provide buyers with more potential for gains and offer better long-term protection for a portfolio.

Corporations on whose stocks the options are written have nothing to do with the option market. Corporations do not raise money in the option market, nor do they have any direct transactions in it. Moreover, option holders do not vote for corporate directors or receive dividends. There have been studies by the SEC and others as to

[7]Insiders who trade illegally generally buy options rather than stock because the leverage inherent in options increases the profit potential. However, it is illegal to use insider information for personal gain, and an insider using such information would be taking advantage of the option seller. Insider trading, in addition to being unfair and essentially equivalent to stealing, hurts the economy: Investors lose confidence in the capital markets and raise their required returns because of an increased element of risk, and this raises the cost of capital and thus reduces the level of real investment.

whether option trading stabilizes or destabilizes the stock market and whether this activity helps or hinders corporations seeking to raise new capital. The studies have not been conclusive, but research on the impact of option trading is ongoing.

Self-Test

What is an option? A call option? A put option?

Define a call option's exercise value. Why is the market price of a call option usually above its exercise value?

Brighton Memory's stock is currently trading at $50 a share. A call option on the stock with a $35 strike price currently sells for $21. What is the exercise value of the call option? **($15.00)** What is the time value? **($6.00)**

8.2 The Single-Period Binomial Option Pricing Approach

We can use a model like the Capital Asset Pricing Model (CAPM) to calculate the required return on a stock and then use that required return to discount its expected future cash flows to find its value. No such model exists for the required return on options, so we must use a different approach to find an option's value. In Section 8.5 we describe the Black-Scholes option pricing model, but in this section we explain the binomial option pricing model. The idea behind this model is different from that of the DCF model used for stock valuation. Instead of discounting cash flows at a required return to obtain a price, as we did with the stock valuation model, we will use the option, shares of stock, and the risk-free rate to construct a portfolio whose value we already know and then deduce the option's price from this portfolio's value.

The following sections describe and apply the binomial option pricing model to Western Cellular, a manufacturer of cell phones. Call options exist that permit the holder to buy 1 share of Western at a strike price, X, of $35. Western's options will expire at the end of 6 months (t is the number of years until expiration, so t = 0.5 for Western's options).Western's stock price, P, is currently $40 per share. Given this background information, we will use the binomial model to determine the call option's value. The first step is to determine the option's possible payoffs, as described in the next section.

Payoffs in a Single-Period Binomial Model

In general, the time until expiration can be divided into many periods, with n denoting the number of periods. But in a single-period model, which we describe in this section, there is only one period. We assume that, at the end of the period, the stock's price can take on only one of two possible values, so this is called the **binomial approach**. For this example, Western's stock will either go up (u) by a factor of 1.25 or go down (d) by a factor of 0.80. If we were considering a riskier stock, then we would have assumed a wider range of ending prices; we will show how to estimate this range later in the chapter. If we let u = 1.25 and d = 0.80, then the ending stock price will be either P(u) = $40(1.25) = $50 or P(d) = $40(0.80) = $32. Figure 8-1 illustrates the stock's possible price paths and contains additional information about the call option that is explained in what follows.

When the option expires at the end of the year, Western's stock will sell for either $50 or $32. As shown in Figure 8-1, if the stock goes up to $50 then the option will have a payoff, C_u, of $15 at expiration because the option is in-the-money: $50 – $35 = $15. If the stock price goes down to $32 then the option's payoff, C_d, will be zero because the option is out-of-the-money.

FIGURE 8-1 Binomial Payoffs from Holding Western Cellular's Stock or Call Option

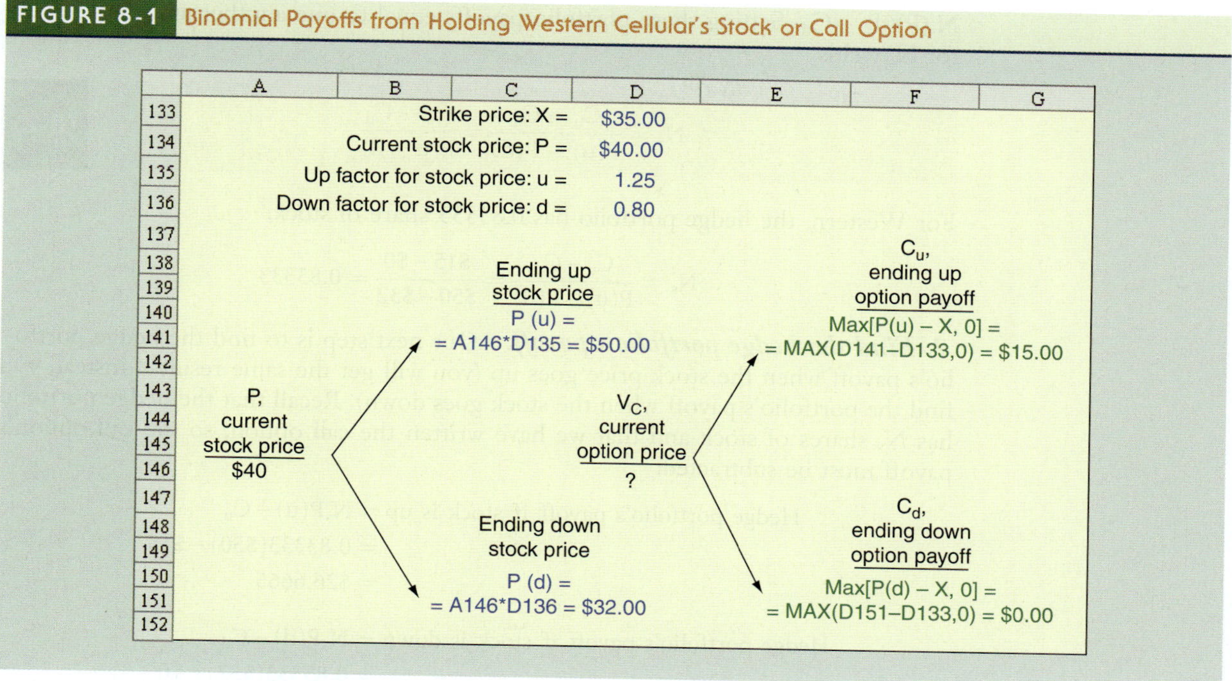

The Hedge Portfolio Approach

Suppose we created a portfolio by writing 1 call option and purchasing 1 share of stock. As Figure 8-1 shows, if the stock price goes up then our portfolio's stock will be worth \$50 but we will owe \$15 on the option, so our portfolio's net payoff is \$35 = \$50 − \$15. If the stock price goes down then our portfolio's stock will be worth only \$32, but the amount we owe on the written option also will fall to zero, leaving the portfolio's net payoff at \$32. The portfolio's end-of-period price range is smaller than if we had just owned the stock, so writing the call option reduces the portfolio's price risk. Taking this further: Is it possible for us to choose the number of shares held by our portfolio so that it will have the same net payoff whether the stock goes up or down? If so, then our portfolio is hedged and will have a riskless payoff when the option expires. Therefore, it is called a **hedge portfolio**.

We are not really interested in investing in the hedge portfolio, but we want to use it to help us determine the value of the option. Notice that if the hedge portfolio has a riskless net payoff when the option expires, then we can find the present value of this payoff by discounting it at the risk-free rate. Our current portfolio value must equal this present value, which allows us to determine the option's value. The following example illustrates the steps in this approach.

1. Find N_s, the number of shares of stock in the hedge portfolio. We want the portfolio's payoff to be the same whether the stock goes up or down. If we write 1 call option and buy N_s shares of stock, then the portfolio's stock will be worth $N_s(P)(u)$ should the stock price go up, so its net payoff will be $N_s(P)(u) - C_u$. The portfolio's stock will be worth $N_s(P)(d)$ if the stock price goes down, so its net payoff will be

$N_s(P)(d) - C_d$. Setting these portfolio payoffs equal to one another and then solving for N_s yields

$$N_s = \frac{C_u - C_d}{P(u) - P(d)} = \frac{C_u - C_d}{P(u - d)} \tag{8-2}$$

For Western, the hedge portfolio has 0.83333 share of stock:[8]

$$N_s = \frac{C_u - C_d}{P(u) - P(d)} = \frac{\$15 - \$0}{\$50 - \$32} = 0.83333$$

2. Find the hedge portfolio's payoff. Our next step is to find the hedge portfolio's payoff when the stock price goes up (you will get the same result if instead you find the portfolio's payoff when the stock goes down). Recall that the hedge portfolio has N_s shares of stock and that we have written the call option, so the call option's payoff must be subtracted:

$$\begin{aligned}\text{Hedge portfolio's payoff if stock is up} &= N_sP(u) - C_u \\ &= 0.83333(\$50) - \$15 \\ &= \$26.6665\end{aligned}$$

$$\begin{aligned}\text{Hedge portfolio's payoff if stock is down} &= N_sP(d) - C_d \\ &= 0.83333(\$32) - \$0 \\ &= \$26.6665\end{aligned}$$

Figure 8-2 illustrates the payoffs of the hedge portfolio.

3. Find the present value of the hedge portfolio's payoff. Because the hedge portfolio's payoff is riskless, the current value of the hedge portfolio must be equal to the present value of its riskless payoff. Option pricing models usually assume continuous compounding, which we discuss in ***Web Extension 4C*** on the textbook's Web site, but daily compounding works well. For a 1-period model, the time to expiration also is the time until the payoff occurs. In a later section we consider more than 1 period prior to expiration, so the time that we discount the payoff is equal to the time until expiration (t) divided by the number of periods until expiration (n). In our example, t = 0.5 and n = 1. Therefore, the present value of the hedge portfolio's payoff is

$$\begin{aligned}\text{PV of riskless payoff} &= \frac{\$26.6665}{\left(1 + \frac{r_{RF}}{365}\right)^{365(t/n)}} = \frac{\$26.6665}{\left(1 + \frac{0.08}{365}\right)^{365(0.5/1)}} \\ &= \$25.621\end{aligned}$$

4. Find the option's value. The current value of the hedge portfolio is the value of the stock, $N_s(P)$, less the value of the call option we wrote. Because the payoff is riskless, the current value of the hedge portfolio must also equal the present value of the riskless payoff:

$$\text{Current value of hedge portfolio} = N_sP - V_c = \text{Present value of riskless payoff}$$

[8]An easy way to remember this formula is to notice that N_s is equal to the range in possible option payoffs divided by the range in possible stock prices.

FIGURE 8-2 Hedge Portfolio with Riskless Payoffs

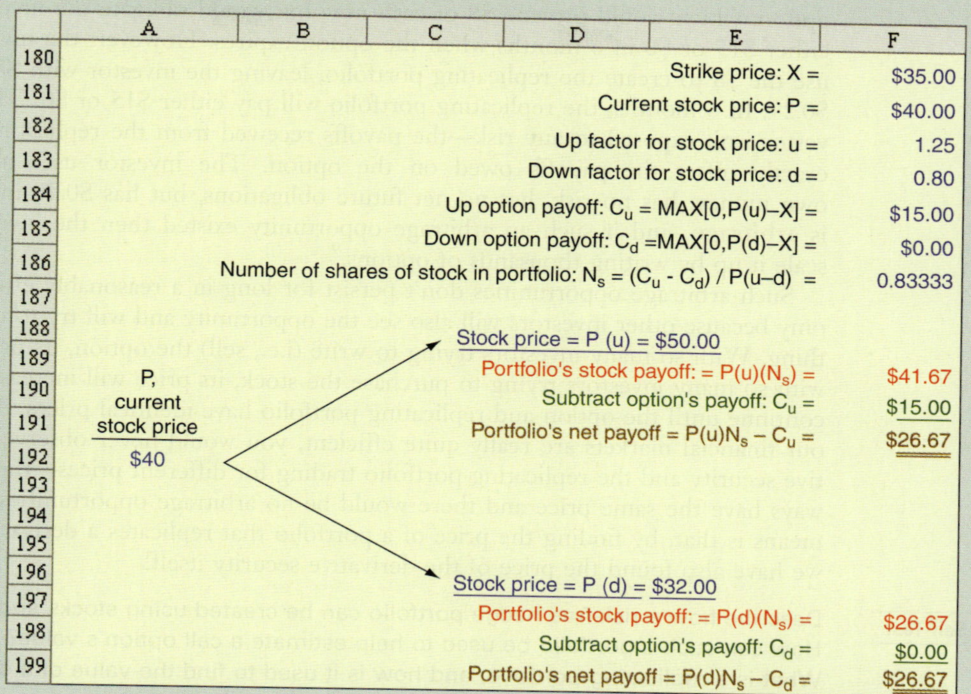

	A	B	C	D	E	F
180					Strike price: X =	$35.00
181					Current stock price: P =	$40.00
182					Up factor for stock price: u =	1.25
183					Down factor for stock price: d =	0.80
184					Up option payoff: C_u = MAX[0,P(u)–X] =	$15.00
185					Down option payoff: C_d =MAX[0,P(d)–X] =	$0.00
186					Number of shares of stock in portfolio: N_s = (C_u - C_d) / P(u–d) =	0.83333
187						
188				Stock price = P (u) = $50.00		
189	P,				Portfolio's stock payoff: = P(u)(N_s) =	$41.67
190	current				Subtract option's payoff: C_u =	$15.00
191	stock price				Portfolio's net payoff = P(u)N_s – C_u =	$26.67
192	$40					
193						
194						
195						
196				Stock price = P (d) = $32.00		
197					Portfolio's stock payoff: = P(d)(N_s) =	$26.67
198					Subtract option's payoff: C_d =	$0.00
199					Portfolio's net payoff = P(d)N_s – C_d =	$26.67

See **Ch08 Tool Kit.xls** on the textbook's Web site.

Solving for the call option's value, we get

$$V_C = N_sP - \begin{matrix}\text{Present value of}\\ \text{riskless payoff}\end{matrix}$$

For Western's option, this is

$$\begin{aligned} V_C &= 0.83333(\$40) - \$25.621 \\ &= \$7.71 \end{aligned}$$

Hedge Portfolios and Replicating Portfolios

In our previous derivation of the call option's value, we combined an investment in the stock with writing a call option to create a risk-free investment. We can modify this approach and create a portfolio that replicates the call option's payoffs. For example, suppose we formed a portfolio by purchasing 0.83333 shares of Western's stock and borrowing $25.621 at the risk-free rate (this is equivalent to selling a T-bill short). In 6 months we would repay $\$25.621(1 + 0.08/365)^{365(0.5/1)} = \$26.6665$. If the stock goes up, our net payoff would be 0.83333($50) – $26.6665 = $15.00. If the stock goes down, our net payoff would be 0.83333($32) – $26.6665 = $0. The portfolio's payoffs are exactly equal to the option's payoffs as shown in Figure 8-1, so our portfolio of 0.83333 shares of stock and the $25.621 that we borrowed would exactly replicate the option's payoffs. Therefore, this is called a **replicating portfolio**. Our cost to create this portfolio is the cost of the stock less the amount we borrowed:

$$\text{Cost of replicating portfolio} = 0.83333(\$40) - \$25.621 = \$7.71$$

If the call option did not sell for exactly $7.71, then a clever investor could make a sure profit. For example, suppose the option sold for $8. The investor would write an option, which would provide $8 of cash now but would obligate the investor to pay either $15 or $0 in 6 months when the option expires. However, the investor could use the $8 to create the replicating portfolio, leaving the investor with $8 – $7.71 = $0.29. In 6 months, the replicating portfolio will pay either $15 or $0. Thus, the investor isn't exposed to any risk—the payoffs received from the replicating portfolio exactly offset the payoffs owed on the option. The investor uses none of his own money, has no risk, has no net future obligations, but has $0.29 in cash. This is **arbitrage**, and if such an arbitrage opportunity existed then the investor would scale it up by writing thousands of options.[9]

Such arbitrage opportunities don't persist for long in a reasonably efficient economy because other investors will also see the opportunity and will try to do the same thing. With so many investors trying to write (i.e., sell) the option, its price will fall; with so many investors trying to purchase the stock, its price will increase. This will continue until the option and replicating portfolio have identical prices. And because our financial markets are really quite efficient, you would never observe the derivative security and the replicating portfolio trading for different prices—they would always have the same price and there would be no arbitrage opportunities. What this means is that, by finding the price of a portfolio that replicates a derivative security, we have also found the price of the derivative security itself!

Self-Test

Describe how a risk-free hedge portfolio can be created using stocks and options. How can such a portfolio be used to help estimate a call option's value?

What is a replicating portfolio, and how is it used to find the value of a derivative security?

What is arbitrage?

Lett Incorporated's stock price is now $50, but it is expected either to rise by a factor of 1.5 or fall by a factor of 0.7 by the end of the year. There is a call option on Lett's stock with a strike price of $55 and an expiration date 1 year from now. What are the stock's possible prices at the end of the year? **($75 or $35)** What is the call option's payoff if the stock price goes up? **($20)** If the stock price goes down? **($0)** If we sell one call option, how many shares of Lett's stock must we buy to create a riskless hedged portfolio consisting of the option position and the stock? **(0.5)** What is the payoff of this portfolio? **($17.50)** If the annual risk free rate is 6%, then how much is the riskless portfolio worth today (assuming daily compounding)? **($16.48)** What is the current value of the call option? **($8.52)**

8.3 The Single-Period Binomial Option Pricing Formula[10]

The hedge portfolio approach works well if you only want to find the value of one type of option with one period until expiration. But in all other situations, the step-by-step approach becomes tedious very quickly. The following sections describe a formula that replaces the step-by-step approach.

---

[9]If the option sold for less than the replicating portfolio, the investor would raise cash by shorting the portfolio and use the cash to purchase the option, again resulting in arbitrage profits.

[10]The material in this section is relatively technical, and some instructors may choose to skip it with no loss in continuity.

The Binomial Option Pricing Formula

With a little (or a lot!) of algebra, we can derive a single formula for a call option. After programming it into *Excel,* which we did for this chapter's ***Tool Kit***, it is easy to change inputs and determine the new value of a call option. Here is the binomial option pricing formula:

$$V_C = \frac{C_u\left[\frac{(1 + r_{RF}/365)^{365(t/n)} - d}{u - d}\right] + C_d\left[\frac{u - (1 + r_{RF}/365)^{365(t/n)}}{u - d}\right]}{(1 + r_{RF}/365)^{365(t/n)}} \tag{8-3}$$

We can apply this formula to Western's call option:

$$V_C = \frac{\$15\left[\frac{(1 + 0.08/365)^{365(0.5/1)} - 0.80}{1.25 - 0.80}\right] + \$0\left[\frac{1.25 - (1 + 0.08/365)^{365(0.5/1)}}{1.25 - 0.80}\right]}{(1 + 0.08/365)^{365(0.5/1)}}$$

$$= \frac{\$15(0.5351) + \$0(0.2092)}{1.040806} = \$7.71$$

Notice that this is the same value that resulted from the step-by-step process shown earlier.

The binomial option pricing formula in Equation 8-3 does not include the actual probabilities that the stock will go up or down, nor does it include the expected stock return, which is not what one might expect. After all, the higher the stock's expected return, the greater the chance that the call will be in-the-money at expiration. Note, however, that the stock's expected return is already indirectly incorporated into the stock price.

If we want to value other Western call options or puts that expire in 6 months, then we can again use Equation 8-3. Observe that for options with the same time left until expiration, C_u and C_d are the only variables that depend on the option itself. The other variables depend only on the stock process (u and d), the risk-free rate, the time until expiration, and the number of periods until expiration. If we group these variables together, we can then define π_u and π_d as

$$\pi_u = \frac{\left[\frac{(1 + r_{RF}/365)^{365(t/n)} - d}{u - d}\right]}{(1 + r_{RF}/365)^{365(t/n)}} \tag{8-4}$$

and

$$\pi_d = \frac{\left[\frac{u - (1 + r_{RF}/365)^{365(t/n)}}{u - d}\right]}{(1 + r_{RF}/365)^{365(t/n)}} \tag{8-5}$$

By substituting these values into Equation 8-3, we obtain an option pricing model that can be applied to all of Western's 6-month options:

$$V_C = C_u\pi_u + C_d\pi_d \tag{8-6}$$

In this example, π_u and π_d are

$$\pi_u = \frac{\left[\dfrac{(1+0.08/365)^{365(0.5/1)} - 0.80}{1.25 - 0.80}\right]}{(1+0.08/365)^{365(0.5/1)}} = 0.5141$$

and

$$\pi_d = \frac{\left[\dfrac{1.25 - (1+0.08/365)^{365(0.5/1)}}{1.25 - 0.80}\right]}{(1+0.08/365)^{365(0.5/1)}} = 0.4466$$

Using Equation 8-6, the value of Western's 6-month call option with a strike price of $35 is

$$\begin{aligned} V_c &= C_u\pi_u + C_d\pi_d \\ &= \$15(0.5141) + \$0(0.4466) \\ &= \$7.71 \end{aligned}$$

Sometimes these π's are called *primitive securities* because π_u is the price of a simple security that pays $1 if the stock goes up and nothing if it goes down; π_u is the opposite. This means that we can use these π's to find the price of any 6-month option on Western. For example, suppose we want to find the value of a 6-month call option on Western but with a strike price of $30. Rather than reinvent the wheel, all we have to do is find the payoffs of this option and use the same values of π_u and π_d in Equation 8-6. If the stock goes up to $50, the option will pay $50 – $30 = $20; if the stock falls to $32, the option will pay $32 – $30 = $2. The value of the call option is:

$$\begin{aligned} \text{Value of 6-month call with \$30 strike price} &= C_u\pi_u + C_d\pi_d \\ &= \$20(0.5141) + \$2(0.4466) \\ &= \$11.18 \end{aligned}$$

It is a bit tedious initially to calculate π_u and π_d, but once you save them it is easy to find the value of any 6-month call or put option on the stock. In fact, you can use these π's to find the value of any security with payoffs that depend on Western's 6-month stock prices, which makes them a very powerful tool.

Self-Test

Yegi's Fine Phones has a current stock price of $30. You need to find the value of a call option with a strike price of $32 that expires in 3 months. Use the binomial model with one period until expiration. The factor for an increase in stock price is u = 1.15; the factor for a downward movement is d = 0.85. What are the possible stock prices at expiration? **($34.50 or $25.50)** What are the option's possible payoffs at expiration? **($2.50 or $0)** What are π_u and π_d? **(0.5422 and 0.4429)** What is the current value of the option (assume each month is 1/12 of a year)? **($1.36)**

8.4 The Multi-Period Binomial Option Pricing Model[11]

Clearly, this example is simplified. Although you could duplicate buying 0.8333 share and writing one option by buying 8,333 shares and writing 10,000 options, the stock price assumptions are unrealistic—Western's stock price could be almost anything

[11]The material in this section is relatively technical, and some instructors may choose to skip it with no loss in continuity.

after 6 months, not just \$50 or \$32. However, if we allowed the stock to move up or down more often, then a more realistic range of ending prices would result. In other words, dividing the time until expiration into more periods would improve the realism of the resulting prices at expiration. The key to implementing a multi-period binomial model is to keep the stock return's annual standard deviation the same no matter how many periods you have during a year. In fact, analysts typically begin with an estimate of the standard deviation and use it to determine u and d. The derivation is beyond the scope of a financial management textbook, but the appropriate equations are

$$u = e^{\sigma\sqrt{t/n}} \tag{8-7}$$

$$d = \frac{1}{u} \tag{8-8}$$

where σ is the annualized standard deviation of the stock's return, t is the time in years until expiration, and n is the number of periods until expiration.

The standard deviation of Western's stock returns is 31.5573%, and application of Equations 8-7 and 8-8 confirms the values of u and d that we used previously:

$$u = e^{0.315573\sqrt{0.5/1}} = 1.25 \text{ and } d = \frac{1}{1.25} = 0.80$$

Now suppose we allow stock prices to change every 3 months (which is 0.25 years). Using Equations 8-7 and 8-8, we estimate u and d to be

$$u = e^{0.315573\sqrt{0.5/2}} = 1.1709 \text{ and } d = \frac{1}{1.1709} = 0.8540$$

At the end of the first 3 months, Western's price would either rise to \$40(1.1709) = \$46.84 or fall to \$40(0.8540) = \$34.16. If the price rises in the first 3 months to \$46.84, then it would either go up to \$46.84(1.1709) = \$54.84 or go down to \$46.84(0.8540) = \$40 at expiration. If instead the price initially falls to \$40(0.8540) = \$34.16 during the first 3 months, then it would either go up to \$34.16(1.1709) = \$40 or go down to \$34.16(0.8540) = \$29.17 by expiration. This pattern of stock price movements is called a **binomial lattice** and is shown in Figure 8-3.

Because the interest rate and the volatility (as defined by u and d) are constant for each period, we can calculate π_u and π_d for any period and apply these same values for each period:[12]

$$\pi_u = \frac{\left[\frac{(1+0.08/365)^{365(0.5/2)} - 0.8540}{1.1709 - 0.8540}\right]}{(1+0.08/365)^{365(0.5/2)}} = 0.51400$$

$$\pi_d = \frac{\left[\frac{1.1709 - (1+0.08/365)^{365(0.5/2)}}{1.1709 - 0.8540}\right]}{(1+0.08/365)^{365(0.5/2)}} = 0.46621$$

[12]These values were calculated in *Excel*, so there may be small differences due to rounding in intermediate steps.

FIGURE 8-3 Two-Period Binomial Lattice and Option Valuation

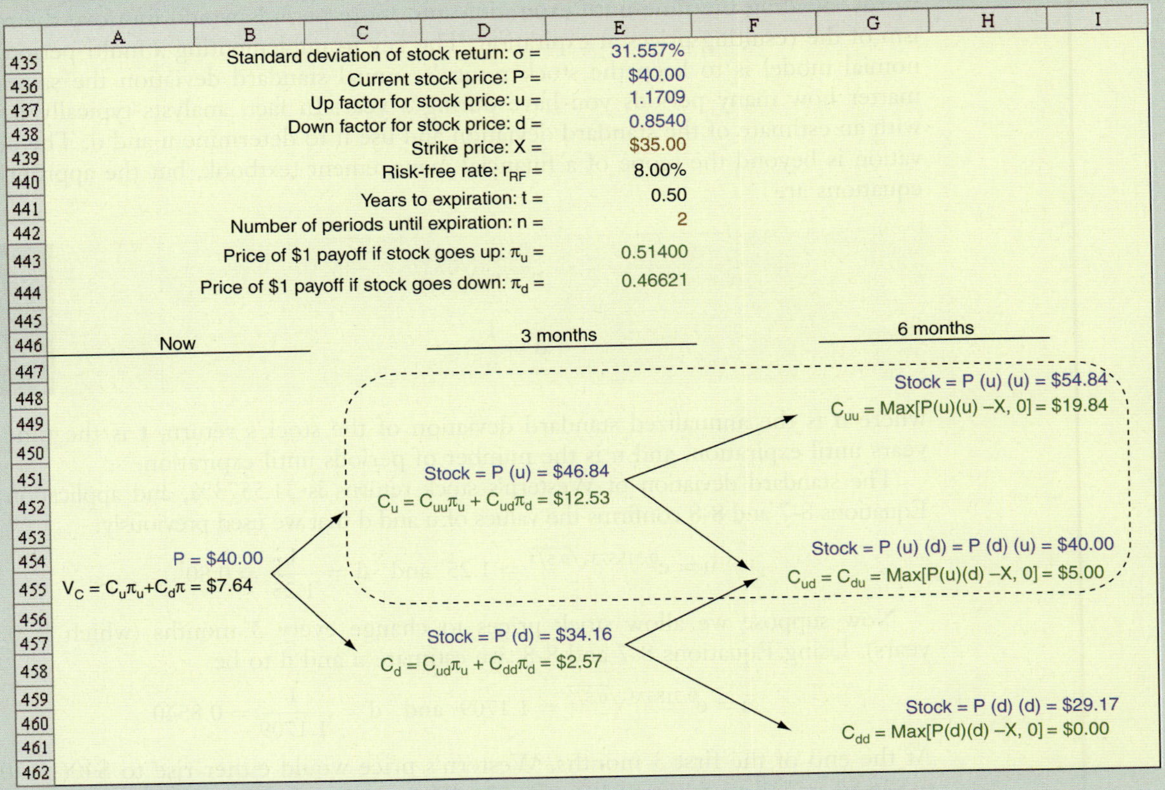

	A	B	C	D	E	F	G	H	I
435		Standard deviation of stock return: σ =			31.557%				
436		Current stock price: P =			\$40.00				
437		Up factor for stock price: u =			1.1709				
438		Down factor for stock price: d =			0.8540				
439		Strike price: X =			\$35.00				
440		Risk-free rate: r_{RF} =			8.00%				
441		Years to expiration: t =			0.50				
442		Number of periods until expiration: n =			2				
443		Price of \$1 payoff if stock goes up: π_u =			0.51400				
444		Price of \$1 payoff if stock goes down: π_d =			0.46621				

Now | 3 months | 6 months

Stock = P (u) (u) = \$54.84
C_{uu} = Max[P(u)(u) −X, 0] = \$19.84

Stock = P (u) = \$46.84
$C_u = C_{uu}\pi_u + C_{ud}\pi_d$ = \$12.53

P = \$40.00
$V_C = C_u\pi_u + C_d\pi$ = \$7.64

Stock = P (u) (d) = P (d) (u) = \$40.00
$C_{ud} = C_{du}$ = Max[P(u)(d) −X, 0] = \$5.00

Stock = P (d) = \$34.16
$C_d = C_{ud}\pi_u + C_{dd}\pi_d$ = \$2.57

Stock = P (d) (d) = \$29.17
C_{dd} = Max[P(d)(d) −X, 0] = \$0.00

These values are shown in Figure 8-3.

The lattice shows the possible stock prices at the option's expiration and we know the strike price, so we can calculate the option payoffs at expiration. Figure 8-3 also shows the option payoffs at expiration. If we focus only on the upper right portion of the lattice shown inside the dotted lines, then it is similar to the single-period problem we solved in Section 8.3. In fact, we can use the binomial option pricing model from Equation 8-6 to determine the value of the option in 3 months given that the stock price increased to \$46.84. As shown in Figure 8-3, the option will be worth \$12.53 in 3 months if the stock price goes up to \$46.84. We can repeat this procedure on the lower right portion of Figure 8-3 to determine the call option's value in 3 months if the stock price falls to \$34.16; in this case, the call's value would be \$2.57. Finally, we can use Equation 8-6 and the 3-month option values just calculated to determine the current price of the option, which is \$7.64. Thus, we are able to find the current option price by solving three simple binomial problems.

If we broke the year into smaller periods and allowed the stock price to move up or down more often, then the lattice would have an even more realistic range of possible ending stock prices. Of course, estimating the current option price would require solving lots of binomial problems within the lattice, but each problem is simple and computers can solve them rapidly. With more outcomes, the resulting estimated option price is more accurate. For example, if we divide the year into 15 periods then the estimated price is $7.42. With 50 periods, the price is $7.39. With 100 periods it is still $7.39, which shows that the solution converges to its final value within a relatively small number of steps. In fact, as we break the time to expiration into smaller and smaller periods, the solution for the binomial approach converges to the Black-Scholes solution, which is described in the next section.

The binomial approach is widely used to value options with more complicated payoffs than the call option in our example, such as employee stock options. This is beyond the scope of a financial management textbook, but if you are interested in learning more about the binomial approach then you should take a look at the textbooks by Don Chance and John Hull cited in footnote 1.

Self-Test

Ringling Cycle's stock price is now $20. You need to find the value of a call option with a strike price of $22 that expires in 2 months. You want to use the binomial model with 2 periods (each period is a month). Your assistant has calculated that u = 1.1553, d = 0.8656, π_u = 0.4838, and π_d = 0.5095. Draw the binomial lattice for stock prices. What are the possible prices after 1 month? **($23.11 or $17.31)** After 2 months? **($26.69, $20, or $14.99)** What are the option's possible payoffs at expiration? **($4.69, $0, or $0)** What will the option's value be in 1 month if the stock goes up? **($2.27)** What will the option's value be in 1 month if the stock price goes down? **($0)** What is the current value of the option (assume each month is 1/12 of a year)? **($1.10)**

8.5 The Black-Scholes Option Pricing Model (OPM)

The **Black-Scholes option pricing model (OPM)**, developed in 1973, helped give rise to the rapid growth in options trading. This model, which has even been programmed into some handheld and Web-based calculators, is widely used by option traders.

OPM Assumptions and Equations

In deriving their option pricing model, Fischer Black and Myron Scholes made the following assumptions.

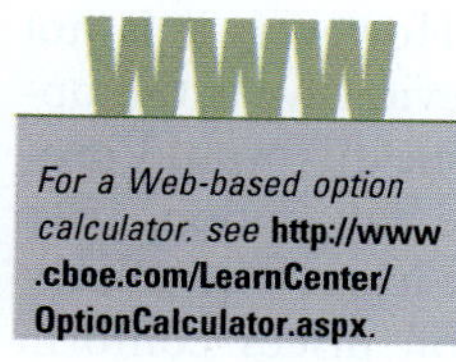

For a Web-based option calculator. see **http://www.cboe.com/LearnCenter/OptionCalculator.aspx.**

1. The stock underlying the call option provides no dividends or other distributions during the life of the option.
2. There are no transaction costs for buying or selling either the stock or the option.
3. The short-term, risk-free interest rate is known and is constant during the life of the option.
4. Any purchaser of a security may borrow any fraction of the purchase price at the short-term, risk-free interest rate.
5. Short selling is permitted, and the short seller will receive immediately the full cash proceeds of today's price for a security sold short.
6. The call option can be exercised only on its expiration date.
7. Trading in all securities takes place continuously, and the stock price moves randomly.

The derivation of the Black-Scholes model rests on the same concepts as the binomial model, except time is divided into such small increments that stock prices change continuously. The Black-Scholes model consists of the following three equations:

$$V_C = P[N(d_1)] - Xe^{-r_{RF}t}[N(d_2)] \tag{8-9}$$

$$d_1 = \frac{\ln(P/X) + [r_{RF} + (\sigma^2/2)]t}{\sigma\sqrt{t}} \tag{8-10}$$

$$d_2 = d_1 - \sigma\sqrt{t} \tag{8-11}$$

The variables used in the Black-Scholes model are explained below.

V_C = Current value of the call option.

P = Current price of the underlying stock.

$N(d_i)$ = Probability that a deviation less than d_i will occur in a standard normal distribution. Thus, $N(d_1)$ and $N(d_2)$ represent areas under a standard normal distribution function.

X = Strike price of the option.

$e \approx 2.7183$.

r_{RF} = Risk-free interest rate.[13]

t = Time until the option expires (the option period).

$\ln(P/X)$ = Natural logarithm of P/X.

σ = Standard deviation of the rate of return on the stock.

WWW

Robert's Online Option Pricer can be accessed at **http://www.intrepid.com/robertl/index.html**. *The site is designed to provide a financial service over the Internet to small investors for option pricing, giving anyone a means to price option trades without having to buy expensive software and hardware.*

The value of the option is a function of five variables: (1) P, the stock's price; (2) t, the option's time to expiration; (3) X, the strike price; (4) σ, the standard deviation of the underlying stock; and (5) r_{RF}, the risk-free rate. We do not derive the Black-Scholes model—the derivation involves some extremely complicated mathematics that go far beyond the scope of this text. However, it is not difficult to use the model. Under the assumptions set forth previously, if the option price is different from the one found by Equation 8-9, then this would provide the opportunity for arbitrage profits, which would force the option price back to the value indicated by the model.[14] As we noted earlier, the Black-Scholes model is widely used by traders because actual option prices conform reasonably well to values derived from the model.

13The risk-free rate should be expressed as a continuously compounded rate. If r is a continuously compounded rate, then the effective annual yield is $e^r - 1.0$. An 8% continuously compounded rate of return yields $e^{0.08} - 1 = 8.33\%$. In all of the Black-Scholes option pricing model examples, we will assume that the rate is expressed as a continuously compounded rate.

14*Programmed trading*, in which stocks are bought and options are sold (or vice versa), is an example of arbitrage between stocks and options.

Application of the Black-Scholes Option Pricing Model

The current stock price (P), the exercise price (X), and the time to maturity (t) can all be obtained from a newspaper, such as *The Wall Street Journal*, or from the Internet, such as the CBOE's Web site. The risk-free rate (r_{RF}) is the yield on a Treasury bill with a maturity equal to the option expiration date. The annualized standard deviation of stock returns (σ) can be estimated from daily stock prices. First, find the stock return for each trading day for a sample period, such as each trading day of the past year. Second, estimate the variance of the daily stock returns. Third, multiply this estimated daily variance by the number of trading days in a year, which is approximately 250.[15] Take the square root of the annualized variance, and the result is an estimate of the annualized standard deviation.

We will use the Black-Scholes model to estimate Western's call option that we discussed previously. Here are the inputs:

See **Ch08 Tool Kit.xls** *on the textbook's Web site for all calculations.*

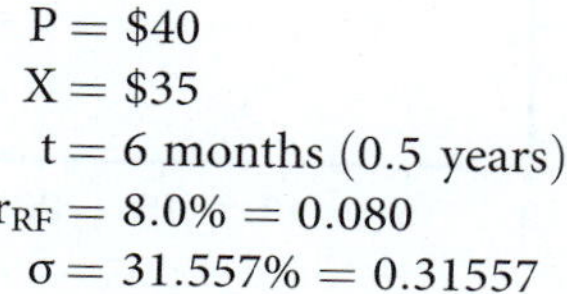

$$P = \$40$$
$$X = \$35$$
$$t = 6 \text{ months } (0.5 \text{ years})$$
$$r_{RF} = 8.0\% = 0.080$$
$$\sigma = 31.557\% = 0.31557$$

Given this information, we first estimate d_1 and d_2 from Equations 8-10 and 8-11:

$$d_1 = \frac{\ln(\$40/\$35) + [0.08 + ((0.31557^2)/2)](0.5)}{0.31557\sqrt{0.5}}$$
$$= \frac{0.13353 + 0.064896}{0.22314} = 0.8892$$
$$d_2 = d_1 - 0.31557\sqrt{0.5} = 0.6661$$

Note that $N(d_1)$ and $N(d_2)$ represent areas under a standard normal distribution function. The easiest way to calculate this value is with *Excel*. For example, we can use the function **=NORMSDIST(0.8892)**, which returns a value of $N(d_1)$ =

---

[15] If stocks traded every single day of the year, then each daily stock return would cover a period of 24 hours. Suppose you take a sample of these 24-hour returns and estimate the variance. There are 365 24-hour periods in a year, so you should multiply the 24-hour variance by 365 to estimate the annual variance. However, stocks don't trade every day because of weekends and holidays. If you excluded weekends from your sample (i.e., if you discarded the returns from the close of trading on Friday to the close of trading on Monday), then each return would be for a 24-hour period. So you should multiply your estimated 24-hour variance by 365 to estimate the annual variance.

If instead you measure returns from the close of one trading day until the close of the next trading day, then some returns are for 24 hours (such as Thursday close to Friday close) and some are for longer periods, like the 72-hour return from Friday close to Monday close. On average, though, five sequential returns cover one week. With roughly 50 weeks of trading in the year (assuming that about 14 weekdays have no trading because of holidays), each of the returns measured from trading day to trading day covers about 1/250 = 1/(5 × 50) year. So if you include returns over weekends and holidays in your sample, you should multiply the variance of daily (i.e., trading-day-to-trading-day) returns by 250 to convert it to an annual variance.

You could use trading-day-to-trading-day returns and adjust them for the length of each period (24 hours, 48, hours, etc.), but most analysts just multiply the variance by 250. Also, some analysts estimate the daily return as $\ln(P_t/P_{t-1})$ instead of estimating the daily return as the percentage change in stock prices.

FIGURE 8-4 Western Cellular's Call Options with a Strike Price of $35

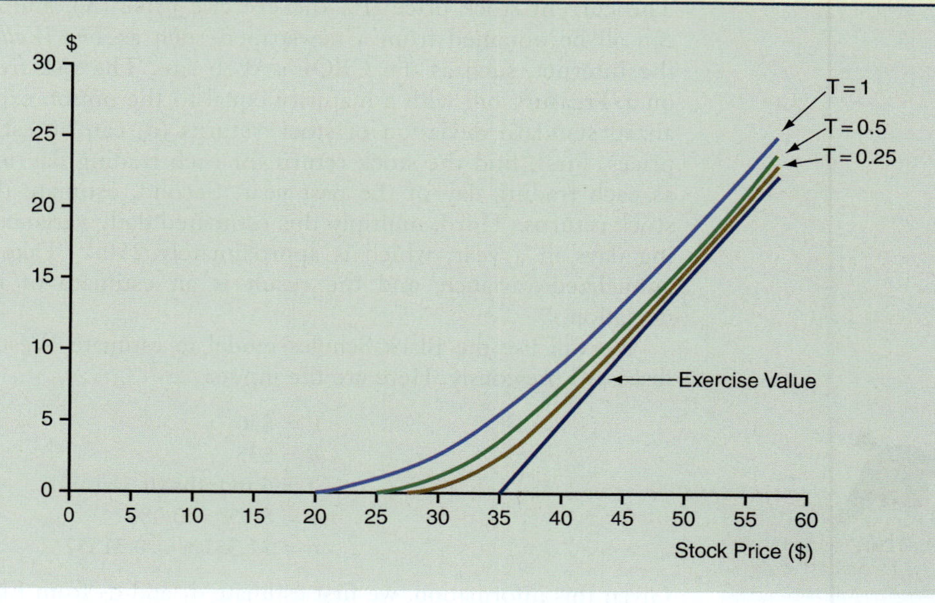

See Ch08 Tool Kit.xls.

N(0.8892) = 0.8131. Similarly, the **NORMSDIST** function returns a value of $N(d_2)$ = 0.7473.[16] We can use those values to solve Equation 8-9:

$$\begin{aligned} V_C &= \$40[N(0.8892)] - \$35e^{-(0.08)(0.5)}[N(0.6661)] \\ &= \$7.39 \end{aligned}$$

Thus, the value of the option is $7.39. This is the same value we found using the binomial approach with 100 periods in the year.

The Five Factors That Affect Option Prices

The Black-Scholes model has five inputs, so there are five factors that affect option prices. Figure 8-4 shows how three of Western Cellular's call options are affected by Western's stock price (all three options have a strike price of $35). The three options expire in 1 year, in 6 months (0.5 years, like the option in our example), and in 3 months (or 0.25 years), respectively.

Figure 8-4 offers several insights regarding option valuation. Notice that for all stock prices, the option prices are always above the exercise value. If this were not true, then an investor could purchase the option and immediately exercise it for a quick profit.

When the stock price falls far below the strike price, the option prices fall toward zero. In other words, options lose value as they become more and more out-of-the-money. When the stock price greatly exceeds the strike price, the option prices fall toward the exercise value. Thus, for very high stock prices, options tend to move up and down by about the same amount as does the stock price.

[16]If you do not have access to *Excel*, then you can use the table in Appendix D. For example, the table shows that the value for d = 0.88 is 0.5000 + 0.3106 = 0.8106 and that the value for d = 0.89 is 0.5000 + 0.3133 = 0.8133, so N(0.8892) lies between 0.8106 and 0.8133. You could interpolate to find a closer value, but we suggest using *Excel* instead.

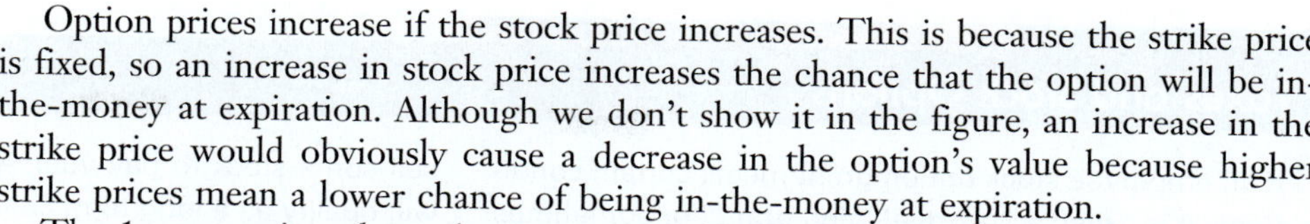

Option prices increase if the stock price increases. This is because the strike price is fixed, so an increase in stock price increases the chance that the option will be in-the-money at expiration. Although we don't show it in the figure, an increase in the strike price would obviously cause a decrease in the option's value because higher strike prices mean a lower chance of being in-the-money at expiration.

The 1-year option always has a greater value than the 6-month option, which always has a greater value than the 3-month option; thus, the longer an option has until expiration, the greater its value. This is because stock prices move up on average, so a longer time until expiration means a greater chance for the option to be in-the-money by its expiration date, making the option more valuable.

See **Ch08 Tool Kit.xls** for all calculations.

Shown in the following table are the Black-Scholes model prices for Western's call option with the original inputs except for standard deviation, which is allowed to vary.

Standard Deviation (σ)	Call Option Price
0.001%	\$ 6.37
10.000	6.22
31.557	7.39
40.000	8.72
60.000	11.91
90.000	16.37

The first row shows the option price if there is very little stock volatility.[17] Notice that as volatility increases, so does the option price. Therefore, the riskier the underlying security, the more valuable the option. To see why this makes sense, suppose you bought a call option with a strike price equal to the current stock price. If the stock had no risk (which means $\sigma = 0$), then there would be a zero probability of the stock going up, hence a zero probability of making money on the option. On the other hand, if you bought an option on a high-variance stock, there would be a higher probability that the stock would go way up and hence that you would make a large profit on the option. Of course, a high-variance stock could go way down, but as an option holder your losses would be limited to the price paid for the option—only the right-hand side of the stock's probability distribution counts. Put another way, an increase in the price of the stock helps option holders more than a decrease hurts them, so the greater the stock's volatility, the greater the value of the option. This makes options on risky stocks more valuable than those on safer, low-risk stocks. For example, an option on Cisco should have a greater value than an otherwise identical option on Kroger, the grocery store chain.

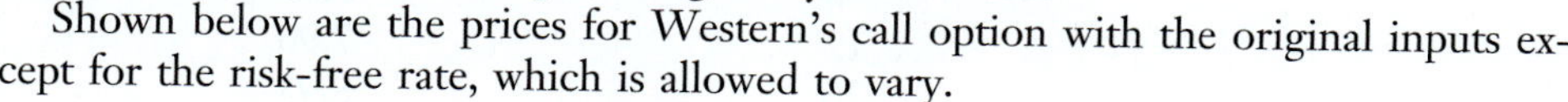

See **Ch08 Tool Kit.xls** for all calculations.

Shown below are the prices for Western's call option with the original inputs except for the risk-free rate, which is allowed to vary.

[17]With such a low standard deviation, the current stock price of \$40 is unlikely to change very much before expiration, so the option will be in-the-money at expiration and the owner will certainly pay the strike price and exercise the option at that time. This means that the present value of the strike price is the cost of exercising expressed in today's dollars. The present value of a stock's expected cash flows is equal to the current stock price. So the value of the option today is approximately equal to the current stock price of \$40 less the present value of the strike price that must be paid when the stock is exercised at expiration. If we assume daily compounding, then the current option price should be:

$$V_C(\text{for } \sigma = 0.001\%) \approx \$40 - \frac{\$35}{\left(1+\frac{0.08}{365}\right)^{365(0.5)}} = \$6.37$$

Observe that this is the same value given by the Black-Scholes model, even though we calculated it more directly. This approach only works if the volatility is almost zero.

Taxes and Stock Options

If an employee stock option grant meets certain conditions, it is called a "tax-qualifying grant" or sometimes an "Incentive Stock Option"; otherwise, it is a "nonqualifying grant." For example, suppose you receive a grant of 1,000 options with an exercise price of $50. If the stock price goes to $110 and you exercise the options, you must pay $50(1,000) = $50,000 for stock that is worth $110,000, which is a sweet deal. But what is your tax liability? If you receive a nonqualifying grant, then you are liable for ordinary income taxes on 1,000($110 − $50) = $60,000 when you exercise the option. But if it is a tax-qualified grant, you owe no regular taxes when exercised. By waiting at least a year and then selling the stock for, say, $150, you would have a long-term capital gain of 1,000($150 − $50) = $100,000, which would be taxed at the lower capital gains rate.

Before you gloat over your newfound wealth, you had better consult your accountant. Your "profit" when you exercise the tax-qualified options isn't taxable under the regular tax code, but it is under the Alternative Minimum Tax (AMT) code. With an AMT tax rate of up to 28%, you might owe as much as 0.28($110 − $50)(1,000) = $16,800. Here's where people get into trouble. The AMT tax isn't due until the following April, so you might think about waiting until then to sell some stock to pay your AMT tax (so that the sale will qualify as a long-term capital gain).

But what happens if the stock price falls to $5 by next April? You can sell your stock, which raises only $5(1,000) = $5,000 in cash. Without going into the details, you will have a long-term capital loss of 1,000 ($50 − $5) = $45,000 but IRS regulations limit your net capital loss in a single year to $3,000. In other words, the cash from the sale and the tax benefit from the capital loss aren't nearly enough to cover the AMT tax. You may be able to reduce your taxes in future years because of the AMT tax you pay this year and the carry-forward of the remaining long-term capital loss, but that doesn't help right now. You lost $45,000 of your original $50,000 investment, you now have very little cash, and—adding insult to injury—the IRS will insist that you also pay the $16,800 AMT tax.

This is exactly what happened to many people who made paper fortunes in the dot-com boom only to see them evaporate in the ensuing bust. They were left with worthless stock but multimillion-dollar AMT tax obligations. In fact, many still have IRS liens garnishing their wages until they eventually pay their AMT tax. So if you receive stock options, we congratulate you. But unless you want to be the next poster child for poor financial planning, we advise you to settle your AMT tax when you incur it.

Risk-Free Rate (r_{RF})	Call Option Price
0%	$6.41
4	6.89
8	7.39
12	7.90
20	8.93

As the risk-free rate increases, the value of the option increases. The principal effect of an increase in r_{RF} is to reduce the present value of the exercise price, which increases the current value of the option. Option prices in general are not very sensitive to interest rate changes, at least not to changes within the ranges normally encountered.

Myron Scholes and Robert Merton (who also was a pioneer in the field of options) were awarded the 1997 Nobel Prize in Economics, and Fischer Black would have been a co-recipient had he still been living. Their work provided analytical tools and methodologies that are widely used to solve many types of financial problems, not just option pricing. Indeed, the entire field of modern risk management is based primarily on their contributions. Although the Black-Scholes model was derived for a European option that can be exercised only on its maturity date, it also applies to

American options that don't pay any dividends prior to expiration. The textbooks by Don Chance and John Hull (cited in footnote 1) show adjusted models for dividend-paying stocks.

Self-Test

What is the purpose of the Black-Scholes option pricing model?

Explain what a "riskless hedge" is and how the riskless hedge concept is used in the Black-Scholes OPM.

Describe the effect of a change in each of the following factors on the value of a call option: (1) stock price, (2) exercise price, (3) option life, (4) risk-free rate, and (5) stock return standard deviation (i.e., risk of stock).

Using an *Excel* worksheet, what is the value of a call option with these data: $P = \$35$, $X = \$25$, $r_{RF} = 6\%$, $t = 0.5$ (6 months), and $\sigma = 0.6$? (\$12.05)

8.6 The Valuation of Put Options

A put option gives its owner the right to sell a share of stock. If the stock pays no dividends and the option can be exercised only upon its expiration date, what is its value? Rather than reinventing the wheel, consider the payoffs for two portfolios at expiration date T, as shown in Table 8-2. The first portfolio consists of a put option and a share of stock; the second has a call option (with the same strike price and expiration date as the put option) and some cash. The amount of cash is equal to the present value of the exercise cost discounted at the continuously compounded risk-free rate, which is $Xe^{-r_{RF}t}$. At expiration, the value of this cash will equal the exercise cost, X.

If P_T, the stock price at expiration date T, is less than X, the strike price when the option expires, then the value of the put option at expiration is $X - P_T$. Therefore, the value of Portfolio 1, which contains the put and the stock, is equal to X minus P_T plus P_T, or just X. For Portfolio 2, the value of the call is zero at expiration (because the call option is out-of-the-money), and the value of the cash is X, for a total value of X. Notice that both portfolios have the same payoffs if the stock price is less than the strike price.

What if the stock price is greater than the strike price at expiration? In this case, the put is worth nothing, so the payoff of Portfolio 1 is equal to P_T, the stock price at expiration. The call option is worth $P_T - X$, and the cash is worth X, so the payoff of Portfolio 2 is P_T. Hence the payoffs of the two portfolios are equal regardless of whether the stock price is below or above the strike price.

If the two portfolios have identical payoffs, then they must have identical values. This is known as the **put–call parity relationship**:

TABLE 8-2 Portfolio Payoffs

		PAYOFF AT EXPIRATION IF:	
		$P_T < X$	$P_T \geq X$
Put		$X - P_T$	0
Stock		P_T	P_T
	Portfolio 1:	X	P_T
Call		0	$P_T - X$
Cash		X	X
	Portfolio 2:	X	P_T

Put option + Stock = Call option + PV of exercise price.

If V_c is the Black-Scholes value of the call option, then the value of a put is[18]

$$\text{Put option} = V_C - P + Xe^{-r_{RF}t} \tag{8-12}$$

For example, consider a put option written on the stock discussed in the previous section. If the put option has the same exercise price and expiration date as the call, then its price is

$$\begin{aligned}\text{Put option} &= \$7.39 - \$40 + \$35e^{-0.08(0.5)}\\ &= \$7.39 - \$40 + \$33.63 = \$1.02\end{aligned}$$

It is also possible to modify the Black-Scholes call option formula to obtain a put option formula:

$$\text{Put option} = P[N(d_1) - 1] - Xe^{-r_{RF}t}[N(d_2) - 1] \tag{8-13}$$

The only difference between this formula for puts and the formula for calls is the subtraction of 1 from $N(d_1)$ and $N(d_2)$ in the call option formula.

Self-Test

In words, what is put–call parity?

A put option written on the stock of Taylor Enterprises (TE) has an exercise price of \$25 and 6 months remaining until expiration. The risk-free rate is 6%. A call option written on TE has the same exercise price and expiration date as the put option. TE's stock price is \$35. If the call option has a price of \$12.05, then what is the price (i.e., value) of the put option? (\$1.31)

8.7 Applications of Option Pricing in Corporate Finance

Option pricing is used in four major areas of corporate finance: (1) real options analysis for project evaluation and strategic decisions, (2) risk management, (3) capital structure decisions, and (4) compensation plans.

Real Options

Suppose a company has a 1-year proprietary license to develop a software application for use in a new generation of wireless cellular telephones. Hiring programmers and marketing consultants to complete the project will cost \$30 million. The good news is that if consumers love the new cell phones, there will be a tremendous demand for the software. The bad news is that if sales of the new cell phones are low, the software project will be a disaster. Should the company spend the \$30 million and develop the software?

Because the company has a license, it has the option of waiting for a year, at which time it might have a much better insight into market demand for the new cell phones. If demand is high in a year, then the company can spend the \$30 million and develop the software. If demand is low, it can avoid losing the \$30 million devel-

[18]This model cannot be applied to an American put option or to a European option on a stock that pays a dividend prior to expiration. For an explanation of valuation approaches in these situations, see the books by Chance and Hull cited in footnote 1.

opment cost by simply letting the license expire. Notice that the license is analogous to a call option: It gives the company the right to buy something (in this case, software for the new cell phones) at a fixed price ($30 million) at any time during the next year. The license gives the company a **real option**, because the underlying asset (the software) is a real asset and not a financial asset.

There are many other types of real options, including the option to increase capacity at a plant, to expand into new geographical regions, to introduce new products, to switch inputs (such as gas versus oil), to switch outputs (such as producing sedans versus SUVs), and to abandon a project. Many companies now evaluate real options with techniques that are similar to those described earlier in the chapter for pricing financial options.

Risk Management

Suppose a company plans to issue $400 million of bonds in 6 months to pay for a new plant now under construction. The plant will be profitable if interest rates remain at current levels, but if rates rise then it will be unprofitable. To hedge against rising rates, the company could purchase a put option on Treasury bonds. If interest rates go up then the company would "lose" because its bonds would carry a high interest rate, but it would have an offsetting gain on its put options. Conversely, if rates fall then the company would "win" when it issues its own low-rate bonds, but it would lose on the put options. By purchasing puts, the company has hedged the risk due to possible interest rate changes that it would otherwise face.

Another example of risk management is a firm that bids on a foreign contract. For example, suppose a winning bid means that the firm will receive a payment of 12 million euros in 9 months. At a current exchange rate of $1.57 per euro, the project would be profitable. But if the exchange rate falls to $1.10 per euro, the project would be a loser. To avoid exchange rate risk, the firm could take a short position in a forward contract that allows it to convert 12 million euros into dollars at a fixed rate of $1.50 per euro in 9 months, which would still ensure a profitable project. This eliminates exchange rate risk if the firm wins the contract, but what if the firm loses the contract? It would still be obligated to sell 12 million euros at a price of $1.50 per euro, which could be a disaster. For example, if the exchange rate rises to $1.75 per euro, then the firm would have to spend $21 million to purchase 12 million euros at a price of $1.75/€ and then sell the euros for $18 million = ($1.50/€)(€12 million), a loss of $3 million.

To eliminate this risk, the firm could instead purchase a currency put option that allows it to sell 12 million euros in 9 months at a fixed price of $1.50 per euro. If the company wins the bid, it will exercise the put option and sell the 12 million euros for $1.50 per euro if the exchange rate has declined. If the exchange rate hasn't declined, then it will sell the euros on the open market for more than $1.50 and let the option expire. On the other hand, if the firm loses the bid, then it has no reason to sell euros and could let the option contract expire. Note, however, that even if the firm doesn't win the contract, it still is gambling on the exchange rate because it owns the put; if the price of euros declines below $1.50, the firm will still make some money on the option. Thus, the company can lock in the future exchange rate if it wins the bid and can avoid any net payment at all if it loses the bid. The total cost in either scenario is equal to the initial cost of the option. In other words, the cost of the option is like insurance that guarantees the exchange rate if the company wins the bid and guarantees no net obligations if it loses the bid.

Many other applications of risk management involve futures contracts and other complex derivatives rather than calls and puts. However, the principles used in pricing derivatives are similar to those used earlier in this chapter for pricing options. Thus, financial options and their valuation techniques play key roles in risk management.

Capital Structure Decisions

Decisions regarding the mix of debt and equity used to finance operations are quite important. One interesting aspect of the capital structure decision is based on option pricing. For example, consider a firm with debt requiring a final principal payment of $60 million in 1 year. If the company's value 1 year from now is $61 million, then it can pay off the debt and have $1 million left for stockholders. If the firm's value is less than $60 million, then it may well file for bankruptcy and turn over its assets to creditors, resulting in stockholders' equity of zero. In other words, the value of the stockholders' equity is analogous to a call option: The equity holders have the right to buy the assets for $60 million (which is the face value of the debt) in 1 year (when the debt matures).

Suppose the firm's owner-managers are considering two projects. One project has very little risk, and it will result in an asset value of either $59 million or $61 million. The other has high risk, and it will result in an asset value of either $20 million or $100 million. Notice that the equity will be worth zero if the assets are worth less than $60 million, so the stockholders will be no worse off if the assets end up at $20 million than if they end up at $59 million. On the other hand, the stockholders would benefit much more if the assets were worth $100 million than $61 million. Thus, the owner-managers have an incentive to choose risky projects, which is consistent with an option's value rising with the risk of the underlying asset. Potential lenders recognize this situation, so they build covenants into loan agreements that restrict managers from making excessively risky investments.

Not only does option pricing theory help explain why managers might want to choose risky projects (consider, for example, the case of Enron) and why debtholders might want restrictive covenants, but options also play a direct role in capital structure choices. For example, a firm could choose to issue convertible debt, which gives bondholders the option to convert their debt into stock if the value of the company turns out to be higher than expected. In exchange for this option, bondholders charge a lower interest rate than for nonconvertible debt. Because owner-managers must share the wealth with convertible-bond holders, they have a smaller incentive to gamble with high-risk projects.

Compensation Plans

Many companies use stock options as a part of their compensation plans. It is important for boards of directors to understand the value of these options before they grant them to employees. We discuss compensation issues associated with stock options in more detail in Chapter 13.

Self-Test

Describe four ways that option pricing is used in corporate finance.

Summary

In this chapter we discussed option pricing topics, which included the following.

- **Financial options** are instruments that (1) are created by exchanges rather than firms, (2) are bought and sold primarily by investors, and (3) are of importance to both investors and financial managers.

- The two primary types of financial options are (1) **call options**, which give the holder the right to purchase a specified asset at a given price (the **exercise**, or **strike, price**) for a given period of time, and (2) **put options**, which give the holder the right to sell an asset at a given price for a given period of time.
- A call option's **exercise value** is defined as the maximum of zero or the current price of the stock less the strike price.
- The **Black-Scholes option pricing model (OPM)** or the **binomial model** can be used to estimate the value of a call option.
- The five inputs to the Black-Scholes model are (1) P, the current stock price; (2) X, the strike price; (3) r_{RF}, the risk-free interest rate; (4) t, the remaining time until expiration; and (5) σ, the standard deviation of the stock's rate of return.
- A call option's value increases if P increases, X decreases, r_{RF} increases, t increases, or σ increases.
- The **put–call parity relationship** states that

  Put option + Stock = Call option + PV of exercise price.

Questions

(8–1) Define each of the following terms:
  a. Option; call option; put option
  a. Exercise value; strike price
  c. Black-Scholes option pricing model

(8–2) Why do options sell at prices higher than their exercise values?

(8–3) Describe the effect on a call option's price that results from an increase in each of the following factors: (1) stock price, (2) strike price, (3) time to expiration, (4) risk-free rate, and (5) standard deviation of stock return.

Self-Test Problems

Solutions Appear in Appendix A

(ST–1) Binomial Option Pricing — The current price of a stock is $40. In 1 year, the price will be either $60 or $30. The annual risk-free rate is 5%. Find the price of a call option on the stock that has an exercise price of $42 and that expires in 1 year. (*Hint:* Use daily compounding.)

(ST–2) Black-Scholes Model — Use the Black-Scholes Model to find the price for a call option with the following inputs: (1) current stock price is $22, (2) strike price is $20, (3) time to expiration is 6 months, (4) annualized risk-free rate is 5%, and (5) standard deviation of stock return is 0.7.

Problems

Answers Appear in Appendix B

Easy Problems 1–2

(8–1) Options — A call option on the stock of Bedrock Boulders has a market price of $7. The stock sells for $30 a share, and the option has a strike price of $25 a share. What is the exercise value of the call option? What is the option's time value?

(8–2) Options

The exercise price on one of Flanagan Company's options is $15, its exercise value is $22, and its time value is $5. What are the option's market value and the price of the stock?

INTERMEDIATE PROBLEMS 3–4

(8–3) Black-Scholes Model

Assume that you have been given the following information on Purcell Industries:

Current stock price = $15	Strike price of option = $15
Time to maturity of option = 6 months	Risk-free rate = 6%
Variance of stock return = 0.12	
d_1 = 0.24495	$N(d_1)$ = 0.59675
d_2 = 0.00000	$N(d_2)$ = 0.50000

According to the Black-Scholes option pricing model, what is the option's value?

(8–4) Put–Call Parity

The current price of a stock is $33, and the annual risk-free rate is 6%. A call option with a strike price of $32 and with 1 year until expiration has a current value of $6.56. What is the value of a put option written on the stock with the same exercise price and expiration date as the call option?

CHALLENGING PROBLEMS 5–7

(8–5) Black-Scholes Model

Use the Black-Scholes Model to find the price for a call option with the following inputs: (1) current stock price is $30, (2) strike price is $35, (3) time to expiration is 4 months, (4) annualized risk-free rate is 5%, and (5) variance of stock return is 0.25.

(8–6) Binomial Model

The current price of a stock is $20. In 1 year, the price will be either $26 or $16. The annual risk-free rate is 5%. Find the price of a call option on the stock that has a strike price of $21 and that expires in 1 year. (*Hint:* Use daily compounding.)

(8–7) Binomial Model

The current price of a stock is $15. In 6 months, the price will be either $18 or $13. The annual risk-free rate is 6%. Find the price of a call option on the stock that has a strike price of $14 and that expires in 6 months. (*Hint:* Use daily compounding.)

SPREADSHEET PROBLEM

(8-8) Build a Model: Black-Scholes Model

Start with the partial model in the file ***Ch08 P08 Build a Model.xls*** on the textbook's Web site. You have been given the following information for a call option on the stock of Puckett Industries: P = $65.00, X = $70.00, t = 0.50, r_{RF} = 5.00% and σ = 50.00%.

a. Use the Black-Scholes option pricing model to determine the value of the call option.

b. Suppose there is a put option on Puckett's stock with exactly the same inputs as the call option. What is the value of the put?

Mini Case

Assume that you have just been hired as a financial analyst by Triple Play Inc., a mid-sized California company that specializes in creating high-fashion clothing. Because no one at Triple Play is familiar with the basics of financial options, you have been asked to prepare a brief report that the firm's executives can use to gain at least a cursory understanding of the topic.

To begin, you gathered some outside materials on the subject and used these materials to draft a list of pertinent questions that need to be answered. In fact, one possible approach to the report is to use a question-and-answer format. Now that the questions have been drafted, you have to develop the answers.

a. What is a financial option? What is the single most important characteristic of an option?

b. Options have a unique set of terminology. Define the following terms:

  (1) Call option
  (2) Put option
  (3) Strike price or exercise price
  (4) Expiration date
  (5) Exercise value
  (6) Option price
  (7) Time value
  (8) Writing an option
  (9) Covered option
  (10) Naked option
  (11) In-the-money call
  (12) Out-of-the-money call
  (13) LEAPS

c. Consider Triple Play's call option with a \$25 strike price. The following table contains historical values for this option at different stock prices:

Stock Price	Call Option Price
\$25	\$ 3.00
30	7.50
35	12.00
40	16.50
45	21.00
50	25.50

  (1) Create a table that shows (a) stock price, (b) strike price, (c) exercise value, (d) option price, and (e) the time value, which is the option's price less its exercise value.
  (2) What happens to the time value as the stock price rises? Why?

d. Consider a stock with a current price of P = \$27. Suppose that over the next 6 months the stock price will either go up by a factor of 1.41 or down by a factor of 0.71. Consider a call option on the stock with a strike price of \$25 that expires in 6 months. The risk-free rate is 6%.

  (1) Using the binomial model, what are the ending values of the stock price? What are the payoffs of the call option?
  (2) Suppose you write 1 call option and buy N_s shares of stock. How many shares must you buy to create a portfolio with a riskless payoff (i.e., a hedge portfolio)? What is the payoff of the portfolio?
  (3) What is the present value of the hedge portfolio? What is the value of the call option?
  (4) What is a replicating portfolio? What is arbitrage?

e. In 1973, Fischer Black and Myron Scholes developed the Black-Scholes option pricing model (OPM).

   (1) What assumptions underlie the OPM?
   (2) Write out the three equations that constitute the model.
   (3) According to the OPM, what is the value of a call option with the following characteristics?

      Stock price = \$27.00
      Strike price = \$25.00
      Time to expiration = 6 months = 0.5 years
      Risk-free rate = 6.0%
      Stock return standard deviation = 0.49

f. What impact does each of the following parameters have on the value of a call option?

   (1) Current stock price
   (2) Strike price
   (3) Option's term to maturity
   (4) Risk-free rate
   (5) Variability of the stock price

g. What is put–call parity?

PART 4

Projects and Their Valuation

CHAPTER 9

The Cost of Capital

Fortune magazine conducts annual surveys of business leaders to identify the most-admired U.S. companies. Since the surveys began, General Electric has consistently ranked either at or close to the top of the list. Although GE's stock has fallen sharply in recent times, like that of most other companies, it was still in eighth place in the March 2009 survey.

GE is the most diversified company in the world. It originally manufactured electric generating equipment and light bulbs. Then it branched into appliances and industrial equipment such as jet engines and locomotives, then into infrastructure, various industrial services, movies, TV, and loans to individuals and businesses. People tend to think of GE as an industrial company, but by far its largest unit is GE Capital, its finance unit. This reliance on GE Capital, combined with uncertainty about potential losses on its huge loan portfolio, was primarily responsible for GE's poor stock price performance in 2008–2009.

A key factor in GE's long-run success has been its financial discipline: the company is reported to have set a uniform "hurdle rate" for potential new investments and then accepted projects if and only if their expected returns exceed that hurdle rate. Historically, the same hurdle rate was used for all projects—apparently the company did not systematically vary the rate to reflect individual projects' perceived risks. Project managers were charged with achieving the rate of return they had forecasted, and careers rose or fell depending on whether or not they "made their numbers."

With 20-20 hindsight, we can see that there was a flaw in GE's logic. The economy enjoyed a strong upward trend from 1945 to 2007, so defaults on mortgages, corporate debt, credit cards, and other debt instruments were relatively low. Moreover, until 2009 GE was one of only six nonfinancial companies with a AAA bond rating, which enabled it to borrow at extremely low rates and then re-lend the money at much higher rates. In that environment, it was easy for GE Capital to forecast returns that exceeded the corporate hurdle rate, and that led to the unit's rapid growth. GE's other units had fewer projects that exceeded the corporate hurdle rate; hence, GE Capital's share of total corporate revenues, profits, and especially debt increased rapidly.

Recently, though, as the economy sank into a recession and the housing market collapsed, investors became worried about all lenders' loans. They started dumping financial stocks—including GE's, which led to its huge stock price decline. If GE's management had looked more closely at the potential effects of GE Capital's increased use of debt to finance the purchase of risky mortgages and other debt, and if it had used risk-adjusted hurdle rates rather than a uniform rate, then some of its pain might have been avoided.

Corporate Valuation and the Cost of Capital

In Chapter 1, we told you that managers should strive to make their firms more valuable and that the value of a firm is determined by the size, timing, and risk of its free cash flows (FCF). Indeed, a firm's intrinsic value is found as the present value of its FCFs, discounted at the weighted average cost of capital (WACC). In previous chapters, we examined the major sources of financing (stocks, bonds, and preferred stock) and the costs of those instruments. In this chapter, we put those pieces together and estimate the WACC that is used to determine intrinsic value.

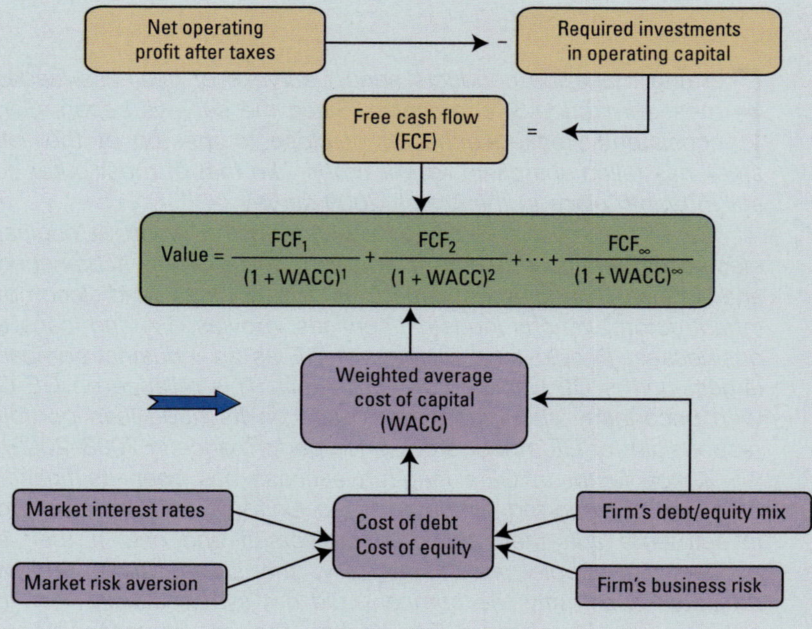

The textbook's Web site contains an Excel file that will guide you through the chapter's calculations. The file for this chapter is **Ch09 Tool Kit.xls**, and we encourage you to open the file and follow along as you read the chapter.

Businesses require capital to develop new products, build factories and distribution centers, install information technology, expand internationally, and acquire other companies. For each of these actions, a company must estimate the total investment required and then decide whether the expected rate of return exceeds the cost of the capital. The cost of capital is also a factor in compensation plans, with bonuses dependent on whether the company's return on invested capital exceeds the cost of that capital. This cost is also a key factor in choosing the firm's mixture of debt and equity and in decisions to lease rather than buy assets. As these examples illustrate, the cost of capital is a critical element in many business decisions.[1]

[1]The cost of capital is also an important factor in the regulation of electric, gas, and water companies. These utilities are natural monopolies in the sense that one firm can supply service at a lower cost than could two or more firms. Because it has a monopoly, an unregulated electric or water company could exploit its customers. Therefore, regulators (1) determine the cost of the capital investors have provided the utility and then (2) set rates designed to permit the company to earn its cost of capital, no more and no less.

9.1 The Weighted Average Cost of Capital

If a firm's only investors were common stockholders, then its cost of capital would be the required rate of return on its equity. However, most firms employ different types of capital, and because of their differences in risk, the different securities have different required rates of return. The required rate of return on each capital component is called its **component cost**, and the cost of capital used to analyze capital budgeting decisions is found as a *weighted average* of the various components' costs. We call this weighted average just that, the **weighted average cost of capital**, or **WACC**.

National Computer Corporation (NCC) is a mid-sized manufacturer of mainframe computers. We will estimate NCC's cost of capital in this chapter. We begin by providing some basic information in Figure 9-1, including: (1) balance sheets; (2) percentages of total liabilities and equity comprised by each item (Column F); (3) percentages of financing in the form of "costly" capital supplied by investors, including banks, bondholders, and stockholders (Column H reports percentages based on book values from the financial statements); (4) percentages of investor-supplied capital based on current market values (Column I); and (5) target capital structure weights that management plans to use when raising new capital in the future (Column L). Following is a brief discussion of this information.

Notice that we exclude accounts payable and accruals in Columns G to L. Capital is provided by *investors*—interest-bearing debt, preferred stock, and common equity. Accounts payable and accruals arise from operating decisions, not from financing decisions. For example, payables and accruals increase automatically when sales increase, so the impact of payables and accruals is incorporated into a firm's free cash flows and a project's cash flows rather than into the cost of capital. Therefore, we consider only investor-supplied capital when we calculate the cost of capital.

Notice that Figure 9-1 (in Columns H, J, and L) reports percentages of financing based on book values, market values, and target weights. We examine the choice of target weights in more detail in Chapter 15, where we discuss the optimal capital structure: one in which the percentages of debt, preferred stock, and common equity maximize the firm's value. As shown in the last column of Figure 9-1, NCC has concluded that it should use 30% debt, 10% preferred stock, and 60% common equity in its target capital structure, and it plans to raise capital in those proportions in the future. Therefore, we use those target weights when calculating NCC's weighted average cost of capital.[2]

Self-Test

What is a component cost?
What is a target capital structure?

[2]We should also note that the weights could be based on either the book or market values of the capital components. The market value of the equity is found by multiplying the stock's price by the number of shares outstanding. Market value weights are theoretically superior. However, accountants show assets on a book value basis, bond rating agencies and security analysts generally focus on book values, and market value weights are quite unstable because stock prices fluctuate so much. If a firm's book and market values differ widely, then often it appears as though management sets *target* weights as a blend of book and market weights. We discuss this more in Chapter 15, but for now just accept the target weights provided in this chapter as determined by management.

FIGURE 9-1 National Computer Corporation: Book Values, Market Values, and Target Capital Structure (Millions of Dollars, December 31, 2010)

	A	B	C	D	E	F	G	H	I	J	K	L
35	Balance Sheets						Investor-Supplied Capital				Target Capital Structure	
36							Book		Market			
37						Percent	Book	Percent	Market	Percent		
38	*Assets*		*Liabilities and Equity*			of Total	Value	of Total	Value	of Total		
39												
40	Cash	$ 65	Accounts payable		$ 650	6.5%						
41	S-T investments	10	Accruals		399	4.0%						
42	Receivables	1,800	Spontaneous liabilities		$1,049	10.5%						
43	Inventories	3,100	Notes payable		350	3.5%	$ 350	3.9%	$ 350	2.2%		
44	Total C.A.	$4,975	Total C.L.		$1,399	14.0%						
45			Long-term debt		4,200	42.0%	4,200	46.9%	4,200	26.0%		
46	Net fixed assets	5,020	Total liabilities		$5,599	56.0%	$4,550	50.9%	$ 4,550	28.2%	w_d =	30.0%
47			Preferred stock		1,200	12.0%	1,200	13.4%	1,200	7.4%	w_{ps} =	10.0%
48			Common stock		650	6.5%	650	7.3%				
49			Retained earnings		2,546	25.5%	2,546	28.5%				
50			Total common equity		$3,196	32.0%	$3,196	35.7%	10,400	64.4%	w_s =	60.0%
51	Total assets	$9,995	Total liabilities and equity		$9,995	100.0%	$8,946	100.0%	$16,150	100.0%		100.0%

Notes:

1. The market value of the notes payable is equal to the book value. Some of NCC's long-term bonds sell at a discount and some sell at a premium, but their aggregate market value is approximately equal to their aggregate book value.
2. The common stock price is $32 per share. There are 325 million shares outstanding, for a total market cap of $32(325) = $10,400 million.
3. The preferred stock price is $100 per share. There are 12 million shares outstanding, for a total market value of $100(12) = $1,200 million.
4. When establishing the target capital structure, no distinction is made between common equity raised by issuing stock versus retaining earnings.
5. The firm assumes that it will eventually replace most notes payable with long-term bonds and that the costs of notes payable and long-term debt are approximately the same; hence it simply uses a 30% weight for all investor-supplied debt (i.e., for the combined notes payable and long-term debt).
6. Accounts payable and accruals are not sources of investor-supplied capital, so we exclude them when calculating the WACC. However, we include the effects of payables and accruals on free cash flow and on a project's cash flows, so we do not ignore payables and accruals when estimating the value of a company or project. See Chapter 16 for more discussion of payables in the context of working capital management.
7. When deciding on a target capital structure, managers consider the firm's current and recent past book and market value structures as well as those of benchmark firms. They also perform stress tests by forecasting financial statements under different assumptions regarding capital structures and different states of the economy. See Chapter 15 for more on setting the target capital structure weights.

9.2 Basic Definitions

Now we define the key terms used in this chapter. Later we describe how to estimate the values of these variables and how to combine them to form the weighted average cost of capital, but an early overview is useful.

r_d = Interest rate on the firm's new debt = before-tax component cost of debt. It can be found in several ways, including calculating the yield to maturity on the firm's currently outstanding bonds.

$r_d(1 - T)$ = After-tax component cost of debt, where T is the firm's marginal tax rate. *$r_d(1 - T)$ is the debt cost used to calculate the weighted average cost of capital.* As we shall see, the after-tax cost of debt is lower than its before-tax cost because interest is tax deductible.

r_{ps} = Component cost of preferred stock, found as the yield investors expect to earn on the preferred stock. Preferred dividends are not tax deductible, so the before-tax and after-tax costs of preferred are equal.

r_s = Component cost of common equity raised by retaining earnings, or *internal equity*. It is the r_s developed in Chapter 7, where it is defined as the rate of return that investors require on a firm's common stock. Most firms, once they have become well established, obtain all of their new equity as retained earnings.

r_e = component cost of *external equity*, or common equity raised by issuing new stock. As we will see, r_e is equal to r_s plus a factor that reflects the cost of issuing new stock. Note, though, that established firms like NCC rarely issue new stock; hence r_e is rarely a relevant consideration except for very young, rapidly growing firms.

$w = w_d, w_{ps}, w_s, w_e$ = target weights of debt, preferred stock, internal equity (retained earnings) and external equity (new issues of common stock). The weights are the percentages of the different types of capital the firm plans to use when it raises capital in the future. Target weights may differ from actual current weights.

WACC = the firm's weighted average, or overall, cost of capital.

The target proportions of debt (w_d), preferred stock (w_{ps}), and common equity (w_s)—along with the costs of those components—are used to calculate the firm's **weighted average cost of capital, WACC:**[3]

$$\begin{aligned}\text{WACC} &= \left(\begin{array}{c}\%\\ \text{of}\\ \text{debt}\end{array}\right)\left(\begin{array}{c}\text{After-tax}\\ \text{cost of}\\ \text{debt}\end{array}\right)+\left(\begin{array}{c}\%\text{ of}\\ \text{preferred}\\ \text{stock}\end{array}\right)\left(\begin{array}{c}\text{Cost of}\\ \text{preferred}\\ \text{stock}\end{array}\right)+\left(\begin{array}{c}\%\text{ of}\\ \text{common}\\ \text{equity}\end{array}\right)\left(\begin{array}{c}\text{Cost of}\\ \text{common}\\ \text{equity}\end{array}\right)\\ &= w_d r_d(1-T) + w_{ps} r_{ps} + w_s r_s\end{aligned} \tag{9-1}$$

In the following sections we explain how to estimate the various components' costs.

Self-Test

Identify the firm's three major capital structure components and give the symbols for their respective costs and weights.

What are the two possible components of new common equity (and hence two possible costs of common equity)? Which one is normally relevant, and why is this so?

[3]We assume at this point that all new common equity is raised internally by retaining earnings, as is true for most companies with moderate or slow sales growth, so the cost of common equity is r_s.

9.3 Cost of Debt, $r_d(1-T)$

The first step in estimating the cost of debt is to determine the rate of return debtholders require, or r_d. Although estimating r_d is conceptually straightforward, some problems arise in practice. Companies use both fixed- and floating-rate debt, both straight and convertible debt, both long- and short-term debt, as well as debt with and without sinking funds. Each type of debt may have a somewhat different cost.

It is unlikely that the financial manager will know at the beginning of a planning period the exact types and amounts of debt that will be used during the period. The type or types used will depend on the specific assets to be financed and on capital market conditions as they develop over time. Even so, the financial manager does know what types of debt are typical for his firm. For example, NCC typically issues commercial paper to raise short-term money to finance working capital, and it issues 30-year bonds to raise long-term debt used to help finance its capital budgeting projects. Since the WACC is used primarily in capital budgeting, NCC's treasurer uses the cost of 30-year bonds in her WACC estimate.

Assume that it is January 2011 and that NCC's treasurer is estimating the WACC for the coming year. How should she calculate the component cost of debt? Most financial managers begin by discussing current and prospective interest rates with their investment bankers. Assume NCC's bankers believe that a new, 30-year, noncallable, straight bond issue would require a 9% coupon rate with semiannual payments. It can be offered to the public at its $1,000 par value. Therefore, their estimate of r_d is 9%.[4]

Note that 9% is the cost of **new**, or **marginal, debt**, and it will probably not be the same as the average rate on NCC's previously issued debt, which is called the **historical**, or **embedded, rate**. The embedded cost is important for some decisions but not for others. For example, the average cost of all the capital raised in the past and still outstanding is used by regulators when they determine the rate of return that a public utility should be allowed to earn. However, in financial management the WACC is used primarily to make investment decisions, and these decisions hinge on projects' expected future returns versus the cost of the new, or marginal, capital that will be used to finance those projects. *Thus, for our purposes, the relevant cost is the marginal cost of new debt to be raised during the planning period.*

Suppose NCC has issued debt in the past and the bonds are publicly traded. The financial staff can use the market price of the bonds to find the yield to maturity (or yield to call, if the bonds sell at a premium and are likely to be called). This yield is the rate of return that current bondholders expect to receive, and it is also a good estimate of r_d, the rate of return that new bondholders will require.

For example, suppose NCC has outstanding bonds with an 8% annual coupon rate, 22 years remaining until maturity, and a face value of $1,000. The bonds make semiannual coupon payments and currently are trading in the market at a price of $904.91. We can find the yield to maturity by using a financial calculator with these inputs: N = 44, PV = −904.91, PMT = 40, and FV = 1000. Solving for the rate, we find I/YR = 4.5%. This is a semiannual periodic rate, so the nominal annual rate is 9.0%. This is consistent with the investment bankers' estimated rate, so 9% is a reasonable estimate for r_d. If NCC had no publicly traded debt, then its staff could still look at the yields on publicly traded debt of similar firms for a reasonable estimate of r_d.

The required return to debtholders, r_d, is not equal to the company's cost of debt because interest payments are deductible, which means the government in effect pays part of the total cost. As a result, the weighted average cost of capital is calculated using the

---

[4]The effective annual rate is $(1 + 0.09/2)^2 - 1 = 9.2\%$, but NCC and most other companies use nominal rates for all component costs.

after-tax cost of debt, $r_d(1 - T)$, which is the interest rate on debt, r_d, less the tax savings that result because interest is deductible. Here T is the firm's marginal tax rate.[5]

$$\begin{aligned}\text{After-tax component cost of debt} &= \text{Interest rate} - \text{Tax savings}\\ &= r_d - r_d T\\ &= r_d(1 - T)\end{aligned} \qquad (9\text{-}2)$$

If we assume that NCC's marginal federal-plus-state tax rate is 40%, then its after-tax cost of debt is 5.4%:[6]

$$\begin{aligned}r_d(1 - T) &= 9\%(1.0 - 0.4)\\ &= 9\%(0.6)\\ &= 5.4\%\end{aligned}$$

Flotation Costs and the Cost of Debt

Most debt offerings have very low flotation costs, especially for privately placed debt. Because flotation costs are usually low, most analysts ignore them when estimating the after-tax cost of debt. However, the following example illustrates the procedure for incorporating flotation costs as well as their impact on the after-tax cost of debt.

Suppose NCC can issue 30-year debt with an annual coupon rate of 9%, with coupons paid semiannually. The flotation costs, F, are equal to 1% of the value of the issue. Instead of finding the pre-tax yield based upon pre-tax cash flows and then adjusting it to reflect taxes, as we did before, we can find the after-tax, flotation-adjusted cost by using this formula:

$$M(1 - F) = \sum_{t=1}^{N} \frac{INT(1 - T)}{[1 + r_d(1 - T)]^t} + \frac{M}{[1 + r_d(1 - T)]^N} \qquad (9\text{-}3)$$

Here M is the bond's maturity (or par) value, F is the **percentage flotation cost** (i.e., the percentage of proceeds paid to the investment bankers), N is the number of payments, T is the firm's tax rate, INT is the dollars of interest per period, and $r_d(1 - T)$ is the after-tax cost of debt adjusted for flotation costs. With a financial calculator, enter N = 60, PV = −1000(1 − 0.01) = −990, PMT = 45(1 − 0.40) = 33, and FV = 1000. Solving for I/YR, we find I/YR = $r_d(1 - T)$ = 2.73%, which is the semiannual after-tax component cost of debt. The nominal after-tax cost of debt is 5.46%. Note that this is quite close to the original 5.40% after-tax cost, so in this instance adjusting for flotation costs doesn't make much difference.[7]

---

[5]The federal tax rate for most corporations is 35%. However, most corporations are also subject to state income taxes, so the marginal tax rate on most corporate income is about 40%. For illustrative purposes, we assume that the effective federal-plus-state tax rate on marginal income is 40%. The effective tax rate is *zero* for a firm with such large current or past losses that it does not pay taxes. In this situation, the after-tax cost of debt is equal to the pre-tax interest rate.

[6]Strictly speaking, the after-tax cost of debt should reflect the *expected* cost of debt. Although NCC's bonds have a promised return of 9%, there is some chance of default and so its bondholders' expected return (and consequently NCC's cost) is a bit less than 9%. However, for a relatively strong company such as NCC, this difference is quite small.

[7]Equation 9-3 produces the correct after-tax cost of debt only for bonds issued at par. For bonds with a price other than par, the after-tax cash flows must be adjusted to take into account the actual taxation of the discount or premium. See ***Web Extension 5A*** on the textbook's Web site for a discussion of the taxation of original issue discount bonds. Also, we ignored the tax shield due to amortization of flotation costs because it has very little effect on the cost of debt; see ***Ch09 Tool Kit.xls*** for an example that incorporates the amortization tax shield.

However, the flotation adjustment would be higher if F were larger or if the bond's life were shorter. For example, if F were 10% rather than 1%, then the nominal annual flotation-adjusted $r_d(1 - T)$ would be 6.13%. With N at 1 year rather than 30 years and F still equal to 1%, the nominal annual $r_d(1 - T) = 6.45\%$. Finally, if F = 10% and N = 1, then the nominal annual $r_d(1 - T) = 16.67\%$. In all of these cases, the effect of flotation costs would be too large to ignore.

As an alternative to adjusting the cost of debt for flotation costs, in some situations it makes sense to instead adjust the project's cash flows. For example, **project financing** is a special situation in which a large project, such as an oil refinery, is financed with debt plus other securities that have a specific claim on the project's cash flows. This is different from the usual debt offering, in which the debt has a claim on all of the corporation's cash flows. Because project financing is funded by securities with claims tied to a particular project, the flotation costs can be included with the project's other cash flows when evaluating the project's value. However, project financing is relatively rare, so when we incorporate the impact of flotation costs, we usually do so by adjusting the component cost of the new debt.

The Cost of Short-Term Debt

As we mentioned earlier, most U.S. companies use short-term debt primarily to finance seasonal working capital needs. Seasonal debt fluctuates during the year, often dropping close to zero, so it is not a permanent source of financing for most U.S. companies. Therefore, we usually do not include short-term debt when estimating the cost of capital.

However, some U.S. companies and many international companies, especially those in Japan, do use relatively large amounts of short-term debt on a consistent basis. For such companies, we should include short-term debt as a capital component when estimating the WACC. Most short-term debt is in the form of bank loans, often with an interest rate that is tied to the prime rate or to the London Interbank Offered Rate (LIBOR). The interest rate on short-term debt is its pre-tax cost, and it must be adjusted to determine its after-tax cost. Also, there are normally no flotation costs for short-term debt, so flotation adjustments are not required.

Self-Test

Why is the after-tax cost of debt, rather than its before-tax cost, used to calculate the weighted average cost of capital?

Is the relevant cost of debt when calculating the WACC the interest rate on already *outstanding* debt or the rate on *new* debt? Why?

A company has outstanding long-term bonds with a face value of $1,000, a 10% coupon rate, 25 years remaining until maturity, and a current market value of $1,214.82. If it pays interest semiannually, then what is the nominal annual pre-tax cost of debt? **(8%)** If the company's tax rate is 40%, what is the after-tax cost of debt? **(4.8%)**

9.4 Cost of Preferred Stock, r_{ps}

Many firms (including NCC) use, or plan to use, preferred stock as part of their financing mix. Preferred dividends are not tax deductible, so the company bears their full cost. Therefore, *no tax adjustment is used when calculating the cost of preferred stock.* Some preferred stocks are issued without a stated maturity date, but today most have a sinking fund that effectively limits their life. Finally, although it is not mandatory that preferred dividends be paid, firms generally have every intention of doing so, because otherwise (1) they cannot pay dividends on their common stock, (2) they will find it difficult to raise additional funds in the capital markets, and (3) in some cases preferred stockholders can take control of the firm.

GE and Warren Buffett: The Cost of Preferred Stock

In October 2008, GE was in serious trouble. Its stock price had been crashing, its sales and earnings were declining, it was having trouble rolling over its commercial paper, and there were rumors that its bonds were about to be downgraded, which would raise its interest expense and exacerbate all its other problems. Then Warren Buffett came to the rescue. Buffett agreed to buy $3 billion of a new GE preferred stock, and he publicly expressed his confidence by asserting that "GE will continue to be successful in the years to come." GE needed a boost, and Buffett's money and endorsement provided it.

However, Buffett didn't exactly give GE something for nothing. The preferred stock carried a 10% coupon, it had a 10% call premium, and it was convertible into GE's common stock during the next 5 years at a rate of 4.4944 shares of common per share of preferred. GE incurred no flotation costs because the deal was worked out between the two parties rather than being sold by underwriters. GE had been financing with commercial paper (until that market dried up) at an after-tax cost of about 2%, and its AAA-rated bonds were yielding about 8%, for an after-tax cost of about 4.8% because interest is tax-deductible. So the 10% coupon cost of Buffett's preferred stock was not cheap.

Buffett actually expected to earn more than 10% on the deal. We don't know what he assumed the stock would do over the next 5 years, but he might have expected it to grow at a rate of 13.3% per year, which would move the stock from its then-current price of $24.50 to $45.74. Given that growth rate, Buffett could earn a tidy 23.3% on his investment by converting to common stock at the end of Year 5. Even if the stock appreciated at only 6% he would still earn 16.78% per year, and if the stock actually declined then he would still earn 10%—provided GE didn't go bankrupt. (The rate of return on the convertible preferred stock is calculated in a Tab in ***Ch09 Tool Kit.xls***.)

Buffett's return is the mirror image of GE's cost. Because GE had been doing most of its financing with commercial paper and long-term debt at much lower rates, using convertible preferred instead was a real shock to its system. Obviously, this raised GE's weighted average cost of capital, and that presumably affected its required return on new assets and thus its capital budget.

The **component cost of preferred stock, r_{ps},** is the cost used in the WACC calculation. For preferred stock with a stated maturity date, we use the same approach as in the previous section for the cost of debt, keeping in mind that a firm has no tax savings with preferred stock. For preferred stock without a stated maturity date, r_{ps} is

$$\text{Component cost of preferred stock} = r_{ps} = \frac{D_{ps}}{P_{ps}(1-F)} \qquad \text{(9-4)}$$

Here D_{ps} is the preferred dividend, P_{ps} is the preferred stock price, and F is the flotation cost as a percentage of proceeds.

To illustrate the calculation, assume NCC has preferred stock that pays an $8 dividend per share and sells for $100 per share. If NCC issued new shares of preferred then it would incur an underwriting (or flotation) cost of 2.5%, or $2.50 per share, so it would net $97.50 per share. Therefore, NCC's cost of preferred stock is 8.2%:

$$r_{ps} = \$8/\$97.50 = 8.2\%$$

If we had not incorporated flotation costs, we would have incorrectly estimated $r_{ps} = \$8/\$100 = 8.0\%$, which is too big a difference to ignore. Therefore, analysts usually include flotation costs when estimating the firm's cost of preferred stock.

Although preferred stock is riskier than debt, NCC's preferred stock has a lower return to investors than does its debt: 8% versus 9%. However, recall that most preferred stock is held by other companies, which are allowed to exclude 70% of preferred stocks' dividends from taxation. Thus, the after-tax return to these investors is higher for preferred stock than for debt, which is consistent with preferred stock being riskier than debt.

Self-Test

Does the component cost of preferred stock include or exclude flotation costs? Explain.

Why is no tax adjustment made to the cost of preferred stock?

A company's preferred stock currently trades for $50 per share and pays a $3 annual dividend. Flotation costs are equal to 3% of the gross proceeds. If the company issues preferred stock, what is the cost of that stock? (6.19%)

9.5 Cost of Common Stock, r_s

Companies can raise common equity in two ways: (1) by selling newly issued shares to the public, and (2) by retaining and reinvesting earnings. If new shares are issued, what rate of return must the company earn to satisfy the new stockholders? In previous chapters we have seen that investors require a return of r_s. However, a company must earn more than r_s on new external equity to provide this rate of return to investors, because there are flotation costs when a firm issues new equity.

Few firms with moderate or slow growth issue new shares of common stock through public offerings.[8] In fact, less than 2% of all new corporate funds come from the external public equity market. There are three reasons for this.

1. As we noted earlier, flotation costs can be quite high.
2. Investors perceive the issuance of common stock as a negative signal about the true value of the company's stock. Investors believe that managers have superior knowledge about companies' future prospects and that managers are most likely to issue new stock when they think the current stock price is above its intrinsic value. Suppose a company has an extremely profitable new project but will have to finance it with external capital. If the firm finances the project with common stock, the new stockholders will share in the windfall when the new project's profits start rolling in. Therefore, it is logical to think that managers will want to finance really good new projects with debt, temporarily increasing the debt ratio but planning to sell stock when profits rise and pull up the stock price. On the other hand, if things look bad, management might want to finance with stock to let new shareholders share in the pain. The net result is that if a mature company announces plans to issue additional shares, investors typically take this as a signal of bad news; as a result, the stock declines.
3. Even without the signaling effect, an increase in the supply of stock will put pressure on the stock's price, forcing the company to sell the new stock at a lower price than existed before the new issue was announced.

In the remainder of this section, we assume that the company does not plan to issue new shares.[9] We will address the impact of flotation costs on the cost of equity in Section 9.10.

Does new equity capital raised by reinvesting earnings have a cost? The answer is a resounding "yes!" If earnings are reinvested, then stockholders will incur an

[8] A few companies issue new shares through new-stock dividend reinvestment plans, which we discuss in Chapter 14. Many companies sell stock to their employees, and companies occasionally issue stock to finance huge projects or mergers. Also, some utilities regularly issue common stock.

[9] There are times when companies should issue stock in spite of these problems; hence, we discuss stock issues and the cost of equity later in the chapter.

opportunity cost—the earnings could have been paid out as dividends or used to repurchase stock, and in either case stockholders would have received funds that they could reinvest in other securities. *Thus, the firm should earn on its reinvested earnings at least as much as its stockholders themselves could earn on alternative investments of equivalent risk.*

What rate of return could stockholders expect to earn on equivalent-risk investments? The answer is r_s, because they could presumably earn that return by simply buying the stock of the firm in question or that of a similar firm. *Therefore, r_s is the cost of common equity raised internally as reinvested earnings.* If a company can't earn at least r_s on reinvested earnings, then it should pass those earnings on to its stockholders and let them invest the money themselves in assets that do yield r_s.

Whereas debt and preferred stock are contractual obligations that have easily determined costs, it is more difficult to estimate r_s. However, we can employ the principles described in Chapters 6 and 7 to produce reasonably good estimates for the cost of equity. Three methods are typically used: (1) the Capital Asset Pricing Model (CAPM), (2) the discounted cash flow (DCF) method, and (3) the over-own-bond-yield-plus-judgmental-risk-premium approach. These methods are not mutually exclusive: When estimating a company's cost of equity, we generally use all three methods and then use an average, weighted on the basis of our confidence in the data used for each method.

Self-Test

What are the two primary sources of equity capital?

Why do most established firms not issue additional shares of common equity?

Explain why there is a cost to using reinvested earnings; that is, why aren't reinvested earnings a free source of capital?

9.6 The CAPM Approach

To estimate the cost of common stock using the Capital Asset Pricing Model as discussed in Chapter 6, we proceed as follows.

1. Estimate the risk-free rate, r_{RF}.
2. Estimate the current market risk premium, RP_M, which is the required market return minus the risk-free rate.
3. Estimate the stock's beta coefficient, b_i, which measures the stock's relative risk. The subscript i signifies Stock i's beta.
4. Use these three values in Equation 9-5 to estimate the stock's required rate of return:

$$r_s = r_{RF} + (RP_M)b_i \qquad (9\text{-}5)$$

Equation 9-5 shows that the CAPM estimate of r_s begins with the risk-free rate, r_{RF}. We then add a risk premium that is equal to the risk premium on the market, RP_M, scaled up or down to reflect the particular stock's risk as measured by its beta coefficient. The following sections explain how to implement this four-step process.

Estimating the Risk-Free Rate

The starting point for the CAPM cost-of-equity estimate is r_{RF}, the risk-free rate. There is no such thing as a truly riskless asset in the U.S. economy. Treasury securities are essentially free of default risk; however, nonindexed long-term T-bonds will suffer capital losses if interest rates rise, indexed long-term bonds will decline if the

To find the rate on a T-bond, go to **http://www.federalreserve.gov**. *Select "Economic Research & Data" and then select "Statistical Releases and Historical Data." Click on "Daily" for "H.15: Selected Interest Rates."*

real rate rises, and a portfolio of short-term T-bills will provide a volatile earnings stream because the rate earned on T-bills varies over time.

Since we cannot, in practice, find a truly riskless rate upon which to base the CAPM, what rate should we use? A survey of highly regarded companies shows that about two-thirds of them use the rate on 10-year Treasury bonds.[10] We agree with their choice, and here are our reasons.

1. Common stocks are long-term securities and—although a particular stockholder may not have a long investment horizon—most stockholders do invest on a relatively long-term basis. Therefore, it is reasonable to think that stock returns embody relatively long-term inflation expectations similar to those reflected in bonds rather than the short-term expectations in bills.
2. Short-term Treasury bill rates are more volatile than are long-term Treasury bond rates and, most experts agree, are more volatile than r_s.[11]
3. In theory, the CAPM is supposed to measure the required return over a particular holding period. When it is used to estimate the cost of equity for a project, the theoretically correct holding period is the life of the project. Since a time period of 10 years is a reasonable average for projects' lives, the return on a 10-year T-bond is a logical choice for the risk-free rate.

T-bond rates can be found in *The Wall Street Journal*, the *Federal Reserve Bulletin*, or on the Internet. Although most analysts use the yield on a 10-year T-bond as a proxy for the risk-free rate, yields on 20- or 30-year T-bonds are also reasonable proxies.

Estimating the Market Risk Premium

Recall from Chapter 6 that the market risk premium, RP_M, is the required return on the stock market minus the risk-free rate, where the risk-free rate usually is defined as the yield on a 10-year Treasury bond. This is also called the **equity risk premium**, or just the **equity premium**. Since most investors are risk averse, they require a higher anticipated return (a risk premium) to induce them to invest in risky equities versus a Treasury bond. Unfortunately, the required return on the market, and hence the equity premium, is not directly observable. Three approaches may be used to estimate the market risk premium: (1) calculate historical premiums and use them to estimate the current premium; (2) use the current value of the market to estimate forward-looking premiums; and (3) survey experts. We proceed with an explanation of each approach.

Historical Risk Premium. Historical risk premium data for U.S. securities, updated annually, are available from many sources, including Ibbotson Associates.[12] Using data from 1926 through the most recent year, Ibbotson calculates the actual realized rate of return each year for the stock market and for long-term government bonds. Ibbotson defines the annual equity risk premium as the difference between

---

[10]See Robert E. Bruner, Kenneth M. Eades, Robert S. Harris, and Robert C. Higgins, "Best Practices in Estimating the Cost of Capital: Survey and Synthesis," *Financial Practice and Education*, Spring/Summer 1998, pp. 13–28.

[11]Economic events usually have a larger impact on short-term rates than on long-term rates. For example, see the analysis of the 1995–1996 federal–debt limit disagreement between the White House and Congress provided in Srinivas Nippani, Pu Liu, and Craig T. Schulman, "Are Treasury Securities Free of Default?" *Journal of Financial and Quantitative Analysis*, June 2001, pp. 251–266.

[12]See *Ibbotson Stocks, Bonds, Bills, and Inflation: 2009 Valuation Yearbook* (Chicago: Morningstar, Inc., 2009) for the most recent estimates.

the historical realized returns on stocks and the historical returns on long-term T-bonds.[13] Ibbotson's 2009 book reported a 6.5% arithmetic average historical risk premium and a 4.4% geometric average. If investor risk aversion had actually been constant during the sample period, then the arithmetic average would be the best estimate for next year's risk premium, whereas the geometric average would be the best estimate for the longer-term risk premium, say, for the next 20 years.

There are several problems with using historical averages to estimate the current risk premium. First, stock returns are quite volatile, which leads to low confidence in estimated averages. For example, the estimated historical average premium is 6.5%, but the 95% confidence interval ranges from about 1.6% to 11.4%. In other words, there is a very good chance that the true risk premium is much different from the calculated 6.5% average.

Second, the historical average is extremely sensitive to the period over which it is calculated. Just 9 years ago the historical average premium was 8.1%, which is substantially different from the current 6.5% average. In fact, over the past 12 years the average T-bond return has been higher than the average stock return, resulting in a negative historical premium. However, the expected premium can't be negative—no one would invest in the stock market expecting to get a return that is less than the risk-free rate.

Third, changes in the risk premium can occur if investors' tolerance for risk changes. This causes problems in interpreting historical returns because a change in the required risk premium causes an *opposite change in the observed* premium. For example, an increase in the required premium means that investors have become more risk averse and require a higher return on stocks. But applying a higher discount rate to a stock's future cash flows causes a decline in stock price. Thus, an *increase* in the required premium causes a simultaneous *decrease* in the observed premium. Part of the market's precipitous decline in 2008 surely was due to investors' increased risk aversion.

Forward-Looking Risk Premiums. An alternative to the historical risk premium is the forward-looking, or ex ante, risk premium. Again, the market risk premium is $RP_M = r_M - r_{RF}$, but r_M and r_{RF} are measured using forward-looking rather than historical data. As explained previously, we can use the yield to maturity on a 10-year T-bond as an estimate of the risk-free rate, which was 2.94% when we wrote this in May 2009. The challenge is to estimate the required return on the market, r_M. The most common approach is to assume that the market is in equilibrium, in which case the required return is equal to the expected return: $r_M = \hat{r}_M$. We can use the discounted cash flow (DCF) model from Chapter 7 to estimate the expected market rate of return, $\hat{r}_M$. If we assume that the market dividend will grow at a constant rate and that the firms that make up the market pay out as dividends all the funds available for distribution (i.e., the firms make no stock repurchases or purchases of short-term investments), then the required return is:

$$\text{Required rate of return} = r_M = \text{Expected rate of return} = \hat{r}_M = \frac{D_1}{P_0} + g \tag{9-6}$$

Thus, the required return on the market can be estimated as the sum of the market's expected dividend yield plus the expected constant growth rate in dividends.

---

[13]The risk premium should be defined using the yield on T-bonds, so Ibbotson actually uses the return on T-bonds due to coupons rather than the total bond return (which includes capital gains and appreciation) as a proxy for the yield.

For current estimates from Standard & Poor's, go to **http://www2.standardandpoors.com/spf/xls/index/SP500EPSEST.XLS**.

It is easy to obtain the market's actual dividend yield; in May 2009, Reuters.com reported a dividend yield of 2.93% for the S&P 500. It is a little more difficult, but not impossible, to find an estimate of the expected dividend yield. In April 2009, Standard & Poor's reported a projected dividend yield of 2.8% for the S&P 500.

We have an estimate of the expected dividend yield to use in Equation 9-6, but where can we get an estimate of the constant dividend growth rate, g? There is no definitive answer to that question, but neither are we totally in the dark. In the long run, constant dividend growth is driven by constant earnings growth, which in turn is driven by constant sales growth; hence it is reasonable to use an estimate of the market's long-term growth rate of sales as a proxy for the dividend growth rate.

Go to the Federal Reserve Web site at **http://www.federalreserve.gov/releases/h15/update/** *for current yields on T-bonds and TIPS.*

Sales revenue growth is determined by growth in prices and units sold. In the long run, price growth will follow inflation. Historically, the average inflation rate has been about 3%. We can get a forward estimate of inflation by subtracting the real interest rate from the yield on a 10-year T-bond. The yield of an inflation-protected Treasury bond (called a TIPS) is a good estimate of the real interest rate. In May 2009, the yield on a 10-year TIPS was 1.69%, so a forward estimate of inflation is 2.94% − 1.69% = 1.25%.[14] This suggests that a reasonable estimate of expected inflation is somewhere between 1.25% and the historical average of 3%. In the long run, quantity growth will be driven by population growth. What is a reasonable estimate of sustainable population growth? There is no definitive answer, but somewhere around 1% to 2.5% is reasonable. Combining long-term population growth with expected inflation suggests that the long-term constant growth rate in sales is around 2.25% to 5.5%.[15]

Using a mid-point of our inflation and population growth estimates, a reasonable estimate of g is about 3.88%. When we combine this with the market's projected dividend yield, our estimate of the expected market risk return is

$$\begin{aligned} r_M = \hat{r}_M &= \frac{D_1}{P_0} + g \\ &= 2.82\% + 3.88\% \\ &= 6.70\% \end{aligned}$$

Given the 10-year T-bond yield of 2.94%, the estimated forward-looking market risk premium is therefore

$$\begin{aligned} RP_M &= r_M - r_{RF} \\ &= 6.70\% - 2.94\% \\ &= 3.76\% \end{aligned}$$

This probably underestimates the market risk premium because it relies on two unrealistic assumptions: (1) firms will not repurchase any stock and (2) growth in dividends will be constant. Let's examine each of these assumptions and see how to incorporate them into the forward-looking approach.

---

[14]The difference in the yield on a T-bond and a TIPS of the same maturity actually includes a risk premium for bearing inflation risk as well as the anticipated inflation, but we assume that anticipated inflation makes up most of the difference.

[15]Our estimates might be a little low because they ignore potential innovation and sustainable productivity growth. Will innovation create net increases in the quantity sold as new products hit the market, or will new products simply replace old products, resulting in no net increase in quantity sold? Real productivity (measured as per capita GDP) in the United States has grown at an average annual rate of about 1.5% to 2.5%. Will this continue, or will the law of diminishing returns cause productivity eventually to level off? If you are optimistic about the positive prospects of innovation and productivity, then you might want to add about 1% to our estimates of long-term sales growth. Keep in mind, though, that there's a reason economics is called "the dismal science"!

In recent years, companies in the S&P 500 have distributed roughly as much cash to shareholders in the form of stock repurchases as in dividends.[16] We define Rep/Div as the dollars used to repurchase stock divided by the dollars paid out in dividends and define Rep_1 as the expected repurchases at Year 1. In this notation, the total dollars paid out in dividends and repurchases will be (1 + Rep/Div)(Div). When stocks are repurchased each year, the number of outstanding shares declines each year, so the long-term growth rate in dividends per share (DPS) no longer is equal to the growth rate in sales. Let g be the long-term growth rate in total payouts (which should be the same as the long-term growth rate in sales and earnings) and let g_{DPS} be the long-term growth in DPS. The expected market return is given by

$$\begin{aligned} r_M = \hat{r}_M &= (1 + \text{Rep/Div})\frac{D_1}{P_0} + g \\ &= \frac{D_1}{P_0} + \frac{\text{Rep}_1}{P_0} + g \\ &= \frac{D_1}{P_0} + g_{DPS} \end{aligned} \tag{9-7}$$

where the actual growth rate in dividends per share, g_{DPS}, is the sum of the repurchase yield (Rep_1/P_0) and the long-term growth rate in sales. All three versions of Equation 9-7 are equivalent, but we usually work with the first line because it's easier to obtain the necessary inputs.

If we assume that companies will, in aggregate, distribute about as many dollars via repurchases as via cash dividends in the future as they have in the recent past, then Rep/Div ≈ 1. Using our previous estimates of the dividend yield and the long-term growth rate, the expected market return and risk premium are

$$\begin{aligned} r_M = \hat{r}_M &= (1 + \text{Rep/Div})\frac{D_1}{P_0} + g \\ &= (1+1)(2.82\%) + 3.88\% = 9.52\%; \\ RP_M &= r_M - r_{RF} = 9.52\% - 2.94\% = 6.98\% \end{aligned}$$

As these equations show, it is fairly easy to incorporate the impact of stock repurchases into our estimated market risk premium. We can also incorporate nonconstant payouts. We do this in ***Web Extension 9A*** and in the tab ***Web 9A*** in ***Ch09 Tool Kit.xls.*** Allowing for nonconstant growth and stock repurchases, we estimate that the required market return is about 8.97%. This would imply a market risk premium of

$$RP_M = r_M - r_{RF} = 8.97\% - 2.94\% = 6.03\%$$

Although this is our best estimate of the market risk premium as of April 2009, the forward-looking approach has some potential problems. First, analysts (and professors!) have a hard time accurately predicting sales, earnings, and payouts for more than a few quarters into the future. Second, the accuracy (and truthfulness) of analysts who work for investment banking firms has been questioned in recent years. This suggests it might be better to use the forecasts of independent analysts, such as those who work for publications like *Value Line*, rather than those who work for the large investment banking firms who sell stocks for a living. Third, different analysts

[16]For example, see the analysis by Douglas J. Skinner, "The Evolving Relation between Earnings, Dividends, and Stock Repurchases," *Journal of Financial Economics*, Vol. 87, 2008, pp. 582–609. We discuss payout strategies in more detail in Chapter 14.

have different estimates for growth, and we don't know which estimate, if any, truly represents the views of the marginal investor.

Surveys of Experts. What do the experts think about the market risk premium? Two professors at Duke University, John Graham and Campbell Harvey (now working in conjunction with *CFO* magazine), have surveyed CFOs quarterly beginning in 2000.[17] One survey question asks CFOs what they expect the S&P 500 return to be over the next year. Their answers over the past 8 years have implied an average expected risk premium of 3.46%. It is interesting that, in the most recent survey (March 2009), CFOs expect the S&P 500 to have a 2.18% return—this is less than the 10-year T-bond rate, which implies a negative market risk premium.

According to recent surveys of professors, the expected market risk premium is around 5.0% to 6.5%, with most professors in 2007 and 2008 indicating that they believe the risk premium has fallen somewhat since 2000.[18]

To muddy the water a bit further, some academics have recently argued for a much lower market risk premium. Professors Eugene Fama and Kenneth French examined earnings and dividend growth rates during the period from 1951 to 2000 and estimated the forward-looking market risk premium to be 2.55%. Similarly, Professor Jay Ritter from the University of Florida argues that the forward-looking market risk premium should be based on inflation-adjusted expected returns, which would make it even lower—closer to 1%.[19]

Our View on the Market Risk Premium. After reading the previous sections, you might well be confused about the best way to estimate the market risk premium. Here's our opinion: The risk premium is driven primarily by investors' attitudes toward risk, and there are good reasons to believe that investors' risk aversion changes over time. Some factors suggest that the premium has declined. The introduction of pension plans, Social Security, health insurance, and disability insurance over the last 50 years means that people today can take more chances with their investments, which should make them less risk averse. Moreover, many households have dual incomes, which also allows investors to take more chances. Finally, the historical average return on the market as Ibbotson measures it is probably too high for two reasons. The first is survivorship bias: the companies that fail had low returns, so excluding them raises the average historical return on stocks, which in turn raises the historical risk premium. The second reason is that increases in required returns cause decreases in observed returns, and vice versa.

On the other hand, we have recently seen a huge plunge in stock and home prices, most of us know people who have recently lost their jobs, and the pundits speak of investors exiting the stock market as a result of recent losses and fears of more losses. And some analysts who were recently extolling the virtues of "stocks for the long run" are now recommending T-bonds and other low-risk assets rather than stock.

Putting it all together, we conclude that the true risk premium in 2009 is lower than Ibbotson's long-term historical average, but it is certainly not negative as suggested by

---

[17]See John Graham and Campbell Harvey, "The Equity Risk Premium in 2008," Working Paper, Duke University, 2008. For updates on the survey, see **http://www.cfosurvey.org**.

[18]See Ivo Welch, "Views of Financial Economists on The Equity Premium and Other Issues," *The Journal of Business*, October 2000, 501–537, with 2009 updates at **http://welch.econ.brown.edu/academics/equpdate-results2009.html**. Also see Pablo Fernaández, "Market Risk Premium Used in 2008 by Professors: A Survey with 1,400 Answers" (April 16, 2009), at SSRN: **http://ssrn.com/abstract=1344209**.

[19]See Eugene F. Fama and Kenneth R. French, "The Equity Premium," *Journal of Finance*, April 2002, pp. 637–659; and Jay Ritter, "The Biggest Mistakes We Teach," *Journal of Financial Research*, Summer 2002, pp. 159–168.

some recent data. But just how low is it? In our consulting, we currently (during the bear market of 2008–2009) use a risk premium of about 6%, but we would have a hard time arguing with someone who used a risk premium anywhere in the range of 3.5% to 6.5%. We believe that investors' aversion to risk is relatively stable much of the time, but it is not absolutely constant from year to year and is certainly not constant during periods of great stress, such as during the 2008–2009 financial crisis. When stock prices are relatively high, investors feel less risk averse, so we would use a risk premium at the low end of our range. Conversely, when prices are depressed, we would use a premium at the high end of the range. The bottom line is that there is no way to prove that a particular risk premium is either right or wrong, though we'd be suspicious of an estimated market premium that is less than 3.0% or greater than 6.5%.[20]

Estimating Beta

To find an estimate of beta, go to **http://www.reuters.com** *and then enter the ticker symbol for a stock quote. Or go to Thomson ONE—Business School Edition. Beta is shown in the Key Fundamentals section.*

Recall from Chapter 6 that beta can be estimated as the slope coefficient in a regression, with the company's stock returns on the y-axis and market returns on the x-axis. The result is called the *historical beta* because it is based on historical data. Although this approach is conceptually straightforward, complications quickly arise in practice.

First, there is no theoretical guidance as to the correct holding period for measuring returns. The returns for a company can be calculated using daily, weekly, or monthly periods, and the resulting betas will differ. Beta is also sensitive to the number of years of data that are used. With too few years, there will be few observations and the regression will not be statistically significant. On the other hand, with too many years the statistical significance may be improved but the "true" beta may have changed over the sample period. In practice, it is common to use either 3 to 5 years of monthly returns, or perhaps 1 to 2 years of weekly returns. Unfortunately, betas calculated in different ways can be different, and it is impossible to know for certain which is correct.

A second problem is that the market return should, in theory, reflect returns on every single asset—even human capital as reflected in people's earning power. In practice, however, it is common to use only an index of common stocks such as the S&P 500, the NYSE Composite, or the Wilshire 5000. Even though these indexes are correlated with one another, using different indexes in the regression will result in a different beta, and we would surely obtain a different beta if we broadened the index to include real estate and other assets.

Third, some organizations modify the calculated historical beta in order to produce what they deem to be a more accurate estimate of the "true" beta, where the true beta is the one that reflects the risk perceptions of the marginal investor. One modification, called an *adjusted beta*, attempts to correct a possible statistical bias by adjusting the historical beta to make it closer to the known average beta of 1.0. A second modification is to estimate a *fundamental beta*, which incorporates known information such as any changes in the company's product lines or capital structure.

Fourth, the estimate of beta for any individual company is statistically imprecise. The average company has an estimated beta of 1.0, but the 95% confidence interval ranges from about 0.6 to 1.4. For most companies, if your regression produces an estimated beta of 1.0, then in general you can only be 95% sure that the true beta lies within the range from 0.6 to 1.4. This isn't a big problem with well-diversified portfolios, but it does add another element of uncertainty when calculating the cost of equity for a single company.

---

[20]For more on estimating the risk premium, see Robert S. Harris and Felicia C. Marston, "Estimating Shareholder Risk Premia Using Analysts' Growth Forecasts," *Financial Management*, Summer 1992, pp. 63–70.

The preceding discussion refers to conditions in the United States and other countries with well-developed financial markets where relatively good data are available. When we consider countries with less-developed financial markets, we are much less certain about the true size of a company's beta. Moreover, further complications arise when we are dealing with multinational companies, especially those that raise equity capital in different parts of the world. We might, for example, be relatively confident in the beta calculated for the parent company in its home country but less confident of the betas for subsidiaries located in other countries. When such complications arise, we are often forced to make "educated guesses" as to the appropriate beta. It would be nice to have exact, precise numbers for everything and thus be able to make decisions with a great deal of confidence, but that's not the way the world is—we are often forced to use judgment and to make educated guesses. Still, our discussion should help improve your judgment regarding the choice of beta for use in cost-of-capital studies, and it should also keep you from being too dogmatic about the accuracy of your beta and therefore your estimated cost of capital.

One More Caveat Regarding the CAPM Approach

We should point out one more potential problem with the CAPM: It has never been proven that investors base their required rates of return on the equation $r_M = r_{RF} + (RP_M)b_i$. Hundreds, perhaps thousands of studies have been conducted to test the validity of the CAPM, but there have been no definitive answers. The principal problem is that the CAPM itself deals only with *expectations*, yet the tests of the theory (such as the Fama-French work described in Chapter 6) have necessarily relied on historical data.

Still, we do know that security analysts and portfolio managers rely on the CAPM for much of their work, and betas are widely publicized. In addition, the CAPM's focus on diversification and systematic risk is quite logical, so it makes sense for people to use it when they make investment decisions. Therefore, it is reasonable to use the CAPM when you estimate the cost of equity, as most academics recommend and most corporate practitioners do. Just recognize that there may be other factors at work and so—even if you could estimate r_{RF}, b_i, and RP_M exactly—your estimate of r_s might still not be exact.

An Illustration of the CAPM Approach

To illustrate the CAPM approach, assume that $r_{RF} = 5\%$, $RP_M = 5.5\%$, and NCC's $b_i = 1.2$. Therefore, NCC is riskier than an average company, and its cost of equity is about 11.6%:

$$\begin{aligned} r_s &= 5\% + (5.5\%)(1.2) \\ &= 5\% + 6.6\% \\ &= 11.6\% \end{aligned}$$

It should be obvious by now that, although the CAPM approach appears to yield precise estimates of r_s, it is impossible to know with certainty the correct values of the required inputs to make it operational; this is because (1) it is impossible to estimate the required inputs precisely and (2) even if we knew the correct inputs, it might still turn out that the CAPM does not perfectly reflect the views of the marginal investor. Still, in our judgment it is possible to develop "reasonable" estimates of the required variables, and we believe that investors do use the CAPM concept when making decisions; thus that it can be used to obtain reasonable estimates of the cost of equity capital. Indeed, despite the difficulties we have pointed out, surveys indicate that the CAPM is the dominant choice for the vast majority of companies in the United States and around the world.

Self-Test

What is generally considered to be the more appropriate estimate of the risk-free rate: the yield on a short-term T-bill or the yield on a 10-year T-bond?

Explain both the historical and the forward-looking approach to estimating the market risk premium.

Describe some problems one encounters when estimating beta.

A company's beta is 1.4, the yield on a 10-year T-bond is 4%, and the market risk premium is 4.5%. What is r_s? **(10.3%)**

9.7 Dividend-Yield-Plus-Growth-Rate, or Discounted Cash Flow (DCF), Approach

In Chapter 7, we saw that if the marginal investor expects dividends to grow at a constant rate and if the company makes all payouts in the form of dividends (the company does not repurchase stock), then the price of a stock can be found as follows:

$$P_0 = \frac{D_1}{r_s - g} \quad (9\text{-}8)$$

Here P_0 is the price of the stock, D_1 is the dividend expected to be paid at the end of Year 1, g is the expected growth rate in dividends, and r_s is the required rate of return. Assuming the stock is in equilibrium, we can solve for r_s to obtain the required rate of return on common equity, which for the marginal investor is also equal to the expected rate of return:

$$\hat{r}_s = r_s = \frac{D_1}{P_0} + \text{Expected } g \quad (9\text{-}9)$$

Thus, investors expect to receive a dividend yield, D_1/P_0, plus a capital gain, g, for a total expected return of $\hat{r}_s$. In equilibrium this expected return is also equal to the required return, r_s. This method of estimating the cost of equity is called the **discounted cash flow**, or **DCF, method**. Henceforth, we will assume that markets are at equilibrium (which means that $r_s = \hat{r}_s$), and this permits us to use the terms r_s and $\hat{r}_s$ interchangeably.

Estimating Inputs for the DCF Approach

Three inputs are required to use the DCF approach: the current stock price, the current dividend, and the marginal investor's expected dividend growth rate. The stock price and the dividend are easy to obtain, but the expected growth rate is difficult to estimate, as we will see in the following sections.

Historical Growth Rates. If earnings and dividend growth rates have been relatively stable in the past, and if investors expect these trends to continue, then the past realized growth rate may be used as an estimate of the expected future growth rate. This is a reasonable proposition, but such situations occur only at a handful of very mature, slow-growing companies. Unfortunately, this limits the usefulness of historical growth rates as predictors of future growth rates for most companies.

Retention Growth Model. Most firms pay out some of their net income as dividends and reinvest, or retain, the rest. The more they retain, and the higher the earned rate of return on those retained earnings, the larger their growth rate. This is the idea behind the retention growth model.

The **payout ratio** is the percent of net income that the firm pays out in dividends, and the **retention ratio** is the complement of the payout ratio: Retention ratio = (1 − Payout ratio). NCC's payout ratio has averaged 63% over the past 15 years, so its retention rate has averaged 1.0 − 0.63 = 0.37 = 37%. Also, NCC's return on equity (ROE) has averaged 14.5% over the past 15 years. We know that, other things held constant, the earnings growth rate depends on the amount of income the firm retains and the rate of return it earns on those retained earnings, and the **retention growth equation** can be expressed as follows:

1- Payout Ratio

$$g = \text{ROE}(\text{Retention ratio}) \quad \text{(9-10)}$$

When we use this equation to estimate the DCF growth rate, we are implicitly making four important assumptions: (1) we expect the payout rate, and thus the retention rate, to remain constant; (2) we expect the ROE on new investments to remain constant and equal to the ROE on existing assets; (3) the firm is not expected to repurchase or issue new common stock, or, if it does, this new stock will be sold at a price equal to its book value; and (4) future projects are expected to have the same degree of risk as the firm's existing assets. Under these assumptions, the earnings growth rate will be constant, and it will also be the dividend growth rate.

Using NCC's 14.5% average ROE and its 37% retention rate, we can use Equation 9-10 to find the estimated g:

$$g = 14.5\%(0.37) = 5.365 \approx 5.4\%$$

Analysts' Forecasts. A third technique calls for using security analysts' forecasts. As we discussed earlier, analysts publish earnings' growth rate estimates for most of the larger publicly owned companies. For example, *Value Line* provides such forecasts on about 1,700 companies, and all of the larger brokerage houses provide similar forecasts. Further, several companies compile analysts' forecasts on a regular basis and provide summary information such as the median and range of forecasts on widely followed companies. These growth rate summaries, such as those compiled by Zacks or by Thomson ONE—BSE, can be found on the Internet. These earnings growth rates are often used as proxies for dividend growth rates.

WWW

For example, see **http://www.zacks.com.**

Note, however, that analysts' forecasts often involve nonconstant growth. For example, one widely followed analyst forecasted that NCC would have a 10.4% annual growth rate in earnings and dividends over the next 5 years, after which the growth rate would decline to 5%. Such nonconstant growth forecasts can be converted to an approximate constant growth rate. Computer simulations indicate that dividends beyond Year 50 contribute very little to the value of any stock—the present value of all dividends beyond Year 50 is virtually zero, so for practical purposes we can ignore anything beyond 50 years. If we consider only a 50-year horizon, then we can develop a weighted average growth rate and use it as a constant growth rate for cost-of-capital purposes. In the NCC case, we assume a growth rate of 10.4% for 5 years followed by a growth rate of 5% for 45 years. We weight the short-term growth by 5/50 = 10% and the long-term growth by 45/50 = 90%. This produces an average growth rate of 0.10(10.4%) + 0.90(5%) = 5.54% ≈ 5.5%.[21]

[21]Instead of converting nonconstant growth estimates into an approximate average growth rate, it is possible to use the nonconstant growth estimates to estimate directly the required return on common stock. See ***Web Extension 9A*** on the textbook's Web site for an explanation of this approach; all calculations are in the worksheet ***Web 9A*** in the file ***Ch09 Tool Kit.xls***.

Applying the DCF Approach. To illustrate the DCF approach, suppose NCC's stock sells for $32, its next expected dividend is $1.82, and its expected growth rate is 5.5%. NCC is not expected to repurchase any stock. NCC's stock is thought to be in equilibrium, so its expected and required rates of return are equal. Based on these assumptions, its estimated DCF cost of common equity is 11.2%:

$$\hat{r}_s = r_s = \frac{\$1.82}{\$32.00} + 5.5\%$$
$$= 5.7\% + 5.5\%$$
$$= 11.2\%$$

Evaluating the Methods for Estimating Growth

Observe that the DCF approach finds the cost of common equity as the dividend yield (the expected dividend divided by the current price) plus the growth rate. The dividend yield can be estimated without much error, but there is uncertainty in the growth estimate. We would like to know the expected average growth rate as forecasted by the marginal investor, but that rate simply cannot be observed. However, we have considered three methods that can be used to estimate expected future growth: (1) historical growth rates, which implicitly assume that investors expect past results to be repeated in the future; (2) the retention growth model, which implicitly assumes that investors expect historical payout ratios and ROEs to be repeated; and (3) analysts' forecasts. Of these three methods, the third is the most logical. Moreover, studies have also shown that analysts' forecasts usually predict actual future growth better than the other methods. We recommend a primary reliance on analysts' forecasts for the growth rate in DCF cost of capital estimates.[22]

Self-Test

What inputs are required for the DCF method?

What are three ways to estimate the expected dividend growth rate, and which of these methods is likely to provide the best estimate?

A company's estimated growth rate in dividends is 6%, its current stock price is $40, and its expected annual dividend is $2. Using the DCF approach, what is the firm's r_s? **(11%)**

9.8 Over-Own-Bond-Yield-Plus-Judgmental-Risk-Premium Approach

Some analysts use a subjective, ad hoc procedure to estimate a firm's cost of common equity: They simply add a judgmental risk premium of 3% to 5% to the interest rate on the firm's own long-term debt. It is logical to think that firms with risky, low-rated, and hence high–interest rate debt will also have risky, high-cost equity, and the procedure for basing the cost of equity on a readily observable debt cost utilizes this logic. In this approach,

$$r_s = \text{Company's own bond yield} + \text{Judgmental risk premium} \quad \text{(9-11)}$$

[22] See Robert Harris, "Using Analysts' Growth Rate Forecasts to Estimate Shareholder Required Rates of Return," *Financial Management*, Spring 1986, pp. 58–67.

NCC's bonds yield 9.0%, so if its over-own-bond-yield judgmental risk premium is estimated as 3% then its estimated cost of equity is 12%:

$$r_s = 9\% + 3\% = 12\%$$

Because the risk premium is a judgmental estimate, the estimated value of r_s is also judgmental. Similarly, though, a lot of judgment goes into the CAPM and DCF estimates of r_s. Empirical work suggests that the risk premium over a firm's own bond yield generally has ranged from 3 to 5 percentage points.[23] Therefore, this method is not likely to produce a precise cost of equity, but it can help "get us into the ballpark."

Self-Test

Explain the reasoning behind the bond-yield-plus-judgmental-risk-premium approach.

A company's bond yield is 7%. If the appropriate over-own-bond-yield risk premium is 3.5%, then what is r_s? **(10.5%)**

9.9 Comparison of the CAPM, DCF, and Over-Own-Bond-Yield-Plus-Judgmental-Risk-Premium Methods

We have discussed three methods for estimating the cost of common stock. For NCC, the CAPM estimate is 11.6%, the DCF constant growth estimate is 11.2%, and the over-own-bond-yield-plus-judgmental-risk-premium estimate is 12%. The overall average of these three methods is (11.6% + 11.2% + 12%)/3 = 11.6%. These results are unusually close, so it would make little difference which one we used. However, if the methods produced widely varied estimates, then a financial analyst would have to use his or her own best judgment regarding the relative merits of each estimate and then choose one that seemed reasonable under the circumstances.

Recent surveys indicate that the CAPM is by far the most widely used method. Although most firms use more than one method, almost 74% of respondents in one survey (and 85% in another) used the CAPM.[24] This is in sharp contrast to a 1982 survey, which found that only 30% of respondents used the CAPM.[25] Only 16% now use the DCF approach, down from 31% in 1982. The bond-yield-plus-judgmental-risk-premium is relied upon primarily by companies that are not publicly traded.

People experienced in estimating the cost of equity recognize that both careful analysis and sound judgment are required. It would be nice to pretend that judgment is unnecessary and to specify an easy, precise way of determining the exact cost of

---

[23]Analysts have surveyed portfolio managers, asking how much more they would have to expect to earn on a firm's stock versus its bonds to induce them to buy the stock. The range we have seen is 3% to 5%, which is what we use. Discussions with financial executives indicate that most are comfortable with this range. All this is purely judgmental, but that's the case for much of finance.

[24]See John R. Graham and Campbell Harvey, "The Theory and Practice of Corporate Finance: Evidence from the Field," *Journal of Financial Economics*, 2001, pp. 187–243, and the paper cited in footnote 10. It is interesting that a growing number of firms (about 34%) also are using CAPM-type models with more than one factor. Of these firms, over 40% include factors for interest rate risk, foreign exchange risk, and business cycle risk (proxied by gross domestic product). More than 20% of these firms include a factor for inflation, size, and exposure to particular commodity prices. Less than 20% of these firms make adjustments due to distress factors, book-to-market ratios, or momentum factors.

[25]See Lawrence J. Gitman and Vincent Mercurio, "Cost of Capital Techniques Used by Major U.S. Firms: Survey Analysis of *Fortune's* 1000," *Financial Management*, 1982, pp. 21–29.

equity capital. Unfortunately, this is not possible—finance is in large part a matter of judgment, and we simply must face that fact.[26]

Self-Test

Which approach for estimating the required return on common stock is used most often by businesses today?

9.10 Adjusting the Cost of Equity for Flotation Costs

As explained earlier, most mature companies rely primarily on reinvesting a large portion of their earnings and hence rarely issue new common stock. However, for those that do, the **cost of new common equity, r_e,** or external equity, is higher than the cost of equity raised internally by reinvesting earnings, r_s, because of the **flotation costs** involved in issuing new common stock. What rate of return must be earned on new investments to make issuing stock worthwhile? Put another way, what is the cost of new common stock?

The answer, for a constant growth firm, is found by applying this formula:

$$r_e = \hat{r}_e = \frac{D_1}{P_0(1-F)} + g \quad (9\text{-}12)$$

In Equation 9-10, F is the percentage flotation cost incurred in selling the new stock, so here $P_0(1 - F)$ is the net price per share received by the company.

Using the same inputs as when we estimated NCC's cost of common equity using the DCF approach—but assuming that NCC incurs a flotation cost of 12.5% to sell new common stock—its cost of new outside equity is calculated as follows:

$$r_e = \frac{\$1.82}{\$32(1-0.125)} + 5.5\%$$

$$= 6.5\% + 5.5\% = 12.0\%$$

As we calculated earlier using the DCF model (but ignoring flotation costs), NCC's stockholders require a return of $r_s = 11.2\%$. However, because of flotation costs the company must earn *more* than 11.2% on the net funds it has to invest if investors are to receive an 11.2% return on the money they actually contributed. Specifically, if the firm earns 12.0% on net funds obtained by issuing new stock, then earnings per share will remain at the previously expected level, the firm's expected dividend can be maintained, and so the price per share will not decline. If it earns less than 12.0% then earnings, dividends, and growth will fall below expectations, which will cause a decline in the stock price. If it earns more than 12.0%, the stock price will rise.

As we noted previously, most analysts use the CAPM to estimate the cost of equity. In an earlier section, we estimated NCC's CAPM cost of equity as 11.6%. How would the analyst incorporate flotation costs into a CAPM cost estimate? If application of the DCF methodology gives a cost of internally generated equity of

[26]One senior executive told us that, in his judgment, the CAPM's popularity was partly the result of lower-level staffers wanting to use methods that can be defended by reference to the finance literature and to "hard" numbers based on published data, like historical betas and risk premiums. His conclusion was that the CAPM's use with historical data is widely discussed in the finance literature and taught in MBA programs, so the result is sort of a self-fulfilling prophecy. He went on to say that in his opinion a great deal of judgment is required; in his company, lower-level staffers derived relatively precise results and then experienced, senior managers applied judgment when making decisions based on those results. He thought this procedure worked out well for his company.

TABLE 9-1 Average Flotation Costs for Debt and Equity

AMOUNT OF CAPITAL RAISED (MILLIONS OF DOLLARS)	AVERAGE FLOTATION COST FOR COMMON STOCK (% OF TOTAL CAPITAL RAISED)	AVERAGE FLOTATION COST FOR NEW DEBT (% OF TOTAL CAPITAL RAISED)
2–9.99	13.28%	4.39%
10–19.99	8.72	2.76
20–39.99	6.93	2.42
40–59.99	5.87	2.32
60–79.99	5.18	2.34
80–99.99	4.73	2.16
100–199.99	4.22	2.31
200–499.99	3.47	2.19
500 and up	3.15	1.64

Source: Inmoo Lee, Scott Lochhead, Jay Ritter, and Quanshui Zhao, "The Costs of Raising Capital," *The Journal of Financial Research*, Spring 1996, pp. 59–74. Reprinted with permission.

11.2% but a cost of 12.0% when flotation costs are involved, then the flotation costs add 0.8 percentage points to the cost of equity. To incorporate flotation costs into the CAPM estimate, we would simply add 0.8% to the 11.6% CAPM estimate, resulting in a 12.4% estimated cost of external equity. As an alternative, you could find the average of the CAPM, DCF, and over-own-bond-yield-plus-judgmental-risk-premium costs of equity (ignoring flotation costs) and then add to it the 0.8 percentage points to adjust for flotation costs.

Table 9-1 shows the average flotation costs for debt and equity issued by U.S. corporations in the 1990s. The common stock flotation costs are for non-IPO issues. For IPOs, flotation costs are higher: about 17% higher if less than \$10 million is raised and higher still as issue size increases. The data in Table 9-1 include both utility and nonutility companies; if utilities had been excluded, the reported flotation costs would have been higher. Table 9-1 shows that flotation costs are significantly higher for equity than for debt. Notice that all flotation costs, as a *percentage* of capital raised, fall as the *amount* of capital raised increases.

The lower cost for issuing debt results from two factors. First, debt is a contractual obligation; hence returns are more predictable, which makes selling debt easier. Second, corporate debt is sold mainly in large blocks to institutional investors, whereas common stock is sold in smaller amounts to many different investors; this imposes higher costs on the investment banks, who pass these costs on to the issuing company.

Self-Test

What are flotation costs?

Why are flotation costs higher for stock than for debt?

A firm has common stock with D_1 = \$3.00; P_0 = \$30; g = 5%; and F = 4%. If the firm must issue new stock, what is its cost of external equity, r_e? **(15.42%)**

9.11 Composite, or Weighted Average, Cost of Capital, WACC

As we saw earlier in this chapter (and as we discuss in more detail in Chapter 15), each firm has an optimal capital structure, which is defined as the mix of debt, preferred, and common equity that maximizes its stock price. Therefore, a value-maximizing firm must attempt to find its *target (or optimal) capital structure* and then raise new capital in a manner that will keep the actual capital structure on target over time. In this chapter, we assume that the firm has identified its optimal capital structure, that it uses this optimum as the target, and that it finances so as to remain constantly on target. How the target is established is examined in Chapter 15. The target proportions of debt, preferred stock, and common equity, along with the component costs of capital, are used to calculate the WACC, as shown previously in Equation 9-1:

$$\text{WACC} = w_d r_d(1-T) + w_{ps} r_{ps} + w_s r_s \quad (9\text{-}1)$$

Here w_d, w_{ps}, and w_s are the target weights for debt, preferred, and common equity, respectively.[27]

To illustrate, we first note that NCC has a target capital structure calling for 30% debt, 10% preferred stock, and 60% common equity. Its before-tax cost of debt, r_d, is 9%; its cost of preferred stock, r_{ps}, is 8.2%; its cost of common equity, r_s, is 11.6%; its marginal tax rate is 40%; and all of its new equity will come from reinvested earnings. We can now calculate NCC's weighted average cost of capital as follows:

$$\begin{aligned} \text{WACC} &= 0.3(9.0\%)(1-0.4) + 0.1(8.2\%) + 0.6(11.6\%) \\ &= 9.4\% \end{aligned}$$

Three points should be noted. First, the WACC is the cost the company would incur to raise each new, or *marginal*, dollar of capital—it is not the average cost of dollars raised in the past. Second, the percentages of each capital component, called *weights*, should be based on management's target capital structure, not on the particular sources of financing in any single year. Third, the target weights should be based on market values and not on book values. We discuss these points in what follows.

Marginal Rates versus Historical Rates

The required rates of return for a company's investors, whether they are new or old, are always marginal rates. For example, a stockholder might have invested in a company last year when the risk-free interest rate was 6% and the required return on equity was 12%. If the risk-free rate subsequently falls and is now 4%, then the investor's required return on equity is now 10% (holding all else constant). This is the same required rate of return that a new equity holder would have, whether the new investor bought stock in the secondary market or through a new equity offering. In other words, whether the shareholders are already equity holders or are brand-new equity holders, they all have the same required rate of return, which is the current required rate of return on equity. The same reasoning applies for the firm's bondholders. All bondholders, whether old or new, have a required rate of return equal to today's yield on the firm's debt, which is based on current market conditions.

Because investors' required rates of return are based on *current* market conditions, not on market conditions when they purchased their securities, it follows that the cost of capital depends on current conditions and not on past market conditions.

---

[27]If a company also used short-term debt as a permanent source of financing, then its cost of capital would be:

$$\text{WACC} = w_d r_d(1-T) + w_{STD} r_{STD}(1-T) + w_{ps} r_{ps} + w_s r_s \quad (9\text{-}1a)$$

where w_{STD} is the percentage of the firm that is financed with short-term debt and r_{STD} is the cost of short-term debt.

Target Weights versus Annual Financing Choices

We have heard managers (and students!) say, "Our debt has a 5% after-tax cost versus a 10% WACC and a 14% cost of equity. Therefore, since we will finance only with debt this year, we should evaluate this year's projects at a 5% cost." There are two flaws in that line of reasoning.

First, suppose the firm exhausts its capacity to issue low-cost debt this year to take on projects with after-tax returns as low as 5.1% (which is slightly higher than the after-tax cost of debt). Then next year, when the firm must finance with common equity, it will have to turn down projects with returns as high as 13.9% (which is slightly lower than the cost of equity). To avoid this problem, a firm that plans to remain in business indefinitely should evaluate all projects using the 10% WACC.

Second, both existing and new investors have claims on *all* future cash flows. For example, if a company raises debt and also invests in a new project that same year, the new debtholders don't have a specific claim on that specific project's cash flows (assuming it is not non-recourse project financing). In fact, new debtholders receive a claim on the cash flows being generated by existing as well as new projects, while old debtholders (and equity holders) have claims on both new and existing projects. Thus, the decision to take on a new project should depend on the project's ability to satisfy all of the company's investors, not just the new debtholders, even if only debt is being raised that year.

Weights for Component Costs: Book Values versus Market Values versus Targets

Our primary reason for calculating the WACC is to use it in capital budgeting or corporate valuation, since we need to compare the expected returns on projects and companies with the cost of the funds used to finance them. As Figure 9-1 showed, accountants report financial statements in book value terms, but financial analysts can convert those numbers into market values.

At one time academics—and, to a lesser extent, financial executives—debated whether we should use book value versus market value weights when estimating the cost of capital. The main arguments in favor of book weights were (1) these are the numbers shown on financial statements, (2) the bond rating agencies seem to focus on book weights, and (3) book values are more stable than market values, so book value weights produce more stable inputs for use in capital budgeting. The main arguments in favor of market value weights were (1) firms raise funds by selling securities at their market values, not at book values, and (2) market values are more consistent with the idea of value maximization.

Market value supporters won the argument, as they should have, but in a dynamic world it is simply not feasible to blindly and mechanically focus on current market value weights (i.e., on the market value weights given in Column J of Figure 9-1). As a result of the stock market crash of 2008–2009, many firms saw their equity ratios drop from about 75% to near 10%, and managers concluded that neither the book value nor market value numbers represented how they wanted to finance in the future. Thus, they didn't want to use either book value or market value weights.

What they did, as we discuss in Chapter 15, was focus on a less mechanical, more judgmental capital structure—the **Target Capital Structure**. At the target structure, the firm uses enough debt to gain the benefits of interest tax shields and also leverages up earnings per share. However, the amount of debt is not so great that it subjects the firm to a high probability of financial distress during a period of economic recession. Managements have some flexibility in setting their target capital

Global Variations in the Cost of Capital

For U.S. firms to be competitive with foreign companies, they must have a cost of capital no greater than that faced by their international competitors. In the past, many experts argued that U.S. firms were at a disadvantage. In particular, Japanese firms enjoyed a very low cost of capital, which lowered their total costs and thus made it hard for U.S. firms to compete with them. Recent events, however, have considerably narrowed cost-of-capital differences between U.S. and Japanese firms. In particular, the U.S. stock market has outperformed the Japanese market in recent years, which has made it easier and cheaper for U.S. firms to raise equity capital.

As capital markets become increasingly integrated, cross-country differences in the cost of capital are declining. Today, most large corporations raise capital throughout the world; hence, we are moving toward one global capital market instead of distinct capital markets in each country. Government policies and market conditions can affect the cost of capital within a given country, but this primarily affects smaller firms that do not have access to global capital markets, and even these differences are becoming less important as time passes. What matters most is the risk of the individual firm, not the market in which it raises capital.

structures, but they are also subject to constraints and market forces. Firms compare their data with those of benchmark firms in their industry; this allows firms to see how they are doing relative to other firms in their industry. If a company uses too little debt then its earnings will be lower than they could have been without subjecting the firm to undue risk, and individual stockholders, private equity firms, or hedge firms will probably challenge management and force it toward the optimal structure. If a company uses too much debt, then lenders will raise interest rates or perhaps refuse to lend at all, rating agencies and analysts will report on its risky situation, the intrinsic value of the firm's stock will decline, and its market value will suffer. Thus, forces exist to compel firms to set their target capital structures at levels that will maximize their intrinsic values and thus their stock prices.

Finally, note that an optimal capital structure in one economic environment may not be optimal under different market conditions. In a dynamic economy it is important to constantly monitor the situation and make adjustments to the target capital structure as circumstances change.

Self-Test

How is the weighted average cost of capital calculated? Write out the equation.

Should the weights used to calculate the WACC be based on book values, market values, or something else? Explain.

A firm has the following data: target capital structure of 25% debt, 10% preferred stock, and 65% common equity; tax rate = 40%; r_d = 7%; r_{ps} = 7.5%; and r_s = 11.5%. Assume the firm will not issue new stock. What is this firm's WACC? **(9.28%)**

9.12 Factors That Affect the WACC

The cost of capital is affected by some factors that are under a firm's control and some that are not.

Three Factors the Firm Cannot Control

Three key determinants of WACC are beyond a firm's control: (1) the state of the financial markets, including stock prices in general and the level of interest rates; (2) investors' aversion to risk and thus the market risk premium; and (3) tax rates as set by Congress.

Stock and Bond Markets. The stock and bond markets, and the market for short-term debt, are normally in equilibrium and thus fairly stable. However, at times the markets are disrupted, making it virtually impossible for a firm to raise capital at reasonable rates. This happened in 2008 and 2009, before the U.S. Treasury and the Federal Reserve intervened to open up the capital markets. During such times, firms tend to cut back on growth plans; if they must raise capital, its cost can be extraordinarily high. For example, see the box "GE and Warren Buffett: The Cost of Preferred Stock" presented earlier in the chapter.

Note also that if interest rates in the economy rise, the costs of both debt and equity will increase. The firm will have to pay bondholders a higher interest rate to obtain debt capital; and, as indicated in our discussion of the CAPM, higher interest rates also increase the cost of equity. Interest rates are heavily influenced by inflation. When inflation hit historic highs in the early 1980s, interest rates followed, but they trended down until the financial crisis in 2008 led to an upward spike. However, strong actions by the federal government in the spring of 2009 brought rates back down. These actions should encourage investment, and there is little doubt that they will eventually lead the economy out of its recession. However, many observers fear that the government's actions will also reignite long-run inflation, which would lead to higher interest rates.[28]

Market Risk Premium. Investors' aversion to risk determines the market risk premium. Individual firms have no control over the RP_M, which affects the cost of equity and thus the WACC.

Tax Rates. Tax rates, which are influenced by the president and set by Congress, have an important effect on the cost of capital. They are used when we calculate the after-tax cost of debt for use in the WACC. In addition, the lower tax rate on dividends and capital gains than on interest income favors financing with stock rather than bonds, as we discuss in detail in Chapter 15.

Three Factors the Firm Can Control

A firm can affect its cost of capital through (1) its capital structure policy, (2) its dividend policy, and (3) its investment (capital budgeting) policy.

Capital Structure Policy. In the current chapter we assume that the firm has a given target capital structure, and we use weights based on that target to calculate its WACC. However, a firm can change its capital structure, and such a change can affect its cost of capital. For example, the after-tax cost of debt is lower than the cost of equity, so if the firm decides to use more debt and less common equity, then this increase in debt will tend to lower the WACC. However, an increased use of debt will increase the risk of debt and the equity, offsetting to some extent the effect due to a greater weighting of debt. In Chapter 15 we discuss this in more depth, and we demonstrate that the optimal capital structure is the one that minimizes the WACC and simultaneously maximizes the intrinsic value of the stock.

Dividend Policy. As we will see in Chapter 14, the percentage of earnings paid out in dividends may affect a stock's required rate of return, r_s. Also, if the payout ratio is so high that the firm must issue new stock to fund its capital budget, then the resulting flotation costs will also affect the WACC.

---

[28]Other things held constant, if the government doubles the money supply then there would be twice as many dollars chasing the same amount of goods, and this would eventually lead to inflation. So one cost of the stimulus program may be higher inflation.

Investment Policy. When we estimate the cost of capital, we use as the starting point the required rates of return on the firm's outstanding stock and bonds, which reflect the risks inherent in the existing assets. Therefore, we are implicitly assuming that new capital will be invested in assets with the same degree of risk as existing assets. This assumption is generally correct, because most firms do invest in assets similar to those they currently use. However, the equal risk assumption is incorrect if a firm dramatically changes its investment policy. For example, if a company invests in an entirely new line of business, then its marginal cost of capital should reflect the risk of that new business. With hindsight we can therefore see that GE's huge investments in the TV and movie businesses, as well as its investment in mortgages, increased its risk and thus its cost of capital.

Self-Test

Name some factors that are generally beyond the firm's control but still affect its cost of capital.

What three policies that are under the firm's control affect its cost of capital?

Explain how a change in interest rates in the economy would be expected to affect each component of the weighted average cost of capital.

9.13 Adjusting the Cost of Capital for Risk

As we have calculated it, the weighted average cost of capital reflects the average risk and overall capital structure of the entire firm. No adjustments are needed when using the WACC as the discount rate when estimating the value of a company by discounting its cash flows. However, adjustments for risk are often needed when evaluating a division or project. For example, what if a firm has divisions in several business lines that differ in risk? Or what if a company is considering a project that is much riskier than its typical project? It is not logical to use the overall cost of capital to discount divisional or project-specific cash flows that don't have the same risk as the company's average cash flows. The following sections explain how to adjust the cost of capital for divisions and for specific projects.

Divisional Costs of Capital

Consider Starlight Sandwich Shops, a company with two divisions—a bakery operation and a chain of cafes. The bakery division is low-risk and has a 10% WACC. The cafe division is riskier and has a 14% WACC. Each division is approximately the same size, so Starlight's overall cost of capital is 12%. The bakery manager has a project with an 11% expected rate of return, and the cafe division manager has a project with a 13% expected return. Should these projects be accepted or rejected? Starlight will create value if it accepts the bakery's project, since its rate of return is greater than its cost of capital (11% > 10%), but the cafe project's rate of return is less than its cost of capital (13% < 14%), so it should reject that project. However, if management simply compared the two projects' returns with Starlight's 12% overall cost of capital, then the bakery's value-adding project would be rejected while the cafe's value-destroying project would be accepted.

Many firms use the CAPM to estimate the cost of capital for specific divisions. To begin, recall that the Security Market Line (SML) equation expresses the risk–return relationship as follows:

$$r_s = r_{RF} + (RP_M)b_i$$

As an example, consider the case of Huron Steel Company, an integrated steel producer operating in the Great Lakes region. For simplicity, assume that Huron has only one division and uses only equity capital, so its cost of equity is also its corporate cost of capital, or WACC. Huron's beta = b = 1.1, r_{RF} = 5%, and RP_M = 6%. Thus, Huron's cost of equity (and WACC) is 11.6%:

$$r_s = 5\% + (6\%)1.1 = 11.6\%$$

This suggests that investors should be willing to give Huron money to invest in new, average-risk projects if the company expects to earn 11.6% or more on this money. By "average risk" we mean projects having risk similar to the firm's existing division.

Now suppose Huron creates a new transportation division consisting of a fleet of barges to haul iron ore, and suppose barge operations typically have betas of 1.5 rather than 1.1. The barge division, with b = 1.5, has a 14.0% cost of capital:

$$r_{Barge} = 5\% + (6\%)1.5 = 14.0\%$$

On the other hand, if Huron adds a low-risk division, such as a new distribution center with a beta of only 0.5, then that division's cost of capital would be 8%:

$$r_{Center} = 5\% + (6\%)0.5 = 8.0\%$$

A firm itself may be regarded as a "portfolio of assets," and since the beta of a portfolio is a weighted average of the betas of its individual assets, adding the barge and distribution center divisions will change Huron's overall beta. The exact value of the new corporate beta would depend on the size of the investments in the new divisions relative to Huron's original steel operations. If 70% of Huron's total value ends up in the steel division, 20% in the barge division, and 10% in the distribution center, then its new corporate beta would be calculated as follows:

$$\text{New beta} = 0.7(1.1) + 0.2(1.5) + 0.1(0.5) = 1.12$$

Thus, investors in Huron's stock would require a return of

$$r_{Huron} = 5\% + (6\%)1.12 = 11.72\%$$

Even though investors require an overall return of 11.72%, they should expect a rate of return on projects in each division at least as high as the division's required return based on the SML. In particular, they should expect a return of at least 11.6% from the steel division, 14.0% from the barge division, and 8.0% from the distribution center.

Obviously, our example suggests a level of precision that is much higher than firms can obtain in the real world. Still, managers should be aware of the logic of our example, and they should strive to measure the required inputs as well as possible.

Techniques for Measuring Divisional Betas

In Chapter 6 we discussed the estimation of betas for stocks and indicated how difficult it is to measure beta precisely. Estimating divisional betas is much more difficult, primarily because divisions do not have their own publicly traded stock.[29] Therefore, we must estimate the beta that the division would have if it were an independent, publicly traded company. Two approaches can be used to estimate divisional betas: the pure play method and the accounting beta method.

The Pure Play Method. In the **pure play method**, the company tries to find the betas of several publicly held specialized companies in the same line of business as the

[29]This same problem applies to privately held companies, which we discuss in Section 9.14.

division being evaluated, and it then averages those betas to determine the cost of capital for its own division. For example, suppose Huron found three companies devoted exclusively to operating barges, and suppose that Huron's management believes its barge division would be subject to the same risks as those firms. Then Huron could use the average beta of those firms as a proxy for its barge division's beta.[30]

The Accounting Beta Method. As noted above, it may be impossible to find specialized publicly traded firms suitable for the pure play approach. If that is the case, we may be able to use the **accounting beta method**. Betas are normally found by regressing the returns of a particular company's *stock* against returns on a *stock market index*. However, we could run a regression of the division's *accounting return on assets* against the *average return on assets* for a large sample of companies, such as those included in the S&P 500. Betas determined in this way (that is, by using accounting data rather than stock market data) are called **accounting betas**.

Estimating the Cost of Capital for Individual Projects

In Chapter 11 we examine ways to estimate the risk inherent in individual projects, but at this point it is useful to consider how project risk is reflected in measures of the firm's cost of capital. First, although it is intuitively clear that riskier projects have a higher cost of capital, it is difficult to measure projects' relative risks. Also, note that three separate and distinct types of risk can be identified as follows.

1. **Stand-alone risk**, which is the variability of the project's expected returns.
2. **Corporate**, or **within-firm, risk**, which is the variability the project contributes to the corporation's returns, giving consideration to the fact that the project represents only one asset of the firm's portfolio of assets and so some of its risk will be diversified away.
3. **Market**, or **beta, risk**, which is the risk of the project as seen by a well-diversified stockholder who owns many different stocks. A project's market risk is measured by its effect on the firm's overall beta coefficient.

Taking on a project with a high degree of either stand-alone or corporate risk will not necessarily increase the corporate beta. However, if the project has highly uncertain returns and if those returns are highly correlated with returns on the firm's other assets and with most other assets in the economy, then the project will have a high degree of all types of risk. For example, suppose General Motors decides to undertake a major expansion to build electric autos. GM is not sure how its technology will work on a mass production basis, so there is much risk in the venture—its stand-alone risk is high. Management also estimates that the project will do best if the economy is strong, for then people will have more money to spend on automobiles. This means that the project will tend to do well if GM's other divisions are doing well but will do poorly if other divisions are doing poorly. This being the case, the project will also have a high degree of corporate risk. Finally, since GM's profits are highly correlated with those of most other firms, the project's beta will also be high. Thus, this project will be risky under all three definitions of risk.

Of the three measures, market risk is theoretically the most relevant because of its direct effect on stock prices. Unfortunately, the market risk for a project is also the

[30] If the pure play firms employ different capital structures than that of Huron, then this must be addressed by adjusting the beta coefficients. See Chapter 15 for a discussion of this aspect of the pure play method. For a technique that can be used when pure play firms are not available, see Yatin Bhagwat and Michael Ehrhardt, "A Full Information Approach for Estimating Divisional Betas," *Financial Management*, Summer 1991, pp. 60–69.

most difficult to estimate. In practice, most decision makers consider all three risk measures in a subjective manner.

The first step is to determine the divisional cost of capital before grouping divisional projects into subjective risk categories. Then, using the divisional WACC as a starting point, **risk-adjusted costs of capital** are developed for each category. For example, a firm might establish three risk classes—high, average, and low—and then assign average-risk projects the divisional cost of capital, higher-risk projects an above-average cost, and lower-risk projects a below-average cost. Thus, if a division's WACC were 10%, its managers might use 10% to evaluate average-risk projects in the division, 12% for high-risk projects, and 8% for low-risk projects. Although this approach is better than ignoring project risk, these adjustments are necessarily subjective and somewhat arbitrary. Unfortunately, given the data, there is no completely satisfactory way to specify exactly how much higher or lower we should go in setting risk-adjusted costs of capital.

Self-Test

Based on the CAPM, how would one adjust the corporation's overall cost of capital to establish the required return for most projects in a low-risk division and in a high-risk division?

Describe the pure play and the accounting beta methods for estimating divisional betas.

What are the three types of risk to which projects are exposed? Which type of risk is theoretically the most relevant? Why?

Describe a procedure firms can use to establish costs of capital for projects with differing degrees of risk.

9.14 Privately Owned Firms and Small Businesses

Up until now, our discussion of the cost of common equity has been focused on publicly owned corporations. When we estimated the rate of return required by public stockholders, we used stock prices as input data for the DCF method and used stock returns to estimate beta as an input for the CAPM approach. But how can one measure the cost of equity for a firm whose stock is not traded? Most analysts begin by identifying one or more publicly traded firms that are in the same industry and that are approximately the same size as the privately owned firm.[31] The analyst then estimates the betas for these publicly traded firms and uses their average beta as an estimate of the beta of the privately owned firm. This is similar to the pure play method discussed earlier for estimating divisional betas. With an estimate of beta, the cost of equity can be estimated using the CAPM approach.

The stock of a privately held firm is less liquid than that of a publicly held firm. Just as investors demand a liquidity premium on thinly traded bonds, they also add a liquidity premium to obtain the required return on a privately held firm's stock.[32] Many analysts make an ad hoc adjustment to reflect this lack of liquidity by adding 1 to 3 percentage points to the firm's cost of equity. This "rule of thumb" is not theoretically satisfying because we don't know exactly how large the liquidity premium should be, but it is logical and is also a common practice.[33]

[31]In Chapter 15 we show how to adjust for differences in capital structures.

[32]See Yakov Amihud and Haim Mendelson, "Liquidity and Cost of Capital: Implications for Corporate Management," *Journal of Applied Corporate Finance*, Fall 1989, pp. 65–73.

[33]In fact, some analysts make a similar liquidity adjustment for any small firm's cost of common equity even if the firm is publicly traded. Ibbotson Association's data, discussed earlier in the chapter in connection with historical risk premiums, support this position: the smaller the firm, the larger the historical risk premiums.

In addition to the difficulty of estimating the cost of equity for small and privately held firms, there are also problems in estimating their proper capital structure weights. These weights should take account of the firm's market value weights. However, a privately held firm can't directly observe its market value, so it can't directly observe its market value weights. To resolve this problem, many analysts begin by making a trial guess as to the value of the firm's equity. The analysts then use this estimated value of equity to estimate the cost of capital, next use the cost of capital to estimate the value of the firm, and finally complete the circle by using the estimated value of the firm to estimate the value of its equity.[34] If this newly estimated equity value is different from their trial guess, analysts repeat the process but start the iteration with the newly estimated equity value as the trial value of equity. After several iterations, the trial value of equity and the resulting estimated equity value usually converge. Although somewhat tedious, this process provides consistent estimates of the weights and the cost of capital.

Self-Test

Identify some problems that occur when estimating the cost of capital for a privately held firm. What are some solutions to these problems?

9.15 Four Mistakes to Avoid

We often see managers and students make the following mistakes when estimating the cost of capital. Although we have discussed these errors previously at separate places in the chapter, they are worth repeating here.

To find the current S&P 500 Market-to-Book ratio, go to **http://www.reuters.com,** *get the stock quote for any company, and select "Ratios." Then look for the Price-to-Book ratio.*

1. *Never base the cost of debt on the coupon rate on a firm's existing debt.* The cost of debt must be based on the interest rate the firm would pay if it issued new debt today.
2. *When estimating the market risk premium for the CAPM method, never use the historical average return on stocks in conjunction with the current return on T-bonds.* The historical average return on bonds should be subtracted from the past average return on stocks to calculate the *historical market risk premium.* On the other hand, it is appropriate to subtract today's yield on T-bonds from an estimate of the expected future return on stocks to obtain the *forward-looking market risk premium.* A case can be made for using either the historical or the current risk premium, but it would be wrong to take the *historical* rate of return on stocks, subtract from it the *current* rate on T-bonds, and then use the difference as the market risk premium.
3. *Never use the current book value capital structure to obtain the weights when estimating the WACC.* Your first choice should be to use the firm's target capital structure for the weights. However, if you are an outside analyst and do not know the target weights, it would probably be best to estimate weights based on the current market values of the capital components. If the company's debt is not publicly traded, then it is reasonable to use the book value of debt to estimate the weights because book and market values of debt, especially short-term debt, are usually close to one another. However, stocks' market values in recent years have generally been at least 2–3 times their book values, so using book values for equity could lead to serious errors. The bottom line: If you don't know the target weights then use the market value, not the book value, of equity when calculating the WACC.
4. *Always remember that capital components are funds that come from investors.* If it's not from an investor, then it's not a capital component. Sometimes the argument is

[34]See Chapter 13 for more discussion on estimating the value of a firm.

made that accounts payable and accruals should be included in the calculation of the WACC. However, these funds are not provided by investors. Instead, they arise from operating relationships with suppliers and employees. Such funds are not included when calculating free cash flows, and they are not included when we calculate the amount of capital needed in a capital budgeting analysis. Therefore, they should not be included when we calculate the WACC.

Self-Test

What four mistakes are commonly made when estimating the WACC?

Summary

This chapter discussed how the cost of capital is developed for use in capital budgeting. The key points covered are listed below.

- Much of the chapter was devoted to pointing out the problems encountered when estimating the cost of capital. Although these problems are not trivial, the state of the art in cost-of-capital estimation is really not in bad shape. The procedures outlined in this chapter can be used to obtain cost-of-capital estimates that are sufficiently accurate for practical purposes.
- The cost of capital used in capital budgeting is a **weighted average** of the types of capital the firm uses—typically debt, preferred stock, and common equity.
- The **component cost of debt** is the **after-tax cost of new debt**. It is found by multiplying the interest rate paid on new debt by 1 – T, where T is the firm's marginal tax rate: $r_d(1 - T)$.
- Most debt is raised directly from lenders without the use of investment bankers, hence no flotation costs are incurred. However, a **debt flotation cost adjustment** should be made if large flotation costs are incurred. We reduce the bond's issue price by the flotation expenses, reduce the bond's cash flows to reflect taxes, and then solve for the after-tax yield to maturity.
- The **component cost of preferred stock** is calculated as the preferred dividend divided by the net price the firm receives after deducting flotation costs: $r_{ps} = D_{ps}/[P_{ps}(1 - F)]$. Flotation costs on preferred stock are usually fairly high, so we typically include the impact of flotation costs when estimating r_{ps}. Also note that if the preferred stock is convertible into common stock, then the true cost of the preferred stock will exceed the flotation-adjusted yield of the preferred dividend.
- The **cost of common equity, r_s**, also called the **cost of common stock**, is the rate of return required by the firm's stockholders, and it can be estimated in three ways: (1) the **CAPM**; (2) the **dividend-yield-plus-growth-rate**, or **DCF**, **approach**; and (3) the **over-own-bond-yield-plus-judgmental-risk-premium approach**.
- To use the **CAPM approach**, we (1) estimate the firm's beta, (2) multiply this beta by the market risk premium to obtain the firm's risk premium, and then (3) add the firm's risk premium to the risk-free rate to obtain its cost of common stock: $r_s = r_{RF} + (RP_M)b_i$.
- The best proxy for the **risk-free rate** is the yield on long-term T-bonds, with 10 years the maturity used most frequently.
- To use the **dividend-yield-plus-growth-rate approach**, which is also called the **discounted cash flow (DCF) approach**, add the firm's expected dividend growth rate to its expected dividend yield: $r_s = \hat{r}_s = D_1/P_0 + g$. ***Web Extension 9A*** shows how to estimate the DCF cost of equity if dividends are not growing at a constant rate.

- The growth rate for use in the DCF model can be based on security analysts' **published forecasts**, on **historical growth rates** of earnings and dividends, or on the **retention growth model**, g = (1 − Payout)(Return on equity).
- The **over-own-bond-yield-plus-judgmental-risk-premium approach** calls for adding a subjective risk premium of 3 to 5 percentage points to the interest rate on the firm's own long-term debt: r_s = Bond yield + Judgmental risk premium.
- When calculating the **cost of new common stock, r_e**, the DCF approach can be used to estimate the flotation cost. For a constant growth stock, the flotation-adjusted cost can be expressed as $r_e = \hat{r}_e = D_1/[P_0(1 - F)] + g$. Note that flotation costs cause r_e to be greater than r_s. We can find the difference between r_e and r_s and then add this differential to the CAPM estimate of r_s to find the CAPM estimate of r_e.
- Each firm has a **target capital structure**, which is defined as the mix of debt, preferred stock, and common equity that minimizes its **weighted average cost of capital (WACC)**:

  $$WACC = w_d r_d (1 - T) + w_{ps} r_{ps} + w_s r_s$$

  We discuss in Chapter 15 how the target weights are determined, but keep in mind that if you don't know the target weights, it's better to calculate WACC using market value than book value weights.
- **Various factors affect a firm's cost of capital.** Some are determined by the financial environment, but the firm can influence others through its financing, investment, and dividend policies.
- Many firms estimate **divisional costs of capital** that reflect each division's risk and capital structure.
- The **pure play** and **accounting beta methods** can be used to estimate betas for large projects or for divisions.
- A project's **stand-alone risk** is the risk the project would have if it were the firm's only asset and if stockholders held only that one stock. Stand-alone risk is measured by the variability of the asset's expected returns.
- **Corporate**, or **within-firm, risk** reflects the effect of a project on the firm's risk, and it is measured by the project's effect on the firm's earnings variability.
- **Market**, or **beta, risk** reflects the effects of a project on stockholders' risk, assuming they hold diversified portfolios. Market risk is measured by the project's effect on the firm's beta coefficient.
- Most decision makers consider all three risk measures in a subjective manner and then classify projects into risk categories. Using the firm's WACC as a starting point, risk-adjusted costs of capital are developed for each category. The **risk-adjusted cost of capital** is the cost of capital appropriate for a given project, given its risk. The greater a project's risk, the higher its cost of capital.
- Firms may be able to use the CAPM to estimate the cost of capital for specific projects or divisions. However, estimating betas for projects is difficult and subjective; hence, project risk adjustments tend to be more subjective than precisely measured.

The cost of capital as developed in this chapter is used in the next two chapters to evaluate potential capital budgeting projects, and it is used later in the text to determine the value of a corporation.

Questions

(9–1) Define each of the following terms:

a. Weighted average cost of capital, WACC; after-tax cost of debt, $r_d(1 - T)$
b. Cost of preferred stock, r_{ps}; cost of common equity (or cost of common stock), r_s
c. Target capital structure
d. Flotation cost, F; cost of new external common equity, r_e

(9–2) How can the WACC be both an average cost and a marginal cost?

(9–3) How would each of the factors in the following table affect a firm's cost of debt, $r_d(1 - T)$; its cost of equity, r_s; and its weighted average cost of capital, WACC? Indicate by a plus (+), a minus (–), or a zero (0) if the factor would raise, lower, or have an indeterminate effect on the item in question. Assume that all other factors are held constant. Be prepared to justify your answer, but recognize that several of the parts probably have no single correct answer; these questions are designed to stimulate thought and discussion.

	EFFECT ON:		
	$r_d(1 - T)$	r_s	WACC
a. The corporate tax rate is lowered.	______	______	______
b. The Federal Reserve tightens credit.	______	______	______
c. The firm uses more debt.	______	______	______
d. The firm doubles the amount of capital it raises during the year.	______	______	______
e. The firm expands into a risky new area.	______	______	______
f. Investors become more risk averse.	______	______	______

(9–4) Distinguish between beta (or market) risk, within-firm (or corporate) risk, and stand-alone risk for a potential project. Of the three measures, which is theoretically the most relevant, and why?

(9–5) Suppose a firm estimates its overall cost of capital for the coming year to be 10%. What might be reasonable costs of capital for average-risk, high-risk, and low-risk projects?

Self-Test Problem

Solution Appears in Appendix A

(ST–1) WACC

Longstreet Communications Inc. (LCI) has the following capital structure, which it considers to be optimal: debt = 25%, preferred stock = 15%, and common stock = 60%. LCI's tax rate is 40%, and investors expect earnings and dividends to grow at a constant rate of 6% in the future. LCI paid a dividend of $3.70 per share last year (D_0), and its stock currently sells at a price of $60 per share. Ten-year Treasury bonds yield 6%, the market risk premium is 5%, and LCI's beta is 1.3. The following terms would apply to new security offerings.

Preferred: New preferred could be sold to the public at a price of $100 per share, with a dividend of $9. Flotation costs of $5 per share would be incurred.
Debt: Debt could be sold at an interest rate of 9%.
Common: New common equity will be raised only by retaining earnings.

a. Find the component costs of debt, preferred stock, and common stock.
b. What is the WACC?

Problems

Answers Appear in Appendix B

EASY PROBLEMS 1–8

(9–1) After-Tax Cost of Debt

Calculate the after-tax cost of debt under each of the following conditions:

a. Interest rate of 13%, tax rate of 0%
b. Interest rate of 13%, tax rate of 20%
c. Interest rate of 13%, tax rate of 35%

(9–2) After-Tax Cost of Debt

LL Incorporated's currently outstanding 11% coupon bonds have a yield to maturity of 8%. LL believes it could issue new bonds at par that would provide a similar yield to maturity. If its marginal tax rate is 35%, what is LL's after-tax cost of debt?

(9–3) Cost of Preferred Stock

Duggins Veterinary Supplies can issue perpetual preferred stock at a price of $50 a share with an annual dividend of $4.50 a share. Ignoring flotation costs, what is the company's cost of preferred stock, r_{ps}?

(9–4) Cost of Preferred Stock with Flotation Costs

Burnwood Tech plans to issue some $60 par preferred stock with a 6% dividend. A similar stock is selling on the market for $70. Burnwood must pay flotation costs of 5% of the issue price. What is the cost of the preferred stock?

(9–5) Cost of Equity: DCF

Summerdahl Resort's common stock is currently trading at $36 a share. The stock is expected to pay a dividend of $3.00 a share at the end of the year (D_1 = $3.00), and the dividend is expected to grow at a constant rate of 5% a year. What is its cost of common equity?

(9–6) Cost of Equity: CAPM

Booher Book Stores has a beta of 0.8. The yield on a 3-month T-bill is 4% and the yield on a 10-year T-bond is 6%. The market risk premium is 5.5%, and the return on an average stock in the market last year was 15%. What is the estimated cost of common equity using the CAPM?

(9–7) WACC

Shi Importer's balance sheet shows $300 million in debt, $50 million in preferred stock, and $250 million in total common equity. Shi's tax rate is 40%, $r_d = 6\%$, $r_{ps} = 5.8\%$, and $r_s = 12\%$. If Shi has a target capital structure of 30% debt, 5% preferred stock, and 65% common stock, what is its WACC?

(9–8) WACC

David Ortiz Motors has a target capital structure of 40% debt and 60% equity. The yield to maturity on the company's outstanding bonds is 9%, and the company's tax rate is 40%. Ortiz's CFO has calculated the company's WACC as 9.96%. What is the company's cost of equity capital?

INTERMEDIATE PROBLEMS 9–14

(9–9) Bond Yield and After-Tax Cost of Debt

A company's 6% coupon rate, semiannual payment, $1,000 par value bond that matures in 30 years sells at a price of $515.16. The company's federal-plus-state tax rate is 40%. What is the firm's after-tax component cost of debt for purposes of calculating the WACC? (*Hint:* Base your answer on the *nominal* rate.)

(9–10) Cost of Equity

The earnings, dividends, and stock price of Shelby Inc. are expected to grow at 7% per year in the future. Shelby's common stock sells for $23 per share, its last dividend was $2.00, and the company will pay a dividend of $2.14 at the end of the current year.

a. Using the discounted cash flow approach, what is its cost of equity?
b. If the firm's beta is 1.6, the risk-free rate is 9%, and the expected return on the market is 13%, then what would be the firm's cost of equity based on the CAPM approach?
c. If the firm's bonds earn a return of 12%, then what would be your estimate of r_s using the over-own-bond-yield-plus-judgmental-risk-premium approach? (*Hint:* Use the midpoint of the risk premium range.)
d. On the basis of the results of parts a through c, what would be your estimate of Shelby's cost of equity?

(9–11) Cost of Equity

Radon Homes' current EPS is $6.50. It was $4.42 five years ago. The company pays out 40% of its earnings as dividends, and the stock sells for $36.

a. Calculate the historical growth rate in earnings. (*Hint:* This is a 5-year growth period.)
b. Calculate the *next* expected dividend per share, D_1. (*Hint:* $D_0 = 0.4(\$6.50) = \$2.60$.) Assume that the past growth rate will continue.
c. What is Radon Homes' cost of equity, r_s?

(9–12) Calculation of g and EPS

Spencer Supplies' stock is currently selling for $60 a share. The firm is expected to earn $5.40 per share this year and to pay a year-end dividend of $3.60.

a. If investors require a 9% return, what rate of growth must be expected for Spencer?
b. If Spencer reinvests earnings in projects with average returns equal to the stock's expected rate of return, then what will be next year's EPS? (*Hint:* g = ROE × Retention ratio.)

(9–13) The Cost of Equity and Flotation Costs

Messman Manufacturing will issue common stock to the public for $30. The expected dividend and the growth in dividends are $3.00 per share and 5%, respectively. If the flotation cost is 10% of the issue's gross proceeds, what is the cost of external equity, r_e?

(9–14) The Cost of Debt and Flotation Costs

Suppose a company will issue new 20-year debt with a par value of $1,000 and a coupon rate of 9%, paid annually. The tax rate is 40%. If the flotation cost is 2% of the issue proceeds, then what is the after-tax cost of debt? Disregard the tax shield from the amortization of flotation costs.

Challenging Problems 15–17

(9–15) WACC Estimation

On January 1, the total market value of the Tysseland Company was $60 million. During the year, the company plans to raise and invest $30 million in new projects. The firm's present market value capital structure, shown below, is considered to be optimal. There is no short-term debt.

Debt	$30,000,000
Common equity	30,000,000
Total capital	$60,000,000

New bonds will have an 8% coupon rate, and they will be sold at par. Common stock is currently selling at $30 a share. The stockholders' required rate of return is estimated to be 12%, consisting of a dividend yield of 4% and an expected constant growth rate of 8%. (The next expected dividend is $1.20, so the dividend yield is $1.20/$30 = 4%.) The marginal tax rate is 40%.

a. In order to maintain the present capital structure, how much of the new investment must be financed by common equity?
b. Assuming there is sufficient cash flow for Tysseland to maintain its target capital structure without issuing additional shares of equity, what is its WACC?
c. Suppose now that there is not enough internal cash flow and the firm must issue new shares of stock. Qualitatively speaking, what will happen to the WACC? No numbers are required to answer this question.

(9–16) Market Value Capital Structure

Suppose the Schoof Company has this *book value* balance sheet:

Current assets	$30,000,000	Current liabilities	$10,000,000
Fixed assets	50,000,000	Long-term debt	30,000,000
		Common equity	
		Common stock	
		(1 million shares)	1,000,000
		Retained earnings	39,000,000
Total assets	$80,000,000	Total claims	$80,000,000

The current liabilities consist entirely of notes payable to banks, and the interest rate on this debt is 10%, the same as the rate on new bank loans. These bank loans are not used for seasonal financing but instead are part of the company's permanent capital structure. The long-term debt consists of 30,000 bonds, each with a par value of $1,000, an annual coupon interest rate of 6%, and a 20-year maturity. The going rate of interest on new long-term debt, r_d, is 10%, and this is the present yield to maturity on the bonds. The common stock sells at a price of $60 per share. Calculate the firm's *market value* capital structure.

(9–17) WACC Estimation

The table below gives the balance sheet for Travellers Inn Inc. (TII), a company that was formed by merging a number of regional motel chains.

Travellers Inn: December 31, 2009 (Millions of Dollars)

Cash	$ 10	Accounts payable	$ 10
Accounts receivable	20	Accruals	10
Inventories	20	Short-term debt	5
Current assets	$ 50	Current liabilities	$ 25
Net fixed assets	50	Long-term debt	30
		Preferred stock	5
		Common equity	
		Common stock	$ 10
		Retained earnings	30
		Total common equity	$ 40
Total assets	$100	Total liabilities and equity	$100

The following facts also apply to TII.

(1) Short-term debt consists of bank loans that currently cost 10%, with interest payable quarterly. These loans are used to finance receivables and inventories on a seasonal basis, so bank loans are zero in the off-season.

(2) The long-term debt consists of 20-year, semiannual payment mortgage bonds with a coupon rate of 8%. Currently, these bonds provide a yield to investors of r_d = 12%. If new bonds were sold, they would have a 12% yield to maturity.
(3) TII's perpetual preferred stock has a $100 par value, pays a quarterly dividend of $2, and has a yield to investors of 11%. New perpetual preferred would have to provide the same yield to investors, and the company would incur a 5% flotation cost to sell it.
(4) The company has 4 million shares of common stock outstanding. P_0 = $20, but the stock has recently traded in the price range from $17 to $23. D_0 = $1 and EPS_0 = $2. ROE based on average equity was 24% in 2008, but management expects to increase this return on equity to 30%; however, security analysts and investors generally are not aware of management's optimism in this regard.
(5) Betas, as reported by security analysts, range from 1.3 to 1.7; the T-bond rate is 10%; and RP_M is estimated by various brokerage houses to be in the range from 4.5% to 5.5%. Some brokerage house analysts report forecasted growth dividend growth rates in the range of 10% to 15% over the foreseeable future.
(6) TII's financial vice president recently polled some pension fund investment managers who hold TII's securities regarding what minimum rate of return on TII's common would make them willing to buy the common rather than TII bonds, given that the bonds yielded 12%. The responses suggested a risk premium over TII bonds of 4 to 6 percentage points.
(7) TII is in the 40% federal-plus-state tax bracket.
(8) TII's principal investment banker predicts a decline in interest rates, with r_d falling to 10% and the T-bond rate to 8%, although the bank acknowledges that an increase in the expected inflation rate could lead to an increase rather than a decrease in interest rates.

Assume that you were recently hired by TII as a financial analyst and that your boss, the treasurer, has asked you to estimate the company's WACC under the assumption that no new equity will be issued. Your cost of capital should be appropriate for use in evaluating projects that are in the same risk class as the assets TII now operates.

Spreadsheet Problem

(9-18)
Build a Model: WACC

Start with the partial model in the file ***Ch09 P18 Build a Model.xls*** on the textbook's Web site. The stock of Gao Computing sells for $50, and last year's dividend was $2.10. A flotation cost of 10% would be required to issue new common stock. Gao's preferred stock pays a dividend of $3.30 per share, and new preferred could be sold at a price to net the company $30 per share. Security analysts are projecting that the common dividend will grow at a rate of 7% a year. The firm can issue additional long-term debt at an interest rate (or a before-tax cost) of 10%, and its marginal tax rate is 35%. The market risk premium is 6%, the risk-free rate is 6.5%, and Gao's beta is 0.83. In its cost-of-capital calculations, Gao uses a target capital structure with 45% debt, 5% preferred stock, and 50% common equity.

a. Calculate the cost of each capital component—in other words, the after-tax cost of debt, the cost of preferred stock (including flotation costs), and the cost of equity (ignoring flotation costs). Use both the DCF method and the CAPM method to find the cost of equity.
b. Calculate the cost of new stock using the DCF model.

c. What is the cost of new common stock based on the CAPM? (*Hint:* Find the difference between r_e and r_s as determined by the DCF method and then add that difference to the CAPM value for r_s.)

d. Assuming that Gao will not issue new equity and will continue to use the same target capital structure, what is the company's WACC?

e. Suppose Gao is evaluating three projects with the following characteristics.

 (1) Each project has a cost of $1 million. They will all be financed using the target mix of long-term debt, preferred stock, and common equity. The cost of the common equity for each project should be based on the beta estimated for the project. All equity will come from reinvested earnings.

 (2) Equity invested in Project A would have a beta of 0.5 and an expected return of 9.0%.

 (3) Equity invested in Project B would have a beta of 1.0 and an expected return of 10.0%.

 (4) Equity invested in Project C would have a beta of 2.0 and an expected return of 11.0%.

f. Analyze the company's situation and explain why each project should be accepted or rejected.

THOMSON ONE | Business School Edition Problem

Use the Thomson ONE—Business School Edition online database to work this chapter's questions.

Calculating 3M's Cost of Capital

In this chapter we described how to estimate a company's WACC, which is the weighted average of its costs of debt, preferred stock, and common equity. Most of the data we need to do this can be found in Thomson ONE. Here, we walk through the steps used to calculate Minnesota Mining & Manufacturing's (MMM) WACC.

Thomson ONE—BSE Discussion Questions

1. As a first step we need to estimate what percentage of MMM's capital comes from long-term debt, preferred stock, and common equity. If we click on FINANCIALS, we can see immediately from the balance sheet the amount of MMM's long-term debt and common equity (as of mid-2008, MMM had no preferred stock). Alternatively, you can click on FUNDAMENTAL RATIOS in the next row of tabs below and then select WORLDSCOPE'S BALANCE SHEET RATIOS. Here, you will also find a recent measure of long-term debt as a percentage of total capital.

 Recall that the weights used in the WACC are based on the company's target capital structure. If we assume the company wants to maintain the same mix of capital that it currently has on its balance sheet, then what weights should you use to estimate the WACC for MMM? (In Chapter 15, we will see that we might arrive at different estimates for these weights if we assume that MMM bases its target capital structure on the market values, rather than the book values, of debt and equity.)

2. Once again, we can use the CAPM to estimate MMM's cost of equity. Thomson ONE provides various estimates of beta; select the measure that you believe is best and combine this with your estimates of the risk-free rate and the market risk premium to obtain an estimate of its cost of equity. (See the Thomson ONE exercise in Chapter 6 for more details.) What is your estimate for the cost of equity? Why might it not make much sense to use the DCF approach to estimate MMM's cost of equity?
3. Next, we need to calculate MMM's cost of debt. Unfortunately, Thomson ONE doesn't provide a direct measure of the cost of debt. However, we can use different approaches to estimate it. One approach is to take the company's long-term interest expense and divide it by the amount of long-term debt. This approach works only if the historical cost of debt equals the yield to maturity in today's market (that is, only if MMM's outstanding bonds are trading at close to par). This approach may produce misleading estimates in the years during which MMM issues a significant amount of new debt.

   For example, if a company issues a lot of debt at the end of the year, then the full amount of debt will appear on the year-end balance sheet, yet we still may not see a sharp increase in interest expense on the annual income statement because the debt was outstanding for only a small portion of the entire year. When this situation occurs, the estimated cost of debt will likely understate the true cost of debt.

   Another approach is to try to find this number in the notes to the company's annual report by accessing the company's home page and its Investor Relations section. Remember that you need the after-tax cost of debt to calculate a firm's WACC, so you will need MMM's average tax rate (which has been about 37% in recent years). What is your estimate of MMM's after-tax cost of debt?
4. Putting all this information together, what is your estimate of MMM's WACC? How confident are you in this estimate? Explain your answer.

Mini Case

During the last few years, Harry Davis Industries has been too constrained by the high cost of capital to make many capital investments. Recently, though, capital costs have been declining, and the company has decided to look seriously at a major expansion program proposed by the marketing department. Assume that you are an assistant to Leigh Jones, the financial vice president. Your first task is to estimate Harry Davis's cost of capital. Jones has provided you with the following data, which she believes may be relevant to your task:

(1) The firm's tax rate is 40%.

(2) The current price of Harry Davis's 12% coupon, semiannual payment, noncallable bonds with 15 years remaining to maturity is $1,153.72. Harry Davis does not use short-term interest-bearing debt on a permanent basis. New bonds would be privately placed with no flotation cost.

(3) The current price of the firm's 10%, $100 par value, quarterly dividend, perpetual preferred stock is $116.95. Harry Davis would incur flotation costs equal to 5% of the proceeds on a new issue.

(4) Harry Davis's common stock is currently selling at $50 per share. Its last dividend (D_0) was $3.12, and dividends are expected to grow at a constant rate of 5.8% in the foreseeable future. Harry Davis's beta is 1.2, the yield on T-bonds is 5.6%, and the market risk premium is estimated to be 6%. For the over-own-bond-yield-plus-judgmental-risk-premium approach, the firm uses a 3.2% risk premium.

(5) Harry Davis's target capital structure is 30% long-term debt, 10% preferred stock, and 60% common equity.

To help you structure the task, Leigh Jones has asked you to answer the following questions.

a. (1) What sources of capital should be included when you estimate Harry Davis's weighted average cost of capital?
   (2) Should the component costs be figured on a before-tax or an after-tax basis?
   (3) Should the costs be historical (embedded) costs or new (marginal) costs?
b. What is the market interest rate on Harry Davis's debt, and what is the component cost of this debt for WACC purposes?
c. (1) What is the firm's cost of preferred stock?
   (2) Harry Davis's preferred stock is riskier to investors than its debt, yet the preferred's yield to investors is lower than the yield to maturity on the debt. Does this suggest that you have made a mistake? (*Hint:* Think about taxes.)
d. (1) What are the two primary ways companies raise common equity?
   (2) Why is there a cost associated with reinvested earnings?
   (3) Harry Davis doesn't plan to issue new shares of common stock. Using the CAPM approach, what is Harry Davis's estimated cost of equity?
e. (1) What is the estimated cost of equity using the discounted cash flow (DCF) approach?
   (2) Suppose the firm has historically earned 15% on equity (ROE) and has paid out 62% of earnings, and suppose investors expect similar values to obtain in the future. How could you use this information to estimate the future dividend growth rate, and what growth rate would you get? Is this consistent with the 5.8% growth rate given earlier?
   (3) Could the DCF method be applied if the growth rate were not constant? How?
f. What is the cost of equity based on the over-own-bond- yield-plus-judgmental-risk-premium method?
g. What is your final estimate for the cost of equity, r_s?
h. What is Harry Davis's weighted average cost of capital (WACC)?
i. What factors influence a company's WACC?
j. Should the company use the overall, or composite, WACC as the hurdle rate for each of its divisions?
k. What procedures can be used to estimate the risk-adjusted cost of capital for a particular division? What approaches are used to measure a division's beta?
l. Harry Davis is interested in establishing a new division that will focus primarily on developing new Internet-based projects. In trying to determine the cost of capital for this new division, you discover that specialized firms involved in similar projects have, on average, the following characteristics: (1) their capital structure is 10% debt and 90% common equity; (2) their cost of debt is typically 12%; and (3) they have a beta of 1.7. Given this information, what would your estimate be for the new division's cost of capital?
m. What are three types of project risk? How can each type of risk be considered when thinking about the new division's cost of capital?
n. Explain in words why new common stock that is raised externally has a higher percentage cost than equity that is raised internally by retaining earnings.
o. (1) Harry Davis estimates that if it issues new common stock, the flotation cost will be 15%. Harry Davis incorporates the flotation costs into the DCF approach. What is the estimated cost of newly issued common stock, taking into account the flotation cost?
   (2) Suppose Harry Davis issues 30-year debt with a par value of $1,000 and a coupon rate of 10%, paid annually. If flotation costs are 2%, what is the after-tax cost of debt for the new bond issue?
p. What four common mistakes in estimating the WACC should Harry Davis avoid?

Selected Additional Cases

The following cases from Textchoice, *Cengage Learning's online library, cover many of the concepts discussed in this chapter and are available at* ***http://www.textchoice2.com****.*

Klein-Brigham Series:
Case 42, "West Coast Semiconductor"; Case 54, "Ace Repair"; Case 55, "Premier Paint & Body"; Case 6, "Randolph Corporation"; Case 75, "The Western Company"; and Case 81, "Pressed Paper Products."

Brigham-Buzzard Series:
Case 5, "Powerline Network Corporation (Determining the Cost of Capital)."

CHAPTER 10

The Basics of Capital Budgeting: Evaluating Cash Flows

FPL Group is a holding company that owns Florida Power & Light, electric generating plants across the country, the nation's largest fleet of wind turbines, and major solar power facilities. It takes up to 10 years to acquire property, obtain the necessary permits, design the plant, arrange the financing, and complete the construction of a large generating plant. Moreover, utilities like FPL are required by law to have electricity available when it is demanded—when people turn on the switch, the utility must have the energy its customers expect or suffer severe fines and other penalties. Thus, FPL must forecast power usage many years in advance and make plans for meeting that demand.

Making a 10-year forecast is always difficult, but the 2008–2009 recession increased this difficulty tremendously. The two most important sectors of Florida's economy are housing and tourism. In 2009 the state had a huge supply of unsold houses and was second only to California in foreclosures, which was driving home prices down and vacancies up. Also, the bad economy was hurting the tourism industry. No one could know when those two industries—and the retail businesses that depend on them—would start to improve. That means no one could accurately forecast electricity usage or, thus, the need for new generating capacity.

Before the economy started downhill, FPL had developed a detailed capital budget for 2009–2011. But as the economy began to decline, its managers had many long, hard meetings to consider modifications. On the one hand, FPL's managers wanted to keep construction on track—it's costly to start and stop large projects because large cancellation fees are imposed if contracts are canceled. Moreover, FPL wanted to move ahead with its wind and solar programs and thus provide more "green" energy. On the other hand, the capital markets were drying up, making it difficult and expensive to acquire the funds FPL needed to finance its capital budget. Even worse, if it charged ahead and completed plants for which there was no demand, then it was possible that interest, depreciation, and maintenance costs could literally drive the company to bankruptcy.

In the end, management compromised—they cut back on the projects that were easiest to defer but went ahead with those for which deferrals would be most costly. The 2009 capital budget was reduced from $7.0 billion to $5.3 billion. Of the $1.7 billion reduction, $1.3 billion was related to wind farms, solar, and other "green" projects. FPL's actions, and similar ones by other utilities across the country, have had effects on the manufacturers of windmills, solar panels, and related products. Those firms have laid off workers, cut back R&D, and in some cases simply gone out of business.

The FPL story is typical, and it illustrates that capital budgeting is critically important both to companies and to the economy. The principles set forth in this chapter will help you make the right choices regarding which projects to accept and which to reject.

Corporate Valuation and Capital Budgeting

You can calculate the cash flows (CF) for a project in much the same way as for a firm. When the project's cash flows are discounted at the appropriate risk-adjusted weighted average cost of capital ("r" for simplicity), the result is the project's value. Note that when valuing an entire firm we discount its free cash flows at the overall weighted average cost of capital, but when valuing a project we discount its cash flows at the project's own risk-adjusted cost of capital. Note also that the firm's free cash flows are the total of all the net cash flows from its past projects. Thus, if a project is accepted and put into operation, it will provide cash flows that add to the firm's free cash flows and thus to the firm's value.

Subtracting the initial cost of the project from the discounted cash flows gives the project's net present value (NPV). A project that has a positive NPV adds value to the firm. In fact, the firm's Market Value Added (MVA) is the sum of all its projects' NPVs. The key point, though, is that the process of evaluating projects, or capital budgeting, is absolutely critical for a firm's success.

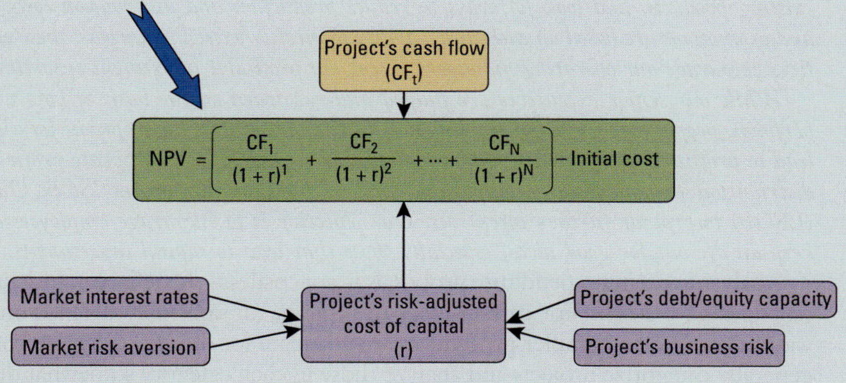

The textbook's Web site contains an Excel file that will guide you through the chapter's calculations. The file for this chapter is **Ch10 Tool Kit.xls**, *and we encourage you to open the file and follow along as you read the chapter.*

In Chapter 10 and Chapter 11 we discuss *capital budgeting*. Here *capital* refers to long-term assets used in production, and a *budget* is a plan that outlines projected expenditures during a future period. Thus, *the capital budget* is a summary of planned investments of assets that will last for more than a year, and **capital budgeting** is the whole process of analyzing projects and deciding which ones to accept and thus include in the capital budget. Chapter 10 focuses on the basics of capital budgeting, especially the primary criteria used to evaluate projects, and it explains why one method—the net present value (NPV)—is the best single criterion. We use simplified examples in this chapter to explain the basic theory and then, in Chapter 11, we go on to discuss how cash flows are estimated, how risk is measured, and how capital budgeting decisions are actually made.

10.1 An Overview of Capital Budgeting

Capital budgeting is based on the same procedures that are used in security valuation, but with two major differences. First, stocks and bonds exist in the securities markets and investors choose from the available set. However, firms actually create capital budgeting projects, so capital budgeting involves project creation. Second, most investors have no influence over the cash flows produced by their investments, whereas corporations do have a major influence on their projects' results. If companies execute their plans well, then capital budgeting projects will be successful, but poor execution will lead to project failures. Still, in both security analysis and capital budgeting, we forecast a set of cash flows, find the present value of those flows, and then make the investment if and only if the PV of the future expected cash flows exceeds the investment's cost.

A firm's growth, and even its ability to remain competitive and to survive, depends on a constant flow of ideas for new products, improvements in existing products, and ways to operate more efficiently. Accordingly, well-managed firms go to great lengths to develop good capital budgeting proposals. For example, the executive vice president of one successful corporation told us that his company takes the following steps to generate projects.

Our R&D department constantly searches for new products and ways to improve existing products. In addition, our Executive Committee, which consists of senior executives in marketing, production, and finance, identifies the products and markets in which our company should compete, and the Committee sets long-run targets for each division. These targets, which are spelled out in the corporation's strategic business plan, provide a general guide to the operating executives who must meet them. The operating executives then seek new products, set expansion plans for existing products, and look for ways to reduce production and distribution costs. Since bonuses and promotions are based on each unit's ability to meet or exceed its targets, these economic incentives encourage our operating managers to seek out profitable investment opportunities.

While our senior executives are judged and rewarded on the basis of how well their units perform, people further down the line are given bonuses and stock options for suggestions that lead to profitable investments. Additionally, a percentage of our corporate profit is set aside for distribution to nonexecutive employees, and we have an Employees' Stock Ownership Plan (ESOP) to provide further incentives. Our objective is to encourage employees at all levels to keep an eye out for good ideas, especially those that lead to capital investments.

Analyzing capital expenditure proposals is not costless—benefits can be gained, but analysis does have a cost. For certain types of projects, an extremely detailed analysis may be warranted, whereas simpler procedures are adequate for other projects. Accordingly, firms generally categorize projects and analyze those in each category somewhat differently:

1. *Replacement needed to continue profitable operations.* An example would be an essential pump on a profitable offshore oil platform. The platform manager could make this investment without an elaborate review process.
2. *Replacement to reduce costs.* An example would be the replacement of serviceable but obsolete equipment in order to lower costs. A fairly detailed analysis would be needed, with more detail required for larger expenditures.
3. *Expansion of existing products or markets.* These decisions require a forecast of growth in demand, so a more detailed analysis is required. Go/no-go decisions are generally made at a higher level than are replacement decisions.
4. *Expansion into new products or markets.* These investments involve strategic decisions that could change the fundamental nature of the business. A detailed analysis is required, and the final decision is made by top officers, possibly with board approval.
5. *Contraction decisions.* Especially during bad recessions, companies often find themselves with more capacity than they are likely to need in the foreseeable future. Then, rather than continue to operate plants at, say, 50% of capacity and incur losses as a result of excessive fixed costs, they decide to downsize. That generally requires payments to laid off workers and additional costs for shutting down selected operations. These decisions are made at the board level.
6. *Safety and/or environmental projects.* Expenditures necessary to comply with environmental orders, labor agreements, or insurance policy terms fall into this category. How these projects are handled depends on their size, with small ones being treated much like the Category 1 projects and large ones requiring expenditures that might even cause the firm to abandon the line of business.

7. *Other*. This catch-all includes items such as office buildings, parking lots, and executive aircraft. How they are handled varies among companies.
8. *Mergers*. Buying a whole firm (or division) is different from buying a machine or building a new plant. Still, basic capital budgeting procedures are used when making merger decisions.

Relatively simple calculations, and only a few supporting documents, are required for most replacement decisions, especially maintenance investments in profitable plants. More detailed analyses are required as we move on to more complex expansion decisions, especially for investments in new products or areas. Also, within each category projects are grouped by their dollar costs: Larger investments require increasingly detailed analysis and approval at higher levels. Thus, a plant manager might be authorized to approve maintenance expenditures up to $10,000 using a simple payback analysis, but the full board of directors might have to approve decisions that involve either amounts greater than $1 million or expansions into new products or markets.

If a firm has capable and imaginative executives and employees, and if its incentive system is working properly, then many ideas for capital investment will be forthcoming. Some ideas will be good and should be funded, but others should be killed. Therefore, the following procedures have been established for screening projects and deciding which to accept or reject:[1]

1. Net Present Value (NPV)
2. Internal Rate of Return (IRR)
3. Modified Internal Rate of Return (MIRR)
4. Profitability Index (PI)
5. Regular Payback
6. Discounted Payback

As we shall see, the NPV is the best single criterion, primarily because it is directly related to the firm's central goal of maximizing the stock's intrinsic value. However, all of the methods provide some useful information, and all are used in practice.

Self-Test

How is capital budgeting similar to security valuation? How is it different?
What are some ways that firms generate ideas for capital projects?
Identify the major project classification categories, and explain how and why they are used.
List six procedures used for screening projects and deciding which to accept or reject.

10.2 Net Present Value (NPV)

The **net present value (NPV)**, defined as the present value of a project's cash inflows minus the present value of its costs, tells us how much the project contributes to shareholder wealth—the larger the NPV, the more value the project adds and thus the higher the stock's price. NPV is generally regarded as the best single screening criterion. We use the data for Projects S and L shown in Figure 10-1 to illustrate the calculations for the NPV and the other criteria. The S stands for *Short* and the L for *Long*: Project S is a short-term project in the sense that most of its cash inflows come in relatively soon; Project L has more total cash inflows, but most are realized in the later years.

[1]One other rarely used criterion, the Accounting Rate of Return, is covered in the chapter's *Excel* ***Tool Kit*** model and ***Web Extension 10A.***

FIGURE 10-1 Cash Flows (CF_t) and Selected Evaluation Criteria for Projects S and L

	A	B	C	D	E	F
23	Panel A: Project Cash Flows and Cost of Capital					
24						
25	Project cost of capital, r, for each project:			10%		
26						
27		Initial Cost	After-Tax, End of Year, Project Cash Flows, CF_t			
28		0	1	2	3	4
29	Project S	−$10,000	$5,000	$4,000	$3,000	$1,000
30	Project L	−$10,000	$1,000	$3,000	$4,000	$6,750
31						
32	Panel B: Summary of Selected Evaluation Criteria					
33						
34			Project S	Project L		
35		NPV	$788.20	$1,004.03		
36		IRR	14.49%	13.55%		
37		MIRR	12.11%	12.66%		
38		PI	1.08	1.10		
39		Payback	2.33	3.30		
40		Discounted Payback	2.95	3.78		

See **Ch10 Tool Kit.xls** *on the textbook's Web site.*

The projects are equally risky, and they both have a 10% cost of capital. Furthermore, the cash flows have been adjusted to incorporate the impact of depreciation, taxes, and salvage values.[2] The investment outlays are shown under Year 0, and they include investments in fixed assets and any necessary working capital. All subsequent cash flows occur at the end of the year. All of the calculations can be done easily with a financial calculator, but since capital budgeting in the real world is generally done using a spreadsheet, we show how problems would be set up in *Excel.*

We can find the NPVs as follows.

1. Calculate the present value of each cash flow discounted at the project's risk-adjusted cost of capital, which is r = 10% in our example.
2. The sum of the discounted cash flows is defined as the project's NPV.

The equation for the NPV, set up with input data for Project S, is

$$\begin{aligned} NPV &= CF_0 + \frac{CF_1}{(1+r)^1} + \frac{CF_2}{(1+r)^2} + \cdots + \frac{CF_N}{(1+r)^N} \\ &= \sum_{t=0}^{N} \frac{CF_t}{(1+r)^t} \end{aligned} \qquad (10\text{-}1)$$

[2]So that we can focus on the capital budgeting decision criteria, we provide the cash flows for each project in this chapter. However, the most difficult aspect of capital budgeting is estimating the "relevant" cash flows, which are defined as the cash flows generated by the project that are available for distribution to investors. In other words, they are the project's free cash flows. Cash flow estimation is simple conceptually but difficult in practice, so we defer its discussion to Chapter 11.

FIGURE 10-2 Finding the NPV for Projects S and L

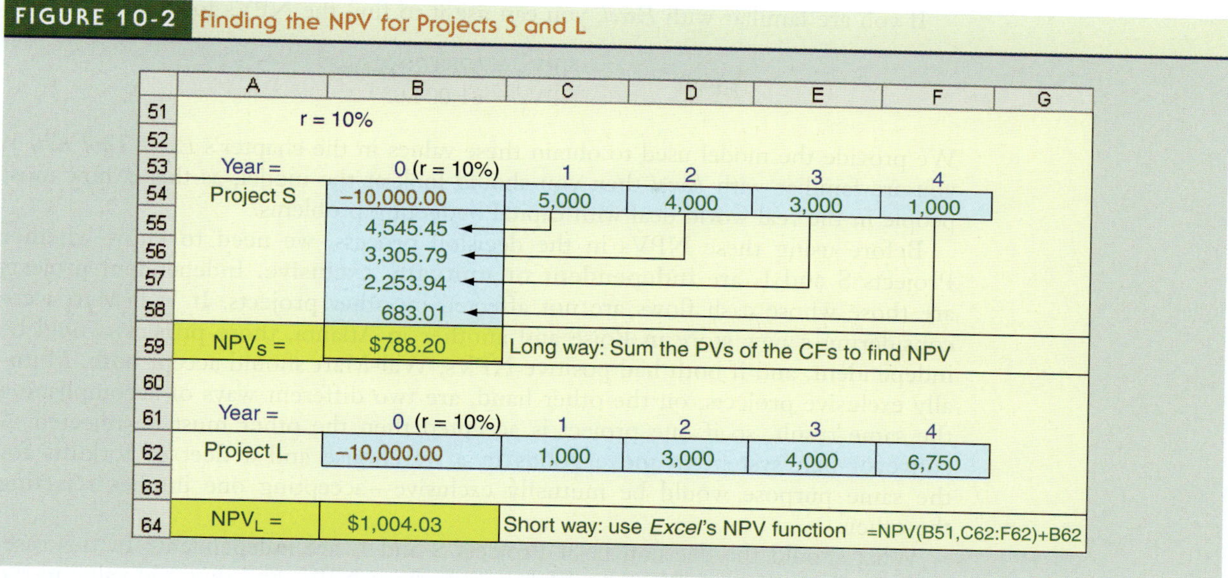

	A	B	C	D	E	F	G
51	r = 10%						
52							
53	Year =	0 (r = 10%)	1	2	3	4	
54	Project S	−10,000.00	5,000	4,000	3,000	1,000	
55		4,545.45					
56		3,305.79					
57		2,253.94					
58		683.01					
59	NPV_S =	$788.20	Long way: Sum the PVs of the CFs to find NPV				
60							
61	Year =	0 (r = 10%)	1	2	3	4	
62	Project L	−10,000.00	1,000	3,000	4,000	6,750	
63							
64	NPV_L =	$1,004.03	Short way: use *Excel*'s NPV function			=NPV(B51,C62:F62)+B62	

Applying Equation 10-1 to Project S, we have

$$\begin{aligned} NPV_S &= -\$10{,}000 + \frac{\$5{,}000}{(1.10)^1} + \frac{\$4{,}000}{(1.10)^2} + \frac{\$3{,}000}{(1.10)^3} + \frac{\$1{,}000}{(1.10)^4} \\ &= -\$10{,}000 + \$4{,}545.45 + \$3{,}305.79 + \$2{,}253.94 + \$683.01 \\ &= \$788.20 \end{aligned}$$

Here CF_t is the expected net cash flow at Time t, r is the project's risk-adjusted cost of capital (or WACC), and N is its life. Projects generally require an initial investment—for example, developing the product, buying the equipment needed to make it, building a factory, and stocking inventory. The initial investment is a negative cash flow. For Projects S and L, only CF_0 is negative, but for a large project such as an FPL power plant, outflows would occur for several years before cash inflows begin.

Figure 10-2 shows, on Row 59, the cash flow time line for project S as taken from Figure 10-1. The cost is –$10,000, which is not discounted because it occurs at t = 0. The PV of each cash inflow, and the sum of the PVs, is shown in Column B. You could find the PVs of the cash flows with a calculator or with *Excel*, and the end result would be the numbers in Column B of the figure. When we sum the PVs of the inflows and subtract the cost, the result is $788.20, which is NPV_S. The NPV for Project L, $1,004.03, can be found similarly.

The step-by-step procedure shown for Project S is useful for illustrating how the NPV is calculated, but in practice (and on exams) it is far more efficient to use a financial calculator or *Excel*.Different calculators are set up somewhat differently, but (as we discussed in Chapter 4) they all have a "cash flow register" that can be used to evaluate uneven cash flows such as those for Projects S and L. Equation 10-1 is actually programmed into these calculators, and all we need to do is enter the cash flows (with the correct signs) along with r = I/YR = 10. Once the data have been entered, you can press the NPV key to get the answer, 788.20, on the screen.[3]

[3]The keystrokes for finding the NPV are shown for several calculators in the calculator tutorials we provide on the textbook's Web site.

If you are familiar with *Excel*, you can use it to find the NPVs for S and L:

$$NPV_S = \$788.20$$
$$NPV_L = \$1{,}004.03$$

We provide the model used to obtain these values in the chapter's *Excel* ***Tool Kit.*** If you are familiar with *Excel* then you should look at the model, as this is how most people in the real world deal with capital budgeting problems.

Before using these NPVs in the decision process, we need to know whether Projects S and L are **independent** or **mutually exclusive**. Independent projects are those whose cash flows are not affected by other projects. If Wal-Mart were considering a new store in Boise and another in Atlanta, those projects would be independent, and if both had positive NPVs, Wal-Mart should accept both. Mutually exclusive projects, on the other hand, are two different ways of accomplishing the same result, so if one project is accepted then the other must be rejected. A conveyor-belt system to move goods in a warehouse and a fleet of forklifts for the same purpose would be mutually exclusive—accepting one implies rejecting the other.

What should the decision be if Projects S and L are independent? In this case, both should be accepted because both have positive NPVs and thus add value to the firm. However, if they are mutually exclusive, then Project L should be chosen because it has the higher NPV and thus adds more value than S. We can summarize these criteria with the following rules.

NPV Decision Rules

Independent projects: If NPV exceeds zero, accept the project. Since S and L both have positive NPVs, accept them both if they are independent.

Mutually exclusive projects: Accept the project with the highest positive NPV. If no project has a positive NPV, then reject them all. If S and L are mutually exclusive, the NPV criterion would select L.

Projects must be either independent or mutually exclusive, so one or the other of these rules applies to every project.[4]

Self-Test

Why is NPV the primary capital budgeting decision criterion?

What is the difference between "independent" and "mutually exclusive" projects?

Projects SS and LL have the following cash flows:

	End-of-Year Cash Flows			
	0	1	2	3
SS	-700	500	300	100
LL	-700	100	300	600

If the cost of capital is 10%, then what are the projects' NPVs? **(NPV_{SS} = $77.61; NPV_{LL} = $89.63)**

What project or set of projects would be in your capital budget if SS and LL were (a) independent or (b) mutually exclusive? **(Both; LL)**

[4]This is a simplification. For example, some projects can benefit others—these are "complementary" projects. Other projects harm others—these are called "cannibalizing" projects. These concepts are addressed in Chapter 11.

10.3 Internal Rate of Return (IRR)

In Chapter 5 we discussed the yield to maturity on a bond, and we explained that if you hold a bond to maturity then you will earn the yield to maturity on your investment. The YTM is found as the discount rate that forces the present value of the cash inflows to equal the price of the bond. This same concept is used in capital budgeting when we calculate a project's **internal rate of return**, or **IRR:**

A project's IRR is the discount rate that forces the PV of the inflows to equal the initial cost (or to equal the PVs of all the costs if costs are incurred over several years). This is equivalent to forcing the NPV to equal zero. The IRR is an estimate of the project's rate of return, and it is comparable to the YTM on a bond.

To calculate the IRR, we begin with Equation 10-1 for the NPV, replace r in the denominator with the term "IRR," and set the NPV equal to zero. This transforms Equation 10-1 into Equation 10-2, the one used to find the IRR. The rate that forces NPV to equal zero is the IRR.[5]

$$\text{NPV} = \text{CF}_0 + \frac{\text{CF}_1}{(1+\text{IRR})^1} + \frac{\text{CF}_2}{(1+\text{IRR})^2} + \cdots + \frac{\text{CF}_N}{(1+\text{IRR})^N} = 0$$
$$= \sum_{t=0}^{N} \frac{\text{CF}_t}{(1+\text{IRR})^t} = 0 \quad \text{(10-2)}$$

See **Ch10 Tool Kit.xls** *on the textbook's Web site.*

For Project S, we have

$$\text{NPV}_s = 0 = -\$10{,}000 + \frac{\$5{,}000}{(1+\text{IRR})^1} + \frac{\$4{,}000}{(1+\text{IRR})^2} + \frac{\$3{,}000}{(1+\text{IRR})^3} + \frac{\$1{,}000}{(1+\text{IRR})^4}$$

Figure 10-3 illustrates the process for finding the IRR of Project S.

FIGURE 10-3 Finding the IRR

	A	B	C	D	E	F
88	r = 14.49%					
89	Year =	0	1	2	3	4
90	Project S	−10,000.00	5,000	4,000	3,000	1,000
91		4,367.24				
92		3,051.64				
93		1,999.09				
94		582.03				
95	Sum of PVs =	$0.00	= NPV at r = 14.489%. NPV = 0, so IRR = 14.489%.			
96						
97	IRR_S =	14.49%	= IRR(B90:F90) using IRR function			
98						
99	Year =	0	1	2	3	4
100	Project L	−10,000.00	1,000	3,000	4,000	6,750
101						
102	IRR_L =	13.55%	= IRR(B100:F100) using IRR function			

[5]For a large, complex project like an FPL power plant, costs are incurred for several years before cash inflows begin. That simply means that we have a number of negative cash flows before the positive cash flows begin.

Three procedures can be used to find the IRR:

1. *Trial-and-error.* We could use a trial-and-error procedure: try a discount rate, see if the equation solves to zero, and if it doesn't, try a different rate. We could then continue until we found the rate that forces the NPV to zero, and that rate would be the IRR. For Project S the IRR is 14.489%. Note, though, that the trial-and-error procedure is so time-consuming that—before computers and financial calculators were available—the IRR was almost never calculated. It's useful to think about the trial-and-error procedure, but it's far better to use either a calculator or *Excel* for the actual calculations.
2. *Calculator solution.* Enter the cash flows into the calculator's cash flow register just as we did to find the NPV, and then press the calculator key labeled "IRR." Instantly, you get the internal rate of return. Here are the values for Projects S and L:[6]

$$IRR_S = 14.489\%$$
$$IRR_L = 13.549\%$$

3. *Excel solution.* It is even easier to find IRRs using *Excel,* as we demonstrate in this chapter's ***Tool Kit.***[7]

Why is the discount rate that causes a project's NPV to equal zero so special? The reason is that the IRR is an estimate of the project's rate of return. If this return exceeds the cost of the funds used to finance the project, then the difference is a bonus that goes to the firm's stockholders and causes the stock's price to rise. Project S has an estimated return of 14.489% versus a 10% cost of capital, so its bonus is 4.489%. On the other hand, if the IRR is less than the cost of capital then stockholders must make up the shortfall, which would hurt the stock price.

Note again that the IRR formula, Equation 10-2, is simply the NPV formula, Equation 10-1, solved for the particular discount rate that forces the NPV to zero. Thus, the same basic equation is used for both methods. The only difference is that with the NPV method, the discount rate is given and we find the NPV, whereas with the IRR method, the NPV is set equal to zero and we find the interest rate that provides this equality.

If the IRR criterion is used to rank projects, then the decision rules are as follows.

Independent projects: If IRR exceeds the project's WACC, then the project should be accepted. If IRR is less than the project's WACC, reject it. Projects S and L both have positive IRRs, so they would both be accepted by the IRR method. Note that both projects were also accepted by the NPV criterion, so the NPV and IRR criteria provide the same result if the projects are independent.

Mutually exclusive projects. Accept the mutually exclusive project with the highest IRR, provided that the project's IRR is greater than its WACC. Reject any

[6]See our calculator tutorials on the textbook's Web site. Note that once the cash flows have been entered into the cash flow register, you can find both the NPV and the IRR. To find the NPV, enter the interest rate (I/YR) and then press the NPV key. Then, with no further entries, press the IRR key to find the IRR. Thus, once you set up the calculator to find the NPV, it is easy to find the IRR. This is one reason most firms calculate both the NPV and the IRR. If you calculate one, it is easy to also calculate the other, and both provide information that decision makers find useful. The same is true with *Excel:* after estimating cash flows, it is easy to calculate both NPV and IRR.

[7]Note that to calculate the IRR with *Excel* the full data range is specified, because *Excel's* IRR function assumes that the first cash flow (the negative $10,000) occurs at t = 0. You can use the function wizard if you don't have the formula memorized.

Why NPV Is Better Than IRR

Buffett University recently hosted a seminar on business methods for managers. A finance professor covered capital budgeting, explaining how to calculate the NPV, and stated that it should be used to screen potential projects. In the Q-and-A session, Ed Wilson, treasurer of an electronics firm, said his firm used the IRR primarily because the CFO and the directors understood about selecting projects based on their rates of return but didn't understand the NPV. Ed had tried to explain why the NPV was better, but it simply confused his bosses, so the company stuck with the IRR. Now a meeting on the firm's capital budget is coming up, and Ed asked the professor for a simple, easy-to-understand explanation of why the NPV is better.

The professor recommended the following extreme example. A firm with adequate access to capital and a 10% WACC is choosing between two equally risky, mutually exclusive projects. Project Large calls for investing $100,000 and then receiving $50,000 per year for 10 years, while Project Small calls for investing $1 and then receiving $0.60 per year for 10 years. Here are the two project's NPVs and IRRs:

Project Large		Project Small	
NPV_L :	**$207,228.36**	NPV_S :	$2.69
IRR_L :	49.1%	**IRR_S :**	**59.4%**

The IRR says choose S, but the NPV says accept L. Intuitively, it's obvious that the firm would be better off choosing the large project in spite of its lower IRR. With a cost of capital of only 10%, a 49% rate of return on a $100,000 investment is much more profitable than a 59% return on a $1 investment.

When Ed gave this example in his firm's executive meeting on the capital budget, the CFO argued that this example was extreme and unrealistic, and no one would choose S in spite of its higher IRR. Ed agreed, but he asked the CFO where the line should be drawn between realistic and unrealistic examples. When he received no answer, he went on to say that (1) it's hard to draw this line, and (2) the NPV is always better because it tells us how much each project will add to the firm's value. The president was listening, and he declared Ed the winner. The company switched from IRR to NPV, and Ed is now the CFO.

project whose best IRR does not exceed the firm's WACC. Since Project S has the higher IRR, it should be accepted (and L rejected) if the projects are mutually exclusive. However, recall that Project L had the larger NPV, so the NPV method ranked L over S and thus would choose L. Therefore, a conflict will exist between the NPV and the IRR criteria if the projects are mutually exclusive.

The IRR is logically appealing—it is useful to know the rates of return on proposed investments. However, as we see from Projects L and S, NPV and IRR can produce conflicting conclusions when one is choosing between mutually exclusive projects, and when conflicts occur the NPV criterion is generally better.

Self-Test

In what sense is a project's IRR similar to the YTM on a bond?

The cash flows for Projects SS and LL are as follows:

	End-of-Year Cash Flows			
	0	1	2	3
SS	−700	500	300	100
LL	−700	100	300	600

Assume that the firm's WACC = r = 10%. What are the two projects' IRRs? (IRR_{SS} = 18.0%; IRR_{LL} = 15.6%)

Which project would the IRR method select if the firm has a 10% cost of capital and the projects are (a) independent or (b) mutually exclusive? (Both; SS)

10.4 Multiple Internal Rates of Return[8]

One problem with the IRR is that, under certain conditions, a project may have more than one IRR. First, note that a project is said to have *normal* cash flows if it has one or more cash outflows (costs) followed by a series of cash inflows. If, however, a cash *outflow* occurs sometime after the inflows have started, meaning that the signs of the cash flows change *more than once*, then the project is said to have *nonnormal* cash flows. Here's an illustration of these concepts:

Normal: − + + + + + or − − − + + + + +
Nonnormal: − + + + + − or − + + + − + + +

An example of a project with nonnormal flows would be a strip coal mine where the company first spends money to buy the property and prepare the site for mining, has positive inflows for several years, and then spends more money to return the land to its original condition. In this case, the project might have two IRRs—that is, **multiple IRRs**.[9]

To illustrate multiple IRRs, suppose a firm is considering a potential strip mine (Project M) that has a cost of $1.6 million, will produce a cash flow of $10 million at the end of Year 1; then, at the end of Year 2, the firm must spend $10 million to restore the land to its original condition. Therefore, the project's expected net cash flows are as follows (in millions):

See **Ch10 Tool Kit.xls** on the textbook's Web site for all calculations.

	Year 0	End of Year 1	End of Year 2
Cash flows	−$1.6	+$10	−$10

We can substitute these values into Equation 10-2 and then solve for the IRR:

$$\text{NPV} = \frac{-\$1.6 \text{ million}}{(1+\text{IRR})^0} + \frac{\$10 \text{ million}}{(1+\text{IRR})^1} + \frac{-\$10 \text{ million}}{(1+\text{IRR})^2} = 0$$

Here the NPV equals 0 when IRR = 25%, but it also equals 0 when IRR = 400%.[10] Therefore, Project M has one IRR of 25% and another of 400%, and we don't know which one to use. This relationship is depicted graphically in Figure 10-4.[11] The graph is constructed by plotting the project's NPV at different discount rates.

Observe that no dilemma regarding Project M would arise if the NPV method were used; we would simply find the NPV at the appropriate cost of capital and use it to evaluate the project. We would see that if Project M's cost of capital were 10% then its NPV would be −$0.774 million and the project should be rejected. If r were between 25% and 400% then the NPV would be positive, but any such number

[8]This section is relatively technical, and some instructors may choose to omit it without loss of continuity.

[9]Equation 10-2 is a polynomial of degree n, so it has n different roots, or solutions. All except one of the roots is an imaginary number when investments have normal cash flows (one or more cash outflows followed by cash inflows), so in the normal case only one value of IRR appears. However, the possibility of multiple real roots, and hence of multiple IRRs, arises when negative net cash flows occur after the project has been placed in operation.

[10]If you attempt to find Project M's IRR with an HP calculator, you will get an error message, whereas TI calculators give only the IRR that's closest to zero. When you encounter either situation, you can find the approximate IRRs by first calculating NPVs using several different values for r = I/YR, constructing a graph with NPV on the vertical axis and cost of capital on the horizontal axis, and then visually determining approximately where NPV = 0. The intersection with the x-axis gives a rough idea of the IRRs' values. With some calculators and also with *Excel*, you can find both IRRs by entering guesses, as we explain in our calculator and *Excel* tutorials.

[11]Figure 10-4 is called a *NPV profile*. Profiles are discussed in more detail in Section 10.7.

FIGURE 10-4 Graph for Multiple IRRs: Project M (Millions of Dollars)

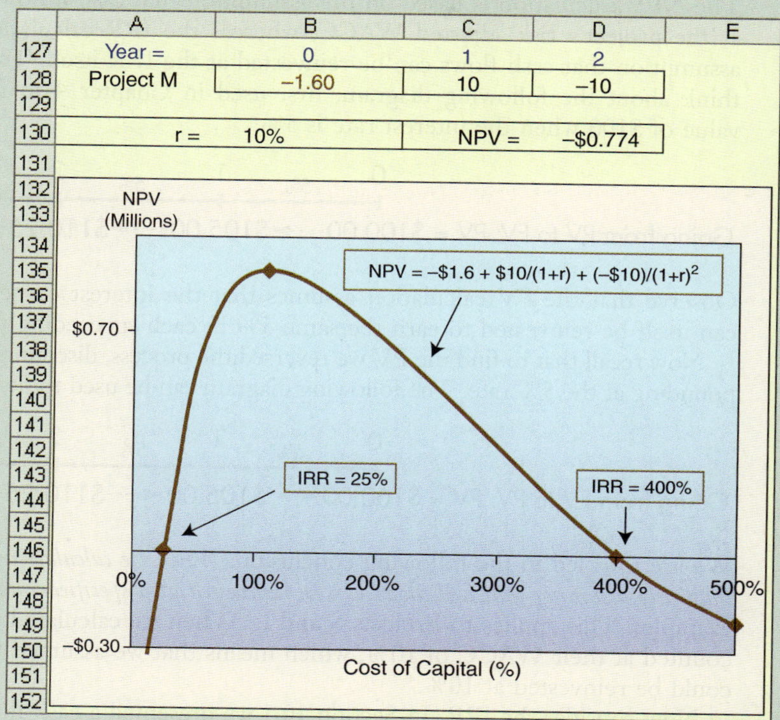

Note: The data table shown below calculates Project M's NPV at the rates shown in the left column. These data are plotted to form the graph shown above. Notice that NPV = 0 at both 25% and 400%. Since the definition of the IRR is the rate at which the NPV = 0, we see that there are two IRRs.

r	NPV	
0%	−$1.600	
10%	−$0.774	
25%	$0.000	= IRR #1 = 25%
110%	$0.894	
400%	$0.000	= IRR #2 = 400%
500%	−$0.211	

See **Ch10 Tool Kit.xls** *on the textbook's Web site.*

would probably not be realistic or useful for anything. (At such a high cost of capital, the firm's typical projects would have negative NPVs.)

Self-Test

What condition regarding cash flows would cause more than one IRR to exist?

Project MM has the following cash flows:

End-of-Year Cash Flows			
0	1	2	3
−$1,000	$2,000	$2,000	−$3,350

Calculate MM's NPV at discount rates of 0%, 10%, 12.2258%, 25%, 122.147%, and 150%. **(−$350; −$46; $0; $165; $0; −$94)** What are MM's IRRs? **(12.23% and 122.15%)** If the cost of capital were 10%, should the project be accepted or rejected? **(Reject because NPV < 0)**

10.5 Reinvestment Rate Assumptions[12]

The NPV calculation is based on the assumption that cash inflows can be reinvested at the project's risk-adjusted WACC, whereas the IRR calculation is based on the assumption that cash flows can be reinvested at the IRR itself. To see why this is so, think about the following diagram, first used in Chapter 4 to illustrate the future value of $100 when the interest rate is 5%:

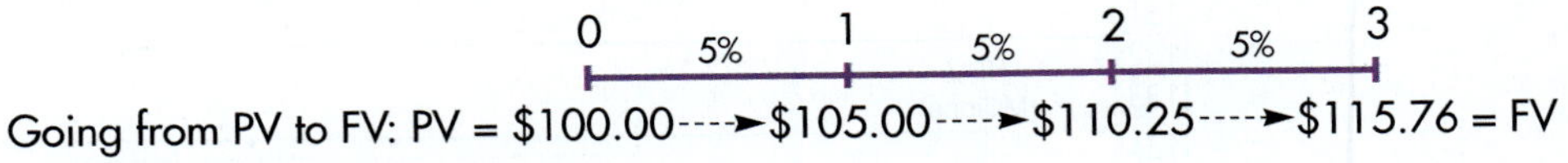

	0	5%	1	5%	2	5%	3	
Going from PV to FV: PV =	$100.00	----►	$105.00	----►	$110.25	----►	$115.76	= FV

Observe that the FV calculation assumes that the interest earned during each year can itself be reinvested to earn the same 5% in each succeeding year.

Now recall that to find the PV we reversed the process, discounting rather than compounding at the 5% rate. The following diagram can be used to demonstrate this point:

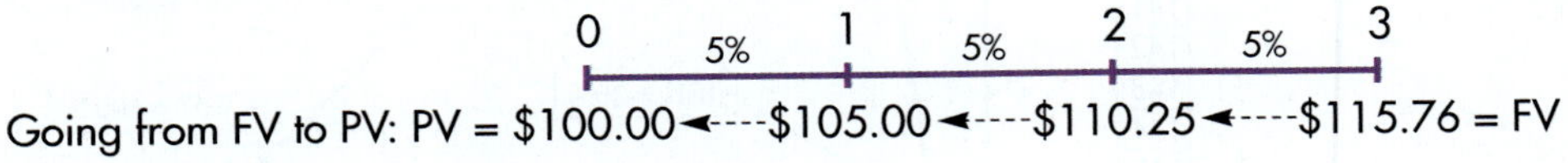

	0	5%	1	5%	2	5%	3	
Going from FV to PV: PV =	$100.00	◄----	$105.00	◄----	$110.25	◄----	$115.76	= FV

We are thus led to the following conclusion: *When we calculate a present value, we are implicitly assuming that cash flows can be reinvested at a specified interest rate* (5% in our example). This applies to Projects S and L: When we calculated their NPVs, we discounted at their WACC of 10%, which means that we assumed that their cash flows could be reinvested at 10%.

Now consider the IRR. In Section 10.3 we presented a cash flow diagram set up to show the PVs of the cash flows when discounted at the IRR. We saw that the sum of the PVs is equal to the cost at a discount rate of 14.489%, so by definition 14.489% is the IRR. Now we can ask this question: What reinvestment rate is built into the IRR?

Because discounting at a given rate assumes that cash flows can be reinvested at that same rate, the IRR assumes that cash flows are reinvested at the IRR itself.

So the NPV assumes reinvestment at the WACC whereas the IRR assumes reinvestment at the IRR itself. Which assumption is more reasonable? For most firms, assuming reinvestment at the WACC is better, for the following reasons.

- If a firm has reasonably good access to the capital markets then it can raise all the capital it needs at the going rate, which in our example is 10%.
- Since the firm can obtain capital at 10%, if it has investment opportunities with positive NPVs then it should take them on, and it can finance them at a 10% cost.
- If we assume that the firm operates in a reasonably competitive industry, then its return on investment opportunities should be relatively close to its cost of capital; if it were much higher, then new firms would enter the market and drive prices (and thus returns) down to near the cost of capital.
- If the firm uses internally generated cash flows from past projects rather than external capital, this will simply save it the 10% cost of capital. Thus, 10% is the *opportunity cost* of the cash flows, and that is the effective return on reinvested funds.

[12]This section gives a theoretical explanation of the key difference between NPV and IRR. However, it is relatively technical, so if time is a constraint then professors may decide to have students skip it and just read the box "Why NPV Is Better Than IRR."

As an illustration, suppose a project's IRR is 50%, the firm's WACC is 10%, and it has good access to the capital markets and operates in a competitive industry. Thus, the firm can raise all the capital it needs at the 10% rate. Given the existence of competition, the 50% return would attract new entry, which would make it hard to find new projects with a similar high return, which is what the IRR assumes. Moreover, even if the firm does find such projects, it would take them on with external capital that costs 10%. The logical conclusion is that the original project's cash flows will simply save the 10% cost of the external capital and that 10%, not 50%, is the effective return on those flows.

If a firm does not have good access to external capital, and if it also has a lot of potential projects with high IRRs, then it might be reasonable to assume that a project's cash flows could be reinvested at rates close to their IRRs. However, that situation rarely occurs, since firms with good investment opportunities generally *do* have good access to debt and equity markets.

Our conclusion is that the assumption built into the IRR—that cash flows can be reinvested at the IRR, no matter how high it is—is flawed, whereas the assumption built into the NPV—that cash flows can be reinvested at the WACC—is generally correct. Moreover, if the true reinvestment rate is less than the IRR, then the true rate of return on the investment must be less than the calculated IRR; thus the IRR is misleading as a measure of a project's profitability. This point is discussed further in the next section.

Self-Test

Why is a reinvestment rate implicitly assumed whenever we find the present value of a future cash flow? Would it be possible to find the PV of a FV without specifying an implicit reinvestment rate?

What reinvestment rate is built into the NPV calculation? The IRR calculation?

For a firm that has adequate access to capital markets, is it more reasonable to assume reinvestment at the WACC or the IRR? Why?

10.6 Modified Internal Rate of Return (MIRR)[13]

It is logical for managers to want to know the expected rate of return on investments, and this is what the IRR is supposed to tell us. However, the IRR is based on the assumption that projects' cash flows can be reinvested at the IRR itself, and this assumption is usually wrong: *The IRR overstates the expected return for accepted projects because cash flows cannot generally be reinvested at the IRR itself.* Therefore, the IRR for accepted projects is generally greater than the true expected rate of return. This imparts an upward bias on corporate projections based on IRRs. Given this fundamental flaw, is there a percentage evaluator that is better than the regular IRR? The answer is "yes": *We can modify the IRR to make it a better measure of profitability.*

This new measure, the **Modified IRR (MIRR)**, is illustrated for Project S in Figure 10-5. It is similar to the regular IRR, except it is based on the assumption that cash flows are reinvested at the WACC (or some other explicit rate if that is a more reasonable assumption). Refer to Figure 10-5 as you read about the construction of this measure.

[13]This section is relatively technical, and some instructors may choose to omit it without loss of continuity.

	A	B	C	D	E	F	G
205							
206	r =	10%					
207							
208	Year =	0 (r =10%)	1	2	3	4	
209	Project S	−10,000	5,000	4,000	3,000	1,000	
210						$3,300	
211						$4,840	
212						$6,655	
213		−10,000		Terminal Value (TV) =		$15,795	
214							
215	Calculator: N = 4, PV = −10000, PMT = 0, FV = 15795. Press I/YR to get:					$MIRR_S$ =	12.11%
216	*Excel* Rate funtion--Easier:		= RATE(F208,0,B209,F213)			$MIRR_S$ =	12.11%
217	*Excel* MIRR function--Easiest:		= MIRR(B209:F209,B206,B206)			$MIRR_S$ =	12.11%
218							
219	Year =	0 (r = 10%)	1	2	3	4	
220	Project L	−10,000	1,000	3,000	4,000	6,750	
221							
222	For Project L, using the MIRR function:			=MIRR(B220:F220,B206,B206)=		$MIRR_L$ =	12.66%

Notes:

1. In this figure we find the rate that forces the present value of the terminal value to equal the project's cost. That rate is defined as the MIRR. We have $\$10{,}000 = TV/(1 + MIRR)^N = \$15{,}795/(1 + MIRR)^4$. We can find the MIRR with a calculator or *Excel*.
2. If S and L are independent, then both should be accepted because both MIRRs exceed the cost of capital. If the projects are mutually exclusive, then L should be chosen because it has the higher MIRR.

See **Ch10 Tool Kit.xls** *on the textbook's Web site.*

1. Project S has just one outflow, a negative \$10,000 at t = 0. Since it occurs at Time 0, it is not discounted, and its PV is –\$10,000. If the project had additional outflows, we would find the PV at t = 0 for each one and then sum them for use in the MIRR calculation.
2. Next, we find the future value of each *inflow*, compounded at the WACC out to the "terminal year," which is the year the last inflow is received. We assume that cash flows are reinvested at the WACC. For Project S, the first cash flow, \$5,000, is compounded at WACC = 10% for 3 years, and it grows to \$6,655.00. The second inflow, \$4,000, grows to \$4,840.00, and the third inflow, \$3,000, grows to \$3,300.00. The last inflow, \$1,000, is received at the end, so it is not compounded at all. The sum of the future values, \$15,795.00, is called the "terminal value," or TV.
3. We now have the cost at t = 0, –\$10,000, and the TV at Year 4, \$15,795.00. There is some discount rate that will cause the PV of the terminal value to equal the cost. *That interest rate is defined as the Modified Internal Rate of Return (MIRR).* In a calculator, enter N = 4, PV = –10000, PMT = 0, and FV = 15795.00. Then pressing the I/YR key yields the MIRR, 12.11%.
4. The MIRR can be found in a number of ways. Figure 10-5 illustrates exactly how the MIRR is calculated: We compound each cash inflow, sum them to determine the TV, and then find the rate that causes the PV of the TV to equal the cost. That rate in this example is 12.11%. However, *Excel* and some of the better calculators have a built-in MIRR function that streamlines the process. We explain how to use the

MIRR function in our calculator tutorials, and we explain how to find MIRR with *Excel* in this chapter's *Excel* model.[14]

The MIRR has two significant advantages over the regular IRR. First, whereas the regular IRR assumes that the cash flows from each project are reinvested at the IRR itself, the MIRR assumes that cash flows are reinvested at the cost of capital (or some other explicit rate). Since reinvestment at the IRR is generally not correct, the MIRR is usually a better indicator of a project's true profitability. Second, the MIRR eliminates the multiple IRR problem—there can never be more than one MIRR, and it can be compared with the cost of capital when deciding to accept or reject projects.

Our conclusion is that the MIRR is better than the regular IRR; however, this question remains: Is MIRR as good as the NPV? Here is our take on the situation.

- For *independent* projects, the NPV, IRR, and MIRR always reach the same accept–reject conclusion, so the three criteria are equally good when evaluating independent projects.
- However, if projects are *mutually exclusive* and if they differ in size, conflicts can arise. In such cases the NPV is best because it selects the project that maximizes value.[15]
- Our overall conclusions are that (1) the MIRR is superior to the regular IRR as an indicator of a project's "true" rate of return, but (2) NPV is better than either IRR or MIRR when choosing among competing projects. If managers want to know the expected rates of return on projects, it would be better to give them MIRRs rather than IRRs because MIRRs are more likely to be the rates that are actually earned.

Self-Test

What's the primary difference between the MIRR and the regular IRR?

Which provides a better estimate of a project's "true" rate of return, the MIRR or the regular IRR? Explain your answer.

Projects A and B have the following cash flows:

	0	1	2
A	–$1,000	$1,150	$ 100
B	–$1,000	$ 100	$1,300

The cost of capital is 10%. What are the projects' IRRs, MIRRs, and NPVs? **(IRR_A = 23.1%, IRR_B = 19.1%; $MIRR_A$ = 16.8%, $MIRR_B$ = 18.7%; NPV_A = $128.10, NPV_B = $165.29)** Which project would each method select? **(IRR: A; MIRR: B; NPV: B)**

[14]If we let COF_t and CIF_t denote cash outflows and inflows, respectively, then Equations 10-2a and 10-2b summarize the steps just described:

$$\sum_{t=0}^{N}\frac{COF_t}{(1+r)^t}=\frac{\sum_{t=0}^{N}CIF_t(1+r)^{N-t}}{(1+MIRR)^N} \quad (10\text{-}2a)$$

$$\text{PV costs}=\frac{TV}{(1+MIRR)^N} \quad (10\text{-}2b)$$

Also, note that there are alternative definitions for the MIRR. One difference relates to whether negative cash flows after the positive cash flows begin should be compounded and treated as part of the TV or discounted and treated as a cost. A related issue is whether negative and positive flows in a given year should be netted or treated separately. For more discussion, see David M. Shull, "Interpreting Rates of Return: A Modified Rate of Return Approach," *Financial Practice and Education*, Fall 1993, pp. 67–71.

[15]For projects of equal size but different lives, the MIRR will always lead to the same decision as the NPV if the MIRRs are both calculated using as the terminal year the life of the longer project. (Just fill in zeros for the shorter project's missing cash flows.)

10.7 NPV Profiles

See **Ch10 Tool Kit.xls** *on the textbook's Web site.*

Figure 10-6 shows the **net present value profile** for Project S. To make the profile, we find the project's NPV at a number of different discount rates and then plot those values to create a graph. Note that, at a zero cost of capital, the NPV is simply the net total of the undiscounted cash flows: \$13,000 – \$10,000 = \$3,000. This value is plotted as the vertical axis intercept. Also, recall that the IRR is the discount rate that causes the NPV to equal zero, so the discount rate at which the profile line crosses the horizontal axis is the project's IRR. When we connect all the data points, we have the NPV profile.[16]

FIGURE 10-6 NPV Profile for Project S

	A	B	C	D	E	F
244	Cost of capital =	10.00%				
245	Year =	0	1	2	3	4
246	Project S	–10,000.00	5,000	4,000	3,000	1,000
247						
248		r	NPV_S			
249		0%	\$3,000.00			
250		5%	1,804.24			
251		10%	788.20			
252		14.489%	0.00	NPV = \$0, so IRR = 14.489%		
253		15%	–83.30			
254		20%	–837.19			

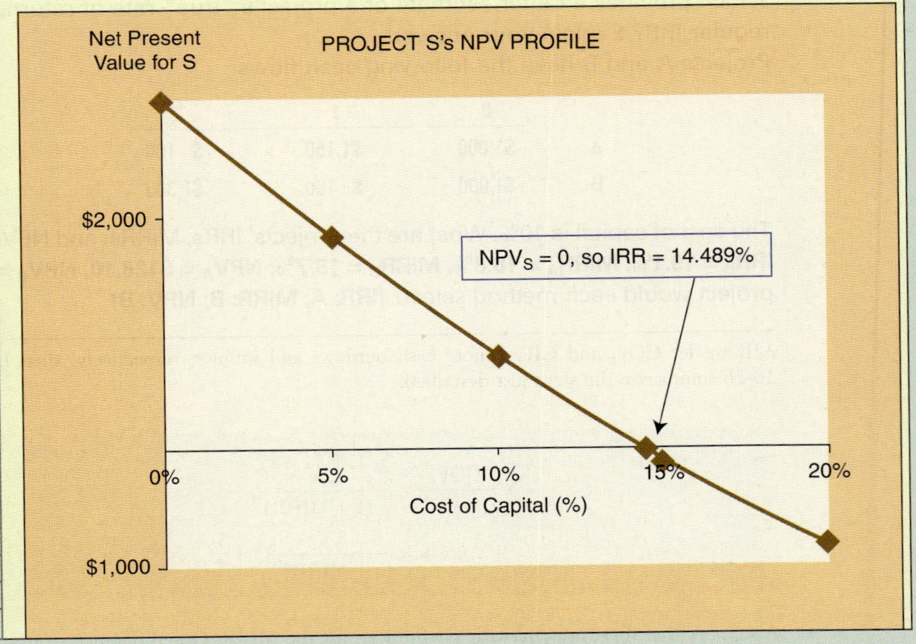

PROJECT S's NPV PROFILE

Net Present Value for S

\$2,000

\$1,000

NPV_S = 0, so IRR = 14.489%

0% 5% 10% 15% 20%

Cost of Capital (%)

[16]The NPV profile is curved—it is *not* a straight line. NPV approaches CF_0, which is the –\$10,000 project cost, as the discount rate increases toward infinity. The reason is that, at an infinitely high cost of capital, the PVs of the inflows would all be zero, so NPV at r = ∞ must be CF_0. We should also remark that under certain conditions the NPV profiles can cross the horizontal axis several times, or never cross it. This point was discussed in Section 10.4.

FIGURE 10-7 NPV Profiles for Projects S and L: Why Conflict Occurs

	A	B	C	D	E
299		Cost of Capital	NPV_S	NPV_L	
300		0%	$3,000.00	$4,750.00	
301		5%	1,804.24	2,682.06	
302		10%	788.20	1,004.03	
303	Crossover =	11.975%	428.38	428.38	$NPV_S = NPV_L$
304	IRR_L =	13.549%	156.40	0.00	$NPV_L = 0$
305	IRR_S =	14.489%	0.00	−243.65	$NPV_S = 0$
306		20%	−$837.19	−$1,513.31	

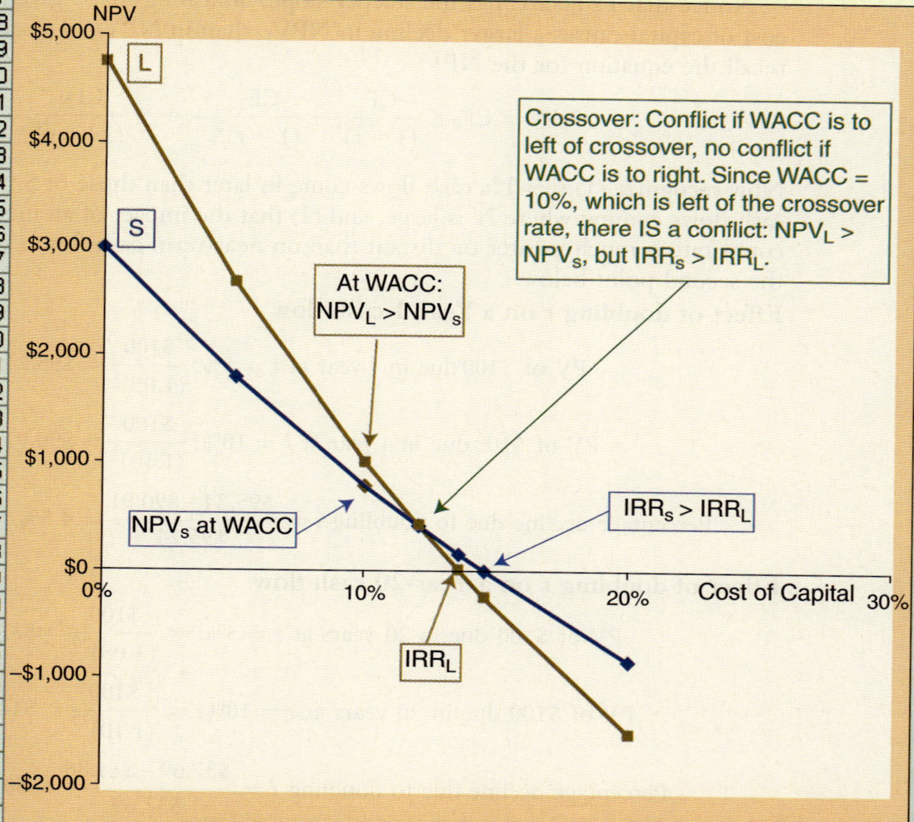

NPV
$5,000
$4,000
$3,000
$2,000
$1,000
$0
−$1,000
−$2,000
0%
10%
20%
Cost of Capital
30%
L
S
At WACC: $NPV_L > NPV_S$
Crossover: Conflict if WACC is to left of crossover, no conflict if WACC is to right. Since WACC = 10%, which is left of the crossover rate, there IS a conflict: $NPV_L > NPV_S$, but $IRR_S > IRR_L$.
NPV_S at WACC
$IRR_S > IRR_L$
IRR_L

See **Ch10 Tool Kit.xls** *on the textbook's Web site.*

Now consider Figure 10-7, which shows two NPV profiles: the one for Project S, as developed in Figure 10-6, and a new one for L. Note the following points.

- The NPVs vary depending on the actual cost of capital—the higher the cost of capital, the lower the NPV. Observe also that L's NPV declines faster than does S's with increases in the cost of capital.
- However, the IRRs are fixed, and S has the higher IRR regardless of the cost of capital.
- The two NPV profile lines cross at a cost of capital of 11.975%, which is called the **crossover rate**. The crossover rate can be found by calculating the IRR of the differences in the projects' cash flows, as demonstrated below:

	0	1	2	3	4
Project S	-\$10,000	\$5,000	\$4,000	\$3,000	\$1,000
Project L	-10,000	1,000	3,000	4,000	6,750
$\Delta = CF_S - CF_L$	\$ 0	\$4,000	\$1,000	-\$1,000	-\$5,750

IRR Δ = 11.975%

- Project L has the higher NPV if the cost of capital is less than the crossover rate, but S has the higher NPV if the cost of capital is greater than that rate.

Notice that Project L has the steeper slope, indicating that a given increase in the cost of capital causes a larger decline in NPV_L than in NPV_S. To see why this is so, recall the equation for the NPV:

$$NPV = CF_0 + \frac{CF_1}{(1+r)^1} + \frac{CF_2}{(1+r)^2} + \cdots + \frac{CF_N}{(1+r)^N}$$

Now recognize (1) that L's cash flows come in later than those of S, with L's highest cash flows coming where N is large, and (2) that the impact of an increase in the discount rate is much greater on distant than on near-term cash flows. We demonstrate the second point below.

Effect of doubling r on a Year-1 cash flow

$$\text{PV of \$100 due in 1 year at } r = 5\%: \frac{\$100}{(1.05)^1} = \$95.24$$

$$\text{PV of \$100 due in 1 year at } r = 10\%: \frac{\$100}{(1.10)^1} = \$90.91$$

$$\text{Percentage decline due to doubling } r = \frac{\$95.24 - \$90.91}{\$95.24} = \mathbf{4.5\%}$$

Effect of doubling r on a Year-20 cash flow

$$\text{PV of \$100 due in 20 years at } r = 5\%: = \frac{\$100}{(1.05)^{20}} = \$37.69$$

$$\text{PV of \$100 due in 20 years at } r = 10\%: = \frac{\$100}{(1.10)^{20}} = \$14.86$$

$$\text{Percentage decline due to doubling } r = \frac{\$37.69 - \$14.86}{\$37.69} = \mathbf{60.6\%}$$

Thus, a doubling of the discount rate results in only a 4.5% decline in the PV of a Year-1 cash flow, but the same increase in discount rate causes the PV of a Year-20 cash flow to fall by more than 60%. Therefore, *a project like L, which has most of its cash flows coming in the later years, will suffer a sharp decline in its NPV if the cost of capital increases; but a project like S, whose cash flows come earlier, will not be severely penalized.* This is why Project L's NPV profile has the steeper slope.

As we have seen, Projects S and L have conflicting rankings when ranked by the NPV versus the IRR. Figure 10-7 can be used to see the conditions under which such conflicts can and cannot arise.

Independent Projects. *If an independent project with normal cash flows is being evaluated, then the NPV and IRR criteria always lead to the same accept/reject decision: If NPV says accept then IRR also says accept, and vice versa.* To see why this is so, look back at

Figure 10-6 and notice (1) that the IRR says accept Project S if the cost of capital is less than (or to the left of) the IRR and (2) that if the cost of capital is less than the IRR then the NPV must be positive. Thus, at any cost of capital less than 14.489%, Project S will be recommended by both the NPV and IRR criteria, but both methods reject the project if the cost of capital is greater than 14.489%. A similar graph could be created for Project L or any other normal project, and we would always reach the same conclusion: *For normal, independent projects, if the IRR says to accept it, then so will the NPV.*

Mutually Exclusive Projects. Now assume that Projects S and L are mutually exclusive rather than independent. Therefore, we can choose either S or L, or we can reject both, but we can't accept both. Now look at Figure 10-7 and note these points.

- As long as the cost of capital is *greater than* the crossover rate of 11.975%, both methods agree that Project S is better: $NPV_S > NPV_L$ and $IRR_S > IRR_L$. Therefore, if r is *greater* than the crossover rate, no conflict occurs.
- However, if the cost of capital is *less than* the crossover rate, a conflict arises: NPV ranks L higher, but IRR ranks S higher.

There are two basic conditions that cause NPV profiles to cross and thus lead to conflicts.[17]

1. *Timing differences.* If most of the cash flows from one project come in early while most of those from the other project come in later, then the NPV profiles may cross and result in a conflict. This is the reason for the conflict between our Projects S and L.
2. *Project size (or scale) differences.* If the amount invested in one project is larger than the other, this can also lead to profiles crossing and a resulting conflict. If you look back at the box titled "Why NPV is Better than IRR," you will see an example of the size difference conflict.

When either size or timing differences occur, the firm will have different amounts of funds to invest in other projects in the various years, depending on which of the two mutually exclusive projects it chooses. If it chooses S, then it will have more funds to invest in Year 1 because S has a larger inflow that year. Similarly, if one project costs more than the other, then the firm will have more money to invest at t = 0 if it selects the smaller project.

Given this situation, the rate of return at which differential cash flows can be reinvested is a critical issue. We saw earlier that the NPV assumes reinvestment at the cost of capital, and that this is generally a more reasonable assumption. Therefore, *whenever conflicts exist between mutually exclusive projects, use the NPV method.*

Self-Test

Describe in words how an NPV profile is constructed. How does one determine the intercepts for the x-axis and the y-axis?

What is the "crossover rate," and how does it interact with the cost of capital to determine whether or not a conflict exists between NPV and IRR?

What two characteristics can lead to conflicts between the NPV and the IRR when evaluating mutually exclusive projects?

---

[17]Also, if mutually exclusive projects have different lives (as opposed to different cash flow patterns over a common life), this introduces further complications; thus, for meaningful comparisons, some mutually exclusive projects must be evaluated over a common life. This point is discussed later in the chapter.

10.8 Profitability Index (PI)

A fourth method used to evaluate projects is the **profitability index (PI):**

$$PI = \frac{\text{PV of future cash flows}}{\text{Initial cost}} = \frac{\sum_{t=1}^{N} \frac{CF_t}{(1+r)^t}}{CF_0} \quad (10\text{-}3)$$

Here CF_t represents the expected future cash flows and CF_0 represents the initial cost. The PI shows the *relative* profitability of any project, or the present value per dollar of initial cost. As we can see from Figure 10-8, the PI for Project S, based on a 10% cost of capital, is $10,788.20/$10,000 = 1.0788; the PI for Project L is 1.1004. Thus, Project S is expected to produce $1.0788 of present value for each $1 of investment whereas L should produce $1.1004 for each dollar invested.

A project is acceptable if its PI is greater than 1.0; and the higher the PI, the higher the project's ranking. Therefore, both S and L would be accepted by the PI criterion if they were independent, and L would be ranked ahead of S if they were mutually exclusive.

Mathematically, the NPV, IRR, MIRR, and PI methods will always lead to the same accept/reject decisions for *normal, independent* projects: If a project's NPV is positive, its IRR and MIRR will always exceed r and its PI will always be greater than 1.0. However, these methods can give conflicting rankings for *mutually exclusive* projects if the projects differ in size or in the timing of cash flows. If the PI ranking conflicts with the NPV, then the NPV ranking should be used.

See **Ch10 Tool Kit.xls** *on the textbook's Web site.*

Self-Test

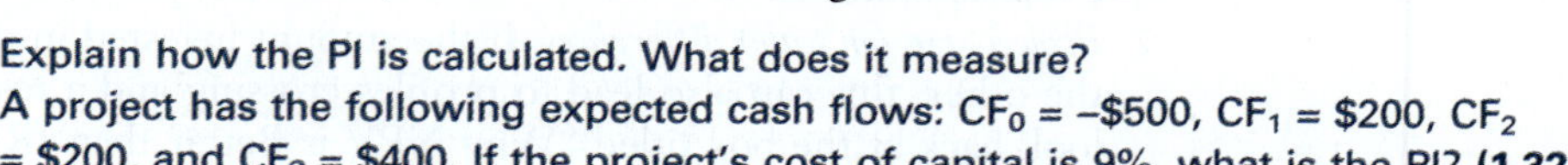
Explain how the PI is calculated. What does it measure?

A project has the following expected cash flows: CF_0 = –$500, CF_1 = $200, CF_2 = $200, and CF_3 = $400. If the project's cost of capital is 9%, what is the PI? (1.32)

FIGURE 10-8 Profitability Index (PI)

	A	B	C	D	E
351	Project S :		PI_S = PV of future cash flows	÷	Initial cost
352			PI_S = $10,788.20	÷	$10,000
353			PI_S = 1.0788		
354					
355	Project L :		PI_L = PV of future cash flows	÷	Initial cost
356			PI_L = $11,004.03	÷	$10,000
357			PI_L = 1.1004		

Notes:

1. If Projects L and S are independent, then both should be accepted because both have PI greater than 1.0. However, if they are mutually exclusive then Project L should be chosen because it has the higher PI.
2. PI and NPV rankings will be consistent if the projects have the same cost, as is true for S and L. However, if they differ in size then conflicts can occur. In the event of a conflict, the NPV ranking should be used.

10.9 Payback Period

NPV and IRR are the most commonly used methods today, but historically the first selection criterion was the **payback period**, defined as the number of years required to recover the funds invested in a project from its operating cash flows. Equation 10-4 is used for the calculation, and the process is diagrammed in Figure 10-9. We start with the project's cost, a negative number, and then add the cash inflow for each year until the cumulative cash flow turns positive. The payback year is the year *prior to* full recovery, plus a fraction equal to the shortfall at the end of the prior year divided by the cash flow during the year when full recovery occurs:[18]

$$\text{Payback} = \begin{array}{c}\text{Number of}\\ \text{years prior to}\\ \text{full recovery}\end{array} + \frac{\begin{array}{c}\text{Unrecovered cost}\\ \text{at start of year}\end{array}}{\begin{array}{c}\text{Cash flow during}\\ \text{full recovery year}\end{array}} \tag{10-4}$$

The cash flows for Projects S and L, together with their paybacks, are shown in Figure 10-9.[19] The shorter the payback, the better the project. Therefore, if the firm requires a payback of 3 years or less, then S would be accepted but L would be rejected. If the projects were mutually exclusive, S would be ranked over L because of its shorter payback.

See **Ch10 Tool Kit.xls** *on the textbook's Web site.*

The regular payback has three flaws: (1) Dollars received in different years are all given the same weight—that is, the time value of money is ignored. (2) Cash flows beyond the payback year are given no consideration whatsoever, regardless of how large they might be. (3) Unlike the NPV or the IRR, which tell us how much wealth a project adds or how much a project's rate of return exceeds the cost of capital, the payback

FIGURE 10-9 Payback Period

	A	B	C	D	E	F	G
386		Years =	0	1	2	3	4
387	Project S	Cash flow	−10,000	5,000	4,000	3,000	1,000
388		Cumulative cash flow	−10,000	−5,000	−1,000	2,000	3,000
389	Intermediate calculation for payback		–	–	–	2.33	5.00
390							
391					Intermediate calculation:		
392	Manual calculation fo Payback S = 2 + $1,000/$3,000 =		2.33		=IF(F388>0,E386+ABS(E388/F387),"–")		
393	*Excel* calculation of Payback S =		2.33			2.33	
394							
395		Years	0	1	2	3	4
396	Project L	Cash flow	−10,000	1,000	3,000	4,000	6,750
397		Cumulative cash flow	−10,000	−9,000	−6,000	−2,000	4,750
398							
399	Manual calculation of Payback L = 3 + $2,000/$6,750 =		3.30		Payback is between negative and positive cumulative cash flow.		
400	Alternative *Excel* calculation of Payback L =						
401	= PERCENTRANK(C397:G397,0,6)*G395 =		3.30				
402							

[18]Equation 10-4 assumes that cash flows come in uniformly during the full recovery year.

[19]There is not an *Excel* function for payback. But if the cash flows are normal then the PERCENTRANK function can be used to find payback, as illustrated in Figures 10-9 and 10-10.

FIGURE 10-10 Discounted Payback

	A	B	C	D	E	F	G
414	WACC = 10%						
415		Years =	0	1	2	3	4
416	Project S	Cash flow	−10,000.00	5,000.00	4,000.00	3,000.00	1,000.00
417		Discounted Cash flow	−10,000.00	4,545.45	3,305.79	2,253.94	683.01
418		Cumulative discounted CF	−10,000.00	−5,454.55	−2,148.76	105.18	788.20
419							
420		Discounted Payback S = 2+ $2,148.76/$2,253.94 =		2.95	Payback is between negative and positive cumulative discounted cash flow.		
421		*Excel* calculation of Discounted Payback S =					
422		= PERCENTRANK(C418:G418,0,6)*G415 =		2.95			
423							
424		Years	0	1	2	3	4
425	Project L	Cash flow	−10,000.00	1,000.00	3,000.00	4,000.00	6,750.00
426		Discounted Cash flow	−10,000.00	909.09	2,479.34	3,005.26	4,610.34
427		Cumulative discounted CF	−10,000.00	−9,090.91	−6,611.57	−3,606.31	1,004.03
428							
429		Discounted Payback L = 3 + $3,606.31/$4,610.34 =		3.78		Payback is between negative and positive cumulative discounted cash flow.	
430		*Excel* calculation of Discounted Payback L =					
431		= PERCENTRANK(C427:G427,0,6)*G424 =		3.78			
432							

See **Ch10 Tool Kit.xls** *on the textbook's Web site.*

merely tells us how long it takes to recover our investment. There is no necessary relationship between a given payback period and investor wealth, so we don't know how to specify an acceptable payback. The firm might use 2 years, 3 years, or any other number as the minimum acceptable payback, but the choice is purely arbitrary.

To counter the first criticism, financial analysts developed the **discounted payback**, where cash flows are discounted at the WACC and then those discounted cash flows are used to find the payback. In Figure 10-10 we calculate the discounted paybacks for S and L, assuming both have a 10% cost of capital. Each inflow is divided by $(1 + r)^t = (1.10)^t$, where t is the year in which the cash flow occurs and r is the project's cost of capital, and then those PVs are used to find the payback. Project S's discounted payback is 2.95 years and L's is 3.78 years.

Note that the payback is a "break-even" calculation in the sense that if cash flows come in at the expected rate, then the project will at least break even. However, since the regular payback doesn't consider the cost of capital, it doesn't specify the true break-even year. The discounted payback does consider capital costs, but it still disregards cash flows beyond the payback year, which is a serious flaw. Further, if mutually exclusive projects vary in size, both payback methods can conflict with the NPV, and that might lead to poor decisions. Finally, there is no way to determine how short the payback periods must be to justify accepting a project.

Although the payback methods have faults as ranking criteria, they do provide information about *liquidity* and *risk*. The shorter the payback, other things held constant, the greater the project's liquidity. This factor is often important for smaller firms that don't have ready access to the capital markets. Also, cash flows expected in the distant future are generally riskier than near-term cash flows, so the payback period is also a risk indicator.

Self-Test

What two pieces of information does the payback method provide that are absent from the other capital budgeting decision methods?

What three flaws does the regular payback method have? Does the discounted payback method correct all of those flaws? Explain.

Project P has a cost of $1,000 and cash flows of $300 per year for 3 years plus another $1,000 in Year 4. The project's cost of capital is 15%. What are P's regular and discounted paybacks? **(3.10, 3.55)** If the company requires a payback of 3 years or less, would the project be accepted? Would this be a good accept/reject decision, considering the NPV and/or the IRR? **(NPV = $256.72, IRR = 24.78%)**

10.10 Conclusions on Capital Budgeting Methods

We have discussed six capital budgeting decision criteria: NPV, IRR, MIRR, PI, payback, and discounted payback. We compared these methods with one another and highlighted their strengths and weaknesses. In the process, we may have created the impression that "sophisticated" firms should use only one method, the NPV. However, virtually all capital budgeting decisions are analyzed by computer, so it is easy to calculate using all six methods. In making the accept–reject decision, large sophisticated firms such as FPL, GE, and Boeing generally calculate and consider all six measures, because each provides a somewhat different piece of information about the decision.

NPV is the single best criterion because it provides a direct measure of the value a project adds to shareholder wealth. IRR and MIRR measure profitability expressed as a percentage rate of return, which decision makers like to consider. The PI also measures profitability but in relation to the amount of the investment. Further, IRR, MIRR, and PI all contain information concerning a project's "safety margin." To illustrate, consider a firm, whose WACC is 10%, that must choose between these two mutually exclusive projects: SS (for small) has a cost of $10,000 and is expected to return $16,500 at the end of one year; LL (for large) has a cost of $100,000 and is expected to return $115,550 at the end of one year. SS has a huge IRR, 65%, while LL's IRR is a more modest 15.6%. The NPV paints a somewhat different picture: at the 10% cost of capital, SS's NPV is $5,000 while LL's is $5,045. By the NPV rule we would choose LL. However, SS's IRR indicates that it has a much larger margin for error: Even if its cash flow were 39% below the $16,500 forecast, the firm would still recover its $10,000 investment. On the other hand, if LL's inflows fell by only 13.5% from its forecasted $115,550, the firm would not recover its investment. Further, if neither project generated any cash flows at all, the firm would lose only $10,000 on SS but would lose $100,000 by accepting LL.

The modified IRR has all the virtues of the IRR, but it incorporates a better reinvestment rate assumption and also avoids the problem of multiple rates of return. So if decision makers want to know projects' rates of return, the MIRR is a better indicator than the regular IRR.

The PI tells a similar story to the IRR. Here PI_{LL} is only 1.05 while PI_{SS} is 1.50. As with the IRR, this indicates that Project SS's cash inflows could decline by 50% before it loses money, whereas a decline of only 5% in LL's cash flows would result in a loss.

Payback and discounted payback provide indications of a project's *liquidity* and *risk*. A long payback means that investment dollars will be locked up for a long time; hence the project is relatively illiquid. In addition, a long payback means that cash flows must be forecast far into the future, and that probably makes the project riskier than one with a shorter payback. A good analogy for this is bond valuation. An investor should never compare the yields to maturity on two bonds without also considering their terms to maturity, because a bond's risk is significantly influenced by its maturity. The same holds true for capital projects.

In summary, the different measures provide different types of useful information. It is easy to calculate all of them: Simply put the cost of capital and the cash flows into an *Excel* model like the one provided in this chapter's ***Tool Kit*** and the model will instantly calculate all six criteria. Therefore, most sophisticated companies consider all six measures when making capital budgeting decisions. For most decisions, the greatest weight should be given to the NPV, but it would be foolish to ignore the information provided by the other criteria.

Just as it would be foolish to ignore these capital budgeting methods, it would also be foolish to make decisions based *solely* on them. One cannot know at Time 0 the exact cost of future capital or the exact future cash flows. These inputs are simply estimates, and if they turn out to be incorrect then so will be the calculated NPVs and IRRs. Thus, *quantitative methods provide valuable information, but they should not be used as the sole criteria for accept–reject decisions* in the capital budgeting process. Rather, managers should use quantitative methods in the decision-making process but should also consider the likelihood that actual results will differ from the forecasts. Qualitative factors, such as the chances of a tax increase, or a war, or a major product liability suit, should also be considered. In summary, *quantitative methods such as NPV and IRR should be considered as an aid to informed decisions but not as a substitute for sound managerial judgment.*

In this same vein, managers should ask sharp questions about any project that has a large NPV, a high IRR, or a high PI. In a perfectly competitive economy, there would be no positive-NPV projects—all companies would have the same opportunities, and competition would quickly eliminate any positive NPV. The existence of positive-NPV projects must be predicated on some imperfection in the marketplace, and the longer the life of the project, the longer that imperfection must last. Therefore, managers should be able to identify the imperfection and explain why it will persist before accepting that a project will really have a positive NPV. Valid explanations might include patents or proprietary technology, which is how pharmaceutical and software firms create positive-NPV projects. Pfizer's Lipitor (a cholesterol-reducing medicine) and Microsoft's Vista operating system are examples. Companies can also create positive NPV by being the first entrant into a new market or by creating new products that meet some previously unidentified consumer needs. The Post-it notes invented by 3M are an example. Similarly, Dell developed procedures for direct sales of microcomputers and, in the process, created projects with enormous NPV. Also, companies such as Southwest Airlines have managed to train and motivate their workers better than their competitors, and this has led to positive-NPV projects. In all of these cases, the companies developed some source of competitive advantage, and that advantage resulted in positive-NPV projects.

This discussion suggests three things: (1) If you can't identify the reason a project has a positive projected NPV, then its actual NPV will probably not be positive. (2) Positive NPV projects don't just happen—they result from hard work to develop some competitive advantage. At the risk of oversimplification, the primary job of a manager is to find and develop areas of competitive advantage. (3) Some competitive advantages last longer than others, with their durability depending on competitors' ability to replicate them. Patents, the control of scarce resources, or large size in an industry where strong economies of scale exist can keep competitors at bay. However, it is relatively easy to replicate product features that cannot be patented. The bottom line is that managers should strive to develop nonreplicable sources of competitive advantage. If such an advantage cannot be demonstrated, then you should question projects with high NPV—especially if they have long lives.

Self-Test

Describe the advantages and disadvantages of the six capital budgeting methods.

Should capital budgeting decisions be made solely on the basis of a project's NPV, with no regard to the other criteria? Explain your answer.

What are some possible reasons that a project might have a high NPV?

TABLE 10-1 Capital Budgeting Methods Used in Practice

	FIRMS' PRIMARY CRITERION			FIRMS USE
	1960	1970	1980	1999
NPV	0%	0%	15%	75%
IRR	20	60	65	76
Payback	35	15	5	57
Discounted Payback	NA	NA	NA	29
Other	45	25	15	NA
Totals	100%	100%	100%	

Sources: The 1999 data are from John R. Graham and Campbell R. Harvey, "The Theory and Practice of Corporate Finance: Evidence from the Field," *Journal of Financial Economics*, 2001, pp. 187–244. Data from prior years are our estimates based on averaging data from these studies: J. S. Moore and A. K. Reichert, "An Analysis of the Financial Management Techniques Currently Employed by Large U.S. Corporations," *Journal of Business Finance and Accounting*, Winter 1983, pp. 623–645; and M. T. Stanley and S. R. Block, "A Survey of Multinational Capital Budgeting," *The Financial Review*, March 1984, pp. 36–51.

10.11 Decision Criteria Used in Practice

Over the years, surveys have been designed and administered to find out which of the criteria managers actually use. Surveys prior to 1999 asked companies to indicate which method they gave the most weight, whereas the most recent one (taken in 1999) asked what method or methods managers actually calculated and used. A summary of all these surveys is shown in Table 10-1, and it reveals some interesting trends.

First, the NPV criterion was not used significantly before the 1980s, but by 1999 it was close to the top in usage. Moreover, informal discussions with companies suggest that if a survey were taken in 2009, NPV would be at the top of this list. Second, the IRR method was used slightly more than the NPV at the time of the last survey (1999), but its recent growth is much less dramatic than that of NPV; if a survey were taken today, we believe that the NPV would predominate. Third, payback was the most important criterion years ago, but its use as the primary criterion had fallen drastically by 1980. Companies still use payback because it is easy to calculate and provides some useful information, but it is rarely used as the primary criterion. Fourth, "other methods," primarily the profitability index and the accounting rate of return (the latter of which is explained in this chapter's ***Tool Kit***), have been fading due to the increased use of IRR and especially NPV.

These trends are consistent with our evaluation of the various methods. NPV is the best single criterion, but all of the methods provide useful information and are easy to calculate. Hence all are used, along with judgment and common sense. We will have more to say about all this in the next chapter.

Self-Test

What trends in capital budgeting methodology can be seen from Table 10-1?

10.12 Other Issues in Capital Budgeting

Three other issues in capital budgeting are discussed in this section: (1) how to deal with mutually exclusive projects whose lives differ; (2) the potential advantage of terminating a project before the end of its physical life; and (3) the optimal capital budget when the cost of capital rises as the size of the capital budget increases.

Mutually Exclusive Projects with Unequal Lives

When choosing between two mutually exclusive alternatives with significantly different lives, an adjustment is necessary. For example, suppose a company is planning to modernize its production facilities and is considering either a conveyor system (Project C) or a fleet of forklift trucks (Project F) for moving materials. The first two sections of Figure 10-11 show the expected net cash flows, NPVs, and IRRs for these two mutually exclusive alternatives. We see that Project C, when discounted at the firm's 12% cost of capital, has the higher NPV and thus appears to be the better project.

Although the NPVs shown in Figure 10-11 suggest that Project C should be selected, this analysis is incomplete, and the decision to choose Project C is actually incorrect. If we choose Project F, we will have an opportunity to make a similar investment in 3 years, and if cost and revenue conditions continue at the levels shown in Figure 10-11, then this second investment will also be profitable. However, if we choose Project C, we cannot make this second investment. Two different approaches can be used to correctly compare Projects C and F, as shown in Figure 10-11 and discussed next.

Replacement Chains. The key to the *replacement chain*, or *common life, approach* is to analyze both projects over an equal life. In our example, Project C has a 6-year life, so we assume that Project F will be repeated after 3 years and then analyze it over the same 6-year period. We can then calculate the NPV of C and compare it to the extended-life NPV of Project F. The NPV for Project C, as shown in Figure 10-11, is already based on the 6-year common life. For Project F, however, we must add in a second project to extend the overall life to 6 years. The time line for this extended project, denoted as "All CFs for FF," is shown in Figure 10-11. Here we assume (1) that Project F's cost and annual cash inflows will not change if the project is repeated in 3 years and (2) that the cost of capital will remain at 12%.

The NPV of this extended Project F is $8,824, and its IRR is 25.2%. (The IRR of two Project Fs is the same as the IRR for one Project F.) However, the $8,824 extended NPV of Project F is greater than Project C's $6,491 NPV, so Project F should be selected.

FIGURE 10-11 Analysis of Projects C and F (r = 12%)

	A	B	C	D	E	F	G	H
467	Data on Project C, Conveyor System:							
468	Year (t)	0	1	2	3	4	5	6
469	CF_t for C	($40,000)	$8,000	$14,000	$13,000	$12,000	$11,000	$10,000
470		NPV_C =	$6,491		IRR_C =	17.5%		
471								
472	Data on Project F, Forklifts:							
473	Year (t)	0	1	2	3			
474	CF_t for F	($20,000)	$7,000	$13,000	$12,000			
475		NPV_F =	$5,155		IRR_F =	25.2%		
476								
477	Common Life Approach with F Repeated (Project FF):							
478	Year (t)	0	1	2	3	4	5	6
479	CF_t for 1st F	($20,000)	$7,000	$13,000	$12,000			
480	CF_t for 2nd F				($20,000)	$7,000	$13,000	$12,000
481	All CFs for FF	($20,000)	$7,000	$13,000	($8,000)	$7,000	$13,000	$12,000
482		NPV_{FF} =	$8,824		IRR_{FF} =	25.2%		

Alternatively, we could recognize that Project F has an NPV of $5,155 at Time 0 and a second NPV of that same amount at Time 3, then find the PV of the second NPV at Time 0, and sum the two to find Project F's extended-life NPV of $8,824.

Equivalent Annual Annuities (EAA). Electrical engineers designing power plants and distribution lines were the first to encounter the unequal life problem. They could install transformers and other equipment that had relatively low initial costs but short lives, or they could use equipment that had higher initial costs but longer lives. The services would be required into the indefinite future, so this was the issue: Which choice would result in a higher NPV in the long run? The engineers converted the annual cash flows under the alternative investments into a constant cash flow stream whose NPV was equal to, or equivalent to, the NPV of the initial stream. This was called the **equivalent annual annuity (EAA) method**. To apply the EAA method to Projects C and F, for each project we simply find the constant payment streams that the projects' NPVs ($6,491 for C and $5,155 for F) would provide over their respective lives. Using a financial calculator for Project C, we enter N = 6, I/YR = 12, PV = −6491, and FV = 0. Then, when we press the PMT key, we find EAA_C = $1,579. For Project F, we enter N = 3, I/YR = 12, PV = −5155, and FV = 0; solving for PMT, we find EAA_F = $2,146. Project F would thus produce a higher cash flow stream over the 6 years, so it is the better project.

Conclusions about Unequal Lives. When should we worry about analysis of unequal lives? The unequal life issue (1) does not arise for independent projects but (2) can arise if mutually exclusive projects with significantly different lives are being compared. However, even for mutually exclusive projects, it is not always appropriate to extend the analysis to a common life. This should be done if and only if there is a high probability that the projects will actually be repeated at the end of their initial lives.

We should note several potentially serious weaknesses inherent in this type of analysis. (1) If inflation occurs, then replacement equipment will have a higher price. Moreover, both sales prices and operating costs would probably change. Thus, the static conditions built into the analysis would be invalid. (2) Replacements that occur down the road would probably employ new technology, which in turn might change the cash flows. (3) It is difficult enough to estimate the lives of most projects, and even more so to estimate the lives of a series of projects. In view of these problems, no experienced financial analyst would be too concerned about comparing mutually exclusive projects with lives of, say, 8 years and 10 years. Given all the uncertainties in the estimation process, such projects would, for all practical purposes, be assumed to have the same life. Still, it is important to recognize that a problem exists if mutually exclusive projects have substantially different lives.

When we encounter situations in practice where significant differences in project lives are encountered, we first use a computer spreadsheet to build expected inflation and/or possible efficiency gains directly into the cash flow estimates and then use the replacement chain approach. We prefer the replacement chain approach for two reasons. First, it is easier to explain to those who are responsible for approving capital budgets. Second, it is easier to build inflation and other modifications into a spreadsheet and then go on to make the replacement chain calculations.

Economic Life versus Physical Life

Projects are normally evaluated under the assumption that the firm will operate them over their full physical lives. However, this may not be the best plan—it may be better to terminate a project before the end of its potential life. For example, the cost of maintenance for trucks and machinery can become quite high if they are used for too many years, so it might be better to replace them before the end of their potential lives.

FIGURE 10-12 Economic Life versus Physical Life

	A	B	C	D	E	F	G
520					PVs of the Cash Flows		
521			Operating	Salvage	Operating	Salvage	
522		Year	Cash Flow	Value	Cash Flow	Value	
523		0	−$4,800				
524		1	2,000	$3,000	$1,818.18	$2,727.27	
525		2	2,000	1,650	1,652.89	1,363.64	
526		3	1,750	0	1,314.80	0.00	
527							
528	WACC: 10%						
529					PV of		PV of
530	NPV at Different Operating Lives:		Initial Cost	+	Operating	+	Salvage
531					Cash Flows		Value
532							
533	Operate for 3 Years:		−$4,800.00	+	$4,785.88	+	$0.00
534	NPV_3:	−$14.12					
535							
536	Operate for 2 Years:		−$4,800.00	+	$3,471.07	+	$1,363.64
537	NPV_2:	$34.71					
538							
539	Operate for 1 Year:		−$4,800.00	+	$1,818.18	+	$2,727.27
540	NPV_1:	−$254.55					

Note: The project is profitable if and only if it is operated for just 2 years.

See ***Ch10 Tool Kit.xls*** *on the textbook's Web site.*

Figure 10-12 provides data for an asset with a physical life of 3 years. However, the project can be terminated at the end of any year and the asset sold at the indicated salvage values. All of the cash flows are after taxes, and the firm's cost of capital is 10%. The undiscounted cash flows are shown in Columns C and D in the upper part of the figure, and the present values of these flows are shown in Columns E and F. We find the project's NPV under different assumptions about how long it will be operated. If the project is operated for its full 3-year life, it will have a negative NPV. The NPV will be positive if it is operated for 2 years and then the asset is sold for a relatively high salvage value; the NPV will be negative if the asset is disposed after only 1 year of operation. Therefore, the project's optimal life is 2 years.

This type of analysis is used to determine a project's **economic life**, which is the life that maximizes the NPV and thus shareholder wealth. For our project, the economic life is 2 years versus the 3-year **physical**, or **engineering, life**. Note that this analysis was based on the expected cash flows and the expected salvage values, and it should always be conducted as a part of the capital budgeting evaluation if salvage values are relatively high.

The Optimal Capital Budget

The **optimal capital budget** is defined as the set of projects that maximizes the value of the firm. Finance theory states that all independent projects with positive NPVs should be accepted, as should the mutually exclusive projects with the highest NPVs. Therefore, the optimal capital budget consists of that set of projects. However, two complications arise in practice: (1) The cost of capital might increase as the size of the capital budget increases, making it hard to know the proper discount rate to use when evaluating projects; and (2) sometimes firms set an upper limit on the size of their capital budgets, which is also known as *capital rationing*.

An Increasing Cost of Capital. The cost of capital may increase as the capital budget increases—this is called an *increasing marginal cost of capital.* As we discussed in Chapter 9, flotation costs associated with issuing new equity can be quite high. This means that the cost of capital will increase once a company has invested all of its internally generated cash and must sell new common stock. In addition, once a firm has used up its normal credit lines and must seek additional debt capital, it may encounter an increase in its cost of debt. This means that a project might have a positive NPV if it is part of a $10 million capital budget but the same project might have a negative NPV if it is part of a $20 million capital budget because the cost of capital might increase.

resource

See **Ch10 Tool Kit.xls** *on the textbook's Web site.*

Fortunately, these problems rarely occur for most firms, especially those that are stable and well established. When a rising cost of capital is encountered, we would proceed as indicated below. You can look at Figure 10-13 as you read through our points.

FIGURE 10-13 IOS and MCC Schedules

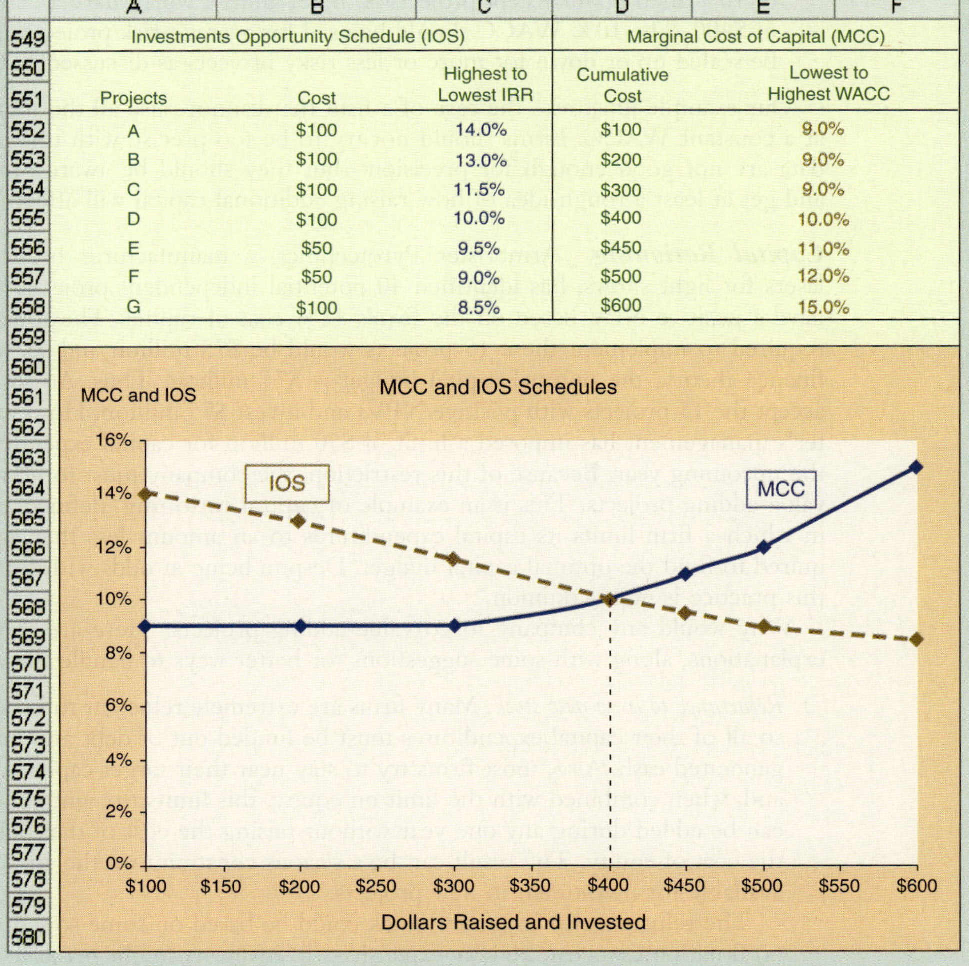

Investments Opportunity Schedule (IOS)			Marginal Cost of Capital (MCC)	
Projects	Cost	Highest to Lowest IRR	Cumulative Cost	Lowest to Highest WACC
A	$100	14.0%	$100	9.0%
B	$100	13.0%	$200	9.0%
C	$100	11.5%	$300	9.0%
D	$100	10.0%	$400	10.0%
E	$50	9.5%	$450	11.0%
F	$50	9.0%	$500	12.0%
G	$100	8.5%	$600	15.0%

Note: Use WACC = 10% as the base rate for finding base risk-adjusted project WACCs.

- Find the IRR (or MIRR) on all potential projects, arrange them in rank order (along with their initial costs), and then plot them on a graph with the IRR on the vertical axis and the cumulative costs on the horizontal axis. The firm's data are shown in Figure 10-13, and the IRRs are plotted in the graph. The line is called the Investment Opportunity Schedule (IOS), and it shows the marginal return on capital.
- Next, determine how much capital can be raised before it is necessary to issue new common stock or go to higher-cost sources of debt, and identify the amounts of higher-cost capital. Use this information to calculate the WACC that corresponds to the different amounts of capital raised. In this example, the firm can raise $300 before the WACC rises, but the WACC increases as additional capital is raised. The increasing WACC represents the marginal cost of capital, and its graph is called the Marginal Cost of Capital (MCC) schedule.
- The intersection of the IOS and MCC schedules indicates the amount of capital the firm should raise and invest, and it is analogous to the familiar marginal cost versus marginal revenue schedule discussed in introductory economics courses. In our example, the firm should have a capital budget of $400; if it uses a WACC of 10% then it will accept projects A, B, C, and D, which have a cumulative cost of $400. The 10% WACC should be used for average-risk projects, but it should be scaled up or down for more or less risky projects as discussed in Chapter 9.

Our example illustrates the case of a firm that cannot raise all the money it needs at a constant WACC. Firms should not try to be too precise with this process—the data are not good enough for precision—but they should be aware of the concept and get at least a rough idea of how raising additional capital will affect the WACC.

Capital Rationing. Armbrister Pyrotechnics, a manufacturer of fireworks and lasers for light shows, has identified 40 potential independent projects, of which 15 have a positive NPV based on the firm's 12% cost of capital. The total investment required to implement these 15 projects would be $75 million and so, according to finance theory, the optimal capital budget is $75 million. Thus, Armbrister should accept the 15 projects with positive NPVs and invest $75 million. However, Armbrister's management has imposed a limit of $50 million for capital expenditures during the upcoming year. Because of this restriction, the company must forgo a number of value-adding projects. This is an example of **capital rationing**, defined as a situation in which a firm limits its capital expenditures to an amount less than would be required to fund the optimal capital budget. Despite being at odds with finance theory, this practice is quite common.

Why would any company forgo value-adding projects? Here are some potential explanations, along with some suggestions for better ways to handle these situations.

1. *Reluctance to issue new stock.* Many firms are extremely reluctant to issue new stock, so all of their capital expenditures must be funded out of debt and internally generated cash. Also, most firms try to stay near their target capital structure, and, when combined with the limit on equity, this limits the amount of debt that can be added during any one year without raising the cost of that debt as well as the cost of equity. The result can be a serious constraint on the amount of funds available for investment in new projects.

   The reluctance to issue new stock could be based on some sound reasons: (a) flotation costs can be very expensive; (b) investors might perceive new stock offerings as a signal that the company's equity is overvalued; and (c) the company might have to reveal sensitive strategic information to investors, thereby reducing some of its competitive advantages. To avoid these costs, many companies simply limit their capital expenditures.

However, rather than placing a somewhat artificial limit on capital expenditures, companies might be better off explicitly incorporating the costs of raising external capital into their costs of capital along the lines shown in Figure 10-13. If there still are positive-NPV projects even with the higher cost of capital, then the company should go ahead and raise external equity and accept the projects.

2. *Constraints on nonmonetary resources*. Sometimes a firm simply doesn't have the necessary managerial, marketing, or engineering talent to immediately accept all positive-NPV projects. In other words, the potential projects may be independent from a demand standpoint but not from an internal standpoint, because accepting them all would raise the firm's costs. To avoid potential problems due to spreading existing talent too thinly, many firms simply limit the capital budget to a size that can be accommodated by their current personnel.

   A better solution might be to employ a technique called **linear programming**. Each potential project has an expected NPV, and each potential project requires a certain level of support by different types of employees. A linear program can identify the set of projects that maximizes NPV *subject to the constraint* that the total amount of support required for these projects does not exceed the available resources.

3. *Controlling estimation bias*. Many managers become overly optimistic when estimating the cash flows for a project. Some firms try to control this estimation bias by requiring managers to use an unrealistically high cost of capital. Others try to control the bias by limiting the size of the capital budget. Neither solution is generally effective, because managers quickly learn the rules of the game and then increase their own estimates of project cash flows, which might have been biased upward to begin with.

   A better solution is to implement a post-audit program and to link the accuracy of forecasts to the compensation of the managers who initiated the projects.

Self-Test

Briefly describe the replacement chain (common life) approach and differentiate it from the Equivalent Annual Annuity (EAA) approach.

Differentiate between a project's *physical* life and its *economic* life.

What factors can lead to an increasing marginal cost of capital? How might this affect capital budgeting?

What is capital rationing?

What are three explanations for capital rationing? How might firms otherwise handle these situations?

Summary

This chapter has described six techniques that are used in capital budgeting analysis: NPV, IRR, MIRR, PI, payback, and discounted payback. Each approach provides a different piece of information, so in this age of computers, managers often look at all of them when evaluating projects. However, NPV is the best single measure, and almost all firms now use NPV. The key concepts covered in this chapter are listed below.

- **Capital budgeting** is the process of analyzing potential projects. Capital budgeting decisions are probably the most important ones that managers must make.
- The **net present value (NPV) method** discounts all cash flows at the project's cost of capital and then sums those cash flows. The project should be accepted if the NPV is positive because such a project increases shareholders' value.

- The **internal rate of return (IRR)** is defined as the discount rate that forces a project's NPV to equal zero. The project should be accepted if the IRR is greater than the cost of capital.
- The NPV and IRR methods make the same accept–reject decisions for **independent projects**, but if projects are **mutually exclusive** then ranking conflicts can arise. In such cases, the NPV method should generally be relied upon.
- The NPV method assumes that cash flows will be reinvested at the firm's cost of capital, whereas the IRR method assumes reinvestment at the project's IRR. *Reinvestment at the cost of capital is generally a better assumption* because it is closer to reality.
- The **modified IRR (MIRR) method** corrects some of the problems with the regular IRR. MIRR involves finding the **terminal value (TV)** of the cash inflows, compounding them at the firm's cost of capital, and then determining the discount rate that forces the present value of the TV to equal the present value of the outflows. Thus, the MIRR assumes reinvestment at the cost of capital, not at the IRR. If management wants to know the rate of return on projects, the MIRR is a better estimate than the regular IRR.
- The **profitability index (PI)** is calculated by dividing the present value of cash inflows by the initial cost, so it measures relative profitability—that is, the amount of the present value per dollar of investment.
- The regular **payback period** is defined as the number of years required to recover a project's cost. The regular payback method has three flaws: It ignores cash flows beyond the payback period, it does not consider the time value of money, and it doesn't give a precise acceptance rule. The payback does, however, provide an indication of a project's risk and liquidity, because it shows how long the invested capital will be tied up.
- The **discounted payback** is similar to the regular payback except that it discounts cash flows at the project's cost of capital. It considers the time value of money, but it still ignores cash flows beyond the payback period.
- The chapter's ***Tool Kit** Excel* model and ***Web Extension 10A*** describe another but seldom-used evaluation method, the **accounting rate of return**.
- If mutually exclusive projects have **unequal lives**, it may be necessary to adjust the analysis to put the projects on an equal-life basis. This can be done using the **replacement chain (common life) approach** or the **equivalent annual annuity (EAA) approach**.
- A project's true value may be greater than the NPV based on its **physical life** if it can be **terminated** at the end of its **economic life**.
- Flotation costs and increased risk associated with unusually large expansion programs can cause the **marginal cost of capital** to increase as the size of the capital budget increases.
- **Capital rationing** occurs when management places a constraint on the size of the firm's capital budget during a particular period.

Questions

(10–1) Define each of the following terms:

a. Capital budgeting; regular payback period; discounted payback period
b. Independent projects; mutually exclusive projects
c. DCF techniques; net present value (NPV) method; internal rate of return (IRR) method; profitability index (PI)

d. Modified internal rate of return (MIRR) method
e. NPV profile; crossover rate
f. Nonnormal cash flow projects; normal cash flow projects; multiple IRRs
g. Reinvestment rate assumption
h. Replacement chain; economic life; capital rationing; equivalent annual annuity (EAA)

(10–2) What types of projects require the least detailed and the most detailed analysis in the capital budgeting process?

(10–3) Explain why the NPV of a relatively long-term project, defined as one for which a high percentage of its cash flows are expected in the distant future, is more sensitive to changes in the cost of capital than is the NPV of a short-term project.

(10–4) When two mutually exclusive projects are being compared, explain why the short-term project might be higher ranked under the NPV criterion if the cost of capital is high whereas the long-term project might be deemed better if the cost of capital is low. Would changes in the cost of capital ever cause a change in the IRR ranking of two such projects?

(10–5) In what sense is a reinvestment rate assumption embodied in the NPV, IRR, and MIRR methods? What is the assumed reinvestment rate of each method?

(10–6) Suppose a firm is considering two mutually exclusive projects. One has a life of 6 years and the other a life of 10 years. Would the failure to employ some type of replacement chain analysis bias an NPV analysis against one of the projects? Explain.

Self-Test Problem

Solution Appears in Appendix A

(ST–1)
Project Analysis

You are a financial analyst for the Hittle Company. The director of capital budgeting has asked you to analyze two proposed capital investments, Projects X and Y. Each project has a cost of \$10,000, and the cost of capital for each is 12%. The projects' expected net cash flows are as follows:

	Expected Net Cash Flows	
Year	**Project X**	**Project Y**
0	–\$10,000	–\$10,000
1	6,500	3,500
2	3,000	3,500
3	3,000	3,500
4	1,000	3,500

a. Calculate each project's payback period, net present value (NPV), internal rate of return (IRR), modified internal rate of return (MIRR), and profitability index (PI).
b. Which project or projects should be accepted if they are independent?
c. Which project should be accepted if they are mutually exclusive?
d. How might a change in the cost of capital produce a conflict between the NPV and IRR rankings of these two projects? Would this conflict exist if r were 5%? (*Hint:* Plot the NPV profiles.)
e. Why does the conflict exist?

Problems

Answers Appear in Appendix B

EASY PROBLEMS 1–7

(10–1) NPV
A project has an initial cost of $52,125, expected net cash inflows of $12,000 per year for 8 years, and a cost of capital of 12%. What is the project's NPV? (*Hint:* Begin by constructing a time line.)

(10–2) IRR
Refer to Problem 10-1. What is the project's IRR?

(10–3) MIRR
Refer to Problem 10-1. What is the project's MIRR?

(10–4) Profitability Index
Refer to Problem 10-1. What is the project's PI?

(10–5) Payback
Refer to Problem 10-1. What is the project's payback period?

(10–6) Discounted Payback
Refer to Problem 10-1. What is the project's discounted payback period?

(10–7) NPV
Your division is considering two investment projects, each of which requires an up-front expenditure of $15 million. You estimate that the investments will produce the following net cash flows:

Year	Project A	Project B
1	$ 5,000,000	$20,000,000
2	10,000,000	10,000,000
3	20,000,000	6,000,000

a. What are the two projects' net present values, assuming the cost of capital is 5%? 10%? 15%?

b. What are the two projects' IRRs at these same costs of capital?

INTERMEDIATE PROBLEMS 8–18

(10–8) NPVs, IRRs, and MIRRs for Independent Projects
Edelman Engineering is considering including two pieces of equipment, a truck and an overhead pulley system, in this year's capital budget. The projects are independent. The cash outlay for the truck is $17,100 and that for the pulley system is $22,430. The firm's cost of capital is 14%. After-tax cash flows, including depreciation, are as follows:

Year	Truck	Pulley
1	$5,100	$7,500
2	5,100	7,500
3	5,100	7,500
4	5,100	7,500
5	5,100	7,500

Calculate the IRR, the NPV, and the MIRR for each project, and indicate the correct accept–reject decision for each.

(10–9) NPVs and IRRs for Mutually Exclusive Projects

Davis Industries must choose between a gas-powered and an electric-powered forklift truck for moving materials in its factory. Since both forklifts perform the same function, the firm will choose only one. (They are mutually exclusive investments.) The electric-powered truck will cost more, but it will be less expensive to operate; it will cost $22,000, whereas the gas-powered truck will cost $17,500. The cost of capital that applies to both investments is 12%. The life for both types of truck is estimated to be 6 years, during which time the net cash flows for the electric-powered truck will be $6,290 per year and those for the gas-powered truck will be $5,000 per year. Annual net cash flows include depreciation expenses. Calculate the NPV and IRR for each type of truck, and decide which to recommend.

(10–10) Capital Budgeting Methods

Project S has a cost of $10,000 and is expected to produce benefits (cash flows) of $3,000 per year for 5 years. Project L costs $25,000 and is expected to produce cash flows of $7,400 per year for 5 years. Calculate the two projects' NPVs, IRRs, MIRRs, and PIs, assuming a cost of capital of 12%. Which project would be selected, assuming they are mutually exclusive, using each ranking method? Which should actually be selected?

(10–11) MIRR and NPV

Your company is considering two mutually exclusive projects, X and Y, whose costs and cash flows are shown below:

Year	X	Y
0	–$1,000	–$1,000
1	100	1,000
2	300	100
3	400	50
4	700	50

The projects are equally risky, and their cost of capital is 12%. You must make a recommendation, and you must base it on the modified IRR (MIRR). Which project has the higher MIRR?

(10–12) NPV and IRR Analysis

After discovering a new gold vein in the Colorado mountains, CTC Mining Corporation must decide whether to go ahead and develop the deposit. The most cost-effective method of mining gold is sulfuric acid extraction, a process that could result in environmental damage. Before proceeding with the extraction, CTC must spend $900,000 for new mining equipment and pay $165,000 for its installation. The gold mined will net the firm an estimated $350,000 each year for the 5-year life of the vein. CTC's cost of capital is 14%. For the purposes of this problem, assume that the cash inflows occur at the end of the year.

a. What are the project's NPV and IRR?
b. Should this project be undertaken if environmental impacts were not a consideration?
c. How should environmental effects be considered when evaluating this, or any other, project? How might these concepts affect the decision in part b?

(10–13) NPV and IRR Analysis

Cummings Products is considering two mutually exclusive investments whose expected net cash flows are as follows:

	EXPECTED NET CASH FLOWS	
Year	**Project A**	**Project B**
0	–$300	–$405
1	–387	134
2	–193	134
3	–100	134
4	600	134
5	600	134
6	850	134
7	–180	0

a. Construct NPV profiles for Projects A and B.
b. What is each project's IRR?
c. If you were told that each project's cost of capital was 10%, which project, if either, should be selected? If the cost of capital were 17%, what would be the proper choice?
d. What is each project's MIRR at the cost of capital of 10%? At 17%? (*Hint:* Consider Period 7 as the end of Project B's life.)
e. What is the crossover rate, and what is its significance?

(10–14)
Timing Differences

The Ewert Exploration Company is considering two mutually exclusive plans for extracting oil on property for which it has mineral rights. Both plans call for the expenditure of $10 million to drill development wells. Under Plan A, all the oil will be extracted in 1 year, producing a cash flow at t = 1 of $12 million; under Plan B, cash flows will be $1.75 million per year for 20 years.

a. What are the annual incremental cash flows that will be available to Ewert Exploration if it undertakes Plan B rather than Plan A? (*Hint:* Subtract Plan A's flows from B's.)
b. If the company accepts Plan A and then invests the extra cash generated at the end of Year 1, what rate of return (reinvestment rate) would cause the cash flows from reinvestment to equal the cash flows from Plan B?
c. Suppose a firm's cost of capital is 10%. Is it logical to assume that the firm would take on all available independent projects (of average risk) with returns greater than 10%? Further, if all available projects with returns greater than 10% have been taken, would this mean that cash flows from past investments would have an opportunity cost of only 10%, because all the firm could do with these cash flows would be to replace money that has a cost of 10%? Finally, does this imply that the cost of capital is the correct rate to assume for the reinvestment of a project's cash flows?
d. Construct NPV profiles for Plans A and B, identify each project's IRR, and indicate the crossover rate.

(10–15)
Scale Differences

The Pinkerton Publishing Company is considering two mutually exclusive expansion plans. Plan A calls for the expenditure of $50 million on a large-scale, integrated plant that will provide an expected cash flow stream of $8 million per year for 20 years. Plan B calls for the expenditure of $15 million to build a somewhat less efficient, more labor-intensive plant that has an expected cash flow stream of $3.4 million per year for 20 years. The firm's cost of capital is 10%.

a. Calculate each project's NPV and IRR.
b. Set up a Project Δ by showing the cash flows that will exist if the firm goes with the large plant rather than the smaller plant. What are the NPV and the IRR for this Project Δ?
c. Graph the NPV profiles for Plan A, Plan B, and Project Δ.
d. Give a logical explanation, based on reinvestment rates and opportunity costs, as to why the NPV method is better than the IRR method when the firm's cost of capital is constant at some value such as 10%.

(10–16) Unequal Lives

Shao Airlines is considering two alternative planes. Plane A has an expected life of 5 years, will cost $100 million, and will produce net cash flows of $30 million per year. Plane B has a life of 10 years, will cost $132 million, and will produce net cash flows of $25 million per year. Shao plans to serve the route for only 10 years. Inflation in operating costs, airplane costs, and fares is expected to be zero, and the company's cost of capital is 12%. By how much would the value of the company increase if it accepted the better project (plane)? What is the equivalent annual annuity for each plane?

(10–17) Unequal Lives

The Perez Company has the opportunity to invest in one of two mutually exclusive machines that will produce a product it will need for the foreseeable future. Machine A costs $10 million but realizes after-tax inflows of $4 million per year for 4 years. After 4 years, the machine must be replaced. Machine B costs $15 million and realizes after-tax inflows of $3.5 million per year for 8 years, after which it must be replaced. Assume that machine prices are not expected to rise because inflation will be offset by cheaper components used in the machines. The cost of capital is 10%. By how much would the value of the company increase if it accepted the better machine? What is the equivalent annual annuity for each machine?

(10–18) Unequal Lives

Filkins Fabric Company is considering the replacement of its old, fully depreciated knitting machine. Two new models are available: Machine 190-3, which has a cost of $190,000, a 3-year expected life, and after-tax cash flows (labor savings and depreciation) of $87,000 per year; and Machine 360-6, which has a cost of $360,000, a 6-year life, and after-tax cash flows of $98,300 per year. Knitting machine prices are not expected to rise, because inflation will be offset by cheaper components (microprocessors) used in the machines. Assume that Filkins's cost of capital is 14%. Should the firm replace its old knitting machine? If so, which new machine should it use? By how much would the value of the company increase if it accepted the better machine? What is the equivalent annual annuity for each machine?

Challenging Problems 19–22

(10–19) Multiple Rates of Return

The Ulmer Uranium Company is deciding whether or not it should open a strip mine whose net cost is $4.4 million. Net cash inflows are expected to be $27.7 million, all coming at the end of Year 1. The land must be returned to its natural state at a cost of $25 million, payable at the end of Year 2.

a. Plot the project's NPV profile.
b. Should the project be accepted if r = 8%? If r = 14%? Explain your reasoning.
c. Can you think of some other capital budgeting situations in which negative cash flows during or at the end of the project's life might lead to multiple IRRs?
d. What is the project's MIRR at r = 8%? At r = 14%? Does the MIRR method lead to the same accept–reject decision as the NPV method?

(10–20)
Present Value of Costs

The Aubey Coffee Company is evaluating the within-plant distribution system for its new roasting, grinding, and packing plant. The two alternatives are (1) a conveyor system with a high initial cost but low annual operating costs, and (2) several forklift trucks, which cost less but have considerably higher operating costs. The decision to construct the plant has already been made, and the choice here will have no effect on the overall revenues of the project. The cost of capital for the plant is 8%, and the projects' expected net costs are listed in the following table:

	Expected Net Cost	
Year	Conveyor	Forklift
0	−$500,000	−$200,000
1	−120,000	−160,000
2	−120,000	−160,000
3	−120,000	−160,000
4	−120,000	−160,000
5	−20,000	−160,000

a. What is the IRR of each alternative?
b. What is the present value of the costs of each alternative? Which method should be chosen?

(10–21)
Payback, NPV, and MIRR

Your division is considering two investment projects, each of which requires an up-front expenditure of $25 million. You estimate that the cost of capital is 10% and that the investments will produce the following after-tax cash flows (in millions of dollars):

Year	Project A	Project B
1	5	20
2	10	10
3	15	8
4	20	6

a. What is the regular payback period for each of the projects?
b. What is the discounted payback period for each of the projects?
c. If the two projects are independent and the cost of capital is 10%, which project or projects should the firm undertake?
d. If the two projects are mutually exclusive and the cost of capital is 5%, which project should the firm undertake?
e. If the two projects are mutually exclusive and the cost of capital is 15%, which project should the firm undertake?
f. What is the crossover rate?
g. If the cost of capital is 10%, what is the modified IRR (MIRR) of each project?

(10–22)
Economic Life

The Scampini Supplies Company recently purchased a new delivery truck. The new truck cost $22,500, and it is expected to generate net after-tax operating cash flows, including depreciation, of $6,250 per year. The truck has a 5-year expected life. The expected salvage values after tax adjustments for the truck are given below. The company's cost of capital is 10%.

Year	Annual Operating Cash Flow	Salvage Value
0	–$22,500	$22,500
1	6,250	17,500
2	6,250	14,000
3	6,250	11,000
4	6,250	5,000
5	6,250	0

a. Should the firm operate the truck until the end of its 5-year physical life? If not, then what is its optimal economic life?
b. Would the introduction of salvage values, in addition to operating cash flows, ever *reduce* the expected NPV and/or IRR of a project?

Spreadsheet Problem

(10-23) Build a Model: Capital Budgeting Tools

Start with the partial model in the file ***Ch10 P23 Build a Model.xls*** on the textbook's Web site. Gardial Fisheries is considering two mutually exclusive investments. The projects' expected net cash flows are as follows:

	Expected Net Cash Flows	
Year	Project A	Project B
0	–$375	–$575
1	–300	190
2	–200	190
3	–100	190
4	600	190
5	600	190
6	926	190
7	–200	0

a. If each project's cost of capital is 12%, which project should be selected? If the cost of capital is 18%, what project is the proper choice?
b. Construct NPV profiles for Projects A and B.
c. What is each project's IRR?
d. What is the crossover rate, and what is its significance?
e. What is each project's MIRR at a cost of capital of 12%? At r = 18%? (*Hint:* Consider Period 7 as the end of Project B's life.)
f. What is the regular payback period for these two projects?
g. At a cost of capital of 12%, what is the discounted payback period for these two projects?
h. What is the profitability index for each project if the cost of capital is 12%?

Mini Case

You have just graduated from the MBA program of a large university, and one of your favorite courses was "Today's Entrepreneurs." In fact, you enjoyed it so much you have decided you want to "be your own boss." While you were in the master's program, your grandfather died and left you $1 million to do with as you please. You are not an inventor, and you do not have a trade skill that you can market; however, you have decided that you would like to purchase at least one established franchise in the fast-foods area, maybe two (if profitable). The problem is that you have never been one to stay with any project for too long, so you figure that your time frame is 3 years. After 3 years you will go on to something else.

You have narrowed your selection down to two choices: (1) Franchise L, Lisa's Soups, Salads, & Stuff, and (2) Franchise S, Sam's Fabulous Fried Chicken. The net cash flows shown below include the price you would receive for selling the franchise in Year 3 and the forecast of how each franchise will do over the 3-year period. Franchise L's cash flows will start off slowly but will increase rather quickly as people become more health-conscious, while Franchise S's cash flows will start off high but will trail off as other chicken competitors enter the marketplace and as people become more health-conscious and avoid fried foods. Franchise L serves breakfast and lunch whereas Franchise S serves only dinner, so it is possible for you to invest in both franchises. You see these franchises as perfect complements to one another: You could attract both the lunch and dinner crowds and the health-conscious and not-so-health-conscious crowds without the franchises directly competing against one another.

Here are the net cash flows (in thousands of dollars):

	Expected Net Cash Flows	
Year	**Franchise L**	**Franchise S**
0	–$100	–$100
1	10	70
2	60	50
3	80	20

Depreciation, salvage values, net working capital requirements, and tax effects are all included in these cash flows.

You also have made subjective risk assessments of each franchise and concluded that both franchises have risk characteristics that require a return of 10%. You must now determine whether one or both of the franchises should be accepted.

a. What is capital budgeting?

b. What is the difference between independent and mutually exclusive projects?

c. (1) Define the term *net present value (NPV)*. What is each franchise's NPV?
   (2) What is the rationale behind the NPV method? According to NPV, which franchise or franchises should be accepted if they are independent? Mutually exclusive?
   (3) Would the NPVs change if the cost of capital changed?

d. (1) Define the term *internal rate of return (IRR)*. What is each franchise's IRR?
   (2) How is the IRR on a project related to the YTM on a bond?
   (3) What is the logic behind the IRR method? According to IRR, which franchises should be accepted if they are independent? Mutually exclusive?
   (4) Would the franchises' IRRs change if the cost of capital changed?

e. (1) Draw NPV profiles for Franchises L and S. At what discount rate do the profiles cross?
   (2) Look at your NPV profile graph without referring to the actual NPVs and IRRs. Which franchise or franchises should be accepted if they are independent? Mutually exclusive? Explain. Are your answers correct at any cost of capital less than 23.6%?

f. (1) What is the underlying cause of ranking conflicts between NPV and IRR?
(2) What is the *reinvestment rate assumption*, and how does it affect the NPV-versus-IRR conflict?
(3) Which method is the best? Why?

g. (1) Define the term *modified IRR (MIRR)*. Find the MIRRs for Franchises L and S.
(2) What are the MIRR's advantages and disadvantages vis-à-vis the regular IRR? What are the MIRR's advantages and disadvantages vis-à-vis the NPV?

h. What does the profitability index (PI) measure? What are the PIs of Franchises S and L?

i. (1) What is the payback period? Find the paybacks for Franchises L and S.
(2) What is the rationale for the payback method? According to the payback criterion, which franchise or franchises should be accepted if the firm's maximum acceptable payback is 2 years and if Franchises L and S are independent? If they are mutually exclusive?
(3) What is the difference between the regular and discounted payback periods?
(4) What is the main disadvantage of discounted payback? Is the payback method of any real usefulness in capital budgeting decisions?

j. As a separate project (Project P), you are considering sponsorship of a pavilion at the upcoming World's Fair. The pavilion would cost $800,000, and it is expected to result in $5 million of incremental cash inflows during its single year of operation. However, it would then take another year, and $5 million of costs, to demolish the site and return it to its original condition. Thus, Project P's expected net cash flows look like this (in millions of dollars):

Year	Net Cash Flows
0	–$0.8
1	5.0
2	–5.0

The project is estimated to be of average risk, so its cost of capital is 10%.
(1) What are normal and nonnormal cash flows?
(2) What is Project P's NPV? What is its IRR? Its MIRR?
(3) Draw Project P's NPV profile. Does Project P have normal or nonnormal cash flows? Should this project be accepted?

k. In an unrelated analysis, you have the opportunity to choose between the following two mutually exclusive projects:

	Expected Net Cash Flows	
Year	**Project S**	**Project L**
0	–$100,000	–$100,000
1	60,000	33,500
2	60,000	33,500
3	—	33,500
4	—	33,500

The projects provide a necessary service, so whichever one is selected is expected to be repeated into the foreseeable future. Both projects have a 10% cost of capital.

(1) What is each project's initial NPV without replication?
(2) What is each project's equivalent annual annuity?
(3) Now apply the replacement chain approach to determine the projects' extended NPVs. Which project should be chosen?
(4) Now assume that the cost to replicate Project S in 2 years will increase to $105,000 because of inflationary pressures. How should the analysis be handled now, and which project should be chosen?

l. You are also considering another project that has a physical life of 3 years; that is, the machinery will be totally worn out after 3 years. However, if the project were terminated prior to the end of 3 years, the machinery would have a positive salvage value. Here are the project's estimated cash flows:

Year	Initial Investment and Operating Cash Flows	End-of-Year Net Salvage Value
0	–$5,000	$5,000
1	2,100	3,100
2	2,000	2,000
3	1,750	0

Using the 10% cost of capital, what is the project's NPV if it is operated for the full 3 years? Would the NPV change if the company planned to terminate the project at the end of Year 2? At the end of Year 1? What is the project's optimal (economic) life?

m. After examining all the potential projects, you discover that there are many more projects this year with positive NPVs than in a normal year. What two problems might this extra-large capital budget cause?

Selected Additional Cases

The following cases from Textchoice, *Cengage Learning's online library, cover many of the concepts discussed in this chapter and are available at* ***http://www.textchoice2.com***.

Klein-Brigham Series:
Case 11, "Chicago Valve Company."

Brigham-Buzzard Series:
Case 6, "Powerline Network Corporation (Basics of Capital Budgeting)."

CHAPTER 11

Cash Flow Estimation and Risk Analysis

In the last chapter we discussed how the recession caused FPL Group to reduce its planned capital expenditures from $7 billion to $5.3 billion. That change rippled through the economy. It reduced FPL's job count, which had a negative effect on housing and retail sales in Florida, where most of its operations are based. It also led to job losses in supplier firms like GE that would have supplied FPL with wind turbines and other materials needed for the canceled projects. It reduced our "green" power and thus increased our reliance on coal and foreign oil. Sales taxes, property taxes, and income taxes also fell, negatively affecting cities and states as well as the federal government.

FPL's experience was matched by thousands of other businesses all over the world; in this way, it exacerbated the global recession and increased the possibilities of a 1930's type depression. Government leaders, from President Obama on down, recognized this, and they authorized spending trillions of dollars on programs designed to push back the tide and get the ship righted and back on course. No one knows either how well the stimulus program will work or how long it will take to get things back on track. Still, companies like FPL, its suppliers, retailers who depend on workers for sales, and governments who depend on all of the above for tax revenues must make decisions based on predictions about the future. This chapter obviously can't teach you how to solve the problems of the world, but it does set forth a framework for making capital expenditure decisions in a world of uncertainty. If companies use the procedures we recommend, this will help avoid serious recessions in the future.

Corporate Valuation, Cash Flows, and Risk Analysis

When we estimate a project's cash flows (CF) and then discount them at the project's risk-adjusted cost of capital, r, the result is the project's NPV, which tells us how much the project increases the firm's value. This chapter focuses on how to estimate the size and risk of a project's cash flows.

Note too that project cash flows, once a project has been accepted and placed in operation, are added to the firm's free cash flows from other sources. Therefore, projects' cash flows essentially determine the firm's free cash flows as discussed in Chapter 2 and thus form the basis for the firm's market value and stock price.

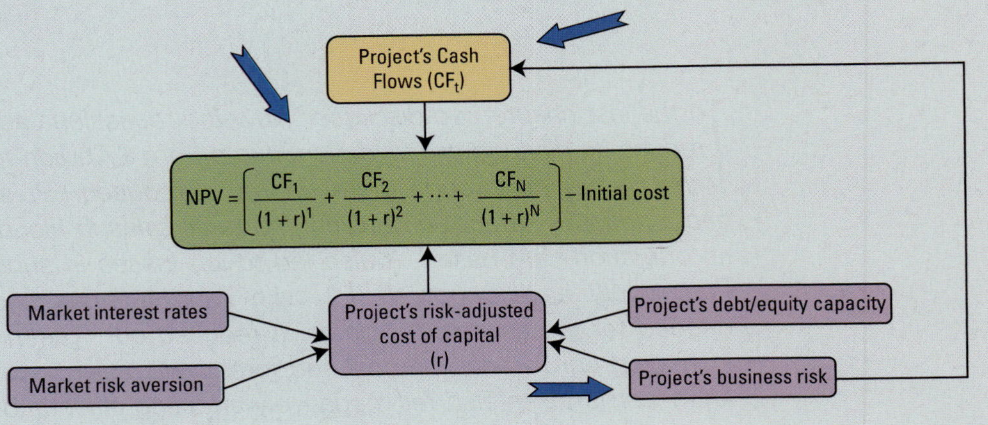

The textbook's Web site contains an Excel *file that will guide you through the chapter's calculations. The file for this chapter is* **Ch11 Tool Kit.xls**, *and we encourage you to open the file and follow along as you read the chapter.*

The basic principles of capital budgeting were covered in Chapter 10. Given a project's expected cash flows, it is easy to calculate its NPV, IRR, MIRR, PI, payback, and discounted payback. Unfortunately, cash flows are rarely just given—rather, managers must estimate them based on information collected from sources both inside and outside the company. Moreover, uncertainty surrounds the cash flow estimates, and some projects are riskier than others. In the first part of this chapter, we develop procedures for estimating the cash flows associated with capital budgeting projects. Then, in the second part, we discuss techniques used to measure and take account of project risk.

11.1 Conceptual Issues

The most important but also the most difficult step in capital budgeting is estimating **project cash flows**. Many variables are involved, and many individuals and departments participate in the process. For example, the forecasts of unit sales and sales prices are normally made by the marketing group based on their knowledge of price elasticity, advertising effects, the state of the economy, competitors' reactions, and trends in consumers' tastes. Similarly, the capital outlays associated with a new product are generally obtained from the engineering and product development staffs, while operating costs are estimated by cost accountants, production experts, personnel specialists, purchasing agents, and so forth.

A proper analysis includes (1) obtaining information from various departments such as engineering and marketing, (2) ensuring that everyone involved with the forecast uses a consistent set of realistic economic assumptions, and (3) making sure that no biases are inherent in the forecasts. This last point is extremely important, because some managers become emotionally involved with pet projects and others push projects in order to build empires. Both problems cause cash flow forecast biases that make bad projects look good—on paper!

A number of conceptual issues arise in the cash flow estimation process. Some of these are covered in the balance of this section. Some of them are illustrated in the examples we explore in the subsequent sections.

Cash Flow versus Accounting Income

We saw in Chapter 2 that free cash flow differs from accounting income: Free cash flow is cash flow that is available for distribution to investors; hence free cash flow is the basis of a firm's value. It is common in the practice of finance to speak of a firm's free cash flow and a project's cash flow (or net cash flow), but these are based on the same concepts. In fact, a project's cash flow is identical to the project's free cash flow, and a firm's total net cash flow from all projects is equal to the firm's free cash flow. We will follow the typical convention and refer to a project's free cash flow simply as project cash flow, but keep in mind that the two concepts are identical.[1]

Because net income is not equal to the cash flow available for distribution to investors, in the last chapter we discounted *net cash flows*, not accounting income, to find projects' NPVs. *For capital budgeting purposes it is the project's net cash flow, not its accounting income, that is relevant.* Therefore, when analyzing a proposed capital budgeting project, disregard the project's net income and focus exclusively on its net cash flow.[2] Be especially alert to the following differences between cash flow and accounting income.

The Cash Flow Effect of Asset Purchases and Depreciation. Most projects require assets, and asset purchases represent *negative* cash flows. Even though the acquisition of assets results in a cash outflow, accountants do not show the purchase of fixed assets as a deduction from accounting income. Instead, they deduct a depreciation expense each year throughout the life of the asset. Depreciation shelters income from taxation, and this has an impact on cash flow, but depreciation itself is not a cash flow. Therefore, depreciation must be added back when estimating a project's operating cash flow.

Depreciation is the most common noncash charge, but there are many other noncash charges that might appear on a company's financial statements. Just as with depreciation, all other noncash charges should be added back when calculating a project's net cash flow.

---

[1]When the financial press refers to a firm's "net cash flow," it is almost always equal to the definition we provide in Chapter 2 (which simply adds back depreciation and any other noncash charges to net income). However, as we explained in Chapter 2, the net cash flow from operations (from the statement of cash flows) and the firm's free cash flow are much more useful measures of cash flow. When financial analysts within a company use the term "a project's net cash flow," they almost always calculate it as we do in this chapter, which is in essence the project's free cash flow. Thus, free cash flow means the same thing whether you calculate it for a firm or for a project. On the other hand, when the financial press talks about a firm's net cash flow or when an internal analysts talks about a project's net cash flow, those "net cash flows" are not the same.

[2]This statement is theoretically correct but sometimes an overstatement in the real world. Stockholders in publicly owned companies do look at accounting income, it affects stock prices, and those prices affect the cost of capital. Therefore, if a project would have a negative effect on net income but a positive effect on cash flows, management should focus primarily on cash flows but try to communicate to investors that (1) the adverse effect on net income is temporary and (2) in the long run, the positive effect on cash flows will show up in future net income. Privately owned companies don't have this problem—they can and do focus almost exclusively on cash flows, and that's a significant advantage of private ownership.

Changes in Net Operating Working Capital. Normally, additional inventories are required to support a new operation, and expanded sales tie up additional funds in accounts receivable. However, payables and accruals increase as a result of the expansion, and this reduces the cash needed to finance inventories and receivables. The difference between the required increase in operating current assets and the increase in operating current liabilities is the change in net operating working capital. If this change is positive, as it generally is for expansion projects, then additional financing—beyond the cost of the fixed assets—will be needed.

Toward the end of a project's life, inventories will be used but not replaced, and receivables will be collected without corresponding replacements. As these changes occur the firm will receive cash inflows; as a result, the investment in net operating working capital will be returned by the end of the project's life.

Interest Charges Are Not Included in Project Cash Flows. Interest is a cash expense, so at first blush it would seem that interest on any debt used to finance a project should be deducted when we estimate the project's net cash flows. However, this is not correct. Recall from Chapter 10 that we discount a project's cash flows by its risk-adjusted cost of capital, which is a weighted average (WACC) of the costs of debt, preferred stock, and common equity, adjusted for the project's risk and debt capacity. This project cost of capital is the rate of return necessary to satisfy *all* of the firm's investors, including stockholders and debtholders. A common mistake made by many students and financial managers is to subtract interest payments when estimating a project's cash flows. This is a mistake because the cost of debt is already embedded in the cost of capital, so subtracting interest payments from the project's cash flows would amount to double-counting interest costs. Therefore, *you should not subtract interest expenses when finding a project's cash flows.*[3]

Timing of Cash Flows: Yearly versus Other Periods

In theory, in capital budgeting analyses we should discount cash flows based on the exact moment when they occur. Therefore, one could argue that daily cash flows would be better than annual flows. However, it would be costly to estimate daily cash flows and laborious to analyze them, and in general the analysis would be no better than one using annual flows because we simply can't make accurate forecasts of daily cash flows more than a couple of months into the future. Therefore, it is generally appropriate to assume that all cash flows occur at the end of the various years. But for projects with highly predictable cash flows, such as constructing a building and then leasing it on a long-term basis (with monthly payments) to a financially sound tenant, we would analyze the project using monthly periods.

Incremental Cash Flows

The relevant cash flows to be used in project analysis are the difference between the cash flows the firm will have if it implements the project versus the cash flows it will have if it rejects the project. These are called **incremental cash flows**:

[3]Some years ago the interest situation was debated in the academic literature. One position was that interest should be deducted, resulting in the net cash flow to stockholders, and then that cash flow should be discounted at the cost of common equity. It was demonstrated that equity flows discounted at the equity cost and operating flows discounted at the WACC led to the same conclusions. Now most academics recommend the operating cash flow approach, and it is practiced by most companies.

$$\text{Incremental cash flows} = \begin{matrix}\text{Company's cash flows} \\ \textit{with} \text{ the project}\end{matrix} - \begin{matrix}\text{Company's cash flows} \\ \textit{without} \text{ the project}\end{matrix}$$

We discuss several types of incremental cash flows in the following sections.

Expansion Projects and Replacement Projects

Two types of projects can be distinguished: (1) *expansion projects*, in which the firm makes an investment in, for example, a new Home Depot store in Seattle; and (2) *replacement projects*, in which the firm replaces existing assets, generally to reduce costs. In expansion projects, the cash expenditures on buildings, equipment, and required working capital are obviously incremental, as are the sales revenues and operating costs associated with the project. The incremental costs associated with replacement projects are not so obvious. For example, Home Depot might replace some of its delivery trucks to reduce fuel and maintenance expenses. Replacement analysis is complicated by the fact that most of the relevant cash flows are the cash flow differences between the existing project and the replacement project. For example, the fuel bill for a more efficient new truck might be \$10,000 per year versus \$15,000 for the old truck, and the \$5,000 fuel savings would be an incremental cash flow associated with the replacement decision. We analyze an expansion and replacement decision later in the chapter.

Sunk Costs

A **sunk cost** is an outlay related to the project that was incurred in the past and cannot be recovered in the future regardless of whether or not the project is accepted. Therefore, sunk costs are *not incremental costs* and thus are not relevant in a capital budgeting analysis.

To illustrate, suppose Home Depot spent \$2 million to investigate sites for a potential new store in a given area. That \$2 million is a sunk cost—the money is gone, and it won't come back regardless of whether or not a new store is built. Therefore, the \$2 million should not be included in a capital budgeting decision.

Improper treatment of sunk costs can lead to bad decisions. For example, suppose Home Depot completed the analysis for a new store and found that it must spend an additional (or incremental) \$17 million to build and supply the store, on top of the \$2 million already spent on the site study. Suppose the present value of future cash flows is \$18 million. Should the project be accepted? If the sunk costs are mistakenly included, the NPV is –\$2 million + (–\$17 million) + \$18 million = –\$1 million and the project would be rejected. However, *that would be a bad decision*. The real issue is whether the *incremental* \$17 million would result in enough *incremental* cash flow to produce a positive NPV. If the \$2 million sunk cost were disregarded, as it should be, then the NPV on an incremental basis would be a *positive* \$1 million.

Opportunity Costs Associated with Assets the Firm Already Owns

Another conceptual issue relates to **opportunity costs** related to assets the firm already owns. Continuing our example, suppose Home Depot (HD) owns land with a current market value of \$2 million that can be used for the new store if it decides to build the store. If HD goes forward with the project, only another \$15 million will be required, not the full \$17 million, because it will not need to buy the required land. Does this mean that HD should use the \$15 million incremental cost as the cost of the new store? The answer is definitely "no." If the new store is *not* built, then HD could sell the land and receive a cash flow of $2 million. This $2 million is an *opportunity cost*—it is cash that HD would not receive if the land is used for the new store. Therefore, the $2 million must be charged to the new project, and failing to do so would cause the new project's calculated NPV to be too high.

Externalities

Another conceptual issue relates to **externalities**, which are the effects of a project on other parts of the firm or on the environment. As explained in what follows, there are three types of externalities: negative within-firm externalities, positive within-firm externalities, and environmental externalities.

Negative *Within-Firm Externalities.* If a retailer like Home Depot opens a new store that is close to its existing stores, then the new store might attract customers who would otherwise buy from the existing stores, reducing the old stores' cash flows. Therefore, the new store's incremental cash flow must be reduced by the amount of the cash flow lost by its other units. This type of externality is called **cannibalization**, because the new business eats into the company's existing business. Many businesses are subject to cannibalization. For example, each new iPod model cannibalizes existing models. Those lost cash flows should be considered, and that means charging them as a cost when analyzing new products.

Dealing properly with negative externalities requires careful thinking. If Apple decided not to come out with a new model of iPod because of cannibalization, another company might come out with a similar new model, causing Apple to lose sales on existing models. Apple must examine the total situation, and this is definitely more than a simple, mechanical analysis. Experience and knowledge of the industry is required to make good decisions in most cases.

One of the best examples of a company getting into trouble as a result of not dealing correctly with cannibalization was IBM's response when personal computers were first developed in the 1970s. IBM's mainframes dominated the computer industry, and they generated huge profits. IBM used its technology to enter the PC market, and initially it was the leading PC company. However, its top managers decided to deemphasize the PC division because they were afraid it would hurt the more profitable mainframe business. That decision opened the door for Apple, Dell, Hewlett Packard, Sony, and Chinese competitors to take PC business away from IBM. As a result, IBM went from being the most profitable firm in the world to one whose very survival was threatened. IBM's experience highlights that, even as it's essential to understand the theory of finance, it is equally important to understand the industry and the long-run consequences of a given decision. Good judgment is an essential element for good financial decisions.

Positive *Within-Firm Externalities.* As we noted earlier, cannibalization occurs when a new product competes with an old one. However, a new project can also be *complementary* to an old one, in which case cash flows in the old operation will be *increased* when the new one is introduced. For example, Apple's iPod was a profitable product, but when Apple considered an investment in its music store it realized that the store would boost sales of iPods. So, even if an analysis of the proposed music store indicated a negative NPV, the analysis would not be complete unless the incremental cash flows that would occur in the iPod division were credited to the music store. Consideration of positive externalities often changes a project's NPV from negative to positive.

Environmental Externalities. The most common type of negative externality is a project's impact on the environment. Government rules and regulations constrain what companies can do, but firms have some flexibility in dealing with the environment. For example, suppose a manufacturer is studying a proposed new plant. The company could meet current environmental regulations at a cost of $1 million, but the plant would still emit fumes that would cause some bad will in its neighborhood. Those ill feelings would not show up in the cash flow analysis, but they should still be considered. Perhaps a relatively small additional expenditure would reduce the emissions substantially, make the plant look good relative to other plants in the area, and provide goodwill that in the future would help the firm's sales and its negotiations with governmental agencies.

Of course, all firms' profits depend on the Earth remaining healthy, so companies have an incentive to do things that protect the environment even though those actions are not currently required. However, if one firm decides to take actions that are good for the environment but quite costly, then either it must raise its prices or suffer a decline in earnings. If its competitors decide to get by with less costly but environmentally unfriendly processes, they can price their products lower and make more money. Of course, the more environmentally friendly companies can advertise their environmental efforts, and this might—or might not—offset their higher costs. All this illustrates why government regulations are often necessary. Finance, politics, and the environment are all interconnected.

Self-Test

Why should companies use a project's net cash flows rather than its accounting income when determining a project's NPV?

Explain the following terms: incremental cash flow, sunk cost, opportunity cost, externality, cannibalization, and complementary project.

Provide an example of a "good" externality—that is, one that increases a project's true NPV over what it would be if just its own cash flows were considered.

11.2 Analysis of an Expansion Project

Chapter 10 assumed that estimated cash flows were already available and then proceeded to illustrate how project cash flows are evaluated. In this chapter, we illustrate how cash flows are estimated by analyzing a project under consideration by Guyton Products Company (GPC). The project is the application of a radically new technology to a new type of solar water heater, which will be manufactured under a 4-year license from a university. It's not clear how well the water heater will work, how strong demand for it will be, how long it will be before the product becomes obsolete, or whether the license can be renewed after the initial 4 years. Still, the water heater has the potential for being quite profitable, though it could also fail miserably. GPC is a relatively large company and this is just one of its projects, so a failure would not bankrupt the firm but would hurt profits and the stock's price.

Cash Flow Projections: Base Case

See **Ch11 Tool Kit.xls** on the textbook's Web site.

We used *Excel* to do the analysis. We could have used a calculator and paper, but *Excel* is *much* easier when dealing with realistic capital budgeting problems. You don't need to know *Excel* to understand our discussion, but if you plan to work in finance—or, really, in any business field—you must know how to use *Excel*, so we recommend that you open the *Excel* ***Tool Kit*** for this chapter and scroll through it as the textbook explains the analysis.

Figure 11-1 shows the base-case inputs used in the analysis. For example, the cost of required equipment to manufacture the water heaters is $3,400 and is shown in

FIGURE 11-1 Analysis of an Expansion Project: Inputs and Key Results (Thousands of Dollars)

	A	B	C	D	E	F	G	H	I
44	Part 1. Inputs and Key Results								
45									
46	Inputs				Base-Case		Key Results		
47	Equipment cost				$3,400		NPV		$36
48	Salvage value, equipment, Year 4				$300		IRR		10.35%
49	Opportunity cost				$0		MIRR		10.23%
50	Externalities (cannibalization)				$0		PI		1.01
51	Units sold, Year 1				550		Payback		3.41
52	Annual change in units sold, after Year 1				4.00%		Discounted payback		3.98
53	Sales price per unit, Year 1				$11.60				
54	Annual change in sales price, after Year 1				2.00%				
55	Variable cost per unit (VC), Year 1				$6.00				
56	Annual change in VC, after Year 1				2.00%				
57	Nonvariable cost (Non-VC), Year 1				$2,000				
58	Annual change in Non-VC, after Year 1				2.00%				
59	Project WACC				10.00%				
60	Tax rate				40.00%				
61	Working capital as % of next year's sales				12.65%				

See **Ch11 Tool Kit.xls** *on the textbook's Web site.*

Cell E47 (all dollar values in Figure 11-1 and in our discussion here are reported in thousands, so the equipment actually costs $3,400,000). If you change the inputs in Cells E47:E61, *Excel* will instantly generate revised cash flows and performance measures (shown in Figure 11-2). We report key results next to the inputs so it is easy to see in real time the effects of changes in assumptions.

The input values from Figure 11-1 are used to calculate cash flows and performance measures, as reported in Figure 11-2. Some values change each year, and we report those in Rows 77 to 80. Annual unit sales are shown on Row 77, and they are projected to grow at 4% per year. The annual sales prices per unit are shown on Row 78, variable costs per unit on Row 79, and nonvariable costs on Row 80. These values are all projected to grow at the rates assumed in Part 1, and the annual values are used in the cash flow forecast.

The initial investments at t = 0 are shown in Cells E83:E85. The initial equipment cost of $3,400 is in Cell E83. Virtually all projects require working capital, and this one is no exception. For example, raw materials must be purchased and replenished each year as they are used. In Part 1 (Figure 11-1) we assume that GPC must have an amount of net operating working capital on hand that is equal to 12.65% of the upcoming year's sales. As we explain below, projected sales in Year 1 are $6,380, so there must be an initial investment in working capital of 12.65%($6,380) = $807; this is shown in Cell E84.[4] There are no opportunity costs in the base-case scenario, so the entry in Cell E85 is zero.

Unit sales and sales prices are multiplied to find the projected sales revenues shown on Row 87. Variable costs per unit multiplied by the number of units gives us total variable costs, as shown on Row 88. Nonvariable costs are shown on Row 89, and depreciation is on Row 90 (we explain the depreciation expense later in this section). Subtracting variable costs, nonvariable costs, and depreciation from sales

[4]Net operating working capital consists of inventories and accounts receivable *less* accounts payable and accruals.

FIGURE 11-2 Analysis of an Expansion Project: Cash Flows and Performance Measures (Thousands of Dollars)

	A–D	E	F	G	H	I
75	Part 2. Cash Flows and Performance Measures					
76	Variables Used in the Cash Flow Forecast	0	1	2	3	4
77	Unit sales		550	572	595	619
78	Sales price per unit		$11.60	$11.83	$12.07	$12.31
79	Variable cost per unit		$6.00	$6.12	$6.24	$6.37
80	Nonvariable costs (excluding depreciation)		$2,000	$2,040	$2,081	$2,122
81			Cash Flows At End of Year			
82	Investment Outlays at Time = 0	0	1	2	3	4
83	Equipment	–$3,400				
84	Initial investment in working capital	–807				
85	Opportunity cost, after taxes	0				
86	Net Cash Flows Over the Project's Life					
87	Sales revenues = Units × Price/unit		$6,380	$6,768	$7,179	$7,616
88	Variable costs = Units × Cost/unit		3,300	3,501	3,713	3,933
89	Nonvariable costs (excluding depreciation)		2,000	2,040	2,081	2,122
90	Depreciation: Accelerated, from table below		1,122	1,530	510	238
91	Operating profit (EBIT)		–$42	–$303	$875	$1,316
92	Taxes on operating profit		–17	–121	350	526
93	Net operating profit after taxes		–$25	–$182	$525	$790
94	Add back depreciation		1,122	1,530	510	238
95	Opportunity cost, after taxes		0	0	0	0
96	Cannibalization or complementary effects, after taxes		0	0	0	0
97	Salvage value (taxed as ordinary income)					300
98	Tax on salvage value (SV is taxed at 40%)					–120
99	Change in WC: Outflow (–) or recovery (+)		–49	–52	–55	963
100						
101	Project net cash flows: Time Line	–$4,207	–$1,048	–$1,296	$980	$2,171
102						

	Project Evaluation	Accelerated		Straight Line
104		Results	Formulas	Results
105	NPV	$36	= NPV(E59,F101:I101)+E101	–$18
106	IRR	10.35%	= IRR(E101:I101)	9.83%
107	MIRR	10.23%	=MIRR(E101:I101,E59,E59)	9.88%
108	Profitability index	1.01	=NPV(E59,F101:I101)/(–E101)	1.00
109	Payback	3.41	=PERCENTRANK(E112:I112,0,6)*I111	3.47
110	Discounted payback	3.98	=PERCENTRANK(E114:I114,0,6)*I111	#N/A

	A–D	E	F	G	H	I
111	Calculations for Payback — Year:	0	1	2	3	4
112	Cumulative cash flows for payback	–$4,207	–$3,159	–$1,863	–$883	–$1,288
113	Discounted cash flows for disc. payback	–$4,207	–$952	–$1,071	$736	–$1,483
114	Cumulative discounted cash flows	–$4,207	–$3,255	–$2,183	–$1,447	–$36
115	Accelerated Depreciation					
116	Depreciable basis: $3,400	Rate/year	33%	45%	15%	7%
117		Dollars/year	$1,122	$1,530	$510	$238

See **Ch11 Tool Kit.xls** on the textbook's Web site.

revenues results in operating profit (EBIT), as shown on Row 91. We calculate taxes on Row 92 and subtract them to get the project's net operating profit after taxes on Row 93. We add back depreciation on Row 94 because it is a noncash expense. There are no annual opportunity costs or cannibalization effects in the base-case scenario; if there were, we would include them on an after-tax basis on Rows 95 and 96.

Because of the license, the project has a 4-year life; at Year 4, the equipment is expected to have a salvage value of $300, which is shown in Cell I97. Because the assets will be fully depreciated by Year 4, the $300 is a gain that is taxed at the firm's ordinary income tax rate of 40%; this tax is shown in Cell I98.[5]

Row 99 shows the annual changes in working capital. GPC will operate the project with net working capital equal to 12.65% of the next year's sales, so as sales grow, the firm will have to increase its net working capital. These increases are shown as negative numbers (investments) on Row 99, Years 1 through 3. Then, at the end of Year 4, all of the investments in working capital will be recovered. Inventories will be sold and not replaced, and all receivables will be collected by the end of Year 4. Total net working capital recovered at t = 4 is the sum of the initial investment at t = 0, $807, plus the additional investments during Years 1 through 3; the total is $963.

We sum Cells E83:E85 to get the total initial investment, and we sum Rows 93 to 99 to get the project's annual net cash flows, set up as a time line on Row 101. These cash flows are then used to calculate NPV, IRR, MIRR, PI, payback, and discounted payback, performance measures that are shown in Cells C105 through C110. (The results Columns H and I are based on straight-line depreciation and are discussed later.) Based on this analysis, the project looks like it is barely breaking even, with an NPV of only $36 as compared with an initial investment of over $4,200. Its IRR and MIRR are both barely greater than the 10% WACC, the PI is barely greater than 1.0, and the payback and discounted payback are almost as long as the project's life. However, before the decision is finalized, we need to look at some additional factors. In particular, we must recognize that the actual outcome could be better or worse than the base-case level, that there might be responses management can make to changing conditions, and that there might be qualitative factors to consider. We examine these concerns later in the chapter, but first we address the following issues associated with the base-case analysis.

Depreciation

The depreciation expense is calculated as the annual rate allowed by the IRS multiplied by the project's depreciable cost basis, which in this case is $3,400.[6] Congress sets the depreciation rates used for tax purposes, which are then used in capital budgeting. The rates for this project are shown on Row 116, and more details are provided in Appendix 11A and in the chapter's ***Tool Kit.*** Congress permits firms to depreciate assets using either the straight-line method or an accelerated method. The results we have discussed thus far were based on accelerated depreciation. We also analyzed the project using straight-line depreciation with the results reported in Figure 11-2 in H105:H110; the full analysis is in the chapter's ***Tool Kit.*** The results indicate that the project is worth less when using straight-line depreciation than when using accelerated depreciation. In general, *profitable firms are better off using accelerated depreciation* because more depreciation is taken in the early years under the accelerated method, so taxes are lower in those years and higher in later years. Total depreciation, total cash flows, and total taxes are the same under both depreciation methods, but receiving the cash earlier under the accelerated method results in a higher NPV, IRR, and MIRR.

Suppose Congress wants to encourage companies to increase their capital expenditures and thereby boost economic growth and employment. What changes in de-

[5]If an asset is sold for less than its book value, the resulting "negative" tax is a credit and would increase the cash flow. If an asset is sold for exactly its book value, there will be no gain or loss and hence no tax liability or credit.

[6]Regardless of whether accelerated or straight-line depreciation is used, the basis is not adjusted by the salvage value when calculating the depreciation expense that is used to determine taxable income.

preciation regulations would have the desired effect? The answer is "Make accelerated depreciation even more accelerated." For example, if GPC could write off equipment at rates of 67%, 22%, 7%, and 4% rather than 33%, 45%, 15%, and 7%, then its early tax payments would be even lower, early cash flows would be even higher, and the project's NPV would exceed the value shown in Figure 11-2.[7]

Taxation of Salvage

In our example, GPC's project was fully depreciated by the end of the project. But suppose instead that GPC terminates operations before the equipment is fully depreciated. The after-tax salvage value depends on the price at which GPC can sell the equipment *and* on the book value of the equipment (i.e., the original basis less all previous depreciation charges). The following table shows the calculations of yearly book values.

	Year			
	1	2	3	4
Beginning book value	$3,400	$2,278	$748	$238
Annual depreciation	1,122	1,530	510	238
Ending book value	$2,278	$ 748	$238	$ 0

Suppose GPC terminates at Year 2, at which time the book value is $748. We consider two cases, gains and losses. In the first case, the salvage value is $898 and so there is a reported gain of $898 – $748 = $150. This gain is taxed as ordinary income, so the tax is 40%($150) = $60. The after-tax cash flow is equal to the sales price less the tax: $898 – $60 = $838.

Now suppose the salvage value at Year 2 is only $98. In this case, there is a reported loss: $98 – $748 = –$650. This is treated as an ordinary expense, so its tax is 40%(–$650) = –$260. This "negative" tax acts as a credit if GPC has other taxable income, so the net after-tax cash flow is $98 – (–$260) = $358.

Externalities: Cannibalization or Complementary Projects

As noted earlier, the solar water heater project does not lead to any cannibalization effects. Suppose, however, that it would reduce the net after-tax cash flows of another GPC division by $50 per year and that no other firm could take on this project if GPC turns it down. In this case, we would use the cannibalization line at Row 96, deducting $50 each year. As a result, the project would have a lower NPV. On the other hand, if the project would cause additional inflows to some other GPC division because it was complementary to that other division's products (i.e., if a positive externality exists), then those after-tax inflows should be attributed to the water heater project and thus shown as a positive inflow on Row 96.

Opportunity Costs

Now suppose the $3,400 initial cost were based on the assumption that the project would use space in a building that GPC now owns and that the space could be leased to another company for $200 per year, after taxes, if the project is rejected. The $200

[7]Indeed, this is exactly what Congress did in 2008 and 2009, in response to the global economic crisis, by establishing a temporary "bonus" depreciation to stimulate investment. The depreciation in the first year is the regular accelerated depreciation plus a bonus of 50% of the original basis. This feature of the tax code is set to expire before this book will be printed, but Congress has extended the bonus once and might extend it again.

would be an *opportunity cost*, and it should be reflected in our calculations. We would subtract the $200 per year on Row 95, causing a decrease in NPV.

Sunk Costs. Now consider a different example. Suppose GPC had spent $100,000 on a marketing study for an oil pump project, and the study was inconclusive. If it abandons the project without going forward, it would show a loss of $100,000. But suppose it could go forward with an additional investment of $500,000, and suppose the NPV on this incremental investment would be $50,000. In the final analysis, this project would be a loser regardless of whether GPC stops or goes forward. With hindsight we can see that the true "NPV" if we go forward would be the calculated NPV of $50,000 minus the $100,000 sunk cost, or $50,000 − $100,000 = −$50,000. A loss of $50,000 is bad, but not as bad as a loss of $100,000, so GPC should go ahead with the oil pump project.

Other Changes to the Inputs

All of the input variables could be changed, and these changes would alter the calculated project cash flows and thus the NPV and other capital budgeting decision criteria. We could increase or decrease the projected unit sales, the sales price, the variable and/or the fixed costs, the initial investment cost, the net working capital requirements, the salvage value, and even the tax rate if we thought Congress was likely to raise or lower taxes. Such changes can be made easily in an *Excel* model, making it possible to immediately see the resulting changes in the decision criteria. This is called *sensitivity analysis*, and we discuss it in Section 11.5.

The Importance of Incorporating Expected Inflation in Prices and Costs

Notice that the model has inputs for annual changes in prices and costs; in other words, it allows for inflation (or deflation) in prices and costs. In Figure 11-2, we let all prices and costs change by 2% annually to keep the example simple, but it is certainly possible that some items (such as energy costs) might experience higher inflation than others (such as CPU prices), so our models always include separate line items for the expected inflation in each price or cost. It is easy to overlook inflation, but it is important to include it. For example, had we forgotten to include inflation in the GPC example, then the estimated NPV would have dropped from +$36 to −$29. Forgetting to include inflation in a capital budgeting analysis typically causes the estimated NPV to be lower than the true NPV, which could cause a company to reject a project that it should have accepted.[8]

Self-Test

In what way is the setup for finding a project's cash flows similar to the projected income statements for a new, single-product firm? In what way would the two statements be different?

Would a project's NPV for a typical firm be higher or lower if the firm used accelerated rather than straight-line depreciation? Explain.

How could the analysis in Figure 11-2 be modified to consider cannibalization, opportunity costs, and sunk costs?

Why does net working capital appear with both negative and positive values in Figure 11-2?

---

[8]The market's estimate of expected inflation is already incorporated into the cost of debt (via the inflation premium) and the cost of equity (via the risk-free rate in the CAPM), so the project's cost of capital includes the effect of expected inflation. If you don't also include the effect of inflation in projected cash flows, then the cash flows will be too low relative to the cost of capital, leading to a downward-biased estimate of NPV.

11.3 Risk Analysis in Capital Budgeting[9]

Projects differ in risk, and risk should be reflected in capital budgeting decisions. There are three separate and distinct types of risk.

1. **Stand-alone risk** is a project's risk assuming (a) that it is the firm's only asset and (b) that each of the firm's stockholders holds only that one stock in his portfolio. Stand-alone risk is based on uncertainty about the project's expected cash flows. It is important to remember that *stand-alone risk ignores diversification by both the firm and its stockholders*.
2. **Within-firm risk** (also called **corporate risk**) is a project's risk to the corporation itself. Within-firm risk recognizes that the project is only one asset in the firm's portfolio of projects; hence some of its risk is eliminated by diversification within the firm. However, *within-firm risk ignores diversification by the firm's stockholders.* Within-firm risk is measured by the project's impact on uncertainty about the firm's future total cash flows.
3. **Market risk** (also called **beta risk**) is the risk of the project as seen by a well-diversified stockholder who recognizes (a) that the project is only one of the firm's projects and (b) that the firm's stock is but one of her stocks. The project's market risk is measured by its effect on the firm's beta coefficient.

Taking on a project with a lot of stand-alone and/or corporate risk will not necessarily affect the firm's beta. However, if the project has high stand-alone risk and if its cash flows are highly correlated with cash flows on the firm's other assets and with cash flows of most other firms in the economy, then the project will have a high degree of all three types of risk. Market risk is, *theoretically*, the most relevant because it is the one that, according to the CAPM, is reflected in stock prices. Unfortunately, market risk is also the most difficult to measure, primarily because new projects don't have "market prices" that can be related to stock market returns.

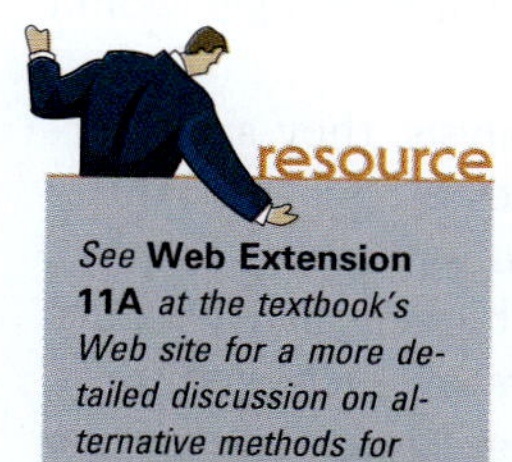

See **Web Extension 11A** *at the textbook's Web site for a more detailed discussion on alternative methods for incorporating project risk into the capital budgeting decision process.*

Most decision makers do a *quantitative* analysis of stand-alone risk and then consider the other two types of risk in a *qualitative* manner. Projects are classified into several categories; then, using the firm's overall WACC as a starting point, a **risk-adjusted cost of capital** is assigned to each category. For example, a firm might establish three risk classes and then assign the corporate WACC to average-risk projects, add a 5% risk premium for higher-risk projects, and subtract 2% for low-risk projects. Under this setup, if the company's overall WACC were 10%, then 10% would be used to evaluate average-risk projects, 15% for high-risk projects, and 8% for low-risk projects. Although this approach is probably better than not making any risk adjustments, these adjustments are highly subjective and difficult to justify. Unfortunately, there's no perfect way to specify how high or low the risk adjustments should be.[10]

---

[9]Some professors may choose to cover some of the risk sections and skip others. We offer a range of choices, and we tried to make the exposition clear enough that interested and self-motivated students can read these sections on their own if they are not assigned.

[10]We should note that the CAPM approach can be used for projects provided there are specialized publicly traded firms in the same business as that of the project under consideration. See the discussion in Chapter 9 regarding techniques for measuring divisional betas.

For more on risk adjustments, see Tarun K. Mukherjee, "Reducing the Uncertainty-Induced Bias in Capital Budgeting Decisions—A Hurdle Rate Approach," *Journal of Business Finance & Accounting*, September 1991, pp. 747–753.

Self-Test

What are the three types of project risk?
Which type is theoretically the most relevant? Why?
Describe a type of classification scheme that firms often use to obtain risk-adjusted costs of capital.

11.4 Measuring Stand-Alone Risk

A project's stand-alone risk reflects uncertainty about its cash flows. The required dollars of investment, unit sales, sales prices, and operating costs as shown in Figure 11-1 for GPC's project are all subject to uncertainty. First-year sales are projected at 550 units to be sold at a price of $11.60 per unit (recall that all dollar values are reported in thousands). However, unit sales will almost certainly be somewhat higher or lower than 550, and the price will probably turn out to be different from the projected $11.50 per unit. Similarly, the other variables would probably differ from their indicated values. Indeed, *all the inputs are expected values, not known values, and actual values can and do vary from expected values.* That's what risk is all about!

Three techniques are used in practice to assess stand-alone risk: (1) sensitivity analysis, (2) scenario analysis, and (3) Monte Carlo simulation. We discuss them in the sections that follow.

Self-Test

What does a project's stand-alone risk reflect?
What three techniques are used to assess stand-alone risk?

11.5 Sensitivity Analysis

Intuitively, we know that a change in a key input variable such as units sold or the sales price will cause the NPV to change. **Sensitivity analysis** *measures the percentage change in NPV that results from a given percentage change in an input variable when other inputs are held at their expected values.* This is by far the most commonly used type of risk analysis. It begins with a base-case scenario in which the project's NPV is found using the base-case value for each input variable. GPC's base-case inputs were given in Figure 11-1, but it's easy to imagine changes in the inputs, and any changes would result in a different NPV.

When GPC's senior managers review a capital budgeting analysis, they are interested in the base-case NPV, but they always go on to ask a series of "what if" questions: "What if unit sales fall to 385?" "What if market conditions force us to price the product at $8.12, not $11.60?" "What if variable costs are higher than we have forecasted?" Sensitivity analysis is designed to provide answers to such questions. Each variable is increased or decreased by a specified percentage from its expected value, holding other variables constant at their base-case levels. Then the NPV is calculated using the changed input. Finally, the resulting set of NPVs is plotted to show how sensitive NPV is to changes in the different variables.

Figure 11-3 shows GPC's project's sensitivity graph for six key variables. The data below the graph give the NPVs based on different values of the inputs, and those NPVs were then plotted to make the graph. Figure 11-3 shows that, as unit sales and the sales price are increased, the project's NPV increases; in contrast, increases in variable costs, fixed costs, equipment costs, and WACC lower the project's NPV. The slopes of the lines in the graph and the ranges in the table below the graph indicate how sensitive NPV is to each input: *The larger the range, the steeper the variable's slope and the more sensitive the NPV is to this variable.* We see that NPV is extremely sensitive to changes in the sales price; fairly sensitive to changes in variable

FIGURE 11-3 Sensitivity Graph for Solar Water Heater Project

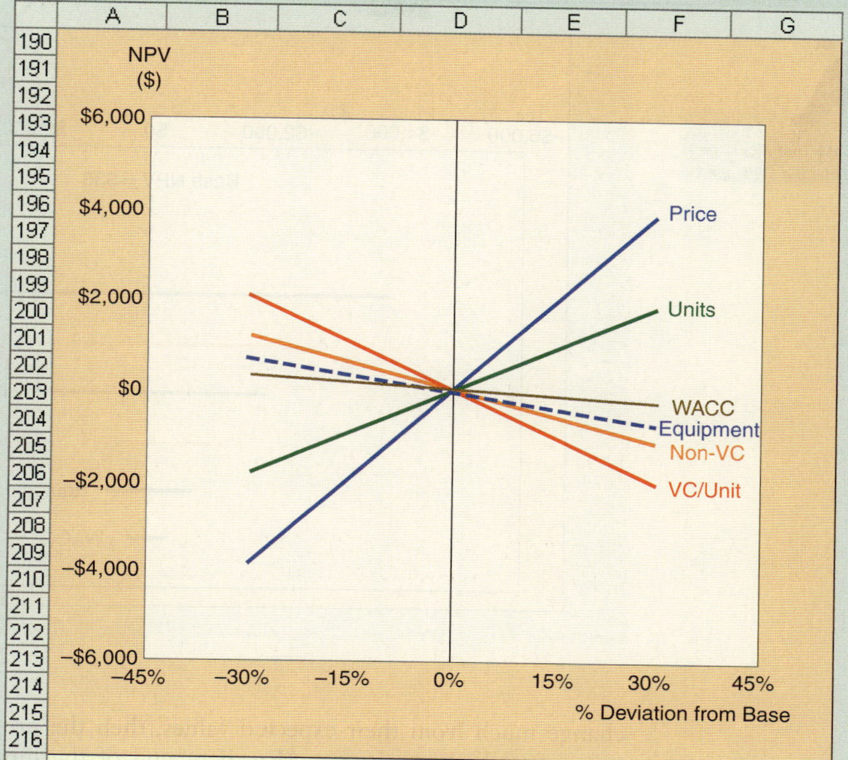

See **Ch11 Tool Kit.xls** on the textbook's Web site.

Data for Sensitivity Graph

Deviation from Base	NPV With Variables At Different Deviations From Base					
	Equipment	Price	Units	VC/Unit	Non-VC	WACC
−30%	$716	−$3,839	−$1,791	−$2,083	$1,209	$361
0%	$36	$36	$36	$36	$36	$36
30%	−$645	$3,910	$1,863	−$2,011	−$1,137	−$254
Range	$1,361	$7,749	$3,655	$4,095	$2,346	$615

costs, units sold, and fixed costs; and not especially sensitive to changes in the equipment's cost and the WACC. Management should, of course, try especially hard to obtain accurate estimates of the variables that have the greatest impact on the NPV.

If we were comparing two projects, then the one with the steeper sensitivity lines would be riskier (other things held constant), because relatively small changes in the input variables would produce large changes in the NPV. Thus, sensitivity analysis provides useful insights into a project's risk.[11] Note, however, that even though NPV may be highly sensitive to certain variables, if those variables are not likely to

[11]Sensitivity analysis is tedious with a regular calculator but easy with a spreadsheet. We used the chapter's *Excel* model to calculate the NPVs and then to draw the graph in Figure 11-3. To conduct such an analysis by hand would be quite time-consuming, and if the basic data were changed even slightly—say, the cost of the equipment was increased slightly—then all of the calculations would have to be redone. With a spreadsheet, we can simply type over the old input with the new one, and presto, the analysis and the graph change instantaneously.

FIGURE 11-4 Tornado Diagram for Solar Water Heater Project: Range of Outcomes for Input Deviations from Base Case (Thousands of Dollars)

See **Ch11 Tool Kit.xls** on the textbook's Web site.

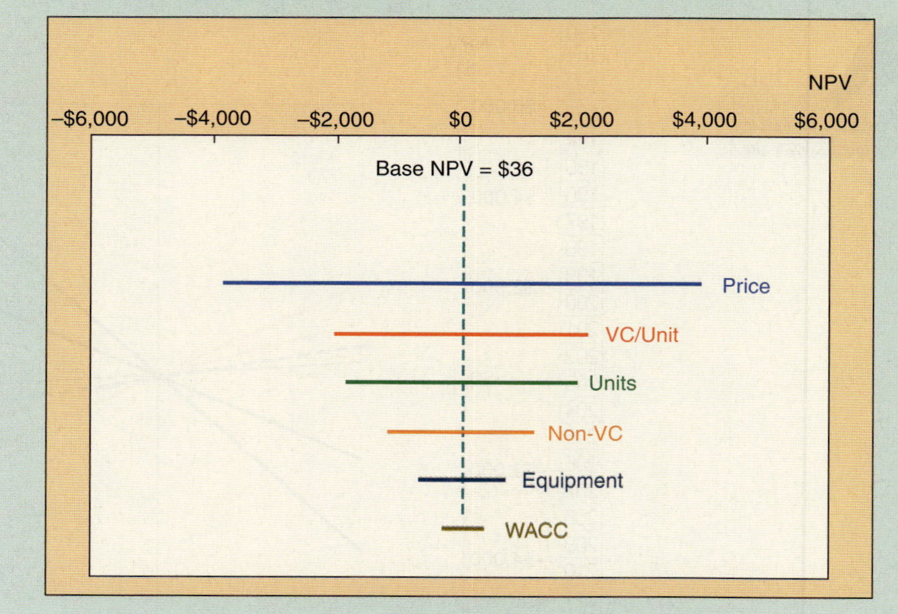

change much from their expected values, then the project may not be very risky in spite of its high sensitivity. Also, if several of the inputs change at the same time, the combined effect on NPV can be much greater than sensitivity analysis suggests.

Tornado Diagrams

Tornado diagrams are another way to present results from sensitivity analysis. The first step is to rank the range of possible NPVs for each of the input variables being changed. In our example, the range for sales price per unit is the largest and the range for WACC is the smallest. The ranges for each variable are then plotted, with the largest range on top and the smallest range on the bottom. It is also helpful to plot a vertical line showing the base-case NPV. We present a tornado diagram in Figure 11-4. Notice that the diagram is like a tornado in the sense that it is widest at the top and smallest at the bottom; hence its name. The tornado diagram makes it immediately obvious which inputs have the greatest impact on NPV: sales price and variable costs.

NPV Break-even Analysis

A special application of sensitivity analysis is called **NPV break-even analysis**. In a break-even analysis, we find the level of an input that produces an NPV of exactly zero. We used *Excel*'s Goal Seek feature to do this. See ***Ch11 Tool Kit.xls*** on the textbook's Web site for an explanation of how to use this *Excel* feature.

Table 11-1 shows the values of the inputs discussed previously that produce a zero NPV. For example, the number of units sold in Year 1 can drop to 547 before the project's NPV falls to zero. Break-even analysis is helpful in determining how bad things can get before the project has a negative NPV.

See **Ch11 Tool Kit.xls** on the textbook's Web site.

TABLE 11-1 NPV Break-even Analysis (Thousands of Dollars)

INPUT	INPUT VALUE THAT PRODUCES ZERO NPV HOLDING ALL ELSE CONSTANT
Sales price per unit, Year 1	\$11.57
Variable cost per unit (VC), Year 1	\$ 6.03
Annual change in units sold after Year 1	3.58%
Units sold, Year 1	547
Nonvariable cost (Non-VC), Year 1	\$2,018
Project WACC	10.35%

Extensions of Sensitivity Analysis. In our examples, we showed how one output, NPV, varied with a change in a single input. Sensitivity analysis can easily be extended to show how multiple outputs, such as NPV and IRR, vary with a change in an input. See ***Ch11 Tool Kit.xls*** on the textbook's Web site for an example showing how to use *Excel*'s Data Table feature to present multiple outputs.

It is also possible to use a Data Table to show how a single output, such as NPV, varies for changes in two inputs, such as the number of units sold and the sales price per unit. See ***Ch11 Tool Kit.xls*** on the textbook's Web site for an example. However, when we examine the impact of a change in more than one input, we usually use scenario analysis, which is described in the following section.

Self-Test

What is sensitivity analysis?

Briefly explain the usefulness of a sensitivity graph.

Discuss the following statement: "A project may not be very risky in spite of its high sensitivity to certain variables."

11.6 Scenario Analysis

In the sensitivity analysis just described, we changed one variable at a time. However, it is useful to know what would happen to the project's NPV if several of the inputs turn out to be better or worse than expected, and this is what we do in a **scenario analysis**. Also, scenario analysis allows us to assign probabilities to the base (or most likely) case, the best case, and the worst case; then we can find the *expected value* of the project's NPV, along with its *standard deviation* and *coefficient of variation*, to get a better idea of the project's risk.

In a scenario analysis, we begin with the base-case scenario, which uses the most likely value for each input variable. We then ask marketing, engineering, and other operating managers to specify a worst-case scenario (low unit sales, low sales price, high variable costs, and so on) and a best-case scenario. Often, the best and worst cases are defined as having a 25% probability of occurring, with a 50% probability for the base-case conditions. Obviously, conditions could take on many more than three values, but such a scenario setup is useful to help get some idea of the project's riskiness.

After much discussion with the marketing staff, engineers, accountants, and other experts in the company, a set of worst-case and best-case values were determined for several key inputs. Figure 11-5, taken from Tab 3 of the chapter ***Tool Kit*** model, shows the probability and inputs assumed for the base-case, worst-case, and best-case scenarios.

FIGURE 11-5 Inputs and Key Results for Each Scenario (Thousands of Dollars)

	A B C D	E	F	G	H	I
33						
34				Scenarios:		
35	Inputs:	Base		Worst		Best
36	Probability of Scenario	50%		25%		25%
37	Equipment cost	$3,400		$4,250		$2,550
38	Salvage value, equipment, Year 4	$300		$300		$300
39	Opportunity cost	$0		$0		$0
40	Externalities (cannibalization)	$0		$0		$0
41	Units sold, Year 1	550		412		688
42	Annual change in units sold, after Year 1	4.00%		−6.00%		14.00%
43	Sales price per unit, Year 1	$11.60		$8.70		$14.50
44	Annual change in sales price, after Year 1	2.00%		2.00%		2.00%
45	Variable cost per unit (VC), Year 1	$6.00		$7.50		$4.50
46	Annual change in VC, after Year 1	2.00%		2.00%		2.00%
47	Nonvariable cost (Non-VC), Year 1	$2,000		$2,500		$1,500
48	Annual change in Non-VC, after Year 1	2.00%		2.00%		2.00%
49	Project WACC	10.00%		10.00%		10.00%
50	Tax rate	40.00%		50.00%		30.00%
51	Working capital as % of next year's sales	12.65%		12.65%		12.65%
52	Key Results:	Base		Worst		Best
53	NPV	$36		−$5,847		$13,379
54	IRR	10.35%		Not found		112.01%
55	MIRR	10.23%		−100.00%		60.30%
56	PI	1.01		−0.24		4.51
57	Payback	3.41		Not found		1.00
58	Discounted payback	3.98		Not found		1.09

See **Ch11 Tool Kit.xls** on the textbook's Web site.

The project's cash flows and performance measures under each scenario are calculated; see the ***Tool Kit*** for the calculations. The cash flows for each scenario are shown in Figure 11-6, along with a probability distribution of the possible outcomes for NPV. If the project is highly successful, then a low initial investment, high sales price, high unit sales, and low production costs would combine to result in a very high NPV, $13,379. However, if things turn out badly, then the NPV would be a *negative* $5,847. This wide range of possibilities, and especially the large potential negative value, suggests that this is a risky project. If bad conditions materialize, the project will not bankrupt the company—this is just one project for a large company. Still, losing $5,847 (actually $5,847,000, since the units are thousands of dollars) would certainly hurt the company's value and the reputation of the project's manager.

If we multiply each scenario's probability by the NPV for that scenario and then sum the products, we will have the project's expected NPV of $1,901, as shown in Figure 11-6. Note that the *expected* NPV differs from the *base-case* NPV. This is not an error—mathematically, they are not equal.[12] We also calculate the standard deviation of the expected NPV; it is $7,049. Dividing the standard deviation by the expected NPV yields the coefficient of variation, 3.71, which is a measure of stand-alone risk. The firm's average project has a coefficient of variation of about 0.50, so

[12]This result occurs because two uncertain variables, sales volume and sales price, are multiplied together to obtain dollar sales, and this process causes the NPV distribution to be skewed to the right. A large number multiplied by another large number produces a very big number, and this in turn causes the average value (or expected value) to increase.

FIGURE 11-6 Scenario Analysis: Expected NPV and Its Risk

	A	B	C	D	E	F	G	H	I
123									
124			Predicted Cash Flows for Alternative Scenarios						
125		Prob:	0	1	2	3	4	WACC	NPV
126	Best	25%	–$3,812	$3,813	$4,634	$5,256	$8,705	10.00%	$13,379
127									
128	Base	50%	–$4,207	$1,048	$1,296	$980	$2,171	10.00%	$36
129									
130	Worst	25%	–$4,703	–$283	–$64	–$737	–$410	10.00%	–$5,847
131								Expected NPV =	$1,901
132								Standard Deviation (SD) =	$7,049
133								Coefficient of Variation (CV) = Std Dev/Expected NPV =	3.71

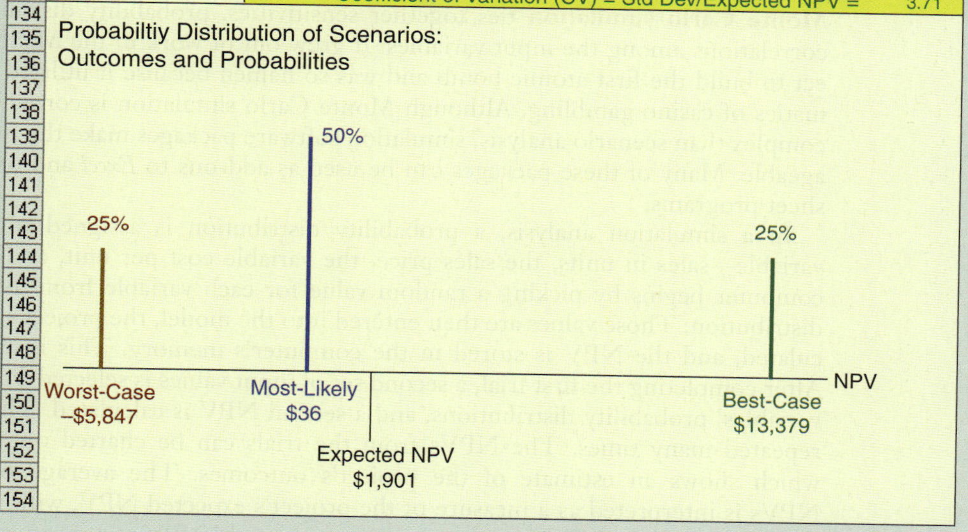

Probabiltiy Distribution of Scenarios:
Outcomes and Probabilities

See **Ch11 Tool Kit.xls** *on the textbook's Web site.*

the 3.71 indicates that this project is much riskier than most of GPC's other typical projects.

GPC's corporate WACC is 9%, so that rate should be used to find the NPV of an average-risk project. However, the water heater project is riskier than average, so a higher discount rate should be used to find its NPV. There is no way to determine the "precisely correct" discount rate—this is a judgment call. Management decided to evaluate the project using a 10% rate.[13]

Note that the base-case results are the same in our sensitivity and scenario analyses, but in the scenario analysis the worst case is much worse than in the sensitivity analysis and the best case is much better. This is because in scenario analysis all of the variables are set at their best or worst levels, whereas in sensitivity analysis only one variable is adjusted and all the others are left at their base-case levels.

[13]One could argue that the best-case scenario should be evaluated with a relatively low WACC, the worst-case scenario with a relatively high WACC, and the base case with the average corporate WACC. However, one could also argue that, at the time of the initial decision, we don't know what case will occur and hence a single rate should be used. Observe that, in the worst-case scenario, all of the cash flows are negative. If we used a high WACC because of this branch's risk, this would lower the PV of these negative cash flows, making the worst case much better than if we used the average WACC. Determining the "right" WACC to use in the analysis is not an easy task!

The project has a positive NPV, but its coefficient of variation (CV) is 3.71, which is almost 8 times higher than the 0.50 CV of an average project. With all that risk, it is not clear if the project should be accepted or not. At this point, GPC's CEO asked the CFO to investigate the risk further by performing a simulation analysis, as described in the next section.

Self-Test

What is scenario analysis?

Differentiate between sensitivity analysis and scenario analysis. What advantage does scenario analysis have over sensitivity analysis?

11.7 Monte Carlo Simulation[14]

Monte Carlo simulation ties together sensitivities, probability distributions, and correlations among the input variables. It grew out of work in the Manhattan Project to build the first atomic bomb and was so named because it utilized the mathematics of casino gambling. Although Monte Carlo simulation is considerably more complex than scenario analysis, simulation software packages make the process manageable. Many of these packages can be used as add-ons to *Excel* and other spreadsheet programs.

In a simulation analysis, a probability distribution is assigned to each input variable—sales in units, the sales price, the variable cost per unit, and so on. The computer begins by picking a random value for each variable from its probability distribution. Those values are then entered into the model, the project's NPV is calculated, and the NPV is stored in the computer's memory. This is called a trial. After completing the first trial, a second set of input values is selected from the input variables' probability distributions, and a second NPV is calculated. This process is repeated many times. The NPVs from the trials can be charted on a histogram, which shows an estimate of the project's outcomes. The average of the trials' NPVs is interpreted as a measure of the project's expected NPV, with the standard deviation (or the coefficient of variation) of the trials' NPV as a measure of the project's risk.

Using this procedure, we conducted a simulation analysis of GPC's solar water heater project. To compare apples and apples, we focused on the same six variables that were allowed to change in the previously conducted scenario analysis. We assumed that each variable can be represented by its own continuous normal distribution with means and standard deviations that are consistent with the base-case scenario. For example, we assumed that the units sold in Year 1 come from a normal distribution with a mean equal to the base-case value of 550. We used the probabilities and outcomes of the three scenarios to estimate the standard deviation (all calculations are in the ***Tool Kit***). The standard deviation of units sold is 98, as calculated using the scenario values. We made similar assumptions for all variables. In addition, we assumed that the annual change in unit sales will be positively correlated with unit sales in the first year: If demand is higher than expected in the first year, it will continue to be higher than expected. In particular, we assume a correlation of 0.65 between units sold in the first year and growth in units sold in later years. For all other variables, we assumed zero correlation. Figure 11-7 shows the inputs used in the simulation analysis.

[14]This section is relatively technical, and some instructors may choose to skip it with no loss in continuity.

FIGURE 11-7 Inputs and Key Results for the Current Simulation Trial (Thousands of Dollars)

	A	B	C	D	E	F
30						
31–33			Inputs for Simulation Probability Distributions		Random Variables Used in Current Simulation Trial	
34–36			Expected Value of input	Standard Deviation of Input	Standard Normal Random Variable	Value used in Current Trial
37	Inputs:					
38	Equipment cost		$3,400	$601	−0.30	$3,217
39	Salvage value, equipment, Year 4					$300
40	Opportunity cost					$0
41	Externalities (cannibalization)					$0
42	Units sold, Year 1		550	98	0.57	606
43	Annual change in units sold, after Year 1		4.00%	7.07%	0.93	10.60%
44	Sales price per unit, Year 1		$11.60	$2.05	−0.24	$11.11
45	Annual change in sales price, after Year 1					2.00%
46	Variable cost per unit (VC), Year 1		$6.60	$1.06	−0.70	$5.25
47	Annual change in VC, after Year 1					2.00%
48	Nonvariable cost (Non-VC), Year 1		$2,000	$354	−0.31	$1,890
49	Annual change in Non-VC, after year 1					2.00%
50	Project WACC					10.00%
51	Tax rate		40.00%	7.07%	1.23	48.67%
52	Working capital as % of next year's sales					12.65%
53–55	Assumed correlation between units sold in Year 1 and annual change in units sold in later years:		ρ =	65.00%		
56–57				Key Results Based on Current Trial		
58				NPV		$1,595
59				IRR		24.67%
60				MIRR		19.48%
61				PI		1.39
62				Payback		2.83
63				Discounted payback		3.24

See **Ch11 Tool Kit.xls** on the textbook's Web site.

Figure 11-7 also shows the current set of random variables that were drawn from the distributions at the time we created the figure for the textbook. We used a two-step procedure to create the random variables for the inputs. First, we used *Excel*'s functions to generate standard normal random variables with a mean of 0 and a standard deviation of 1; these are shown in Cells E38:E51.[15] To create the random values for the inputs used in the analysis, we multiplied a random standard normal variable by the standard deviation and added the expected value. For

[15]See the ***Tool Kit*** for detailed explanations on using *Excel* to generate random variables.

FIGURE 11-8 Summary of Simulation Results (Thousands of Dollars)

	A	B	C	D	E	F	G	H	I
156	Number of Trials =	5,000							
157		Simulated Input Variables							
158–161		Equipment cost	Units sold, Year 1	Annual change in units sold, after Year 1	Sales price per unit, Year 1	Variable cost per unit (VC), Year 1	Nonvariable cost (Non- VC), Year 1	Tax rate	Key Results: NPV
162	Mean	$3,382	550	4.1%	$11.63	$5.99	$1,998	39.9%	$215
163	Standard deviation	603	99	7.2%	2.05	1.06	357	7.2%	$3,275
164	Maximum	5,565	925	34.6%	18.64	9.76	3,234	66.4%	$25,523
165	Minimum	1,130	212	−18.3%	3.18	1.78	670	11.1%	−$10,246
166	Correlation with unit sales			64.4%					
167	Median								−$51
168	Probability of NPV > 0								49.5%
169	Coefficient of variation								15.24

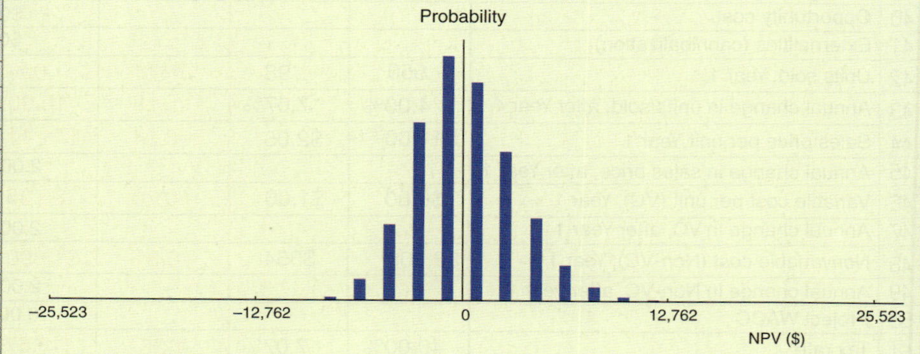

See **Ch11 Tool Kit.xls** *on the textbook's Web site.*

example, *Excel* drew the value 0.57 for first-year unit sales (Cell E42) from a standard normal distribution. We calculated the value for first-year unit sales to use in the current trial as 550 + 98(0.57) = 606, which is shown in Cell F42.[16]

We used the inputs in Cells F38:F52 to generate cash flows and to calculate performance measures for the project (the calculations are in the ***Tool Kit***). For the trial reported in Figure 11-7, the NPV is $1,595. We used a Data Table in the ***Tool Kit*** to generate additional trials. For each trial, the Data Table saved the value of the input variables and the value of the trial's NPV. Figure 11-8 presents selected results from the simulation for 5,000 trials. (The ***Tool Kit*** shows only 100 trials because simulating 5,000 trials reduces *Excel*'s speed when performing other calculations in the worksheet.)

After running a simulation, the first thing we do is verify that the results are consistent with our assumptions. The resulting sample mean and standard deviation of units sold in the first year are 550 and 99, which are virtually identical to our assumptions in Figure 11-7. The same is true for all the other inputs, so we can be reasonably confident that the simulation is doing what we are asking.

---

[16]We used a slightly more complicated procedure to generate a random variable for the annual change in sales to ensure that it had 0.65 correlation with the first-year units sold. See the ***Tool Kit*** for details.

THE GLOBAL ECONOMIC CRISIS

Are Bank Stress Tests Stressful Enough?

In late February of 2009, President Obama's newly appointed financial team—consisting of leaders of the Treasury, the Federal Reserve, and the FDIC—announced that the 19 largest U.S. banks (including Citi, JPMorgan Chase, and Bank of America) would have to undergo "stress tests." If its test indicated that a bank has a high probability of failure under possible conditions, then it would be forced to raise new capital. Investors would be reluctant to provide capital to a bank deemed likely to fail, so the capital would have to come from the Treasury. That would mean that the U.S. government would then own most of the equity and would control the bank, and the bank's top managers would likely be fired.

Just what is a stress test? In medicine, people are connected to a device that monitors their heart, then put on a treadmill, and then tested to see how well their heart takes the stress of a brisk uphill jog. In engineering, beams are subjected to pressure to see how much weight they can hold before breaking. In finance, scenario and simulation analyses like those described in this chapter are conducted to see what would happen under unfavorable conditions. The "worst-case" scenario we described earlier amounts to a stress test for an individual project, and similar tests can be conducted at the corporate level to answer questions like this: "Could we make the required interest and principal payments on our debt if sales fall by 50%?" Well-run companies are constantly stress-testing projects, divisions, and the entire corporation; then, as a result of these tests, managers take actions such as rejecting projects that are too risky or financing with stock rather than debt.

Banks and other financial institutions have been leaders in risk management, which includes stress-testing, but as we know all too well, those tests failed in the 2008–2009 recession. Banks grossly underestimated the combined effects of too much consumer and corporate debt, too much homebuilding, inadequate supervision of mortgage lenders, too many exotic derivatives whose risks the bankers did not fully understand, and so on. In a nutshell, banks throughout the world simply failed to test and plan for the level of economic distress that actually materialized, and the result was a meltdown of the worldwide financial system.

Regulators today are determined not to let that situation occur again; hence the administration mandated that the banks undergo stress tests under governmental supervision. Some of the parameters that the banks must test for include a 3.3% decline in GDP in 2009 followed by no growth in 2010, an additional 22% decline in housing prices, and a 10.3% unemployment rate by 2010. These conditions are worse than the consensus of economic forecasters, but the economists were much too optimistic in the months leading up to our current plight. Indeed, a number of analysts think the government's stress test is not nearly stressful enough and that, if "realistic" parameters were used, then most of the large banks would fail. If such information were released, this would set off a panic that would make the recession worse. Therefore, government officials have announced that no banks will be declared to have failed, just that they need more capital, and even that information may not be released.

A stress test makes sense, but—as with all forecasting—it may or may not do what it is supposed to do. This is true in capital budgeting, and it is even truer for the hugely important job of bank regulation. A failure to develop accurate forecasts of a project's returns could hurt a manager's chances for promotion, but the failure to develop accurate forecasts for our largest banks could do irreparable harm to our entire nation.

Figure 11-8 also reports summary statistics for the project's NPV. The mean is \$215, which suggests that the project should be accepted. However, the range of outcomes is quite large, from a loss of \$10,246 to a gain of \$25,523, so the project is clearly risky. The standard deviation of \$3,275 indicates that losses could easily occur, which is consistent with this wide range of possible outcomes.[17] Figure 11-8 also reports a median NPV of −$51, which means that half the time the project will have an NPV of less than −$51. In other words, most of the time the project will lose money.

A picture is worth a thousand words, and Figure 11-8 shows the probability distribution of the outcomes. Note that the distribution of outcomes is skewed to the right. As the figure shows, the potential downside losses are not as large as the potential upside gains. Our conclusion is that this is a very risky project, as indicated by the coefficient of variation, but it does have a positive expected NPV and the potential to be a "home run."

Self-Test

What is Monte Carlo simulation?

11.8 Project Risk Conclusions

We have discussed the three types of risk normally considered in capital budgeting: stand-alone risk, within-firm (or corporate) risk, and market risk. However, two important questions remain: (1) Should firms care at all about stand-alone and corporate risk, given that finance theory says that market (beta) risk is the only relevant risk? (2) What do we do when the stand-alone, within-firm, and market risk assessments lead to different conclusions?

There are no easy answers to these questions. Strict adherents of the CAPM would argue that well-diversified investors are concerned only with market risk, that managers should be concerned only with maximizing stock price, and thus that market (beta) risk ought to be given virtually all the weight in capital budgeting decisions. However, we know that not all investors are well diversified, that the CAPM does not operate exactly as the theory says it does, and that measurement problems keep managers from having complete confidence in the CAPM inputs. In addition, the CAPM ignores bankruptcy costs, even though such costs can be substantial, and the probability of bankruptcy depends on a firm's corporate risk, not on its beta risk. Therefore, even well-diversified investors should want a firm's management to give at least some consideration to a project's corporate risk, and that means giving some consideration to stand-alone project risk.

Although it would be nice to reconcile these problems and to measure risk on some absolute scale, the best we can do in practice is to estimate risk in a somewhat nebulous, relative sense. For example, we can generally say with a fair degree of confidence that a particular project has more, less, or about the same stand-alone risk as the firm's average project. Then, since stand-alone and corporate risk are generally correlated, the project's stand-alone risk is generally a reasonably good measure of its corporate risk. Finally, assuming that market risk and corporate risk are correlated, as is true for most companies, a project with a relatively high or low corporate risk will also have a relatively high or low market risk. We wish we could be more specific, but one simply must use a lot of judgment when assessing projects' risks.

---

[17]Note that the standard deviation of NPV in the simulation is much smaller than the standard deviation in the scenario analysis. In the scenario analysis, we assumed that all of the poor outcomes would occur together in the worst-case scenario and that all of the positive outcomes would occur together in the best-case scenario. In other words, we implicitly assumed that all of the risky variables were perfectly positively correlated. In the simulation, we assumed that the variables were independent (except for the correlation between unit sales and growth). The independence of variables in the simulation reduces the range of outcomes. For example, in the simulation, sometimes the sales price is high but the sales growth is low. In the scenario analysis, a high sales price is always coupled with high growth. Because the scenario analysis assumption of perfect correlation is unlikely, simulation may provide a better estimate of project risk. However, if the standard deviations and correlations used as inputs in the simulation are inaccurately estimated, then the simulation output will likewise be inaccurate.

Capital Budgeting Practices in the Asian/Pacific Region

A recent survey of executives in Australia, Hong Kong, Indonesia, Malaysia, the Philippines, and Singapore asked several questions about companies' capital budgeting practices. The study yielded the results summarized below.

Techniques for Evaluating Corporate Projects

Consistent with U.S. companies, most companies in this region evaluate projects using IRR, NPV, and payback. For IRR, usage ranges from 96% (in Australia) to 86% (in Hong Kong); NPV usage ranges from 96% (in Australia) to 81% (in the Philippines); and payback usage ranges from 100% (in Hong Kong and the Philippines) to 81% (in Indonesia).

Techniques for Estimating the Cost of Equity Capital

Recall from Chapter 9 that three basic approaches can be used to estimate the cost of equity: CAPM, dividend yield plus growth (DCF), and cost of own debt plus a risk premium. The use of these methods varies considerably from country to country (see Table A). The CAPM is used most often by U.S. firms. This is also true for Australian firms, but not for the other Asian/Pacific firms, which instead more often use the DCF and risk premium approaches.

Techniques for Assessing Risk

Firms in the Asian/Pacific region rely heavily on scenario and sensitivity analyses. They also use decision trees and Monte Carlo simulation, but much less frequently (see Table B).

TABLE A

Method	Australia	Hong Kong	Indonesia	Malaysia	Philippines	Singapore
CAPM	72.7%	26.9%	0.0%	6.2%	24.1%	17.0%
Dividend yield plus growth rate	16.4	53.8	33.3	50.0	34.5	42.6
Cost of debt plus risk premium	10.9	23.1	53.4	37.5	58.6	42.6

TABLE B

Risk Assessment Technique	Australia	Hong Kong	Indonesia	Malaysia	Philippines	Singapore
Scenario analysis	96%	100%	94%	80%	97%	90%
Sensitivity analysis	100	100	88	83	94	79
Decision-tree analysis	44	58	50	37	33	46
Monte Carlo simulation	38	35	25	9	24	35

Source: Adapted from George W. Kester et al., "Capital Budgeting Practices in the Asia-Pacific Region: Australia, Hong Kong, Indonesia, Malaysia, Philippines, and Singapore," *Financial Practice and Education,* Vol. 9, No. 1, Spring/Summer 1999, pp. 25–33.

Self-Test

In theory, should a firm be equally concerned with stand-alone, corporate, and market risk? Would your answer be the same if we substituted "In practice" for "In theory"? Explain your answers.

If a project's stand-alone, corporate, and market risk are known to be highly correlated, would this make the task of evaluating the project's risk easier or harder? Explain.

11.9 Replacement Analysis

In the previous sections we assumed that the solar water heater project was an entirely new project, so all of its cash flows were incremental—they would occur if and only if the project were accepted. However, for replacement projects we must find the cash flow *differentials* between the new and old projects, and these differentials are the *incremental cash flows* that we must analyze.

See **Ch11 Tool Kit.xls** on the textbook's Web site.

We evaluate a replacement decision in Figure 11-9, which is set up much like Figures 11-1 and 11-2 but with data on both a new, highly efficient machine (which will be depreciated on an accelerated basis) and data on the old machine (which is being depreciated on a straight-line basis). In Part I we show the key inputs in the analysis, including depreciation on the new and old machines. In Part II

FIGURE 11-9 Replacement Analysis

	A B C	D	E	F	G	H	I
16	Part I. Inputs:		Both Machines	Old Machine	New Machine		
17	Cost of new machine		$2,000				
18	After-tax salvage value old machine		$400				
19	Sales revenues (fixed)		$2,500				
20	Annual operating costs except depreciation			$1,200	$280		
21	Tax rate		40%				
22	WACC		10%				
23	Depreciation	1	2	3	4	Totals:	
24	Depr. rates (new machine)	33%	45%	15%	7%	100%	
25	Depreciation on new machine	$660	$900	$300	$140	$2,000	
26	Depreciation on old machine	–$400	–$400	–$400	–$400	–$1,600	
27	Δ: Change in depreciation	$260	$500	–$100	–$260	–$400	
28	Part II. Net Cash Flows Before Replacement: Old Machine						
29			0	1	2	3	4
30	Sales revenues			$2,500	$2,500	$2,500	$2,500
31	Operating costs except depreciation			1,200	1,200	1,200	1,200
32	Depreciation			–400	–400	–400	–400
33	Total operating costs			$800	$800	$800	$800
34	Operating income			$1,700	$1,700	$1,700	$1,700
35	Taxes 40%			680	680	680	680
36	After-tax operating income			$1,020	$1,020	$1,020	$1,020
37	Add back depreciation			–400	–400	–400	–400
38	Net cash flows **before** replacement		$0	$620	$620	$620	$620
39	Part III. Net Cash Flows After Replacement: New Machine						
40			0	1	2	3	4
41	New machine cost:		–$2,000				
42	After-tax salvage value, old machine		$400				
43	Sales revenues			–$2,500	–$2,500	–$2,500	–$2,500
44	Operating costs except depreciation			280	280	280	280
45	Depreciation			660	900	300	140
46	Total operating costs			$940	$1,180	$580	$420
47	Operating income			–$1,560	–$1,320	–$1,920	–$2,080
48	Taxes 40%			624	528	768	832
49	After-tax operating income			$936	$792	–$1,152	–$1,248
50	Add back depreciation			660	900	300	140
51	Net cash flows **after** replacement		–$1,600	$1,596	$1,692	$1,452	$1,388
52	Part IV. Incremental CF: Row 51–Row 38		–$1,600	$976	$1,072	$832	$768
53	Part V. Evaluation	NPV =	$1,322.87	IRR =	46.36%	MIRR =	27.88%

we find the cash flows the firm will have if it continues to use the old machine, and in Part III we find the cash flows if the firm replaces the old machine. Then, in Part IV, we subtract the old flows from the new to arrive at the *incremental cash flows*, and we evaluate those flows in Part V to find the NPV, IRR, and MIRR. Replacing the old machine appears to be a good decision.[18]

In some instances, replacements add capacity as well as lower operating costs. In this case, sales revenues in Part III would be increased, and if that leads to a need for more working capital, then this would be shown as a Time-0 expenditure along with a recovery at the end of the project's life. These changes would, of course, be reflected in the incremental cash flows on Row 52.

Self-Test

How are incremental cash flows found in a replacement analysis?

If you were analyzing a replacement project and suddenly learned that the old equipment could be sold for $1,000 rather than $400, would this new information make the replacement look better or worse? Explain.

In Figure 11-9 we assumed that output would remain stable if the old machine were replaced. Suppose output would actually double. How would this change be dealt with in the framework of Figure 11-9?

11.10 Real Options

According to traditional capital budgeting theory, a project's NPV is the present value of its expected future cash flows, discounted at a rate that reflects the riskiness of those cash flows. Note, however, that this says nothing about actions that can be taken *after* the project has been accepted and placed in operation that might lead to an increase in the cash flows. In other words, traditional capital budgeting theory assumes that a project is like a roulette wheel. A gambler can choose whether or not to spin the wheel, but once the wheel has been spun, nothing can be done to influence the outcome. Once the game begins, the outcome depends purely on chance, and no skill is involved.

Contrast roulette with a game such as poker. Chance plays a role in poker, and it continues to play a role after the initial deal because players receive additional cards throughout the game. However, poker players are able to respond to their opponents' actions, so skilled players usually win.

Capital budgeting decisions have more in common with poker than roulette because (1) chance plays a continuing role throughout the life of the project, but (2) managers can respond to changing market conditions and to competitors' actions. Opportunities to respond to changing circumstances are called **managerial options** because they give managers a chance to influence the outcome of a project. They are also called **strategic options** because they are often associated with large, strategic projects rather than routine maintenance projects. Finally, they are called **real options** to differentiate them from financial options because they involve real, rather than financial, assets. The following sections describe projects with several types of **embedded options**.

[18]The same sort of risk analysis discussed in previous sections can be applied to replacement decisions. One of our MBA graduates was hired as a financial analyst with a company that manufactured products for sale to other businesses. He took our *Excel* replacement model, obtained input data from several of his firm's customers, and analyzed how his firm's products would help the customers. In several cases, his analysis helped nail down a sale. He then instructed the firm's sales reps on how to use the model to stimulate sales. This effort was highly successful, so our student got a nice bonus and was promoted in the company.

Investment Timing Options

Conventional NPV analysis implicitly assumes that projects either will be accepted or rejected, which implies they will be undertaken now or never. In practice, however, companies sometimes have a third choice—delay the decision until later, when more information is available. Such **investment timing options** can dramatically affect a project's estimated profitability and risk, as we saw in our example of GPC's solar water heater project.

Keep in mind, though, that the *option to delay* is valuable only if it more than offsets any harm that might result from delaying. For example, while one company delays, some other company might establish a loyal customer base that makes it difficult for the first company to enter the market later. The option to delay is usually most valuable to firms with proprietary technology, patents, licenses, or other barriers to entry, because these factors lessen the threat of competition. The option to delay is valuable when market demand is uncertain, but it is also valuable during periods of volatile interest rates, since the ability to wait can allow firms to delay raising capital for a project until interest rates are lower.

Growth Options

A **growth option** allows a company to increase its capacity if market conditions are better than expected. There are several types of growth options. One lets a company *increase the capacity of an existing product line*. A "peaking unit" power plant illustrates this type of growth option. Such units have high variable costs and are used to produce additional power only if demand, and thus prices, are high.

The second type of growth option allows a company to *expand into new geographic markets*. Many companies are investing in China, Eastern Europe, and Russia even though standard NPV analysis produces negative NPVs. However, if these developing markets really take off, the option to open more facilities could be quite valuable.

The third type of growth option is the opportunity to *add new products*, including complementary products and successive "generations" of the original product. Auto companies are losing money on their first electric autos, but the manufacturing skills and consumer recognition those cars will provide should help turn subsequent generations of electric autos into money makers.

Abandonment Options

Section 11.11 estimates the value of an **abandonment option** for GPC's solar water heater project. The standard DCF analysis we first employed assumed that the assets would be used over a specified economic life. But even though some projects must be operated over their full economic life—in spite of deteriorating market conditions and hence lower than expected cash flows—other projects can be abandoned. Smart managers negotiate the right to abandon if a project turns out to be unsuccessful as a condition for undertaking the project.

Note, too, that some projects can be structured so that they provide the option to *reduce capacity* or *temporarily suspend operations*. Such options are common in the natural resources industry, including mining, oil, and timber, and they should be reflected in the analysis when NPVs are being estimated.

Flexibility Options

Many projects offer **flexibility options** that permit the firm to alter operations depending on how conditions change during the life of the project. Typically, either inputs or outputs (or both) can be changed. BMW's Spartanburg, South Carolina, auto assembly plant provides a good example of output flexibility. BMW needed the plant to produce sports coupes. If it built the plant configured to produce only these vehicles, the construction cost would be minimized. However, the company thought that later on it might want to switch production to some other vehicle type, and that would be difficult if the plant were designed just for coupes. Therefore, BMW decided to spend additional funds to construct a more flexible plant: one that could produce different types of vehicles should demand patterns shift. Sure enough, things did change. Demand for coupes dropped a bit and demand for sport-utility vehicles soared. But BMW was ready, and the Spartanburg plant began spewing out hot-selling SUVs. The plant's cash flows were much higher than they would have been without the flexibility option that BMW "bought" by paying more to build a more flexible plant.

Electric power plants provide an example of input flexibility. Utilities can build plants that generate electricity by burning coal, oil, or natural gas. The prices of those fuels change over time in response to events in the Middle East, changing environmental policies, and weather conditions. Some years ago, virtually all power plants were designed to burn just one type of fuel, because this resulted in the lowest construction costs. However, as fuel cost volatility increased, power companies began to build higher-cost but more flexible plants, especially ones that could switch from oil to gas and back again depending on relative fuel prices.

Valuing Real Options

A full treatment of real option valuation is beyond the scope of this chapter, but there are some things we can say. First, if a project has an embedded real option, then management should at least recognize and articulate its existence. Second, we know that a financial option is more valuable if it has a long time until maturity or if the underlying asset is very risky. If either of these characteristics applies to a project's real option, then management should know that its value is probably relatively high. Third, management might be able to model the real option along the lines of a decision tree, as we illustrate in the following section.

Self-Test

Explain the relevance of the following statement: "Capital budgeting decisions have more in common with poker than roulette."

What are managerial options? Strategic options?

Identify some different types of real options and differentiate among them.

11.11 Phased Decisions and Decision Trees

Up to this point we have focused primarily on techniques for estimating a project's risk. Although this is an integral part of capital budgeting, managers are just as interested in *reducing* risk as in *measuring* it. One way to reduce risk is to structure projects so that expenditures can be made in stages over time rather than all at once. This gives managers the opportunity to reevaluate decisions using new information and then to either invest additional funds or terminate the project. This type of analysis involves the use of *decision trees*.

The Basic Decision Tree

GPC's analysis of the solar water heater project thus far has assumed that the project cannot be abandoned once it goes into operation, even if the worst-case situation arises. However, GPC is considering the possibility of terminating (abandoning) the

FIGURE 11-10 Simple Decision Tree: Abandoning Project in Worst-Case Scenario

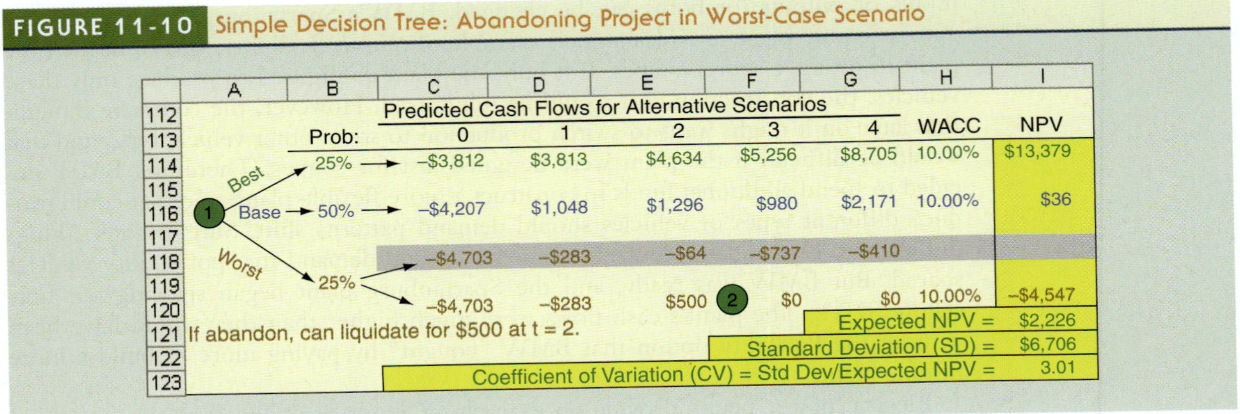

	A	B	C	D	E	F	G	H	I
112			Predicted Cash Flows for Alternative Scenarios						
113		Prob:	0	1	2	3	4	WACC	NPV
114		25%	−$3,812	$3,813	$4,634	$5,256	$8,705	10.00%	$13,379
115	Best								
116	1 Base	50%	−$4,207	$1,048	$1,296	$980	$2,171	10.00%	$36
117									
118	Worst		−$4,703	−$283	−$64	−$737	−$410		
119		25%							
120			−$4,703	−$283	$500 (2)	$0	$0	10.00%	−$4,547
121	If abandon, can liquidate for $500 at t = 2.							Expected NPV =	$2,226
122								Standard Deviation (SD) =	$6,706
123								Coefficient of Variation (CV) = Std Dev/Expected NPV =	3.01

project at Year 2 if the demand is low. The net after-tax cash flow from salvage, legal fees, liquidation of working capital, and all other termination costs and revenues is $500. Using these assumptions, the GPC ran a new scenario analysis; the results are shown in Figure 11-10, which is a simple decision tree.

1. Here we assume that, if the worst case materializes, then this will be recognized after the negative Year-1 operating loss and GPC will abandon the project. Rather than continue realizing negative cash flows in Years 2, 3, and 4, the company will shut down the operation and liquidate the project for $500 at t = 2. Now the expected NPV rises from $1,901 to $2,226 and the CV declines from 3.71 to 3.01. So, securing the right to abandon the project if things don't work out raised the project's expected return and lowered its risk. This will give you an approximate value, but keep in mind that you may not have a good estimate of the appropriate discount rate because the real option changes the risk, and hence the required return, of the project.[19]

After the management team thought about the decision-tree approach, other ideas for improving the project emerged. The marketing manager stated that for $100,000 she could undertake a study that would give the firm a better idea of demand for the product, and the design engineer stated that he could build a prototype solar water heater that could be used to gauge consumer reactions to the actual product, which would provide even more information about the final demand and production costs. This led the CEO to discuss with the local university the possibility of delaying a final decision on the project until another type of analysis could be done, a full-blown **staged decision-tree analysis**, which is shown in Figure 11-11.

Decision trees such as the one in Figure 11-11 are often used to analyze multistage, or sequential, decisions. Each circle represents a decision point, also known as a **decision node**. The dollar value to the left of each decision node represents the net cash flow at that point, and the cash flows shown under t = 3, 4, 5, and 6 represent the cash inflows if the project is pushed on to completion. Each diagonal line leads to a **branch** of the decision tree, and each branch has an estimated probability. For example, if the firm decides to "go" with the project at Decision Point 1, then it will

[19]For more on real option valuation, see M. Amram and N. Kulatilaka, *Real Options: Managing Strategic Investment in an Uncertain World* (Boston: Harvard Business School Press, 1999); and H. Smit and L. Trigeorgis, *Strategic Investments: Real Options and Games* (Princeton, NJ: Princeton University Press, 2004).

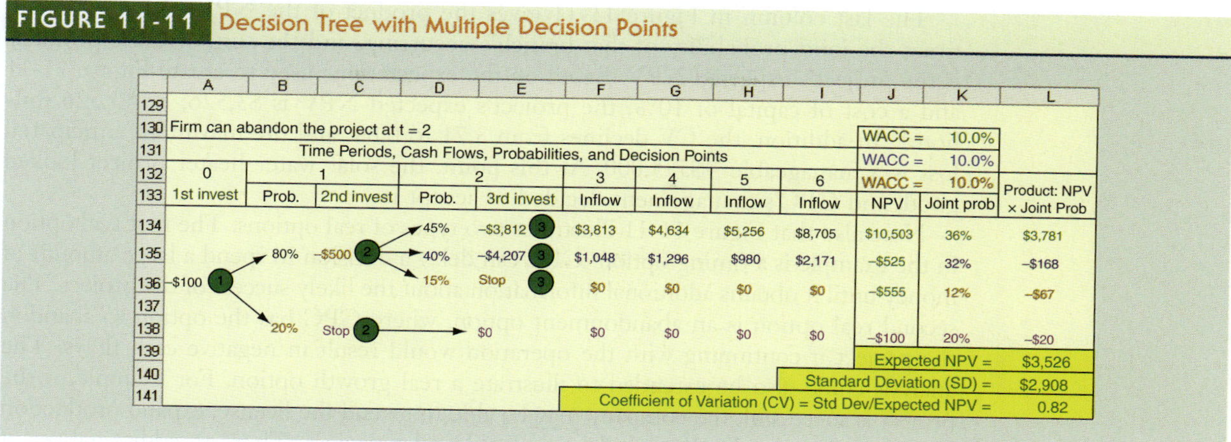

FIGURE 11-11 Decision Tree with Multiple Decision Points

	A	B	C	D	E	F	G	H	I	J	K	L
129												
130	Firm can abandon the project at t = 2									WACC =	10.0%	
131	Time Periods, Cash Flows, Probabilities, and Decision Points									WACC =	10.0%	
132	0	1		2		3	4	5	6	WACC =	10.0%	Product: NPV × Joint Prob
133	1st invest	Prob.	2nd invest	Prob.	3rd invest	Inflow	Inflow	Inflow	Inflow	NPV	Joint prob	
134				45%	−$3,812 (3)	$3,813	$4,634	$5,256	$8,705	$10,503	36%	$3,781
135		80%	−$500 (2)	40%	−$4,207 (3)	$1,048	$1,296	$980	$2,171	−$525	32%	−$168
136	−$100 (1)			15%	Stop (3)	$0	$0	$0	$0	−$555	12%	−$67
137												
138		20%	Stop (2)		$0	$0	$0	$0	$0	−$100	20%	−$20
139										Expected NPV =		$3,526
140									Standard Deviation (SD) =			$2,908
141						Coefficient of Variation (CV) = Std Dev/Expected NPV =						0.82

See **Ch11 Tool Kit.xls** on the textbook's Web site.

spend \$100,000 on the marketing study.[20] Management estimates that there is a 0.8 probability that the study will produce *positive* results, leading to the decision to make an additional investment and thus move on to Decision Point 2, and a 0.2 probability that the marketing study will produce *negative* results, indicating that the project should be canceled after Stage 1. If the project is canceled, the cost to the company will be the \$100,000 spent on the initial marketing study.

If the marketing study yields positive results, then the firm will spend \$500,000 on the prototype water heater at Decision Point 2. Management estimates (even before making the initial \$100,000 investment) that there is a 45% probability of the pilot project yielding good results, a 40% probability of average results, and a 15% probability of bad results. If the prototype works well, then the firm will spend several millions more at Decision Point 3 to build a production plant, buy the necessary inventory, and commence operations. The operating cash flows over the project's 4-year life will be good, average, or bad, and these cash flows are shown under Years 3 through 6.

The column of joint probabilities in Figure 11-11 gives the probability of occurrence of each branch—and hence of each NPV. Each joint probability is obtained by multiplying together all the probabilities on that particular branch. For example, the probability that the company will, if Stage 1 is undertaken, move through Stages 2 and 3, and that a strong demand will produce the indicated cash flows, is (0.8)(0.45) = 0.36 = 36.0%. There is a 32% probability of average results, a 12% probability of building the plant and then getting bad results, and a 20% probability of getting bad initial results and stopping after the marketing study.

The NPV of the top (most favorable) branch as shown in Column J is \$10,503, calculated as follows:

$$\text{NPV} = -\$100 - \frac{\$500}{(1.10)^1} - \frac{\$3{,}812}{(1.10)^2} + \frac{\$3{,}813}{(1.10)^3} + \frac{\$4{,}634}{(1.10)^4} + \frac{\$5{,}256}{(1.10)^5} + \frac{\$8{,}705}{(1.10)^6}$$

$$= \$10{,}503$$

The NPVs for the other branches are calculated similarly.[21]

[20] GPC might also have to pay the university an additional licensing fee. Such a fee could be added to the \$100,000 marketing study cost.

[21] The calculations in *Excel* use nonrounded annual cash flows, so there may be small differences when calculating by hand with rounded annual cash flows.

The last column in Figure 11-11 gives the product of the NPV for each branch times the joint probability of that branch's occurring, and the sum of these products is the project's expected NPV. Based on the expectations used to create Figure 11-11 and a cost of capital of 10%, the project's expected NPV is $3,526, or $3.526 million.[22] In addition, the CV declines from 3.71 to 0.84, and the maximum anticipated loss is a manageable –$555,000. At this point, the solar water heater project looked good, and GPC's management decided to accept it.

Note also that Figure 11-11 illustrates two types of real options. The first real option in the example is a timing option: GPC can delay a decision to spend a large amount of money until it obtains additional information about the likely success of the project. The second real option is an abandonment option, where GPC has the option to abandon the project if continuing with the operation would result in negative cash flows. The analysis could also be extended to illustrate a real growth option. For example, if the project is successful, the company may be able to extend the license, expand production of this project, or develop another profitable solar project. Thus, an additional set of branches might be extended out from Cell I134, where the company would invest in one or more other projects that offer potentially high NPVs. If one or more promising growth options can be identified, then the project's expected NPV might be higher yet.

As this example shows, decision-tree analysis requires managers to explicitly articulate the types of risk a project faces and to develop responses to potential scenarios. Note also that our example could be extended to cover many other types of decisions and could even be incorporated into a simulation analysis. All in all, decision-tree analysis is a valuable tool for analyzing project risks.[23]

Self-Test

What is a decision tree? A branch? A node?

If a firm can structure a project such that expenditures can be made in stages rather than all at the beginning, how would this affect the project's risk and expected NPV? Explain.

Summary

In this chapter, we developed a framework for analyzing a project's cash flows and its risk. The key concepts covered are listed below.

- The most important (and most difficult) step in analyzing a capital budgeting project is **estimating the incremental after-tax cash flows** the project will produce.
- A project's **net cash flow** is different from its accounting income. Project net cash flow reflects (1) cash outlays for fixed assets, (2) sales revenues, (3) operating costs, (4) the tax shield provided by depreciation, and (5) cash flows due to changes in net working capital. A project's net cash flow does *not* include interest payments, since they are accounted for by the discounting process. If we deducted interest and then discounted cash flows at the WACC, this would double-count interest charges.

[22]As we mentioned concerning the abandonment option, the presence of the real options in Figure 11-11 might cause the discount rate to change.

[23]In this example we glossed over an important issue: the appropriate cost of capital for the project. Adding decision nodes to a project clearly changes its risk, so we would expect the cost of capital for a project with few decision nodes to have a different risk than one with many nodes. If this is so then the projects should have different costs of capital. In fact, we might expect the cost of capital to change over time as the project moves to different stages, since the stages themselves differ in risk.

- In determining incremental cash flows, **opportunity costs** (the cash flows forgone by using an asset) must be included, but **sunk costs** (cash outlays that have been made and that cannot be recouped) are not included. Any **externalities** (effects of a project on other parts of the firm) should also be reflected in the analysis. Externalities can be *positive* or *negative* and may be *environmental*.
- **Cannibalization** is an important type of externality that occurs when a new project leads to a reduction in sales of an existing product.
- **Tax laws** affect cash flow analysis in two ways: (1) taxes reduce operating cash flows, and (2) tax laws determine the depreciation expense that can be taken in each year.
- The incremental cash flows from a typical project can be classified into three categories: (1) **initial investment outlay**, (2) **operating cash flows over the project's life**, and (3) **terminal year cash flows**.
- **Price level changes** (**inflation** or **deflation**) must be considered in project analysis. The best procedure is to build expected price changes into the cash flow estimates. Recognize that output prices and costs for a product can decline over time even though the economy is experiencing inflation.
- The chapter illustrates both **expansion projects**, in which the investment generates new sales, and **replacement projects**, where the primary purpose of the investment is to operate more efficiently and thus reduce costs.
- We discuss three types of risk: **Stand-alone risk, corporate** (or **within-firm**) **risk** and **market** (or **beta**) **risk**. Stand-alone risk does not consider diversification at all; corporate risk considers risk among the firm's own assets; and market risk considers risk at the stockholder level, where stockholders' own diversification is considered.
- **Risk** is important because it affects the discount rate used in capital budgeting; in other words, a project's WACC depends on its risk.
- Assuming the CAPM holds true, **market risk** is the most important risk because (according to the CAPM) it is the risk that affects stock prices. However, usually *it is difficult to measure a project's market risk.*
- **Corporate risk** is important because it influences the firm's ability to use low-cost debt, to maintain smooth operations over time, and to avoid crises that might consume management's energy and disrupt its employees, customers, suppliers, and community. Also, a project's corporate risk is generally easier to measure than its market risk; and, because corporate and market risks are generally thought to be correlated, corporate risk can often serve as a proxy for market risk.
- **Stand-alone risk** is easier to measure than either market or corporate risk. Also, most of a firm's projects' cash flows are correlated with one another, and the firm's total cash flows are correlated with those of most other firms. These correlations mean that a project's stand-alone risk can generally be used as a proxy for hard-to-measure market and corporate risk. As a result, most risk analysis in capital budgeting focuses on stand-alone risk.
- **Sensitivity analysis** is a technique that shows how much a project's NPV will change in response to a given change in an input variable, such as sales, when all other factors are held constant.
- **Scenario analysis** is a risk analysis technique in which the best- and worst-case NPVs are compared with the project's base-case NPV.

- **Monte Carlo simulation** is a risk analysis technique that uses a computer to simulate future events and thereby estimate a project's profitability and riskiness.
- The **risk-adjusted discount rate**, or **project cost of capital**, is the rate used to evaluate a particular project. It is based on the corporate WACC, a value that is increased for projects that are riskier than the firm's average project and decreased for less risky projects.
- **A decision tree** shows how different decisions during a project's life can affect its value.
- A **staged decision-tree analysis** divides the analysis into different phases. At each phase a decision is made either to proceed or to stop the project. These decisions are represented on the decision trees by circles and are called **decision nodes**.
- Opportunities to respond to changing circumstances are called **real,** or **managerial, options** because they give managers the option to influence the returns on a project. They are also called **strategic options** if they are associated with large, strategic projects rather than routine maintenance projects. Finally, they are also called "real" options because they involve "real" (or "physical") rather than "financial" assets. Many projects include a variety of these **embedded options** that can dramatically affect the true NPV.
- An **investment timing option** involves the possibility of delaying major expenditures until more information on likely outcomes is known. The opportunity to delay can dramatically change a project's estimated value.
- A **growth option** occurs if an investment creates the opportunity to make other potentially profitable investments that would not otherwise be possible. These include (1) options to expand the original project's output, (2) options to enter a new geographical market, and (3) options to introduce complementary products or successive generations of products.
- An **abandonment option** is the ability to discontinue a project if the operating cash flow turns out to be lower than expected. It reduces the risk of a project and increases its value. Instead of total abandonment, some options allow a company to reduce capacity or temporarily suspend operations.
- A **flexibility option** is the option to modify operations depending on how conditions develop during a project's life, especially the type of output produced or the inputs used.
- The **option value** can be determined by comparing the project's expected NPV with and without the option. If an initial cost is required to obtain a real option, then that cost can be compared to the calculated value of the option as a part of the overall analysis.

Questions

(11–1) Define each of the following terms:

a. Project cash flow; accounting income
b. Incremental cash flow; sunk cost; opportunity cost; externality; cannibalization; expansion project; replacement project
c. Net operating working capital changes; salvage value
d. Stand-alone risk; corporate (within-firm) risk; market (beta) risk
e. Sensitivity analysis; scenario analysis; Monte Carlo simulation analysis

f. Risk-adjusted discount rate; project cost of capital
g. Decision tree; staged decision-tree analysis; decision node; branch
h. Real options; managerial options; strategic options; embedded options
i. Investment timing option; growth option; abandonment option; flexibility option

(11–2) Operating cash flows, rather than accounting profits, are used in project analysis. What is the basis for this emphasis on cash flows as opposed to net income?

(11–3) Why is it true, in general, that a failure to adjust expected cash flows for expected inflation biases the calculated NPV downward?

(11–4) Explain why sunk costs should not be included in a capital budgeting analysis but opportunity costs and externalities should be included.

(11–5) Explain how net operating working capital is recovered at the end of a project's life and why it is included in a capital budgeting analysis.

(11–6) Define (a) simulation analysis, (b) scenario analysis, and (c) sensitivity analysis.

(11–7) Why are interest charges not deducted when a project's cash flows are calculated for use in a capital budgeting analysis?

(11–8) Most firms generate cash inflows every day, not just once at the end of the year. In capital budgeting, should we recognize this fact by estimating daily project cash flows and then using them in the analysis? If we do not, will this bias our results? If it does, would the NPV be biased up or down? Explain.

(11–9) What are some differences in the analysis for a replacement project versus that for a new expansion project?

(11–10) Distinguish among beta (or market) risk, within-firm (or corporate) risk, and stand-alone risk for a project being considered for inclusion in a firm's capital budget.

(11–11) In theory, market risk should be the only "relevant" risk. However, companies focus as much on stand-alone risk as on market risk. What are the reasons for the focus on stand-alone risk?

Self-Test Problems

Solutions Appear in Appendix A

(ST–1) New-Project Analysis

You have been asked by the president of the Farr Construction Company to evaluate the proposed acquisition of a new earth mover. The mover's basic price is $50,000, and it would cost another $10,000 to modify it for special use. Assume that the mover falls into the MACRS 3-year class (see Appendix 11A), that it would be sold after 3 years for $20,000, and that it would require an increase in net working capital (spare parts inventory) of $2,000. The earth mover would have no effect on revenues, but it is expected to save the firm $20,000 per year in before-tax operating costs, mainly labor. The firm's marginal federal-plus-state tax rate is 40%.

a. What are the Year-0 cash flows?
b. What are the operating cash flows in Years 1, 2, and 3?
c. What are the additional (nonoperating) cash flows in Year 3?
d. If the project's cost of capital is 10%, should the earth mover be purchased?

(ST–2) Corporate Risk Analysis

The staff of Porter Manufacturing has estimated the following net after-tax cash flows and probabilities for a new manufacturing process:

	Net After-Tax Cash Flows		
Year	**P = 0.2**	**P = 0.6**	**P = 0.2**
0	–$100,000	–$100,000	–$100,000
1	20,000	30,000	40,000
2	20,000	30,000	40,000
3	20,000	30,000	40,000
4	20,000	30,000	40,000
5	20,000	30,000	40,000
5*	0	20,000	30,000

Line 0 gives the cost of the process, Lines 1 through 5 give operating cash flows, and Line 5* contains the estimated salvage values. Porter's cost of capital for an average-risk project is 10%.

a. Assume that the project has average risk. Find the project's expected NPV. (*Hint:* Use expected values for the net cash flow in each year.)
b. Find the best-case and worst-case NPVs. What is the probability of occurrence of the worst case if the cash flows are perfectly dependent (perfectly positively correlated) over time? If they are independent over time?
c. Assume that all the cash flows are perfectly positively correlated. That is, assume there are only three possible cash flow streams over time—the worst case, the most likely (or base) case, and the best case—with respective probabilities of 0.2, 0.6, and 0.2. These cases are represented by each of the columns in the table. Find the expected NPV, its standard deviation, and its coefficient of variation.

Problems

Answers Appear in Appendix B

Easy Problems 1–4

(11–1) Investment Outlay

Talbot Industries is considering an expansion project. The necessary equipment could be purchased for $9 million, and the project would also require an initial $3 million investment in net operating working capital. The company's tax rate is 40%.

a. What is the initial investment outlay?
b. The company spent and expensed $50,000 on research related to the project last year. Would this change your answer? Explain.
c. The company plans to house the project in a building it owns but is not now using. The building could be sold for $1 million after taxes and real estate commissions. How would this affect your answer?

(11–2) Operating Cash Flow

Cairn Communications is trying to estimate the first-year operating cash flow (at t = 1) for a proposed project. The financial staff has collected the following information:

Projected sales	$10 million
Operating costs (not including depreciation)	$ 7 million
Depreciation	$ 2 million
Interest expense	$ 2 million

The company faces a 40% tax rate. What is the project's operating cash flow for the first year (t = 1)?

(11–3) Net Salvage Value

Allen Air Lines is now in the terminal year of a project. The equipment originally cost $20 million, of which 80% has been depreciated. Carter can sell the used equipment today to another airline for $5 million, and its tax rate is 40%. What is the equipment's after-tax net salvage value?

(11–4) Replacement Analysis

The Chen Company is considering the purchase of a new machine to replace an obsolete one. The machine being used for the operation has both a book value and a market value of zero; it is in good working order, however, and will last physically for at least another 10 years. The proposed replacement machine will perform the operation so much more efficiently that Chen's engineers estimate it will produce after-tax cash flows (labor savings and depreciation) of $9,000 per year. The new machine will cost $40,000 delivered and installed, and its economic life is estimated to be 10 years. It has zero salvage value. The firm's WACC is 10%, and its marginal tax rate is 35%. Should Chen buy the new machine?

Intermediate Problems 5–11

(11–5) Depreciation Methods

Wendy is evaluating a capital budgeting project that should last for 4 years. The project requires $800,000 of equipment. She is unsure what depreciation method to use in her analysis, straight-line or the 3-year MACRS accelerated method. Under straight-line depreciation, the cost of the equipment would be depreciated evenly over its 4-year life (ignore the half-year convention for the straight-line method). The applicable MACRS depreciation rates are 33%, 45%, 15%, and 7%, as discussed in Appendix 11A. The company's WACC is 10%, and its tax rate is 40%.

a. What would the depreciation expense be each year under each method?
b. Which depreciation method would produce the higher NPV, and how much higher would it be?

(11–6) New-Project Analysis

The Campbell Company is evaluating the proposed acquisition of a new milling machine. The machine's base price is $108,000, and it would cost another $12,500 to modify it for special use. The machine falls into the MACRS 3-year class, and it would be sold after 3 years for $65,000. The machine would require an increase in net working capital (inventory) of $5,500. The milling machine would have no effect on revenues, but it is expected to save the firm $44,000 per year in before-tax operating costs, mainly labor. Campbell's marginal tax rate is 35%.

a. What is the net cost of the machine for capital budgeting purposes? (That is, what is the Year-0 net cash flow?)
b. What are the net operating cash flows in Years 1, 2, and 3?

c. What is the additional Year-3 cash flow (i.e., the after-tax salvage and the return of working capital)?
d. If the project's cost of capital is 12%, should the machine be purchased?

(11–7)
New-Project Analysis

You have been asked by the president of your company to evaluate the proposed acquisition of a new spectrometer for the firm's R&D department. The equipment's basic price is $70,000, and it would cost another $15,000 to modify it for special use by your firm. The spectrometer, which falls into the MACRS 3-year class, would be sold after 3 years for $30,000. Use of the equipment would require an increase in net working capital (spare parts inventory) of $4,000. The spectrometer would have no effect on revenues, but it is expected to save the firm $25,000 per year in before-tax operating costs, mainly labor. The firm's marginal federal-plus-state tax rate is 40%.

a. What is the net cost of the spectrometer? (That is, what is the Year-0 net cash flow?)
b. What are the net operating cash flows in Years 1, 2, and 3?
c. What is the additional (nonoperating) cash flow in Year 3?
d. If the project's cost of capital is 10%, should the spectrometer be purchased?

(11–8)
Inflation Adjustments

The Rodriguez Company is considering an average-risk investment in a mineral water spring project that has a cost of $150,000. The project will produce 1,000 cases of mineral water per year indefinitely. The current sales price is $138 per case, and the current cost per case is $105. The firm is taxed at a rate of 34%. Both prices and costs are expected to rise at a rate of 6% per year. The firm uses only equity, and it has a cost of capital of 15%. Assume that cash flows consist only of after-tax profits, since the spring has an indefinite life and will not be depreciated.

a. Should the firm accept the project? (*Hint:* The project is a perpetuity, so you must use the formula for a perpetuity to find its NPV.)
b. Suppose that total costs consisted of a fixed cost of $10,000 per year plus variable costs of $95 per unit, and suppose that only the variable costs were expected to increase with inflation. Would this make the project better or worse? Continue to assume that the sales price will rise with inflation.

(11–9)
Replacement Analysis

The Taylor Toy Corporation currently uses an injection-molding machine that was purchased 2 years ago. This machine is being depreciated on a straight-line basis, and it has 6 years of remaining life. Its current book value is $2,100, and it can be sold for $2,500 at this time. Thus, the annual depreciation expense is $2,100/6 = $350 per year. If the old machine is not replaced, it can be sold for $500 at the end of its useful life.

Taylor is offered a replacement machine that has a cost of $8,000, an estimated useful life of 6 years, and an estimated salvage value of $800. This machine falls into the MACRS 5-year class, so the applicable depreciation rates are 20%, 32%, 19%, 12%, 11%, and 6%. The replacement machine would permit an output expansion, so sales would rise by $1,000 per year; even so, the new machine's much greater efficiency would reduce operating expenses by $1,500 per year. The new machine would require that inventories be increased by $2,000, but accounts payable would simultaneously increase by $500. Taylor's marginal federal-plus-state tax rate is 40%, and its WACC is 15%. Should it replace the old machine?

(11–10)
Replacement Analysis

St. Johns River Shipyards is considering the replacement of an 8-year-old riveting machine with a new one that will increase earnings before depreciation from $27,000 to $54,000 per year. The new machine will cost $82,500, and it will have an estimated life of 8 years and no salvage value. The new machine will be depreciated over its 5-year MACRS recovery period, so the applicable depreciation rates are 20%, 32%, 19%, 12%, 11%, and 6%. The applicable corporate tax rate is 40%, and the firm's WACC is 12%. The old machine has been fully depreciated and has no salvage value. Should the old riveting machine be replaced by the new one?

Challenging Problems 11–17

(11–11)
Scenario Analysis

Shao Industries is considering a proposed project for its capital budget. The company estimates the project's NPV is $12 million. This estimate assumes that the economy and market conditions will be average over the next few years. The company's CFO, however, forecasts there is only a 50% chance that the economy will be average. Recognizing this uncertainty, she has also performed the following scenario analysis:

Economic Scenario	Probability of Outcome	NPV
Recession	0.05	–$70 million
Below average	0.20	–25 million
Average	0.50	12 million
Above average	0.20	20 million
Boom	0.05	30 million

What is the project's expected NPV, its standard deviation, and its coefficient of variation?

(11–12)
New-Project Analysis

Madison Manufacturing is considering a new machine that costs $250,000 and would reduce pre-tax manufacturing costs by $90,000 annually. Madison would use the 3-year MACRS method to depreciate the machine, and management thinks the machine would have a value of $23,000 at the end of its 5-year operating life. The applicable depreciation rates are 33%, 45%, 15%, and 7%, as discussed in Appendix 11A. Working capital would increase by $25,000 initially, but it would be recovered at the end of the project's 5-year life. Madison's marginal tax rate is 40%, and a 10% WACC is appropriate for the project.

a. Calculate the project's NPV, IRR, MIRR, and payback.
b. Assume management is unsure about the $90,000 cost savings—this figure could deviate by as much as plus or minus 20%. What would the NPV be under each of these extremes?
c. Suppose the CFO wants you to do a scenario analysis with different values for the cost savings, the machine's salvage value, and the working capital (WC) requirement. She asks you to use the following probabilities and values in the scenario analysis:

Scenario	Probability	Cost Savings	Salvage Value	WC
Worst case	0.35	$ 72,000	$18,000	$30,000
Base case	0.35	90,000	23,000	25,000
Best case	0.30	108,000	28,000	20,000

Calculate the project's expected NPV, its standard deviation, and its coefficient of variation. Would you recommend that the project be accepted?

(11–13)
Replacement Analysis

The Everly Equipment Company purchased a machine 5 years ago at a cost of $90,000. The machine had an expected life of 10 years at the time of purchase, and it is being depreciated by the straight-line method by $9,000 per year. If the machine is not replaced, it can be sold for $10,000 at the end of its useful life.

A new machine can be purchased for $150,000, including installation costs. During its 5-year life, it will reduce cash operating expenses by $50,000 per year. Sales are not expected to change. At the end of its useful life, the machine is estimated to be worthless. MACRS depreciation will be used, and the machine will be depreciated over its 3-year class life rather than its 5-year economic life, so the applicable depreciation rates are 33%, 45%, 15%, and 7%.

The old machine can be sold today for $55,000. The firm's tax rate is 35%, and the appropriate WACC is 16%.

a. If the new machine is purchased, what is the amount of the initial cash flow at Year 0?
b. What are the incremental net cash flows that will occur at the end of Years 1 through 5?
c. What is the NPV of this project? Should Everly replace the old machine?

(11–14)
Replacement Analysis

The Balboa Bottling Company is contemplating the replacement of one of its bottling machines with a newer and more efficient one. The old machine has a book value of $600,000 and a remaining useful life of 5 years. The firm does not expect to realize any return from scrapping the old machine in 5 years, but it can sell it now to another firm in the industry for $265,000. The old machine is being depreciated by $120,000 per year, using the straight-line method.

The new machine has a purchase price of $1,175,000, an estimated useful life and MACRS class life of 5 years, and an estimated salvage value of $145,000. The applicable depreciation rates are 20%, 32%, 19%, 12%, 11%, and 6%. It is expected to economize on electric power usage, labor, and repair costs, as well as to reduce the number of defective bottles. In total, an annual savings of $255,000 will be realized if the new machine is installed. The company's marginal tax rate is 35%, and it has a 12% WACC.

a. What is the initial net cash flow if the new machine is purchased and the old one is replaced?
b. Calculate the annual depreciation allowances for both machines, and compute the change in the annual depreciation expense if the replacement is made.
c. What are the incremental net cash flows in Years 1 through 5?
d. Should the firm purchase the new machine? Support your answer.
e. In general, how would each of the following factors affect the investment decision, and how should each be treated?
   (1) The expected life of the existing machine decreases.
   (2) The WACC is not constant but is increasing as Balboa adds more projects into its capital budget for the year.

(11–15)
Risky Cash Flows

The Bartram-Pulley Company (BPC) must decide between two mutually exclusive investment projects. Each project costs $6,750 and has an expected life of 3 years. Annual net cash flows from each project begin 1 year after the initial investment is made and have the following probability distributions:

Project A		Project B	
Probability	Net Cash Flows	Probability	Net Cash Flows
0.2	$ 6,000	0.2	$ 0
0.6	6,750	0.6	6,750
0.2	7,500	0.2	18,000

BPC has decided to evaluate the riskier project at a 12% rate and the less risky project at a 10% rate.

a. What is the expected value of the annual net cash flows from each project? What is the coefficient of variation (CV)? (*Hint:* σ_B = $5,798 and CV_B = 0.76.)
b. What is the risk-adjusted NPV of each project?
c. If it were known that Project B is negatively correlated with other cash flows of the firm whereas Project A is positively correlated, how would this affect the decision? If Project B's cash flows were negatively correlated with gross domestic product (GDP), would that influence your assessment of its risk?

(11–16) Simulation

Singleton Supplies Corporation (SSC) manufactures medical products for hospitals, clinics, and nursing homes. SSC may introduce a new type of X-ray scanner designed to identify certain types of cancers in their early stages. There are a number of uncertainties about the proposed project, but the following data are believed to be reasonably accurate.

Probability	Developmental Costs	Random Numbers
0.3	$2,000,000	00–29
0.4	4,000,000	30–69
0.3	6,000,000	70–99

Probability	Project Life	Random Numbers
0.2	3 years	00–19
0.6	8 years	20–79
0.2	13 years	80–99

Probability	Sales in Units	Random Numbers
0.2	100	00–19
0.6	200	20–79
0.2	300	80–99

Probability	Sales Price	Random Numbers
0.1	$13,000	00–09
0.8	13,500	10–89
0.1	14,000	90–99

Probability	Cost per Unit (Excluding Developmental Costs)	Random Numbers
0.3	$5,000	00–29
0.4	6,000	30–69
0.3	7,000	70–99

SSC uses a cost of capital of 15% to analyze average-risk projects, 12% for low-risk projects, and 18% for high-risk projects. These risk adjustments primarily reflect the uncertainty about each project's NPV and IRR as measured by their coefficients of variation. The firm is in the 40% federal-plus-state income tax bracket.

a. What is the expected IRR for the X-ray scanner project? Base your answer on the expected values of the variables. Also, assume the after-tax "profits" figure that you develop is equal to annual cash flows. All facilities are leased, so depreciation may be disregarded. Can you determine the value of σ_{IRR} short of actual simulation or a fairly complex statistical analysis?
b. Assume that SSC uses a 15% cost of capital for this project. What is the project's NPV? Could you estimate σ_{NPV} without either simulation or a complex statistical analysis?
c. Show the process by which a computer would perform a simulation analysis for this project. Use the random numbers 44, 17, 16, 58, 1; 79, 83, 86; and 19, 62, 6 to illustrate the process with the first computer run. Actually calculate the first-run NPV and IRR. Assume the cash flows for each year are independent of cash flows for other years. Also, assume the computer operates as follows: (1) A developmental cost and a project life are estimated for the first run using the first two random numbers. (2) Next, sales volume, sales price, and cost per unit are estimated using the next three random numbers and used to derive a cash flow for the first year. (3) Then, the next three random numbers are used to estimate sales volume, sales price, and cost per unit for the second year, hence the cash flow for the second year. (4) Cash flows for other years are developed similarly, on out to the first run's estimated life. (5) With the developmental cost and the cash flow stream established, NPV and IRR for the first run are derived and stored in the computer's memory. (6) The process is repeated to generate perhaps 500 other NPVs and IRRs. (7) Frequency distributions for NPV and IRR are plotted by the computer, and the distributions' means and standard deviations are calculated.

(11–17) Decision Tree

The Yoran Yacht Company (YYC), a prominent sailboat builder in Newport, may design a new 30-foot sailboat based on the "winged" keels first introduced on the 12-meter yachts that raced for the America's Cup.

First, YYC would have to invest $10,000 at t = 0 for the design and model tank testing of the new boat. YYC's managers believe there is a 60% probability that this phase will be successful and the project will continue. If Stage 1 is not successful, the project will be abandoned with zero salvage value.

The next stage, if undertaken, would consist of making the molds and producing two prototype boats. This would cost $500,000 at t = 1. If the boats test well, YYC would go into production. If they do not, the molds and prototypes could be sold for $100,000. The managers estimate the probability is 80% that the boats will pass testing and that Stage 3 will be undertaken.

Stage 3 consists of converting an unused production line to produce the new design. This would cost $1 million at t = 2. If the economy is strong at this point, the net value of sales would be $3 million; if the economy is weak, the net value would be $1.5 million. Both net values occur at t = 3, and each state of the economy has a probability of 0.5. YYC's corporate cost of capital is 12%.

a. Assume this project has average risk. Construct a decision tree and determine the project's expected NPV.
b. Find the project's standard deviation of NPV and coefficient of variation of NPV. If YYC's average project had a CV of between 1.0 and 2.0, would this project be of high, low, or average stand-alone risk?

SPREADSHEET PROBLEM

(11-18) Build a Model: Issues in Capital Budgeting

Start with the partial model in the file ***Ch11 P18 Build a Model.xls*** on the textbook's Web site. Webmasters.com has developed a powerful new server that would be used for corporations' Internet activities. It would cost $10 million at Year 0 to buy the equipment necessary to manufacture the server. The project would require net working capital at the beginning of a year in an amount equal to 10% of the year's projected sales: $NOWC_0$ = 10%($Sales_1$). The servers would sell for $24,000 per unit, and Webmasters believes that variable costs would amount to $17,500 per unit. After Year 1, the sales price and variable costs will increase at the inflation rate of 3%. The company's nonvariable costs would be $1 million at Year 1 and would increase with inflation.

The server project would have a life of 4 years. If the project is undertaken, it must be continued for the entire 4 years. Also, the project's returns are expected to be highly correlated with returns on the firm's other assets. The firm believes it could sell 1,000 units per year.

The equipment would be depreciated over a 5-year period, using MACRS rates. The estimated market value of the equipment at the end of the project's 4-year life is $500,000. Webmasters' federal-plus-state tax rate is 40%. Its cost of capital is 10% for average-risk projects, defined as projects with an NPV coefficient of variation between 0.8 and 1.2. Low-risk projects are evaluated with a WACC of 8% and high-risk projects at 13%.

a. Develop a spreadsheet model, and use it to find the project's NPV, IRR, and payback.

b. Now conduct a sensitivity analysis to determine the sensitivity of NPV to changes in the sales price, variable costs per unit, and number of units sold. Set these variables' values at 10% and 20% above and below their base-case values. Include a graph in your analysis.

c. Now conduct a scenario analysis. Assume that there is a 25% probability that best-case conditions, with each of the variables discussed in part b being 20% better than its base-case value, will occur. There is a 25% probability of worst-case conditions, with the variables 20% worse than base, and a 50% probability of base-case conditions.

d. If the project appears to be more or less risky than an average project, find its risk-adjusted NPV, IRR, and payback.

e. On the basis of information in the problem, would you recommend that the project be accepted?

Mini Case

Shrieves Casting Company is considering adding a new line to its product mix, and the capital budgeting analysis is being conducted by Sidney Johnson, a recently graduated MBA. The production line would be set up in unused space in Shrieves's main plant. The machinery's invoice price would be approximately $200,000, another $10,000 in shipping charges would be required, and it would cost an additional $30,000 to install the equipment. The machinery has an economic life of 4 years, and Shrieves has obtained a special tax ruling that places the equipment in the MACRS 3-year class. The machinery is expected to have a salvage value of $25,000 after 4 years of use.

The new line would generate incremental sales of 1,250 units per year for 4 years at an incremental cost of $100 per unit in the first year, excluding depreciation. Each unit can be sold for $200 in the first year. The sales price and cost are both expected to increase by 3% per year due to inflation. Further, to handle the new line, the firm's net working capital would have to increase by an amount equal to 12% of sales revenues. The firm's tax rate is 40%, and its overall weighted average cost of capital is 10%.

a. Define "incremental cash flow."

(1) Should you subtract interest expense or dividends when calculating project cash flow?

(2) Suppose the firm had spent $100,000 last year to rehabilitate the production line site. Should this be included in the analysis? Explain.

(3) Now assume the plant space could be leased out to another firm at $25,000 per year. Should this be included in the analysis? If so, how?

(4) Finally, assume that the new product line is expected to decrease sales of the firm's other lines by $50,000 per year. Should this be considered in the analysis? If so, how?

b. Disregard the assumptions in part a. What is Shrieves's depreciable basis? What are the annual depreciation expenses?

c. Calculate the annual sales revenues and costs (other than depreciation). Why is it important to include inflation when estimating cash flows?

d. Construct annual incremental operating cash flow statements.

e. Estimate the required net working capital for each year and the cash flow due to investments in net working capital.

f. Calculate the after-tax salvage cash flow.

g. Calculate the net cash flows for each year. Based on these cash flows, what are the project's NPV, IRR, MIRR, PI, payback, and discounted payback? Do these indicators suggest that the project should be undertaken?

h. What does the term "risk" mean in the context of capital budgeting; to what extent can risk be quantified; and, when risk is quantified, is the quantification based primarily on statistical analysis of historical data or on subjective, judgmental estimates?

i. (1) What are the three types of risk that are relevant in capital budgeting?

(2) How is each of these risk types measured, and how do they relate to one another?

(3) How is each type of risk used in the capital budgeting process?

j. (1) What is sensitivity analysis?

(2) Perform a sensitivity analysis on the unit sales, salvage value, and cost of capital for the project. Assume each of these variables can vary from its base-case, or expected, value by ±10%, ±20%, and ±30%. Include a sensitivity diagram, and discuss the results.

(3) What is the primary weakness of sensitivity analysis? What is its primary usefulness?

k. Assume that Sidney Johnson is confident in her estimates of all the variables that affect the project's cash flows except unit sales and sales price. If product acceptance is poor, unit sales would be only 900 units a year and the unit price would only be $160; a strong consumer response would produce sales of 1,600 units and a unit price of $240. Johnson believes there is a 25% chance of poor acceptance, a 25% chance of excellent acceptance, and a 50% chance of average acceptance (the base case).

(1) What is scenario analysis?

(2) What is the worst-case NPV? The best-case NPV?

(3) Use the worst-, base-, and best-case NPVs and probabilities of occurrence to find the project's expected NPV, as well as the NPV's standard deviation and coefficient of variation.

l. Are there problems with scenario analysis? Define simulation analysis, and discuss its principal advantages and disadvantages.

m. (1) Assume Shrieves's average project has a coefficient of variation in the range of 0.2 to 0.4. Would the new line be classified as high risk, average risk, or low risk? What type of risk is being measured here?

(2) Shrieves typically adds or subtracts 3 percentage points to the overall cost of capital to adjust for risk. Should the new line be accepted?

(3) Are there any subjective risk factors that should be considered before the final decision is made?

n. What is a real option? What are some types of real options?

Selected Additional Cases

The following cases from Textchoice, *Cengage Learning's online library, cover many of the concepts discussed in this chapter and are available at* ***http://www.textchoice2.com.***

Klein-Brigham Series:
Case 12, "Indian River Citrus Company (A)," Case 44, "Cranfield, Inc. (A)," and Case 14, "Robert Montoya, Inc.," focus on cash flow estimation. Case 13, "Indian River Citrus (B)," Case 45, "Cranfield, Inc. (B)," Case 58, "Tasty Foods (B)," Case 60, "Heavenly Foods," and Case 15, "Robert Montoya, Inc. (B)," illustrate project risk analysis. Cases 75, 76, and 77, "The Western Company (A and B)," are comprehensive cases.

Brigham-Buzzard Series:
Case 7, "Powerline Network Corporation (Risk and Real Options in Capital Budgeting)."

APPENDIX 11A
Tax Depreciation

Companies often calculate depreciation one way when figuring taxes and another way when reporting income to investors: Many use the **straight-line method** for stockholder reporting (or "book" purposes), but they use the fastest rate permitted by law for tax purposes. Under the straight-line method used for stockholder reporting, one normally takes the cost of the asset, subtracts its estimated salvage value, and divides the net amount by the asset's useful economic life. For example, consider an asset with a 5-year life that costs $100,000 and has a $12,500 salvage value; its annual straight-line depreciation charge is ($100,000 − $12,500)/5 = $17,500. Note, however, as we stated earlier, salvage value is a factor in financial reporting but it is *not* considered for tax depreciation purposes.

For tax purposes, Congress changes the permissible tax depreciation methods from time to time. Prior to 1954, the straight-line method was required for tax purposes, but in 1954 **accelerated methods** (double-declining balance and sum-of-years'-digits) were permitted. Then, in 1981, the old accelerated methods were replaced by a simpler procedure known as the Accelerated Cost Recovery System (ACRS). The ACRS system was changed again in 1986 as a part of the Tax Reform Act, and it is now known as the **Modified Accelerated Cost Recovery System (MACRS)**; a 1993 tax law made further changes in this area.

Note that U.S. tax laws are complicated, and in this text we can provide only an overview of MACRS that will give you a basic understanding of the impact of depreciation on capital budgeting decisions. Further, the tax laws change so often that the numbers we present may be outdated before the book is even published. Thus, when dealing with tax depreciation in real-world situations, current Internal Revenue Service (IRS) publications or individuals with expertise in tax matters should be consulted.

For tax purposes, the entire cost of an asset is expensed over its depreciable life. Historically, an asset's depreciable life was set equal to its estimated useful economic life; it was intended that an asset would be fully depreciated at approximately the same time that it reached the end of its useful economic life. However, MACRS totally abandoned that practice and set simple guidelines that created several classes of assets, each with a more-or-less arbitrarily prescribed life called a *recovery period* or *class life*. The MACRS class lives bear only a rough relationship to assets' expected useful economic lives.

A major effect of the MACRS system has been to shorten the depreciable lives of assets, thus giving businesses larger tax deductions early in the assets' lives and thereby increasing the present value of the cash flows. Table 11A-1 describes the types of property that fit into the different class life groups, and Table 11A-2 sets forth the MACRS recovery allowance percentages (depreciation rates) for selected classes of investment property.

TABLE 11A-1 Major Classes and Asset Lives for MACRS

CLASS	TYPE OF PROPERTY
3-year	Certain special manufacturing tools
5-year	Automobiles, light-duty trucks, computers, and certain special manufacturing equipment
7-year	Most industrial equipment, office furniture, and fixtures
10-year	Certain longer-lived types of equipment
27.5-year	Residential rental real property such as apartment buildings
39-year	All nonresidential real property, including commercial and industrial buildings

TABLE 11A-2 Recovery Allowance Percentage for Personal Property

OWNERSHIP YEAR	CLASS OF INVESTMENT			
	3-YEAR	5-YEAR	7-YEAR	10-YEAR
1	33%	20%	14%	10%
2	45	32	25	18
3	15	19	17	14
4	7	12	13	12
5		11	9	9
6		6	9	7
7			9	7
8			4	7
9				7
10				6
11				3
	100%	100%	100%	100%

Notes:

[a]We developed these recovery allowance percentages based on the 200% declining balance method prescribed by MACRS, with a switch to straight-line depreciation at some point in the asset's life. For example, consider the 5-year recovery allowance percentages. The straight-line percentage would be 20% per year, so the 200% declining balance multiplier is 2.0(20%) = 40% = 0.4. However, because the half-year convention applies, the MACRS percentage for Year 1 is 20%. For Year 2, there is 80% of the depreciable basis remaining to be depreciated, so the recovery allowance percentage is 0.40(80%) = 32%. In Year 3, 20% + 32% = 52% of the depreciation has been taken, leaving 48%, so the percentage is 0.4(48%) ≈ 19%. In Year 4, the percentage is 0.4(29%) ≈ 12%. After 4 years, straight-line depreciation exceeds the declining balance depreciation, so a switch is made to straight-line (which is permitted under the law). However, the half-year convention must also be applied at the end of the class life, and the remaining 17% of depreciation must be taken (amortized) over 1.5 years. Thus, the percentage in Year 5 is 17%/1.5 ≈ 11%, and in Year 6 it is 17% − 11% = 6%. Although the tax tables carry the allowance percentages out to two decimal places, we have rounded to the nearest whole number for ease of illustration. See the worksheet ***7. App. A*** in the file ***Ch11 Tool Kit.xls*** on the textbook's Web site for the exact recovery percentages specified by the IRS.

[b]Residential rental property (apartments) is depreciated over a 27.5-year life, whereas commercial and industrial structures are depreciated over 39 years. In both cases, straight-line depreciation must be used. The depreciation allowance for the first year is based, pro rata, on the month the asset was placed in service, with the remainder of the first year's depreciation being taken in the 28th or 40th year. A half-month convention is assumed; that is, an asset placed in service in February would receive 10.5 months of depreciation in the first year.

*See **Ch11 Tool Kit.xls** on the textbook's Web site for all calculations.*

Consider Table 11A-1, which gives the MACRS class lives and the types of assets that fall into each category. Property in the 27.5- and 39-year categories (real estate) must be depreciated by the straight-line method, but 3-, 5-, 7-, and 10-year property (personal property) can be depreciated either by the accelerated method set forth in Table 11A-2 or by the straight-line method.[1]

As we saw earlier in the chapter, higher depreciation expenses result in lower taxes in the early years and hence lead to a higher present value of cash flows. Therefore, since a firm has the choice of using straight-line rates or the accelerated rates shown in Table 11A-2, most elect to use the accelerated rates.

The yearly recovery allowance, or depreciation expense, is determined by multiplying each asset's *depreciable basis* by the applicable recovery percentage shown in Table 11A-2. You might be wondering why 4 years of deprecation rates are shown for property in the 3-year class. Under MACRS, the assumption is generally made that property is placed in service in the middle of the first year. Thus, for 3-year-class property, the recovery period begins in the middle of the year the asset is placed in service and ends 3 years later. The effect of the *half-year convention* is to extend the recovery period out one more year, so 3-year-class property is depreciated over 4 calendar years, 5-year property is depreciated over 6 calendar years, and so on. This convention is incorporated into Table 11A-2's recovery allowance percentages.[2]

Self-Test

What do the acronyms ACRS and MACRS stand for?

Briefly describe the tax depreciation system under MACRS.

---

[1]The Tax Code currently (for 2009) permits companies to *expense*, which is equivalent to depreciating over 1 year, up to $125,000 of equipment; see IRS Publication 946 for details. This is a benefit primarily for small companies. Thus, if a small company bought one asset worth up to $125,000, it could write the asset off in the year it was acquired. This is called "Section 179 expensing." We shall disregard this provision throughout the book. Also, Congress enacted the Job Creation and Worker Assistance Act of 2002 following the terrorist attacks on the World Trade Center and Pentagon. This act, among other things, temporarily changed how depreciation is charged for property acquired after September 10, 2001, and before September 11, 2004, and put in service before January 1, 2005. We shall disregard this provision throughout the book as well.

[2]The half-year convention also applies if the straight-line alternative is used, with half of one year's depreciation taken in the first year, a full year's depreciation taken in each of the remaining years of the asset's class life, and the remaining half-year's depreciation taken in the year following the end of the class life. You should recognize that virtually all companies have computerized depreciation systems. Each asset's depreciation pattern is programmed into the system at the time of its acquisition, and the computer aggregates the depreciation allowances for all assets when the accountants close the books and prepare financial statements and tax returns.

PART 5

Corporate Valuation and Governance

CHAPTER 12

Financial Planning and Forecasting Financial Statements

A recent survey of CFOs disclosed a paradox regarding financial planning. On the one hand, almost all CFOs stated that financial planning is both important and highly useful for allocating resources. On the other hand, 45% also said that budgeting is "contentious, political, and time-consuming," and 53% went on to say that the budgeting process can encourage undesirable behavior among managers as they negotiate budgets to meet their own rather than the company's objectives. Further, they also said that instead of basing growth and incentive compensation targets on an analysis of what markets and competitors are likely to do in the future, firms often set their targets at last year's levels plus a percentage increase, which is dangerous in a dynamic economy.

To help resolve these issues, companies are developing a variety of new strategies. For example, demand-pull budgeting links the budget to a sales forecast, and the sales forecast is updated as needed to reflect changing economic conditions. This approach is often augmented with a rolling forecast, in which companies make 1- and 5-year forecasts but then modify the 1-year forecast each month as new operating results become available. Also, some companies have switched to activity-based budgeting, which allocates costs and revenues by products and services rather than by traditional departments.

A recent survey shows that high-performance companies also focus on the links between forecasting, planning, and business strategy rather than on just cost management and cost accounting. According to John McMahan of the Hackett Group, such changes are leading to greater forecasting accuracy, higher employee morale, and better corporate performance. These issues are often thought of as "management" rather than "finance," but this is a false distinction. Much of finance is numbers-oriented, but as any CFO will tell you, his or her primary job is to help the firm as a whole achieve good results. The procedures discussed in this chapter can help firms improve their operations and results.

Sources: J. McCafferty, "Planning for the Best," CFO, *February 2007, p. 24; and Don Durfee, "Alternative Budgeting,"* CFO, *June 2006, p. 28.*

Corporate Valuation and Financial Planning

The value of a firm is determined by the size, timing, and risk of its expected future free cash flows (FCF). This chapter explains how to project financial statements and use them to calculate expected future free cash flows under different operating plans. The next chapter takes the analysis further, showing how to identify optimal plans and then design incentive compensation systems that will lead to optimal results.

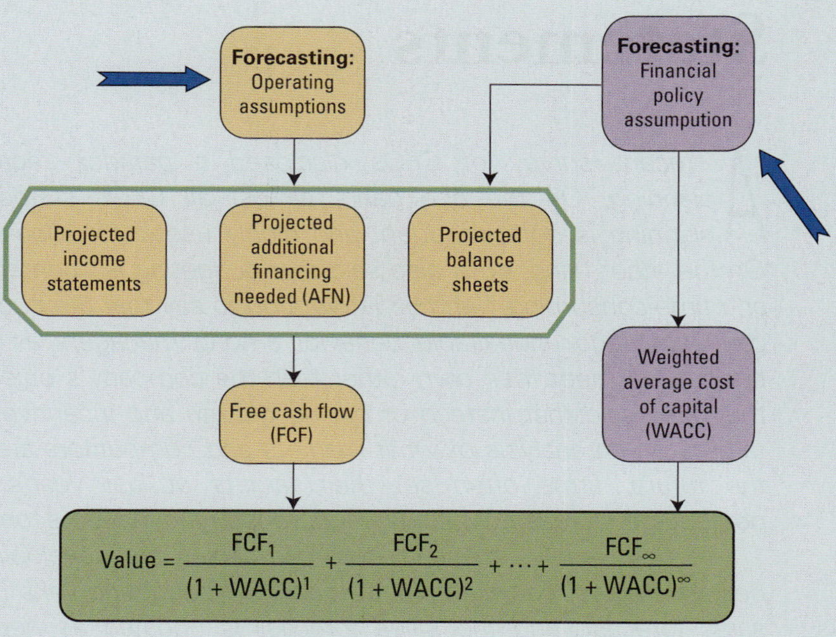

The textbook's Web site contains an Excel *file that will guide you through the chapter's calculations. The file for this chapter is* **Ch12 Tool Kit.xls**, *and we encourage you to open the file and follow along as you read the chapter.*

Our primary objective in this book is to explain how financial managers can make their companies more valuable. However, value creation is impossible unless the company has well-designed strategic and tactical operating plans. As Yogi Berra once said, "You've got to be careful if you don't know where you're going, because you might not get there."

12.1 Overview of Financial Planning

Most companies have strategic plans, operating plans, and financial plans.

Strategic Plans

Strategic plans usually have statements for mission, corporate scope, corporate objectives, and strategies.

Mission Statement. Strategic plans usually begin with a *mission statement*, which is a statement of the firm's overall purpose. Many companies are very clear about their corporate mission, and for most this is typical: "Our mission is to maximize shareowner value over time." Before the economic crisis of 2008 and 2009, many companies forgot about the "over time" part, focusing instead on "maximizing the stock price on the date the CEO's options vest." Stockholders and directors have, fortunately, brought "over time" back into focus.

The goal of creating wealth for the company's owners is not as common abroad as it is in the United States. For example, Veba AG, one of Germany's largest companies, created a stir when it made the following statement in its annual report: "Our commitment is to create value for you, our shareholders." This was quite different from the usual German model, for German companies generally have representatives from labor on their boards of directors and explicitly state their commitments to labor and a variety of other stakeholders. As one might expect, Veba's stock has consistently outperformed the average German stock. As the trend in international investing continues, more and more non-U.S. companies are adopting a corporate purpose similar to that of Veba.

Corporate Scope. A firm's corporate scope defines its line or lines of business and its geographic area of operations. For example, Coca-Cola limits its products to soft drinks, but it operates on a global scale. PepsiCo followed Coke's lead by spinning off its food service businesses, as several studies have found that the market tends to value focused firms more highly than diversified ones.[1] During the bull market that led up to the 2008–2009 crash, many companies expanded willy-nilly into things that management knew little about, seeking sales growth as much or more than profits. For example, electric utilities bought insurance companies, and conservative banks bought gun-slinging mortgage companies. Those misguided ventures led to many disasters, so today companies are paying more attention to having a reasonable corporate scope.

Statement of Corporate Objectives. This statement sets forth specific goals or targets to help operating managers focus on the firm's primary objectives. Most organizations have both quantitative and qualitative objectives. A typical quantitative objective might be attaining a 50% market share, a 20% ROE, and a 10% earnings growth rate. Qualitatively, their stated objective might be: "To provide better information systems to lower the cost and improve the efficiency of the U.S. medical system."

Corporate Strategies. Once a firm has defined its purpose, scope, and objectives, it must develop a strategy for achieving its goals. Corporate strategies are broad approaches rather than detailed plans. For example, one airline may have a strategy of offering no-frills service to a limited number of cities, while another's strategy may be to offer "a stateroom in the sky." Any such strategy should, of course, be compatible with the firm's purpose, scope, and objectives.

Overall, the strategic plan provides a "vision" of what the firm's top management expects, and without such a vision, the firm is not likely to be successful.

Operating Plans

Operating plans provide detailed implementation guidance to help the firm realize its strategic vision. These plans can be developed for any time horizon, but most companies use a 5-year horizon, with the plan being quite detailed for the first year but less and less specific for each succeeding year. The plan explains who is responsible for each particular function, when specific tasks are to be accomplished, targets for sales and profits, and the like. Large, multidivisional companies such as General Electric break their operating plans down by divisions, so each division has its own goals,

---

[1] See, for example, Philip G. Berger and Eli Ofek, "Diversification's Effect on Firm Value," *Journal of Financial Economics*, January 1995, pp. 39–66; and Larry Lang and René Stulz, "Tobin's Q, Corporate Diversification, and Firm Performance," *Journal of Political Economy*, Vol. 102, 1994, pp. 1248–1280.

mission, and plan for meeting its objectives. These plans are then consolidated to form the overall corporate plan.

The Financial Plan

The financial planning process generally involves five steps.

1. The firm forecasts financial statements under alternative versions of the operating plan in order to analyze the effects of different operating procedures on projected profits and financial ratios.
2. Next, it determines the amount of capital that will be needed to support the plan; that is, it finds out how much the new assets needed to achieve the target sales will cost, since without adequate capital, the plan obviously cannot be realized.
3. Then the firm forecasts the funds that will be generated internally. If internal funds are insufficient to cover the required new investment, then it must identify sources from which the required external capital can be raised, taking account of any constraints due to bond covenants that limit its debt ratio and other financial ratios. Market conditions must also be recognized. For example, in 2009 banks reduced many firms' lines of credit and also increased the fees and interest rates on such lines. This surprised firms that were not keeping up with conditions in financial markets.
4. The firm establishes a performance-based management compensation system that rewards employees for creating shareholder wealth. The emphasis here should be on the long run, not on profits over the next few quarters or even years. A failure in this area was perhaps the most important factor leading to the worldwide financial and economic crisis that hit in 2008 and 2009.
5. Finally, management must monitor operations after implementing the plan to spot any deviations and then take corrective actions. Computer software is helping greatly here, and it's changing the way companies do business. In particular, corporate information systems are reducing the need for "middle managers" and flattening firms' management structures.

In the remainder of this chapter, we explain how to create a financial plan, including its three key components: (1) the sales forecast, (2) forecasted financial statements, and (3) methods for raising any needed external financing. Then, in Chapter 13, we discuss in more detail the relationships among incentives, compensation, and performance.

Self-Test

Briefly explain the following terms: (1) mission statement, (2) corporate scope, (3) corporate objectives, and (4) corporate strategies.

Briefly describe the key elements of an operating plan.

Identify the five steps involved in the financial planning process as discussed in this section.

12.2 Sales Forecast

The **sales forecast** generally starts with a review of sales during the past 5 to 10 years, expressed in a graph such as that in Figure 12-1. The first part of the graph shows 5 years of historical sales for MicroDrive, the fictional firm we discussed in Chapters 2 and 3. The graph could have contained 10 years of sales data, but MicroDrive typically focuses on sales for the latest 5 years because its studies have shown that its future growth is more closely related to recent events than to the distant past.

Entire courses are devoted to forecasting sales, so we only touch on the basic elements here. However, forecasting the future sales growth rate always begins with a

FIGURE 12-1 MicroDrive Inc.: Historical Sales (Millions of Dollars)

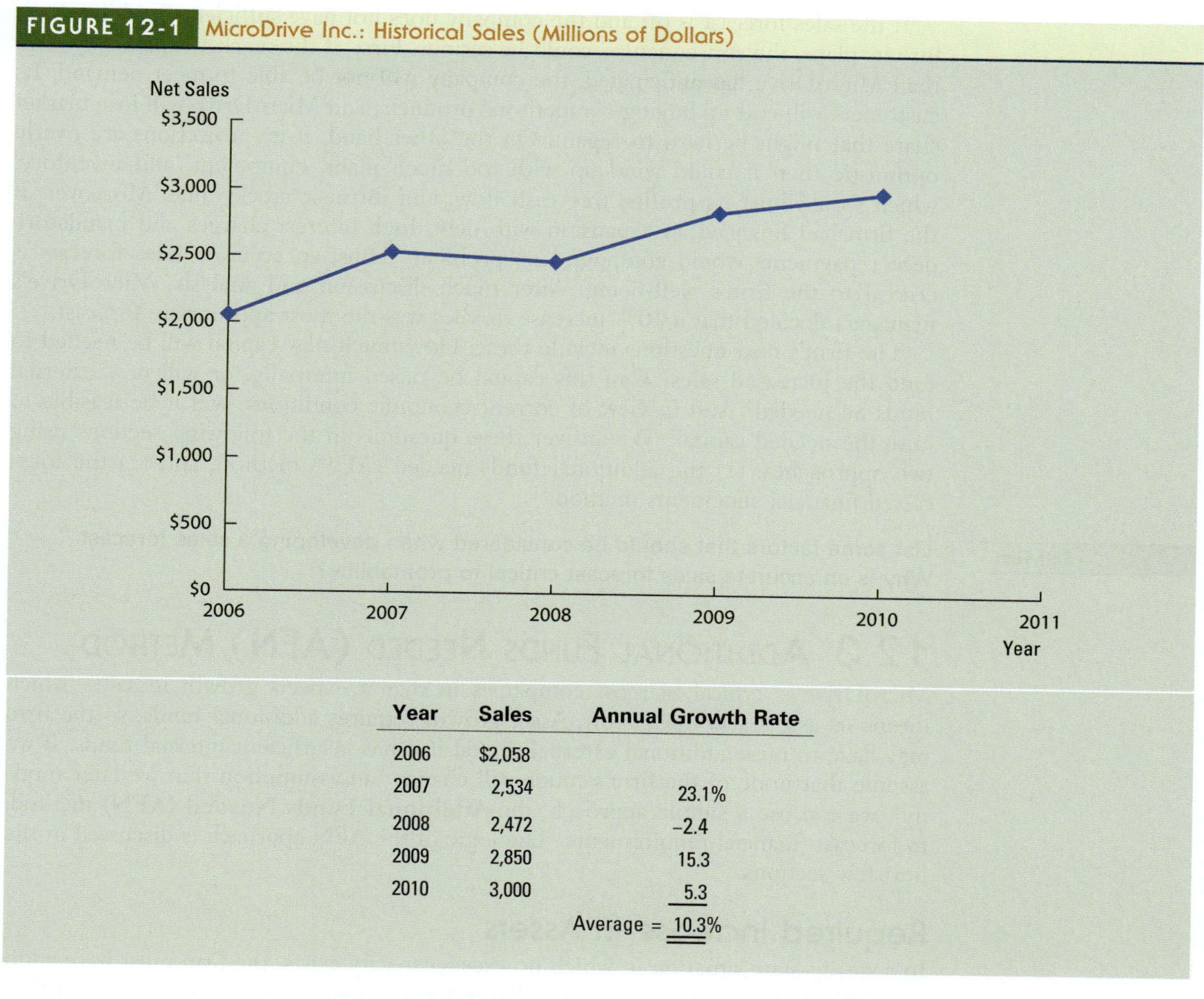

Year	Sales	Annual Growth Rate
2006	$2,058	
2007	2,534	23.1%
2008	2,472	−2.4
2009	2,850	15.3
2010	3,000	5.3
		Average = 10.3%

look at past growth. MicroDrive's recent annual growth rates have averaged 10.3%, and the compound growth rate from 2006 to 2010 is the value for g in this equation:[2]

$$\$2{,}058(1+g)^4 = \$3{,}000$$

The value of g can be found by solving the equation with a financial calculator. Enter N = 4, PV = −2058, PMT = 0, and FV = 3000; then press I/YR to get g = 9.9%.[3]

No sensible manager would ever just forecast a continuation of past sales growth without taking account of current conditions in both the national and global economies, the firm's and its competitors' new products, planned advertising programs, and so on. But in the end, a sales forecast will emerge. In MicroDrive's case, the conclusion is that sales are most likely to grow at a 10% rate. Note, though, that actual sales could turn out to be materially higher or lower, depending on a number of factors that cannot be forecasted at this time.

[2]Unless we indicate otherwise, we report values from MicroDrive's financial statements in millions of dollars, as shown in Figure 12-1.

[3]See this chapter's *Excel **Tool Kit*** for an explanation of projecting sales using a trend line or the average exponential growth rate.

If the sales forecast is off and the company does not have sufficient flexibility built into its plans, the consequences could be serious. First, if the market expands by *more* than MicroDrive has anticipated, the company will not be able to meet demand. Its customers will end up buying competitors' products, and MicroDrive will lose market share that might be hard to regain. On the other hand, if its projections are overly optimistic then it could wind up with too much plant, equipment, and inventory, which would hurt its profits, free cash flow, and intrinsic stock value. Moreover, if the firm had financed an expansion with debt, high interest charges and mandatory debt repayments would compound its problem. Thus, an accurate sales forecast is critical to the firm's well-being. After much discussion and analysis, MicroDrive's managers decided that a 10% increase in sales was the most appropriate forecast.

The firm's next questions include these: How much new capital will be needed to fund the increased sales? Can this capital be raised internally, or will new external funds be needed? And in view of current economic conditions, will it be feasible to raise the needed capital? We answer these questions in the following sections using two approaches: (1) the additional funds needed (AFN) method, and (2) the forecasted financial statements method.

Self-Test

List some factors that should be considered when developing a sales forecast.
Why is an accurate sales forecast critical to profitability?

12.3 Additional Funds Needed (AFN) Method

MicroDrive is typical of most companies in that it expects growth in sales, which means its assets also must grow. Asset growth requires additional funds, so the firm may have to raise additional external capital if it has insufficient internal funds. If we assume that none of the firm's ratios will change (an assumption that we later modify), we can use a simple approach, the **Additional Funds Needed (AFN)** method, to forecast financial requirements. The logic of the AFN approach is discussed in the next few sections.

Required Increase in Assets

In a steady-state situation in which no excess capacity exists, the firm must have additional plant and equipment, more delivery trucks, higher inventories, and so forth if sales are to increase. In addition, more sales will lead to more accounts receivable, and those receivables must be financed from the time of the sale until they are collected. Therefore, both fixed and current assets must increase if sales are to increase. Of course, if assets are to increase, liabilities and equity must also increase by a like amount to make the balance sheet balance.

Spontaneous Liabilities

The first sources of expansion funding are the "spontaneous" increases that will occur in MicroDrive's accounts payable and accrued wages and taxes. The company's suppliers give it 10 days to pay for inventory purchases, and since purchases will increase with sales, accounts payable will automatically rise. For example, if sales rise by 10% then inventory purchases will also rise by 10%, and this will cause accounts payable to rise spontaneously by the same 10%. Similarly, because the company pays workers every two weeks, more workers and a larger payroll will mean more accrued wages payable. Finally, higher expected income will mean more accrued income taxes, and its higher wage bill will mean more accrued withholding taxes. No interest normally is paid on these spontaneous funds, but their amount is limited by credit terms, contracts with workers, and tax laws. Therefore, *spontaneous funds will thus be used to the extent possible, but there is little flexibility in their usage.*

Addition to Retained Earnings

The second source of funds for expansion comes from net income. Part of MicroDrive's profit will be paid out in dividends, but the remainder will be reinvested in operating assets, as shown in the Assets section of the balance sheet; a corresponding amount will be reported as an addition to retained earnings in the Liabilities and equity section of the balance sheet. There is some flexibility in the amount of funds that will be generated from new reinvested earnings because dividends can be increased or decreased, but if the firm plans to hold its dividend steady or to increase it at a target rate, as most do, then flexibility is limited.

Calculating Additional Funds Needed (AFN)

If we start with the required new assets and then subtract both spontaneous funds and additions to retained earnings, we are left with the Additional Funds Needed, or AFN. The AFN must come from *external sources*; hence it is sometimes called EFN. The typical sources of external funds are bank loans, new long-term bonds, new preferred stock, and newly issued common stock. The mix of the external funds used should be consistent with the firm's financial policies, especially its target debt ratio.

Using MicroDrive's Data to Implement the AFN Method

Figure 12-2 reports MicroDrive's 2009 and 2010 financial statements.

FIGURE 12-2 MicroDrive's Most Recent Financial Statements (Millions of Dollars, Except for Per Share Data)

	A / B	C	D	E / F	G	H
103	INCOME STATEMENTS	2009	2010	BALANCE SHEETS	2009	2010
104				*Assets*		
105	Sales	$2,850.0	$3,000.0	Cash	$15.0	$10.0
106	Costs except depreciation	2,497.0	2,616.2	ST Investments	65.0	0.0
107	Depreciation	90.0	100.0	Accounts receivable	315.0	375.0
108	Total operating costs	$2,587.0	$2,716.2	Inventories	415.0	615.0
109	EBIT	263.0	283.8	Total current assets	$810.0	$1,000.0
110	Less interest (INT)	60.0	88.0	Net plant and equip.	870.0	1,000.0
111	Earnings before taxes (EBT)	$203.0	$195.8	Total assets	$1,680.0	$2,000.0
112	Taxes (40%)	81.2	78.3			
113	Income before pref. dividends	$121.8	$117.5	*Liabilities and equity*		
114	Preferred dividends	4.0	4.0	Accounts payable	$30.0	$60.0
115	Net income for common (NI)	$117.8	$113.5	Accruals	130.0	140.0
116				Notes payable	60.0	110.0
117	Dividends to common (DIVs)	$53.0	$57.5	Total current liab.	$220.0	$310.0
118	Add. to retained earnings:			Long-term bonds	580.0	754.0
119	(NI – DIVs)	$64.8	$56.0	Total liabilities	$800.0	$1,064.0
120	Shares of common stock	50	50	Preferred stock	40.0	40.0
121	Earnings per share (EPS)	$2.36	$2.27	Common stock	130.0	130.0
122	Dividends per share (DPS)	$1.06	$1.15	Retained earnings	710.0	766.0
123	Price per share (P)	$26.00	$23.00	Total common equity	$840.0	$896.0
124				Total liab. & equity	$1,680.0	$2,000.0
125						

FIGURE 12-3 Additional Funds Needed (AFN) (Millions of Dollars)

	A	B	C	D	E	F	G	H	I
131	Part I. Inputs and Definitions								
132	S_0:		Last year's sales, i.e., 2010 sales:						\$3,000
133	g:		Forecasted growth rate in sales:						10.000000%
134	S_1:		Coming year's sales, i.e., 2011 sales = $S_0 \times (1 + g)$:						\$3,000
135	gS_0:		Change in sales = $S_1 - S_2 = \Delta S$:						\$300
136	A_0^*:		Assets that must increase to support the increase in sales:						\$2,000
137	A_0^* / S_0:		Required assets per dollar of sales:						66.67%
138	L_0^*:		Last year's spontaneous assets, i.e., payables + accruals:						\$200
139	L_0^* / S_0:		Spontaneous liabilities per dollar of sales:						6.67%
140	Profit margin (M):		2010 profit margin = net income/sales:						3.78%
141	Payout ratio (POR):		Last year's dividends / net income = % of income paid out:						50.67%
142									
143	Part II. Additional Funds Needed (AFN) to Support Growth								
144									
145	AFN =	Required Increase in Assets		–	Spontaneous Increase		–	Addition to Retained	
146	=	$(A_0^*/S_0)\Delta S$		–	$(L_0^*/S_0)\Delta S$		–	$S_1 \times M \times (1 - POR)$	
147				–			–		
148	=	$(A_0^*/S_0)(gS_0)$		–	$(L_0^*/S_0)(gS_0)$		–	$(1{+}g)S_0 \times M \times (1 - POR)$	
149				–			–		
150	=	(0.667)(\$300)		–	(0.667)(\$300)		–	\$3,300(0.0378)(1 – 0.507)	
151	=	\$200		–	\$20.00		–	\$61.58	
152	AFN =	\$118.42 million							

Notes:

1. Under the assumed conditions, the firm must raise \$118.42 million externally to support its planned growth. However, the model assumes (1) that no excess capacity existed in 2010, so all assets were needed to produce the indicated sales; and (2) that the key ratios will remain constant at their 2010 levels. We explain later how to relax these assumptions, but it is better to use forecasted financial statements to deal with these issues, as we do on ***Tab 2*** of the *Excel* ***Tool Kit*** model.
2. Under the conditions set forth in Figure 12-3, a growth rate of 3.21% could be achieved without any AFN. This 3.21% is called the "sustainable growth rate," and we explain how it is calculated in a later section and also in the chapter's *Excel* ***Tool Kit*** model.

Equation 12-1 summarizes the logic underlying the AFN method. Figure 12-3 defines the notation in Equation 12-1 and applies it to identify MicroDrive's AFN.

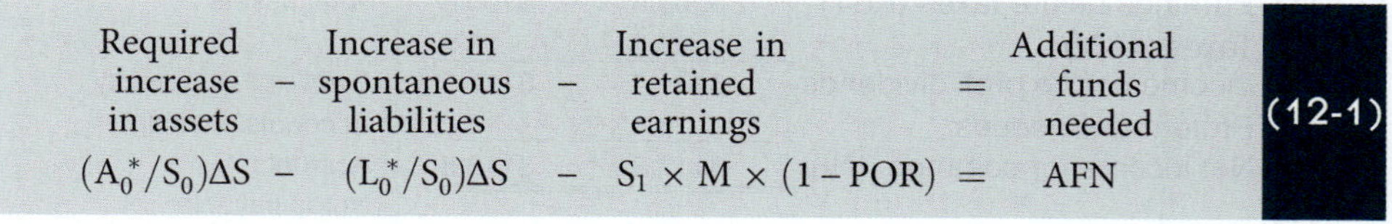

$$\begin{array}{ccccccc} \text{Required increase in assets} & - & \text{Increase in spontaneous liabilities} & - & \text{Increase in retained earnings} & = & \text{Additional funds needed} \\ (A_0^*/S_0)\Delta S & - & (L_0^*/S_0)\Delta S & - & S_1 \times M \times (1 - POR) & = & AFN \end{array} \tag{12-1}$$

We see from Part II of Figure 12-3 that, for sales to increase by \$300 million, MicroDrive must increase assets by \$200 million. Therefore, liabilities and capital must also increase by \$200 million. Of this total, \$20 million will come from spontaneous liabilities, and another \$61.58 million will come from new retained earnings. The remaining \$118.42 million must be raised from external sources—probably some combination of short-term bank loans, long-term bonds, preferred stock, and common stock.

Key Factors in the AFN Equation

The AFN equation shows that external financing requirements depend on five key factors.

1. **Sales growth (g).** Rapidly growing companies require large increases in assets and a corresponding large amount of external financing, other things held constant. When capital is in short supply, as was the case during the financial crisis of 2009, companies may be forced to limit their growth.
2. **Capital intensity (A_0*/S_0).** The amount of assets required per dollar of sales, A_0*/S_0, is the **capital intensity ratio**, which has a major effect on capital requirements. Companies with relatively high assets-to-sales ratios require a relatively large amount of new assets for any given increase in sales; hence they have a greater need for external financing. If a firm can find a way to lower this ratio—for instance, by adopting a just-in-time inventory system, by going to two shifts in its manufacturing plants, or by outsourcing rather than manufacturing parts—then it can achieve a given level of growth with fewer assets and thus less new external capital.
3. **Spontaneous liabilities-to-sales ratio (L_0*/S_0).** If a company can increase its spontaneously generated liabilities, this will reduce its need for external financing. One way of raising this ratio is by paying suppliers in, say, 20 days rather than 10 days. Such a change may be possible but, as we shall see in Chapter 16, it would probably have serious adverse consequences.
4. **Profit margin (M = Net Income/Sales).** The higher the profit margin, the more net income is available to support increases in assets—and hence the less the need for external financing. A firms' profit margin is normally as high as management can get it, but sometimes a change in operations can boost the sales price or reduce costs, thus raising the margin further. If so, this will permit a faster growth rate with less external capital.
5. **Payout Ratio (POR = DPS/EPS).** The less of its income a company distributes as dividends, the larger its addition to retained earnings—and hence the less its need for external capital. Companies typically like to keep their dividends stable or to increase them at a steady rate—stockholders like stable, dependable dividends, so such a dividend policy will generally lower the cost of equity and thus maximize the stock price. So even though reducing the dividend is one way a company can reduce its need for external capital, companies generally resort to this method only if they are under financial duress.

The Self-Supporting Growth Rate

One interesting question is: "What is the maximum growth rate the firm could achieve if it had no access to external capital?" This rate is called the "self-supporting growth rate," and it can be found as the value of g that, when used in the AFN equation, results in an AFN of zero. We first replace ΔS in the AFN equation with gS_0 and S_1 with $(1+g)S_0$ so that the only unknown is g; then we then solve for g to obtain the following equation for the self-supporting growth rate:

$$\text{Self-supporting g} = \frac{M(1 - POR)(S_0)}{A_0* - L_0* - M(1 - POR)(S_0)} \quad (12\text{-}2)$$

The definitions of the terms used in this equation are shown in Figure 12-3.

If the firm has any positive earnings and pays out less than 100% in dividends, then it will have some additions to retained earnings, and those additions could be combined with spontaneous funds to enable the company to grow at some rate without having to raise external capital. As explained in the chapter's *Excel* ***Tool Kit***, this value can be found either algebraically or with *Excel*'s Goal Seek function. For MicroDrive, the self-supporting growth rate is 3.21%; this means it could grow at that rate even if capital markets dried up completely, with everything else held constant.

See **Ch12 Tool Kit.xls** *on the textbook's Web site for details.*

A Potential Problem with the AFN Equation: Excess Capacity

As noted previously, when we use the AFN equation we are implicitly assuming that the key ratios remain constant at their base-year levels. However, this assumption may not always be true. For example, in 2010 many firms were operating at significantly less than their full capacity because of the recession. Let's suppose MicroDrive had been operating its fixed assets at only 50% of capacity. It could then double its sales, which is a 100% increase, without adding any fixed assets at all. Similarly, if it had 25% more inventories at the start of the year than it required, it could increase sales by 25% without increasing its inventories. We could adjust the AFN equation to account for excess capacity, and we explain how to do so in the ***Tool Kit.*** However, a far better procedure is simply to recognize that while the AFN is useful for quickly obtaining a "back of the envelope" estimate of external financing requirements, the forecasted financial statements method, which is explained in the next section, is vastly superior for realistic financial planning.

Self-Test

If all ratios are expected to remain constant, an equation can be used to forecast AFN. Write out the equation and briefly explain it.

Describe how do the following factors affect external capital requirements: (1) payout ratio, (2) capital intensity, (3) profit margin.

In what sense do accounts payable and accruals provide "spontaneous funds" to a growing firm?

Is it possible for the calculated AFN to be negative? If so, what would this imply?

Refer to data in the MicroDrive example presented, but now assume that MicroDrive's growth rate in sales is forecasted to be 15% rather than 10%. If all ratios remain constant, what would the AFN be? **($205.62 million)**

12.4 Forecasted Financial Statements Method

As its name implies, the objective of the **forecasted financial statements (FFS) method** is to project a complete set of financial statements. Because financial statements contain numerous accounts, forecasting is almost always done using computer software such as *Excel.* As you have probably experienced in your own spreadsheets, there are many different ways to solve a particular problem, and this is also true when forecasting financial statements. In fact, entire books have been written on the topic.[4] In the following analysis, we explain one particular approach that we have found to be effective, particularly for a company considering changes to its capital structures

[4]For a much more detailed treatment of financial forecasting, see P. Daves, M. Ehrhardt, and R. Shrieves, *Corporate Valuation: A Guide for Managers and Investors* (Mason, OH: Thomson/South-Western, 2004).

or dividend policy.[5] In addition, it is easy to modify this forecasting approach to incorporate changes in assumptions.

Forecasting financial statements is conceptually similar to the AFN equation, but it is easy to get lost in the details. *Excel*'s calculations don't necessarily follow this sequence, but keep these conceptual steps in mind as we describe MicroDrive's forecasted financial statements.

1. Forecast the operating items on the income statement and balance sheet; these include sales, costs, operating assets, and spontaneous operating liabilities. Notice that these are the items required to calculate free cash flow.
2. Forecast items that depend on the firm's choice of financial policies, such as the dividend payout policy and the planned financing from debt and equity.
3. Forecast interest expense and preferred dividends, given the levels of debt and preferred stock that were forecast according to the financing plan.
4. Use the forecasted interest expense and preferred dividends to complete the income statement.
5. Determine the total common dividend payments.
6. Issue or repurchase additional common stock to make the balance sheets balance.

Forecasting is an iterative process. It begins with a set of initial operating assumptions and financial policies. The resulting forecasted statements are used to estimate free cash flow, EPS, and financial ratios. Managers then go through a set of "what if" questions and examine their operating assumptions and financial policies, as we describe next.

Background on the Company and the Forecast

MicroDrive's board recently installed a new management team: a new CEO, CFO, marketing manager, sales manager, inventory manager, and credit manager—only the production manager was retained. The new team was charged with improving the company's performance. As we noted in Chapter 3, many of MicroDrive's ratios are below industry averages.

The management team met in late 2010, when the industry was in a recession, for a 3-day retreat. The new CFO developed an *Excel* model to forecast financial statements under several different sets of assumptions, or scenarios. The first scenario assumes that operations maintain the status quo, the second that operations improve, and the third that conditions deteriorate. During the 3-day meeting, the CFO developed a fourth scenario based on discussions among the managers regarding changes that could be made to improve the firm's performance. (We report the details of these discussions in a later section.) They concluded that many changes could be implemented almost immediately and that the effects of those changes would be reflected in the 2011 results.

[5]One point about *Excel* models is worth noting. It is generally fairly easy to set up a model to study a given issue, but the complexity of the model rises exponentially as you attempt to deal with more and more different issues within the model. Therefore, in our experience it's generally better to develop limited-scope, single-issue models and then modify them to create new models—rather than trying to develop one model that can "do everything." Also, and crucially, it's much easier to debug single-purpose models than all-inclusive ones. Furthermore, if others are planning to use and perhaps modify the model, it's far easier for them to work with a simple model. There have been numerous occasions when we were given a complex model, had a hard time understanding it, and then abandoned it to make our own model that could do what we needed. These statements about "keeping it simple" are, of course, more appropriate for time-constrained students than for business people.

See **Ch12 Tool Kit.xls** on the textbook's Web site for details.

Input Data for the Forecast: Alternative Scenarios

The forecast begins with Figure 12-4, which shows the data used in the three preliminary forecasts as well as the final forecast. Industry averages and MicroDrive's actual operating and financial data for the most recent year are given in Columns C and D. Ignore Column E for the moment and look at Columns F, G, H, and I, which show the inputs used in four alternative scenarios.

Inputs for the Status Quo Scenario. The Status Quo scenario in Column F assumes that the firm in 2011 has essentially the same operating and financial ratios as it had in 2010, except that its rate of sales growth increases from 5.26% to 10%. Operating costs, operating assets, and operating spontaneous liabilities are assumed to be the same percentage of sales in 2011 as in 2010. Depreciation is assumed to be a fixed percentage of the net plant and equipment.

The components of MicroDrive's investor-supplied capital are notes payable, long-term bonds, preferred stock, and common equity. For this initial forecast, the target proportions of these components as percentages of total investor-supplied capital are held constant. The interest rates on its debt and the dividend rate on its preferred stock are assumed to remain at 2010 levels. The payout ratio for total common dividends is also assumed to stay at the 2010 level in the Status Quo scenario.

If additional financing is needed, it is assumed that new shares of common stock can be issued at $23 per share, the 2010 year-end price. If a surplus of funds arises, then MicroDrive will pay down some of its debt and repurchase shares of preferred and common stock.

Inputs for the Best-Case Scenario. The data in Column G are for the Best case. Here the CEO assumes that MicroDrive is able to achieve industry average operating

FIGURE 12-4 Input Data for the Forecast (Millions, Except for Percentages and Per Share Data)

	A	B	C	D	E	F	G	H	I
85			2010			2011			
86	Inputs		Actual Values			Forecasted Input Values for Scenarios			
87					Active				
88			Industry	MicroDrive	Scenario:				
89	Operating Ratios:				Final	Status Quo	Best	Worst	Final
90	Growth rate in sales		10.00%	5.26%	10.00%	10.00%	10.00%	−10.00%	10.00%
91	Op costs except depr'n / Sales		83.00%	87.21%	86.00%	87.21%	83.00%	92.21%	86.00%
92	Depr'n / Net plant & equip.		10.20%	10.00%	10.20%	10.00%	10.00%	10.00%	10.20%
93	Cash / Sales		0.25%	0.33%	0.25%	0.33%	0.33%	0.33%	0.25%
94	Accounts Rec. / Sales		9.80%	12.50%	11.00%	12.50%	9.80%	15.00%	11.00%
95	Inventory / Sales		11.11%	20.50%	16.00%	20.50%	11.11%	25.50%	16.00%
96	Net plant & equip. / Sales		33.33%	33.33%	33.33%	33.33%	33.33%	40.00%	33.33%
97	Accounts Pay. / Sales		2.00%	2.00%	2.00%	2.00%	2.00%	2.00%	2.00%
98	Accruals / Sales		4.00%	4.67%	4.00%	4.67%	2.00%	4.67%	4.00%
99	Tax rate:		40.00%	40.00%	40.00%	40.00%	40.00%	40.00%	40.00%
100	Financing Data:								
101	Notes payable/Investor-sup cap		5.00%	6.11%	5.00%	6.11%	6.11%	6.11%	5.00%
102	LT bonds/Investor-sup capital		32.00%	41.89%	37.00%	41.89%	41.89%	41.89%	37.00%
103	Pref.stock/Investor-sup cap.		3.00%	2.22%	3.00%	2.22%	2.22%	2.22%	3.00%
104	Comm equity/Investor-sup cap		60.00%	49.78%	55.00%	49.78%	49.78%	49.78%	55.00%
105	Interest rate on notes payable		8.00%	9.00%	8.50%	9.00%	8.50%	11.00%	8.50%
106	Interest rate on L-T bonds		10.00%	11.00%	10.50%	11.00%	10.50%	11.50%	10.50%
107	Dividend rate on pfd stock		9.00%	10.00%	9.50%	10.00%	9.50%	10.00%	9.50%
108	Target dividend payout ratio		40.00%	50.67%	40.00%	50.67%	50.67%	50.67%	40.00%

results immediately. However, the CEO also assumes that the company continues to use its current capital structure, which calls for more debt than the industry average. The improved operating performance would lower the costs of debt and preferred stock. However, the higher than average debt level would offset this factor to some extent, so the end result would be somewhat higher than industry average cost rates for notes payable, long-term debt, and preferred stock.

Inputs for the Worst-Case Scenario. The data in Column H, the Worst case, assume a continued long, bad recession, in which case the growth rate would be negative and the operating and financial ratios would be poor. It is likely that the stock price would decline during the year, but the CFO assumes that new shares could still have been issued at the beginning of the year for $23 per share, before investors and managers learned how bad things were going to get.

Inputs for the Final Scenario. The fourth set of input data, given in Column I and called "Final," was developed during the 3-day management conference held in late 2010. All of the operating executives were there, and all aspects of the business (including the ratios shown in Figure 12-4) were discussed. Some of the executives were relatively optimistic while others were relatively pessimistic, but all tried their best to be realistic. We will discuss these Final inputs in the next section.

Inputs for the Active Scenario. Now look at Column E in Figure 12-4, the one labeled "Active Scenario: Final." With *Excel*'s Scenario Manager, you choose a scenario and *Excel* replaces the input date in Column E with the data for the chosen scenario (we had chosen the Final scenario when we created Figure 12-4, so that is the scenario showing in Column E). These inputs are then linked to the section of the spreadsheet where the financial statements are forecast. (The forecasted statements are shown in Figure 12-5.)

After forecasting the financial statements, the model calculates performance measures, including the forecasted free cash flow (FCF), return on invested capital (ROIC), EPS, ROE, number of shares at the end of the year, and DPS. These six key results are shown in Figure 12-6; we will discuss them later.

Discussion of the Forecasted Operating Input Data

The CFO had taken a two-part computer course in college. The first module was taught by a computer science expert who focused on the mechanics of programming and computer usage in general. The second module was taught by an economist who discussed how to apply computers to specific tasks, including various types of forecasting. The economist's favorite term was GIGO, which stands for "garbage in, garbage out," and she repeated it constantly. No matter how well a model is set up, if the inputs used aren't accurate then the output won't be accurate, either. The CFO began the discussion by reminding the management team of this critical fact.

The sales growth rate is the first input item shown in Figure 12-4 and is followed by the most important driver of profitability, the ratio of operating costs (excluding depreciation) to sales. MicroDrive's 2010 operating cost ratio was 87.21%, well above the 83% industry average. This ratio is affected by operating costs, sales prices, and unit sales, and it was discussed at length during the planning conference. The CFO showed the forecasted results for the status quo, best-case, and worst-case scenarios, after which the CEO led a discussion of what the firm could actually achieve in 2011. After much discussion, the management team concluded that, because of licensing fees and other costs, it was not feasible for the firm to achieve the industry average operating cost ratio of 83% in the foreseeable future. However, the team believed that a figure of 86%, down from 2010's 87.21%, was "attainable." They agreed that over time it might be possible to reduce this ratio a bit further, but that 86% was the most realistic choice to use in the forecast.

Intrinsic value is affected by many factors, including the level of inventory. If MicroDrive carries too much inventory then storage costs, deterioration, and obsolescence will drive up operating costs. The CFO had studied the inventory/sales ratio earlier and had pointed out that MicroDrive had almost twice as much inventory for its sales as an average firm in the industry. The CEO stated that the production, sales, and purchasing managers were jointly responsible for inventory in MicroDrive's supply chain. The managers said that they had already been working on a plan to fix this problem. Because MicroDrive's production facilities are farther from their suppliers and customers than are those of most other firms in the industry, MicroDrive must hold a higher than average level of inventory to avoid running out of stock if sales surge. In the end, it was agreed that the inventory/sales ratio could be lowered from 20.5% to 16%, a significant improvement but still above the 11.11% industry average.

The CFO also pointed out that accounts receivable were much higher than the industry average level. This meant that too much capital was tied up in receivables. If a firm continues to sell to a customer who does not pay on time, the account balance will rise significantly, and if the customer then defaults, the selling firm will suffer a larger bad debt loss than if it had stopped selling to the customer sooner. In addition, collection costs rise with the amount of old receivables, which is another reason to keep a tight rein on credit operations. During the discussion, the sales manager noted that tightening its credit policy would lose the firm some sales. However, the lost sales would not be excessive, because most of the late-paying customers were financially sound but were just taking advantage of the "float" MicroDrive was giving them. After the discussion, the credit manager, sales manager, and treasurer jointly agreed that it would be feasible to reduce the receivables/sales ratio to 11% in 2011. That was still above the 9.8% industry average but below MicroDrive's 2010 level of 12.5%. Therefore, 11% was built into the final forecast.

The CFO also brought up the net plant/sales ratio but noted that this ratio was in line with the industry average—the production manager, who was not replaced during the management change, had been forecasting sales accurately and holding equipment purchases to the level actually required. This was facilitated by the outsourcing of production to make up for shortfalls if more orders came during a given period than had been expected. This smart use of outsourcing enabled the firm to operate without carrying excess capacity in "normal" times in order to meet demand when orders surged. Thus, the 2010 ratio of 33.3% for net plant and equipment to sales was used in the forecast.

Financial Policy Issues

The discussion next turned to two key financial policies: capital structure and dividends. The CFO noted that MicroDrive's debt ratio was significantly above the industry average. This high leverage boosted ROE and EPS during good times, but it also raised the interest rates for debt as well as the required return on common stock. Further, an excessive amount of debt increased the risk of bankruptcy and reduced the firm's ability to maintain stable operations in times of stress. The treasurer noted that the company's banks were concerned about its high debt usage and that banks nationwide were reducing the credit lines of companies deemed to have too much debt. MicroDrive's credit lines had not been reduced to date, but if the firm were to have even one bad quarter then a reduction might well occur, and that would be devastating. Credit is the lifeblood of a business, and if its credit were curtailed then MicroDrive might not be able to purchase supplies, pay workers, and so on, which would be fatal. After this discussion, the decision was made to increase the common equity ratio from its current 49.8% level of investor-supplied capital to 55.0%.[6]

The discussion then turned to dividend policy. In recent years, MicroDrive has been increasing the dividend by about 8% per year, and the board of directors has stated that it would like to continue this policy. However, the CFO recently disclosed to the board that many companies that formerly increased their dividends at a steady rate had re-examined that policy and had lowered the targeted rate of increase. An 8% annual increase during the long boom from the 1980s until 2008 had been feasible, but in the current and likely future economic climate a different policy might be necessary. The CFO also pointed out that the average mature firm in the industry was distributing about 40% of its earnings as dividends, compared with MicroDrive's 50.7%. At the conclusion of this discussion, it was decided to use the 40% industry average payout for the forecast, determine the resulting dividend per share, review the resulting performance measures, and then discuss the recommended dividend policy recommendation with the board. The CEO agreed with this plan but clearly hoped that the forecast would support a dividend growth rate of 8% or more.

The next item discussed was the timing of new financing. The treasurer argued that it would be best to issue any required new stock early in the year to ensure that these funds would be available—stock prices are volatile, and the market for new stock could slam shut later in the year. Also, if the firm raised equity early, that would make it easier to issue new debt later. The CFO and CEO agreed, so the decision was made to sell any required new stock early and to borrow throughout the year as needed.

A question was asked about the price at which new stock would be sold. The CFO noted that the most recent price was $23 per share, and that was the most likely price at which new shares could be sold early in the year. Interest rates on the existing debt floated, moving up and down with rates in the general economy and the company's financial condition.[7] The CFO thought interest rates probably would fluctuate to some extent, but there was no more reason to believe that rates would go up than go down. However, by mid-year the company's own financial condition would be known sufficiently well to influence its cost of debt. Therefore, as indicated in Figure 12-4, the rates vary depending on the scenarios—low rates under good conditions and high rates under bad conditions. The preferred dividend also floated, so its rate also varied with the scenarios.

See **Ch12 Tool Kit.xls** *on the textbook's Web site for details.*

Based on an earlier back-of-the-envelope calculation using the AFN model, the CFO had concluded that if operations improved significantly, the firm might not need any new external funds and might even have a surplus. For example, if the profit margin could be increased, this would lower external capital requirements. Even more importantly, if the ratios of inventories and accounts receivable to sales could be lowered, as the management team had discussed earlier, then this would greatly reduce the need for new capital, especially during 2011. Those considerations prompted the CEO to raise the following question: "If excess funds become available, what should we do with them?" The CFO had actually considered several

[6]Capital structure decisions are discussed in detail in Chapter 15.

[7]All of the debt—both short-term bank loans and long-term bonds—had floating rates. The spread between the bank loan rate and the London Interbank Offered Rate (LIBOR) was based on the firm's coverage ratio (EBIT to interest charges). The long-term bond rate was determined similarly. The bank loan rate was reset quarterly, and the long-term rate was reset every 6 months.

possibilities: (1) increase the dividend, (2) repurchase stock and repay debt in amounts that would keep the capital structure constant, (3) invest excess funds in marketable securities, or (4) embark on a merger program to acquire other firms. They decided that the best alternative for modeling purposes was to simply use surplus funds to repay debt and buy back stock. If the surplus was projected to extend on into the long run, then a strategic decision would have to be made regarding what to do with it, but that would require input from the board.

Debt could be repaid at book value and preferred stock repurchased at close to book value. If the repurchase occurred early in the year, then it could probably be bought at close to the current price. This brought up the question of when any surplus funds would actually be available—would they be available early or late, or would they come in regularly throughout the year? It might make sense to *raise* new funds early, but excess funds could not be *used* until they were actually in hand, and that would probably occur throughout the year. The decision was made to repurchase stock early in the year and repay debt later in the year. The CFO also planned to revisit this issue when developing the projected 2011 cash budget. (Cash budgets are discussed in Chapter 16; they are typically done on a monthly basis.)

The Forecasted Financial Statements

resource

See **Ch12 Tool Kit.xls** *on the textbook's Web site for details.*

Using input from the Final scenario as shown in column E of Figure 12-4, MicroDrive's forecasted financial statements (balance sheet and income statement) are reported in Figure 12-5.[8] The following points explain how to forecast the statements shown in Figure 12-5.

1. Forecast next year's sales based on the assumed growth rate: $S_{2011} = S_{2010} \times (1 + g)$.
2. Forecast each of the operating assets (cash, accounts receivable, inventories, and net plant and equipment) and the spontaneous current liabilities (accounts payable and accruals) as a percentage of forecasted sales. This completes the assets section of the balance sheet and partially completes the liabilities section.
3. Use the forecasted operating data from Step 2 to calculate the required investor-supplied capital, which is found as Total assets − (Accounts payable + Accruals).
4. Multiply the investor-supplied capital found in Step 3 by the inputs for the target capital structure percentages shown in Figure 12-4 to forecast the amounts of notes payable, long-term bonds, preferred stock, and total common equity. This completes the balance sheet except for dividing the forecasted total common equity into its two components, common stock and retained earnings.
5. Calculate operating costs as a percentage of forecasted sales and calculate depreciation as a percentage of forecasted net plant and equipment. Subtract these costs from sales to find EBIT.
6. It is assumed that new debt will be borrowed throughout the year, so interest expenses will be based on the average amount of debt outstanding during the year. This amount is equal to the average of the beginning-of-year debt and the end-of-year debt forecast in Step 4. Multiply this average by the interest rate to determine the forecasted interest expense. Observe that the income statement shows separate lines for the interest expense due to notes payable and long-term bonds—we find that we make fewer errors if we have more lines in a spreadsheet but less complicated formulas in each cell.

[8]Columns E and I are identical in Figure 12-4. *Excel*'s Scenario Manager replaces the values in Column E with the values shown in Column I when the Final scenario is selected. Similarly, the Scenario Manager replaces data in Column E with the values shown in Columns F, G, or H when those scenarios are selected.

FIGURE 12-5 Forecasted Financial Statements (Millions of Dollars, Except for Per Share Data)

	A	B	C	D	E	F	G
129	Scenario Shown:	Final					
130			Most Recent				Final Forecast
131	Part 1. Balance Sheet		2010	Factors	Basis for 2011 Forecast		2011
132	*Assets*						
133	Cash		$10.0	0.25%	Factor × 2011 Sales		$8.25
134	Accounts receivable		375.0	11.00%	Factor × 2011 Sales		363.00
135	Inventories		615.0	16.00%	Factor × 2011 Sales		528.00
136	Total current assets		$1,000.0				$899.25
137	Net plant and equipment		1,000.0	33.33%	Factor × 2011 Sales		1,100.00
138	Total assets (TA)		$2,000.0				$1,999.25
139	*Liabilities and equity*						
140	Accounts payable		$60.0	2.00%	Factor × 2011 Sales		$66.00
141	Accruals		140.0	4.00%	Factor × 2011 Sales		132.00
142	Notes payable[a]		110.0	5.00%	% of investor-sup. cap.		90.06
143	Total current liabilities		$310.0				$288.06
144	Long-term bonds[a]		754.0	37.00%	% of investor-sup. cap.		666.46
145	Total liabilities		$1,064.0				$954.52
146	Preferred stock[a]		40.0	3.00%	% of investor-sup. cap.		$54.04
147	Common stock		130.0		Tot. Com–Eq – Ret. Earn		131.37
148	Retained earnings		766.0		Old RE + Add. to RE		859.32
149	Total common equity[a]		$896.0	55.00%	% of investor -sup. cap.		$990.69
150	Total liabilities and equity		$2,000.0				$1,999.25
151	[a]Investor-supplied capital		$1,800.0		TA – accts. pay. – accrual		$1,801.25
152	Scenario Shown:	Final					
153			Most Recent				Final Forecast
154	Part 2. Income Statement		2010	Factors	Basis for 2011 Forecast		2011
155	Sales		$3,000.0	110%	Factor × 2010 Sales		$3,300.0
156	Costs except depreciation		2,616.2	86.00%	Factor × 2011 Sales		2,838.0
157	Depreciation		100.0	10.20%	Factor × 2011 Net plant		112.2
158	Total operating costs		$2,716.2				$2,950.2
159	EBIT		$283.8				$349.8
160	Less: Interest on notes		9.9	8.50%	Interest rate × Avg notes		8.5
161	Interest on bonds		78.1	10.50%	Interest rate × Avg bonds		74.6
162	Earnings before taxes (EBT)		$195.8				$266.7
163	Taxes (40%)		78.3	40.00%	Tax rate × 2011 EBT		106.7
164	NI before preferred dividends		$117.5				$160.0
165	Preferred dividends		4.0	9.50%	Pfd div rate × Avg preferred		4.5
166	NI available to common		$113.5				$155.6
167	Dividends paid out		$57.5	40.00%	Net income × Payout rate		$62.2
168	Addition to retained earnings		$56.0		Net income – Dividends		$93.3
169	Change in shares outstanding				(Change in com.stk.)/P_{2010}		0.06
170	Ending shares outstanding		50.00		$Shares_{2010}$ + Δ shares		50.06
171	Earnings per share, EPS		$2.27		Net income/Total shares		$3.11
172	Dividends per share, DPS		$1.15		Total dividends/Total shares		$1.24

Note: Calculations in the model have been shown to one decimal, so rounding differences may occur.

7. Subtract interest expense from EBIT to find taxable income (EBT). Calculate taxes and subtract them from EBT to get net income before preferred dividends.
8. Forecast preferred dividends in a similar manner as the forecasted interest expense in Step 6: (1) find the average amount of preferred stock outstanding during the year and then (2) multiply it by the preferred stock's dividend rate.

9. Subtract the forecasted preferred dividends from the net income before preferred dividends to find the net income available to common stockholders.
10. Multiply the net income by the target payout ratio to forecast the total amount of common dividends paid. If net income is negative, set common dividends to zero.
11. Subtract common dividends from net income to find the addition to retained earnings.
12. The forecasted total retained earnings shown on the balance sheet is equal to the prior year's retained earnings plus the addition to retained earnings calculated in Step 11.
13. The forecasted total common stock must be equal to the difference between forecasted total common equity from Step 4 and the forecasted retained earnings balance from Step 12: Common stock = Total common equity − Retained earnings.
14. The required additional dollars of common stock issued or repurchased are equal to the change in common stock: Additional dollars of stock issued or repurchased = Common stock in 2011 − Common stock in 2010. If the amount is negative, it means that stock will be repurchased rather than issued.
15. The number of new shares either issued or repurchased is equal to the additional dollars of common stock found in Step 14 divided by the price per share. Because the stock is assumed to be sold at the beginning of 2011, the assumed stock price is $23, the price at the end of 2010. We calculate this as: Change in shares = (Additional dollars of common stock) ÷ (Stock price at the beginning of the year).
16. The number of shares outstanding at the end of the year is equal to the number of outstanding shares at the beginning of the year plus the change in the number of shares calculated in Step 15.

Analyzing the Forecasted Results

After the Final set of inputs had been chosen, the CFO created a summary sheet showing key results for the different scenarios, as shown in Figure 12-6. After projecting the key results on a big screen, the team discussed each of the scenarios. Everyone dismissed the worst-case results, because if things started getting that bad there would be an emergency meeting in which actions would be taken to modify the plan. Similarly, the status quo and best-case results were given short shrift, and then the team focused on the Final scenario results.

The jump in EPS looked good, and even with the assumed 40% payout ratio, DPS rose by about 8%, which pleased the CEO.

The ROE improved nicely, rising from 12.7% to 15.7%, which exceeded the industry average. However, the CFO pointed out that the firm's debt ratio, even after the capital structure change, still exceeded the industry average, and that its greater leverage was largely responsible for the above-average ROE.

Free cash flow was projected to make a tremendous improvement, from −$175 million in 2010 to +$209 million in 2011. The CFO noted, though, that a similar improvement would not occur in the future, because most of the gain in free cash flow was attributable to the one-time reduction in inventories and accounts receivable. AFN, the last item in Figure 12-6, turned out to be negative, indicating that a surplus of funds would exist in 2011 and for the same reason that free cash flow rose—the reduction in inventories and accounts receivable. The lower payout and higher profit margin also helped reduce the AFN, but the one-time reduction in inventories and receivables was the key driver here.

FIGURE 12-6 Summary of Key Results for Forecasted Scenarios (Millions, Except for Percentages and Per Share Data)

	A B	C	D	E	F	G	H
240		2010 Actual		2011 Forecasts			
241		Industry	MicroDrive				
242	Key Results			Final	Status Quo	Best	Worst
243	Net operating profit after taxes	NA	$170	$210	$187	$271	$61
244	Net operating working capital	NA	$800	$701	$880	$569	$922
245	Total operating capital	NA	$1,800	$1,801	$1,980	$1,669	$2,002
246	FCF = NOPAT − Δ op capital	NA	−$175	$209	$7	$402	−$141
247	Return on invested capital	11.0%	9.5%	11.7%	9.5%	16.2%	3.1%
248	EPS	NA	$2.27	$3.11	$2.43	$5.07	−$0.10
249	DPS	NA	$1.15	$1.24	$1.23	$2.57	$0.00
250	Return on equity (ROE)	15.0%	12.7%	15.7%	12.6%	26.0%	−0.5%
251	Return on assets (ROA)	9.0%	5.7%	7.8%	5.7%	12.0%	−0.2%
252	Inventory turnover	9.0	4.9	6.3	4.9	9.0	3.9
253	Days sales outstanding	36.0	45.6	40.2	45.6	35.8	54.8
254	Total liabilities / TA	46.0%	53.2%	47.7%	53.2%	51.8%	52.3%
255	Times interest earned	6.0	3.2	4.2	3.2	5.3	1.0
256	Shares outstanding	NA	50.00	50.06	51.22	42.54	54.62
257	Payout ratio	40.0%	50.7%	4.0%	50.7%	50.7%	0.0%
258	AFN[a]	NA	$224	−$92	$119	−$237	$208
259							

260 [a] Unlike the AFN equation, the approach used to forecast the statements in these scenarios determines the
261 total amount of financing (the sum of notes payable, bonds, preferred stock, and common equity) rather than
262 the additional financing needed in comparison to the financing used in the most recent year. Therefore, the
263 additional financing needed is calculated directly from the changes in notes payable, bonds, preferred
264 stock, and common stock.

The forecasted statement of cash flows in Figure 12-7 tells a similar story: (1) cash flow from operations is positive and large (with large cash flows resulting from improved asset utilization; (2) cash flow from investments is negative because of the expansion in fixed assets needed to support growth; and (3) the cash flow from financing activities shows that MicroDrive would be able to pay large dividends and reduce its debt.

At the conclusion of the CFO's summary, the CEO said that the firm would be in great shape and that nice bonuses and stock options would result if the targets were met and maintained over the long run.

Alternative Financial Policies and Multi-Year Forecasts

When the CEO and CFO presented the plan to the board of directors, the board was pleased overall but had a few questions. Several board members, including the chairman and founder of the company, were concerned that the plan included issuing new shares of common stock. They were also uneasy about the assumed price at which shares of stock could be repurchased later in the year if there were surplus funds. In addition, the board thought that determining dividends as a fixed percentage payout of net income might introduce quite a bit of volatility in DPS. Because of these concerns, the board asked the CFO to provide forecasted statements using the following different assumptions regarding the financial policies.

For the purposes of this additional forecast, the board specified the following financial policies: (1) let the regular DPS grow at a specified rate; (2) do not change the level of existing notes payable; and (3) do not issue or repurchase bonds, preferred stock, or common stock. If additional financing is needed, the board suggested forecasting the AFN as a draw against an existing line of credit on a temporary basis

FIGURE 12-7 Forecasted Statement of Cash Flows (Millions of Dollars, Except for Per Share Data)

	A	B	C	D	E	F
268	Scenario Shown: Final				Actual 2010	Forecast 2011
269						
270	Operating Activities					
271	Net Income before preferred dividends				$117.5	$160.0
272	Noncash adjustments					
273	Depreciation and amortization				100.0	112.2
274	Due to changes in working capital					
275	Increase(–)/Decrease (+) in accounts receivable				–60.0	12.0
276	Increase(–)/Decrease (+) in inventories				–200.0	87.0
277	Increase(–)/Decrease (+) in payables				30.0	6.0
278	Increase(–)/Decrease (+) in accruals				10.0	–8.0
279	Net cash provided by operating activities				–$2.5	$369.2
280						
281	Long-term investing activities					
282	Cash used to acquire fixed assets				–$230.0	–$212.2
283	Sale of short-term investments				65.0	0.0
284	Net cash provided by financing activities				–$165.0	–$212.2
285						
286	Financing Activities					
287	Increase(+)/Decrease(–) in notes payable				$50.0	–$19.9
288	Increase(+)/Decrease(–) in bonds				174.0	–87.0
289	Preferred stock issue (+) / repurchase(–)				0.0	14.0
290	Payment of common and preferred dividends				–61.5	–66.7
291	Common stock issue (+) / repurchase (–)				0.0	1.4
292	Net cash provided by financing activities				$162.5	–$158.8
293						
294	Net cash flow				–$5.0	–$1.7
295	Cash at beginning of the year				15.0	10.0
296	Cash at end of the year				$10.0	$8.3

(even though the interest rate would be high) until the board could meet and decide on a final financing plan. If instead a surplus of funds is available at the end of the year, the board suggested that the surplus be paid to shareholders in the form of a special dividend.[9]

The board asked to see two scenarios. The first is similar to the Status Quo scenario previously discussed, except that the board's three financial policies just described are employed (the board suggested a zero growth rate for regular DPS). Because there is no change in operating performance, this is called the Maintain scenario. The second scenario is similar to the Final scenario discussed earlier, except that the board's financial policy is applied (the board suggested an 8% growth in regular DPS for this scenario). Because there are significant improvements in operating performance, this is called the Improve scenario. The board asked to see the Maintain scenario first, which is shown in Figure 12-8 (see ***Tab 3*** in ***Ch12 Tool Kit.xls*** for details).

The operating items are forecasted in the same way as shown before. All liabilities and equity accounts (except the line of credit) are planned in the sense that they are specified by the financial policies. For the policies used here, there are no changes in notes payable, bonds, or common stock; in addition, regular dividends are specified, so the addition to retained earnings is specified. Column F in Figure 12-8 shows

[9]In actuality, the board would decide at that time whether to repurchase shares of stock instead, if that seemed preferable given the prevailing stock price.

FIGURE 12-8 One-Year Forecasted Financial Statements under an Alternative Financial Policy: Scenario = Maintain (Millions, Except for Per Share Data)

	A	B	C	D	E	F	G	H
94	Scenario Shown:	Maintain				Planned		With
95		Actual	Factor	Basis for		(w/o AFN)	AFN	AFN
96	Balance Sheet	2010	or Rate	2011 forecast		2011	Adjust.	2011
97	*Assets*							
98	Cash	$10.0	0.33%	× 2011 Sales		$11.0		$11.0
99	Acc. rec.	375.0	12.50%	× 2011 Sales		412.5		412.5
100	Inventories	615.0	20.50%	× 2011 Sales		676.5		676.5
101	Total CA	$1,000.0				$1,100.0		$1,100.0
102	Net plant & equip.	1,000.0	33.33%	× 2011 Sales		1,100.0		1,100.0
103	Total assets (TA)	$2,000.0				$2,200.0		$2,200.0
104	*Liab. & equity*							
105	Accounts payable	$60.0	2.00%	× 2011 Sales		$66.0		$66.0
106	Accruals	140.0	4.67%	× 2011 Sales		154.1		154.1
107	Notes pay. (NP)	110.0		Carry over		110.0		110.0
108	Line of credit (LOC)[a]			Blank			$109.8	109.8
109	Total CL	$310.0				$330.1		$440.0
110	LT bonds	754.0		Carry over		754.0		754.0
111	Tot. liab.	$1,064.0				$1,084.1		$1,194.0
112	Pref. stock	40.0		Carry over		40.0		40.0
113	Com. stock	130.0		Carry over		130.0		130.0
114	Ret. earnings	766.0		2010 RE+ ΔRE		836.0		836.0
115	Total CE	$896.0				$966.0		$966.0
116	Total L&E	$2,000.0				$2,090.1		$2,200.0
117								
118	AFN[b]		= TA − Planned total liabilities & equity				$109.8	
119	Line of credit[c]		= AFN if AFN > 0 (additional financing needed)				$109.8	
120	Special dividend[d]		= −AFN if AFN ≤ 0 (surplus funds available)				$0.0	
121								
122	Scenario Shown:	Maintain				Planned		With
123		Actual	Factor	Basis for		(w/o AFN)	AFN	AFN
124	Income Statement	2010	or Rate	2011 forecast		2011	Adjust.	2011
125	Sales	$3,000.0	1.10	× 2010 Sales		$3,300.0		$3,300.0
126	Costs (excl. depr.)	2,616.2	87.21%	× 2011 Sales		2,877.9		2,877.9
127	Depreciation	100.0	10.00%	× 2011 Net plant		110.0		110.0
128	Total op. costs	$2,716.2				$2,987.9		$2,987.9
129	EBIT	$283.8				$312.1		$312.1
130	Int. on planned NP	9.9	9.00%	× Avg notes		9.9		9.9
131	Int. on planned bonds	78.1	11.00%	× Avg bonds		82.9		82.9
132	Int. on LOC[e]		9.00%	Blank			$0.0	0.0
133	EBT	$195.8				$219.2		$219.2
134	Taxes (T = 40%)	78.3	40.00%	× 2011 EBT		87.7		87.7
135	NI before pref. div.	$117.5				$131.5		$131.5
136	Pref. div.	4.0	10.00%	× Avg preferred		4.0		4.0
137	NI to common	$113.5				$127.5		$127.5
138								
139	# of shares (n)	50.0		Carry over		50.0		50.0
140	Regular DPS	$1.15	1.00	× 2010 DPS		$1.15		$1.15
141	Regular dividends	$57.5		n × 2011 DPS		$57.5		$57.5
142	Special dividend[f]	0.0				0.0	$0.0	0.0
143	Add. To RE (ΔRE)	$56.0		NI − Dividends		$70.0		$70.0

Notes:

[a]If additional financing is needed, notes payable will be added on a temporary basis.

[b]The AFN in forecasted financial statements is equal to the required assets minus the planned liabilities and equity (i.e., the liabilities and equity assuming AFN is zero).

[c]If AFN > 0, then additional financing will be raised by borrowing via notes payable.

[d]If AFN ≤ 0, then surplus funds will be used to pay a special dividend.

[e]This forecast assumes that any temporary notes payable will be raised at the end of the year; thus, there will be no additional interest expense.

[f]Any surplus funds will be paid out as a special dividend.

these planned forecasts, but notice that the balance sheets don't balance: The total assets line equals \$2,200, but total liabilities and equity sum only to \$2,090.1. Thus, there is a \$2,200 − \$2,090.1 = \$109.9 million shortfall. In other words, the AFN is \$109.9, as shown in Row 118. Because additional financing is needed, there will be an adjustment to the statements by borrowing \$109.9 through the line of credit, as shown in Column G. Because we assume that the borrowing occurs at the end of the year, there will be no additional interest in this forecast. Column H shows the forecasted statements after including the AFN.

Figure 12-9 reports the forecasted statements for the Improve scenario. The balance sheets in Column F again do not balance, but this is because there is more financing (total liabilities and equity = \$2,088.8) than assets (total assets = \$1,999.2). Thus, Row 118 shows a negative AFN, −\$89.6 million. This will be paid out as a special dividend, as shown in Column G. Column H reports the forecasted statements after including the AFN.

The board expressed two additional concerns. First, they thought it unrealistic to assume that the line of credit was only used on the last day of the year and thus caused no additional interest expense. The board felt it would be more appropriate to assume that the line of credit was accessed at regular intervals throughout the year, which would lead to additional interest expense. The CFO explained that when the AFN leads to additional interest expense it reduces net income, which reduces the addition to retained earnings and then increases the AFN, with the cycle being repeated in a circular manner. This is called **financing feedback,** and there are a variety of ways to incorporate feedback effects into the forecast. The CFO agreed that adding debt throughout the year was a more realistic assumption but said that the end-of-year assumption usually produced results fairly close to those that incorporated feedback effects. However, the CFO agreed to incorporate financing feedback in the next set of forecasts, but rather than use valuable board time explaining feedback adjustments in detail, the CFO suggested that interested board members take a look at ***Tab 4*** in ***Ch12 Tool Kit.xls.***

The board also wanted to see multi-year projections. After updating the forecasting model to incorporate feedback effects and multi-year forecasts, the CFO returned to the board meeting and presented the results shown in Figure 12-10. (See ***Tab 5*** in ***Ch12 Tool Kit.xls*** for calculations.)

The dramatic increase in FCF during 2011 would be a result of the improved operations, including less inventory and fewer receivables. After this one-time improvement, FCF drops in 2012 but then increases each year. The improved operations are reflected in the increased return on invested capital, which in turn leads to strong growth in EPS and thus enables growth in DPS. With the projected increase in the times interest earned ratio and the decrease in the ratio of total liabilities to total assets, the board discussed whether MicroDrive could support more debt. They decided to discuss a possible recapitalization at their next meeting, in which MicroDrive might issue bonds and use the proceeds to pay off the line of credit and possibly repurchase shares of stock, topics we discuss in Chapter 14 and Chapter 15.

Self-Test

Is the AFN as calculated using the forecasted financial statements method, with all the ratios held constant, the same (except for rounding errors) as the AFN found using the AFN equation? Explain.

Why does the text argue that the forecasted financial statements method is preferable to the AFN equation method?

What does the acronym GIGO stand for? Is this important for forecasting?

FIGURE 12-9 One-Year Forecasted Financial Statements under an Alternative Financial Policy: Scenario = Improve (Millions, Except for Per Share Data)

	A	B	C	D	E	F	G	H
94	Scenario Shown:	Improve				Planned		With
95		Actual	Factor	Basis for		(w/o AFN)	AFN	AFN
96	Balance Sheet	2010	or Rate	2011 forecast		2011	Adjust.	2011
97	*Assets*							
98	Cash	$10.0	0.25%	× 2011 Sales		$8.3		$8.3
99	Acc. rec.	375.0	11.00%	× 2011 Sales		363.0		363.0
100	Inventories	615.0	16.00%	× 2011 Sales		568.0		568.0
101	Total CA	$1,000.0				$899.3		$899.3
102	Net plant & equip.	1,000.0	33.33%	× 2011 Sales		1,100.0		1,100.0
103	Total assets (TA)	$2,000.0				$1,992.2		$1,999.2
104	*Liab. & equity*							
105	Accounts payable	$60.0	2.00%	× 2011 Sales		$66.0		$66.0
106	Accruals	140.0	4.67%	× 2011 Sales		132.0		132.0
107	Notes pay. (NP)	110.0		Carry over		110.0		110.0
108	Line of credit (LOC)[a]			Blank			$0.0	0.0
109	Total CL	$310.0				$308.0		$308.0
110	LT bonds	754.0		Carry over		754.0		754.0
111	Tot. liab.	$1,064.0				$1,062.0		$1,062.0
112	Pref. stock	40.0		Carry over		40.0		40.0
113	Com. stock	130.0		Carry over		130.0		130.0
114	Ret. earnings	766.0		2010 RE+ ΔRE		856.8		767.2
115	Total CE	$896.0				$986.8		$897.2
116	Total L&E	$2,000.0				$2,088.8		$1,999.2
117								
118	AFN[b]	= TA − Planned total liabilities & equity					−$89.6	
119	Line of credit[c]	= AFN if AFN > 0 (additional financing needed)					$0.0	
120	Special dividend[d]	= −AFN if AFN ≤ 0 (surplus funds available)					$89.6	
121								
122	Scenario Shown:	Improve				Planned		With
123		Actual	Factor	Basis for		(w/o AFN)	AFN	AFN
124	Income Statement	2010	or Rate	2011 forecast		2011	Adjust.	2011
125	Sales	$3,000.0	1.10	× 2010 Sales		$3,300.0		$3,300.0
126	Costs (excl. depr.)	2,616.2	86.00%	× 2011 Sales		2,838.0		2,838.0
127	Depreciation	100.0	10.20%	× 2011 Net plant		112.2		112.2
128	Total op. costs	$2,716.2				$2,950.2		$2,950.2
129	EBIT	$283.8				$349.8		$349.8
130	Int. on planned NP	9.9	8.50%	× Avg notes		9.4		9.4
131	Int. on planned bonds	78.1	10.50%	× Avg bonds		79.2		79.2
132	Int. on LOC[e]		8.50%	Blank			$0.0	0.0
133	EBT	$195.8				$261.3		$261.3
134	Taxes (T = 40%)	78.3	40.00%	× 2011 EBT		104.5		104.5
135	NI before pref. div.	$117.5				$156.8		$156.8
136	Pref. div.	4.0	9.50%	× Avg preferred		3.8		3.8
137	NI to common	$113.5				$153.0		$153.0
138								
139	# of shares (n)	50.0		Carry over		50.0		50.0
140	Regular DPS	$1.15	1.08	× 2010 DPS		$1.24		$1.24
141	Regular dividends	$57.5		n × 2011 DPS		$62.1		$62.1
142	Special dividend[f]	0.0				0.0	$89.6	89.6
143	Add. To RE (ΔRE)	$56.0		NI − Dividends		$90.9		$1.3

Notes:

[a]If additional financing is needed, notes payable will be added on a temporary basis.

[b]The AFN in forecasted financial statements is equal to the required assets minus the planned liabilities and equity (i.e., the liabilities and equity assuming AFN is zero).

[c]If AFN > 0, then additional financing will be raised by borrowing via notes payable.

[d]If AFN ≤ 0, then surplus funds will be used to pay a special dividend.

[e]This forecast assumes that any temporary notes payable will be raised at the end of the year; thus, there will be no additional interest expense.

[f]Any surplus funds will be paid out as a special dividend.

FIGURE 12-10 Summary of Forecasted Key Results for the "Improve" Scenario (Millions, Except for Percentages and Per Share Data)

	A	B	C	D	E	F	G	H	I
211			Actual		Forecast	Forecast	Forecast	Forecast	Forecast
212			2010		2011	2012	2013	2014	2015
213			Industry	MicroDrive	Improve	Improve	Improve	Improve	Improve
214	Key Results								
215	Net operating profit after taxes		NA	\$170	\$210	\$231	\$254	\$279	\$307
216	Net operating working capital		NA	\$800	\$701	\$771	\$849	\$933	\$1,027
217	Total operating capital		NA	\$1,800	\$1,801	\$1,981	\$2,180	\$2,397	\$2,637
218	FCF = NOPAT − Δ op capital		NA	−\$175	\$209	\$51	\$56	\$61	\$68
219	Return on invested capital		11.0%	9.5%	11.7%	11.7%	11.7%	11.7%	11.7%
220	EPS		NA	\$2.27	\$3.06	\$3.43	\$3.79	\$4.18	\$4.62
221	DPS		NA	\$1.15	\$1.24	\$1.34	\$1.45	\$1.56	\$1.69
222	Return on equity (ROE)		15.0%	12.7%	17.0%	17.1%	16.9%	16.7%	16.6%
223	Return on assets (ROA)		9.0%	5.7%	7.7%	7.8%	7.8%	7.9%	7.9%
224	Inventory turnover		9.0	4.9	6.3	6.3	6.3	6.3	6.3
225	Days sales outstanding		36.0	45.6	40.2	40.2	40.2	40.2	40.2
226	Total liabilities / TA		46.0%	53.2%	53.1%	52.6%	52.1%	51.5%	50.9%
227	Times interest earned		6.0	3.2	4.0	4.3	4.8	5.3	5.8
228	Shares outstanding		NA	50.00	50.00	50.00	50.00	50.00	50.00
229	Payout ratio		40.0%	50.7%	40.6%	39.1%	38.3%	37.4%	36.5%
230	AFN		NA	\$224	−\$90	\$76	\$157	\$244	\$337

12.5 Forecasting When the Ratios Change

The AFN equation assumes that the ratios of assets and liabilities to sales (A_0^*/S_0 and L_0^*/S_0) remain constant over time. This assumption can be relaxed when we use the forecasted financial statement method, but in our forecast we made a one-time change in these ratios and then held them constant thereafter. This implies that each "spontaneous" asset and liability item increases at the same rate as sales. In graph form, this implies the type of relationship shown in Panel a of Figure 12-11, a relationship whose graph (1) is linear and (2) passes through the origin. Under those conditions, if the company's sales increase from \$200 million to \$400 million, or by 100%, then inventory will also increase by 100%, from \$100 million to \$200 million.

The assumption of constant ratios and identical growth rates is appropriate at times, but there are times when it is incorrect. Three such conditions are described in the following sections.

Economies of Scale

There are economies of scale in the use of many kinds of assets, and when economies of scale occur, the ratios are likely to change over time as the size of the firm increases. For example, retailers often need to maintain base stocks of different inventory items even if current sales are quite low. As sales expand, inventories may then grow less rapidly than sales, so the ratio of inventory to sales (I/S) declines. This situation is depicted in Panel b of Figure 12-11. Here we see that the inventory/sales ratio is 1.5 (or 150%) when sales are \$200 million but declines to 1.0 when sales climb to \$400 million.

The relationship in Panel b is linear, but nonlinear relationships often exist. Indeed, if the firm uses one popular model for establishing inventory levels (the Economic Ordering Quantity, or EOQ, model), its inventories will rise with the *square root* of sales. This situation is shown in Panel c of Figure 12-11, which shows a

FIGURE 12-11 Four Possible Ratio Relationships (Millions of Dollars)

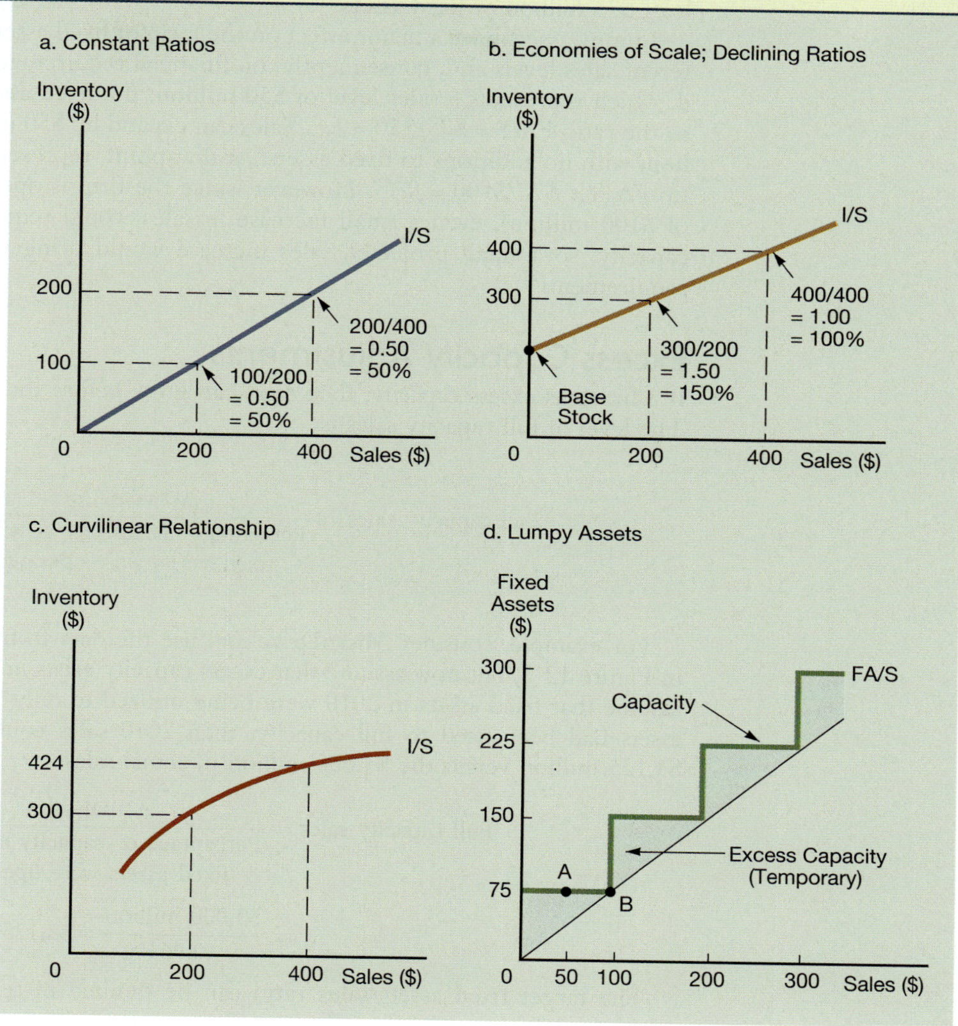

curved line whose slope decreases at higher sales levels. In this situation, very large increases in sales would require very little additional inventory.[10]

Lumpy Assets

In many industries, technological considerations dictate that if a firm is to be competitive, it must add fixed assets in large, discrete units; such assets are often referred to as **lumpy assets.** In the paper industry, for example, there are strong economies of scale in basic paper mill equipment, so when a paper company expands capacity, it must do so in large, lumpy increments. This type of situation is depicted in Panel d of Figure 12-11. Here we assume that the minimum economically efficient plant has a cost of \$75 million, and that such a plant can produce enough output to reach a

[10]See *Web Extension 12A* for more on forecasting when things like inventories are not constant in relation to sales.

sales level of $100 million. If the firm is to be competitive, it simply must have at least $75 million of fixed assets.

Lumpy assets have a major effect on the ratio of fixed assets to sales (FA/S) at different sales levels and, consequently, on financial requirements. At Point A in Panel d, which represents a sales level of $50 million, the fixed assets are $75 million and so the ratio FA/S = $75/$50 = 1.5. Sales can expand by $50 million, out to $100 million, with no additions to fixed assets. At that point, represented by Point B, the ratio FA/S = $75/$100 = 0.75. However, since the firm is operating at capacity (sales of $100 million), even a small increase in sales would require a doubling of plant capacity, so a small projected sales increase would bring with it a large financial requirement.[11]

Excess Capacity Adjustments

If a firm has excess capacity, then sales can grow before the firm must add capacity. The level of full capacity sales is

$$\text{Full capacity sales} = \frac{\text{Actual sales}}{\text{Percentage of capacity at which fixed assets were operated}} \tag{12-3}$$

For example, consider MicroDrive and use the data from its financial statements in Figure 12-2, but now assume that excess capacity exists in fixed assets. Specifically, assume that fixed assets in 2010 were being utilized to only 96% of capacity. If fixed assets had been used to full capacity, then 2010 sales could have been as high as $3,125 million versus the $3,000 million in actual sales:

$$\begin{aligned}\text{Full capacity sales} &= \frac{\text{Actual sales}}{\text{Percentage of capacity at which fixed assets were operated}}\\ &= \frac{\$3{,}000\text{ million}}{0.96} = \$3{,}125\text{ million}\end{aligned}$$

The target fixed assets/sales ratio can be defined in terms of the full capacity sales:

$$\text{Target fixed assets/Sales} = \frac{\text{Actual fixed assets}}{\text{Full capacity sales}} \tag{12-4}$$

[11]Several other points should be noted about Panel d of Figure 12-11. First, if the firm is operating at a sales level of $100 million or less, then any expansion that calls for a sales increase of more than $100 million would require a *doubling* of the firm's fixed assets. A much smaller percentage increase would be involved if the firm were large enough to be operating a number of plants. Second, firms generally go to multiple shifts and take other actions to minimize the need for new fixed asset capacity as they approach Point B. However, these efforts can only go so far, and eventually a fixed asset expansion will be required. Third, firms often make arrangements to share excess capacity with other firms in their industry. For example, the situation in the electric utility industry is very much like that depicted in Panel d. However, electric companies often build jointly owned plants, or else they "take turns" building plants, and then they buy power from or sell power to other utilities to avoid building new plants that would be underutilized.

MicroDrive's target fixed assets/sales ratio should be 32% rather than 33.3%:

$$\text{Target fixed assets/Sales} = \frac{\text{Actual fixed assets}}{\text{Full capacity sales}}$$

$$= \frac{\$1{,}000}{\$3{,}125} = 0.32 = 32\%$$

The required level of fixed assets depends upon this target fixed assets/sales ratio:

$$\begin{matrix}\text{Required level} \\ \text{of fixed assets}\end{matrix} = \left(\frac{\text{Target fixed assets}}{\text{Sales}}\right)\left(\begin{matrix}\text{Projected} \\ \text{sales}\end{matrix}\right) \quad \text{(12-5)}$$

Therefore, if MicroDrive's sales increase to $3,300 million, its fixed assets would have to increase to $1,056 million:

$$\begin{matrix}\text{Required level} \\ \text{of fixed assets}\end{matrix} = \left(\frac{\text{Target fixed assets}}{\text{Sales}}\right)\left(\begin{matrix}\text{Projected} \\ \text{sales}\end{matrix}\right)$$

$$= 0.32(\$3{,}300) = \$1{,}056 \text{ million}$$

We previously forecasted that MicroDrive would need to increase fixed assets at the same rate as sales, or by 10%. That meant an increase of $100 million, from $1,000 million to $1,100 million. Under the new assumptions, the actual required increase in fixed assets is only from $1,000 million to $1,056 million, or $56 million. Thus, the capacity-adjusted forecast is $100 − $56 = $44 million less than the earlier forecast. With a smaller fixed asset requirement, the projected AFN would decline from an estimated $118 million to $118 − $44 = $74 million.

Note also that when excess capacity exists, sales can grow to the capacity sales as calculated above with no increase in fixed assets, but sales beyond that level would require additions of fixed assets as in our example. The same situation could occur with respect to inventories, and the required additions would be determined in exactly the same manner as for fixed assets. Theoretically, the same situation could occur with other types of assets, but as a practical matter excess capacity normally exists only with respect to fixed assets and inventories.

Self-Test

How do economies of scale and lumpy assets affect financial forecasting?

Summary

- **Financial forecasting** generally begins with a forecast of the firm's sales in terms of both units and dollars.
- Either the **forecasted financial statements (FFS) method** or the **additional funds needed (AFN) equation** can be used to forecast financial requirements. If conditions are likely to change, the financial statements method is more reliable, and it also provides ratios and other data that can be used to evaluate alternative business plans. The AFN equation is typically used to arrive at an approximation for AFN.
- A firm can determine its **AFN** by estimating the amount of new assets necessary to support the forecasted level of sales and then subtracting from this amount the spontaneous funds that will be generated from operations. The firm can then plan how to raise the AFN most efficiently.

- The higher a firm's **sales growth rate** and the higher its **payout ratio,** the greater will be its need for additional financing.
- The greatest benefit of the forecasted financial statements method is its use in **planning to optimize operations and thereby increase the firm's intrinsic value** and thus its stock price.
- Adjustments must be made if **economies of scale** exist in the use of assets, if **excess capacity** exists, or if growth must occur in large increments **(lumpy assets).**
- **Linear regression** and **excess capacity adjustments** can be used to forecast asset requirements in situations in which assets are not expected to grow at the same rate as sales. See ***Web Extension 12A*** for more discussion of these issues.

Questions

(12–1) Define each of the following terms:

a. Mission statement; corporate scope; statement of corporate objectives; corporate strategies
b. Operating plan; financial plan; sales forecast
c. Spontaneous liabilities; profit margin; payout ratio
d. Additional funds needed (AFN); AFN equation; capital intensity ratio; self-supporting growth rate
e. Forecasted financial statement approach
f. Excess capacity; lumpy assets; economies of scale
g. Full capacity sales; target fixed assets/sales ratio; required level of fixed assets
h. Financing feedback effects

(12–2) Some liability and net worth items increase spontaneously with increases in sales. Put a check (✓) by those items listed below that typically increase spontaneously:

Accounts payable	______	Mortgage bonds	______
Notes payable to banks	______	Common stock	______
Accrued wages	______	Retained earnings	______
Accrued taxes	______		

(12–3) The following equation is sometimes used to forecast financial requirements:

$$AFN = (A_0^*/S_0)(\Delta S) - (L_0^*/S_0)(\Delta S) - MS_1(1 - POR)$$

What key assumption do we make when using this equation? Under what conditions might this assumption not hold true?

(12–4) Name five key factors that affect a firm's external financing requirements.

(12–5) What is meant by the term "self-supporting growth rate?" How is this rate related to the AFN equation, and how can that equation be used to calculate the self-supporting growth rate?

(12–6) Suppose a firm makes the policy changes listed below. If a change means that external, nonspontaneous financial requirements (AFN) will increase, indicate this by a (+); indicate a decrease by a (–); and indicate no effect or an indeterminate effect by a (0). Think in terms of the *immediate, short-run* effect on funds requirements.

a. The dividend payout ratio is increased. ________
b. The firm decides to pay all suppliers on delivery, rather than after a 30-day delay, to take advantage of discounts for rapid payment. ________
c. The firm begins to offer credit to its customers, whereas previously all sales had been on a cash basis. ________
d. The firm's profit margin is eroded by increased competition, although sales hold steady. ________
e. The firm sells its manufacturing plants for cash to a contractor and simultaneously signs an outsourcing contract to purchase from that contractor goods that the firm formerly produced. ________
f. The firm negotiates a new contract with its union that lowers its labor costs without affecting its output. ________

(12–7) Assume that you recently received your MBA and now work as assistant to the CFO of a relatively large corporation. Your boss has asked you to prepare a financial forecast for the coming year, using an *Excel* model, and then to present your forecast to the firm's executive committee. Describe how you would deal with the following issues.

a. Would you want to set up the model with a number of scenarios whose results could be presented to the executives?
b. What are "financing feedbacks," and what are the pros and cons of incorporating such feedbacks into your model?
c. What are the pros and cons of assuming that all necessary outside funds are obtained from a single source (such as a bank loan) versus assuming that a mix of funds is raised so as to keep the capital structure at its target level?
d. What are the pros and cons of providing the capability to examine the results of changing dividend policy and capital structure policy as well as various operating policies such as credit policy, outsourcing policy, and so forth?
e. What does the acronym GIGO stand for, and how important is this for someone who is developing a financial model? For someone using a forecasting model? How might post-audits and incentive compensation plans help reduce GIGO?

Self-Test Problems

Solutions Appear in Appendix A

(ST–1) Self-Supporting Growth Rate

The Barnsdale Corporation has the following ratios: $A_0^*/S_0 = 1.6$; $L_0^*/S_0 = 0.4$; profit margin = 0.10; and dividend payout ratio = 0.45, or 45%. Sales last year were \$100 million. Assuming that these ratios will remain constant, use the AFN equation to determine the firm's self-supporting growth rate—in other words, the maximum growth rate Barnsdale can achieve without having to employ nonspontaneous external funds.

(ST–2) AFN Equation

Refer to Problem ST-1, and suppose Barnsdale's financial consultants report (1) that the inventory turnover ratio (sales/inventory) is 3, compared with an industry average of 4, and (2) that Barnsdale could reduce inventories and thus raise its turnover ratio to 4 without affecting its sales, profit margin, or other asset turnover ratios. Under these conditions, use the AFN equation to determine the amount of additional funds Barnsdale would require during each of the next 2 years if sales grow at a rate of 20% per year.

(ST–3) Excess Capacity

Van Auken Lumber's 2010 financial statements are shown below.

Van Auken Lumber: Balance Sheet as of December 31, 2010 (Thousands of Dollars)

Cash	$ 1,800	Accounts payable	$ 7,200
Receivables	10,800	Notes payable	3,472
Inventories	12,600	Accruals	2,520
Total current assets	$25,200	Total current liabilities	$13,192
Net fixed assets	21,600	Mortgage bonds	5,000
		Common stock	2,000
		Retained earnings	26,608
Total assets	$46,800	Total liabilities and equity	$46,800

Van Auken Lumber: Income Statement for December 31, 2010 (Thousands of Dollars)

Sales	$36,000
Operating costs	30,783
Earnings before interest and taxes	$ 5,217
Interest	717
Earnings before taxes	$ 4,500
Taxes (40%)	1,800
Net income	$ 2,700
Dividends (60%)	$ 1,620
Addition to retained earnings	$ 1,080

a. Assume that the company was operating at full capacity in 2010 with regard to all items *except* fixed assets, which in 2010 were being utilized to only 75% of capacity. By what percentage could 2011 sales increase over 2010 sales without the need for an increase in fixed assets?

b. Now suppose that 2011 sales increase by 25% over 2010 sales. Use the forecasted financial statement method to forecast a 12/31/11 balance sheet and 2011 income statement, assuming that (1) the historical ratios of operating costs/sales, cash/sales, receivables/sales, inventories/sales, accounts payable/sales, and accruals/sales remain constant; (2) Van Auken cannot sell any of its fixed assets; (3) any required financing is done at the *end* of 2011 as notes payable; (4) the firm earns no interest on its cash; and (5) the interest rate on all of its debt is 12%. Van Auken pays out 60% of its net income as dividends and has a tax rate of 40%. How much additional external capital will be required? (*Hints:* Base the forecasted interest expense on the amount of debt at the beginning of the year, because any new debt is added at the end of the year; also, use the forecasted income statement to determine the addition to retained earnings for use in the balance sheet.)

Problems

Answers Appear in Appendix B

EASY PROBLEMS 1–3

(12–1) AFN Equation

Baxter Video Products's sales are expected to increase by 20% from $5 million in 2010 to $6 million in 2011. Its assets totaled $3 million at the end of 2010. Baxter is already at full capacity, so its assets must grow at the same rate as projected sales. At the end of 2010, current liabilities were $1 million, consisting of $250,000 of accounts payable, $500,000 of notes payable, and $250,000 of accruals. The after-tax profit margin is forecasted to be 5%, and the forecasted payout ratio is 70%. Use the AFN equation to forecast Baxter's additional funds needed for the coming year.

(12–2) AFN Equation

Refer to Problem 12-1. What would be the additional funds needed if the company's year-end 2010 assets had been $4 million? Assume that all other numbers, including sales, are the same as in Problem 12-1 and that the company is operating at full capacity. Why is this AFN different from the one you found in Problem 12-1? Is the company's "capital intensity" ratio the same or different?

(12–3) AFN Equation

Refer to Problem 12-1. Return to the assumption that the company had $3 million in assets at the end of 2010, but now assume that the company pays no dividends. Under these assumptions, what would be the additional funds needed for the coming year? Why is this AFN different from the one you found in Problem 12-1?

INTERMEDIATE PROBLEMS 4–6

(12–4) Sales Increase

Bannister Legal Services generated $2,000,000 in sales during 2010, and its year-end total assets were $1,500,000. Also, at year-end 2010, current liabilities were $500,000, consisting of $200,000 of notes payable, $200,000 of accounts payable, and $100,000 of accruals. Looking ahead to 2011, the company estimates that its assets must increase at the same rate as sales, its spontaneous liabilities will increase at the same rate as sales, its profit margin will be 5%, and its payout ratio will be 60%. How large a sales increase can the company achieve without having to raise funds externally; that is, what is its self-supporting growth rate?

(12–5) Long-Term Financing Needed

At year-end 2010, Bertin Inc.'s total assets were $1.2 million and its accounts payable were $375,000. Sales, which in 2010 were $2.5 million, are expected to increase by 25% in 2011. Total assets and accounts payable are proportional to sales, and that relationship will be maintained. Bertin typically uses no current liabilities other than accounts payable. Common stock amounted to $425,000 in 2010, and retained earnings were $295,000. Bertin has arranged to sell $75,000 of new common stock in 2011 to meet some of its financing needs. The remainder of its financing needs will be met by issuing new long-term debt at the end of 2011. (Because the debt is added at the end of the year, there will be no additional interest expense due to the new debt.) Its profit margin on sales is 6%, and 40% of earnings will be paid out as dividends.

a. What were Bertin's total long-term debt and total liabilities in 2010?

b. How much new long-term debt financing will be needed in 2011? (*Hint:* AFN − New stock = New long-term debt.)

(12-6) Additional Funds Needed

The Booth Company's sales are forecasted to double from $1,000 in 2010 to $2,000 in 2011. Here is the December 31, 2010, balance sheet:

Cash	$ 100	Accounts payable	$ 50
Accounts receivable	200	Notes payable	150
Inventories	200	Accruals	50
Net fixed assets	500	Long-term debt	400
		Common stock	100
		Retained earnings	250
Total assets	$1,000	Total liabilities and equity	$1,000

Booth's fixed assets were used to only 50% of capacity during 2010, but its current assets were at their proper levels in relation to sales. All assets except fixed assets must increase at the same rate as sales, and fixed assets would also have to increase at the same rate if the current excess capacity did not exist. Booth's after-tax profit margin is forecasted to be 5% and its payout ratio to be 60%. What is Booth's additional funds needed (AFN) for the coming year?

CHALLENGING PROBLEMS 7–9

(12-7) Forecasted Statements and Ratios

Upton Computers makes bulk purchases of small computers, stocks them in conveniently located warehouses, ships them to its chain of retail stores, and has a staff to advise customers and help them set up their new computers. Upton's balance sheet as of December 31, 2010, is shown here (millions of dollars):

Cash	$ 3.5	Accounts payable	$ 9.0
Receivables	26.0	Notes payable	18.0
Inventories	58.0	Accruals	8.5
Total current assets	$ 87.5	Total current liabilities	$ 35.5
Net fixed assets	35.0	Mortgage loan	6.0
		Common stock	15.0
		Retained earnings	66.0
Total assets	$122.5	Total liabilities and equity	$122.5

Sales for 2010 were $350 million and net income for the year was $10.5 million, so the firm's profit margin was 3.0%. Upton paid dividends of $4.2 million to common stockholders, so its payout ratio was 40%. Its tax rate is 40%, and it operated at full capacity. Assume that all assets/sales ratios, spontaneous liabilities/sales ratios, the profit margin, and the payout ratio remain constant in 2011.

a. If sales are projected to increase by $70 million, or 20%, during 2011, use the AFN equation to determine Upton's projected external capital requirements.

b. Using the AFN equation, determine Upton's self-supporting growth rate. That is, what is the maximum growth rate the firm can achieve without having to employ nonspontaneous external funds?

c. Use the forecasted financial statement method to forecast Upton's balance sheet for December 31, 2011. Assume that all additional external capital is raised as a bank loan at the end of the year and is reflected in notes payable (because the debt is added at the end of the year, there will be no additional interest expense due to the new debt). Assume Upton's profit margin and dividend payout ratio will be the same in 2011 as they were in 2010. What is the amount of notes payable reported on the 2011 forecasted balance sheets? (*Hint:* You don't need to forecast the income statements because you are given the projected sales, profit margin, and dividend payout ratio; these figures allow you to calculate the 2011 addition to retained earnings for the balance sheet.)

(12–8) Additional Funds Needed

Stevens Textiles's 2010 financial statements are shown below:

Balance Sheet as of December 31, 2010 (Thousands of Dollars)

Cash	$ 1,080	Accounts payable	$ 4,320
Receivables	6,480	Accruals	2,880
Inventories	9,000	Notes payable	2,100
Total current assets	$16,560	Total current liabilities	$ 9,300
Net fixed assets	12,600	Mortgage bonds	3,500
		Common stock	3,500
		Retained earnings	12,860
Total assets	$29,160	Total liabilities and equity	$29,160

Income Statement for December 31, 2010 (Thousands of Dollars)

Sales	$36,000
Operating costs	32,440
Earnings before interest and taxes	$ 3,560
Interest	460
Earnings before taxes	$ 3,100
Taxes (40%)	1,240
Net income	$ 1,860
Dividends (45%)	$ 837
Addition to retained earnings	$ 1,023

a. Suppose 2011 sales are projected to increase by 15% over 2010 sales. Use the forecasted financial statement method to forecast a balance sheet and income statement for December 31, 2011. The interest rate on all debt is 10%, and cash earns no interest income. Assume that all additional debt is added at the end of the year, which means that you should base the forecasted interest expense on the balance of debt at the beginning of the year. Use the forecasted income statement to determine the addition to retained earnings. Assume that the company was operating at full capacity in 2010, that it cannot sell off any of its fixed assets, and that any required financing will be borrowed as notes payable. Also, assume that assets, spontaneous liabilities, and operating costs are expected to increase by the same percentage as sales. Determine the additional funds needed.

b. What is the resulting total forecasted amount of notes payable?

c. In your answers to Parts a and b, you should not have charged any interest on the additional debt added during 2011 because it was assumed that the new debt was added at the end of the year. But now suppose that the new debt is added throughout the year. Don't do any calculations, but how would this change the answers to parts a and b?

(12–9) Additional Funds Needed

Garlington Technologies Inc.'s 2010 financial statements are shown below:

Balance Sheet as of December 31, 2010

Cash	$ 180,000	Accounts payable	$ 360,000
Receivables	360,000	Notes payable	156,000
Inventories	720,000	Accruals	180,000
Total current assets	$1,260,000	Total current liabilities	$ 696,000
Fixed assets	1,440,000	Common stock	1,800,000
		Retained earnings	204,000
Total assets	$2,700,000	Total liabilities and equity	$2,700,000

Income Statement for December 31, 2010

Sales	$3,600,000
Operating costs	3,279,720
EBIT	$ 320,280
Interest	18,280
EBT	$ 302,000
Taxes (40%)	120,800
Net income	$ 181,200
Dividends	$ 108,000

Suppose that in 2011 sales increase by 10% over 2010 sales and that 2011 dividends will increase to $112,000. Forecast the financial statements using the forecasted financial statement method. Assume the firm operated at full capacity in 2010. Use an interest rate of 13%, and assume that any new debt will be added at the end of the year (so forecast the interest expense based on the debt balance at the beginning of the year). Cash does not earn any interest income. Assume that the AFN will be in the form of notes payable.

Spreadsheet Problems

(12-10) Build a Model: Forecasting Financial Statements

Start with the partial model in the file ***Ch12 P10 Build a Model.xls*** on the textbook's Web site, which contains the 2010 financial statements of Zieber Corporation. Forecast Zeiber's 2011 income statement and balance sheets. Use the following assumptions: (1) Sales grow by 6%. (2) The ratios of expenses to sales, depreciation to fixed assets, cash to sales, accounts receivable to sales, and inventories to sales will be the same in 2011 as in 2010. (3) Zeiber will not issue any new stock or new long-term bonds. (4) The interest rate is 9% for short-term debt and 11% for long-term debt. (5) No interest is earned on cash. (6) Dividends grow at an 8% rate. (6) Calculate the additional funds needed (AFN). If new financing is required, assume it will be raised as notes payable. Assume that any new notes payable will be borrowed on the last day of the year, so there will be no additional interest expense for the new notes payable. If surplus funds are available, pay a special dividend.

a. What are the forecasted levels of notes payable and special dividends?

b. Now assume that the growth in sales is only 3%. What are the forecasted levels of notes payable and special dividends?

(12-11)
Build a Model: Forecasting Financial Statements

Start with the partial model in the file ***Ch12 P11 Build a Model.xls*** on the textbook's Web site, which shows Matthews Industries's most recent balance sheet, income statement, and other data. Matthews Industries's financial planners must forecast the company's financial results for the coming year. The forecast will be based on the forecasted financial statement method, and any additional funds needed will be obtained by using notes payable. Complete the partial model and answer the following questions.

a. Assume that the firm's 2010 profit margin, payout ratio, capital intensity ratio, and spontaneous liabilities-to-sales ratio remain constant. If sales grow by 10% in 2011, what is the required external capital the firm will need in 2011 as calculated by the AFN equation?

b. If 2010 ratios remain constant, what is Matthews's self-supporting growth rate? Describe how the self-supporting growth rate will change in response to each of the following: (1) the profit margin declines, (2) the payout ratio increases, (3) the capital intensity ratio declines.

c. Matthews's management has reviewed its financial statements and arrived at two possible scenarios for 2011. The first scenario assumes a steady state while the second scenario, the target scenario, shows some improvement in ratios toward industry average values. Forecasted values for the scenarios are shown in the partially completed file ***Ch12 P11 Build a Model.xls.*** If Matthews assumes that external financing is achieved through notes payable and that financing feedbacks are not considered because the new notes payable are added at the end of the year, then what are the firm's forecasted AFN, EPS, DPS, and year-end stock price under each scenario?

d. Matthews's management realizes that interest for additional notes payable should be included in the analysis. Assume that notes will be issued midway through the year, so that interest on these notes is incurred for only half the year. If Matthews assumes now that external financing is achieved through notes payable and if financing feedbacks are considered, then what are the firm's forecasted AFN, EPS, DPS, and year-end stock price under each scenario?

THOMSON ONE | Business School Edition Problem

Use the Thomson ONE—Business School Edition online database to work this chapter's questions.

Forecasting the Future Performance of Abercrombie & Fitch

Clothing retailer Abercrombie & Fitch enjoyed phenomenal success in the late 1990s. Between 1996 and 2000, its sales grew almost fourfold, from $335 million to more than $1.2 billion, and its stock price soared by more than 500%. More recently, however, its growth rate has begun to slow down, and Abercrombie has had a hard time meeting its quarterly earnings targets. As a result, the stock price in late 2002 was about half of what it was 3 years earlier. Abercrombie's struggles resulted from increased competition, a sluggish economy, and the challenges of staying ahead of the fashion curve.

Since 2002, the company's stock has rebounded strongly but questions remain about the firm's long-term growth prospects. Given the questions about Abercrombie's future growth rate, analysts have focused on the company's earnings reports. Thomson ONE provides a convenient and detailed summary of the company's recent earnings history along with a summary of analysts' earnings forecasts.

To access this information, we begin by entering the company's ticker symbol, ANF, on Thomson ONE's main screen and then selecting GO. This takes us to an overview of the company's recent performance. After checking out the overview, you should click on the tab labeled Estimates, near the top of your screen. Here you will find a wide range of information about the company's past and projected earnings.

Thomson ONE—BSE Discussion Questions

1. What are the mean and median forecasts for Abercrombie's earnings per share over the next fiscal year?
2. Based on analysts' forecasts, what is the firm's expected long-term growth rate in earnings?
3. Have analysts made any significant changes to their forecasted earnings for Abercrombie & Fitch in the past few months?
4. Historically, have Abercrombie's reported earnings generally met, exceeded, or fallen short of analysts' forecasted earnings?
5. How has Abercrombie's stock performed this year relative to the S&P 500?

Mini Case

Hatfield Medical Supplies's stock price had been lagging its industry averages, so its board of directors brought in a new CEO, Adam Lee. Lee asked for the company's long-run strategic plan; when he learned that no formal plan existed, he decided to develop one himself. Lee had brought in Rick Novak, a finance MBA who had been working for a consulting company, to replace the old CFO, and he asked Rick to develop the financial planning section of the strategic plan. In his previous job, Novak's primary task had been to help clients develop financial forecasts, and that was one reason Lee hired him.

Novak began as he always did, by comparing Hatfield's financial ratios to the industry averages. If any ratio was substandard, he discussed it with the responsible manager to see what could be done to improve the situation. Figure MC-1 provides Hatfield's latest financial statements plus some ratios and other data that Novak plans to use in his analysis. Notice that the figure is extracted from an *Excel* spreadsheet. Novak learned back in his university days that, because of interactions among variables, any realistic financial forecast must be based on a computer model. (The model is available to your instructor on the textbook's Web site.) Of course, he is also aware of the well-known computer axiom—garbage in, garbage out (GIGO). Novak therefore plans to discuss the model's inputs carefully with Hatfield's operating managers, individually and also collectively in the company's financial planning conference.

a. Do you think Adam Lee should develop a strategic plan for the company? Why? What are the central elements of such a plan? What is the role of finance in a strategic plan?
b. Given the data in Figure MC-1, how well run would you say Hatfield appears to be in comparison with other firms in its industry? What are its primary strengths and weaknesses? Be specific in your answer, and point to various ratios that support your position. Also, use the Du Pont equation (see Chapter 3) as one part of your analysis.
c. Use the AFN equation to estimate Hatfield's required new external capital for 2011 if the 15% expected growth takes place. Assume that the firm's 2010 ratios will remain the same in 2011.
d. Define the term *capital intensity*. Explain how a decline in capital intensity would affect the AFN, other things held constant. Would economies of scale combined with rapid growth affect capital intensity, other things held constant? Also, explain how changes in each of the following would affect AFN, holding other things constant: the growth rate, the amount of accounts payable, the profit margin, and the payout ratio.

FIGURE MC-1 Financial Statements and Other Data (Millions, Except for Per Share Data)

	A	B	C	D	E	F	G
4							
5	Balance Sheet, Hatfield, 12/31/10				Income Statement, Hatfield, 2010		
6	Cash and securities		$20		Sales		$2,000
7	Accounts receivable		290		Total operating costs		1,900
8	Inventories		390		EBIT		$100
9	Total current assets		$700		Interest		60
10	Net fixed assests		500		EBT		$40
11	Total assets		$1,200		Taxes (40%)		16
12					Net income		$24
13	Accounts pay. + accruals		$100		Dividends		$9
14	Notes payable		80		Add'n to retain. earnings		$15
15	Total current liabilities		$180		Shares outstanding		10
16	Long-term debt		520		EPS		$2.40
17	Total liabilities		$700		DPS		$0.90
18	Common stock		300		Year-end stock price		$24.00
19	Retained earnings		200				
20	Total common equity		$500				
21	Total liab. & equity		$1,200				

	A	B	C	D	E	F	G
23	Selected Ratios and Other Data, 2010			Hatfield	Industry		
24			Sales, 2010 (S_0)	$2.000	$2.000	Sales set equal to Hatfield to make the data comparable.	
25			Expected growth in sales:	15.0%	15.0%		
26			Profit margin (M):	1.2%	2.74%		
27			Assests/Sales (A_0*S_0):	60.0%	50.0%		
28			Payout ratio (POR):	67.5%	35.0%		
29			Equity multiplier (Assets/Equity):	2.40	2.13		
30			Total liability/Total assets	58.3%	53.0%		
31			Times interest earned (EBIT/Interest):	1.67	5.20		
32			Increase in sales ($\Delta S = gS_0$):	$300	$300		
33			(Payables + Accruals)/Sales (L_0*S_0)	5.0%	4.0%		
34			Operating costs/Sales:	95.0%	93.0%		
35			Cash/Sales:	1.0%	1.0%		
36			Receivables/Sales:	14.5%	11.0%		
37			Inventories/Sales:	19.5%	15.0%		
38			Fixed assets/Sales:	25.0%	23.0%		
39			Tax rate:	40.0%	40.0%		
40			Interest rate on all debt:	10.00%	9.5%		
41			Price/Earning (P/E):	10.0	12.0		
42			ROE (Net income/Common equity):	4.80%	11.64%		

Note: Hatfield was operating at full capacity in 2010.

e. Define the term *self-supporting growth rate*. Based on the Figure MC-1 data, what is Hatfield's self-supporting growth rate? Would the self-supporting growth rate be affected by a change in the capital intensity ratio or the other factors mentioned in question d? Other things held constant, would the calculated capital intensity ratio change over time if the company were growing and were also subject to economies of scale and/or lumpy assets?

f. Forecast the financial statements for 2011 using the following assumptions. (1) Operating ratios remain unchanged. (2) No additional notes payable, LT bonds, or common stock will be issued. (3) The interest rate on all debt is 10%. (4) If additional financing is needed, then it will be raised through a line of credit. The line of credit would be tapped on the last day of the year, so it would create no additional interest expenses for that year. (5) Interest expenses for notes payable and LT bonds are based on the average balances during the year. (6) If surplus funds are available, the surplus will be paid out as a special dividend payment. (7) Regular dividends will grow by 15%. (8) Sales will grow by 15%. We call this the Steady scenario because operations remain unchanged.

1. How much new capital will the firm need (i.e., what is the forecasted AFN); how does it compare with the amount you calculated using the AFN equation; and why does any difference exist?
2. Calculate the firm's free cash flow, return on invested capital, EPS, DPS, ROE, and any other ratios you think would be useful in considering the situation.
3. Assuming all of the inputs turn out to be exactly correct, would these answers also be exactly correct? If not, why not?

g. Repeat the analysis performed for Question f but now assume that Hatfield is able to achieve industry averages for the following input variables: operating costs/sales, receivables/sales, inventories/sales, and fixed assets/sales. Answer parts (1) and (2) of f under the new assumptions.
h. Could a strategic plan that included an incentive compensation program affect the firm's ability to move toward industry average operating performance?
i. What is financing feedback?

Selected Additional Cases

The following cases from Textchoice, *Cengage Learning's online library, cover many of the concepts discussed in this chapter and are available at* **http://www.textchoice2.com**.

Klein-Brigham Series:
Case 37, "Space-Age Materials, Inc."; Case 38, "Automated Banking Management, Inc."; Case 52, "Expert Systems"; and Case 69, "Medical Management Systems, Inc."

CHAPTER 13

Corporate Valuation, Value-Based Management and Corporate Governance

The year 2008 was a grim one for many companies, with the average stock (as measured by the NYSE Composite Index) losing about 40% of its value. There are only three possible explanations for this decline.

1. *The market price did not reflect intrinsic value—at the beginning of the year, at the end of the year, or possibly both. In other words, the market might have been overvalued in early 2008, undervalued at the end of 2008, or both. This implies that investors were (and perhaps still are) irrational.*
2. *Companies' expected future free cash flows fell sharply when investors revised their estimates downward as information about the pending economic crisis unfolded.*
3. *The cost of capital went up, which could have been due to an increase in investors' risk aversion.*

These explanations aren't mutually exclusive, so the explanation for the market decline is likely some mix of the three reasons. Keep the stock market's performance in mind as you read the first half of this chapter, which explains how the intrinsic values of a company and its stock are determined.

The global economic crisis also has caused widespread attention on corporate governance, with governments now taking ownership/leadership positions at many companies ranging from Fannie Mae to Citigroup to General Motors. As we write this, governments all over the world are struggling to determine the type and degree of regulation that will prevent future meltdowns yet still promote innovation. CEOs and board directors are in the news daily, with many poorly performing CEOs being replaced and many boards assuming additional responsibilities. There is a spotlight on executive compensation, with the federal government limiting compensation to bailout recipients and Congress proposing laws to "claw back" some compensation already paid. In summary, there is a worldwide focus on corporate governance, so think about these examples when reading the second half of this chapter.

Corporate Valuation: Putting the Pieces Together

The intrinsic value of a firm is determined by the size, timing, and risk of its expected future free cash flows (FCF). Chapter 12 showed how to project financial statements, and Chapter 2 showed how to calculate free cash flows. Chapter 9 explained how to estimate the weighted average cost of capital. This chapter puts the pieces together and shows how to calculate the value of a firm. It also shows how to use the valuation model as a guide for choosing among different corporate strategies and operating tactics.

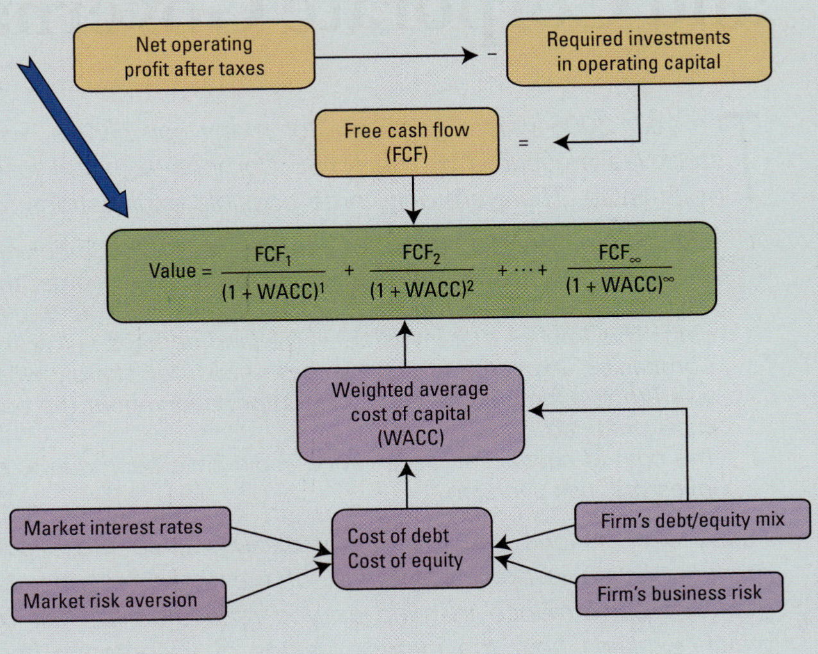

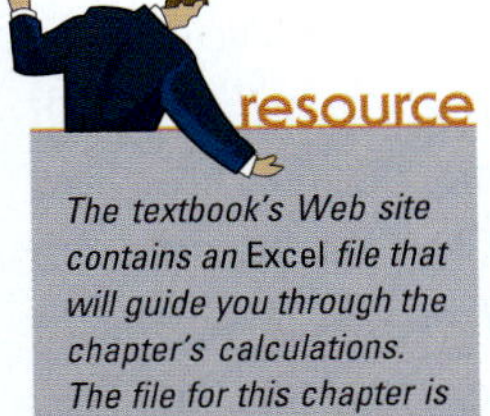

The textbook's Web site contains an Excel file that will guide you through the chapter's calculations. The file for this chapter is **Ch13 Tool Kit.xls**, *and we encourage you to open the file and follow along as you read the chapter.*

As we have emphasized throughout the book, maximizing intrinsic value should be management's primary objective. However, to maximize value, managers need a tool for estimating the effects of alternative strategies. In this chapter, we develop and illustrate such a tool—the **corporate valuation model**, which is the present value of expected future free cash flows discounted at the weighted average cost of capital. In a sense, the corporate valuation model is the culmination of all the material covered thus far, because it pulls together financial statements, cash flows, financial projections, time value of money, risk, and the cost of capital. Some companies practice **value-based management** by systematically using the corporate valuation model to guide their decisions. The degree to which a company employs principles of value-based management often depends on its **corporate governance**, which is the set of laws, rules, and procedures that influence its operations and the decisions made by its managers. This chapter addresses all these topics, beginning with corporate valuation.

13.1 Overview of Corporate Valuation

As stated earlier, managers should evaluate the effects of alternative strategies on their firms' values. This really means forecasting financial statements under alternative strategies, finding the present value of each strategy's cash flow stream, and then choosing the strategy that provides the maximum value. The financial statements should be projected using the techniques and procedures discussed in Chapter 12, and the discount rate should be the risk-adjusted cost of capital as discussed in Chapter 9. But what model should managers use to discount the cash flows? One possibility is the dividend growth model from Chapter 7. However, that model is often unsuitable for managerial purposes. For example, suppose a start-up company is formed to develop and market a new product. Its managers will focus on product development, marketing, and raising capital. They will probably be thinking about an eventual IPO, or perhaps the sale of the company to a larger firm—Cisco, Microsoft, Intel, IBM, or another of the industry leaders that buy hundreds of successful new companies each year. For the managers of such a start-up, the decision to initiate dividend payments in the foreseeable future will be totally off the radar screen. Thus, the dividend growth model is not useful for valuing most start-up companies.

Also, many established firms pay no dividends. Investors may expect them to pay dividends sometime in the future—but when, and how much? As long as internal opportunities and acquisitions are so attractive, the initiation of dividends will be postponed, and this makes the dividend growth model of little use. Even Microsoft, one of the world's most successful companies, paid no dividends until 2003.

Finally, the dividend growth model is generally of limited use for internal management purposes, even for a dividend-paying company. If the firm consisted of just one big asset and if that asset produced all of the cash flows used to pay dividends, then alternative strategies could be judged through the use of the dividend growth model. However, most firms have several different divisions with many assets, so the corporation's value depends on the cash flows from many different assets and on the actions of many managers. These managers need a way to measure the effects of their decisions on corporate value, but the discounted dividend model isn't very useful because individual divisions don't pay dividends.

Fortunately, the corporate valuation model does not depend on dividends, and it can be applied to divisions and subunits as well as to the entire firm.

Another important aspect of value-based management is the concept of corporate governance. The corporate valuation model shows how corporate decisions affect *stockholders*. However, corporate decisions are made by managers, not stockholders, and maximizing shareholder wealth is not the same as individual managers maximizing their own "satisfaction." Thus, a key aspect of value-based management is making sure that managers focus on the goal of maximizing stockholder wealth. The set of laws, rules, and procedures that influence a company's operations and motivate its managers falls under the general heading of *corporate governance*.

This chapter discusses the corporate valuation model, value-based management, and corporate governance, beginning with the corporate valuation model.

Self-Test

Why is the corporate valuation model applicable in more circumstances than the dividend growth model?

What is value-based management?

What is corporate governance?

13.2 The Corporate Valuation Model

There are two types of corporate assets: **operating** and **nonoperating**. Operating assets, in turn, take two forms: **assets-in-place** and **growth options**. Assets-in-place include such tangible assets as land, buildings, machines, and inventory as well as intangible assets such as patents, customer lists, reputation, and general know-how. Growth options are opportunities to expand that arise from the firm's current operating knowledge, experience, and other resources. The assets-in-place provide an expected stream of cash flows, and so do the growth options. For instance, Wal-Mart has stores, inventory, widespread name recognition, a reputation for low prices, and considerable expertise in business processes. These tangible and intangible assets produce current sales and cash flows, and they also provide opportunities for new investments that will produce additional cash flows in the future. Similarly, Merck owns manufacturing plants, patents, and other real assets; it also has a knowledge base that facilitates the development of new drugs and thus new cash flow streams.

Most companies also own some nonoperating assets, which come in two forms. The first is a marketable securities portfolio over and above the cash needed to operate the business. For example, Ford Motor Company's automotive operation held about $9.2 billion in marketable securities at the end of December 2008, and this was in addition to $6.4 billion in cash. Second, Ford also had $1.1 billion of investments in other businesses, which were reported on the asset side of the balance sheet as "Equity in Net Assets of Affiliated Companies." In total, Ford had $9.2 + $1.1 = $10.3 billion of nonoperating assets, amounting to 14% of its $73.8 billion of total automotive assets. For most companies, the percentage is much lower. For example, as of the end of January, 2009, Wal-Mart's percentage of nonoperating assets was less than 1%, which is more typical.

We see, then, that for most companies operating assets are far more important than nonoperating assets. Moreover, companies can influence the values of their operating assets, whereas the values of nonoperating assets are largely beyond their direct control. Therefore, value-based management—and hence this chapter—focuses on operating assets.

Estimating the Value of Operations

Tables 13-1 and 13-2 contain the actual 2010 and projected 2011 to 2014 financial statements for MagnaVision Inc., which produces optical systems for use in medical photography. (See Chapter 12 for more details on how to project financial statements.) Growth has been rapid in the past, but the market is becoming saturated, so the sales growth rate is expected to decline from 21% in 2011 to a sustainable rate of 5% in 2014 and beyond. Profit margins are expected to improve as the production process becomes more efficient and because MagnaVision will no longer be incurring marketing costs associated with the introduction of a major product. All items on the financial statements are projected to grow at a 5% rate after 2014. Note that the company does not pay a dividend, but it is expected to start paying out about 75% of its earnings beginning in 2013. (Chapter 14 explains in more detail how companies decide how much to pay out in dividends.)

Recall that free cash flow (FCF) is the cash from operations that is actually available for distribution to investors, including stockholders, bondholders, and preferred stockholders. The value of operations is the present value of the free cash flows the firm is expected to generate out into the future. Therefore, MagnaVision's value can be calculated as the present value of its expected future free cash flows from operations, discounted at its weighted average cost of capital (WACC), plus the value of its

TABLE 13-1 MagnaVision Inc.: Income Statements (Millions of Dollars, Except for Per Share Data)

	ACTUAL	PROJECTED			
	2010	2011	2012[a]	2013	2014
Net sales	$700.0	$850.0	$1,000.0	$1,100.0	$1,155.0
Costs (except depreciation)	599.0	734.0	911.0	935.0	982.0
Depreciation	28.0	31.0	34.0	36.0	38.0
Total operating costs	$627.0	$765.0	$ 945.0	$ 971.0	$1,020.0
Earnings before interest and taxes (EBIT)	$ 73.0	$ 85.0	$ 55.0	$ 129.0	$ 135.0
Less: Net interest[b]	13.0	15.0	16.0	17.0	19.0
Earnings before taxes	$ 60.0	$ 70.0	$ 39.0	$ 112.0	$ 116.0
Taxes (40%)	24.0	28.0	15.6	44.8	46.4
Net income before preferred dividends	$ 36.0	$ 42.0	$ 23.4	$ 67.2	$ 69.6
Preferred dividends	6.0	7.0	7.4	8.0	8.3
Net income available for common dividends	$ 30.0	$ 35.0	$ 16.0	$ 59.2	$ 61.3
Common dividends	—	—	—	$ 44.2	$ 45.3
Addition to retained earnings	$ 30.0	$ 35.0	$ 16.0	$ 15.0	$ 16.0
Number of shares	100.0	100.0	100.0	100.0	100.0
Dividends per share	—	—	—	$ 0.442	$ 0.453

Notes:

[a]Net income is projected to decline in 2012. This is due to the projected cost for a one-time marketing program in that year.

[b]"Net interest" is interest paid on debt minus interest earned on marketable securities. Both items could be shown separately on the income statements, but for this example we combine them and show net interest. MagnaVision pays more interest than it earns; hence its net interest is subtracted.

nonoperating assets. Here is the equation for the value of operations, which is the firm's value as a going concern:

$$\text{Value of operations} = V_{op} = \text{PV of expected future free cash flows}$$
$$= \frac{FCF_1}{(1+WACC)^1} + \frac{FCF_2}{(1+WACC)^2} + \cdots + \frac{FCF_\infty}{(1+WACC)^\infty} \quad \textbf{(13-1)}$$
$$= \sum_{t=1}^{\infty} \frac{FCF_t}{(1+WACC)^t}$$

MagnaVision's cost of capital is 10.84%. To find its value of operations as a going concern, we use an approach similar to the nonconstant dividend growth model for stocks in Chapter 7 and proceed as follows.

1. Assume that the firm will experience nonconstant growth for N years, after which it will grow at some constant rate.
2. Calculate the expected free cash flow for each of the N nonconstant growth years.
3. Recognize that growth after Year N will be constant, so we can use the constant growth formula to find the firm's value at Year N. This is the sum of the PVs for year N + 1 and all subsequent years, discounted back to Year N.
4. Find the PV of the free cash flows for each of the N nonconstant growth years. Also, find the PV of the firm's value at Year N.

TABLE 13-2 MagnaVision Inc.: Balance Sheets (Millions of Dollars)

	ACTUAL	PROJECTED			
	2010	2011	2012	2013	2014
Assets					
Cash	$ 17.0	$ 20.0	$ 22.0	$ 23.0	$ 24.0
Marketable securities[a]	63.0	70.0	80.0	84.0	88.0
Accounts receivable	85.0	100.0	110.0	116.0	121.0
Inventories	170.0	200.0	220.0	231.0	243.0
Total current assets	$335.0	$390.0	$432.0	$454.0	$476.0
Net plant and equipment	279.0	310.0	341.0	358.0	376.0
Total assets	$614.0	$700.0	$773.0	$812.0	$852.0
Liabilities and Equity					
Accounts payable	$ 17.0	$ 20.0	$ 22.0	$ 23.0	$ 24.0
Notes payable	123.0	140.0	160.0	168.0	176.0
Accruals	43.0	50.0	55.0	58.0	61.0
Total current liabilities	$183.0	$210.0	$237.0	$249.0	$261.0
Long-term bonds	124.0	140.0	160.0	168.0	176.0
Preferred stock	62.0	70.0	80.0	84.0	88.0
Common stock[b]	200.0	200.0	200.0	200.0	200.0
Retained earnings	45.0	80.0	96.0	111.0	127.0
Common equity	$245.0	$280.0	$296.0	$311.0	$327.0
Total liabilities and equity	$614.0	$700.0	$773.0	$812.0	$852.0

Notes:
[a]All assets except marketable securities are operating assets required to support sales. The marketable securities are financial assets not required in operations.
[b]Par plus paid-in capital.

5. Now sum all the PVs, those of the annual free cash flows during the nonconstant period plus the PV of the Year-N value, to find the firm's value of operations.

Figure 13-1 calculates free cash flow for each year, using procedures discussed in Chapter 2. Line 1, with data for 2010 from the balance sheets in Table 13-2, shows the required net operating working capital, or operating current assets minus operating current liabilities, for 2010:

$$\begin{aligned}\begin{matrix}\text{Required net}\\ \text{operating}\\ \text{working capital}\end{matrix} &= \begin{pmatrix}\text{Cash}\\ +\text{ Accounts receivable}\\ +\text{ Inventories}\end{pmatrix} - \begin{pmatrix}\text{Accounts payable}\\ +\text{ Accruals}\end{pmatrix}\\ &= (\$17.00 + \$85.00 + \$170.00) - (\$17.00 + \$43.00)\\ &= \$212.00\end{aligned}$$

Line 2 shows required net plant and equipment; Line 3, which is the sum of Lines 1 and 2, shows the required net operating assets, also called total net operating capital or just operating capital. For 2010, operating capital is $212 + $279 = $491 million.

Line 4 shows the required annual addition to operating capital, found as the change in operating capital from the previous year. For 2011, the required investment in operating capital is $560 − $491 = $69 million.

FIGURE 13-1 Calculating MagnaVision's Expected Free Cash Flow (Millions of Dollars)

	A	B	C	D	E	F	G
72			Actual		Projected		
73	Step 1: Calculate FCF		2010	2011	2012	2013	2014
74	1. Net operating working capital		$212.00	$250.00	$275.00	$289.00	$303.00
75	2. Net plant and equipment		279.00	310.00	341.00	358.00	376.00
76	3. Net operating capital		$491.00	$560.00	$616.00	$647.00	$679.00
77	4. Investment in operating capital			69.00	56.00	31.00	32.00
78	5. NOPAT		$43.80	$51.00	$33.00	$77.40	$81.00
79	6. Less: Investment in op. capital			69.00	56.00	31.00	32.00
80	7. Free cash flow			–$18.00	–$23.00	$46.40	$49.00

[a]We use the terms "total net operating capital," "operating capital," and "net operating assets" interchangeably.
[b]NOPAT declines in 2012 because of a marketing expenditure projected for that year. See Note a in Table 13-1.

See **Ch13 Tool Kit.xls** on the textbook's Web site.

Line 5 shows NOPAT, or net operating profit after taxes. Note that EBIT is operating earnings *before* taxes, while NOPAT is operating earnings *after* taxes. Therefore, NOPAT = EBIT(1 − T). With a 2011 EBIT of $85 million (as shown in Table 13-1) and a tax rate of 40%, the NOPAT projected for 2011 is $51 million:

$$\text{NOPAT} = \text{EBIT}(1 - \text{T}) = \$85(1.0 - 0.4) = \$51 \text{ million}$$

Although MagnaVision's operating capital is projected to produce $51 million of after-tax profits in 2011, the company must invest $69 million in new operating capital in 2011 to support its growth plan. Therefore, the free cash flow for 2011, shown on Line 7, is a negative $18 million:

$$\text{Free cash flow (FCF)} = \$51 - \$69 = -\$18 \text{ million}$$

This negative free cash flow in the early years is typical for young, high-growth companies. Even though net operating profit after taxes (NOPAT) is positive in all years, free cash flow is negative because of the need to invest in operating assets. The negative free cash flow means the company will have to obtain new funds from investors, and the balance sheets in Table 13-2 show that notes payable, long-term bonds, and preferred stock all increase from 2010 to 2011. Stockholders will also help fund MagnaVision's growth—they will receive no dividends until 2013, so all of the net income from 2011 and 2012 will be reinvested. However, as growth slows, free cash flow will become positive, and MagnaVision plans to use some of its FCF to pay dividends beginning in 2013.[1]

A variant of the constant growth dividend model is shown as Equation 13-2. This equation can be used to find the value of MagnaVision's operations at time N, when its free cash flows stabilize and begin to grow at a constant rate. This is the value of all FCFs beyond time N, discounted back to time N (which is 2014 for MagnaVision):

$$V_{op(\text{at time N})} = \sum_{t=N+1}^{\infty} \frac{FCF_t}{(1 + WACC)^{t-N}} = \frac{FCF_{N+1}}{WACC - g} = \frac{FCF_N(1 + g)}{WACC - g} \qquad (13\text{-}2)$$

[1]Magna Vision plans to increase its debt and preferred stock each year so as to maintain a constant capital structure. We discuss capital structure in detail in Chapter 15.

Based on a 10.84% cost of capital, $49 million of free cash flow in 2014, and a 5% growth rate, the value of MagnaVision's operations as of December 31, 2014, is forecasted to be $880.99 million:

See **Ch13 Tool Kit.xls** *on the textbook's Web site.*

$$V_{op(12/31/14)} = \frac{FCF_{12/31/14}(1+g)}{WACC - g} = \frac{\$49(1+0.05)}{0.1084-0.05} = \frac{\$51.45}{0.1084-0.05} = \$880.99 \quad (13\text{-}2a)$$

This $880.99 million figure is called the company's **terminal**, or **horizon, value**, because it is the value at the end of the forecast period. It is also sometimes called a **continuing value**. It is the amount that MagnaVision could expect to receive if it sold its operating assets on December 31, 2014.

Figure 13-2 shows the free cash flow for each year during the nonconstant growth period along with the horizon value of operations in 2014. To find the value of operations as of "today," December 31, 2010, we find the PV of the horizon value and each annual free cash flow in Figure 13-2, discounting at the 10.84% cost of capital:

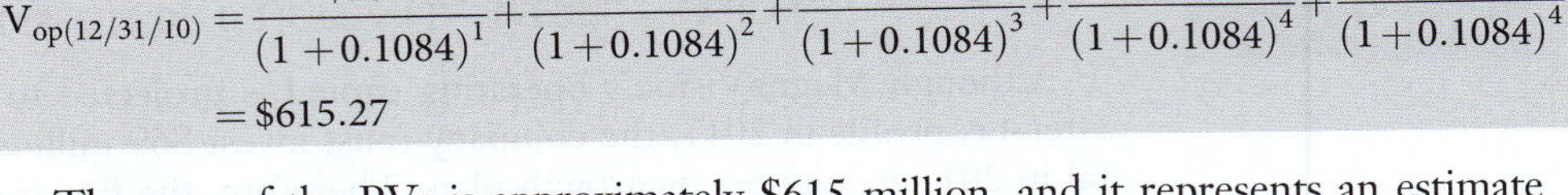

$$V_{op(12/31/10)} = \frac{-\$18.00}{(1+0.1084)^1} + \frac{-\$23.00}{(1+0.1084)^2} + \frac{\$46.40}{(1+0.1084)^3} + \frac{\$49.00}{(1+0.1084)^4} + \frac{\$880.99}{(1+0.1084)^4}$$
$$= \$615.27$$

The sum of the PVs is approximately $615 million, and it represents an estimate of the price MagnaVision could expect to receive if it sold its operating assets "today," December 31, 2010.

See **Ch13 Tool Kit.xls** *on the textbook's Web site.*

Estimating the Price Per Share

The total value of any company is the value of its operations plus the value of its nonoperating assets.[2] As the shown in the Table 13-2 balance sheet for December 31,

FIGURE 13-2 MagnaVision's Value of Operations (Millions of Dollars)

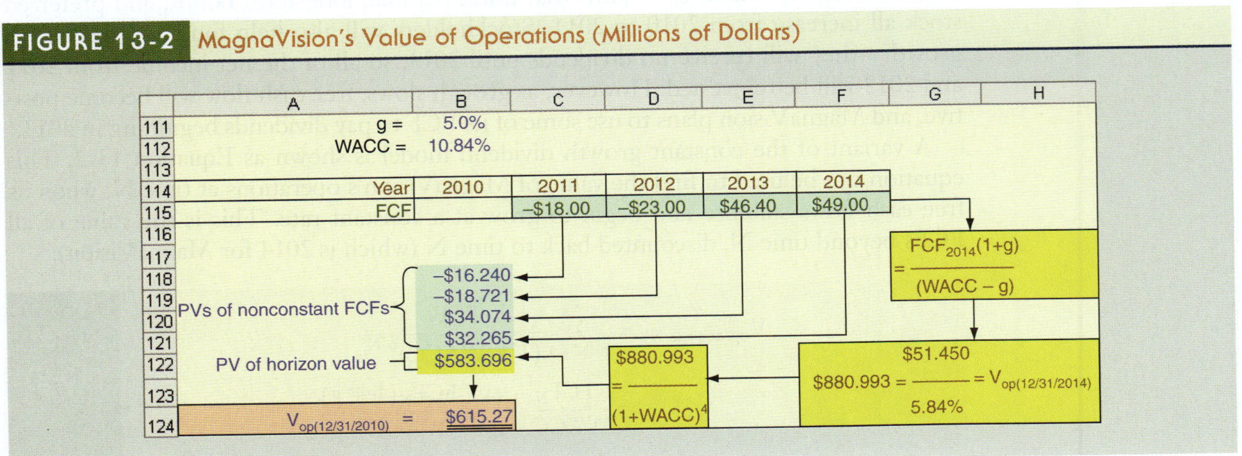

	A	B	C	D	E	F	G	H
111	g =	5.0%						
112	WACC =	10.84%						
113								
114	Year	2010	2011	2012	2013	2014		
115	FCF		−$18.00	−$23.00	$46.40	$49.00		
116								
117							FCF2014(1+g)	
118		−$16.240					= ————	
119	PVs of nonconstant FCFs	−$18.721					(WACC − g)	
120		$34.074						
121		$32.265						
122	PV of horizon value	$583.696		$880.993			$51.450	
123				= ————			$880.993 = ———— = Vop(12/31/2014)	
124	Vop(12/31/2010) =	$615.27		(1+WACC)4			5.84%	

[2]The total value also includes the value of growth options not associated with assets-in-place, but MagnaVision has no such options.

FIGURE 13-3 MagnaVision's Value as of December 31, 2010

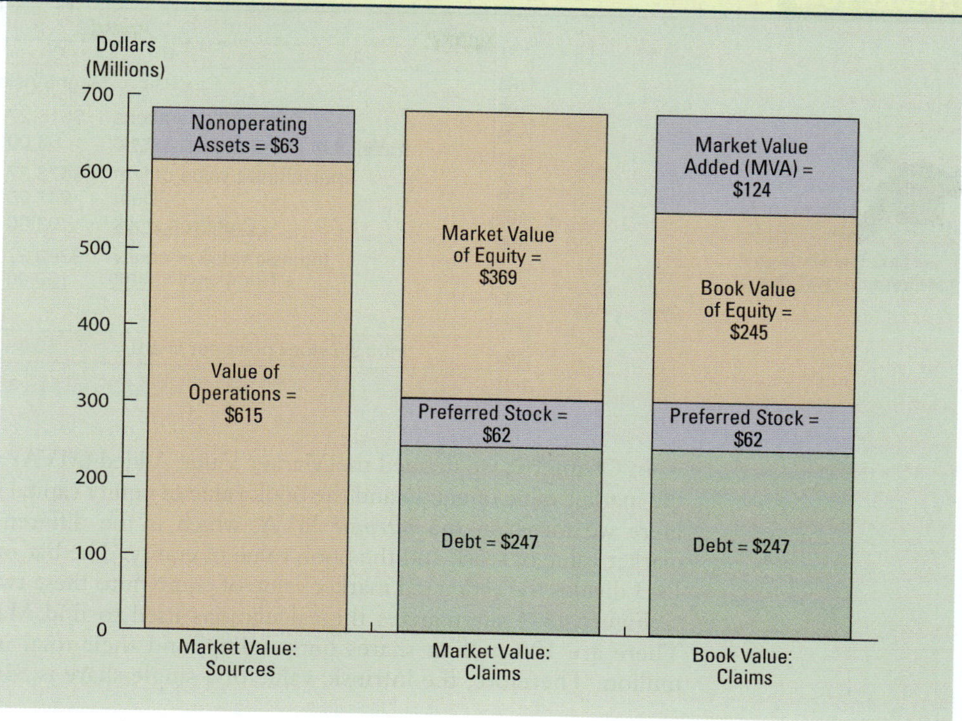

2010, MagnaVision had $63 million of marketable securities on that date. Unlike for operating assets, we don't need to calculate a present value for marketable securities because short-term financial assets as reported on the balance sheet are at (or close to) their market value. Therefore, MagnaVision's total value on December 31, 2010, is $615.27 + $63 = $678.27 million.

If the company's total value on December 31, 2010, is $678.27 million, then what is the value of its common equity? First, the sum of notes payable and long-term debt is $123 + $124 = $247 million, and these securities have the first claim on assets and income.[3] The preferred stock has a claim of $62 million, and it also ranks above the common. Therefore, the value left for common stockholders is $678.27 − $247 − $62 = $369.27 million.

Figure 13-3 is a bar chart that provides a breakdown of MagnaVision's value. The left bar shows the company's total value as the sum of its nonoperating assets and its value of operations. Next, the middle bar shows the claim of each class of investors on that total value. Debtholders have the highest priority claim, and MagnaVision owes $123 million on notes payable and $124 million on long-term bonds for a total of $247 million. The preferred stockholders have the next claim, $62 million. The remaining value belongs to the common equity, and it amounts to $678.27 − $247 − $62 = $369.27 million.[4] This is MagnaVision's intrinsic value of equity.

[3]Accounts payable and accruals were part of the calculation of FCF, so their impact on value is already incorporated into the valuation of the company's operations. It would be double-counting to subtract them now from the value of operations.

[4]When estimating the intrinsic market value of equity, it would be better to subtract the market values of debt and preferred stock rather than their book values. However, in most cases (including this one), the book values of fixed-income securities are close to their market values. When this is true, one can simply use book values.

FIGURE 13-4 Finding the Value of MagnaVision's Intrinsic Stock Price (Millions, Except for Per Share Data)

	A	B	C	D
184		Process	MagnaVision	
185		Value of operations	$615.27	
186		+ Value of nonoperating assets	63.00	
187		Total intrinsic value of firm	$678.27	
188		− Debt	247.00	
189		− Preferred stock	62.00	
190		Intrinsic value of equity	$369.27	
191		÷ Number of shares	100.00	
192				
193				
194	Intrinsic stock price per share =		$3.69	

In Chapter 2, we defined the Market Value Added (MVA) as the difference between the market value of equity and the book value of equity capital supplied by shareholders. Here we focus on the *intrinsic* MVA, which is the difference between the intrinsic market value of stock and the book value of equity. The bar on the right side of Figure 13-3 divides the estimated market value of equity into these two components.

Figure 13-4 summarizes the calculations used to find MagnaVision's stock value. There are 100 million shares outstanding, and their total intrinsic value is $369.27 million. Therefore, the intrinsic value of a single share is $369.27/100 = $3.69.

The Dividend Growth Model Applied to MagnaVision

MagnaVision has not yet begun to pay dividends. However, as we saw in Table 13-1, a cash dividend of $0.442 per share is forecasted for 2013. The dividend is expected to grow by about 2.5% in 2014 and at a constant 5% rate thereafter. MagnaVision's cost of equity is 14%. In this situation, we can apply the nonconstant dividend growth model as developed earlier in Chapter 7. Figure 13-5 shows that the value of MagnaVision's stock, based on this model, is $3.70 per share, which is the same (except for a rounding difference) as the value found using the corporate valuation model.[5]

Comparing the Corporate Valuation and Dividend Growth Models

Because the corporate valuation and dividend growth models give the same answer, does it matter which model you choose? In general, it does. For example, if you were a financial analyst estimating the value of a mature company whose dividends are expected to grow steadily in the future, it would probably be more efficient to use the dividend growth model. In this case you would need to estimate only the growth rate in dividends, not the entire set of forecasted financial statements.

However, if a company is paying a dividend but is still in the high-growth stage of its life cycle, you would need to project the future financial statements before you could make a reasonable estimate of future dividends. Then, because you would have already estimated future financial statements, it would be a toss-up as to whether the corporate valuation model or the dividend growth model would be easier to apply. Intel, which pays a dividend of about 52 cents per share on earnings of about $1.25 per share, is an example of a company to which you could apply either model.

[5]The small difference is due to rounding the cost of capital to four significant digits.

FIGURE 13-5 Using the DCF Dividend Model to Find MagnaVision's Stock Value

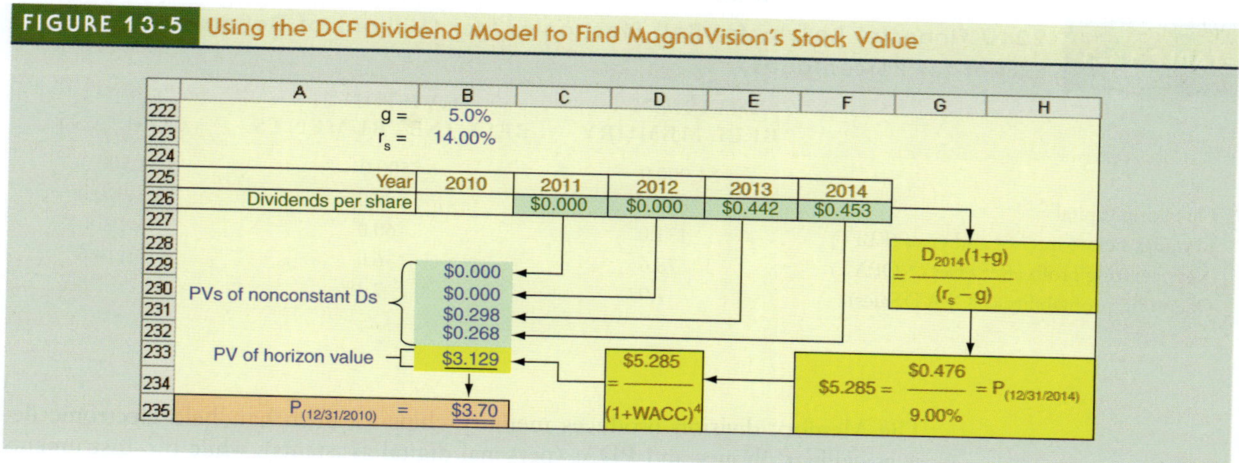

Now suppose you were trying to estimate the value of a company that has never paid a dividend, or a new firm that is about to go public, or a division that GE or some other large company is planning to sell. In each of these situations there would be no choice: You would have to estimate future financial statements and use the corporate valuation model.

Actually, much can be learned from the corporate valuation model even if a company is paying steady dividends; hence, many analysts today use it for all valuation analyses. The process of projecting future financial statements can reveal quite a bit about a company's operations and financing needs. Also, such an analysis can provide insights into actions that might be taken to increase the company's value. This is the essence of value-based management, which we discuss in the next section.[6]

Self-Test

Give some examples of assets-in-place, growth options, and nonoperating assets.
Write out the equation for the value of operations.
What is the *terminal,* or *horizon, value?* Why is it also called the *continuing value?*
Explain how to estimate the price per share using the corporate valuation model.
A company expects FCF of –$10 million at Year 1 and FCF of $20 million at Year 2; after Year 2, FCF is expected to grow at a 5% rate. If the WACC is 10%, then what is the horizon value of operations, $V_{op(Year\ 2)}$? ($420 million) What is the current value of operations, $V_{op(Year\ 0)}$? ($354.55 million)
A company has a current value of operations of $800 million, and it holds $100 million in short-term investments. If the company has $400 million in debt and has 10 million shares outstanding, what is the price per share? ($50.00)

13.3 Value-Based Management

Bell Electronics Inc. has two divisions, Memory and Instruments, with total sales of $1.5 billion and operating capital of $1.07 billion. Based on its current stock and bond prices, the company's total market value is about $1.215 billion, giving it an MVA of $145 million: $1.215 – $1.070 = $0.145 billion = $145 million. Because it has a positive MVA, Bell has created value for its investors. Even so, management is considering several new strategic plans in its efforts to increase the firm's value. All of Bell's assets are used in operations.

[6]For a more detailed explanation of corporate valuation, see P. Daves, M. Ehrhardt, and R. Shrieves, *Corporate Valuation: A Guide for Managers and Investors* (Mason, OH: Thomson/South-Western, 2004).

TABLE 13-3 2010 Financial Results for Bell Electronics Inc. (Millions of Dollars, Except for Percentages)

	DIVISION 1: BELL MEMORY	DIVISION 2: BELL INSTRUMENTS	TOTAL COMPANY
Sales	$1,000.0	$500.0	$1,500.0
Operating capital	870.0	200.0	1,070.0
Earnings before interest and taxes (EBIT)	131.0	60.0	191.0
Net operating profit after taxes (NOPAT)	78.6	36.0	114.6
Operating profitability (NOPAT/Sales)	7.9%	7.2%	7.6%

The Memory division produces memory chips for such handheld electronic devices as cellular phones and PDAs (personal digital assistants), while the Instruments division produces devices for measuring and controlling sewage and water treatment facilities. Table 13-3 shows the latest financial results for the two divisions and for the company as a whole.

As the table shows, Bell Memory is the larger of the two divisions, with higher sales and more operating capital. Bell Memory is also more profitable, with a NOPAT/Sales ratio of 7.9% versus 7.2% for Bell Instruments. This year, as in other recent years, the focus of the initial strategic planning sessions was on the Memory division. Bell Memory has grown rapidly because of the phenomenal growth in consumer electronics, and this division rocketed past Instruments several years ago. Although Memory's growth has tapered off, senior management generally agreed that this division should receive the lion's share of corporate attention and resources because it is larger, more profitable, and, frankly, more exciting. After all, Bell Memory is associated with the glamorous market for telecommunications and personal electronic devices, whereas Bell Instruments is associated with sewage and sludge.

The financial assumptions and projections associated with the preliminary strategic plans for the two divisions are shown in Tables 13-4 and 13-5. The initial strategic plans project that each division will have 5% annual growth for the next 5 years and thereafter. These plans also assume that the cost structures of the two divisions will remain unchanged from the current year, 2010. Only partial financial projections are shown in Tables 13-4 and 13-5. However, when Bell's management decides on a final strategic plan, it will develop complete financial statements for the company as a whole and use them to determine financing requirements, as described in Chapter 12.

To evaluate the plans, Bell's management applied the corporate valuation model to each division, thus valuing them using the free cash flow valuation technique. Each division has a WACC of 10.5%, and Table 13-6 shows the results. The three key items are NOPAT, the required investment in operating capital, and the resulting free cash flows for each year. In addition, the table shows each division's horizon value of operations at 2015, which is the end of the 5 years of explicit forecasts, as calculated via Equation 13-2. The value of operations at 2010 is the present value of the free cash flows and the horizon value, discounted at the weighted average cost of capital. As expected, Bell Memory has the greater value of operations, $709.6 million versus $505.5 million for Bell Instruments. However, the managers were surprised to see that Bell Memory's Market Value Added (MVA) is *negative:* $709.6 value of operations

TABLE 13-4 Initial Projections for the Bell Memory Division (Millions of Dollars, Except for Percentages)

	ACTUAL	PROJECTED[a]				
	2010	2011	2012	2013	2014	2015
Panel A: Inputs						
Sales growth rate		5%	5%	5%	5%	5%
Costs/Sales	81%	81	81	81	81	81
Depreciation/Net plant	10	10	10	10	10	10
Cash/Sales	1	1	1	1	1	1
Accounts receivable/Sales	8	8	8	8	8	8
Inventories/Sales	30	30	30	30	30	30
Net plant/Sales	59	59	59	59	59	59
Accounts payable/Sales	5	5	5	5	5	5
Accruals/Sales	6	6	6	6	6	6
Tax rate	40	40	40	40	40	40
Panel B: Partial Income Statement						
Net sales	$1,000.0	$1,050.0	$1,102.5	$1,157.6	$1,215.5	$1,276.3
Costs (except depreciation)	$ 810.0	$ 850.5	$ 893.0	$ 937.7	$ 984.6	$1,033.8
Depreciation	59.0	62.0	65.0	68.3	71.7	75.3
Total operating costs	$ 869.0	$ 912.5	$ 958.1	$1,006.0	$1,056.3	$1,109.1
EBIT	$ 131.0	$ 137.6	$ 144.4	$ 151.6	$ 159.2	$ 167.2
Panel C: Partial Balance Sheets						
Operating Assets						
Cash	$ 10.0	$ 10.5	$ 11.0	$ 11.6	$ 12.2	$ 12.8
Accounts receivable	80.0	84.0	88.2	92.6	97.2	102.1
Inventories	300.0	315.0	330.8	347.3	364.7	382.9
Operating current assets	$ 390.0	$ 409.5	$ 430.0	$ 451.5	$ 474.0	$ 497.7
Net plant and equipment	$ 590.0	$ 619.5	$ 650.5	$ 683.0	$ 717.1	$ 753.0
Operating Liabilities						
Accounts payable	$ 50.0	$ 52.5	$ 55.1	$ 57.9	$ 60.8	$ 63.8
Accruals	60.0	63.0	66.2	69.5	72.9	76.6
Operating current liabilities	$ 110.0	$ 115.5	$ 121.3	$ 127.3	$ 133.7	$ 140.4

[a]Projected figures may not total exactly because of rounding.

− $870.0 operating capital = −$160.4 million.[7] In contrast, Bell Instruments' MVA is positive: $505.5 value of operations − $200 operating capital = $305.5 million.

[7]Earlier in this chapter we estimated MVA as the estimated value of equity minus the book value of equity. We can also define MVA as

$$\text{MVA} = \text{Total market value} - \text{Total capital}$$

(see Chapter 2). By subtracting the value of any short-term investments from total market value, we get the value of operations. If we subtract short-term investments from total capital, we get investor-supplied operating capital. Therefore, MVA can be estimated as

$$\text{MVA} = \text{Value of operations} - \text{Investor-supplied operating capital}$$

Recall from Chapter 2 that investor-supplied operating capital is equal to total net operating capital, which we also call total capital. Therefore, we can estimate MVA for a division or for a privately held company as

$$\text{MVA} = \text{Value of operations} - \text{Total capital}$$

TABLE 13-5 Initial Projections for the Bell Instruments Division (Millions of Dollars, Except for Percentages)

	ACTUAL	PROJECTED[a]				
	2010	2011	2012	2013	2014	2015
Panel A: Inputs						
Sales growth rate		5%	5%	5%	5%	5%
Costs/Sales	85%	85	85	85	85	85
Depreciation/Net plant	10	10	10	10	10	10
Cash/Sales	1	1	1	1	1	1
Accounts receivable/Sales	5	5	5	5	5	5
Inventories/Sales	15	15	15	15	15	15
Net plant/Sales	30	30	30	30	30	30
Accounts payable/Sales	5	5	5	5	5	5
Accruals/Sales	6	6	6	6	6	6
Tax rate	40	40	40	40	40	40
Panel B: Partial Income Statement						
Net sales	$500.0	$525.0	$551.3	$578.8	$607.8	$638.1
Costs (except depreciation)	$425.0	$446.3	$468.6	$492.0	$516.6	$542.4
Depreciation	15.0	15.8	16.5	17.4	18.2	19.1
Total operating costs	$440.0	$462.0	$485.1	$509.4	$534.8	$561.6
EBIT	$ 60.0	$ 63.0	$ 66.2	$ 69.5	$ 72.9	$ 76.6
Panel C: Partial Balance Sheets						
Operating Assets						
Cash	$ 5.0	$ 5.3	$ 5.5	$ 5.8	$ 6.1	$ 6.4
Accounts receivable	25.0	26.3	27.6	28.9	30.4	31.9
Inventories	75.0	78.8	82.7	86.8	91.2	95.7
Operating current assets	$105.0	$110.3	$115.8	$121.6	$127.6	$134.0
Net plant and equipment	$150.0	$157.5	$165.4	$173.6	$182.3	$191.4
Operating Liabilities						
Accounts payable	$ 25.0	$ 26.3	$ 27.6	$ 28.9	$ 30.4	$ 31.9
Accruals	30.0	31.5	33.1	34.7	36.5	38.3
Operating current liabilities	$ 55.0	$ 57.8	$ 60.6	$ 63.7	$ 66.9	$ 70.2

[a]Projected figures may not total exactly because of rounding.

A second strategic planning meeting was called to address this unexpected result. In it, Bell Memory's managers proposed a $20 million marketing campaign to boost their sales growth rate from 5% to 6%. They argued that because Bell Memory is so profitable, its value would be much higher if they could push up sales. Before accepting this proposal, though, the proposed changes were run through the valuation model. The managers changed the Bell Memory division's growth rate from 5% to 6%; see the file ***Ch13 Tool Kit.xls*** on the textbook's Web site for details. To their surprise, the division's value of operations fell to $691.5 million, and its MVA also declined, from –$160.4 million to –$178.5 million. Although Bell Memory was profitable, increasing its sales growth actually reduced its value!

See ***Ch13 Tool Kit.xls*** *on the textbook's Web site.*

TABLE 13-6 Initial FCF Valuation of Each Division (Millions of Dollars, Except for Percentages)

	ACTUAL	PROJECTED				
	2010	2011	2012	2013	2014	2015
Panel A: FCF Valuation of the Bell Memory Division						
Calculation of FCF						
Net operating working capital	$ 280.0	$294.0	$308.7	$ 324.1	$ 340.3	$ 357.4
Net plant	590.0	619.5	650.5	683.0	717.1	753.0
Net operating capital	$ 870.0	$913.5	$959.2	$1,007.1	$1,057.5	$1,110.4
Investment in operating capital		$ 43.5	$ 45.7	$ 48.0	$ 50.4	$ 52.9
NOPAT	$ 78.6	$ 82.5	$ 86.7	$ 91.0	$ 95.5	$ 100.3
Free cash flow		$ 39.0	$ 41.0	$ 43.0	$ 45.2	$ 47.4
Growth in FCF			5.0%	5.0%	5.0%	5.0%
Value of Operations						
Horizon value						$ 905.7
Value of operations	$ 709.6					
Divisional MVA						
(Value of operations − Capital)	($160.4)					
Panel B: FCF Valuation of the Bell Instruments Division						
Calculation of FCF						
Net operating working capital	$ 50.0	$ 52.5	$ 55.1	$ 57.9	$ 60.8	$ 63.8
Net plant	150.0	157.5	165.4	173.6	182.3	191.4
Net operating capital	$ 200.0	$210.0	$220.5	$ 231.5	$ 243.1	$ 255.3
Investment in operating capital		$ 10.0	$ 10.5	$ 11.0	$ 11.6	$ 12.2
NOPAT	$ 36.0	$ 37.8	$ 39.7	$ 41.7	$ 43.8	$ 45.9
Free cash flow		$ 27.8	$ 29.2	$ 30.6	$ 32.2	$ 33.8
Growth in FCF			5.0%	5.0%	5.0%	5.0%
Value of Operations						
Horizon value						$ 645.1
Value of operations	$ 505.5					
Divisional MVA						
(Value of operations − Capital)	$ 305.5					

Notes: The WACC is 10.5% for each division. The horizon value (HV) at 2015 is calculated using Equation 13-2, the constant growth formula for free cash flows:

$$HV_{2015} = [FCF_{2015}(1 + g)] \div (WACC - g)$$

The value of operations is the present value of the horizon value and the free cash flows discounted at the WACC; it is calculated in a manner similar to Figure 13-1. Projected figures may not total exactly because of rounding. See ***Ch13 Tool Kit.xls*** on the textbook's Web site for all calculations.

To better understand these results, we can express the firm's value in terms of four fundamental wealth drivers:

$$g = \text{Growth in sales}$$
$$OP = \text{Operating profitability}(OP) = \text{NOPAT/Sales}$$
$$CR = \text{Capital requirements}(CR) = \text{Operating capital/Sales}$$
$$WACC = \text{Weighted average cost of capital}$$

How do these drivers affect the value of a firm? First, the sales growth rate usually (but not always) has a positive effect on value, provided the company is profitable enough. However, the effect can be negative if growth requires a great deal of capital and if the cost of capital is high. Second, operating profitability, which measures the after-tax profit per dollar of sales, always has a positive effect—the higher the better. Third, the capital requirements ratio, which measures how much operating capital is needed to generate a dollar of sales, also has a consistent effect: the lower the CR the better, since a low CR means that the company can generate new sales with smaller amounts of new capital. Finally, the fourth factor, the WACC, also has a consistent effect: the lower it is, the higher the firm's value.

Another important metric in the corporate valuation model is the **expected return on invested capital (EROIC)**, defined as the expected NOPAT for the coming year divided by the amount of operating capital at the beginning of the year (which is the end of the preceding year). It can also be defined in terms of the fundamental value drivers for profitability (OP) and capital requirements (CR). Thus, EROIC represents the expected return on the capital that has already been invested:

$$\text{EROIC}_N = \frac{\text{NOPAT}_{N+1}}{\text{Capital}_N} = \frac{\text{OP}_{N+1}}{\text{CR}_N} \quad \text{(13-3)}$$

To illustrate, the EROIC of the Bell Memory division for 2015, the last year in the forecast period, is

See **Ch13 Tool Kit.xls** on the textbook's Web site for details.

$$\text{EROIC}_{2015} = \frac{\text{NOPAT}_{2016}}{\text{Capital}_{2015}} = \frac{\text{NOPAT}_{2015}(1+g)}{\text{Capital}_{2015}} = \frac{\$100.3(1.05)}{\$1,110.4} = 9.5\%$$

To see exactly how the four value drivers and EROIC determine value for a constant growth firm, we can start with Equation 13-2 (which we repeat here),

$$V_{op(\text{at time N})} = \frac{\text{FCF}_{N+1}}{\text{WACC} - g} \quad \text{(13-2)}$$

and rewrite it in terms of the value drivers:

$$V_{op(\text{at time N})} = \text{Capital}_N + \left\{ \left[\frac{\text{Sales}_N(1+g)}{\text{WACC} - g} \right] \left[\text{OP} - \text{WACC}\left(\frac{\text{CR}}{1+g} \right) \right] \right\} \quad \text{(13-4)}$$

Equation 13-4 shows that the value of operations can be divided into two components: (1) the dollars of operating capital that investors have provided; and (2) the additional value that management has added or subtracted, which is equivalent to MVA.

Note that the first [bracketed] fraction in Equation 13-4 represents the present value of growing sales, discounted at the WACC. This would be the MVA of a firm that has no costs and that never needs to invest additional capital. But firms do have costs and capital requirements, and their effect is captured by the term in the second set of brackets. Here we see that, holding g constant, MVA will improve if operating profitability (OP) increases, if WACC decreases, and/or if capital requirements (CR) decrease.

Observe that an increase in growth will not necessarily increase value. OP could be positive, but if CR is quite high—meaning that a lot of new capital is needed to support a given increase in sales—then the second bracketed term can be negative. In this situation, growth causes first bracketed term to increase; however, since it's being multiplied by a negative term (the second bracket), the net result will be a decrease in MVA.

We can also rewrite Equation 13-2 in terms of EROIC (or profitability and capital requirements) as follows:

$$\begin{aligned} V_{op(\text{at time N})} &= \text{Capital}_N + \frac{\text{Capital}_N(\text{EROIC}_N - \text{WACC})}{\text{WACC} - g} \\ &= \text{Capital}_N + \frac{\text{Capital}_N\left(\frac{\text{OP}_{N+1}}{\text{CR}_N} - \text{WACC}\right)}{\text{WACC} - g} \end{aligned} \quad (13\text{-}5)$$

Equation 13-5 also breaks value into two components, the value of capital and the MVA, shown in the second term. This term for MVA shows that value depends on the EROIC, the WACC, and the spread between the expected return on invested capital. Notice that the EROIC in turn depends on profitability and required capital. If the combination of profitability and required capital produces an EROIC greater than WACC, then the return on capital is greater than the return investors expect and management is adding value. In this case, an increase in the growth rate causes value to go up. If EROIC is exactly equal to WACC then the firm is, in an economic sense, "breaking even." It has positive accounting profits and cash flow, but these cash flows are just sufficient to satisfy investors, causing value to exactly equal the amount of capital that has been provided. If EROIC is less than WACC then the term in parentheses is negative, management is destroying value, and growth is harmful. This is one case where the faster the growth rate, the lower the firm's value.

We should also note that the insights from Equations 13-4 and 13-5 apply to all firms, but the equations themselves can be applied only to relatively stable firms whose growth has leveled out at a constant rate. For example, in 2008 Qualcomm's sales grew at 25% per year, so we cannot apply Equations 13-4 and 13-5 directly (although we could always apply Equation 13-1). Qualcomm's NOPAT/Sales ratio was an outstanding 27.6%, but even though Qualcomm was profitable, it had a negative free cash flow of about \$3.9 billion! If Qualcomm can maintain profitability as its growth slows to sustainable levels, it will generate huge amounts of FCF. This explains why its MVA was over \$38 billion in 2008 even though its FCF was negative.

Table 13-7 shows the value drivers for Bell's two divisions as measured at 2015, the end of the forecast period. We report these for the *end* of the forecast period

TABLE 13-7 Bell Electronics' Forecasted Value Drivers for 2015

	DIVISION 1: BELL MEMORY	DIVISION 2:BELL INSTRUMENTS
Growth: g	5.0%	5.0%
Profitability: ($NOPAT_{2015}/Sales_{2015}$)	7.9	7.2
Capital requirement: ($Capital_{2015}/ Sales_{2015}$)	87.0	40.0
WACC	10.5	10.5
Expected return on invested capital, EROIC: $NOPAT_{2015}(1 + g)/Capital_{2015}$	9.5	18.9

because ratios can change during the forecast period in response to input changes. By the end of the forecast period, however, all inputs and ratios should be stable.

Both divisions have the same growth rate and the same WACC, as shown in Table 13-7. Bell Memory is more profitable, but it also has much higher capital requirements. The result is that Bell Memory's EROIC is only 9.5%, well below its 10.5% WACC. Thus, growth doesn't help Bell Memory—indeed, it reduces the division's value.

Based on this analysis, Bell Memory's managers decided not to request funds for a marketing campaign. Instead, they developed a plan to reduce capital requirements. The new plan called for spending $50 million on an integrated supply chain information system that would allow them to cut their inventory/sales ratio from 30% to 20% and also reduce the ratio of net plant to sales from 59% to 50%. Table 13-8 shows projected operating results based on this new plan. The value of operations would increase from $709.6 million to $1.1574 billion, or by $447.8 million. Because this amount is well over the $50 million required to implement the plan, top management decided to approve it. Note also that the plan shows MVA becoming positive at $287.4 million (a substantial improvement on the preliminary plan's negative $160.4 million) and the divisional EROIC rising to 13.0%, well over the 10.5% WACC.

Bell Instruments's managers also used the valuation model to assess changes in plans for their division. Given their high EROIC, the Instruments division proposed (1) an aggressive marketing campaign and (2) an increase in inventories that would allow faster delivery and fewer stockouts. Together, these changes would boost the growth rate from 5% to 6%. The direct cost to implement the plan was $20 million, but there was also an indirect cost in that more inventories would have to be carried: The ratio of inventories to sales was forecasted to increase from 15% to 16%.

Should Instruments's new plan be implemented? Table 13-8 shows the forecasted results. The capital requirements associated with the increased inventory caused the EROIC to fall from 18.9% to 18.6%, but (1) the 18.6% return greatly exceeds the 10.5% WACC, and (2) the spread between 18.6% and 10.5% would be earned on additional capital. This caused the forecasted value of operations to increase from $505.5 to $570.1 million, or by $64.6 million. An 18.6% return on $274.3 million of capital is more valuable than an 18.9% return on $255.3 million of capital.[8] (To see this, note that you, or one of Bell's stockholders, would surely rather have an asset that provides a 50% return on an investment of $1,000 than one that provides

[8]A potential fly in the ointment is that Bell's compensation plan might be based on rates of return and not on changes in wealth. In such a plan, which is fairly typical, the managers might reject the new proposed strategic plan if it lowers ROIC and hence their bonuses, even though the plan is good for the company's stockholders. We discuss the effect of compensation plans in more detail later in the chapter.

TABLE 13-8 Comparison of the Preliminary and Final Plans (Millions of Dollars, Except for Percentages)

	BELL MEMORY		BELL INSTRUMENTS	
	PRELIMINARY	FINAL	PRELIMINARY	FINAL
Inputs				
Sales growth rate, g	5%	5%	5%	6%
Inventories/Sales	30	20	15	16
Net plant/Sales	59	50	30	30
Results				
EROIC (2015)[a]	9.5%	13.0%	18.9%	18.6%
Invested (operating) capital (2015)[a]	$1,110.4	$ 867.9	$255.3	$274.3
Current value of operations (2010)[b]	709.6	1,157.4	505.5	570.1
Current MVA (2010)[b]	(160.4)	287.4	305.5	370.1

Notes:

[a]We report EROIC and capital for the end of the forecast period because ratios can change during the forecast period if inputs change during that period. By the end of the forecast period, however, all inputs and ratios should be stable.

[b]We report the value of operations and the MVA as of the current date, 2010, because we want to see what effect the proposed plans would have on the current value of the divisions.

a 100% return on an investment of $1.) Therefore, the new plan should be accepted, even though it lowers the Instruments division's EROIC.

Sometimes companies focus on their profitability and growth without giving adequate consideration to their capital requirements. This is a big mistake—*all* the wealth creation drivers, not just growth, must be taken into account. Fortunately for Bell's investors, the revised plan was accepted. However, as this example illustrates, it is easy for a company to mistakenly focus only on profitability and growth. They are important, but so are the other value drivers: capital requirements and the weighted average cost of capital. Value-based management explicitly includes the effects of all the value drivers because it uses the corporate valuation model, and the drivers are all embodied in that model.[9]

Self-Test

What are the four drivers of value?

How is it possible for sales growth to *decrease* the value of a profitable firm?

You are given the following forecasted information for a constant growth company: sales = $10 million, operating profitability (OP) = 5%, capital requirements (CR) = 40%, growth (g) = 6%, and the weighted average cost of capital (WACC) = 10%. What is the current level of capital? **($4 million)** What is the current level of NOPAT? **($0.5 million)** What is the EROIC? **(13.25%)** What is the value of operations? **($7.25 million)**

[9]For more on corporate valuation and value-based management, see Sheridan Titman and John D. Martin, *Valuation: The Art and Science of Corporate Investment Decisions* (Boston: Pearson/Addison-Wesley, 2008); Tim Koller, Marc Goedhart, and David Wessels, *Valuation: Measuring and Managing the Value of Companies*, 4th ed. (Hoboken, NJ: John Wiley & Sons, 2005); John D. Martin and J. William Petty, *Value Based Management: The Corporate Response to the Shareholder Revolution* (Boston: Harvard Business School Press, 2000); John D. Martin, J. William Petty, and James S. Wallace, *Value Based Management with Corporate Social Responsibility* (New York: Oxford University Press, 2009); James M. McTaggart, Peter W. Kontes, and Michael C. Mankins, *The Value Imperative* (New York: The Free Press, 1994); and G. Bennett Stewart, *The Quest for Value* (New York: Harper Collins, 1991). For an application to small-firm valuation, see Michael S. Long and Thomas A. Bryant, *Valuing the Closely Held Firm*, (New York: Oxford University Press, 2008).

13.4 Managerial Behavior and Shareholder Wealth

For excellent discussions of corporate governance, see the Web pages of CalPERS (the California Public Employees' Retirement System), **http://www.calpers.org**, *and TIAA-CREF (Teachers Insurance and Annuity Association College Retirement Equity Fund),* **http://www.tiaa-cref.org.**

Shareholders want companies to hire managers who are able and willing to take legal and ethical actions to maximize intrinsic stock prices.[10] This obviously requires managers with technical competence, but it also requires managers who are willing to put forth the extra effort necessary to identify and implement value-adding activities. However, managers are people, and people have both personal and corporate goals. Logically, therefore, managers can be expected to act in their own self-interests, and if their self-interests are not aligned with those of stockholders, then corporate value will not be maximized. There are six ways in which a manager's behavior might harm a firm's intrinsic value.

1. Managers might not expend the time and effort required to maximize firm value. Rather than focusing on corporate tasks, they might spend too much time on external activities, such as serving on boards of other companies, or on nonproductive activities, such as golfing, lunching, and traveling.
2. Managers might use corporate resources on activities that benefit themselves rather than shareholders. For example, they might spend company money on such perquisites as lavish offices, memberships at country clubs, museum-quality art for corporate apartments, large personal staffs, and corporate jets. Because these perks are not actually cash payments to the managers, they are called **nonpecuniary benefits**.
3. Managers might avoid making difficult but value-enhancing decisions that harm friends in the company. For example, a manager might not close a plant or terminate a project if the manager has personal relationships with those who are adversely affected by such decisions, even if termination is the economically sound action.
4. Managers might take on too much risk or they might not take on enough risk. For example, a company might have the opportunity to undertake a risky project with a positive NPV. If the project turns out badly, then the manager's reputation will be harmed and the manager might even be fired. Thus, a manager might choose to avoid risky projects even if they are desirable from a shareholder's point of view. On the other hand, a manager might take on projects with too much risk. Consider a project that is not living up to expectations. A manager might be tempted to invest even more money in the project rather than admit that the project is a failure. Or a manager might be willing to take on a second project with a negative NPV if it has even a slight chance of a very positive outcome, since hitting a home run with this second project might cover up the first project's poor performance. In other words, the manager might throw good money after bad.
5. If a company is generating positive free cash flow, a manager might "stockpile" it in the form of marketable securities instead of returning FCF to investors. This

---

[10]Notice that we said both legal and ethical actions. The accounting frauds perpetrated by Enron, WorldCom, and others that were uncovered in 2002 raised stock prices in the short run, but only because investors were misled about the companies' financial positions. Then, when the correct financial information was finally revealed, the stocks tanked. Investors who bought shares based on the fraudulent financial statements lost tens of billions of dollars. Releasing false financial statements is illegal. Aggressive earnings management and the use of misleading accounting tricks to pump up reported earnings is unethical, and executives can go to jail as a result of their shenanigans. When we speak of taking actions to maximize stock prices, we mean making operational or financial changes designed to maximize intrinsic stock value, not fooling investors with false or misleading financial reports.

potentially harms investors because it prevents them from allocating these funds to other companies with good growth opportunities. Even worse, positive FCF often tempts a manager into paying too much for the acquisition of another company. In fact, most mergers and acquisitions end up as break-even deals, at best, for the acquiring company because the premiums paid for the targets are often very large.

Why would a manager be reluctant to return cash to investors? First, extra cash on hand reduces the company's risk, which appeals to many managers. Second, a large distribution of cash to investors is an admission that the company doesn't have enough good investment opportunities. Slow growth is normal for a maturing company, but it isn't very exciting for a manager to admit this. Third, there is a lot of glamour associated with making a large acquisition, and this can provide a large boost to a manager's ego. Fourth, compensation usually is higher for executives at larger companies; cash distributions to investors make a company smaller, not larger.

6. Managers might not release all the information that is desired by investors. Sometimes, they might withhold information to prevent competitors from gaining an advantage. At other times, they might try to avoid releasing bad news. For example, they might "massage" the data or "manage the earnings" so that the news doesn't look so bad. If investors are unsure about the quality of information provided by managers, they tend to discount the company's expected free cash flows at a higher cost of capital, which reduces the company's intrinsic value.

If senior managers believe there is little chance that they will be removed, we say that they are *entrenched*. Such a company faces a high risk of being poorly run, because entrenched managers are able to act in their own interests rather than in the interests of shareholders.

Self-Test

Name six types of managerial behaviors that can reduce a firm's intrinsic value.

13.5 Corporate Governance

A key requirement for successful implementation of value-based management is to influence executives and other managers so that they do not behave in the ways described in the previous section but instead behave in a way that maximizes a firm's intrinsic value. Corporate governance can provide just such an influence. Corporate governance can be defined as the set of laws, rules, and procedures that influence a company's operations and the decisions made by its managers. At the risk of oversimplification, most corporate governance provisions come in two forms, sticks and carrots. The primary stick is the *threat of removal*, either as a decision by the board of directors or as the result of a hostile takeover. If a firm's managers are maximizing the value of the resources entrusted to them, they need not fear the loss of their jobs. On the other hand, if managers are not maximizing value, they should be removed by their own boards of directors, by dissident stockholders, or by other companies seeking to profit by installing a better management team. The main carrot is *compensation*. Managers have greater incentives to maximize intrinsic stock value if their compensation is linked to their firm's performance rather than being strictly in the form of salary.

Almost all corporate governance provisions affect either the threat of removal or compensation. Some provisions are internal to a firm and are under its control.[11]

[11]We have adapted this framework from the one provided by Stuart L. Gillan, "Recent Developments in Corporate Governance: An Overview," *Journal of Corporate Finance*, June 2006, pp. 381–402. Gillan provides an excellent discussion of the issues associated with corporate governance, and we highly recommend this article to the reader who is interested in an expanded discussion of the issues in this section.

These internal provisions and features can be divided into five areas: (1) monitoring and discipline by the board of directors, (2) charter provisions and bylaws that affect the likelihood of hostile takeovers, (3) compensation plans, (4) capital structure choices, and (5) accounting control systems. In addition to the corporate governance provisions that are under a firm's control, there are also environmental factors outside of a firm's control, such as the regulatory environment, block ownership patterns, competition in the product markets, the media, and litigation. Our discussion begins with the internal provisions.

Monitoring and Discipline by the Board of Directors

Shareholders are a corporation's owners, and they elect the board of directors to act as agents on their behalf. In the United States, it is the board's duty to monitor senior managers and discipline them if they do not act in the interests of shareholders, either by removal or by a reduction in compensation.[12] This is not necessarily the case outside the United States. For example, many companies in Europe are required to have employee representatives on the board. Also, many European and Asian companies have bank representatives on the board. But even in the United States, many boards fail to act in the shareholders' best interests. How can this be?

Consider the election process. The board of directors has a nominating committee. These directors choose the candidates for the open director positions, and the ballot for a board position usually lists only one candidate. Although outside candidates can run a "write-in" campaign, only those candidates named by the board's nominating committee are on the ballot.[13] At many companies, the CEO is also the chairman of the board and has considerable influence on this nominating committee. This means that in practice it often is the CEO who, in effect, nominates candidates for the board. High compensation and prestige go with a position on the board of a major company, so board seats are prized possessions. Board members typically want to retain their positions, and they are grateful to whomever helped get them on the board. Thus, the nominating process often results in a board that is favorably disposed to the CEO.

At most companies, a candidate is elected simply by having a majority of votes cast. The proxy ballot usually lists all candidates, with a box for each candidate to check if the shareholder votes "For" the candidate and a box to check if the shareholder "withholds" a vote on the candidate—you can't actually vote "No"; you can only withhold your vote. In theory, a candidate could be elected with a single "For" vote if all other votes were withheld. In practice, though, most shareholders either vote "For" or assign to management their right to vote (proxy is defined as the authority to act for another, which is why it is called a proxy statement). In practice, then, the nominated candidates virtually always receive a majority of votes and are thus elected.

Occasionally there is a "Just vote no" campaign in which a large investor (usually an institution such as a pension fund) urges stockholders to withhold their votes for one or more directors. Although such campaigns do not directly affect the director's election, they do provide a visible way for investors to express their dissatisfaction. Recent evidence shows that "Just vote no" campaigns at poorly performing firms lead to better subsequent firm performance and a greater probability that the CEO will be dismissed.[14]

---

[12]There are a few exceptions to this rule. For example, some states have laws allowing the board to take into consideration the interests of other stakeholders, such as employees and members of the community.

[13]There is currently (early 2009) a movement under way to allow also shareholders to nominate candidates for the board, but only time will tell whether this movement is successful.

[14]See Diane Del Guercio, Laura Seery, and Tracie Woidtke, "Do Boards Pay Attention When Institutional Investor Activists 'Just Vote No'?" *Journal of Financial Economics,* October 2008, pp. 84–103.

Let's Go to Miami! IBM's 2009 Annual Meeting

IBM invited its stockholders to its annual meeting held on April 28, 2009, in Miami. The agenda included election of each board member for a 1-year term, ratification of PricewaterhouseCoopers as its independent auditing firm, approval of long-term incentive plans for executives, and three stockholder proposals: (1) adopt cumulative voting; (2) remove consideration of pension income that does not reflect operating performance from the measure of income used for bonuses; (3) adopt an advisory shareholder vote each year ratifying (or not) executive compensation. IBM's board recommended that shareholders vote against all three proposals.

About 8 pages of the proxy statement described nominees for the board and their compensation, about 53 pages explained executive compensation, and about 4½ pages covered the stockholders' proposals, with much of that being management's explanation for why it opposed them.

Stockholders were permitted to vote over the Web, by telephone, by mail, or in person at the meeting. When the result were tallied, IBM revealed that all board nominees had been elected by a majority and that all three stockholder proposals had been defeated, although the last two proposals garnered over 43% of the votes in their favor.[a]

IBM's annual meeting might not have been as exciting as the TV show *CSI: Miami*, but we think the evidence shows that there will be more stockholder proposals in the future and that many will win approval.

[a]IBM had not released the actual vote count for any directors at the time this was written, but the results will be in IBM's 10-Q report for the quarter ending in June 2009.

Voting procedures also affect the ability of outsiders to gain positions on the board. If the charter specifies cumulative voting, then each shareholder is given a number of votes equal to his or her shares multiplied by the number of board seats up for election. For example, the holder of 100 shares of stock will receive 1,000 votes if 10 seats are to be filled. Then, the shareholder can distribute those votes however he or she sees fit. One hundred votes could be cast for each of 10 candidates, or all 1,000 votes could be cast for one candidate. If noncumulative voting is used, our hypothetical stockholder cannot concentrate votes in this way—no more than 100 votes can be cast for any one candidate.

With noncumulative voting, if management controls 51% of the shares then they can fill every seat on the board, leaving dissident stockholders without any representation on the board. With cumulative voting, however, if 10 seats are to be filled then dissidents could elect a representative, provided they have 10% plus 1 additional share of the stock.

Note also that bylaws specify whether the entire board is to be elected annually or if directors are to have staggered terms with, say, one-third of the seats to be filled each year and directors to serve three-year terms. With staggered terms, fewer seats come up each year, making it harder for dissidents to gain representation on the board. Staggered boards are also called **classified boards**.

Many board members are "insiders"—that is, people who hold managerial positions within the company, such as the CFO. Because insiders report to the CEO, it may be difficult for them to oppose the CEO at a board meeting. To help mitigate this problem, several exchanges, such as the NYSE and Nasdaq, now require that listed companies have a majority of outside directors.

Some "outside" board members often have strong connections with the CEO through professional relationships, personal friendships, and consulting or other fee-generating activities. In fact, outsiders sometimes have very little expert business knowledge but have "celebrity" status from nonbusiness activities. Some companies also have **interlocking boards of directors**, where Company A's CEO sits on Company B's board and B's CEO sits on A's board. In these situations, even the outside directors are not truly independent and impartial.

Large boards (those with more than about ten members) often are less effective than smaller boards. As anyone who has been on a committee can attest, individual participation tends to fall as committee size increases. Thus, there is a greater likelihood that members of a large board will be less active than those on smaller boards.

The compensation of board members has an impact on the board's effectiveness. When board members have exceptionally high compensation, the CEO also tends to have exceptionally high compensation. This suggests that such boards tend to be too lenient with the CEO.[15] The form of board compensation also affects board performance. Rather than compensating board members with only salary, many companies now include restricted stock grants or stock options in an effort to better align board members with stockholders.

Studies show that corporate governance usually improves if (1) the CEO is not also the chairman of the board, (2) the board has a majority of true outsiders who bring some type of business expertise to the board and are not too busy with other activities, (3) the board is not too large, and (4) board members are compensated appropriately (not too high and not all cash, but including exposure to equity risk through options or stock). The good news for the shareholder is that the boards at many companies have made significant improvements in these directions during the past decade. Fewer CEOs are also board chairmen and, as power has shifted from CEOs to boards as a whole, there has been a tendency to replace insiders with strong, independent outsiders. Today, the typical board has about one-third insiders and two-thirds outsiders, and most outsiders are truly independent. Moreover, board members are compensated primarily with stock or options rather than a straight salary. These changes clearly have decreased the patience of boards with poorly performing CEOs. Within the past several years the CEOs of Wachovia, Sprint Nextel, Gap, Hewlett-Packard, Home Depot, Citigroup, Pfizer, Ford and Dynegy, to name just a few, have been removed by their boards. This would have been unheard of 30 years ago.

Charter Provisions and Bylaws That Affect the Likelihood of Hostile Takeovers

Hostile takeovers usually occur when managers have not been willing or able to maximize the profit potential of the resources under their control. In such a situation, another company can acquire the poorly performing firm, replace its managers, increase free cash flow, and improve MVA. The following paragraphs describe some provisions that can be included in a corporate charter to make it harder for poorly performing managers to remain in control.[16]

A shareholder-friendly charter should ban **targeted share repurchases**, also known as **greenmail**. For example, suppose a company's stock is selling for $20 per

---

[15]See I. E. Brick, O. Palmon, and J. Wald, "CEO Compensation, Director Compensation, and Firm Performance: Evidence of Cronyism?" *Journal of Corporate Finance*, June 2006, pp. 403–423.

[16]Some states have laws that go further than others to protect management. This is one reason that many companies are incorporated in manager-friendly Delaware. Some companies have even shifted their state of incorporation to Delaware because their managers felt that a hostile takeover attempt was likely. Note that a "shareholder-friendly charter" could and would waive the company's right to strong anti-takeover protection, even if the state allowed it.

share. Now a hostile bidder, or raider, who plans to replace management if the takeover is successful, buys 5% of the company's stock at the $20 price.[17] The raider then makes an offer to purchase the remainder of the stock for $30 per share. The company might offer to buy back the raider's stock at a price of, say, $35 per share. This is called a targeted share repurchase since the stock will be purchased only from the raider and not from any other shareholders. A raider who paid only $20 per share for the stock would be making a quick profit of $15 per share, which could easily total several hundred million dollars. As a part of the deal, the raider would sign a document promising not to attempt to take over the company for a specified number of years; hence the buyback also is called greenmail. Greenmail hurts shareholders in two ways. First, they are left with $20 stock when they could have received $30 per share. Second, the company purchased stock from the bidder at $35 per share, which represents a direct loss by the remaining shareholders of $15 for each repurchased share.

Managers who buy back stock in targeted repurchases typically argue that their firms are worth more than the raiders offered and that, in time, the "true value" will be revealed in the form of a much higher stock price. This situation might be true if a company were in the process of restructuring itself, or if new products with high potential were in the pipeline. But if the old management had been in power for a long time and had a history of making empty promises, then one should question whether the true purpose of the buyback was to protect stockholders or management.

Another characteristic of a stockholder-friendly charter is that it does not contain a **shareholder rights provision**, better described as a **poison pill**. These provisions give the shareholders of target firms the right to buy a specified number of shares in the company at a very low price if an outside group or firm acquires a specified percentage of the firm's stock. Therefore, if a potential acquirer tries to take over a company, its other shareholders will be entitled to purchase additional shares of stock at a bargain price, thus seriously diluting the holdings of the raider. For this reason, these clauses are called poison pills, because if they are in the charter, the acquirer will end up swallowing a poison pill if the acquisition is successful. Obviously, the existence of a poison pill makes a takeover more difficult, and this helps to entrench management.

A third management entrenchment tool is a **restricted voting rights** provision, which automatically cancels the voting rights of any shareholder who owns more than a specified amount of the company's stock. The board can grant voting rights to such a shareholder, but this is unlikely if that shareholder plans to take over the company.

Using Compensation to Align Managerial and Shareholder Interests

The typical CEO today receives a fixed salary, a cash bonus based on the firm's performance, and stock-based compensation, either in the form of stock grants or option grants. Cash bonuses often are based upon short-run operating factors, such as this year's growth in earnings per share, or medium-term operating performance, such as earnings growth over the past 3 years.

Stock-based compensation is often in the form of options. Chapter 8 explains option valuation in detail, but here we discuss how a standard **stock option**

[17]Someone can, under the law, acquire up to 5% of a firm's stock without announcing the acquisition. Once the 5% limit has been hit, the acquirer has 10 days to "announce" the acquisition by filing Schedule 13D with the SEC. Schedule 13D reports not only the acquirer's number of shares but also his or her intentions, such as a passive investment or a takeover. These reports are monitored closely, so as soon as one is filed, management is alerted to the possibility of an imminent takeover.

THE GLOBAL ECONOMIC CRISIS

Would the U.S. Government Be an Effective Board Director?

In response to the global economic crisis that began with the recession of 2007, many governments are becoming major stakeholders in heretofore publicly traded companies. For example, the U.S. government has invested billions in Fannie Mae and Freddie Mac, taking them into conservatorship and having a direct say in the companies' leadership and operations, including the dismissal of former Fannie Mae CEO Daniel Mudd in 2008.

The U.S. government has made multibillon-dollar investments in banks (about $50 billion to Citigroup, $45 billion to Bank of America, and $25 billion each to JP Morgan Chase and Wells Fargo), insurance companies (almost $70 billion to AIG), and auto companies ($16 billion to GM and $7 billion to Chrysler). Much of this has been in the form of preferred stock, which does not give the government any direct voting or decision-making authority. However, the government has certainly applied moral suasion, as evidenced by the removal of GM's former CEO Rick Wagoner. The government is also imposing limits on executive compensation at firms receiving additional government funds.

For the most part, however, the government does not have voting rights at bailout recipients, nor does it have representation on their boards of directors. It will be interesting to see if this changes and if the government takes a more direct role in corporate governance.

Sources: See http://projects.nytimes.com/creditcrisis/recipients/table for updates on TARP recipients.

compensation plan works. Suppose IBM decides to grant an option to an employee, allowing her to purchase a specified number of IBM shares at a fixed price, called the **strike price** (or **exercise price**), regardless of the actual price of the stock. The strike price is usually set equal to the current stock price at the time the option is granted. Thus, if IBM's current price were $100, then the option would have an exercise price of $100. Options usually cannot be exercised until after some specified period (the **vesting period**), which is usually 1 to 5 years. Some grants have **cliff vesting**, which means that all the granted options vest at the same date, such as 3 years after the grant. Other grants have **annual vesting**, which means that a certain percentage vest each year. For example, one-third of the options in the grant might vest each year. The options have an **expiration date**, usually 10 years after issue. For our IBM example, assume that the options have cliff vesting in 3 years and have an expiration date in 10 years. Thus, the employee can exercise the option 3 years after issue or wait as long as 10 years. Of course, the employee would not exercise unless IBM's stock is above the $100 exercise price, and if the price never rose above $100, the option would expire unexercised. However, if the stock price were above $100 on the expiration date, the option would surely be exercised.

Suppose the stock price had grown to $134 after 5 years, at which point the employee decided to exercise the option. She would buy stock from IBM for $100, so IBM would get only $100 for stock worth $134. The employee would (probably) sell the stock the same day she exercised the option and hence would receive in cash the $34 difference between the $134 stock price and the $100 exercise price. There are two important points to note in this example. First, most employees sell stock soon after exercising the option. Thus, the incentive effects of an option grant typically end when the option is exercised. Second, option pricing theory shows that it is not optimal to exercise a conventional call option on stock that does not pay dividends before the option expires: An investor is always better off selling the option in the marketplace rather than exercising it. But because employee stock options are not tradable, grantees often exercise the options well before they expire. For example, people often time the exercise of options to the purchase of a new home or some other large expenditure. But early exercise occurs not just for liquidity reasons, such as needing cash to purchase a house, but also because of behavioral reasons. For example, exercises occur more frequently after stock run-ups, which suggests that grantees view the stock as overpriced.

In theory, stock options should align a manager's interests with those of shareholders, influencing the manager to behave in a way that maximizes the company's value. But in practice there are two reasons why this does not always occur.

First, suppose a CEO is granted options on 1 million shares. If we use the same stock prices as in our previous example then the grantee would receive \$34 for each option, or a total of \$34 million. Keep in mind that this is in addition to an annual salary and cash bonuses. The logic behind employee options is that they motivate people to work harder and smarter, thus making the company more valuable and benefiting shareholders. But take a closer look at this example. If the risk-free rate is 5.5%, the market risk premium is 6%, and IBM's beta is 1.19, then the expected return, based on the CAPM, is 5.5% + 1.19(6%) = 12.64%. IBM's dividend yield is only 0.8%, so the expected annual price appreciation must be about 11.84% (12.64% − 0.8% = 11.84%). Now note that if IBM's stock price grew from \$100 to \$134 over 5 years, that would translate to an annual growth rate of only 6%, not the 11.84% shareholders expected. Thus, the executive would receive \$34 million for helping run a company that performed below shareholders' expectations. As this example illustrates, standard stock options do not necessarily link executives' wealth with that of shareholders.

Second, and even worse, the events of the early 2000s showed that some executives were willing to illegally falsify financial statements in order to drive up stock prices just prior to exercising their stock options.[18] In some notable cases, the subsequent stock price drop and loss of investor confidence have forced firms into bankruptcy. Such behavior is certainly not in shareholders' best interests!

As a result, companies today are experimenting with different types of compensation plans that involve different vesting periods and different measures of performance. For example, from a legal standpoint it is more difficult to manipulate EVA (Economic Value Added) than earnings per share.[19] Therefore, many companies incorporate EVA-type measures in their compensation systems. Also, many companies have quit granting options and instead are granting restricted stock that cannot be sold until it has vested.

Just as "all ships rise in a rising tide," so too do most stocks rise in a bull market such as that of 2003–2007. In a strong market, even the stocks of companies whose performance ranks in the bottom 10% of their peer group can rise and thus trigger handsome executive bonuses. This situation is leading to compensation plans that are based on *relative* as opposed to *absolute* stock price performance. For example, some

---

[18]Several academic studies show that option-based compensation leads to a greater likelihood of earnings restatements (which means having to refile financial statements with the SEC because there was a material error) and outright fraud. See A. Agrawal and S. Chadha, "Corporate Governance and Accounting Scandals," *Journal of Law and Economics*, 2006, pp. 371–406; N. Burns and S. Kedia, "The Impact of Performance-Based Compensation on Misreporting," *Journal of Financial Economics*, January 2006, pp. 35–67; and D. J. Denis, P. Hanouna, and A. Sarin, "Is There a Dark Side to Incentive Compensation?" *Journal of Corporate Finance*, June 2006, pp. 467–488.

[19]For a discussion of EVA, see Al Ehrbar, *EVA: The Real Key to Creating Wealth* (New York: John Wiley & Sons, 1998); and Pamela P. Peterson and David R. Peterson, *Company Performance and Measures of Value Added* (The Research Foundation of the Institute of Chartered Financial Analysts, 1996).

THE GLOBAL ECONOMIC CRISIS

Shareholder Reactions to the Crisis

It is safe to say that shareholders were dismayed by the market's decline in 2008, and it looks like they are seeking more control. RiskMetrics Group provides data on the shareholder proposals that are included in proxy statements, with votes tallied at the annual meetings. The 2009 proxy season saw an enormous number of proposals related to corporate governance, especially compensation, as shown below.

It will be interesting to see how companies respond to these votes and whether more shareholder power translates into better performance.

Sources: RiskMetrics Group, **http://www.riskmetrics.com/knowledge/proxy_season_scorecard_2009.**

	Number of proposals
Executive Pay Issues	
Advisory vote on compensation	85
Vote on golden parachutes	9
Anti–gross-ups policy	2
Vote on executive death benefits	12
Retention period for stock awards	14
Establish bonus banks	3
Board Issues	
Independent board chairman	33
Allow for cumulative voting	34
Require majority vote to elect directors	51
Takeover Defenses/Other	
Right to call special meeting	61
End supermajority vote requirement	15
Repeal classified board	71

compensation plans have indexed options whose exercise prices depend on the performance of the market or a subset of competitors.

Finally, the empirical results from academic studies show that the correlation between executive compensation and corporate performance is mixed. Some studies suggest that the type of compensation plan used affects company performance, while others find little effect, if any. But we can say with certainty that managerial compensation plans will continue to receive lots of attention from researchers, the popular press, and boards of directors.

Capital Structure and Internal Control Systems

Capital structure decisions can affect managerial behavior. As the debt level increases, so does the probability of bankruptcy. This increased threat of bankruptcy brings with it two effects on behavior. First, as discussed earlier in this chapter, managers may waste money on unnecessary expenditures and perquisites. This behavior is more likely when times are good and firms are flush with cash; it is less likely in the face of high debt levels and possible bankruptcy. Thus high levels of debt tend to reduce managerial waste. Second, however, high levels of debt may also reduce a manager's willingness to undertake positive-NPV but risky projects. Most managers have their personal reputation and wealth tied to a single company. If that company has a lot of debt then a particularly risky project, even if it has a positive-NPV, may be just too risky for the manager to tolerate because a bad outcome could lead to bankruptcy and loss of the manager's job. Stockholders, on the other hand, are diversified and would want the manager to invest in positive-NPV projects even if they are risky. When managers forgo risky but value-adding projects, the resulting **underinvestment problem** reduces firm value. So increasing debt might increase firm value by reducing wasteful expenditures, but it also might reduce value by inducing underinvestment by managers. Empirical tests have not been able to establish exactly which effect dominates.

Internal control systems have become an increasingly important issue since the passage of the Sarbanes-Oxley Act of 2002. Section 404 of the act requires companies to establish effective internal control systems. The Securities and Exchange Commission, which is charged with the implementation of Sarbanes-Oxley, defines an effective internal control system as one that provides "reasonable assurance regarding the reliability of financial reporting and the preparation of financial statements for external purposes in accordance with generally accepted accounting principles." In other words, investors should be able to trust a company's reported financial statements.

Environmental Factors Outside of a Firm's Control

As noted earlier, corporate governance is also affected by environmental factors that are outside of a firm's control, including the regulatory/legal environment, block ownership patterns, competition in the product markets, the media, and litigation.

Regulations and Laws. The regulatory/legal environment includes the agencies that regulate financial markets, such as the SEC. Even though the fines and penalties levied on firms for financial misrepresentation by the SEC are relatively small, the damage to a firm's reputation can have significant costs, leading to extremely large reductions in the firm's value.[20] Thus, the regulatory system has an enormous impact on corporate governance and firm value.

The regulatory/legal environment also includes the laws and legal system under which a company operates. These vary greatly from country to country. Studies show that firms located in countries with strong legal protection for investors have stronger corporate governance and that this is reflected in better access to financial markets, a lower cost of equity, increases in market liquidity, and less noise in stock prices.[21]

Block Ownership Patterns. Prior to the 1960s, most U.S. stock was owned by a large number of individual investors, each of whom owned a diversified portfolio of stocks. Because each individual owned a small amount of any given company's stock, there was little that he or she could do to influence its operations. Also, with such a small investment, it was not cost effective for the investor to monitor companies closely. Indeed dissatisfied stockholders would typically just "vote with their feet" by selling the stock. This situation began to change as institutional investors such

[20]For example, see Jonathan M. Karpoff, D. Scott Lee, and Gerald S. Martin, "The Cost to Firms of Cooking the Books," *Journal of Financial and Quantitative Analysis*, September 2008, pp. 581–612.

[21]For example, see R. La Porta, F. Lopez-de-Silanes, A. Shleifer, and R. Vishny, "Legal Determinants of External Finance," *Journal of Finance*, January 1997, pp. 1131–1150; Hazem Daouk, Charles M. C. Lee, and David Ng, "Capital Market Governance: How Do Security Laws Affect Market Performance?" *Journal of Corporate Finance*, June 2006, pp. 560–593; and Li Jin and Stewart C. Myers, "R^2 Around the World: New Theory and New Tests," *Journal of Financial Economics*, February 2006, pp. 257–292.

The Sarbanes-Oxley Act of 2002 and Corporate Governance

In 2002 Congress passed the Sarbanes-Oxley Act, known in the industry as SOX, as a measure to improve transparency in financial accounting and to prevent fraud. SOX consists of eleven chapters, or *titles*, which establish wide-ranging new regulations for auditors, CEOs and CFOs, boards of directors, investment analysts, and investment banks. These regulations are designed to ensure that (a) companies that perform audits are sufficiently independent of the companies that they audit, (b) a key executive in each company *personally* certifies that the financial statements are complete and accurate, (c) the board of directors' audit committee is relatively independent of management, (d) financial analysts are relatively independent of the companies they analyze, and (e) companies publicly and promptly release all important information about their financial condition. The individual titles are briefly summarized below.

Title I establishes the Public Company Accounting Oversight Board, whose charge is to oversee auditors and establish quality control and ethical standards for audits.

Title II requires that auditors be independent of the companies that they audit. Basically this means they can't provide consulting services to the companies they audit. The purpose is to remove financial incentives for auditors to help management cook the books.

Title III requires that the board of directors' audit committee must be composed of "independent" members. Section 302 requires that the CEO and CFO must review the annual and quarterly financial statements and reports and personally certify that they are complete and accurate. Penalties for certifying reports that executives know are false range up to a $5 million fine, 20 years in prison, or both. Under Section 304, if the financial statements turn out to be false and must be *restated,* then certain bonuses and equity-based compensation that executives earn must be reimbursed to the company.

Title IV's Section 401(a) requires prompt disclosure and more extensive reporting on off–balance sheet transactions. Section 404 requires that management evaluate its internal financial controls and report whether they are "effective." The external auditing firm must also indicate whether it agrees with management's evaluation of its internal controls. Section 409 requires that a company disclose to the public promptly and *in plain English* any material changes to its financial condition. Title IV also places restrictions on the loans that a company can make to its executives.

Title V addresses the relationship between financial analysts, the investment banks they work for, and the companies they cover. It requires that analysts and brokers who make stock recommendations disclose any conflicts of interest they might have concerning the stocks they recommend.

Titles VI and VII are technical in nature, dealing with the SEC's budget and powers and requiring that several studies be undertaken by the SEC.

Title VIII establishes penalties for destroying or falsifying audit records. It also provides "whistle-blower protection" for employees who report fraud.

Title IX increases the penalties for a variety of white-collar crimes associated with securities fraud, such as mail and wire fraud. Section 902 also makes it a crime to alter, destroy, or hide documents that might be used in an investigation. It also makes it a crime to conspire to do so.

Title X requires that the CEO sign the company's federal income tax return.

Title XI provides penalties for obstructing an investigation and grants the SEC authority to remove officers or directors from a company if they have committed fraud.

as pension funds and mutual funds gained control of larger and larger shares of investment capital—and as they then acquired larger and larger percentages of all outstanding stock. Given their large block holdings, it now makes sense for institutional investors to monitor management, and they have the clout to influence the board. In some cases, they have actually elected their own representatives to the board. For example, when TIAA-CREF, a huge private pension fund, became frustrated with the performance and leadership of Furr's/Bishop, a cafeteria chain, the fund led a fight that ousted the entire board and then elected a new board consisting only of outsiders.

In general, activist investors with large blocks in companies have been good for all shareholders. They have searched for firms with poor profitability and then replaced management with new teams that are well versed in value-based management techniques, thereby improving profitability. Not surprisingly, stock prices usually rise on the news that a well-known activist investor has taken a major position in an underperforming company.

Note that activist investors can improve performance even if they don't go so far as to take over a firm. More often, they either elect their own representatives to the board or simply point out the firm's problems to other board members. In such cases, boards often change their attitudes and become less tolerant when they realize that the management team is not following the dictates of value-based management. Moreover, the firm's top managers recognize what will happen if they don't whip the company into shape, and they go about doing just that.

Competition in Product Markets. The degree of competition in a firm's product market has an impact on its corporate governance. For example, companies in industries with lots of competition don't have the luxury of tolerating poorly performing CEOs. As might be expected, CEO turnover is higher in competitive industries than in those with less competition.[22] When most firms in an industry are fairly similar, you might expect it to be easier to find a qualified replacement from another firm for a poorly performing CEO. This is exactly what the evidence shows: As industry homogeneity increases, so does the incidence of CEO turnover.[23]

The Media and Litigation. Corporate governance, especially compensation, is a hot topic in the media. The media can have a positive impact by discovering or reporting corporate problems, such as the Enron scandal. Another example is the extensive coverage that was given to option backdating, in which the exercise prices of executive stock options were set *after* the options officially were granted. Because the exercise prices were set at the lowest stock price during the quarter in which the options were granted, the options were in-the-money and more valuable when their "official" lives began. Several CEOs have already lost their jobs over this practice, and more firings are likely.

However, the media can also hurt corporate governance by focusing too much attention on a CEO. Such "superstar" CEOs often command excessive compensation packages and spend too much time on activities outside the company, resulting in too much pay for too little performance.[24]

In addition to penalties and fines from regulatory bodies such as the SEC, civil litigation also occurs when companies are suspected of fraud. Recent research indicates that such suits lead to improvements in corporate governance.[25]

---

[22]See M. De Fond and C. Park, "The Effect of Competition on CEO Turnover," *Journal of Accounting and Economics*, Vol. 27, 1999, pp. 35–56; and T. Fee and C. Hadlock, "Management Turnover and Product Market Competition: Empirical Evidence from the U.S. Newspaper Industry," *Journal of Business*, April 2000, pp. 205–243.

[23]See R. Parrino, "CEO Turnover and Outside Succession: A Cross-Sectional Analysis," *Journal of Financial Economics*, Vol. 46, 1997, pp. 165–197.

[24]See U. Malmendier and G. A. Tate, "Superstar CEOs," *Quarterly Journal of Economics*, forthcoming.

[25]For example, see D. B. Farber, "Restoring Trust after Fraud: Does Corporate Governance Matter?" *Accounting Review*, April 2005, pp. 539–561; and Stephen P. Ferris, Tomas Jandik, Robert M. Lawless, and Anil Makhija, "Derivative Lawsuits as a Corporate Governance Mechanism: Empirical Evidence on Board Changes Surrounding Filings," *Journal of Financial and Quantitative Analysis*, March 2007, pp. 143–166.

International Corporate Governance

Corporate governance includes the following factors: (1) the likelihood that a poorly performing firm can be taken over; (2) whether the board of directors is dominated by insiders or outsiders; (3) the extent to which most of the stock is held by a few large "blockholders" versus many small shareholders; and (4) the size and form of executive compensation. An interesting study compared corporate governance in Germany, Japan, and the United States.

First, note from the accompanying table that the threat of a takeover serves as a stick in the United States but not in Japan or Germany. This threat, which reduces management entrenchment, should benefit shareholders in the United States relative to the other two countries. Second, German and Japanese boards are larger than those in the United States. Japanese boards consist primarily of insiders, unlike German and American boards, which have similar inside/outside mixes. It should be noted, though, that the boards of most large German corporations include representatives of labor, whereas U.S. boards represent only shareholders. Thus, it would appear that U.S. boards, with a higher percentage of outsiders, would have interests most closely aligned with those of shareholders.

German and Japanese firms are also more likely to be controlled by large blocks of stock than those in the United States. Although pension and mutual funds, as well as other institutional investors, are increasingly important in the United States, block ownership is still less prevalent than in Germany and Japan. In both Germany and Japan, banks often own large blocks of stock, something that is not permitted by law in the United States, and corporations also own large blocks of stock in other corporations. In Japan, combinations of companies, called **keiretsus**, have cross-ownership of stock among the member companies, and these interlocking blocks distort the definition of an outside board member. For example, when the performance of a company in a keiretsu deteriorates, new directors are often appointed from the staffs of other members of the keiretsu. Such appointees might be classified officially as insiders, but they represent interests other than those of the troubled company's CEO.

In general, large blockholders are better able to monitor management than are small investors, so one might expect the blockholder factor to favor German and Japanese shareholders. However, these blockholders have other relationships with the company that might be detrimental to outside shareholders. For example, if one company buys from another, transfer pricing might be used to shift wealth to a favored company, or a company might be forced to buy from a sister company in spite of the availability of lower-cost resources from outside the group.

Executive compensation packages differ dramatically across the three countries, with U.S. executives receiving by far the highest compensation. However, compensation plans are remarkably similar in terms of how sensitive total compensation is to corporate performance.

Which country's system of corporate governance is best from the standpoint of a shareholder whose goal is stock price maximization? There is no definitive answer. U.S. stocks have had the best performance in recent years. Moreover, German and Japanese companies are slowly moving toward the U.S. system with respect to size of compensation, and compensation plans in all three countries are being linked ever more closely to performance. At the same time, however, U.S. companies are moving toward the others in the sense of having larger ownership blocks; because those blocks are primarily held by pension and mutual funds (rather than banks and related corporations), they better represent the interests of shareholders.

Sources: Steven N. Kaplan, "Top Executive Incentives in Germany, Japan, and the USA: A Comparison," in *Executive Compensation and Shareholder Value,* Jennifer Carpenter and David Yermack, eds. (Boston: Kluwer Academic Publishers, 1999), pp. 3–12. Reprinted by permission of Springer Science and Business Media.

International Characteristics of Corporate Governance

	Germany	Japan	United States
Threat of a takeover	Moderate	Low	High
Board of directors			
Size of board	26	21	14
Percent insiders	27%	91%	33%
Percent outsiders	73%	9%	67%
Are large blocks of stock typically owned by			
A controlling family?	Yes	No	No
Another corporation?	Yes	Yes	No
A bank?	Yes	Yes	No
Executive compensation			
Amount of compensation	Moderate	Low	High
Sensitivity to performance	Low to moderate	Low to moderate	Low to moderate

Self-Test

What are the two primary forms of corporate governance provisions that correspond to the stick and the carrot?

What factors improve the effectiveness of a board of directors?

What are three provisions in many corporate charters that deter takeovers?

Describe how a typical stock option plan works. What are some problems with a typical stock option plan?

13.6 Employee Stock Ownership Plans (ESOPs)

See **http://www.esopassociation.org** *for more on ESOPs.*

Studies show that 90% of the employees who receive stock under option plans sell the stock as soon as they exercise their options, so the plans motivate employees only for a limited period.[26] Moreover, many companies limit their stock option plans to key managers and executives. To help provide long-term productivity gains and improve retirement incomes for all employees, Congress authorized the use of **Employee Stock Ownership Plans (ESOPs)**. Today about 9,000 privately held companies and 1,000 publicly held firms have ESOPs, and more are being created every day. Typically, the ESOP's major asset is shares of the common stock of the company that created it, and of the 10,000 total ESOPs, about 2,500 of them actually own a majority of their company's stock.[27]

To illustrate how an ESOP works, consider Gallagher & Abbott Inc. (G&A), a construction company located in Knoxville, Tennessee. G&A's simplified balance sheet is shown below:

[26] See Gary Laufman, "To Have and Have Not," *CFO*, March 1998, pp. 58–66.

[27] See Eugene Pilotte, "Employee Stock Ownership Plans, Management Motives, and Shareholder Wealth: A Review of the Evidence," *Journal of Financial Education*, Spring 1997, pp. 41–46; and Daniel Eisenberg, "No ESOP Fable," *Time*, May 10, 1999, p. 95.

G&A's Balance Sheet prior to ESOP (Millions of Dollars)

Assets		Liabilities and Equity	
Cash	$ 10	Debt	$100
Other	190	Equity (1 million shares)	100
Total	$200	Total	$200

Now G&A creates an ESOP, which is a new legal entity. The company issues 500,000 shares of new stock at $100 per share, or $50 million in total, which it sells to the ESOP. The company's employees are the ESOP's stockholders, and each employee receives an ownership interest based on the size of his or her salary and years of service. The ESOP borrows the $50 million to buy the newly issued stock.[28] Financial institutions are willing to lend the ESOP the money because G&A signs a guarantee for the loan. Here is the company's new balance sheet:

G&A's Balance Sheet after the ESOP (Millions of Dollars)

Assets		Liabilities and Equity	
Cash	$ 60	Debt[a]	$100
Other	190	Equity (1.5 million shares)	150
Total	$250	Total	$250

[a]The company has guaranteed the ESOP's loan, and it has promised to make payments to the ESOP sufficient to retire the loan, but this does not show up on the balance sheet.

The company now has an additional $50 million of cash and $50 million more of book equity, but it has a de facto liability owing to its guarantee of the ESOP's debt. It could use the cash to finance an expansion, but many companies use the cash to repurchase their own common stock, so we assume that G&A will do likewise. The company's new balance sheets, and that of the ESOP, are shown below:

G&A's Balance Sheet after the ESOP and Share Repurchase (Millions of Dollars)

Assets		Liabilities and Equity	
Cash	$ 10	Debt	$100
Other	190	Equity (1 million shares)	150
		Treasury stock	(50)
Total	$200	Total	$200

ESOP's Initial Balance Sheet (Millions of Dollars)

Assets		Liabilities and Equity	
G&A stock	$50	Debt	$50
		Equity	0
Total	$50	Total	$50

[28]Our description is somewhat simplified. Technically, the stock would be placed in a suspense account and then be allocated to employees as the debt is repaid.

Note that although the company's balance sheet looks exactly as it did initially, there is actually a huge difference—the company has guaranteed the ESOP's debt and hence it has an off–balance sheet liability of $50 million. Moreover, because the ESOP has no equity, the guarantee is very real indeed. Finally, observe that operating assets have not been increased at all, but the total debt outstanding supported by those assets has increased by $50 million.[29]

If this were the whole story, then there would be no reason to have an ESOP. However, G&A has promised to make payments to the ESOP in sufficient amounts to enable the ESOP to pay interest and principal charges on the debt, amortizing it over 15 years. Thus, after 15 years, the debt will be paid off and the ESOP's equity holders (the employees) will have equity with a book value of $50 million and a market value that could be much higher if G&A's stock increases, as it should over time. Then, as employees retire, the ESOP will distribute a pro rata amount of the G&A stock to each employee, who can then use it as a part of his or her retirement plan.

An ESOP is clearly beneficial for employees, but why would a company want to establish one? There are five primary reasons.

1. Congress passed the enabling legislation in hopes of enhancing employees' productivity and thus making the economy more efficient. In theory, employees who have equity in the enterprise will work harder and smarter. Note too that if employees are more productive and creative then this will benefit outside shareholders, because productivity enhancements that benefit ESOP shareholders also benefit outside shareholders.
2. The ESOP represents additional compensation to employees: in our example, there is a $50 million (or more) transfer of wealth from existing shareholders to employees over the 15-year period. Presumably, if the ESOP were not created then some other form of compensation would have been required, and that alternative compensation might not have the secondary benefit of enhancing productivity. Also note that the ESOP's payments to employees (as opposed to the payment by the company) come primarily at retirement, and Congress wanted to boost retirement incomes.
3. Depending on when an employee's rights to the ESOP are vested, the ESOP may help the firm retain employees.
4. There are strong tax incentives that encourage a company to form an ESOP. First, Congress decreed that when the ESOP owns 50% or more of the company's common stock, financial institutions that lend money to ESOPs can exclude from taxable income 50% of the interest they receive on the loan. This improves the financial institutions' after-tax returns, which allows them to lend to ESOPs at below-market rates. Therefore, a company that establishes an ESOP can borrow through the ESOP at a lower rate than would otherwise be available—in our example, the $50 million of debt would be at a reduced rate.

   There is also a second tax advantage. If the company were to borrow directly, it could deduct interest but not principal payments from its taxable income. However, companies typically make the required payments to their ESOPs in the form of cash dividends. Dividends are not normally deductible from taxable income, but *cash dividends paid on ESOP stock are deductible if the dividends are paid to plan participants or are used to repay the loan.* Thus, companies whose ESOPs

[29]We assumed that the company used the $50 million paid to it by the ESOP to repurchase common stock and thus to increase its de facto debt. It could have used the $50 million to retire debt, in which case its true debt ratio would remain unchanged, or it could have used the money to support an expansion.

own 50% of their stock can in effect borrow on ESOP loans at subsidized rates and then deduct both the interest and principal payments made on the loans. American Airlines and Publix Supermarkets are two of the many firms that have used ESOPs to obtain this benefit, along with motivating employees by giving them an equity interest in the enterprise.

5. A less desirable use of ESOPs is to help companies avoid being acquired by another company. The company's CEO, or someone appointed by the CEO, typically acts as trustee for its ESOP, and the trustee is supposed to vote the ESOP's shares according to the will of the plan participants. Moreover, the participants, who are the company's employees, usually oppose takeovers because they frequently involve labor cutbacks. Therefore, if an ESOP owns a significant percentage of the company's shares, then management has a powerful tool for warding off takeovers. This is not good for outside stockholders.

Are ESOPs good for a company's shareholders? In theory, ESOPs motivate employees by providing them with an ownership interest. That should increase productivity and thereby enhance stock values. Moreover, tax incentives mitigate the costs associated with some ESOPs. However, an ESOP can be used to help entrench management, and that could hurt stockholders. How do the pros and cons balance out? The empirical evidence is not entirely clear, but certain findings are worth noting. First, if an ESOP is established to help defend against a takeover, then the firm's stock price typically falls when plans for the ESOP are announced. The market does not like the prospect of entrenching management and having to give up the premium normally associated with a takeover. However, if the ESOP is established for tax purposes and/or to motivate employees, the stock price generally goes up at the time of the announcement. In these cases, the company typically has a subsequent improvement in sales per employee and other long-term performance measures, which stimulates the stock price. Indeed, a study showed that companies with ESOPs enjoyed a 26% average annual stock return compared to a return of only 19% for peer companies without ESOPs.[30] It thus appears that ESOPs, if used appropriately, can be a powerful tool for creating shareholder value.

Self-Test What are ESOPs? What are some of their advantages and disadvantages?

Summary

- **Corporate assets** consist of operating assets and financial, or nonoperating, assets.
- **Operating assets** take two forms: assets-in-place and growth options.
- **Assets-in-place** include the land, buildings, machines, and inventory that the firm uses in its operations to produce products and services.
- **Growth options** refer to opportunities the firm has to increase sales. They include opportunities arising from R&D expenditures, customer relationships, and the like.
- **Financial**, or **nonoperating**, **assets** are distinguished from operating assets and include items such as investments in marketable securities and noncontrolling interests in the stock of other companies.
- The **value of nonoperating assets** is usually close to the figure reported on the balance sheet.

[30]See Daniel Eisenberg, "No ESOP Fable," *Time*, May 10, 1999, p. 95.

- The **value of operations** is the present value of all the future free cash flows expected from operations when discounted at the weighted average cost of capital:

$$V_{op(at\ time\ 0)} = \sum_{t=1}^{\infty} \frac{FCF_t}{(1 + WACC)^t}$$

- The **terminal**, or **horizon**, **value** is the value of operations at the end of the explicit forecast period. It is also called the **continuing value**, and it is equal to the present value of all free cash flows beyond the forecast period, discounted back to the end of the forecast period at the weighted average cost of capital:

$$\text{Continuing value} = V_{op(at\ time\ N)} = \frac{FCF_{N+1}}{WACC - g} = \frac{FCF_N(1 + g)}{WACC - g}$$

- The **corporate valuation model** can be used to calculate the total value of a company by finding the value of operations plus the value of nonoperating assets.
- The intrinsic **value of equity** is the total value of the company minus the value of the debt and preferred stock. The intrinsic **price per share** is the total value of the equity divided by the number of shares.
- **Value-based management** involves the systematic use of the corporate valuation model to evaluate a company's potential decisions.
- The four **value drivers** are (1) the growth rate (g) of sales; (2) operating profitability (OP), which is measured by the ratio of NOPAT to sales; (3) capital requirements (CR), as measured by the ratio of operating capital to sales; and (4) the weighted average cost of capital (WACC).
- **Expected return on invested capital (EROIC)** is equal to expected NOPAT divided by the amount of capital that is available at the beginning of the year.
- A company creates value when the spread between EROIC and WACC is positive—that is, when EROIC − WACC > 0.
- **Corporate governance** involves the manner in which shareholders' objectives are implemented, and it is reflected in a company's policies and actions.
- The two primary mechanisms used in corporate governance are (1) the threat of removal of a poorly performing CEO and (2) the type of plan used to compensate executives and managers.
- Poorly performing managers can be removed either by a takeover or by the company's own board of directors. Provisions in the corporate charter affect the difficulty of a successful takeover, and the composition of the board of directors affects the likelihood of a manager being removed by the board.
- **Managerial entrenchment** is most likely when a company has a weak board of directors coupled with strong anti-takeover provisions in its corporate charter. In this situation, the likelihood that badly performing senior managers will be fired is low.
- **Nonpecuniary benefits** are noncash perks such as lavish offices, memberships at country clubs, corporate jets, foreign junkets, and the like. Some of these expenditures may be cost effective, but others are wasteful and simply reduce profits. Such fat is almost always cut after a hostile takeover.
- **Targeted share repurchases**, also known as **greenmail**, occur when a company buys back stock from a potential acquirer at a price higher than the market price. In return, the potential acquirer agrees not to attempt to take over the company.

- **Shareholder rights provisions**, also known as **poison pills**, allow existing shareholders to purchase additional shares of stock at a price lower than the market value if a potential acquirer purchases a controlling stake in the company.
- A **restricted voting rights** provision automatically deprives a shareholder of voting rights if he or she owns more than a specified amount of stock.
- **Interlocking boards of directors** occur when the CEO of Company A sits on the board of Company B and also B's CEO sits on A's board.
- A **stock option** provides for the purchase of a share of stock at a fixed price, called the **exercise price**, no matter what the actual price of the stock is. Stock options have an **expiration date**, after which they cannot be exercised.
- An **Employee Stock Ownership Plan**, or **ESOP**, is a plan that facilitates employees' ownership of stock in the company for which they work.

Questions

(13–1) Define each of the following terms:

a. Assets-in-place; growth options; nonoperating assets
b. Net operating working capital; operating capital; NOPAT; free cash flow
c. Value of operations; horizon value; corporate valuation model
d. Value-based management; value drivers; EROIC
e. Managerial entrenchment; nonpecuniary benefits
f. Greenmail; poison pills; restricted voting rights
g. Stock option; ESOP

(13–2) Explain how to use the corporate valuation model to find the price per share of common equity.

(13–3) Explain how it is possible for sales growth to decrease the value of a profitable company.

(13–4) What are some actions an entrenched management might take that would harm shareholders?

(13–5) How is it possible for an employee stock option to be valuable even if the firm's stock price fails to meet shareholders' expectations?

Self-Test Problem

Solution Appears in Appendix A

(ST–1) Corporate Valuation

Watkins Inc. has never paid a dividend, and it's not known when the firm might begin paying dividends. Its current free cash flow is \$100,000, and this FCF is expected to grow at a constant 7% rate. The weighted average cost of capital is WACC = 11%. Watkins currently holds \$325,000 of nonoperating marketable securities. Its long-term debt is \$1,000,000, but it has never issued preferred stock. Watkins has 50,000 shares of stock outstanding.

a. Calculate Watkins's value of operations.
b. Calculate the company's total value.
c. Calculate the intrinsic value of its common equity.
d. Calculate the intrinsic per share stock price.

Problems

Answers Appear in Appendix B

EASY PROBLEMS 1–5

(13–1) Free Cash Flow

Use the following income statements and balance sheets to calculate Garnet Inc.'s free cash flow for 2011.

Garnet Inc.

Income Statement	**2011**	**2010**
Net sales	$530.0	$500.0
Costs (except depreciation)	400.0	380.0
Depreciation	30.0	25.0
Total operating costs	$430.0	$405.0
Earnings before interest and taxes (EBIT)	100.0	95.0
Less interest	23.0	21.0
Earnings before taxes	$ 77.0	$ 74.0
Taxes (40%)	30.8	29.6
Net income	$ 46.2	$ 44.4

Balance Sheet	**2011**	**2010**
Assets		
Cash	$ 28.0	$ 27.0
Marketable securities	69.0	66.0
Accounts receivable	84.0	80.0
Inventories	112.0	106.0
Total current assets	$293.0	$279.0
Net plant and equipment	281.0	265.0
Total assets	$574.0	$544.0
Liabilities and Equity		
Accounts payable	$ 56.0	$ 52.0
Notes payable	138.0	130.0
Accruals	28.0	28.0
Total current liabilities	$222.0	$210.0
Long-term bonds	173.0	164.0
Common stock	100.0	100.0
Retained earnings	79.0	70.0
Common equity	$179.0	$170.0
Total liabilities and equity	$574.0	$544.0

(13–2) Value of Operations of Constant Growth Firm

EMC Corporation has never paid a dividend. Its current free cash flow of $400,000 is expected to grow at a constant rate of 5%. The weighted average cost of capital is WACC = 12%. Calculate EMC's value of operations.

(13–3) Horizon Value

Current and projected free cash flows for Radell Global Operations are shown below. Growth is expected to be constant after 2012, and the weighted average cost of capital is 11%. What is the horizon (continuing) value at 2012?

	Actual	Projected		
	2010	2011	2012	2013
Free cash flow (millions of dollars)	\$606.82	\$667.50	\$707.55	\$750.00

(13–4) EROIC and MVA of Constant Growth Firm

A company has capital of \$200 million. It has an EROIC of 9%, forecasted constant growth of 5%, and a WACC of 10%. What is its value of operations? What is its intrinsic MVA? (*Hint:* Use Equation 13-5.)

(13–5) Value Drivers and Horizon Value of Constant Growth Firm

You are given the following forecasted information for the year 2014: sales = \$300,000,000, operating profitability (OP) = 6%, capital requirements (CR) = 43%, growth (g) = 5%, and the weighted average cost of capital (WACC) = 9.8%. If these values remain constant, what is the horizon value (i.e., the 2014 value of operations)? (*Hint:* Use Equation 13-4.)

INTERMEDIATE PROBLEMS 6–7

(13–6) Value of Operations

Brooks Enterprises has never paid a dividend. Free cash flow is projected to be \$80,000 and \$100,000 for the next 2 years, respectively; after the second year, FCF is expected to grow at a constant rate of 8%. The company's weighted average cost of capital is 12%.

a. What is the terminal, or horizon, value of operations? (*Hint:* Find the value of all free cash flows beyond Year 2 discounted back to Year 2.)
b. Calculate the value of Brooks's operations.

(13–7) Corporate Valuation

Dozier Corporation is a fast-growing supplier of office products. Analysts project the following free cash flows (FCFs) during the next 3 years, after which FCF is expected to grow at a constant 7% rate. Dozier's weighted average cost of capital is WACC = 13%.

	Year		
	1	2	3
Free cash flow (\$ millions)	–\$20	\$30	\$40

a. What is Dozier's terminal, or horizon, value? (*Hint:* Find the value of all free cash flows beyond Year 3 discounted back to Year 3.)
b. What is the current value of operations for Dozier?
c. Suppose Dozier has \$10 million in marketable securities, \$100 million in debt, and 10 million shares of stock. What is the intrinsic price per share?

CHALLENGING PROBLEMS 8–10

(13–8) Value of Equity

The balance sheet of Hutter Amalgamated is shown below. If the 12/31/2010 value of operations is \$756 million, what is the 12/31/2010 intrinsic market value of equity?

Balance Sheet, December 31, 2010 (Millions of Dollars)

Assets		Liabilities and Equity	
Cash	$ 20.0	Accounts payable	$ 19.0
Marketable securities	77.0	Notes payable	151.0
Accounts receivable	100.0	Accruals	51.0
Inventories	200.0	Total current liabilities	$ 221.0
Total current assets	$ 397.0	Long-term bonds	190.0
Net plant and equipment	279.0	Preferred stock	76.0
		Common stock (par plus PIC)	100.0
		Retained earnings	89.0
		Common equity	$ 189.0
Total assets	$ 676.0	Total liabilities and equity	$ 676.0

(13–9) Price per Share

The balance sheet of Roop Industries is shown below. The 12/31/2010 value of operations is $651 million, and there are 10 million shares of common equity. What is the intrinsic price per share?

Balance Sheet, December 31, 2010 (Millions of Dollars)

Assets		Liabilities and Equity	
Cash	$ 20.0	Accounts payable	$ 19.0
Marketable securities	47.0	Notes payable	65.0
Accounts receivable	100.0	Accruals	51.0
Inventories	200.0	Total current liabilities	$135.0
Total current assets	$367.0	Long-term bonds	131.0
Net plant and equipment	279.0	Preferred stock	33.0
		Common stock (par plus PIC)	160.0
		Retained earnings	187.0
		Common equity	$347.0
Total assets	$646.0	Total liabilities and equity	$646.0

(13–10) Corporate Valuation

The financial statements of Lioi Steel Fabricators are shown below—both the actual results for 2010 and the projections for 2011. Free cash flow is expected to grow at a 6% rate after 2011. The weighted average cost of capital is 11%.

a. If operating capital as of 12/31/2010 is $502.2 million, what is the free cash flow for 12/31/2011?
b. What is the horizon value as of 12/31/2011?
c. What is the value of operations as of 12/31/2010?
d. What is the total value of the company as of 12/31/2010?
e. What is the intrinsic price per share for 12/31/2010?

Income Statements for the Year Ending December 31 (Millions of Dollars Except for Per Share Data)

	Actual 2010	Projected 2011
Net sales	$ 500.0	$ 530.0
Costs (except depreciation)	360.0	381.6
Depreciation	37.5	39.8
Total operating costs	$ 397.5	$ 421.4
Earnings before interest and taxes	$ 102.5	$ 108.6
Less interest	13.9	16.0
Earnings before taxes	$ 88.6	$ 92.6
Taxes (40%)	35.4	37.0
Net income before preferred dividends	$ 53.2	$ 55.6
Preferred dividends	6.0	7.4
Net income available for common dividends	$ 47.2	$ 48.2
Common dividends	$ 40.8	$ 29.7
Addition to retained earnings	$ 6.4	$ 18.5
Number of shares	10	10
Dividends per share	$ 4.08	$ 2.97

Balance Sheets for December 31 (Millions of Dollars)

	Actual 2010	Projected 2011
Assets		
Cash	$ 5.3	$ 5.6
Marketable securities	49.9	51.9
Accounts receivable	53.0	56.2
Inventories	106.0	112.4
Total current assets	$ 214.2	$ 226.1
Net plant and equipment	375.0	397.5
Total assets	$ 589.2	$ 623.6
Liabilities and Equity		
Accounts payable	$ 9.6	$ 11.2
Notes payable	69.9	74.1
Accruals	27.5	28.1
Total current liabilities	$ 107.0	$ 113.4
Long-term bonds	140.8	148.2
Preferred stock	35.0	37.1
Common stock (par plus PIC)	160.0	160.0
Retained earnings	146.4	164.9
Common equity	$ 306.4	$ 324.9
Total liabilities and equity	$ 589.2	$ 623.6

SPREADSHEET PROBLEM

(13-11) Build a Model: Corporate Valuation

resource

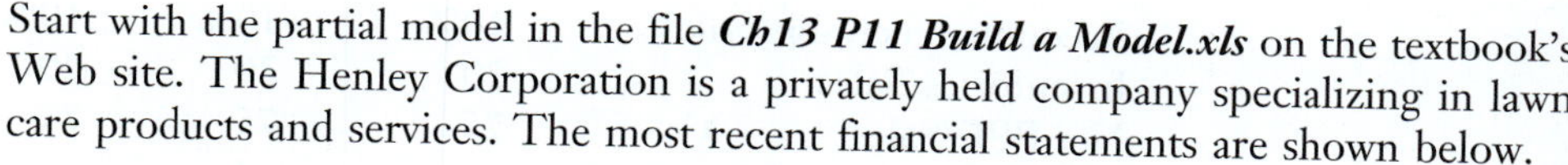

Start with the partial model in the file ***Ch13 P11 Build a Model.xls*** on the textbook's Web site. The Henley Corporation is a privately held company specializing in lawn care products and services. The most recent financial statements are shown below.

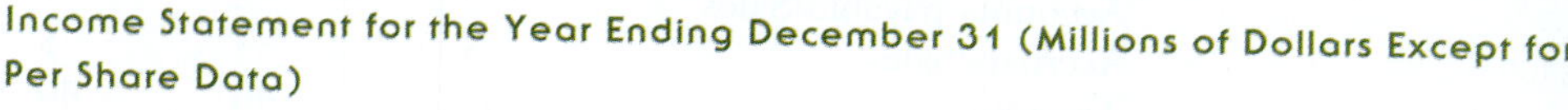

Income Statement for the Year Ending December 31 (Millions of Dollars Except for Per Share Data)

	2010
Net sales	$ 800.0
Costs (except depreciation)	576.0
Depreciation	60.0
Total operating costs	$ 636.0
Earnings before interest and taxes	$ 164.0
Less interest	32.0
Earnings before taxes	$ 132.0
Taxes (40%)	52.8
Net income before preferred dividends	$ 79.2
Preferred dividends	1.4
Net income available for common dividends	$ 77.9
Common dividends	$ 31.1
Addition to retained earnings	$ 46.7
Number of shares (in millions)	10
Dividends per share	$ 3.11

Balance Sheet for December 31 (Millions of Dollars)

Assets	2010	Liabilities and Equity	2010
Cash	$ 8.0	Accounts payable	$ 16.0
Marketable securities	20.0	Notes payable	40.0
Accounts receivable	80.0	Accruals	40.0
Inventories	160.0	Total current liabilities	$ 96.0
Total current assets	$268.0	Long-term bonds	300.0
Net plant and equipment	600.0	Preferred stock	15.0
		Common stock (par plus PIC)	257.0
		Retained earnings	200.0
		Common equity	$457.0
Total assets	$868.0	Total liabilities and equity	$868.0

Projected ratios and selected information for the current and projected years are shown below.

	Actual	Projected			
	2010	2011	2012	2013	2014
Sales growth rate		15%	10%	6%	6%
Costs/Sales	72%	72	72	72	72
Depreciation/Net PPE	10	10	10	10	10
Cash/Sales	1	1	1	1	1

	Actual	Projected			
	2010	2011	2012	2013	2014
Accounts receivable/Sales	10%	10%	10%	10%	10%
Inventories/Sales	20	20	20	20	20
Net PPE/Sales	75	75	75	75	75
Accounts payable/Sales	2	2	2	2	2
Accruals/Sales	5	5	5	5	5
Tax rate	40	40	40	40	40
Weighted average cost of capital (WACC)	10.5	10.5	10.5	10.5	10.5

a. Forecast the parts of the income statement and balance sheet that are necessary for calculating free cash flow.

b. Calculate free cash flow for each projected year. Also calculate the growth rates of free cash flow each year to ensure that there is constant growth (that is, the same as the constant growth rate in sales) by the end of the forecast period.

c. Calculate operating profitability (OP = NOPAT/Sales), capital requirements (CR = Operating capital/Sales), and expected return on invested capital (EROIC = Expected NOPAT/Operating capital at beginning of year). Based on the spread between EROIC and WACC, do you think that the company will have a positive Market Value Added (MVA = Market value of company − Book value of company = Value of operations − Operating capital)?

d. Calculate the value of operations and MVA. (*Hint*: First calculate the horizon value at the end of the forecast period, which is equal to the value of operations at the end of the forecast period.) Assume that the annual growth rate beyond the horizon is 6%.

e. Calculate the price per share of common equity as of 12/31/2010.

Mini Case

You have been hired as a consultant to Kulpa Fishing Supplies (KFS), a company that is seeking to increase its value. The company's CEO and founder, Mia Kulpa, has asked you to estimate the value of two privately held companies that KFS is considering acquiring. But first, the senior management of KFS would like for you to explain how to value companies that don't pay any dividends. You have structured your presentation around the following items.

a. List the two types of assets that companies own.

b. What are assets-in-place? How can their value be estimated?

c. What are nonoperating assets? How can their value be estimated?

d. What is the total value of a corporation? Who has claims on this value?

e. The first acquisition target is a privately held company in a mature industry owned by two brothers, each with 5 million shares of stock. The company currently has free cash flow of $20 million. Its WACC is 11%, and the FCF is expected to grow at a constant rate of 5%. The company owns marketable securities of $100 million. It is financed with $200 million of debt, $50 million of preferred stock, and $210 million of book equity.

(1) What is its value of operations?
(2) What is its total corporate value?
(3) What is its intrinsic value of equity?
(4) What is its intrinsic stock price per share?
(5) What is its intrinsic MVA (MVA = Total corporate value − Total book value of capital supplied by investors)?

f. The second acquisition target is a privately held company in a growing industry. The target has recently borrowed $40 million to finance its expansion; it has no other debt or preferred stock. It pays no dividends and currently has no marketable securities. KFS expects the company to produce free cash flows of –$5 million in 1 year, $10 million in 2 years, and $20 million in 3 years. After 3 years, free cash flow will grow at a rate of 6%. The target's WACC is 10% and it currently has 10 million shares of stock outstanding.
   (1) What is the company's horizon value (i.e., its value of operations at Year 3)? What is its current value of operations (i.e., at Time 0)?
   (2) What is its intrinsic value of equity on a price-per-share basis?

g. KFS is also interested in applying value-based management to its own divisions. Explain what value-based management is.

h. What are the four value drivers? How does each of them affect value?

i. What is expected return on invested capital (EROIC)? Why is the spread between EROIC and WACC so important?

j. KFS has two divisions. Both have current sales of $1,000, current expected growth of 5%, and a WACC of 10%. Division A has high profitability (OP = 6%) but high capital requirements (CR = 78%). Division B has low profitability (OP = 4%) but low capital requirements (CR = 27%). Given the current growth rate of 5%, determine the intrinsic MVA of each division. What is the intrinsic MVA of each division if growth is instead 6%?

k. What is the EROIC of each division for 5% growth and for 6% growth? How is this related to intrinsic MVA?

l. List six potential managerial behaviors that can harm a firm's value.

m. The managers at KFS have heard that corporate governance can affect shareholder value. What is corporate governance? List five corporate governance provisions that are internal to a firm and are under its control.

n. What characteristics of the board of directors usually lead to effective corporate governance?

o. List three provisions in the corporate charter that affect takeovers.

p. Briefly describe the use of stock options in a compensation plan. What are some potential problems with stock options as a form of compensation?

q. What is block ownership? How does it affect corporate governance?

r. Briefly explain how regulatory agencies and legal systems affect corporate governance.

Selected Additional Cases

The following cases from Textchoice, *Cengage Learning's online library, cover many of the concepts discussed in this chapter and are available at* **http://www.textchoice2.com**.

Klein-Brigham Series:

Case 41, "Advanced Fuels Corporation," and Case 93, "Electro Technology Corporation," discuss financing and valuing a new venture.

Brigham-Buzzard Series:

Case 14, "Maris Distributing Company," discusses valuation techniques used in a court case.

PART 6
Cash Distributions and Capital Structure

CHAPTER 14

Distributions to Shareholders: Dividends and Repurchases

Mature companies with stable cash flows and limited growth opportunities tend to return large amounts of their cash flows to shareholders, either by paying dividends or by using the cash to repurchase common stock. In contrast, rapidly growing companies with good investment opportunities are prone to invest most of their available cash flows in new projects and thus are less likely to pay dividends or repurchase stock. Microsoft, which was long regarded as the epitome of a growth company, illustrates this pattern. Its sales grew from $786 million in 1989 to $28.365 billion as of June 30, 2002, which translates to an annual growth rate of nearly 32%. Much of this growth came from investments in new products and technology, and given its emphasis on growth, Microsoft paid no dividends.

Market saturation and competition (including piracy) have caused its sales growth to slow. In May, 2009, Microsoft reported annual sales growth during the previous 12 months of about 5.6%, far short of its spectacular earlier growth rates. As growth slowed, Microsoft's cash flows increased, and its cash flow from operating activities was on pace to reach about $18 billion for 2009.

As companies tend to do when growth slows and cash flows increase, Microsoft first began paying a regular dividend in 2003. It stunned the world with a huge special dividend in 2005, which—when combined with its regular dividend—totaled more than $36 billion. Perhaps not coincidentally, Microsoft's decision to pay dividends coincided with a change in the Tax Code that lowered the tax rate on dividends from 35% to 15% for most investors.

In the first three quarters of its 2009 fiscal year, Microsoft paid regular dividends of $3.3 billion and also repurchased $8.9 billion in stock, for a total cash flow to shareholders of $12.2 billion. Microsoft still had over $25 billion in cash and marketable securities on its balance sheets, so investors might expect more large cash distributions in the future.

As you read this chapter, think about Microsoft's decisions to initiate regular dividend payments, occasionally use special dividends, and frequently repurchase stocks.

Uses of Free Cash Flow: Distributions to Shareholders

Free cash flow is generated from operations and is available for distribution to all investors. This chapter focuses on the distributions of FCF to shareholders in the form of dividends and stock repurchases.

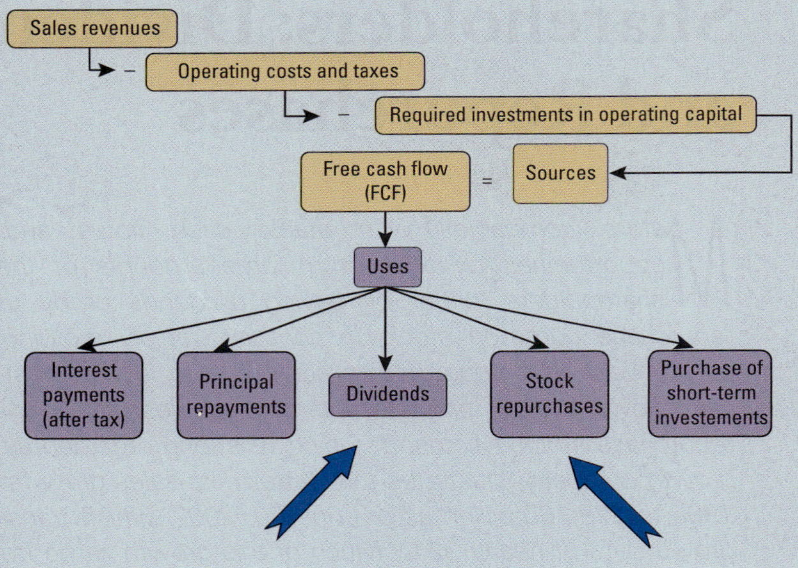

The textbook's Web site contains an Excel file that will guide you through the chapter's calculations. The file for this chapter is **Ch14 Tool Kit.xls**, *and we encourage you to open the file and follow along as you read the chapter.*

Because a company's value depends on its ability to generate free cash flow (FCF), most of this book has focused on aspects of FCF generation, including measurement, forecasts, and risk analysis. In contrast, this chapter focuses on the use of FCF for cash distributions to shareholders. Here are the central issues addressed in this chapter: Can a company increase its value through its choice of **distribution policy,** defined as (1) the *level* of distributions, (2) the *form* of distributions (cash dividends versus stock repurchases), and (3) the *stability* of distributions? Do different groups of shareholders prefer one form of distribution over the other? Do shareholders perceive distributions as signals regarding a firm's risk and expected future free cash flows?

Before addressing these questions, let's take a look at the big picture regarding cash distributions.

14.1 An Overview of Cash Distributions

At the risk of stating the obvious, a company must have cash before it can make a cash distribution to shareholders. Occasionally the cash comes from a recapitalization or the sale of an asset, but in most cases it comes from the company's internally generated free cash flow. Recall that FCF is defined as the amount of cash flow available for distribution to investors after expenses, taxes, and the necessary investments in operating capital. Thus, the *source* of FCF depends on a company's investment opportunities and its effectiveness in turning those opportunities into realities. Notice that a company with many opportunities will have large investments in operating capital and might have negative FCF even if the company is profitable. But when growth begins to slow, a profitable company's FCF will be positive and very large.

Home Depot and Microsoft are good examples of once-fast-growing companies that are now generating large amounts of free cash flows.

After FCF becomes positive, how should a company use it? There are only five potentially "good" ways to use free cash flow: (1) pay interest expenses, (2) pay down the principal on debt, (3) pay dividends, (4) repurchase stock, or (5) buy non-operating assets such as Treasury bills or other marketable securities.[1] Let's examine each of these uses.

A company's capital structure choice determines its payments for interest expenses and debt principal. A company's value typically increases over time, even if the company is mature, which implies its debt will also increase over time if the company maintains a target capital structure. If a company instead were to pay off its debt, then it would lose valuable tax shields associated with the deductibility of interest expenses. Therefore, most companies make net additions to debt over time rather than net repayments, even if FCF is positive. This "negative use" of FCF provides even more FCF for the other uses. We discuss capital structure choices in more detail in Chapter 15.

A company's working capital policies determine its level of marketable securities. Chapter 16 discusses marketable securities in more detail, but for now you should recognize that the decision involves a trade-off between the benefits and costs of having a large investment in marketable securities. In terms of benefits, a large investment in marketable securities reduces the risk of financial distress should there be an economic downturn. Also, if investment opportunities turn out to be better than expected, marketable securities provide a ready source of funding that will not incur the flotation or signaling costs due to raising external funds. However, there is a potential agency cost: If a company has a large investment in marketable securities, then managers might be tempted to squander the money on perks (such as corporate jets) or high-priced acquisitions.

In summary, a company's investment opportunities and operating plans determine its level of FCF. The company's capital structure policy determines the amount of debt and interest payments. Working capital policy determines the investment in marketable securities. The remaining FCF should be distributed to shareholders, with the only question being how much to distribute in the form of dividends versus stock repurchases.

Obviously this is a simplification, since companies (1) sometimes scale back their operating plans for sales and asset growth if such reductions are needed to maintain an existing dividend, (2) temporarily adjust their current financing mix in response to market conditions, and (3) often use marketable securities as shock absorbers for fluctuations in short-term cash flows. Still, there is an interdependence among operating plans (which have the biggest impact on free cash flow), financing plans (which have the biggest impact on the cost of capital), working capital policies (which determine the target level of marketable securities), and shareholder distributions.

Self-Test

What are the five uses of free cash flows?

How do a company's investment opportunities, capital structure, and working capital policies affect its distributions to shareholders?

[1] Recall from Chapter 2 that the company's cost of paying interest is on an after-tax basis. Recall also that a company doesn't *spend* FCF on operating assets (such as the acquisition of another company), because those expenditures were already deducted when calculating FCF. In other words, the purchase of an operating asset (even if it is another company) is not a *use* of FCF; instead, it is a *source* of FCF (albeit a "negative source").

14.2 Procedures for Cash Distributions

An excellent source of recent dividend news for major corporations is available on the Web site of Corporate Financials Online at **http://cfonews.com/scs**. *By clicking the down arrow of the "News Category" box on the left side of the screen, you may select "Dividends" to receive a list of companies with dividend news. Click on any company, and you will see its latest dividend news.*

Companies can distribute cash to shareholders via cash dividends or stock repurchases. In this section we describe the actual procedures used to make cash distributions.

Dividend Payment Procedures

Dividends are normally paid quarterly, and, if conditions permit, the dividend is increased once each year. For example, Katz Corporation paid a $0.50 dividend per share in each quarter of 2010, for an annual dividend per share of $2.00. In common financial parlance, we say that in 2010 Katz's *regular quarterly dividend* was $0.50, and its *annual dividend* was $2.00. In late 2010, Katz's board of directors met, reviewed projections for 2011, and decided to keep the 2011 dividend at $2.00. The directors announced the $2 rate, so stockholders could count on receiving it unless the company experienced unanticipated operating problems.

The actual payment procedure is as follows.

1. *Declaration date*. On the **declaration date**—say, on Thursday, November 11—the directors meet and declare the regular dividend, issuing a statement similar to the following: "On November 11, 2010, the directors of Katz Corporation met and declared the regular quarterly dividend of 50 cents per share, payable to holders of record as of Friday, December 10, payment to be made on Friday, January 7, 2011." For accounting purposes, the declared dividend becomes an actual liability on the declaration date. If a balance sheet were constructed, an amount equal to $\$0.50 \times n_0$, where n_0 is the number of shares outstanding, would appear as a current liability, and retained earnings would be reduced by a like amount.
2. *Holder-of-record date*. At the close of business on the **holder-of-record date**, December 10, the company closes its stock transfer books and makes up a list of shareholders as of that date. If Katz Corporation is notified of the sale before 5 p.m. on December 10, then the new owner receives the dividend. However, if notification is received after 5 p.m. on December 10, the previous owner gets the dividend check.
3. *Ex-dividend date*. Suppose Jean Buyer buys 100 shares of stock from John Seller on December 7. Will the company be notified of the transfer in time to list Buyer as the new owner and thus pay the dividend to her? To avoid conflict, the securities industry has set up a convention under which the right to the dividend remains with the stock until two business days prior to the holder-of-record date; on the second day before that date, the right to the dividend no longer goes with the shares. The date when the right to the dividend leaves the stock is called the **ex-dividend date**. In this case, the ex-dividend date is two days prior to December 10, which is December 8:

Dividend goes with stock:	Tuesday, December 7
Ex-dividend date:	Wednesday, December 8
	Thursday, December 9
Holder-of-record date:	Friday, December 10

Therefore, if Buyer is to receive the dividend, she must buy the stock on or before December 7. If she buys it on December 8 or later, Seller will receive the dividend because he will be the official holder of record.

Katz's dividend amounts to $0.50, so the ex-dividend date is important. Barring fluctuations in the stock market, we would normally expect the price of a stock to drop by approximately the amount of the dividend on the ex-dividend date. Thus, if Katz closed at $30.50 on December 7, it would probably open at about $30 on December 8.

4. *Payment date*. The company actually pays the dividend on January 7, the **payment date,** to the holders of record.

Stock Repurchase Procedures

Stock repurchases occur when a company buys back some of its own outstanding stock.[2] Three situations can lead to stock repurchases. First, a company may decide to increase its leverage by issuing debt and using the proceeds to repurchase stock; we discuss recapitalizations in more detail in Chapter 15. Second, many firms have given their employees stock options, and companies often repurchase their own stock to sell to employees when employees exercise the options. In this case, the number of outstanding shares reverts to its pre-repurchase level after the options are exercised. Third, a company may have excess cash. This may be due to a one-time cash inflow, such as the sale of a division, or the company may simply be generating more free cash flow than it needs to service its debt.[3]

Stock repurchases are usually made in one of three ways. (1) A publicly owned firm can buy back its own stock through a broker on the open market.[4] (2) The firm can make a tender offer, under which it permits stockholders to send in (that is, "tender") shares in exchange for a specified price per share. In this case, the firm generally indicates it will buy up to a specified number of shares within a stated time period (usually about two weeks). If more shares are tendered than the company wants to buy, purchases are made on a pro rata basis. (3) The firm can purchase a block of shares from one large holder on a negotiated basis. This is a targeted stock repurchase, as discussed in Chapter 13.

Patterns of Cash Distributions

The occurrence of dividends versus stock repurchases has changed dramatically during the past 30 years. First, total cash distributions as a percentage of net income have remained fairly stable at around 26% to 28%, but the mix of dividends and repurchases has changed.[5] The average dividend payout ratio fell from 22.3% in 1974 to 13.8% in 1998, while the average repurchase payout as a percentage of net income rose from 3.7% to 13.6%. Since 1985, large companies have repurchased more shares than they have

---

[2]The repurchased stock is called "treasury stock" and is shown as a negative value on the company's detailed balance sheet. On the consolidated balance sheet, treasury shares are deducted to find shares outstanding, and the price paid for the repurchased shares is deducted when determining common equity.

[3]See Benton Gup and Doowoo Nam, "Stock Buybacks, Corporate Performance, and EVA," *Journal of Applied Corporate Finance*, Spring 2001, pp. 99–110. The authors show that the firms that repurchase stock have superior operating performance to those that do not buy back stock, which is consistent with the notion that firms buy back stock when they generate additional free cash flow. They also show that operating performance improves in the year after the buyback, indicating that the superior performance is sustainable.

[4]Many firms announce their plans to repurchase stock on the open market. For example, a company might announce it plans to repurchase 4 million shares of stock. However, companies usually don't buy back all the shares they announce but instead repurchase only about 80% of the announced number. See Clifford Stephens and Michael Weisbach, "Actual Share Reacquisitions in Open-Market Repurchase Programs," *Journal of Finance*, February 1998, pp. 313–333.

[5]See Gustavo Grullon and Roni Michaely, "Dividends, Share Repurchases, and the Substitution Hypothesis," Journal of Finance, August 2002, pp. 1649–1684; and Eugene Fama and Kenneth French, "Disappearing Dividends: Changing Firm Characteristics or Lower Propensity to Pay?" *Journal of Applied Corporate Finance*, Spring 2001, pp. 67–79.

TABLE 14-1 Dividend Payouts (March 2009)

COMPANY	INDUSTRY	DIVIDEND PAYOUT	DIVIDEND YIELD
Empire District Electric (EDE)	Electric utility	109%	8.7%
Rayonier Inc. (RYN.N)	Forest products	99	6.7
Regions Financial Corp. (RF)	Regional banks	NM	8.5
Reynolds American Inc. (RAI)	Tobacco products	74	9.0
WD-40 Company (WDFC)	Household products	56	4.2
Harley-Davidson Inc. (HOG)	Recreational products	46	2.8
Ingles Markets Inc. (IMKTA)	Retail (grocery)	30	4.1
Microsoft Corp. (MSFT)	Software and programming	25	2.9
Tiffany and Company (TIF)	Specialty retail	38	3.0
Aaron Rents Inc. (RNT)	Rental and leasing	4	0.3
Papa John's Intl. Inc. (PZZA)	Restaurants	0	NM

Source: **http://www.reuters.com**, March 2009.

Notes: Regions Financial's payout ratio is not meaningful (NM) because Regions has negative net income. Papa John's dividend yield is not meaningful because it pays no dividend.

issued. Since 1998, more cash has been returned to shareholders in repurchases than as dividend payments.

Second, companies today are less likely to pay a dividend. In 1978, about 66.5% of NYSE, AMEX, and Nasdaq firms paid a dividend. In 1999, only 20.8% paid a dividend. Part of this reduction can be explained by the large number of IPOs in the 1990s, since young firms rarely pay a dividend. However, that doesn't explain the entire story, as many mature firms now do not pay dividends. For example, consider the way in which a maturing firm will make its first cash distribution. In 1973, 73% of firms making an initial distribution did so with a dividend. By 1998, only 19% initiated distributions with dividends.[6]

Third, the aggregate dividend payouts have become more concentrated in the sense that a relatively small number of older, more established, and more profitable firms accounts for most of the cash distributed as dividends.[7]

Fourth, Table 14-1 shows there is considerable variation in distribution policies, with some companies paying a high percentage of their income as dividends and others paying none. The next section discusses some theories about distribution policies.

Self-Test

Explain the procedures used to actually pay the dividend.
Why is the ex-dividend date important to investors?
What are the three ways in which a company can repurchase stock?

14.3 Cash Distributions and Firm Value

A company can change its value of operations only if it changes the cost of capital or investors' perceptions regarding expected free cash flow. This is true for all corporate

[6]See Gustavo Grullon and David Ikenberry, "What Do We Know about Stock Repurchases?" *Journal of Applied Corporate Finance*, Spring 2000, pp. 31–51.

[7]For example, see Harry DeAngelo, Linda DeAngelo, and Douglas J. Skinner, "Are Dividends Disappearing? Dividend Concentration and the Consolidation of Earnings," *Journal of Financial Economics*, June 2004, pp. 425–456.

decisions, including the distribution policy. Is there an **optimal distribution policy** that maximizes a company's intrinsic value?

The answer depends in part on investors' preferences for returns in the form of dividend yields versus capital gains. The relative mix of dividend yields and capital gains is determined by the **target distribution ratio**, which is the percentage of net income distributed to shareholders through cash dividends or stock repurchases, and the **target payout ratio**, which is the percentage of net income paid as a cash dividend. Notice that the payout ratio must be less than the distribution ratio because the distribution ratio includes stock repurchases as well as cash dividends.

A high distribution ratio and a high payout ratio mean that a company pays large dividends and has small (or zero) stock repurchases. In this situation, the dividend yield is relatively high and the expected capital gain is low. If a company has a large distribution ratio but a small payout ratio, then it pays low dividends but regularly repurchases stock, resulting in a low dividend yield but a relatively high expected capital gain yield. If a company has a low distribution ratio, then it must also have a relatively low payout ratio, again resulting in a low dividend yield and, it is hoped, a relatively high capital gain.

In this section, we examine three theories of investor preferences for dividend yield versus capital gains: (1) the dividend irrelevance theory, (2) the dividend preference theory (also called the "bird in the hand" theory), and (3) the tax effect theory.

Dividend Irrelevance Theory

The original proponents of the **dividend irrelevance theory** were Merton Miller and Franco Modigliani (MM).[8] They argued that the firm's value is determined only by its basic earning power and its business risk. In other words, MM argued that the value of the firm depends only on the income produced by its assets, not on how this income is split between dividends and retained earnings.

To understand MM's argument, recognize that any shareholder can in theory construct his own dividend policy. For example, if a firm does not pay dividends, a shareholder who wants a 5% dividend can "create" it by selling 5% of his stock. Conversely, if a company pays a higher dividend than an investor desires, the investor can use the unwanted dividends to buy additional shares of the company's stock. If investors could buy and sell shares and thus create their own dividend policy without incurring costs, then the firm's dividend policy would truly be irrelevant.

In developing their dividend theory, MM made a number of important assumptions, especially the absence of taxes and brokerage costs. If these assumptions are not true, then investors who want additional dividends must incur brokerage costs to sell shares and must pay taxes on any capital gains. Investors who do not want dividends must incur brokerage costs to purchase shares with their dividends. Because taxes and brokerage costs certainly exist, dividend policy may well be relevant. We will discuss empirical tests of MM's dividend irrelevance theory shortly.

Dividend Preference (Bird-in-the-Hand) Theory

The principal conclusion of MM's dividend irrelevance theory is that dividend policy does not affect a stock's value or risk. Therefore, it does not affect the required rate of return on equity, r_s. In contrast, Myron Gordon and John Lintner both argued

---

[8]See Merton H. Miller and Franco Modigliani, "Dividend Policy, Growth, and the Valuation of Shares," *Journal of Business*, October 1961, pp. 411–433. However, their conclusion is valid only if investors expect managers eventually to pay out the equivalent of the present value of all future free cash flows; see Harry DeAngelo and Linda DeAngelo, "The Irrelevance of the MM Dividend Irrelevance Theorem," *Journal of Financial Economics*, Vol. 79, 2006, pp. 293–315.

that a stock's risk declines as dividends increase: A return in the form of dividends is a sure thing, but a return in the form of capital gains is risky. In other words, a **bird in the hand** is worth more than two in the bush. Therefore, shareholders prefer dividends and are willing to accept a lower required return on equity.[9]

The possibility of agency costs leads to a similar conclusion. First, high payouts reduce the risk that managers will squander cash because there is less cash on hand. Second, a high-payout company must raise external funds more often than a low-payout company, all else held equal. If a manager knows that the company will receive frequent scrutiny from external markets, then the manager will be less likely to engage in wasteful practices. Therefore, high payouts reduce the risk of agency costs. With less risk, shareholders are willing to accept a lower required return on equity.

Tax Effect Theory: Capital Gains Are Preferred

Before 2003, individual investors paid ordinary income taxes on dividends but lower rates on long-term capital gains. The Jobs and Growth Act of 2003 changed this, reducing the tax rate on dividend income to the same as on long-term capital gains.[10] However, there are two reasons why stock price appreciation still is taxed more favorably than dividend income. First, the time value of money means that a dollar of taxes paid in the future has a lower effective cost than a dollar paid today. So even when dividends and gains are taxed equally, capital gains are never taxed sooner than dividends. Second, if a stock is held until the shareholder dies, then no capital gains tax is due at all: the beneficiaries who receive the stock can use its value on the date of death as their cost basis and thus completely escape the capital gains tax.

Because dividends are in some cases taxed more highly than capital gains, investors might require a higher pre-tax rate of return to induce them to buy dividend-paying stocks. Therefore, investors may prefer that companies minimize dividends. If so, then investors should be willing to pay more for low-payout companies than for otherwise similar high-payout companies.[11]

Empirical Evidence on Distribution Policies

It is very difficult to construct a perfect empirical test of the relationship between payout policy and the required rate of return on stock. First, all factors other than distribution level should be held constant; that is, the sample companies should differ only in their distribution levels. Second, each firm's cost of equity should be measured with

---

[9]Myron J. Gordon, "Optimal Investment and Financing Policy," *Journal of Finance*, May 1963, pp. 264–272; and John Lintner, "Dividends, Earnings, Leverage, Stock Prices, and the Supply of Capital to Corporations," *Review of Economics and Statistics*, August 1962, pp. 243–269.

[10]Of course, nothing involving taxes is quite this simple. The dividend must be from a domestic company, and the investor must own the stock for more than 60 days during the 120-day period beginning 60 days before the ex-dividend date. There are other restrictions for dividends other than regular cash dividends. The Tax Increase Prevention and Reconciliation Act of 2005 cut the long-term capital gains tax rate to zero for low-income investors (that is, those whose marginal tax rate is 15% or less) and kept it at 15% for those with more income. After 2010, unless Congress again extends the provisions, the capital gains rates will revert to 10% and 20%, which were the capital gains rates in effect prior to the 2003 Act. Also, the Alternative Minimum Tax (AMT) increases the effective tax rate on dividends and capital gains by 7% for some moderately high-income earners. See Leonard Burman, William Gale, Greg Leiserson, and Jeffrey Rohaly, "The AMT: What's Wrong and How to Fix It," *National Tax Journal*, September 2007, pp. 385–405.

[11]For more on tax-related issues, see Eli Talmor and Sheridan Titman, "Taxes and Dividend Policy," *Financial Management*, Summer 1990, pp. 32–35; and Rosita P. Chang and S. Ghon Rhee, "The Impact of Personal Taxes on Corporate Dividend Policy and Capital Structure Decisions," *Financial Management*, Summer 1990, pp. 21–31.

a high degree of accuracy. Unfortunately, we cannot find a set of publicly owned firms that differ only in their distribution levels, nor can we obtain precise estimates of the cost of equity. Therefore, no one has yet identified a completely unambiguous relationship between the distribution level and the cost of equity or firm value.

Although none of the empirical tests is perfect, recent evidence does suggest that firms with higher dividend payouts also have higher required returns.[12] This tends to support the tax effect hypothesis, although the size of the required return is too high to be fully explained by taxes.

Agency costs should be most severe in countries with poor investor protection. In such countries, companies with high dividend payouts should be more highly valued than those with low payouts because high payouts limit the extent to which managers can expropriate shareholder wealth. Recent research shows that this is the case, which supports the dividend preference hypothesis in the case of companies with severe agency problems.[13]

Although the evidence from these studies is mixed as to whether the *average* investor uniformly prefers either higher or lower distribution levels, other research does show that *individual* investors have strong preferences. Also, other research shows that investors prefer stable, predictable dividend payouts (regardless of the payout level) and that they interpret dividend changes as signals about firms' future prospects. We discuss these issues in the next several sections.

Self-Test

What did Modigliani and Miller assume about taxes and brokerage costs when they developed their dividend irrelevance theory?

How did the bird-in-the-hand theory get its name?

What have been the results of empirical tests of the dividend theories?

14.4 Clientele Effect

As we indicated earlier, different groups, or *clienteles*, of stockholders prefer different dividend payout policies. For example, retired individuals, pension funds, and university endowment funds generally prefer cash income, so they may want the firm to pay out a high percentage of its earnings. Such investors are often in low or even zero tax brackets, so taxes are of no concern. On the other hand, stockholders in their peak earning years might prefer reinvestment, because they have less need for current investment income and would simply reinvest dividends received—after first paying income taxes on those dividends.

WWW

For updates of industry payout ratios, go to **http://www.reuters.com/finance/stocks.** *After picking a company, select Ratios.*

If a firm retains and reinvests income rather than paying dividends, those stockholders who need current income would be disadvantaged. The value of their stock might increase, but they would be forced to go to the trouble and expense of selling some of their shares to obtain cash. Also, some institutional investors (or trustees for individuals) would be legally precluded from selling stock and then "spending capital." On the other hand, stockholders who are saving rather than spending dividends might favor the low-dividend policy: the less the firm pays out in dividends, the less these stockholders will have to pay in current taxes, and the less trouble and expense they will have to go through to reinvest their after-tax dividends. Therefore, investors who want current investment income should own shares in high–dividend

[12]See A. Naranjo, N. Nimalendran, and M. Ryngaert, "Stock Returns, Dividend Yields, and Taxes," *Journal of Finance*, December 1998, pp. 2029–2057.

[13]See L. Pinkowitz, R. Stulz, and R. Williamson, "Does the Contribution of Corporate Cash Holdings and Dividends to Firm Value Depend on Governance? A Cross-Country Analysis," *Journal of Finance*, December 2006, pp. 2725–2751.

payout firms, while investors with no need for current investment income should own shares in low–dividend payout firms. For example, investors seeking high cash income might invest in electric utilities, which averaged a 32% payout in March 2009, while those favoring growth could invest in the software industry, which paid out only 2.5% during the same time period.

To the extent that stockholders can switch firms, a firm can change from one dividend payout policy to another and then let stockholders who do not like the new policy sell to other investors who do. However, frequent switching would be inefficient because of (1) brokerage costs, (2) the likelihood that stockholders who are selling will have to pay capital gains taxes, and (3) a possible shortage of investors who like the firm's newly adopted dividend policy. Thus, management should be hesitant to change its dividend policy, because a change might cause current shareholders to sell their stock, forcing the stock price down. Such a price decline might be temporary but might also be permanent—if few new investors are attracted by the new dividend policy, then the stock price would remain depressed. Of course, the new policy might attract an even larger clientele than the firm had before, in which case the stock price would rise.

Evidence from several studies suggests that there is, in fact, a **clientele effect.**[14] It's been argued by MM and others that one clientele is as good as another, so the existence of a clientele effect does not necessarily imply that one dividend policy is better than any other. However, MM may be wrong, and neither they nor anyone else can prove that the aggregate makeup of investors permits firms to disregard clientele effects. This issue, like most others in the dividend arena, is still up in the air.

Self-Test

Define the clientele effect and explain how it affects dividend policy.

14.5 Information Content, or Signaling, Hypothesis

When MM set forth their dividend irrelevance theory, they assumed that everyone—investors and managers alike—has identical information regarding a firm's future earnings and dividends. In reality, however, different investors have different views on both the level of future dividend payments and the uncertainty inherent in those payments, and managers have better information about future prospects than public stockholders.

It has been observed that an increase in the dividend is often accompanied by an increase in the price of a stock and that a dividend cut generally leads to a stock price decline. Some have argued this indicates that investors prefer dividends to capital gains. However, MM saw this differently. They noted the well-established fact that corporations are reluctant to cut dividends, which implies that corporations do not raise dividends unless they anticipate higher earnings in the future. Thus, MM argued that a higher than expected dividend increase is a signal to investors that the firm's management forecasts good future earnings. Conversely, a dividend reduction, or a smaller than expected increase, is a signal that management is forecasting poor earnings in the future. Thus, MM argued that investors' reactions to changes in dividend policy do not necessarily show that investors prefer dividends to retained earnings. Rather, they argue that price changes following dividend actions simply indicate that there is important **information**, or **signaling, content** in dividend announcements.

---

[14]For example, see R. Richardson Pettit, "Taxes, Transactions Costs and the Clientele Effect of Dividends," *Journal of Financial Economics*, December 1977, pp. 419–436.

The initiation of a dividend by a firm that formerly paid no dividend is certainly a significant change in distribution policy. It appears that initiating firms' future earnings and cash flows are less risky than before the initiation. However, the evidence is mixed regarding the future profitability of initiating firms: Some studies find slightly higher earnings after the initiation but others find no significant change in earnings.[15] What happens when firms with existing dividends unexpectedly increase or decrease the dividend? Early studies, using small data samples, concluded that unexpected dividend changes did not provide a signal about future earnings.[16] However, more recent data with larger samples provide mixed evidence.[17] On average, firms that cut dividends had poor earnings in the years directly preceding the cut but actually improved earnings in subsequent years. Firms that increased dividends had earnings increases in the years preceding the increase but did not appear to have subsequent earnings increases. However, neither did they have subsequent declines in earnings, so it appears that the increase in dividends is a signal that past earnings increases were not temporary. Also, a relatively large number of firms that expect a large permanent increase in cash flow (as opposed to earnings) do in fact increase their dividend payouts in the year prior to the cash flow increase.

All in all, there is clearly some information content in dividend announcements: Stock prices tend to fall when dividends are cut, even if they don't always rise when dividends are increased. However, this doesn't necessarily validate the signaling hypothesis, because it is difficult to tell whether any stock price change following a change in dividend policy reflects only signaling effects or reflects both signaling and dividend preferences.

Self-Test

Define signaling content, and explain how it affects dividend policy.

14.6 Implications for Dividend Stability

The clientele effect and the information content in dividend announcements definitely have implications regarding the desirability of stable versus volatile dividends. For example, many stockholders rely on dividends to meet expenses, and they would be seriously inconvenienced if the dividend stream were unstable. Further, reducing dividends to make funds available for capital investment could send incorrect signals to investors, who might push down the stock price because they interpret the dividend cut to mean that the company's future earnings prospects have been diminished. Thus, maximizing its stock price probably requires a firm to maintain a steady dividend policy. Because sales and earnings are expected to grow for most firms, a stable dividend policy means a company's regular cash dividends should also

---

15 See Edward Dyl and Robert Weigand, "The Information Content of Dividend Initiations: Additional Evidence," *Financial Management*, Autumn 1998, pp. 27–35; P. Asquith and D. Mullins, "The Impact of Initiating Dividend Payments on Shareholders' Wealth," *Journal of Business*, January 1983, pp. 77–96; and P. Healy and K. Palepu, "Earnings Information Conveyed by Dividend Initiations and Omissions," *Journal of Financial Economics*, September 1988, pp. 149–175.

16 For example, see N. Gonedes, "Corporate Signaling, External Accounting, and Capital Market Equilibrium: Evidence of Dividends, Income, and Extraordinary Items," *Journal of Accounting Research*, Spring 1978, pp. 26–79; and R. Watts, "The Information Content of Dividends," *Journal of Business*, April 1973, pp. 191–211.

17 See Shlomo Benartzi, Roni Michaely, and Richard Thaler, "Do Changes in Dividends Signal the Future or the Past?" *Journal of Finance*, July 1997, pp. 1007–1034; and Yaron Brook, William Charlton Jr., and Robert J. Hendershott, "Do Firms Use Dividends to Signal Large Future Cash Flow Increases?" *Financial Management*, Autumn 1998, pp. 46–57.

THE GLOBAL ECONOMIC CRISIS

Will Dividends Ever Be the Same?

The global economic crisis has had dramatic effects on dividend policies. According to Standard & Poor's, companies announcing dividend increases have exceeded those announcing decreases by a factor of 15 to 1 since 1955—at least until the first 5 months of 2009. Out of 7,000 publicly traded companies, only 283 announced dividend increases in the first quarter of 2009 while 367 cut dividends, a stunning reversal in the normal ratio of increasers to decreasers. Even the S&P 500 companies weren't immune to the crisis, with only 74 increasing dividends as compared with 54 cutting dividends and 9 suspending dividend payments altogether. To put this in perspective, only *one* S&P 500 company cut its dividend during the first quarter of 2007. The dividend decreases in 2009 aren't minor cuts, either. Howard Silverblatt, a Senior Index Analyst at Standard & Poor's, estimates the cuts add up to $77 billion.

How has the market reacted to cuts by these companies? JPMorgan Chase's stock price went up on the announcement, presumably because investors thought a stronger balance sheet at JPM would increase its intrinsic value by more than the loss investors incurred because of the lower dividend. On the other hand, GE's stock fell by more than 6% on the news of its 68% dividend cut, perhaps because investors feared this was a signal that GE's plight was worse than they had expected.

One thing is for certain, though: The days of large "permanent" dividends are over!

Source: "S&P: Q1 Worst Quarter for Dividends Since 1955; Companies Reduce Shareholder Payments by $77 Billion," press release, April 7, 2009; also see **http://www2.standardandpoors.com/spf/xls/index/INDICATED_RATE_ CHANGE.xls.**

grow at a steady, predictable rate.[18] But as we explain in the next section, most companies will probably move toward small, sustainable, regular cash dividends that are supplemented by stock repurchases.

Self-Test

Why do the clientele effect and the information content hypotheses imply that investors prefer stable dividends?

14.7 Setting the Target Distribution Level: The Residual Distribution Model

When deciding how much cash to distribute to stockholders, two points should be kept in mind: (1) The overriding objective is to maximize shareholder value, and (2) the firm's cash flows really belong to its shareholders, so a company should refrain from retaining income unless its managers can reinvest that income to produce returns higher than shareholders could themselves earn by investing the cash in investments of equal risk. On the other hand, recall from Chapter 9 that internal equity (reinvested earnings) is cheaper than external equity (new common stock issues)

[18]For more on announcements and stability, see Jeffrey A. Born, "Insider Ownership and Signals—Evidence from Dividend Initiation Announcement Effects," *Financial Management*, Spring 1988, pp. 38–45; Chinmoy Ghosh and J. Randall Woolridge, "An Analysis of Shareholder Reaction to Dividend Cuts and Omissions," *Journal of Financial Research*, Winter 1988, pp. 218–294; C. Michael Impson and Imre Karafiath, "A Note on the Stock Market Reaction to Dividend Announcements," *Financial Review*, May 1992, pp. 259–271; James W. Wansley, C. F. Sirmans, James D. Shilling, and Young-jin Lee, "Dividend Change Announcement Effects and Earnings Volatility and Timing," *Journal of Financial Research*, Spring 1991, pp. 37–49; and J. Randall Woolridge and Chinmoy Ghosh, "Dividend Cuts: Do They Always Signal Bad News?" *Midland Corporate Finance Journal*, Summer 1985, pp. 20–32.

because it avoids flotation costs and adverse signals. This encourages firms to retain earnings so as to avoid having to issue new stock.

When establishing a distribution policy, one size does not fit all. Some firms produce a lot of cash but have limited investment opportunities—this is true for firms in profitable but mature industries in which few opportunities for growth exist. Such firms typically distribute a large percentage of their cash to shareholders, thereby attracting investment clienteles that prefer high dividends. Other firms generate little or no excess cash because they have many good investment opportunities. Such firms generally don't distribute much cash but do enjoy rising earnings and stock prices, thereby attracting investors who prefer capital gains.

As Table 14-1 suggests, dividend payouts and dividend yields for large corporations vary considerably. Generally, firms in stable, cash-producing industries such as utilities, financial services, and tobacco pay relatively high dividends, whereas companies in rapidly growing industries such as computer software tend to pay lower dividends.

For a given firm, the optimal distribution ratio is a function of four factors: (1) investors' preferences for dividends versus capital gains, (2) the firm's investment opportunities, (3) its target capital structure, and (4) the availability and cost of external capital. The last three elements are combined in what we call the **residual distribution model.** Under this model a firm follows these four steps when establishing its target distribution ratio: (1) it determines the optimal capital budget; (2) it determines the amount of equity needed to finance that budget, given its target capital structure (we explain the choice of target capital structures in Chapter 15); (3) it uses reinvested earnings to meet equity requirements to the extent possible; and (4) it pays dividends or repurchases stock only if more earnings are available than are needed to support the optimal capital budget. The word *residual* implies "leftover," and the residual policy implies that distributions are paid out of "leftover" earnings.

If a firm rigidly follows the residual distribution policy, then distributions paid in any given year can be expressed as follows:

$$\begin{aligned}\text{Distributions} &= \text{Net income} - \begin{matrix}\text{Retained earnings needed to}\\ \text{finance new investments}\end{matrix} \\ &= \text{Net income} - [(\text{Target equity ratio}) \times (\text{Total capital budget})]\end{aligned} \tag{14-1}$$

As an illustration, consider the case of Texas and Western (T&W) Transport Company, which has \$60 million in net income and a target capital structure of 60% equity and 40% debt.

If T&W forecasts poor investment opportunities, then its estimated capital budget will be only \$40 million. To maintain the target capital structure, 40% (\$16 million) of this capital must be raised as debt and 60% (\$24 million) must be equity. If it followed a strict residual policy, T&W would retain \$24 million of its \$60 million earnings to help finance new investments and then distribute the remaining \$36 million to shareholders:

$$\begin{aligned}\text{Distributions} &= \text{Net income} - [(\text{Target equity ratio})(\text{Total capital budget})] \\ &= \$60 - [(60\%)(\$40)] \\ &= \$60 - \$24 = \$36\end{aligned}$$

Under this scenario, the company's distribution ratio would be \$36 million ÷ \$60 million = 0.6 = 60%. These results are shown in Table 14-2.

TABLE 14-2 T&W's Distribution Ratio with $60 Million of Net Income and a 60% Target Equity Ratio When Faced with Different Investment Opportunities (Millions of Dollars)

	INVESTMENT OPPORTUNITIES		
	POOR	AVERAGE	GOOD
Capital budget	$40	$70	$150
Net income	60	60	60
Required equity (0.6 × Capital budget)	24	42	90
Distributions paid (NI – Required equity)	$36	$18	–$ 30[a]
Distribution ratio (Dividend/NI)	60%	30%	0%

[a]With a $150 million capital budget, T&W would retain all of its earnings and also issue $30 million of new stock.

In contrast, if the company's investment opportunities are average, its optimal capital budget would rise to $70 million. Here it would require $42 million of retained earnings, so distributions would be $60 – $42 = $18 million, for a ratio of $18/$60 = 30%. Finally, if investment opportunities are good then the capital budget would be $150 million, which would require 0.6($150) = $90 million of equity. In this case, T&W would retain all of its net income ($60 million) and thus make no distributions. Moreover, since the required equity exceeds the retained earnings, the company would have to issue some new common stock to maintain the target capital structure.

Because investment opportunities and earnings will surely vary from year to year, a strict adherence to the residual distribution policy would result in unstable distributions. One year the firm might make no distributions because it needs the money to finance good investment opportunities, but the next year it might make a large distribution because investment opportunities are poor and so it does not need to retain much. Similarly, fluctuating earnings could also lead to variable distributions, even if investment opportunities were stable. Until now, we have not said whether distributions should be in the form of dividends, stock repurchases, or some combination. The next sections discuss specific issues associated with dividend payments and stock repurchases; this is followed by a comparison of their relative advantages and disadvantages.

Self-Test

Explain the logic of the residual dividend model and the steps a firm would take to implement it.

Hamilton Corporation has a target equity ratio of 65%, and its capital budget is $2 million. If Hamilton has net income of $1.6 million and follows a residual distribution model, how much will its distribution be? **($300,000)**

14.8 The Residual Distribution Model in Practice

If distributions were solely in the form of dividends, then rigidly following the residual policy would lead to fluctuating, unstable dividends. Since investors dislike volatile regular dividends, r_s would be high and the stock price low. Therefore, firms should proceed as follows:

1. Estimate earnings and investment opportunities, on average, for the next 5 or so years.
2. Use this forecasted information and the target capital structure to find the average residual model distributions and dollars of dividends during the planning period.
3. Set a *target payout ratio* based on the average projected data.

Thus, *firms should use the residual policy to help set their long-run target distribution ratios, but not as a guide to the distribution in any one year.*

Companies often use financial forecasting models in conjunction with the residual distribution model discussed here to help understand the determinants of an optimal dividend policy. Most large corporations forecast their financial statements over the next 5 to 10 years. Information on projected capital expenditures and working capital requirements is entered into the model, along with sales forecasts, profit margins, depreciation, and the other elements required to forecast cash flows. The target capital structure is also specified, and the model shows the amount of debt and equity that will be required to meet the capital budgeting requirements while maintaining the target capital structure. Then, dividend payments are introduced. Naturally, the higher the payout ratio, the greater the required external equity. Most companies use the model to find a dividend pattern over the forecast period (generally 5 years) that will provide sufficient equity to support the capital budget without forcing them to sell new common stock or move the capital structure ratios outside their optimal range.

Some companies set a very low "regular" dividend and then supplement it with an "extra" dividend when times are good, such as Microsoft now does. This **low-regular-dividend-plus-extras policy** ensures that the regular dividend can be maintained "come hell or high water" and that stockholders can count on receiving that dividend under all conditions. Then, when times are good and profits and cash flows are high, the company can either pay a specially designated extra dividend or repurchase shares of stock. Investors recognize that the extras might not be maintained in the future, so they do not interpret them as a signal that the companies' earnings are going up permanently; nor do they take the elimination of the extra as a negative signal.

Self-Test

Why is the residual model more often used to establish a long-run payout target than to set the actual year-by-year dividend payout ratio?

How do firms use planning models to help set dividend policy?

14.9 A Tale of Two Cash Distributions: Dividends versus Stock Repurchases

Benson Conglomerate, a prestigious publishing house with several Nobel laureates among its authors, recently began generating positive free cash flow and is analyzing the impact of different distribution policies. Benson anticipates extremely stable cash flows and will use the residual model to determine the level of distributions, but it has not yet chosen the form of the distribution. In particular, Benson is comparing distributions via dividends versus repurchases and wants to know the impact the different methods will have on financial statements, shareholder wealth, the number of outstanding shares, and the stock price.

The Impact on Financial Statements

Consider first the case in which distributions are in the form of dividends. Figure 14-1 shows the most recent financial statements and the inputs we will use to forecast its financial statements. The forecasted financial statements for the next two years are shown in the figure. (The file ***Ch14 Tool Kit.xls*** shows four years of projected statements.) Benson has no debt, so its interest expense is zero.

Calculations to ensure the balance sheets do in fact balance are shown in Panel d of Figure 14-1. Required operating assets are the sum of cash, accounts receivable,

FIGURE 14-1 Projecting Benson Conglomerate's Financial Statements: Distributions as Dividends (Millions of Dollars)

	A	B	C	D	E	F	G
				Projected			
79	*Panel a: Inputs*		Actual				
80			12/31/2010	2011		2012	
81	Sales growth rate			5%		5%	
82	Costs / Sales		70%	70%		70%	
83	Depreciation / Net PPE		10%	10%		10%	
84	Cash / Sales		1%	1%		1%	
85	Acct. rec. / Sales		15%	15%		15%	
86	Inventories / Sales		12%	12%		12%	
87	Net PPE / Sales		85%	85%		85%	
88	Acct. pay. / Sales		8%	8%		8%	
89	Accruals / Sales		2%	2%		2%	
90	Tax rate		40%	40%		40%	
91							
92	*Panel b: Income Statement*		12/31/2010	12/31/2011		12/31/2012	
93	Net Sales		$8,000.0	$8,400.0		$8,820.0	
94	Costs (except depreciation)		5,600.0	5,880.0		6,174.0	
95	Depreciation		680.0	714.0		749.7	
96	Earning before int. & tax		$1,720.0	$1,806.0		$1,896.3	
97	Interest expense[b]		0.0	0.0		0.0	
98	Earnings before taxes		$1,720.0	$1,806.0		$1,896.3	
99	Taxes		688.0	722.4		758.5	
100	Net income		$1,032.0	$1,083.6		$1,137.8	
101							
102	*Panel c: Balance Sheets*			2011		2012	
103	*Assets*		12/31/2010	12/30	12/31	12/30	12/31
104	Cash		$80.0	$84.0	$84.0	$88.2	$88.2
105	Short-term investments[c]		0.0	671.6	0.0	705.2	0.0
106	Accounts receivable		1,200.0	1,260.0	1,260.0	1,323.0	1,323.0
107	Inventories		960.0	1,008.0	1,008.0	1,058.4	1,058.4
108	Total current assets		$2,240.0	$3,023.6	$2,352.0	$3.174.8	$2.469.6
109	Net plant and equipment		6,800.0	7,140.0	7,140.0	7,497.0	7,497.0
110	Total assets		$9,040.0	$10,163.6	$9,492.0	$10,671.8	$9,966.6
111	*Liabilities & Equity*						
112	Accounts payable		$640.0	$672.0	$672.0	$705.6	$705.6
113	Accruals		160.0	168.0	168.0	176.4	176.4
114	Short-term debt		0.0	0.0	0.0	0.0	0.0
115	Total current liabilities		$800.0	$840.0	$840.0	$882.0	$882.0
116	Long-term debt		0.0	0.0	0.0	0.0	0.0
117	Total liabilities		$800.0	$840.0	$840.0	$882.0	$882.0
118	Preferred stock		0.0	0.0	0.0	0.0	0.0
119	Common stock		2,400.0	2,400.0	2,400.0	2,400.0	2,400.0
120	Retained earnings[d]		5,840.0	6,923.6	6,252.0	7,389.8	6,684.6
121	Total common equity		$8,240.0	$9,323.6	$8,652.0	$9,789.8	$9,084.6
122	Total liabilities & equity		$9,040.0	$10,163.6	$9,492.0	$10,671.8	$9,966.6
123							
124	*Panel d: Plugging to balance*			12/30/2011		12/30/2012	
125	Required operating assets:			$9,492.0		$9,966.6	
126	Liabilities & equity before distribution			$10,163.6		$10,671.8	
127	AFN: Addition funds needed			−$671.6		−$705.2	

Notes:

[a]All calculations are in the file ***Ch14 Tool Kit.xls.*** *Excel* uses all significant digits in calculations, but numbers in the figure are rounded and so columns may not total exactly.

[b]To simplify the example, we assume that any short-term investments are held for only part of the year and earn no interest.

[c]A negative AFN means there are extra funds available. These are held as short-term investments through December 30. The funds are distributed to investors on December 31, so the balance of short-term investments goes to zero on December 31.

[d]Because no funds have been paid out in dividends as of December 30, the retained earnings balance for that date is equal to the previous year's retained earnings balance plus the current year's net income. When short-term investments are sold and their proceeds are used to make the cash dividend payments on December 31, the balance of retained earnings is reduced by the amount of the total dividend payments (which is equal to the reduction in short-term investments).

See **Ch14 Tool Kit.xls** *on the textbook's Web site.*

inventories, and net plant and equipment. We show balance sheets in Figure 14-1 for both December 30 and 31 of each year; this is to better illustrate the impact of the distribution, which we assume occurs once each year on December 31.[19] Liabilities and equity on December 30 (before the distribution) are the sum of accounts payable, accruals, short-term debt, long-term debt, preferred stock, common stock, the previous year's retained earnings balance, and the current year's net income. The amount of additional funds needed (AFN) is equal to the required operating assets minus liabilities and equity. Notice that a *negative* AFN is projected, which indicates additional funds are available rather than needed.

We assume that the extra funds temporarily are used to purchase short-term investments to be held until the distribution to shareholders. At that time, all short-term investments will be converted to cash and paid out as dividends. Thus, the 2011 short-term investments total \$671.6 on December 30 and drop to zero on December 31, when they are distributed to investors.[20] Observe that the retained earnings account also drops by \$671.6 on December 31 as funds that were previously retained are paid out as dividends.

Now let's consider the case of stock repurchases. The projected income statements and asset portion of the balance sheets are the same whether the distribution is in the form of dividends or repurchases, but this is not true for the liabilities-and-equity side of the balance sheet. Figure 14-2 reports the case in which distributions are in the form of stock repurchases. As in the case of dividend distributions, the December 30 balance of the retained earnings account is equal to the previous retained earnings balance plus the year's net income, because all income is retained. However, when funds in the short-term investments account are used to repurchase stock on December 31, the repurchase is shown as negative entry in the treasury stock account.

To summarize, the projected income statements and assets are identical whether the distribution is made in the form of dividends or stock repurchases. There also is no difference in liabilities. However, distributions as dividends reduce the retained earnings account, whereas stock repurchases reduce the treasury stock account.

The Residual Distribution Model

Figures 14-1 and 14-2 illustrate the residual distribution model in Equation 14-1 as applied to entire financial statements. The projected capital budget is equal to the net

[19]As we noted earlier in the chapter, when dividends are declared, a new current liability called "dividends payable" would be added to current liabilities and then retained earnings would be reduced by that amount. To simplify the example, we ignore that provision and assume that there is no balance sheet effect on the declaration date.

[20]As explained previously, there is a difference between the actual payment date and the ex-dividend date. To simplify the example, we assume that the dividends are paid on the ex-dividend date to the shareholder owning the stock the day before it goes ex-dividend.

FIGURE 14-2 Projecting Benson Conglomerate's Liabilities & Equity: Distributions as Stock Repurchases (Millions of Dollars)

	A	B	C	D	E	F	G
147				Projected			
148				2011		2012	
149	*Liabilities & Equity*[a]		12/31/2010	12/30	12/31	12/30	12/31
150	Accounts payable		$640.0	$672.0	$672.0	$705.6	$705.6
151	Accruals		160.0	168.0	168.0	176.4	176.4
152	Short-term debt		0.0	0.0	0.0	0.0	0.0
153		Total current liabilities	$800.0	$840.0	$840.0	$882.0	$882.0
154	Long-term debt		0.0	0.0	0.0	0.0	0.0
155		Total liabilities	$800.0	$840.0	840.0	882.0	882.0
156	Preferred stock		0.0	0.0	0.0	0.0	0.0
157	Common stock		2,400.0	2,400.0	2,400.0	2,400.0	2,400.0
158	Treasury stock[b]		0.0	0.0	(671.6)	(671.6)	(1,376.8)
159	Retained earnings[c]		5,840.0	6,923.6	6,923.6	8,061.4	8,061.4
160		Total common equity	$8,240.0	$9,323.6	8,652.0	9,789.8	9,084.6
		Total liabilities & equity	$9,040.0	$10,163.6	9,492.0	10,671.8	9,966.6
161							

Notes:

[a]All calculations are in the file ***Ch14 Tool Kit.xls***. *Excel* uses all significant digits in calculations, but numbers in the figure are rounded and so columns may not total exactly. See Figure 14-1 for income statements and assets.

[b]When distributions are made as repurchases, the treasury stock account is reduced by the dollar value of the repurchase at the time of the repurchase, which occurs when short-term investments are liquidated and used to repurchase stock.

[c]No funds are paid out in dividends, so the retained earnings balance is equal to the previous balance plus the year's net income (all net income is being retained).

See **Ch14 Tool Kit.xls** *on the textbook's Web site.*

addition to total operating capital from the projected balance sheets in Figure 14-1. For example, for 2011 the capital budget is:

$$\begin{aligned}\text{Capital budget} &= (\Delta\text{Cash} + \Delta\text{Accounts receivable} + \Delta\text{Inventories} \\ &\quad + \Delta\text{Net plant \& equipment}) \\ &\quad - (\Delta\text{Accounts payable} + \Delta\text{Accruals}) \\ &= (\$84 - \$80) + (\$1{,}260 - \$1{,}200) + (\$1{,}008 - \$960) \\ &\quad + (\$7{,}140 - \$6{,}800) - (\$672 - \$640) - (\$168 - \$160) \\ &= \$452 - \$40 = \$412\end{aligned}$$

With a 100% target equity ratio and net income of $1,083.6, the residual is $1,083.6 - $412 = $671.6, as shown in Figure 14-3. Notice that this is the same as the AFN we calculated in Figure 14-1.

The Impact of Distributions on Intrinsic Value

What is the impact of cash distributions on intrinsic value? We devote the rest of this section to answering that question.

Free Cash Flow. We begin by calculating expected free cash flows and performance measures as shown in Figure 14-4. Notice that Benson's expected return on invested capital is greater than the cost of capital, indicating that the managers are creating value for their shareholders. Also notice that the company is beyond its high-growth phase, so FCF is positive and growing at a constant rate of 5%. Therefore, Benson has cash flow available for distribution to investors.

FIGURE 14-3 Illustration of the Residual Distribution Model as Applied to Benson Conglomerate (Millions of Dollars): Determining the Level of the Distribution

	A	B	C	D	E	F	G
179							
180				Projected			
				12/31/2011		12/31/2012	
181	Capital budget[a]			$412.0		$432.6	
182	Target equity ratio			100%		100%	
183	Net income[b]			$1,083.6		$1,137.8	
184	Required additional equity[c]			$412.0		$432.6	
185	Residual distribution: NI – Req. equ.			$671.6		$705.2	

Notes:

[a]See Figure 14-1 for balance sheet projections. The capital budget is equal to the net addition to total operating capital: (ΔCash + ΔAccts. rec. + ΔInventories + ΔNet plant & equipment) – (ΔAccts. pay. + ΔAccruals).

[b]See Figure 14-1 for income statement projections.

[c]Required additional equity = Capital budget × Target equity ratio.

See **Ch14 Tool Kit.xls** on the textbook's Web site.

The Value of Operations. Figure 14-4 also shows the value of operations for each year. (See the ***Tool Kit*** for the full 4-year projections.) Recall from Chapter 13 that we can use the projected FCFs to determine the horizon value at the end of the projections and then estimate the value of operations for each year prior to the horizon. For Benson, the horizon value on December 31, 2012, is

$$V_{op(12/31/12)} = \frac{FCF_{12/31/12}(1+g)}{WACC - g}$$

$$= \frac{\$705.18(1+0.05)}{0.12 - 0.05} = \$10{,}577.70$$

The value of operations at the end of the previous year is equal to the value of operations 1 year ahead plus the free cash flow 1 year ahead, discounted back 1 year at the cost of capital. For example, the value of operations on December 31, 2011, is

$$V_{op(12/31/11)} = \frac{V_{op(12/31/12)} + FCF_{12/31/12}}{(1+WACC)}$$

$$= \frac{\$10{,}577.7 + \$705.18}{1+0.12} = \$10{,}074.00$$

We can repeat this process to obtain the current value of operations (i.e., as of December 31, 2010): $9,549.29.

Notice that the choice of how to distribute the residual does not affect the value of operations because the distribution choice does not affect the projected free cash flows.

The Intrinsic Stock Price: Distributions as Dividends. Figure 14-5 shows the intrinsic stock price each year using the corporate valuation approach described in Chapter 13. Panel a provides calculations assuming cash is distributed via dividends. (See ***Ch14 Tool Kit.xls*** for projections for 4 years.) Notice that on

FIGURE 14-4 Illustration of the Residual Distribution Model as Applied to Benson Conglomerate (Millions of Dollars): Valuation Analysis

	A	B	C	D	E	F	G
201	WACC = 12.0%						
202				Projected			
203	*Calculation of Free Cash Flow*		12/31/2010	12/31/2011		12/31/2012	
204	Operating current assets[a]		$2,240.00	$2,352.00		$2,469.60	
205	Operating current liabilities[b]		800.00	840.00		882.00	
206	NOWC[c]		$1,440.00	$1,512.00		$1,587.60	
207	Net plant & equipment		6,800.00	7,140.00		7,497.00	
208	Net operating capital[d]		$8,240.00	$8,652.00		$9,084.60	
209	NOPAT[e]		$1,032.00	$1,083.60		$1,137.78	
210	Inv. in operating capital[f]			412.00		432.60	
211	Free cash flow (FCF)[g]			$671.60		$705.18	
212							
213	*Performance Measures*						
214	Expected ROIC[h]			13.15%		13.15%	
215	Growth in FCF			na		5.00%	
216	Growth in sales			5.00%		5.00%	
217							
218	*Valuation*						
219	Horizon value[i]					$10,577.70	
220	Value of operations[j]		$9,594.29	$10,074.00		$10,577.70	

Notes:

[a]Sum of cash, accounts receivable, and inventories.

[b]Sum of accounts payable and accruals.

[c]Net operating working capital is equal to operating current assets minus operating current liabilities.

[d]Sum of NOWC and net plant & equipment.

[e]Net operating profit after taxes = (EBIT)(1 − T). In this example, NOPAT is equal to net income because there is no interest expense or interest income.

[f]Change in net operating capital from previous year.

[g]FCF = NOPAT − Investment in operating capital.

[h]Expected return on invested capital = NOPAT divided by beginning capital.

[i]Horizon value at T = $V_{op(T)} = [FCF_T (1 + g)]/(WACC - g)$.

[j]Value of operations before horizon = $V_{op(t)} = (V_{op(t+1)} + FCF_{t+1})/(1 + WACC)$.

See **Ch14 Tool Kit.xls** *on the textbook's Web site.*

December 31 the intrinsic value of equity drops because the firm no longer owns the short-term investments. This causes the intrinsic stock price also to drop. In fact, the drop in stock price is equal to the dividend per share. For example, the 2011 dividend per share (DPS) is \$0.67 and the drop in stock price is \$10.75 − \$10.07 = \$0.68 ≈ \$0.67. (The penny difference here is due to rounding in intermediate steps.)

Notice that if the stock price did *not* fall by the amount of the DPS then there would be an opportunity for arbitrage. If the price were to drop by less than the DPS—say, by \$0.50 to \$10.25, then you could buy the stock on December 30 for \$10.75, receive a DPS of \$0.67 on December 31, and then immediately sell the stock for \$10.25, reaping a sure profit of −\$10.75 + \$0.67 + \$10.25 = \$0.17. Of course, you'd want to implement this strategy with a million shares, not just a single share. But if everyone tried to use this strategy, the increased demand would drive up the stock price on December 30 until there was no more sure

FIGURE 14-5 Illustration of the Residual Distribution Model as Applied to Benson Conglomerate (Millions of Dollars): Distributions as Dividends versus Stock Repurchases

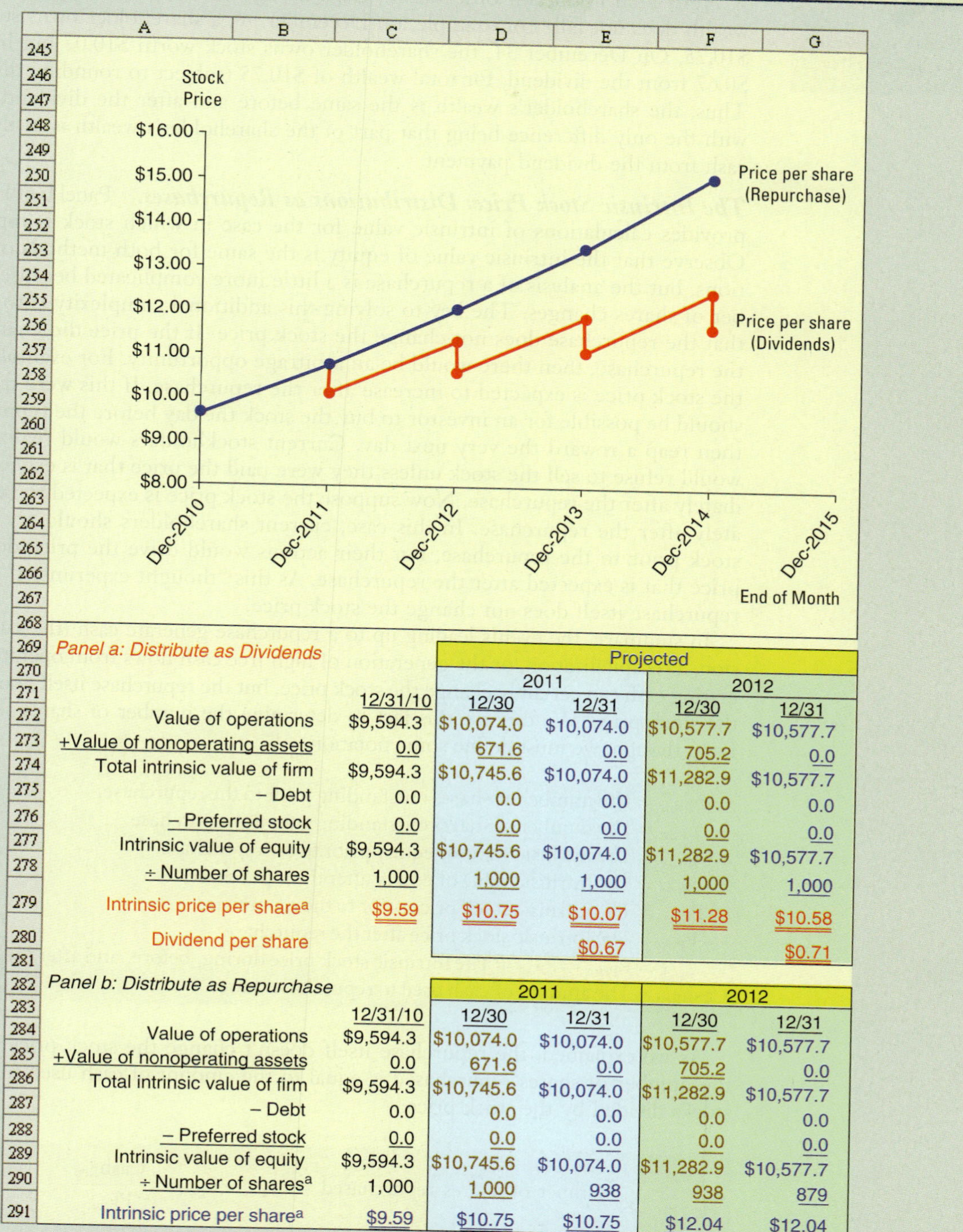

Panel a: Distribute as Dividends

		Projected			
		2011		2012	
	12/31/10	12/30	12/31	12/30	12/31
Value of operations	$9,594.3	$10,074.0	$10,074.0	$10,577.7	$10,577.7
+Value of nonoperating assets	0.0	671.6	0.0	705.2	0.0
Total intrinsic value of firm	$9,594.3	$10,745.6	$10,074.0	$11,282.9	$10,577.7
− Debt	0.0	0.0	0.0	0.0	0.0
− Preferred stock	0.0	0.0	0.0	0.0	0.0
Intrinsic value of equity	$9,594.3	$10,745.6	$10,074.0	$11,282.9	$10,577.7
÷ Number of shares	1,000	1,000	1,000	1,000	1,000
Intrinsic price per share[a]	$9.59	$10.75	$10.07	$11.28	$10.58
Dividend per share			$0.67		$0.71

Panel b: Distribute as Repurchase

		2011		2012	
	12/31/10	12/30	12/31	12/30	12/31
Value of operations	$9,594.3	$10,074.0	$10,074.0	$10,577.7	$10,577.7
+Value of nonoperating assets	0.0	671.6	0.0	705.2	0.0
Total intrinsic value of firm	$9,594.3	$10,745.6	$10,074.0	$11,282.9	$10,577.7
− Debt	0.0	0.0	0.0	0.0	0.0
− Preferred stock	0.0	0.0	0.0	0.0	0.0
Intrinsic value of equity	$9,594.3	$10,745.6	$10,074.0	$11,282.9	$10,577.7
÷ Number of shares[a]	1,000	1,000	938	938	879
Intrinsic price per share[a]	$9.59	$10.75	$10.75	$12.04	$12.04

Notes:

[a]The projected intrinsic stock prices for 4 years are shown in ***Ch14 Tool Kit.xls.***

[b]The number of shares after the repurchase is: $n_{Post} = n_{Prior} - (Cash_{Rep}/P_{Prior})$. In this example, the entire amount of ST investments (i.e., the balance of nonoperating assets) is used to repurchase stock.

See **Ch14 Tool Kit.xls** on the textbook's Web site.

profit to be made. The reverse would happen if investors expected the stock price to fall by more than the DPS.[21]

Here is an important observation: Even though the stock price falls, shareholder wealth does not fall. For example, on December 30, a shareholder owns stock worth \$10.75. On December 31, the shareholder owns stock worth \$10.07 but has cash of \$0.67 from the dividend, for total wealth of \$10.75 (subject to rounding differences). Thus, the shareholder's wealth is the same before and after the dividend payment, with the only difference being that part of the shareholder's wealth is in the form of cash from the dividend payment.

The Intrinsic Stock Price: Distributions as Repurchases. Panel b of Figure 14-5 provides calculations of intrinsic value for the case in which stock is repurchased. Observe that the intrinsic value of equity is the same for both methods of distributions, but the analysis of a repurchase is a little more complicated because the number of shares changes. The key to solving this additional complexity is to recognize that the repurchase does not change the stock price. If the price did change due to the repurchase, then there would be an arbitrage opportunity. For example, suppose the stock price is expected to increase after the repurchase. If this were true, then it should be possible for an investor to buy the stock the day before the repurchase and then reap a reward the very next day. Current stockholders would realize this and would refuse to sell the stock unless they were paid the price that is expected immediately after the repurchase. Now suppose the stock price is expected to fall immediately after the repurchase. In this case, current shareholders should try to sell the stock prior to the repurchase, but their actions would drive the price down to the price that is expected after the repurchase. As this "thought experiment" shows, the repurchase itself does not change the stock price.

In summary, the events leading up to a repurchase generate cash (the sale of a division, a recapitalization, or the generation of high free cash flows from operations). Generating cash can certainly change the stock price, but the repurchase itself doesn't change the stock price. We can use this fact to determine the number of shares repurchased. First, though, we must define some notation.

n_{Prior} = The number of shares outstanding prior to the repurchase.
n_{Post} = The number of shares outstanding after the repurchase.
S_{Prior} = The intrinsic value of equity prior to the repurchase.
S_{Post} = The intrinsic value of equity after the repurchase.
P_{Prior} = The intrinsic stock price prior to the repurchase.
P_{Post} = The intrinsic stock price after the repurchase.
$P = P_{Prior} = P_{Post}$ = The intrinsic stock price during, before, and after the repurchase.
$Cash_{Rep}$ = The amount of cash used to repurchase shares.

As we explained, the repurchase itself doesn't change the stock price. Therefore, the number of shares repurchased is equal to the amount of cash used to repurchase stocks divided by the stock price:

$$\text{Number of shares repurchased} = n_{Prior} - n_{Post} = \frac{Cash_{Rep}}{P_{Prior}} \qquad (14\text{-}2)$$

[21]We ignore taxes in this description. Empirical evidence suggests that the actual drop in stock price is equal to about 90% of the DPS, with all pre-tax profit being eliminated by taxes.

We can rewrite Equation 14-2 to find an expression for the number of shares after the repurchase:

$$\begin{aligned} n_{Post} &= n_{Prior} - \frac{Cash_{Rep}}{P_{Prior}} \\ &= n_{Prior} - \frac{Cash_{Rep}}{S_{Prior}/n_{Prior}} \\ &= n_{Prior}\left(1 - \frac{Cash_{Rep}}{S_{Prior}}\right) \end{aligned} \qquad (14\text{-}3)$$

For example, as shown in Panel b of Figure 14-5, the intrinsic stock price on December 30, 2011, the day before the repurchase, is \$10.75, and there are 1,000 shares of stock. Using Equation 14-3, the number of shares after the repurchase is equal to:

$$\begin{aligned} n_{Post} &= n_{Prior} - \frac{Cash_{Rep}}{P_{Prior}} \\ &= 1{,}000 - \frac{\$671.6}{\$10.75} \\ &= 1{,}000 - 62.47 = 937.5 \end{aligned}$$

Panel b of Figure 14-5 also shows that on December 31, 2011, the intrinsic value of equity prior to the repurchase, S_{Prior}, drops from \$10,745.6 to a value after the repurchase, S_{Post}, of \$10,074.0. This decrease in the intrinsic value of equity is equal to the amount of the cash used in the repurchase, \$671.6. However, the stock price remains at \$10.75 after the repurchase because the number of shares also drops:

$$P_{Post} = \frac{S_{Post}}{n_{Post}} = \frac{\$10{,}074}{937.5} = \$10.75$$

How does the repurchase affect shareholder wealth? The aggregate value of outstanding stock drops after the repurchase, but the aggregate wealth of the shareholders remains unchanged. Before the repurchase, shareholders own a total of equity worth S_{Prior}, \$10,745.6. After the repurchase, shareholders own a total of equity worth S_{Post}, \$10,074, but they also own cash (received in the repurchase) in the amount of \$671.6, for a total wealth of \$10,745.6. Thus, the repurchase does not change shareholders' aggregate wealth, it only changes the form in which they hold wealth (all stock versus a combination of stock and cash).

Comparing Intrinsic Stock Prices: Distributions as Repurchases. The chart at the top of Figure 14-5 shows the projected intrinsic stock prices for the two different distribution methods. Notice that the prices begin at the same level (because Benson has not yet begun making any distributions). The price for the repurchase scenario climbs smoothly and grows to a higher level than does the price for the dividend scenario, which drops by the DPS each time it is paid. However, the number of shares falls in the repurchase scenario. As shown in Rows 277 and 289 of the figure, the intrinsic values of equity are identical for both distribution methods.

This example illustrates three key results: (1) Ignoring possible tax effects and signals, the total market value of equity will be the same whether a firm pays dividends or repurchases stock. (2) The repurchase itself does not change the stock price (compared with using the cash to buy marketable securities) at the time of the repurchase, although it does reduce the number of outstanding shares. (3) Because a company that repurchases stock will have fewer shares than an otherwise identical company that pays dividends, the stock price of a repurchasing company will climb faster than that of the dividend-paying company. However, the total return to the two companies' shareholders will be the same.[22]

Self-Test

Explain how a repurchase changes the number of shares but not the stock price.

A firm's most recent FCF was $2.4 million, and its FCF is expected to grow at a constant rate of 5%. The firm's WACC is 14% and it has 2 million shares outstanding. The firm has $12 million in short-term investments that it plans to liquidate and then distribute in a stock repurchase; the firm has no other financial investments or debt. Verify that the value of operations is $28 million. Immediately prior to the repurchase, what are the intrinsic value of equity and the intrinsic stock price? **($40 million; $20/share)** How many shares will be repurchased? **(0.6 million)** How many shares will remain after the repurchase? **(1.4 million)** Immediately after the repurchase, what are the intrinsic value of equity and the intrinsic stock price? **($28 million; $20/share)**

14.10 The Pros and Cons of Dividends and Repurchases

The advantages of repurchases can be listed as follows.

1. Repurchase announcements are viewed as positive signals by investors because the repurchase is often motivated by management's belief that the firm's shares are undervalued.
2. Stockholders have a choice when the firm distributes cash by repurchasing stock —they can sell or not sell. Those stockholders who need cash can sell back some of their shares while others can simply retain their stock. With a cash dividend, on the other hand, stockholders must accept a dividend payment.
3. Dividends are "sticky" in the short run because management is usually reluctant to raise the dividend if the increase cannot be maintained in the future, and cutting cash dividends is always avoided because of the negative signal it gives. Hence, if the excess cash flow is thought to be only temporary, management may prefer making the distribution in the form of a stock repurchase to declaring an increased cash dividend that cannot be maintained.
4. Companies can use the residual model to set a *target cash distribution* level and then divide the distribution into a *dividend component* and a *repurchase component*. The dividend payout ratio will be relatively low, but the dividend itself will be relatively secure, and it will grow as a result of the declining number of shares outstanding. The company has more flexibility in adjusting the total distribution than it would if the entire distribution were in the form of cash dividends,

[22]For more on repurchases, see David J. Denis, "Defensive Changes in Corporate Payout Policy: Share Repurchases and Special Dividends," *Journal of Finance*, December 1990, pp. 1433–1456; Gerald D. Gay, Jayant R. Kale, and Thomas H. Noe, "Share Repurchase Mechanisms: A Comparative Analysis of Efficacy, Shareholder Wealth and Corporate Control Effects," *Financial Management*, Spring 1991, pp. 44–59; Jeffry M. Netter and Mark L. Mitchell, "Stock-Repurchase Announcements and Insider Transactions after the October 1987 Stock Market Crash," *Financial Management*, Autumn 1989, pp. 84–96; William Pugh and John S. Jahera, Jr., "Stock Repurchases and Excess Returns: An Empirical Examination," *The Financial Review*, February 1990, pp. 127–142; and James W. Wansley, William R. Lane, and Salil Sarkar, "Managements' View on Share Repurchase and Tender Offer Premiums," *Financial Management*, Autumn 1989, pp. 97–110.

because repurchases can be varied from year to year without giving off adverse signals. This procedure, which is what Florida Power & Light employed, has much to recommend it, and it is one reason for the dramatic increase in the total volume of stock repurchases.

5. Repurchases can be used to produce large-scale changes in capital structures. For example, several years ago Consolidated Edison decided to borrow $400 million and use the funds to repurchase some of its common stock. Thus, Con Ed was able to quickly change its capital structure.
6. Companies that use stock options as an important component of employee compensation usually repurchase shares in the secondary market and then use those shares when employees exercise their options. This technique allows companies to avoid issuing new shares and thus diluting earnings.

Repurchases have three principal disadvantages.

1. Stockholders may not be indifferent between dividends and capital gains, and the price of the stock might benefit more from cash dividends than from repurchases. Cash dividends are generally dependable, but repurchases are not.
2. The *selling* stockholders may not be fully aware of all the implications of a repurchase, or they may not have all the pertinent information about the corporation's present and future activities. However, in order to avoid potential stockholder suits, firms generally announce repurchase programs before embarking on them.
3. The corporation may pay too much for the repurchased stock—to the disadvantage of remaining stockholders. If the firm seeks to acquire a relatively large amount of its stock, then the price may be bid above its equilibrium level and then fall after the firm ceases its repurchase operations.

When all the pros and cons on stock repurchases versus dividends have been totaled, where do we stand? Our conclusions may be summarized as follows.

1. Because of the deferred tax on capital gains, repurchases have a tax advantage over dividends as a way to distribute income to stockholders. This advantage is reinforced by the fact that repurchases provide cash to stockholders who want cash while allowing those who do not need current cash to delay its receipt. On the other hand, dividends are more dependable and thus are better suited for those who need a steady source of income.
2. The danger of signaling effects requires that a company not have volatile dividend payments, which would lower investors' confidence in the company and adversely affect its cost of equity and its stock price. However, cash flows vary over time, as do investment opportunities, so the "proper" dividend in the residual model sense varies. To get around this problem, a company can set its dividend low enough to keep dividend payments from constraining operations and then use repurchases on a more or less regular basis to distribute excess cash. Such a procedure will provide regular, dependable dividends plus additional cash flow to those stockholders who want it.
3. Repurchases are also useful when a firm wants to make a large shift in its capital structure, wants to distribute cash from a one-time event such as the sale of a division, or wants to obtain shares for use in an employee stock option plan.

Self-Test

What are some advantages and disadvantages of stock repurchases?

How can stock repurchases help a company operate in accordance with the residual distribution model?

Dividend Yields around the World

Dividend yields vary considerably in different stock markets throughout the world. In 1999, dividend yields in the United States averaged 1.6% for the large blue-chip stocks in the Dow Jones Industrials, 1.2% for a broader sample of stocks in the S&P 500, and 0.3% for stocks in the Nasdaq, where high-tech firms predominate. Outside the United States, average dividend yields ranged from 5.7% in New Zealand to 0.7% in Taiwan. The accompanying table summarizes the dividend picture in 1999.

World Stock Market (Index)	Dividend Yield	World Stock Market (Index)	Dividend Yield
New Zealand	5.7%	United States (Dow Jones Industrials)	1.6%
Australia	3.1	Canada (TSE 300)	1.5
Britain FTSE 100	2.4	United States (S&P 500)	1.2
Hong Kong	2.4	Mexico	1.1
France	2.1	Japan Nikkei	0.7
Germany	2.1	Taiwan	0.7
Belgium	2.0	United States (Nasdaq)	0.3
Singapore	1.7		

Source: From Alexandra Eadie, "On the Grid Looking for Dividend Yield around the World," *The Globe and Mail*, June 23, 1999, p. B16 Eadie's source was Bloomberg Financial Services. Reprinted with permission from *The Globe and Mail*.

14.11 Other Factors Influencing Distributions

In this section, we discuss several other factors that affect the dividend decision. These factors may be grouped into two broad categories: (1) constraints on dividend payments and (2) availability and cost of alternative sources of capital.

Constraints

Constraints on dividend payments can affect distributions, as the following examples illustrate.

1. *Bond indentures*. Debt contracts often limit dividend payments to earnings generated after the loan was granted. Also, debt contracts often stipulate that no dividends can be paid unless the current ratio, times-interest-earned ratio, and other safety ratios exceed stated minimums.
2. *Preferred stock restrictions*. Typically, common dividends cannot be paid if the company has omitted its preferred dividend. The preferred arrearages must be satisfied before common dividends can be resumed.
3. *Impairment of capital rule*. Dividend payments cannot exceed the balance sheet item "retained earnings." This legal restriction, known as the "impairment of capital rule," is designed to protect creditors. Without the rule, a company in trouble might distribute most of its assets to stockholders and leave its debtholders out in the cold. (*Liquidating dividends* can be paid out of capital, but they must be indicated as such and must not reduce capital below the limits stated in debt contracts.)
4. *Availability of cash*. Cash dividends can be paid only with cash, so a shortage of cash in the bank can restrict dividend payments. However, the ability to borrow can offset this factor.

5. *Penalty tax on improperly accumulated earnings.* To prevent wealthy individuals from using corporations to avoid personal taxes, the Tax Code provides for a special surtax on improperly accumulated income. Thus, if the IRS can demonstrate that a firm's dividend payout ratio is being deliberately held down to help its stockholders avoid personal taxes, the firm is subject to heavy penalties. This factor is generally relevant only to privately owned firms.

Alternative Sources of Capital

The second factor that influences the dividend decision is the cost and availability of alternative sources of capital.

1. *Cost of selling new stock.* If a firm needs to finance a given level of investment, it can obtain equity by retaining earnings or by issuing new common stock. If flotation costs (including any negative signaling effects of a stock offering) are high then r_e will be well above r_s, making it better to set a low payout ratio and to finance through retention rather than through the sale of new common stock. On the other hand, a high dividend payout ratio is more feasible for a firm whose flotation costs are low. Flotation costs differ among firms—for example, the flotation percentage is generally higher for small firms, so they tend to set low payout ratios.
2. *Ability to substitute debt for equity.* A firm can finance a given level of investment with either debt or equity. As just described, low stock flotation costs permit a more flexible dividend policy because equity can be raised either by retaining earnings or by selling new stock. A similar situation holds for debt policy: If the firm can adjust its debt ratio without raising costs sharply, then it can pay the expected dividend—even if earnings fluctuate—by increasing its debt ratio.
3. *Control.* If management is concerned about maintaining control, it may be reluctant to sell new stock; hence the company may retain more earnings than it otherwise would. However, if stockholders want higher dividends and a proxy fight looms, then the dividend will be increased.

Self-Test

What constraints affect dividend policy?
How do the availability and cost of outside capital affect dividend policy?

14.12 Summarizing the Distribution Policy Decision

In practice, the distribution decision is made jointly with capital structure and capital budgeting decisions. The underlying reason for joining these decisions is asymmetric information, which influences managerial actions in two ways.

1. In general, managers do not want to issue new common stock. First, new common stock involves issuance costs—commissions, fees, and so on—and those costs can be avoided by using retained earnings to finance equity needs. Second, as we will explain in Chapter 15, asymmetric information causes investors to view new common stock issues as negative signals and thus lowers expectations regarding the firm's future prospects. The end result is that the announcement of a new stock issue usually leads to a decrease in the stock price. Considering the total costs due to issuance and asymmetric information, managers prefer to use retained earnings as the primary source of new equity.
2. Dividend changes provide signals about managers' beliefs concerning their firms' future prospects. Thus, dividend reductions generally have a significant negative effect on a firm's stock price. Since managers recognize this, they try to

set dollar dividends low enough that there is only a remote chance the dividend will have to be reduced in the future.

The effects of asymmetric information suggest that, to the extent possible, managers should avoid both new common stock sales and dividend cuts, because both actions tend to lower the stock price. Thus, in setting distribution policy, managers should begin by considering the firm's future investment opportunities relative to its projected internal sources of funds. The target capital structure also plays a part, but because it is a *range*, firms can vary their actual capital structures somewhat from year to year. Since it is best to avoid issuing new common stock, the target long-term payout ratio should be designed to permit the firm to meet all of its equity capital requirements with retained earnings. In effect, *managers should use the residual model to set dividends, but in a long-term framework*. Finally, the current dollar dividend should be set so that there is an extremely low probability that the dividend, once set, will ever have to be lowered or omitted.

Of course, the dividend decision is made during the planning process, so there is uncertainty about future investment opportunities and operating cash flows. The actual payout ratio in any year will therefore likely be above or below the firm's long-range target. However, the dollar dividend should be maintained, or increased as planned, unless the firm's financial condition deteriorates to the point at which the planned policy simply cannot be maintained. A steady or increasing stream of dividends over the long run signals that the firm's financial condition is under control. Moreover, investor uncertainty is decreased by stable dividends, so a steady dividend stream reduces the negative effect of a new stock issue—should one become absolutely necessary.

In general, firms with superior investment opportunities should set lower payouts, and hence retain more earnings, than firms with poor investment opportunities. The degree of uncertainty also influences the decision. If there is a great deal of uncertainty regarding the forecasts of free cash flows, which are defined here as the firm's operating cash flows minus mandatory equity investments, then it is best to be conservative and to set a lower current dollar dividend. Also, firms with postponable investment opportunities can afford to set a higher dollar dividend, because in times of stress investments can be postponed for a year or two, thus increasing the cash available for dividends. Finally, firms whose cost of capital is largely unaffected by changes in the debt ratio can also afford to set a higher payout ratio, because in times of stress they can more easily issue additional debt to maintain the capital budgeting program without having to cut dividends or issue stock.

The net result of these factors is that many firms' dividend policies are consistent with the life-cycle theory in which younger firms with many investment opportunities but relatively low cash flows reinvest their earnings so that they can avoid the large flotation costs associated with raising external capital.[23] As firms mature and begin to generate more cash flow, they tend to pay more dividends and issue more debt as a way to "bond" their cash flows (as described in Chapter 15) and thereby reduce the agency costs of free cash flow.

What do executives think? A recent survey indicates financial executives believe that it is extremely important to *maintain* dividends but much less important to initiate or increase dividend payments. In general, they view the cash distribution decision as being much less important than capital budgeting decisions. Managers like

---

[23]For a test of the life-cycle theory, see Harry DeAngelo, Linda DeAngelo, and René Stulz, "Dividend Policy and the Earned/Contributed Capital Mix: A Test of the Life-Cycle Theory," *Journal of Financial Economics*, August 2006, pp. 227–254.

the flexibility provided by repurchases instead of regular dividends. They tend to repurchase shares when they believe their stock price is undervalued, and they believe that shareholders view repurchases as positive signals. In general, the different taxation of dividends and repurchases is not a major factor when a company chooses how to distribute cash to investors.[24]

Self-Test

Describe the decision process for distribution policy and dividend payout. Be sure to discuss all the factors that influence this decision.

14.13 Stock Splits and Stock Dividends

The rationale for stock splits and dividends can best be explained through an example. We will use Porter Electronic Controls Inc., a $700 million electronic components manufacturer, for this purpose. Since its inception, Porter's markets have been expanding, and the company has enjoyed growth in sales and earnings. Some of its earnings have been paid out in dividends, but some are also retained each year, causing its earnings per share and stock price to grow. The company began its life with only a few thousand shares outstanding, and after some years of growth the stock price was high. Porter's CFO thought this high price limited the number of investors who could buy the stock, which reduced demand for the stock and thus kept the firm's total market value below what it could be if there were more shares, at a lower price, outstanding. To correct this situation, Porter "split its stock," as we describe next.

Stock Splits

Although there is little empirical evidence to support the contention, there is nevertheless a widespread belief in financial circles that an *optimal price range* exists for stocks. "Optimal" means that if the price is within this range, the firm's value will be maximized. Many observers, including Porter's management, believe the best range for most stocks is from $20 to $80 per share. Accordingly, if the price of Porter's stock rose to $80, management would probably declare a 2-for-1 **stock split,** thus doubling the number of shares outstanding, halving the earnings and dividends per share, and thereby lowering the stock price. Each stockholder would have more shares, but each share would be worth less. If the post-split price were $40, then Porter's stockholders would be exactly as well off as before the split. However, if the stock price were to stabilize above $40, stockholders would be better off. Stock splits can be of any size—for example, the stock could be split 2-for-1, 3-for-1, 1.5-for-1, or in any other way.

Sometimes a company will have a **reverse split.** For example, International Pictures Corp. (IPIX) developed the iPIX computer imaging technology, which allows a user to "walk through" a 360-degree view. Its stock price was in the $30 range prior to the dot-com crash of April 2000, but by August 2001 its price had fallen to $0.20 per share. One of Nasdaq's listing requirements is that the stock price must be above $1 per share, and Nasdaq was threatening to delist IPIX. To drive its price up, IPIX had a 1-10 reverse stock split before trading began on August 23, 2001, with its shareholders exchanging 10 shares of stock for a single new share. In theory, the stock price should have increased by a factor of 10, to around $2, but IPIX closed that day at a price of $1.46. Evidently, investors saw the reverse split as a negative signal. IPIX continued to struggle and declared bankruptcy in 2006, eventually auctioning off virtually all of its assets.

[24]See Alon Brav, John R. Graham, Campbell R. Harvey, and Roni Michaely, "Payout Policy in the 21st Century," *Journal of Financial Economics*, September 2005, pp. 483–527.

THE GLOBAL ECONOMIC CRISIS

Talk about a Split Personality!

Sun Microsystems once was among the highest of the high-flying companies in the tech boom of the 1990s. Sun went public in 1986 and its stock price grew rapidly, with Sun declaring seven different 2-1 stock splits between 1988 and 2000. Without these splits, Sun's stock price would have grown from about $30 in late 1988 to over $1,700 in mid-2000, a staggering return of over 40% per year! However, Sun's fortunes fell when the tech bubble burst, and Sun never recovered. With its stock price languishing around $5, Sun declared a 1-4 reverse stock split in late 2007, which boosted the stock price to over $20, but subsequently it sank into the $3–$4 range by the spring of 2009. In April 2009, Sun announced that it had agreed to be acquired by Oracle for about $9.50 per share. This would have been only $2.375 = $9.50/4 if not for the reverse split in 2007, quite a fall from its former highs.

Reverse splits were rare when Sun Microsystems declared its split in 2007, but now Sun might have plenty of company caused by the economic crisis. In May 2009, many firms were considering reverse splits, including AIG, GM, Rite Aid, and Citigroup. In fact, over 340 companies had stock prices of less than a dollar per share in May 2009, including such familiar names as Sirius XM Radio, Vonage, and Blockbuster. Because so many firms have such low stock prices, the NYSE and Nasdaq temporarily suspended their requirement that listed companies maintain a stock price of over $1 per share.

Stock Dividends

Stock dividends are similar to stock splits in that they "divide the pie into smaller slices" without affecting the fundamental position of the current stockholders. On a 5% stock dividend, the holder of 100 shares would receive an additional 5 shares (without cost); on a 20% stock dividend, the same holder would receive 20 new shares; and so on. Again, the total number of shares is increased, so earnings, dividends, and price per share all decline.

If a firm wants to reduce the price of its stock, should it use a stock split or a stock dividend? Stock splits are generally used after a sharp price run-up to produce a large price reduction. Stock dividends used on a regular annual basis will keep the stock price more or less constrained. For example, if a firm's earnings and dividends were growing at about 10% per year, its stock price would tend to go up at about that same rate, and it would soon be outside the desired trading range. A 10% annual stock dividend would maintain the stock price within the optimal trading range. Note, however, that small stock dividends create bookkeeping problems and unnecessary expenses, so firms today use stock splits far more often than stock dividends.[25]

Effect on Stock Prices

If a company splits its stock or declares a stock dividend, will this increase the market value of its stock? Many empirical studies have sought to answer this question. Here is a summary of their findings.

[25]Accountants treat stock splits and stock dividends somewhat differently. For example, in a 2-for-1 stock split, the number of shares outstanding is doubled and the par value is halved, and that's about all there is to it. With a stock dividend, a bookkeeping entry is made transferring "retained earnings" to "common stock.."

1. On average, the price of a company's stock rises shortly after it announces a stock split or a stock dividend.
2. However, these price increases are probably due to signaling rather than a desire for stock splits or dividends per se. Only managers who think future earnings will be higher tend to split stocks, so investors often view the announcement of a stock split as a positive signal. Thus, it is the signal of favorable prospects for earnings and dividends that causes the price to increase.
3. If a company announces a stock split or stock dividend, its price will tend to rise. However, if during the next few months it does not announce an increase in earnings and dividends, then its stock price will drop back to the earlier level.
4. As we noted earlier, brokerage commissions are generally higher in percentage terms on lower-priced stocks. This means that it is more expensive to trade low-priced than high-priced stocks—which, in turn, means that stock splits may reduce the liquidity of a company's shares. This particular piece of evidence suggests that stock splits/dividends might actually be harmful, although a lower price does mean that more investors can afford to trade in round lots (100 shares), which carry lower commissions than do odd lots (fewer than 100 shares).

What can we conclude from all this? From a purely economic standpoint, stock dividends and splits are just additional pieces of paper. However, they provide management with a relatively low-cost way of signaling that the firm's prospects look good.[26] Further, we should note that since few large, publicly owned stocks sell at prices above several hundred dollars, we simply do not know what the effect would be if Microsoft, Wal-Mart, Hewlett-Packard, and other highly successful firms had never split their stocks and consequently sold at prices in the thousands or even tens of thousands of dollars. All in all, it probably makes sense to employ stock splits (or stock dividends) when a firm's prospects are favorable, especially if the price of its stock has gone beyond the normal trading range.[27]

Self-Test

What are stock splits and stock dividends?

How do stock splits and dividends affect stock prices?

In what situations should managers consider the use of stock splits?

In what situations should managers consider the use of stock dividends?

Suppose you have 1,000 common shares of Burnside Bakeries. The EPS is $6.00, the DPS is $3.00, and the stock sells for $90 per share. Burnside announces a 3-for-1 split. Immediately after the split, how many shares will you have? (3,000) What will the adjusted EPS and DPS be? ($2 and $1) What would you expect the stock price to be? ($30)

---

[26]For more on stock splits and stock dividends, see H. Kent Baker, Aaron L. Phillips, and Gary E. Powell, "The Stock Distribution Puzzle: A Synthesis of the Literature on Stock Splits and Stock Dividends," *Financial Practice and Education*, Spring/Summer 1995, pp. 24–37; Maureen McNichols and Ajay Dravid, "Stock Dividends, Stock Splits, and Signaling," *Journal of Finance*, July 1990, pp. 857–879; and David R. Peterson and Pamela P. Peterson, "A Further Understanding of Stock Distributions: The Case of Reverse Stock Splits," *Journal of Financial Research*, Fall 1992, pp. 189–205.

[27]It is interesting to note that Berkshire Hathaway (controlled by billionaire Warren Buffett) has never had a stock split, and its stock (BRKa) sold on the NYSE for $85,500 per share in March 2009. Yet in response to investment trusts that were being formed in 1996 to sell fractional units of the stock and thus—in effect—split it, Buffett himself created a new class of Berkshire Hathaway stock (Class B) worth about 1/30 of a Class A (regular) share.

14.14 Dividend Reinvestment Plans

During the 1970s, most large companies instituted **dividend reinvestment plans (DRIPs)**, under which stockholders can choose to automatically reinvest their dividends in the stock of the paying corporation. Today most large companies offer DRIPs; participation rates vary considerably, but about 25% of the average firm's shareholders are enrolled. There are two types of DRIPs: (1) plans that involve only "old stock" that is already outstanding and (2) plans that involve newly issued stock. In either case, the stockholder must pay taxes on the amount of the dividends, even though stock rather than cash is received.

Under both types of DRIPs, stockholders choose between continuing to receive dividend checks or having the company use the dividends to buy more stock in the corporation. Under the "old stock" type of plan, if a stockholder elects reinvestment then a bank, acting as trustee, takes the total funds available for reinvestment, purchases the corporation's stock on the open market, and allocates the shares purchased to the participating stockholders' accounts on a pro rata basis. The transaction costs of buying shares (brokerage costs) are low because of volume purchases, so these plans benefit small stockholders who do not need cash dividends for current consumption.

The "new stock" type of DRIP uses the reinvested funds to buy newly issued stock; hence these plans raise new capital for the firm. AT&T, Union Carbide, and many other companies have used new stock plans to raise substantial amounts of new equity capital. No fees are charged to stockholders, and many companies offer stock at a discount of 3% to 5% below the actual market price. The companies offer discounts as a trade-off against flotation costs that would have been incurred if new stock had been issued through investment bankers instead of through the dividend reinvestment plans.

One interesting aspect of DRIPs is that they cause corporations to re-examine their basic dividend policies. A high participation rate in a DRIP suggests that stockholders might be better off if the firm simply reduced cash dividends, which would save stockholders some personal income taxes. Quite a few firms are surveying their stockholders to learn more about their preferences and to find out how they would react to a change in dividend policy. A more rational approach to basic dividend policy decisions may emerge from this research.

Note that companies start or stop using new stock DRIPs depending on their need for equity capital. For example, Union Carbide and AT&T recently stopped offering new stock DRIPs with a 5% discount because their needs for equity capital declined.

Some companies have expanded their DRIPs by moving to "open enrollment," whereby anyone can purchase the firm's stock directly and thus bypass brokers' commissions. ExxonMobil not only allows investors to buy their initial shares at no fee but also lets them pick up additional shares through automatic bank account withdrawals. Several plans, including ExxonMobil's, offer dividend reinvestment for individual retirement accounts, and some, such as U.S. West's, allow participants to invest weekly or monthly rather than on the quarterly dividend schedule. In all of these plans, and many others, stockholders can invest more than the dividends they are forgoing—they simply send a check to the company and buy shares without a brokerage commission. According to First Chicago Trust, which handles the paperwork for 13 million shareholder DRIP accounts, at least half of all DRIPs will offer open enrollment, extra purchases, and other expanded services within the next few years.

Self-Test

What are dividend reinvestment plans?

What are their advantages and disadvantages from both the stockholders' and the firm's perspectives?

Summary

- **Distribution policy** involves three issues: (1) What fraction of earnings should be distributed? (2) Should the distribution be in the form of cash dividends or stock repurchases? (3) Should the firm maintain a steady, stable dividend growth rate?
- The **optimal distribution policy** strikes a balance between current dividends and future growth so as to maximize the firm's stock price.
- Miller and Modigliani (MM) developed the **dividend irrelevance theory**, which holds that a firm's dividend policy has no effect on either the value of its stock or its cost of capital.
- The **dividend preference theory**, also called the **bird-in-the-hand theory**, holds that the firm's value will be maximized by a high dividend payout ratio, because investors regard cash dividends as being less risky than potential capital gains.
- The **tax effect theory** states that because long-term capital gains are subject to lower taxes than dividends, investors prefer to have companies retain earnings rather than pay them out as dividends.
- Dividend policy should take account of the **information content of dividends (signaling)** and the **clientele effect.** The information content, or signaling, effect stems from investors regarding an unexpected dividend change as a signal of management's forecast of future earnings. The clientele effect suggests that a firm will attract investors who like the firm's dividend payout policy. Both factors should be taken into account by firms that are considering a change in dividend policy.
- In practice, dividend-paying firms follow a policy of paying a **steadily increasing dividend.** This policy provides investors with stable, dependable income, and departures from it give investors signals about management's expectations for future earnings.
- Most firms use the **residual distribution model** to set the long-run target distribution ratio at a level that will permit the firm to meet its equity requirements with retained earnings.
- Under a **stock repurchase plan**, a firm buys back some of its outstanding stock, thereby decreasing the number of shares but leaving the stock price unchanged.
- **Legal constraints**, **investment opportunities**, **availability and cost of funds from other sources**, and **taxes** are also considered when firms establish dividend policies.
- A **stock split** increases the number of shares outstanding. Normally, splits reduce the price per share in proportion to the increase in shares because splits merely "divide the pie into smaller slices." However, firms generally split their stocks only if (1) the price is quite high and (2) management thinks the future is bright. Therefore, stock splits are often taken as positive signals and thus boost stock prices.
- A **stock dividend** is a dividend paid in additional shares rather than in cash. Both stock dividends and splits are used to keep stock prices within an "optimal" trading range.
- A **dividend reinvestment plan (DRIP)** allows stockholders to have the company automatically use dividends to purchase additional shares. DRIPs are popular because they allow stockholders to acquire additional shares without brokerage fees.

Questions

(14–1) Define each of the following terms:

a. Optimal distribution policy
b. Dividend irrelevance theory; bird-in-the-hand theory; tax effect theory
c. Information content, or signaling, hypothesis; clientele effect
d. Residual distribution model; extra dividend
e. Declaration date; holder-of-record date; ex-dividend date; payment date
f. Dividend reinvestment plan (DRIP)
g. Stock split; stock dividend; stock repurchase

(14–2) How would each of the following changes tend to affect aggregate payout ratios (that is, the average for all corporations), other things held constant? Explain your answers.

a. An increase in the personal income tax rate
b. A liberalization of depreciation for federal income tax purposes—that is, faster tax write-offs
c. A rise in interest rates
d. An increase in corporate profits
e. A decline in investment opportunities
f. Permission for corporations to deduct dividends for tax purposes as they now do interest charges
g. A change in the Tax Code so that both realized and unrealized capital gains in any year were taxed at the same rate as dividends

(14–3) What is the difference between a stock dividend and a stock split? As a stockholder, would you prefer to see your company declare a 100% stock dividend or a 2-for-1 split? Assume that either action is feasible.

(14–4) One position expressed in the financial literature is that firms set their dividends as a residual after using income to support new investments. Explain what a residual policy implies (assuming that all distributions are in the form of dividends), illustrating your answer with a table showing how different investment opportunities could lead to different dividend payout ratios.

(14–5) Indicate whether the following statements are true or false. If the statement is false, explain why.

a. If a firm repurchases its stock in the open market, the shareholders who tender the stock are subject to capital gains taxes.
b. If you own 100 shares in a company's stock and the company's stock splits 2-for-1, then you will own 200 shares in the company following the split.
c. Some dividend reinvestment plans increase the amount of equity capital available to the firm.
d. The Tax Code encourages companies to pay a large percentage of their net income in the form of dividends.
e. A company that has established a clientele of investors who prefer large dividends is unlikely to adopt a residual dividend policy.
f. If a firm follows a residual dividend policy then, holding all else constant, its dividend payout will tend to rise whenever the firm's investment opportunities improve.

Self-Test Problem

Solution Appears in Appendix A

(ST–1) Residual Dividend

Components Manufacturing Corporation (CMC) has 1 million shares of stock outstanding. CMC has a target capital structure with 60% equity and 40% debt. The company projects net income of $5 million and investment projects requiring $6 million in the upcoming year.

a. CMC uses the residual distribution model and pays all distributions in the form of dividends. What is the projected DPS?
b. What is the projected payout ratio?

Problems

Answers Appear in Appendix B

EASY PROBLEMS 1–5

(14–1) Residual Distribution Model

Axel Telecommunications has a target capital structure that consists of 70% debt and 30% equity. The company anticipates that its capital budget for the upcoming year will be $3 million. If Axel reports net income of $2 million and follows a residual distribution model with all distributions as dividends, what will be its dividend payout ratio?

(14–2) Residual Distribution Policy

Petersen Company has a capital budget of $1.2 million. The company wants to maintain a target capital structure which is 60% debt and 40% equity. The company forecasts that its net income this year will be $600,000. If the company follows a residual distribution model and pays all distributions as dividends, what will be its payout ratio?

(14–3) Dividend Payout

The Wei Corporation expects next year's net income to be $15 million. The firm's debt ratio is currently 40%. Wei has $12 million of profitable investment opportunities, and it wishes to maintain its existing debt ratio. According to the residual distribution model (assuming all payments are in the form of dividends), how large should Wei's dividend payout ratio be next year?

(14–4) Stock Repurchase

A firm has 10 million shares outstanding with a market price of $20 per share. The firm has $25 million in extra cash (short-term investments) that it plans to use in a stock repurchase; the firm has no other financial investments or any debt. What is the firm's value of operations, and how many shares will remain after the repurchase?

(14–5) Stock Split

Gamma Medical's stock trades at $90 a share. The company is contemplating a 3-for-2 stock split. Assuming the stock split will have no effect on the total market value of its equity, what will be the company's stock price following the stock split?

INTERMEDIATE PROBLEMS 6–9

(14–6) External Equity Financing

Northern Pacific Heating and Cooling Inc. has a 6-month backlog of orders for its patented solar heating system. To meet this demand, management plans to expand production capacity by 40% with a $10 million investment in plant and machinery. The firm wants to maintain a 40% debt-to-total-assets ratio in its capital structure; it also wants to maintain its past dividend policy of distributing 45% of last year's net income. In 2010, net income was $5 million. How much external equity must Northern Pacific seek at the beginning of 2011 in order to expand capacity as desired?

(14–7) Stock Split

Suppose you own 2,000 common shares of Laurence Incorporated. The EPS is $10.00, the DPS is $3.00, and the stock sells for $80 per share. Laurence announces a 2-for-1 split. Immediately after the split, how many shares will you have, what will the adjusted EPS and DPS be, and what would you expect the stock price to be?

(14–8) Stock Split

After a 5-for-1 stock split, the Strasburg Company paid a dividend of $0.75 per new share, which represents a 9% increase over last year's pre-split dividend. What was last year's dividend per share?

(14–9) Residual Distribution Policy

The Welch Company is considering three independent projects, each of which requires a $5 million investment. The estimated internal rate of return (IRR) and cost of capital for these projects are as follows:

Project H (high risk):	Cost of capital = 16%; IRR = 20%
Project M (medium risk):	Cost of capital = 12%; IRR = 10%
Project L (low risk):	Cost of capital = 8%; IRR = 9%

Note that the projects' cost of capital varies because the projects have different levels of risk. The company's optimal capital structure calls for 50% debt and 50% common equity. Welch expects to have net income of $7,287,500. If Welch bases its dividends on the residual model (all distributions are in the form of dividends), what will its payout ratio be?

Challenging Problems 10–11

(14–10) Alternative Dividend Policies

In 2010, the Keenan Company paid dividends totaling $3.6 million on net income of $10.8 million. The year was a normal one, and earnings have grown at a constant rate of 10% for the past 10 years. However, in 2011, earnings are expected to jump to $14.4 million, and the firm expects to have profitable investment opportunities of $8.4 million. It is predicted that Keenan will not be able to maintain the 2011 level of earnings growth—the high 2011 projected earnings level is due to an exceptionally profitable new product line to be introduced that year—and then the company will return to its previous 10% growth rate. Keenan's target debt ratio is 40%.

a. Calculate Keenan's total dividends for 2011 if it follows each of the following policies:
   (1) Its 2011 dividend payment is set to force dividends to grow at the long-run growth rate in earnings.
   (2) It continues the 2010 dividend payout ratio.
   (3) It uses a pure residual policy with all distributions in the form of dividends (40% of the $8.4 million investment is financed with debt).
   (4) It employs a regular-dividend-plus-extras policy, with the regular dividend being based on the long-run growth rate and the extra dividend being set according to the residual policy.

b. Which of the preceding policies would you recommend? Restrict your choices to the ones listed, but justify your answer.

c. Does a 2011 dividend of $9 million seem reasonable in view of your answers to parts a and b? If not, should the dividend be higher or lower?

(14–11) Residual Distribution Model

Buena Terra Corporation is reviewing its capital budget for the upcoming year. It has paid a $3 dividend per share (DPS) for the past several years, and its shareholders expect the dividend to remain constant for the next several years. The company's target capital structure is 60% equity and 40% debt, it has 1 million shares of common equity outstanding, and its net income is $8 million. The company forecasts it would require $10 million to fund all of its profitable (i.e., positive-NPV) projects for the upcoming year.

a. If Buena Terra follows the residual model and makes all distributions as dividends, how much retained earnings will it need to fund its capital budget?
b. If Buena Terra follows the residual model with all distributions in the form of dividends, what will be the company's dividend per share and payout ratio for the upcoming year?
c. If Buena Terra maintains its current $3 DPS for next year, how much retained earnings will be available for the firm's capital budget?
d. Can the company maintain its current capital structure, maintain the $3 DPS, and maintain a $10 million capital budget *without* having to raise new common stock?
e. Suppose Buena Terra's management is firmly opposed to cutting the dividend; that is, it wishes to maintain the $3 dividend for the next year. Suppose also that the company is committed to funding all profitable projects and is willing to issue more debt (along with the available retained earnings) to help finance the company's capital budget. Assume the resulting change in capital structure has a minimal impact on the company's composite cost of capital, so that the capital budget remains at $10 million. What portion of this year's capital budget would have to be financed with debt?
f. Suppose once again that Buena Terra's management wants to maintain the $3 DPS. In addition, the company wants to maintain its target capital structure (60% equity, 40% debt) and its $10 million capital budget. What is the minimum dollar amount of new common stock the company would have to issue in order to meet all of its objectives?
g. Now consider the case in which Buena Terra's management wants to maintain the $3 DPS and its target capital structure but also wants to avoid issuing new common stock. The company is willing to cut its capital budget in order to meet its other objectives. Assuming the company's projects are divisible, what will be the company's capital budget for the next year?
h. If a firm follows the residual distribution policy, what actions can it take when its forecasted retained earnings are less than the retained earnings required to fund its capital budget?

(14–12)
Stock Repurchase

Bayani Bakery's most recent FCF was $48 million; the FCF is expected to grow at a constant rate of 6%. The firm's WACC is 12% and it has 15 million shares of common stock outstanding. The firm has $30 million in short-term investments, which it plans to liquidate and distribute to common shareholders via a stock repurchase; the firm has no other nonoperating assets. It has $368 million in debt and $60 million in preferred stock.

a. What is the value of operations?
b. Immediately prior to the repurchase, what is the intrinsic value of equity?
c. Immediately prior to the repurchase, what is the intrinsic stock price?
d. How many shares will be repurchased? How many shares will remain after the repurchase?
e. Immediately after the repurchase, what is the intrinsic value of equity? The intrinsic stock price?

Spreadsheet Problem

(14-13)
Build a Model: Distributions as Dividends or Repurchases

Start with the partial model in the file ***Ch14 P13 Build a Model.xls*** on the textbook's Web site. J. Clark Inc. (JCI), a manufacturer and distributor of sports equipment, has grown until it has become a stable, mature company. Now JCI is planning its first distribution to shareholders. (See the file for the most recent year's financial statements and projections for the next year, 2011; JCI's fiscal year ends on June 30.) JCI plans to liquidate and distribute $500 million of its short-term securities on July 1, 2011, the first day of the next fiscal year, but has not yet decided whether to distribute with dividends or with stock repurchases.

a. Assume first that JCI distributes the $500 million as dividends. Fill in the missing values in the file's balance sheet column for July 1, 2011, that is labeled Distribute as Dividends. (*Hint:* Be sure that the balance sheets balance after you fill in the missing items.) Assume that JCI did not have to establish an account for dividends payable prior to the distribution.

b. Now assume that JCI distributes the $500 million through stock repurchases. Fill in the missing values in the file's balance sheet column for July 1, 2011, that is labeled Distribute as Repurchase. (*Hint:* Be sure that the balance sheets balance after you fill in the missing items.)

c. Calculate JCI's projected free cash flow; the tax rate is 40%.

d. What is JCI's current intrinsic stock price (the price on 6/30/2010)? What is the projected intrinsic stock price for 6/30/2011?

e. What is the projected intrinsic stock price on 7/1/2011 if JCI distributes the cash as dividends?

f. What is the projected intrinsic stock price on 7/1/2011 if JCI distributes the cash through stock repurchases? How many shares will remain outstanding after the repurchase?

THOMSON ONE | Business School Edition Problem

Use the Thomson ONE—Business School Edition online database to work this chapter's questions.

Microsoft's Dividend Policy

Let's find out what has happened to Microsoft's (MSFT) dividend policy since its 2003 announcement to initiate dividends. We can address this issue by relying on the data that are provided to you in Thomson ONE.

Thomson ONE—BSE Discussion Questions

1. To get information about MSFT's dividend policy, enter its ticker and select OVERVIEW>FULL REPORTS>WORLDSCOPE FULL REPORTS>FULL COMPANY REPORT. Click on STOCK & EARNINGS DATA, and scroll down to the Annual Historical Data section. What has happened to MSFT's dividend per share, dividend yield, and dividend payout over the past 5 years? Do you have any explanations?
2. Compare this with other firms in the same industry. To see how MSFT stacks up against its peers, select PEERS>OVERVIEWS>PER SHARE DATA to get MSFT's peers' last annual dividends. Accessing PEER>OVERVIEWS>

ABSOLUTE RANKINGS will give their dividend yields. You can also get this information from the VALUATION COMPARISON in this same section. Has MSFT behaved differently from its peers, or have there been industry-wide shifts?

3. Refer back to the FULL COMPANY REPORT used in Question 1. Manually plot earnings and dividends over time. In the text, we point out that dividends are often much more stable than earnings. Do you see a similar pattern for MSFT?
4. In the Interim Financial Data section of the FULL COMPANY REPORT, identify the dividend declared date, the ex dividend date, and the pay date. Explain the significance of these dates. Go back to Overview and access the Interactive Price Chart. Can you observe price shifts around these dates? Explain what price shifts you might expect to see.
5. Investors are more concerned with future dividends than historical dividends, so go to ESTIMATES and scroll down to the Consensus Estimates section. Click on the Available Measures menu to toggle between earnings per share and dividends per share. What do analysts expect MSFT's payout policy to be in the future?
6. Refer back to the FULL COMPANY REPORT, and scroll down to the 5 Yr Annual Balance Sheet section. Does it appear that MSFT has been repurchasing any stock, or has it been issuing new stock?

Mini Case

Southeastern Steel Company (SSC) was formed 5 years ago to exploit a new continuous casting process. SSC's founders, Donald Brown and Margo Valencia, had been employed in the research department of a major integrated-steel company, but when that company decided against using the new process (which Brown and Valencia had developed), they decided to strike out on their own. One advantage of the new process was that it required relatively little capital in comparison with the typical steel company, so Brown and Valencia have been able to avoid issuing new stock and thus own all of the shares. However, SSC has now reached the stage at which outside equity capital is necessary if the firm is to achieve its growth targets. Therefore, Brown and Valencia have decided to take the company public. Until now, Brown and Valencia have paid themselves reasonable salaries but routinely reinvested all after-tax earnings in the firm, so dividend policy has not been an issue. However, before talking with potential outside investors, they must decide on a dividend policy.

Assume you were recently hired by Pierce Westerfield Carney (PWC), a national consulting firm that has been asked to help SSC prepare for its public offering. Martha Millon, the senior PWC consultant in your group, has asked you to make a presentation to Brown and Valencia in which you review the theory of dividend policy and discuss the following issues.

a. (1) What is meant by the term "distribution policy"? How has the mix of dividend payouts and stock repurchases changed over time?
   (2) The terms "irrelevance," "dividend preference, or bird-in-the-hand," and "tax effect" have been used to describe three major theories regarding the way dividend payouts affect a firm's value. Explain what these terms mean, and briefly describe each theory.
   (3) What do the three theories indicate regarding the actions management should take with respect to dividend payouts?
   (4) What results have empirical studies of the dividend theories produced? How does all this affect what we can tell managers about dividend payouts?

b. Discuss (1) the information content, or signaling, hypothesis, (2) the clientele effect, and (3) their effects on distribution policy.

c. (1) Assume that SSC has completed its IPO and has a \$112.5 million capital budget planned for the coming year. You have determined that its present capital structure (80% equity and 20% debt) is optimal, and its net income is forecasted at \$140 million. Use the residual distribution approach to determine SSC's total dollar distribution.

Assume for now that the distribution is in the form of a dividend. Suppose SSC has 100 million shares of stock outstanding. What is the forecasted dividend payout ratio? What is the forecasted dividend per share? What would happen to the payout ratio and DPS if net income were forecasted to decrease to $90 million? To increase to $160 million?

(2) In general terms, how would a change in investment opportunities affect the payout ratio under the residual distribution policy?

(3) What are the advantages and disadvantages of the residual policy? (*Hint:* Don't neglect signaling and clientele effects.)

d. (1) Describe the procedures a company follows when it make a distribution through dividend payments.

(2) What is a stock repurchase? Describe the procedures a company follows when it make a distribution through a stock repurchase.

e. Discuss the advantages and disadvantages of a firm repurchasing its own shares.

f. Suppose SSC has decided to distribute $50 million, which it presently is holding in very liquid short-term investments. SSC's value of operations is estimated to be about $1,937.5 million, and it has $387.5 million in debt (it has no preferred stock). As mentioned previously, SSC has 100 million shares of stock outstanding.

(1) Assume that SSC has not yet made the distribution. What is SSC's intrinsic value of equity? What is its intrinsic stock price per share?

(2) Now suppose that SSC has just made the $50 million distribution in the form of dividends. What is SSC's intrinsic value of equity? What is its intrinsic stock price per share?

(3) Suppose instead that SSC has just made the $50 million distribution in the form of a stock repurchase. Now what is SSC's intrinsic value of equity? How many shares did SSC repurchase? How many shares remained outstanding after the repurchase? What is its intrinsic stock price per share after the repurchase?

g. Describe the series of steps that most firms take when setting dividend policy.

h. What are stock splits and stock dividends? What are the advantages and disadvantages of each?

i. What is a dividend reinvestment plan (DRIP), and how does it work?

Selected Additional Cases

The following cases from Textchoice, *Cengage Learning's online library, cover many of the concepts discussed in this chapter and are available at* **http://www.textchoice2.com**.

Klein-Brigham Series:
Case 19, "Georgia Atlantic Company," Case 20, "Bessemer Steel Products, Inc.," Case 47, "Floral Fragrance, Inc.," and Case 80, "The Western Company," all illustrate the dividend policy decision.

Brigham-Buzzard Series:
Case 9, "Powerline Network Corporation (Dividend Policy)."

CHAPTER 15
Capital Structure Decisions

What is the difference between bankruptcy and a liquidity crisis? Although that question may sound like the first line of a joke, the answer isn't very funny for many companies. An economic bankruptcy *means that the market value of a company's assets (which is determined by the cash flows those assets are expected to produce) is less than the amount owed to creditors. A* legal bankruptcy *occurs when a filing is made in bankruptcy court to protect a company from its creditors until an orderly reorganization or liquidation can be arranged.*

A liquidity crisis *occurs when a company doesn't have access to enough cash to make payments to creditors as the payments come due in the near future. In normal times, a strong company (one whose market value of assets far exceeds the amount owed to creditors) can usually borrow money in the short-term credit markets to meet any urgent liquidity needs. Thus, a liquidity crisis usually doesn't trigger a bankruptcy.*

However, 2008 and the first half of 2009 were anything but usual. Many companies had loaded up on debt during the boom years prior to 2007, and much of that was short-term debt. When the mortgage crisis began in late 2007 and spread like wildfire through the financial sector, many financial institutions virtually stopped providing short-term credit as they tried to stave off their own bankruptcies. As a result, many nonfinancial companies faced liquidity crises. Even worse, consumer demand began to drop and investors' risk aversion began to rise, leading to falling market values of assets and triggering economic and legal bankruptcy for many companies.

Lehman Brothers and Washington Mutual each filed for bankruptcy in 2008 and have the distinction of being the two largest firms to fail, with assets of $691 billion and $328 billion, respectively. But the economic crisis has claimed plenty of nonfinancial firms, too, such as General Motors, Chrysler, Masonite Corporation, Trump Entertainment Resorts, Pilgrim's Pride, and Circuit City.

Many other companies are scrambling to reduce their liquidity problems. For example, in early 2009, Black & Decker issued about $350 million in 5-year notes and used the proceeds to pay off some of its commercial paper. Even though the interest rate on Black & Decker's 5-year notes was higher than the rates on its commercial paper, B&D doesn't have to repay the note until 2014, whereas it had to refinance the commercial paper each time it came due.

As you read the chapter, think of these companies that suffered or failed because they mismanaged their capital structure decisions.

Sources: See ***www.bankruptcydata.com*** *and the Black & Decker press release of April 23, 2009.*

Corporate Valuation and Capital Structure

A firm's financing choices obviously have a direct effect on the weighted average cost of capital (WACC). Financing choices also have an indirect effect on the costs of debt and equity because they change the risk and required returns of debt and equity. Financing choices can also affect free cash flows if the probability of bankruptcy becomes high. This chapter focuses on the debt–equity choice and its effect on value.

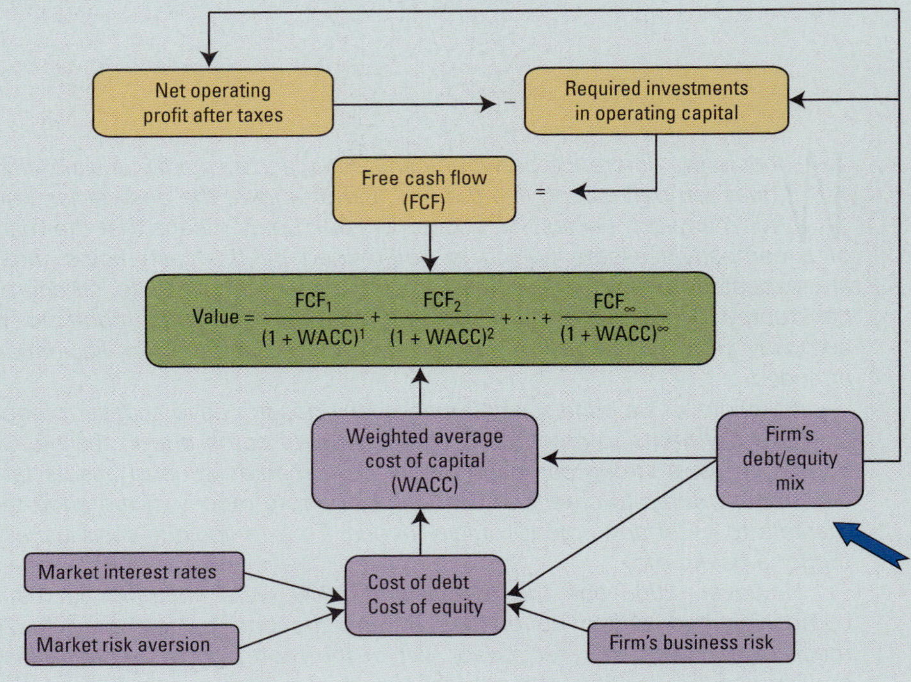

The textbook's Web site contains an Excel *file that will guide you through the chapter's calculations. The file for this chapter is* **Ch15 Tool Kit.xls**, *and we encourage you to open the file and follow along as you read the chapter.*

As we saw in Chapters 12 and 13, growth in sales requires growth in operating capital, often requiring that external funds must be raised through a combination of equity and debt. The firm's mixture of debt and equity is called its **capital structure.** Although actual levels of debt and equity may vary somewhat over time, most firms try to keep their financing mix close to a **target capital structure.** A firm's **capital structure decision** includes its choice of a target capital structure, the average maturity of its debt, and the specific types of financing it decides to use at any particular time. As with operating decisions, managers should make capital structure decisions that are designed to maximize the firm's intrinsic value.

15.1 A Preview of Capital Structure Issues

Recall from Chapter 13 that the value of a firm's operations is the present value of its expected future free cash flows (FCF) discounted at its weighted average cost of capital (WACC):

$$V_{op} = \sum_{t=1}^{\infty} \frac{FCF_t}{(1+WACC)^t} \quad (15\text{-}1)$$

The WACC depends on the percentages of debt and common equity (w_d and w_s), the cost of debt (r_d), the cost of stock (r_s), and the corporate tax rate (T):

$$WACC = w_d(1 - T)r_d + w_s r_s \quad (15\text{-}2)$$

As these equations show, the only way any decision can change a firm's value is by affecting either free cash flows or the cost of capital. We discuss below some of the ways that a higher proportion of debt can affect WACC and/or FCF.

Debt Increases the Cost of Stock, r_s

Debtholders have a claim on the company's cash flows that is prior to shareholders, who are entitled only to any residual cash flow after debtholders have been paid. As we show later in a numerical example, the "fixed" claim of the debtholders causes the "residual" claim of the stockholders to become riskier, and this increases the cost of stock, r_s.

Debt Reduces the Taxes a Company Pays

Imagine that a company's cash flows are a pie and that three different groups get pieces of the pie. The first piece goes to the government in the form of taxes, the second goes to debtholders, and the third to shareholders. Companies can deduct interest expenses when calculating taxable income, which reduces the government's piece of the pie and leaves more pie available to debtholders and investors. This reduction in taxes reduces the after-tax cost of debt, as shown in Equation 15-2.

The Risk of Bankruptcy Increases the Cost of Debt, r_d

As debt increases, the probability of financial distress, or even bankruptcy, goes up. With higher bankruptcy risk, debtholders will insist on a higher interest rate, which increases the pre-tax cost of debt, r_d.

The Net Effect on the Weighted Average Cost of Capital

As Equation 15-2 shows, the WACC is a weighted average of relatively low-cost debt and high-cost equity. If we increase the proportion of debt, then the weight of low-cost debt (w_d) increases and the weight of high-cost equity (w_s) decreases. If all else remained the same, then the WACC would fall and the value of the firm in Equation 15-1 would increase. But the previous paragraphs show that all else doesn't remain the same: both r_d and r_s increase. It should be clear that changing the capital structure affects all the variables in the WACC equation, but it's not easy to say whether those changes increase the WACC, decrease it, or balance out exactly and thus leave the WACC unchanged. We'll return to this issue later when discussing capital structure theory.

Bankruptcy Risk Reduces Free Cash Flow

As the risk of bankruptcy increases, some customers may choose to buy from another company, which hurts sales. This, in turn, decreases net operating profit after taxes (NOPAT), thus reducing FCF. Financial distress also hurts the productivity of workers and managers, who spend more time worrying about their next job than attending to their current job. Again, this reduces NOPAT and FCF. Finally, suppliers tighten their credit standards, which reduces accounts payable and causes net operating working capital to increase, thus reducing FCF. Therefore, the risk of bankruptcy can decrease FCF and reduce the value of the firm.

Bankruptcy Risk Affects Agency Costs

Higher levels of debt may affect the behavior of managers in two opposing ways. First, when times are good, managers may waste cash flow on perquisites and unnecessary expenditures. This is an agency cost, as described in Chapter 13. The good news is that the threat of bankruptcy reduces such wasteful spending, which increases FCF.

But the bad news is that a manager may become gun-shy and reject positive-NPV projects if they are risky. From the stockholder's point of view, it would be unfortunate if a risky project caused the company to go into bankruptcy, but note that other companies in the stockholder's portfolio may be taking on risky projects that turn out to be successful. Since most stockholders are well diversified, they can afford for a manager to take on risky but positive-NPV projects. But a manager's reputation and wealth are generally tied to a single company, so the project may be unacceptably risky from the manager's point of view. Thus, high debt can cause managers to forgo positive-NPV projects unless they are extremely safe. This is called the **underinvestment problem**, and it is another type of agency cost. Notice that debt can reduce one aspect of agency costs (wasteful spending) but may increase another (underinvestment), so the net effect on value isn't clear.

Issuing Equity Conveys a Signal to the Marketplace

Managers are in a better position to forecast a company's free cash flow than are investors, and academics call this **informational asymmetry**. Suppose a company's stock price is $50 per share. If managers are willing to issue new stock at $50 per share, investors reason that no one would sell anything for less than its true value. Therefore, the true value of the shares as seen by the managers with their superior information must be less than or equal to $50. Thus, investors perceive an equity issue as a negative signal, and this usually causes the stock price to fall.[1]

In addition to affecting investors' perceptions, capital structure choices also affect FCF and risk, as discussed earlier. The following section focuses on the way that capital structure affects risk.

A Quick Overview of Actual Debt Ratios

For the average company in the S&P 500, the ratio of long-term debt to equity was about 92% in the summer of 2009. This means that the typical company had about $0.92 in debt for every dollar of equity. However, Table 15-1 shows that there are wide divergences in the average ratios for different business sectors and for different companies within a sector. For example, the technology sector has a very low average ratio (23%) while the utilities sector has a much higher ratio (177%). Even so, within each sector there are some companies with low levels of debt and others with high

[1] An exception to this rule is any situation with little informational asymmetry, such as a regulated utility. Also, some companies, such as start-ups or high-tech ventures, are unable to find willing lenders and therefore must issue equity; we discuss this later in the chapter.

TABLE 15-1 Long-Term Debt-to-Equity Ratios for Selected Firms and Industries

SECTOR AND COMPANY	LONG-TERM DEBT-TO-EQUITY RATIO	SECTOR AND COMPANY	LONG-TERM DEBT-TO-EQUITY RATIO
Technology	**23%**	**Capital Goods**	**38%**
Microsoft (MSFT)	0	Winnebago Industries (WGO)	0
Ricoh (RICTEYR.Lp)	25	Caterpillar Inc. (CAT)	375
Energy	**64**	**Consumer/Noncyclical**	**38**
ExxonMobil (XOM)	6	Starbucks (SBUX)	21
Chesapeake Energy (CHK)	87	Kellogg Company (K)	280
Transportation	**84**	**Services**	**84**
United Parcel Service (UPS)	115	Administaff, Inc. (ASF)	0
Continental Airlines (CAL)	5,115	Republic Services (RSG)	99
Basic Materials	**45**	**Utilities**	**177**
Anglo American PLC (AAUK)	36	Reliant Energy, Inc. (RRI)	96
Century Aluminum (CENX)	29	CMS Energy (CMS)	227

Source: For updates on a company's ratio, go to **http://www.reuters.com** and enter the ticker symbol for a stock quote. Click on Ratios (on the left) for updates on the sector ratio.

levels. For example, the average debt ratio for the consumer/noncyclical sector is 38%, but in this sector Starbucks has a ratio of 21% while Kellogg has a ratio of 280%. Why do we see such variation across companies and business sectors? Can a company make itself more valuable through its choice of debt ratio? We address those questions in the rest of this chapter, beginning with a description of business risk and financial risk.

Self-Test

Briefly describe some ways in which the capital structure decision can affect the WACC and FCF.

15.2 Business Risk and Financial Risk

Business risk and financial risk combine to determine the total risk of a firm's future return on equity, as we explained in the next sections.

Business Risk

Business risk is the risk a firm's common stockholders would face if the firm had no debt. In other words, it is the risk inherent in the firm's operations, which arises from uncertainty about future operating profits and capital requirements.

Business risk depends on a number of factors, beginning with variability in product demand. For example, General Motors has more demand variability than does Kroger: When times are tough, consumers quit buying cars but they still buy food. Second, most firms are exposed to variability in sales prices and input costs. Some firms with strong brand identity like Apple may be able to pass unexpected costs through to their customers, and firms with strong market power like Wal-Mart may be able to keep their input costs low, but variability in prices and costs adds significant risk to most firms' operations. Third, firms that are slower to bring new products to market have greater business risk: Think of GM's relatively sluggish time to bring a new model to the market versus that of Toyota. Being faster to the market allows Toyota to more quickly respond to changes in consumer desires. Fourth, international operations add the risk of currency fluctuations and political risk. Fifth, if a high percentage of a firm's costs are fixed and hence do not decline when demand falls, then the firm has high *operating leverage*, which increases its business risk. We focus on operating leverage in the next section.

Operating Leverage

A high degree of **operating leverage** implies that a relatively small change in sales results in a relatively large change in EBIT, net operating profits after taxes (NOPAT), and return on invested capital (ROIC). Other things held constant, the higher a firm's fixed costs, the greater its operating leverage. Higher fixed costs are generally associated with (1) highly automated, capital intensive firms; (2) businesses that employ highly skilled workers who must be retained and paid even when sales are low; and (3) firms with high product development costs that must be maintained to complete ongoing R&D projects.

To illustrate the relative impact of fixed versus variable costs, consider Strasburg Electronics Company, a manufacturer of components used in cell phones. Strasburg is considering several different operating technologies and several different financing alternatives. We will analyze its financing choices in the next section, but for now we focus on its operating plans.

Each of Strasburg's plans requires a capital investment of $200 million; assume for now that Strasburg will finance its choice entirely with equity.[2] Each plan is expected to produce 100 million units per year at a sales price of $2 per unit. As shown in Figure 15-1, Plan A's technology requires a smaller annual fixed cost than Plan U's, but Plan A has higher variable costs. (We denote the second plan with U because it has no financial leverage, and we denote the third plan with L because it does have financial leverage; Plan L is discussed in the next section.) Figure 15-1 also shows the projected income statements and selected performance measures for the first year. Notice that Plan U has higher net income, higher net operating profit after taxes (NOPAT), higher return on equity (ROE), and higher return on invested capital than does Plan A. So at first blush it seems that Strasburg should accept Plan U instead of Plan A.

Notice that the projections in Figure 15-1 are based on the 110 million units that are expected to be sold. But what if demand is lower than expected? It often is useful to know how far sales can fall before operating profits become negative. The **operating break-even point** occurs when earnings before interest and taxes (EBIT) equal zero (P, Q, V, and F are defined in Figure 15-1):[3]

$$\text{EBIT} = PQ - VQ - F = 0 \qquad \textbf{(15-3)}$$

[2]Strasburg has improved its supply chain operations to such an extent that its operating current assets are not larger than its operating current liabilities. In fact, its Op CA = Op CL = $10 million. Recall that net operating working capital (NOWC) is the difference between Op CA and Op CL, so Strasburg has NOWC = 0. Even though Strasburg's plans require $210 million in assets, they also generate $10 million in spontaneous operating liabilities, so Strasburg's investors must put up only $200 million in some combination of debt and equity.

[3]This definition of the break-even point does not include any fixed financial costs because it focuses on operating profits. We could also examine net income, in which case a levered firm would suffer an accounting loss even at the operating break-even point. We introduce financial costs shortly.

FIGURE 15-1 Illustration of Operating and Financial Leverage (Millions of Dollars and Millions of Units, Except Per Unit Data)

	A	B	C	D	E
23	***Input Data***		Plan A	Plan U	Plan L
24	Required capital		\$200	\$200	\$200
25	Book equity		\$200	\$200	\$150
26	Debt				\$50
27	Interest rate		8%	8%	8%
28	Sales price (P)		\$2.00	\$2.00	\$2.00
29	Tax rate (T)		40%	40%	40%
30	Expected units sold (Q)		110	110	110
31	Fixed costs (F)		\$20	\$60	\$60
32	Variable costs (V)		\$1.50	\$1.00	\$1.00
33					
34	***Income Statements***		Plan A	Plan U	Plan L
35	Sales revenue (P×Q)		\$220.0	\$220.0	\$220.0
36	Fixed costs		\$20.0	\$60.0	\$60.0
37	Variable costs (V×Q)		\$165.0	\$110.0	\$110.0
38	EBIT		\$35.0	\$50.0	\$50.0
39	Interest		\$0.0	\$0.0	\$4.0
40	EBT		\$35.0	\$50.0	\$46.0
41	Tax		\$14.0	\$20.0	\$18.4
42	Net income		\$21.0	\$30.0	\$27.6
43					
44	***Key Performance Measures***		Plan A	Plan U	Plan L
45	NOPAT = EBIT(1−T)		\$21.0	\$30.0	\$30.0
46	ROIC = NOPAT/Capital		10.5%	15.0%	15.0%
47	ROE = NI/Equity		10.5%	15.0%	18.4%

If we solve for the break-even quantity, Q_{BE}, we get this expression:

$$Q_{BE} = \frac{F}{P - V} \tag{15-4}$$

The break-even quantities for Plans A and U are

$$\text{Plan A: } Q_{BE} = \frac{\$20{,}000}{\$2.00 - \$1.50} = 40{,}000 \text{ units}$$

$$\text{Plan U: } Q_{BE} = \frac{\$60{,}000}{\$2.00 - \$1.00} = 60{,}000 \text{ units}$$

Plan A will be profitable if unit sales are above 40,000, whereas Plan U requires sales of 60,000 units before it is profitable. This difference is because Plan U has higher fixed costs, so more units must be sold to cover these fixed costs. Panel a of Figure 15-2 illustrates the operating profitability of these two plans for different levels of unit sales. (We discuss Panel b in the next section.) Suppose sales are at 80 million units. In this case, the NOPAT is identical for each plan. As unit sales begin to climb above 80 million, both plans increase in profitability, but

FIGURE 15-2 Operating Leverage and Financial Leverage

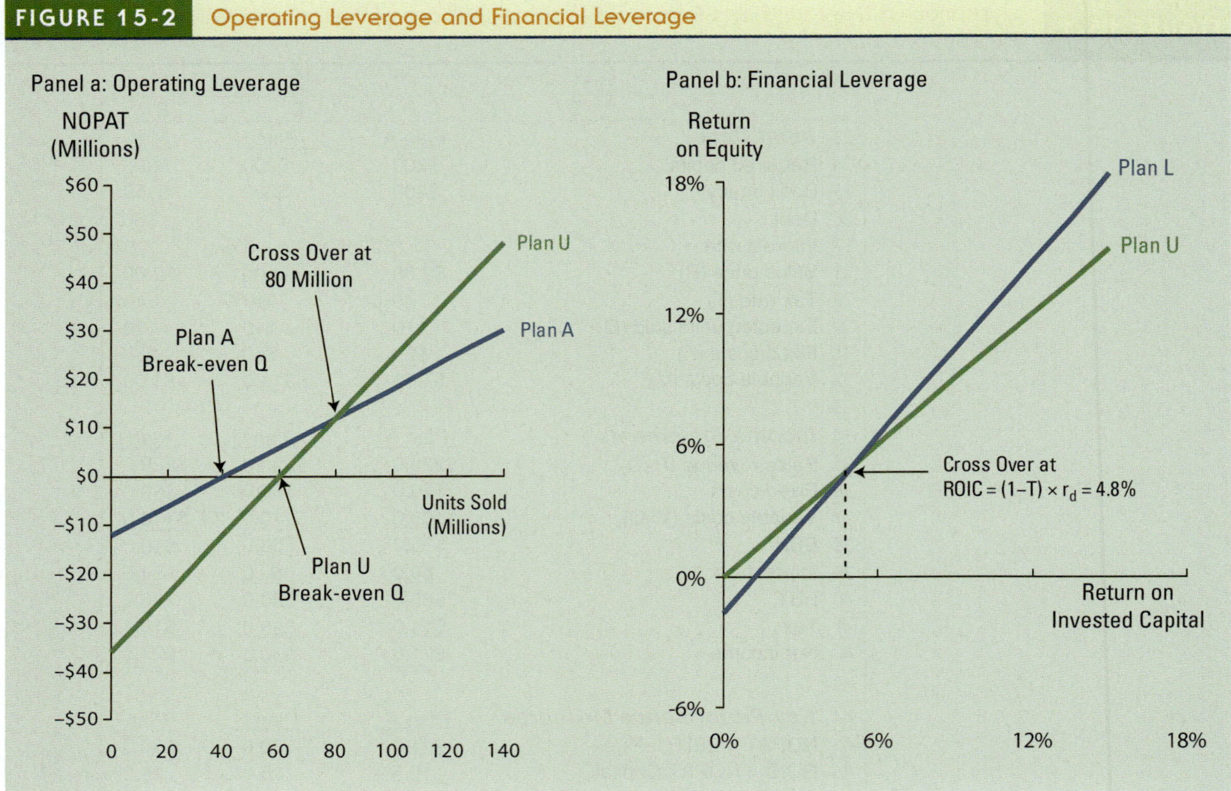

NOPAT increases more for Plan U than for Plan A. If sales fall below 80 million then both plans become less profitable, but NOPAT decreases more for Plan U than for Plan A. This illustrates that the combination of higher fixed costs and lower variable costs of Plan U magnifies its gain or loss relative to Plan A. In other words, because Plan U has higher operating leverage, it also has greater business risk.

Notice that business risk is being driven by variability in the number of units that can be sold. It would be straightforward to estimate a probability for each possible level of sales and then calculate the standard deviation of the resulting NOPATs in exactly the same way that we calculated project risk using scenario analysis in Chapter 11. This would produce a quantitative estimate of business risk.[4] However, for most purposes it is sufficient to recognize that business risk increases if operating leverage increases and then use that insight qualitatively rather than quantitatively when evaluating plans with different degrees of operating leverage.

[4]For this example, we could also directly express the standard deviation of NOPAT, σ_{NOPAT}, in terms of the standard deviation of unit sales, σ_Q: $\sigma_{NOPAT} = (P - V)(1 - T) \times \sigma_Q$. We could also express the standard deviation of ROIC as $\sigma_{ROIC} = [(P - V)(1 - T)/\text{Capital}] \times \sigma_Q$. As this shows, volatility in NOPAT (and ROIC) is driven by volatility in unit sales, with a bigger spread between price and variable costs leading to higher volatility. Also, there are several other ways to calculate measures of operating leverage, as we explain in ***Web Extension 15A.***

Financial Risk

Financial risk is the additional risk placed on the common stockholders as a result of the decision to finance with debt.[5] Conceptually, stockholders face a certain amount of risk that is inherent in a firm's operations—this is its business risk, which is defined as the uncertainty in projections of future EBIT, NOPAT, and ROIC. If a firm uses debt (financial leverage), then the business risk is concentrated on the common stockholders. To illustrate, suppose ten people decide to form a corporation to manufacture flash memory drives. There is a certain amount of business risk in the operation. If the firm is capitalized only with common equity and if each person buys 10% of the stock, then each investor shares equally in the business risk. However, suppose the firm is capitalized with 50% debt and 50% equity, with five of the investors putting up their money by purchasing debt and the other five putting up their money by purchasing equity. In this case, the five debtholders are paid before the five stockholders, so *virtually all* of the business risk is borne by the stockholders. Thus, the use of debt, or **financial leverage**, concentrates business risk on stockholders.[6]

To illustrate the impact of financial risk, we can extend the Strasburg Electronics example. Strasburg initially decided to use the technology of Plan U, which is unlevered (financed with all equity), but now it's considering financing the technology with $150 million of equity and $50 million of debt at an 8% interest rate, as shown for Plan L in Figure 15-1 (recall that L denotes leverage). Compare Plans U and L. Notice that the ROIC of 15% is the same for the two plans because the financing choice doesn't affect operations. Plan L has lower net income ($27.6 million versus $30 million) because it must pay interest, but it has a higher ROE (18.4%) because the net income is shared over a smaller equity base.[7]

Suppose Strasburg is a zero-growth company and pays out all net income as dividends. This means that Plan U has net income of $30 million available for distribution to its investors. Plan L has $27.6 million net income available to pay as dividends and it already pays $4 million in interest to its debtholders, so its total distribution is $27.6 + $4 = $31.6 million. How is it that Plan L is able to distribute a larger total amount to investors? Look closely at the taxes paid under the two plans. Plan L pays only $18.4 million in tax while Plan U pays $20 million. The $1.6 million difference is because interest payments are deductible for tax purposes. Because Plan L pays less in taxes, an extra $1.6 million is available to distribute to investors. If our analysis ended here, we would choose Plan L over Plan U because Plan L distributes more cash to investors and provides a higher ROE for its equity holders.

But there is more to the story. Just as operating leverage adds risk, so does financial leverage. We used the Data Table feature in the file ***Ch15 Tool Kit.xls*** to generate performance measures for plans U and L at different levels of unit sales, which lead to different levels of ROIC. Panel b of Figure 15-2 shows the ROE of Plan L versus its ROIC. (Keep in mind that the ROIC for Plan U is the same as for Plan L because leverage doesn't affect operating performance; also, Plan U's ROE is the same as its ROIC because it has no leverage.)

---

[5]Preferred stock also adds to financial risk. To simplify matters, we examine only debt and common equity in this chapter.

[6]Holders of corporate debt generally do bear some business risk, because they may lose some of their investment if the firm goes bankrupt. We discuss this in more depth later in the chapter.

[7]Recall that Strasburg's operating CA are equal to its operating CL. Strasburg has no short-term investments, so its book values of debt and equity must sum up to the amount of operating capital it uses.

Notice that for an ROIC of 4.8%, which is the after-tax cost of debt, Plan U (with no leverage) and Plan L (with leverage) have the same ROE. As ROIC increases above 6%, the ROE increases for each plan, but more for Plan L than for Plan U. However, if ROIC falls below 6%, then the ROE falls further for Plan L than for Plan U. Thus, financial leverage magnifies the ROE for good or ill, depending on the ROIC, and so increases the risk of a levered firm relative to an unlevered firm.[8]

We see, then, that using leverage has both good and bad effects: If expected ROIC is greater than the after-tax cost of debt, then higher leverage increases expected ROE but also increases risk.

Strasburg's Valuation Analysis

Strasburg decided to go with Plan L, the one with high operating leverage and $50 million in debt financing. This resulted in a stock price of $20 per share. With 10 million shares, Strasburg's market value of equity is $20(10) = $200 million. Strasburg has no short-term investments, so Strasburg's total enterprise value is the sum of its debt and equity: V = $50 + $200 = $250 million. Notice that this is greater than the required investment, which means that the plan has a positive NPV; another way to view this is that Strasburg's Market Value Added (MVA) is positive. In terms of market values, Strasburg's capital structure has 20% debt (w_d = $50/$250 = 0.20) and 80% equity (w_s = $200/$250 = 0.80). These calculations are reported in Figure 15-3.

Is this the optimal capital structure? We will address the question in more detail later, but for now let's focus on understanding Strasburg's current valuation, beginning with its cost of capital. Strasburg has a beta of 1.25. We can use the Capital Asset Pricing Model (CAPM) to estimate the cost of equity. The risk-free rate, r_{RF}, is 6.3% and the market risk premium, RP_M, is 6%, so the cost of equity is

$$r_s = r_{RF} + b(RP_M) = 6.3\% + 1.25(6\%) = 13.8\%$$

The weighted average cost of capital is

$$\begin{aligned} \text{WACC} &= w_d(1 - T)r_d + w_s r_s \\ &= 20\%(1 - 0.40)(8\%) + 80\%(13.8\%) \\ &= 12\% \end{aligned}$$

As shown in Figure 15-1, Plan L has a NOPAT of $30 million. Strasburg expects zero growth, which means there are no required investments in capital. Therefore, FCF is equal to NOPAT. Using the constant growth formula, the value of operations is

$$V_{op} = \frac{\text{FCF}(1 + g)}{\text{WACC} - g} = \frac{\$30(1 + 0)}{0.12 - 0} = \$250$$

Figure 15-3 illustrates the calculation of the intrinsic stock price. For Strasburg, the intrinsic stock price and the market price are each equal to $20. Can Strasburg increase its value by changing its capital structure? The next section discusses how the trade-off between risk and return affects the value of the firm, and Section 15.5 estimates the optimal capital structure for Strasburg.

---

[8]We could also express the standard deviation of ROE, σ_{ROE}, in terms of the standard deviation of ROIC: σ_{ROE} = (Capital/Equity) × σ_{ROIC} = (Capital/Equity) × [(P − V)(1 − T)/Capital]× σ_Q. Thus, volatility in ROE is due to the amount of financial leverage, the amount of operating leverage, and the underlying risk in units sold. This is similar in spirit to the Du Pont model discussed in Chapter 3.

FIGURE 15-3 Strasburg's Valuation Analysis (Millions of Dollars Except Per Share Data)

	A	B	C	D
103	Input Data (Millions Except Per Share Data)			
104	Tax rate			40.00%
105	Debt (D)			\$50.00
106	Number of shares (n)			10.00
107	Stock price per share (P)			\$20.00
108	NOPAT			\$30.00
109	Free Cash Flow (FCF)			\$30.00
110	Growth rate in FCF			0.00%
111				
112	Capital Structure (Millions Except Per Share Data)			
113	Market value of equity ($S = P \times n$)			\$200.00
114	Total value ($V = D + S$)			\$250.00
115	Percent financed with debt ($w_d = D/V$)			20%
116	Percent financed with stock ($w_s = S/V$)			80%
117				
118	Cost of Capital			
119	Cost of debt (r_d)			8.00%
120	Beta (b)			1.25
121	Risk-free rate (r_{RF})			6.30%
122	Market risk premium (RP_M)			6.00%
123	Cost of equity ($r_s = r_{RF} + b \times RP_M$)			13.80%
124	WACC			12.00%
125				
126	Intrinsic Valuation (Millions Except Per Share Data)			
127				
128			Value of operations:	
129			$V_{op} = [FCF(1+g)]/(WACC-g)$	\$250.00
130			+ Value of ST investments	\$0.00
131			Total intrinsic value of firm	\$250.00
132			− Debt	\$50.00
133			Intrinsic value of equity	\$200.00
134			÷ Number of shares	10.00
135			Intrinsic price per share	\$20.00

Self-Test

What is business risk, and how can it be measured?
What are some determinants of business risk?
How does operating leverage affect business risk?
What is financial risk, and how does it arise?
Explain this statement: "Using leverage has both good and bad effects."
A firm has fixed operating costs of \$100,000 and variable costs of \$4 per unit. If it sells the product for \$6 per unit, what is the break-even quantity? **(50,000)**

15.3 Capital Structure Theory

In the previous section, we showed how capital structure choices affect a firm's ROE and its risk. For a number of reasons, we would expect capital structures to vary considerably across industries. For example, pharmaceutical companies generally have very different capital structures than airline companies. Moreover, capital structures vary among firms within a given industry. What factors explain these differences? In an attempt to answer this question, academics and practitioners have developed a number of theories, and the theories have been subjected to many empirical tests. The following sections examine several of these theories.[9]

Modigliani and Miller: No Taxes

Modern capital structure theory began in 1958, when Professors Franco Modigliani and Merton Miller (hereafter MM) published what has been called the most influential finance article ever written.[10] MM's study was based on some strong assumptions, which included the following:

1. There are no brokerage costs.
2. There are no taxes.
3. There are no bankruptcy costs.
4. Investors can borrow at the same rate as corporations.
5. All investors have the same information as management about the firm's future investment opportunities.
6. EBIT is not affected by the use of debt.

Modigliani and Miller imagined two hypothetical portfolios. The first contains all the equity of an unlevered firm, so the portfolio's value is V_U, the value of an unlevered firm. Because the firm has no growth (which means it does not need to invest in any new net assets) and because it pays no taxes, the firm can pay out all of its EBIT in the form of dividends. Therefore, the cash flow from owning this first portfolio is equal to EBIT.

Now consider a second firm that is identical to the unlevered firm *except* that it is partially financed with debt. The second portfolio contains all of the levered firm's stock (S_L) and debt (D), so the portfolio's value is V_L, the total value of the levered firm. If the interest rate is r_d, then the levered firm pays out interest in the amount r_dD. Because the firm is not growing and pays no taxes, it can pay out dividends in the amount EBIT − r_dD. If you owned all of the firm's debt and equity, your cash flow would be equal to the sum of the interest and dividends: $r_dD + (EBIT - r_dD) = EBIT$. Therefore, the cash flow from owning this second portfolio is equal to EBIT.

Notice that the cash flow of each portfolio is equal to EBIT. Thus, MM concluded that two portfolios producing the same cash flows must have the same value:[11]

$$V_L = V_U = S_L + D \tag{15-5}$$

[9]For additional discussion of capital structure theories, see John C. Easterwood and Palani-Rajan Kadapakkam, "The Role of Private and Public Debt in Corporate Capital Structures," *Financial Management*, Autumn 1991, pp. 49–57; Gerald T. Garvey, "Leveraging the Underinvestment Problem: How High Debt and Management Shareholdings Solve the Agency Costs of Free Cash Flow," *Journal of Financial Research*, Summer 1992, pp. 149–166; Milton Harris and Artur Raviv, "Capital Structure and the Informational Role of Debt," *Journal of Finance*, June 1990, pp. 321–349; and Ronen Israel, "Capital Structure and the Market for Corporate Control: The Defensive Role of Debt Financing," *Journal of Finance*, September 1991, pp. 1391–1409.

[10]Franco Modigliani and Merton H. Miller, "The Cost of Capital, Corporation Finance, and the Theory of Investment," *American Economic Review*, June 1958, pp. 261–297. Modigliani and Miller each won a Nobel Prize for their work.

[11]They actually showed that if the values of the two portfolios differed, then an investor could engage in riskless arbitrage: The investor could create a trading strategy (buying one portfolio and selling the other) that had no risk, required none of the investor's own cash, and resulted in a positive cash flow for the investor. This would be such a desirable strategy that everyone would try to implement it. But if everyone tries to buy the same portfolio, its price will be driven up by market demand, and if everyone tries to sell a portfolio, its price will be driven down. The net result of the trading activity would be to change the portfolio's values until they were equal and no more arbitrage was possible.

Yogi Berra on the MM Proposition

When a waitress asked Yogi Berra (Baseball Hall of Fame catcher for the New York Yankees) whether he wanted his pizza cut into four pieces or eight, Yogi replied: "Better make it four. I don't think I can eat eight."[a]

Yogi's quip helps convey the basic insight of Modigliani and Miller. The firm's choice of leverage "slices" the distribution of future cash flows in a way that is like slicing a pizza. MM recognized that holding a company's investment activities fixed is like fixing the size of the pizza; no information costs means that everyone sees the same pizza; no taxes means the IRS gets none of the pie; and no "contracting costs" means nothing sticks to the knife.

So, just as the substance of Yogi's meal is unaffected by whether the pizza is sliced into four pieces or eight, the economic substance of the firm is unaffected by whether the liability side of the balance sheet is sliced to include more or less debt—at least under the MM assumptions.

[a]Lee Green, *Sportswit* (New York: Fawcett Crest, 1984), p. 228.

Source: "Yogi Berra on the MM Proposition," *Journal of Applied Corporate Finance*, Winter 1995, p. 6. Reprinted by permission of Stern Stewart Management.

Given their assumptions, MM proved that a firm's value is unaffected by its capital structure.

Recall that the WACC is a combination of the cost of debt and the relatively higher cost of equity, r_s. As leverage increases, more weight is given to low-cost debt but equity becomes riskier, which drives up r_s. Under MM's assumptions, r_s increases by exactly enough to keep the WACC constant. Put another way: If MM's assumptions are correct, then it doesn't matter how a firm finances its operations and so capital structure decisions are irrelevant.

Even though some of their assumptions are obviously unrealistic, MM's irrelevance result is extremely important. By indicating the conditions under which capital structure is irrelevant, MM also provided us with clues about what is required for capital structure to be relevant and hence to affect a firm's value. The work of MM marked the beginning of modern capital structure research, and subsequent research has focused on relaxing the MM assumptions in order to develop a more realistic theory of capital structure.

Modigliani and Miller's thought process was just as important as their conclusion. It seems simple now, but their idea that two portfolios with identical cash flows must also have identical values changed the entire financial world because it led to the development of options and derivatives. It is no surprise that Modigliani and Miller received Nobel awards for their work.

Modigliani and Miller II: The Effect of Corporate Taxes

In 1963, MM published a follow-up paper in which they relaxed the assumption that there are no corporate taxes.[12] The Tax Code allows corporations to deduct interest payments as an expense, but dividend payments to stockholders are not deductible. The differential treatment encourages corporations to use debt in their capital structures. This means that interest payments reduce the taxes paid by a corporation, and if a corporation pays less to the government then more of its cash flow is available for its investors. In other words, the tax deductibility of the interest payments shields the firm's pre-tax income.

[12]Franco Modigliani and Merton H. Miller, "Corporate Income Taxes and the Cost of Capital: A Correction," *American Economic Review*, June 1963, pp. 433–443.

As in their earlier paper, MM introduced a second important way of looking at the effect of capital structure: The value of a levered firm is the value of an otherwise identical unlevered firm plus the value of any "side effects." While others have expanded on this idea by considering other side effects, MM focused on the tax shield:

$$V_L = V_U + \text{Value of side effects} = V_U + \text{PV of tax shield} \quad \textbf{(15-6)}$$

Under their assumptions, they showed that the present value of the tax shield is equal to the corporate tax rate, T, multiplied by the amount of debt, D:

$$V_L = V_U + TD \quad \textbf{(15-7)}$$

With a tax rate of about 40%, this implies that every dollar of debt adds about 40 cents of value to the firm, and this leads to the conclusion that the optimal capital structure is virtually 100% debt. MM also showed that the cost of equity, r_s, increases as leverage increases but that it doesn't increase quite as fast as it would if there were no taxes. As a result, under MM with corporate taxes the WACC falls as debt is added.

Miller: The Effect of Corporate and Personal Taxes

Merton Miller (this time without Modigliani) later brought in the effects of personal taxes.[13] The income from bonds is generally interest, which is taxed as personal income at rates (T_d) going up to 35%, while income from stocks generally comes partly from dividends and partly from capital gains. Long-term capital gains are taxed at a rate of 15%, and this tax is deferred until the stock is sold and the gain realized. If stock is held until the owner dies, no capital gains tax whatsoever must be paid. So, on average, returns on stocks are taxed at lower effective rates (T_s) than returns on debt.[14]

Because of the tax situation, Miller argued that investors are willing to accept relatively low before-tax returns on stock relative to the before-tax returns on bonds. (The situation here is similar to that with tax-exempt municipal bonds as discussed in Chapter 5 and preferred stocks held by corporate investors as discussed in Chapter 7.) For example, an investor might require a return of 10% on Strasburg's bonds, and if stock income were taxed at the same rate as bond income, the required rate of return on Strasburg's stock might be 16% because of the stock's greater risk. However, in view of the favorable treatment of income on the stock, investors might be willing to accept a before-tax return of only 14% on the stock.

Thus, as Miller pointed out, (1) the *deductibility of interest* favors the use of debt financing, but (2) the *more favorable tax treatment of income from stock* lowers the required rate of return on stock and thus favors the use of equity financing.

Miller showed that the net impact of corporate and personal taxes is given by this equation:

---

[13]See Merton H. Miller, "Debt and Taxes," *Journal of Finance*, May 1977, pp. 261–275.

[14]The Tax Code isn't quite as simple as this. An increasing number of investors face the Alternative Minimum Tax (AMT); see ***Web Extension 2A*** for a discussion. The AMT imposes a 28% tax rate on most income and an effective rate of 22% on long-term capital gains and dividends. Under the AMT there is still a spread between the tax rates on interest income and stock income, but the spread is narrower. See Leonard Burman, William Gale, Greg Leiserson, and Jeffrey Rohaly, "The AMT: What's Wrong and How to Fix It," *National Tax Journal*, September 2007, pp. 385–405.

$$V_L = V_U + \left[1 - \frac{(1 - T_c)(1 - T_s)}{(1 - T_d)}\right]D \qquad (15\text{-}8)$$

Here T_c is the corporate tax rate, T_s is the personal tax rate on income from stocks, and T_d is the tax rate on income from debt. Miller argued that the marginal tax rates on stock and debt balance out in such a way that the bracketed term in Equation 15-8 is zero and so $V_L = V_U$, but most observers believe there is still a tax advantage to debt if reasonable values of tax rates are assumed. For example, if the marginal corporate tax rate is 40%, the marginal rate on debt is 30%, and the marginal rate on stock is 12%, then the advantage of debt financing is

$$\begin{aligned} V_L &= V_U + \left[1 - \frac{(1 - 0.40)(1 - 0.12)}{(1 - 0.30)}\right]D \\ &= V_U + 0.25D \end{aligned} \qquad (15\text{-}8a)$$

Thus it appears that the presence of personal taxes reduces but does not completely eliminate the advantage of debt financing.

Trade-off Theory

The results of Modigliani and Miller also depend on the assumption that there are no **bankruptcy costs.** However, bankruptcy can be quite costly. Firms in bankruptcy have very high legal and accounting expenses, and they also have a hard time retaining customers, suppliers, and employees. Moreover, bankruptcy often forces a firm to liquidate or sell assets for less than they would be worth if the firm were to continue operating. For example, if a steel manufacturer goes out of business it might be hard to find buyers for the company's blast furnaces. Such assets are often illiquid because they are configured to a company's individual needs and also because they are difficult to disassemble and move.

Note, too, that the *threat of bankruptcy*, not just bankruptcy per se, causes many of these same problems. Key employees jump ship, suppliers refuse to grant credit, customers seek more stable suppliers, and lenders demand higher interest rates and impose more restrictive loan covenants if potential bankruptcy looms.

Bankruptcy-related problems are most likely to arise when a firm includes a great deal of debt in its capital structure. Therefore, bankruptcy costs discourage firms from pushing their use of debt to excessive levels.

Bankruptcy-related costs have two components: (1) the probability of financial distress and (2) the costs that would be incurred if financial distress does occur. Firms whose earnings are more volatile, all else equal, face a greater chance of bankruptcy and should therefore use less debt than more stable firms. This is consistent with our earlier point that firms with high operating leverage, and thus greater business risk, should limit their use of financial leverage. Likewise, firms that would face high costs in the event of financial distress should rely less heavily on debt. For example, firms whose assets are illiquid and thus would have to be sold at "fire sale" prices should limit their use of debt financing.

The preceding arguments led to the development of what is called the trade-off theory of leverage, in which firms trade off the benefits of debt financing (favorable corporate tax treatment) against higher interest rates and bankruptcy costs. In essence, the **trade-off theory** says that the value of a levered firm is equal to the

FIGURE 15-4 Effect of Financial Leverage on Value

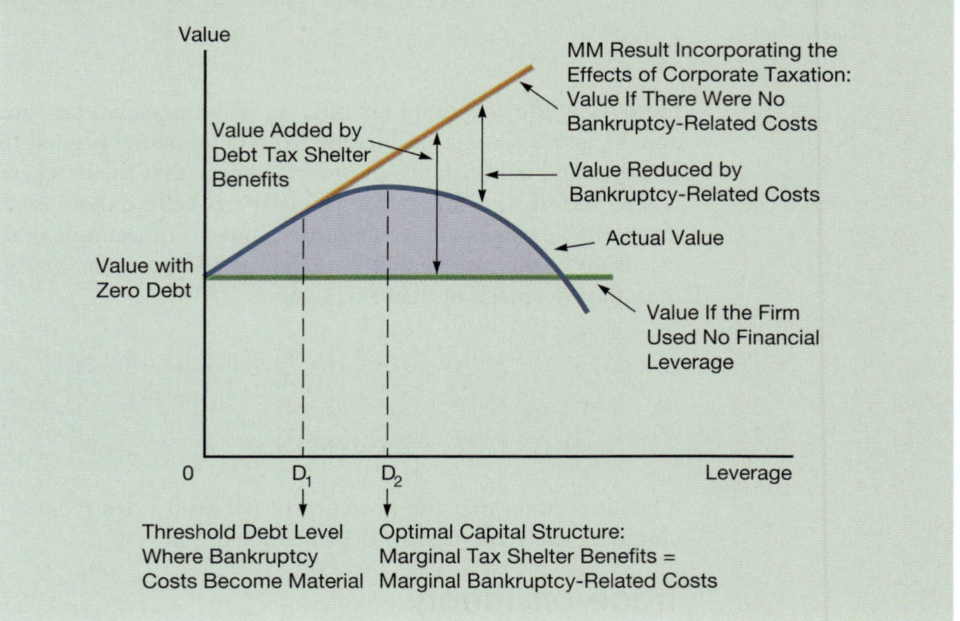

value of an unlevered firm plus the value of any side effects, which include the tax shield and the expected costs due to financial distress. A summary of the trade-off theory is expressed graphically in Figure 15-4, and a list of observations about the figure follows here.

1. Under the assumptions of the MM model with corporate taxes, a firm's value increases linearly for every dollar of debt. The line labeled "MM Result Incorporating the Effects of Corporate Taxation" in Figure 15-4 expresses the relationship between value and debt under those assumptions.
2. There is some threshold level of debt, labeled D_1 in Figure 15-4, below which the probability of bankruptcy is so low as to be immaterial. Beyond D_1, however, expected bankruptcy-related costs become increasingly important, and they reduce the tax benefits of debt at an increasing rate. In the range from D_1 to D_2, expected bankruptcy-related costs reduce but do not completely offset the tax benefits of debt, so the stock price rises (but at a decreasing rate) as the debt ratio increases. However, beyond D_2, expected bankruptcy-related costs exceed the tax benefits, so from this point on increasing the debt ratio lowers the value of the stock. Therefore, D_2 is the optimal capital structure. Of course, D_1 and D_2 vary from firm to firm, depending on their business risks and bankruptcy costs.
3. Although theoretical and empirical work confirm the general shape of the curve in Figure 15-4, this graph must be taken as an approximation and not as a precisely defined function.

Signaling Theory

It was assumed by MM that investors have the same information about a firm's prospects as its managers—this is called **symmetric information.** However, managers in fact often have better information than outside investors. This is called **asymmetric information,** and it has an important effect on the optimal capital structure. To see why, consider two situations, one in which the company's managers know that its prospects are extremely positive (Firm P) and one in which the managers know that the future looks negative (Firm N).

Suppose, for example, that Firm P's R&D labs have just discovered a nonpatentable cure for the common cold. They want to keep the new product a secret as long as possible to delay competitors' entry into the market. New plants must be built to make the new product, so capital must be raised. How should Firm P's management raise the needed capital? If it sells stock then, when profits from the new product start flowing in, the price of the stock would rise sharply and the purchasers of the new stock would make a bonanza. The current stockholders (including the managers) would also do well, but not as well as they would have done if the company had not sold stock before the price increased, because then they would not have had to share the benefits of the new product with the new stockholders. Therefore, *we should expect a firm with very positive prospects to avoid selling stock and instead to raise required new capital by other means, including debt usage beyond the normal target capital structure.*[15]

Now let's consider Firm N. Suppose its managers have information that new orders are off sharply because a competitor has installed new technology that has improved its products' quality. Firm N must upgrade its own facilities, at a high cost, just to maintain its current sales. As a result, its return on investment will fall (but not by as much as if it took no action, which would lead to a 100% loss through bankruptcy). How should Firm N raise the needed capital? Here the situation is just the reverse of that facing Firm P, which did not want to sell stock so as to avoid having to share the benefits of future developments. *A firm with negative prospects would want to sell stock, which would mean bringing in new investors to share the losses!*[16] The conclusion from all this is that firms with extremely bright prospects prefer not to finance through new stock offerings, whereas firms with poor prospects like to finance with outside equity. How should you, as an investor, react to this conclusion? You ought to say: "If I see that a company plans to issue new stock, this should worry me because I know that management would not want to issue stock if future prospects looked good. However, management *would* want to issue stock if things looked bad. Therefore, I should lower my estimate of the firm's value, other things held constant, if it plans to issue new stock."

If you gave this answer then your views are consistent with those of sophisticated portfolio managers. In a nutshell: *The announcement of a stock offering is generally taken as a* ***signal*** *that the firm's prospects as seen by its own management are not good; conversely, a debt offering is taken as a positive signal.* Notice that Firm N's managers cannot make a false signal to investors by mimicking Firm P and issuing debt. With its unfavorable future prospects, issuing debt could soon force Firm N into bankruptcy. Given the resulting damage to the personal wealth and reputations of N's managers, they cannot afford to mimic Firm P. All of this suggests that when a firm announces a new stock offering, more often than not the price of its stock will decline. Empirical studies have shown that this is indeed true.

Reserve Borrowing Capacity

Because issuing stock sends a negative signal and tends to depress the stock price even if the company's true prospects are bright, a company should try to maintain a **reserve**

---

[15]It would be illegal for Firm P's managers to personally purchase more shares on the basis of their inside knowledge of the new product.

[16]Of course, Firm N would have to make certain disclosures when it offered new shares to the public, but it might be able to meet the legal requirements without fully disclosing management's worst fears.

borrowing capacity so that debt can be used if an especially good investment opportunity comes along. This means that *firms should, in normal times, use more equity and less debt than is suggested by the tax benefit–bankruptcy cost trade-off model depicted in Figure 15-4.*

The Pecking Order Hypothesis

The presence of flotation costs and asymmetric information may cause a firm to raise capital according to a **pecking order.** In this situation, a firm first raises capital internally by reinvesting its net income and selling its short-term marketable securities. When that supply of funds has been exhausted, the firm will issue debt and perhaps preferred stock. Only as a last resort will the firm issue common stock.[17]

Using Debt Financing to Constrain Managers

Agency problems may arise if managers and shareholders have different objectives. Such conflicts are particularly likely when the firm's managers have too much cash at their disposal. Managers often use excess cash to finance pet projects or for perquisites such as nicer offices, corporate jets, and sky boxes at sports arenas—none of which have much to do with maximizing stock prices. Even worse, managers might be tempted to pay too much for an acquisition, something that could cost shareholders hundreds of millions of dollars. By contrast, managers with limited "excess cash flow" are less able to make wasteful expenditures.

Firms can reduce excess cash flow in a variety of ways. One way is to funnel some of it back to shareholders through higher dividends or stock repurchases. Another alternative is to shift the capital structure toward more debt in the hope that higher debt service requirements will force managers to be more disciplined. If debt is not serviced as required then the firm will be forced into bankruptcy, in which case its managers would likely lose their jobs. Therefore, a manager is less likely to buy an expensive new corporate jet if the firm has large debt service requirements that could cost the manager his or her job. In short, high levels of debt **bond the cash flow**, since much of it is precommitted to servicing the debt.

A **leveraged buyout (LBO)** is one way to bond cash flow. In an LBO, a large amount of debt and a small amount of cash are used to finance the purchase of a company's shares, after which the firm "goes private." The first wave of LBOs was in the mid-1980s; private equity funds led the buyouts of the late 1990s and early 2000s. Many of these LBOs were specifically designed to reduce corporate waste. As noted, high debt payments force managers to conserve cash by eliminating unnecessary expenditures.

Of course, increasing debt and reducing the available cash flow has its downside: It increases the risk of bankruptcy. Ben Bernanke, current (summer 2009) chairman of the Fed, has argued that adding debt to a firm's capital structure is like putting a dagger into the steering wheel of a car.[18] The dagger—which points toward your stomach—motivates you to drive more carefully, but you may get stabbed if someone runs into you—even if you are being careful. The analogy applies to corporations in the following sense: Higher debt forces managers to be more careful with shareholders' money, but even well-run firms could face bankruptcy (get stabbed) if some event beyond their control occurs: a war, an earthquake, a strike, or a recession. To complete the analogy, the capital structure decision comes down to deciding how long a dagger stockholders should use to keep managers in line.

[17]For more information, see Jonathon Baskin, "An Empirical Investigation of the Pecking Order Hypothesis," *Financial Management*, Spring 1989, pp. 26–35.

[18]See Ben Bernanke, "Is There Too Much Corporate Debt?" *Federal Reserve Bank of Philadelphia Business Review*, September/October 1989, pp. 3–13.

Finally, too much debt may overconstrain managers. A large portion of a manager's personal wealth and reputation is tied to a single company, so managers are not well diversified. When faced with a positive-NPV project that is risky, a manager may decide that it's not worth taking on the risk even though well-diversified stockholders would find the risk acceptable. As previously mentioned, this is an underinvestment problem. The more debt the firm has, the greater the likelihood of financial distress and thus the greater the likelihood that managers will forgo risky projects even if they have positive NPVs.

The Investment Opportunity Set and Reserve Borrowing Capacity

Bankruptcy and financial distress are costly, and, as just reiterated, this can discourage highly levered firms from undertaking risky new investments. If potential new investments, although risky, have positive net present values, then high levels of debt can be doubly costly—the expected financial distress and bankruptcy costs are high, and the firm loses potential value by not making some potentially profitable investments. On the other hand, if a firm has very few profitable investment opportunities then high levels of debt can keep managers from wasting money by investing in poor projects. For such companies, increases in the debt ratio can actually increase the value of the firm.

Thus, in addition to the tax, signaling, bankruptcy, and managerial constraint effects discussed previously, the firm's optimal capital structure is related to its set of investment opportunities. Firms with many profitable opportunities should maintain their ability to invest by using low levels of debt, which is also consistent with maintaining reserve borrowing capacity. Firms with few profitable investment opportunities should use high levels of debt (which have high interest payments) to impose managerial constraint.[19]

Windows of Opportunity

If markets are efficient, then security prices should reflect all available information; hence they are neither underpriced nor overpriced (except during the time it takes prices to move to a new equilibrium caused by the release of new information). The *windows of opportunity theory* states that managers don't believe this and supposes instead that stock prices and interest rates are sometimes either too low or too high relative to their true fundamental values. In particular, the theory suggests that managers issue equity when they believe stock market prices are abnormally high and issue debt when they believe interest rates are abnormally low. In other words, they try to time the market.[20] Notice that this differs from signaling theory because no asymmetric information is involved: These managers aren't basing their beliefs on insider information, just on a difference of opinion with the market consensus.

Self-Test

Why does the MM theory with corporate taxes lead to 100% debt?

Explain how *asymmetric information* and *signals* affect capital structure decisions.

What is meant by *reserve borrowing capacity,* and why is it important to firms?

How can the use of debt serve to discipline managers?

---

[19]See Michael J. Barclay and Clifford W. Smith, Jr., "The Capital Structure Puzzle: Another Look at the Evidence," *Journal of Applied Corporate Finance*, Spring 1999, pp. 8–20.

[20]See Malcolm Baker and Jeffrey Wurgler, "Market Timing and Capital Structure," *Journal of Finance*, February 2002, pp. 1–32.

15.4 Capital Structure Evidence and Implications

There have been hundreds, perhaps even thousands, of papers testing the capital structure theories described in the previous section. We can cover only the highlights here, beginning with the empirical evidence.[21]

Empirical Evidence

Studies show that firms do benefit from the tax deductibility of interest payments, with a typical firm increasing in value by about $0.10 for every dollar of debt. This is much less than the corporate tax rate, which supports the Miller model (with corporate and personal taxes) more than the MM model (with only corporate taxes). Recent evidence shows that the cost of bankruptcies can be as much as 10% to 20% of the firm's value.[22] Thus, the evidence shows the existence of tax benefits and financial distress costs, which provides support for the trade-off theory.

A particularly interesting study by Professors Mehotra, Mikkelson, and Partch examined the capital structure of firms that were spun off from their parents.[23] The financing choices of existing firms might be influenced by their past financing choices and by the costs of moving from one capital structure to another, but because spin-offs are newly created companies, managers can choose a capital structure without regard to these issues. The study found that more profitable firms (which have a lower expected probability of bankruptcy) and more asset-intensive firms (which have better collateral and thus a lower cost of bankruptcy should one occur) have higher levels of debt. These findings support the trade-off theory.

However, there is also evidence that is inconsistent with the static optimal target capital structure implied by the trade-off theory. For example, stock prices are volatile, which frequently causes a firm's actual market-based debt ratio to deviate from its target. However, such deviations don't cause firms to immediately return to their target by issuing or repurchasing securities. Instead, firms tend to make a partial adjustment each year, moving about one-third of the way toward their target capital structure.[24] This evidence supports the idea of a more dynamic trade-off theory in which firms have target capital structures but don't strive to maintain them too closely.

If a stock price has a big run-up, which reduces the debt ratio, then the trade-off theory suggests that the firm should issue debt to return to its target. However, firms tend to do the opposite, issuing stock after big run-ups. This is much more consistent with the windows of opportunity theory, with managers trying to time the market by issuing stock when they perceive the market to be overvalued. Furthermore, firms tend to issue debt when stock prices and interest rates are low. The maturity of the issued debt seems to reflect an attempt to time interest rates: Firms tend to issue short-term debt if the term structure is upward sloping but long-term debt if the

---

[21]This section also draws heavily from Barclay and Smith, "The Capital Structure Puzzle," cited in footnote 19; Jay Ritter, ed., *Recent Developments in Corporate Finance* (Northampton, MA: Edward Elgar Publishing Inc., 2005); and a presentation by Jay Ritter at the 2003 FMA meeting, "The Windows of Opportunity Theory of Capital Structure."

[22]The *expected cost* of financial distress is the product of bankruptcy costs and the probability of bankruptcy. At moderate levels of debt with low probabilities of bankruptcy, the expected cost of financial distress would be much less than the actual bankruptcy costs if the firm failed.

[23]See V. Mehotra, W. Mikkelson, and M. Partch, "The Design of Financial Policies in Corporate Spin-offs," *Review of Financial Studies*, Winter 2003, pp. 1359–1388.

[24]See Mark Flannery and Kasturi Rangan, "Partial Adjustment toward Target Capital Structures," *Journal of Financial Economics*, Vol. 79, 2006, pp. 469–506.

term structure is flat. Again, these facts suggest that managers try to time the market, which is consistent with the windows of opportunity theory.

Firms issue equity much less frequently than debt. On the surface, this seems to support both the pecking order hypothesis and the signaling hypothesis. The pecking order hypothesis predicts that firms with a high level of informational asymmetry, which causes equity issuances to be costly, should issue debt before issuing equity. Yet we often see the opposite, with high-growth firms (which usually have greater informational asymmetry) issuing more equity than debt. Also, many highly profitable firms could afford to issue debt (which comes before equity in the pecking order) but instead choose to issue equity. With respect to the signaling hypothesis, consider the case of firms that have large increases in earnings that were unanticipated by the market. If managers have superior information, then they will anticipate these upcoming performance improvements and issue debt before the increase. Such firms do, in fact, tend to issue debt slightly more frequently than other firms, but the difference isn't economically meaningful.

Many firms have less debt than might be expected, and many have large amounts of short-term investments. This is especially true for firms with high market/book ratios (which indicate many growth options as well as informational asymmetry). This behavior is consistent with the hypothesis that investment opportunities influence attempts to maintain reserve borrowing capacity. It is also consistent with tax considerations, since low-growth firms (which have more debt) are more likely to benefit from the tax shield. This behavior is not consistent with the pecking order hypothesis, where low-growth firms (which often have high free cash flow) would be able to avoid issuing debt by raising funds internally.

To summarize these results, it appears that firms try to capture debt's tax benefits while avoiding financial distress costs. However, they also allow their debt ratios to deviate from the static optimal target ratio implied by the trade-off theory. There is a little evidence indicating that firms follow a pecking order and use security issuances as signals, but there is much more evidence in support of the windows of opportunity theory. Finally, it appears that firms often maintain reserve borrowing capacity, especially firms with many growth opportunities or problems with informational asymmetry.[25]

Implications for Managers

Managers should explicitly consider tax benefits when making capital structure decisions. Tax benefits obviously are more valuable for firms with high tax rates. Firms can utilize tax loss carryforwards and carrybacks, but the time value of money means that tax benefits are more valuable for firms with stable, positive pre-tax income. Therefore, a firm whose sales are relatively stable can safely take on more debt and incur higher fixed charges than a company with volatile sales. Other things being equal, a firm with less operating leverage is better able to employ financial leverage because it will have less business risk and less volatile earnings.

---

[25]For more on empirical tests of capital structure theory, see Gregor Andrade and Steven Kaplan, "How Costly Is Financial (Not Economic) Distress? Evidence from Highly Leveraged Transactions That Became Distressed," *Journal of Finance*, Vol. 53, 1998, pp. 1443–1493; Malcolm Baker, Robin Greenwood, and Jeffrey Wurgler, "The Maturity of Debt Issues and Predictable Variation in Bond Returns," *Journal of Financial Economics*, November 2003, pp. 261–291; Murray Z. Frank and Vidhan K. Goyal, "Testing the Pecking Order Theory of Capital Structure," *Journal of Financial Economics*, February 2003, pp. 217–248; and Michael Long and Ileen Malitz, "The Investment-Financing Nexus: Some Empirical Evidence," *Midland Corporate Finance Journal*, Fall 1985, pp. 53–59.

Taking a Look at Global Capital Structures

To what extent does capital structure vary across different countries? The accompanying table, which is taken from a study by Raghuram Rajan and Luigi Zingales, gives the median debt ratios of firms in the largest industrial countries.

Rajan and Zingales show that there is considerable variation in capital structure among firms within each of the seven countries. However, they also show that capital structures for the firms in each country are generally determined by a similar set of factors: firm size, profitability, market-to-book ratio, and the ratio of fixed assets to total assets. All in all, the Rajan–Zingales study suggests that the points developed in the chapter apply to firms around the world.

Median Percentage of Debt to Total Assets in Different Countries

Country	Book Value Debt Ratio
Canada	32%
France	18
Germany	11
Italy	21
Japan	21
United Kingdom	10
United States	25

Source: Raghuram G. Rajan and Luigi Zingales, "What Do We Know about Capital Structure? Some Evidence from International Data," *The Journal of Finance,* Vol. 50, no. 5 (December 1995), pp. 1421-1460. Reprinted by permission of John Wiley & Sons, Inc.

Managers should also consider the expected cost of financial distress, which depends on the probability and cost of distress. Notice that stable sales and lower operating leverage provide tax benefits but also reduce the *probability* of financial distress. One *cost* of financial distress comes from lost investment opportunities. Firms with profitable investment opportunities need to be able to fund them, either by holding higher levels of marketable securities or by maintaining excess borrowing capacity. An astute corporate treasurer made this statement to the authors:

> *Our company can earn a lot more money from good capital budgeting and operating decisions than from good financing decisions. Indeed, we are not sure exactly how financing decisions affect our stock price, but we know for sure that having to turn down a promising venture because funds are not available will reduce our long-run profitability.*

Another cost of financial distress is the possibility of being forced to sell assets to meet liquidity needs. General-purpose assets that can be used by many businesses are relatively liquid and make good collateral, in contrast to special-purpose assets. Thus, real estate companies are usually highly leveraged whereas companies involved in technological research are not.

Asymmetric information also has a bearing on capital structure decisions. For example, suppose a firm has just successfully completed an R&D program, and it forecasts higher earnings in the immediate future. However, the new earnings are not yet anticipated by investors and hence are not reflected in the stock price. This company should not issue stock—it should finance with debt until the higher earnings materialize and are reflected in the stock price. Then it could issue common stock, retire the debt, and return to its target capital structure.

Managers should consider conditions in the stock and bond markets. For example, during a recent credit crunch, the junk bond market dried up and there was simply no market at a "reasonable" interest rate for any new long-term bonds rated below BBB. Therefore, low-rated companies in need of capital were forced to go to the stock market or to the short-term debt market, regardless of their target capital structures. When conditions eased, however, these companies sold bonds to get their capital structures back on target.

Finally, managers should always consider lenders' and rating agencies' attitudes. For example, one large utility was recently told by Moody's and Standard & Poor's that its bonds would be downgraded if it issued more debt. This influenced the utility's decision to finance its expansion with common equity. This doesn't mean that managers should never increase debt if it will cause their bond rating to fall, but managers should always factor this into their decision making.[26]

Self-Test

Which capital structure theories does the empirical evidence seem to support?
What issues should managers consider when making capital structure decisions?

15.5 Estimating the Optimal Capital Structure

Managers should choose the capital structure that maximizes shareholders' wealth. The basic approach is to consider a trial capital structure, based on the market values of the debt and equity, and then estimate the wealth of the shareholders under this capital structure. This approach is repeated until an optimal capital structure is identified. There are several steps in the analysis of each potential capital structure: (1) Estimate the interest rate the firm will pay. (2) Estimate the cost of equity. (3) Estimate the weighted average cost of capital. (4) Estimate the value of operations, which is the present value of free cash flows discounted by the new WACC. The objective is to find the amount of debt financing that maximizes the value of operations. As we will show, this is also the capital structure that maximizes shareholder wealth and the intrinsic stock price. The following sections explain each of these steps, using the company we considered earlier, Strasburg Electronics.

Estimating the Cost of Debt, r_d

Recall that Strasburg chose Plan L, with high operating leverage and a capital structure consisting of 20% debt. The CFO asked Strasburg's investment bankers to estimate the cost of debt at different capital structures. The investment bankers began by analyzing industry conditions and prospects. They appraised Strasburg's business risk based on its past financial statements and its current technology and customer base. The bankers also forecasted financial statements with different capital structures and analyzed such key ratios as the current ratio and the times-interest-earned ratio. Finally, they factored in current conditions in the financial markets, including interest rates paid by firms in Strasburg's industry. Based on their analysis and judgment, they estimated interest rates at various capital structures as shown in Row 2 of Figure 15-5, starting with a 7.7% cost of debt for the first dollar of debt. This rate increases to 16% if the firm finances 60% of its capital structure with debt. Strasburg's current situation is in Column D and is shown in blue. (We will explain all the rows in Figure 15-5 in the following discussion.)

Estimating the Cost of Equity, r_s

An increase in the debt ratio also increases the risk faced by shareholders, and this has an effect on the cost of equity, r_s. Recall from Chapter 6 that a stock's beta is the relevant measure of risk for diversified investors. Moreover, it has been

[26]For some insights into how practicing financial managers view the capital structure decision, see John Graham and Campbell Harvey, "The Theory and Practice of Corporate Finance: Evidence from the Field," *Journal of Financial Economics*, Vol. 60, 2001, pp. 187–243; Ravindra R. Kamath, "Long-Term Financing Decisions: Views and Practices of Financial Managers of NYSE Firms," *Financial Review*, May 1997, pp. 331–356; and Edgar Norton, "Factors Affecting Capital Structure Decisions," *Financial Review*, August 1991, pp. 431–446.

FIGURE 15-5 Estimating Strasburg's Optimal Capital Structure (Millions of Dollars)

	A	B	C	D	E	F	G	H
151		Percent of Firm Financed with Debt (w_d)						
152		0%	10%	20%	30%	40%	50%	60%
153								
154	1. w_s	100.00%	90.00%	80.00%	70.00%	60.00%	50.00%	40.00%
155	2. r_d	7.70%	7.80%	8.00%	8.50%	9.90%	12.00%	16.00%
156	3. b	1.09	1.16	1.25	1.37	1.52	1.74	2.07
157	4. r_s	12.82%	13.26%	13.80%	14.50%	15.43%	16.73%	18.69%
158	5. r_d (1−T)	4.62%	4.68%	4.80%	5.10%	5.94%	7.20%	9.60%
159	6. WACC	12.82%	12.40%	12.00%	11.68%	11.63%	11.97%	13.24%
160	7. V_{op}	$233.98	$241.96	$250.00	$256.87	$257.86	$250.68	$226.65
161	8. Debt	$0.00	$24.20	$50.00	$77.06	$103.14	$125.34	$135.99
162	9. Equity	$233.98	$217.76	$200.00	$179.81	$154.72	$125.34	$90.66
163	10. # shares	12.72	11.34	10.00	8.69	7.44	6.25	5.13
164	11. Stock price	$18.40	$19.20	$20.00	$20.69	$20.79	$20.07	$17.66
165	12. Net income	$30.00	$28.87	$27.60	$26.07	$23.87	$20.98	$16.95
166	13. EPS	$2.36	$2.54	$2.76	$3.00	$3.21	$3.36	$3.30

Notes:

1. The percent financed with equity is: $w_s = 1 - w_d$.
2. The interest rate on debt, r_d, is obtained from investment bankers.
3. Beta is estimated using Hamada's formula, the unlevered beta of 1.09, and a tax rate of 40%: $b = b_U \times [1 + (1 - T) \times (w_d/w_s)]$.
4. The cost of equity is estimated using the CAPM formula with a risk-free rate of 6.3% and a market risk premium of 6%: $r_s = r_{RF} + (RP_M)b$.
5. The after-tax cost of debt is: $r_d(1 - T)$, where T = 40%.
6. The weighted average cost of capital is calculated as WACC = $w_s r_s + w_d r_d(1 - T)$.
7. The value of the firm's operations is calculated as $V_{op} = [FCF(1 + g)]/(WACC - g)$, where FCF = $30 million and g = 0.
8. Debt = $w_d \times V_{op}$.
9. The intrinsic value of equity after the recapitalization and repurchase is $S_{Post} = w_s \times V_{op}$.
10. The number of shares after the recap has been completed is found using this equation: $n_{Post} = n_{Prior} \times [(V_{opNew} - D_{New})/(V_{opNew} - D_{Old})$. The subscript "Old" indicates values from the original capital structure, where w_d = 20%; the subscript "New" indicates values at the current capital structure after the recap and repurchase; and the subscript "Post" indicates values after the recap and repurchase.
11. The price after the recap and repurchase is $P_{Post} = S_{Post}/n_{Post}$, but we can also find the price as $P_{Post} = (V_{opNew} - D_{Old})/n_{Prior}$.
12. EBIT is $50 million; see Figure 15-1. Net income is NI = $(EBIT - r_d D)(1 - T)$.
13. Earnings per share is EPS = NI/n_{Post}.

demonstrated, both theoretically and empirically, that beta increases with financial leverage. The Hamada equation specifies the effect of financial leverage on beta:[27]

$$b = b_U[1 + (1 - T)(D/S)] \quad (15\text{-}9)$$

Here D is the market value of the debt and S is the market value of the equity. The Hamada equation shows how increases in the market value debt/equity ratio increase beta. Here b_U is the firm's **unlevered beta** coefficient—that is, the beta it would have if it had no debt. In that case, beta would depend entirely on business risk and thus be a measure of the firm's "basic business risk."

[27]See Robert S. Hamada, "Portfolio Analysis, Market Equilibrium, and Corporation Finance," *Journal of Finance*, March 1969, pp. 13–31. For a comprehensive framework, see Robert A. Taggart, Jr., "Consistent Valuation and Cost of Capital Expressions with Corporate and Personal Taxes," *Financial Management*, Autumn 1991, pp. 8–20.

Sometimes it is more convenient to work with the percentages of debt and equity at which the firm is financed (w_d and w_s) rather than the dollar values of D and S. Notice that w_d and w_s are defined as D/(D + S) and S/(D + S), respectively. This means that the ratio w_d/w_s is equal to the ratio D/S. Substituting these values gives us another form of Hamada's formula:

$$b = b_U[1 + (1 - T)(w_d/w_s)] \tag{15-9a}$$

Often we know the current capital structure and beta but wish to know the unlevered beta. We find this by rearranging Equation 15-9a as follows:

$$b_U = b/[1 + (1 - T)(w_d/w_s)] \tag{15-10}$$

For Strasburg, the unlevered beta is

$$\begin{aligned} b_U &= 1.25/[1 + (1 - 0.40)(0.20/0.80)] \\ &= 1.087 \end{aligned}$$

Using this unlevered beta, we can then apply Hamada's formula in Equation 15-9a to determine estimates of Strasburg's beta for different capital structures. These results are reported in Line 3 of Figure 15-5.

Recall from Section 15.2 that the risk-free rate is 6.3% and the market risk premium is 6%. We can use the CAPM and the previously estimated betas to estimate Strasburg's cost of equity for different capital structures (which cause Strasburg's beta to change). These results are shown in Line 4 of Figure 15-5. As expected, Strasburg's cost of equity increases as its debt increases. Figure 15-6 graphs Strasburg's required return on equity at different debt ratios. Observe that the cost of equity consists of the 6.3% risk-free rate, a

FIGURE 15-6 Strasburg's Required Rate of Return on Equity at Different Debt Levels

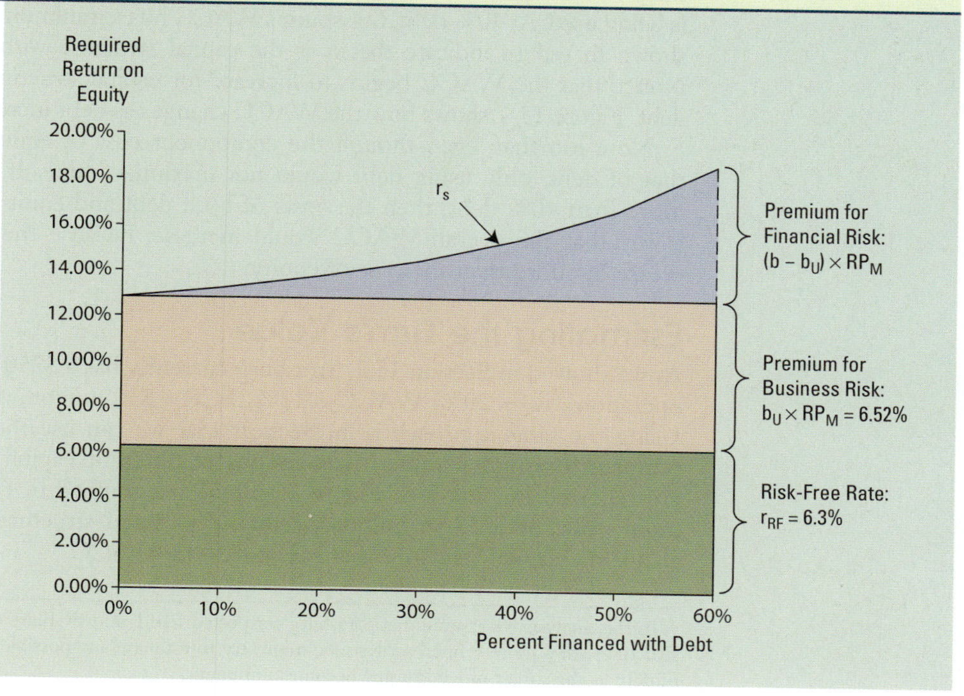

FIGURE 15-7 Effects of Capital Structure on the Cost of Capital

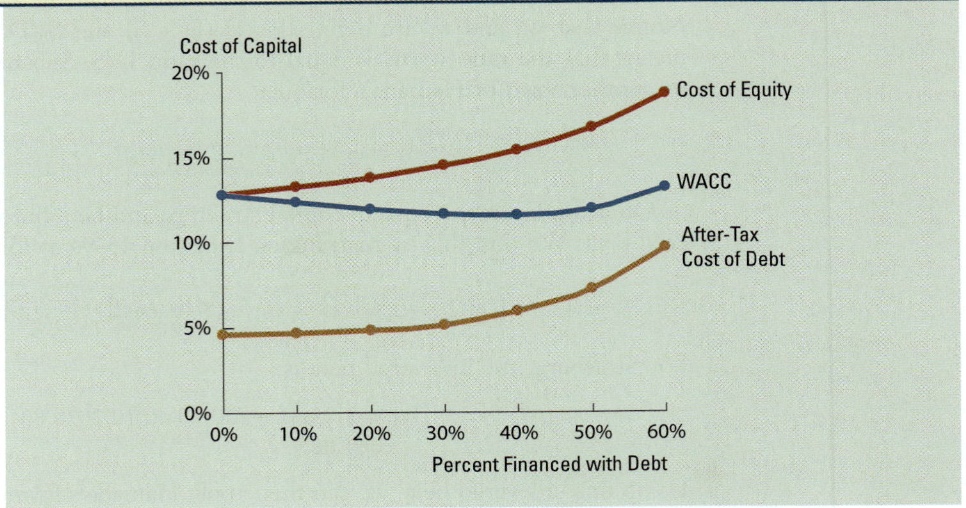

constant premium for business risk in the amount of $RP_M(b_U) = 6.522\%$, and a premium for financial risk in the amount of $RP_M(b - b_U)$ that starts at zero (because $b = b_U$ for zero debt) but rises at an increasing rate as the debt ratio increases.

Estimating the Weighted Average Cost of Capital, WACC

Line 6 of Figure 15-5 shows Strasburg's weighted average cost of capital, WACC, at different capital structures. As the debt ratio increases, the costs of both debt and equity rise, at first slowly but then at an accelerating rate. Eventually, the increasing costs of these two components offset the fact that more debt (which is still less costly than equity) is being used. At 40% debt, Strasburg's WACC hits a minimum of 11.63%; Column F is shown in red to indicate that it is the capital structure with the minimum WACC. Notice that the WACC begins to increase for capital structures with more than 40% debt. Figure 15-7 shows how the WACC changes as debt increases.

Note too that, even though the component cost of equity is always higher than that of debt, only using debt would not maximize value. If Strasburg were to issue more than 40% debt, then the costs of both debt and equity would increase in such a way that the overall WACC would increase, because the cost of debt would increase by more than the cost of equity.

Estimating the Firm's Value

As we showed in Section 15.2, Strasburg currently has a \$250 million intrinsic value of operations: $w_d = 20\%$, WACC = 12%, FCF = \$30 million, and zero growth in FCF. Using the same approach as in Section 15.2 we can use the data in Figure 15-5 to estimate Strasburg's value of operations at different capital structures; these results are reported in Line 7 of Figure 15-5 and are graphed in Figure 15-8.[28] The maximum value of \$257.86 million occurs at a capital structure with 40% debt, which also is the capital structure that minimizes the WACC.

[28]In this analysis we assume that Strasburg's expected EBIT and FCF are constant for the various capital structures. In a more refined analysis we might try to estimate any possible declines in FCF at high levels of debt as the threat of bankruptcy becomes imminent.

FIGURE 15-8 Effects of Capital Structure on the Value of Operations

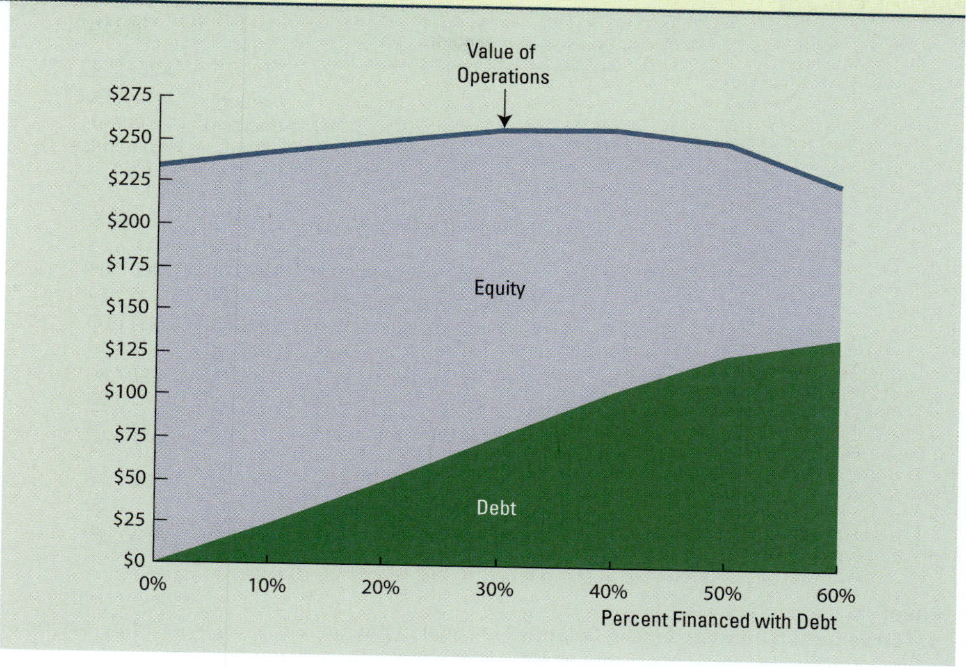

Notice that the value of the firm initially increases but then begins to fall. As discussed earlier, the value initially rises because the WACC initially falls. But the rising costs of equity and debt eventually cause the WACC to increase, causing the value of the firm to fall. Notice how flat the curve is around the optimal level of debt. Thus, it doesn't make a great deal of difference whether Strasburg's capital structure has 30% debt or 40% debt. Also, notice that the maximum value is about 10% greater than the value with no debt. Although this example is for a single company, the results are typical: The optimal capital structure can add 7% to 15% more value relative to zero debt, and there is a fairly wide range of w_d (from about 20% to 50%) over which value changes very little.

Figures 15-5 and 15-8 also show the values of debt and equity for each capital structure. The value of debt is found by multiplying the value of operations by the percentage of the firm that is financed by debt: Debt = $w_d \times V_{op}$. The intrinsic value of equity is found in a similar manner: $S = w_s \times V_{op}$. Even though the intrinsic value of equity falls as debt increases, the wealth of shareholders is maximized at the maximum value of operations, as we explain in the next section.

Self-Test

What happens to the costs of debt and equity when the leverage increases? Explain.

Use the Hamada equation to calculate the unlevered beta for JAB Industries, assuming the following data: Levered beta = b = 1.4; T = 40%; w_d = 45%. **(0.939)**

Suppose r_{RF} = 6% and RP_M = 5%. What would be the cost of equity for JAB Industries if it had no debt? **(10.7%)** If w_d were 45%? **(13.0%)**

15.6 Anatomy of a Recapitalization

Strasburg should **recapitalize**, meaning that it should issue enough additional debt to optimize its capital structure, and then use the debt proceeds to repurchase stock. As shown in Figure 15-5, a capital structure with 40% debt is optimal. But before

FIGURE 15-9 Anatomy of a Recapitalization (Millions, Except Per Share Data)

	Before Issuing Additional Debt (1)	After Debt Issue, But Prior to Repurchase (2)	Post Repurchase (3)
Percent financed with debt: w_d	20%	40%	40%
Value of operations	$250.00	$257.86	$257.86
+ Value of ST investments	0.00	53.14	0.00
Total intrinsic value of firm	$250.00	$311.00	$257.86
− Debt	50.00	103.14	103.14
Intrinsic value of equity	$200.00	$207.86	$154.72
÷ Number of shares	10.00	10.00	7.44
Intrinsic price per share	$20.00	$20.79	$20.79
Value of stock	$200.00	$207.86	$154.72
+ Cash distributed in repurchase	0.00	0.00	53.14
Wealth of shareholders	$200.00	$207.86	$207.86

Notes:

1. The value of ST investments in Column 2 is equal to the amount of cash raised by issuing additional debt but that has not been used to repurchase shares: ST investments = $D_{New} - D_{Old}$.
2. The value of ST investments in Column 3 is zero because the funds have been used to repurchase shares of stock.
3. The number of shares in Column 3 reflects the shares repurchased: $n_{Post} = n_{Prior} - (Cash_{Rep}/P_{Prior}) = n_{Prior} - [(D_{New} - D_{Old})/P_{Prior}]$.

tackling the **recap**, as it is commonly called, let's consider the sequence of events, starting with the situation before Strasburg issues any additional debt. Figure 15-3 shows the valuation analysis of Strasburg at a capital structure consisting of 20% debt and 80% equity. These results are repeated in Column 1 of Figure 15-9, along with the shareholder wealth, which consists entirely of $200 million in stock before the repurchase. The next step is to examine the impact of Strasburg's debt issuance.

Strasburg Issues New Debt but Has Not Yet Repurchased Stock

The next step in the recap is to issue debt and announce the firm's intent to repurchase stock with the newly issued debt. At the optimal capital structure of 40% debt, the value of the firm's operations is $257.86 million, as calculated in Figure 15-5 and repeated in Column 2 of Figure 15-9. This value of operations is greater than the $250 million value of operations for w_d = 20% because the WACC is lower. Notice that Strasburg raised its debt from $50 million to $103.14 million, an increase of $53.14 million. Because Column 2 reports data prior to the repurchase, Strasburg has short-term investments in the amount of $53.14 million, the amount that was raised in the debt issuance but that has not yet been used to repurchase stock.[29] As Figure 15-9 shows, Strasburg's intrinsic value of equity is $207.86 million.

[29]These calculations are shown in the *Excel* file ***Ch15 Tool Kit.xls*** on the textbook's Web site. The values reported in the text are rounded, but the values used in calculations in the spreadsheet are not rounded.

Because Strasburg has not yet repurchased any stock, it still has 10 million shares outstanding. Therefore, the price per share after the debt issue but prior to the repurchase is

$$\begin{aligned} P_{Prior} &= S_{Prior}/n_{Prior} \\ &= \$207.86/10 = \$20.79 \end{aligned}$$

Column 2 of Figure 15-9 summarizes these calculations and also shows the wealth of the shareholders. The shareholders own Strasburg's equity, which is worth \$207.86 million. Strasburg has not yet made any cash distributions to shareholders, so the total wealth of shareholders is \$207.86 million. The new wealth of \$207.86 million is greater than the initial wealth of \$200 million, so the recapitalization has added value to Strasburg's shareholders. Notice also that the recapitalization caused the intrinsic stock price to increase from \$20.00 to \$20.79.

Summarizing these results, we see that the issuance of debt and the resulting change in the optimal capital structure caused (1) the WACC to decrease, (2) the value of operations to increase, (3) shareholder wealth to increase, and (4) the stock price to increase.

Strasburg Repurchases Stock

What happens to the stock price during the repurchase? Recall from Chapter 14 that a repurchase does not change the stock price. It is true that the additional debt will change the WACC and the stock price prior to the repurchase (P_{Prior}), but the subsequent repurchase itself will not affect the post-repurchase stock price (P_{Post}).[30] Therefore, $P_{Post} = P_{Prior}$. (Keep in mind that P_{Prior} is the price immediately prior to the repurchase, not the price prior to the event that led to the cash available for the repurchase, such as the issuance of debt in this example.)

Strasburg uses the entire amount of cash raised by the debt issue to repurchase stock. The total cash raised is equal to $D_{New} - D_{Old}$. The number of shares repurchased is equal to the cash raised by issuing debt divided by the repurchase price:

$$\text{Number of shares repurchased} = \frac{D_{New} - D_{Old}}{P_{Prior}} \tag{15-11}$$

Strasburg repurchases (\$103.14 – \$50)/\$20.79 = 2.56 million shares of stock.

The number of remaining shares after the repurchase, n_{Post}, is equal to the initial number of shares minus the number that is repurchased:

$$\begin{aligned} n_{Post} &= \text{Number of outstanding shares remaining after the repurchase} \\ &= n_{Prior} - \text{Number of shares repurchased} \\ &= n_{Prior} - \frac{D_{New} - D_{Old}}{P_{Prior}} \end{aligned} \tag{15-12}$$

For Strasburg, the number of remaining shares after the repurchase is

$$\begin{aligned} n_{Post} &= n_{Prior} - (D_{New} - D_{Old})/P_{Prior} \\ &= 10 - (\$103.14 - \$50)/\$20.79 \\ &= 7.44 \text{ million} \end{aligned}$$

[30]As we discussed in Chapter 14, a stock repurchase may be a signal of a company's future prospects or it may be the way a company "announces" a change in capital structure, and either of these situations could have an impact on estimated free cash flows or WACC. However, neither situation applies to Strasburg.

Column 3 of Figure 15-9 summarizes these post-repurchase results. The repurchase doesn't change the value of operations, which remains at \$257.86 million. However, the short-term investments are sold and the cash is used to repurchase stock. Strasburg is left with no short-term investments, so the intrinsic value of equity is:

$$S_{Post} = \$257.86 - \$103.14 = \$154.72 \text{ million}$$

After the repurchase, Strasburg has 7.44 million shares of stock. We can verify that the intrinsic stock price has not changed:[31]

$$P_{Post} = S_{Post}/n_{Post} = \$154.72/7.44 = \$20.79$$

Shareholders now own an equity position in the company worth only \$154.72 million, but they have received a cash distribution in the amount of \$53.14 million, so their total wealth is equal to the value of their equity plus the amount of cash they received: \$154.72 + \$53.14 = \$207.86.

Here are some points worth noting. As shown in Column 3 of Figure 15-9, the change in capital structure clearly added wealth to the shareholders, increased the price per share, and increased the cash (in the form of short-term investments) temporarily held by the company. However, the repurchase itself did not affect shareholder wealth or the price per share. The repurchase did reduce the cash held by the company and the number of shares outstanding, but shareholder wealth stayed constant. After the repurchase, shareholders directly own the funds used in the repurchase; before the repurchase, shareholders indirectly own the funds. In either case, shareholders own the funds. The repurchase simply takes them out of the company's account and puts them into the shareholders' personal accounts.

The approach we've described here is based on the corporate valuation model, and it will always provide the correct value for S_{Post}, and n_{Post}, and P_{Post}. However, there is a quicker way to calculate these values if the firm has no short-term investments either before or after the recap (other than the temporary short-term investments held between the time debt was issued and shares repurchased). After the recap is completed, the percentage of equity in the capital structure, based on market values, is equal to $1 - w_d$ if the firm holds no other short-term investments. Therefore, the value of equity after the repurchase is

$$S_{Post} = V_{opNew}(1 - w_d) \tag{15-13}$$

where we use the subscript "New" to indicate the value of operations at the new capital structure and the subscript "Post" to indicate the post-repurchase intrinsic value of equity.

The post-repurchase number of shares can found using this equation:

$$n_{Post} = n_{Prior}\left[\frac{V_{opNew} - D_{New}}{V_{opNew} - D_{Old}}\right] \tag{15-14}$$

Given the value of equity and the number of shares, it is straightforward to calculate the intrinsic price per share as $P_{Post} = S_{Post}/n_{Post}$. But we can also calculate the post-repurchase price using

[31]There may be a small rounding difference due to using rounded numbers in intermediate steps. See the *Excel* file ***Ch15 Tool Kit.xls*** for the exact calculations.

FIGURE 15-10 Effects of Capital Structure on Stock Price and Earnings per Share

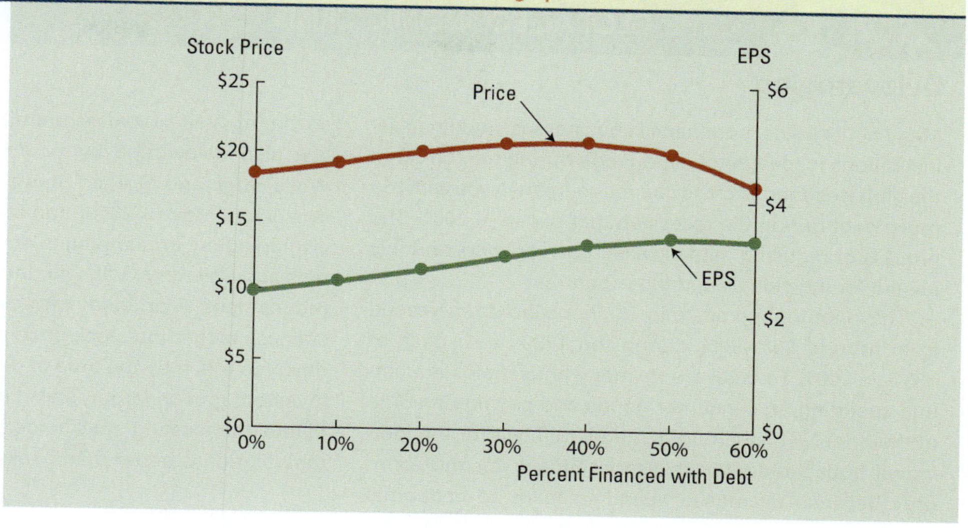

$$P_{Post} = \frac{V_{opNew} - D_{Old}}{n_{Prior}} \qquad (15\text{-}15)$$

Figure 15-5 reports the number of shares and the intrinsic price per share in Lines 9–10. Notice that the number of shares goes down as debt goes up because the debt proceeds are used to buy back stock. Notice also that the capital structure that maximizes stock price, $w_d = 40\%$, is the same capital structure that optimizes the WACC and the value of operations.

Figure 15-5 also reports the earnings per share for the different levels of debt. Figure 15-10 graphs the intrinsic price per share and the earnings per share. Notice that the maximum earnings per share is at 50% debt even though the optimal capital structure is at 40% debt. This means that maximizing EPS will not maximize shareholder wealth.

Recapitalizations: A Post-Mortem

In Chapter 13, we looked at value-based management and saw how companies can increase their value by improving their operations. Yet there is good news and bad news regarding this connection. The good news is that small improvements in operations can lead to huge increases in value. The bad news is that it's often difficult to improve operations, especially if the company is already well managed and is in a competitive industry.

If instead you seek to increase a firm's value by changing its capital structure, we again have good news and bad news. The good news is that changing capital structure is easy—just call an investment banker and issue debt (or issue equity if the firm has too much debt). The bad news is that this will add only a relatively small amount of value. Of course, any additional value is better than none, so it's hard to understand why there are some mature firms with zero debt.

THE GLOBAL ECONOMIC CRISIS

Deleveraging

Many households, nonfinancial businesses, and financial institutions loaded up on easy credit during the run-up to the global economic crisis and found themselves with too much debt during the recession that began in 2007. The process of reducing debt is called *deleveraging,* and it is painful for individuals and the economy.

The debt-to-income ratio for households increased from around 80%–90% during the 1990s to a peak of 133% in 2007. To deleverage, many households are cutting spending on consumer goods and paying off some of their debt. This belt-tightening is difficult for the individual households, but it also is difficult for the economy because decreased spending leads to economic contraction and job losses. Other households are deleveraging by declaring bankruptcy, with over 1.4 million people filing in 2008 and even more expected to file by the end of 2009.

Like individuals, business can deleverage by paying off debt or by declaring bankruptcy, and many are doing so during this global economic crisis. But businesses can also deleverage by issuing equity. For example, Wells Fargo and Morgan Stanley issued over $12 billion in stock in May of 2009; nonfinancial companies either issuing equity or planning to do so include Vulcan Materials and Callaway Golf, with the proceeds being used to reduce debt. A problem with deleveraging via stock issuances is that the stock price usually has been beaten down so much by the time of deleveraging that the new investors get a larger stake in the company, which dilutes the existing stockholders. But the bottom line is that dilution is better than bankruptcy!

Sources: Reuven Glick and Kevin J. Lansing, "U.S. Household Deleveraging and Future Consumption Growth," FRBSF Economic Letter, May 15, 2009, ***http://www.frbsf.org/publications/economics/letter/2009/el2009-16.pdf****; and BankruptcyAction.com,* ***http://www.bankruptcyaction.com/USbankstats.htm****, May 2009.*

Finally, some firms have more debt than is optimal and should recapitalize to a lower debt level. This is called *deleveraging.* We can use exactly the same approach and the same formulas as we used for Strasburg. The difference is that the debt will go down and the number of shares will go up. In other words, the company will issue new shares of stock and then use the proceeds to pay off debt, resulting in a capital structure with less debt and lower interest payments.

Self-Test

A firm's value of operations is equal to $800 million after a recapitalization (the firm had no debt before the recap). The firm raised $200 million in new debt and used this to buy back stock. The firm had no short-term investments before or after the recap. After the recap, w_d = 25%. The firm had 10 million shares before the recap. What is S (the value of equity after the recap)? **($600 million)** What is P (the stock price after the recap)? **($80/share)** What is n (the number of remaining shares after the recap)? **(7.5 million)**

Summary

This chapter examined the effects of financial leverage on stock prices, earnings per share, and the cost of capital. The key concepts covered are listed below.

- A firm's **optimal capital structure** is the mix of debt and equity that maximizes the stock price. At any point in time, management has a specific **target capital structure** in mind, presumably the optimal one, although this target may change over time.

- Several factors influence a firm's capital structure. These include its (1) **business risk**, (2) **tax position**, (3) need for **financial flexibility**, (4) **managerial conservatism or aggressiveness**, and (5) **growth opportunities.**
- **Business risk** is the risk inherent in the firm's operations if it uses no debt. A firm will have little business risk if the demand for its products is stable, if the prices of its inputs and products remain relatively constant, if it can adjust its prices freely if costs increase, and if a high percentage of its costs are variable and hence will decrease if sales decrease. Other things the same, the lower a firm's business risk, the higher its optimal debt ratio.
- **Financial leverage** is the extent to which fixed-income securities (debt and preferred stock) are used in a firm's capital structure. **Financial risk** is the added risk borne by stockholders as a result of financial leverage.
- **Operating leverage** is the extent to which fixed costs are used in a firm's operations. In business terminology, a high degree of operating leverage, other factors held constant, implies that a relatively small change in sales results in a large change in ROIC. ***Web Extension 15A*** describes additional measures of operating and financial leverage.
- Modigliani and Miller showed that if there are no taxes, then the value of a levered firm is equal to the value of an otherwise identical but unlevered firm:

$$V_L = V_U$$

- If there are only corporate taxes, Modigliani and Miller showed that a firm's value increases as it adds debt due to the interest rate deductibility of debt:

$$V_L = V_U + TD$$

- If there are personal and corporate taxes, Miller showed that

$$V_L = V_U + \left[1 - \frac{(1 - T_c)(1 - T_s)}{(1 - T_d)}\right] D$$

- The **Hamada equation** shows the effect of financial leverage on beta as follows:

$$b = b_U[1 + (1 - T)(D/S)]$$

  Firms can use their current beta, tax rate, and debt/equity ratio to derive their **unlevered beta**, $\mathbf{b_U}$, as follows:

$$b_U = b/[1 + (1 - T)(D/S)] = b/[1 + (1 - T)(w_d/w_s)]$$

- **The trade-off theory of capital structure** states that debt initially adds value because interest is **tax deductible** but that debt also brings costs associated with actual or potential bankruptcy. The optimal capital structure strikes a balance between the tax benefits of debt and the costs associated with bankruptcy.
- A firm's decision to use debt versus stock to raise new capital sends a **signal** to investors. A stock issue is viewed as a negative signal, whereas a debt issuance is a positive (or at least a neutral) signal. As a result, companies try to avoid having to issue stock by maintaining a **reserve borrowing capacity**, and this means using less debt in "normal" times than the trade-off theory would suggest.
- A firm's owners may decide to use a relatively large amount of debt to constrain the managers. A **high debt ratio raises the threat of bankruptcy**, which not only carries a cost but also forces managers to be more careful and less wasteful with shareholders' money. Many of the corporate takeovers and leveraged buyouts in recent years were designed to improve efficiency by reducing the cash flow available to managers.

Questions

(15–1) Define each of the following terms:
  a. Capital structure; business risk; financial risk
  b. Operating leverage; financial leverage; break-even point
  c. Reserve borrowing capacity

(15–2) What term refers to the uncertainty inherent in projections of future ROIC?

(15–3) Firms with relatively high nonfinancial fixed costs are said to have a high degree of what?

(15–4) "One type of leverage affects both EBIT and EPS. The other type affects only EPS." Explain this statement.

(15–5) Why is the following statement true? "Other things being the same, firms with relatively stable sales are able to carry relatively high debt ratios."

(15–6) Why do public utility companies usually have capital structures that are different from those of retail firms?

(15–7) Why is EBIT generally considered to be independent of financial leverage? Why might EBIT actually be influenced by financial leverage at high debt levels?

(15–8) If a firm went from zero debt to successively higher levels of debt, why would you expect its stock price to first rise, then hit a peak, and then begin to decline?

Self-Test Problems

Solutions Appear in Appendix A

(ST–1) Optimal Capital Structure

The Rogers Company is currently in this situation: (1) EBIT = \$4.7 million; (2) tax rate, T = 40%; (3) value of debt, D = \$2 million; (4) r_d = 10%; (5) r_s = 15%; (6) shares of stock outstanding, n = 600,000; and stock price, P = \$30. The firm's market is stable and it expects no growth, so all earnings are paid out as dividends. The debt consists of perpetual bonds.

  a. What is the total market value of the firm's stock, S, and the firm's total market value, V?
  b. What is the firm's weighted average cost of capital?
  c. Suppose the firm can increase its debt so that its capital structure has 50% debt, based on market values (it will issue debt and buy back stock). At this level of debt, its cost of equity rises to 18.5% and its interest rate on all debt will rise to 12% (it will have to call and refund the old debt). What is the WACC under this capital structure? What is the total value? How much debt will it issue, and what is the stock price after the repurchase? How many shares will remain outstanding after the repurchase?

(ST–2) Hamada Equation

Lighter Industrial Corporation (LIC) is considering a large-scale recapitalization. Currently, LIC is financed with 25% debt and 75% equity. LIC is considering increasing its level of debt until it is financed with 60% debt and 40% equity. The beta on its common stock at the current level of debt is 1.5, the risk-free rate is 6%, the market risk premium is 4%, and LIC faces a 40% federal-plus-state tax rate.

  a. What is LIC's current cost of equity?
  b. What is LIC's unlevered beta?
  c. What will be the new beta and new cost of equity if LIC recapitalizes?

Problems

Answers Appear in Appendix B

EASY PROBLEMS 1–6

(15–1) Break-even Quantity

Shapland Inc. has fixed operating costs of $500,000 and variable costs of $50 per unit. If it sells the product for $75 per unit, what is the break-even quantity?

(15–2) Unlevered Beta

Counts Accounting has a beta of 1.15. The tax rate is 40%, and Counts is financed with 20% debt. What is Counts's unlevered beta?

(15–3) Premium for Financial Risk

Ethier Enterprise has an unlevered beta of 1.0. Ethier is financed with 50% debt and has a levered beta of 1.6. If the risk-free rate is 5.5% and the market risk premium is 6%, how much is the additional premium that Ethier's shareholders require to be compensated for financial risk?

(15–4) Value of Equity after Recapitalization

Nichols Corporation's value of operations is equal to $500 million after a recapitalization (the firm had no debt before the recap). It raised $200 million in new debt and used this to buy back stock. Nichols had no short-term investments before or after the recap. After the recap, w_d = 40%. What is S (the value of equity after the recap)?

(15–5) Stock Price after Recapitalization

Lee Manufacturing's value of operations is equal to $900 million after a recapitalization (the firm had no debt before the recap). Lee raised $300 million in new debt and used this to buy back stock. Lee had no short-term investments before or after the recap. After the recap, w_d = 1/3. The firm had 30 million shares before the recap. What is P (the stock price after the recap)?

(15–6) Shares Remaining after Recapitalization

Dye Trucking raised $150 million in new debt and used this to buy back stock. After the recap, Dye's stock price is $7.50. If Dye had 60 million shares of stock before the recap, how many shares does it have after the recap?

INTERMEDIATE PROBLEMS 7–8

(15–7) Break-even Point

Schweser Satellites Inc. produces satellite earth stations that sell for $100,000 each. The firm's fixed costs, F, are $2 million, 50 earth stations are produced and sold each year, profits total $500,000, and the firm's assets (all equity financed) are $5 million. The firm estimates that it can change its production process, adding $4 million to investment and $500,000 to fixed operating costs. This change will (1) reduce variable costs per unit by $10,000 and (2) increase output by 20 units, but (3) the sales price on all units will have to be lowered to $95,000 to permit sales of the additional output. The firm has tax loss carryforwards that render its tax rate zero, its cost of equity is 16%, and it uses no debt.

a. What is the incremental profit? To get a rough idea of the project's profitability, what is the project's expected rate of return for the next year (defined as the incremental profit divided by the investment)? Should the firm make the investment?
b. Would the firm's break-even point increase or decrease if it made the change?
c. Would the new situation expose the firm to more or less business risk than the old one?

(15–8) Capital Structure Analysis

The Rivoli Company has no debt outstanding, and its financial position is given by the following data:

Assets (book = market)	\$3,000,000
EBIT	\$500,000
Cost of equity, r_s	10%
Stock price, P_0	\$15
Shares outstanding, n_0	200,000
Tax rate, T (federal-plus-state)	40%

The firm is considering selling bonds and simultaneously repurchasing some of its stock. If it moves to a capital structure with 30% debt based on market values, its cost of equity, r_s, will increase to 11% to reflect the increased risk. Bonds can be sold at a cost, r_d, of 7%. Rivoli is a no-growth firm. Hence, all its earnings are paid out as dividends. Earnings are expected to be constant over time.

a. What effect would this use of leverage have on the value of the firm?
b. What would be the price of Rivoli's stock?
c. What happens to the firm's earnings per share after the recapitalization?
d. The \$500,000 EBIT given previously is actually the expected value from the following probability distribution:

Probability	EBIT
0.10	(\$ 100,000)
0.20	200,000
0.40	500,000
0.20	800,000
0.10	1,100,000

Determine the times-interest-earned ratio for each probability. What is the probability of not covering the interest payment at the 30% debt level?

Challenging Problems 9–11

(15–9) Capital Structure Analysis

Pettit Printing Company has a total market value of \$100 million, consisting of 1 million shares selling for \$50 per share and \$50 million of 10% perpetual bonds now selling at par. The company's EBIT is \$13.24 million, and its tax rate is 15%. Pettit can change its capital structure either by increasing its debt to 70% (based on market values) or decreasing it to 30%. If it decides to *increase* its use of leverage, it must call its old bonds and issue new ones with a 12% coupon. If it decides to *decrease* its leverage, it will call its old bonds and replace them with new 8% coupon bonds. The company will sell or repurchase stock at the new equilibrium price to complete the capital structure change.

The firm pays out all earnings as dividends; hence its stock is a zero-growth stock. Its current cost of equity, r_s, is 14%. If it increases leverage, r_s will be 16%. If it decreases leverage, r_s will be 13%. What is the firm's WACC and total corporate value under each capital structure?

(15–10) Optimal Capital Structure with Hamada

Beckman Engineering and Associates (BEA) is considering a change in its capital structure. BEA currently has \$20 million in debt carrying a rate of 8%, and its stock price is \$40 per share with 2 million shares outstanding. BEA is a zero-growth firm and pays out all of its earnings as dividends. The firm's EBIT is \$14.933 million, and it faces a 40% federal-plus-state tax rate. The market risk premium is 4%, and the risk-free rate is 6%. BEA is considering increasing its debt level to a capital structure with 40% debt, based on market values, and repurchasing shares with the extra money that it borrows. BEA will have to retire the old debt in order to issue new debt, and the rate on the new debt will be 9%. BEA has a beta of 1.0.

a. What is BEA's unlevered beta? Use market value D/S when unlevering.
b. What are BEA's new beta and cost of equity if it has 40% debt?
c. What are BEA's WACC and total value of the firm with 40% debt?

(15–11) WACC and Optimal Capital Structure

Elliott Athletics is trying to determine its optimal capital structure, which now consists of only debt and common equity. The firm does not currently use preferred stock in its capital structure, and it does not plan to do so in the future. To estimate how much its debt would cost at different debt levels, the company's treasury staff has consulted with investment bankers and, on the basis of those discussions, has created the following table:

Market Debt-to-Value Ratio (w_d)	Market Equity-to-Value Ratio (w_s)	Market Debt-to-Equity Ratio (D/S)	Bond Rating	Before-Tax Cost of Debt (r_d)
0.0	1.0	0.00	A	7.0%
0.2	0.8	0.25	BBB	8.0
0.4	0.6	0.67	BB	10.0
0.6	0.4	1.50	C	12.0
0.8	0.2	4.00	D	15.0

Elliott uses the CAPM to estimate its cost of common equity, r_s. The company estimates that the risk-free rate is 5%; the market risk premium is 6%, and the company's tax rate is 40%. Elliott estimates that if it had no debt, its "unlevered" beta, b_U, would be 1.2. Based on this information, what is the firm's optimal capital structure, and what would be the weighted average cost of capital at the optimal capital structure?

Spreadsheet Problem

(15-12) Build a Model: WACC and Optimal Capital Structure

Start with the partial model in the file ***Ch15 P12 Build a Model.xls*** on the textbook's Web site. Reacher Technology has consulted with investment bankers and determined the interest rate it would pay for different capital structures, as shown in the following table. Data for the risk-free rate, the market risk premium, an estimate of Reacher's unlevered beta, and the tax rate are also shown. Based on this information, what is the firm's optimal capital structure, and what is the weighted average cost of capital at the optimal structure?

Percent Financed with Debt (w_d)	Before-Tax Cost Debt (r_d)
0%	6.0%
10	6.1
20	7.0
30	8.0
40	10.0
50	12.5
60	15.5
70	18.0

Input Data	
Risk-free rate	4.5%
Market risk premium	5.5%
Unlevered beta	0.8
Tax rate	40.0%

THOMSON ONE | Business School Edition Problem

Use the Thomson ONE—Business School Edition online database to work this chapter's questions.

EXPLORING THE CAPITAL STRUCTURES FOR THREE GLOBAL AUTO COMPANIES

The following discussion questions demonstrate how we can evaluate the capital structures for three global automobile companies: Ford (F), BMW (BMW), and Toyota (J:TYMO). As you gather information on these companies, be mindful of the currencies in which these companies' financial data are reported.

Thomson ONE—BSE Discussion Questions

1. To get an overall picture of each company's capital structure, it is helpful to see a chart that summarizes the company's capital structure over the past decade. To obtain this chart, choose a company to start with and select FINANCIALS. Next, select MORE>THOMSON REPORTS & CHARTS>CAPITAL STRUCTURE. This should generate a chart that plots the company's long-term debt, common equity, and total current liabilities over the past decade. What, if any, are the major trends that emerge from looking at these charts? Do these companies tend to have relatively high or relatively low levels of debt? Do these companies have significant levels of current liabilities? Have their capital structures changed over time? (Note that an alternative chart can be found by selecting FINANCIALS>FUNDAMENTAL RATIOS>WORLDSCOPE RATIOS>DEBT TO ASSETS & EQUITY RATIOS.)
2. To obtain more details about the companies' capital structures over the past five years, select FINANCIALS>FUNDAMENTAL RATIOS>THOMSON RATIOS. From here you can select ANNUAL RATIOS and/or 5 YEAR AVERAGE RATIOS REPORT. In each case, you can scroll down and look for Leverage Ratios. Here you will find a variety of leverage ratios for the past 5 years. (Notice that these two pages offer different information. The ANNUAL RATIOS page offers year-end leverage ratios, whereas the 5 YEAR AVERAGE RATIOS REPORT offers the average ratio over the previous 5 years for each calendar date. In other words, the 5 YEAR AVERAGE RATIOS REPORT smoothes the changes in capital structure over the reporting period.) Do these ratios suggest that the company has significantly changed its capital structure over the past 5 years? If so, what factors could possibly explain this shift? (Financial statements might be useful for detecting any shifts that may have led to the company's changing capital structure. You may also consult the company's annual report to see if there is any discussion and/or explanation for these changes. Both the historical financial statements and annual report information can be found via Thomson ONE).
3. Repeat this procedure for the other auto companies. Do you find similar capital structures for each of the four companies? Do you find that the capital structures have moved in the same direction over the past 5 years, or have the different companies changed their capital structures in different ways over the past 5 years?
4. The financial ratios investigated thus far are based on book values of debt and equity. Determine whether using the market value of equity (market capitalization found on the OVERVIEW page) makes a significant difference in the most recent year's "LT

Debt Pct Common Equity" and "Total Debt Pct Total Assets." (*Note:* "LT Debt" is defined by Thomson ONE as the "Long Term Debt" listed on the balance sheet, while "Total Debt" is defined as "Long Term Debt" plus "ST Debt & Current Portion Due LT Debt.") Are there big differences between the capital structures measured on a book or market basis?

5. You can also use Thomson ONE to search for companies with either very large or very small debt ratios. For example, if you want to find the top 50 companies with the highest debt ratio, select: SEARCH FOR COMPANIES>ADVANCED SEARCH>ALL COMPANIES>THOMSON FINANCIAL>RATIOS>LEVERAGE. From here, select "LT Debt Pct Total Cap 5 Yr. Avg." (This will focus in on the average capital structure over the past 5 years, which may give us a better indication of the company's long-run target capital structure.) Once you click on SELECT, you should see the Search Expression Builder screen. From here, you go to Rank and select the top 50 by typing "50" in the box below rank and then clicking on ADD. You can easily change this to also select the bottom 50 (or perhaps the bottom 5% or 10%). Take a close look at the resulting firms by clicking on SEARCH. Do you observe any differences between the types of firms that have high debt levels and the types of firms that have low debt levels? Are these patterns similar to what you expect after reading the chapter? (As a quick review, you may want to look at the average capital structures for different industries, which are summarized in the text.) *Note:* The searches are cumulative, so that if you ask for the top 10% of the database and follow that by asking for the bottom 5%, you will be shown the bottom 5% of the top 10%. In other words, you would only see a small subset of the firms you are asking for. Hence, *when beginning a new search, clear all existing searches first.*
6. From the submenu just above the list of firms, you may choose a number of options. "List" displays a list of the firms and allows you to access a firm report. "Profiles" provides key information about the firms, such as ticker, country, exchange, and industry code. "Financials" gives a couple of key financial figures (expressed in U.S. dollars) from the firms' balance sheets and income statements. "Market Data" includes the firms' market capitalization, current price, P/E ratio, EPS, and so forth. "Report Writer" allows you to create customized company reports.

Mini Case

Assume you have just been hired as a business manager of PizzaPalace, a regional pizza restaurant chain. The company's EBIT was $50 million last year and is not expected to grow. The firm is currently financed with all equity, and it has 10 million shares outstanding. When you took your corporate finance course, your instructor stated that most firms' owners would be financially better off if the firms used some debt. When you suggested this to your new boss, he encouraged you to pursue the idea. As a first step, assume that you obtained from the firm's investment banker the following estimated costs of debt for the firm at different capital structures:

Percent Financed with Debt, w_d	r_d
0%	—
20	8.0%
30	8.5
40	10.0
50	12.0

If the company were to recapitalize, then debt would be issued and the funds received would be used to repurchase stock. PizzaPalace is in the 40% state-plus-federal corporate tax bracket, its beta is 1.0, the risk-free rate is 6%, and the market risk premium is 6%.

a. Provide a brief overview of capital structure effects. Be sure to identify the ways in which capital structure can affect the weighted average cost of capital and free cash flows.
b. (1) What is business risk? What factors influence a firm's business risk?
   (2) What is operating leverage, and how does it affect a firm's business risk? Show the operating break-even point if a company has fixed costs of $200, a sales price of $15, and variable costs of $10.
c. Now, to develop an example that can be presented to PizzaPalace's management to illustrate the effects of financial leverage, consider two hypothetical firms: Firm U, which uses no debt financing, and Firm L, which uses $10,000 of 12% debt. Both firms have $20,000 in assets, a 40% tax rate, and an expected EBIT of $3,000.
   (1) Construct partial income statements, which start with EBIT, for the two firms.
   (2) Now calculate ROE for both firms.
   (3) What does this example illustrate about the impact of financial leverage on ROE?
d. Explain the difference between financial risk and business risk.
e. What happens to ROE for Firm U and Firm L if EBIT falls to $2,000? What does this imply about the impact of leverage on risk and return?
f. What does capital structure theory attempt to do? What lessons can be learned from capital structure theory? Be sure to address the MM models.
g. What does the empirical evidence say about capital structure theory? What are the implications for managers?
h. With the preceding points in mind, now consider the optimal capital structure for PizzaPalace.
   (1) For each capital structure under consideration, calculate the levered beta, the cost of equity, and the WACC.
   (2) Now calculate the corporate value for each capital structure.
i. Describe the recapitalization process and apply it to PizzaPalace. Calculate the resulting value of the debt that will be issued, the resulting market value of equity, the price per share, the number of shares repurchased, and the remaining shares. Considering only the capital structures under analysis, what is PizzaPalace's optimal capital structure?

Selected Additional Cases

The following cases from Textchoice, *Cengage Learning's online library, cover many of the concepts discussed in this chapter and are available at* **http://www.textchoice2.com**.

Klein-Brigham Series:
Case 9, "Kleen Kar, Inc.," Case 43, "Mountain Springs, Inc.," and Case 57, "Greta Cosmetics, Inc.," each present a situation similar to the Strasburg example in the text. Case 74, "The Western Company," and Case 99, "Moore Plumbing Supply," explore capital structure policies.

Brigham-Buzzard Series:
Case 8, "Powerline Network Corporation (Operating Leverage, Financial Leverage, and the Optimal Capital Structure)."

PART 7

Managing Global Operations

CHAPTER 16

Working Capital Management

What do U.S. Airways, Apple Computer, Clorox, Kellogg, Dow Chemical, and Family Dollar Stores have in common? Each led its industry in the latest CFO Magazine *annual survey of working capital management, which covered the 1,000 largest U.S. publicly traded firms. Each company is rated on its "days of working capital," which is the amount of net operating working capital required per dollar of daily sales:*

$$\text{Days of working capital (DWC)} = \frac{\text{Receivables} + \text{Inventory} - \text{Payables}}{\text{Average daily sales}}$$

The average U.S. firm's DWC was 51 days, and the range was from a low of −154 for CIGNA, a health care provider that collects premiums in advance of payouts, to +475 for Toll Brothers, a homebuilder with a huge inventory of unsold houses. Tiffany, the jeweler, had a ratio of 207 due to its policy of extending credit to boost sales, while Apple achieved a ratio of −29 largely by making Internet sales and being paid by credit cards well in advance of shipping products and paying its suppliers.

Variations across industries reflect different operating conditions, but there are also huge differences within industries. For example, the leader in the semiconductor sector, MEMC Electronic Materials, had an investment of only 21 days sales in working capital versus 111 days for another semiconductor firm, Novellus Systems. Ken Hannah, MEMC's CFO, made this statement to CFO Magazine: *"Every dollar we free up from working capital can be deployed back into the business." He went on to say that MEMC managed to trim its working capital by 26 days, which released about $340 million. Assuming this money was used to repay debt that cost 6%, this would boost before-tax profits by $20.4 million.*

How can a company lower its DWC? MEMC reduced its inventories by adopting just-in-time manufacturing processes, and it lowered receivables by requiring customers to pay for goods before they were shipped. It did not "stretch" its own payables. Rather, it asked for and received discounts of as much as 10% in exchange for early payments, which actually raised its DWC but also increased its net income. Keep MEMC's actions in mind as you read this chapter.

Sources: Various issues of CFO, *including an article by Randy Myers, "Cleaner (Balance) Sheets: The 2009 Working Capital Scorecard,"* CFO, *June 2009. For an update on* CFO*'s survey, go to* **http://www.cfo.com** *and look for "Working Capital Scorecard" under the "Special Reports" tab.*

Corporate Valuation and Working Capital Management

Superior working capital management can dramatically reduce required investments in operating capital, which can lead in turn to larger free cash flows and greater firm value.

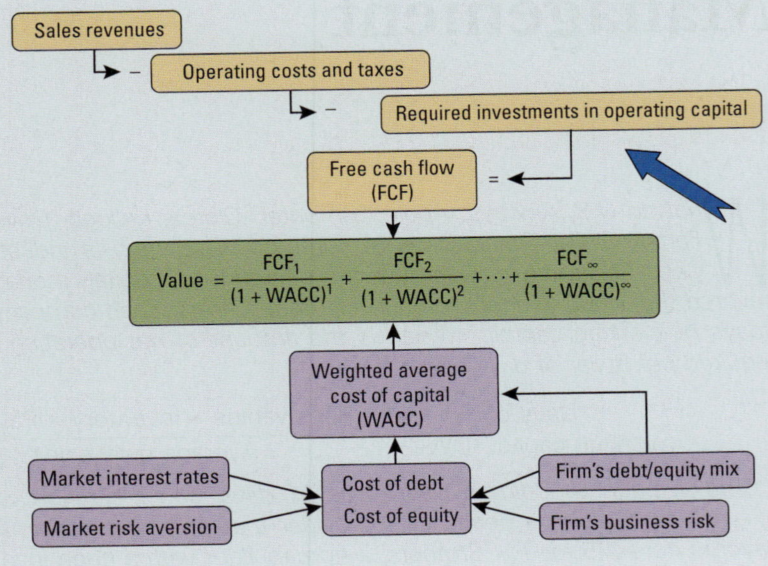

The textbook's Web site contains an Excel *file that will guide you through the chapter's calculations. The file for this chapter is* **Ch16 Tool Kit.xls**, *and we encourage you to open the file and follow along as you read the chapter.*

Working capital management involves two basic questions: (1) What is the appropriate amount of working capital, both in total and for each specific account, and (2) how should working capital be financed? Note that sound working capital management goes beyond finance. Indeed, improving the firm's working capital position generally comes from improvements in the operating divisions. For example, experts in logistics, operations management, and information technology often work with engineers and production specialists to develop ways to speed up the manufacturing process and thus reduce the goods-in-process inventory. Similarly, marketing managers and logistics experts cooperate to develop better ways to deliver the firm's products to its customers. Finance comes into play in evaluating how effective the firm's operating departments are relative to other firms in its industry and also in evaluating the profitability of alternative proposals for improving working capital management. In addition, financial managers decide how much cash their companies should keep on hand and how much short-term financing should be used to finance their working capital.

Here are some basic definitions and concepts.

1. **Working capital**, sometimes called *gross working capital*, simply refers to current assets used in operations.[1]
2. **Net working capital** is defined as current assets minus all current liabilities.

[1]The term "working capital" originated with the old Yankee peddler, who would load his wagon with pots and pans and then take off to peddle his wares. His horse and wagon were his fixed assets, while his merchandise was sold, or turned over at a profit, and thus was called his *working capital*.

3. **Net operating working capital (NOWC)** is defined as current *operating* assets minus current *operating* liabilities. Generally, NOWC is equal to cash required in operations, accounts receivable, and inventories, less accounts payable and accruals. Marketable securities not used in operations, cash in excess of operating needs, and other short-term investments are generally not considered to be operating current assets, so they are typically excluded when NOWC is calculated. The firm itself determines how much of its cash is required for operations, but all of the cash of most firms is used in operations.

16.1 Current Asset Holdings

Current assets can be divided into two categories, operating and nonoperating. Operating current assets consist of cash plus marketable securities held as a substitute for operating cash, inventories, and accounts receivable. These are assets that are necessary to operate the business. Nonoperating current assets consist of any other current assets, principally short-term securities in excess of what is required in operations, funds held in case a good merger opportunity arises, cash from the sale of a stock or bond issue before the funds can be invested in fixed assets, or funds held in case the firm loses a lawsuit and is required to compensate the winning party. *Our focus in this section is strictly on operating current assets.*

The amount of operating current assets held is a policy decision, and one that affects profitability. Figure 16-1 shows three alternative policies regarding the size of the firm's operating current assets. The top line has the steepest slope, which indicates that the firm holds a lot of cash, marketable securities, receivables, and inventories relative to its sales. If receivables are high, the firm has a liberal credit policy that results in a high level of accounts receivable. This is a **relaxed policy**. On the other hand, if a firm has a **restricted**, *tight*, or *"lean-and-mean"* **policy**, holdings of current assets are minimized. A **moderate policy** lies between the two extremes.

We can use the Du Pont equation to demonstrate how working capital management affects the return on equity:

$$
\begin{aligned}
\text{ROE} &= \text{Profit margin} \times \text{Total assets turnover} \times \text{Equity multiplier} \\
&= \frac{\text{Net income}}{\text{Sales}} \times \frac{\text{Sales}}{\text{Assets}} \times \frac{\text{Assets}}{\text{Equity}}
\end{aligned}
$$

A relaxed policy means a high level of assets and hence a low total assets turnover ratio; this results in a low ROE, other things held constant. Conversely, a restricted policy results in low current assets, a high turnover, and hence a relatively high ROE. However, the restricted policy exposes the firm to risk, because shortages can lead to work stoppages, unhappy customers, and serious long-run problems. The moderate policy falls between the two extremes. The optimal strategy is the one that management believes will maximize the firm's long-run earnings and thus the stock's intrinsic value.

Note that changing technologies can lead to changes in the optimal policy. For example, if a new technology makes it possible for a manufacturer to produce a given product in 5 rather than 10 days, then work-in-progress inventories can be cut in half. Similarly, retailers such as Wal-Mart and Home Depot have inventory management systems that use bar codes on all merchandise. These codes are read at the cash register, this information is transmitted electronically to a computer that adjusts the remaining stock of the item, and the computer automatically places an order with the supplier's computer when the stock falls to a specified level. This process lowers the "safety stocks" that would otherwise be necessary to avoid running out of stock. Such systems have dramatically lowered inventories and thus boosted profits.

FIGURE 16-1 Current Asset Investment Policies (Millions of Dollars)

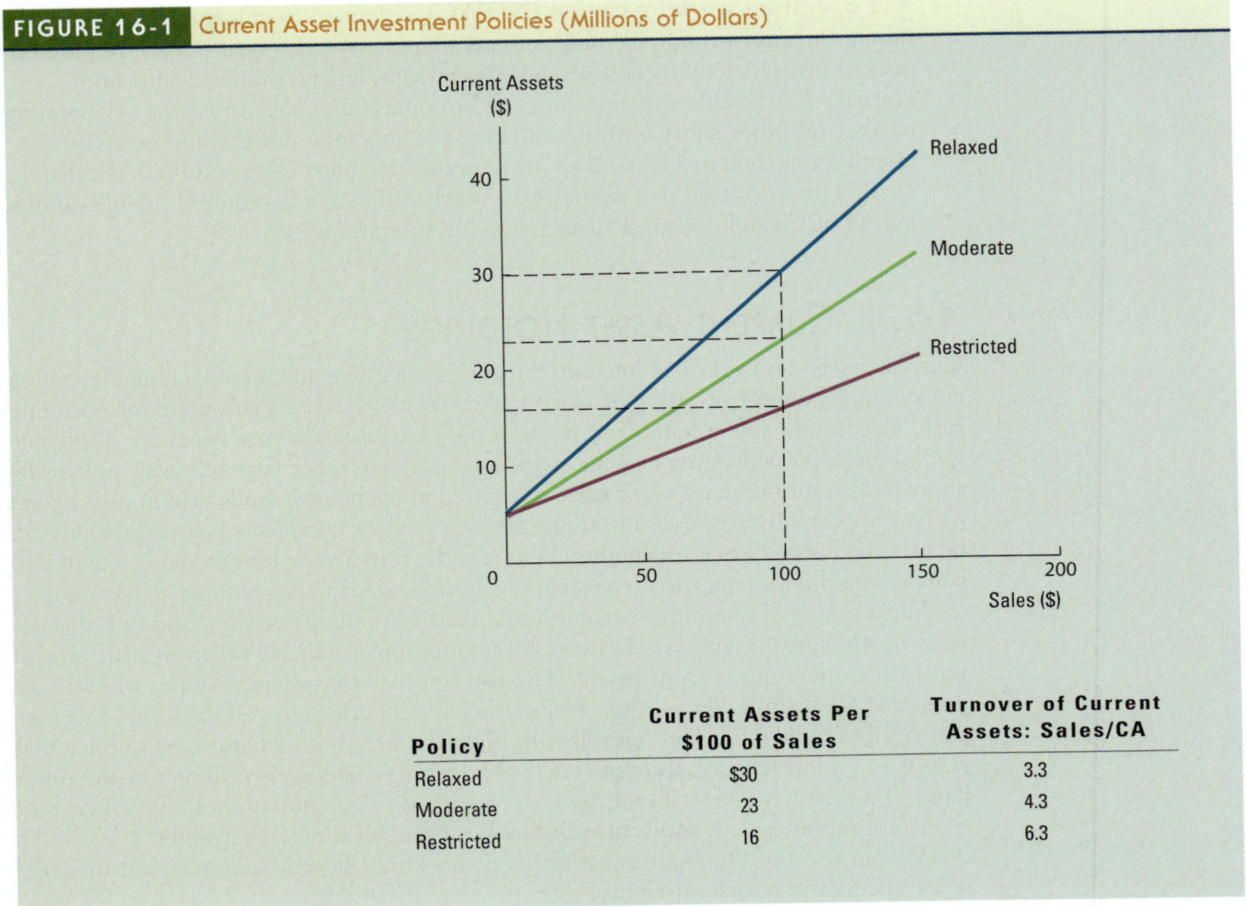

Policy	Current Assets Per $100 of Sales	Turnover of Current Assets: Sales/CA
Relaxed	$30	3.3
Moderate	23	4.3
Restricted	16	6.3

Self-Test

Identify and explain three alternative current asset investment policies.
Use the Du Pont equation to show how working capital policy can affect a firm's expected ROE.
What are the reasons for not wanting to hold too little working capital? For not wanting to hold too much?

16.2 Current Assets Financing Policies

Investments in operating current assets must be financed, and the primary sources of funds include bank loans, credit from suppliers (accounts payable), accrued liabilities, long-term debt, and common equity. Each of those sources has advantages and disadvantages, so a firm must decide which sources are best for it.

To begin, note that most businesses experience seasonal and/or cyclical fluctuations. For example, construction firms tend to peak in the summer, retailers peak around Christmas, and the manufacturers who supply both construction companies and retailers follow related patterns. Similarly, the sales of virtually all businesses increase when the economy is strong, so they increase current operating assets during booms but let inventories and receivables fall during recessions. However, current assets rarely drop to zero—companies maintain some **permanent current operating assets**, which are the current operating assets needed even at the low point of the business cycle. For a growing firm in a growing economy, permanent current assets tend to increase over time. Also, as sales increase during a cyclical upswing, current assets are increased; these extra current assets are defined as **temporary current operating assets** as opposed to permanent current assets. The way permanent and temporary current assets are financed is called the firm's **current operating assets financing policy**. Three alternative policies are discussed next.

Maturity Matching, or "Self-Liquidating," Approach

The **maturity matching**, or **"self-liquidating," approach** calls for matching asset and liability maturities as shown in Panel a of Figure 16-2. All of the fixed assets plus the permanent current assets are financed with long-term capital, but temporary current assets are financed with short-term debt. Inventory expected to be sold in 30 days would be financed with a 30-day bank loan; a machine expected to last for 5 years would be financed with a 5-year loan; a 20-year building would be financed with a 20-year mortgage bond; and so on. Actually, two factors prevent an exact maturity matching: (1) The lives of assets are uncertain. For example, a firm might finance inventories with a 30-day bank loan, expecting to sell the inventories and use the cash to retire the loan. But if sales are slow, then the cash would not be forthcoming and the firm might not be able to pay off the loan when it matures. (2) Some common equity must be used, and common equity has no maturity. Still, if a firm attempts to match or come close to matching asset and liability maturities, this is defined as a *moderate current asset financing policy*.

Aggressive Approach

Panel b of Figure 16-2 illustrates the situation for a more aggressive firm that finances some of its permanent assets with short-term debt. Note that we used the term "relatively" in the title for Panel b because there can be different *degrees* of aggressiveness. For example, the dashed line in Panel b could have been drawn *below* the line designating fixed assets, indicating that all of the current assets—both permanent and temporary—and part of the fixed assets were financed with short-term credit. This policy would be a highly aggressive, extremely nonconservative position, and the firm would be subject to dangers from loan renewal as well as rising interest rate problems. However, short-term interest rates are generally lower than long-term rates, and some firms are willing to gamble by using a large amount of low-cost, short-term debt in hopes of earning higher profits.

A possible reason for adopting the aggressive policy is to take advantage of an upward sloping yield curve, for which short-term rates are lower than long-term rates. However, as many firms learned during the financial crisis of 2009, a strategy of financing long-term assets with short-term debt is really quite risky. As an illustration, suppose a company borrowed $1 million on a 1-year basis and used the funds to buy machinery that would lower labor costs by $200,000 per year for 10 years.[2] Cash flows from the equipment would not be sufficient to pay off the loan at the end of only one year, so the loan would have to be renewed. If the economy were in a recession like that of 2009, the lender might refuse to renew the loan, and that could lead to bankruptcy. Had the firm matched maturities and financed the equipment with a 10-year loan, then the annual loan payments would have been lower and better matched with the cash flows, and the loan renewal problem would not have arisen.

---

[2]We are oversimplifying here. Few lenders would explicitly lend money for one year to finance a 10-year asset. What would actually happen is that the firm would borrow on a 1-year basis for "general corporate purposes" and then actually use the money to purchase the 10-year machinery.

FIGURE 16-2 Alternative Current Operating Assets Financing Policies

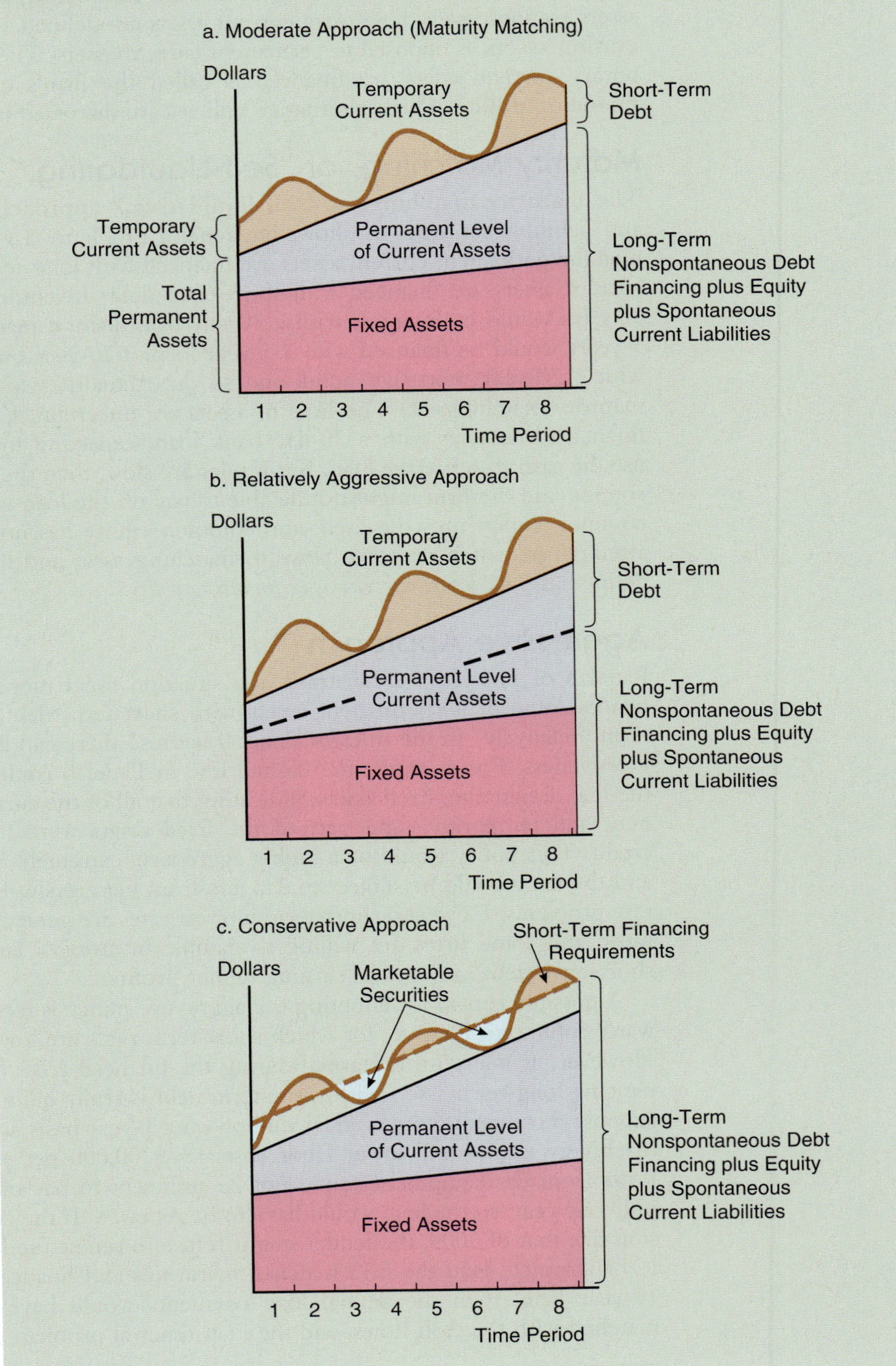

Under some circumstances even maturity matching can be risky, as many firms that thought they were conservatively financed learned in 2009. If a firm borrowed on a 30-day bank loan to finance inventories that it expected to sell within 30 days but then sales dropped, as they did for many firms in 2009, the funds needed to pay off the maturing bank loan might not be available. Then the bank might not extend the loan, and if it did not then the firm could be forced into bankruptcy. This happened to many firms in 2009, and it was exacerbated by the banks' own problems. The banks had lost billions on mortgages, mortgage-backed bonds, and other bad investments, which led banks to restrict credit to their normal business customers in order to conserve their own cash.

Conservative Approach

Panel c of the figure shows the dashed line *above* the line designating permanent current assets, indicating that long-term capital is used to finance all permanent assets and also to meet some seasonal needs. In this situation, the firm uses a small amount of short-term credit to meet its peak requirements, but it also meets a part of its seasonal needs by "storing liquidity" in the form of marketable securities. The humps above the dashed line represent short-term financings, while the troughs below the dashed line represent short-term security holdings. This conservative financing policy is fairly safe, and the wisdom of using it was demonstrated in 2009: when credit dried up, firms with adequate cash holdings were able to operate more effectively than those that were forced to cut back their operations because they couldn't order new inventories or pay their normal workforce.

Choosing among the Approaches

Because the yield curve is normally upward sloping, *the cost of short-term debt is generally lower than that of long-term debt*. However, *short-term debt is riskier to the borrowing firm* for two reasons: (1) If a firm borrows on a long-term basis then its interest costs will be relatively stable over time, but if it uses short-term credit then its interest expense can fluctuate widely—perhaps reaching such high levels that profits are extinguished.[3] (2) If a firm borrows heavily on a short-term basis, then a temporary recession may adversely affect its financial ratios and render it unable to repay its debt. Recognizing this fact, the lender may not renew the loan if the borrower's financial position is weak, which could force the borrower into bankruptcy.

Note also that *short-term loans can generally be negotiated much faster* than long-term loans. Lenders need to make a thorough financial examination before extending long-term credit, and the loan agreement must be spelled out in great detail because a lot can happen during the life of a 10- to 20-year loan.

Finally, *short-term debt generally offers greater flexibility*. If the firm thinks that interest rates are abnormally high and due for a decline, it may prefer short-term credit because prepayment penalties are often attached to long-term debt. Also, if its needs for funds are seasonal or cyclical, then the firm may not want to commit itself to long-term debt because of its underwriting costs and possible prepayment penalties. Finally, long-term loan agreements generally contain provisions, or *covenants*, that constrain the firm's future actions in order to protect the lender, whereas short-term credit agreements generally have fewer restrictions.

---

[3]The prime interest rate—the rate banks charge very good customers—hit 21% in the early 1980s. This produced a level of business bankruptcies that was not seen again until 2009. The primary reason for the very high interest rate was that the inflation rate was up to 13%, and high inflation must be compensated by high interest rates. Also, the Federal Reserve was tightening credit in order to hold down inflation, and it was encouraging banks to restrict their lending.

All things considered, it is not possible to state that either long-term or short-term financing is generally better. The firm's specific conditions will affect its decision, as will the risk preferences of managers. Optimistic and/or aggressive managers will lean more toward short-term credit to gain an interest cost advantage, whereas more conservative managers will lean toward long-term financing to avoid potential renewal problems. The factors discussed here should be considered, but the final decision will reflect managers' personal preferences and subjective judgments.

Self-Test

Differentiate between permanent current operating assets and temporary current operating assets.

What does maturity matching mean, and what is the logic behind this policy?

What are some advantages and disadvantages of short-term versus long-term debt?

16.3 The Cash Conversion Cycle

All firms follow a "working capital cycle" in which they purchase or produce inventory, hold it for a time, and then sell it and receive cash. This process is known as the **cash conversion cycle (CCC)**.

Calculating the Target CCC

Assume that Great Basin Medical Equipment (GBM) is just starting in business, buying orthopedic devices from a manufacturer in China and selling them through distributors in the United States, Canada, and Mexico. Its business plan calls for it to purchase $10,000,000 of merchandise at the start of each month and have it sold within 50 days. The company will have 40 days to pay its suppliers, and it will give its customers 60 days to pay for their purchases. GBM expects to just break even during its first few years and so its monthly sales will be $10,000,000, the same as its purchases (or cost of goods sold). For simplicity, assume that there are no administrative costs. Also, any funds required to support operations will be obtained from the bank, and those loans must be repaid as soon as cash becomes available.

This information can be used to calculate GBM's target, or theoretical, cash conversion cycle, which "nets out" the three time periods described below.[4]

1. **Inventory conversion period**. For GBM, this is the 50 days it expects to take to sell the equipment, converting it from equipment to accounts receivable.[5]
2. **Average collection period (ACP)**. This is the length of time customers are given to pay for goods following a sale. The ACP is also called the *days sales outstanding* (DSO). GBM's business plan calls for an ACP of 60 days based on its 60-day credit terms. This is also called the *receivables conversion period*, as it is supposed to take 60 days to collect and thus convert receivables to cash.
3. **Payables deferral period**. This is the length of time GBM's suppliers give it to pay for its purchases, which in our example is 40 days.

On Day 1, GBM expects to buy merchandise, and it expects to sell the goods and thus convert them to accounts receivable within 50 days. It should then take 60 days to collect the receivables, making a total of 110 days between receiving merchandise and collecting cash. However, GBM is able to defer its own payments for only 40 days.

---

[4]See Verlyn D. Richards and Eugene J. Laughlin, "A Cash Conversion Cycle Approach to Liquidity Analysis," *Financial Management*, Spring 1980, pp. 32–38.

[5]If GBM were a manufacturer, the inventory conversion period would be the time required to convert raw materials into finished goods and then to sell those goods.

FIGURE 16-3 The Cash Conversion Cycle

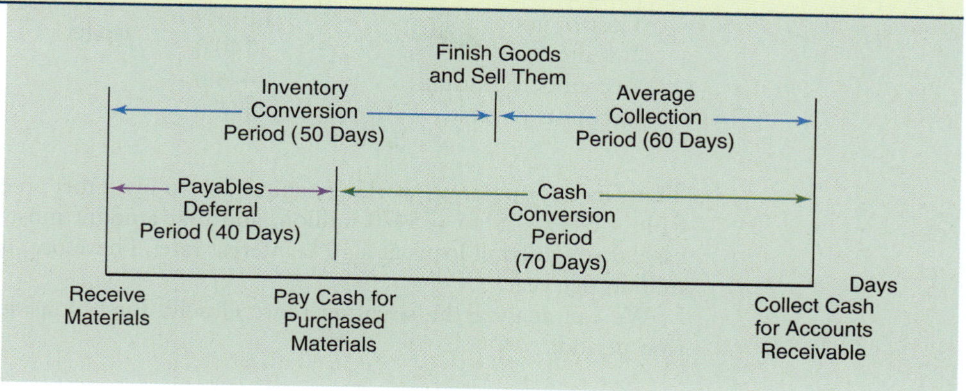

We can combine these three periods to find the theoretical, or target, cash conversion cycle, shown below as an equation and diagrammed in Figure 16-3.

$$\begin{array}{c} \text{Inventory} \\ \text{conversion} \\ \text{period} \end{array} + \begin{array}{c} \text{Average} \\ \text{collection} \\ \text{period} \end{array} - \begin{array}{c} \text{Payables} \\ \text{deferral} \\ \text{period} \end{array} = \begin{array}{c} \text{Cash} \\ \text{conversion} \\ \text{cycle} \end{array} \quad (16\text{-}1)$$

$$50 \quad + \quad 60 \quad - \quad 40 \quad = \quad 70 \text{ days}$$

Although GBM is supposed to pay its suppliers $10,000,000 after 40 days, it does not expect to receive any cash until 50 + 60 = 110 days into the cycle. Therefore, it will have to borrow the $10,000,000 cost of the merchandise from its bank on Day 40, and it does not expect to be able to repay the loan until it collects on Day 110. Thus, for 110 − 40 = 70 days—which is the theoretical cash conversion cycle (CCC)—it will owe the bank $10,000,000 and it will be paying interest on this debt. The shorter the cash conversion cycle the better, because a shorter CCC means lower interest charges.

Observe that if GBM could sell goods faster, collect receivables faster, or defer its payables longer without hurting sales or increasing operating costs, then its CCC would decline, its expected interest charges would be reduced, and its expected profits and stock price would be improved.

Calculating the Actual CCC from Financial Statements

So far we have illustrated the CCC from a theoretical standpoint. However, in practice we would generally calculate the CCC based on the firm's financial statements, and the actual CCC would almost certainly differ from the theoretical value because of real-world complexities such as shipping delays, sales slowdowns, and slow-paying customers. Moreover, a firm such as GBM would be continually starting new cycles before the earlier ones ended, and this too would muddy the waters.

To see how the CCC is calculated in practice, assume that GBM has been in business for several years and is in a stable position, placing orders, making sales, receiving payments, and making its own payments on a recurring basis. The following data were taken from its latest financial statements, in millions:

Annual sales	\$1,216.7
Cost of goods sold	1,013.9
Inventories	140.0
Accounts receivable	445.0
Accounts payable	115.0

Thus, its net operating working capital due to inventory, receivables, and payables is \$140 + \$445 − \$115 = \$470 million, and that amount must be financed—in GBM's case, through bank loans at a 10% interest rate. Therefore, its interest expense is \$47 million per year.

We can analyze the situation more closely. First, consider the inventory conversion period:[6]

$$\text{Inventory conversion period} = \frac{\text{Inventory}}{\text{Cost of goods sold per day}} \tag{16-2}$$

$$= \frac{\$140.0}{\$1{,}013.9/365} = 50.4 \text{ days}$$

Thus, it takes GBM an average of 50.4 days to sell its merchandise, which is very close to the 50 days called for in the business plan. Note also that inventory is carried at cost, which explains why the denominator in Equation 16-2 is the cost of goods sold per day, not daily sales.

The average collection period (or days sales outstanding) is calculated next:

$$\text{Average collection period} = \text{ACP(or DSO)} = \frac{\text{Receivables}}{\text{Sales}/365} \tag{16-3}$$

$$= \frac{\$445.0}{\$1{,}216.7/365} = 133.5 \text{ days}$$

Thus, it takes GBM 133.5 days after a sale to receive cash, not the 60 days called for in its business plan. Because receivables are recorded at the sales price, we use daily sales (rather than the cost of goods sold per day) in the denominator for the ACP.

The payables deferral period is found as follows, again using daily cost of goods sold in the denominator because payables are recorded at cost:

$$\begin{matrix}\text{Payables}\\ \text{deferral period}\end{matrix} = \frac{\text{Payables}}{\text{Purchases per day}} = \frac{\text{Payables}}{\text{Cost of goods sold}/365} \tag{16-4}$$

$$= \frac{\$115.0}{\$1{,}013.9/365} = 41.4 \text{ days}$$

[6]In past editions of this book we divided inventories by daily sales to be consistent with many reported data sources. We believe that dividing by daily cost of goods sold provides a more meaningful cash conversion period, so we changed the formula in this edition.

GBM is supposed to pay its suppliers after 40 days, but it actually pays on average just after Day 41. This slight delay is normal, since mail delays and time for checks to be cashed generally slow payments down a bit.

We can now combine the three periods to calculate GBM's actual cash conversion cycle:

See **Ch16 Tool Kit.xls** *on the textbook's Web site for details.*

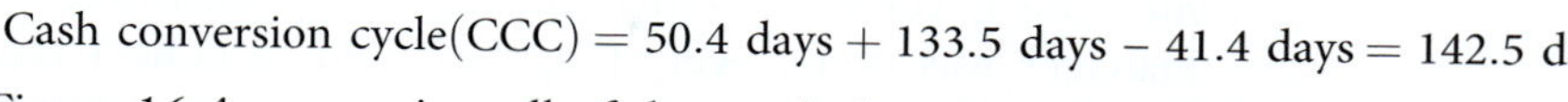

$$\text{Cash conversion cycle(CCC)} = 50.4 \text{ days} + 133.5 \text{ days} - 41.4 \text{ days} = 142.5 \text{ days}$$

Figure 16-4 summarizes all of these calculations and then analyzes why the actual CCC exceeds the theoretical CCC by such a large amount. It is clear from the figure that the firm's inventory control is working as expected in that sales match the inflow of new inventory items quite well. Also, its own payments match reasonably well the terms under which it buys. However, its accounts receivable are much higher than they should be, indicating that its customers are not paying on time. In fact, they

FIGURE 16-4 Summary of the Cash Conversion Cycle (Millions of Dollars)

	A	B	C	D	E	F	G
9	Panel a. Target CCC: Based on Planned Conditions						
10	Cash Conversion Cycle (CCC)	=	Planned Inventory Conversion Period (ICP)	+	Credit Terms Offered to Our Customers	–	Credit Terms Our Supplier Offers Us
11		=	50.0	+	60.0	–	40.0
12							
13	Target CCC	=	70.0				
14							
15	Panel b. Actual CCC: Based on Financial Statements						
16							
17	Sales	$1,216.7					
18	COGS	$1,013.9					
19	Inventories	$140.0					
20	Receivables	$445.0					
21	Payables	$115.0					
22	Days/year	365					
23	Actual CCC	=	Inventory ÷ COGS/365	+	Receivables ÷ Sales/365	–	Payables ÷ COGS/365
24		=	$140 ÷ ($1,013.9/365)	+	$445 ÷ ($1,216.7/365)	–	$115 ÷ ($1,013.9/365)
25		=	50.4	+	133.5	–	41.4
26							
27	Actual CCC	=	142.5				
28							
29	Panel c. Actual versus Target components						
30			ICP		ACP		PDP
31	Actual - Target	=	50.4 – 50.0		133.5 – 60.0		41.4 – 40.0
32		=	0.4	+	73.5	–	1.4
33	% Difference	=	0.8%		122.5%		3.5%
34			OK		VERY BAD		OK

Note: GBM's inventories are in line with its plans, and it's paying its suppliers nearly on time. However, some of its customers are paying quite late, so its average collection period (or DSO) is 133.5 days even though all customers are supposed to pay by Day 60.

are paying 73.5 days late, which is increasing GBM's working capital. Because working capital must be financed, the collections delay is lowering the firm's profits and presumably hurting its stock price.

When the CFO reviewed the situation, she discovered that GBM's customers—doctors, hospitals, and clinics—were themselves reimbursed by insurance companies and government units, and those organizations were paying late. The credit manager was doing everything he could to collect faster, but the customers said that they just could not make their own payments until they themselves were paid. If GBM wanted to keep making sales, it seemed that it would have to accept late-paying customers. However, the CFO wondered if collections might come in faster if GBM offered substantial discounts for early payments. We will take up this issue later in the chapter.

Benefits of Reducing the CCC

As we have seen, GBM currently has a CCC of 142.5 days, which results in $470 million being tied up in net operating working capital. Assuming that its cost of debt to carry working capital is 10%, this means that the firm is incurring interest charges of $47 million per year to carry its working capital. Now suppose the company can speed up its sales enough to reduce the inventory conversion period from 50.4 to 35.0 days. In addition, it begins to offer discounts for early payment and thereby reduces its average collection period to 40 days. Finally, assume that it could negotiate a change in its own payment terms from 40 to 50 days. The "New" column of Figure 16-5 shows the net effects of these improvements: a 117.5-day reduction in the cash conversion cycle and a reduction in net operating working capital from $470.0 to $91.7 million, which saves $37.8 million of interest.

Recall also that free cash flow (FCF) is equal to NOPAT minus the net new investment in operating capital. Therefore, if working capital *decreases* by a given amount while other things remain constant, then FCF *increases* by that same amount—$378.3 million in the GBM example. If sales remained constant in the fol-

FIGURE 16-5 Benefits from Reducing the Cash Conversion Cycle (Millions of Dollars)

	A	B	C	D	E	F	G
44					Old (Actual)		New (Target)
45	Inventory conversion period (ICP, days)				50.4		35.0
46	Average collection period (ACP, days)				133.5		40.0
47	Payable deferral period (PDP, days)				−41.4		−50.0
48	Cash Collection Cycle (CCC, days)				142.5		25.0
49							
50	Reduction in CCC					117.5	
51							
52	Effects of the CCC Reduction						
53	Annual sales				$1,216.7		$1,216.7
54	Costs of goods sold (COGS)				$1,013.9		$1,013.9
55	Inventory = Actual Old, New = new ICP(COGS/365)				$140.0		$97.2
56	Receivables = Actual Old, New = new ACP(Sales/365)				445.0		133.3
57	Payables = Actual Old, New = new PDP(COGS/365)				−115.0		−138.9
58	Net operating WC = Inv + Receivables − Payables				$470.0		$91.7
59							
60	Reduction in NOWC					$378.3	
61	Reduction in interest expense @ 10%					$37.8	

Some Firms Operate with Negative Working Capital!

Some firms are able to operate with zero or even negative net working capital. Dell Computer and Amazon.com are examples. When customers order computers from Dell's Web site or books from Amazon, they must provide a credit card number. Dell and Amazon then receive next-day cash, even before the product is shipped and even before they have paid their own suppliers. This results in a negative CCC, which means that working capital *provides* cash rather than using it.

In order to grow, companies normally need cash for working capital. However, if the CCC is negative then growth in sales *provides* cash rather than *uses* it. This cash can be invested in plant and equipment, research and development, or for any other corporate purpose. Analysts recognize this point when they value Dell and Amazon, and it certainly helps their stock prices.

lowing years, then this reduction in working capital would simply be a one-time cash inflow. However, suppose sales grow in future years. When a company improves its working capital management, the components (inventory conversion period, collection period, and payments period) usually remain at their improved levels, which means the NOWC/Sales ratio remains at its new level. With an improved NOWC/Sales ratio, less working capital will be required to support future sales, leading to higher annual FCFs than would have otherwise existed.

Thus, an improvement in working capital management creates a large one-time increase in FCF at the time of the improvement as well as higher FCF in future years. Therefore, an improvement in working capital management is a gift that keeps on giving.

These benefits can add substantial value to the company. Professors Hyun-Han Shin and Luc Soenen studied more than 2,900 companies over a 20-year period, finding a strong relationship between a company's cash conversion cycle and its stock performance.[7] For an average company, a 10-day improvement in its CCC was associated with an increase in pre-tax operating profit margin from 12.76% to 13.02%. Moreover, companies with cash conversion cycles 10 days shorter than the average for their industry had annual stock returns that were 1.7 percentage points higher than the average company. Given results like these, it's no wonder firms place so much emphasis on working capital management![8]

Self-Test

Define the following terms: inventory conversion period, average collection period, and payables deferral period. Give the equation for each term.

What is the cash conversion cycle? What is its equation?

What should a firm's goal be regarding the cash conversion cycle, holding other things constant? Explain your answer.

What are some actions a firm can take to shorten its cash conversion cycle?

A company has $20 million of inventory, $5 million of receivables, and $4 million of payables. Its annual sales revenue is $80 million, and its cost of goods sold is $60 million. What is its CCC? **(120.15)**

---

[7]Hyun-Han Shin and Luc Soenen, "Efficiency of Working Capital Management and Corporate Profitability," *Financial Practice and Education*, Fall/Winter 1998, pp. 37–45.

[8]For more on the CCC, see James A. Gentry, R. Vaidyanathan, and Hei Wai Lee, "A Weighted Cash Conversion Cycle," *Financial Management*, Spring 1990, pp. 90–99.

16.4 The Cash Budget

See **Ch16 Tool Kit.xls** on the textbook's Web site for details.

Firms must forecast their cash flows. If they are likely to need additional cash then they should line up funds well in advance, yet if they are likely to generate surplus cash then they should plan for its productive use. The primary forecasting tool is the cash budget, illustrated in Figure 16-6, which is a printout from the chapter's *Excel* ***Tool Kit*** model. The illustrative company is Educational Products Corporation (EPC), which supplies educational materials to schools and retailers in the Midwest. Sales are cyclical, peaking in September and then declining for the balance of the year.

FIGURE 16-6 EPC's Cash Budget, July–December 2011 (Millions of Dollars)

	A–E	F	G	H	I	J	K	L	M
73	Base Case	May	June	July	August	Sept	Oct	Nov	Dec
74	Forecasted gross sales (manual inputs):	$200.0	$250.0	$300.0	$400.0	$500.0	$350.0	$250.0	$200.0
75	Adjustment: % deviation from forecast	0%	0%	0%	0%	0%	0%	0%	0%
76	Adjusted gross sales forecast	$200.0	$250.0	$300.0	$400.0	$500.0	$350.0	$250.0	$200.0
77									
78	Collections on sales:								
79	During sales' month: 0.2 (Sales)(1 – discount %)			$58.8	$78.4	$98.0	$68.6	$49.0	$39.2
80	During 2nd month: 0.7(prior month's sales)			175.0	210.0	280.0	350.0	245.0	175.0
81	Due in 3rd month: 0.1(sales 2 months ago)			20.0	25.0	30.0	40.0	50.0	35.0
82	Less bad debts (BD% × Sales 2 months ago)			0.0	0.0	0.0	0.0	0.0	0.0
83	Total collections			$253.8	$313.4	$408.0	$458.6	$344.0	$249.2
84									
85	Purchases: 60% of next month's sales		$180.0	$240.0	$300.0	$210.0	$150.0	$120.0	$120.0
86	Payments								
87	Pmt for last month's purchases (30 days of credit)			$180.0	$240.0	$300.0	$210.0	$150.0	$120.0
88	Wages and salaries			30.0	40.0	50.0	40.0	30.0	30.0
89	Lease payments			30.0	30.0	30.0	30.0	30.0	30.0
90	Other payments (interest on LT bonds, dividends, etc.)			30.0	30.0	30.0	30.0	30.0	30.0
91	Taxes					30.0			30.0
92	Payment for plant construction					150.0			
93	Total payments			$270.0	$340.0	$590.0	$310.0	$240.0	$240.0
94									
95	Net cash flows:								
96	Assumed excess cash on hand at start of forecast period			$0.0					
97	Net cash flow (NCF): Total collections – Total pmts			–16.2	–26.6	–182.0	148.6	104.0	9.2
98	Cumulative NCF: Prior month cum plus this month's NCF			–$16.2	–$42.8	–$224.8	–$76.2	$27.8	$37.0
99									
100	Cash surplus (or loan requirement)								
101	Target cash balance			$10.0	$10.0	$10.0	$10.0	$10.0	$10.0
102	Surplus cash or loan needed: Cum NCF – Target cash			–$26.2	–$52.8	–$234.8	–$86.2	$17.8	$27.0
103									
104	Max required loan (most negative on Row 102)	$234.8							
105	Max investable funds (most positive on Row 102)	$27.0							

Notes:

1. Although the budget period is July through December, sales and purchases data for May and June are needed to determine collections and payments during July and August.
2. Firms can both borrow and pay off commercial loans on a daily basis, so the $26.2 million loan needed for July would likely be gradually borrowed as needed on a daily basis, and during October the $234.8 million loan that presumably existed at the beginning of the month would be reduced daily to the $86.2 million ending balance—which in turn, would be completely paid off sometime during November.
3. The data in the figure are for EPC's base-case forecast. Data for alternative scenarios are shown in the chapter's Excel ***Tool Kit*** model.

Monthly Cash Budgets

Cash budgets can be of any length, but EPC and most companies use a monthly cash budget such as the one in Figure 16-6, but set up for 12 months. We used only 6 months for the purpose of illustration. The monthly budget is used for longer-range planning, but a daily cash budget is also prepared at the start of each month to provide a more precise picture of the daily cash flows for use in scheduling actual payments on a day-by-day basis.

The cash budget focuses on cash flows, but it also includes information on forecasted sales, credit policy, and inventory management. Since the statement is a forecast and not a report on historical results, actual results could vary from the figures given. Therefore, the cash budget is generally set up as an expected, or base-case, forecast, but it is created with a model that makes it easy to generate alternative forecasts to see what would happen under different conditions.

Figure 16-6 begins with a forecast of sales for each month on Row 74. Then, on Row 75, it shows possible percentage deviations from the forecasted sales. Since we are showing the base-case forecast, no adjustments are made, but the model is set up to show the effects if sales increase or decrease and so result in "adjusted sales" that are above or below the forecasted levels.

The company sells on terms of "2/10, net 60." This means that a 2% discount is given if payment is made within 10 days; otherwise, the full amount is due in 60 days. However, like most companies, EPC finds that some customers pay late. Experience shows that 20% of customers pay during the month of the sale and take the discount. Another 70% pay during the month immediately following the sale, and 10% are late, paying in the second month after the sale.[9]

The statement (Line 85) next shows forecasted materials purchases, which equal 60% of the following month's sales. EPC buys on terms of net 30, meaning that it receives no discounts and is required to pay for its purchases within 30 days of the purchase date. The purchases information is followed by forecasted payments for materials, labor, leases, other payments such as dividends and interest on long-term bonds, taxes (due in September and December), and a payment of $150 million in September for a new plant that is being constructed.

When the total forecasted payments are subtracted from the forecasted collections, the result is the expected net cash gain or loss for each month. This gain or loss is added to or subtracted from the excess cash on hand at the start of the forecast (which we assume was zero), and the result—the *cumulative net cash flow*—is the amount of cash the firm would have on hand at the end of the month if it neither borrowed nor invested.

EPC's target cash balance is $10 million, and it plans either to borrow to meet this target or to invest surplus funds if it generates more cash than it needs. How the target cash balance is determined is discussed later in the chapter, but EPC believes that it needs $10 million.

By subtracting the target cash balance from the cumulative cash flow, we calculate the *loan needed or surplus cash*, as shown on Row 102. A negative number indicates that we need a loan, whereas a positive number indicates that we forecast surplus cash that is available for investment or other uses.

---

[9]A negligible percentage of sales results in bad debts. The low bad-debt losses evident here result from EPC's careful screening of customers and its generally tight credit policies. However, the cash budget model is able to show the effects of bad debts, so EPC's CFO could show top management how cash flows would be affected if the firm relaxed its credit policy in order to stimulate sales or if the recession worsened and more customers were forced to delay payments.

If we total the net cash flows on Row 97 then the sum is $37 million, the cumulative NCF as shown in Cell M98. Because this number is positive, it indicates that EPC's cash flow is positive. Also, note that EPC borrows on a basis that allows it to borrow or repay loans on a daily basis. Thus, it would borrow a total of $26.2 million in July, increasing the loan daily, and would continue to build up the loan through September. Then, when its cash flows turn positive in October, it would start repaying the loan on a daily basis and completely pay it off sometime in November, assuming that everything works out as forecasted.

Note that our cash budget is incomplete in that it shows neither interest paid on the working capital loans nor interest earned on the positive cash balances. These amounts could be added to the budget simply by adding rows and including them. Similarly, if the firm makes quarterly dividend payments, principal payments on its long-term bonds, or any other payments, or if it has investment income, then those cash flows also could be added to the statement. In our simplified statement, we just lumped all such payments into "other payments."

Under the base-case forecast, the CFO will need to arrange a line of credit so that the firm can borrow up to $234.8 million, increasing the loan over time as funds are needed and repaying it later when cash flows become positive. The treasurer would show the cash budget to the bankers when negotiating for the line of credit. Lenders would want to know how much the firm expects to need, when the funds will be needed, and when the loan will be repaid. The lenders—and EPC's top executives—would question the treasurer about the budget, and they would want to know how the forecasts would be affected if sales were higher or lower than those projected, how changes in customers' payment times would affect the forecasts, and the like. The focus would be on these two questions: *How accurate is the forecast likely to be? What would be the effects of significant errors?* The first question could best be answered by examining historical forecasts, and the second by running different scenarios as we do in the *Excel* ***Tool Kit*** model.

See **Ch16 Tool Kit.xls** *on the textbook's Web site for details.*

No matter how hard we try, no forecast will ever be exactly correct, and this includes cash budgets. You can imagine the bank's reaction if the company negotiated a loan of $235 million and then came back a few months later saying that it had underestimated its requirements and needed to boost the loan to say $260 million. The banker might well refuse, thinking the company was not very well managed. Therefore, EPC's treasurer would undoubtedly want to build a cushion into the line of credit—say, a maximum commitment of $260 million rather than the forecasted requirement of $234.8 million. However, as we discuss later in the chapter, banks charge commitment fees for guaranteed lines of credit; thus, the higher the cushion built into the line of credit, the more costly the credit will be. This is another reason why it is important to develop accurate forecasts.

Cash Budgets versus Income Statements and Free Cash Flows

If you look at the cash budget, it looks similar to an income statement. However, the two statements are quite different. Here are some key differences: (1) In an income statement, the focus would be on sales, not collections. (2) An income statement would show accrued taxes, wages, and so forth, not the actual payments. (3) An income statement would show depreciation as an expense, but it would not show expenditures on new fixed assets. (4) An income statement would show a cost for goods purchased when those goods were sold, not for when they were ordered or paid.

These are obviously large differences, so it would be a big mistake to confuse a cash budget with an income statement. Also, the cash flows shown on the cash budget are different from the firm's free cash flows, because FCF reflects after-tax operating income and the investments required to maintain future operations whereas the cash budget reflects only the actual cash inflows and outflows during a particular period.

The bottom line is that cash budgets, income statements, and free cash flows are all important and are related to one another, but they are also quite different. Each is designed for a specific purpose, and the main purpose of the cash budget is to forecast the firm's liquidity position, not its profitability.

Daily Cash Budgets

Note that if cash inflows and outflows do not occur uniformly during each month, then the actual funds needed might be quite different from the indicated amounts. The data in Figure 16-6 show the situation on the last day of each month, and we see that the maximum projected loan during the forecast period is $234.8 million. Yet if all payments had to be made on the 1st of the month but most collections came on the 30th, then EPC would have to make $270 million of payments in July before it received the $253.8 million from collections. In that case, the firm would need to borrow about $270 million in July, not the $26.2 million shown in Figure 16-6. This would make the bank unhappy—perhaps so unhappy that it would not extend the requested credit. A daily cash budget would have revealed this situation.

See **Ch16 Tool Kit.xls** *on the textbook's Web site for details.*

Figure 16-6 was prepared using *Excel*, which makes it easy to change the assumptions. In the ***Tool Kit*** model we examine the cash flow effects of changes in sales, in customers' payment patterns, and so forth. Also, the effects of changes in credit policy and inventory management could be examined through the cash budget.

Self-Test

How could the cash budget be used when negotiating the terms of a bank loan?

How would a shift from a tight credit policy to a relaxed policy be likely to affect a firm's cash budget?

How would the cash budget be affected if our firm's suppliers offered us terms of "2/10, net 30," rather than "net 30," and we decided to take the discount?

Suppose a firm's cash flows do not occur uniformly throughout the month. What effect would this have on the accuracy of the forecasted borrowing requirements based on a monthly cash budget? How could the firm deal with this problem?

16.5 Cash Management and the Target Cash Balance

Cash is needed to pay for labor and raw materials, to purchase fixed assets, to pay taxes, to service debt, to pay dividends, and so on, but cash itself (and the money in most commercial checking accounts) earns no interest. Thus, the goal of the cash manager is to minimize the cash amount the firm must hold for conducting its normal business activities while continuing to maintain a sufficient cash reserve to (1) take trade discounts, (2) pay promptly and thus maintain its credit rating, and (3) meet any unexpected cash needs. We begin our analysis with a discussion of the traditional reasons for holding cash.

Reasons for Holding Cash

Firms hold cash for two primary reasons:

1. *Transactions, both routine and precautionary.* Cash balances are necessary in business operations. Payments must be made in cash, and receipts are

The *CFO* Cash Management Scorecard

Each year *CFO Magazine* publishes a cash management scorecard, prepared by REL Consultancy Group, based on the 1,000 largest publicly traded U.S. companies. On the one hand, if a company holds more cash than needed to support its operations, its return on invested capital (ROIC) will be dragged down because cash earns a low rate of return. On the other hand, if a company doesn't have enough cash, then it might experience financial distress if there is an unexpected downturn in business. How much cash is enough?

Although the optimum level of cash depends on a company's unique set of circumstances, REL defines industry benchmarks as that quartile of firms in an industry that have the lowest cash/sales ratios—on the theory that these firms have the best cash management procedures. A recent average benchmark cash/sales ratio was 5.6%, whereas the average firm had a ratio of 10.4%. This suggests that many firms had a lot more cash than they actually needed.

It's one thing to talk about reducing cash, but how can a company do it? A good relationship with its banks is one key to keeping low cash levels. Jim Hopwood, treasurer of Wickes, says, "We have a credit revolver if we ever need it." The same is true at Havertys Furniture, where CFO Dennis Fink says that if you have solid bank commitments, "You don't have to worry about predicting short-term fluctuations in cash flow."

Sources: Randy Myers, "Tight Makes Right," *CFO*, December 2008, pp. 64–70; D. M. Katz, "Cash Scorecard: Unleash the Hoards," *CFO.com*, October 17, 2006, **http://www.cfo.com/article.cfm/8048654?f=search**; Randy Myers, "Stuck on Yellow," *CFO*, October 2005, pp. 81–90; and S. L. Mintz, "Lean Green Machine," *CFO*, July 2000, pp. 76–94. For updates, go to **http://ww.cfo.com** and search for "cash management."

deposited in the cash account. Cash balances associated with routine payments and collections are known as **transactions balances**. Cash inflows and outflows are unpredictable, and the degree of predictability varies among firms and industries. Therefore, firms need to hold some cash to meet random, unforeseen fluctuations in inflows and outflows. These "safety stocks" are called **precautionary balances**, and the less predictable the firm's cash flows, the larger such balances should be.

2. *Compensation to banks for providing loans and services.* A bank makes money by lending out funds that have been deposited with it, so the larger its deposits, the better the bank's profit position. If a bank is providing services to a customer then it may require that customer to leave a minimum balance on deposit to help offset the costs of providing those services. Also, banks may require borrowers to hold their transactions deposits at the bank. Both types of deposits are called **compensating balances**. In a 1979 survey, 84.7% of responding companies reported they were required to maintain compensating balances to help pay for bank services; only 13.3% reported paying direct fees for banking services.[10] By 1996, those findings were reversed: Only 28% paid for bank services with compensating balances, while 83% paid direct fees.[11] Although the use of compensating balances to pay for services has declined, these balances improve a firm's relationship with its bank and are still a reason why some companies hold additional cash.

In addition to holding cash for transactions, precautionary, and compensating balances, it is essential that the firm have sufficient cash to take **trade discounts**. Sup-

[10] See Lawrence J. Gitman, E. A. Moses, and I. T. White, "An Assessment of Corporate Cash Management Practices," *Financial Management*, Spring 1979, pp. 32–41.

[11] See Charles E. Maxwell, Lawrence J. Gitman, and Stephanie A. M. Smith, "Working Capital Management and Financial-Service Consumption Preferences of US and Foreign Firms: A Comparison of 1979 and 1996 Preferences," *Financial Practice and Education*, Fall/Winter 1998, pp. 46–52.

pliers frequently offer customers discounts for early payment of bills. As we will see later in this chapter, the cost of not taking discounts is sometimes very high, so firms should have enough cash to permit payment of bills in time to take discounts.

Finally, for a number of reasons firms often hold short-term investments in excess of the cash needed to support operations. We discuss short-term investments later in the chapter.

Self-Test

Why is cash management important?
What are the primary motives for holding cash?

16.6 Cash Management Techniques

In terms of dollar volume, most business is conducted by large firms, many of which operate nationally or globally. They collect cash from many sources and make payments from a number of different cities or even countries. For example, companies such as IBM, General Electric, and Hewlett-Packard have manufacturing plants all around the world, even more sales offices, and bank accounts in virtually every city where they do business. Their collection centers follow sales patterns. However, while some disbursements are made from local offices, most are made in the cities where manufacturing occurs or else from the home office. Thus, a major corporation might have hundreds or even thousands of bank accounts located in cities all over the globe, but there is no reason to think that inflows and outflows will balance in each account. Therefore, a system must be in place to transfer funds from where they come in to where they are needed, to arrange loans to cover net corporate shortfalls, and to invest net corporate surpluses without delay. Some commonly used techniques for accomplishing these tasks are discussed next.[12]

Synchronizing Cash Flow

If you as an individual were to receive income once a year, then you would probably put it in the bank, draw down your account periodically, and have an average balance for the year equal to about half of your annual income. If instead you received income weekly and paid rent, tuition, and other charges on a daily basis, then your average bank balance would still be about half of your periodic receipts and thus only 1/52 as large as if you received income only once annually.

Exactly the same situation holds for businesses: By timing their cash receipts to coincide with their cash outlays, firms can hold their transactions balances to a minimum. Recognizing this fact, firms such as utilities, oil companies, and credit card companies arrange to bill customers—and to pay their own bills—on regular "billing cycles" throughout the month. This **synchronization of cash flows** provides cash when it is needed and thus enables firms to reduce their average cash balances.

Speeding Up the Check-Clearing Process

When a customer writes and mails a check, the funds are not available to the receiving firm until the **check-clearing process** has been completed. First, the check must be delivered through the mail. Checks received from customers in distant cities are especially subject to mail delays.

When a customer's check is written on one bank and a company deposits the check in another bank, the company's bank must verify that the check is valid before

[12]For more information on cash management, see Bruce J. Summers, "Clearing and Payment Systems: The Role of the Central Bank," *Federal Reserve Bulletin*, February 1991, pp. 81–91.

the payee can use those funds. Checks are generally cleared through the Federal Reserve System or through a clearinghouse set up by the banks in a particular city.[13] Before 2004, this process sometimes took 2 to 5 days. But with the passage of a federal law in 2004 known as "Check 21," banks can exchange digital images of checks. This means that most checks now clear in a single day.

Using Float

Float is defined as the difference between the balance shown in a firm's (or individual's) checkbook and the balance on the bank's records. Suppose a firm writes, on average, checks in the amount of $5,000 each day, and suppose it takes 6 days for these checks to clear and be deducted from the firm's bank account. This will cause the firm's own checkbook to show a balance that is $30,000 smaller than the balance on the bank's records; this difference is called **disbursement float**. Now suppose the firm also receives checks in the amount of $5,000 daily but that it loses 4 days while those checks are being deposited and cleared. This will result in $20,000 of **collections float**. In total, the firm's **net float**—the difference between the $30,000 positive disbursement float and the $20,000 negative collections float—will be $10,000. In sum, collections float is bad, disbursement float is good, and positive net float is even better.

Delays that cause float will occur because it takes time for checks to (1) travel through the mail (mail float), (2) be processed by the receiving firm (processing float), and (3) clear through the banking system (clearing, or availability, float). Basically, the size of a firm's net float is a function of its ability to speed up collections on checks it receives and to slow down collections on checks it writes. Efficient firms go to great lengths to speed up the processing of incoming checks, thus putting the funds to work faster, and they try to stretch their own payments out as long as possible, sometimes by disbursing checks from banks in remote locations.

Speeding Up Collections

Two major techniques are used to speed collections and to get funds where they are needed: lockboxes and electronic transfers.

Lockboxes. A **lockbox system** is one of the oldest cash management tools. In a lockbox system, incoming checks are sent to post office boxes rather than to the firm's corporate headquarters. For example, a firm headquartered in New York City might have its West Coast customers send their payments to a post office box in San Francisco, its customers in the Southwest send their checks to Dallas, and so on, rather than having all checks sent to New York City. Several times a day, a local bank will empty the lockbox and deposit the checks into the company's local account. The bank then provides the firm with a daily record of the receipts collected, usually via an electronic data transmission system in a format that permits online updating of the firm's accounts receivable records.

---

[13]For example, suppose a check for $100 is written on Bank A and deposited at Bank B. Bank B will usually contact either the Federal Reserve System or a clearinghouse to which both banks belong. The Fed or the clearinghouse will then verify with Bank A that the check is valid and that the account has sufficient funds to cover the check. Bank A's account with the Fed or the clearinghouse is then reduced by $100, and Bank B's account is increased by $100. Of course, if the check is deposited in the same bank on which it was drawn, that bank merely transfers funds by bookkeeping entries from one depositor to another.

A lockbox system reduces the time required to receive incoming checks, to deposit them, and to get them cleared through the banking system and available for use. Lockbox services can make funds available as many as 2 to 5 days faster than via the "regular" system.

Payment by Wire or Automatic Debit. Firms are increasingly demanding payments of larger bills by wire or by automatic electronic debits. Under an electronic debit system, funds are automatically deducted from one account and added to another. This is, of course, the ultimate in a speeded-up collection process, and computer technology is making such a process increasingly feasible and efficient, even for retail transactions.

Self-Test

What is float? How do firms use float to increase cash management efficiency?
What are some methods firms can use to accelerate receipts?

16.7 Inventory Management

Inventory management techniques are covered in depth in production management courses. Still, financial managers have a responsibility for raising the capital needed to carry inventory and for overseeing the firm's overall profitability, so it is appropriate that we cover the financial aspects of inventory management here.

The twin goals of inventory management are (1) to ensure that the inventories needed to sustain operations are available, but (2) to hold the costs of ordering and carrying inventories to the lowest possible level. While analyzing improvements in the cash conversion cycle, we identified some of the cash flows associated with a reduction in inventory. In addition to the points made earlier, lower inventory levels reduce costs due to storage and handling, insurance, property taxes, spoilage, and obsolescence.

Before the computer age, companies used such simple inventory control techniques as the "red line" system, where a red line was drawn around the inside of a bin holding inventory items; when the actual stock declined to the level where the red line showed, inventory would be reordered. But now computers have taken over, and supply chains have been established that provide inventory items just before they are needed—the *just-in-time* system. For example, consider Trane Corporation, which makes air conditioners and currently uses just-in-time procedures. In the past, Trane produced parts on a steady basis, stored them as inventory, and had them ready whenever the company received an order for a batch of air conditioners. However, the company's inventory eventually covered an area equal to three football fields, and it still could take as long as 15 days to fill an order. To make matters worse, occasionally some of the necessary components simply could not be located; in other instances, the components were located but found to have been damaged from long storage.

Then Trane adopted a new inventory policy—it began producing components only after receiving an order and then sending the parts directly from the machines that make them to the final assembly line. The net effect: Inventories fell nearly 40% even as sales were increasing by 30%.

Such improvements in inventory management can free up considerable amounts of cash. For example, suppose a company has sales of \$120 million and an inventory turnover ratio of 3. This means the company has an inventory level of

$$\begin{aligned}\text{Inventory} &= \text{Sales}/(\text{Inventory turnover ratio})\\ &= \$120/3 = \$40 \text{ million}\end{aligned}$$

If the company can improve its inventory turnover ratio to 4, then its inventory will fall to

$$\text{Inventory} = \$120/4 = \$30 \text{ million}$$

This \$10 million reduction in inventory boosts free cash flow by \$10 million.

Supply Chain Management

Herman Miller Inc. manufactures a wide variety of office furniture, and a typical order from a single customer might require work at five different plants. Each plant uses components from different suppliers, and each plant works on orders for many customers. Imagine all the coordination that is required. The sales force generates the order, the purchasing department orders components from suppliers, and the suppliers must order materials from their own suppliers. The suppliers make and then ship the components to Herman Miller, the factory builds the products, the different products are gathered together to complete the order, and then the order is shipped to the customer. If one part of that process malfunctions, then the order will be delayed, inventory will pile up, extra costs to expedite the order will be incurred, and the customer's goodwill will be damaged, hurting future growth.

To prevent such consequences, many companies employ supply chain management (SCM). The key element in SCM is sharing information all the way back from the retailer where the product is sold, to the company's own plant, then back to the firm's suppliers, and even back to the suppliers' suppliers. SCM requires special computer software, but even more important is that it requires cooperation among the different companies and departments in the supply chain. This culture of open communication is often difficult for many companies, which can be reluctant to divulge operating information. For example, EMC Corp., a manufacturer of data storage systems, has become deeply involved in the design processes and financial controls of its key suppliers. Many of EMC's suppliers were initially wary of these new relationships. However, SCM has been a win–win proposition, with higher profits for both EMC and its suppliers.

The same is true at many other companies. After implementing SCM, Herman Miller was able to reduce its days of inventory on hand by a week and to cut 2 weeks off of delivery times to customers. It was also able to operate its plants at a 20% higher volume without additional capital expenditures, because downtime due to inventory shortages was virtually eliminated. As another example, Heineken USA can now get beer from its Dutch breweries to its customers' shelves in less than 6 weeks, compared with 10 to 12 weeks before implementing SCM. As these and other companies have found, SCM increases free cash flows, and that leads to more profits and higher stock prices.

Sources: Elaine L. Appleton, "Supply Chain Brain," *CFO*, July 1997, pp. 51–54; and Kris Frieswick, "Up Close and Virtual," *CFO*, April 1998, pp. 87–91.

However, there are costs associated with holding too little inventory, and these costs can be severe. If a business lowers its inventories then it must reorder frequently, which increases ordering costs. Even worse, if stocks become depleted then firms can miss out on profitable sales and also suffer lost goodwill, which may lead to lower future sales. Therefore, it is important to have enough inventory on hand to meet customer demands but not so much as to incur the costs we discussed previously. Inventory optimization models have been developed, but the best approach—and the one most firms today are following—is to use supply chain management and monitor the system closely.[14]

Self-Test

What are some costs associated with high inventories? With low inventories?

What is a "supply chain," and how are supply chains related to just-in-time inventory procedures?

A company has $20 million in sales and an inventory turnover ratio of 2.0. If it can reduce its inventory and improve its inventory turnover ratio to 2.5 with no loss in sales, by how much will FCF increase? ($2 million)

[14]For additional insights into the problems of inventory management, see Richard A. Followill, Michael Schellenger, and Patrick H. Marchard, "Economic Order Quantities, Volume Discounts, and Wealth Maximization," *The Financial Review*, February 1990, pp. 143–152.

16.8 Receivables Management

Firms would, in general, rather sell for cash than on credit, but competitive pressures force most firms to offer credit for substantial purchases, especially to other businesses. Thus, goods are shipped, inventories are reduced, and an **account receivable** is created.[15] Eventually, the customer will pay the account, at which time (1) the firm will receive cash and (2) its receivables will decline. Carrying receivables has both direct and indirect costs, but selling on credit also has an important benefit: increased sales.

Receivables management begins with the firm's credit policy, but a monitoring system is also important to keep tabs on whether the terms of credit are being observed. Corrective action is often needed, and the only way to know whether the situation is getting out of hand is with a good receivables control system.[16]

Credit Policy

The success or failure of a business depends primarily on the demand for its products—as a rule, high sales lead to larger profits and a higher stock price. Sales, in turn, depend on a number of factors: some, like the state of the economy, are exogenous, but others are under the firm's control. The major controllable factors are sales prices, product quality, advertising, and the firm's **credit policy**. Credit policy, in turn, consists of the following four variables.

1. *Credit period.* A firm might sell on terms of "net 30," which means that the customer must pay within 30 days.
2. *Discounts.* If the credit terms are stated as "2/10, net 30," then buyers may deduct 2% of the purchase price if payment is made within 10 days; otherwise, the full amount must be paid within 30 days. Thus, these terms allow a discount to be taken.
3. *Credit standards.* How much financial strength must a customer show to qualify for credit? Lower credit standards boost sales, but they also increase bad debts.
4. *Collection policy.* How tough or lax is a company in attempting to collect slow-paying accounts? A tough policy may speed up collections, but it might also anger customers and cause them to take their business elsewhere.

The credit manager is responsible for administering the firm's credit policy. However, because of the pervasive importance of credit, the credit policy itself is normally established by the executive committee, which usually consists of the president plus the vice presidents of finance, marketing, and production.

The Accumulation of Receivables

The total amount of accounts receivable outstanding at any given time is determined by two factors: (1) the credit sales per day and (2) the average length of time it takes to collect cash on accounts receivable:

---

[15]Whenever goods are sold on credit, two accounts are created—an asset item entitled *accounts receivable* appears on the books of the selling firm, and a liability item called *accounts payable* appears on the books of the purchaser. At this point, we are analyzing the transaction from the viewpoint of the seller, so we are concentrating on the variables under its control (i.e., the receivables). We examine the transaction from the viewpoint of the purchaser later in this chapter, where we discuss accounts payable as a source of funds and consider their cost.

[16]For more on credit policy and receivables management, see Shehzad L. Mian and Clifford W. Smith, "Extending Trade Credit and Financing Receivables," *Journal of Applied Corporate Finance*, Spring 1994, pp. 75–84; and Paul D. Adams, Steve B. Wyatt, and Yong H. Kim, "A Contingent Claims Analysis of Trade Credit," *Financial Management*, Autumn 1992, pp. 104–112.

$$\text{Accounts receivable} = \text{Credit sales per day} \times \text{Length of collection period} \quad (16\text{-}5)$$

For example, suppose Boston Lumber Company (BLC), a wholesale distributor of lumber products, opens a warehouse on January 1 and, starting the first day, makes sales of $1,000 each day. For simplicity, we assume that all sales are on credit and that customers are given 10 days to pay. At the end of the first day, accounts receivable will be $1,000; they will rise to $2,000 by the end of the second day; and by January 10, they will have risen to 10($1,000) = $10,000. On January 11, another $1,000 will be added to receivables, but payments for sales made on January 1 will be collected and thus will reduce receivables by $1,000, so total accounts receivable will remain constant at $10,000. Once the firm's operations have stabilized, the following situation will exist:

$$\begin{aligned}\text{Accounts receivable} &= \text{Credit sales per day} \times \text{Length of collection period}\\ &= \$1{,}000 \times 10 \text{ days} = \$10{,}000\end{aligned}$$

If either credit sales or the collection period changes, these changes will be reflected in the accounts receivable balance.

Monitoring the Receivables Position

Both investors and bank loan officers should pay close attention to accounts receivable, because what you see on a financial statement is not necessarily what you end up getting. To see why, consider how the accounting system operates. When a credit sale is made, these events occur: (1) inventories are reduced by the cost of goods sold; (2) accounts receivable are increased by the sales price; and (3) the difference is reported as a profit, which is adjusted for taxes and then added to the previous retained earnings balance. If the sale is for cash, then the cash from the sale has actually been received by the firm and the scenario just described is completely valid. If the sale is on credit, however, then the firm will not receive the cash from the sale unless and until the account is collected. Firms have been known to encourage "sales" to weak customers in order to report high current profits. This could boost the firm's stock price—but only for a short time. Eventually, credit losses will lower earnings, at which time the stock price will fall. This is another example of how differences between a firm's stock price and its intrinsic value can arise, and it is something that security analysts must keep in mind.

An analysis along the lines suggested in the following sections will detect any such questionable practice, and it will also help a firm's management learn of problems that might be arising. Such early detection helps both investors and bankers avoid losses, and it also helps a firm's management maximize intrinsic values.

Days Sales Outstanding (DSO). Suppose Super Sets Inc., a television manufacturer, sells 200,000 television sets a year at a price of $198 each. Assume that all sales are on credit under the terms 2/10, net 30. Finally, assume that 70% of the customers take the discount and pay on Day 10 and that the other 30% pay on Day 30.[17]

---

[17]Unless otherwise noted, we assume throughout that payments are made either on the *last day* for taking discounts or on the *last day* of the credit period. It would be foolish to pay on (say) the 5th day or on the 20th day if the credit terms were 2/10, net 30.

Supply Chain Finance

In our global economy, companies purchase parts and materials from suppliers located all over the world. For small and mid-size suppliers, especially those in less developed economies, selling to international customers can lead to cash flow problems. First, many suppliers have no way of knowing when their invoices have been approved by their customers. Second, they have no way of knowing when they will actually receive payment from their customers. With a 4–5-month lag between the time an order is received and the time the payment occurs, many suppliers resort to expensive local financing that can add as much as 4% to their costs. Even worse, some suppliers go out of business, which reduces competition and ultimately leads to higher prices.

Although most companies now work very hard with their suppliers to improve their supply chain operations, which is at the heart of supply management, a recent poll shows that only 13% actively use supply chain finance (SCF) techniques. However, that figure is likely to rise in the near future. For example, Big Lots joined a Web-based service operated by PrimeRevenue that works like this: First, invoices received by Big Lots are posted to the system as soon as they are approved. The supplier doesn't need specialized software but can check its invoices using a Web browser. Second, the supplier has the option of selling the approved invoices at a discount to financial institutions and banks that have access to the PrimeRevenue network. A further advantage to the supplier is that it receives cash within a day of the invoices' approval. In addition, the effective interest rate built into the discounted price is based on the credit rating of Big Lots, not that of the supplier.

As Big Lots treasurer Jared Poff puts it, this allows vendors to "compete on their ability to make the product and not on their ability to access financing."

Sources: Kate O'Sullivan, "Financing the Chain," *CFO*, February 2007, pp. 46–53.

Super Sets's **days sales outstanding (DSO)**, sometimes called the *average collection period (ACP)*, is 16 days:

$$\text{DSO} = \text{ACP} = 0.7(10 \text{ days}) + 0.3(30 \text{ days}) = 16 \text{ days}$$

Super Sets's *average daily sales (ADS)* is \$108,493:

$$\text{ADS} = \frac{\text{Annual sales}}{365} = \frac{(\text{Units sold})(\text{Sales price})}{365} \quad \text{(16-6)}$$

$$= \frac{200{,}000(\$198)}{365} = \frac{\$39{,}600{,}000}{365} = \$108{,}493$$

Super Sets's accounts receivable—assuming a constant, uniform rate of sales throughout the year—will at any point in time be \$1,735,888:

$$\text{Receivables} = (\text{DSO})\ (\text{ADS}) \quad \text{(16-7)}$$

$$= (\$108{,}493)(16) = \$1{,}735{,}888$$

Note that DSO, or average collection period, is a measure of the average length of time it takes the firm's customers to pay off their credit purchases. Super Sets's DSO is 16 days versus an industry average of 25 days, so either Super Sets has a higher percentage of discount customers or else its credit department is exceptionally good at ensuring prompt payment.

TABLE 16-1 Aging Schedules

AGE OF ACCOUNT (DAYS)	SUPER SETS		WONDER VISION	
	VALUE OF ACCOUNT	PERCENTAGE OF TOTAL VALUE	VALUE OF ACCOUNT	PERCENTAGE OF TOTAL VALUE
0–10	$1,215,122	70%	$ 815,867	47%
11–30	520,766	30	451,331	26
31–45	0	0	260,383	15
46–60	0	0	173,589	10
Over 60	0	0	34,718	2
Total receivables	$1,735,888	100%	$1,735,888	100%

Finally, note that you can derive both the annual sales and the receivables balance from the firm's financial statements, so you can calculate DSO as follows:

$$\text{DSO} = \frac{\text{Receivables}}{\text{Sales per day}} = \frac{\$1{,}735{,}888}{\$108{,}493} = 16 \text{ days}$$

The DSO can also be compared with the firm's own credit terms. For example, suppose Super Sets's DSO had been averaging 35 days. With a 35-day DSO, some customers obviously are taking more than 30 days to pay their bills. In fact, if many customers are paying by Day 10 to take advantage of the discount, then the others must be taking, on average, *much* longer than 35 days. A way to check this possibility is to use an aging schedule, as described next.

Aging Schedules. An **aging schedule** breaks down a firm's receivables by age of account. Table 16-1 shows the December 31, 2009, aging schedules of two television manufacturers, Super Sets and Wonder Vision. Both firms offer the same credit terms, and they have the same total receivables. Super Sets's aging schedule indicates that all of its customers pay on time: 70% pay by Day 10 and 30% pay by Day 30. In contrast, Wonder Vision's schedule, which is more typical, shows that many of its customers are not paying on time: 27% of its receivables are more than 30 days old, even though Wonder Vision's credit terms call for full payment by Day 30.

Aging schedules cannot be constructed from the type of summary data reported in financial statements; rather, they must be developed from the firm's accounts receivable ledger. However, well-run firms have computerized their accounts receivable records, so it is easy to determine the age of each invoice, to sort electronically by age categories, and thus to generate an aging schedule.

Management should constantly monitor both the DSO and the aging schedule to detect any trends, to see how the firm's collections experience compares with its credit terms, and to see how effectively the credit department is operating in comparison with other firms in the industry. If the DSO starts to lengthen or the aging schedule begins to show an increasing percentage of past-due accounts, then the credit manager should examine why these changes are occurring.

Although increases in the DSO and the aging schedule are warning signs, this does not necessarily indicate the firm's credit policy has weakened. If a firm experiences sharp seasonal variations or if it is growing rapidly, then both the aging schedule and the DSO may be distorted. To see this point, note that the DSO is calculated as follows:

$$\text{DSO} = \frac{\text{Accounts receivable}}{\text{Annual Sales}/365}$$

Receivables at any point in time reflect sales in the past 1 or 2 months, but sales as shown in the denominator are for the past 12 months. Therefore, a seasonal increase in sales will increase the numerator more than the denominator and hence will raise the DSO, even if customers continue to pay just as quickly as before. Similar problems arise with the aging schedule, because if sales are rising then the percentage in the 0–10-day category will be high, and the reverse will occur if sales are falling. Therefore, a change in either the DSO or the aging schedule should be taken as a signal to investigate further; it is not necessarily a sign that the firm's credit policy has weakened.

Self-Test

Explain how a new firm's receivables balance is built up over time.

Define days sales outstanding (DSO). What can be learned from it? How is it affected by sales fluctuations?

What is an aging schedule? What can be learned from it? How is it affected by sales fluctuations?

A company has annual sales of $730 million. If its DSO is 35, what is its average accounts receivables balance? ($70 million).

16.9 Accruals and Accounts Payable (Trade Credit)

Recall that net operating working capital is equal to operating current assets minus operating current liabilities. The previous sections discussed the management of operating current assets (cash, inventory, and accounts receivable), and the following sections discuss the two major types of operating current liabilities: accruals and accounts payable.[18]

Accruals

Firms generally pay employees on a weekly, biweekly, or monthly basis, so the balance sheet will typically show some accrued wages. Similarly, the firm's own estimated income taxes, employment and income taxes withheld from employees, and sales taxes collected are generally paid on a weekly, monthly, or quarterly basis. Therefore, the balance sheet will typically show some accrued taxes along with accrued wages.

These **accruals** can be thought of as short-term, interest-free loans from employees and taxing authorities, and they increase automatically (that is, *spontaneously*) as a firm's operations expand. However, a firm cannot ordinarily control its accruals: The timing of wage payments is set by economic forces and industry norms, and tax payment dates are established by law. Thus, firms generally use all the accruals they can, but they have little control over the levels of these accounts.

Accounts Payable (Trade Credit)

Firms generally make purchases from other firms on credit, recording the debt as an *account payable*. Accounts payable, or **trade credit**, is the largest single operating

[18]For more on accounts payable management, see James A. Gentry and Jesus M. De La Garza, "Monitoring Accounts Payables," *Financial Review*, November 1990, pp. 559–576.

current liability, representing about 40% of the current liabilities for an average non-financial corporation. The percentage is somewhat larger for smaller firms: Because small companies often have difficulty obtaining financing from other sources, they rely especially heavily on trade credit.

Trade credit is a spontaneous source of financing in the sense that it arises from ordinary business transactions. For example, suppose a firm makes average purchases of $2,000 a day on terms of net 30, meaning that it must pay for goods 30 days after the invoice date. On average, it will owe 30 times $2,000, or $60,000, to its suppliers. If its sales, and consequently its purchases, were to double, then its accounts payable would also double, to $120,000. So simply by growing, the firm would spontaneously generate an additional $60,000 of financing. Similarly, if the terms under which the firm buys were extended from 30 to 40 days, then its accounts payable would expand from $60,000 to $80,000 even with no growth in sales. Thus, both expanding sales and lengthening the credit period generate additional amounts of financing via trade credit.

The Cost of Trade Credit

Firms that sell on credit have a *credit policy* that includes their *terms of credit*. For example, Microchip Electronics sells on terms of 2/10, net 30: it gives customers a 2% discount if they pay within 10 days of the invoice date, but the full invoice amount is due and payable within 30 days if the discount is not taken.

The "true price" of Microchip's products is the net price, or 0.98 times the list price, because any customer can purchase an item at that price as long as payment is made within 10 days. Now consider Personal Computer Company (PCC), which buys its memory chips from Microchip. One chip is listed at $100, so its "true" price to PCC is $98. Now if PCC wants an additional 20 days of credit beyond the 10-day discount period, it must incur a finance charge of $2 per chip for that credit. Thus, the $100 list price consists of two components:

$$\text{List price} = \$98 \text{ true price} + \$2 \text{ finance charge}$$

The question PCC must ask before it turns down the discount to obtain the additional 20 days of credit is this: Could credit be obtained at a lower cost from a bank or some other lender?

Now assume that PCC buys $11,923,333 of memory chips from Microchip each year at the net, or true, price. This amounts to $11,923,333/365 = $32,666.67 per day. For simplicity, assume that Microchip is PCC's only supplier. If PCC decides not to take the additional 20 days of trade credit—that is, if it pays on the 10th day and takes the discount—then its payables will average 10($32,666.67) = $326,667. Thus, PCC will be receiving $326,667 of credit from Microchip.

Now suppose PCC decides to take the additional 20 days credit and so must pay the full list price. Since PCC will now pay on the 30th day, its accounts payable will increase to 30($32,666.67) = $980,000.[19] Microchip will now be supplying PCC with an additional $980,000 − $326,667 = $653,333 of credit, which PCC could use to build up its cash account, to pay off debt, to expand inventories, or even to extend credit to its own customers, hence increasing its own accounts receivable.

---

[19]A question arises here: Should accounts payable reflect gross purchases or purchases net of discounts? Generally accepted accounting principles permit either treatment if the difference is not material, but if the discount is material then the transaction must be recorded net of discounts, or at "true" prices. Then, the higher payment that results from not taking discounts is reported as an expense called "discounts lost." Therefore, *we show accounts payable net of discounts even if the company does not expect to take discounts.*

Thus the additional trade credit offered by Microchip has a cost: PCC must pay a finance charge equal to the 2% discount it is forgoing. PCC buys $11,923,333 of chips at the true price, so the added finance charge would increase the total cost to $11,923,333/0.98 = $12,166,666. Therefore, the annual financing cost is $12,166,666 – $11,923,333 = $243,333. Dividing the $243,333 financing cost by the $653,333 of additional credit, we calculate the nominal annual cost rate of the additional trade credit to be 37.2%:

$$\text{Nominal annual costs} = \frac{\$243{,}333}{\$653{,}333} = 37.2\%$$

If PCC can borrow from its bank (or some other source) at an interest rate less than 37.2%, then it should take the 2% discount and forgo the additional trade credit.

The following equation can be used to calculate the nominal cost (on an annual basis) of not taking discounts, illustrated with terms of 2/10, net 30:

$$\begin{array}{c}\text{Nominal cost}\\ \text{of trade credit}\end{array} = \text{Cost per period} \times \text{Number of periods per year}$$

$$\begin{array}{c}\text{Nominal cost}\\ \text{of trade credit}\end{array} = \frac{\text{Discount percentage}}{100 - \begin{array}{c}\text{Discount}\\ \text{percentage}\end{array}} \times \frac{365}{\begin{array}{c}\text{Days credit is}\\ \text{outstanding}\end{array} - \begin{array}{c}\text{Discount}\\ \text{period}\end{array}} \tag{16-8}$$

$$= \frac{2}{98} \times \frac{365}{20} = 2.04\% \times 18.25 = 37.2\%$$

The numerator of the first term, Discount percentage, is the cost per dollar of credit, while the denominator, 100 – Discount percentage, represents the funds made available by not taking the discount. Thus, the first term, 2.04%, is the cost per period for the trade credit. The denominator of the second term is the number of days of extra credit obtained by not taking the discount, so the entire second term shows how many times each year the cost is incurred—18.25 times in this example.

This nominal annual cost formula does not consider the compounding of interest. In terms of effective annual interest, the cost of trade credit is even higher:

$$\text{Effective annual rate} = (1.0204)^{18.25} - 1.0 = 1.4459 - 1.0 = 44.6\%$$

Thus, the 37.2% nominal cost calculated with Equation 16-8 actually understates the true cost.

Note, however, that the calculated cost of trade credit can be reduced by paying late. Thus, if PCC could get away with paying in 60 days rather than the specified 30 days, then the effective credit period would become 60 – 10 = 50 days, the number of times the discount would be lost would fall to 365/50 = 7.3, and the nominal cost would drop from 37.2% to 2.04% × 7.3 = 14.9%. Then the effective annual rate would drop from 44.6% to 15.9%:

$$\text{Effective annual rate} = (1.0204)^{7.3} - 1.0 = 1.1589 - 1.0 = 15.9\%$$

In periods of excess capacity, firms may be able to get away with deliberately paying late, or **stretching accounts payable**. However, they will also suffer a variety of problems associated with being a "slow payer." These problems are discussed later in the chapter.

FIGURE 16-7 Varying Credit Terms and Their Associated Costs

See **Ch16 Tool Kit.xls** on the textbook's Web site for details.

	A	B	C	D	E	F
31						
32			Days in year:	365	Cost of additional credit	
33						
34	Credit terms	Discount	Discount period	Net period	Nominal	Effective
35	1/10, net 20	1%	10	20	36.87%	44.32%
36	1/10, net 30	1%	10	30	18.43%	20.13%
37	1/10, net 90	1%	10	90	4.61%	4.69%
38	2/10, net 20	2%	10	20	74.49%	109.05%
39	2/10, net 30	2%	10	30	37.24%	44.59%
40	3/15, net 45	3%	15	45	37.63%	44.86%

The costs of the additional trade credit from forgoing discounts under some other purchase terms are taken from the chapter's *Excel **Tool Kit*** model and shown here as Figure 16-7. As these numbers indicate, the cost of not taking discounts can be substantial.

On the basis of the preceding discussion, trade credit can be divided into two components: (1) **free trade credit**, which involves credit received during the discount period, and (2) **costly trade credit**, which involves credit in excess of the free trade credit and whose cost is an implicit one based on the forgone discounts. *Firms should always use the free component, but they should use the costly component only after analyzing the cost of this capital to make sure it is less than the cost of funds that could be obtained from other sources.* Under the terms of trade found in most industries, the costly component is relatively expensive, so stronger firms generally avoid using it.

Note, though, that firms sometimes offer favorable credit terms in order to stimulate sales. For example, suppose a firm has been selling on terms of 2/10, net 30, with a nominal cost of 37.24%, but a recession has reduced sales and the firm now has excess capacity. It wants to boost the sales of its product without cutting the list price, so it might offer terms of 1/10, net 90, which implies a nominal cost of additional credit of only 4.61%. In this situation, its customers would probably be wise to take the additional credit and reduce their reliance on banks and other lenders. So, turning down discounts is not always a bad decision.

Self-Test

What are accruals? How much control do managers have over accruals?
What is trade credit?
What's the difference between free trade credit and costly trade credit?
How does the cost of costly trade credit generally compare with the cost of short-term bank loans?
A company buys on terms of 2/12, net 28. What is its nominal cost of trade credit? **(46.6%)** The effective cost? **(58.5%)**

16.10 Short-Term Marketable Securities

Short-term marketable securities are held for two separate and distinct purposes: (1) to provide liquidity, as a substitute for cash; and (2) as a nonoperating investment, generally on a temporary basis while awaiting deployment for long-term, permanent investments. Of course, it is difficult to separate these two purposes, because securities held while awaiting reinvestment are available for liquidity purposes.

For updates, see **http://finance.yahoo.com**, *get a quote for MRK, and take a look at its balance sheets.*

Marketable securities typically provide much lower yields than operating assets. For example, in January 2009 Merck held approximately $1.1 billion in short-term marketable securities in addition to $4.4 billion in cash and cash equivalents. Two years earlier, in 2007, it held $2.8 billion of short-term securities plus $5.9 billion of cash and cash equivalents. Why would Merck hold such a large amount of low-yielding assets?

Consider first the *reduction* in cash and securities from 2007 to 2009. At the earlier date, Merck was in the midst of a series of trials over allegations that its drug Vioxx had caused a number of fatal heart attacks. This case was settled in 2008, so the cash and securities it had been holding to cover potential losses could be reduced. This demonstrates one reason why firms sometimes hold what seems to be an excessive amount of cash and securities. Other reasons include needing to pay off maturing bonds or paying for plants under construction.

With regard to operating funds, companies typically lump liquid marketable securities in with currency and bank demand deposits and call the total "cash and cash equivalents." These are the current assets that the firm needs to carry in its operations on an uninterrupted basis. If the company needs to write checks in amounts greater than its demand deposits, it simply makes a phone call to a broker and places a market sell order; the broker in turn will sell the securities, and almost immediately the sale proceeds will be deposited in the firm's bank account. Because cash and most commercial checking accounts yield nothing whereas marketable securities provide at least a modest return, firms choose to hold part of their liquid assets as marketable securities rather than pure cash balances.

Note also that firms' cash and equivalents holdings can be reduced by having unused credit lines with banks. A firm can negotiate a line of credit under which it can borrow immediately if it needs cash for transactions. It can simply call the bank, ask to "take down" a portion of its line, and the bank will immediately deposit funds in its account that can then be used for writing checks.

There are both benefits and costs associated with holding marketable securities. The benefits are twofold: (1) the firm reduces risk and transaction costs, because it won't have to issue securities or borrow as frequently to raise cash; and (2) it will have ready cash to take advantage of bargain purchases or growth opportunities. Funds held for the second reason are called **speculative balances**. The primary disadvantage is that the after-tax return on short-term securities is very low. Thus, firms face a trade-off between benefits and costs.

Recent research supports this trade-off hypothesis as an explanation for firms' cash holdings.[20] Firms with high growth opportunities suffer the most if they don't have ready cash to quickly take advantage of an opportunity, and the data show that these firms do hold relatively high levels of marketable securities. Firms with volatile cash flows are the ones most likely to run low on cash, so they tend to hold high levels of cash. In contrast, cash holdings are less important to large firms with high credit ratings, because they have quick and inexpensive access to capital markets. As expected, such firms hold relatively low levels of cash. Of course, there will always be outliers such as Microsoft, which is large, strong, and cash-rich, but volatile firms with good growth opportunities are still the ones that hold the most marketable securities, on average.

---

[20]See Tim Opler, Lee Pinkowitz, René Stulz, and Rohan Williamson, "The Determinants and Implications of Corporate Cash Holdings," *Journal of Financial Economics*, 1999, pp. 3–46. For additional insights into maturity choice, see Karlyn Mitchell, "The Debt Maturity Choice: An Empirical Investigation," *Journal of Financial Research*, Winter 1993, pp. 309–320.

Self-Test Why might a company hold low-yielding marketable securities when it could earn a much higher return on operating assets?

16.11 Short-Term Financing

The three possible short-term financing policies described earlier in the chapter were distinguished by the relative amounts of short-term debt used under each policy. The aggressive policy called for the greatest use of short-term debt, and the conservative policy called for using the least; maturity matching fell in between. Although short-term credit is generally riskier than long-term credit, using short-term funds does have some significant advantages. The pros and cons of short-term financing are considered in this section.

Advantages of Short-Term Financing

First, a short-term loan can be obtained much faster than long-term credit. Lenders will insist on a more thorough financial examination before extending long-term credit, and the loan agreement will have to be spelled out in considerable detail because a lot can happen during the life of a 10- to 20-year loan. Therefore, if funds are needed in a hurry, the firm should look to the short-term markets.

Second, if its needs for funds are seasonal or cyclical, then a firm may not want to commit itself to long-term debt. There are three reasons for this: (1) Flotation costs are higher for long-term debt than for short-term credit. (2) Although long-term debt can be repaid early (provided the loan agreement includes a prepayment provision), prepayment penalties can be expensive. Accordingly, if a firm thinks its need for funds will diminish in the near future, it should choose short-term debt. (3) Long-term loan agreements always contain provisions, or covenants, that constrain the firm's future actions. Short-term credit agreements are generally less restrictive.

The third advantage is that, because the yield curve is normally upward sloping, interest rates are generally lower on short-term debt. Thus, under normal conditions, interest costs at the time the funds are obtained will be lower if the firm borrows on a short-term rather than a long-term basis.

Disadvantages of Short-Term Debt

Even though short-term rates are often lower than long-term rates, using short-term credit is riskier for two reasons: (1) If a firm borrows on a long-term basis then its interest costs will be relatively stable over time, but if it uses short-term credit then its interest expense will fluctuate widely, at times going quite high. For example, the rate banks charged large corporations for short-term debt more than tripled over a 2-year period in the 1980s, rising from 6.25% to 21%. Many firms that had borrowed heavily on a short-term basis simply could not meet their rising interest costs; as a result, bankruptcies hit record levels during that period. (2) If a firm borrows heavily on a short-term basis, a temporary recession may render it unable to repay this debt. If the borrower is in a weak financial position then the lender may not extend the loan, which could force the firm into bankruptcy.

Self-Test What are the advantages and disadvantages of short-term debt compared with long-term debt?

16.12 Short-Term Bank Loans

Loans from commercial banks generally appear on balance sheets as notes payable. A bank's importance is actually greater than it appears from the dollar amounts shown on balance sheets because banks provide *nonspontaneous* funds. As a firm's financing needs increase, it requests additional funds from its bank. If the request is denied, the firm may be forced to abandon attractive growth opportunities. The key features of bank loans are discussed in the following paragraphs.

Maturity

Although banks do make longer-term loans, *the bulk of their lending is on a short-term basis*—about two-thirds of all bank loans mature in a year or less. Bank loans to businesses are frequently written as 90-day notes, so the loan must be repaid or renewed at the end of 90 days. Of course, if a borrower's financial position has deteriorated then the bank may refuse to renew the loan. This can mean serious trouble for the borrower.

Promissory Notes

When a bank loan is approved, the agreement is executed by signing a **promissory note**. The note specifies (1) the amount borrowed, (2) the interest rate, (3) the repayment schedule, which can call for either a lump sum or a series of installments, (4) any collateral that might have to be put up as security for the loan, and (5) any other terms and conditions to which the bank and the borrower have agreed. When the note is signed, the bank credits the borrower's checking account with the funds; hence both cash and notes payable increase on the borrower's balance sheet.

Compensating Balances

Banks sometimes require borrowers to maintain an average demand deposit (checking account) balance of 10% to 20% of the loan's face amount. This is called a compensating balance, and such balances raise the effective interest rate on the loans. For example, if a firm needs $80,000 to pay off outstanding obligations but it must maintain a 20% compensating balance, then it must borrow $100,000 to obtain a usable $80,000. If the stated annual interest rate is 8%, the effective cost is actually 10%: $8,000 interest divided by $80,000 of usable funds equals 10%.[21]

As we noted earlier in the chapter, recent surveys indicate that compensating balances are much less common now than earlier. In fact, compensating balances are now illegal in many states. Despite this trend, some small banks in states where compensating balances are legal still require their customers to maintain them.

Informal Line of Credit

A **line of credit** is an informal agreement between a bank and a borrower indicating the maximum credit the bank will extend to the borrower. For example, on December 31, a bank loan officer might indicate to a financial manager that the bank regards the firm as being "good" for up to $80,000 during the forthcoming year, provided the borrower's financial condition does not deteriorate. If on January 10 the financial manager signs a 90-day promissory note for $15,000, this would be called "taking down" $15,000 of the total line of credit. This amount would be credited to the firm's checking account at the bank, and the firm could borrow additional amounts up to a total of $80,000 outstanding at any one time.

[21]Note, however, that the compensating balance may be set as a minimum monthly *average*, and if the firm would maintain this average anyway then the compensating balance requirement would not raise the effective interest rate. Also, note that these loan compensating balances are *added to* any compensating balances that the firm's bank may require for services performed, such as clearing checks.

Revolving Credit Agreement

A **revolving credit agreement** is a formal line of credit often used by large firms. To illustrate, suppose in 2010 Texas Petroleum Company negotiated a revolving credit agreement for $100 million with a group of banks. The banks were formally committed for 4 years to lend the firm up to $100 million if the funds were needed. Texas Petroleum, in turn, paid an annual commitment fee of 0.25% on the unused balance of the commitment to compensate the banks for making the commitment. Thus, if Texas Petroleum did not take down any of the $100 million commitment during a year, it would still be required to pay a $250,000 annual fee, normally in monthly installments of $20,833.33. If it borrowed $50 million on the first day of the agreement, then the unused portion of the line of credit would fall to $50 million and the annual fee would fall to $125,000. Of course, interest would also have to be paid on the money Texas Petroleum actually borrowed. As a general rule, the interest rate on "revolvers" is pegged to the London Interbank Offered Rate (LIBOR), the T-bill rate, or some other market rate, so the cost of the loan varies over time as interest rates change. The interest that Texas Petroleum must pay was set at the prime lending rate plus 1.0%.

Observe that a revolving credit agreement is similar to an informal line of credit but has an important difference: The bank has a *legal obligation* to honor a revolving credit agreement, and it receives a commitment fee. Neither the legal obligation nor the fee exists under the informal line of credit.

Often a line of credit will have a **cleanup clause** that requires the borrower to reduce the loan balance to zero at least once a year. Keep in mind that a line of credit typically is designed to help finance seasonal or cyclical peaks in operations, not as a source of permanent capital. For example, our cash budget for Educational Products Corporation showed negative flows from July through September but positive flows from October through December. Also, the cumulative net cash flow goes positive in November, indicating that the firm could pay off its loan at that time. If the cumulative flows were always negative, this would indicate that the firm was using its credit lines as a permanent source of financing.

Costs of Bank Loans

The costs of bank loans vary for different types of borrowers at any given point in time and for all borrowers over time. Interest rates are higher for riskier borrowers, and rates are also higher on smaller loans because of the fixed costs involved in making and servicing loans. If a firm can qualify as a "prime credit" because of its size and financial strength, it can borrow at the **prime rate**, which at one time was the lowest rate banks charged. Rates on other loans are generally scaled up from the prime rate. Loans to large, strong customers are made at rates tied to LIBOR; and the costs of such loans are generally well below prime:

Rates on June 28, 2009	
Prime	3.25%
1-Year LIBOR	1.520%

The rate to smaller, riskier borrowers is generally stated something like "prime plus 1.0%"; but for a larger borrower it is generally stated as something like "LIBOR plus 1.5%."

Bank rates vary widely over time depending on economic conditions and Federal Reserve policy. When the economy is weak, loan demand is usually slack, inflation is low, and the Fed makes plenty of money available to the system. As a result, rates on all types of loans are relatively low. Conversely, when the economy is booming, loan demand is typically strong, the Fed restricts the money supply to fight inflation, and the result is high interest rates. As an indication of the kinds of fluctuations that can occur, the prime rate during 1980 rose from 11% to 21% in just four months; during 1994, it rose from 6% to 9%.

Calculating Banks' Interest Charges: Regular (or "Simple") Interest. Banks calculate interest in several different ways. In this section we explain the procedure used for most business loans. For illustration purposes, we assume a loan of $10,000 at the prime rate, currently 3.25%, with a 360-day year. Interest must be paid monthly, and the principal is payable "on demand" if and when the bank wants to end the loan. Such a loan is called a **regular** (or **simple**) **interest** loan.

We begin by dividing the nominal interest rate (3.25% in this case) by 360 to obtain the rate per day. This rate is expressed as a *decimal fraction*, not as a percentage:

$$\text{Simple interest rate per day} = \frac{\text{Nominal rate}}{\text{Days in year}}$$
$$= 0.0325/360 = 0.000090278$$

To find the monthly interest payment, the daily rate is multiplied by the amount of the loan, then by the number of days during the payment period. For our illustrative loan, the daily interest charge would be $0.902777778, and the total for a 30-day month would be $27.08:

$$\text{Interest charge for month} = (\text{Rate per day})(\text{Amount of loan})(\text{Days in month})$$
$$= (0.000090278)(\$10{,}000)(30 \text{ days}) = \$27.08$$

The *effective interest rate* on a loan depends on how frequently interest must be paid—the more frequently interest is paid, the higher the effective rate. If interest is paid once per year, then the nominal rate is also the effective rate. However, if interest must be paid monthly, then the effective rate is $(1 + 0.0325/12)^{12} - 1 = 3.2989\%$.

Calculating Banks' Interest Charges: Add-on Interest. Banks and other lenders typically use **add-on interest** for automobiles and other types of installment loans. The term *add-on* means that the interest is calculated and then added to the amount borrowed to determine the loan's face value. To illustrate, suppose you borrow $10,000 on an add-on basis at a nominal rate of 7.25% to buy a car, with the loan to be repaid in 12 monthly installments. At a 7.25% add-on rate, you would make total interest payments of $10,000(0.0725) = $725. However, since the loan is paid off in monthly installments, you would have the use of the full $10,000 for only the first month; then the outstanding balance would decline until, during the last month, only 1/12 of the original loan was still outstanding. Thus, you would be paying $725 for the use of only about half the loan's face amount, since the average usable funds would be only about $5,000. Therefore, we can calculate the approximate annual rate as 14.5%:

$$\text{Approximate annual rate}_{\text{Add-on}} = \frac{\text{Interest paid}}{(\text{Amount received})/2} = \frac{\$725}{\$10{,}000/2} = 14.5\% \qquad (16\text{-}9)$$

The annual percentage rate (APR) the bank would provide to the borrower would be 13.12%, and the true effective annual rate would be 13.94%.[22] Both of these rates are much higher than the nominal 7.25%.

Self-Test

What is a promissory note, and what are some terms that are normally included in promissory notes?
What is a line of credit? A revolving credit agreement?
What's the difference between simple interest and add-on interest?
Explain how a firm that expects to need funds during the coming year might make sure the that needed funds will be available.
How does the cost of costly trade credit generally compare with the cost of short-term bank loans?
If a firm borrowed $500,000 at a rate of 10% simple interest with monthly interest payments and a 365-day year, what would be the required interest payment for a 30-day month? **($4,109.59)** If interest must be paid monthly, what would be the effective annual rate? **(10.47%)**
If this loan had been made on a 10% add-on basis, payable in 12 end-of-month installments, what would be the monthly payment amount? **($45,833.33)** What is the annual percentage rate? **(17.97%)** The effective annual rate? **(19.53%)**

WWW

For updates on the outstanding balances of commercial paper, go to **http://www.federalreserve.gov/releases** *and check out the daily releases for Commercial Paper and the weekly releases for Assets and Liabilities of Commercial Banks in the United States.*

16.13 Commercial Paper

Commercial paper is a type of unsecured promissory note issued by large, strong firms and sold primarily to other business firms, to insurance companies, to pension funds, to money market mutual funds, and to banks. In March 2009, there was approximately $1.4 trillion of commercial paper outstanding, versus nearly $1.5 trillion of commercial and industrial bank loans. Most, but not all, commercial paper outstanding is issued by financial institutions.

Maturity and Cost

Maturities of commercial paper generally vary from 1 day to 9 months, with an average of about 5 months.[23] The interest rate on commercial paper fluctuates with supply and demand conditions—it is determined in the marketplace, varying daily as conditions change. Recently, commercial paper rates have ranged from 1.5 to 3.5 percentage points below the stated prime rate and up to half of a percentage point above the T-bill rate. For example, in March 2009, the average rate on 3-month commercial paper was 0.60%, the prime rate was 3.25%, and the 3-month T-bill rate was 0.22%.

WWW

For current rates, see **http://www.federalreserve.gov/releases** *and look at the Daily Releases for Selected Interest Rates.*

Use of Commercial Paper

The use of commercial paper is restricted to a comparatively small number of very large concerns that are exceptionally good credit risks. Dealers prefer to handle the

[22]To find the annual percentage rate and the effective rate on an add-on loan, we first find the payment per month, $10,725/12 = $893.75. With a financial calculator, enter N = 12, PV = 10000, PMT = −893.75, and FV = 0; then press I/YR to obtain 1.093585%. This is a monthly rate, so multiply by 12 to get 13.12%, which is the APR the bank would report to the borrower. The effective annual rate would then be (1.010936) − 1 = 13.94%, quite a bit above the APR.

[23]The maximum maturity without SEC registration is 270 days. Also, commercial paper can be sold only to "sophisticated" investors; otherwise, SEC registration would be required even for maturities of 270 days or less.

paper of firms whose net worth is $100 million or more and whose annual borrowing exceeds $10 million. One potential problem with commercial paper is that a debtor who is in temporary financial difficulty may receive little help because commercial paper dealings are generally less personal than are bank relationships. Thus, banks are generally more able and willing to help a good customer weather a temporary storm than is a commercial paper dealer. On the other hand, using commercial paper permits a corporation to tap a wide range of credit sources, including financial institutions outside its own area and industrial corporations across the country, and this can reduce interest costs.

Self-Test

What is commercial paper?
What types of companies can use commercial paper to meet their short-term financing needs?
How does the cost of commercial paper compare with the cost of short-term bank loans? With the cost of Treasury bills?

16.14 Use of Security in Short-Term Financing

Thus far, we have not addressed the question of whether or not short-term loans should be secured. Commercial paper is never secured, but other types of loans can be secured if this is deemed necessary or desirable. Other things held constant, it is better to borrow on an unsecured basis, since the bookkeeping costs of **secured loans** are often high. However, firms often find that they can borrow only if they put up some type of collateral to protect the lender or that, by using security, they can borrow at a much lower rate.

Several different kinds of collateral can be employed, including marketable stocks or bonds, land or buildings, equipment, inventory, and accounts receivable. Marketable securities make excellent collateral, but few firms that need loans also hold portfolios of stocks and bonds. Similarly, real property (land and buildings) and equipment are good forms of collateral, but they are generally used as security for long-term loans rather than for working capital loans. Therefore, most secured short-term business borrowing involves the use of accounts receivable and inventories as collateral.

For a more detailed discussion of secured financing, see **Web Extension 16A** *on the textbook's Web site.*

To understand the use of security, consider the case of a Chicago hardware dealer who wanted to modernize and expand his store. He requested a $200,000 bank loan. After examining the business's financial statements, his bank indicated that it would lend him a maximum of $100,000 and that the effective interest rate would be 9%. The owner had a substantial personal portfolio of stocks, and he offered to put up $300,000 of high-quality stocks to support the $200,000 loan. The bank then granted the full $200,000 loan at the prime rate of 3.25%. The store owner might also have used his inventories or receivables as security for the loan, but processing costs would have been high.[24]

Self-Test

What is a secured loan?
What are some types of current assets that are pledged as security for short-term loans?

[24]The term "asset-based financing" is often used as a synonym for "secured financing." In recent years, accounts receivable have been used as security for long-term bonds, permitting corporations to borrow from lenders such as pension funds rather than just from banks and other traditional short-term lenders.

Summary

This chapter discussed working capital management and short-term financing. The key concepts covered are listed below.

- **Working capital** refers to current assets used in operations, and **net working capital** is defined as current assets minus all current liabilities. **Net operating working capital** is defined as operating current assets minus operating current liabilities.
- Under a **relaxed working capital policy**, a firm would hold relatively large amounts of each type of current asset. Under a **restricted working capital policy**, the firm would hold minimal amounts of these items.
- A **moderate** approach to short-term financing involves matching, to the extent possible, the maturities of assets and liabilities, so that temporary current operating assets are financed with short-term debt and permanent current operating assets and fixed assets are financed with long-term debt or equity. Under an **aggressive** approach, some permanent current operating assets, and perhaps even some fixed assets, are financed with short-term debt. A **conservative** approach would be to use long-term sources to finance all permanent operating capital and some of the temporary current operating assets.
- **Permanent current operating assets** are the operating current assets the firm holds even during slack times, whereas **temporary current operating assets** are the additional operating current assets needed during seasonal or cyclical peaks. The methods used to finance permanent and temporary current operating assets define the firm's **short-term financing policy**.
- The **inventory conversion period** is the average time required to convert materials into finished goods and then to sell those goods:

$$\text{Inventory conversion period} = \text{Inventory} \div \text{Cost of goods sold per day}$$

- The **average collection period** is the average length of time required to convert the firm's receivables into cash—that is, to collect cash following a sale:

$$\text{Average collection period} = \text{DSO} = \text{Receivables} \div (\text{Sales}/365)$$

- The **payables deferral period** is the average length of time between the purchase of materials and labor and the payment of cash for them:

$$\text{Payables deferral period} = \text{Payables} \div \text{Cost of goods sold per day}$$

- The **cash conversion cycle (CCC)** is the length of time between the firm's actual cash expenditures to pay for productive resources (materials and labor) and its own cash receipts from the sale of products (that is, the length of time between paying for labor and materials and collecting on receivables):

$$\begin{matrix}\text{Cash} \\ \text{conversion} \\ \text{cycle}\end{matrix} = \begin{matrix}\text{Inventory} \\ \text{conversion} \\ \text{period}\end{matrix} + \begin{matrix}\text{Average} \\ \text{collection} \\ \text{period}\end{matrix} - \begin{matrix}\text{Payables} \\ \text{deferral} \\ \text{period}\end{matrix}$$

- A **cash budget** is a schedule showing projected cash inflows and outflows over some period. The cash budget is used to predict cash surpluses and deficits, and it is the primary cash management planning tool.
- The **primary goal of cash management** is to minimize the amount of cash the firm must hold for conducting its normal business activities while at the same

time maintaining a sufficient cash reserve to take discounts, pay bills promptly, and meet any unexpected cash needs.

- The **transactions balance** is the cash necessary to conduct routine day-to-day business; **precautionary balances** are cash reserves held to meet random, unforeseen needs. A **compensating balance** is a minimum checking account balance that a bank requires as compensation either for services provided or as part of a loan agreement.
- The twin goals of **inventory management** are (1) to ensure that the inventories needed to sustain operations are available, but (2) to hold the costs of ordering and carrying inventories to the lowest possible level.
- When a firm sells goods to a customer on credit, an **account receivable** is created.
- A firm can use an **aging schedule** and the **days sales outstanding (DSO)** to monitor its receivables balance and to help avoid an increase in bad debts.
- A firm's **credit policy** consists of four elements: (1) credit period, (2) discounts given for early payment, (3) credit standards, and (4) collection policy.
- **Accounts payable**, or **trade credit**, arises spontaneously as a result of credit purchases. Firms should use all the **free trade credit** they can obtain, but they should use **costly trade credit** only if it is less expensive than other forms of short-term debt. Suppliers often offer discounts to customers who pay within a stated period. The following equation may be used to calculate the nominal cost, on an annual basis, of not taking such discounts:

$$\text{Nominal annual cost of trade credit} = \frac{\text{Discount percentage}}{100 - \text{Discount percentage}} \times \frac{365}{\text{Days credit is outstanding} - \text{Discount period}}$$

- The advantages of short-term credit are (1) the **speed** with which short-term loans can be arranged, (2) increased **flexibility**, and (3) generally **lower interest rates** than with long-term credit. The principal disadvantage of short-term credit is the **extra risk** the borrower must bear because (1) the lender can demand payment on short notice, and (2) the cost of the loan will increase if interest rates rise.
- **Bank loans** are an important source of short-term credit. When a bank loan is approved, a **promissory note** is signed. It specifies: (1) the amount borrowed, (2) the percentage interest rate, (3) the repayment schedule, (4) the collateral, and (5) any other conditions to which the parties have agreed.
- Banks sometimes require borrowers to maintain **compensating balances**, which are deposit requirements set at between 10% and 20% of the loan amount. Compensating balances raise the effective interest rate on bank loans.
- A **line of credit** is an informal agreement between the bank and the borrower indicating the maximum amount of credit the bank will extend to the borrower.
- A **revolving credit agreement** is a formal line of credit often used by large firms; it involves a **commitment fee**.
- A **simple interest** loan is one in which interest must be paid monthly and the principal is payable "on demand" if and when the bank wants to end the loan.
- An **add-on interest loan** is one in which interest is calculated and added to the funds received to determine the face amount of the installment loan.
- **Commercial paper** is unsecured short-term debt issued by large, financially strong corporations. Although the cost of commercial paper is lower than the cost of bank loans, it can be used only by large firms with exceptionally strong credit ratings.

- Sometimes a borrower will find it is necessary to borrow on a **secured basis**, in which case the borrower pledges assets such as real estate, securities, equipment, inventories, or accounts receivable as collateral for the loan. For a more detailed discussion of secured financing, see ***Web Extension 16A.***

Questions

(16–1) Define each of the following terms:

a. Working capital; net working capital; net operating working capital
b. Relaxed policy; restricted policy; moderate policy
c. Permanent current operating assets; temporary current operating assets
d. Moderate (maturity matching) financing policy; aggressive financing policy; conservative financing policy
e. Inventory conversion period; average collection period; payables deferral period; cash conversion cycle
f. Cash budget; target cash balance
g. Transactions balances; compensating balances; precautionary balances
h. Trade discounts
i. Credit policy; credit period; credit standards; collection policy; cash discounts
j. Account receivable; days sales outstanding; aging schedule
k. Accruals; trade credit
l. Stretching accounts payable; free trade credit; costly trade credit
m. Promissory note; line of credit; revolving credit agreement
n. Commercial paper; secured loan

(16–2) What are the two principal reasons for holding cash? Can a firm estimate its target cash balance by summing the cash held to satisfy each of the two reasons?

(16–3) Is it true that, when one firm sells to another on credit, the seller records the transaction as an account receivable while the buyer records it as an account payable and that, disregarding discounts, the receivable typically exceeds the payable by the amount of profit on the sale?

(16–4) What are the four elements of a firm's credit policy? To what extent can firms set their own credit policies as opposed to accepting policies that are dictated by its competitors?

(16–5) What are the advantages of matching the maturities of assets and liabilities? What are the disadvantages?

(16–6) From the standpoint of the borrower, is long-term or short-term credit riskier? Explain. Would it ever make sense to borrow on a short-term basis if short-term rates were above long-term rates?

(16–7) Discuss this statement: "Firms can control their accruals within fairly wide limits."

(16–8) Is it true that most firms are able to obtain some free trade credit and that additional trade credit is often available, but at a cost? Explain.

(16–9) What kinds of firms use commercial paper?

Self-Test Problems

Solutions Appear in Appendix A

(ST–1) Working Capital Policy

The Calgary Company is attempting to establish a current assets policy. Fixed assets are $600,000, and the firm plans to maintain a 50% debt-to-assets ratio. Calgary has no operating current liabilities. The interest rate is 10% on all debt. Three alternative current asset policies are under consideration: 40%, 50%, and 60% of projected sales. The company expects to earn 15% before interest and taxes on sales of $3 million. Calgary's effective federal-plus-state tax rate is 40%. What is the expected return on equity under each asset policy?

(ST–2) Current Asset Financing

Vanderheiden Press Inc. and the Herrenhouse Publishing Company had the following balance sheets as of December 31, 2010 (thousands of dollars):

	Vanderheiden Press	Herrenhouse Publishing
Current assets	$100,000	$ 80,000
Fixed assets (net)	100,000	120,000
Total assets	$200,000	$200,000
Current liabilities	$ 20,000	$ 80,000
Long-term debt	80,000	20,000
Common stock	50,000	50,000
Retained earnings	50,000	50,000
Total liabilities and equity	$200,000	$200,000

Earnings before interest and taxes for both firms are $30 million, and the effective federal-plus-state tax rate is 40%.

a. What is the return on equity for each firm if the interest rate on current liabilities is 10% and the rate on long-term debt is 13%?

b. Assume that the short-term rate rises to 20%, that the rate on new long-term debt rises to 16%, and that the rate on existing long-term debt remains unchanged. What would be the return on equity for Vanderheiden Press and Herrenhouse Publishing under these conditions?

c. Which company is in a riskier position? Why?

Problems

Answers Appear in Appendix B

Easy Problems 1–5

(16–1) Cash Management

Williams & Sons last year reported sales of $10 million and an inventory turnover ratio of 2. The company is now adopting a new inventory system. If the new system is able to reduce the firm's inventory level and increase the firm's inventory turnover ratio to 5 while maintaining the same level of sales, how much cash will be freed up?

(16–2) Receivables Investment

Medwig Corporation has a DSO of 17 days. The company averages $3,500 in credit sales each day. What is the company's average accounts receivable?

(16–3) Cost of Trade Credit

What is the nominal and effective cost of trade credit under the credit terms of 3/15, net 30?

(16–4) Cost of Trade Credit

A large retailer obtains merchandise under the credit terms of 1/15, net 45, but routinely takes 60 days to pay its bills. (Because the retailer is an important customer, suppliers allow the firm to stretch its credit terms.) What is the retailer's effective cost of trade credit?

(16–5) Accounts Payable

A chain of appliance stores, APP Corporation, purchases inventory with a net price of $500,000 each day. The company purchases the inventory under the credit terms of 2/15, net 40. APP always takes the discount but takes the full 15 days to pay its bills. What is the average accounts payable for APP?

INTERMEDIATE PROBLEMS 6–12

(16–6) Receivables Investment

McDowell Industries sells on terms of 3/10, net 30. Total sales for the year are $912,500. Forty percent of customers pay on the 10th day and take discounts; the other 60% pay, on average, 40 days after their purchases.

a. What is the days sales outstanding?
b. What is the average amount of receivables?
c. What would happen to average receivables if McDowell toughened its collection policy with the result that all nondiscount customers paid on the 30th day?

(16–7) Cost of Trade Credit

Calculate the nominal annual cost of nonfree trade credit under each of the following terms. Assume that payment is made either on the discount date or on the due date.

a. 1/15, net 20
b. 2/10, net 60
c. 3/10, net 45
d. 2/10, net 45
e. 2/15, net 40

(16–8) Cost of Trade Credit

a. If a firm buys under terms of 3/15, net 45, but actually pays on the 20th day and *still takes the discount*, what is the nominal cost of its nonfree trade credit?
b. Does it receive more or less credit than it would if it paid within 15 days?

(16–9) Cost of Trade Credit

Grunewald Industries sells on terms of 2/10, net 40. Gross sales last year were $4,562,500 and accounts receivable averaged $437,500. Half of Grunewald's customers paid on the 10th day and took discounts. What are the nominal and effective costs of trade credit to Grunewald's nondiscount customers? (*Hint:* Calculate sales/day based on a 365-day year, then calculate average receivables of discount customers, and then find the DSO for the nondiscount customers.)

(16–10) Effective Cost of Trade Credit

The D.J. Masson Corporation needs to raise $500,000 for 1 year to supply working capital to a new store. Masson buys from its suppliers on terms of 3/10, net 90, and it currently pays on the 10th day and takes discounts. However, it could forgo the discounts, pay on the 90th day, and thereby obtain the needed $500,000 in the form of costly trade credit. What is the effective annual interest rate of this trade credit?

(16–11) Cash Conversion Cycle

The Zocco Corporation has an inventory conversion period of 60 days, an average collection period of 38 days, and a payables deferral period of 30 days. Assume that cost of goods sold is 75% of sales.

a. What is the length of the firm's cash conversion cycle?
b. If Zocco's annual sales are $3,421,875 and all sales are on credit, what is the firm's investment in accounts receivable?
c. How many times per year does Zocco turn over its inventory?

(16–12)
Working Capital Cash Flow Cycle

The Christie Corporation is trying to determine the effect of its inventory turnover ratio and days sales outstanding (DSO) on its cash flow cycle. Christie's sales last year (all on credit) were $150,000, and it earned a net profit of 6%, or $9,000. It turned over its inventory 7.5 times during the year, and its DSO was 36.5 days. Its annual cost of goods sold was $121,667. The firm had fixed assets totaling $35,000. Christie's payables deferral period is 40 days.
a. Calculate Christie's cash conversion cycle.
b. Assuming Christie holds negligible amounts of cash and marketable securities, calculate its total assets turnover and ROA.
c. Suppose Christie's managers believe the annual inventory turnover can be raised to 9 times without affecting sales. What would Christie's cash conversion cycle, total assets turnover, and ROA have been if the inventory turnover had been 9 for the year?

CHALLENGING PROBLEMS
13–17

(16–13)
Working Capital Policy

The Rentz Corporation is attempting to determine the optimal level of current assets for the coming year. Management expects sales to increase to approximately $2 million as a result of an asset expansion presently being undertaken. Fixed assets total $1 million, and the firm wishes to maintain a 60% debt ratio. Rentz's interest cost is currently 8% on both short-term and longer-term debt (both of which the firm uses in its permanent capital structure). Three alternatives regarding the projected current asset level are available to the firm: (1) a tight policy requiring current assets of only 45% of projected sales, (2) a moderate policy of 50% of sales in current assets, and (3) a relaxed policy requiring current assets of 60% of sales. The firm expects to generate earnings before interest and taxes at a rate of 12% on total sales.
a. What is the expected return on equity under each current asset level? (Assume a 40% effective federal-plus-state tax rate.)
b. In this problem, we have assumed that the level of expected sales is independent of current asset policy. Is this a valid assumption?
c. How would the overall riskiness of the firm vary under each policy?

(16–14)
Cash Budgeting

Dorothy Koehl recently leased space in the Southside Mall and opened a new business, Koehl's Doll Shop. Business has been good, but Koehl has frequently run out of cash. This has necessitated late payment on certain orders, which is beginning to cause a problem with suppliers. Koehl plans to borrow from the bank to have cash ready as needed, but first she needs a forecast of just how much she should borrow. Accordingly, she has asked you to prepare a cash budget for the critical period around Christmas, when needs will be especially high.

Sales are made on a cash basis only. Koehl's purchases must be paid for during the following month. Koehl pays herself a salary of $4,800 per month, and the rent is $2,000 per month. In addition, she must make a tax payment of $12,000 in December. The current cash on hand (on December 1) is $400, but Koehl has agreed to maintain an average bank balance of $6,000—this is her target cash balance. (Disregard cash in the till, which is insignificant because Koehl keeps only a small amount on hand in order to lessen the chances of robbery.)

The estimated sales and purchases for December, January, and February are shown below. Purchases during November amounted to $140,000.

	Sales	Purchases
December	$160,000	$40,000
January	40,000	40,000
February	60,000	40,000

a. Prepare a cash budget for December, January, and February.
b. Now suppose that Koehl starts selling on a credit basis on December 1, giving customers 30 days to pay. All customers accept these terms, and all other facts in the problem are unchanged. What would the company's loan requirements be at the end of December in this case? (*Hint:* The calculations required to answer this question are minimal.)

(16–15) Cash Discounts

Suppose a firm makes purchases of $3.65 million per year under terms of 2/10, net 30, and takes discounts.

a. What is the average amount of accounts payable net of discounts? (Assume the $3.65 million of purchases is net of discounts—that is, gross purchases are $3,724,489.80, discounts are $74,489.80, and net purchases are $3.65 million.)
b. Is there a cost of the trade credit the firm uses?
c. If the firm did not take discounts but did pay on the due date, what would be its average payables and the cost of this nonfree trade credit?
d. What would be the firm's cost of not taking discounts if it could stretch its payments to 40 days?

(16–16) Trade Credit

The Thompson Corporation projects an increase in sales from $1.5 million to $2 million, but it needs an additional $300,000 of current assets to support this expansion. Thompson can finance the expansion by no longer taking discounts, thus increasing accounts payable. Thompson purchases under terms of 2/10, net 30, but it can delay payment for an additional 35 days—paying in 65 days and thus becoming 35 days past due—without a penalty because its suppliers currently have excess capacity. What is the effective, or equivalent, annual cost of the trade credit?

(16–17) Bank Financing

The Raattama Corporation had sales of $3.5 million last year, and it earned a 5% return (after taxes) on sales. Recently, the company has fallen behind in its accounts payable. Although its terms of purchase are net 30 days, its accounts payable represent 60 days' purchases. The company's treasurer is seeking to increase bank borrowings in order to become current in meeting its trade obligations (that is, to have 30 days' payables outstanding). The company's balance sheet is as follows (in thousands of dollars):

Cash	$ 100	Accounts payable	$ 600
Accounts receivable	300	Bank loans	700
Inventory	1,400	Accruals	200
Current assets	$1,800	Current liabilities	$1,500
Land and buildings	600	Mortgage on real estate	700
Equipment	600	Common stock, $0.10 par	300
		Retained earnings	500
Total assets	$3,000	Total liabilities and equity	$3,000

a. How much bank financing is needed to eliminate the past-due accounts payable?
b. Assume that the bank will lend the firm the amount calculated in part a. The terms of the loan offered are 8%, simple interest, and the bank uses a 360-day year for the interest calculation. What is the interest charge for one month? (Assume there are 30 days in a month.)
c. Now ignore part b and assume that the bank will lend the firm the amount calculated in part a. The terms of the loan are 7.5%, add-on interest, to be repaid in 12 monthly installments.
   1. What is the total loan amount?
   2. What are the monthly installments?
   3. What is the APR of the loan?
   4. What is the effective rate of the loan?
d. Would you, as a bank loan officer, make this loan? Why or why not?

Spreadsheet Problem

(16-18) Build a Model: Cash Budgeting

resource

Start with the partial model in the file ***Ch16 P18 Build a Model.xls*** on the textbook's Web site. Helen Bowers, owner of Helen's Fashion Designs, is planning to request a line of credit from her bank. She has prepared the following sales forecasts for parts of 2011 and 2012:

	Sales	Labor and Raw Materials
May 2011	$180,000	$ 90,000
June	180,000	90,000
July	360,000	126,000
August	540,000	882,000
September	720,000	306,000
October	360,000	234,000
November	360,000	162,000
December	90,000	90,000
January 2012	180,000	NA

Estimates obtained from the credit and collection department are as follows: collections within the month of sale, 10%; collections during the month following the sale, 75%; collections the second month following the sale, 15%. Payments for labor and raw materials are typically made during the month following the one in which these costs were incurred. Total costs for labor and raw materials are estimated for each month as shown in the table.

General and administrative salaries will amount to approximately $27,000 a month; lease payments under long-term lease contracts will be $9,000 a month; depreciation charges will be $36,000 a month; miscellaneous expenses will be $2,700 a month; income tax payments of $63,000 will be due in both September and December; and a progress payment of $180,000 on a new design studio must be paid in October. Cash on hand on July 1 will amount to $132,000, and a minimum cash balance of $90,000 will be maintained throughout the cash budget period.

a. Prepare a monthly cash budget for the last 6 months of 2011.
b. Prepare an estimate of the required financing (or excess funds)—that is, the amount of money Bowers will need to borrow (or will have available to invest)—for each month during that period.

c. Assume that receipts from sales come in uniformly during the month (i.e., cash receipts come in at the rate of 1/30 each day) but that all outflows are paid on the 5th of the month. Will this have an effect on the cash budget—in other words, would the cash budget you have prepared be valid under these assumptions? If not, what can be done to make a valid estimate of peak financing requirements? No calculations are required, although calculations can be used to illustrate the effects.

d. Bowers produces on a seasonal basis, just ahead of sales. Without making any calculations, discuss how the company's current ratio and debt ratio would vary during the year assuming all financial requirements were met by short-term bank loans. Could changes in these ratios affect the firm's ability to obtain bank credit?

e. If its customers began to pay late, this would slow down collections and thus increase the required loan amount. Also, if sales dropped off, this would have an effect on the required loan amount. Perform a sensitivity analysis that shows the effects of these two factors on the maximum loan requirement.

Mini Case

Dan Barnes, financial manager of Ski Equipment Inc. (SKI), is excited but apprehensive. The company's founder recently sold his 51% controlling block of stock to Kent Koren, who is a big fan of EVA (Economic Value Added). EVA is found by taking the net operating profit after taxes (NOPAT) and then subtracting the dollar cost of all the capital the firm uses:

$$\begin{aligned} \text{EVA} &= \text{NOPAT} - \text{Capital costs} \\ &= \text{EBIT}(1 - \text{T}) - \text{WACC}(\text{Total capital employed}) \end{aligned}$$

If EVA is positive then the firm's management is creating value. On the other hand, if EVA is negative, then the firm is not covering its cost of capital and stockholders' value is being eroded. Koren rewards managers handsomely if they create value, but those whose operations produce negative EVAs are soon looking for work. Koren frequently points out that if a company could generate its current level of sales with fewer assets, it would need less capital. This would, other things held constant, lower capital costs and increase its EVA.

Shortly after taking control of SKI, Kent Koren met with SKI's senior executives to tell them of his plans for the company. First, he presented some EVA data that convinced everyone that SKI had not been creating value in recent years. He then stated, in no uncertain terms, that this situation must change. He noted that SKI's designs of skis, boots, and clothing are acclaimed throughout the industry but claimed that something was seriously amiss elsewhere in the company. Costs are too high, prices are too low, or the company employs too much capital, and Koren wants SKI's managers to correct the problem—or else.

Barnes has long felt that SKI's working capital situation should be studied. The company may have the optimal amounts of cash, securities, receivables, and inventories, but it may also have too much or too little of these items. In the past, the production manager resisted Barnes's efforts to question his holdings of raw materials, the marketing manager resisted questions about finished goods, the sales staff resisted questions about credit policy (which affects accounts receivable), and the treasurer did not want to talk about her cash and securities balances. Koren's speech made it clear that such resistance would no longer be tolerated.

Barnes also knows that decisions about working capital cannot be made in a vacuum. For example, if inventories could be lowered without adversely affecting operations, then less capital would be required, the dollar cost of capital would decline, and EVA would increase. However, lower raw materials inventories might lead to production slowdowns and higher costs, and lower finished goods inventories might lead to the loss of profitable sales. So, before inventories are changed, it will be necessary to study operating as well as financial effects. The situation is the same with regard to cash and receivables. Barnes begins by collecting the ratios shown below. (The partial cash budget shown after the ratios is used later in this mini case.)

	SKI	Industry
Current	1.75	2.25
Quick	0.92	1.16
Total liabilities/assets	58.76%	50.00%
Turnover of cash and securities	16.67	22.22
Days sales outstanding (365-day basis)	45.63	32.00
Inventory turnover	6.00	8.00
Fixed assets turnover	7.75	13.220
Total assets turnover	2.08	3.00
Profit margin on sales	2.07%	3.50%
Return on equity (ROE)	10.45%	21.00%
Payables deferral period	30.00	33.00

	Cash Budget (Thousands of Dollars)	Nov	Dec	Jan	Feb	Mar	Apr
	Sales Forecast						
(1)	Sales (gross)	$71,218.00	$68,212.00	$65,213.00	$52,475.00	$42,909.00	$30,524.00
	Collections						
(2)	During month of sale: (0.2)(0.98)(month's sales)			12,781.75	10,285.10		
(3)	During first month after sale: (0.7)(previous month's sales)			47,748.40	45,649.10		
(4)	During second month after sale: (0.1)(sales 2 months ago)			7,121.80	6,821.20		
(5)	Total collections (Lines 2 + 3 + 4)			$67,651.95	$62,755.40		
	Purchases						
(6)	(0.85)(forecasted sales 2 months from now)		$44,603.75	$36,472.65	$25,945.40		
	Payments						
(7)	Payments (1-month lag)			44,603.75	36,472.65		
(8)	Wages and salaries			6,690.56	5,470.90		
(9)	Rent			2,500.00	2,500.00		
(10)	Taxes						
(11)	Total payments			$53,794.31	$44,443.55		
	NCFs						
(12)	Cash on hand at start of forecast			$ 3,000.00			
(13)	NCF: Coll. − Pmts. = Line 5 − Line 11			$13,857.64	$18,311.85		
(14)	Cum NCF: Prior + this mos. NCF			$16,857.64	$ 35169.49		
	Cash Surplus (or Loan Requirement)						
(15)	Target cash balance			1,500.00	1,500.00		
(16)	Surplus cash or loan needed			$15,357.64	$33,669.49		

a. Barnes plans to use the preceding ratios as the starting point for discussions with SKI's operating executives. He wants everyone to think about the pros and cons of changing each type of current asset and how changes would interact to affect profits and EVA. Based on the data, does SKI seem to be following a relaxed, moderate, or restricted working capital policy?
b. How can one distinguish between a relaxed but rational working capital policy and a situation in which a firm simply has excessive current assets because it is inefficient? Does SKI's working capital policy seem appropriate?
c. Calculate the firm's cash conversion cycle given that annual sales are $660,000 and cost of goods sold represents 90% of sales. Assume a 365-day year.
d. What might SKI do to reduce its cash without harming operations? In an attempt to better understand SKI's cash position, Barnes developed a cash budget. Data for the first 2 months of the year are shown above. (Note that Barnes's preliminary cash budget does not account for interest income or interest expense.) He has the figures for the other months, but they are not shown.
e. Should depreciation expense be explicitly included in the cash budget? Why or why not?
f. In his preliminary cash budget, Barnes has assumed that all sales are collected and thus that SKI has no bad debts. Is this realistic? If not, how would bad debts be dealt with in a cash budgeting sense? (*Hint:* Bad debts will affect collections but not purchases.)
g. Barnes's cash budget for the entire year, although not given here, is based heavily on his forecast for monthly sales. Sales are expected to be extremely low between May and September but then to increase dramatically in the fall and winter. November is typically the firm's best month, when SKI ships equipment to retailers for the holiday season. Barnes's forecasted cash budget indicates that the company's cash holdings will exceed the targeted cash balance every month except for October and November, when shipments will be high but collections will not be coming in until later. Based on the ratios shown earlier, does it appear that SKI's target cash balance is appropriate? In addition to possibly lowering the target cash balance, what actions might SKI take to better improve its cash management policies, and how might that affect its EVA?
h. What reasons might SKI have for maintaining a relatively high amount of cash?
i. Is there any reason to think that SKI may be holding too much inventory? If so, how would that affect EVA and ROE?
j. If the company reduces its inventory without adversely affecting sales, what effect should this have on the company's cash position (1) in the short run and (2) in the long run? Explain in terms of the cash budget and the balance sheet.
k. Barnes knows that SKI sells on the same credit terms as other firms in its industry. Use the ratios presented earlier to explain whether SKI's customers pay more or less promptly than those of its competitors. If there are differences, does that suggest SKI should tighten or loosen its credit policy? What four variables make up a firm's credit policy, and in what direction should each be changed by SKI?
l. Does SKI face any risks if it tightens its credit policy?
m. If the company reduces its DSO without seriously affecting sales, what effect would this have on its cash position (1) in the short run and (2) in the long run? Answer in terms of the cash budget and the balance sheet. What effect should this have on EVA in the long run?

In addition to improving the management of its current assets, SKI is also reviewing the ways in which it finances its current assets. With this concern in mind, Barnes is also trying to answer the following questions.

n. Is it likely that SKI could make significantly greater use of accruals?
o. Assume that SKI purchases $200,000 (net of discounts) of materials on terms of 1/10, net 30, but that it can get away with paying on the 40th day if it chooses not to take discounts. How much free trade credit can the company get from its equipment supplier, how much costly trade credit can it get, and what is the nominal annual interest rate of the costly credit? Should SKI take discounts?
p. SKI tries to match the maturity of its assets and liabilities. Describe how SKI could adopt either a more aggressive or a more conservative financing policy.
q. What are the advantages and disadvantages of using short-term debt as a source of financing?
r. Would it be feasible for SKI to finance with commercial paper?

Selected Additional Cases

The following cases from Textchoice, *Cengage Learning's online case library, cover many of the concepts discussed in this chapter and are available at* **http://www.textchoice2.com**.

Klein-Brigham Series:
Case 29, "Office Mates, Inc.," which illustrates how changes in current asset policy affect expected profitability and risk; Case 32, "Alpine Wear, Inc.," which illustrates the mechanics of the cash budget and the rationale behind its use; Case 50, "Toy World, Inc.," and Case 66, "Sorenson Stove Company," which deal with cash budgeting; Case 33, "Upscale Toddlers, Inc.," which deals with credit policy changes; and Case 34, "Texas Rose Company," which focuses on receivables management.

Brigham-Buzzard Series:
Case 11, "Powerline Network Corporation (Working Capital Management)."

CHAPTER 17
Multinational Financial Management*

The United States has had plenty of company in the global economic crisis. According to the International Monetary Fund (IMF), 2008 was a terrible year globally. World output (measured by real GDP) averaged 4% growth per year from 1999 to 2007 but grew by only 3.2% in 2008. Most of the 2008 growth was due to the BRIC countries (Brazil, Russia, India, and China), which averaged almost 7% growth. In contrast, the U.S. economy grew by only 1.1% in 2008.

But as bad as 2008 was, the IMF predicted a much worse 2009: the world's real GDP was forecast to fall by 1.3%, making this the first year since World War II to exhibit worldwide contraction. The IMF predicts positive growth in 2009 for some countries (including Qatar, China, and India), but 78 of 182 countries it tracks are predicted to have declines in real GDP, including the following:

Country	2009 (Predicted) Change in Real GDP
United States	−2.8%
Germany	−5.6
Japan	−6.2
Brazil	−1.3
Russia	−6.0
Botswana	−10.4
Iceland	−10.6
Latvia	−12.0

The IMF predicts that it will be 2011 before the world economy returns to its 2008 level and that the United States won't make up its lost ground until 2012.

According to the United Nations, corporations retrenched by cutting their foreign direct investments (such as factories, warehouses, and retail operations in foreign countries) by 54% in the first quarter of 2009. Cross-border mergers and acquisitions dropped by a whopping 77% in the same period.

Is this retrenching short-sighted? Foreign operations are risky, but that is where the IMF predicts the most economic growth. As you read this chapter, think about the risks and rewards of international business ventures.

Sources: International Monetary Fund, World Economic Outlook, *April 2009,* **http://www.imf.org/external/pubs/ft/weo/2009/01/pdf/text.pdf**; *Laurence Chandy, Geoffrey Gertz, and Johannes Linn, "Tracking the Global Financial Crisis: An Analysis of the IMF's World Economic Outlook," Wolfensohn Center for Development at Brookings, May 2009; and UNCTAD, "Global Flows Halved in 1st Quarter of 2009," press release, June 24, 2009.*

*Earlier editions of this chapter benefited from the help of Professor Roy Crum of the University of Florida and Subu Vemkataraman of Morgan Stanley.

Corporate Valuation in a Global Context

The intrinsic value of a firm is determined by the size, timing, and risk of its expected future free cash flows (FCF). This is true for foreign as well as domestic operations, but the FCF of a foreign operation is affected by exchange rates, cultural differences, and the host country's regulatory environment. In addition, global financial markets and political risk can affect the cost of capital.

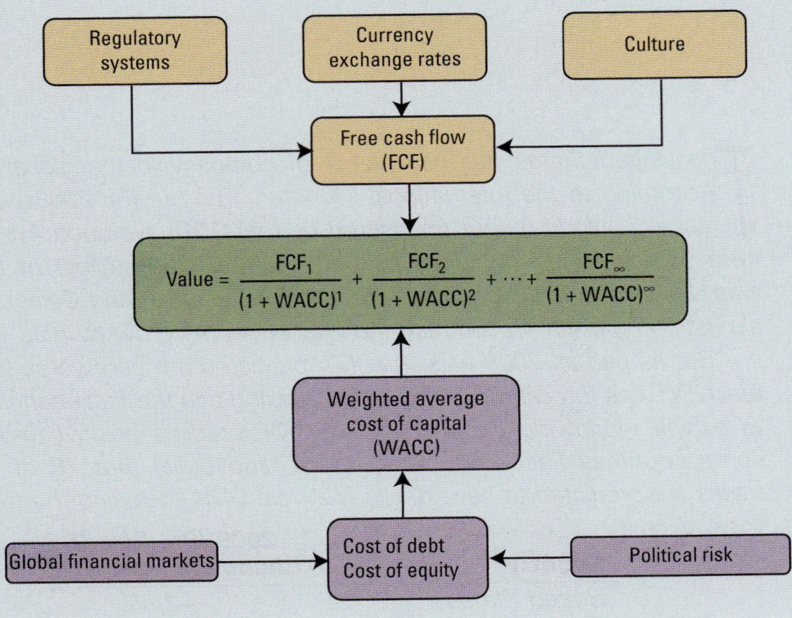

The textbook's Web site contains an Excel file *that will guide you through the chapter's calculations. The file for this chapter is* **Ch17 Tool Kit.xls**, *and we encourage you to open the file and follow along as you read the chapter.*

Managers of multinational companies must deal with a wide range of issues that are not present when a company operates in a single country. In this chapter, we highlight the key differences between multinational and domestic corporations, and we discuss the effects these differences have on the financial management of multinational businesses.

17.1 Multinational, or Global, Corporations

The terms **multinational corporations**, **transnational corporations**, and **global corporations** are used to describe firms that operate in an integrated fashion in a number of countries. Rather than merely buying resources from and selling goods to foreign nations, multinational firms often make direct investments in fully integrated operations, from extraction of raw materials, through the manufacturing process, and to distribution to consumers throughout the world. Today, multinational corporate networks control a large and growing share of the world's technological, marketing, and productive resources.

Companies "go global" for many reasons, including the following.

1. *To broaden their markets.* After a company has saturated its home market, growth opportunities are often better in foreign markets. Thus, such homegrown firms as Coca-Cola and McDonald's are aggressively expanding into overseas markets,

and foreign firms such as Sony and Toshiba now dominate the U.S. consumer electronics market.

2. *To seek raw materials.* Many U.S. oil companies, such as ExxonMobil, have major subsidiaries around the world to ensure access to the basic resources needed to sustain the companies' primary business lines.
3. *To seek new technology.* No single nation holds a commanding advantage in all technologies, so companies scour the globe for leading scientific and design ideas. For example, Xerox has introduced more than 80 different office copiers in the United States that were engineered and built by its Japanese joint venture, Fuji Xerox.
4. *To seek production efficiency.* Companies in high-cost countries are shifting production to low-cost regions. For example, GE has production and assembly plants in Mexico, South Korea, and Singapore; Japanese manufacturers are shifting some of their production to lower-cost countries in the Pacific Rim.
5. *To avoid political and regulatory hurdles.* For example, when Germany's BASF launched biotechnology research at home, it confronted legal and political challenges from the environmentally conscious Green movement. In response, BASF shifted its cancer and immune system research to two laboratories in the Boston suburbs. This location is attractive not only because of its large number of engineers and scientists but also because the Boston area has resolved many controversies involving safety, animal rights, and the environment.
6. *To diversify.* By establishing worldwide production facilities and markets, firms can cushion the impact of adverse economic trends in any single country. In general, geographic diversification helps because the economic ups and downs of different countries are not perfectly correlated.

Interesting reports about the effect of trade on the U.S. economy can be found on the United States Trade Representative's home page at **http://www.ustr.gov**.

Self-Test

What is a multinational corporation?
Why do companies "go global"?

17.2 Multinational versus Domestic Financial Management

In theory, the concepts and procedures discussed in earlier chapters are valid for both domestic and multinational operations. However, six major factors distinguish financial management in firms operating entirely within a single country from that of firms operating globally.

1. *Different currency denominations.* Cash flows in various parts of a multinational corporate system will be denominated in different currencies. Hence, the effects of exchange rates must be addressed in all financial analyses.
2. *Economic and legal ramifications.* Each country has its own unique economic and legal systems, and these differences can cause significant problems when a corporation tries to coordinate and control its worldwide operations. For example, differences in tax laws among countries can cause a given economic transaction to have strikingly different after-tax consequences, depending on where the transaction occurs. Similarly, differences in legal systems of host nations, such as the Common Law of Great Britain versus the French Civil Law, complicate matters ranging from the simple recording of business transactions to the role played by the judiciary in resolving conflicts. Such differences can restrict multinational corporations' flexibility in deploying resources and can even make procedures that are required in one part of the company illegal in another part. These differences also make it difficult for executives trained in one country to move easily to another.

3. *Language differences*. The ability to communicate is critical in all business transactions, and here U.S. citizens are often at a disadvantage because they are generally fluent only in English, whereas European and Japanese businesspeople are usually fluent in several languages, including English.
4. *Cultural differences*. Even within geographic regions that are considered relatively homogeneous, different countries have unique cultural heritages that shape values and influence the conduct of business. Multinational corporations find that matters such as defining the appropriate goals of the firm, attitudes toward risk, dealings with employees, and the ability to curtail unprofitable operations vary dramatically from one country to the next.
5. *Role of governments*. In a foreign country, the terms under which companies compete, the actions that must be taken or avoided, and the terms of trade on various transactions often are determined not in the marketplace but by direct negotiation between host governments and multinational corporations.
6. *Political risk*. A nation might place constraints on the transfer of corporate resources or even expropriate assets within its boundaries. This is political risk, and it varies from country to country. Another aspect of political risk is terrorism against U.S. firms or executives. For example, U.S. and Japanese executives are at risk of being kidnapped in Mexico and several South American countries.

These factors complicate financial management, and they increase the risks faced by multinational firms. However, the prospects for high returns and better diversification make it worthwhile for firms to accept these risks and learn how to manage them.

Self-Test

Identify and briefly discuss six major factors that complicate financial management in multinational firms.

17.3 Exchange Rates

WWW

The Bloomberg World Currency Values site provides up-to-the-minute foreign currency values versus the U.S. dollar. The site can be accessed at **http://www.bloomberg.com/markets/currencies/fxc.html**.

An **exchange rate** specifies the number of units of a given currency that can be purchased with one unit of another currency. Exchange rates appear daily in the financial sections of newspapers, such as *The Wall Street Journal*, and on financial Web sites, such as **http://www.bloomberg.com.** The values shown in Column 1 of Table 17-1 are the number of U.S. dollars required to purchase one unit of a foreign currency; this is called a **direct quotation.** Direct quotations have a dollar sign in their quotation and state the number of dollars per foreign currency unit, such as dollars per euro. Thus, the direct U.S. dollar quotation for the euro is $1.3276, because one euro could be bought for 1.3276 dollars.

The exchange rates given in Column 2 represent the number of units of a foreign currency that can be purchased for one U.S. dollar; these are called **indirect quotations.** Indirect quotations often begin with the foreign currency's equivalent to the dollar sign and express the foreign currency per dollar, such as euros per dollar. Thus, the indirect quotation for the euro is €0.7532. (The "€" stands for *euro*, and it is analogous to the symbol "$.")

Normal practice in currency trading centers is to use the indirect quotations (Column 2) for all currencies other than British pounds and euros, for which the direct quotations are given. Thus, we speak of the pound as "selling at 1.4915 dollars, or at $1.4915," and the euro as "selling at $1.3276." For all other currencies, the normal convention is to use indirect quotations. For example, for the Japanese yen, we would quote the dollar as "being at ¥98.8600," where the "¥" stands for *yen*. This conven-

TABLE 17-1 Selected Exchange Rates

	DIRECT QUOTATION: U.S. DOLLARS REQUIRED TO BUY ONE UNIT OF FOREIGN CURRENCY (1)	INDIRECT QUOTATION: NUMBER OF UNITS OF FOREIGN CURRENCY PER U.S. DOLLAR (2)
Canadian dollar	0.8238	1.2139
Japanese yen	0.0101	98.8600
Mexican peso	0.0758	13.1978
Swiss franc	0.8795	1.1370
U.K. (British) pound	1.4915	0.6705
Euro	1.3276	0.7532

Note: The financial press usually quotes British pounds and euros as direct quotations, so Column 2 equals 1.0 divided by Column 1 for these currencies. The financial press usually quotes all other currencies as indirect quotations, so Column 1 equals 1.0 divided by Column 2 for these currencies.

Source: The Wall Street Journal, **http://online.wsj.com**; quotes for April 14, 2009.

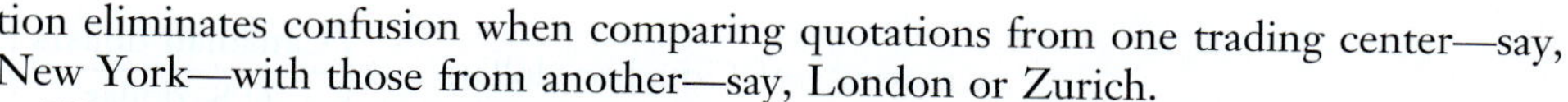

tion eliminates confusion when comparing quotations from one trading center—say, New York—with those from another—say, London or Zurich.

See **Ch17 Tool Kit.xls** *on the textbook's Web site for all calculations.*

We can use the data in Table 17-1 to show how to work with exchange rates. Suppose a tourist flies from New York to London, then to Paris, and then on to Geneva. She then flies to Montreal, and finally back to New York. Her tour includes lodging, food, and transportation, but she must pay for any other expenses. When she arrives at London's Heathrow Airport, she goes to the bank to check the foreign exchange listings. The rate she observes for U.S. dollars is \$1.4915, which means that £1 will cost \$1.4915. Assume that she exchanges \$3,000. How many pounds will she get?

$$\text{Pounds} = \frac{\text{Dollars}}{\text{Dollars/pound}}$$
$$= \frac{\$3,000}{\$1.4915 \text{ per pound}} = £2,011.40$$

She then enjoys a week's vacation in London, ending with £1,000.

After taking a train under the Channel to France, she realizes that she needs to exchange her 1,000 remaining pounds for euros. However, what she sees on the board is the direct quotation for dollars per pound and the direct quotation for dollars per euro. The exchange rate between any two currencies other than dollars is called a **cross rate.** Cross rates are actually calculated on the basis of various currencies relative to the U.S. dollar. For example, the cross rate between British pounds and euros is computed as follows:

$$\text{Cross rate of euros per pound} = \frac{\text{Dollars/Pound}}{\text{Dollars/Euro}} = \frac{\text{Euros}}{\text{Pound}}$$
$$= \frac{\$1.4915 \text{ per pound}}{\$1.3276 \text{ per euro}} = 1.1235 \text{ euros per pound}$$

She would receive 1.1235 euros for every British pound, so she would receive 1,123.50 euros = (1.1235 euros/pound)(1,000 pounds).

She has 800 euros remaining when she finishes touring in France and arrives in Geneva. She again needs to determine a cross rate, this time between euros and Swiss francs. The quotes she sees, as shown in Table 17-1, are a direct quote for euros ($1.3276 per euro) and an indirect quote for Swiss francs (SFr 1.1370 per dollar). To find the cross rate for Swiss francs per euro, she makes the following calculation:

$$\begin{aligned}\text{Cross rate of Swiss francs per euro} &= \left(\frac{\text{Swiss francs}}{\text{Dollar}}\right)\left(\frac{\text{Dollars}}{\text{Euro}}\right)\\ &= (\text{SFr } 1.1370 \text{ per dollar})(\$1.3276 \text{ per euro})\\ &= 1.5095 \text{ Swiss francs per euro}\end{aligned}$$

For a nice currency calculator to determine the exchange rate between any two currencies, see **http://finance.yahoo.com/currency**.

Therefore, for every euro she would receive 1.5095 Swiss francs, so she would receive 1,207.60 Swiss francs = (1.5095 Swiss francs per euro)(800 euros).

She has 500 Swiss francs remaining when she leaves Geneva and arrives in Montreal. She again needs to determine a cross rate, this time between Swiss francs and Canadian dollars. The quotes she sees, as shown in Table 17-1, are an indirect quote for Swiss francs (SFr 1.1370 per dollar) and an indirect quote for Canadian dollars (1.2139 Canadian dollars per U.S. dollar). To find the cross rate for Canadian dollars per Swiss franc, she makes the following calculation:

$$\begin{aligned}\text{Cross rate of Canadian dollars per Swiss franc} &= \frac{\left(\dfrac{\text{Canadian dollars}}{\text{U.S. dollar}}\right)}{\left(\dfrac{\text{Swiss francs}}{\text{U.S. dollar}}\right)}\\ &= \frac{1.2139 \text{ Canadian dollars per U.S. dollar}}{\text{SFr } 1.1370 \text{ per U.S. dollar}}\\ &= 1.0676 \text{ Canadian dollars per Swiss franc}\end{aligned}$$

Therefore, she would receive 533.80 Canadian dollars = (1.0676 Canadian dollars per Swiss franc)(500 Swiss francs).

After leaving Montreal and arriving at New York, she has 100 Canadian dollars remaining. She sees the indirect quote for Canadian dollars and converts the 100 Canadian dollars to U.S. dollars as follows:

$$100 \text{ Canadian dollars} = \frac{100 \text{ Canadian dollars}}{1.2139 \text{ Canadian dollars per U.S. dollar}} = \$82.38$$

In this example, we made three assumptions. First, we assumed that our traveler had to calculate all of the cross rates. For retail transactions, it is customary to display the cross rates directly instead of a series of dollar rates. Second, we assumed that exchange rates remain constant over time. Actually, exchange rates vary every day, often dramatically. We will have more to say about exchange rate fluctuations in the next section. Finally, we assumed that there were no transaction costs involved in exchanging currencies. In reality, small retail exchange transactions such as those in our example usually involve fixed and/or sliding-scale fees that can easily consume 5% or more of the transaction amount. However, credit card purchases minimize these fees.

Major business publications, such as *The Wall Street Journal*, and Web sites, such as **http://www.bloomberg.com**, regularly report cross rates among key currencies. A set of cross rates is given in Table 17-2. When examining the table, note the following points.

TABLE 17-2 Key Currency Cross Rates

	DOLLAR	EURO	POUND	SFRANC	PESO	YEN	CdnDlr
Canada	1.2139	1.6116	1.8105	1.0676	0.0920	0.0123	—
Japan	98.8600	131.2465	147.4497	86.9481	7.4906	—	81.4400
Mexico	13.1978	17.5214	19.6845	11.6076	—	0.1335	10.8722
Switzerland	1.1370	1.5095	1.6958	—	0.0862	0.0115	0.9367
United Kingdom	0.6705	0.8901	—	0.5897	0.0508	0.0068	0.5523
Euro	0.7532	—	1.1235	0.6625	0.0571	0.0076	0.6205
United States	—	1.3276	1.4915	0.8795	0.0758	0.0101	0.8238

Source: Derived from Table 17-1; quotes for April 14, 2009.

1. Column 1 gives indirect quotes for dollars—that is, units of a foreign currency that can be bought with one U.S. dollar. Examples: $1 will buy 0.7532 euro or 1.1370 Swiss francs. This is consistent with Table 17-1, Column 2.
2. Other columns show number of units of other currencies that can be bought with one pound, one Swiss franc, etc. For example, the euro column shows that 1 euro will buy 1.6116 Canadian dollars, 131.2465 Japanese yen, or 1.3276 U.S. dollars.
3. The rows show direct quotes—that is, the number of units of the currency of the country listed in the left column required to buy one unit of the currency listed in the top row. The bottom row is particularly important for U.S. companies, as it shows the direct quotes for the U.S. dollar. This row is consistent with Column 1 of Table 17-1.
4. Observe that the values on the bottom row of Table 17-2 are reciprocals of the corresponding values in the first column. For example, the U.K. row in the first column shows 0.6705 pound per dollar, and the pound column in the bottom row shows 1/0.6705 = 1.4915 dollars per pound.
5. By reading down the euro column, you can see that 1 euro is worth 1.5095 Swiss francs. This is the same cross rate that we calculated for the U.S. tourist in our example.

The tie-in with the dollar ensures that all currencies are related to one another in a consistent manner—if this consistency did not exist, then currency traders could profit by buying undervalued and selling overvalued currencies. This process, known as *arbitrage*, works to bring about an equilibrium wherein the same relationship described earlier exists. Currency traders are constantly operating in the market, seeking small inconsistencies from which they can profit. The traders' existence enables the rest of us to assume that currency markets are in equilibrium and that, at any moment in time, cross rates are all internally consistent.[1]

[1]For more discussion of exchange rates, see Jongmoo Jay Choi and Anita Mehra Prasad, "Exchange Risk Sensitivity and Its Determinants: A Firm and Industry Analysis of U.S. Multinationals," *Financial Management*, Autumn 1995, pp. 77–88; Jerry A. Hammer, "Hedging Performance and Hedging Objectives: Tests of New Performance Measures in the Foreign Currency Market," *Journal of Financial Research*, Winter 1990, pp. 307–323; and William C. Hunter and Stephen G. Timme, "A Stochastic Dominance Approach to Evaluating Foreign Exchange Hedging Strategies," *Financial Management*, Autumn 1992, pp. 104–112.

Self-Test

What is an exchange rate?
Explain the difference between direct and indirect quotations.
What is a cross rate?
Assume that the indirect quote is for 10.0 Mexican pesos per U.S. dollar. What is the direct quote for dollars per peso? **(0.10 dollars/peso)**
Assume that the indirect quote is for 115 Japanese yen per U.S. dollar and that the direct quote is for 1.25 U.S. dollars per euro. What is the yen per euro exchange rate? **(143.75 yen per euro)**

17.4 Exchange Rates and International Trade

Just as the demand for consumer goods such as Tommy Hilfiger clothing and Nike shoes changes over time, so does the demand for currency. One factor affecting currency demand is the balance of trade between two countries. For example, U.S. importers must buy yen to pay for Japanese goods, whereas Japanese importers must buy U.S. dollars to pay for U.S. goods. If U.S. imports from Japan were to exceed U.S. exports to Japan, then the U.S. would have a **trade deficit** with Japan, and there would be a greater demand for yen than for dollars. Capital movements also affect currency demand. For example, suppose interest rates in the United States were higher than those in Japan. To take advantage of high U.S. interest rates, Japanese banks, corporations, and sophisticated individuals would buy dollars with yen and then use those dollars to purchase high-yielding U.S. securities. This would create greater demand for dollars than for yen.

Without any government intervention, the relative prices of yen and dollars would fluctuate in response to changes in supply and demand in much the same way that prices of consumer goods fluctuate. For example, if U.S. consumers were to increase their demand for Japanese electronic products, then the accompanying increase in demand for the yen would cause its value to increase relative to the dollar. In this situation, the strong yen would be due to fundamental economic forces.

However, governments can and do intervene. A country's central bank can artificially prop up its currency by using its reserves of gold or foreign currencies to purchase its own currency in the open market. This creates artificial demand for its own currency, thus causing its value to be artificially high. A central bank can also keep its currency at an artificially low value by selling its own currency in the open markets. This increases the currency's supply, which reduces its price.

Why might an artificially low currency be a problem? After all, a cheap currency makes it less expensive for other nations to purchase the country's goods, which creates jobs in the exporting country. However, an artificially low currency value raises the cost of imports, which increases inflation. In addition, high import prices allow competing domestic manufacturers to raise their prices as well, further boosting inflation. The government intervention that causes the artificially low value also contributes to inflation: When a government creates currency to sell in the open markets, this increases the money supply, and, all else held constant, an increasing money supply leads to still more inflation. Thus, artificially holding down the value of a currency stimulates exports but at the expense of potentially overheating and inflating the economy. Also, other countries—whose economies are being weakened because their manufacturers cannot compete against the artificially low prices—may retaliate and impose tariffs or other restrictions on the country that is holding its currency value down.

For example, China had for many years artificially held down the value of the yuan (also called the rinminbi). This helped make China the world's largest exporter and greatly stimulated its economy. However, by 2004 the Chinese economy was growing at an unsustainably high rate, and inflation was rising rapidly. The United States and other nations began urging the Chinese government to allow the yuan to rise, which would help their economies by slowing Chinese exports and stimulating their own exports to China. On July 21, 2005, the Chinese government suddenly announced that it was changing the exchange rate to allow the yuan's value to rise by 2.1%. The Chinese government has continued to allow the yuan to appreciate slowly, and it now (June 2009) stands at about 0.1466 dollars/yuan versus 0.1217 dollars/yuan in June 2005. Notice that this change has made it somewhat cheaper for Chinese to buy from America (a yuan now buys more dollars) and more expensive for Americans to buy from China.

A currency that is artificially high has the opposite effects: Inflation will be held down and citizens can purchase imported goods at low domestic prices, but exporting industries are hurt, as are domestic industries that compete with the cheap imports. Because there is relatively little external demand for the currency, the government will have to create demand by purchasing its own currency, paying with either gold or foreign currencies held by its central bank. Over time, supporting an inflated currency can deplete the gold and foreign currency reserves, making it impossible to continue propping up the currency.

The following sections describe ways that governments handle changes in currency demands.

Self-Test

What is the effect on a country's economy of an artificially low exchange rate? Of an artificially high exchange rate?

17.5 The International Monetary System and Exchange Rate Policies

The International Monetary Fund reports a full listing of exchange rate arrangements. See **http://www.imf.org/external/np/mfd/er/index.asp**. *The IMF also publishes a more detailed listing in its Annual Report on Exchange Arrangements and Exchange Restrictions. For another listing of world currencies, see* **http://fx.sauder.ubc.ca/currency_table.html**.

Every nation has a monetary system and a monetary authority. In the United States, the Federal Reserve is our monetary authority, and its task is to hold down inflation while promoting economic growth and raising our national standard of living. Moreover, if countries are to trade with one another, we must have some sort of system designed to facilitate payments between nations. The international monetary system is the framework within which exchange rates are determined. As we describe in this section, there are several different policies used by various countries to determine exchange rates.[2]

A Short History Lesson: The Bretton Woods Fixed Exchange Rate System

From the end of World War II until August 1971, most of the industrialized world operated under the Bretton Woods **fixed exchange rate system** administered by the International Monetary Fund (IMF). Under this system, the U.S. dollar was linked to gold (at $35 per ounce), and other currencies were then tied to the dollar. The United States took actions to keep the price of gold at $35 per ounce, and central

[2]For a comprehensive history of the international monetary system and details of how it has evolved, consult one of the many economics books on the subject, which include Robert Carbaugh, *International Economics* (Mason, OH: South-Western Cengage Learning, 2008); Mordechai Kreinin, *International Economics: A Policy Approach*, 10th ed. (Mason, OH: Thomson/South-Western, 2006); Jeff Madura, *International Financial Management* (Mason, OH: Thomson/South-Western, 2008); and Joseph P. Daniels and David D. Van Hoose, *International Monetary and Financial Economics*, 3rd ed. (Mason, OH: South-Western, 2005).

banks acted to keep exchange rates between other currencies and the dollar within narrow limits. For example, when the demand for pounds was falling, the Bank of England would step in and buy pounds to push up their price, offering gold or foreign currencies in exchange for pounds. Conversely, when the demand for pounds was too high, the Bank of England would sell pounds for dollars or gold. The Federal Reserve in the United States performed the same functions, and central banks of other countries operated similarly. These actions artificially matched supply and demand, keeping exchange rates stable, but they didn't address the underlying imbalance. For example, if the high demand for pounds occurred because British productivity was rising and British goods were improving in quality, then the underlying demand for pounds would continue in spite of central bank intervention. In such a situation, the Bank of England would find it necessary to continually sell pounds. If the central bank stopped selling pounds then their value would rise; that is, the pound would strengthen and exceed the agreed-upon limits.

Many countries found it difficult and economically painful to maintain the fixed exchange rates required by Bretton Woods. This system began to crumble in August 1971, and it was abandoned completely by the end of 1973. The following sections describe several modern exchange rate systems.

Freely, or Independently, Floating Rates

In the early 1970s, the U.S. dollar was cut loose from the gold standard and, in effect, allowed to "float" in response to supply and demand caused by international trade and international investing activities. According to the International Monetary Fund, about 42 countries currently operate under a system of **floating exchange rates,** whereby currency prices are allowed to seek their own levels, with only modest central bank intervention to smooth out extreme exchange rate fluctuations. The IMF reports that about 31 currencies have freely, or independently, floating exchange rates; these currencies include the dollar, euro, pound, and yen.

Currency Appreciation and Depreciation. Suppose the dollar cost of a pound is $1.4915, as shown in Table 17-1. If there were increased demand for pounds caused by a U.S. trade deficit with Great Britain, then the price of pounds might increase to $2.5. In this situation the pound is said to be *appreciating,* because a pound would now buy more dollars. In other words, a pound would now be worth more than it previously was. This is called **currency appreciation.** Conversely, the dollar would be *depreciating* because the dollar now buys fewer pounds (a dollar would previously buy 1/1.4915 = 0.6705 pounds, but afterward it would buy only 1/2.5 = 0.4 pounds). This is called **currency depreciation.** Notice that the more costly pound would make British imports more expensive to U.S. consumers, which would reduce imports—and, consequently, the demand for pounds—until the exchange rate reached equilibrium.

Exchange Rate Risk. Exchange rate fluctuations can have a profound effect on profits and trade. For example, in 2002 the euro exchange rate was about $0.87 (i.e., 0.87 dollars per euro). In 2009, the exchange rate was about $1.33. Consider the impact this has on profits and trade. For example, a hand-blown glass from the Italian island of Murano cost about €50 in 2002. Ignoring shipping costs and taxes, a consumer in the United States could have purchased this glass for €50($0.87/€) = $43.50. Assuming the price in 2009 still was €50, it would cost €50($1.33/€) = $57.86. Thus, the change in exchange rates obviously hurt Italian exports to the United States.

On the other hand, U.S. vintners were able to export wines to Italy much more profitably in 2009 than in 2002. For example, suppose a bottle of Pinot Noir cost a California vineyard \$10 to produce in 2002 but could be sold for €17 in Europe. In 2002, the profit would have been €17(\$0.87/€) − \$10 = \$14.79 − \$10 = \$4.79. Assuming no change in production costs, the bottle's profit in 2009 is €17(\$1.33/€) − \$10 = \$22.61 − \$10 = \$12.61. Thus, U.S. exporters to Europe have benefited by the change in exchange rates.

The volatility of exchange rates under a floating system increases the uncertainty of the cash flows for a multinational corporation. Because its cash flows are generated in many parts of the world, they are denominated in many different currencies. When exchange rates change, the dollar-equivalent value of the company's consolidated cash flows also fluctuates. This is known as **exchange rate risk,** and it is a major factor differentiating a global company from a purely domestic one.

Managed Floating Rates

In a **managed floating rate** system, there is significant government intervention to manage the exchange rate by manipulating the currency's supply and demand. The government rarely reveals its target exchange rate levels if it uses a managed float regime because this would make it too easy for currency speculators to profit. According to the IMF, about 53 countries have a managed floating rate system, including Colombia, India, Singapore, and Burundi.

Pegged Exchange Rates

In a **pegged exchange rates** system, a country locks, or "pegs," its currency's exchange rate to another currency or basket of currencies. It is common for a country with a pegged exchange rate to allow its currency to vary within specified limits or bands (often set at ±1% of the target rate) before the country intervenes to force the currency back within the limits. Examples in which a currency is pegged to another country's currency include Bhutan's ngultrum, which is pegged to the Indian rupee; the Falkland Islands' pound, which is pegged to the British pound; and Barbados's dollar, which is pegged to the U.S. dollar. An example of a currency being pegged to a basket is China, where the yuan is no longer just pegged to the U.S. dollar but rather to a basket of currencies. The Chinese government will not reveal exactly which currencies make up the basket, but the U.S. dollar, the euro, the yen, and the South Korean won are certainly components.

Currency Devaluation and Revaluation. As indicated previously, countries with pegged exchange rates establish a fixed exchange rate with some other major currency or basket of currencies. When a government reduces its target fixed exchange rate, the result is a currency **devaluation**; increasing the rate results in a currency **revaluation.** For example, from 1991 through early 2002, Argentina had a fixed exchange rate of 1 peso per U.S. dollar. Imports were high, exports were low, and the Argentinean government had to purchase huge amounts of pesos to maintain that artificially high exchange rate. The government borrowed heavily to finance these purchases, and eventually it was unable to continue supporting the peso. (Indeed, the government defaulted on some of its obligations.) As a result, the government had to devalue the peso to 1.4 pesos per dollar in early 2002. Notice that this made the peso weaker: Before the devaluation, 1 peso would buy 1 dollar, but afterward 1 peso would buy only 71 cents (1.4 pesos per dollar = 1/1.4 = 0.71 dollar per peso). The devaluation lowered the prices of Argentine goods on the world market, which helped its exporters, but prices rose for imported goods, including oil. The initial shock to the Argentine economy was severe, as employment fell in those industries that were not exporters. The problem was exacerbated because many Argentine companies and individuals had incurred debt that was denominated in dollars, which instantly cost much more to service. However, the economy gradually improved, aided by increased exports, tourism, and employment rates. Still, the initial pain caused by devaluation helps explain why many countries with fixed exchange rates tend to postpone needed measures until economic pressures build to explosive levels.

Given the expense of maintaining an artificially high exchange rate and the pain of large devaluations, many countries that once had pegged exchange rates now allow their currencies to float. For example, Mexico had a pegged exchange rate prior to 1994, but it depleted its foreign reserves trying to support the peso and was forced to devalue it. Mexico's currency now floats, as does that of Argentina.

Convertible versus Nonconvertible Securities. A pegged exchange rate isn't necessarily a deterrent to direct investment in the country by foreign corporations—as long as the local government's central bank supports the currency and devaluations are unlikely. This was generally the case in the Bretton Woods era, so those currencies were considered to be **convertible** because the nation that issued them allowed them to be traded in the currency markets and was willing to redeem them at market rates. This is true today for all floating-rate currencies, which are also called **hard currencies** because of their convertibility. Some pegged currencies are also at least partially convertible, because their central banks will redeem them at market rates under specified conditions.

However, some countries set the exchange rate but do not allow their currencies to be traded on world markets. For example, the Chinese yuan is allowed to float in a very narrow band against a basket of securities. However, the yuan can be legally used and exchanged only within China. Furthermore, the Chinese government imposes restrictions on both residents and nonresidents from freely converting their holdings of yuans into another currency. Thus, the yuan is a **nonconvertible currency**, also called a **soft currency**. When official exchange rates differ from "market rates" or when there are restrictions on convertibility, a black market will often arise. For example, in mid-2008 Venezuela's official exchange rate was about 2.15 bolivars per dollar, but black market prices were estimated to be around 3.25.

A nonconvertible currency creates problems for foreign companies looking to make direct investments. Consider the situation faced by Pizza Hut when it wanted to open a chain of restaurants in the former Soviet Union. The Russian ruble was not convertible, so Pizza Hut could not take the profits from its restaurants out of the Soviet Union in the form of dollars. Because there was no mechanism to exchange the rubles it earned in Russia for dollars, it seemed that investing in the Soviet Union was essentially worthless to a U.S. company. However, Pizza Hut arranged to use the ruble profit from the restaurants to buy Russian vodka, which it then shipped to the United States and sold for dollars. Pizza Hut managed to find a solution, but lack of convertibility significantly inhibits the ability of a country to attract foreign investment.

No Local Currency

A few countries don't have their own separate legal tender but instead use the currency of another nation. For example, Ecuador has used the U.S. dollar since September 2000. Other countries belong to a monetary union, such as the 16 European Monetary Union nations in 2009 whose currency is the euro, which is allowed to float. In contrast, member nations of the Eastern Caribbean Currency Union, the West African Economic and Monetary Union (WAEMU), and the Central African

Economic and Monetary Community (CAEMC) use their respective union's currency, which is itself pegged to some other currency. For example, the Eastern Caribbean dollar is pegged to the U.S. dollar, and the CFA franc (used by both the WAEMU and CAEMC) is pegged to the euro.[3]

Self-Test

What is the difference between a fixed exchange rate system and a floating rate system?
What are pegged exchange rates?
What does it mean to say that the dollar is depreciating with respect to the euro?
What is a convertible currency?

17.6 Trading in Foreign Exchange

Importers, exporters, tourists, and governments buy and sell currencies in the foreign exchange market. For example, when a U.S. trader imports automobiles from Japan, payment will probably be made in Japanese yen. The importer buys yen (through its bank) in the foreign exchange market, much as one buys common stocks on the New York Stock Exchange or pork bellies on the Chicago Mercantile Exchange. However, whereas stock and commodity exchanges have organized trading floors, the foreign exchange market consists of a network of brokers and banks based in New York, London, Tokyo, and other financial centers. Most buy and sell orders are conducted by computer and telephone.

Spot Rates and Forward Rates

WWW

Currency futures prices are available from the Chicago Mercantile Exchange (CME) on their Web site at **http://www.cme.com**. *Currency spot and forward rates are available from the Bank of Montreal Financial Group at* **http://www4.bmo.com**

The exchange rates shown in Tables 17-1 and 17-2 are known as **spot rates**, which means the rate paid for delivery of the currency "on the spot" or, in reality, no more than two days after the day of the trade. For most of the world's major currencies, it is also possible to buy (or sell) currencies for delivery at some agreed-upon future date, usually 30, 90, or 180 days from the day the transaction is negotiated. This rate is known as the **forward exchange rate**.

For example, suppose that a U.S. firm must pay 500 million yen to a Japanese firm in 30 days and that the current spot rate is 98.8600 yen per dollar. If spot rates remain constant, then the U.S. firm will pay the Japanese firm the equivalent of $5.058 million (500 million yen divided by 98.8600 yen per dollar) in 30 days. But if the spot rate falls to, say, 90 yen per dollar, then the U.S. firm will have to pay the equivalent of $5/(90 ¥/$) = $5.56 million. If the spot rate increases to 109, the firm will pay only $5/(109 ¥/$) = $4.587 million. The treasurer of the U.S. firm can avoid this variability by entering into a 30-day forward exchange contract. Suppose this contract promises delivery of yen to the U.S. firm in 30 days at a guaranteed price of 98.8100 yen per dollar. No cash changes hands at the time the treasurer signs the forward contract, although the U.S. firm might have to put some collateral down as a guarantee against default. Yet because the firm can use an interest-bearing instrument for the collateral, this requirement is not costly. The counterparty to the forward contract must deliver the yen to the U.S. firm in 30 days, and the U.S. firm is obligated to purchase the 500 million yen at the previously agreed-upon rate of 98.8100 yen per dollar. Therefore, the treasurer of the U.S. firm is able to lock in a payment

[3]A few countries, such as Bosnia and Herzegovina, have currency board arrangements. Under this system, a country technically has its own currency but commits to exchange it for a specified foreign money unit at a fixed exchange rate. This requires it to impose domestic currency restrictions unless it has the foreign currency reserves to cover requested exchanges.

TABLE 17-3 Selected Spot and Forward Exchange Rates, Indirect Quotation: Number of Units of Foreign Currency per U.S. Dollar

	SPOT RATE	FORWARD RATES[a] 30 DAYS	90 DAYS	180 DAYS	FORWARD RATE AT A PREMIUM OR DISCOUNT[b]
Britain (Pound)	0.6705	0.6705	0.6705	0.6702	Premium
Canada (Dollar)	1.2139	1.2137	1.2129	1.2111	Premium
Japan (Yen)	98.8600	98.8100	98.7100	98.4900	Premium
Switzerland (Franc)	1.1370	1.1365	1.1352	1.1331	Premium

Notes:

[a] These are representative quotes as provided by a sample of New York banks. Forward rates for other currencies and for other lengths of time can often be negotiated.

[b] When it takes more units of a foreign currency to buy a dollar in the future, then the value of the foreign currency is less in the forward market than in the spot market; hence the forward rate is at a *discount* to the spot rate. When it takes fewer units of a foreign currency to buy a dollar in the future, the forward rate is at a *premium.*

Source: The Wall Street Journal, **http://online.wsj.com**; quotes for April 14, 2009.

equivalent to \$5.060 million = (¥500 million)/(98.8100 ¥/\$), no matter what happens to spot rates. This technique is called *hedging.*

Forward rates for 30-, 90-, and 180-day delivery, along with the current spot rates for some commonly traded currencies, are given in Table 17-3. If you can obtain *more* of the foreign currency for a dollar in the forward than in the spot market, then the forward currency is less valuable than the spot currency and the forward currency is said to be selling at a **discount.** In other words, if the foreign currency is expected to depreciate (based on the forward rates), then the forward currency is at a discount. Conversely, since a dollar would buy *fewer* yen and francs in the forward than in the spot market, the forward yen and francs are selling at a **premium.**

Self-Test

Differentiate between spot and forward exchange rates.

Explain what it means for a forward currency to sell at a discount and at a premium.

17.7 Interest Rate Parity

Market forces determine whether a currency sells at a forward premium or a discount, and the general relationship between spot and forward exchange rates is specified by a concept called "interest rate parity."

Interest rate parity means that investors should expect to earn the same return on security investments in all countries after adjusting for risk. It recognizes that when you invest in a country other than your home country, you are affected by two forces—returns on the investment itself and changes in the exchange rate. It follows that your overall return will be higher than the investment's stated return if the currency in which your investment is denominated appreciates relative to your home currency. Likewise, your overall return will be lower if the foreign currency that you receive declines in value.

To illustrate interest rate parity, consider the case of a U.S. investor who can buy default-free 180-day Swiss bonds that promise a 4% nominal annual return. The

180-day foreign (Swiss) interest rate, r_f, is 4% ÷ 2 = 2% because 180 days is one-half of a 360-day year. Assume also that the indirect quotation for the spot exchange rate is 1.1370 Swiss francs per dollar, as shown in Table 17-3. Finally, assume that the 180-day forward exchange rate is 1.1331 Swiss francs per dollar, which means that in 180 days the investor can exchange 1 dollar for 1.1331 Swiss francs.

The U.S. investor could receive a 4% annualized return denominated in Swiss francs, but if he ultimately wants to consume goods in the United States, then those Swiss francs must be converted to dollars. The dollar return on the investment depends, therefore, on what happens to exchange rates over the next 6 months. However, the investor can lock in the dollar return by selling the foreign currency in the forward market. For example, the investor could simultaneously do the following:

1. Convert $1,000 to 1,137.00 Swiss francs in the spot market: $1,000(1.1370 Swiss francs per dollar) = 1,137.00 Swiss francs.
2. Invest the Swiss francs in a 180-day Swiss bond that has a 4% annual return, or a 2% semiannual return. This investment will pay 1,137.00(1.02) = 1,159.74 Swiss francs in 180 days.
3. Agree today to exchange the Swiss francs in 180 days at the forward rate of 1.1331 Swiss francs per dollar, for a total of (1,159.74 Swiss francs) ÷ (1.1331 Swiss francs per dollar) = $1,023.51.

Hence this investment has an expected 180-day return in dollars of $23.51/$1,000 = 2.351%, which translates into a nominal annual return of 2(2.351%) = 4.702%. In this case, 4% of the expected 4.702% is coming from the bond itself while 0.702% arises because the market believes that the Swiss franc will strengthen relative to the dollar. Observe that, by locking in the forward rate today, the investor has eliminated all exchange rate risk. And since the Swiss bond is assumed to be default-free, the investor is certain to earn a 4.702% annual dollar return.

Interest rate parity implies that an investment in the United States with the same risk as the Swiss bond should also have a return of 4.702%. When we express interest rates as periodic rates, we can express interest rate parity by the following equation (later in the chapter we will use a slightly different version of interest rate parity when we consider multi-year cash flows):

$$\frac{\text{Forward exchange rate}}{\text{Spot exchange rate}} = \frac{1 + r_h}{1 + r_f} \tag{17-1}$$

Here r_h is the periodic interest rate in the home country, r_f is the periodic interest rate in the foreign country, and the forward and exchange rates are expressed as direct quotations (that is, dollars per foreign currency).

Using Table 17-3, the direct spot quotation is 0.87951 dollar per Swiss franc = (1/1.1370 Swiss francs per dollar), and the direct 180-day forward quotation is 0.88253 = (1/1.1331). Using Equation 17-1, we can solve for the equivalent home rate, r_h:

$$\frac{\text{Forward exchange rate}}{\text{Spot exchange rate}} = \frac{1 + r_h}{1 + r_f} = \frac{1 + r_h}{1 + 0.02} = \frac{0.88253}{0.87951}$$

$$1 + r_h = \left(\frac{0.88253}{0.87951}\right)(1 + 0.02) = 1.023502 \tag{17-1a}$$

The periodic home interest rate is 2.3502%, and the annualized home interest rate is (2.3502%)(2) = 4.700%, the same value we found before excepting a slight difference due to rounding.

After accounting for exchange rates, interest rate parity states that bonds in the home country and the foreign country must have the same actual rate of return in the investor's currency. In this example, the U.S. bond must yield 4.700% to provide the same return as the 4% Swiss bond. If one bond provides a higher return, then investors will sell their low-return bond and flock to the high-return bond. This activity will cause the price of the low-return bond to fall (which pushes up its yield) and the price of the high-return bond to increase (driving down its yield). These effects will continue until the two bonds again have the same returns after accounting for exchange rates.

In other words, interest rate parity implies that an investment in the United States with the same risk as a Swiss bond should have a dollar value return of 4.700%. Solving for r_h in Equation 17-1, we indeed find that the predicted interest rate in the United States is 4.702%, the same return except for the slight rounding difference.

Interest rate parity shows why a particular currency might be at a forward premium or discount. Note that a currency is at a forward premium whenever domestic interest rates are higher than foreign interest rates. Discounts prevail if domestic interest rates are lower than foreign interest rates. If these conditions do not hold, then arbitrage will soon force interest rates and exchange rates back to parity.

Self-Test

What is interest rate parity?

Assume that interest rate parity holds. When a currency trades at a forward premium, what does that imply about domestic rates relative to foreign interest rates? What does it imply when a currency trades at a forward discount?

Assume that 90-day U.S. securities have a 4.5% annualized interest rate whereas 90-day Swiss securities have a 5% annualized interest rate. In the spot market, 1 U.S. dollar can be exchanged for 1.2 Swiss francs. If interest rate parity holds, what is the 90-day forward rate exchange between U.S. and Swiss francs? **(0.8323 $/SFr or 1.2015 SFr/$)**

On the basis of your answer to the previous question, is the Swiss franc selling at a premium or discount on the forward rate? **(Discount)**

17.8 Purchasing Power Parity

We have discussed exchange rates in some detail, and we have considered the relationship between spot and forward exchange rates. However, we have not yet addressed the fundamental question: What determines the spot level of exchange rates in each country? Although exchange rates are influenced by a multitude of factors that are difficult to predict, particularly on a day-to-day basis, market forces over the long run work to ensure that similar goods sell for similar prices in different countries after taking exchange rates into account. This relationship is known as "purchasing power parity."

Purchasing power parity (PPP), sometimes referred to as the *law of one price*, implies that the levels of exchange rates and prices adjust so as to cause identical goods to cost the same amount in different countries. For instance, if a pair of tennis shoes costs $150 in the United States and 100 pounds in Britain, then PPP implies that the exchange rate must be \$1.50 per pound. Consumers could purchase the shoes in Britain for 100 pounds, or they could exchange their 100 pounds for \$150 and then purchase the same shoes in the United States at the same effective cost (assuming no transaction or transportation costs). Here is the equation for purchasing power parity:

$$P_h = (P_f)(\text{Spot rate}) \quad (17\text{-}2)$$

or

$$\text{Spot rate} = \frac{P_h}{P_f} \quad (17\text{-}3)$$

Here

P_h = The price of the good in the home country (\$150 in our example, assuming the United States is the home country).

P_f = The price of the good in the foreign country (100 pounds).

Note that the spot market exchange rate is expressed as the number of units of home currency that can be exchanged for one unit of foreign currency (\$1.50 per pound).

Purchasing power parity assumes that market forces will eliminate situations in which the same product sells at a different price overseas. For example, if the shoes cost \$140 in the United States then importers/exporters could purchase them in the United States for \$140, sell them for 100 pounds in Britain, exchange the 100 pounds for \$150 in the foreign exchange market, and earn a profit of \$10 on every pair of shoes. Ultimately, this trading activity would increase the demand for shoes in the United States and thus raise P_h, increase the supply of shoes in Britain and thus reduce P_f, and increase the demand for dollars in the foreign exchange market and thus reduce the spot rate. Each of these actions works to restore PPP.

Note that PPP assumes that there are no transportation or transaction costs and no import restrictions, all of which limit the ability to ship goods between countries. In many cases, these assumptions are incorrect, which explains why PPP is often violated. An additional problem for empirical tests of the PPP theorem is that products in different countries are rarely identical. There are frequently real or perceived differences in quality that can lead to price differences in different countries.

Still, the concepts of interest rate parity and purchasing power parity are vitally important to those engaged in international activities. Companies and investors must anticipate changes in interest rates, inflation, and exchange rates, and they often try to hedge the risks of adverse movements in these factors. The parity relationships are extremely useful when anticipating future conditions.

Self-Test

What is meant by purchasing power parity?

A computer sells for \$1,500 U.S. dollars. In the spot market, \$1 = 115 Japanese yen. If purchasing power parity holds, what should be the price (in yen) of the same computer in Japan? **(¥172,500)**

Hungry for a Big Mac? Go To Malaysia!

Purchasing power parity (PPP) implies that the same product will sell for the same price in every country after adjusting for current exchange rates. One problem when testing to see if PPP holds is that it assumes that goods consumed in different countries are of the same quality. For example, if you find that a product is more expensive in Switzerland than it is in Canada, one explanation is that PPP fails to hold, but another explanation is that the product sold in Switzerland is of a higher quality and therefore deserves a higher price.

One way to test for PPP is to find goods that have the same quality worldwide. With this in mind, *The Economist* magazine occasionally compares the prices of a well-known good whose quality is the same in nearly 120 different countries: the McDonald's Big Mac hamburger.

The accompanying table provides information collected during early 2009. The second column shows the price of a Big Mac in local currency. For example, a Big Mac costs 62 rubles in Russia. The second column shows the cost in dollars (based on the actual exchange rate in the fourth column), which is the amount you would pay in that country if you exchanged dollars for local currency and then purchased a Big Mac at the local price. For example, the exchange rate is 35.7 rubles per dollar, which means that a Big Mac in Russia costs \$1.73 = (62 rubles) ÷ (35.7 rubles per dollar), subject to rounding in the exchange rate used by *The Economist.*

The third column backs out the implied exchange rate that would hold under PPP. For example, the 62-ruble price of a Big Mac in Russia compared to the \$3.54 price in the United States gives us the implied PPP exchange rate of (62 rubles per Big Mac) ÷ (\$3.54 per Big Mac) = 17.5 rubles per dollar. The last column shows how much the local currency is overvalued or undervalued relative to the dollar. The ruble is undervalued by 51%: (17.5 − 35.7)/35.7 = −0.51.

The evidence suggests that strict PPP does not hold, but the Big Mac test may shed some insights about where exchange rates are headed. Most European currencies are overvalued against the dollar, while most other currencies are undervalued. The Big Mac 2009 test suggests that European currencies will fall over the next year or so but that most others will rise.

One last benefit of the Big Mac test is that it tells us the cheapest places to find a Big Mac. According to the data, if you are looking for a Big Mac, head to Malaysia and avoid Switzerland.

	Big Mac prices				
	in local currency	in dollars	Implied PPP* of the Dollar	Actual exchange rate: Jan 30th	Under (−)/Over (+) Valuation against the dollar,%
United States†	\$3.54	3.54	-	-	
Argentina	Peso 11.50	3.30	3.25	3.49	−7
Australia	A\$3.45	2.19	0.97	1.57	−38
Brazil	Real 8.02	3.45	2.27	2.32	−2
Britain	£2.29	3.30	1.55‡	1.44‡	−7
Canada	C\$4.16	3.36	1.18	1.24	−5
Chile	Peso 1,550	2.51	438	617	−29
China	Yuan 12.5	1.83	3.53	6.84	−48
Czech Republic	Koruna 65.94	3.02	18.6	21.9	−15
Denmark	DK 29.5	5.07	8.33	5.82	43
Egypt	Pound 13.0	2.34	3.67	5.57	−34
Euro Area§	€3.42	4.38	1.04**	1.28**	24
Hong Kong	HK\$13.3	1.72	3.76	7.75	−52
Hungary	Forint 680	2.92	192	233	−18
Indonesia	Rupiah 19,800	1.74	5,593	11,380	−51
Israel	Shekel 15.0	3.69	4.24	4.07	4

	Big Mac prices				
	in local currency	in dollars	Implied PPP* of the Dollar	Actual exchange rate: Jan 30th	Under (–)/Over (+) Valuation against the dollar,%
Japan	¥290	3.23	81.9	89.8	-9
Malaysia	Ringgit 5.50	1.52	1.55	3.61	-57
Mexico	Peso 33.0	2.30	9.32	14.4	-35
New Zealand	NZ$4.90	2.48	1.38	1.97	-30
Norway	Kroner 40.0	5.79	11.3	6.91	63
Peru	Sol 8.06	2.54	2.28	3.18	-28
Philippines	Peso 98.0	2.07	27.7	47.4	-42
Poland	Zloty 7.00	2.01	1.98	3.48	-43
Russia	Ruble 62.0	1.73	17.5	35.7	-51
Saudi Arabia	Riyal 10.0	2.66	2.82	3.75	-25
Singapore	S$3.95	2.61	1.12	1.51	-26
South Africa	Rand 16.95	1.66	4.79	10.2	-53
South Korea	Won 3,300	2.39	932	1,380	-32
Sweden	SKR 38.0	4.58	10.7	8.30	29
Switzerland	CHF 6.50	5.60	1.84	1.16	58
Taiwan	NT$75.0	2.23	21.2	33.6	-37
Thailand	Baht 62.0	1.77	17.5	35.0	-50
Turkey	Lire 5.15	3.13	1.45	1.64	-12

*Purchasing-power parity: local price divided by price in the United States
†Average of New York, Chicago, Atlanta, and San Francisco ‡Dollars per pound
§Weighted average of prices in euro area **Dollars per euro.

Source: The Economist, Feb. 4, 2009. **www.economist.com.**

17.9 Inflation, Interest Rates, and Exchange Rates

For current international interest rates, go to **http://www.bloomberg.com** *and select Market Data. Then select Rates and Bonds.*

Relative inflation rates, or the rates of inflation in foreign countries compared with that in the home country, have many implications for multinational financial decisions. Obviously, relative inflation rates will greatly influence future production costs at home and abroad. Equally important, inflation has a dominant influence on relative interest rates and exchange rates. Both of these factors influence decisions by multinational corporations for financing their foreign investments, and both have an important effect on the profitability of foreign investments.

The currencies of countries with higher inflation rates than that of the United States will by definition *depreciate* over time against the dollar. Countries where this has occurred include Mexico and all the South American nations. On the other hand, the currencies of Switzerland and Japan, which have had less inflation than the United States, have generally *appreciated* against the dollar. In fact, *a foreign currency will, on average, depreciate or appreciate against the U.S. dollar at a percentage rate approximately equal to the amount by which its inflation rate exceeds or is less than the U.S. rate.*

Relative inflation rates also affect interest rates. The interest rate in any country is largely determined by its inflation rate. Therefore, countries currently experiencing higher rates of inflation than the United States also tend to have higher interest rates. The reverse is true for countries with lower inflation rates.

It is tempting for a multinational corporation to borrow in countries with the lowest interest rates. However, this is not always a good strategy. Suppose, for example, that interest rates in Switzerland are lower than those in the United States because of Switzerland's lower inflation rate. A U.S. multinational firm could therefore save interest by borrowing in Switzerland. However, because of relative inflation rates, the Swiss franc will probably appreciate in the future, causing the dollar cost of annual interest and principal payments on Swiss debt to rise over time. Thus, *the lower interest rate could be more than offset by losses from currency appreciation*. Similarly, multinational corporations should not necessarily avoid borrowing in a country such as Brazil, where interest rates have been very high, because future depreciation of the Brazilian real could make such borrowing end up being relatively inexpensive.

Self-Test

What effects do relative inflation rates have on relative interest rates?

What happens over time to the currencies of countries with higher inflation rates than that of the United States? To those with lower inflation rates?

Why might a multinational corporation decide to borrow in a country such as Brazil, where interest rates are high, rather than in a country like Switzerland, where interest rates are low?

17.10 International Money and Capital Markets

One way for U.S. citizens to invest in world markets is to buy the stocks of U.S. multinational corporations that invest directly in foreign countries. Another way is to purchase foreign securities—stocks, bonds, or money market instruments issued by foreign companies. Security investments are known as *portfolio investments*, and they are distinguished from *direct investments* in physical assets by U.S. corporations.

From World War II through the 1960s, the U.S. capital markets dominated world markets. Today, however, the value of U.S. securities represents less than one-fourth the value of all securities. Given this situation, it is important for both corporate managers and investors to have an understanding of international markets. Moreover, these markets often offer better opportunities for raising or investing capital than are available domestically.

Eurodollar Market

A **Eurodollar** is a U.S. dollar deposited in a bank outside the United States. (Although they are called Eurodollars because they originated in Europe, Eurodollars are actually any dollars deposited in any part of the world other than the United States.) The bank in which the deposit is made may be a non-U.S. bank, such as Barclays Bank in London; the foreign branch of a U.S. bank, such as Citibank's Paris branch; or even a foreign branch of a third-country bank, such as Barclays' Munich branch. Most Eurodollar deposits are for $500,000 or more, and they have maturities ranging from overnight to about 1 year.

The major difference between Eurodollar deposits and regular U.S. time deposits is their geographic locations. The two types of deposits do not involve different currencies—in both cases, dollars are on deposit. However, Eurodollars are outside the direct control of the U.S. monetary authorities, so U.S. banking regulations, including reserve requirements and FDIC insurance premiums, do not apply. The absence of these costs means that the interest rate paid on Eurodollar deposits can be higher than domestic U.S. rates on equivalent instruments.

The dollar is the leading international currency. However, British pounds, euros, Swiss francs, Japanese yen, and other currencies are also deposited outside their home countries; these *Eurocurrencies* are handled in exactly the same way as Eurodollars.

Greasing the Wheels of International Business

What do bribery and tax shelters have in common? Both are targets of international regulation.

Thirty-seven countries have now signed the Organization for Economic Cooperation and Development's Anti-Bribery Convention. This requires each country to pass legislation making it a crime for companies to bribe public officials. The United States, which signed the convention, has been the most aggressive in prosecuting violators. It is interesting that this prosecution has not been limited to U.S. companies but also has extended to foreign companies whose stocks are listed in the United States. For example, Statoil, a Norwegian firm, was fined $10.5 million in 2006 for bribing Iranian officials. Subsidiaries of Vetco International, headquartered in the United Kingdom, were fined $26 million in 2007 for bribing Nigerian officials. Siemens, a German company, holds the record for the largest fine paid to date (2009), with over *$1.6 billion* paid to regulatory agencies in the United States and Germany.

Among the international organizations striving to reform global taxation and eliminate tax-shelter abuse are the Joint International Tax Shelter Information Centre, the Seven Country Working Group, and the Leeds Castle Group. Their goals include improving transparency, eliminating double taxation, and abolishing tax havens.

What does the reformation of tax havens have in common with the elimination of bribery? First, both of these problems distract companies from focusing on their core business issues, and both create uneven playing fields where providing the best product at the best price isn't as important as who you know (and bribe!) or how clever your lawyers are. Second, these problems reduce transparency in capital markets, making it harder for investors to identify the best firms. When investors are uncertain about a company, the cost of capital goes up. Thus, there is a direct link between transparency and a company's ability to raise capital at a fair price.

Sources: Janet Kersnar, "View from Europe," *CFO*, June 2007, p. 25; and Kayleigh Karutis, *CFO*, "Global Norming," May 2007, p. 22.

Eurodollars are borrowed by U.S. and foreign corporations for various purposes but especially to pay for goods imported from the United States and to invest in U.S. security markets. Also, U.S. dollars are used as an international currency or medium of exchange, and many Eurodollars are also used for this purpose. It is interesting to note that Eurodollars were actually "invented" by the Soviets in 1946. International merchants did not trust the Soviets or their rubles, so the Soviets bought some dollars (for gold), deposited them in a Paris bank, and then used these dollars to buy goods in the world markets. Others found it convenient to use dollars this same way, and soon the Eurodollar market was in full swing.

Eurodollars are usually held in interest-bearing accounts. The interest rate paid on these deposits depends (1) on the bank's lending rate, since the interest a bank earns on loans determines its willingness and ability to pay interest on deposits, and (2) on rates of return available on U.S. money market instruments. If money market rates in the United States were above Eurodollar deposit rates then these dollars would be sent back and invested in the United States, whereas if Eurodollar deposit rates were significantly above U.S. rates, which is more often the case, then more dollars would be sent out of the United States to become Eurodollars. Given the existence of the Eurodollar market and the electronic flow of dollars to and from the United States, it is easy to see why interest rates in the United States cannot be insulated from those in other parts of the world.

Interest rates on Eurodollar deposits (and loans) are tied to a standard rate known by the acronym **LIBOR,** which stands for **London Interbank Offered Rate.** LIBOR is the rate of interest offered by the largest and strongest London banks on dollar deposits of significant size. On May 8, 2009, LIBOR rates were just a little above domestic U.S. bank rates on time deposits of the same maturity—0.75% for 3-month CDs versus 0.99% for LIBOR CDs. The Eurodollar market is essentially a short-term market; most loans and deposits are for less than 1 year.

International Bond Markets

Any bond sold outside the country of the borrower is called an *international bond*. However, there are two important types of international bonds: foreign bonds and Eurobonds. **Foreign bonds** are bonds sold by a foreign borrower but denominated in the currency of the country in which the issue is sold. For instance, Nortel Networks (a Canadian company) may need U.S. dollars to finance the operations of its subsidiaries in the United States. If it decides to raise the needed capital in the United States, then the bond would be underwritten by a syndicate of U.S. investment bankers, denominated in U.S. dollars, and sold to U.S. investors in accordance with SEC and applicable state regulations. Except for the foreign origin of the borrower, this bond would be indistinguishable from those issued by equivalent U.S. corporations. However, since Nortel is a foreign corporation, the bond would be a foreign bond. Furthermore, because it is denominated in dollars and sold in the United States under SEC regulations, it is also called a **Yankee bond.** In contrast, if Nortel issued bonds in Mexico that were denominated in pesos then they would be foreign bonds, not Yankee bonds.

The term **Eurobond** is used to designate any bond issued in one country but denominated in the currency of some other country. Examples include a Ford Motor Company issue denominated in dollars and sold in Germany and a British firm's sale of euro-denominated bonds in Switzerland. The institutional arrangements by which Eurobonds are marketed are different than those for most other bond issues, with the most important distinction being a far lower level of required disclosure than is usually found for bonds issued in domestic markets, particularly in the United States. Governments tend to be less strict when regulating securities denominated in foreign currencies, because the bonds' purchasers are generally more "sophisticated." The lower disclosure requirements result in lower total transaction costs for Eurobonds.

Eurobonds appeal to investors for several reasons. Generally, they are issued in bearer form rather than as registered bonds, so the names and nationalities of investors are not recorded. Individuals who desire anonymity, whether for privacy reasons or for tax avoidance, like Eurobonds. Similarly, most governments do not withhold taxes on interest payments associated with Eurobonds. If the investor requires an effective yield of 10%, then a Eurobond that is exempt from tax withholding would simply need a coupon rate of 10%. Another type of bond—for instance, a domestic issue subject to a 30% withholding tax on interest paid to foreigners—would need a coupon rate of 14.3% to yield an after-withholding rate of 10%. Investors who desire secrecy would not want to file for a refund of the tax, so they would prefer to hold the Eurobond.

More than half of all Eurobonds are denominated in dollars. Bonds in Japanese yen, German marks, and Dutch guilders account for most of the rest. Although centered in Europe, Eurobonds are truly international. Their underwriting syndicates include investment bankers from all parts of the world, and the bonds are sold to investors not only in Europe but also in such faraway places as Bahrain and Singapore. Up to a few years ago, Eurobonds were issued solely by multinational firms, by international financial institutions, or by national governments. Today, however, the Eurobond market is also being tapped by purely domestic U.S. firms, which often find they can lower their debt costs by borrowing overseas.

Stock Market Indices around the World

In the United States, the Dow Jones Industrial Average (^DJI) is the most well-known stock market index. Similar indices also exist for each major world financial center. As shown in the accompanying table, India's market has had the strongest performance during the past 10 years while Japan's has had the weakest.

Hong Kong (^HSI)

In Hong Kong, the primary stock index is the Hang Seng. Created by HSI Services Limited, the Hang Seng index is composed of 33 large stocks.

Great Britain (^FTSE)

The FT-SE 100 Index (pronounced "footsie") is the most widely followed indicator of equity investments in Great Britain. It is a value-weighted index composed of the 100 largest companies on the London Stock Exchange.

Japan (^N225)

In Japan, the principal barometer of stock performance is the Nikkei 225 Index. The index consists of highly liquid equity issues thought to be representative of the Japanese economy.

Germany (^GDAXI)

The Deutscher Aktienindex, commonly called the DAX, is an index composed of the 30 largest companies trading on the Frankfurt Stock Exchange.

India (^BSESN)

Of the 22 stock exchanges in India, the Bombay Stock Exchange (BSE) is the largest, with more than 6,000 listed stocks and approximately two-thirds of the country's total trading volume. Established in 1875, the exchange is also the oldest in Asia. Its yardstick is the BSE Sensex, an index of 30 publicly traded Indian stocks that account for one-fifth of the BSE's market capitalization.

Note: For easy access to world indices, see **http://finance.yahoo.com/m2** and use the ticker symbols shown above in parentheses.

Relative 10-Year Performance (Starting Values = 100)

	United States	Germany	Great Britain	Hong Kong	India	Japan
May 1999	100	100	100	100	100	100
May 2009	80	97	71	150	369	57

International Stock Markets

New issues of stock are sold in international markets for a variety of reasons. For example, a non-U.S. firm might sell an equity issue in the United States because it can tap a much larger source of capital than in its home country. Also, a U.S. firm might tap a foreign market because it wants to create an equity market presence to accompany its operations in that country. Large multinational companies also occasionally issue new stock simultaneously in multiple countries. For example, Alcan Aluminum, a Canadian company, issued new stock in Canada, Europe, and the United States simultaneously, using different underwriting syndicates in each market.

In addition to new issues, outstanding stocks of large multinational companies are increasingly being listed on multiple international exchanges. For example, Coca-Cola's stock is traded on six stock exchanges in the United States, four stock exchanges in Switzerland, and the Frankfurt stock exchange in Germany. Some 500 foreign stocks are listed in the United States—an example here is Royal Dutch Petroleum, which is listed on the New York Stock Exchange. U.S. investors can also invest in foreign companies through American Depository Receipts (ADRs), which are certificates representing ownership of foreign stock held in trust. About 1,700 ADRs are now available in the United States, with most of them traded on the over-the-counter

(OTC) market. However, more and more ADRs are being listed on the NYSE, including England's British Airways, Japan's Honda Motors, and Italy's Fiat Group.[4]

Self-Test

Differentiate between foreign portfolio investments and direct foreign investments.
What are Eurodollars?
Has the development of the Eurodollar market made it easier or more difficult for the Federal Reserve to control U.S. interest rates?
Differentiate between foreign bonds and Eurobonds.
Why do Eurobonds appeal to investors?

17.11 Multinational Capital Budgeting

Until now we've discussed the general environment in which multinational firms operate. In the remainder of the chapter, we see how international factors affect key corporate decisions, beginning with capital budgeting. Although the same basic principles apply to capital budgeting for both foreign and domestic operations, there are some key differences. These include the types of risks faced by the firm, cash flow estimation, and project analysis.[5]

Risk Exposure

Foreign projects may be more or less risky than equivalent domestic projects, and that can lead to differences in the cost of capital. Higher risk for foreign projects tends to result from two primary sources: (1) exchange rate risk and (2) political risk. However, international diversification might result in a lower risk.

Exchange rate risk concerns the value of the basic cash flows in the parent company's home currency. Foreign currency cash flows turned over to the parent must be converted into U.S. dollars, so projected cash flows must be translated to dollars at the expected future exchange rates. An analysis should be conducted to ascertain the effects of exchange rate variations on dollar cash flows; then, on the basis of this analysis, an exchange rate risk premium should be added to the domestic cost of capital. It is sometimes possible to hedge against exchange rate risk, but it may not be possible to hedge completely, especially on long-term projects. If hedging is used, then the costs of doing so must be subtracted from the project's operating cash flows.

Political risk refers to potential actions by a host government that would reduce the value of a company's investment. It includes at one extreme expropriation of the subsidiary's assets without compensation, but it also includes less drastic actions that reduce the value of the parent firm's investment in the foreign subsidiary.[6] Included here are higher taxes, tighter repatriation or currency controls, and restrictions on prices charged. The risk of expropriation is small in traditionally friendly and stable

[4]For an interesting discussion of ADRs and the costs faced by listing companies when the ADR is underwritten by investment banks, see Hsuen-Chi Chen, Larry Fauver, and Pei-Ching Yang, "What Do Investment Banks Charge to Underwrite American Depository Receipts?" *Journal of Banking and Finance,* April 2009, pp. 609–618.

[5]Many domestic companies form joint ventures with foreign companies; see Insup Lee and Steve B. Wyatt, "The Effects of International Joint Ventures on Shareholder Wealth," *Financial Review,* November 1990, pp. 641–649. For a discussion of the Japanese cost of capital, see Jeffrey A. Frankel, "The Japanese Cost of Finance," *Financial Management,* Spring 1991, pp. 95–127. For a discussion of financial practices in the Pacific basin, see George W. Kester, Rosita P. Chang, and Kai-Chong Tsui, "Corporate Financial Policy in the Pacific Basin: Hong Kong and Singapore," *Financial Practice and Education,* Spring/Summer 1994, pp. 117–127.

[6]For an interesting article on expropriation, see Arvind Mahajan, "Pricing Expropriation Risk," *Financial Management,* Winter 1990, pp. 77–86.

Consumer Finance in China

The financial frontier for consumer finance is in China, where applicants must often wait more than a month to get a credit card and even longer for car loans or home mortgages. But that is changing quickly, as GE Money (formerly known as GE Capital) is among a host of financial players looking to partner with or become part owners of Chinese banks. Other foreign investors include financial institutions from all over the world, such as Citigroup (United States), ING Group (Netherlands), Hang Seng Bank (Hong Kong), and the Royal Bank of Scotland. Even investment banks (Goldman Sachs) and private equity firms (Newbridge Capital) are in the hunt.

What makes Chinese banks attractive? First, China is now allowing foreign-owned banks to make direct loans to Chinese customers. Second, China has a huge consumer base with a growing middle class that is purchasing homes, cars, and other consumer goods. Third, many Chinese banks might be considered "fixer-uppers" because they hold too many uncollectible loans (up to 9.2% of their loan portfolios), have weak information technology systems, and provide poor customer service. These problems are viewed as opportunities by GE Money, which brings considerable business expertise (in addition to cash) to the partnership. For example, GE Money helped Shenzhen Development Bank (SDB) introduce a Wal-Mart credit card, an Auchen credit card (Auchen is a large French retailer), and various mortgage services. All the results aren't yet in, but GE has helped SDB reduce the time to get a credit card from over a month to just 5 days.

Investing in China isn't without risks, with an estimated 60% of partnerships not providing the return that was anticipated at the deal's inception. Problems include insufficient pre-deal planning, a lack of focus and traction in the immediate post-deal period, a failure to integrate cultures, and a lack of flexibility in adapting to local conditions. Still, the potential rewards are enormous, so you should expect to see more foreign investment in China.

Source: Don Durfee, "Give Them Credit," *CFO*, July 2007, pp. 50–57.

countries such as Great Britain or Switzerland. However, in Latin America, Africa, the Far East, and Eastern Europe, the risk may be substantial. Past expropriations include those of ITT and Anaconda Copper in Chile; Gulf Oil in Bolivia; Occidental Petroleum in Libya; Enron Corporation in Peru; BP, ConocoPhillips, ExxonMobil, and Chevron in Venezuela; and the assets of many companies in Iraq, Iran, and Cuba.

Note that companies can take steps to reduce the potential loss from expropriation, including one or more of the following.

1. Finance the subsidiary with local capital.
2. Structure operations so that the subsidiary has value only as a part of the integrated corporate system.
3. Obtain insurance against economic losses from expropriation from a source such as the Overseas Private Investment Corporation (OPIC).

If OPIC insurance is purchased, then the premiums paid must be added to the project's cost.

Several organizations rate countries according to different aspects of risk. For example, Transparency International (TI) ranks countries based on perceived corruption, which is an important part of political risk. Table 17-4 shows selected countries. Denmark, New Zealand, and Sweden are rated by TI as the most honest countries, while Somalia is the most dishonest. The United States is ranked eighteenth.

Cash Flow Estimation

Cash flow estimation is more complex for foreign than domestic investments. Most multinational firms set up separate subsidiaries in each foreign country in which they operate, and the relevant cash flows for the parent company are the dividends

TABLE 17-4 The 2008 Transparency International Corruption Perceptions Index (CPI)

TOP-RANKED COUNTRIES			BOTTOM-RANKED COUNTRIES		
RANK	COUNTRY	2008 CPI SCORE	RANK	COUNTRY	2008 CPI SCORE
1 (tie)	Denmark	9.3	147 (tie)	Bangladesh	2.1
	New Zealand	9.3		Kenya	2.1
	Sweden	9.3		Russia	2.1
4	Singapore	9.2		Syria	2.1
5 (tie)	Finland	9.0	166 (tie)	Cambodia	1.8
	Switzerland	9.0		Kyrgyzstan	1.8
7 (tie)	Iceland	8.9		Turkmenistan	1.8
	Netherlands	8.9		Uzbekistan	1.8
9 (tie)	Australia	8.7		Zimbabwe	1.8
	Canada	8.7	173 (tie)	Chad	1.6
11	Luxembourg	8.3		Guinea	1.6
12 (tie)	Austria	8.1		Sudan	1.6
	Hong Kong	8.1	176	Afghanistan	1.5
14 (tie)	Germany	7.9	180	Somalia	1.0

Source: **http://www.transparency.org.**

and royalties paid by the subsidiaries to the parent, translated into dollars. Dividends and royalties are normally taxed by both foreign and home country governments, although the home country may allow credits for some or all of the foreign taxes paid. Furthermore, a foreign government may restrict the amount of the cash that may be **repatriated** to the parent company. For example, some governments place a ceiling, stated as a percentage of the company's net worth, on the amount of cash dividends that a subsidiary can pay to its parent. Such restrictions are normally intended to force multinational firms to reinvest earnings in the foreign country, although restrictions are sometimes imposed to prevent large currency outflows, which might disrupt the exchange rate.

Whatever the host country's motivation for blocking repatriation of profits, the result is that the parent corporation cannot use cash flows blocked in the foreign country to pay dividends to its shareholders or to invest elsewhere in the business. Hence, from the perspective of the parent organization, the cash flows relevant for foreign investment analysis are the cash flows that the subsidiary is actually expected to send back to the parent. Note, though, that if returns on investments in the foreign country are attractive and if blockages are expected to be lifted in the future, then current blockages may not be bad; however, dealing with this situation does complicate the process of cash flow estimation.

Some companies attempt to circumvent repatriation restrictions (and to lower their taxes) through the use of transfer pricing. For example, a foreign subsidiary might obtain raw materials or other input components from the parent. The price the subsidiary pays the parent is called a **transfer price.** If the transfer price is high then the foreign subsidiary's costs will be high, leaving little or no profit to repatriate. However, the parent's profit will be higher because it sold to the subsidiary at an inflated transfer price. The net result is that the parent receives cash flows from the subsidiary via transfer pricing rather than as repatriated dividends. Transfer pricing can also be used to shift profits from high-tax to low-tax jurisdictions. Of course, governments are well aware of these possibilities, so governmental auditors are on guard to prevent abusive transfer pricing.

Project Analysis

First, consider a domestic project that requires foreign raw materials, or one where the finished product will be sold in a foreign market. Because the operation is based in the United States, any projected nondollar cash flows—costs in the first example and revenues in the second—should be converted into dollars. This conversion does not present much of a problem for cash flows to be paid or received in the short run, but there is a significant problem in estimating exchange rates for converting long-term foreign cash flows into dollars because forward exchange rates are usually not available for more than 180 days into the future. However, long-term expected forward exchange rates can be estimated using the idea behind the interest rate parity relationship. For example, if a foreign cash flow is expected to occur in 1 year, then the 1-year forward exchange rate can be estimated using domestic and foreign government bonds maturing in 1 year. Similarly, the 2-year exchange rate can be estimated using 2-year bonds. Thus, foreign cash flows can be converted into dollars and added to the project's other projected cash flows, and then the project's NPV can be calculated based on its cost of capital.

Now consider a project to be based overseas, so that most expected future cash flows will be denominated in a foreign currency. Two approaches can be used to estimate such a project's NPV. Both begin by forecasting the future cash flows denominated in the foreign currency and then determining the annual repatriations to the United States, denominated in the foreign currency. Under the first approach, we convert the expected future repatriations to dollars (as described earlier) and then find the NPV using the project's cost of capital. Under the second approach, we take the projected repatriations (denominated in the foreign currency) and then discount them at the foreign cost of capital, which reflects foreign interest rates and relevant risk premiums. This produces an NPV denominated in the foreign currency, which can be converted into a dollar-denominated NPV using the spot exchange rate.

The following example illustrates the first approach. A U.S. company has the opportunity to lease a manufacturing facility in Great Britain for 3 years. The company must spend £20 million initially to refurbish the plant. The expected net cash flows from the plant for the next 3 years, in millions, are CF_1 = £7, CF_2 = £9, and CF_3 = £11. A similar project in the United States would have a risk-adjusted cost of capital of 10%. The first step is to estimate the expected exchange rates at the end of 1, 2, and 3 years using the multi-year interest rate parity equation:

$$\text{Expected t-year forward exchange rate} = (\text{Spot exchange rate})\left(\frac{1 + r_h}{1 + r_f}\right)^t \qquad (17\text{-}4)$$

where the exchange rates are expressed in direct quotations and the interest rates are expressed as annual rates, not periodic rates. We are using the interest rate parity equation to estimate expected forward rates because market-based forward rates for maturities longer than a year are generally not available.

Suppose the spot exchange rate is 1.8000 dollars per pound. Interest rates on U.S. and U.K. government bonds are shown below, along with the expected forward rate implied by the multi-year interest rate parity relationship in Equation 17-4:

TABLE 17-5 Net Present Value of International Investment (Cash Flows in Millions)

	YEAR			
	0	1	2	3
Cash flows in pounds	–£20	£7	£9	£11
Expected exchange rates (pounds/dollar)	1.8000	1.7553	1.7254	1.7141
Cash flows in dollars	–$36.00	$12.29	$15.53	$18.86
Project cost of capital	10%			
NPV	$2.18			

	Maturity (Years)		
	1	2	3
r_h (annualized)	2.0%	2.8%	3.5%
r_f (annualized)	4.6%	5.0%	5.2%
Spot rate ($/£)	1.8000	1.8000	1.8000
Expected forward rate based on Equation 17-4 ($/£)	1.7553	1.7254	1.7141

The current dollar cost of the project is £20(1.8000 $/£) = $36 million. The Year-1 cash flow in dollars is £7(1.7553 $/£) = $12.29 million. Table 17-5 shows the complete time line and the net present value of $2.18 million.

Self-Test

List some key differences in capital budgeting as applied to foreign versus domestic operations.

What are the relevant cash flows for an international investment: the cash flow produced by the subsidiary in the country where it operates, or the cash flows in dollars that it sends to its parent company?

Why might the cost of capital for a foreign project differ from that of an equivalent domestic project? Could it be lower?

What adjustments might be made to the domestic cost of capital for a foreign investment that are due to exchange rate risk and political risk?

17.12 International Capital Structures

Companies' capital structures vary among countries. For example, the Organization for Economic Cooperation and Development (OECD) recently reported that, on average, Japanese firms use 85% debt to total assets (in book value terms), German firms use 64%, and U.S. firms use 55%. One problem when interpreting these numbers is that different countries often use different accounting conventions with regard to (1) reporting assets on the basis of historical versus replacement cost, (2) the treatment of leased assets, (3) pension plan funding, and (4) capitalizing versus expensing R&D costs. These differences make it difficult to compare capital structures.

A study by Raghuram Rajan and Luigi Zingales of the University of Chicago attempted to account for differences in accounting practices. In their study, Rajan and Zingales used a database that covered fewer firms than the OECD but that provided a more complete breakdown of balance sheet data. They concluded that differences in accounting practices can explain much of the cross-country variation in capital structures.

TABLE 17-6 Median Capital Structures among Large Industrialized Countries (Measured in Terms of Book Value)

COUNTRY	TOTAL LIABILITIES TO TOTAL ASSETS (UNADJUSTED FOR ACCOUNTING DIFFERENCES) (1)	INTEREST-BEARING DEBT TO TOTAL ASSETS (UNADJUSTED FOR ACCOUNTING DIFFERENCES) (2)	TOTAL LIABILITIES TO TOTAL ASSETS (ADJUSTED FOR ACCOUNTING DIFFERENCES) (3)	DEBT TO TOTAL ASSETS (ADJUSTED FOR ACCOUNTING DIFFERENCES) (4)	TIMES-INTEREST-EARNED (TIE) RATIO (5)
Canada	56%	32%	48%	32%	1.55
France	71	25	69	18	2.64
Germany	73	16	50	11	3.20
Italy	70	27	68	21	1.81
Japan	69	35	62	21	2.46
United Kingdom	54	18	47	10	4.79
United States	58	27	52	25	2.41
Mean	64%	26%	57%	20%	2.69
Standard deviation	8%	7%	10%	8%	1.07

Source: Raghuram Rajan and Luigi Zingales, "What Do We Know about Capital Structure? Some Evidence from International Data," *The Journal of Finance*, Vol. 50, no. 5 (December 1995), pp. 1421-1460. Reprinted by permission of John Wiley & Sons, Inc.

Rajan and Zingales's results are summarized in Table 17-6. There are a number of different ways to measure capital structure. One measure is the average ratio of total liabilities to total assets—this is similar to the measure used by the OECD, and it is reported in Column 1. Based on this measure, German and Japanese firms appear to be more highly levered than U.S. firms. However, if you look at Column 2, where capital structure is measured by interest-bearing debt to total assets, it appears that German firms use less leverage than U.S. and Japanese firms. What explains these conflicting results? Rajan and Zingales argue that much of the difference is explained by the way German firms account for pension liabilities. German firms generally include all pension liabilities (and their offsetting assets) on the balance sheet, whereas firms in other countries (including the United States) generally "net out" pension assets and liabilities on their balance sheets. To see the importance of this difference, consider a firm with \$10 million in liabilities (not including pension liabilities) and \$20 million in assets (not including pension assets). Assume that the firm has \$10 million in pension liabilities that are fully funded by \$10 million in pension assets. Therefore, net pension liabilities are zero. If this firm were in the United States, it would report a ratio of total liabilities to total assets equal to 50% (\$10 million/\$20 million). By contrast, if this firm operated in Germany, both its pension assets and liabilities would be reported on the balance sheet. The firm would have \$20 million in liabilities and \$30 million in assets—or a 67% (\$20 million/\$30 million) ratio of total liabilities to total assets. Total debt is the sum of short-term debt and long-term debt and *excludes* other liabilities, including pension liabilities. Therefore, the measure of total debt to total assets provides a more comparable measure of leverage across different countries.

Rajan and Zingales also make a variety of adjustments that attempt to control for other differences in accounting practices. The effects of these adjustments are reported in Columns 3 and 4. Overall, the evidence suggests that companies in Germany and the United Kingdom tend to have less leverage, and that firms in Canada appear to have more leverage, than firms in the United States, France, Italy, and Japan. This conclusion is supported by data in the final column, which shows the average times-interest-earned ratio for firms in a number of different countries. Recall from Chapter 3 that the times-interest-earned ratio is the ratio of operating income (EBIT) to interest expense. This measure indicates how much cash the firm has available to service its interest expense. In general, firms with more leverage have a lower times-interest-earned ratio. The data indicate that this ratio is highest in the United Kingdom and Germany and lowest in Canada.

Self-Test

Are there international differences in firms' financial leverage? Explain.

17.13 Multinational Working Capital Management

Working capital management in a multinational setting involves more complexity than purely domestic working capital management. We discuss some of these differences in this section.

Cash Management

The goals of cash management in a multinational corporation are similar to those in a purely domestic corporation: (1) to speed up collections, slow down disbursements, and thus maximize net float; (2) to shift cash as rapidly as possible from those parts of the business where it is not needed to those parts where it is needed; and (3) to maximize the risk-adjusted, after-tax rate of return on temporary cash balances. Multinational companies use the same general procedures for achieving these goals as domestic firms, but the longer distances and more serious mail delays make such devices as lockbox systems and electronic funds transfers especially important.

Although multinational and domestic corporations have the same objectives and use similar procedures, multinational corporations face a far more complex task. As noted earlier in our discussion of political risk, foreign governments often place restrictions on transfers of funds out of the country. So even though IBM can transfer money from its Salt Lake City office to its New York concentration bank just by pressing a few buttons, a similar transfer from its Buenos Aires office is far more complex. Buenos Aires funds must be converted to dollars before the transfer. If there is a shortage of dollars in Argentina or if the Argentinean government wants to conserve dollars so they will be available for the purchase of strategic materials, then conversion, and hence the transfer, may be blocked. Even if no dollar shortage exists in Argentina, the government may still restrict funds outflows if those funds represent profits or depreciation rather than payments for purchased materials or equipment, because many countries—especially those that are less developed—want profits reinvested in the country in order to stimulate economic growth.

Once it has been determined what funds can be transferred, the next task is to get those funds to locations where they will earn the highest returns. Whereas domestic corporations tend to think in terms of domestic securities, multinationals are more likely to be aware of investment opportunities all around the world. Most multinational corporations use one or more global concentration banks, located in money centers such as London, New York, Tokyo, Zurich, or Singapore, and their staffs in those cities, working with international bankers, are able to take advantage of the best rates available anywhere in the world.

Credit Management

Consider the international cash conversion cycle for a foreign company importing from the United States: The order is placed, the goods are shipped, an account payable is created for the importer and an account receivable is created for the exporter, the goods arrive in the foreign country, the importer sells them, and the importer collects on the sales. At some point in this process, the importer pays off the account payable, which is usually before the importer collects on its own sales. Notice that the importer must finance the transaction from the time it pays the account payable until it collects on its sales. In many poorer, less-developed nations, the capital markets are not adequate to enable the importer to finance the cash conversion cycle. Even when foreign capital markets are available, the additional shipping time might lengthen the cash conversion cycle to such an extent that the importer can't afford the financing costs. Thus, there is enormous pressure on the exporter to grant credit, often with very lengthy payment periods.

But now consider the situation from the exporter's point of view. First, it is much more difficult for the exporter to perform a credit analysis on a foreign customer. Second, the exporter must also worry about exchange-rate fluctuations between the time of the sale and the time the receivable is collected. For example, if IBM sold a computer to a Japanese customer for 90 million yen when the exchange rate was 90 yen to the dollar, IBM would obtain 90,000,000/90 = $1,000,000 for the computer. However, if it sold the computer on terms of net/6 months and if the yen then fell against the dollar, so that 1 dollar would now buy 112.5 yen, IBM would end up realizing only 90,000,000/112.5 = $800,000 when it collected the receivable. Hedging with forward contracts can reduce this exchange rate risk, but what about the credit risk?

One possibility is for the importer to obtain a letter of credit from its bank whereby the bank certifies that the importer will meet the terms of the account payable or else the bank will pay. However, the importer often must pay the bank a relatively large fee for the letter of credit, and letters of credit might not be available to companies in developing countries.

A second option is for the importer to essentially write a check to the exporter at the time of the purchase, but one that is postdated so that it cannot be cashed until the account payable's due date. If the importer's bank promises that it will "accept" the check even if there are insufficient funds in the importer's account, then the check becomes a financial instrument that is called a **banker's acceptance.** If the bank is strong, then this virtually eliminates the credit risk. In addition, the exporter can then sell this banker's acceptance in the secondary market if it needs funds immediately. Of course, it must sell the banker's acceptance at a discount to reflect the time value of money, because the banker's acceptance is essentially a short-term financial security that pays no interest, similar to a T-bill. Financing an international transaction via a banker's acceptance has many benefits for the exporter, but the importer often must pay the bank a relatively large fee, and this service might not be available to companies in developing countries.

A third alternative is for the exporter to purchase export credit insurance, in which an insurer makes a commitment to pay the exporter even if the importer defaults. Sometimes the "insurer" is a government agency, such as the Japanese Ministry of International Trade and Industry (MITI) or the United States Export-Import Bank. Other times, the insurer is a private insurance company. These large insurance companies have developed expertise in international credit analysis, and they can spread the risk over a large number of customers. These advantages allow them to offer credit insurance at rates that often make it less costly than either letters of credit or bankers' acceptances. In fact, export credit insurance has been so successful that it has virtually killed the market for bankers' acceptances and has become the primary method companies use to manage the credit risk of international sales.

Inventory Management

As with most other aspects of finance, inventory management for a firm in a multinational setting is similar to but more complex than for a purely domestic firm. First, there is the matter of the physical location of inventories. For example, where should ExxonMobil keep its stockpiles of crude oil and refined products? It has refineries and marketing centers located worldwide, and one alternative is to keep items concentrated in a few strategic spots from which they can then be shipped as needs arise. Such a strategy might minimize the total amount of inventories needed and thus might minimize the investment in inventories. Note, though, that consideration will have to be given to potential delays in getting goods from central storage locations to user locations all around the world. Both working stocks and safety stocks would have to be maintained at each user location as well as at the strategic storage centers. Problems like the Iraqi occupation of Kuwait in 1990 and the subsequent trade embargo, which brought with it the potential for a shutdown of production of about 25% of the world's oil supply, complicate matters further.

Exchange rates also influence inventory policy. If a local currency—say, the Danish krone—were expected to rise in value against the dollar, then a U.S. company operating in Denmark would want to increase stocks of local products before the rise in the krone, and vice versa if the krone were expected to fall.

Another factor that must be considered is the possibility of import or export quotas or tariffs. For example, Apple Computer Company was buying certain memory chips from Japanese suppliers at a bargain price. Then U.S. chipmakers accused the Japanese of dumping chips in the U.S. market at prices below cost, and they sought to force the Japanese to raise their prices.[7] This led Apple to increase its chip inventory. Then computer sales slacked off, and Apple ended up with an oversupply of obsolete computer chips. As a result, Apple's profits were hurt and its stock price fell, demonstrating once more the importance of careful inventory management.

As mentioned earlier, another danger in certain countries is the threat of expropriation. If that threat is large, then inventory holdings will be minimized and goods will be brought in only as needed. Similarly, if the operation involves extraction of raw materials such as oil or bauxite, processing plants may be moved offshore rather than located close to the production site.

Taxes have two effects on multinational inventory management. First, countries often impose property taxes on assets, including inventories; when this is done, the

[7]The term "dumping" warrants explanation, because the practice can be so important in international markets. Suppose Japanese chipmakers have excess capacity. A particular chip has a variable cost of $25, and its "fully allocated cost," which is the $25 plus total fixed cost per unit of output, is $40. Now suppose the Japanese firm can sell chips in the United States at $35 per unit, but if it charges $40 then it won't make any sales because U.S. chipmakers sell for $35.50. If the Japanese firm sells at $35, it will cover variable costs plus make a contribution to fixed overhead, so selling at $35 makes sense. Continuing, if the Japanese firm can sell in Japan at $40 but U.S. firms are excluded from Japanese markets by import duties or other barriers, then the Japanese will have a huge advantage over U.S. manufacturers. This practice of selling goods at lower prices in foreign markets than at home is called "dumping." U.S. firms are required by antitrust laws to offer the same price to all customers and, therefore, cannot engage in dumping.

tax is based on holdings as of a specific date, such as January 1 or March 1. Such rules make it advantageous for a multinational firm (1) to schedule production so that inventories are low on the assessment date, and (2) if assessment dates vary among countries in a region, to hold safety stocks in different countries at different times during the year.

Finally, multinational firms may consider the possibility of at-sea storage. Oil, chemical, grain, and other companies that deal in a bulk commodity that must be stored in some type of tank can often buy tankers at a cost not much greater—or perhaps even less, considering land cost—than land-based facilities. Loaded tankers can then be kept at sea or at anchor in some strategic location. This eliminates the danger of expropriation, minimizes the property tax problem, and maximizes flexibility with regard to shipping to areas where needs are greatest or prices highest.

This discussion has only scratched the surface of inventory management in the multinational corporation—the task is much more complex than for a purely domestic firm. However, the greater the degree of complexity, the greater the rewards from superior performance, so if you are willing to take challenges along with potentially high rewards then look to the international arena.

Self-Test

What are some factors that make cash management more complicated in a multinational corporation than in a purely domestic corporation?
Why is granting credit riskier in an international context?
Why is inventory management especially important for a multinational firm?

Summary

Multinational companies have more opportunities but also face different risks than do companies that operate only in their home market. This chapter discussed many of the key trends affecting the global markets today, and it described the most important differences between multinational and domestic financial management. The key concepts are listed below.

- **International operations** are becoming increasingly important to individual firms and to the national economy. A multinational, transnational, or **global corporation** is a firm that operates in an integrated fashion in a number of countries.
- Companies "go global" for these reasons: (1) to expand their markets, (2) to obtain raw materials, (3) to seek new technology, (4) to lower production costs, (5) to avoid trade barriers, and (6) to diversify.
- Several major factors distinguish financial management as practiced by domestic firms from that practiced by multinational corporations: (1) different currency denominations, (2) different economic and legal structures, (3) languages, (4) cultural differences, (5) role of governments, and (6) political risk.
- When discussing **exchange rates,** the number of U.S. dollars required to purchase one unit of a foreign currency is called a **direct quotation,** while the number of units of foreign currency that can be purchased for one U.S. dollar is an **indirect quotation.**
- **Exchange rate fluctuations** make it difficult to estimate the dollars that overseas operations will produce.
- Prior to August 1971, the world was on a **fixed exchange rate system** whereby the U.S. dollar was linked to gold and other currencies were then tied to the dollar. After August 1971, the world monetary system changed to a **floating**

system under which major world currency rates float with market forces, largely unrestricted by governmental intervention. The central bank of each country does operate in the foreign exchange market, buying and selling currencies to smooth out exchange rate fluctuations, but only to a limited extent.

- **Pegged exchange rates** occur when a country establishes a fixed exchange rate with a major currency. Consequently, the values of pegged currencies move together over time.
- A **convertible currency** is one that may be readily exchanged for other currencies.
- **Spot rates** are the rates paid for delivery of currency "on the spot," whereas the **forward exchange rate** is the rate paid for delivery at some agreed-upon future date—usually 30, 90, or 180 days from the day the transaction is negotiated. The forward rate can be at either a **premium** or a **discount** to the spot rate.
- **Interest rate parity** holds that investors should expect to earn the same risk-free return in all countries after adjusting for exchange rates.
- **Purchasing power parity,** sometimes referred to as the *law of one price*, implies that the level of exchange rates adjusts so that identical goods cost the same in different countries.
- Granting credit is more risky in an international context because, in addition to the normal risks of default, the multinational firm must worry about **exchange rate changes** between the time a sale is made and the time a receivable is collected.
- Credit policy is important for a multinational firm for two reasons: (1) Much trade is with less-developed nations, and in such situations granting credit is a necessary condition for doing business. (2) The governments of nations such as Japan, whose economic health depends on exports, often help their firms compete by granting credit to foreign customers.
- Foreign investments are similar to domestic investments, but political risk and exchange rate risk must be considered. **Political risk** is the risk that the foreign government will take some action that will decrease the value of the investment; **exchange rate risk** is the risk of losses due to fluctuations in the value of the dollar relative to the values of foreign currencies.
- Investments in **international capital projects** expose firms to exchange rate risk and political risk. The relevant cash flows in international capital budgeting are the dollars that can be **repatriated** to the parent company.
- **Eurodollars** are U.S. dollars deposited in banks outside the United States. Interest rates on Eurodollars are tied to **LIBOR,** the **London Interbank Offered Rate**.
- U.S. firms often find that they can raise long-term capital at a lower cost outside the United States by selling bonds in the **international capital markets.** International bonds may be either **foreign bonds**, which are exactly like regular domestic bonds except that the issuer is a foreign company, or **Eurobonds,** which are bonds sold in a foreign country but denominated in the currency of the issuing company's home country.

Questions

(17–1) Define each of the following terms:

a. Multinational corporation
b. Exchange rate; fixed exchange rate system; floating exchange rates
c. Trade deficit; devaluation; revaluation

d. Exchange rate risk; convertible currency; pegged exchange rates
e. Interest rate parity; purchasing power parity
f. Spot rate; forward exchange rate; discount on forward rate; premium on forward rate
g. Repatriation of earnings; political risk
h. Eurodollar; Eurobond; international bond; foreign bond
i. The euro

(17–2) Under the fixed exchange rate system, what was the currency against which all other currency values were defined? Why?

(17–3) Exchange rates fluctuate under both the fixed exchange rate and floating exchange rate systems. What, then, is the difference between the two systems?

(17–4) If the Swiss franc depreciates against the U.S. dollar, can a dollar buy more or fewer Swiss francs as a result?

(17–5) If the United States imports more goods from abroad than it exports, then foreigners will tend to have a surplus of U.S. dollars. What will this do to the value of the dollar with respect to foreign currencies? What is the corresponding effect on foreign investments in the United States?

(17–6) Why do U.S. corporations build manufacturing plants abroad when they could build them at home?

(17–7) Should firms require higher rates of return on foreign projects than on identical projects located at home? Explain.

(17–8) What is a Eurodollar? If a French citizen deposits $10,000 in Chase Bank in New York, have Eurodollars been created? What if the deposit is made in Barclays Bank in London? Chase's Paris branch? Does the existence of the Eurodollar market make the Federal Reserve's job of controlling U.S. interest rates easier or more difficult? Explain.

(17–9) Does interest rate parity imply that interest rates are the same in all countries?

(17–10) Why might purchasing power parity fail to hold?

Self-Test Problem

Solution Appears in Appendix A

(ST–1) Cross Rates

Suppose the exchange rate between U.S. dollars and euros is €0.98 = $1.00 and the exchange rate between the U.S. dollar and the Canadian dollar is $1.00 = C$1.50. What is the cross rate of euros to Canadian dollars?

Problems

Answers Appear in Appendix B

Easy Problems 1–4

(17–1) Cross Rates

A currency trader observes that, in the spot exchange market, 1 U.S. dollar can be exchanged for 9 Mexican pesos or for 111.23 Japanese yen. What is the cross rate between the yen and the peso; that is, how many yen would you receive for every peso exchanged?

(17–2) Interest Rate Parity

Six-month T-bills have a nominal rate of 7%, while default-free Japanese bonds that mature in 6 months have a nominal rate of 5.5%. In the spot exchange market, 1 yen equals $0.009. If interest rate parity holds, what is the 6-month forward exchange rate?

(17–3) Purchasing Power Parity

A television set costs $500 in the United States. The same set costs 550 euros in France. If purchasing power parity holds, what is the spot exchange rate between the euro and the dollar?

(17–4) Exchange Rate

If British pounds sell for $1.50 (U.S.) per pound, what should dollars sell for in pounds per dollar?

INTERMEDIATE PROBLEMS 5–8

(17–5) Currency Appreciation

Suppose that 1 Swiss franc could be purchased in the foreign exchange market for 60 U.S. cents today. If the franc appreciated 10% tomorrow against the dollar, how many francs would a dollar buy tomorrow?

(17–6) Cross Rates

Suppose the exchange rate between U.S. dollars and the Swiss franc is SFr1.6 = $1 and the exchange rate between the dollar and the British pound is £1 = $1.50. What then is the cross rate between francs and pounds?

(17–7) Interest Rate Parity

Assume that interest rate parity holds. In both the spot market and the 90-day forward market, 1 Japanese yen equals 0.0086 dollar. In Japan, 90-day risk-free securities yield 4.6%. What is the yield on 90-day risk-free securities in the United States?

(17–8) Purchasing Power Parity

In the spot market, 7.8 pesos can be exchanged for 1 U.S. dollar. A compact disc costs $15 in the United States. If purchasing power parity holds, what should be the price of the same disc in Mexico?

CHALLENGING PROBLEMS 9–14

(17–9) Exchange Gains and Losses

You are the vice president of International InfoXchange, headquartered in Chicago. All shareholders of the firm live in the United States. Earlier this month, you obtained a loan of 5 million Canadian dollars from a bank in Toronto to finance the construction of a new plant in Montreal. At the time the loan was received, the exchange rate was 75 U.S. cents to the Canadian dollar. By the end of the month, it has unexpectedly dropped to 70 cents. Has your company made a gain or loss as a result, and by how much?

(17–10) Results of Exchange Rate Changes

Early in September 1983, it took 245 Japanese yen to equal $1. More than 20 years later, that exchange rate had fallen to 108 yen to $1. Assume that the price of a Japanese-manufactured automobile was $8,000 in September 1983 and that its price changes were in direct relation to exchange rates.

a. Has the price (in dollars) of the automobile increased or decreased during the 20-year period because of changes in the exchange rate?
b. What would the dollar price of the car be, assuming the car's price changes only with exchange rates?

(17–11) Spot and Forward Rates

Boisjoly Watch Imports has agreed to purchase 15,000 Swiss watches for 1 million francs at today's spot rate. The firm's financial manager, James Desreumaux, has noted the following current spot and forward rates:

	U.S. Dollar/Franc	Franc/U.S. Dollar
Spot	1.6590	0.6028
30-day forward	1.6540	0.6046
90-day forward	1.6460	0.6075
180-day forward	1.6400	0.6098

On the same day, Desreumaux agrees to purchase 15,000 more watches in 3 months at the same price of 1 million francs.

a. What is the price of the watches, in U.S. dollars, if purchased at today's spot rate?
b. What is the cost, in dollars, of the second 15,000 batch if payment is made in 90 days and the spot rate at that time equals today's 90-day forward rate?
c. If the exchange rate for the Swiss franc is 0.50 to $1 in 90 days, how much will Desreumaux have to pay (in dollars) for the watches?

(17–12) Interest Rate Parity

Assume that interest rate parity holds and that 90-day risk-free securities yield 5% in the United States and 5.3% in Germany. In the spot market, 1 euro equals $0.80 dollar.

a. Is the 90-day forward rate trading at a premium or a discount relative to the spot rate?
b. What is the 90-day forward rate?

(17–13) Foreign Investment Analysis

After all foreign and U.S. taxes, a U.S. corporation expects to receive 3 pounds of dividends per share from a British subsidiary this year. The exchange rate at the end of the year is expected to be $1.60 per pound, and the pound is expected to depreciate 5% against the dollar each year for an indefinite period. The dividend (in pounds) is expected to grow at 10% a year indefinitely. The parent U.S. corporation owns 10 million shares of the subsidiary. What is the present value, in dollars, of its equity ownership of the subsidiary? Assume a cost of equity capital of 15% for the subsidiary.

(17–14) Foreign Capital Budgeting

Solitaire Machinery is a Swiss multinational manufacturing company. Currently, Solitaire's financial planners are considering whether to undertake a 1-year project in the United States. The project's expected dollar-denominated cash flows consist of an initial investment of $1,000 and a cash inflow the following year of $1,200. Solitaire estimates that its risk-adjusted cost of capital is 14%. Currently, 1 U.S. dollar will buy 1.62 Swiss francs. In addition, 1-year risk-free securities in the United States are yielding 7.25%, while similar securities in Switzerland are yielding 4.5%.

a. If this project were instead undertaken by a similar U.S.-based company with the same risk-adjusted cost of capital, what would be the net present value and rate of return generated by this project?
b. What is the expected forward exchange rate 1 year from now?
c. If Solitaire undertakes the project, what is the net present value and rate of return of the project for Solitaire?

Spreadsheet Problem

(17–15) Build a Model: Multinational Financial Management

Start with the partial model in the file ***Ch17 P15 Build a Model.xls*** on the textbook's Web site. Yohe Telecommunications is a multinational corporation that produces and distributes telecommunications technology. Although its corporate headquarters are located in Maitland, Florida, Yohe usually must buy its raw materials in several different foreign countries using several different foreign currencies. The matter is further

complicated because Yohe usually sells its products in other foreign countries. One product in particular, the SY-20 radio transmitter, draws its principal components—Component X, Component Y, and Component Z—from Germany, Mexico, and England, respectively. Specifically, Component X costs 84 euros, Component Y costs 650 Mexican pesos, and Component Z costs 105 British pounds. The largest market for the SY-20 is in Japan, where it sells for 38,000 Japanese yen. Naturally, Yohe is intimately concerned with economic conditions that could adversely affect dollar exchange rates. You will find Tables 17-1, 17-2, and 17-3 useful for this problem.

a. How much, in dollars, does it cost for Yohe to produce the SY-20? What is the dollar sale price of the SY-20?
b. What is the dollar profit that Yohe makes on the sale of the SY-20? What is the percentage profit?
c. If the U.S. dollar were to weaken by 10% against all foreign currencies, what would be the dollar profit for the SY-20?
d. If the U.S. dollar were to weaken by 10% only against the Japanese yen and remained constant relative to all other foreign currencies, what would be the dollar and percentage profits for the SY-20?
e. Using the forward exchange information from Table 17-3, calculate the return on 90-day securities in England if the rate of return on 90-day securities in the United States is 4.9%.
f. Assuming that purchasing power parity (PPP) holds, what would be the sale price of the SY-20 if it were sold in England rather than in Japan?

Mini Case

Citrus Products Inc. is a medium-sized producer of citrus juice drinks with groves in Indian River County, Florida. Until now, the company has confined its operations and sales to the United States, but its CEO, George Gaynor, wants to expand into Europe. The first step would be to set up sales subsidiaries in Spain and Sweden, then to set up a production plant in Spain, and finally to distribute the product throughout the European common market. The firm's financial manager, Ruth Schmidt, is enthusiastic about the plan, but she is worried about the implications of the foreign expansion on the firm's financial management process. She has asked you, the firm's most recently hired financial analyst, to develop a 1-hour tutorial package that explains the basics of multinational financial management. The tutorial will be presented at the next board of directors' meeting. To get you started, Schmidt has supplied you with the following list of questions.

a. What is a multinational corporation? Why do firms expand into other countries?
b. What are the six major factors that distinguish multinational financial management from financial management as practiced by a purely domestic firm?
c. Consider the following illustrative exchange rates.

	U.S. Dollars Required to Buy 1 Unit of Foreign Currency
Euro	1.2500
Swedish krona	0.1481

(1) Are these currency prices direct quotations or indirect quotations?
(2) Calculate the indirect quotations for euros and kronor (the plural of krona is kronor).
(3) What is a cross rate? Calculate the two cross rates between euros and kronor.
(4) Assume Citrus Products can produce a liter of orange juice and ship it to Spain for $1.75. If the firm wants a 50% markup on the product, what should the orange juice sell for in Spain?

(5) Now assume that Citrus Products begins producing the same liter of orange juice in Spain. The product costs 2 euros to produce and ship to Sweden, where it can be sold for 20 kronor. What is the dollar profit on the sale?

(6) What is exchange rate risk?

d. Briefly describe the current international monetary system. How does the current system differ from the system that was in place prior to August 1971?

e. What is a convertible currency? What problems arise when a multinational company operates in a country whose currency is not convertible?

f. What is the difference between spot rates and forward rates? When is the forward rate at a premium to the spot rate? At a discount?

g. What is interest rate parity? Currently, you can exchange 1 euro for 1.27 dollars in the 180-day forward market, and the risk-free rate on 180-day securities is 6% in the United States and 4% in Spain. Does interest rate parity hold? If not, which securities offer the highest expected return?

h. What is purchasing power parity? If grapefruit juice costs $2 a liter in the United States and purchasing power parity holds, what should be the price of grapefruit juice in Spain?

i. What effect does relative inflation have on interest rates and exchange rates?

j. Briefly discuss the international capital markets.

k. To what extent do average capital structures vary across different countries?

l. Briefly describe special problems that occur in multinational capital budgeting, and describe the process for evaluating a foreign project. Now consider the following project: A U.S. company has the opportunity to lease a manufacturing facility in Japan for 2 years. The company must spend ¥1 billion initially to refurbish the plant. The expected net cash flows from the plant for the next 2 years, in millions, are CF_1 = ¥500 and CF_2 = ¥800. A similar project in the United States would have a risk-adjusted cost of capital of 10%. In the United States, a 1-year government bond pays 2% interest and a 2-year bond pays 2.8%. In Japan, a 1-year bond pays 0.05% and a 2-year bond pays 0.26%. What is the project's NPV?

m. Briefly discuss special factors associated with the following areas of multinational working capital management:

(1) Cash management

(2) Credit management

(3) Inventory management

Selected Additional Case

The following case from Textchoice, *Cengage Learning's online library, covers many of the concepts discussed in this chapter and is available at* **http://www.textchoice2.com.**

Klein-Brigham Series:
Case 18, "Alaska Oil Corporation."

APPENDIX A

Solutions to Self-Test Problems

Chapter 2

ST-1 a.

EBIT	\$5,000,000
Interest	1,000,000
EBT	\$4,000,000
Taxes (40%)	1,600,000
Net income	\$2,400,000

b.

$$\begin{aligned} \text{NCF} &= \text{NI} + \text{DEP and AMORT} \\ &= \$2{,}400{,}000 + \$1000{,}000 = \$3{,}400{,}000 \end{aligned}$$

c.

$$\begin{aligned} \text{NOPAT} &= \text{EBIT}(1 - \text{T}) \\ &= \$5{,}000{,}000(0.6) \\ &= \$3{,}000{,}000 \end{aligned}$$

d.

$$\begin{aligned} \text{NOWC} &= \text{Operating current assets} - \text{Operating current liabilities} \\ &= (\text{Cash} + \text{Accounts receivable} + \text{Inventory}) \\ &\quad - (\text{Accounts payable} + \text{Accruals}) \\ &= \$14{,}000{,}000 - \$4{,}000{,}000 \\ &= \$10{,}000{,}000 \\ \text{Total net operating capital} &= \text{NOWC} + \text{Operating long-term assets} \\ &= \$10{,}000{,}000 + \$15{,}000{,}000 \\ &= \$25{,}000{,}000 \end{aligned}$$

e.

$$\begin{aligned} \text{FCF} &= \text{NOPAT} - \text{Net investment in operating capital} \\ &= \$3{,}000{,}000 - (\$25{,}000{,}000 - \$24{,}000{,}000) \\ &= \$2{,}000{,}000 \end{aligned}$$

f.

$$\begin{aligned} \text{EVA} &= \text{EBIT}(1 - \text{T}) - (\text{Total capital})(\text{After-tax cost of capital}) \\ &= \$5{,}000{,}000(0.6) - (\$25{,}000{,}000)(0.10) \\ &= \$3{,}000{,}000 - \$2{,}500{,}000 = \$500{,}000 \end{aligned}$$

Chapter 3

ST-1 Argent paid \$2 in dividends and retained \$2 per share. Since total retained earnings rose by \$12 million, there must be 6 million shares outstanding. With a book value of \$40 per share, total common equity must be \$40(6 million) = \$240 million. Since Argent has \$120 million of debt, its debt ratio must be 33.3%:

$$\frac{\text{Debt}}{\text{Assets}} = \frac{\text{Debt}}{\text{Debt + Equity}} = \frac{\$120 \text{ million}}{\$120 \text{ million} + \$240 \text{ million}}$$
$$= 0.333 = 33.3\%$$

ST-2 a. In answering questions such as this, always begin by writing down the relevant definitional equations and then start filling in numbers. Note that the extra zeros indicating millions have been deleted in the calculations below.

(1)
$$\text{DSO} = \frac{\text{Accounts receivable}}{\text{Sales}/365}$$
$$40.55 = \frac{\text{AR}}{\text{Sales}/365}$$
$$\text{AR} = 40.55(\$2.7397) = \$111.1 \text{ million}$$

(2)
$$\text{Quick ratio} = \frac{\text{Current assets} - \text{Inventories}}{\text{Current liabilities}} = 2.0$$
$$= \frac{\text{Cash and marketable securities} + \text{AR}}{\text{Current liabilities}} = 2.0$$
$$2.0 = \frac{\$100.0 + \$111.1}{\text{Current liabilities}}$$
$$\text{Current liabilities} = (\$100.0 + \$111.1)/2 = \$105.5 \text{ million}$$

(3)
$$\text{Current ratio} = \frac{\text{Current assets}}{\text{Current liabilities}} = 3.0$$
$$= \frac{\text{Current assets}}{\$105.5} = 3.0$$
$$\text{Current assets} = 3.0(\$105.5) = \$316.50 \text{ million}$$

(4)
$$\text{Total assets} = \text{Current assets} + \text{Fixed assets}$$
$$= \$316.5 + \$283.5 = \$600 \text{ million}$$

(5)
$$\text{ROA} = \text{Profit margin} \times \text{Total assets turnover}$$
$$= \frac{\text{Net income}}{\text{Sales}} \times \frac{\text{Sales}}{\text{Total assets}}$$
$$= \frac{\$50}{\$1{,}000} \times \frac{\$1{,}000}{\$600}$$
$$= 0.05 \times 1.667 = 0.083333 = 8.3333\%$$

(6)

$$\text{ROE} = \text{ROA} \times \frac{\text{Assets}}{\text{Equity}}$$

$$12.0\% = 8.3333\% \times \frac{\$600}{\text{Equity}}$$

$$\text{Equity} = \frac{(8.3333\%)(\$600)}{12.0\%}$$

$$= \$416.67 \text{ million}$$

(7)

$$\text{Total assets} = \text{Total claims} = \$600 \text{ million}$$
$$\text{Current liabilities} + \text{Long-term debt} + \text{Equity} = \$600 \text{ million}$$
$$\$105.5 + \text{Long-term debt} + \$416.67 = \$600 \text{ million}$$
$$\text{Long-term debt} = \$600 - \$105.5 - \$416.67 = \$77.83 \text{ million}$$

Note: We could also have found equity as follows:

$$\text{ROE} = \frac{\text{Net income}}{\text{Equity}}$$

$$12.0\% = \frac{\$50}{\text{Equity}}$$

$$\text{Equity} = \$50/0.12$$

$$= \$416.67 \text{ million}$$

Then we could have gone on to find long-term debt.

b. Jacobus's average sales per day were $1,000/365 = $2.7397 million. Its DSO was 40.55, so accounts receivable equal 40.55($2.7397) = $111.1 million. Its new DSO of 30.4 would cause AR = 30.4($2.7397) = $83.3 million. The reduction in receivables would be $111.1 – $83.3 = $27.8 million, which would equal the amount of cash generated.

(1)

$$\text{New equity} = \text{Old equity} - \text{Stock bought back}$$
$$= \$416.7 - \$27.8$$
$$= \$388.9 \text{ million}$$

Thus,

$$\text{New ROE} = \frac{\text{Net income}}{\text{New equity}}$$

$$= \frac{\$50}{\$388.9}$$

$$= 12.86\% \text{ (versus old ROE of12.0\%)}$$

(2)

$$\text{New ROA} = \frac{\text{Net income}}{\text{Total assets} - \text{Reduction in AR}}$$

$$= \frac{\$50}{\$600 - \$27.8}$$

$$= 8.74\% \text{ (versus old ROA of 8.33\%)}$$

(3) The old debt is the same as the new debt:

$$\text{Debt} = \text{Total claims} - \text{Equity}$$
$$= \$600 - \$416.7 = \$183.3 \text{ million}$$

$$\text{New total assets} = \text{Old total assets} - \text{Reduction in AR}$$
$$= \$600 - \$27.8$$
$$= \$572.2 \text{ million}$$

Therefore,

$$\frac{\text{Debt}}{\text{Old total assets}} = \frac{\$183.3}{\$600} = 30.6\%$$

while

$$\frac{\text{New debt}}{\text{New total assets}} = \frac{\$183.3}{\$572.2} = 32.0\%$$

Chapter 4

ST-1 a.

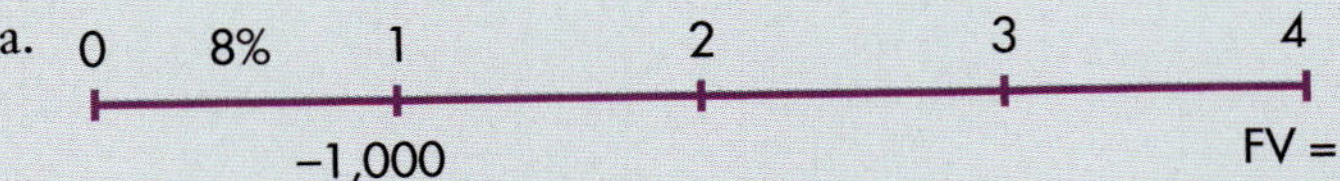

\$1,000 is being compounded for 3 years, so your balance at Year 4 is \$1,259.71:

$$FV_N = PV(1 + I)^N = \$1{,}000(1 + 0.08)^3 = \$1{,}259.71$$

Alternatively, using a financial calculator, input N = 3, I/YR = 8, PV =−1000, and PMT = 0; then solve for FV = \$1,259.71.

b.

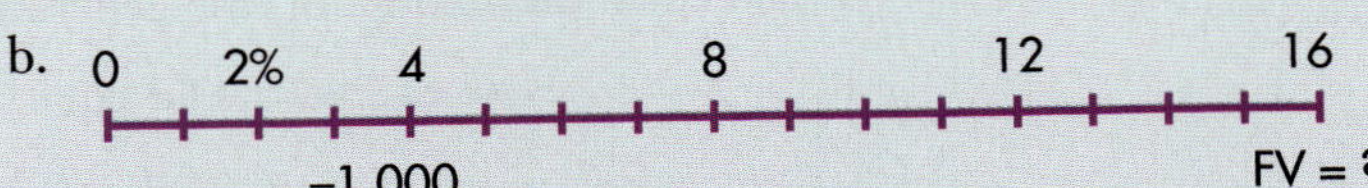

There are 12 compounding periods from Quarter 4 to Quarter 16.

$$FV_N = PV\left(1 + \frac{I_{NOM}}{M}\right)^{NM} = FV_{12} = \$1{,}000(1.02)^{12} = \$1{,}268.24$$

Alternatively, using a financial calculator, input N = 12, I/YR = 2, PV = −1000, and PMT = 0; then solve for FV = \$1,268.24.

c.

0 8% 1 2 3 4

250 250 250 250

FV = ?

$$FVA_4 = \$250\left[\frac{(1 + 0.08)^4}{0.08} - \frac{1}{0.08}\right] = \$1{,}126.53$$

Using a financial calculator, input N = 4, I/YR = 8, PV = 0, and PMT = −250; then solve for FV = \$1,126.53.

d. 0 8% 1 2 3 4

? ? ? ?

FV = 1,259.71

$$\text{PMT}\left[\frac{(1+0.08)^4}{0.08}-\frac{1}{0.08}\right] = \$1,259.71$$

$$\text{PMT}(4.5061) = \$1,259.71$$

$$\text{PMT} = \$279.56$$

Using a financial calculator, input N = 4, I/YR = 8, PV = 0, and FV = 1259.71; then solve for PMT = –$279.56.

ST-2 a. Set up a time line like the one in the preceding problem:

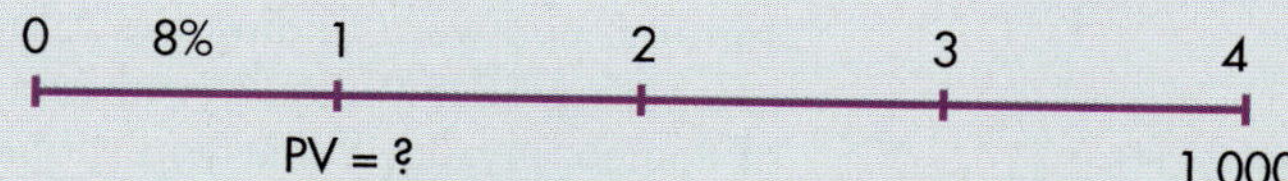

Note that your deposit will grow for 3 years at 8%. The deposit at Year 1 is the PV, and the FV is $1,000. Here is the solution:

N = 3, I/YR = 8, PMT = 0, FV = 1000; then PV = $793.83.

Alternatively,

$$\text{PV} = \frac{\text{FV}_\text{N}}{(1+\text{I})^\text{N}} = \frac{\$1,000}{(1+0.08)^3} = \$793.83$$

b. 0 8% 1 2 3 4

? ? ? ?

FV = 1,000

Here we are dealing with a 4-year annuity whose first payment occurs 1 year from today and whose future value must equal $1,000. Here is the solution: N = 4; I/YR = 8; PV = 0; FV = 1000; then PMT = $221.92. Alternatively,

$$\text{PMT}\left[\frac{(1+0.08)^4}{0.08}-\frac{1}{0.08}\right] = \$1,000$$

$$\text{PMT}(4.5061) = \$1,000$$

$$\text{PMT} = \$222.92$$

c. This problem can be approached in several ways. Perhaps the simplest is to ask this question: "If I received $750 1 year from now and deposited it to earn 8%, would I have the required $1,000 4 years from now?" The answer is "no":

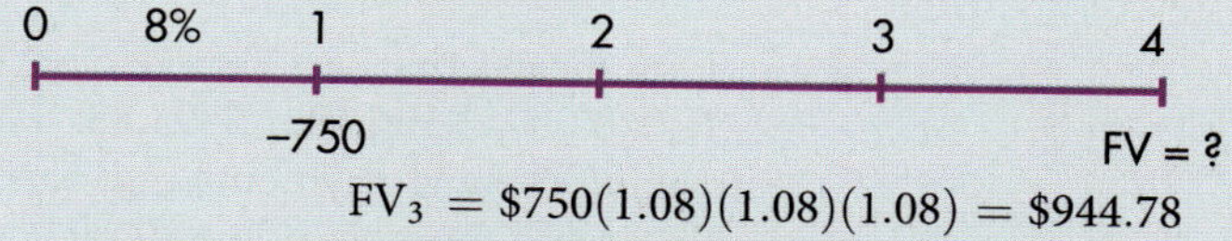

$$\text{FV}_3 = \$750(1.08)(1.08)(1.08) = \$944.78$$

This indicates that you should let your father make the payments rather than accept the lump sum of $750.

You could also compare the \$750 with the PV of the payments:

0 8% 1 2 3 4

221.92 221.92 221.92 221.92

N = 4, I/YR = 8, PMT = −221.92, FV = 0; then PV = \$735.03.

Alternatively,

$$\text{PVA}_4 = \$221.92\left[\frac{1}{0.08} - \frac{1}{(0.08)(1+0.08)^4}\right] = \$735.03$$

This is less than the \$750 lump sum offer, so your initial reaction might be to accept the lump sum of \$750. However, it would be a mistake to do so. The problem is that, when you found the \$735.03 PVof the annuity, you were finding the value of the annuity *today*. You were comparing \$735.03 today with the lump sum of \$750 in 1 year. This is, of course, invalid. What you should have done was take the \$735.03, recognize that this is the PV of an annuity as of today, multiply \$735.03 by 1.08 to get \$793.83, and compare this \$793.83 with the lump sum of \$750. You would then take your father's offer to make the payments rather than take the lump sum 1 year from now.

d. 0 I = ? 1 2 3 4

−750 1,000

N = 3, PV = −750, PMT = 0, FV = 1000; then I/YR = 10.0642%.

e. 0 I = ? 1 2 3 4

186.29 186.29 186.29 186.29

FV = 1,000

N = 4, PV = 0, PMT = −186.29, FV = 1000; then I/YR = 19.9997%.

You might be able to find a borrower willing to offer you a 20% interest rate, but there would be some risk involved—he or she might not actually pay you your \$1,000!

f. 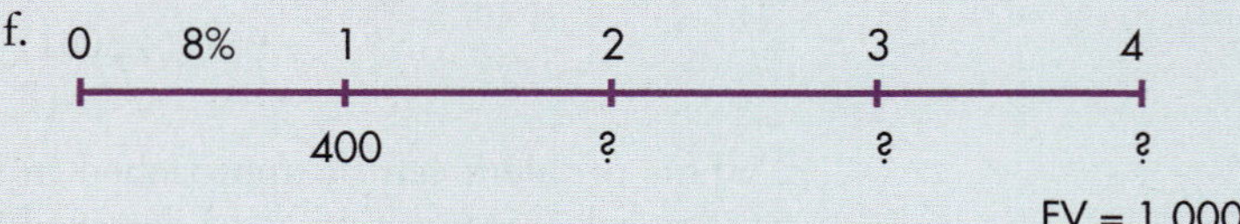

Find the future value of the original \$400 deposit:

$$\text{FV}_6 = \text{PV}(1+\text{I})^6 = 400(1+0.04)^6 = \$400(1.2653) = \$506.12.$$

This means that, at Year 4, you need an additional sum of \$493.88: \$1,000.00 − \$506.12 = \$493.88. This amount will be accumulated by making 6 equal payments that earn 8% compounded semiannually, or 4% each 6 months: N = 6, I/YR = 4, PV = 0, FV = 493.88; then PMT = \$74.46. Alternatively,

$$\text{PMT}\left[\frac{(1+0.04)^6}{0.04}-\frac{1}{0.04}\right] = \$493.88$$
$$\text{PMT}(6.6330) = \$493.88$$
$$\text{PMT} = \$74.46$$

g.
$$\text{EFF\%} = \left(1+\frac{I_{NOM}}{M}\right)^M -1.0$$
$$= \left(1+\frac{0.08}{2}\right)^2 -1.0$$
$$= 1.0816 - 1 = 0.0816 = 8.16\%$$

ST-3 Bank A's effective annual rate is 8.24%:

$$\text{EFF\%} = \left(1+\frac{0.08}{4}\right)^4 -1.0$$
$$= 1.0824 - 1 = 0.0824 = 8.24\%$$

Now Bank B must have the same effective annual rate:

$$\left(1+\frac{I}{12}\right)^{12} -1.0 = 0.0824$$
$$\left(1+\frac{I}{12}\right)^{12} = 1.0824$$
$$1+\frac{I}{12} = (1.0824)^{1/12}$$
$$1+\frac{I}{12} = 1.00662$$
$$\frac{I}{12} = 0.00662$$
$$I = 0.07944 = 7.94\%$$

Thus, the two banks have different quoted rates—Bank A's quoted rate is 8%, whereas Bank B's quoted rate is 7.94%—yet both banks have the same effective annual rate of 8.24%. The difference in their quoted rates is due to the difference in compounding frequency.

Chapter 5

ST-1 a. Pennington's bonds were sold at par; therefore, the original YTM equaled the coupon rate of 12%.

b.
$$V_B = \sum_{t=1}^{50}\frac{\$120/2}{\left(1+\frac{0.10}{2}\right)^t}+\frac{\$1{,}000}{\left(1+\frac{1.10}{2}\right)^{50}}$$
$$= \$60\left[\frac{1}{0.05}-\frac{1}{0.05(1+0.05)^{50}}\right]+\frac{\$1{,}000}{(1+0.05)^{50}}$$
$$= \$1{,}182.56$$

Alternatively, with a financial calculator, input the following: N = 50, I/YR = 5, PMT = 60, and FV = 1000; solve for PV = – $1,182.56.

c.

$$\begin{aligned}\text{Current yield} &= \text{Annual coupon payment} \div \text{Price}\\ &= \$120/\$1{,}182.56\\ &= 0.1015 = 10.15\%\\ \text{Capital gains yield} &= \text{Total yield} - \text{Current yield}\\ &= 10\% - 10.15\% = -0.15\%\\ \text{Total yield} &= \text{Current yield} + \text{Capital gains yield}\\ &= 10.15\% + (-0.15\%) = 10.00\%\end{aligned}$$

d.

$$\$916.42 = \sum_{t=1}^{13} \frac{\$60}{(1 + r_d/2)^t} + \frac{\$1000}{(1 + r_d/2)^{13}}$$

With a financial calculator, input the following: N = 13, PV = −916.42, PMT = 60, and FV = 1000; then solve for = I/YR = $r_d/2$ = 7.00%. Therefore, r_d = 14.00%.

$$\begin{aligned}\text{Current yield} &= \$120/\$916.42 = 13.09\%\\ \text{Capital gains yield} &= 14\%-13.09\% = \underline{0.91\%}\\ \text{Total yield} &= 14.00\%\end{aligned}$$

e. The following time line illustrates the years to maturity of the bond:

1/1/10 — 3/1/10 — 6/30/10 — 12/31/10 — 6/30/11 — ... — 12/31/16

Thus, on March 1, 2010, there were 13⅔ periods left before the bond matured. Bond traders actually use the following procedure to determine the price of the bond.

(1) Find the price of the bond immediately after the next coupon is paid on June 30, 2010:

$$V_B = \$60\left[\frac{1}{0.0775} - \frac{1}{0.0775(1 + 0.0775)^{13}}\right] + \frac{\$1{,}000}{(1 + 0.0775)^{13}}$$

$$= \$859.76$$

Using a financial calculator, input N = 13, I/YR = 7.75, PMT = 60, and FV = 1000; then solve for PV = −$859.76.

(2) Add the coupon, $60, to the bond price to get the total value, TV, of the bond on the next interest payment date: TV = $859.76 + $60.00 = $919.76.

(3) Discount this total value back to the purchase date:

$$\text{Value at purchase date (March 1, 2010)} = \frac{\$919.76}{(1 + 0.0775)^{(4/6)}}$$

$$= \$875.11$$

Using a financial calculator, input N = 4/6, I/YR = 7.75, PMT = 0, and FV = 919.76; then solve for PV = $875.11.

(4) Therefore, you would have written a check for $875.11 to complete the transaction. Of this amount, $20 = (⅓)($60) would represent

accrued interest and \$855.11 would represent the bond's basic value. This breakdown would affect both your taxes and those of the seller.

(5) This problem could be solved *very* easily using a spreadsheet or a financial calculator with a bond valuation function.

Chapter 6

ST-1 a. The average rate of return for each stock is calculated simply by averaging the returns over the 5-year period. The average return for Stock A is

$$r_{Avg\ A} = (-18\% + 44\% - 22\% + 22\% + 34\%)/5$$
$$= 12\%$$

The realized rate of return on a portfolio made up of Stock A and Stock B would be calculated by finding the average return in each year as

$$r_A(\%\text{ of Stock A}) + r_B(\%\text{ of Stock B})$$

and then averaging these annual returns:

Year	Portfolio AB's Return, r_{AB}
2006	−21%
2007	34
2008	−13
2009	15
2010	45
r_{Avg} =	12%

b. The standard deviation of returns is estimated as follows:

$$\text{Estimated } \sigma = S = \sqrt{\frac{\sum_{t=1}^{N}(\bar{r}_t - \bar{r}_{Avg})^2}{N-1}}$$

For Stock A, the estimated σ is about 30%:

$$\sigma_A = \sqrt{\frac{(-0.18-0.12)^2 + (0.44-0.12)^2 + (-0.22-0.12)^2 + (0.22-0.12)^2 + (0.34-0.12)^2}{5-1}}$$
$$= 0.30265 \approx 30\%$$

The standard deviations of returns for Stock B and for the portfolio are similarly determined, and they are as follows:

	Stock A	Stock B	Portfolio AB
Standard deviation	30%	30%	29%

c. Because the risk reduction from diversification is small (σ_{AB} falls only from 30% to 29%), the most likely value of the correlation coefficient is 0.8. If the correlation coefficient were −0.8, then the risk reduction would be much larger. In fact, the correlation coefficient between Stocks A and B is 0.8.

d. If more randomly selected stocks were added to a portfolio, σ_P would decline to somewhere in the vicinity of 20%. The value of σ_P would remain constant only if the correlation coefficient were +1.0, which is most unlikely. The value of σ_P would decline to zero only if (1) the correlation coefficient ρ were equal to zero and a large number of stocks were added to the portfolio or (2) the proper proportions were held in a two-stock portfolio with $\rho = -1.0$.

ST-2 a.
$$b = (0.6)(0.70) + (0.25)(0.90) + (0.1)(1.30) + (0.05)(1.50)$$
$$= 0.42 + 0.225 + 0.13 + 0.075 = 0.85$$

b.
$$r_{RF} = 6\%;\ RP_M = 5\%;\ b = 0.85$$
$$r_p = 6\% + (5\%)(0.85)$$
$$= 10.25\%$$

c.
$$b_N = (0.5)(0.70) + (0.25)(0.90) + (0.1)(1.30) + (0.15)(1.50)$$
$$= 0.35 + 0.225 + 0.13 + 0.225$$
$$= 0.93$$
$$r = 6\% + (5\%)(0.93)$$
$$= 10.65\%$$

Chapter 7

ST-1 The first step is to solve for g, the unknown variable, in the constant growth equation. Since D_1 is unknown but D_0 is known, substitute $D_0(1 + g)$ as follows:

$$\hat{P}_0 = P_0 = \frac{D_1}{r_s - g} = \frac{D_0(1+g)}{r_s - g}$$

$$\$36 = \frac{\$2.40(1+g)}{0.12 - g}.$$

Solving for g, we find the growth rate to be 5%:

$$\$4.32 - \$36g = \$2.40 + \$2.40g$$
$$\$38.4g = \$1.92$$
$$g = 0.05 = 5\%$$

The next step is to use the growth rate to project the stock price 5 years hence:

$$\hat{P}_5 = \frac{D_0(1+g)^6}{r_s - g}$$
$$= \frac{\$2.40(1.05)^6}{0.12 - 0.05}$$
$$= \$45.95$$

(Alternatively, $\hat{P}_5 = \$36(1.05)^5 = \$45.95$.) Therefore, Ewald Company's expected stock price 5 years from now, $\hat{P}_5$, is \$45.95.

ST-2 a. (1) Calculate the PV of the dividends paid during the supernormal growth period:

$$D_1 = \$1.1500(1.15) = \$1.3225$$
$$D_2 = \$1.3225(1.15) = \$1.5209$$
$$D_3 = \$1.5209(1.13) = \$1.7186$$

$$\text{PV of Div} = \$1.3225/(1.12) + \$1.5209/(1.12)^2 + \$1.7186/(1.12)^3$$
$$= \$3.6167 \approx \$3.62$$

(2) Find the PV of Snyder's stock price at the end of Year 3:

$$\hat{P}_3 = \frac{D_4}{r_s - g} = \frac{D_3(1+g)}{r_s - g}$$
$$= \frac{\$1.7186(1.06)}{0.12 - 0.06}$$
$$= \$30.36$$
$$\text{PV of } \hat{P}_3 = \$30.36/(1.12)^3 = \$21.61$$

(3) Sum the two components to find the value of the stock today:

$$\hat{P}_0 = \$3.62 + \$21.61 = \$25.23$$

Alternatively, the cash flows can be placed on a time line as follows:

0	12%	1	2	3	4
	g = 15%	g = 15%	g = 13%	g = 6%	
		1.3225	1.5209	1.7186	1.8217

$$30.3617 = \frac{\$1.8217}{0.12 - 0.06}$$

32.0803

Enter the cash flows into the cash flow register (CF_0 = 0, CF_1 = 1.3225, CF_2 = 1.5209, CF_3 = 32.0803) and I/YR = 12; then press the NPV key to obtain $\hat{P}_0$ = \$25.23.

b. $\hat{P}_1 = \$1.5209/(1.12) + \$1.7186/(1.12)^2 + \$30.36/(1.12)^2$

$= \$26.9311 \approx \$26.93$

(Calculator solution: \$26.93.)

$\hat{P}_2 = \$1.7186/(1.12) + \$30.36/(1.12)$

$= \$28.6429 \approx \$28.64$

(Calculator solution: \$28.64.)

c.

Year	Dividend Yield	+	Capital Gains Yield	=	Total Return
1	$\frac{\$1.3225}{\$25.23} \approx 5.24\%$	+	$\frac{\$26.93 - \$25.23}{\$25.23} \approx 6.74\%$	≈	12%
2	$\frac{\$1.5209}{\$26.93} \approx 5.65\%$	+	$\frac{\$28.64 - \$26.93}{\$26.93} \approx 6.35\%$	≈	12%
3	$\frac{\$1.7186}{\$28.64} \approx 6.00\%$	+	$\frac{\$30.36 - \$28.64}{\$28.64} \approx 6.00\%$	≈	12%

Chapter 8

ST-1 The option will pay off \$60 – \$42 = \$18 if the stock price is up. The option pays off nothing (\$0) if the stock price is down. Find the number of shares in the hedge portfolio:

$$N = \frac{C_u - C_d}{P_u - P_d} = \frac{\$18 - \$0}{\$60 - \$30} = 0.60$$

With 0.6 shares, the stock's payoff will be either 0.6($60) = $36 or 0.6($30) = $18. The portfolio's payoff will be $36 − $18 = $18, or $18 − 0 = $18.

The present value of $18 at the daily compounded risk-free rate is PV = $18 / $[1 + (0.05/365)]^{365}$ = $17.12. The option price is the current value of the stock in the portfolio minus the PV of the payoff:

$$V = 0.6(\$40) - \$17.12 = \$6.88$$

ST-2

$$d_1 = \frac{\ln(P/X) + [r_{RF} + (\sigma^2/2)]t}{\sigma\sqrt{t}}:$$

$$= \frac{\ln(\$22/\$20) + [0.05 + (0.49/2)](0.5)}{0.7\sqrt{0.5}}$$

$$= 0.4906$$

$$d_2 = d_1 - \sigma(t)^{0.5} = 0.4906 - 0.7(0.5)^{0.5} = -0.0044$$

$N(d_1) = 0.6881$ (from *Excel* NORMSDIST function)

$N(d_2) = 0.4982$ (from *Excel* NORMSDIST function)

$$V = P[N(d_1)] - Xe^{-r_{RF}t}[N(d_2)]$$
$$= \$22(0.6881) - \$20e^{(-0.05)(0.5)}(0.4982)$$
$$= \$5.42$$

Chapter 9

ST-1 a. Component costs are as follows:

Debt at r_d = 9%:

$$r_d(1 - T) = 9\%(0.6) = 5.4\%$$

Preferred with F = 5%:

$$r_{ps} = \frac{\text{Preferred dividend}}{P_{ps}(1 - F)} = \frac{\$9}{\$100(0.95)} = 9.5\%.$$

Common with DCF:

$$r_s = \frac{D_1}{P_0} + g = \frac{\$3.922}{\$60} + 6\% = 12.5\%.$$

Common with CAPM:

$$r_s = 6\% + 1.3(5\%) = 12.5\%$$

b.
$$\text{WACC} = w_d r_d(1 - T) + w_{ps} r_{ps} + w_s r_s$$
$$= 0.25(9\%)(1 - T) + 0.15(9.5\%) + 0.60(12.5\%)$$
$$= 10.275\%$$

Chapter 10

ST-1 a. **Payback:**

To determine the payback, construct the cumulative cash flows for each project as follows.

Year	Cumulative Cash Flows	
	Project X	Project Y
0	−$10,000	−$10,000
1	−3,500	−6,500
2	−500	−3,000
3	2,500	500
4	3,500	4,000

$$\text{Payback}_X = 2 + \frac{\$500}{\$3,000} = 2.17 \text{ years}$$

$$\text{Payback}_Y = 2 + \frac{\$3,000}{\$3,500} = 2.86 \text{ years}$$

Net present value (NPV):

$$\text{NPV}_X = -\$10,000 + \frac{\$6,500}{(1.12)^1} + \frac{\$3,000}{(1.12)^2} + \frac{\$3,000}{(1.12)^3} + \frac{\$1,000}{(1.12)^4} = \$966.01$$

$$\text{NPV}_Y = -\$10,000 + \frac{\$3,500}{(1.12)^1} + \frac{\$3,500}{(1.12)^2} + \frac{\$3,500}{(1.12)^3} + \frac{\$3,500}{(1.12)^4} = \$630.72$$

Alternatively, using a financial calculator, input the cash flows into the cash flow register, enter I/YR = 12, and then press the NPV key to obtain NPV_X = \$966.01 and NPV_Y = \$630.72.

Internal rate of return (IRR):

To solve for each project's IRR, find the discount rates that equate each NPV to zero:

$$\text{IRR}_X = 18.0\%$$
$$\text{IRR}_Y = 15.0\%$$

Modified Internal Rate of Return (MIRR):

To obtain each project's MIRR, begin by finding each project's terminal value (TV) of cash inflows:

$$\text{TV}_X = \$6,500(1.12)^3 + \$3,000(1.12)^2 + \$3,000(1.12)^1 + \$1,000 = \$17,255.23$$

$$\text{TV}_Y = \$3,500(1.12)^3 + \$3,500(1.12)^2 + \$3,500(1.12)^1 + \$3,500 = \$16,727.65$$

Now, each project's MIRR is the discount rate that equates the PV of the TV to each project's cost, \$10,000:

$$\text{MIRR}_X = 14.61\%$$
$$\text{MIRR}_Y = 13.73\%$$

Profitability index (PI):

To obtain each project's PI, divide its present value of future cash flows by its initial cost. The PV of future cash flows can be found from the NPV calculated earlier:

$$\text{PV}_X = \text{NPV}_X + \text{Cost of X} = \$966.01 + \$10,000 = \$10,966.01$$
$$\text{PV}_Y = \text{NPV}_Y + \text{Cost of Y} = \$630.72 + \$10,000 = \$10,630.72$$
$$\text{PI}_X = \text{PV}_X/\text{Cost of X} = \$10,966.01/\$10,000 = 1.097$$
$$\text{PI}_Y = \text{PV}_Y/\text{Cost of Y} = \$10,630.72/\$10,000 = 1.063$$

b. The following table summarizes the project rankings by each method:

	Project That Ranks Higher
Payback	X
NPV	X
IRR	X
MIRR	X

Note that all methods rank Project X over Project Y. Because both projects are acceptable under the NPV, IRR, and MIRR criteria, both should be accepted if they are independent.

c. In this case, we would choose the project with the higher NPV at r = 12%, or Project X.

d. To determine the effects of changing the cost of capital, plot the NPV profiles of each project. The crossover rate occurs at about 6% to 7% (6.2%). See the graph below.

If the firm's cost of capital is less than 6.2%, then a conflict exists because $NPV_Y > NPV_X$ but $IRR_X > IRR_Y$. Therefore, if r were 5% then a conflict would exist. Note, however, that when r = 5.0% we have $MIRR_X$ = 10.64% and $MIRR_Y$ = 10.83%; hence, the modified IRR ranks the projects correctly even if r is to the left of the crossover point.

e. The basic cause of the conflict is differing reinvestment rate assumptions between NPV and IRR: NPV assumes that cash flows can be reinvested at the cost of capital, whereas IRR assumes that reinvestment yields the (generally) higher IRR. The high reinvestment rate assumption under IRR makes early cash flows especially valuable, so short-term projects look better under IRR.

NPV Profiles for Projects X and Y

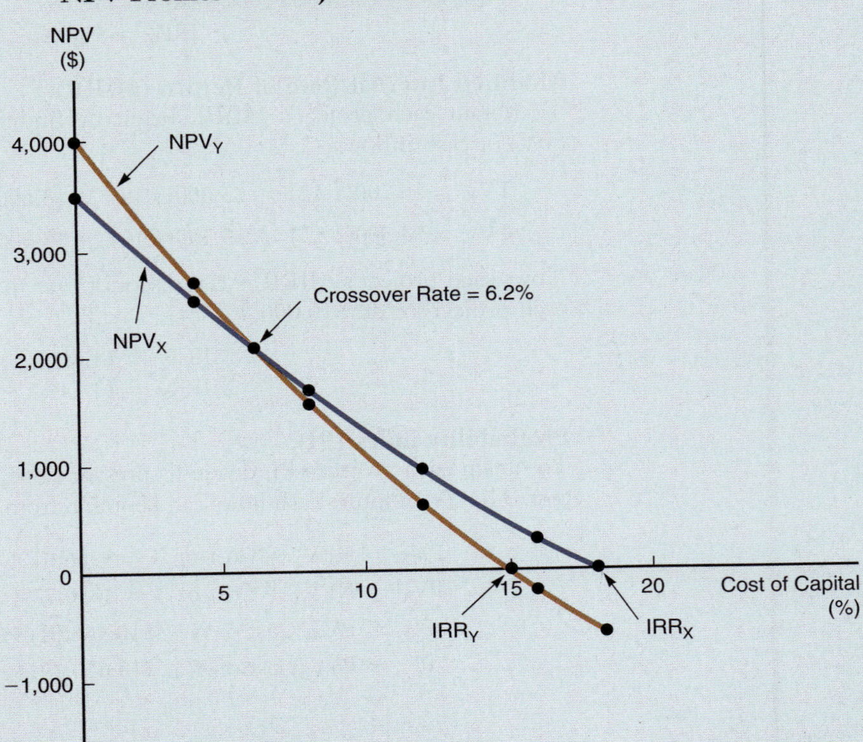

Cost of Capital	NPV_X	NPV_Y
0%	\$3,500	\$4,000
4	2,545	2,705
8	1,707	1,592
12	966	631
16	307	(206)
18	5	(585)

CHAPTER 11

ST-1 a. **Estimated Investment Requirements:**

Price	–\$50,000
Modification	–10,000
Change in net working capital	–2,000
Total investment	–\$62,000

b. **Operating Cash Flows:**

	Year 1	Year 2	Year 3
1. After-tax cost savings[a]	\$12,000	\$12,000	\$12,000
2. Depreciation[b]	19,800	27,000	9,000
3. Depreciation tax savings[c]	7,920	10,800	3,600
Operating cash flow (1 + 3)	\$19,920	\$22,800	\$15,600

[a]\$20,000(1 – T).

[b]Depreciable basis = \$60,000; the MACRS percentage allowances are 0.33, 0.45, and 0.15 in Years 1, 2, and 3, respectively; hence, depreciation in Year 1 = 0.33(\$60,000) = \$19,800, and so on. There will remain \$4,200, or 7%, undepreciated after Year 3; it would normally be taken in Year 4.

[c]Depreciation tax savings = T(Depreciation) = 0.4(\$19,800) = \$7,920 in Year 1, and so forth.

c. **Termination Cash Flow:**

Salvage value	\$20,000
Tax on salvage value[a]	–6,320
Net working capital recovery	2,000
Termination cash flow	\$15,680

[a]Calculation of tax on salvage value:

Book value = Depreciation basis – Accumulated depreciation
= \$60,000 – \$55,800 = \$4,200

Sales price	\$20,000
Less book value	4,200
Taxable income	\$15,800
Tax at 40%	\$ 6,320

d. **Project NPV:**

	0	10%	1	2	3
Project Cash Flows	−62,000		19,920	22,800	31,280

$$\begin{aligned} NPV &= -\$62{,}000 + \frac{\$19{,}920}{(1.10)^1} + \frac{\$22{,}800}{(1.10)^2} + \frac{\$31{,}280}{(1.10)^3} \\ &= -\$1{,}547 \end{aligned}$$

Alternatively, using a financial calculator, input the cash flows into the cash flow register, enter I/YR = 10, and then press the NPV key to obtain NPV = −$1,547. Because the earth mover has a negative NPV, it should not be purchased.

ST-2 a. First, find the expected cash flows:

Year	Expected Cash Flows				
0	0.2(−$100,000)	+ 0.6(−$100,000)	+ 0.2(−$100,000)	=	−$100,000
1	0.2($20,000)	+ 0.6($30,000)	+ 0.2($40,000)	=	$ 30,000
2	0.2($20,000)	+ 0.6($30,000)	+ 0.2($40,000)	=	$ 30,000
3	0.2($20,000)	+ 0.6($30,000)	+ 0.2($40,000)	=	$ 30,000
4	0.2($20,000)	+ 0.6($30,000)	+ 0.2($40,000)	=	$ 30,000
5	0.2($20,000)	+ 0.6($30,000)	+ 0.2($40,000)	=	$ 30,000
5*	0.2($0)	+ 0.6($20,000)	+ 0.2($30,000)	=	$ 18,000

0	10%	1	2	3	4	5
−$100,000		30,000	30,000	30,000	30,000	48,000

Next, determine the NPV based on the expected cash flows:

$$\begin{aligned} NPV = -\$100{,}000 &+ \frac{\$30{,}000}{(1.10)^1} + \frac{\$30{,}000}{(1.10)^2} + \frac{\$30{,}000}{(1.10)^3} \\ &+ \frac{\$30{,}000}{(1.10)^4} + \frac{\$48{,}000}{(1.10)^5} = \$24{,}900 \end{aligned}$$

Alternatively, using a financial calculator, input the cash flows in the cash flow register, enter I/YR = 10, and then press the NPV key to obtain NPV = $24,900.

b. For the worst case, the cash flow values from the cash flow column farthest on the left are used to calculate NPV:

0	10%	1	2	3	4	5
−$100,000		20,000	20,000	20,000	20,000	20,000

$$\begin{aligned} NPV = -\$100{,}000 &+ \frac{\$20{,}000}{(1.10)^1} + \frac{\$20{,}000}{(1.10)^2} + \frac{\$20{,}000}{(1.10)^3} \\ &+ \frac{\$20{,}000}{(1.10)^4} + \frac{\$20{,}000}{(1.10)^5} = -\$24{,}184 \end{aligned}$$

Similarly, for the best case, use the values from the column farthest on the right. Here the NPV is $70,259.

If the cash flows are perfectly dependent, then the low cash flow in the first year will mean a low cash flow in every year. Thus, the probability of the worst case occurring is the probability of getting the \$20,000 net cash flow in Year 1, or 20%. If the cash flows are independent, then the cash flow in each year can be low, high, or average and so the probability of getting all low cash flows will be

$$(0.2)(0.2)(0.2)(0.2)(0.2) = 0.2^5 = 0.00032 = 0.032\%$$

c. The base-case NPV is found using the most likely cash flows and is equal to \$26,142. This value differs from the expected NPV of \$24,900 because the Year-5 cash flows are not symmetric. Under these conditions, the NPV distribution is as follows:

P	NPV
0.2	–\$24,184
0.6	26,142
0.2	70,259

Thus, the expected NPV is 0.2(–\$24,184) + 0.6(\$26,142) + 0.2(\$70,259) = \$24,900. As is always the case, the expected NPV is the same as the NPV of the expected cash flows found in part a. The standard deviation is \$29,904:

$$\begin{aligned}\sigma^2_{NPV} &= 0.2(-\$24{,}184 - \$24{,}900)^2 + 0.6(\$26{,}142 - \$24{,}900)^2 \\ &\quad + 0.2(\$70{,}259 - \$24{,}900)^2 \\ &= \$894{,}261{,}126 \\ \sigma_{NPV} &= \sqrt{\$894{,}261{,}126} = \$29{,}904.\end{aligned}$$

The coefficient of variation, CV, is \$29,904/\$24,900 = 1.20.

Chapter 12

ST-1 To solve this problem, we first define ΔS as the change in sales and g as the growth rate in sales. Then we use the three following equations:

$$\begin{aligned}\Delta S &= S_0 g \\ S_1 &= S_0(1+g) \\ AFN &= (A^*/S_0)(\Delta S) - (L^*/S_0)(\Delta S) - MS_1(1 - \text{Payout ratio})\end{aligned}$$

Set AFN = 0; substitute in known values for A^*/S_0, L^*/S_0, M, d, and S_0; and then solve for g:

$$\begin{aligned}0 &= 1.6(\$100g) - 0.4(\$100g) - 0.10[\$100(1+g)](0.55) \\ &= \$160g - \$40g - 0.055(\$100 + \$100g) \\ &= \$160g - \$40g - \$5.5 - \$5.5g \\ \$114.5g &= \$5.5 \\ g &= \$5.5/\$114.5 = 0.048 = 4.8\% \\ &= \text{Maximum growth rate without external financing}\end{aligned}$$

ST-2 Assets consist of cash, marketable securities, receivables, inventories, and fixed assets. Therefore, we can break the A^*/S_0 ratio into its components—cash/sales, inventories/sales, and so forth. Then,

$$\frac{A^*}{S_0} = \frac{A^* - \text{Inventories}}{S_0} + \frac{\text{Inventories}}{S_0} = 1.6$$

We know that the inventory turnover ratio is sales/inventories = 3 times, so inventories/sales = 1/3 = 0.3333. Further, if the inventory turnover ratio can be increased to 4 times, then the inventory/sales ratio will fall to 1/4 = 0.25, a difference of 0.3333 − 0.2500 = 0.0833. This, in turn, causes the A^*/S_0 ratio to fall from $A^*/S_0 = 1.6$ to $A^*/S_0 = 1.6 - 0.0833 = 1.5167$. This change has two effects: First, it changes the AFN equation; and second, it means that Barnsdale currently has excessive inventories. Because it is costly to hold excess inventories, Barnsdale will want to reduce its inventory holdings by not replacing inventories until the excess amounts have been used. We can account for this by setting up the revised AFN equation (using the new A^*/S_0 ratio), estimating the funds that will be needed next year if no excess inventories are currently on hand, and then subtracting out the excess inventories that are currently on hand:

Present Conditions:

$$\frac{\text{Sales}}{\text{Inventories}} = \frac{\$100}{\text{Inventories}} = 3$$

so

$$\text{Inventories} = \$100/3 = \$33.3 \text{ million at present}$$

New Conditions:

$$\frac{\text{Sales}}{\text{Inventories}} = \frac{\$100}{\text{Inventories}} = 4$$

so

$$\text{New level of inventories} = \$100/4 = \$25 \text{ million}$$

Therefore,

$$\text{Excess inventories} = \$33.3 - \$25 = \$8.3 \text{ million}$$

Forecast of Funds Needed, First Year:

$$\begin{aligned}\Delta S \text{ in first year} &= 0.2(\$100 \text{ million}) = \$20 \text{ million}\\ \text{AFN} &= 1.5167(\$20) - 0.4(\$20) - 0.1(0.55)(\$120) - \$8.3\\ &= \$30.3 - \$8 - \$6.6 - \$8.3\\ &= \$7.4 \text{ million}\end{aligned}$$

Forecast of Funds Needed, Second Year:

$$\begin{aligned}\Delta S \text{ in second year} &= gS_1 = 0.2(\$120 \text{ million}) = \$24 \text{ million}\\ \text{AFN} &= 1.5167(\$24) - 0.4(\$24) - 0.1(0.55)(\$144)\\ &= \$36.4 - \$9.6 - \$7.9\\ &= \$18.9 \text{ million}\end{aligned}$$

ST-3 a. $$\text{Full capacity sales} = \frac{\text{Current sales}}{\text{Percentage of capacity at which FA were operated}} = \frac{\$36,000}{0.75} = \$48,000$$

$$\text{Percentage increase} = \frac{\text{New sales} - \text{Old sales}}{\text{Old sales}} = \frac{\$48,000 - \$36,000}{\$36,000} = 0.33 = 33\%$$

Therefore, sales could expand by 33% before Van Auken Lumber would need to add fixed assets.

b.

Van Auken Lumber: Projected Income Statement for December 31, 2011 (Thousands of Dollars)

	2010	FORECAST BASIS	2011
Sales	$36,000	1.25($Sales_{10}$)	$45,000
Operating costs	30,783	85.508%($Sales_{11}$)	38,479
EBIT	$ 5,217		$ 6,521
Interest	717	12%($Debt_{10}$)	1,017
EBT	$ 4,500		$ 5,504
Taxes (40%)	1,800		2,202
Net income	$ 2,700		$ 3,302
Dividends (60%)	$ 1,620		$ 1,981
Additions to RE	$ 1,080		$ 1,321

Van Auken Lumber: Projected Balance Sheet for December 31, 2011 (Thousands of Dollars)

	2010	PERCENT OF 2011 SALES	ADDITIONS	2011	AFN	2011 AFTER AFN
Cash	$ 1,800	5.000%		$ 2,250		$ 2,250
Receivables	10,800	30.000		13,500		13,500
Inventories	12,600	35.000		15,750		15,750
Total current assets	$25,200			$31,500		$31,500
Net fixed assets	21,600			21,600[a]		21,600
Total assets	$46,800			$53,100		$53,100
Accounts payable	$ 7,200	20.000		$ 9,000		$ 9,000
Notes payable	3,472			3,472	+2,549	6,021
Accruals	2,520	7.000		3,150		3,150
Total current liabilities	$13,192			$15,622		$18,171
Mortgage bonds	5,000			5,000		5,000
Common stock	2,000			2,000		2,000
Retained earnings	26,608		1,321[b]	27,929		27,929
Total liabilities and equity	$46,800			$50,551		$53,100
AFN =				$ 2,549		

[a]From part a we know that sales can increase by 33% before additions to fixed assets are needed.
[b]See income statement

Chapter 13

ST-1 a. $$V_{op} = \frac{FCF(1+g)}{WACC - g} = \frac{\$100{,}000(1+0.07)}{0.11 - 0.07} = \$2{,}675{,}000$$

b. Total value = Value of operations + Value of nonoperating assets

= $2,675,000 + $325,000 = $3,000,000

c. Value of equity = Total value − Value of debt
= $3,000,000 − $1,000,000 = $2,000,000

d. Price per share = Value of equity ÷ Number of shares
= $2,000,000/50,000 = $40

CHAPTER 14

ST-1 a.

Capital investments	$6,000,000
Projected net income	$5,000,000
Required equity = 40%(Capital inv.)	$2,400,000
Available residual	$2,600,000
Shares outstanding	1,000,000

DPS = $2,600,000/1,000,000 shares = $2.60

b. EPS = $5,000,000/1,000,000 shares = $5.00
Payout ratio = DPS/EPS = $2.6/$5 = 52%, or
Total dividends÷NI = $2,600,000/$5,000,000 = 52%

CHAPTER 15

ST-1 a. $S = P(n) = \$30(600{,}000) = \$18{,}000{,}000$
$V = D + S = \$2{,}000{,}000 + \$18{,}000{,}000 = \$20{,}000{,}000$

b. $w_d = D/V = \$2{,}000{,}000/\$20{,}000{,}000 = 0.10$
$w_s = S/V = \$18{,}000{,}000/\$20{,}000{,}000 = 0.90$
$\text{WACC} = w_d\, r_d(1 - T) + w_s\, r_s$
$= (0.10)(10\%)(0.60) + (0.90)(15\%) = 14.1\%$

c. $\text{WACC} = (0.50)(12\%)(0.60) + (0.50)(18.5\%) = 12.85\%$
Since g = 0, it follows that FCF = NOPAT.

$V_{opNew} = \text{FCF/WACC} = \text{EBIT}(1-T)/0.1285 = \$4{,}700{,}000(0.60)/0.1285$
$= \$21{,}945{,}525.292$

$D = w_d(V_{op}) = 0.50(\$21{,}945{,}525.292) = \$10{,}972{,}762.646$

Since it started with $2 million debt, it will issue
$D_{New} - D_{Old} = \$8{,}972{,}762.646 = \$10{,}972{,}762.646 - \$2{,}000{,}000.$
$S_{Post} = V_{opNew} - D_{New} = \$21{,}945{,}525.292 - \$10{,}972{,}762.646 = \$10{,}972{,}762.646$

(Alternatively, $S_{Post} = w_s(V_{opNew}) = 0.50(\$21{,}945{,}525.292) = \$10{,}972{,}762.646.$)

$$n_{Post} = n_{Prior}\left[\frac{V_{opNew} - D_{New}}{V_{opNew} - D_{Old}}\right]$$

$$= 600{,}000\left[\frac{\$21{,}945{,}525.292 - \$10{,}972{,}762.646}{\$21{,}945{,}525.292 - \$2{,}000{,}000}\right]$$

$$= 600{,}000\left[\frac{\$10{,}972{,}762.646}{\$19{,}945{,}525.292}\right]$$

$$= 330{,}082$$

$$P_{Post} = (V_{opNew} - D_{Old})/n_{Prior}$$
$$= (\$21{,}945{,}525.292 - \$2{,}000{,}000)/600{,}000$$
$$= \$33.2425$$

Alternatively, after issuing debt and before repurchasing stock, the firm's equity, S_{Prior}, is worth $V_{opNew} + (D_{New} - D_{Old}) - D_{New}$ = \$21,945,525.292 + \$8,972,762.646 − \$10,972,762.646 = \$19,945,525.29. The stock price prior to the repurchase is $P_{Prior} = S_{Prior}/n_{Prior}$ = \$19,945,525.29/600,000 = \$33.242542. The firm used the proceeds of the new debt, \$8,972,762.646, to repurchase X shares of stock at a price of \$33.242542 per share. The number of shares it will repurchase is X = \$8,972,762.646/\$33.242542 = 269,918.07. Thus, there are 600,000 − 269,918.07 = 330,082 shares remaining. As a check, the stock price should equal the market value of equity (S) divided by the number of shares: P_0 = \$10,972,762.646/330,082 = \$33.2425.

ST-2 a. LIC's current cost of equity is

$$r_s = 6\% + 1.5(4\%) = 12\%$$

b. LIC's unlevered beta is

$$b_U = 1.5/[1 + (1 - 0.40)(25\%/75\%)] = 1.5/1.2 = 1.25$$

c. LIC's levered beta at D/S = 60%/40% = 1.5 is

$$b = 1.25[1 + (1 - 0.40)(60/40)] = 2.375$$

LIC's new cost of capital will be

$$r_s = 6\% + (2.375)(4\%) = 15.5\%$$

CHAPTER 16

ST-1 The Calgary Company: Alternative Balance Sheets

	RESTRICTED (40%)	MODERATE (50%)	RELAXED (60%)
Current assets (% of sales)	\$1,200,000	\$1,500,000	\$1,800,000
Fixed assets	600,000	600,000	600,000
Total assets	\$1,800,000	\$2,100,000	\$2,400,000
Debt	\$ 900,000	\$1,050,000	\$1,200,000
Equity	900,000	1,050,000	1,200,000
Total liabilities and equity	\$1,800,000	\$2,100,000	\$2,400,000

The Calgary Company: Alternative Income Statements

	RESTRICTED	MODERATE	RELAXED
Sales	$3,000,000	$3,000,000	$3,000,000
EBIT	450,000	450,000	450,000
Interest (10%)	90,000	105,000	120,000
Earnings before taxes	$ 360,000	$ 345,000	$ 330,000
Taxes (40%)	144,000	138,000	132,000
Net income	$ 216,000	$ 207,000	$ 198,000
ROE	24.0%	19.7%	16.5%

ST-2 a. and b.

Income Statements for Year Ended December 31, 2010 (Thousands of Dollars)

	VANDERHEIDEN PRESS		HERRENHOUSE PUBLISHING	
	a	b	a	b
EBIT	$ 30,000	$ 30,000	$ 30,000	$ 30,000
Interest	12,400	14,400	10,600	18,600
Taxable income	$ 17,600	$ 15,600	$ 19,400	$ 11,400
Taxes (40%)	7,040	6,240	7,760	4,560
Net income	$ 10,560	$ 9,360	$ 11,640	$ 6,840
Equity	$100,000	$100,000	$100,000	$100,000
Return on equity	10.56%	9.36%	11.64%	6.84%

The Vanderheiden Press has a higher ROE when short-term interest rates are high, whereas Herrenhouse Publishing does better when rates are lower.

c. Herrenhouse's position is riskier. First, its profits and return on equity are much more volatile than Vanderheiden's. Second, Herrenhouse must renew its large short-term loan every year, and if the renewal comes up at a time when money is tight or when its business is depressed or both, then Herrenhouse could be denied credit, which could put it out of business.

Chapter 17

ST-1

$$\frac{\text{Euros}}{\text{C\$}} = \frac{\text{Euros}}{\text{US\$}} \times \frac{\text{US\$}}{\text{C\$}}$$

$$= \frac{0.98}{\$1} \times \frac{\$1}{1.5} = \frac{0.98}{1.5} = 0.6533 \text{ euros per Canadian dollar}$$

APPENDIX B

Answers to End-of-Chapter Problems

We present here some intermediate steps and final answers to selected end-of-chapter problems. Please note that your answer may differ slightly from ours because of rounding differences. Also, although we hope not, some of the problems may have more than one correct solution, depending on what assumptions are made when working the problem. Finally, many of the problems involve some verbal discussion as well as numerical calculations; this verbal material is not presented here.

2-1 5.8%.

2-2 25%.

2-3 $1,000,000.

2-4 $2,500,000.

2-5 $3,600,000.

2-6 $20,000,000.

2-7 Tax = $107,855;
NI = $222,145;
Marginal tax rate = 39%;
Average tax rate = 33.8%.

2-8 a. Tax = $3,575,000.
b. Tax = $350,000.
c. Tax = $105,000.

2-9 AT&T bond = 4.875%;
AT&T preferred stock = 5.37%;
Florida bond = 5%.

2-10 NI = $450,000;
NCF = $650,000.

2-11 a. $2,400,000.
b. NI = $0;
NCF = $3,000,000.
c. NI = $1,350,000;
NCF = $2,100,000.

2-12 a. NOPAT = $756 million.
b. $NOWC_{09}$ = $3.0 billion;
$NOWC_{10}$ = $3.3 billion.
c. Op. $capital_{09}$ = $6.5 billion;
Op. $capital_{10}$ = $7.15 billion.
d. FCF = $106 million.
e. ROIC = 10.57%.
f. Answers in millions:
A-T int. = $72.
Inc. in debt = –$284.
Div. = $220.
Rep. stock = $88.
Purch. ST inv. = $10.

2-13 Refund = $120,000.
Future taxes = $0; $0; $40,000; $60,000; $60,000.

3-1 AR = $400,000.

3-2 D/A = 60%.

3-3 M/B = 10.

3-4 P/E = 16.0.

3-5 ROE = 12%.

3-6 S/TA = 5; TA/E = 1.5.

3-7 CL = $2,000,000;
Inv = $1,000,000.

3-8 Net profit margin = 2%;
D/A = 40%.

3-9 $262,500; 1.19.

3-10 TIE = 3.86.

3-11 A/P = $90,000;
Inv. = $90,000;
FA = $138,000.

3-12 Sales = $2,592,000;
DSO = 36.33 days.

3-13 a. Current ratio = 1.98;
DSO = 76 days;
TA turnover = 1.7;
Debt ratio = 61.9%.

3-14 a. Quick ratio = 0.8;
DSO = 37 days;
ROE = 13.1%;
Debt ratio = 54.8%.

4-1 FV_5 = $16,105.10.

4-2 PV = $1,292.10.

4-3 I/YR = 8.01%.

4-4 N = 11.01 years.

4-5 N = 11 years.

4-6 FVA_5 = $1,725.22;
$FVA_{5\ Due}$ = $1,845.99.

4-7 PV = \$923.98;
FV = \$1,466.24.

4-8 PMT = \$444.89;
EAR = 12.6825%.

4-9 a. \$530.
b. \$561.80.
c. \$471.70.
d. \$445.00.

4-10 a. \$895.42.
b. \$1,552.92.
c. \$279.20.
d. \$160.99.

4-11 a. N = 10.24 ≈ 10 years.
b. N = 7.27 ≈ 7 years.
c. N = 4.19 ≈ 4 years.
d. N = 1.00 ≈ 1 year.

4-12 a. \$6,374.97.
b. \$1,105.13.
c. \$2,000.00.
d. (1) \$7,012.46.
(2) \$1,160.38.
(3) \$2,000.00.

4-13 a. \$2,457.83.
b. \$865.90.
c. \$2,000.00.
d. (1) \$2,703.61.
(2) \$909.19.
(3) \$2,000.00.

4-14 a. PV_A = \$1,251.25.
PV_B = \$1,300.32.
b. PV_A = \$1,600.
PV_B = \$1,600.

4-15 a. 7%.
b. 7%.
c. 9%.
d. 15%.

4-16 a. \$881.17.
b. \$895.42.
c. \$903.06.
d. \$908.35.

4-17 a. \$279.20.
b. \$276.84.
c. \$443.72.

4-18 a. \$5,272.32.
b. \$5,374.07.

4-19 a. Universal, EAR = 7%;
Regional, EAR = 6.14%.

4-20 a. PMT = \$6,594.94;
Interest_1 = \$2,500;
Interest_2 = \$2,090.51.
b. \$13,189.87.
c. \$8,137.27.

4-21 a. I = 14.87% ≈ 15%.

4-22 I = 7.18%.

4-23 I = 9%.

4-24 a. \$33,872.11.
b. (1) \$26,243.16.
(2) \$0.

4-25 N = 14.77 ≈ 15 years.

4-26 6 years; \$1,106.01.

4-27 (1) \$1,428.57.
(2) \$714.29.

4-28 \$893.26.

4-29 \$984.88.

4-30 57.18%.

4-31 a. \$1,432.02.
b. \$93.07.

4-32 I_{NOM} = 15.19%.

4-33 PMT = \$36,949.61.

4-34 First PMT = \$9,736.96.

5-1 \$928.39.

5-2 12.48%.

5-3 8.55%.

5-4 7%; 7.33%.

5-5 2.5%.

5-6 0.3%.

5-7 \$1,085.80.

5-8 YTM = 6.62%;
YTC = 6.49%.

5-9 a. 5%: V_L = \$1,518.98;
V_S = \$1,047.62.
8%: V_L = \$1,171.19;
V_S = \$1,018.52.
12%: V_L = \$863.78;
V_S = \$982.14.

5-10 a. YTM at \$829 = 13.98%;
YTM at \$1,104 = 6.50%.

5-11 14.82%.

5-12 a. 10.37%.
b. 10.91%.
c. −0.54%.
d. 10.15%.

5-13 8.65%.

5-14 10.78%.

5-15 YTC = 6.47%.

5-16 a. 10-year, 10% coupon = 6.75%;
10-year zero = 9.75%;
5-year zero = 4.76%;
30-year zero = 32.19%;
\$100 perpetuity = 14.29%.

5-17 C_0 = \$1,012.79;
Z_0 = \$693.04;
C_1 = \$1,010.02;
Z_1 = \$759.57;
C_2 = \$1,006.98;
Z_2 = \$832.49;
C_3 = \$1,003.65;
Z_3 = \$912.41;
C_4 = \$1,000.00;
Z_4 = \$1,000.00.

5-18 5.8%.

5-19 1.5%.

5-20 6.0%.

5-21 a. \$1,251.22.
b. \$898.94.

5-22 a. 8.02%.
b. 7.59%.

5-23 a. r_1 = 9.20%; r_5 = 7.20%.

6-1 b = 1.12.

6-2 r_s = 10.90%.

6-3 r_M = 11%; r_s = 12.2%.

6-4 $\hat{r}$ = 11.40%; σ = 26.69%;
CV = 2.34.

6-5 a. $\hat{r}_M$ = 13.5%; $\hat{r}_j$ = 11.6%.
b. σ_M = 3.85%; σ_j = 6.22%.
c. CV_M = 0.29; CV_j = 0.54.

6-6 a. b_A = 1.40.
b. r_A = 15%.

6-7 a. r_i = 15.5%.
b. (1) r_M = 15%; r_i = 16.5%.
(2) r_M = 13%; r_i = 14.5%.
c. (1) r_i = 18.1%.
(2) r_i = 14.2%.

6-8 b_N = 1.16.

6-9 $b_p = 0.7625$; $r_p = 12.1\%$.

6-10 $b_N = 1.1250$.

6-11 4.5%.

6-12 a. $\bar{r}_A = 11.30\%$; $\bar{r}_B = 11.30\%$.
b. $\bar{r}_P = 11.30\%$.
c. $\sigma_A = 20.8\%$; $\sigma_B = 20.8\%$; $\sigma_B = 20.1\%$;
d. $CV_A = 1.84$; $CV_B = 1.84$; $CV_p = 1.78$.

6-13 a. $b_X = 1.3471$; $b_Y = 0.6508$.
b. $r_X = 12.7355\%$; $r_Y = 9.254\%$.
c. $r_p = 12.04\%$.

7-1 $D_1 = \$1.5750$; $D_3 = \$1.7364$; $D_5 = \$2.1011$.

7-2 $\hat{P}_0 = \$18.75$.

7-3 $\hat{P}_1 = \$22.00$; $\hat{r}_s = 15.50\%$.

7-4 $r_{ps} = 10\%$.

7-5 \$50.50.

7-6 $g = 9\%$.

7-7 $\hat{P}_3 = \$27.32$.

7-8 a. 13.3%.
b. 10%.
c. 8%.
d. 5.7%.

7-9 \$25.26.

7-10 a. $r_C = 10.6\%$; $r_D = 7\%$.

7-11 \$25.03.

7-12 $\hat{P}_0 = \$19.89$.

7-13 a. \$125.
b. \$83.33.

7-14 a. 7%.
b. 5%.
c. 12%.

7-15 a. (1) \$9.50.
(2) \$13.33.
b. (1)Undefined.

7-16 a. $\hat{P}_0 = \$21.43$.
b. $\hat{P}_0 = \$26.47$.
c. $\hat{P}_0 = \$32.14$.
d. $\hat{P}_0 = \$40.54$.

7-17 b. PV = \$5.29.
d. \$30.01.

7-18 a. $D_5 = \$3.52$.
b. $\hat{P}_0 = \$39.42$.
c. $D_1/P_0 = 5.10\%$; $D_6/P_5 = 7.00\%$.

7-19 $\hat{P}_0 = \$54.11$.

8-1 \$5; \$2.

8-2 \$27.00; \$37.00.

8-3 \$1.67.

8-4 \$3.70.

8-5 \$1.90.

8-6 \$2.39.

8-7 \$1.91.

9-1 a. 13%.
b. 10.4%.
c. 8.45%.

9-2 5.2%.

9-3 9%.

9-4 5.41%.

9-5 13.33%.

9-6 10.4%.

9-7 9.17%.

9-8 13%.

9-9 7.2%.

9-10 a. 16.3%.
b. 15.4%.
c. 16%.

9-11 a. 8%.
b. \$2.81.
c. 15.81%.

9-12 a. $g = 3\%$.
b. $EPS_1 = \$5.562$.

9-13 16.1%.

9-14 $(1 - T)r_d = 5.57\%$.

9-15 a. \$15,000,000.
b. 8.4%.

9-16 Short-term debt = 11.14%; Long-term debt = 22.03%; Common equity = 66.83%.

9-17 $w_{d(Short)} = 0\%$; $w_{d(Long)} = 20\%$; $w_{ps} = 4\%$; $w_s = 76\%$; $r_d(\text{After-tax}) = 7.2\%$; $r_{ps} = 11.6\%$; $r_s \approx 17.5\%$.

10-1 NPV = \$7,486.68.

10-2 IRR = 16%.

10-3 MIRR = 13.89%.

10-4 PI = 1.14.

10-5 4.34 years.

10-6 6.51 years.

10-7 5%: $NPV_A = \$16,108,952$; $NPV_B = \$18,300,939$.
10%: $NPV_A = \$12,836,213$; $NPV_B = \$15,954,170$.
15%: $NPV_A = \$10,059,587$; $NPV_B = \$13,897,838$.

10-8 $NPV_T = \$409$; $IRR_T = 15\%$; $MIRR_T = 14.54\%$; Accept. $NPV_P = \$3,318$; $IRR_P = 20\%$; $MIRR_P = 17.19\%$; Accept.

10-9 $NPV_E = \$3,861$; $IRR_E = 18\%$; $NPV_G = \$3,057$; $IRR_G = 18\%$; Purchase electric-powered forklift, since it has a higher NPV.

10-10 $NPV_S = \$814.33$; $NPV_L = \$1,675.34$; $IRR_S = 15.24\%$; $IRR_L = 14.67\%$; $MIRR_S = 13.77\%$; $MIRR_L = 13.46\%$; $PI_S = 1.081$; $PI_L = 1.067$.

10-11 $MIRR_X = 13.59\%$; $MIRR_Y = 13.10\%$.

10-12 a. NPV = \$136,578; IRR = 19.22%.

10-13 b. $IRR_A = 18.1\%$; $IRR_B = 24.0\%$.

c. 10%: PV_A = \$283.34;
NPV_B = \$178.60.
17%: PV_A = \$31.05;
NPV_B = \$75.95.
d. (1) $MIRR_A$ = 14.07%;
$MIRR_B$ = 15.89%.
(2) $MIRR_A$ = 17.57%;
$MIRR_B$ = 19.91%.

10-14 a. \$0; –\$10,250,000; \$1,750,000.
b. 16.07%.

10-15 a. NPV_A = \$18,108,510; NPV_B = \$13,946,117; IRR_A = 15.03%; IRR_B = 22.26%.
b. NPV_Δ = \$4,162,393; IRR_Δ = 11.71%.

10-16 Extended NPV_A = \$12.76 million; Extended NPV_B = \$9.26 million.
EAA_A = \$2.26 million;
EAA_B = \$1.64 million.

10-17 Extended NPV_A = \$4.51 million.
EAA_A = \$0.85 million;
EAA_B = \$0.69 million.

10-18 NPV of 360-6 = \$22,256.
Extended NPV of 190-3 = \$20,070.
EAA of 360-6 = \$5,723.30;
EAA of 190-3 = \$5,161.02.

10-19 d. 7.61%; 15.58%.

10-20 a. Undefined.
b. NPV_C = –\$911,067; NPV_F = –\$838,834.

10-21 a. A = 2.67 years; B = 1.5 years.
b. A = 3.07 years; B = 1.825 years.
c. NPV_A = \$12,739,908; Choose both.
d. NPV_A = \$18,243,813; Choose A.
e. NPV_B = \$8,643,390; Choose B.
f. 13.53%.
g. $MIRR_A$ = 21.93%; $MIRR_B$ = 20.96%.

10-22 a. 3 years.
b. No.

11-1 a. \$12,000,000.
b. No.
c. Yes; add \$1 million to initial investment outlay.

11-2 \$2,600,000.

11-3 \$4,600,000.

11-4 NPV = \$15,301.10

11-5 a. SL: \$200,000 per year. MACRS: \$264,000; \$360,000; \$120,000; \$56,000.
b. MACRS, \$12,781.64 higher.

11-6 a. –\$126,000.
b. \$42,518; \$47,579; \$34,926.
c. \$50,702.
d. NPV = \$10,841; Purchase.

11-7 a. –\$89,000
b. \$26,220; \$30,300; \$20,100.
c. \$24,380.
d. NPV = –\$6,704; Don't purchase.

11-8 a. NPV = \$106,537.

11-9 NPV of replace = \$921.

11-10 NPV of replace = \$22,329.

11-11 E(NPV) = \$3 million;
σ_{NPV} = \$23.622 million;
CV_{NPV} = 7.874.

11-12 a. NPV = \$37,035.13;
IRR = 15.30%;
MIRR = 12.81%;
Payback = 3.33 years.
b. \$77,976; –\$3,905.
c. E(NPV) = \$34,800;
σ_{NPV} = \$35,968;
CV = 1.03.

11-13 a. –\$98,500.
b. \$46,675; \$52,975; \$37,225; \$33,025; \$22,850.
c. \$34,073.

11-14 a. –\$792,750.
b. \$115,000; \$256,000; \$103,250; \$21,000; \$9,250.
c. \$206,000; \$255,350; \$201,888; \$173,100; \$287,913.
d. NPV = \$11,820.

11-15 a. Expected CF_A = \$6,750;
Expected CF_B = \$7,650;
CV_A = 0.0703.
b. NPV_A = \$10,036;
NPV_B = \$11,624.

11-16 a. E(IRR) ≈ 15.3%.
b. \$38,589.

11-17 a. \$117,779.
b. σ_{NPV} = \$445,060;
CV_{NPV} = 3.78.

12-1 AFN = \$410,000.

12-2 AFN = \$610,000.

12-3 AFN = \$200,000.

12-4 ΔS = \$68,965.52.

12-5 a. \$105,000; \$480,000.
b. \$18,750.

12-6 AFN = \$360.

12-7 a. \$13.44 million.
b. 6.38%.
c. Notes payable = \$31.44 million.

12-8 a. Total assets = \$33,534;
AFN = \$2,128.
b. Notes payable = \$4,228.

12-9 a. AFN = \$128,783.
b. Notes payable = \$284,783.

13-1 FCF = \$37.0.

13-2 V_{op} = \$6,000,000.

13-3 V_{op} at 2010 = $15,000.

13-4 V_{op} = $160,000,000; MVA = −$40,000,000.

13-5 $259,375,000.

13-6 a. HV_2 = $2,700,000.
b. $2,303,571.43.

13-7 a. $713.33.
b. $527.89.
c. $43.79.

13-8 $416 million.

13-9 $46.90.

13-10 a. $34.96 million.
b. $741.152 million.
c. $699.20 million.
d. $749.10 million.
e. $50.34.

14-1 Payout = 55%.

14-2 Payout = 20%.

14-3 Payout = 52%.

14-4 V_{op} = $175 million; n = 8.75 million.

14-5 P_0 = $60.

14-6 $3,250,000.

14-7 n = 4,000; EPS = $5.00; DPS = $1.50; P = $40.00.

14-8 D_0 = $3.44.

14-9 Payout = 31.39%.

14-10 a. (1) $3,960,000.
(2) $4,800,000.
(3) $9,360,000.
(4) Regular = $3,960,000; Extra = $5,400,000.

14-11 a. $6,000,000.
b. DPS = $2.00; Payout = 25%.
c. $5,000,000.
d. No.
e. 50%.
f. $1,000,000.
g. $8,333,333.

14-12 a. $848 million.
b. $450 million.
c. $30.
d. 1 million; 14 million.
e. $420 million; $30.

15-1 20,000.

15-2 1.0.

15-3 3.6%.

15-4 $300 million.

15-5 $30.

15-6 40 million.

15-7 a. ΔProfit = $850,000; Return = 21.25% > r_s = 15%.
b. $Q_{BE,Old}$ = 40; $Q_{BE,New}$ = 45.45.

15-8 a. V = $3,348,214.
b. $16.74.
c. $1.84.
d. 10%.

15-9 30% debt:

WACC = 11.14%; V = $101.023 million.

50% debt:

WACC = 11.25%; V = $100 million.

70% debt:

WACC = 11.94%; V = $94.255 million.

15-10 a. 0.870.
b. b = 1.218; r_s = 10.872%.
c. WACC = 8.683%; V = $103.188 million.

15-11 11.45%.

16-1 $3,000,000.

16-2 AR = $59,500.

16-3 r_{NOM} = 75.26%; EAR = 109.84%.

16-4 EAR = 8.49%.

16-5 $7,500,000.

16-6 a. DSO = 28 days.
b. AR = $70,000.
c. AR = $55,000.

16-7 a. 73.74%.
b. 14.90%.
c. 32.25%.
d. 21.28%.
e. 29.80%.

16-8 a. 45.15%.

16-9 Nominal cost = 14.90%; Effective cost = 15.89%.

16-10 14.91%.

16-11 a. 68 days.
b. $356,250.
c. 8.1.

16-12 a. 56.5 days.
b. (1) 2.1429.
(2) 12.86%.
c. (1) 46.5 days.
(2) 2.25.
(3) 13.5%.

16-13 a. ROE_T = 11.75%; ROE_M = 10.80%; ROE_R = 9.16%.

16-14 a. Feb. surplus = $2,000.
b. $164,400.

16-15 a. $100,000.
c. (1) $300,000.
(2) Nominal cost = 37.24%; Effective cost = 44.59%.
d. Nominal cost = 24.83%; Effective cost = 27.86%.

16-16 a. 14.35%.

16-17 a. $300,000.
b. $2,000.
c. (1) $322,500.
(2) $26,875.
(3) 13.57%.
(4) 14.44%.

17-1 12.358 yen per peso.

17-2 f_t = $0.00907.

17-3 1 euro = \$0.9091 or \$1 = 1.1 euros.

17-4 0.6667 pounds per dollar.

17-5 1.5152 SFr.

17-6 2.4 Swiss francs per pound.

17-7 $r_{NOM-U.S.}$ = 4.6%.

17-8 117 pesos.

17-9 +\$250,000.

17-10 b. \$18,148.00.

17-11 a. \$1,659,000.
b. \$1,646,000.
c. \$2,000,000.

17-12 b. f_t = \$0.7994.

17-13 \$468,837,209.

17-14 a. \$52.63; 20%.
b. 1.5785 SFr per U.S. dollar.
c. 41.54 Swiss francs; 16.92%.

APPENDIX C

Selected Equations and Data

CHAPTER 1

$$\text{Value} = \frac{FCF_1}{(1+WACC)^1} + \frac{FCF_2}{(1+WACC)^2} + \frac{FCF_3}{(1+WACC)^3} + \cdots + \frac{FCF_\infty}{(1+WACC)^\infty}$$

CHAPTER 2

EBIT = Earnings before interest and taxes = Sales revenues − Operating costs

$$\begin{aligned}\text{EBITDA} &= \text{Earnings before interest, taxes, depreciation and amortization}\\ &= \text{EBIT} + \text{Depreciation} + \text{Amortization}\end{aligned}$$

Net cash flow = Net income + Depreciation and amortization

$$\begin{aligned}\text{NOWC} &= \text{Net operating working capital}\\ &= \text{Operating current assets} - \text{Operating current liabilities}\\ &= \begin{pmatrix}\text{Cash + Accounts receivable}\\ \text{+ Inventories}\end{pmatrix} - \begin{pmatrix}\text{Accounts payable}\\ \text{+ Accruals}\end{pmatrix}\end{aligned}$$

Total net operating capital = Net operating working capital + Operating long-term assets

NOPAT = Net operating profit after taxes = EBIT(1 − Tax rate)

$$\begin{aligned}\text{Free cash flow (FCF)} &= \text{NOPAT} - \text{Net investment in operating capital}\\ &= \text{NOPAT} - \begin{pmatrix}\text{Current year's total} & - & \text{Previous year's total}\\ \text{net operating capital} & & \text{net operating capital}\end{pmatrix}\end{aligned}$$

Operating cash flow = NOPAT + Depreciation and amortization

$$\begin{matrix}\text{Gross investment in}\\ \text{operating capital}\end{matrix} = \begin{matrix}\text{Net investment}\\ \text{in operating capital}\end{matrix} + \text{Depreciation}$$

$$\text{FCF} = \text{Operating cash flow} - \begin{matrix}\text{Gross investment}\\ \text{in operating capital}\end{matrix}$$

$$\text{Return on invested capital (ROIC)} = \frac{\text{NOPAT}}{\text{Total net operating capital}}$$

$$\text{MVA} = \text{Market value of stock} - \text{Equity capital supplied by shareholders}$$

$$= (\text{Shares outstanding})(\text{Stock price}) - \text{Total common equity}$$

$$\text{MVA} = \text{Total market value} - \text{Total investor-supplied capital}$$

$$= \begin{pmatrix}\text{Market value of stock}\\ + \text{Market value of debt}\end{pmatrix} - \text{Total investor-supplied capital}$$

$$\text{EVA} = \begin{pmatrix}\text{Net operating profit}\\ \text{after taxes(NOPAT)}\end{pmatrix} - \begin{pmatrix}\text{After-tax dollar cost of capital}\\ \text{used to support operations}\end{pmatrix}$$

$$= \text{EBIT}(1 - \text{Tax rate}) - (\text{Total net operating capital})(\text{WACC})$$

$$\text{EVA} = (\text{Total net operating capital})(\text{ROIC} - \text{WACC})$$

Chapter 3

$$\text{Current ratio} = \frac{\text{Current assets}}{\text{Current liabilities}}$$

$$\text{Quick, or acid test, ratio} = \frac{\text{Current assets} - \text{Inventories}}{\text{Current liabilities}}$$

$$\text{Inventory turnover ratio} = \frac{\text{Sales}}{\text{Inventories}}$$

$$\text{DSO} = \text{Days sales outstanding} = \frac{\text{Receivables}}{\text{Average sales per day}} = \frac{\text{Receivables}}{\text{Annual sales}/365}$$

$$\text{Fixed assets turnover ratio} = \frac{\text{Sales}}{\text{Net fixed assets}}$$

$$\text{Total assets turnover ratio} = \frac{\text{Sales}}{\text{Total assets}}$$

$$\text{Debt ratio} = \frac{\text{Total liabilities}}{\text{Total assets}}$$

$$\text{Market debt ratio} = \frac{\text{Total liabilities}}{\text{Total liabilities} + \text{Market value of equity}}$$

$$\text{Debt-to-equity ratio} = \frac{\text{Total liabilities}}{\text{Total assets} - \text{Total liabilities}}$$

$$\text{Debt-to-equity} = \frac{\text{Debt ratio}}{1 - \text{Debt ratio}} \text{ and Debt ratio} = \frac{\text{Debt-to-equity}}{1 + \text{Debt-to-equity}}$$

$$\text{Equity multiplier} = \frac{\text{Total assets}}{\text{Common equity}}$$

$$\text{Debt ratio} = 1 - \frac{1}{\text{Equity multiplier}}$$

$$\text{Times-interest-earned (TIE) ratio} = \frac{\text{EBIT}}{\text{Interest charges}}$$

$$\text{EBITDA coverage ratio} = \frac{\text{EBITDA} + \text{Lease payments}}{\text{Interest} + \text{Principal payments} + \text{Lease payments}}$$

$$\text{Net profit margin} = \frac{\text{Net income available to common stockholders}}{\text{Sales}}$$

$$\text{Operating profit margin} = \frac{\text{EBIT}}{\text{Sales}}$$

$$\text{Gross profit margin} = \frac{\text{Sales} - \text{Cost of goods sold}}{\text{Sales}}$$

$$\text{Return on total assets (ROA)} = \frac{\text{Net income available to common stockholders}}{\text{Total assets}}$$

$$\text{Basic earning power (BEP) ratio} = \frac{\text{EBIT}}{\text{Total assets}}$$

$$\text{ROA} = \text{Profit margin} \times \text{Total assets turnover} = \frac{\text{Net income}}{\text{Sales}} \times \frac{\text{Sales}}{\text{Total assets}}$$

$$\text{Return on common equity (ROE)} = \frac{\text{Net income available to common stockholders}}{\text{Common equity}}$$

$$\begin{aligned}\text{ROE} &= \text{ROA} \times \text{Equity multiplier}\\ &= \text{Profit margin} \times \text{Total assets turnover} \times \text{Equity multiplier}\\ &= \frac{\text{Net income}}{\text{Sales}} \times \frac{\text{Sales}}{\text{Total assets}} \times \frac{\text{Total assets}}{\text{Common equity}}\end{aligned}$$

$$\text{Price/earnings (P/E) ratio} = \frac{\text{Price per share}}{\text{Earnings per share}}$$

$$\text{Price/cash flow ratio} = \frac{\text{Price per share}}{\text{Cash flow per share}}$$

$$\text{Book value per share} = \frac{\text{Common equity}}{\text{Shares outstanding}}$$

$$\text{Market/book (M/B) ratio} = \frac{\text{Market price per share}}{\text{Book value per share}}$$

Chapter 4

$$FV_N = PV(1 + I)^N$$

$$PV = \frac{FV_N}{(1 + I)^N}$$

$$FVA_N = PMT\left[\frac{(1+I)^N}{I} - \frac{1}{I}\right] = PMT\left[\frac{(1+I)^N - 1}{I}\right]$$

$$FVA_{due} = FVA_{ordinary}(1+I)$$

$$PVA_N = PMT\left[\frac{1}{I} - \frac{1}{I(1+I)^N}\right] = PMT\left[\frac{1 - \frac{1}{(1+I)^N}}{I}\right]$$

$$PVA_{Due} = PVA_{Ordinary}(1+I)$$

$$\text{PV of a perpetuity} = \frac{PMT}{I}$$

$$PV_{\text{Uneven stream}} = \sum_{t=1}^{N} \frac{CF_t}{(1+I)^t}$$

$$FV_{\text{Uneven stream}} = \sum_{t=1}^{N} CF_t(1+I)^{N-t}$$

$$I_{PER} = \frac{I_{NOM}}{M}$$

$$APR = (I_{PER})M$$

$$\text{Number of periods} = NM$$

$$FV_N = PV(1+I_{PER})^{\text{Number of periods}} = PV\left(1 + \frac{I_{NOM}}{M}\right)^{MN}$$

$$EFF\% = \left(1 + \frac{I_{NOM}}{M}\right)^M - 1.0$$

CHAPTER 5

$$V_B = \sum_{t=1}^{N} \frac{INT}{(1+r_d)^t} + \frac{M}{(1+r_d)^N}$$

$$\text{Semiannual payments: } V_B = \sum_{t=1}^{2N} \frac{INT/2}{(1+r_d/2)^t} + \frac{M}{(1+r_d/2)^{2N}}$$

$$\text{Yield to maturity: Bond price} = \sum_{t=1}^{N} \frac{INT}{(1+YTM)^t} + \frac{M}{(1+YTM)^N}$$

$$\text{Price of callable bond (if called at N)} = \sum_{t=1}^{N} \frac{INT}{(1+r_d)^t} + \frac{\text{Call price}}{(1+r_d)^N}$$

$$\text{Current yield} = \frac{\text{Annual interest}}{\text{Bond's current price}}$$

Current yield + Capital gains yield = Yield to maturity

$$r_d = r^* + IP + DRP + LP + MRP$$

$$r_{RF} = r^* + IP$$

$$r_d = r_{RF} + DRP + LP + MRP$$

$$IP_N = \frac{I_1 + I_2 + \cdots + I_N}{N}$$

Chapter 6

$$\text{Expected rate of return} = \hat{r} = \sum_{i=1}^{n} P_i r_i$$

$$\text{Historical average, } \bar{r}_{Avg} = \frac{\sum_{t=1}^{n} \bar{r}_t}{n}$$

$$\text{Variance} = \sigma^2 = \sum_{i=1}^{n} (r_i - \hat{r})^2 P_i$$

$$\text{Standard deviation} = \sigma = \sqrt{\sum_{i=1}^{n} (r_i - \hat{r})^2 P_i}$$

$$\text{Historical estimated } \sigma = S = \sqrt{\frac{\sum_{t=1}^{n} (\bar{r}_t - \bar{r}_{Avg})^2}{n-1}}$$

$$CV = \sigma / \hat{r}$$

$$\hat{r}_p = \sum_{i=1}^{n} w_i \hat{r}_i$$

$$\sigma_p = \sqrt{\sum_{i=1}^{n} (r_{pi} - \hat{r}_p)^2 P_i}$$

$$\text{Estimated } \rho = R = \frac{\sum_{t=1}^{n} (\bar{r}_{i,t} - \bar{r}_{i,Avg})(\bar{r}_{j,t} - \bar{r}_{j,Avg})}{\sqrt{\sum_{t=1}^{n} (\bar{r}_{i,t} - \bar{r}_{i,Avg})^2 \sum_{t=1}^{n} (\bar{r}_{j,t} - \bar{r}_{j,Avg})^2}}$$

$$COV_{iM} = \rho_{iM} \sigma_i \sigma_M$$

$$b_i = \left(\frac{\sigma_i}{\sigma_M}\right) \rho_{iM} = \frac{COV_{iM}}{\sigma_M^2}$$

$$b_p = \sum_{i=1}^{n} w_i b_i$$

Required return on stock market $= r_M$

Market risk premium $= RP_M = r_M - r_{RF}$

$RP_i = (r_M - r_{RF})b_i = (RP_M)b_i$

SML $= r_i = r_{RF} + (r_M - r_{RF})b_i = r_{RF} + RP_M b_i$

Chapter 7

$$\hat{P}_0 = \text{PV of expected future dividends} = \sum_{t=1}^{\infty} \frac{D_t}{(1 + r_s)^t}$$

$$\text{Constant growth}: \hat{P}_0 = \frac{D_0(1+g)}{r_s - g} = \frac{D_1}{r_s - g}$$

$$\hat{r}_s = \frac{D_1}{P_0} + g$$

$$\text{Capital gains yield} = \frac{\hat{P}_1 - P_0}{P_0}$$

$$\text{Dividend yield} = \frac{D_1}{P_0}$$

$$\text{For a zero growth stock, } \hat{P}_0 = \frac{D}{r_s}$$

$$\text{Horizon value} = \text{Terminal value} = \hat{P}_N = \frac{D_{N+1}}{r_s - g}$$

$$V_{ps} = \frac{D_{ps}}{r_{ps}}$$

$$\hat{r}_{ps} = \frac{D_{ps}}{V_{ps}}$$

$$\bar{r}_s = \text{Actual dividend yield} + \text{Actual capital gains yield}$$

CHAPTER 8

$$\text{Exercise value} = \text{Current price of stock} - \text{Strike price}$$

$$\text{Number of stock shares in hedged portfolio} = N = \frac{C_u - C_d}{P_u - P_d}$$

$$V_C = P[N(d_1)] - Xe^{-r_{RF}t}[N(d_2)]$$

$$d_1 = \frac{\ln(P/X) + [r_{RF} + (\sigma^2/2)]t}{\sigma\sqrt{t}}$$

$$d_2 = d_1 - \sigma\sqrt{t}$$

$$\text{Put–call parity: Put option} = V_C - P + Xe^{-r_{RF}t}$$

$$\text{V of put} = P[N(d_1) - 1] - Xe^{-r_{RF}t}[N(d_2) - 1]$$

CHAPTER 9

$$\text{After-tax component cost of debt} = r_d(1 - T)$$

$$M(1-F) = \sum_{t=1}^{N} \frac{INT(1 - T)}{[1 + r_d(1 - T)]^t} + \frac{M}{[1 + r_d(1 - T)]^N}$$

$$r_{ps} = \frac{D_{ps}}{P_{ps}(1 - F)}$$

$$\text{Market equilibrium: } \begin{matrix}\text{Expected}\\ \text{rate of return}\end{matrix} = \hat{r}_M = \frac{D_1}{P_0} + g = r_{RF} + RP_M = r_M = \begin{matrix}\text{Required}\\ \text{rate of return}\end{matrix},$$

where D_1, P_0, and g for the market, not an individual company

Rep/Div = ratio of payouts via repurchases to payouts via dividends

$r_M = \hat{r}_M = (1 + \text{Rep/Div})\frac{D_1}{P_0} + g$, where g is long-term growth rate in total payouts for the market and where D_1 and P_0 are for the market, not an individual company

CAPM: $r_s = r_{RF} + b_i(RP_M)$

DCF: $r_s = \hat{r}_s = \frac{D_1}{P_0} + \text{Expected g in dividends per share}$

$$r_s = \frac{\text{Company's own}}{\text{bond yield}} + \frac{\text{Judgmental}}{\text{risk premium}}$$

$g = (\text{Retention rate})(\text{ROE}) = (1.0 - \text{Payout rate})(\text{ROE})$

$$r_e = \hat{r}_e = \frac{D_1}{P_0(1-F)} + g$$

$\text{WACC} = w_d r_d(1 - T) + w_{ps} r_{ps} + w_s r_s$

Chapter 10

$$\text{NPV} = CF_0 + \frac{CF_1}{(1+r)^1} + \frac{CF_2}{(1+r)^2} + \cdots + \frac{CF_N}{(1+r)^N}$$

$$= \sum_{t=0}^{N} \frac{CF_t}{(1+r)^t}$$

$$\text{IRR: } CF_0 + \frac{CF_1}{(1+\text{IRR})^1} + \frac{CF_2}{(1+\text{IRR})^2} + \cdots + \frac{CF_N}{(1+\text{IRR})^N} = 0$$

$$\text{NPV} = \sum_{t=0}^{N} \frac{CF_t}{(1+\text{IRR})^t} = 0$$

MIRR: PV of costs = PV of terminal value

$$\sum_{t=0}^{N} \frac{COF_t}{(1+r)^t} = \frac{\sum_{t=0}^{N} CIF_t(1+r)^{N-t}}{(1+\text{MIRR})^N}$$

$$\text{PV of costs} = \frac{\text{Terminal value}}{(1+\text{MIRR})^N}$$

$$\text{PI} = \frac{\text{PV of future cash flows}}{\text{Initial cost}} = \frac{\sum_{t=1}^{N} \frac{CF_t}{(1+r)^t}}{CF_0}$$

$$\text{Payback} = \begin{array}{c}\text{Number of}\\ \text{years prior to}\\ \text{full recovery}\end{array} + \frac{\begin{array}{c}\text{Unrecovered cost}\\ \text{at start of year}\end{array}}{\begin{array}{c}\text{Cash flow during}\\ \text{full recovery year}\end{array}}$$

Chapter 11

$$\text{Project cash flow} = \text{FCF} = \frac{\text{Investment outlay}}{\text{cash flow}} + \frac{\text{Operating}}{\text{cash flow}} + \frac{\text{NOWC}}{\text{cash flow}} + \frac{\text{Salvage}}{\text{cash flow}}$$

$$\text{Expected NPV} = \sum_{i=1}^{n} P_i(\text{NPV}_i)$$

$$\sigma_{NPV} = \sqrt{\sum_{i=1}^{n} P_i(\text{NPV}_i - \text{Expected NPV})^2}$$

$$CV_{NPV} = \frac{\sigma_{NPV}}{E(\text{NPV})}$$

Chapter 12

$$\begin{matrix}\text{Additional} \\ \text{funds} \\ \text{needed}\end{matrix} = \begin{matrix}\text{Required} \\ \text{asset} \\ \text{increase}\end{matrix} - \begin{matrix}\text{Spontaneous} \\ \text{liability} \\ \text{increase}\end{matrix} - \begin{matrix}\text{Increase in} \\ \text{retained} \\ \text{earnings}\end{matrix}$$

$$\text{AFN} = (A^*/S_0)\Delta S - (L^*/S_0)\Delta S - MS_1(1 - \text{Payout ratio})$$

$$\begin{matrix}\text{Full} \\ \text{capacity} \\ \text{sales}\end{matrix} = \frac{\text{Actual sales}}{\begin{matrix}\text{Percentage of capacity} \\ \text{at which fixed assets} \\ \text{were operated}\end{matrix}}$$

$$\text{Target fixed assets/Sales} = \frac{\text{Actual fixed assets}}{\text{Full capacity sales}}$$

$$\begin{matrix}\text{Required level} \\ \text{of fixed assets}\end{matrix} = (\text{Target fixed assets/Sales})(\text{Projected sales})$$

Chapter 13

$$\begin{aligned} V_{op} &= \text{Value of operations} \\ &= \text{PV of expected future free cash flows} \\ &= \sum_{t=1}^{\infty} \frac{\text{FCF}_t}{(1 + \text{WACC})^t} \end{aligned}$$

$$\text{Horizon value: } V_{op(\text{at time N})} = \frac{\text{FCF}_{N+1}}{\text{WACC} - g} = \frac{\text{FCF}_N(1 + g)}{\text{WACC} - g}$$

$$\text{Total value} = V_{op} + \text{Value of nonoperating assets}$$

$$\text{Value of equity} = \text{Total value} - \text{Preferred stock} - \text{Debt}$$

$$\text{Operating profitability (OP)} = \text{NOPAT/Sales}$$

$$\text{Capital requirements (CR)} = \text{Operating capital/Sales}$$

$$\begin{aligned}\text{EROIC}_t &= \text{Expected return on invested capital}\\ &= \text{NOPAT}_{t+1}/\text{Capital}_t\\ &= \text{NOPAT}_t(1+g)/\text{Capital}_t\\ &= \text{OP}_{t+1}/\text{CR}_t\end{aligned}$$

For constant growth:

$$\begin{aligned}V_{op(\text{at time N})} &= \text{Capital}_N + \left[\frac{\text{Sales}_N(1+g)}{\text{WACC}-g}\right]\left[\text{OP} - \text{WACC}\left(\frac{\text{CR}}{1+g}\right)\right]\\ &= \text{Capital}_N + \frac{\text{Capital}_N(\text{EROIC}_N - \text{WACC})}{\text{WACC}-g}\\ &= \text{Capital}_N + \frac{\text{Capital}_N\left(\frac{\text{OP}_{N+1}}{\text{CR}_N} - \text{WACC}\right)}{\text{WACC}-g}\end{aligned}$$

Chapter 14

Residual distribution = Net income − [(Target equity ratio)(Total capital budget)]

$$\text{Number of shares repurchased} = n_{Prior} - n_{Post} = \frac{\text{Cash}_{Rep}}{P_{Prior}}$$

$$n_{Post} = n_{Prior} - \frac{\text{Cash}_{Rep}}{P_{Prior}} = n_{Prior} - \frac{\text{Cash}_{Rep}}{S_{Prior}/n_{Prior}} = n_{Prior}\left(1 - \frac{\text{Cash}_{Rep}}{S_{Prior}}\right)$$

Chapter 15

$$V_{op} = \sum_{t=1}^{\infty}\frac{\text{FCF}_t}{(1+\text{WACC})^t}$$

$$\text{WACC} = w_d(1-T)r_d + w_s r_s$$

$$\text{ROIC} = \frac{\text{NOPAT}}{\text{Capital}} = \frac{\text{EBIT}(1-T)}{\text{Capital}}$$

$$\text{EBIT} = PQ - VQ - F$$

$$Q_{BE} = \frac{F}{P-V}$$

$$V_L = D + S$$

MM, no taxes: $V_L = V_U$

MM, corporate taxes: $V_L = V_U + TD$

Miller, corporate and personal taxes: $V_L = V_U + \left[1 - \frac{(1-T_c)(1-T_s)}{(1-T_d)}\right]D$

$b = b_U[1 + (1 - T)(D/S)]$

$b_U = b/[1 + (1 - T)(D/S)]$

$r_s = r_{RF} + RP_M(b)$

$r_s = r_{RF}$ + Premium for business risk + Premium for financial risk

$$\text{If } g = 0\text{: } V_{op} = \frac{FCF}{WACC} = \frac{NOPAT}{WACC} = \frac{EBIT(1 - T)}{WACC}$$

Total corporate value = V_{op} + Value of short-term investments

S = Total corporate value − Value of all debt

$D = w_d V_{op}$

$S = (1 - w_d)V_{op}$

Cash raised by issuing debt = $D - D_0$

$P_{Prior} = S_{Prior}/n_{Prior}$

$P_{Post} = P_{Prior}$

$$n_{Post} = n_{Prior}\left[\frac{V_{opNew} - D_{New}}{V_{opNew} - D_{Old}}\right]$$

$$n_{Post} = n_{Prior} - (D_{New} - D_{Old})/P_{Prior}$$

$$P_{Post} = \frac{V_{opNew} - D_{Old}}{n_{Prior}}$$

$NI = (EBIT - r_d D)(1 - T)$

$EPS = NI/n$

Chapter 16

$$\text{Inventory conversion period} = \frac{\text{Inventory}}{(\text{Cost of goods sold})/365}$$

$$\text{Receivables collection period} = DSO = \frac{\text{Receivables}}{\text{Sales}/365}$$

$$\text{Payables deferral period} = \frac{\text{Payables}}{(\text{Cost of goods sold})/365}$$

$$\text{Cash conversion cycle} = \text{Inventory conversion period} + \text{Average collection period} - \text{Payables deferral period}$$

$$\text{Accounts receivable} = \text{Credit sales per day} \times \text{Length of collection period}$$

$$ADS = \frac{(\text{Units sold})(\text{Sales price})}{365} = \frac{\text{Annual sales}}{365}$$

Receivables = (ADS)(DSO)

$$\text{Nominal annual cost of trade credit} = \frac{\text{Discount percentage}}{100 - \text{Discount percentage}} \times \frac{365}{\text{Days credit is outstanding} - \text{Discount period}}$$

CHAPTER 17

$$\text{Single-period interest rate parity}: \frac{\text{Forward exchange rate}}{\text{Spot exchange rate}} = \frac{1 + r_h}{1 + r_f}$$

$$\text{Expected t-year forward exchange rate} = (\text{Spot rate})\left(\frac{1 + r_h}{1 + r_f}\right)^t$$

$$P_h = (P_f)(\text{Spot rate})$$

$$\text{Spot rate} = \frac{P_h}{P_f}$$

APPENDIX D

Values of the Areas under the Standard Normal Distribution Function

TABLE D-1 Values of the Areas under the Standard Normal Distribution Function

Z	0.00	0.01	0.02	0.03	0.04	0.05	0.06	0.07	0.08	0.09
0.0	.0000	.0040	.0080	.0120	.0160	.0199	.0239	.0279	.0319	.0359
0.1	.0398	.0438	.0478	.0517	.0557	.0596	.0636	.0675	.0714	.0753
0.2	.0793	.0832	.0871	.0910	.0948	.0987	.1026	.1064	.1103	.1141
0.3	.1179	.1217	.1255	.1293	.1331	.1368	.1406	.1443	.1480	.1517
0.4	.1554	.1591	.1628	.1664	.1700	.1736	.1772	.1808	.1844	.1879
0.5	.1915	.1950	.1985	.2019	.2054	.2088	.2123	.2157	.2190	.2224
0.6	.2257	.2291	.2324	.2357	.2389	.2422	.2454	.2486	.2517	.2549
0.7	.2580	.2611	.2642	.2673	.2704	.2734	.2764	.2794	.2823	.2852
0.8	.2881	.2910	.2939	.2967	.2995	.3023	.3051	.3078	.3106	.3133
0.9	.3159	.3186	.3212	.3238	.3264	.3289	.3315	.3340	.3365	.3389
1.0	.3413	.3438	.3461	.3485	.3508	.3531	.3554	.3577	.3599	.3621
1.1	.3643	.3665	.3686	.3708	.3729	.3749	.3770	.3790	.3810	.3830
1.2	.3849	.3869	.3888	.3907	.3925	.3944	.3962	.3980	.3997	.4015
1.3	.4032	.4049	.4066	.4082	.4099	.4115	.4131	.4147	.4162	.4177
1.4	.4192	.4207	.4222	.4236	.4251	.4265	.4279	.4292	.4306	.4319
1.5	.4332	.4345	.4357	.4370	.4382	.4394	.4406	.4418	.4429	.4441
1.6	.4452	.4463	.4474	.4484	.4495	.4505	.4515	.4525	.4535	.4545
1.7	.4554	.4564	.4573	.4582	.4591	.4599	.4608	.4616	.4625	.4633
1.8	.4641	.4649	.4656	.4664	.4671	.4678	.4686	.4693	.4699	.4706
1.9	.4713	.4719	.4726	.4732	.4738	.4744	.4750	.4756	.4761	.4767
2.0	.4773	.4778	.4783	.4788	.4793	.4798	.4803	.4808	.4812	.4817
2.1	.4821	.4826	.4830	.4834	.4838	.4842	.4846	.4850	.4854	.4857
2.2	.4861	.4864	.4868	.4871	.4875	.4878	.4881	.4884	.4887	.4890
2.3	.4893	.4896	.4898	.4901	.4904	.4906	.4909	.4911	.4913	.4916
2.4	.4918	.4920	.4922	.4925	.4927	.4929	.4931	.4932	.4934	.4936
2.5	.4938	.4940	.4941	.4943	.4945	.4946	.4948	.4949	.4951	.4952
2.6	.4953	.4955	.4956	.4957	.4959	.4960	.4961	.4962	.4963	.4964
2.7	.4965	.4966	.4967	.4968	.4969	.4970	.4971	.4972	.4973	.4974
2.8	.4974	.4975	.4976	.4977	.4977	.4978	.4979	.4979	.4980	.4981
2.9	.4981	.4982	.4982	.4982	.4984	.4984	.4985	.4985	.4986	.4986
3.0	.4987	.4987	.4987	.4988	.4988	.4989	.4989	.4989	.4990	.4990

Glossary

A

abandonment option Allows a company to reduce the capacity of its output in response to changing market conditions. This includes the option to contract production or abandon a project if market conditions deteriorate too much.

account receivable Created when a good is shipped or a service is performed, and payment for that good is made on a credit basis, not on a cash basis.

accounting income Income as defined by Generally Accepted Accounting Principles (GAAP).

accounting profit A firm's net income as reported on its income statement.

actual, or realized, rate of return, $\bar{r}_s$ The rate of return that was actually realized at the end of some holding period.

additional funds needed (AFN) Those funds required from external sources to increase the firm's assets to support a sales increase. A sales increase will normally require an increase in assets. However, some of this increase is usually offset by a spontaneous increase in liabilities as well as by earnings retained in the firm. Those funds that are required but not generated internally must be obtained from external sources.

agency cost or problem An expense, either direct or indirect, that is borne by a principal as a result of having delegated authority to an agent. An example is the costs borne by shareholders to encourage managers to maximize a firm's stock price rather than act in their own self-interests. These costs may also arise from lost efficiency and the expense of monitoring management to ensure that debtholders' rights are protected.

aggressive short-term financing policy Refers to a policy in which a firm finances all of its fixed assets with long-term capital but part of its permanent current assets with short-term, nonspontaneous credit.

aging schedule Breaks down accounts receivable according to how long they have been outstanding. This gives the firm a more complete picture of the structure of accounts receivable than that provided by days sales outstanding.

amortization A noncash charge against intangible assets, such as goodwill.

amortization schedule A table that breaks down the periodic fixed payment of an installment loan into its principal and interest components.

amortized loan A loan that is repaid in equal periodic amounts (or "killed off") over time.

annual report A report issued annually by a corporation to its stockholders. It contains basic financial statements as well as management's opinion of the past year's operations and the firm's future prospects.

annuity A series of payments of a fixed amount for a specified number of periods.

annuity due An annuity with payments occurring at the beginning of each period.

APR The nominal annual interest rate is also called the annual percentage rate, or APR.

asset management ratios A set of ratios that measure how effectively a firm is managing its assets.

assets-in-place Refers to the land, buildings, machines, and inventory that the firm uses in its operations to produce its products and services. Also known as operating assets.

asymmetric information theory Assumes managers have more complete information than investors and leads to a preferred "pecking order" of financing: (1) retained earnings, followed by (2) debt, and then (3) new common stock. Also known as signaling theory.

average tax rate Calculated by taking the total amount of tax paid divided by taxable income.

B

balance sheet A statement of the firm's financial position at a specific point in time. The firm's assets are listed on the left-hand side of the balance sheet; the right-hand side shows its liabilities and equity, or the claims against these assets.

basic earning power (BEP) ratio Calculated by dividing earnings before interest and taxes by total assets. This ratio shows the raw earning power of the firm's assets before the influence of taxes and leverage.

benchmarking When a firm compares its ratios to other leading companies in the same industry.

beta coefficient, b A measure of a stock's market risk, or the extent to which the returns on a given stock move with the stock market.

bird-in-the-hand theory Assumes that investors value a dollar of dividends more highly than a dollar of expected capital gains, because a certain dividend is less risky than a possible capital gain. This theory implies that a high-dividend stock has a higher price and lower required return, all else held equal.

Black-Scholes option pricing model A model to estimate the value of a call option. It is widely used by options traders.

bond A promissory note issued by a business or a governmental unit.

book value per share Common equity divided by the number of shares outstanding.

break-even point The level of unit sales at which costs equal revenues.

business risk The risk inherent in the operations of the firm, prior to the financing decision. Thus, business risk is the uncertainty inherent in future operating income or earnings before interest and taxes. Business risk is caused by many factors; two of the most important are sales variability and operating leverage.

C

call option An option that allows the holder to buy the asset at some predetermined price within a specified period of time.

call provision Gives the issuing corporation the right to call the bonds for redemption. The call provision generally states that if the bonds are called then the company must pay the bondholders an amount greater than the par value, or a call premium. Most bonds contain a call provision.

Capital Asset Pricing Model (CAPM) A model based on the proposition that any stock's required rate of return is equal to the risk-free rate of return plus a risk premium reflecting only the risk remaining after diversification. The CAPM equation is $r_i = r_{RF} + b_i(r_M - r_{RF})$.

capital budget Outlines the planned expenditures on fixed assets.

capital budgeting The whole process of analyzing projects and deciding whether they should be included in the capital budget.

capital gain (loss) The profit (loss) from the sale of a capital asset for more (less) than its purchase price.

capital gains yield Results from changing prices and is calculated as $(P_1 - P_0)/P_0$, where P_0 is the beginning-of-period price and P_1 is the end-of-period price.

capital intensity ratio The dollar amount of assets required to produce a dollar of sales. The capital intensity ratio is the reciprocal of the total assets turnover ratio.

capital market Capital markets are the financial markets for long-term debt and corporate stocks. The New York Stock Exchange is an example of a capital market.

capital rationing Occurs when management places a constraint on the size of the firm's capital budget during a particular period.

capital structure The manner in which a firm's assets are financed; that is, the right side of the balance sheet. Capital structure is normally expressed as the percentage of each type of capital used by the firm such as debt, preferred stock, and common equity.

cash budget A schedule showing cash flows (receipts, disbursements, and cash balances) for a firm over a specified period.

cash conversion cycle The length of time between the firm's actual cash expenditures on productive resources (materials and labor) and its own cash receipts from the sale of products (that is, the length of time between paying for labor and materials and collecting on receivables). Thus, the cash conversion cycle equals the length of time the firm has funds tied up in current assets.

cash discounts The amount by which a seller is willing to reduce the invoice price in order to be paid immediately, rather than in the future. A cash discount might be 2/10, net 30, which means a 2% discount if the bill is paid within 10 days and otherwise the entire amount is due within 30 days.

charter The legal document that is filed with the state to incorporate a company.

classified stock Sometimes created by a firm to meet special needs and circumstances. Generally, when special classifications of stock are used, one type is designated "Class A," another as "Class B," and so on. For example, Class A might be entitled to receive dividends before dividends can be paid on Class B stock. Class B might have the exclusive right to vote.

clientele effect The attraction of companies with specific dividend policies to those investors whose needs are best served by those policies. Thus, companies with high dividends will have a clientele of investors with low marginal tax rates and strong desires for current income. Conversely, companies with low dividends will have a clientele of investors with high marginal tax rates and little need for current income.

closely held corporation Refers to companies that are so small that their common stocks are not actively traded; they are owned by only a few people, usually the companies' managers.

coefficient of variation, CV Equal to the standard deviation divided by the expected return; it is a standardized risk measure that allows comparisons between investments having different expected returns and standard deviations.

collection policy The procedure for collecting accounts receivable. A change in collection policy will affect sales, days sales outstanding, bad debt losses, and the percentage of customers taking discounts.

commercial paper Unsecured, short-term promissory notes of large firms, usually issued in denominations of $100,000 or more and having an interest rate somewhat below the prime rate.

common stockholders' equity (net worth) The capital supplied by common stockholders—capital stock, paid-in capital, retained earnings, and (occasionally) certain reserves. Paid-in capital is the difference between the stock's par value and what stockholders paid when they bought newly issued shares.

comparative ratio analysis Compares a firm's own ratios to other leading companies in the same industry. This technique is also known as benchmarking.

compensating balance (CB) A minimum checking account balance that a firm must maintain with a bank to compensate the bank for services rendered or for making a loan; generally equal to 10%–20% of the loans outstanding.

compounding The process of finding the future value of a single payment or series of payments.

computer/telephone network A computer/telephone network, such as Nasdaq, consists of all the facilities that provide for security transactions not conducted at a physical location exchange. These facilities are, basically, the communications networks that link buyers and sellers.

conservative short-term financing policy Refers to using permanent capital to finance all permanent asset requirements as well as to meet some or all of the seasonal demands.

consol A type of perpetuity. Consols were originally bonds issued by England in the mid-1700s to consolidate past debt.

continuous probability distribution Contains an infinite number of outcomes and is graphed from $-\infty$ and $+\infty$.

convertible bond Security that is convertible into shares of common stock, at a fixed price, at the option of the bondholder.

convertible currency A currency that can be traded in the currency markets and can be redeemed at current market rates.

corporate bond Debt issued by corporations and exposed to default risk. Different corporate bonds have different levels of default risk, depending on the issuing company's characteristics and on the terms of the specific bond.

corporate governance The set of rules that control a company's behavior toward its directors, managers, employees, shareholders, creditors, customers, competitors, and community.

corporate valuation model Defines the total value of a company as the value of operations plus the value of nonoperating assets plus the value of growth options.

corporation A corporation is a legal entity created by a state. The corporation is separate and distinct from its owners and managers.

correlation The tendency of two variables to move together.

correlation coefficient, ρ (rho) A standardized measure of how two random variables covary. A correlation coefficient (ρ) of +1.0 means that the two variables move up and down in perfect synchronization, whereas a coefficient of –1.0 means the variables always move in opposite directions. A correlation coefficient of zero suggests that the two variables are not related to one another; that is, they are independent.

cost of common stock, r_s The return required by the firm's common stockholders. It is usually calculated using Capital Asset Pricing Model or the dividend growth model.

cost of new external common equity, r_e A project financed with external equity must earn a higher rate of return because it must cover the flotation costs. Thus, the cost of new common equity is higher than that of common equity raised internally by reinvesting earnings.

cost of preferred stock, r_{ps} The return required by the firm's preferred stockholders. The cost of preferred stock, r_{ps}, is the cost to the firm of issuing new preferred stock. For perpetual preferred, it is the preferred dividend, D_{ps}, divided by the net issuing price, P_n.

costly trade credit Credit taken (in excess of free trade credit) whose cost is equal to the discount lost.

coupon interest rate Stated rate of interest on a bond; defined as the coupon payment divided by the par value.

coupon payment Dollar amount of interest paid to each bondholder on the interest payment dates.

coverage ratio Similar to the times-interest-earned ratio, but it recognizes that many firms lease assets and also must make sinking fund payments. It is found by adding earnings before interest, taxes, depreciation, amortization (EBITDA), and lease payments and then dividing this total by interest charges, lease payments, and sinking fund payments over 1 – T (where T is the tax rate).

credit period The length of time for which credit is extended. If the credit period is lengthened then sales will generally increase, as will accounts receivable. This will increase the firm's financing needs and possibly increase bad debt losses. A shortening of the credit period will have the opposite effect.

credit policy The firm's policy on granting and collecting credit. There are four elements of credit policy, or credit policy variables: credit period, credit standards, collection policy, and discounts.

credit standards The financial strength and creditworthiness that qualifies a customer for a firm's regular credit terms.

credit terms Statements of the credit period and any discounts offered—for example, 2/10, net 30.

cross rate The exchange rate between two non-U.S. currencies.

crossover rate The cost of capital at which the NPV profiles for two projects intersect.

current ratio Indicates the extent to which current liabilities are covered by those assets expected to be converted to cash in the near future; it is found by dividing current assets by current liabilities.

current yield (on a bond) The annual coupon payment divided by the current market price.

D

days sales outstanding (DSO) Used to appraise accounts receivable and indicates the length of time the firm must wait after making a sale before receiving cash. It is found by dividing receivables by average sales per day.

DCF (discounted cash flow) techniques The net present value (NPV) and internal rate of return (IRR) techniques are discounted cash flow (DCF) evaluation techniques. These are called DCF methods because they explicitly recognize the time value of money.

dealer market In a dealer market, a dealer holds an inventory of the security and makes a market by offering to buy or sell. Others who wish to buy or sell can see the offers made by the dealers and can contact the dealer of their choice to arrange a transaction.

debenture An unsecured bond; as such, it provides no lien against specific property as security for the obligation. Debenture holders are therefore general creditors whose claims are protected by property not otherwise pledged.

debt ratio The ratio of total liabilities to total assets, it measures the percentage of funds provided by creditors.

decision trees A form of scenario analysis in which different actions are taken in different scenarios.

declaration date The date on which a firm's directors issue a statement declaring a dividend.

default risk The risk that a borrower may not pay the interest and/or principal on a loan when it becomes due. If the issuer defaults, investors receive less than the promised return on the bond. Default risk is influenced by the financial strength of the issuer and also by the terms of the bond contract, especially whether collateral has been pledged to secure the bond. The greater the default risk, the higher the bond's yield to maturity.

default risk premium (DRP) The premium added to the real risk-free rate to compensate investors for the risk that a borrower may fail to pay the interest and/or principal on a loan when they become due.

depreciation A noncash charge against tangible assets, such as buildings or machines. It is taken for the purpose of showing an asset's estimated dollar cost of the capital equipment used up in the production process.

derivatives Claims whose value depends on what happens to the value of some other asset. Futures and options are two important types of derivatives, and their values depend on what happens to the prices of other assets. Therefore, the value of a derivative security is derived from the value of an underlying real asset or other security.

devaluation The lowering, by governmental action, of the price of its currency relative to another currency. For example, in 1967 the British pound was devalued from $2.80 per pound to $2.50 per pound.

development bond A tax-exempt bond sold by state and local governments whose proceeds are made available to corporations for specific uses deemed (by Congress) to be in the public interest.

discount bond Bond prices and interest rates are inversely related; that is, they tend to move in the opposite direction from one another. A fixed-rate bond will sell at par when its coupon interest rate is equal to the going rate of interest, r_d. When the going rate of interest is above the coupon rate, a fixed-rate bond will sell at a "discount" below its par value. If current interest rates are below the coupon rate, a fixed-rate bond will sell at a "premium" above its par value.

discount on forward rate Occurs when the forward exchange rate differs from the spot rate. When the forward rate is below the spot rate, the forward rate is said to be at a discount.

discounted payback period The number of years it takes a firm to recover its project investment based on discounted cash flows.

discounting The process of finding the present value of a single payment or series of payments.

distribution policy The policy that sets the level of distributions and the form of the distributions (dividends and stock repurchases).

diversifiable risk Refers to that part of a security's total risk associated with random events not affecting the market as a whole. This risk can be eliminated by proper diversification. Also known as company-specific risk.

dividend irrelevance theory Holds that dividend policy has no effect on either the price of a firm's stock or its cost of capital.

dividend reinvestment plan (DRIP) Allows stockholders to automatically purchase shares of common stock of the paying corporation in lieu of receiving cash dividends. There are two types of plans: one involves only stock that is already outstanding; the other involves newly issued stock. In the first type, the dividends of all participants are pooled and the stock is purchased on the open market. Participants benefit from lower transaction costs. In the second type, the company issues new shares to the participants. Thus, the company issues stock in lieu of the cash dividend.

dividend yield Defined as either the end-of-period dividend divided by the beginning-of-period price or as the ratio of the current dividend to the current price. Valuation formulas use the former definition.

DuPont chart A chart designed to show the relationships among return on investment, asset turnover, the profit margin, and leverage.

DuPont equation A formula showing that the rate of return on equity can be found as the profit margin multiplied by the product of total assets turnover and the equity multiplier.

E

EBITDA Earnings before interest, taxes, depreciation, and amortization.

ECN In an ECN (electronic communications network), orders from potential buyers and sellers are automatically matched and the transaction is automatically completed.

economic life The number of years a project should be operated to maximize its net present value; often less than the maximum potential life.

Economic Value Added (EVA) A method used to measure a firm's true profitability. EVA is found by taking the firm's after-tax operating profit and subtracting the annual cost of all the capital a firm uses. If the firm generates a positive EVA, its management has created value for its shareholders. If the EVA is negative, management has destroyed shareholder value.

effective (or equivalent) annual rate (EAR or EFF%) The effective annual rate is the rate that, under annual compounding, would have produced the same future value at the end of 1 year as was produced by more frequent compounding, say quarterly. If the compounding occurs annually, then the effective annual rate and the nominal rate are the same. If compounding occurs more frequently, then the effective annual rate is greater than the nominal rate.

Efficient Markets Hypothesis (EMH) States (1) that stocks are always in equilibrium and (2) that it is impossible for an investor to consistently "beat the market." The EMH assumes that all important information regarding a stock is reflected in the price of that stock.

embedded options Options that are a part of another project. Also called real options, managerial options, and strategic options.

entrenchment Occurs when a company has such a weak board of directors and has such strong anti-takeover provisions in its corporate charter that senior managers feel there is little chance of being removed.

equilibrium The condition under which the intrinsic value of a security is equal to its price; also, when a security's expected return is equal to its required return.

ESOP (employee stock ownership plan) A type of retirement plan in which employees own stock in the company.

euro The currency used by nations in the European Monetary Union.

Eurobond Any bond sold in some country other than the one in whose currency the bond is denominated. Thus, a U.S. firm selling dollar bonds in Switzerland is selling Eurobonds.

Eurodollar A U.S. dollar on deposit in a foreign bank or a foreign branch of a U.S. bank. Eurodollars are used to conduct transactions throughout Europe and the rest of the world.

exchange rate Specifies the number of units of a given currency that can be purchased for one unit of another currency.

exchange rate risk Refers to the fluctuation in exchange rates between currencies over time.

ex-dividend date The date when the right to the dividend leaves the stock. This date was established by stockbrokers to avoid confusion, and it is four business days prior to the holder-of-record date. If the stock sale is made prior to the ex-dividend date, then the dividend is paid to the buyer; if the stock is bought on or after the ex-dividend date, the dividend is paid to the seller.

exercise price The price stated in the option contract at which the security can be bought (or sold). Also called the strike price.

exercise value Equal to the current price of the stock (underlying the option) minus the strike price of the option.

expectations theory States that the slope of the yield curve depends on expectations about future inflation rates and interest rates. Thus, if the annual rate of inflation and future interest rates are expected to increase, then the yield curve will be upward sloping; the curve will be downward sloping if the annual rates are expected to decrease.

expected rate of return, $\hat{r}_s$ The rate of return expected on a stock given its current price and expected future cash flows. If the stock is in equilibrium, the required rate of return will equal the expected rate of return.

extra dividend A dividend paid, in addition to the regular dividend, when earnings permit. Firms with volatile earnings may have a low regular dividend that can be maintained even in years of low profit (or high capital investment) but is supplemented by an extra dividend when excess funds are available.

F

financial distress costs Incurred when a leveraged firm facing a decline in earnings is forced to take actions to avoid bankruptcy. These costs may be the result of delays in the liquidation of assets, legal fees, the effects on product quality from cutting costs, and evasive actions by suppliers and customers.

financial intermediary Intermediary that buys securities with funds that it obtains by issuing its own securities. An example is a common stock mutual fund that buys common stocks with funds obtained by issuing shares in the mutual fund.

financial leverage The extent to which fixed-income securities (debt and preferred stock) are used in a firm's capital structure. If a high percentage of a firm's capital structure is in the form of debt and preferred stock, then the firm is said to have a high degree of financial leverage.

financial risk The risk added by the use of debt financing. Debt financing increases the variability of earnings before taxes (but after interest); thus, along with business risk, it contributes to the uncertainty of net income and earnings per share. Business risk plus financial risk equals total corporate risk.

financial service corporation A corporation that offers a wide range of financial services such as brokerage operations, insurance, and commercial banking.

fixed assets turnover ratio The ratio of sales to net fixed assets; it measures how effectively the firm uses its plant and equipment.

fixed exchange rate system The system in effect from the end of World War II until August 1971. Under the system, the U.S. dollar was linked to gold at the rate of $35 per ounce, and other currencies were then tied to the dollar.

floating exchange rates The system currently in effect, where the forces of supply and demand are allowed to determine currency prices with little government intervention.

floating-rate bond A bond whose coupon payment may vary over time. The coupon rate is usually linked to the rate on some other security, such as a Treasury security, or to some other rate, such as the prime rate or LIBOR.

flotation cost, F Those costs occurring when a company issues a new security, including fees to an investment banker and legal fees.

forecasted financial statements approach A method of forecasting financial statements to determine the additional funds needed. Many items on the income statement and balance sheets are assumed to increase proportionally with sales. As sales increase, these items that are tied to sales also increase, and the values of these items for a particular year are estimated as percentages of the forecasted sales for that year.

foreign bond A bond sold by a foreign borrower but denominated in the currency of the country in which the issue is sold. Thus, a U.S. firm selling bonds denominated in Swiss francs in Switzerland is selling foreign bonds.

foreign trade deficit A deficit that occurs when businesses and individuals in the United States import more goods from foreign countries than are exported.

forward exchange rate The prevailing exchange rate for exchange (delivery) at some agreed-upon future date, which is usually 30, 90, or 180 days from the day the transaction is negotiated.

founders' shares Stock owned by the firm's founders that have sole voting rights but restricted dividends for a specified number of years.

free cash flow (FCF) The cash flow actually available for distribution to all investors after the company has made all investments in fixed assets and working capital necessary to sustain ongoing operations.

free trade credit Credit received during the discount period.

FVA_N The future value of a stream of annuity payments, where N is the number of payments of the annuity.

$FVIFA_{I,N}$ The future value interest factor for an ordinary annuity of N periodic payments paying I percent interest per period.

$FVIF_{I,N}$ The future value interest factor for a lump sum left in an account for N periods paying I percent interest per period.

FV_N The future value of an initial single cash flow, where N is the number of periods the initial cash flow is compounded.

G

going public The act of selling stock to the public at large by a closely held corporation or its principal stockholders.

greenmail Targeted share repurchases that occur when a company buys back stock from a potential acquirer at a higher than fair-market price. In return, the potential acquirer agrees not to attempt to take over the company.

growth option Occurs if an investment creates the opportunity to make other potentially profitable investments that would not otherwise be possible, including options to expand output, to enter a new geographical market, and to introduce complementary products or successive generations of products.

H

holder-of-record date If a company lists the stockholder as an owner on the holder-of-record date, then the stockholder receives the dividend.

horizon value The value of operations at the end of the explicit forecast period. It is equal to the present value of all free cash flows beyond the forecast period, discounted back to the end of the forecast period at the weighted average cost of capital.

hurdle rate The project cost of capital, or discount rate. It is the rate used to discount future cash flows in the net present value method or to compare with the internal rate of return.

I

improper accumulation The retention of earnings by a business for the purpose of enabling stockholders to avoid personal income taxes on dividends.

income bond Pays interest only if the interest is earned. These securities cannot bankrupt a company, but from an investor's standpoint, they are riskier than "regular" bonds.

income statement Summarizes the firm's revenues and expenses over an accounting period. Net sales are shown at the top of each statement, after which various costs, including income taxes, are subtracted to obtain the net income available to common stockholders. The bottom of the statement reports earnings and dividends per share.

incremental cash flow Those cash flows that arise solely from the asset that is being evaluated.

indentures A legal document that spells out the rights of both bondholders and the issuing corporation.

independent projects Projects that can be accepted or rejected individually.

indexed, or purchasing power, bond The interest rate of such a bond is based on an inflation index such as the consumer price index (CPI), so the interest paid rises automatically when the inflation rate rises, thus protecting the bondholders against inflation.

inflation premium (IP) The premium added to the real risk-free rate of interest to compensate for the expected loss of purchasing power. The inflation premium is the average rate of inflation expected over the life of the security.

information content, or signaling, hypothesis A theory that holds that investors regard dividend changes as "signals" of management forecasts. Thus, when dividends are raised, this is viewed by investors as recognition by management of future earnings increases. Therefore, if a firm's stock price increases with a dividend increase, the reason may not be investor preference for dividends but rather expectations of higher future earnings. Conversely, a dividend reduction may signal that management is forecasting poor earnings in the future.

initial public offering (IPO) Occurs when a closely held corporation or its principal stockholders sell stock to the public at large.

initial public offering (IPO) market Going public is the act of selling stock to the public at large by a closely held corporation or its principal stockholders, and this market is often termed the initial public offering market.

I_{NOM} The nominal, or quoted, interest rate.

interest rate parity Holds that investors should expect to earn the same return in all countries after adjusting for risk.

interest rate risk Arises from the fact that bond prices decline when interest rates rise. Under these circumstances, selling a bond prior to maturity will result in a capital loss; the longer the term to maturity, the larger the loss.

internal rate of return (IRR) method The discount rate that equates the present value of the expected future cash inflows and outflows. IRR measures the rate of return on a project, but it assumes that all cash flows can be reinvested at the IRR rate.

international bond Any bond sold outside of the country of the borrower. There are two types of international bonds: Eurobonds and foreign bonds.

intrinsic (or fundamental) value, $\hat{P}_0$ The present value of a firm's expected future free cash flows.

inventory conversion period The average length of time to convert materials into finished goods and then to sell them; calculated by dividing total inventory by sales per day.

inventory turnover ratio Sales divided by inventories.

inverted (abnormal) yield curve A downward-sloping yield curve.

investment bank A firm that assists in the design of an issuing firm's corporate securities and in the sale of the new securities to investors in the primary market.

investment grade bond Securities with ratings of Baa/BBB or above.

investment timing option Gives companies the option to delay a project rather than implement it immediately. This option to wait allows a company to reduce the uncertainty of market conditions before it decides to implement the project.

J

Jensen's alpha Measures the vertical distance of a portfolio's return above or below the Security Market Line; first suggested by Professor Michael Jensen, it became popular because of its ease of calculation.

junk bond High-risk, high-yield bond issued to finance leveraged buyouts, mergers, or troubled companies.

L

limited liability partnership A limited liability partnership (LLP), sometimes called a limited liability company (LLC), combines the limited liability advantage of a corporation with the tax advantages of a partnership.

limited partnership A partnership in which limited partners' liabilities, investment returns, and control are limited; general partners have unlimited liability and control.

line of credit An arrangement in which a bank agrees to lend up to a specified maximum amount of funds during a designated period.

liquidity Liquidity refers to a firm's cash and marketable securities position and to its ability to meet maturing obligations. A liquid asset is any asset that can be quickly sold and converted to cash at its "fair" value. Active markets provide liquidity.

liquidity premium (LP) A liquidity premium is added to the real risk-free rate of interest, in addition to other premiums, if a security is not liquid.

liquidity ratio A ratio that shows the relationship of a firm's cash and other current assets to its current liabilities.

lumpy assets Those assets that cannot be acquired smoothly and instead require large, discrete additions. For example, an electric utility that is operating at full capacity cannot add a small amount of generating capacity, at least not economically.

M

managerial options Options that give opportunities to managers to respond to changing market conditions. Also called real options.

marginal tax rate The tax rate on the last unit of income.

market portfolio A portfolio consisting of all stocks.

market risk That part of a security's total risk that cannot be eliminated by diversification; measured by the beta coefficient.

market risk premium, RP_M The difference between the expected return on the market and the risk-free rate.

Market Value Added (MVA) The difference between the market value of the firm (that is, the sum of the market value of common equity, the market value of debt, and the market value of preferred stock) and the book value of the firm's common equity, debt, and preferred stock. If the book values of debt and preferred stock are equal to their market values, then MVA is also equal to the difference between the market value of equity and the amount of equity capital that investors supplied.

market value ratios Relate the firm's stock price to its earnings and book value per share.

maturity date The date when the bond's par value is repaid to the bondholder. Maturity dates generally range from 10 to 40 years from the time of issue.

maturity matching short-term financing policy A policy that matches asset and liability maturities. It is also referred to as the moderate, or self-liquidating, approach.

maturity risk premium (MRP) The premium that must be added to the real risk-free rate of interest to compensate for interest rate risk, which depends on a bond's maturity. Interest rate risk arises from the fact that bond prices decline when interest rates rise. Under these circumstances, selling a bond prior to maturity will result in a capital loss; the longer the term to maturity, the larger the loss.

Miller model Introduces the effect of personal taxes into the valuation of a levered firm, which reduces the advantage of corporate debt financing.

MM Proposition I with corporate taxes $V_L = V_U + TD$. Thus, firm value increases with leverage and the optimal capital structure is virtually all debt.

MM Proposition I without taxes $V_L = V_U = EBIT/r_{sU}$. Since both EBIT and r_{sU} are constant, firm value is also constant and capital structure is irrelevant.

moderate net operating working capital policy A policy that matches asset and liability maturities. It is also referred to as maturity matching or self-liquidating approach.

Modified Internal Rate of Return (MIRR) method Assumes that cash flows from all projects are reinvested at the cost of capital, not at the project's own IRR. This makes the modified internal rate of return a better indicator of a project's true profitability.

money market A financial market for debt securities with maturities of less than 1 year (short-term). The New York money market is the world's largest.

money market fund A mutual fund that invests in short-term debt instruments and offers investors check-writing privileges; thus, it amounts to an interest-bearing checking account.

Monte Carlo simulation analysis A risk analysis technique in which a computer is used to simulate probable future events and thus to estimate the likely profitability and risk of a project.

mortgage bond A bond for which a corporation pledges certain assets as security. All such bonds are written subject to an indenture.

multinational (or global) corporation A corporation that operates in two or more countries.

municipal bond Issued by state and local governments. The interest earned on most municipal bonds is exempt from federal taxes and also from state taxes if the holder is a resident of the issuing state.

municipal bond insurance An insurance company guarantees to pay the coupon and principal payments should the issuer of the bond (the municipality) default. This reduces the risk to investors who are willing to accept a lower coupon rate for an insured bond issue compared to an uninsured issue.

mutual fund A corporation that sells shares in the fund and uses the proceeds to buy stocks, long-term bonds, or short-term debt instruments. The resulting dividends, interest, and capital gains are distributed to the fund's shareholders after the deduction of operating expenses. Some funds specialize in certain types of securities, such as growth stocks, international stocks, or municipal bonds.

mutually exclusive projects Projects that cannot be performed at the same time. A company could choose either Project 1 or Project 2, or it can reject both, but it cannot accept both projects.

N

net cash flow The sum of net income plus noncash adjustments.

net operating working capital (NOWC) Operating current assets minus operating current liabilities. Operating current assets are the current assets used to support operations, such as cash, accounts receivable, and inventory. They do not include short-term investments. Operating current liabilities are the current liabilities that are a natural consequence of the firm's operations, such as accounts payable and accruals. They do not include notes payable or any other short-term debt that charges interest.

net present value (NPV) method Used to assess the present value of the project's expected future cash flows, discounted at the appropriate cost of capital. NPV is a direct measure of the value of the project to shareholders.

net working capital Current assets minus current liabilities.

nominal (quoted) interest rate, I_{NOM} The rate of interest stated in a contract. If the compounding occurs annually, the effective annual rate and the nominal rate are the same. If compounding occurs more frequently, the effective annual rate is greater than the nominal rate. The nominal annual interest rate is also called the annual percentage rate, or APR.

nominal rate of return, r_n Includes an inflation adjustment (premium). Thus, if nominal rates of return are used in the capital budgeting process, then the net cash flows must also be nominal.

nominal risk-free rate of interest, r_{RF} The real risk-free rate plus a premium for expected inflation. The short-term nominal risk-free rate is usually approximated by the U.S. Treasury bill rate, and the long-term nominal risk-free rate is approximated by the rate on U.S. Treasury bonds.

nonnormal cash flow projects Projects with a large cash outflow either sometime during or at the end of their lives. A common problem encountered when evaluating projects with nonnormal cash flows is multiple internal rates of return.

nonoperating assets Include investments in marketable securities and noncontrolling interests in the stock of other companies.

nonpecuniary benefits Perks that are not actual cash payments, such as lavish offices, memberships at country clubs, corporate jets, and excessively large staffs.

NOPAT (net operating profit after taxes) The amount of profit a company would generate if it had no debt and no financial assets.

normal cash flow project A project with one or more cash outflows (costs) followed by a series of cash inflows.

normal yield curve When the yield curve slopes upward it is said to be "normal," because it is like this most of the time.

O

open outcry auction A method of matching buyers and sellers in which the buyers and sellers are face-to-face, all stating a price at which they will buy or sell.

operating capital The sum of net operating working capital and operating long-term assets, such as net plant and equipment. Operating capital also is equal to the net amount of capital raised from investors. This is the amount of interest-bearing debt plus preferred stock plus common equity minus short-term investments. Also called total net operating capital, net operating capital, or net operating assets.

operating current assets The current assets used to support operations, such as cash, accounts receivable, and inventory. It does not include short-term investments.

operating current liabilities The current liabilities that are a natural consequence of the firm's operations, such as accounts payable and accruals. It does not include notes payable or any other short-term debt that charges interest.

operating leverage The extent to which fixed costs are used in a firm's operations. If a high percentage of a firm's total costs are fixed costs, then the firm is said to have a high degree of operating leverage. Operating leverage is a measure of one element of business risk but does not include the second major element, sales variability.

opportunity cost A cash flow that a firm must forgo in order to accept a project. For example, if the project requires the use of a building that could otherwise be sold, then the market value of the building is an opportunity cost of the project.

opportunity cost rate The rate of return available on the best alternative investment of similar risk.

optimal distribution policy The distribution policy that maximizes the value of the firm by choosing the optimal level and form of distributions (dividends and stock repurchases).

optimal dividend policy The dividend policy that strikes a balance between current dividends and future growth and maximizes the firm's stock price.

option A contract that gives its holder the right to buy or sell an asset at some predetermined price within a specified period of time.

ordinary (deferred) annuity An annuity with a fixed number of equal payments occurring at the end of each period.

original issue discount (OID) bond In general, any bond originally offered at a price that is significantly below its par value.

P

par value The nominal or face value of a stock or bond. The par value of a bond generally represents the amount of money that the firm borrows and promises to repay at some future date. The par value of a bond is often $1,000, but it can be $5,000 or more.

partnership A partnership exists when two or more persons associate to conduct a business.

payables deferral period The average length of time between a firm's purchase of materials and labor and the payment of cash for them. It is calculated by dividing accounts payable by credit purchases per day (i.e., cost of goods sold ÷ 365).

payback period The number of years it takes a firm to recover its project investment. Payback does not capture a project's entire cash flow stream and is thus not the preferred evaluation method. Note, however, that the payback does measure a project's liquidity, so many firms use it as a risk measure.

payment date The date on which a firm actually mails dividend checks.

payment, PMT Equal to the dollar amount of an equal or constant cash flow (an annuity).

pegged exchange rates Rates that are fixed against a major currency such as the U.S. dollar. Consequently, the values of the pegged currencies move together over time.

periodic rate, I_{PER} The rate charged by a lender or paid by a borrower each period. It can be a rate per year, per 6-month period, per quarter, per month, per day, or per any other time interval (usually 1 year or less).

permanent net operating working capital The NOWC required when the economy is weak and seasonal sales are at their low point. Thus, this level of NOWC always requires financing and can be regarded as permanent.

perpetuity A series of payments of a fixed amount that continue indefinitely.

physical location exchanges Exchanges, such as the New York Stock Exchange, that facilitate trading of securities at a particular location.

poison pills Shareholder rights provisions that allow existing shareholders in a company to purchase additional shares of stock at a lower-than-market value if a potential acquirer purchases a controlling stake in the company.

political risk Refers to the possibility of expropriation and the unanticipated restriction of cash flows to the parent by a foreign government.

post-audit The final aspect of the capital budgeting process. The post-audit is a feedback process in which the actual results are compared with those predicted in the original capital budgeting analysis. The post-audit has several purposes, of which the most important are to improve forecasts and operations.

precautionary balance A cash balance held in reserve for random, unforeseen fluctuations in cash inflows and outflows.

preemptive right Gives the current shareholders the right to purchase any new shares issued in proportion to their current holdings. The preemptive right enables current owners to maintain their proportionate share of ownership and control of the business.

preferred stock A hybrid security that is similar to bonds in some respects and to common stock in other respects. Preferred dividends are similar to interest payments on bonds in that they are fixed in amount and generally must be paid before common stock dividends can be paid. If the preferred dividend is not earned, the directors can omit it without throwing the company into bankruptcy.

premium bond Bond prices and interest rates are inversely related; that is, they tend to move in the opposite direction from one another. A fixed-rate bond will sell at par when its coupon interest rate is equal to the going rate of interest, r_d. When the going rate of interest is above the coupon rate, a fixed-rate bond will sell at a "discount" below its par value. If current interest rates are below the coupon rate, a fixed-rate bond will sell at a "premium" above its par value.

premium on forward rate Occurs when the forward exchange rate differs from the spot rate. When the forward rate is above the spot rate, it is said to be at a premium.

price/cash flow ratio Calculated by dividing price per share by cash flow per share. This shows how much investors are willing to pay per dollar of cash flow.

price/earnings (P/E) ratio Calculated by dividing price per share by earnings per share. This shows how much investors are willing to pay per dollar of reported profits.

primary market Markets in which newly issued securities are sold for the first time.

private markets Markets in which transactions are worked out directly between two parties and structured in any manner that appeals to them. Bank loans and private placements of debt with insurance companies are examples of private market transactions.

probability distribution A listing, chart, or graph of all possible outcomes, such as expected rates of return, with a probability assigned to each outcome.

professional corporation (PC) Has most of the benefits of incorporation but the participants are not relieved of professional (malpractice) liability; known in some states as a professional association (PA).

profit margin on sales Calculated by dividing net income by sales; gives the profit per dollar of sales.

profitability index Found by dividing the project's present value of future cash flows by its initial cost. A profitability index greater than 1 is equivalent to a project's having positive net present value.

profitability ratios Ratios that show the combined effects of liquidity, asset management, and debt on operations.

progressive tax A tax system in which the higher one's income, the larger the percentage paid in taxes.

project cost of capital The risk-adjusted discount rate for that project.

projected (pro forma) financial statement Shows how an actual statement would look if certain assumptions are realized.

promissory note A document specifying the terms and conditions of a loan, including the amount, interest rate, and repayment schedule.

proprietorship A business owned by one individual.

proxy A document giving one person the authority to act for another, typically the power to vote shares of common stock.

proxy fight An attempt to take over a company in which an outside group solicits existing shareholders' proxies, which are authorizations to vote shares in a shareholders' meeting, in an effort to overthrow management and take control of the business.

public markets Markets in which standardized contracts are traded on organized exchanges. Securities that are issued in public markets, such as common stock and corporate bonds, are ultimately held by a large number of individuals.

publicly owned corporation Corporation in which the stock is owned by a large number of investors, most of whom are not active in management.

purchasing power parity Implies that the level of exchange rates adjusts so that identical goods cost the same in different countries. Sometimes referred to as the "law of one price."

put option Allows the holder to sell the asset at some predetermined price within a specified period of time.

PV The value today of a future payment, or stream of payments, discounted at the appropriate rate of interest. PV is also the beginning amount that will grow to some future value.

PVA_N The value today of a future stream of N equal payments at the end of each period (an ordinary annuity).

$PVIFA_{I,N}$ The present value interest factor for an ordinary annuity of N periodic payments discounted at I percent interest per period.

$PVIF_{I,N}$ The present value interest factor for a lump sum received N periods in the future discounted at I percent per period.

Q

quick, or acid test, ratio Found by taking current assets less inventories and then dividing by current liabilities.

R

real options Occur when managers can influence the size and risk of a project's cash flows by taking different actions during the project's life. They are referred to as real options because they deal with real as opposed to financial assets. They are also called managerial options because they give opportunities to managers to respond to changing market conditions. Sometimes they are called strategic options because they often deal with strategic issues. Finally, they are also called embedded options because they are a part of another project.

real rate of return, r_r Contains no adjustment for expected inflation. If net cash flows from a project do not include inflation adjustments, then the cash flows should be discounted at the real cost of capital. In a similar manner, the internal rate of return resulting from real net cash flows should be compared with the real cost of capital.

real risk-free rate of interest, r^* The interest rate on a risk-free security in an economy with zero inflation. The real risk-free rate could also be called the pure rate of interest since it is the rate of interest that would exist on very short-term, default-free U.S. Treasury securities if the expected rate of inflation were zero.

realized rate of return, $\bar{r}$ The actual return an investor receives on his or her investment. It can be quite different than the expected return.

receivables collection period The average length of time required to convert a firm's receivables into cash. It is calculated by dividing accounts receivable by sales per day.

redeemable bond Gives investors the right to sell the bonds back to the corporation at a price that is usually close to the par value. If interest rates rise, then investors can redeem the bonds and reinvest at the higher rates.

reinvestment rate risk Occurs when a short-term debt security must be "rolled over." If interest rates have fallen then the reinvestment of principal will be at a lower rate, with correspondingly lower interest payments and ending value.

relaxed net operating working capital policy A policy under which relatively large amounts of cash, marketable securities, and inventories are carried and under which sales are stimulated by a liberal credit policy, resulting in a high level of receivables.

repatriation of earnings The cash flow, usually in the form of dividends or royalties, from the foreign branch or subsidiary to the parent company. These cash flows must be converted to the currency of the parent and thus are subject to future exchange rate changes. A foreign government may restrict the amount of cash that may be repatriated.

replacement chain (common life) approach A method of comparing mutually exclusive projects that have unequal lives. Each project is replicated so that they will both terminate in a common year. If projects with lives of 3 years and 5 years are being evaluated, then the 3-year project would be replicated 5 times and the 5-year project replicated

3 times; thus, both projects would terminate in 15 years.

required rate of return, r_s The minimum acceptable rate of return, considering both its risk and the returns available on other investments.

reserve borrowing capacity Exists when a firm uses less debt under "normal" conditions than called for by the trade-off theory. This allows the firm some flexibility to use debt in the future when additional capital is needed.

residual distribution model In this model, firms should pay dividends only when more earnings are available than needed to support the optimal capital budget.

restricted net operating working capital policy A policy under which holdings of cash, securities, inventories, and receivables are minimized.

restricted voting rights A provision that automatically deprives a shareholder of voting rights if the shareholder owns more than a specified amount of stock.

retained earnings The portion of the firm's earnings that have been saved rather than paid out as dividends.

return on common equity (ROE) Found by dividing net income by common equity.

return on invested capital (ROIC) Net operating profit after taxes divided by the operating capital.

return on total assets (ROA) The ratio of net income to total assets.

revaluation Occurs when the relative price of a currency is increased. It is the opposite of devaluation.

revolving credit agreement A formal, committed line of credit extended by a bank or other lending institution.

risk aversion A risk-averse investor dislikes risk and requires a higher rate of return as an inducement to buy riskier securities.

risk premium for Stock i, RP_i The extra return that an investor requires to hold risky Stock i instead of a risk-free asset.

risk-adjusted discount rate Incorporates the risk of the project's cash flows. The cost of capital to the firm reflects the average risk of the firm's existing projects. Thus, new projects that are riskier than existing projects should have a higher risk-adjusted discount rate. Conversely, projects with less risk should have a lower risk-adjusted discount rate.

S

S corporation A small corporation that, under Subchapter S of the Internal Revenue Code, elects to be taxed as a proprietorship or a partnership yet retains limited liability and other benefits of the corporate form of organization.

salvage value The market value of an asset after its useful life.

scenario analysis A shorter version of simulation analysis that uses only a few outcomes. Often the outcomes are for three scenarios: optimistic, pessimistic, and most likely.

seasonal effects on ratios Seasonal factors can distort ratio analysis. At certain times of the year, a firm may have excessive inventories in preparation of a "season" of high demand. Therefore, an inventory turnover ratio taken at this time will be radically different than one taken after the season.

secondary market Markets in which securities are resold after initial issue in the primary market. The New York Stock Exchange is an example.

secured loan A loan backed by collateral, which is often in the form of inventories or receivables.

Security Market Line (SML) Represents, in a graphical form, the relationship between the risk of an asset as measured by its beta and the required rates of return for individual securities. The SML equation is one of the key results of the CAPM: $r_i = r_{RF} + b_i(r_M - r_{RF})$.

semistrong form of market efficiency States that current market prices reflect all publicly available information. Therefore, the only way to gain abnormal returns on a stock is to possess inside information about the company's stock.

sensitivity analysis Indicates exactly how much net present value will change in response to a given change in an input variable, other things held constant. Sensitivity analysis is sometimes called "what if" analysis because it answers this type of question.

sinking fund Facilitates the orderly retirement of a bond issue. This can be achieved in one of two ways:

(1) the company can call in for redemption (at par value) a certain percentage of bonds each year; or (2) the company may buy the required amount of bonds on the open market.

spontaneously generated funds Funds generated if a liability account increases spontaneously (automatically) as sales increase. An increase in a liability account is a source of funds, thus funds have been generated. Two examples of spontaneous liability accounts are accounts payable and accrued wages. Notes payable, although a current liability account, is not a spontaneous source of funds because an increase in notes payable requires a specific action between the firm and a creditor.

spot rate The exchange rate that applies to "on the spot" trades or, more precisely, to exchanges that occur two days following the day of trade (in other words, current exchanges).

stand-alone risk The risk an investor takes by holding only one asset.

standard deviation, σ A statistical measure of the variability of a set of observations. It is the square root of the variance.

statement of cash flows Reports the impact of a firm's operating, investing, and financing activities on cash flows over an accounting period.

statement of stockholders' equity Statement showing the beginning stockholders' equity, any changes due to stock issues/repurchases, the amount of net income that is retained, and the ending stockholders' equity.

stock dividend Increases the number of shares outstanding but at a slower rate than splits. Current shareholders receive additional shares on some proportional basis. Thus, a holder of 100 shares would receive 5 additional shares at no cost if a 5% stock dividend were declared.

stock option Allows its owner to purchase a share of stock at a fixed price, called the strike price or the exercise price, no matter what the actual price of the stock is. Stock options always have an expiration date, after which they cannot be exercised.

stock repurchase Occurs when a firm repurchases its own stock. These shares of stock are then referred to as treasury stock.

stock split Current shareholders are given some number (or fraction) of shares for each stock share owned. Thus, in a 3-for-1 split, each shareholder would receive three new shares in exchange for each old share, thereby tripling the number of shares outstanding. Stock splits usually occur when the stock price is outside of the optimal trading range.

strategic options Options that often deal with strategic issues. Also called real options, embedded options, and managerial options.

stretching accounts payable The practice of deliberately paying accounts late.

strike (or exercise) price The price stated in the option contract at which the security can be bought (or sold).

strong form of market efficiency Assumes that all information pertaining to a stock, whether public or inside information, is reflected in current market prices. Thus, no investors would be able to earn abnormal returns in the stock market.

subordinated debenture Debentures that have claims on assets, in the event of bankruptcy, only after senior debt (as named in the subordinated debt's indenture) has been paid off. Subordinated debentures may be subordinated to designated notes payable or to all other debt.

sunk cost A cost that has already occurred and is not affected by the capital project decision. Sunk costs are not relevant to capital budgeting decisions.

T

takeover An action whereby a person or group succeeds in ousting a firm's management and taking control of the company.

target capital structure The relative amount of debt, preferred stock, and common equity that the firm desires. The weighted average cost of capital should be based on these target weights.

target cash balance The desired cash balance that a firm plans to maintain in order to conduct business.

tax loss carryback and carryforward Ordinary corporate operating losses can be carried backward for 2 years or forward for 20 years to offset taxable income in a given year.

tax preference theory Proposes that investors prefer capital gains over dividends, because capital gains taxes can be deferred into the future but taxes on dividends must be paid as the dividends are received.

taxable income Gross income less a set of exemptions and deductions that are spelled out in the instructions to the tax forms that individuals must file.

temporary net operating working capital The NOWC required above the permanent level when the economy is strong and/or seasonal sales are high.

term structure of interest rates The relationship between yield to maturity and term to maturity for bonds of a single risk class.

time line A graphical representation used to show the timing of cash flows.

times-interest-earned (TIE) ratio Determined by dividing earnings before interest and taxes by the interest charges. This ratio measures the extent to which operating income can decline before the firm is unable to meet its annual interest costs.

total assets turnover ratio Measures the turnover of all the firm's assets; it is calculated by dividing sales by total assets.

trade credit Debt arising from credit sales and recorded as an account receivable by the seller and as an account payable by the buyer.

trade deficit Occurs when a country imports more goods from abroad than it exports.

trade discounts Price reductions that suppliers offer customers for early payment of bills.

trade-off model The addition of financial distress and agency costs to either the MM tax model or the Miller model. In this model, the optimal capital structure can be visualized as a trade-off between the benefit of debt (the interest tax shelter) and the costs of debt (financial distress and agency costs).

transactions balance The cash balance associated with payments and collections; the balance necessary for day-to-day operations.

Treasury bond Bonds issued by the federal government; sometimes called T-bonds or government bonds. Treasury bonds have no default risk.

trend analysis An analysis of a firm's financial ratios over time. It is used to estimate the likelihood of improvement or deterioration in its financial situation.

V

value drivers The four value drivers are the growth rate in sales (g), operating profitability (OP = NOPAT/Sales), capital requirements (CR = Capital/Sales), and the weighted average cost of capital (WACC).

value of operations (V_{op}) The present value of all expected future free cash flows when discounted at the weighted average cost of capital.

value-based management Managing a firm with shareholder value in mind. It typically involves use of a model of shareholder value, such as the corporate value model.

variance, σ^2 A measure of the distribution's variability. It is the sum of the squared deviations about the expected value.

W

warrant A call option, issued by a company, that allows the holder to buy a stated number of shares of stock from the company at a specified price. Warrants are generally distributed with debt, or preferred stock, to induce investors to buy those securities at lower cost.

weak form of market efficiency Assumes that all information contained in past price movements is fully reflected in current market prices. Thus, information about recent trends in a stock's price is of no use in selecting a stock.

weighted average cost of capital (WACC) The weighted average of the after-tax component costs of capital—debt, preferred stock, and common equity. Each weighting factor is the proportion of that type of capital in the optimal, or target, capital structure.

window dressing Techniques employed by firms to make their financial statements look better than they really are.

working capital A firm's investment in short-term assets—cash, marketable securities, inventory, and accounts receivable.

Y

yield curve The curve that results when yield to maturity is plotted on the y-axis with term to maturity on the x-axis.

yield to call (YTC) The rate of interest earned on a bond if it is called. If current interest rates are well below an outstanding callable bond's coupon rate, then the YTC may be a more relevant estimate of expected return than the YTM because the bond is likely to be called.

yield to maturity (YTM) The rate of interest earned on a bond if it is held to maturity.

Z

zero coupon bond Pays no coupons at all but is offered at a substantial discount below its par value and hence provides capital appreciation rather than interest income.

Name Index

V

W

X

Y

Z

Subject Index

A

D

J

K

L

Q

R

S

T

U

V

W